JAVA™

HOW TO PROGRAM

SEVENTH EDITION

Pearson International Edition

Deitel® Ser

How To Program Series

Advanced Java™ 2 Platform How to Program

C How to Program, 5/E

C++ How to Program, 5/E

e-Business and e-Commerce How to Program

Internet and World Wide Web How to Program, 3/E

Java How to Program, 7/E

Small Java™ How to Program, 6/E

Perl How to Program

Python How to Program

Visual C++® .NET How to Program

Visual Basic® 6 How to Program

Visual Basic® 2005 How to Program, 3/E

Visual C#® 2005 How to Program, 2/E

Wireless Internet & Mobile Business How to Program

XML How to Program

Simply Series

Simply C++: An Application-Driven Tutorial Approach

Simply C#: An Application-Driven Tutorial Approach

Simply Java™ Programming: An Application-Driven Tutorial Approach

Simply Visual Basic® .NET: An Application-Driven Tutorial Approach (Visual Studio .NET 2003 Edition)

Simply Visual Basic® 2005, 2/E: An Application-Driven Tutorial Approach

ies Page

SafariX Web Books

www.deitel.com/books/SafariX.html

C++ How to Program, 5/e	Small C++ How to Program, 5/e
Java How to Program, 6/e	Small Java How to Program, 5/e
Simply C++: An Application-Driven Tutorial Approach	Visual Basic 2005 How to Program, 3/e
	Visual C# 2005 How to Program, 2/e

To follow the Deitel publishing program, please register for the free *DEITEL® BUZZ ONLINE* e-mail newsletter at:

www.deitel.com/newsletter/subscribe.html

To communicate with the authors, send e-mail to:

deitel@deitel.com

For information on corporate on-site seminars offered by Deitel & Associates, Inc. worldwide, visit:

www.deitel.com

or write to

deitel@deitel.com

For continuing updates on Prentice Hall/Deitel publications visit:

www.deitel.com
www.prenhall.com/deitel
www.InformIT.com/deitel

Check out our new Resource Centers for valuable web resources that will help you master Java, other important programming languages and Web 2.0 topics:

www.deitel.com/ResourceCenters.html

Vice President and Editorial Director, ECS: *Marcia J. Horton*
Associate Editor: *Jennifer Cappello*
Assistant Editor: *Carole Snyder*
Executive Managing Editor: *Vince O'Brien*
Managing Editor: *Bob Engelhardt*
Production Editors: *Donna M. Crilly, Marta Samsel*
Director of Creative Services: *Paul Belfanti*
A/V Production Editor: *Xiaohong Zhu*
Art Studio: *Artworks, York, PA*
Creative Director: *Juan López*
Art Director: *Kristine Carney*
Cover Design: *Abbey S. Deitel, Harvey M. Deitel, Francesco Santalucia, Kristine Carney*
Interior Design: *Harvey M. Deitel, Kristine Carney*
Manufacturing Manager: *Alexis Heydt-Long*
Manufacturing Buyer: *Lisa McDowell*
Executive Marketing Manager: *Robin O'Brien*

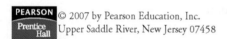 © 2007 by Pearson Education, Inc.
Upper Saddle River, New Jersey 07458

Printed in Singapore

10 9 8 7 6 5 4 3 2 1

ISBN 0-13-613247-2

Pearson Education Ltd., *London*
Pearson Education Australia Pty. Ltd., *Sydney*
Pearson Education Singapore, Pte. Ltd.
Pearson Education North Asia Ltd., *Hong Kong*
Pearson Education Canada, Inc., *Toronto*
Pearson Educación de Mexico, S.A. de C.V.
Pearson Education–Japan, *Tokyo*
Pearson Education Malaysia, Pte. Ltd.
Pearson Education, Inc., *Upper Saddle River, New Jersey*

JAVA™

HOW TO PROGRAM

SEVENTH EDITION

Pearson International Edition

P. J. Deitel
Deitel & Associates, Inc.

H. M. Deitel
Deitel & Associates, Inc.

Pearson Education International

Trademarks

DEITEL, the double-thumbs-up bug and DIVE INTO are registered trademarks of Deitel and Associates, Inc.

Java and all Java-based marks are trademarks or registered trademarks of Sun Microsystems, Inc. in the United States and other countries. Pearson Education is independent of Sun Microsystems, Inc.

Microsoft, Internet Explorer and the Windows logo are either registered trademarks or trademarks of Microsoft Corporation in the United States and/or other countries.

UNIX is a registered trademark of The Open Group.

To Vince O'Brien,
Director of Project Management, Prentice Hall:

It is a privilege for us to work with a consummate professional.
With our best wishes for your continued success.

Paul and Harvey

Deitel Resource Centers

Our Resource Centers focus on the vast amounts of free content available online. Start your search here for resources, downloads, tutorials, documentation, books, e-books, journals, articles, blogs, RSS feeds and more on many of today's hottest programming and technology topics. For the most up-to-date list of our Resource Centers, visit:

www.deitel.com/ResourceCenters.html

Let us know what other Resource Centers you'd like to see! Also, please register for the free *DEITEL® BUZZ ONLINE* e-mail newsletter at:

www.deitel.com/newsletter/subscribe.html

Programming
AJAX
Apache
ASP.NET
C
C++
C#
Code Search Engines and Code Sites
Eclipse™
Game Programming
Java™
Java Certification and Assessment Testing
Java Design Patterns
Java EE 5
Java SE 6 Mustang
JavaScript
Linux
MySQL®
.NET
Open Source
OpenGL®
Perl
PHP
Programming Projects
Python™
Ruby
Visual Basic®
Web Services
Windows Vista™
WinFX
XML

Web 2.0
Affiliate Programs
Alert Services
Attention Economy
Building Web Communities
DotNetNuke™
Firefox®
Google Adsense
Google Analytics
Google Base
Google Services
Google Video
Google Web Toolkit
IE7
Internet Advertising
Internet Business Initiative
Internet Video
Mashups
Microformats
Ning™
Recommender Systems
Podcasting
RSS
Search Engine Optimization
Search Engines
Skype™
Virtual Worlds
Web 2.0
Web 3.0

Other Topics
Computer Games
Gadgets and Gizmos
Sudoku

Contents

6 Methods: A Deeper Look   236

7 Arrays   291

12 Graphics and Java 2D™   602

13 Exception Handling   645

14 Files and Streams   679

28 JAX-WS Web Services   1352

29 Formatted Output   1422

30 Strings, Characters and Regular Expressions 1446

A Operator Precedence Chart 1493

B ASCII Character Set 1495

C Keywords and Reserved Words 1496

D Primitive Types 1497

Web Bonus Appendices

Appendices I–Q are available as PDF documents at www.deitel.com/jhtp7/.

Q   Using the Debugger   XCVII

Index   1537

Preface

"Live in fragments no longer, only connect."
—Edgar Morgan Foster

Welcome to Java and *Java How to Program, Seventh Edition*! At Deitel & Associates, we write programming language textbooks and professional books for Prentice Hall, deliver corporate training worldwide and develop Internet businesses. This book was a joy to create. It reflects significant changes to the Java language and to the preferred ways of teaching and learning programming. All of the chapters have been significantly tuned.

New and Updated Features

Here's a list of updates we've made to the sixth and seventh editions of *Java How to Program*:

- We updated the entire book to the new Java Standard Edition 6 ("Mustang") and carefully audited the manuscript against the *Java Language Specification*.

- We audited the presentation against the ACM/IEEE curriculum recommendations and the Computer Science Advanced Placement Examination.

- We reinforced our early classes and objects pedagogy, paying careful attention to the guidance of the college instructors on our review teams to ensure that we got the conceptual level right. The book is object-oriented throughout and the treatment of OOP is clear and accessible. We introduce the basic concepts and terminology of object technology in Chapter 1. Students develop their first customized classes and objects in Chapter 3. Presenting objects and classes in the early chapters gets students "thinking about objects" immediately and mastering these concepts more thoroughly.

- The early classes and objects presentation features Time, Employee and GradeBook class case studies that weave their way through multiple sections and chapters, gradually introducing deeper OO concepts.

- Instructors teaching introductory courses have a broad choice of the amount of GUI and graphics to cover—from none, to a ten-brief-sections introductory sequence, to a deep treatment in Chapters 11, 12 and 22, and Appendix F.

- We tuned our object-oriented presentation to use the latest version of the *UML™ (Unified Modeling Language™)*—the *UML™ 2*—the industry-standard graphical language for modeling object-oriented systems.

- We introduced and tuned the optional OOD/UML 2 automated teller machine (ATM) case study in Chapters 1–8 and 10. We include a web bonus appendix with the complete code implementation. Check out the back cover testimonials.

- We added several substantial object-oriented web programming case studies.

- We updated Chapter 25, Accessing Databases with JDBC, to include JDBC 4 and to use the new Java DB/Apache Derby database management system, in addition to MySQL. The chapter features an OO case study on developing a database-driven address book that demonstrates prepared statements and JDBC 4's automatic driver discovery.

- We added Chapters 26 and 27, Web Applications: Parts 1 and 2, which introduce JavaServer Faces (JSF) technology and use it with Sun Java Studio Creator 2 to build web applications quickly and easily. Chapter 26 includes examples on building web application GUIs, handling events, validating forms and session tracking. The JSF material replaces our previous chapters on servlets and JavaServer Pages (JSP).

- We added Chapter 27, Web Applications: Part 2, that discusses developing Ajax-enabled web applications, using JavaServer Faces and Java BluePrints technology. The chapter features a database-driven multitier web address book application that allows users to add contacts, search for contacts and display contacts' addresses on Google™ Maps. This Ajax-enabled application gives the reader a real sense of Web 2.0 development. The application uses Ajax-enabled JSF components to suggest contact names while the user types a name to locate, and to display a located address on a Google Map.

- We added Chapter 28, JAX-WS Web Services, which uses a tools-based approach to creating and consuming web services—a signature Web 2.0 capability. Case studies include developing blackjack and airline reservation web services.

- We use the new tools-based approach for rapid web applications development; all the tools are available free for download.

- We launched the Deitel Internet Business Initiative with 60 new Resource Centers to support our academic and professional readers. Check out our new Resource Centers (www.deitel.com/resourcecenters.html) including Java SE 6 (Mustang), Java, Java Assessment and Certification, Java Design Patterns, Java EE 5, Code Search Engines and Code Sites, Game programming, Programming Projects and many more. Sign up for the free *Deitel® Buzz Online* e-mail newsletter (www.deitel.com/newsletter/subscribe.html)—each week we announce our latest Resource Center(s) and include other items of interest to our readers.

- We discuss key software engineering community concepts, such as Web 2.0, Ajax, SOA, web services, open source software, design patterns, mashups, refactoring, extreme programming, agile software development, rapid prototyping and more.

- We completely reworked Chapter 23, Multithreading [special thanks to Brian Goetz and Joseph Bowbeer—co-authors of *Java Concurrency in Practice*, Addison-Wesley, 2006].

- We discuss the new SwingWorker class for developing multithreaded user interfaces.

- We discuss the new Java Desktop Integration Components (JDIC), such as splash screens and interactions with the system tray.

- We discuss the new `GroupLayout` layout manager in the context of the NetBeans 5.5 Matisse GUI design tool to create portable GUIs that adhere to the underlying platform's GUI design guidelines.

- We present the new `JTable` sorting and filtering capabilities which allow the user to re-sort the data in a `JTable` and filter it by regular expressions.

- We present an in-depth treatment of generics and generic collections.

- We introduce mashups—applications typically built by calling the web services (and/or using the RSS feeds) of two or more other sites—another Web 2.0 signature capability.

- We discuss the new `StringBuilder` class, which performs better than `StringBuffer` in non-threaded applications.

- We present annotations, which greatly reduce the amount of code you have to write to build applications.

Capabilities introduced in Java How to Program, Sixth Edition include:

- obtaining formatted input with class `Scanner`
- displaying formatted output with the `System.out` object's `printf` method
- enhanced `for` statements to process array elements and collections
- declaring methods with variable-length argument lists ("varargs")
- using `enum` classes that declare sets of constants
- importing the `static` members of one class for use in another
- converting primitive-type values to type-wrapper objects and vice versa, using autoboxing and auto-unboxing, respectively
- using generics to create general models of methods and classes that can be declared once, but used with many different data types
- using the generics-enhanced data structures of the Collections API
- using the Concurrency API to implement multithreaded applications
- using JDBC `RowSets` to access data in a database

All of this has been carefully reviewed by distinguished academics and industry developers who worked with us on *Java How to Program, 6/e* and *Java How to Program, 7/e.*

We believe that this book and its support materials will provide students and professionals with an informative, interesting, challenging and entertaining Java educational experience. The book includes a comprehensive suite of ancillary materials that help instructors maximize their students' learning experience.

Java How to Program, 7/e presents hundreds of complete, working Java programs and depicts their inputs and outputs. This is our signature "live-code" approach—we present most Java programming concepts in the context of complete working programs.

As you read this book, if you have questions, send an e-mail to deitel@deitel.com; we'll respond promptly. For updates on this book and the status of all supporting Java software, and for the latest news on all Deitel publications and services, visit www.deitel.com.

Sign up at www.deitel.com/newsletter/subscribe.html for the free *Deitel® Buzz Online* e-mail newsletter and check out www.deitel.com/resourcecenters.html for our growing list of Resource Centers.

Using the UML 2 to Develop an Object-Oriented Design of an ATM. UML 2 has become the preferred graphical modeling language for designing object-oriented systems. All the UML diagrams in the book comply with the UML 2 specification. We use UML activity diagrams to demonstrate the flow of control in each of Java's control statements, and we use UML class diagrams to visually represent classes and their inheritance relationships.

We include an optional (but highly recommended) case study on object-oriented design using the UML. The case study was reviewed by a distinguished team of OOD/ UML academic and industry professionals, including leaders in the field from Rational (the creators of the UML) and the Object Management Group (responsible for evolving the UML). In the case study, we design and fully implement the software for a simple automated teller machine (ATM). The Software Engineering Case Study sections at the ends of Chapters 1–8 and 10 present a carefully paced introduction to object-oriented design using the UML. We introduce a concise, simplified subset of the UML 2, then guide the reader through a first design experience intended for the novice. The case study is not an exercise; rather, it is an end-to-end learning experience that concludes with a detailed walkthrough of the complete Java code. The Software Engineering Case Study sections help students develop an object-oriented design to complement the object-oriented programming concepts they begin learning in Chapter 1 and implementing in Chapter 3. In the first of these sections at the end of Chapter 1, we introduce basic concepts and terminology of OOD. In the optional Software Engineering Case Study sections at the ends of Chapters 2–5, we consider more substantial issues, as we undertake a challenging problem with the techniques of OOD. We analyze a typical requirements document that specifies a system to be built, determine the objects needed to implement that system, determine the attributes these objects need to have, determine the behaviors these objects need to exhibit, and specify how the objects must interact with one another to meet the system requirements. In a web bonus appendix, we include a complete Java code implementation of the object-oriented system that we designed in the earlier chapters. This case study helps prepare students for the kinds of substantial projects they will encounter in industry. We employ a carefully developed, incremental object-oriented design process to produce a UML 2 model for our ATM system. From this design, we produce a substantial working Java implementation using key object-oriented programming notions, including classes, objects, encapsulation, visibility, composition, inheritance and polymorphism.

Dependency Chart

The chart on the next page shows the dependencies among the chapters to help instructors plan their syllabi. *Java How to Program, 7/e* is a large book which is appropriate for a variety of programming courses at various levels. Chapters 1–14 form an accessible elementary programming sequence with a solid introduction to object-oriented programming. Chapters 11, 12, 20, 21 and 22 form a substantial GUI, graphics and multimedia sequence. Chapters 15–19 form a nice data structures sequence. Chapters 24–28 form a clear database-intensive web development sequence.

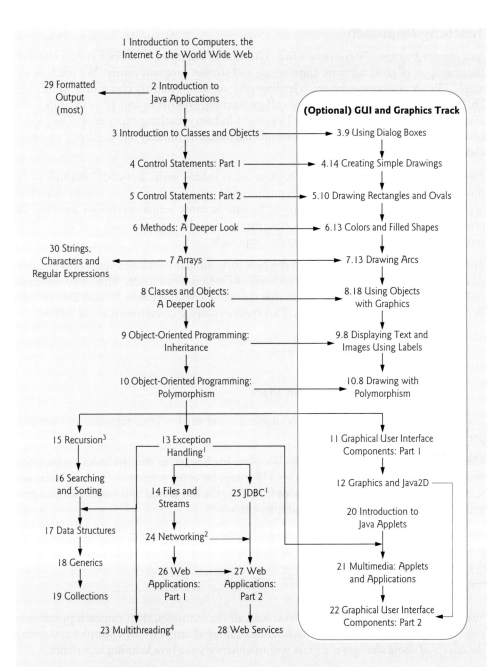

1 Introduction to Computers, the
Internet & the World Wide Web

29 Formatted
Output
(most)

2 Introduction to
Java Applications

3 Introduction to Classes and Objects

4 Control Statements: Part 1

5 Control Statements: Part 2

6 Methods: A Deeper Look

30 Strings,
Characters and
Regular Expressions

7 Arrays

8 Classes and Objects:
A Deeper Look

9 Object-Oriented Programming:
Inheritance

10 Object-Oriented Programming:
Polymorphism

15 Recursion[3]

16 Searching
and Sorting

17 Data Structures

18 Generics

19 Collections

13 Exception
Handling[1]

14 Files and
Streams

25 JDBC[1]

24 Networking[2]

26 Web
Applications:
Part 1

27 Web
Applications:
Part 2

23 Multithreading[4]

28 Web Services

(Optional) GUI and Graphics Track

3.9 Using Dialog Boxes

4.14 Creating Simple Drawings

5.10 Drawing Rectangles and Ovals

6.13 Colors and Filled Shapes

7.13 Drawing Arcs

8.18 Using Objects
with Graphics

9.8 Displaying Text and
Images Using Labels

10.8 Drawing with
Polymorphism

11 Graphical User Interface
Components: Part 1

12 Graphics and Java2D

20 Introduction to
Java Applets

21 Multimedia: Applets
and Applications

22 Graphical User Interface
Components: Part 2

1. Chapters 13 and 25 are dependent on Chapter 11 for GUI used in one example.
2. Chapter 24 is dependent on Chapter 20 for one example that uses an applet. The large case study at the end of this chapter depends on Chapter 22 for GUI and Chapter 23 for multithreading.
3. Chapter 15 is dependent on Chapters 11 and 12 for GUI and graphics used in one example.
4. Chapter 23 is dependent on Chapter 11 for GUI used in one example, and Chapters 18–19 for one example.

Teaching Approach

Java How to Program, 7/e contains a rich collection of examples. The book concentrates on the principles of good software engineering and stresses program clarity. We teach by example. We are educators who teach leading-edge topics in industry classrooms worldwide. Dr. Harvey M. Deitel has 20 years of college teaching experience and 17 years of industry teaching experience. Paul Deitel has 15 years of industry teaching experience. The Deitels have taught courses at all levels to government, industry, military and academic clients of Deitel & Associates.

Live-Code Approach. *Java How to Program, 7/e* is loaded with "live-code" examples—by this we mean that each new concept is presented in the context of a complete working Java application that is immediately followed by one or more actual executions showing the program's inputs and outputs. This style exemplifies the way we teach and write about programming; we call this the "live-code" approach.

Syntax Coloring. We syntax color all the Java code, similar to the way most Java integrated-development environments and code editors syntax color code. This improves code readability—an important goal, given that this book contains about 20,000 lines of code in complete, working Java programs. Our syntax-coloring conventions are as follows:

```
comments appear in green
keywords appear in dark blue
errors appear in red
constants and literal values appear in light blue
all other code appears in black
```

Code Highlighting. We place gray rectangles around the key code segments in each program.

Using Fonts and Colors for Emphasis. We place the key terms and the index's page reference for each defining occurrence in bold blue text for easier reference. We emphasize on-screen components in the **bold Helvetica** font (e.g., the **File** menu) and emphasize Java program text in the Lucida font (for example, int x = 5).

Web Access. All of the source-code examples for *Java How to Program, 7/e* (and for our other publications) are available for download from:

```
www.deitel.com/books/jhtp7
www.prenhall.com/deitel
```

Site registration is quick and easy. Download all the examples, then run each program as you read the corresponding text discussions. Making changes to the examples and seeing the effects of those changes is a great way to enhance your Java learning experience.

Objectives. Each chapter begins with a statement of objectives. This lets you know what to expect and gives you an opportunity, after reading the chapter, to determine if you have met the objectives.

Quotations. The learning objectives are followed by quotations. Some are humorous, philosophical or offer interesting insights. We hope that you enjoy relating the quotations to the chapter material.

Outline. The chapter outline helps you approach the material in a top-down fashion, so you can anticipate what is to come and set a comfortable and effective learning pace.

Illustrations/Figures. Abundant charts, tables, line drawings, programs and program output are included. We model the flow of control in control statements with UML activity diagrams. UML class diagrams model the fields, constructors and methods of classes. We make extensive use of six major UML diagram types in the optional OOD/UML 2 ATM case study.

Programming Tips. We include programming tips to help you focus on important aspects of program development. These tips and practices represent the best we have gleaned from a combined six decades of programming and teaching experience. One of our students—a mathematics major—told us that she feels this approach is like the highlighting of axioms, theorems and corollaries in mathematics books; it provides a basis on which to build good software.

Good Programming Practice

Good Programming Practices *call attention to techniques that will help you produce programs that are clearer, more understandable and more maintainable.*

Common Programming Error

Students tend to make certain kinds of errors frequently. Pointing out these Common Programming Errors *reduces the likelihood that you'll make the same mistakes.*

Error-Prevention Tip

These tips contain suggestions for exposing bugs and removing them from your programs; many describe aspects of Java that prevent bugs from getting into programs in the first place.

Performance Tip

Students like to "turbo charge" their programs. These tips highlight opportunities for making your programs run faster or minimizing the amount of memory that they occupy.

Portability Tip

We include Portability Tips *to help you write code that will run on a variety of platforms and to explain how Java achieves its high degree of portability.*

Software Engineering Observation

The Software Engineering Observations *highlight architectural and design issues that affect the construction of software systems, especially large-scale systems.*

Look-and-Feel Observations

We provide Look-and-Feel Observations *to highlight graphical-user-interface conventions. These observations help you design attractive, user-friendly graphical user interfaces that conform to industry norms.*

Wrap-Up Section. Each of the chapters ends with a brief "wrap-up" section that recaps the chapter content and transitions to the next chapter.

Summary Bullets. Each chapter ends with additional pedagogical devices. We present a thorough, bullet-list-style summary of the chapter, section by section.

Terminology. We include an alphabetized list of the important terms defined in each chapter. Each term also appears in the index, with its defining occurrence highlighted with a bold, blue page number.

Self-Review Exercises and Answers. Extensive self-review exercises and answers are included for self-study.

Exercises. Each chapter concludes with a substantial set of exercises including simple recall of important terminology and concepts; identifying the errors in code samples, writing individual program statements; writing small portions of methods and Java classes; writing complete methods, Java classes and programs; and building major term projects. The large number of exercises enables instructors to tailor their courses to the unique needs of their students and to vary course assignments each semester. Instructors can use these exercises to form homework assignments, short quizzes, major examinations and term projects. [*NOTE:* **Please do not write to us requesting access to the Prentice Hall Instructor's Resource Center. Access is limited strictly to college instructors teaching from the book. Instructors may obtain access only through their Prentice Hall representatives.**] Be sure to check out our Programming Projects Resource Center (`http://www.deitel.com/ProgrammingProjects/`) for lots of additional exercise and project possibilities.

Thousands of Index Entries. We have included an extensive index which is especially useful when you use the book as a reference.

"Double Indexing" of Java Live-Code Examples. For every source-code program in the book, we index the figure caption both alphabetically and as a subindex item under "Examples." This makes it easier to find examples using particular features.

Student Resources Included with *Java How to Program, 7/e*

A number of for-sale Java development tools are available, but you do not need any of these to get started with Java. We wrote *Java How to Program, 7/e* using only the new free Java Standard Edition Development Kit (JDK), version 6.0. The current JDK version can be downloaded from Sun's Java website `java.sun.com/javase/downloads/index.jsp`. This site also contains the JDK documentation downloads.

The CDs that accompany *Java How to Program, 7/e* contain the NetBeans™ 5.5 Integrated Development Environment (IDE) for developing all types of Java applications and Sun Java™ Studio Creator 2 Update 1 for web-application development. Windows and Linux versions of MySQL® 5.0 Community Edition 5.0.27 and MySQL Connector/J 5.0.4 are provided for the database processing performed in Chapters 25–28.

The CD also contains the book's examples and a web page with links to the Deitel & Associates, Inc. website and the Prentice Hall website. This web page can be loaded into a web browser to afford quick access to all the resources.

You can find additional resources and software downloads in our Java SE 6 (Mustang) Resource Center at:

> `www.deitel.com/JavaSE6Mustang/`

Instructor Resources for *Java How to Program, 7/e*

Java How to Program, 7/e has extensive instructor resources. The Prentice Hall *Instructor's Resource Center* contains the *Solutions Manual* with solutions to the vast majority of the end-of-chapter exercises, a *Test Item File* of multiple-choice questions (approximately two per book section) and PowerPoint® slides containing all the code and figures in the text, plus bulleted items that summarize the key points in the text. Instructors can customize the slides. If you are not already a registered faculty member, contact your Prentice Hall representative or visit `vig.prenhall.com/replocator/`.

Computer Science AP Courses

Java How to Program, 7/e is a suitable textbook for teaching AP Computer Science classes and for preparing students to take the corresponding exams. *Java How to Program, 7/e* covers the vast majority of the information required for the exams. For detailed information on the Computer Science AP curriculum, please visit

> `apcentral.collegeboard.com`

Deitel® Buzz Online Free E-mail Newsletter

Each week, the *Deitel® Buzz Online* announces our latest Resource Center(s) and includes commentary on industry trends and developments, links to free articles and resources from our published books and upcoming publications, product-release schedules, errata, challenges, anecdotes, information on our corporate instructor-led training courses and more. It's also a good way for you to keep posted about issues related to *Java How to Program, 7/e*. To subscribe, visit

> `www.deitel.com/newsletter/subscribe.html`

What's New at Deitel

Resource Centers and the Deitel Internet Business Initiative. We have created many online Resource Centers (at `www.deitel.com/resourcecenters.html`) to enhance your Java learning experience. We announce new Resource Centers in each issue of the *Deitel® Buzz Online*. Those of particular interest to readers of this book include Java, Java Certification, Java Design Patterns, Java EE 5, Java SE 6, AJAX, Apache, Code Search Engines and Code Sites, Eclipse, Game Programming, Mashups, MySQL, Open Source, Programming Projects, Web 2.0, Web 3.0, Web Services and XML. Additional Deitel Resource Centers include Affiliate Programs, Alert Services, ASP.NET, Attention Economy, Building Web Communities, C, C++, C#, Computer Games, DotNetNuke, Firefox, Gadgets, Google AdSense, Google Analytics, Google Base, Google Services, Google Video, Google Web Toolkit, IE7, Internet Business Initiative, Internet Advertising, Internet Video, Linux, Microformats, .NET, Ning, OpenGL, Perl, PHP, Podcasting, Python, Recommender Systems, RSS, Ruby, Search Engines, Search Engine Optimization, Skype, Sudoku, Virtual Worlds, Visual Basic, Wikis, Windows Vista, WinFX and many more coming.

Free Content Initiative. We are pleased to bring you guest articles and free tutorials selected from our current and forthcoming publications as part of our Free Content Initiative. In each issue of the *Deitel® Buzz Online* newsletter, we announce the latest additions to our free content library.

Acknowledgments

It is a great pleasure to acknowledge the efforts of many people whose names may not appear on the cover, but whose hard work, cooperation, friendship and understanding were crucial to the production of the book. Many people at Deitel & Associates, Inc. devoted long hours to this project—thanks especially to Abbey Deitel and Barbara Deitel.

We'd also like to thank two participants of our Honors Internship program who contributed to this publication—Megan Schuster, a computer science major at Swarthmore College, and Henry Klementowicz, a computer science major at Columbia University.

We'd like to mention again our colleagues who made substantial contributions to *Java How to Program 6/e:* Andrew B. Goldberg, Jeff Listfield, Su Zhang, Cheryl Yaeger, Jing Hu, Sin Han Lo, John Paul Casiello, and Christi Kelsey.

We are fortunate to have worked on this project with the talented and dedicated team of publishing professionals at Prentice Hall. We appreciate the extraordinary efforts of Marcia Horton, Editorial Director of Prentice Hall's Engineering and Computer Science Division. Jennifer Cappello and Dolores Mars did an extraordinary job recruiting the book's review team and managing the review process. Francesco Santalucia (an independent artist) and Kristine Carney of Prentice Hall did a wonderful job designing the book's cover; we provided the concept, and they made it happen. Vince O'Brien, Bob Engelhardt, Donna Crilly and Marta Samsel did a marvelous job managing the book's production.

We wish to acknowledge the efforts of our reviewers. Adhering to a tight time schedule, they scrutinized the text and the programs, providing countless suggestions for improving the accuracy and completeness of the presentation.

We sincerely appreciate the efforts of our sixth edition post-publication reviewers and our seventh edition reviewers:

Java How to Program, 7/e Reviewers (including 6/e Post-Publication Reviewers)
Sun Microsystems Reviewers: Lance Andersen (JDBC/Rowset Specification Lead, Java SE Engineering), Ed Burns, Ludovic Champenois (Sun's Application Server for Java EE programmers with Sun Application Server and tools—NetBeans, Studio Enterprise and Studio Creator), James Davidson, Vadiraj Deshpande (Java Enterprise System Integration Group, Sun Microsystems India), Sanjay Dhamankar (Core Developer Platform Group), Jesse Glick (NetBeans Group), Brian Goetz (author of *Java Concurrency in Practice,* Addison-Wesley, 2006), Doug Kohlert (Web Technologies and Standards Group), Sandeep Konchady (Java Software Engineering Organization), John Morrison (Sun Java System Portal Server Product Group), Winston Prakash, Brandon Taylor (SysNet group within the Software Division), and Jayashri Visvanathan (Sun Microsystems Java Studio Creator Team). **Academic and Industry Reviewers:** Akram Al-Rawi (King Faisal University), Mark Biamonte (DataDirect), Ayad Boudiab (International School of Choueifat, Lebanon), Joe Bowbeer (Mobile App Consulting), Harlan Brewer (Select Engineering Services), Marita Ellixson (Eglin AFB, Indiana Wesleyan University, Lead Facilitator), John Goodson (DataDirect), Anne Horton (Lockheed Martin), Terrell Regis Hull (Logicalis Integration Solutions), Clark Richey (RABA Technologies, LLC, Java Sun Champion), Manfred Riem (Utah Interactive, LLC, Java Sun Champion), Karen Tegtmeyer (Model Technologies, Inc.), David Wolff (Pacific Lutheran University), and Hua Yan (Borough of Manhattan Community College, City University of New York). **Java How to Program, 6/e Post-Publication Reviewers:** Anne Horton (Lockheed Martin), William Martz (Uni-

versity of Colorado at Colorado Springs), Bill O'Farrell (IBM), Jeffry Babb (Virginia Commonwealth University), Jeffrey Six (University of Delaware, Adjunct Faculty), Jesse Glick (Sun Microsystems), Karen Tegtmeyer (Model Technologies, Inc.), Kyle Gabhart (L-3 Communications), Marita Ellixson (Eglin AFB, Indiana Wesleyan University, Lead Facilitator), and Sean Santry (Independent Consultant).

Java How to Program, 6/e Reviewers (Including 5/e Post-Publication Reviewers)
Academic Reviewers: Karen Arlien (Bismarck State College), Ben Blake (Cleveland State University), Walt Bunch (Chapman University), Marita Ellixson (Eglin AFB/University of Arkansas), Ephrem Eyob (Virginia State University), Bjorn Foss (Florida Metropolitan University), Bill Freitas (The Lawrenceville School), Joe Kasprzyk (Salem State College), Brian Larson (Modesto Junior College), Roberto Lopez-Herrejon (University of Texas at Austin), Dean Mellas (Cerritos College), David Messier (Eastern University), Andy Novobilski (University of Tennessee, Chattanooga), Richard Ord (University of California, San Diego), Gavin Osborne (Saskatchewan Institute of Applied Science & Technology), Donna Reese (Mississippi State University), Craig Slinkman (University of Texas at Arlington), Sreedhar Thota (Western Iowa Tech Community College), Mahendran Velauthapillai (Georgetown University), Loran Walker (Lawrence Technological University), and Stephen Weiss (University of North Carolina at Chapel Hill). **Industry Reviewers:** Butch Anton (Wi-Tech Consulting), Jonathan Bruce (Sun Microsystems, Inc.—JCP Specification Lead for JDBC), Gilad Bracha (Sun Microsystems, Inc.—JCP Specification Lead for Generics), Michael Develle (Independent Consultant), Jonathan Gadzik (Independent Consultant), Brian Goetz (Quiotix Corporation (JCP Concurrency Utilities Specification Expert Group Member), Anne Horton (AT&T Bell Laboratories), James Huddleston (Independent Consultant), Peter Jones (Sun Microsystems, Inc.), Doug Kohlert (Sun Microsystems, Inc.), Earl LaBatt (Altaworks Corp./ University of New Hampshire), Paul Monday (Sun Microsystems, Inc.), Bill O'Farrell (IBM), Cameron Skinner (Embarcadero Technologies, Inc.), Brandon Taylor (Sun Microsystems, Inc.), and Karen Tegtmeyer (Independent Consultant). **OOD/UML Optional Case Study Reviewers:** Sinan Si Alhir (Independent Consultant), Gene Ames (Star HRG), Jan Bergandy (University of Massachusetts at Dartmouth), Marita Ellixson (Eglin AFB/University of Arkansas), Jonathan Gadzik (Independent Consultant), Thomas Harder (ITT ESI, Inc.), James Huddleston (Independent Consultant), Terrell Hull (Independent Consultant), Kenneth Hussey (IBM), Joe Kasprzyk (Salem State College), Dan McCracken (City College of New York), Paul Monday (Sun Microsystems, Inc.), Davyd Norris (Rational Software), Cameron Skinner (Embarcadero Technologies, Inc.), Craig Slinkman (University of Texas at Arlington), and Steve Tockey (Construx Software).

These reviewers scrutinized every aspect of the text and made countless suggestions for improving the accuracy and completeness of the presentation.

Well, there you have it! Java is a powerful programming language that will help you write programs quickly and effectively. It scales nicely into the realm of enterprise systems development to help organizations build their critical information systems. As you read the book, we would sincerely appreciate your comments, criticisms, corrections and suggestions for improving the text. Please address all correspondence to:

deitel@deitel.com

We'll respond promptly, and post corrections and clarifications on:

www.deitel.com/books/jHTP7/

We hope you enjoy reading *Java How to Program, Seventh Edition* as much as we enjoyed writing it!

Paul J. Deitel
Dr. Harvey M. Deitel

Maynard, Massachusetts
December 2006

About the Authors

Paul J. Deitel, CEO and Chief Technical Officer of Deitel & Associates, Inc., is a graduate of MIT's Sloan School of Management, where he studied Information Technology. He holds the Java Certified Programmer and Java Certified Developer certifications, and has been designated by Sun Microsystems as a Java Champion. Through Deitel & Associates, Inc., he has delivered Java, C, C++, C# and Visual Basic courses to industry clients, including IBM, Sun Microsystems, Dell, Lucent Technologies, Fidelity, NASA at the Kennedy Space Center, the National Severe Storm Laboratory, White Sands Missile Range, Rogue Wave Software, Boeing, Stratus, Cambridge Technology Partners, Open Environment Corporation, One Wave, Hyperion Software, Adra Systems, Entergy, CableData Systems, Nortel Networks, Puma, iRobot, Invensys and many more. He has also lectured on Java and C++ for the Boston Chapter of the Association for Computing Machinery. He and his father, Dr. Harvey M. Deitel, are the world's best-selling programming language textbook authors.

    Dr. Harvey M. Deitel, Chairman and Chief Strategy Officer of Deitel & Associates, Inc., has 45 years of academic and industry experience in the computer field. Dr. Deitel earned B.S. and M.S. degrees from the MIT and a Ph.D. from Boston University. He has 20 years of college teaching experience, including earning tenure and serving as the Chairman of the Computer Science Department at Boston College before founding Deitel & Associates, Inc., with his son, Paul J. Deitel. He and Paul are the co-authors of several dozen books and multimedia packages and they are writing many more. With translations published in Japanese, German, Russian, Spanish, Traditional Chinese, Simplified Chinese, Korean, French, Polish, Italian, Portuguese, Greek, Urdu and Turkish, the Deitels' texts have earned international recognition. Dr. Deitel has delivered hundreds of professional seminars to major corporations, academic institutions, government organizations and the military.

About Deitel & Associates, Inc.

Deitel & Associates, Inc., is an internationally recognized corporate training and content-creation organization specializing in computer programming languages, Internet and World Wide Web software technology, object technology education and Internet business development through its Internet Business Initiative. The company provides instructor-led courses on major programming languages and platforms, such as Java, Advanced Java,

C, C++, C#, Visual C++, Visual Basic, XML, Perl, Python, object technology and Internet and World Wide Web programming. The founders of Deitel & Associates, Inc., are Dr. Harvey M. Deitel and Paul J. Deitel. The company's clients include many of the world's largest companies, government agencies, branches of the military, and academic institutions. Through its 30-year publishing partnership with Prentice Hall, Deitel & Associates, Inc. publishes leading-edge programming textbooks, professional books, interactive multimedia *Cyber Classrooms*, *Complete Training Courses*, Web-based training courses and e-content for the popular course management systems WebCT, Blackboard and Pearson's CourseCompass. Deitel & Associates, Inc., and the authors can be reached via e-mail at:

deitel@deitel.com

To learn more about Deitel & Associates, Inc., its publications and its worldwide *DIVE INTO*® Series Corporate Training curriculum, visit:

www.deitel.com

and subscribe to the free *Deitel*® *Buzz Online* e-mail newsletter at:

www.deitel.com/newsletter/subscribe.html

Check out the growing list of online Deitel Resource Centers at:

www.deitel.com/resourcecenters.html

Individuals wishing to purchase Deitel publications can do so through:

www.deitel.com/books/index.html

Bulk orders by corporations, the government, the military and academic institutions should be placed directly with Prentice Hall. For more information, visit

www.prenhall.com/mischtm/support.html#order

Before You Begin

Please follow the instructions in this section to ensure that Java is installed properly on your computer before you begin using this book.

Font and Naming Conventions

We use fonts to distinguish between on-screen components (such as menu names and menu items) and Java code or commands. Our convention is to emphasize on-screen components in a sans-serif bold **Helvetica** font (for example, **File** menu) and to emphasize Java code and commands in a sans-serif Lucida font (for example, System.out.println()).

Java Standard Edition Development Kit (JDK) 6

The examples in this book were developed with the Java Standard Edition Development Kit (JDK) 6. You can download the latest version of JDK 6 and its documentation from

> java.sun.com/javase/6/download.jsp

If you have any questions, please feel free to email us at deitel@deitel.com. We will respond promptly.

Software and Hardware System Requirements

- 500 MHz (minimum) Pentium III or faster processor; Sun® Java™ Studio Creator 2 Update 1 requires a 1 GHz Intel Pentium 4 processor (or equivalent)
- Microsoft Windows Server 2003, Windows XP (with Service Pack 2), Windows 2000 Professional (with Service Pack 4) or
- One of the following Linux distributions: Red Hat® Enterprise Linux 3, or Red Hat Fedora Core 3
- Minimum of 512 MB of RAM; Sun Java Studio Creator 2 Update 1 requires 1 GB of RAM
- Minimum of 1.5 GB of hard disk space
- CD-ROM drive
- Internet connection
- Web browser, Adobe® Acrobat® Reader® and a zip decompression utility

Using the CDs

The examples for *Java How To Program, Seventh Edition* are included on the CDs (Windows and Linux) that accompany this book. Follow the steps in the next section, *Copying the Book Examples from the CD*, to copy the examples directory from the appropriate CD to your hard drive. We suggest that you work from your hard drive rather than your CD drive for two reasons: The CDs are read-only, so you cannot save your applications to the CDs, and files can be accessed faster from a hard drive than from a CD. The examples from the book are also available for download from:

```
www.deitel.com/books/jhtp7/
www.prenhall.com/deitel/
```

The interface to the contents of the Microsoft® Windows® CD is designed to start automatically through the AUTORUN.EXE file. If a startup screen does not appear when you insert the CD into your computer, double click the welcome.htm file to launch the Student CD's interface or refer to the file readme.txt on the CD. To launch the Linux CD's interface, double click the welcome.htm file.

Copying the Book Examples from the CD

Screen shots in this section might differ slightly from what you see on your computer, depending on your operating system and web browser. The instructions in the following steps assume you are running Microsoft Windows.

1. *Inserting the CD.* Insert the CD that accompanies *Java How To Program, Seventh Edition* into your computer's CD drive. The welcome.htm web page (Fig. 1) should automatically appear on Windows. You can also use Windows Explorer to view the CD's contents and double click welcome.htm to display this page.

2. *Opening the CD-ROM directory.* Click the **Browse CD Contents** link (Fig. 1) to view the CD's contents.

3. *Copying the* examples *directory.* Right click the examples directory (Fig. 2), then select **Copy**. Next, use Windows Explorer to view the contents of your **C:** drive. (You may need to click a link to display the drive's contents.) Once the contents are displayed, right click anywhere and select the **Edit** menu's **Paste** option to copy the examples directory from the CD to your **C:** drive. [*Note*: We save the

Fig. 1 | Welcome page for *Java How to Program* CD.

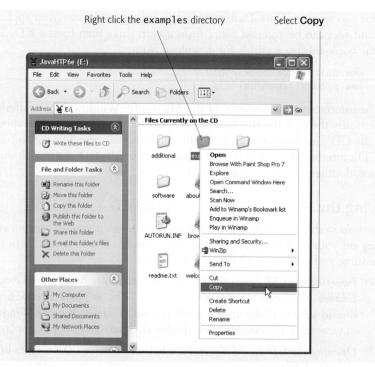

Right click the `examples` directory   Select **Copy**

Fig. 2 | Copying the **examples** directory.

examples to the **C:** drive directly and refer to this drive throughout the text. You may choose to save your files to a different drive based on your computer's set up, the setup in your school's lab or personal preferences. If you are working in a computer lab, please see your instructor for more information to confirm where the examples should be saved.]

Changing the Read-Only Property of Files

The example files you copied to your computer from the CD are read-only. Next, you will remove the read-only property so you can modify and run the examples.

1. *Opening the Properties dialog.* Right click the `examples` directory and select **Properties** from the menu. The **examples Properties** dialog appears (Fig. 3).

2. *Changing the read-only property.* In the **Attributes** section of this dialog, click the box next to **Read-only** to remove the check mark (Fig. 4). Click **Apply** to apply the changes.

3. *Changing the property for all files.* Clicking **Apply** will display the **Confirm Attribute Changes** window (Fig. 5). In this window, click the radio button next to **Apply changes to this folder, subfolders and files** and click **OK** to remove the read-only property for all of the files and directories in the **examples** directory.

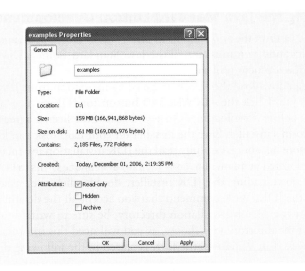

Fig. 3 | **examples Properties** dialog.

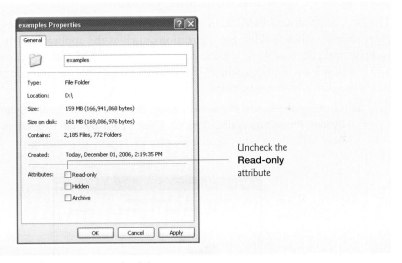

Uncheck the
Read-only
attribute

Fig. 4 | Unchecking the **Read-only** check box.

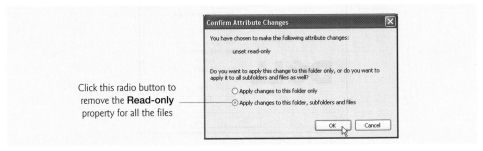

Click this radio button to
remove the **Read-only**
property for all the files

Fig. 5 | Removing read-only for all the files in the **examples** directory.

Installing the Java Standard Edition Development Kit (JDK)

Before you can run the applications in *Java How To Program, Seventh Edition* or build your own applications, you must install the Java Standard Edition Development Kit (JDK) 6 or a Java development tool that supports Java SE 6.

You can download the JDK 6 and its documentation from java.sun.com/javase/6/download.jsp. Click the » **DOWNLOAD** button for JDK 6. You must accept the license agreement before downloading. Once you accept the license agreement, click the link for your platform's installer. Save the installer on your hard disk and keep track of where you save it. Before installing, carefully read the JDK installation instructions for your platform, which are located at java.sun.com/javase/6/webnotes/install/index.html.

After downloading the JDK installer, double click the installer program to begin installing the JDK. We recommend that you accept all the default installation options. If you change the default installation directory, be sure to write down the exact name and location of the directory you choose, as you will need this information later in the installation process. On Windows, the JDK is placed in the following directory by default:

```
C:\Program Files\Java\jdk1.6.0
```

Setting the PATH Environment Variable

The PATH environment variable on your computer designates which directories the computer searches when looking for applications, such as the applications that enable you to compile and run your Java applications (called javac.exe and java.exe, respectively). You will now learn how to set the PATH environment variable on your computer to indicate where the JDK's tools are installed.

1. *Opening the System Properties dialog.* **Start > Control Panel > Sytem** to display the **System Properties** dialog (Fig. 6). [*Note*: Your **System Properties** dialog may appear different than the one shown in Fig. 6, depending on your version of

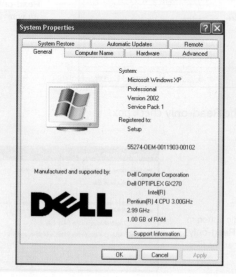

Fig. 6 | **System Properties** dialog.

Microsoft Windows. This particular dialog is from a computer running Microsoft Windows XP. Your dialog might include different information.]

2. *Opening the Environment Variables dialog.* Select the **Advanced** tab at the top of the **System Properties** dialog (Fig. 7). Click the **Environment Variables** button to display the **Environment Variables** dialog (Fig. 8).

3. *Editing the **PATH** variable.* Scroll down inside the **System variables** box to select the PATH variable. Click the **Edit** button. This will cause the **Edit System Variable** dialog to appear (Fig. 9).

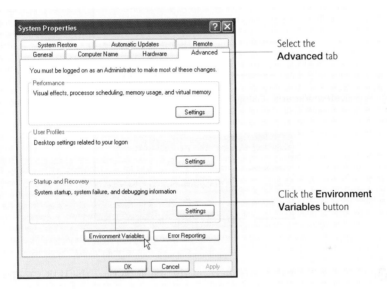

Fig. 7 | Advanced tab of **System Properties** dialog.

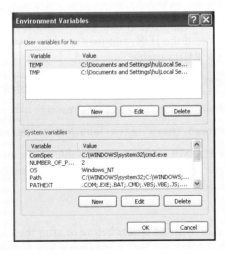

Fig. 8 | Environment Variables dialog.

4. *Changing the PATH.* Place the cursor inside the **Variable Value** field. Use the left-arrow key to move the cursor to the beginning of the list. At the beginning of the list, type the name of the directory in which you placed the JDK followed by \bin; (Fig. 10). Add C:\Program Files\Java\jdk1.6.0\bin; to the PATH variable, if you chose the default installation directory. *Do not place any spaces before or after what you type.* Spaces are not allowed before or after each value in an environment variable. Click the **OK** button to apply your changes to the PATH variable.

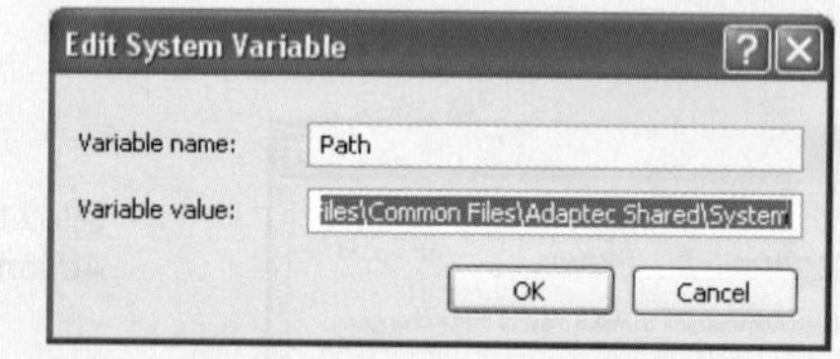

Fig. 9 | Edit **System Variable** dialog.

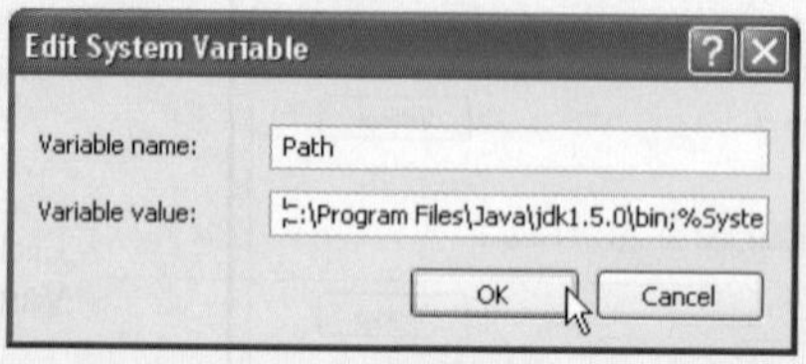

Fig. 10 | Editing the PATH variable.

If you do not set the PATH variable correctly, when you use the JDK's tools, you will receive a message like:

```
'java' is not recognized as an internal or external command,
operable program or batch file.
```

In this case, go back to the beginning of this section and recheck your steps. If you've downloaded a newer version of the JDK, you may need to change the name of the JDK's installation directory in the PATH variable.

Setting the CLASSPATH Environment Variable

If you attempt to run a Java program and receive a message like

```
Exception in thread "main" java.lang.NoClassDefFoundError: YourClass
```

then your system has a CLASSPATH environment variable that must be modified. To fix the preceding error, follow the steps in setting the PATH environment variable, to locate the CLASSPATH variable, then edit the variable's value to include

```
.;
```

at the beginning of its value (with no spaces before or after these characters).

You are now ready to begin your Java studies with *Java How to Program, Seventh Edition.* We hope you enjoy the book!

Introduction to Computers, the Internet and the Web

OBJECTIVES

In this chapter you will learn:

- Basic computer hardware and software concepts.
- Basic object technology concepts, such as classes, objects, attributes, behaviors, encapsulation, inheritance and polymorphism.
- The different types of programming languages.
- Which programming languages are most widely used.
- A typical Java program development environment.
- Java's role in developing distributed client/server applications for the Internet and the web.
- The history of UML—the industry-standard object-oriented design language, the UML.
- The history of the Internet and the World Wide Web.
- To test-drive Java applications.

1.1 Introduction

Welcome to Java! We have worked hard to create what we hope you'll find to be an informative, entertaining and challenging learning experience. Java is a powerful computer programming language that is fun for novices to learn, and appropriate for experienced programmers to use in building substantial information systems. *Java How to Program, Seventh Edition* is an effective learning tool for each of these audiences.

Pedagogy

The core of the book emphasizes achieving program *clarity* through the proven techniques of *object-oriented programming*. Nonprogrammers will learn programming the right way from the beginning. The presentation is clear, straightforward and abundantly illustrated. It includes hundreds of complete working Java programs and shows the outputs produced when those programs are run on a computer. We teach Java features in the context of complete working Java programs—we call this the live-code approach. The example programs are included on the CD that accompanies this book. You may also download them from www.deitel.com/books/jhtp7/ or www.prenhall.com/deitel.

Fundamentals

The early chapters introduce the fundamentals of computers, computer programming and the Java programming language, providing a solid foundation for the deeper treatment of Java in the later chapters. Experienced programmers tend to read the early chapters quickly and find the treatment of Java in the later chapters rigorous and challenging.

Most people are familiar with the exciting tasks computers perform. Using this textbook, you'll learn how to command computers to perform those tasks. It is software (i.e., the instructions you write to command computers to perform **actions** and make **decisions**) that controls computers (often referred to as hardware). Java, developed by Sun Microsystems, is one of today's most popular software development languages.

Java Standard Edition 6 (Java SE 6) and the Java Development Kit 6 (JDK 6)

This book is based on Sun's **Java Standard Edition 6 (Java SE 6)**, also known as Mustang. Sun provides a Java SE 6 implementation, called the **Java Development Kit (JDK)**, that includes the tools you need to write software in Java. We used JDK version 6.0 for the programs in this book. Sun updates the JDK on a regular basis to fix bugs. To download the most recent version of JDK 6, visit `java.sun.com/javase/6/download.jsp`.

Evolution of Computing and Programming

Computer use is increasing in almost every field of endeavor. Computing costs have been decreasing dramatically due to rapid developments in both hardware and software technologies. Computers that might have filled large rooms and cost millions of dollars decades ago can now be inscribed on silicon chips smaller than a fingernail, costing perhaps a few dollars each. Fortunately, silicon is one of the most abundant materials on earth—it is an ingredient in common sand. Silicon chip technology has made computing so economical that about a billion general-purpose computers are in use worldwide, helping people in business, industry and government, and in their personal lives. The number could easily double in the next few years.

Over the years, many programmers learned the programming methodology called structured programming. You will learn structured programming and an exciting newer methodology, **object-oriented programming**. Why do we teach both? Object orientation is the key programming methodology used by programmers today. You will create and work with many software objects in this text. But you will discover that their internal structure is often built using structured-programming techniques. Also, the logic of manipulating objects is occasionally expressed with structured programming.

Language of Choice for Networked Applications

Java has become the language of choice for implementing Internet-based applications and software for devices that communicate over a network. Stereos and other devices in homes are now being networked together by Java technology. At the May 2006 JavaOne conference, Sun announced that there were one billion java-enabled mobile phones and handheld devices! Java has evolved rapidly into the large-scale applications arena. It's the preferred language for meeting many organizations' enterprise-wide programming needs.

Java has evolved so rapidly that this seventh edition of *Java How to Program* was published just 10 years after the first edition was published. Java has grown so large that it has two other editions. The **Java Enterprise Edition (Java EE)** is geared toward developing large-scale, distributed networking applications and web-based applications. The **Java Micro Edition (Java ME)** is geared toward developing applications for small, memory-constrained devices, such as cell phones, pagers and PDAs.

Staying in Touch with Us

You are embarking on a challenging and rewarding path. As you proceed, if you would like to communicate with us, please send e-mail to `deitel@deitel.com` or browse our website at www.deitel.com. We will respond promptly. To keep up to date with Java developments at Deitel & Associates, please register for our free e-mail newsletter, the *Deitel® Buzz Online*, at

> www.deitel.com/newsletter/subscribe.html

For lots of additional Java material, please visit our growing list of Java Resource centers at www.deitel.com/ResourceCenters.html. We hope that you will enjoy learning with *Java How to Program, Seventh Edition.*

1.2 What Is a Computer?

A computer is a device capable of performing computations and making logical decisions at speeds millions (even billions) of times faster than human beings can. For example, many of today's personal computers can perform several billion calculations in one second. A person operating a desk calculator could not perform that many calculations in a lifetime. (Points to ponder: How would you know whether the person added the numbers correctly? How would you know whether the computer added the numbers correctly?) Today's fastest supercomputers are already performing *trillions* of instructions per second!

Computers process data under the control of sets of instructions called computer programs. These programs guide the computer through orderly sets of actions specified by people called computer programmers.

A computer consists of various devices referred to as hardware (e.g., the keyboard, screen, mouse, disks, memory, DVD, CD-ROM and processing units). The programs that run on a computer are referred to as software. Hardware costs have been declining dramatically in recent years, to the point that personal computers have become a commodity. In this book, you'll learn proven methodologies that *can* reduce software development costs—object-oriented programming and (in our optional Software Engineering Case Study in Chapters 2–8 and 10) object-oriented design.

1.3 Computer Organization

Regardless of differences in physical appearance, virtually every computer may be envisioned as divided into six logical units or sections:

1. *Input unit.* This "receiving" section obtains information (data and computer programs) from input devices and places this information at the disposal of the other units so that it can be processed. Most information is entered into computers through keyboards and mouse devices. Information also can be entered in many other ways, including by speaking to your computer, by scanning images and by having your computer receive information from a network, such as the Internet.

2. *Output unit.* This "shipping" section takes information that the computer has processed and places it on various output devices to make the information available for use outside the computer. Most information output from computers today is displayed on screens, printed on paper or used to control other devices. Computers also can output their information to networks, such as the Internet.

3. *Memory unit.* This rapid-access, relatively low-capacity "warehouse" section retains information that has been entered through the input unit, so that it will be immediately available for processing when needed. The memory unit also retains

processed information until it can be placed on output devices by the output unit. Information in the memory unit is typically lost when the computer's power is turned off. The memory unit is often called either memory or primary memory.

4. *Arithmetic and logic unit (ALU).* This "manufacturing" section is responsible for performing calculations, such as addition, subtraction, multiplication and division. It contains the decision mechanisms that allow the computer, for example, to compare two items from the memory unit to determine whether they are equal.

5. *Central processing unit (CPU).* This "administrative" section coordinates and supervises the operation of the other sections. The CPU tells the input unit when information should be read into the memory unit, tells the ALU when information from the memory unit should be used in calculations and tells the output unit when to send information from the memory unit to certain output devices. Many of today's computers have multiple CPUs and, hence, can perform many operations simultaneously—such computers are called multiprocessors.

6. *Secondary storage unit.* This is the long-term, high-capacity "warehousing" section. Programs or data not actively being used by the other units normally are placed on secondary storage devices (e.g., your hard drive) until they are again needed, possibly hours, days, months or even years later. Information in secondary storage takes much longer to access than information in primary memory, but the cost per unit of secondary storage is much less than that of primary memory. Examples of secondary storage devices include CDs and DVDs, which can hold up to hundreds of millions of characters and billions of characters, respectively.

1.4 Early Operating Systems

Early computers could perform only one job or task at a time. This is often called single-user batch processing. The computer runs a single program at a time while processing data in groups or batches. In these early systems, users generally submitted their jobs to a computer center on decks of punched cards and often had to wait hours or even days before printouts were returned to their desks.

Software systems called operating systems were developed to make using computers more convenient. Early operating systems smoothed and speeded up the transition between jobs, increasing the amount of work, or throughput, computers could process.

As computers became more powerful, it became evident that single-user batch processing was inefficient, because so much time was spent waiting for slow input/output devices to complete their tasks. It was thought that many jobs or tasks could *share* the resources of the computer to achieve better utilization. This is called multiprogramming. Multiprogramming involves the simultaneous operation of many jobs that are competing to share the computer's resources. With early multiprogramming operating systems, users still submitted jobs on decks of punched cards and waited hours or days for results.

In the 1960s, several groups in industry and the universities pioneered timesharing operating systems. Timesharing is a special case of multiprogramming in which users access the computer through terminals, typically devices with keyboards and screens. Dozens or even hundreds of users share the computer at once. The computer actually does not run them all simultaneously. Rather, it runs a small portion of one user's job, then moves on to service the next user, perhaps providing service to each user several times per second. Thus, the users' programs *appear* to be running simultaneously. An advantage of timesharing is that user requests receive almost immediate responses.

1.5 Personal, Distributed and Client/Server Computing

In 1977, Apple Computer popularized personal computing. Computers became so economical that people could buy them for their own personal or business use. In 1981, IBM, the world's largest computer vendor, introduced the IBM Personal Computer. This quickly legitimized personal computing in business, industry and government organizations.

These computers were "standalone" units—people transported disks back and forth between them to share information (often called "sneakernet"). Although early personal computers were not powerful enough to timeshare several users, these machines could be linked together in computer networks, sometimes over telephone lines and sometimes in local area networks (LANs) within an organization. This led to the phenomenon of distributed computing, in which an organization's computing, instead of being performed only at some central computer installation, is distributed over networks to the sites where the organization's work is performed. Personal computers were powerful enough to handle the computing requirements of individual users as well as the basic communications tasks of passing information between computers electronically.

Today's personal computers are as powerful as the million-dollar machines of just a few decades ago. The most powerful desktop machines—called workstations—provide individual users with enormous capabilities. Information is shared easily across computer networks where computers called servers store data that may be used by client computers distributed throughout the network, hence the term client/server computing. Java has become widely used for writing software for computer networking and for distributed client/server applications. Today's popular operating systems, such as Linux, Apple's Mac OS X (pronounced "O-S ten") and Microsoft Windows, provide the kinds of capabilities discussed in this section.

1.6 The Internet and the World Wide Web

The Internet—a global network of computers—has its roots in the 1960s with funding supplied by the U.S. Department of Defense. Originally designed to connect the main computer systems of about a dozen universities and research organizations, the Internet is accessible by more than a billion computers and computer-controlled devices worldwide.

With the introduction of the World Wide Web—which allows computer users to locate and view multimedia-based documents on almost any subject over the Internet— the Internet has exploded into one of the world's premier communication mechanisms.

The Internet and the World Wide Web are surely among humankind's most important and profound creations. In the past, most computer applications ran on computers that were not connected to one another. Today's applications can be written to communicate among the world's computers. The Internet mixes computing and communications technologies. It makes our work easier. It makes information instantly and conveniently accessible worldwide. It enables individuals and local small businesses to get worldwide exposure. It is changing the way business is done. People can search for the best prices on virtually any product or service. Special-interest communities can stay in touch with one another. Researchers can be made instantly aware of the latest breakthroughs.

Java How to Program, 7/e presents programming techniques that allow Java applications to use the Internet and the web to interact with other applications. These capabilities and others allow Java programmers to develop the kind of enterprise-level distributed applications that are used in industry today. Java applications can be written to execute on every major type of computer, greatly reducing the time and cost of systems development. If you are interested in developing applications to run over the Internet and the web, learning Java may be the key to rewarding career opportunities for you.

1.7 Machine Languages, Assembly Languages and High-Level Languages

Programmers write instructions in various programming languages, some directly understandable by computers and others requiring intermediate translation steps. Hundreds of computer languages are in use today. These may be divided into three general types:

1. Machine languages

2. Assembly languages

3. High-level languages

Any computer can directly understand only its own machine language. Machine language is the "natural language" of a computer and as such is defined by its hardware design. Machine languages generally consist of strings of numbers (ultimately reduced to 1s and 0s) that instruct computers to perform their most elementary operations one at a time. Machine languages are machine dependent (i.e., a particular machine language can be used on only one type of computer). Such languages are cumbersome for humans, as illustrated by the following section of an early machine-language program that adds overtime pay to base pay and stores the result in gross pay:

```
+1300042774
+1400593419
+1200274027
```

Machine-language programming was simply too slow and tedious for most programmers. Instead of using the strings of numbers that computers could directly understand, programmers began using English-like abbreviations to represent elementary operations. These abbreviations formed the basis of assembly languages. Translator programs called assemblers were developed to convert early assembly-language programs to machine language at computer speeds. The following section of an assembly-language program also adds overtime pay to base pay and stores the result in gross pay:

```
load     basepay
add      overpay
store    grosspay
```

Although such code is clearer to humans, it is incomprehensible to computers until translated to machine language.

Computer usage increased rapidly with the advent of assembly languages, but programmers still had to use many instructions to accomplish even the simplest tasks. To speed the programming process, high-level languages were developed in which single statements could be written to accomplish substantial tasks. Translator programs called compilers convert high-level language programs into machine language. High-level languages allow programmers to write instructions that look almost like everyday English and contain commonly used mathematical notations. A payroll program written in a high-level language might contain a statement such as

```
grossPay = basePay + overTimePay
```

Obviously, high-level languages are preferable to machine and assembly language from the programmer's standpoint. C, C++, Microsoft's .NET languages (e.g., Visual Basic .NET, Visual C++ .NET and C#) are among the most widely used high-level programming languages; Java is *the* most widely used.

The process of compiling a high-level language program into machine language can take a considerable amount of computer time. Interpreter programs were developed to execute high-level language programs directly, although more slowly. Interpreters are popular in program-development environments in which new features are being added and errors corrected. Once a program is fully developed, a compiled version can be produced to run most efficiently.

You now know that there are ultimately two ways to translate a high-level language program into a form that the computer understands—compilation and interpretation. As you will learn in Section 1.13, Java uses a clever mixture of these technologies.

1.8 History of C and C++

Java evolved from C++, which evolved from C, which evolved from BCPL and B. BCPL was developed in 1967 by Martin Richards as a language for writing operating systems software and compilers. Ken Thompson modeled many features in his language B after their counterparts in BCPL, using B to create early versions of the UNIX operating system at Bell Laboratories in 1970.

The C language was evolved from B by Dennis Ritchie at Bell Laboratories and was originally implemented in 1972. It initially became widely known as the development language of the UNIX operating system. Today, most of the code for general-purpose operating systems (e.g., those found in notebooks, desktops, workstations and small servers) is written in C or C++.

C++, an extension of C, was developed by Bjarne Stroustrup in the early 1980s at Bell Laboratories. C++ provides a number of features that "spruce up" the C language, but more important, it provides capabilities for *object-oriented programming* (discussed in more detail in Section 1.16 and throughout this book). C++ is a hybrid language—it is possible to program in either a C-like style, an object-oriented style or both.

A revolution is brewing in the software community. Building software quickly, correctly and economically remains an elusive goal at a time when demands for new and more powerful software are soaring. *Objects*, or more precisely—as we will see in Section 1.16—the classes objects come from, are essentially reusable software components. There are date objects, time objects, audio objects, automobile objects, people objects and so on. In fact, almost any noun can be represented as a software object in terms of attributes (e.g., name, color and size) and behaviors (e.g., calculating, moving and communicating). Software developers are discovering that using a modular, object-oriented design and implementation approach can make software-development groups much more productive than was possible with earlier popular programming techniques like structured programming.

Object-oriented programs are often easier to understand, correct and modify. Java is the world's most widely used object-oriented programming language.

1.9 History of Java

The microprocessor revolution's most important contribution to date is that it made possible the development of personal computers, which now number about a billion worldwide. Personal computers have profoundly affected people's lives and the ways organizations conduct and manage their business.

Microprocessors are having a profound impact in intelligent consumer-electronic devices. Recognizing this, Sun Microsystems in 1991 funded an internal corporate research project code-named Green, which resulted in a C++-based language that its creator, James Gosling, called Oak after an oak tree outside his window at Sun. It was later discovered that there already was a computer language by that name. When a group of Sun people visited a local coffee shop, the name Java was suggested, and it stuck.

The Green project ran into some difficulties. The marketplace for intelligent consumer-electronic devices was not developing in the early 1990s as quickly as Sun had anticipated. The project was in danger of being canceled. By sheer good fortune, the World Wide Web exploded in popularity in 1993, and Sun people saw the immediate potential of using Java to add dynamic content, such as interactivity and animations, to web pages. This breathed new life into the project.

Sun formally announced Java at an industry conference in May 1995. Java garnered the attention of the business community because of the phenomenal interest in the World Wide Web. Java is now used to develop large-scale enterprise applications, to enhance the functionality of web servers (the computers that provide the content we see in our web browsers), to provide applications for consumer devices (e.g., cell phones, pagers and personal digital assistants) and for many other purposes.

1.10 Java Class Libraries

Java programs consist of pieces called classes. Classes include pieces called methods that perform tasks and return information when they complete them. Programmers can create each piece they need to form Java programs. However, most Java programmers take advantage of the rich collections of existing classes in the Java class libraries, which are also known as the Java APIs (Application Programming Interfaces). Thus, there are really two aspects to learning the Java "world." The first is the Java language itself, so that you can program your own classes, and the second is the classes in the extensive Java class libraries. Throughout this book, we discuss many library classes. Class libraries are provided primarily by compiler vendors, but many are supplied by independent software vendors (ISVs).

Software Engineering Observation 1.1

Use a building-block approach to create programs. Avoid reinventing the wheel—use existing pieces wherever possible. This software reuse *is a key benefit of object-oriented programming.*

We include many tips such as these Software Engineering Observations throughout the book to explain concepts that affect and improve the overall architecture and quality of software systems. We also highlight other kinds of tips, including Good Programming Practices (to help you write programs that are clearer, more understandable, more maintainable and easier to test and debug, i.e., remove programming errors), Common Programming Errors (problems to watch out for and avoid), Performance Tips (techniques for writing programs that run faster and use less memory), Portability Tips (techniques to help you write programs that can run, with little or no modification, on a variety of computers—these tips also include general observations about how Java achieves its high degree of portability), Error-Prevention Tips (techniques for removing bugs from your programs and, more important, techniques for writing bug-free programs in the first place) and Look-and-Feel Observations (techniques to help you design the "look" and "feel" of your applications' user interfaces for appearance and ease of use). Many of these are only guidelines. You will, no doubt, develop your own preferred programming style.

Software Engineering Observation 1.2

When programming in Java, you will typically use the following building blocks: classes and methods from class libraries, classes and methods you create yourself and classes and methods that others create and make available to you.

The advantage of creating your own classes and methods is that you know exactly how they work and you can examine the Java code. The disadvantage is the time-consuming and potentially complex effort that is required.

Performance Tip 1.1

Using Java API classes and methods instead of writing your own versions can improve program performance, because they are carefully written to perform efficiently. This technique also shortens program development time.

Portability Tip 1.1

Using classes and methods from the Java API instead of writing your own improves program portability, because they are included in every Java implementation.

Software Engineering Observation 1.3

Extensive class libraries of reusable software components are available over the Internet and the web, many at no charge.

To download the Java API documentation, go to the Sun Java site java.sun.com/javase/6/download.jsp.

1.11 Fortran, COBOL, Pascal and Ada

Hundreds of high-level languages have been developed, but only a few have achieved broad acceptance. Fortran (FORmula TRANslator) was developed by IBM Corporation in the mid-1950s to be used for scientific and engineering applications that require complex mathematical computations. Fortran is still widely used in engineering applications.

COBOL (COmmon Business Oriented Language) was developed in the late 1950s by computer manufacturers, the U.S. government and industrial computer users. COBOL is used for commercial applications that require precise and efficient manipulation of large amounts of data. Much business software is still programmed in COBOL.

During the 1960s, many large software-development efforts encountered severe difficulties. Software deliveries were typically late, costs greatly exceeded budgets and the finished products were unreliable. People began to realize that software development was a far more complex activity than they had imagined. Research in the 1960s resulted in the evolution of structured programming—a disciplined approach to writing programs that are clearer, easier to test and debug and easier to modify than large programs produced with previous techniques.

One of the more tangible results of this research was the development of the Pascal programming language by Professor Niklaus Wirth in 1971. Named after the seventeenth-century mathematician and philosopher Blaise Pascal, it was designed for teaching structured programming in academic environments and rapidly became the preferred programming language in most colleges. Pascal lacks many features needed to make it useful in commercial, industrial and government applications, so it has not been widely accepted in these environments.

The Ada programming language was developed under the sponsorship of the U.S. Department of Defense (DOD) during the 1970s and early 1980s. Hundreds of separate languages were being used to produce the DOD's massive command-and-control software systems. The DOD wanted a single language that would fill most of its needs. The Ada language was named after Lady Ada Lovelace, daughter of the poet Lord Byron. Lady Lovelace is credited with writing the world's first computer program in the early 1800s (for the Analytical Engine mechanical computing device designed by Charles Babbage). One important capability of Ada, called multitasking, allows programmers to specify that many activities are to occur in parallel. Java, through a technique called *multithreading*, also enables programmers to write programs with parallel activities.

1.12 BASIC, Visual Basic, Visual C++, C# and .NET

The BASIC (Beginner's All-Purpose Symbolic Instruction Code) programming language was developed in the mid-1960s at Dartmouth College as a means of writing simple programs. BASIC's primary purpose was to familiarize novices with programming techniques.

Microsoft's Visual Basic language was introduced in the early 1990s to simplify the development of Microsoft Windows applications and is one of the world's most popular programming languages.

Microsoft's latest development tools are part of its corporate-wide strategy for integrating the Internet and the web into computer applications. This strategy is implemented in Microsoft's .NET platform, which provides developers with the capabilities they need to create and run computer applications that can execute on computers distributed across the Internet. Microsoft's three primary programming languages are Visual Basic .NET (based on the original BASIC), Visual C++ .NET (based on C++) and C# (based on C++ and Java, and developed expressly for the .NET platform). Developers using .NET can write software components in the language they are most familiar with then form applications by combining those components with components written in any .NET language.

1.13 Typical Java Development Environment

We now explain the commonly used steps in creating and executing a Java application using a Java development environment (illustrated in Fig. 1.1).

Java programs normally go through five phases—edit, compile, load, verify and execute. We discuss these phases in the context of the JDK 6.0 from Sun Microsystems, Inc., You can download the most up-to-date JDK and its documentation from java.sun.com/

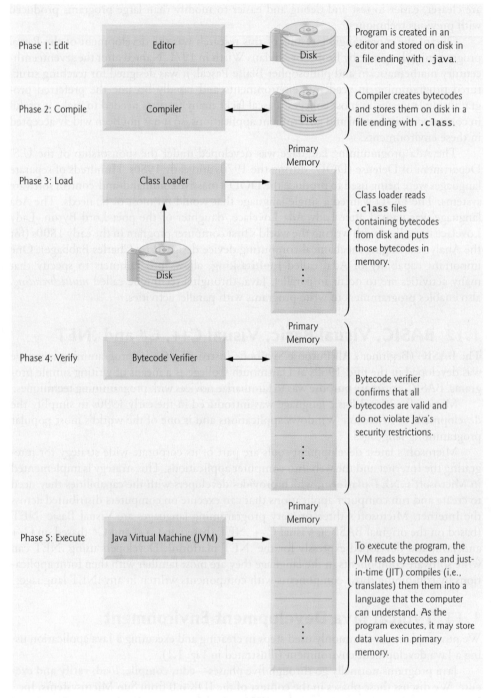

Phase 1: Edit | Editor | Disk — Program is created in an editor and stored on disk in a file ending with .java.

Phase 2: Compile | Compiler | Disk — Compiler creates bytecodes and stores them on disk in a file ending with .class.

Phase 3: Load | Class Loader | Primary Memory | Disk — Class loader reads .class files containing bytecodes from disk and puts those bytecodes in memory.

Phase 4: Verify | Bytecode Verifier | Primary Memory — Bytecode verifier confirms that all bytecodes are valid and do not violate Java's security restrictions.

Phase 5: Execute | Java Virtual Machine (JVM) | Primary Memory — To execute the program, the JVM reads bytecodes and just-in-time (JIT) compiles (i.e., translates) them them into a language that the computer can understand. As the program executes, it may store data values in primary memory.

Fig. 1.1 | Typical Java development environment.

javase/6/download.jsp. Carefully follow the installation instructions for the JDK provided in the Before You Begin *section of this book (or at* java.sun.com/javase/6/webnotes/ install/index.html*) to ensure that you set up your computer properly to compile and execute Java programs.* You may also want to visit Sun's New to Java Center at:

java.sun.com/developer/onlineTraining/new2java/index.html

[*Note:* This website provides installation instructions for Windows, Linux and Mac OS X. If you are not using one of these operating systems, refer to the manuals for your system's Java environment or ask your instructor how to accomplish these tasks based on your computer's operating system. In addition, please keep in mind that web links occasionally break as companies evolve their websites. If you encounter a problem with this link or any other links referenced in this book, please check www.deitel.com for errata and please notify us by e-mail at deitel@deitel.com. We will respond promptly.]

Phase 1: Creating a Program

Phase 1 consists of editing a file with an editor program (normally known simply as an editor). You type a Java program (typically referred to as source code) using the editor, make any necessary corrections and save the program on a secondary storage device, such as your hard drive. A file name ending with the .java extension indicates that the file contains Java source code. We assume that the reader knows how to edit a file.

Two editors widely used on Linux systems are vi and emacs. On Windows, a simple editing program like Windows Notepad will suffice. Many freeware and shareware editors are also available for download from the Internet on sites like www.download.com.

For organizations that develop substantial information systems, integrated development environments (IDEs) are available from many major software suppliers, including Sun Microsystems. IDEs provide tools that support the software development process, including editors for writing and editing programs and debuggers for locating logic errors.

Popular IDEs include Eclipse (www.eclipse.org), NetBeans (www.netbeans.org), JBuilder (www.borland.com), JCreator (www.jcreator.com), BlueJ (www.bluej.org), jGRASP (www.jgrasp.org) and jEdit (www.jedit.org). Sun Microsystems's Java Studio Enterprise (developers.sun.com/prodtech/javatools/jsenterprise/index.jsp) is an enhanced version of NetBeans. [*Note:* Most of our example programs should operate properly with any Java integrated development environment that supports the JDK 6.]

Phase 2: Compiling a Java Program into Bytecodes

In Phase 2, the programmer uses the command javac (the Java compiler) to compile a program. For example, to compile a program called Welcome.java, you would type

```
javac Welcome.java
```

in the command window of your system (i.e., the MS-DOS prompt in Windows 95/98/ME, the Command Prompt in Windows NT/2000/XP, the shell prompt in Linux or the Terminal application in Mac OS X). If the program compiles, the compiler produces a .class file called Welcome.class that contains the compiled version of the program.

The Java compiler translates Java source code into bytecodes that represent the tasks to execute in the execution phase (Phase 5). Bytecodes are executed by the Java Virtual Machine (JVM)—a part of the JDK and the foundation of the Java platform. A virtual machine (VM) is a software application that simulates a computer, but hides the underlying operating system and hardware from the programs that interact with the VM. If the same VM is implemented on many computer platforms, applications that it executes can be used on all those platforms. The JVM is one of the most widely used virtual machines.

Unlike machine language, which is dependent on specific computer hardware, byte-codes are platform-independent instructions—they are not dependent on a particular hardware platform. So Java's bytecodes are portable—that is, the same bytecodes can execute on any platform containing a JVM that understands the version of Java in which the bytecodes were compiled. The JVM is invoked by the `java` command. For example, to execute a Java application called Welcome, you would type the command

```
java Welcome
```

in a command window to invoke the JVM, which would then initiate the steps necessary to execute the application. This begins Phase 3.

Phase 3: Loading a Program into Memory
In Phase 3, the program must be placed in memory before it can execute—known as loading. The class loader takes the .class files containing the program's bytecodes and transfers them to primary memory. The class loader also loads any of the .class files provided by Java that your program uses. The .class files can be loaded from a disk on your system or over a network (e.g., your local college or company network, or the Internet).

Phase 4: Bytecode Verification
In Phase 4, as the classes are loaded, the bytecode verifier examines their bytecodes to ensure that they are valid and do not violate Java's security restrictions. Java enforces strong security, to make sure that Java programs arriving over the network do not damage your files or your system (as computer viruses and worms might).

Phase 5: Execution
In Phase 5, the JVM executes the program's bytecodes, thus performing the actions specified by the program. In early Java versions, the JVM was simply an interpreter for Java bytecodes. This caused most Java programs to execute slowly because the JVM would interpret and execute one bytecode at a time. Today's JVMs typically execute bytecodes using a combination of interpretation and so-called just-in-time (JIT) compilation. In this process, The JVM analyzes the bytecodes as they are interpreted, searching for hot spots—parts of the bytecodes that execute frequently. For these parts, a just-in-time (JIT) compiler—known as the Java HotSpot compiler—translates the bytecodes into the underlying computer's machine language. When the JVM encounters these compiled parts again, the faster machine-language code executes. Thus Java programs actually go through two compilation phases—one in which source code is translated into bytecodes (for portability across JVMs on different computer platforms) and a second in which, during execution, the bytecodes are translated into machine language for the actual computer on which the program executes.

Problems That May Occur at Execution Time
Programs might not work on the first try. Each of the preceding phases can fail because of various errors that we'll discuss throughout this book. For example, an executing program might try to divide by zero (an illegal operation for whole-number arithmetic in Java).

This would cause the Java program to display an error message. If this occurs, you would have to return to the edit phase, make the necessary corrections and proceed through the remaining phases again to determine that the corrections fix the problem(s). [*Note:* Most programs in Java input or output data. When we say that a program displays a message, we normally mean that it displays that message on your computer's screen. Messages and other data may be output to other devices, such as disks and hardcopy printers, or even to a network for transmission to other computers.]

Common Programming Error 1.1

Errors like division by zero occur as a program runs, so they are called runtime errors or execution-time errors. Fatal runtime errors cause programs to terminate immediately without having successfully performed their jobs. Nonfatal runtime errors allow programs to run to completion, often producing incorrect results.

1.14 Notes about Java and *Java How to Program, 7/e*

Java is a powerful programming language. Experienced programmers sometimes take pride in creating weird, contorted, convoluted usage of a language. This is a poor programming practice. It makes programs more difficult to read, more likely to behave strangely, more difficult to test and debug, and more difficult to adapt to changing requirements. This book stresses *clarity.* The following is our first Good Programming Practice tip.

Good Programming Practice 1.1

Write your Java programs in a simple and straightforward manner. This is sometimes referred to as KIS ("keep it simple"). Do not "stretch" the language by trying bizarre usages.

You have heard that Java is a portable language and that programs written in Java can run on many different computers. In general, *portability is an elusive goal.*

Portability Tip 1.2

Although it is easier to write portable programs in Java than in most other programming languages, differences between compilers, JVMs and computers can make portability difficult to achieve. Simply writing programs in Java does not guarantee portability.

Error-Prevention Tip 1.1

Always test your Java programs on all systems on which you intend to run them, to ensure that they will work correctly for their intended audiences.

We audited our presentation against Sun's Java documentation for completeness and accuracy. However, Java is a rich language, and no textbook can cover every topic. A web-based version of the Java API documentation can be found at java.sun.com/javase/6/docs/api/index.html or you can download this documentation to your own computer from java.sun.com/javase/6/download.jsp. For additional technical details on many aspects of Java development, visit java.sun.com/reference/docs/index.html.

Good Programming Practice 1.2

Read the documentation for the version of Java you are using. Refer to it frequently to be sure you are aware of the rich collection of Java features and are using them correctly.

Good Programming Practice 1.3

Your computer and compiler are good teachers. If, after carefully reading your Java documentation, you are not sure how a feature of Java works, experiment and see what happens. Study each error or warning message you get when you compile your programs (called compile-time errors *or* compilation errors*), and correct the programs to eliminate these messages.*

Software Engineering Observation 1.4

Some programmers like to read the source code for the Java API classes to determine how the classes work and to learn additional programming techniques.

1.15 Test-Driving a Java Application

In this section, you'll run and interact with your first Java application. You'll begin by running an ATM application that simulates the transactions that take place when using an ATM machine (e.g., withdrawing money, making deposits and checking account balances). You'll learn how to build this application in the optional, object-oriented case study included in Chapters 1–8 and 10. Figure 1.10 at the end of this section suggests other interesting applications that you may also want to test-drive after completing the ATM test-drive. For the purpose of this section, we assume you are running Microsoft Windows.

In the following steps, you'll run the application and perform various transactions. The elements and functionality you see in this application are typical of what you'll learn to program in this book. [*Note:* We use fonts to distinguish between features you see on a screen (e.g., the **Command Prompt**) and elements that are not directly related to a screen. Our convention is to emphasize screen features like titles and menus (e.g., the **File** menu) in a semibold **sans-serif Helvetica** font and to emphasize non-screen elements, such as file names or input (e.g., ProgramName.java) in a sans-serif Lucida font. As you have already noticed, the defining occurrence of each term is set in bold blue. In the figures in this section, we highlight in yellow the user input required by each step and point out significant parts of the application with lines and text. To make these features more visible, we have modified the background color of the **Command Prompt** windows.]

1. *Checking your setup.* Read the *Before You Begin* section of the book to confirm that you have set up Java properly on your computer and that you have copied the book's examples to your hard drive.

2. *Locating the completed application.* Open a **Command Prompt** window. This can be done by selecting **Start > All Programs > Accessories > Command Prompt**. Change to the ATM application directory by typing cd C:\examples\ch01\ATM, then press *Enter* (Fig. 1.2). The command cd is used to change directories.

Using the cd command to
change directories   File location of the ATM application

```
Command Prompt                                                          _ □ ×
C:\>cd C:\examples\ch01\ATM
C:\examples\ch01\ATM>
```

Fig. 1.2 | Opening a Windows XP **Command Prompt** and changing directories.

3. *Running the ATM application.* Type the command java ATMCaseStudy (Fig. 1.3) and press *Enter*. Recall that the java command, followed by the name of the application's .class file (in this case, ATMCaseStudy), executes the application. Specifying the .class extension when using the java command results in an error. [*Note:* Java commands are case sensitive. It is important to type the name of this application with a capital A, T and M in "ATM," a capital C in "Case" and a capital S in "Study." Otherwise, the application will not execute.] If you receive the error message, "Exception in thread "main" java.lang.NoClassDefFound-Error: ATMCaseStudy," your system has a CLASSPATH problem. Please refer to the *Before You Begin* section of the book for instructions to help you fix this problem.

4. *Entering an account number.* When the application first executes, it displays a "Welcome!" greeting and prompts you for an account number. Type 12345 at the "Please enter your account number:" prompt (Fig. 1.4) and press *Enter*.

5. *Entering a PIN.* Once a valid account number is entered, the application displays the prompt "Enter your PIN:". Type "54321" as your valid PIN (Personal Identification Number) and press *Enter*. The ATM main menu containing a list of options will be displayed (Fig. 1.5).

Fig. 1.3 | Using the java command to execute the ATM application.

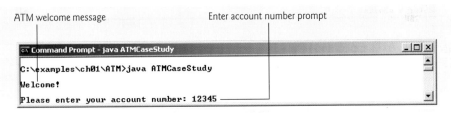

Fig. 1.4 | Prompting the user for an account number.

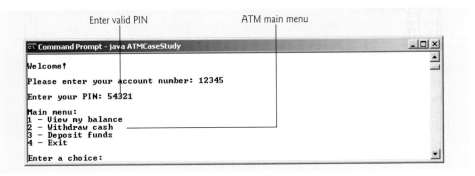

Fig. 1.5 | Entering a valid PIN number and displaying the ATM application's main menu.

6. *Viewing the account balance.* Select option 1, "View my balance", from the ATM menu (Fig. 1.6). The application then displays two numbers—the Available balance ($1000.00) and the Total balance ($1,200.00). The available balance is the maximum amount of money in your account which is available for withdrawal at a given time. In some cases, certain funds, such as recent deposits, are not immediately available for the user to withdraw, so the available balance may be less than the total balance, as it is here. After the account balance information is shown, the application's main menu is displayed again.

7. *Withdrawing money from the account.* Select option 2, "Withdraw cash", from the application menu. You are then presented (Fig. 1.7) with a list of dollar amounts (e.g., 20, 40, 60, 100 and 200). You are also given the option to cancel the transaction and return to the main menu. Withdraw $100 by selecting option 4. The application displays "Please take your cash now." and returns to the main menu. [*Note:* Unfortunately, this application only *simulates* the behavior of a real ATM and thus does not actually dispense money.]

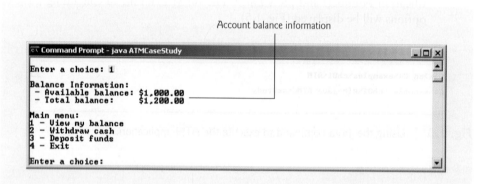

Fig. 1.6 | ATM application displaying user account balance information.

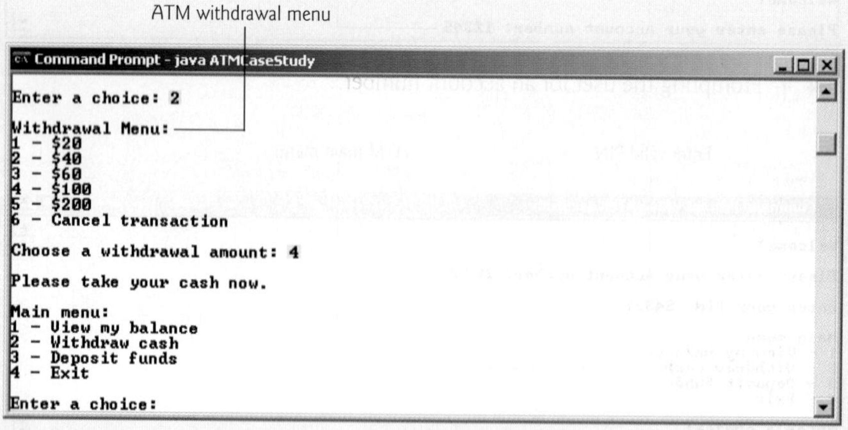

Fig. 1.7 | Withdrawing money from the account and returning to the main menu.

8. *Confirming that the account information has been updated.* From the main menu, select option 1 again to view your current account balance (Fig. 1.8). Note that both the available balance and the total balance have been updated to reflect your withdrawal transaction.

9. *Ending the transaction.* To end your current ATM session, select option 4, "Exit" from the main menu (Fig. 1.9). The ATM will exit the system and display a goodbye message to the user. The application will then return to its original prompt asking for the next user's account number.

10. *Exiting the ATM application and closing the* Command Prompt *window.* Most applications provide an option to exit and return to the Command Prompt directory from which the application was run. A real ATM does not provide a user with the option to turn off the ATM machine. Rather, when a user has completed all desired transactions and chooses the menu option to exit, the ATM resets itself and displays a prompt for the next user's account number. As Fig. 1.9 illustrates, the ATM application here behaves similarly. Choosing the menu option to exit ends only the current user's ATM session, not the entire ATM application. To actually exit the ATM application, click the close (**x**) button in the upper-right corner of the Command Prompt window. Closing the window causes the running application to terminate.

Confirming updated account balance
information after withdrawal transaction

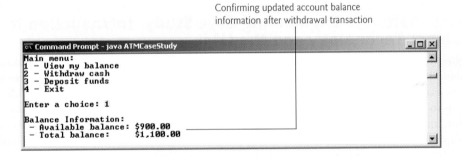

Fig. 1.8 | Checking the new balance.

ATM goodbye message   Account number prompt for next user

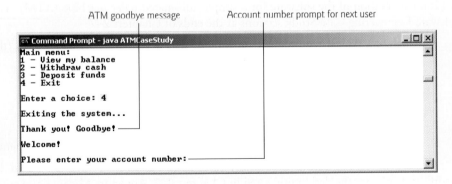

Fig. 1.9 | Ending an ATM transaction session.

Additional Applications Found in **Java How to Program,** 7/e

Figure 1.10 lists a few of the hundreds of applications found in the book's examples and exercises. These programs introduce many of the powerful and fun features of Java. Run these programs to see more of the types of applications you'll learn how to build in this textbook. The examples folder for this chapter contains all the files required to run each application. Simply type the commands listed in Fig. 1.10 in a **Command Prompt** window.

Application Name	Chapter Location	Commands to Run
Tic-Tac-Toe	Chapters 8 and 24	`cd C:\examples\ch01\Tic-Tac-Toe` `java TicTacToeTest`
Guessing Game	Chapter 11	`cd C:\examples\ch01\GuessGame` `java GuessGame`
Logo Animator	Chapter 21	`cd C:\examples\ch01\LogoAnimator` `java LogoAnimator`
Bouncing Ball	Chapter 23	`cd C:\examples\ch01\BouncingBall` `java BouncingBall`

Fig. 1.10 | Examples of additional Java applications found in *Java How to Program, 7/e.*

1.16 Software Engineering Case Study: Introduction to Object Technology and the UML

Now we begin our early introduction to object orientation, a natural way of thinking about the world and writing computer programs. Chapters 1–8 and 10 all end with a brief Software Engineering Case Study section in which we present a carefully paced introduction to object orientation. Our goal here is to help you develop an object-oriented way of thinking and to introduce you to the Unified Modeling Language™ (UML™)—a graphical language that allows people who design software systems to use an industry standard notation to represent them.

In this only required section (1.16), we introduce object-oriented concepts and terminology. The optional sections in Chapters 2–8 and 10 present an object-oriented design and implementation of the software for a simple automated teller machine (ATM). The Software Engineering Case Study sections at the ends of Chapters 2–7

- analyze a typical requirements document that describes a software system (the ATM) to be built
- determine the objects required to implement that system
- determine the attributes the objects will have
- determine the behaviors these objects will exhibit
- specify how the objects interact with one another to meet the system requirements.

The Software Engineering Case Study sections at the ends of Chapters 8 and 10 modify and enhance the design presented in Chapters 2–7. Appendix M contains a complete, working Java implementation of the object-oriented ATM system.

You will experience a concise, yet solid introduction to object-oriented design with the UML. Also, you'll sharpen your code-reading skills by touring the complete, carefully written and well-documented Java implementation of the ATM in Appendix M.

Basic Object Technology Concepts

We begin our introduction to object orientation with some key terminology. Everywhere you look in the real world you see objects—people, animals, plants, cars, planes, buildings, computers and so on. Humans think in terms of objects. Telephones, houses, traffic lights, microwave ovens and water coolers are just a few more objects. Computer programs, such as the Java programs you'll read in this book and the ones you'll write, are composed of lots of interacting software objects.

We sometimes divide objects into two categories: animate and inanimate. Animate objects are "alive" in some sense—they move around and do things. Inanimate objects, on the other hand, do not move on their own. Objects of both types, however, have some things in common. They all have attributes (e.g., size, shape, color and weight), and they all exhibit behaviors (e.g., a ball rolls, bounces, inflates and deflates; a baby cries, sleeps, crawls, walks and blinks; a car accelerates, brakes and turns; a towel absorbs water). We will study the kinds of attributes and behaviors that software objects have.

Humans learn about existing objects by studying their attributes and observing their behaviors. Different objects can have similar attributes and can exhibit similar behaviors. Comparisons can be made, for example, between babies and adults and between humans and chimpanzees.

Object-oriented design (OOD) models software in terms similar to those that people use to describe real-world objects. It takes advantage of class relationships, where objects of a certain class, such as a class of vehicles, have the same characteristics—cars, trucks, little red wagons and roller skates have much in common. OOD also takes advantage of inheritance relationships, where new classes of objects are derived by absorbing characteristics of existing classes and adding unique characteristics of their own. An object of class "convertible" certainly has the characteristics of the more general class "automobile," but more specifically, the roof goes up and down.

Object-oriented design provides a natural and intuitive way to view the software design process—namely, modeling objects by their attributes and behaviors just as we describe real-world objects. OOD also models communication between objects. Just as people send messages to one another (e.g., a sergeant commands a soldier to stand at attention), objects also communicate via messages. A bank account object may receive a message to decrease its balance by a certain amount because the customer has withdrawn that amount of money.

OOD encapsulates (i.e., wraps) attributes and operations (behaviors) into objects—an object's attributes and operations are intimately tied together. Objects have the property of information hiding. This means that objects may know how to communicate with one another across well-defined interfaces, but normally they are not allowed to know how other objects are implemented—implementation details are hidden within the objects themselves. We can drive a car effectively, for instance, without knowing the details of how engines, transmissions, brakes and exhaust systems work internally—as long as we know how to use the accelerator pedal, the brake pedal, the wheel and so on. Information hiding, as we will see, is crucial to good software engineering.

Languages like Java are **object oriented**. Programming in such a language is called **object-oriented programming** (OOP), and it allows computer programmers to implement an object-oriented design as a working system. Languages like C, on the other hand, are **procedural**, so programming tends to be **action oriented**. In C, the unit of programming is the **function**. Groups of actions that perform some common task are formed into functions, and functions are grouped to form programs. In Java, the unit of programming is the class from which objects are eventually **instantiated** (created). Java classes contain **methods** (which implement operations and are similar to functions in C) as well as **fields** (which implement attributes).

Java programmers concentrate on creating classes. Each class contains fields, and the set of methods that manipulate the fields and provide services to **clients** (i.e., other classes that use the class). The programmer uses existing classes as the building blocks for constructing new classes.

Classes are to objects as blueprints are to houses. Just as we can build many houses from one blueprint, we can instantiate (create) many objects from one class. You cannot cook meals in the kitchen of a blueprint; you can cook meals in the kitchen of a house.

Classes can have relationships with other classes. For example, in an object-oriented design of a bank, the "bank teller" class needs to relate to the "customer" class, the "cash drawer" class, the "safe" class, and so on. These relationships are called **associations**.

Packaging software as classes makes it possible for future software systems to **reuse** the classes. Groups of related classes are often packaged as reusable **components**. Just as realtors often say that the three most important factors affecting the price of real estate are "location, location and location," people in the software community often say that the three most important factors affecting the future of software development are "reuse, reuse and reuse." Reuse of existing classes when building new classes and programs saves time and effort. Reuse also helps programmers build more reliable and effective systems, because existing classes and components often have gone through extensive testing, debugging and performance tuning.

Indeed, with object technology, you can build much of the software you will need by combining classes, just as automobile manufacturers combine interchangeable parts. Each new class you create will have the potential to become a valuable software asset that you and other programmers can use to speed and enhance the quality of future software development efforts.

Introduction to Object-Oriented Analysis and Design (OOAD)

Soon you will be writing programs in Java. How will you create the code for your programs? Perhaps, like many beginning programmers, you will simply turn on your computer and start typing. This approach may work for small programs (like the ones we present in the early chapters of the book), but what if you were asked to create a software system to control thousands of automated teller machines for a major bank? Or suppose you were asked to work on a team of 1,000 software developers building the next U.S. air traffic control system. For projects so large and complex, you could not simply sit down and start writing programs.

To create the best solutions, you should follow a detailed process for **analyzing** your project's **requirements** (i.e., determining *what* the system is supposed to do) and developing a **design** that satisfies them (i.e., deciding *how* the system should do it). Ideally, you would go through this process and carefully review the design (or have your design reviewed by other software professionals) before writing any code. If this process involves analyzing and designing your system from an object-oriented point of view, it is called an **object-oriented analysis and design (OOAD) process**. Experienced programmers know that analysis and design can save many hours by helping them to avoid an ill-planned system-development approach that has to be abandoned part of the way through its implementation, possibly wasting considerable time, money and effort.

OOAD is the generic term for the process of analyzing a problem and developing an approach for solving it. Small problems like the ones discussed in these first few chapters do not require an exhaustive OOAD process. It may be sufficient to write **pseudocode** before we begin writing Java code—pseudocode is an informal means of expressing program logic. It is not actually a programming language, but we can use it as a kind of outline to guide us as we write our code. We introduce pseudocode in Chapter 4.

As problems and the groups of people solving them increase in size, the methods of OOAD become more appropriate than pseudocode. Ideally, a group should agree on a strictly defined process for solving its problem and a uniform way of communicating the results of that process to one another. Although many different OOAD processes exist, a single graphical language for communicating the results of *any* OOAD process has come into wide use. This language, known as the Unified Modeling Language (UML), was developed in the mid-1990s under the initial direction of three software methodologists—Grady Booch, James Rumbaugh and Ivar Jacobson.

History of the UML

In the 1980s, increasing numbers of organizations began using OOP to build their applications, and a need developed for a standard OOAD process. Many methodologists—including Booch, Rumbaugh and Jacobson—individually produced and promoted separate processes to satisfy this need. Each process had its own notation, or "language" (in the form of graphical diagrams), to convey the results of analysis and design.

By the early 1990s, different organizations, and even divisions within the same organization, were using their own unique processes and notations. At the same time, these organizations also wanted to use software tools that would support their particular processes. Software vendors found it difficult to provide tools for so many processes. A standard notation and standard processes were needed.

In 1994, James Rumbaugh joined Grady Booch at Rational Software Corporation (now a division of IBM), and the two began working to unify their popular processes. They soon were joined by Ivar Jacobson. In 1996, the group released early versions of the UML to the software engineering community and requested feedback. Around the same time, an organization known as the **Object Management Group™ (OMG™)** invited submissions for a common modeling language. The OMG (www.omg.org) is a nonprofit organization that promotes the standardization of object-oriented technologies by issuing guidelines and specifications, such as the UML. Several corporations—among them HP, IBM, Microsoft, Oracle and Rational Software—had already recognized the need for a common modeling language. In response to the OMG's request for proposals, these companies formed **UML Partners**—the consortium that developed the UML version 1.1 and submitted it to the OMG. The OMG accepted the proposal and, in 1997, assumed responsibility for the continuing maintenance and revision of the UML. The UML version 2 now available marks the first major revision of the UML since the 1997 version 1.1 standard. We present UML 2 terminology and notation throughout this book.

What Is the UML?

The UML is now the most widely used graphical representation scheme for modeling object-oriented systems. It has indeed unified the various popular notational schemes. Those who design systems use the language (in the form of diagrams) to model their systems.

An attractive feature of the UML is its flexibility. The UML is extensible (i.e., capable of being enhanced with new features) and is independent of any particular OOAD process. UML modelers are free to use various processes in designing systems, but all developers can now express their designs with one standard set of graphical notations.

The UML is a complex, feature-rich graphical language. In our Software Engineering Case Study sections, we present a simple, concise subset of these features. We then use this subset to guide you through a first design experience with the UML intended for novice object-oriented programmers in first- or second-semester programming courses.

Web UML Resources

For more information about the UML, refer to the following websites:

`www.uml.org`

This UML resource page from the Object Management Group (OMG) provides specification documents for the UML and other object-oriented technologies.

`www.ibm.com/software/rational/uml`

This is the UML resource page for IBM Rational—the successor to the Rational Software Corporation (the company that created the UML).

`en.wikipedia.org/wiki/Unified_Modeling_Language`

Wikipedia's definition of the UML. This site also provides links to many additional UML resources.

Recommended Readings

The following books provide information about object-oriented design with the UML:

Ambler, S. *The Object Primer: Agile Model-Driven Development with UML 2.0, Third Edition.* New York: Cambridge University Press, 2005.

Arlow, J., and I. Neustadt. *UML and the Unified Process: Practical Object-Oriented Analysis and Design, Second Edition.* Boston: Addison-Wesley Professional, 2006.

Fowler, M. *UML Distilled, Third Edition: A Brief Guide to the Standard Object Modeling Language.* Boston: Addison-Wesley Professional, 2004.

Rumbaugh, J., I. Jacobson and G. Booch. *The Unified Modeling Language User Guide, Second Edition.* Boston: Addison-Wesley Professional, 2006.

Section 1.16 Self-Review Exercises

1.1   List three examples of real-world objects that we did not mention. For each object, list several attributes and behaviors.

1.2   Pseudocode is _____.
   a) another term for OOAD
   b) a programming language used to display UML diagrams
   c) an informal means of expressing program logic
   d) a graphical representation scheme for modeling object-oriented systems

1.3   The UML is used primarily to _____.
   a) test object-oriented systems
   b) design object-oriented systems
   c) implement object-oriented systems
   d) Both a and b

Answers to Section 1.16 Self-Review Exercises

1.1   [*Note:* Answers may vary.] a) A television's attributes include the size of the screen, the number of colors it can display, its current channel and its current volume. A television turns on and off, changes channels, displays video and plays sounds. b) A coffee maker's attributes include the maximum volume of water it can hold, the time required to brew a pot of coffee and the temperature of the heating plate under the coffee pot. A coffee maker turns on and off, brews coffee and heats coffee. c) A turtle's attributes include its age, the size of its shell and its weight. A turtle walks, retreats into its shell, emerges from its shell and eats vegetation.

1.2   c.

1.3   b.

1.17 Web 2.0

The web literally exploded in the mid-to-late 1990s, but hard times hit in the early 2000s due to the dot com economic bust. The resurgence that began in 2004 or so, has been named Web 2.0. The first Web 2.0 Conference was held in 2004. A year into its life, the term "Web 2.0" garnered about 10 million hits on the Google search engine, growing to 60 million a year later. Google is widely regarded as the signature company of Web 2.0. Some others are Craigslist (free classified listings), Flickr (photo sharing), del.icio.us (social bookmarking), YouTube (video sharing), MySpace and FaceBook (social networking), Salesforce (business software offered as an online service), Second Life (a virtual world), Skype (Internet telephony) and Wikipedia (a free online encyclopedia).

At Deitel & Associates, we launched our Web 2.0-based Internet Business Initiative in 2005. We're researching the key technologies of Web 2.0 and using them to build Internet businesses. We're sharing our research in the form of Resource Centers at www.deitel.com/resourcecenters.html. Each week, we announce the latest Resource Centers in our newsletter, the *Deitel® Buzz Online* (www.deitel.com/newsletter/subscribe.html). Each lists many links to free content and software on the Internet.

We include a substantial treatment of web services (Chapter 28) and introduce the new applications development methodology of mashups (Appendix H) in which you can rapidly develop powerful and intriguing applications by combining complementary web services and other forms of information feeds of two or more organizations. A popular mashup is www.housingmaps.com which combines the real estate listings of www.craigslist.org with the mapping capabilities of Google Maps to offer maps that show the locations of apartments for rent in a given area.

Ajax is one of the premier technologies of Web 2.0. Though the term's use exploded in 2005, it's just a term that names a group of technologies and programming techniques that have been in use since the late 1990s. Ajax helps Internet-based applications perform like desktop applications—a difficult task, given that such applications suffer transmission delays as data is shuttled back and forth between your computer and other computers on the Internet. Using Ajax, applications like Google Maps have achieved excellent performance and the look and feel of desktop applications. Although we don't discuss "raw" Ajax programming (which is quite complex) in this text, we do show in Chapter 27 how to build Ajax-enabled applications using JavaServer Faces (JSF) Ajax-enabled components.

Blogs are web sites (currently about 60 million of them) that are like online diaries, with the most recent entries appearing first. Bloggers quickly post their opinions about news, product releases, political candidates, controversial issues, and just about everything else. The collection of all blogs and the blogging community is called the **blogosphere** and is becoming increasingly influential. **Technorati** is the leading blog search engine.

RSS feeds enable sites to push information to subscribers. A common use of RSS feeds is to deliver the latest blog postings to people who subscribe to blogs. The RSS information flows on the Internet are growing exponentially.

Web 3.0 is another name for the next generation of the web also called the **Semantic Web**. Web 1.0 was almost purely HTML-based. Web 2.0 is making increasing use of XML, especially in technologies like RSS feeds. Web 3.0 will make deep use of XML, creating a "web of meaning." If you're a student looking for a great research paper or thesis topic, or an entrepreneur looking for business opportunities, check out our Web 3.0 Resource Center.

To follow the latest developments in Web 2.0, read `www.techcrunch.com` and `www.slashdot.org` and check out the growing list of Web 2.0-related Resource Centers at `www.deitel.com/resourcecenters.html`.

1.18 Software Technologies

In this section, we discuss a number of software engineering buzzwords that you'll hear in the software development community. We've created Resource Centers on most of these topics, with many more on the way.

Agile Software Development is a set of methodologies that try to get software implemented quickly with fewer resources then previous methodologies. Check out the Agile Alliance (`www.agilealliance.org`) and the Agile Manifesto (`www.agilemanifesto.org`).

Extreme programming (XP) is one of many agile development methodologies. It tries to develop software quickly. The software is released frequently in small increments to encourage rapid user feedback. XP recognizes that the users' requirements change often and that software must meet those new requirements quickly. Programmers work in pairs at one machine so code review is done immediately as the code is created. Everyone on the team should be able to work on any part of the code.

Refactoring involves reworking code to make it clearer and easier to maintain while preserving its functionality. It's widely employed with agile development methodologies. Many refactoring tools are available to do major portions of the reworking automatically.

Design patterns are proven architectures for constructing flexible and maintainable object-oriented software (see web bonus Appendix P). The field of design patterns tries to enumerate those recurring patterns, and encourage software designers to reuse them to develop better quality software with less time, money and effort.

Game programming. The computer game business is larger than the first-run movie business. College courses and even majors are now devoted to the sophisticated software techniques used in game programming. Check out our Game Programming and Programming Projects Resource Centers.

Open source software is a style of developing software in contrast to proprietary development that dominated software's early years. With open source development, individuals and companies contribute their efforts in developing, maintaining and evolving software in exchange for the right to use that software for their own purposes, typically at no charge. Open source code generally gets scrutinized by a much larger audience than proprietary software, so bugs get removed faster. Open source also encourages more innovation. Sun recently announced that it is open sourcing Java. Some organizations you'll hear a lot about in the open source community are the Eclipse Foundation (the Eclipse IDE is popular for Java software development), the Mozilla Foundation (creators of the Firefox browser), the Apache Software Foundation (creators of the Apache web server) and SourceForge (which provides the tools for managing open source projects and currently has over 100,000 open source projects under development).

Linux is an open source operating system and one of the greatest successes of the open source movement. MySQL is an open source database management system. PHP is the most popular open source server-side Internet "scripting" language for developing Internet-based applications. LAMP is an acronym for the set of open source technologies that many developers used to build web applications—it stands for Linux, Apache, MySQL and PHP (or Perl or Python—two other languages used for similar purposes).

Ruby on Rails combines the scripting language Ruby with the Rails web application framework developed by the company 37Signals. Their book, *Getting Real*, is a must read for today's web application developers; read it free at `gettingreal.37signals.com/toc.php`. Many Ruby on Rails developers have reported significant productivity gains over using other languages when developing database-intensive web applications.

Software has generally been viewed as a product; most software still is offered this way. If you want to run an application, you buy a software package from a software vendor. You then install that software on your computer and run it as needed. As new versions of the software appear you upgrade your software, often at significant expense. This process can become cumbersome for organizations with tens of thousands of systems that must be maintained on a diverse array of computer equipment. With Software as a Service (SAAS) the software runs on servers elsewhere on the Internet. When that server is updated, all clients worldwide see the new capabilities; no local installation is needed. You access the service through a browser—these are quite portable so you can run the same applications on different kinds of computers from anywhere is the world. Salesforce.com, Google, and Microsoft's Office Live and Windows Live all offer SAAS.

1.19 Wrap-Up

This chapter introduced basic hardware and software concepts, and basic object technology concepts, including classes, objects, attributes, behaviors, encapsulation, inheritance and polymorphism. We discussed the different types of programming languages and which are most widely used. You learned the steps for creating and executing a Java application using Sun's JDK 6. The chapter explored the history of the Internet and the World Wide Web, and Java's role in developing distributed client/server applications for the Internet and the web. You also learned about the history and purpose of the UML—the industry-standard graphical language for modeling software systems. Finally, you "test drove" one or more sample Java applications similar to the types of applications you will learn to program in this book.

In Chapter 2, you'll create your first Java applications. You'll see examples that show how programs display messages and obtain information from the user for processing. We analyze and explain each example to help ease your way into Java programming.

1.20 Web Resources

This section provides many resources that will be useful to you as you learn Java. The sites include Java resources, Java development tools for students and professionals, and our own websites where you can find downloads and resources associated with this book. We also provide a link where you can subscribe to our free *Deitel® Buzz Online* e-mail newsletter.

Deitel & Associates Websites

www.deitel.com
Contains updates, corrections and additional resources for all Deitel publications.

www.deitel.com/newsletter/subscribe.html
Subscribe to the free *Deitel® Buzz Online* e-mail newsletter to follow the Deitel & Associates publishing program, including updates and errata to this book.

www.prenhall.com/deitel
Prentice Hall's home page for Deitel publications. Here you will find detailed product information, sample chapters and *Companion Websites* with resources for students and instructors.

www.deitel.com/books/jhtp7/
The Deitel & Associates home page for *Java How to Program, Seventh Edition*. Here you'll find links to the book's examples (also included on the CD that accompanies the book) and other resources.

Deitel Java Resource Centers

www.deitel.com/Java/
Our Java Resource Center focuses on the enormous amount of Java free content available online. Start your search here for resources, downloads, tutorials, documentation, books, e-books, journals, articles, blogs and more that will help you develop Java applications.

www.deitel.com/JavaSE6Mustang/
Our Java SE 6 (Mustang) Resource Center is your guide to the latest release of Java. The site includes the best resources we found online to help you get started with Java SE 6 development.

www.deitel.com/JavaEE5/
Our Java Enterprise Edition 5 (Java EE 5) Resource Center.

www.deitel.com/JavaCertification/
Our Java Certification and Assessment Testing Resource Center.

www.deitel.com/JavaDesignPatterns/
Our Java Design Patterns Resource Center. In their book, *Design Patterns: Elements of Reusable Object-Oriented Software* (Boston: Addison-Wesley Professional, 1995), the "Gang of Four" (E. Gamma, R. Helm, R. Johnson, and J. Vlissides) describe 23 design patterns that provide proven architectures for building object-oriented software systems. In this resource center, you'll find discussions of many of these and other design patterns.

www.deitel.com/CodeSearchEngines/
Our Code Search Engines and Code Sites Resource Center includes resources developers use to find source code online.

www.deitel.com/ProgrammingProjects/
Our Programming Projects Resource Center is your guide to student programming projects online.

Sun Microsystems Websites

java.sun.com/developer/onlineTraining/new2java/index.html
The "New to Java Center" on the Sun Microsystems website features online training resources to help you get started with Java programming.

`java.sun.com/javase/6/download.jsp`
The download page for the Java Development Kit 6 (JDK 6) and its documentation. The JDK includes everything you need to compile and execute your Java SE 6 (Mustang) applications.

`java.sun.com/javase/6/webnotes/install/index.html`
Instructions for installing JDK 6 on Solaris, Windows and Linux platforms.

`java.sun.com/javase/6/docs/api/index.html`
The online site for the Java SE 6 API documentation.

`java.sun.com/javase`
The home page for the Java Standard Edition platform.

`java.sun.com`
Sun's Java technology home page provides downloads, references, forums, online tutorials and more.

`java.sun.com/reference/docs/index.html`
Sun's documentation site for all Java technologies.

`developers.sun.com`
Sun's home page for Java developers provides downloads, APIs, code samples, articles with technical advice and other resources on the best Java development practices.

Editors and Integrated Development Environments

`www.eclipse.org`
The Eclipse development environment can be used to develop code in any programming language. You can download the environment and several Java plug-ins to develop your Java programs.

`www.netbeans.org`
The NetBeans IDE. One of the most widely used, freely distributed Java development tools.

`borland.com/products/downloads/download_jbuilder.html`
Borland provides a free Foundation Edition version of its popular Java IDE JBuilder. The site also provides 30-day trial versions of the Enterprise and Developer editions.

`www.blueJ.org`
BlueJ—a free tool designed to help teach object-oriented Java to new programmers.

`www.jgrasp.org`
jGRASP downloads, documentation and tutorials. This tool displays visual representations of Java programs to aid comprehension.

`www.jedit.org`
jEdit—a text editor written in Java.

`developers.sun.com/prodtech/javatools/jsenterprise/index.jsp`
Sun Java Studio Enterprise IDE—the Sun Microsystems enhanced version of NetBeans.

`www.jcreator.com`
JCreator—a popular Java IDE. JCreator Lite Edition is available as a free download. A 30-day trial version of JCreator Pro Edition is also available.

`www.textpad.com`
TextPad—compile, edit and run your Java programs from this editor that provides syntax coloring and an easy-to-use interface.

`www.download.com`
A site that contains freeware and shareware application downloads, including, editor programs.

Additional Java Resource Sites

`www.javalobby.org`
Provides up-to-date Java news, forums where developers can exchange tips and advice, and a comprehensive Java knowledge base organizing articles and downloads from across the web.

www.jguru.com

Provides forums, downloads, articles, online courses and a large collection of Java FAQs (Frequently Asked Questions).

www.javaworld.com

Provides resources for Java developers, such as articles, indices of popular Java books, tips and FAQs.

www.ftponline.com/javapro

JavaPro magazine features monthly articles, programming tips, book reviews and more.

sys-con.com/java/

Java Developer's Journal from Sys-Con Media provides articles, e-books and other Java resources.

Summary

Section 1.1 Introduction

- Java has become the language of choice for implementing Internet-based applications and software for devices that communicate over a network.

- Java Enterprise Edition (Java EE) is geared toward developing large-scale, distributed networking applications and web-based applications.

- Java Micro Edition (Java ME) is geared toward developing applications for small, memory-constrained devices, such as cell phones, pagers and PDAs.

Section 1.2 What Is a Computer?

- A computer is a device capable of performing computations and making logical decisions at speeds millions (even billions) of times faster than human beings can.

- Computers process data under the control of sets of instructions called computer programs. Programs guide computers through actions specified by people called computer programmers.

- A computer consists of various devices referred to as hardware. The programs that run on a computer are referred to as software.

Section 1.3 Computer Organization

- Virtually every computer may be envisioned as divided into six logical units or sections.

- The input unit obtains information from input devices and places this information at the disposal of the other units so that it can be processed.

- The output unit takes information that the computer has processed and places it on various output devices to make the information available for use outside the computer.

- The memory unit is the rapid-access, relatively low-capacity "warehouse" section of the computer. It retains information that has been entered through the input unit, so that it will be immediately available for processing when needed. It also retains processed information until it can be placed on output devices by the output unit.

- The arithmetic and logic unit (ALU) is responsible for performing calculations (such as addition, subtraction, multiplication and division) and making decisions.

- The central processing unit (CPU) coordinates and supervises the operation of the other sections. The CPU tells the input unit when information should be read into the memory unit, tells the ALU when information from the memory unit should be used in calculations and tells the output unit when to send information from the memory unit to certain output devices.

- Multiprocessors have multiple CPUs and, hence, can perform many operations simultaneously.

- The secondary storage unit is the long-term, high-capacity "warehousing" section of the computer. Programs or data not actively being used by the other units normally are placed on secondary storage devices until they are again needed.

Section 1.4 Early Operating Systems
- Early computers could perform only one job or task at a time.
- Operating systems were developed to make using computers more convenient.
- Multiprogramming involves the simultaneous operation of many jobs.
- With timesharing, the computer runs a small portion of one user's job, then moves on to service the next user, perhaps providing service to each user several times per second.

Section 1.5 Personal, Distributed and Client/Server Computing
- In 1977, Apple Computer popularized personal computing.
- In 1981, IBM, the world's largest computer vendor, introduced the IBM Personal Computer, which quickly legitimized personal computing in business, industry and government.
- In distributed computing, instead of computing being performed only at a central computer, it is distributed over networks to the sites where the organization's work is performed.
- Servers store data that may be used by client computers distributed throughout the network, hence the term client/server computing.
- Java has become widely used for writing software for computer networking and for distributed client/server applications.

Section 1.6 The Internet and the World Wide Web
- The Internet is accessible by more than a billion computers and computer-controlled devices.
- With the introduction of the World Wide Web the Internet has exploded into one of the world's premier communication mechanisms.

Section 1.7 Machine Languages, Assembly Languages and High-Level Languages
- Any computer can directly understand only its own machine language.
- Machine language is the "natural language" of a computer.
- Machine languages generally consist of strings of numbers (ultimately reduced to 1s and 0s) that instruct computers to perform their most elementary operations one at a time.
- Machine languages are machine dependent.
- Programmers began using English-like abbreviations to represent elementary operations. These abbreviations formed the basis of assembly languages.
- Translator programs called assemblers were developed to convert early assembly-language programs to machine language at computer speeds.
- High-level languages allow programmers to write instructions that look almost like everyday English and contain commonly used mathematical notations.
- Java is the most widely used high-level programming language.
- Interpreter programs execute high-level language programs directly.

Section 1.8 History of C and C++
- Java evolved from C++, which evolved from C, which evolved from BCPL and B.
- The C language was developed by Dennis Ritchie at Bell Laboratories. It initially became widely known as the development language of the UNIX operating system.

- C++, an extension of C, was developed by Bjarne Stroustrup in the early 1980s at Bell Laboratories. C++ provides a number of features that "spruce up" the C language, and capabilities for object-oriented programming.

Section 1.9 History of Java

- Java is used to develop large-scale enterprise applications, to enhance the functionality of web servers, to provide applications for consumer devices and for many other purposes.
- Java programs consist of pieces called classes. Classes include pieces called methods that perform tasks and return information when the tasks are completed.

Section 1.10 Java Class Libraries

- Most Java programmers take advantage of the rich collections of existing classes in the Java class libraries, which are also known as the Java APIs (Application Programming Interfaces).
- The advantage of creating your own classes and methods is that you know how they work and can examine the code. The disadvantage is the time-consuming and potentially complex effort.

Section 1.11 Fortran, COBOL, Pascal and Ada

- Fortran (FORmula TRANslator) was developed by IBM Corporation in the mid-1950s for use in scientific and engineering applications that require complex mathematical computations.
- COBOL (COmmon Business Oriented Language) is used for commercial applications that require precise and efficient manipulation of large amounts of data.
- Research in the 1960s resulted in structured programming—an approach to writing programs that are clearer, and easier to test, debug and modify than those produced with earlier techniques.
- Pascal was designed for teaching structured programming in academic environments and rapidly became the preferred programming language in most colleges.
- The Ada programming language was developed under the sponsorship of the U.S. Department of Defense (DOD) to fill most of its needs. An Ada capability called multitasking allows programmers to specify that activities are to occur in parallel. Java, through a technique called *multithreading*, also enables programmers to write programs with parallel activities.

Section 1.12 BASIC, Visual Basic, Visual C++, C# and .NET

- BASIC was developed in the mid-1960s for writing simple programs.
- Microsoft's Visual Basic language simplifies the development of Windows applications.
- Microsoft's .NET platform integrates the Internet and the web into computer applications.

Section 1.13 Typical Java Development Environment

- Java programs normally go through five phases—edit, compile, load, verify and execute.
- Phase 1 consists of editing a file with an editor. You type a program using the editor, make corrections and save the program on a secondary storage device, such as your hard drive.
- A file name ending with the .java extension indicates that the file contains Java source code.
- Integrated development environments (IDEs) provide tools that support software development, including editors for writing and editing programs and debuggers for locating logic errors.
- In Phase 2, the programmer uses the command javac to compile a program.
- If a program compiles, the compiler produces a .class file that contains the compiled program.
- The Java compiler translates Java source code into bytecodes that represent the tasks to be executed. Bytecodes are executed by the Java Virtual Machine (JVM).

- In Phase 3, loading, the class loader takes the `.class` files containing the program's bytecodes and transfers them to primary memory.
- In Phase 4, as the classes are loaded, the bytecode verifier examines their bytecodes to ensure that they are valid and do not violate Java's security restrictions.
- In Phase 5, the JVM executes the program's bytecodes.

Section 1.16 Software Engineering Case Study: Introduction to Object Technology and the UML (Required)

- The Unified Modeling Language (UML) is a graphical language that allows people who build systems to represent their object-oriented designs in a common notation.
- Object-oriented design (OOD) models software components in terms of real-world objects.
- Objects have the property of information hiding—objects of one class are normally not allowed to know how objects of other classes are implemented.
- Object-oriented programming (OOP) implements object-oriented designs.
- Java programmers concentrate on creating their own user-defined types called classes. Each class contains data and methods that manipulate that data and provide services to clients.
- The data components of a class are attributes or fields; the operation components are methods.
- Classes can have relationships with other classes; these relationships are called associations.
- Packaging software as classes makes it possible for future software systems to reuse the classes.
- An instance of a class is called an object.
- The process of analyzing and designing a system from an object-oriented point of view is called object-oriented analysis and design (OOAD).

Terminology

Ada
ALU (arithmetic and logic unit)
ANSI C
arithmetic and logic unit (ALU)
assembler
assembly language
attribute
BASIC
behavior
bytecode
bytecode verifier
C
C#
C++
central processing unit (CPU)
class
.class file
class libraries
class loader
client/server computing
COBOL
compile phase
compiler

compile-time error
computer
computer program
computer programmer
CPU (central processing unit)
disk
distributed computing
dynamic content
edit phase
editor
encapsulation
execute phase
execution-time error
fatal runtime error
file server
Fortran
hardware
high-level language
HotSpot™ compiler
HTML (Hypertext Markup Language)
IDE (Integrated Development Environment)
information hiding
inheritance

input device
input unit
input/output (I/O)
Internet
interpreter
Java
Java API (Java Application Programming Interface)
Java Development Kit (JDK)
Java Enterprise Edition (Java EE)
.java file-name extension
java interpreter
Java Micro Edition (Java ME)
Java Standard Edition (Java SE)
Java Virtual Machine (JVM)
javac compiler
JIT (just-in-time) compiler
KIS ("keep it simple")
LAN (local area network)
legacy system
live-code approach
load phase
machine language
memory unit
method
Microsoft Internet Explorer web browser
modeling
multiprocessor
multiprogramming
multithreading
.NET
nonfatal runtime error

object
object-oriented design (OOD)
object-oriented programming (OOP)
operating system
output device
output unit
Pascal
personal computing
platform
portability
primary memory
problem statement
procedural programming
programmer-defined type
pseudocode
requirements document
reusable componentry
runtime error
secondary storage unit
software
software reuse
structured programming
Sun Microsystems
throughput
timesharing
translation
translator program
Unified Modeling Language (UML)
verify phase
Visual Basic .NET
Visual C++ .NET
World Wide Web

Self-Review Exercises

1.1 Fill in the blanks in each of the following statements:
   a) The company that popularized personal computing was _____.
   b) The computer that made personal computing legitimate in business and industry was the _____.
   c) Computers process data under the control of sets of instructions called _____.
   d) The six key logical units of the computer are the _____, _____, _____, _____, _____ and _____.
   e) The three types of languages discussed in the chapter are _____, _____ and _____.
   f) The programs that translate high-level language programs into machine language are called _____.
   g) The _____ allows computer users to locate and view multimedia-based documents on almost any subject over the Internet.
   h) _____ allows a Java program to perform multiple activities in parallel.

1.2 Fill in the blanks in each of the following sentences about the Java environment:
   a) The _____ command from the JDK executes a Java application.

b) The _____ command from the JDK compiles a Java program.
c) A Java program file must end with the _____ file extension.
d) When a Java program is compiled, the file produced by the compiler ends with the _____ file extension.
e) The file produced by the Java compiler contains _____ that are executed by the Java Virtual Machine.

1.3 Fill in the blanks in each of the following statements (based on Section 1.16):

a) Objects have the property of _____—although objects may know how to communicate with one another across well-defined interfaces, they normally are not allowed to know how other objects are implemented.
b) Java programmers concentrate on creating _____, which contain fields and the set of methods that manipulate those fields and provide services to clients.
c) Classes can have relationships with other classes called _____.
d) The process of analyzing and designing a system from an object-oriented point of view is called _____.
e) OOD takes advantage of _____ relationships, where new classes of objects are derived by absorbing characteristics of existing classes then adding unique characteristics of their own.
f) _____ is a graphical language that allows people who design software systems to use an industry standard notation to represent them.
g) The size, shape, color and weight of an object are considered _____ of the object.

Answers to Self-Review Exercises

1.1 a) Apple. b) IBM Personal Computer. c) programs. d) input unit, output unit, memory unit, arithmetic and logic unit, central processing unit, secondary storage unit. e) machine languages, assembly languages, high-level languages. f) compilers. g) World Wide Web. h) Multithreading.

1.2 a) `java`. b) `javac`. c) `.java`. d) `.class`. e) bytecodes.

1.3 a) information hiding. b) classes. c) associations. d) object-oriented analysis and design (OOAD). e) inheritance. f) The Unified Modeling Language (UML). g) attributes.

Exercises

1.4 Categorize each of the following items as either hardware or software:
a) CPU
b) Java compiler
c) JVM
d) input unit
e) editor

1.5 What is the difference between fatal errors and nonfatal errors? Why might you prefer to experience a fatal error rather than a nonfatal error?

1.6 Fill in the blanks in each of the following statements (based on Section 1.13):
a) Java programs normally go through five phases—_____, _____, _____, _____ and _____.
b) A(n) _____ provides many tools that support the software development process, such as editors for writing and editing programs, debuggers for locating logic errors in programs, and many other features.
c) The command java invokes the _____, which executes Java programs.

   d) A(n) _____ is a software application that simulates a computer, but hides the underlying operating system and hardware from the programs that interact with the VM.

   e) A(n) _____ program can run on multiple platforms.

   f) The _____ takes the .class files containing the program's bytecodes and transfers them to primary memory.

   g) The _____ examines bytecodes to ensure that they are valid.

1.7 Explain the two compilation phases of Java programs.

Introduction to Java Applications

OBJECTIVES

In this chapter you will learn:

- To write simple Java applications.
- To use input and output statements.
- Java's primitive types.
- Basic memory concepts.
- To use arithmetic operators.
- The precedence of arithmetic operators.
- To write decision-making statements.
- To use relational and equality operators.

2.1 Introduction

We now introduce Java application programming, which facilitates a disciplined approach to program design. Most of the Java programs you will study in this book process information and display results. We present six examples that demonstrate how your programs can display messages and how they can obtain information from the user for processing. We begin with several examples that simply display messages on the screen. We then demonstrate a program that obtains two numbers from a user, calculates their sum and displays the result. You will learn how to perform various arithmetic calculations and save their results for later use. The last example in this chapter demonstrates decision-making fundamentals by showing you how to compare numbers, then display messages based on the comparison results. For example, the program displays a message indicating that two numbers are equal only if they have the same value. We analyze each example one line at a time to help you ease your way into Java programming. To help you apply the skills you learn here, we provide many challenging and entertaining problems in the chapter's exercises.

2.2 A First Program in Java: Printing a Line of Text

Every time you use a computer, you execute various applications that perform tasks for you. For example, your e-mail application helps you send and receive e-mail, and your web browser lets you view web pages from websites around the world. Computer programmers create such applications by writing **computer programs**.

A Java **application** is a computer program that executes when you use the java command to launch the Java Virtual Machine (JVM). Let us consider a simple application that displays a line of text. (Later in this section we will discuss how to compile and run an application.) The program and its output are shown in Fig. 2.1. The output appears in the light blue box at the end of the program. The program illustrates several important Java language features. Java uses notations that may look strange to nonprogrammers. In addition, for your convenience, each program we present in this book includes line numbers, which are not part of actual Java programs. We will soon see that line 9 does the real work of the program—namely, displaying the phrase `Welcome to Java Programming!` on the screen. We now consider each line of the program in order.

```
1    // Fig. 2.1: Welcome1.java
2    // Text-printing program.
3
4    public class Welcome1
5    {
6       // main method begins execution of Java application
7       public static void main( String args[] )
8       {
9          System.out.println( "Welcome to Java Programming!" );
10
11      } // end method main
12
13   } // end class Welcome1
```

```
Welcome to Java Programming!
```

Fig. 2.1 | Text-printing program.

Line 1

```
// Fig. 2.1: Welcome1.java
```

begins with //, indicating that the remainder of the line is a **comment**. Programmers insert comments to **document programs** and improve their readability. This helps other people read and understand your programs. The Java compiler ignores comments, so they do not cause the computer to perform any action when the program is run. By convention, we begin every program with a comment indicating the figure number and file name.

A comment that begins with // is called an **end-of-line** (or **single-line**) **comment**, because the comment terminates at the end of the line on which it appears. A // comment also can begin in the middle of a line and continue until the end of that line (as in lines 11 and 13).

Traditional comments (also called **multiple-line comments**), such as

```
/* This is a traditional
   comment. It can be
   split over many lines */
```

can be spread over several lines. This type of comment begins with the delimiter /* and ends with */. All text between the delimiters is ignored by the compiler. Java incorporated traditional comments and end-of-line comments from the C and C++ programming languages, respectively. In this book, we use end-of-line comments.

Java also provides **Javadoc comments** that are delimited by /** and */. As with traditional comments, all text between the Javadoc comment delimiters is ignored by the compiler. Javadoc comments enable programmers to embed program documentation directly in their programs. Such comments are the preferred Java documenting format in industry. The **javadoc** utility program (part of the Java SE Development Kit) reads Javadoc comments and uses them to prepare your program's documentation in HTML format. We demonstrate Javadoc comments and the javadoc utility in Appendix K, Creating Documentation with javadoc. For complete information, visit Sun's javadoc Tool Home Page at java.sun.com/javase/6/docs/technotes/guides/javadoc/index.html.

Common Programming Error 2.1

Forgetting one of the delimiters of a traditional or Javadoc comment is a syntax error. The syntax of a programming language specifies the rules for creating a proper program in that language. A syntax error occurs when the compiler encounters code that violates Java's language rules (i.e., its syntax). In this case, the compiler issues an error message to help the programmer identify and fix the incorrect code. Syntax errors are also called compiler errors, compile-time errors or compilation errors, because the compiler detects them during the compilation phase. You will be unable to execute your program until you correct all the syntax errors in it.

Line 2

```
// Text-printing program.
```

is an end-of-line comment that describes the purpose of the program.

Good Programming Practice 2.1

Every program should begin with a comment that explains the purpose of the program, the author and the date and time the program was last modified. (We are not showing the author, date and time in this book's programs because this information would be redundant.)

Line 3 is a blank line. Programmers use blank lines and space characters to make programs easier to read. Together, blank lines, space characters and tab characters are known as white space. (Space characters and tabs are known specifically as white-space characters.) White space is ignored by the compiler. In this chapter and the next several chapters, we discuss conventions for using white space to enhance program readability.

Good Programming Practice 2.2

Use blank lines and space characters to enhance program readability.

Line 4

```
public class Welcome1
```

begins a class declaration for class Welcome1. Every program in Java consists of at least one class declaration that is defined by you—the programmer. These are known as programmer-defined classes or user-defined classes. The **class** keyword introduces a class declaration in Java and is immediately followed by the class name (Welcome1). Keywords (sometimes called reserved words) are reserved for use by Java (we discuss the various keywords throughout the text) and are always spelled with all lowercase letters. The complete list of Java keywords is shown in Appendix C.

By convention, all class names in Java begin with a capital letter and capitalize the first letter of each word they include (e.g., SampleClassName). A Java class name is an identifier—a series of characters consisting of letters, digits, underscores (_) and dollar signs ($) that does not begin with a digit and does not contain spaces. Some valid identifiers are Welcome1, $value, _value, m_inputField1 and button7. The name 7button is not a valid identifier because it begins with a digit, and the name input field is not a valid identifier because it contains a space. Normally, an identifier that does not begin with a capital letter is not the name of a Java class. Java is case sensitive—that is, uppercase and lowercase letters are distinct, so a1 and A1 are different (but both valid) identifiers.

Good Programming Practice 2.3

By convention, always begin a class name's identifier with a capital letter and start each subsequent word in the identifier with a capital letter. Java programmers know that such identifiers normally represent Java classes, so naming your classes in this manner makes your programs more readable.

Common Programming Error 2.2

Java is case sensitive. Not using the proper uppercase and lowercase letters for an identifier normally causes a compilation error.

In Chapters 2–7, every class we define begins with the `public` keyword. For now, we will simply require this keyword. When you save your `public` class declaration in a file, the file name must be the class name followed by the `.java` file-name extension. For our application, the file name is `Welcome1.java`. You will learn more about `public` and non-`public` classes in Chapter 8.

Common Programming Error 2.3

A `public` class must be placed in a file that has the same name as the class (in terms of both spelling and capitalization) plus the `.java` extension; otherwise, a compilation error occurs.

Common Programming Error 2.4

It is an error not to end a file name with the `.java` extension for a file containing a class declaration. The Java compiler compiles only files with the `.java` extension.

A left brace (at line 5 in this program), {, begins the body of every class declaration. A corresponding right brace (at line 13), }, must end each class declaration. Note that lines 6–11 are indented. This indentation is one of the spacing conventions mentioned earlier. We define each spacing convention as a Good Programming Practice.

Good Programming Practice 2.4

Whenever you type an opening left brace, {, in your program, immediately type the closing right brace, }, then reposition the cursor between the braces and indent to begin typing the body. This practice helps prevent errors due to missing braces.

Good Programming Practice 2.5

Indent the entire body of each class declaration one "level" of indentation between the left brace, {, and the right brace, }, that delimit the body of the class. This format emphasizes the class declaration's structure and makes it easier to read.

Good Programming Practice 2.6

Set a convention for the indent size you prefer, and then uniformly apply that convention. The Tab key may be used to create indents, but tab stops vary among text editors. We recommend using three spaces to form a level of indent.

Common Programming Error 2.5

It is a syntax error if braces do not occur in matching pairs.

Line 6

```
// main method begins execution of Java application
```

is an end-of-line comment indicating the purpose of lines 7–11 of the program. Line 7

```
public static void main( String args[] )
```

is the starting point of every Java application. The parentheses after the identifier main indicate that it is a program building block called a method. Java class declarations normally contain one or more methods. For a Java application, exactly one of the methods must be called main and must be defined as shown in line 7; otherwise, the JVM will not execute the application. Methods are able to perform tasks and return information when they complete their tasks. Keyword void indicates that this method will perform a task but will not return any information when it completes its task. Later, we will see that many methods return information when they complete their task. You will learn more about methods in Chapters 3 and 6. For now, simply mimic main's first line in your Java applications. In line 7, the String args[] in parentheses is a required part of the method main's declaration. We discuss this in Chapter 7, Arrays.

The left brace, {, in line 8 begins the body of the method declaration. A corresponding right brace, }, must end the method declaration's body (line 11 of the program). Note that line 9 in the body of the method is indented between the braces.

Good Programming Practice 2.7

Indent the entire body of each method declaration one "level" of indentation between the left brace, {, and the right brace, }, that define the body of the method. This format makes the structure of the method stand out and makes the method declaration easier to read.

Line 9

```
System.out.println( "Welcome to Java Programming!" );
```

instructs the computer to perform an action—namely, to print the string of characters contained between the double quotation marks (but not the quotation marks themselves). A string is sometimes called a character string, a message or a string literal. We refer to characters between double quotation marks simply as strings. White-space characters in strings are not ignored by the compiler.

System.out is known as the standard output object. System.out allows Java applications to display sets of characters in the command window from which the Java application executes. In Microsoft Windows 95/98/ME, the command window is the MS-DOS prompt. In more recent versions of Microsoft Windows, the command window is the Command Prompt. In UNIX/Linux/Mac OS X, the command window is called a terminal window or a shell. Many programmers refer to the command window simply as the command line.

Method System.out.println displays (or prints) a line of text in the command window. The string in the parentheses in line 9 is the argument to the method. Method System.out.println performs its task by displaying (also called outputting) its argument in the command window. When System.out.println completes its task, it positions the output cursor (the location where the next character will be displayed) to the beginning of the next line in the command window. (This move of the cursor is similar to when a user presses the *Enter* key while typing in a text editor—the cursor appears at the beginning of the next line in the file.)

The entire line 9, including `System.out.println`, the argument `"Welcome to Java Programming!"` in the parentheses and the semicolon (`;`), is called a **statement**. Each statement ends with a semicolon. When the statement in line 9 of our program executes, it displays the message `Welcome to Java Programming!` in the command window. As we will see in subsequent programs, a method is typically composed of one or more statements that perform the method's task.

Common Programming Error 2.6

Omitting the semicolon at the end of a statement is a syntax error.

Error-Prevention Tip 2.1

When learning how to program, sometimes it is helpful to "break" a working program so you can familiarize yourself with the compiler's syntax-error messages. These messages do not always state the exact problem in the code. When you encounter such syntax-error messages in the future, you will have an idea of what caused the error. Try removing a semicolon or brace from the program of Fig. 2.1, then recompile the program to see the error messages generated by the omission.

Error-Prevention Tip 2.2

When the compiler reports a syntax error, the error may not be on the line number indicated by the error message. First, check the line for which the error was reported. If that line does not contain syntax errors, check several preceding lines.

Some programmers find it difficult when reading or writing a program to match the left and right braces (`{` and `}`) that delimit the body of a class declaration or a method declaration. For this reason, some programmers include an end-of-line comment after a closing right brace (`}`) that ends a method declaration and after a closing right brace that ends a class declaration. For example, line 11

```
} // end method main
```

specifies the closing right brace (`}`) of method `main`, and line 13

```
} // end class Welcome1
```

specifies the closing right brace (`}`) of class `Welcome1`. Each comment indicates the method or class that the right brace terminates.

Good Programming Practice 2.8

Following the closing right brace (}) of a method body or class declaration with an end-of-line comment indicating the method or class declaration to which the brace belongs improves program readability.

Compiling and Executing Your First Java Application

We are now ready to compile and execute our program. For this purpose, we assume you are using the Sun Microsystems' Java SE Development Kit 6.0 (JDK 6.0). In our Java Resource Centers at www.deitel.com/ResourceCenters.html, we provide links to tutorials that help you get started with several popular Java development tools.

To prepare to compile the program, open a command window and change to the directory where the program is stored. Most operating systems use the command **cd** to change directories. For example,

```
cd c:\examples\ch02\fig02_01
```

changes to the fig02_01 directory on Windows. The command

```
cd ~/examples/ch02/fig02_01
```

changes to the fig02_01 directory on UNIX/Linux/Max OS X.

To compile the program, type

```
javac Welcome1.java
```

If the program contains no syntax errors, the preceding command creates a new file called Welcome1.class (known as the class file for Welcome1) containing the Java bytecodes that represent our application. When we use the java command to execute the application, these bytecodes will be executed by the JVM.

Error-Prevention Tip 2.3

When attempting to compile a program, if you receive a message such as "bad command or file-name," "javac: command not found" or "'javac' is not recognized as an internal or external command, operable program or batch file," then your Java software installation was not completed properly. If you are using the JDK, this indicates that the system's PATH environment variable was not set properly. Please review the installation instructions in the Before You Begin section of this book carefully. On some systems, after correcting the PATH, you may need to reboot your computer or open a new command window for these settings to take effect.

Error-Prevention Tip 2.4

The Java compiler generates syntax-error messages when the syntax of a program is incorrect. Each error message contains the file name and line number where the error occurred. For example, Welcome1.java:6 indicates that an error occurred in the file Welcome1.java at line 6. The remainder of the error message provides information about the syntax error.

Error-Prevention Tip 2.5

The compiler error message "Public class ClassName must be defined in a file called ClassName.java" indicates that the file name does not exactly match the name of the public class in the file or that you typed the class name incorrectly when compiling the class.

Figure 2.2 shows the program of Fig. 2.1 executing in a Microsoft® Windows® XP **Command Prompt** window. To execute the program, type java Welcome1. This launches the JVM, which loads the ".class" file for class Welcome1. Note that the ".class" file-name extension is omitted from the preceding command; otherwise, the JVM will not execute the program. The JVM calls method main. Next, the statement at line 9 of main displays "Welcome to Java Programming!" [*Note:* Many environments show command prompts with black backgrounds and white text. We adjusted these settings in our environment to make our screen captures more readable.]

You type this command to
execute the application

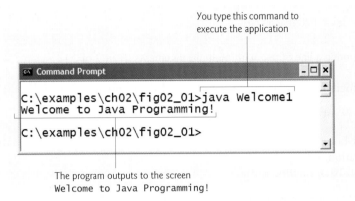

The program outputs to the screen
Welcome to Java Programming!

Fig. 2.2 | Executing Welcome1 in a Microsoft Windows XP **Command Prompt** window.

Error-Prevention Tip 2.6

When attempting to run a Java program, if you receive a message such as "Exception in thread "main" java.lang.NoClassDefFoundError: Welcome1," your CLASSPATH environment variable has not been set properly. Please review the installation instructions in the Before You Begin section of this book carefully. On some systems, you may need to reboot your computer or open a new command window after configuring the CLASSPATH.

2.3 Modifying Our First Java Program

This section continues our introduction to Java programming with two examples that modify the example in Fig. 2.1 to print text on one line by using multiple statements and to print text on several lines by using a single statement.

Displaying a Single Line of Text with Multiple Statements

Welcome to Java Programming! can be displayed several ways. Class Welcome2, shown in Fig. 2.3, uses two statements to produce the same output as that shown in Fig. 2.1. From this point forward, we highlight the new and key features in each code listing, as shown in lines 9–10 of this program.

```java
1  // Fig. 2.3: Welcome2.java
2  // Printing a line of text with multiple statements.
3
4  public class Welcome2
5  {
6     // main method begins execution of Java application
7     public static void main( String args[] )
8     {
9        System.out.print( "Welcome to " );
10       System.out.println( "Java Programming!" );
11
12    } // end method main
13
14 } // end class Welcome2
```

Fig. 2.3 | Printing a line of text with multiple statements. (Part 1 of 2.)

```
Welcome to Java Programming!
```

Fig. 2.3 | Printing a line of text with multiple statements. (Part 2 of 2.)

The program is similar to Fig. 2.1, so we discuss only the changes here. Line 2

```
// Printing a line of text with multiple statements.
```

is an end-of-line comment stating the purpose of this program. Line 4 begins the Welcome2 class declaration.

Lines 9–10 of method main

```
System.out.print( "Welcome to " );
System.out.println( "Java Programming!" );
```

display one line of text in the command window. The first statement uses System.out's method print to display a string. Unlike println, after displaying its argument, print does not position the output cursor at the beginning of the next line in the command window—the next character the program displays will appear immediately after the last character that print displays. Thus, line 10 positions the first character in its argument (the letter "J") immediately after the last character that line 9 displays (the space character before the string's closing double-quote character). Each print or println statement resumes displaying characters from where the last print or println statement stopped displaying characters.

Displaying Multiple Lines of Text with a Single Statement

A single statement can display multiple lines by using **newline characters**, which indicate to System.out's print and println methods when they should position the output cursor at the beginning of the next line in the command window. Like blank lines, space characters and tab characters, newline characters are white-space characters. Figure 2.4 outputs four lines of text, using newline characters to determine when to begin each new line. Most of the program is identical to those in Fig. 2.1 and Fig. 2.3, so we discuss only the changes here.

```
1   // Fig. 2.4: Welcome3.java
2   // Printing multiple lines of text with a single statement.
3
4   public class Welcome3
5   {
6      // main method begins execution of Java application
7      public static void main( String args[] )
8      {
9         System.out.println( "Welcome\nto\nJava\nProgramming!" );
10
11     } // end method main
12
13  } // end class Welcome3
```

Fig. 2.4 | Printing multiple lines of text with a single statement. (Part 1 of 2.)

```
Welcome
to
Java
Programming!
```

Fig. 2.4 | Printing multiple lines of text with a single statement. (Part 2 of 2.)

Line 2

```
// Printing multiple lines of text with a single statement.
```

is a comment stating the program's purpose. Line 4 begins the Welcome3 class declaration. Line 9

```
System.out.println( "Welcome\nto\nJava\nProgramming!" );
```

displays four separate lines of text in the command window. Normally, the characters in a string are displayed exactly as they appear in the double quotes. Note, however, that the two characters \ and n (repeated three times in the statement) do not appear on the screen. The backslash (\) is called an escape character. It indicates to System.out's print and println methods that a "special character" is to be output. When a backslash appears in a string of characters, Java combines the next character with the backslash to form an escape sequence. The escape sequence \n represents the newline character. When a newline character appears in a string being output with System.out, the newline character causes the screen's output cursor to move to the beginning of the next line in the command window. Figure 2.5 lists several common escape sequences and describes how they affect the display of characters in the command window. For the complete list of escape sequences, visit java.sun.com/docs/books/jls/third_edition/html/lexical.html#3.10.6.

Escape sequence	Description
\n	Newline. Position the screen cursor at the beginning of the next line.
\t	Horizontal tab. Move the screen cursor to the next tab stop.
\r	Carriage return. Position the screen cursor at the beginning of the current line—do not advance to the next line. Any characters output after the carriage return overwrite the characters previously output on that line.
\\	Backslash. Used to print a backslash character.
\"	Double quote. Used to print a double-quote character. For example, `System.out.println( "\"in quotes\"" );` displays `"in quotes"`

Fig. 2.5 | Some common escape sequences.

2.4 Displaying Text with `printf`

Java SE 5.0 added the `System.out.printf` method for displaying formatted data—the `f` in the name `printf` stands for "formatted." Figure 2.6 outputs the strings `"Welcome to"` and `"Java Programming!"` with `System.out.printf`.

Lines 9–10

```
System.out.printf( "%s\n%s\n",
    "Welcome to", "Java Programming!" );
```

call method `System.out.printf` to display the program's output. The method call specifies three arguments. When a method requires multiple arguments, the arguments are separated with commas (,)—this is known as a comma-separated list.

Good Programming Practice 2.9

Place a space after each comma (,) in an argument list to make programs more readable.

Remember that all statements in Java end with a semicolon (;). Therefore, lines 9–10 represent only one statement. Java allows large statements to be split over many lines. However, you cannot split a statement in the middle of an identifier or in the middle of a string.

Common Programming Error 2.7

Splitting a statement in the middle of an identifier or a string is a syntax error.

Method `printf`'s first argument is a format string that may consist of fixed text and format specifiers. Fixed text is output by `printf` just as it would be output by `print` or `println`. Each format specifier is a placeholder for a value and specifies the type of data to output. Format specifiers also may include optional formatting information.

```
1   // Fig. 2.6: Welcome4.java
2   // Printing multiple lines in a dialog box.
3
4   public class Welcome4
5   {
6      // main method begins execution of Java application
7      public static void main( String args[] )
8      {
9         System.out.printf( "%s\n%s\n",
10           "Welcome to", "Java Programming!" );
11
12     } // end method main
13
14  } // end class Welcome4
```

```
Welcome to
Java Programming!
```

Fig. 2.6 | Displaying multiple lines with method `System.out.printf`.

Format specifiers begin with a percent sign (%) and are followed by a character that represents the data type. For example, the format specifier %s is a placeholder for a string. The format string in line 9 specifies that printf should output two strings and that each string should be followed by a newline character. At the first format specifier's position, printf substitutes the value of the first argument after the format string. At each subsequent format specifier's position, printf substitutes the value of the next argument in the argument list. So this example substitutes "Welcome to" for the first %s and "Java Programming!" for the second %s. The output shows that two lines of text were displayed.

We introduce various formatting features as they are needed in our examples. Chapter 29 presents the details of formatting output with printf.

2.5 Another Java Application: Adding Integers

Our next application reads (or inputs) two integers (whole numbers, like –22, 7, 0 and 1024) typed by a user at the keyboard, computes the sum of the values and displays the result. This program must keep track of the numbers supplied by the user for the calculation later in the program. Programs remember numbers and other data in the computer's memory and access that data through program elements called variables. The program of Fig. 2.7 demonstrates these concepts. In the sample output, we use highlighting to differentiate between the user's input and the program's output.

```java
1  // Fig. 2.7: Addition.java
2  // Addition program that displays the sum of two numbers.
3  import java.util.Scanner; // program uses class Scanner
4
5  public class Addition
6  {
7     // main method begins execution of Java application
8     public static void main( String args[] )
9     {
10        // create Scanner to obtain input from command window
11        Scanner input = new Scanner( System.in );
12
13        int number1; // first number to add
14        int number2; // second number to add
15        int sum; // sum of number1 and number2
16
17        System.out.print( "Enter first integer: " ); // prompt
18        number1 = input.nextInt(); // read first number from user
19
20        System.out.print( "Enter second integer: " ); // prompt
21        number2 = input.nextInt(); // read second number from user
22
23        sum = number1 + number2; // add numbers
24
25        System.out.printf( "Sum is %d\n", sum ); // display sum
26
27     } // end method main
28
29  } // end class Addition
```

Fig. 2.7 | Addition program that displays the sum of two numbers. (Part I of 2.)

```
Enter first integer: 45
Enter second integer: 72
Sum is 117
```

Fig. 2.7 | Addition program that displays the sum of two numbers. (Part 2 of 2.)

Lines 1–2

```
// Fig. 2.7: Addition.java
// Addition program that displays the sum of two numbers.
```

state the figure number, file name and purpose of the program. Line 3

```
import java.util.Scanner; // program uses class Scanner
```

is an **import declaration** that helps the compiler locate a class that is used in this program. A great strength of Java is its rich set of predefined classes that you can reuse rather than "reinventing the wheel." These classes are grouped into **packages**—named collections of related classes—and are collectively referred to as the **Java class library**, or the **Java Application Programming Interface (Java API)**. Programmers use import declarations to identify the predefined classes used in a Java program. The import declaration in line 3 indicates that this example uses Java's predefined Scanner class (discussed shortly) from package java.util. Then the compiler attempts to ensure that you use class Scanner correctly.

Common Programming Error 2.8

All import declarations must appear before the first class declaration in the file. Placing an import declaration inside a class declaration's body or after a class declaration is a syntax error.

Error-Prevention Tip 2.7

Forgetting to include an import declaration for a class used in your program typically results in a compilation error containing a message such as "cannot resolve symbol." When this occurs, check that you provided the proper import declarations and that the names in the import declarations are spelled correctly, including proper use of uppercase and lowercase letters.

Line 5

```
public class Addition
```

begins the declaration of class Addition. The file name for this public class must be Addition.java. Remember that the body of each class declaration starts with an opening left brace (line 6), {, and ends with a closing right brace (line 29), }.

The application begins execution with method main (lines 8–27). The left brace (line 9) marks the beginning of main's body, and the corresponding right brace (line 27) marks the end of main's body. Note that method main is indented one level in the body of class Addition and that the code in the body of main is indented another level for readability.

Line 11

```
Scanner input = new Scanner( System.in );
```

is a **variable declaration statement** (also called a **declaration**) that specifies the name (input) and type (Scanner) of a variable that is used in this program. A **variable** is a location in the computer's memory where a value can be stored for use later in a program. All variables must be declared with a **name** and a **type** before they can be used. A variable's name enables the program to access the value of the variable in memory. A variable's name can be any valid identifier. (See Section 2.2 for identifier naming requirements.) A variable's type specifies what kind of information is stored at that location in memory. Like other statements, declaration statements end with a semicolon (;).

The declaration in line 11 specifies that the variable named input is of type Scanner. A Scanner enables a program to read data (e.g., numbers) for use in a program. The data can come from many sources, such as a file on disk or the user at the keyboard. Before using a Scanner, the program must create it and specify the source of the data.

The equal sign (=) in line 11 indicates that Scanner variable input should be **initialized** (i.e., prepared for use in the program) in its declaration with the result of the expression new Scanner(System.in) to the right of the equal sign. This expression creates a Scanner object that reads data typed by the user at the keyboard. Recall that the standard output object, System.out, allows Java applications to display characters in the command window. Similarly, the **standard input object**, System.in, enables Java applications to read information typed by the user. So, line 11 creates a Scanner that enables the application to read information typed by the user at the keyboard.

The variable declaration statements at lines 13–15

```
int number1; // first number to add
int number2; // second number to add
int sum; // sum of number1 and number2
```

declare that variables number1, number2 and sum hold data of type **int**—these variables can hold **integer** values (whole numbers such as 7, –11, 0 and 31,914). These variables are not yet initialized. The range of values for an int is –2,147,483,648 to +2,147,483,647. We'll soon discuss types **float** and **double**, for holding real numbers, and type **char**, for holding character data. Real numbers are numbers that contain decimal points, such as 3.4, 0.0 and –11.19. Variables of type char represent individual characters, such as an uppercase letter (e.g., A), a digit (e.g., 7), a special character (e.g., * or %) or an escape sequence (e.g., the newline character, \n). Types such as int, float, double and char are called **primitive types** or **built-in types**. Primitive-type names are keywords and therefore must appear in all lowercase letters. Appendix D, Primitive Types, summarizes the characteristics of the eight primitive types (boolean, byte, char, short, int, long, float and double).

Variable declaration statements can be split over several lines, with the variable names separated by commas (i.e., a comma-separated list of variable names). Several variables of the same type may be declared in one declaration or in multiple declarations. For example, lines 13–15 can also be written as a single statement as follows:

```
int number1, // first number to add
    number2, // second number to add
    sum; // sum of number1 and number2
```

Note that we used end-of-line comments in lines 13–15. This use of comments is a common programming practice for indicating the purpose of each variable in the program.

Good Programming Practice 2.10

Declare each variable on a separate line. This format allows a descriptive comment to be easily inserted next to each declaration.

Good Programming Practice 2.11

Choosing meaningful variable names helps a program to be self-documenting (i.e., one can understand the program simply by reading it rather than by reading manuals or viewing an excessive number of comments).

Good Programming Practice 2.12

By convention, variable-name identifiers begin with a lowercase letter, and every word in the name after the first word begins with a capital letter. For example, variable-name identifier firstNumber has a capital N in its second word, Number.

Line 17

```
System.out.print( "Enter first integer: " ); // prompt
```

uses System.out.print to display the message "Enter first integer: ". This message is called a **prompt** because it directs the user to take a specific action. Recall from Section 2.2 that identifiers starting with capital letters represent class names. So, System is a class. Class System is part of package java.lang. Notice that class System is not imported with an import declaration at the beginning of the program.

Software Engineering Observation 2.1

By default, package java.lang is imported in every Java program; thus, classes in java.lang are the only ones in the Java API that do not require an import declaration.

Line 18

```
number1 = input.nextInt(); // read first number from user
```

uses Scanner object input's nextInt method to obtain an integer from the user at the keyboard. At this point the program waits for the user to type the number and press the *Enter* key to submit the number to the program.

Technically, the user can type anything as the input value. Our program assumes that the user enters a valid integer value as requested. In this program, if the user types a non-integer value, a runtime logic error will occur and the program will terminate. Chapter 13, Exception Handling, discusses how to make your programs more robust by enabling them to handle such errors. This is also known as making your program **fault tolerant**.

In line 18, the result of the call to method nextInt (an int value) is placed in variable number1 by using the **assignment operator**, =. The statement is read as "number1 gets the value of input.nextInt()." Operator = is called a **binary operator** because it has two operands—number1 and the result of the method call input.nextInt(). This statement is called an **assignment statement** because it assigns a value to a variable. Everything to the right of the assignment operator, =, is always evaluated before the assignment is performed.

Good Programming Practice 2.13

Place spaces on either side of a binary operator to make it stand out and make the program more readable.

Line 20

```
System.out.print( "Enter second integer: " ); // prompt
```

prompts the user to input the second integer.

Line 21

```
number2 = input.nextInt(); // read second number from user
```

reads the second integer and assigns it to variable number2.

Line 23

```
sum = number1 + number2; // add numbers
```

is an assignment statement that calculates the sum of the variables number1 and number2 and assigns the result to variable sum by using the assignment operator, =. The statement is read as "sum gets the value of number1 + number2." Most calculations are performed in assignment statements. When the program encounters the addition operation, it uses the values stored in the variables number1 and number2 to perform the calculation. In the preceding statement, the addition operator is a binary operator—its two operands are number1 and number2. Portions of statements that contain calculations are called **expressions**. In fact, an expression is any portion of a statement that has a value associated with it. For example, the value of the expression number1 + number2 is the sum of the numbers. Similarly, the value of the expression input.nextInt() is an integer typed by the user.

After the calculation has been performed, line 25

```
System.out.printf( "Sum is %d\n", sum ); // display sum
```

uses method System.out.printf to display the sum. The format specifier **%d** is a placeholder for an int value (in this case the value of sum)—the letter d stands for "decimal integer." Note that other than the %d format specifier, the remaining characters in the format string are all fixed text. So method printf displays "Sum is ", followed by the value of sum (in the position of the %d format specifier) and a newline.

Note that calculations can also be performed inside printf statements. We could have combined the statements at lines 23 and 25 into the statement

```
System.out.printf( "Sum is %d\n", ( number1 + number2 ) );
```

The parentheses around the expression number1 + number2 are not required—they are included to emphasize that the value of the expression is output in the position of the %d format specifier.

Java API Documentation

For each new Java API class we use, we indicate the package in which it is located. This package information is important because it helps you locate descriptions of each package and class in the **Java API documentation**. A Web-based version of this documentation can be found at

```
java.sun.com/javase/6/docs/api/
```

Also, you can download this documentation to your own computer from

```
java.sun.com/javase/downloads/ea.jsp
```

The download is approximately 53 megabytes (MB). Appendix J, Using the Java API Documentation, describes how to use the Java API documentation.

2.6 **Memory Concepts**

Variable names such as number1, number2 and sum actually correspond to locations in the computer's memory. Every variable has a name, a type, a size and a value.

In the addition program of Fig. 2.7, when the following statement (line 18) executes

```
number1 = input.nextInt(); // read first number from user
```

the number typed by the user is placed into a memory location to which the compiler assigned the name number1. Suppose that the user enters 45. The computer places that integer value into location number1, as shown in Fig. 2.8. Whenever a value is placed in a memory location, the value replaces the previous value in that location. The previous value is lost.

When the statement (line 21)

```
number2 = input.nextInt(); // read second number from user
```

executes, suppose that the user enters 72. The computer places that integer value into location number2. The memory now appears as shown in Fig. 2.9.

After the program of Fig. 2.7 obtains values for number1 and number2, it adds the values and places the sum into variable sum. The statement (line 23)

```
sum = number1 + number2; // add numbers
```

performs the addition, then replaces sum's previous value. After sum has been calculated, memory appears as shown in Fig. 2.10. Note that the values of number1 and number2 appear exactly as they did before they were used in the calculation of sum. These values were used, but not destroyed, as the computer performed the calculation. Thus, when a value is read from a memory location, the process is nondestructive.

number1	45

Fig. 2.8 | Memory location showing the name and value of variable number1.

number1	45
number2	72

Fig. 2.9 | Memory locations after storing values for **number1** and **number2**.

number1	45
number2	72
sum	117

Fig. 2.10 | Memory locations after storing the sum of **number1** and **number2**.

2.7 Arithmetic

Most programs perform arithmetic calculations. The arithmetic operators are summarized in Fig. 2.11. Note the use of various special symbols not used in algebra. The asterisk (*) indicates multiplication, and the percent sign (%) is the remainder operator (called modulus in some languages), which we will discuss shortly. The arithmetic operators in Fig. 2.11 are binary operators because they each operate on two operands. For example, the expression f + 7 contains the binary operator + and the two operands f and 7.

Integer division yields an integer quotient—for example, the expression 7 / 4 evaluates to 1, and the expression 17 / 5 evaluates to 3. Any fractional part in integer division is simply discarded (i.e., truncated)—no rounding occurs. Java provides the remainder operator, %, which yields the remainder after division. The expression x % y yields the remainder after x is divided by y. Thus, 7 % 4 yields 3, and 17 % 5 yields 2. This operator is most commonly used with integer operands but can also be used with other arithmetic types. In this chapter's exercises and in later chapters, we consider several interesting applications of the remainder operator, such as determining whether one number is a multiple of another.

Arithmetic Expressions in Straight-Line Form

Arithmetic expressions in Java must be written in straight-line form to facilitate entering programs into the computer. Thus, expressions such as "a divided by b" must be written as a / b, so that all constants, variables and operators appear in a straight line. The following algebraic notation is generally not acceptable to compilers:

$$\frac{a}{b}$$

Parentheses for Grouping Subexpressions

Parentheses are used to group terms in Java expressions in the same manner as in algebraic expressions. For example, to multiply a times the quantity b + c, we write

    a * (b + c)

If an expression contains nested parentheses, such as

    ((a + b) * c)

the expression in the innermost set of parentheses (a + b in this case) is evaluated first.

Java operation	Arithmetic operator	Algebraic expression	Java expression
Addition	+	$f + 7$	f + 7
Subtraction	–	$p - c$	p – c
Multiplication	*	bm	b * m
Division	/	x / y or $\frac{x}{y}$ or $x \div y$	x / y
Remainder	%	$r \bmod s$	r % s

Fig. 2.11 | Arithmetic operators.

Rules of Operator Precedence

Java applies the operators in arithmetic expressions in a precise sequence determined by the following rules of operator precedence, which are generally the same as those followed in algebra (Fig. 2.12):

1. Multiplication, division and remainder operations are applied first. If an expression contains several such operations, the operators are applied from left to right. Multiplication, division and remainder operators have the same level of precedence.

2. Addition and subtraction operations are applied next. If an expression contains several such operations, the operators are applied from left to right. Addition and subtraction operators have the same level of precedence.

These rules enable Java to apply operators in the correct order. When we say that operators are applied from left to right, we are referring to their associativity. You will see that some operators associate from right to left. Figure 2.12 summarizes these rules of operator precedence. The table will be expanded as additional Java operators are introduced. A complete precedence chart is included in Appendix A, Operator Precedence Chart.

Sample Algebraic and Java Expressions

Now let us consider several expressions in light of the rules of operator precedence. Each example lists an algebraic expression and its Java equivalent. The following is an example of an arithmetic mean (average) of five terms:

Algebra: $m = \dfrac{a + b + c + d + e}{5}$

Java: `m = ( a + b + c + d + e ) / 5;`

The parentheses are required because division has higher precedence than addition. The entire quantity (a + b + c + d + e) is to be divided by 5. If the parentheses are erroneously omitted, we obtain a + b + c + d + e / 5, which evaluates as

$$a + b + c + d + \dfrac{e}{5}$$

Operator(s)	Operation(s)	Order of evaluation (precedence)
* / %	Multiplication Division Remainder	Evaluated first. If there are several operators of this type, they are evaluated from left to right.
+ -	Addition Subtraction	Evaluated next. If there are several operators of this type, they are evaluated from left to right.

Fig. 2.12 | Precedence of arithmetic operators.

The following is an example of the equation of a straight line:

Algebra: $y = mx + b$

Java: y = m * x + b;

No parentheses are required. The multiplication operator is applied first because multiplication has a higher precedence than addition. The assignment occurs last because it has a lower precedence than multiplication or addition.

The following example contains remainder (%), multiplication, division, addition and subtraction operations:

Algebra: $z = pr\%q + w/x - y$

Java: z = p * r % q + w / x - y;
                      6   1   2   4   3   5

The circled numbers under the statement indicate the order in which Java applies the operators. The multiplication, remainder and division operations are evaluated first in left-to-right order (i.e., they associate from left to right), because they have higher precedence than addition and subtraction. The addition and subtraction operations are evaluated next. These operations are also applied from left to right.

Evaluation of a Second-Degree Polynomial

To develop a better understanding of the rules of operator precedence, consider the evaluation of a second-degree polynomial ($y = ax^2 + bx + c$):

y = a * x * x + b * x + c;
    6   1   2   4   3   5

The circled numbers indicate the order in which Java applies the operators. The multiplication operations are evaluated first in left-to-right order (i.e., they associate from left to right), because they have higher precedence than addition. The addition operations are evaluated next and are applied from left to right. There is no arithmetic operator for exponentiation in Java, so x^2 is represented as x * x. Section 5.4 shows an alternative for performing exponentiation in Java.

Suppose that a, b, c and x in the preceding second-degree polynomial are initialized (given values) as follows: a = 2, b = 3, c = 7 and x = 5. Figure 2.13 illustrates the order in which the operators are applied.

As in algebra, it is acceptable to place unnecessary parentheses in an expression to make the expression clearer. These are called redundant parentheses. For example, the preceding statement might be parenthesized as follows:

y = (a * x * x) + (b * x) + c;

Good Programming Practice 2.14

Using parentheses for complex arithmetic expressions, even when the parentheses are not necessary, can make the arithmetic expressions easier to read.

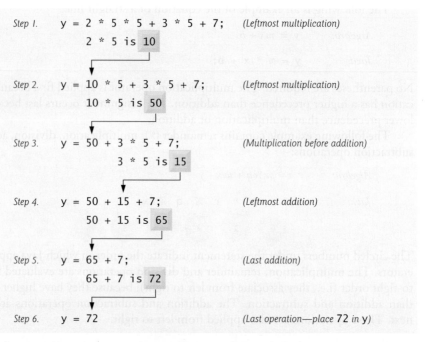

Step 1.   y = 2 * 5 * 5 + 3 * 5 + 7;   *(Leftmost multiplication)*

2 * 5 is 10

Step 2.   y = 10 * 5 + 3 * 5 + 7;   *(Leftmost multiplication)*

10 * 5 is 50

Step 3.   y = 50 + 3 * 5 + 7;   *(Multiplication before addition)*

3 * 5 is 15

Step 4.   y = 50 + 15 + 7;   *(Leftmost addition)*

50 + 15 is 65

Step 5.   y = 65 + 7;   *(Last addition)*

65 + 7 is 72

Step 6.   y = 72   *(Last operation—place 72 in y)*

Fig. 2.13 | Order in which a second-degree polynomial is evaluated.

2.8 Decision Making: Equality and Relational Operators

A condition is an expression that can be either true or false. This section introduces Java's if statement that allows a program to make a decision based on a condition's value. For example, the condition "grade is greater than or equal to 60" determines whether a student passed a test. If the condition in an if statement is true, the body of the if statement executes. If the condition is false, the body does not execute. We will see an example shortly.

Conditions in if statements can be formed by using the equality operators (== and !=) and relational operators (>, <, >= and <=) summarized in Fig. 2.14. Both equality operators have the same level of precedence, which is lower than that of the relational operators. The equality operators associate from left to right. The relational operators all have the same level of precedence and also associate from left to right.

Standard algebraic equality or relational operator	Java equality or relational operator	Sample Java condition	Meaning of Java condition
Equality operators			
=	==	x == y	x is equal to y
≠	!=	x != y	x is not equal to y

Fig. 2.14 | Equality and relational operators. (Part 1 of 2.)

Standard algebraic equality or relational operator	Java equality or relational operator	Sample Java condition	Meaning of Java condition
Relational operators			
>	>	x > y	x is greater than y
<	<	x < y	x is less than y
≥	>=	x >= y	x is greater than or equal to y
≤	<=	x <= y	x is less than or equal to y

Fig. 2.14 | Equality and relational operators. (Part 2 of 2.)

The application of Fig. 2.15 uses six `if` statements to compare two integers input by the user. If the condition in any of these `if` statements is true, the assignment statement associated with that `if` statement executes. The program uses a `Scanner` to input the two integers from the user and store them in variables `number1` and `number2`. Then the program compares the numbers and displays the results of the comparisons that are true.

The declaration of class `Comparison` begins at line 6

```
public class Comparison
```

The class's `main` method (lines 9–41) begins the execution of the program. Line 12

```
Scanner input = new Scanner( System.in );
```

declares `Scanner` variable `input` and assigns it a `Scanner` that inputs data from the standard input (i.e., the keyboard).

```
1   // Fig. 2.15: Comparison.java
2   // Compare integers using if statements, relational operators
3   // and equality operators.
4   import java.util.Scanner; // program uses class Scanner
5
6   public class Comparison
7   {
8      // main method begins execution of Java application
9      public static void main( String args[] )
10     {
11        // create Scanner to obtain input from command window
12        Scanner input = new Scanner( System.in );
13
14        int number1; // first number to compare
15        int number2; // second number to compare
16
17        System.out.print( "Enter first integer: " ); // prompt
18        number1 = input.nextInt(); // read first number from user
```

Fig. 2.15 | Equality and relational operators. (Part 1 of 2.)

```
19
20          System.out.print( "Enter second integer: " ); // prompt
21          number2 = input.nextInt(); // read second number from user
22
23          if ( number1 == number2 )
24             System.out.printf( "%d == %d\n", number1, number2 );
25
26          if ( number1 != number2 )
27             System.out.printf( "%d != %d\n", number1, number2 );
28
29          if ( number1 < number2 )
30             System.out.printf( "%d < %d\n", number1, number2 );
31
32          if ( number1 > number2 )
33             System.out.printf( "%d > %d\n", number1, number2 );
34
35          if ( number1 <= number2 )
36             System.out.printf( "%d <= %d\n", number1, number2 );
37
38          if ( number1 >= number2 )
39             System.out.printf( "%d >= %d\n", number1, number2 );
40
41       } // end method main
42
43   } // end class Comparison
```

```
Enter first integer: 777
Enter second integer: 777
777 == 777
777 <= 777
777 >= 777
```

```
Enter first integer: 1000
Enter second integer: 2000
1000 != 2000
1000 < 2000
1000 <= 2000
```

```
Enter first integer: 2000
Enter second integer: 1000
2000 != 1000
2000 > 1000
2000 >= 1000
```

Fig. 2.15 | Equality and relational operators. (Part 2 of 2.)

Lines 14–15

```
int number1; // first number to compare
int number2; // second number to compare
```

declare the int variables used to store the values input from the user.

Lines 17–18

```
System.out.print( "Enter first integer: " ); // prompt
number1 = input.nextInt(); // read first number from user
```

prompt the user to enter the first integer and input the value, respectively. The input value is stored in variable `number1`.

Lines 20–21

```
System.out.print( "Enter second integer: " ); // prompt
number2 = input.nextInt(); // read second number from user
```

prompt the user to enter the second integer and input the value, respectively. The input value is stored in variable `number2`.

Lines 23–24

```
if ( number1 == number2 )
   System.out.printf( "%d == %d\n", number1, number2 );
```

declare an `if` statement that compares the values of the variables `number1` and `number2` to determine whether they are equal. An `if` statement always begins with keyword `if`, followed by a condition in parentheses. An `if` statement expects one statement in its body. The indentation of the body statement shown here is not required, but it improves the program's readability by emphasizing that the statement in line 24 is part of the `if` statement that begins at line 23. Line 24 executes only if the numbers stored in variables `number1` and `number2` are equal (i.e., the condition is true). The `if` statements at lines 26–27, 29–30, 32–33, 35–36 and 38–39 compare `number1` and `number2` with the operators !=, <, >, <= and >=, respectively. If the condition in any of the `if` statements is true, the corresponding body statement executes.

Common Programming Error 2.9

Forgetting the left and/or right parentheses for the condition in an `if` statement is a syntax error—the parentheses are required.

Common Programming Error 2.10

Confusing the equality operator, ==, with the assignment operator, =, can cause a logic error or a syntax error. The equality operator should be read as "is equal to," and the assignment operator should be read as "gets" or "gets the value of." To avoid confusion, some people read the equality operator as "double equals" or "equals equals."

Common Programming Error 2.11

It is a syntax error if the operators ==, !=, >= and <= contain spaces between their symbols, as in = =, ! =, > = and < =, respectively.

Common Programming Error 2.12

Reversing the operators !=, >= and <=, as in =!, => and =<, is a syntax error.

Good Programming Practice 2.15

Indent an `if` statement's body to make it stand out and to enhance program readability.

Good Programming Practice 2.16

Place only one statement per line in a program. This format enhances program readability.

Note that there is no semicolon (;) at the end of the first line of each if statement. Such a semicolon would result in a logic error at execution time. For example,

```
if ( number1 == number2 ); // logic error
    System.out.printf( "%d == %d\n", number1, number2 );
```

would actually be interpreted by Java as

```
if ( number1 == number2 )
    ; // empty statement

System.out.printf( "%d == %d\n", number1, number2 );
```

where the semicolon on the line by itself—called the empty statement—is the statement to execute if the condition in the if statement is true. When the empty statement executes, no task is performed in the program. The program then continues with the output statement, which always executes, regardless of whether the condition is true or false, because the output statement is not part of the if statement.

Common Programming Error 2.13

Placing a semicolon immediately after the right parenthesis of the condition in an if statement is normally a logic error.

Note the use of white space in Fig. 2.15. Recall that white-space characters, such as tabs, newlines and spaces, are normally ignored by the compiler. So statements may be split over several lines and may be spaced according to the programmer's preferences without affecting the meaning of a program. It is incorrect to split identifiers and strings. Ideally, statements should be kept small, but this is not always possible.

Good Programming Practice 2.17

A lengthy statement can be spread over several lines. If a single statement must be split across lines, choose breaking points that make sense, such as after a comma in a comma-separated list, or after an operator in a lengthy expression. If a statement is split across two or more lines, indent all subsequent lines until the end of the statement.

Figure 2.16 shows the precedence of the operators introduced in this chapter. The operators are shown from top to bottom in decreasing order of precedence. All these operators, with the exception of the assignment operator, =, associate from left to right. Addition is left associative, so an expression like x + y + z is evaluated as if it had been written as (x + y) + z. The assignment operator, =, associates from right to left, so an expression like x = y = 0 is evaluated as if it had been written as x = (y = 0), which, as we will soon see, first assigns the value 0 to variable y and then assigns the result of that assignment, 0, to x.

Good Programming Practice 2.18

Refer to the operator precedence chart (Appendix A) when writing expressions containing many operators. Confirm that the operations in the expression are performed in the order you expect. If you are uncertain about the order of evaluation in a complex expression, use parentheses to force the order, exactly as you would do in algebraic expressions. Observe that some operators, such as assignment, =, associate from right to left rather than from left to right.

Operators				Associativity	Type
*	/	%		left to right	multiplicative
+	-			left to right	additive
<	<=	>	>=	left to right	relational
==	!=			left to right	equality
=				right to left	assignment

Fig. 2.16 | Precedence and associativity of operations discussed.

2.9 (Optional) Software Engineering Case Study: Examining the Requirements Document

Now we begin our optional object-oriented design and implementation case study. The Software Engineering Case Study sections at the ends of this and the next several chapters will ease you into object orientation by examining an automated teller machine (ATM) case study. This case study will provide you with a concise, carefully paced, complete design and implementation experience. In Chapters 3–8 and 10, we will perform the various steps of an object-oriented design (OOD) process using the UML while relating these steps to the object-oriented concepts discussed in the chapters. Appendix M implements the ATM using the techniques of object-oriented programming (OOP) in Java. We present the complete case-study solution. This is not an exercise; rather, it is an end-to-end learning experience that concludes with a detailed walkthrough of the Java code that implements our design. It will acquaint you with the kinds of substantial problems encountered in industry and their potential solutions. We hope you enjoy this learning experience.

We begin our design process by presenting a **requirements document** that specifies the overall purpose of the ATM system and *what* it must do. Throughout the case study, we refer to the requirements document to determine precisely what functionality the system must include.

Requirements Document

A local bank intends to install a new automated teller machine (ATM) to allow users (i.e., bank customers) to perform basic financial transactions (Fig. 2.17). Each user can have only one account at the bank. ATM users should be able to view their account balance, withdraw cash (i.e., take money out of an account) and deposit funds (i.e., place money into an account). The user interface of the automated teller machine contains the following components:

- a screen that displays messages to the user
- a keypad that receives numeric input from the user
- a cash dispenser that dispenses cash to the user and
- a deposit slot that receives deposit envelopes from the user.

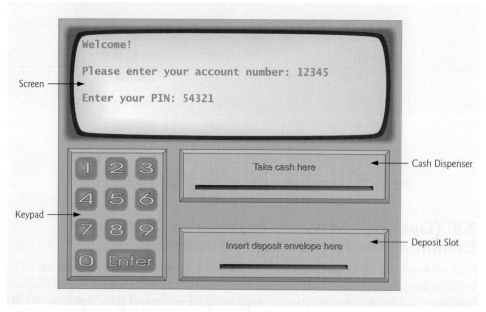

Fig. 2.17 | Automated teller machine user interface.

The cash dispenser begins each day loaded with 500 $20 bills. [*Note:* Due to the limited scope of this case study, certain elements of the ATM described here do not accurately mimic those of a real ATM. For example, a real ATM typically contains a device that reads a user's account number from an ATM card, whereas this ATM asks the user to type the account number on the keypad. A real ATM also usually prints a receipt at the end of a session, but all output from this ATM appears on the screen.]

The bank wants you to develop software to perform the financial transactions initiated by bank customers through the ATM. The bank will integrate the software with the ATM's hardware at a later time. The software should encapsulate the functionality of the hardware devices (e.g., cash dispenser, deposit slot) within software components, but it need not concern itself with how these devices perform their duties. The ATM hardware has not been developed yet, so instead of writing your software to run on the ATM, you should develop a first version of the software to run on a personal computer. This version should use the computer's monitor to simulate the ATM's screen, and the computer's keyboard to simulate the ATM's keypad.

An ATM session consists of authenticating a user (i.e., proving the user's identity) based on an account number and personal identification number (PIN), followed by creating and executing financial transactions. To authenticate a user and perform transactions, the ATM must interact with the bank's account information database (i.e., an organized collection of data stored on a computer). For each bank account, the database stores an account number, a PIN and a balance indicating the amount of money in the account. [*Note:* We assume that the bank plans to build only one ATM, so we do not need to worry about multiple ATMs accessing this database at the same time. Furthermore, we assume that the bank does not make any changes to the information in the database while a user is accessing the ATM. Also, any business system like an ATM faces reasonably complicated security issues that are beyond the scope of a first or second programming course. We make the simplifying assumption, however, that the bank trusts the ATM to access and manipulate the information in the database without significant security measures.]

Upon first approaching the ATM (assuming no one is currently using it), the user should experience the following sequence of events (shown in Fig. 2.17):

1. The screen displays a welcome message and prompts the user to enter an account number.

2. The user enters a five-digit account number using the keypad.

3. The screen prompts the user to enter the PIN (personal identification number) associated with the specified account number.

4. The user enters a five-digit PIN using the keypad.

5. If the user enters a valid account number and the correct PIN for that account, the screen displays the main menu (Fig. 2.18). If the user enters an invalid account number or an incorrect PIN, the screen displays an appropriate message, then the ATM returns to *Step 1* to restart the authentication process.

After the ATM authenticates the user, the main menu (Fig. 2.18) should contain a numbered option for each of the three types of transactions: balance inquiry (option 1), withdrawal (option 2) and deposit (option 3). The main menu also should contain an option to allow the user to exit the system (option 4). The user then chooses either to perform a transaction (by entering 1, 2 or 3) or to exit the system (by entering 4).

If the user enters 1 to make a balance inquiry, the screen displays the user's account balance. To do so, the ATM must retrieve the balance from the bank's database.

Fig. 2.18 | ATM main menu.

The following steps describe the actions that occur when the user enters 2 to make a withdrawal:

1. The screen displays a menu (shown in Fig. 2.19) containing standard withdrawal amounts: $20 (option 1), $40 (option 2), $60 (option 3), $100 (option 4) and $200 (option 5). The menu also contains an option to allow the user to cancel the transaction (option 6).

2. The user enters a menu selection using the keypad.

3. If the withdrawal amount chosen is greater than the user's account balance, the screen displays a message stating this and telling the user to choose a smaller amount. The ATM then returns to *Step 1*. If the withdrawal amount chosen is less than or equal to the user's account balance (i.e., an acceptable amount), the ATM proceeds to *Step 4*. If the user chooses to cancel the transaction (option 6), the ATM displays the main menu and waits for user input.

4. If the cash dispenser contains enough cash to satisfy the request, the ATM proceeds to *Step 5*. Otherwise, the screen displays a message indicating the problem and telling the user to choose a smaller withdrawal amount. The ATM then returns to *Step 1*.

5. The ATM debits the withdrawal amount from the user's account in the bank's database (i.e., subtracts the withdrawal amount from the user's account balance).

6. The cash dispenser dispenses the desired amount of money to the user.

7. The screen displays a message reminding the user to take the money.

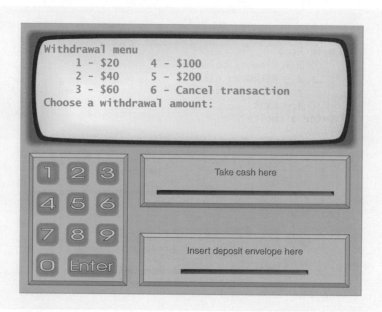

Fig. 2.19 | ATM withdrawal menu.

The following steps describe the actions that occur when the user enters 3 to make a deposit:

1. The screen prompts the user to enter a deposit amount or type 0 (zero) to cancel the transaction.

2. The user enters a deposit amount or 0 using the keypad. [*Note:* The keypad does not contain a decimal point or a dollar sign, so the user cannot type a real dollar amount (e.g., $1.25). Instead, the user must enter a deposit amount as a number of cents (e.g., 125). The ATM then divides this number by 100 to obtain a number representing a dollar amount (e.g., $125 \div 100 = 1.25$).]

3. If the user specifies a deposit amount, the ATM proceeds to *Step 4*. If the user chooses to cancel the transaction (by entering 0), the ATM displays the main menu and waits for user input.

4. The screen displays a message telling the user to insert a deposit envelope into the deposit slot.

5. If the deposit slot receives a deposit envelope within two minutes, the ATM credits the deposit amount to the user's account in the bank's database (i.e., adds the deposit amount to the user's account balance). [*Note:* This money is not immediately available for withdrawal. The bank first must physically verify the amount of cash in the deposit envelope, and any checks in the envelope must clear (i.e., money must be transferred from the check writer's account to the check recipient's account). When either of these events occurs, the bank appropriately updates the user's balance stored in its database. This occurs independently of the ATM system.] If the deposit slot does not receive a deposit envelope within this time period, the screen displays a message that the system has canceled the transaction due to inactivity. The ATM then displays the main menu and waits for user input.

After the system successfully executes a transaction, it should return to the main menu so that the user can perform additional transactions. If the user chooses to exit the system, the screen should display a thank you message, then display the welcome message for the next user.

Analyzing the ATM System

The preceding statement is a simplified example of a requirements document. Typically, such a document is the result of a detailed process of **requirements gathering** that might include interviews with possible users of the system and specialists in fields related to the system. For example, a systems analyst who is hired to prepare a requirements document for banking software (e.g., the ATM system described here) might interview financial experts to gain a better understanding of what the software must do. The analyst would use the information gained to compile a list of system requirements to guide systems designers as they design the system.

The process of requirements gathering is a key task of the first stage of the software life cycle. The software life cycle specifies the stages through which software goes from the time it is first conceived to the time it is retired from use. These stages typically include: analysis, design, implementation, testing and debugging, deployment, maintenance and retirement. Several software life-cycle models exist, each with its own preferences and specifications for when and how often software engineers should perform each of these stages. Waterfall models perform each stage once in succession, whereas iterative models may repeat one or more stages several times throughout a product's life cycle.

The analysis stage of the software life cycle focuses on defining the problem to be solved. When designing any system, one must *solve the problem right*, but of equal importance, one must *solve the right problem*. Systems analysts collect the requirements that indicate the specific problem to solve. Our requirements document describes the requirements of our ATM system in sufficient detail that you do not need to go through an extensive analysis stage—it has been done for you.

To capture what a proposed system should do, developers often employ a technique known as use case modeling. This process identifies the use cases of the system, each of which represents a different capability that the system provides to its clients. For example, ATMs typically have several use cases, such as "View Account Balance," "Withdraw Cash," "Deposit Funds," "Transfer Funds Between Accounts" and "Buy Postage Stamps." The simplified ATM system we build in this case study allows only the first three use cases.

Each use case describes a typical scenario for which the user uses the system. You have already read descriptions of the ATM system's use cases in the requirements document; the lists of steps required to perform each transaction type (i.e., balance inquiry, withdrawal and deposit) actually described the three use cases of our ATM—"View Account Balance," "Withdraw Cash" and "Deposit Funds," respectively.

Use Case Diagrams

We now introduce the first of several UML diagrams in the case study. We create a use case diagram to model the interactions between a system's clients (in this case study, bank customers) and its use cases. The goal is to show the kinds of interactions users have with a system without providing the details—these are provided in other UML diagrams (which we present throughout this case study). Use case diagrams are often accompanied by informal text that describes the use cases in more detail—like the text that appears in the requirements document. Use case diagrams are produced during the analysis stage of the software life cycle. In larger systems, use case diagrams are indispensable tools that help system designers remain focused on satisfying the users' needs.

Figure 2.20 shows the use case diagram for our ATM system. The stick figure represents an actor, which defines the roles that an external entity—such as a person or another system—plays when interacting with the system. For our automated teller machine, the actor is a User who can view an account balance, withdraw cash and deposit funds from the ATM. The User is not an actual person, but instead comprises the roles that a real person—when playing the part of a User—can play while interacting with the ATM. Note that a use case diagram can include multiple actors. For example, the use case diagram for a real bank's ATM system might also include an actor named Administrator who refills the cash dispenser each day.

Our requirements document supplies the actors—"ATM users should be able to view their account balance, withdraw cash and deposit funds." Therefore, the actor in each of the three use cases is the user who interacts with the ATM. An external entity—a real person—plays the part of the user to perform financial transactions. Figure 2.20 shows one actor, whose name, User, appears below the actor in the diagram. The UML models each use case as an oval connected to an actor with a solid line.

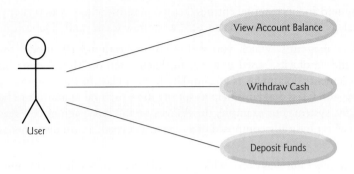

Fig. 2.20 | Use case diagram for the ATM system from the User's perspective.

Software engineers (more precisely, systems designers) must analyze the requirements document or a set of use cases and design the system before programmers implement it in a particular programming language. During the analysis stage, systems designers focus on understanding the requirements document to produce a high-level specification that describes *what* the system is supposed to do. The output of the design stage—a design specification—should specify clearly *how* the system should be constructed to satisfy these requirements. In the next several Software Engineering Case Study sections, we perform the steps of a simple object-oriented design (OOD) process on the ATM system to produce a design specification containing a collection of UML diagrams and supporting text. The UML is designed for use with any OOD process. Many such processes exist, the most well-known of which is the Rational Unified Process™ (RUP) developed by Rational Software Corporation. RUP is a rich process intended for designing "industrial strength" applications. For this case study, we present our own simplified design process, designed for students in first and second programming courses.

Designing the ATM System
We now begin the design stage of our ATM system. A system is a set of components that interact to solve a problem. For example, to perform the ATM system's designated tasks, our ATM system has a user interface (Fig. 2.17), contains software that executes financial transactions and interacts with a database of bank account information. System structure describes the system's objects and their interrelationships. System behavior describes how the system changes as its objects interact with one another. Every system has both structure and behavior—designers must specify both. There are several distinct types of system structures and behaviors. For example, the interactions among objects in the system differ from those between the user and the system, yet both constitute a portion of the system behavior.

The UML 2 standard specifies 13 diagram types for documenting the system models. Each models a distinct characteristic of a system's structure or behavior—six diagrams relate to system structure; the remaining seven relate to system behavior. We list here only the six types used in our case study—one of these (class diagrams) models system structure, whereas the remaining five model system behavior. We overview the remaining seven UML diagram types in Appendix O, UML 2: Additional Diagram Types.

1. **Use case diagrams**, such as the one in Fig. 2.20, model the interactions between a system and its external entities (actors) in terms of use cases (system capabilities, such as "View Account Balance," "Withdraw Cash" and "Deposit Funds").

2. **Class diagrams**, which you will study in Section 3.10, model the classes, or "building blocks," used in a system. Each noun or "thing" described in the requirements document is a candidate to be a class in the system (e.g., Account, Keypad). Class diagrams help us specify the structural relationships between parts of the system. For example, the ATM system class diagram will specify that the ATM is physically composed of a screen, a keypad, a cash dispenser and a deposit slot.

3. **State machine diagrams**, which you will study in Section 5.11, model the ways in which an object changes state. An object's **state** is indicated by the values of all the object's attributes at a given time. When an object changes state, that object may behave differently in the system. For example, after validating a user's PIN, the ATM transitions from the "user not authenticated" state to the "user authenticated" state, at which point the ATM allows the user to perform financial transactions (e.g., view account balance, withdraw cash, deposit funds).

4. **Activity diagrams**, which you will also study in Section 5.11, model an object's **activity**—the object's workflow (sequence of events) during program execution. An activity diagram models the actions the object performs and specifies the order in which the object performs these actions. For example, an activity diagram shows that the ATM must obtain the balance of the user's account (from the bank's account information database) before the screen can display the balance to the user.

5. **Communication diagrams** (called **collaboration diagrams** in earlier versions of the UML) model the interactions among objects in a system, with an emphasis on *what* interactions occur. You will learn in Section 7.14 that these diagrams show which objects must interact to perform an ATM transaction. For example, the ATM must communicate with the bank's account information database to retrieve an account balance.

6. **Sequence diagrams** also model the interactions among the objects in a system, but unlike communication diagrams, they emphasize *when* interactions occur. You will learn in Section 7.14 that these diagrams help show the order in which interactions occur in executing a financial transaction. For example, the screen prompts the user to enter a withdrawal amount before cash is dispensed.

In Section 3.10, we continue designing our ATM system by identifying the classes from the requirements document. We accomplish this by extracting key nouns and noun phrases from the requirements document. Using these classes, we develop our first draft of the class diagram that models the structure of our ATM system.

Internet and Web Resources
The following URLs provide information on object-oriented design with the UML.
www-306.ibm.com/software/rational/uml/
Lists frequently asked questions (FAQs) about the UML, provided by IBM Rational.

`www.douglass.co.uk/documents/softdocwiz.com.UML.htm`
Hosts the Unified Modeling Language Dictionary, which lists and defines all terms used in the UML.

`www-306.ibm.com/software/rational/offerings/design.html`
Provides information about IBM Rational software available for designing systems. Provides downloads of 30-day trial versions of several products, such as IBM Rational Rose® XDE Developer.

`www.embarcadero.com/products/describe/index.html`
Provides a free 14-day license to download a trial version of Describe™—a UML modeling tool from Embarcadero Technologies®.

`www.borland.com/us/products/together/index.html`
Provides a free 30-day license to download a trial version of Borland® Together® Control-Center™—a software-development tool that supports the UML.

`www.ilogix.com/sublevel.aspx?id=53`
Provides a free 30-day license to download a trial version of I-Logix Rhapsody®—a UML 2 based model-driven development environment.

`argouml.tigris.org`
Contains information and downloads for ArgoUML, a free open-source UML tool written in Java.

`www.objectsbydesign.com/books/booklist.html`
Lists books on the UML and object-oriented design.

`www.objectsbydesign.com/tools/umltools_byCompany.html`
Lists software tools that use the UML, such as IBM Rational Rose, Embarcadero Describe, Sparx Systems Enterprise Architect, I-Logix Rhapsody and Gentleware Poseidon for UML.

`www.ootips.org/ood-principles.html`
Provides answers to the question, "What Makes a Good Object-Oriented Design?"

`parlezuml.com/tutorials/umlforjava.htm`
Provides a UML tutorial for Java developers that presents UML diagrams side by side with the Java code that implements them.

`www.cetus-links.org/oo_uml.html`
Introduces the UML and provides links to numerous UML resources.

`www.agilemodeling.com/essays/umlDiagrams.htm`
Provides in-depth descriptions and tutorials on each of the 13 UML 2 diagram types.

Recommended Readings

The following books provide information on object-oriented design with the UML.

Booch, G. *Object-Oriented Analysis and Design with Applications*. 3rd Ed. Boston: Addison-Wesley, 2004.

Eriksson, H., et al. *UML 2 Toolkit*. New York: John Wiley, 2003.

Kruchten, P. *The Rational Unified Process: An Introduction*. Boston: Addison-Wesley, 2004.

Larman, C. *Applying UML and Patterns: An Introduction to Object-Oriented Analysis and Design*. 2nd Ed. Upper Saddle River, NJ: Prentice Hall, 2002.

Roques, P. *UML in Practice: The Art of Modeling Software Systems Demonstrated Through Worked Examples and Solutions*. New York: John Wiley, 2004.

Rosenberg, D., and K. Scott. *Applying Use Case Driven Object Modeling with UML: An Annotated e-Commerce Example*. Reading, MA: Addison-Wesley, 2001.

Rumbaugh, J., I. Jacobson and G. Booch. *The Complete UML Training Course.* Upper Saddle River, NJ: Prentice Hall, 2000.

Rumbaugh, J., I. Jacobson and G. Booch. *The Unified Modeling Language Reference Manual.* Reading, MA: Addison-Wesley, 1999.

Rumbaugh, J., I. Jacobson and G. Booch. *The Unified Software Development Process.* Reading, MA: Addison-Wesley, 1999.

Software Engineering Case Study Self-Review Exercises

2.1   Suppose we enabled a user of our ATM system to transfer money between two bank accounts. Modify the use case diagram of Fig. 2.20 to reflect this change.

2.2   _____ model the interactions among objects in a system with an emphasis on *when* these interactions occur.
   a) Class diagrams
   b) Sequence diagrams
   c) Communication diagrams
   d) Activity diagrams

2.3   Which of the following choices lists stages of a typical software life cycle in sequential order?
   a) design, analysis, implementation, testing
   b) design, analysis, testing, implementation
   c) analysis, design, testing, implementation
   d) analysis, design, implementation, testing

Answers to Software Engineering Case Study Self-Review Exercises

2.1   Figure 2.21 contains a use case diagram for a modified version of our ATM system that also allows users to transfer money between accounts.

2.2   b.

2.3   d.

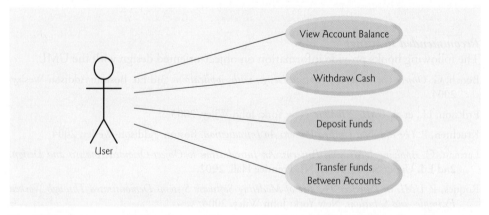

Fig. 2.21 | Use case diagram for a modified version of our ATM system that also allows users to transfer money between accounts.

2.10 Wrap-Up

You learned many important features of Java in this chapter, including displaying data on the screen in a Command Prompt, inputting data from the keyboard, performing calculations and making decisions. The applications presented here were meant to introduce you to basic programming concepts. As you will see in Chapter 3, Java applications typically contain just a few lines of code in method `main`—these statements normally create the objects that perform the work of the application. In Chapter 3, you will learn how to implement your own classes and use objects of those classes in applications.

Summary

Section 2.2 A First Program in Java: Printing a Line of Text

- Computer programmers create applications by writing computer programs. A Java application is a computer program that executes when you use the `java` command to launch the JVM.

- Programmers insert comments to document programs and improve their readability. The Java compiler ignores comments.

- A comment that begins with `//` is called an end-of-line (or single-line) comment because the comment terminates at the end of the line on which it appears.

- Traditional (multiple-line) comments can be spread over several lines and are delimited by `/*` and `*/`. All text between the delimiters is ignored by the compiler.

- Javadoc comments are delimited by `/**` and `*/`. Javadoc comments enable programmers to embed program documentation directly in their programs. The `javadoc` utility program generates HTML documentation based on Javadoc comments.

- A programming language's syntax specifies the rules for creating a proper program in that language.

- A syntax error (also called a compiler error, compile-time error or compilation error) occurs when the compiler encounters code that violates Java's language rules.

- Programmers use blank lines and space characters to make programs easier to read. Together, blank lines, space characters and tab characters are known as white space. Space characters and tabs are known specifically as white-space characters. White space is ignored by the compiler.

- Every program in Java consists of at least one class declaration that is defined by the programmer (also known as a programmer-defined class or a user-defined class).

- Keywords are reserved for use by Java and are always spelled with all lowercase letters.

- Keyword `class` introduces a class declaration and is immediately followed by the class name.

- By convention, all class names in Java begin with a capital letter and capitalize the first letter of each word they include (e.g., `SampleClassName`).

- A Java class name is an identifier—a series of characters consisting of letters, digits, underscores (`_`) and dollar signs (`$`) that does not begin with a digit and does not contain spaces. Normally, an identifier that does not begin with a capital letter is not the name of a Java class.

- Java is case sensitive—that is, uppercase and lowercase letters are distinct.

- The body of every class declaration is delimited by braces, `{` and `}`.

- A `public` class declaration must be saved in a file with the same name as the class followed by the ".java" file-name extension.

- Method main is the starting point of every Java application and must begin with

      public static void main(String args[])

  otherwise, the JVM will not execute the application.

- Methods are able to perform tasks and return information when they complete their tasks. Keyword void indicates that a method will perform a task but will not return any information.

- Statements instruct the computer to perform actions.

- A sequence of characters in double quotation marks is called a string, a character string, a message or a string literal.

- System.out, the standard output object, allows Java applications to display characters in the command window.

- Method System.out.println displays its argument in the command window followed by a newline character to position the output cursor to the beginning of the next line.

- Every statement ends with a semicolon.

- Most operating systems use the command cd to change directories in the command window.

- You compile a program with the command javac. If the program contains no syntax errors, a class file containing the Java bytecodes that represent the application is created. These bytecodes are interpreted by the JVM when we execute the program.

Section 2.3 Modifying Our First Java Program

- System.out.print displays its argument and positions the output cursor immediately after the last character displayed.

- A backslash (\) in a string is an escape character. It indicates that a "special character" is to be output. Java combines the next character with the backslash to form an escape sequence. The escape sequence \n represents the newline character, which positions the cursor on the next line.

Section 2.4 Displaying Text with *printf*

- System.out.printf method (f means "formatted") displays formatted data.

- When a method requires multiple arguments, the arguments are separated with commas (,)—this is known as a comma-separated list.

- Method printf's first argument is a format string that may consist of fixed text and format specifiers. Fixed text is output by printf just as it would be output by print or println. Each format specifier is a placeholder for a value and specifies the type of data to output.

- Format specifiers begin with a percent sign (%) and are followed by a character that represents the data type. The format specifier %s is a placeholder for a string.

- At the first format specifier's position, printf substitutes the value of the first argument after the format string. At each subsequent format specifier's position, printf substitutes the value of the next argument in the argument list.

Section 2.5 Another Java Application: Adding Integers

- Integers are whole numbers, such as –22, 7, 0 and 1024.

- An import declaration helps the compiler locate a class that is used in a program.

- Java provides a rich set of predefined classes that programmers can reuse rather than "reinventing the wheel." These classes are grouped into packages—named collections of classes.

- Collectively, Java's packages are referred to as the Java class library, or the Java Application Programming Interface (Java API).

- A variable declaration statement specifies the name and type of a variable.

- A variable is a location in the computer's memory where a value can be stored for use later in a program. All variables must be declared with a name and a type before they can be used.

- A variable's name enables the program to access the value of the variable in memory. A variable name can be any valid identifier.

- Like other statements, variable declaration statements end with a semicolon (;).

- A Scanner (package java.util) enables a program to read data for use in a program. The data can come from many sources, such as a file on disk or the user at the keyboard. Before using a Scanner, the program must create it and specify the source of the data.

- Variables should be initialized to prepare them for use in a program.

- The expression new Scanner(System.in) creates a Scanner that reads from the keyboard. The standard input object, System.in, enables Java applications to read data typed by the user.

- Data type int is used to declare variables that will hold integer values. The range of values for an int is –2,147,483,648 to +2,147,483,647.

- Types float and double specify real numbers, and type char specifies character data. Real numbers are numbers that contain decimal points, such as 3.4, 0.0 and –11.19. Variables of type char data represent individual characters, such as an uppercase letter (e.g., A), a digit (e.g., 7), a special character (e.g., * or %) or an escape sequence (e.g., the newline character, \n).

- Types such as int, float, double and char are often called primitive types or built-in types. Primitive-type names are keywords; thus, they must appear in all lowercase letters.

- A prompt directs the user to take a specific action.

- Scanner method nextInt obtains an integer for use in a program.

- The assignment operator, =, enables the program to give a value to a variable. Operator = is called a binary operator because it has two operands. An assignment statement uses an assignment operator to assign a value to a variable.

- Portions of statements that have values are called expressions.

- The format specifier %d is a placeholder for an int value.

Section 2.6 Memory Concepts
- Variable names correspond to locations in the computer's memory. Every variable has a name, a type, a size and a value.

- Whenever a value is placed in a memory location, the value replaces the previous value in that location. The previous value is lost.

Section 2.7 Arithmetic
- Most programs perform arithmetic calculations. The arithmetic operators are + (addition), - (subtraction, * (multiplication), / (division) and % (remainder).

- Integer division yields an integer quotient.

- The remainder operator, %, yields the remainder after division.

- Arithmetic expressions in Java must be written in straight-line form.

- If an expression contains nested parentheses, the innermost set of parentheses is evaluated first.

- Java applies the operators in arithmetic expressions in a precise sequence determined by the rules of operator precedence.

- When we say that operators are applied from left to right, we are referring to their associativity. Some operators associate from right to left.

- Redundant parentheses in an expression can make an expression clearer.

Section 2.8 Decision Making: Equality and Relational Operators

- A condition is an expression that can be either true or false. Java's if statement allows a program to make a decision based on the value of a condition.

- Conditions in if statements can be formed by using the equality (== and !=) and relational (>, <, >= and <=) operators.

- An if statement always begins with keyword if, followed by a condition in parentheses, and expects one statement in its body.

- The empty statement is a statement that does not perform a task.

Terminology

addition operator (+)
application
argument
arithmetic operators (*, /, %, + and -)
assignment operator (=)
assignment statement
associativity of operators
backslash (\) escape character
binary operator
body of a class declaration
body of a method declaration
built-in type
case sensitive
cd command to change directories
char primitive type
character string
class declaration
class file
.class file extension
class keyword
class name
comma-separated list
command line
Command Prompt
command window
comment
compilation error
compile-time error
compiler error
computer program
condition
%d format specifier
decision
division operator (/)
document a program
double primitive type
empty statement (;)
end-of-line comment (//)

equality operators
  == "is equal to"
  != "is not equal to"
escape character
escape sequence
false
fault tolerant
fixed text in a format string
float primitive type
format specifier
format string
identifier
if statement
import declaration
int (integer) primitive type
integer
integer division
Java API documentation
Java Application Programming Interface (API)
Java class library
.java file extension
java command
Javadoc comment (/** */)
javadoc utility program
java.lang package
left brace ({)
location of a variable
main method
memory location
message
method
multiple-line comment (/* */)
MS-DOS prompt
multiplication operator (*)
name of a variable
nested parentheses
newline character (\n)
object

operand
operator
output cursor
package
parentheses ()
perform an action
precedence
primitive type
programmer-defined class
prompt
`public` keyword
redundant parentheses
relational operators
    < "is less than"
    <= "is less than or equal to"
    > "is greater than"
    >= "is greater than or equal to"
remainder operator (%)
reserved words
right brace (})
rules of operator precedence
%s format specifier
Scanner class
self-documenting
semicolon (;)
shell
single-line comment (//)
size of a variable

standard input object (`System.in`)
standard output object (`System.out`)
statement
straight-line form
string
string literal
subtraction operator (-)
syntax
syntax error
`System.in` (standard input) object
`System.out` (standard output) object
`System.out.print` method
`System.out.printf` method
`System.out.println` method
terminal window
traditional comment (/* */)
true
type of a variable
user-defined class
variable
variable declaration
variable declaration statement
variable name
variable value
`void` keyword
white space
white-space characters

Self-Review Exercises

2.1   Fill in the blanks in each of the following statements:

    a) A(n) _____ begins the body of every method, and a(n) _____ ends the body of every method.

    b) Every statement ends with a(n) _____.

    c) The _____ statement is used to make decisions.

    d) _____ begins an end-of-line comment.

    e) _____, _____, _____ and _____ are called white space.

    f) _____ are reserved for use by Java.

    g) Java applications begin execution at method _____.

    h) Methods _____, _____ and _____ display information in the command window.

2.2   State whether each of the following is *true* or *false*. If *false*, explain why.

    a) Comments cause the computer to print the text after the // on the screen when the program executes.

    b) All variables must be given a type when they are declared.

    c) Java considers the variables number and NuMbEr to be identical.

    d) The remainder operator (%) can be used only with integer operands.

    e) The arithmetic operators *, /, %, + and - all have the same level of precedence.

2.3   Write statements to accomplish each of the following tasks:

a) Declare variables c, thisIsAVariable, q76354 and number to be of type int.

b) Prompt the user to enter an integer.

c) Input an integer and assign the result to int variable value. Assume Scanner variable input can be used to read a value from the keyboard.

d) If the variable number is not equal to 7, display "The variable number is not equal to 7".

e) Print "This is a Java program" on one line in the command window.

f) Print "This is a Java program" on two lines in the command window. The first line should end with Java. Use method System.out.println.

g) Print "This is a Java program" on two lines in the command window. The first line should end with Java. Use method System.out.printf and two %s format specifiers.

2.4   Identify and correct the errors in each of the following statements:

a) if (c < 7);
          System.out.println("c is less than 7");

b) if (c => 7)
          System.out.println("c is equal to or greater than 7");

2.5   Write declarations, statements or comments that accomplish each of the following tasks:

a) State that a program will calculate the product of three integers.

b) Create a Scanner that reads values from the standard input.

c) Declare the variables x, y, z and result to be of type int.

d) Prompt the user to enter the first integer.

e) Read the first integer from the user and store it in the variable x.

f) Prompt the user to enter the second integer.

g) Read the second integer from the user and store it in the variable y.

h) Prompt the user to enter the third integer.

i) Read the third integer from the user and store it in the variable z.

j) Compute the product of the three integers contained in variables x, y and z, and assign the result to the variable result.

k) Display the message "Product is" followed by the value of the variable result.

2.6   Using the statements you wrote in Exercise 2.5, write a complete program that calculates and prints the product of three integers.

Answers to Self-Review Exercises

2.1   a) left brace ({), right brace (}). b) semicolon (;). c) if. d) //. e) Blank lines, space characters, newline characters and tab characters. f) Keywords. g) main. h) System.out.print, System.out.println and System.out.printf.

2.2   a) False. Comments do not cause any action to be performed when the program executes. They are used to document programs and improve their readability.

b) True.

c) False. Java is case sensitive, so these variables are distinct.

d) False. The remainder operator can also be used with noninteger operands in Java.

e) False. The operators *, / and % are on the same level of precedence, and the operators + and - are on a lower level of precedence.

2.3   a) int c, thisIsAVariable, q76354, number;
     or
     int c;
     int thisIsAVariable;
     int q76354;
     int number;

b) `System.out.print( "Enter an integer: " );`

c) `value = input.nextInt();`

d) `if ( number != 7 )`
   `    System.out.println( "The variable number is not equal to 7" );`

e) `System.out.println( "This is a Java program" );`

f) `System.out.println( "This is a Java\nprogram" );`

g) `System.out.printf( "%s\n%s\n", "This is a Java", "program" );`

2.4 The solutions to Self-Review Exercise 2.4 are as follows:

a) Error: Semicolon after the right parenthesis of the condition (`c < 7`) in the `if`.
   Correction: Remove the semicolon after the right parenthesis. [*Note:* As a result, the output statement will execute regardless of whether the condition in the `if` is true.]

b) Error: The relational operator `=>` is incorrect. Correction: Change `=>` to `>=`.

2.5 a) `// Calculate the product of three integers`

b) `Scanner input = new Scanner( System.in );`

c) `int x, y, z, result;`
   or
   `int x;`
   `int y;`
   `int z;`
   `int result;`

d) `System.out.print( "Enter first integer: " );`

e) `x = input.nextInt();`

f) `System.out.print( "Enter second integer: " );`

g) `y = input.nextInt();`

h) `System.out.print( "Enter third integer: " );`

i) `z = input.nextInt();`

j) `result = x * y * z;`

k) `System.out.printf( "Product is %d\n", result );`

2.6 The solution to Self-Review Exercise 2.6 is as follows:

```
1   // Ex. 2.6: Product.java
2   // Calculate the product of three integers.
3   import java.util.Scanner; // program uses Scanner
4
5   public class Product
6   {
7      public static void main( String args[] )
8      {
9         // create Scanner to obtain input from command window
10        Scanner input = new Scanner( System.in );
11
12        int x; // first number input by user
13        int y; // second number input by user
14        int z; // third number input by user
15        int result; // product of numbers
16
17        System.out.print( "Enter first integer: " ); // prompt for input
18        x = input.nextInt(); // read first integer
19
20        System.out.print( "Enter second integer: " ); // prompt for input
21        y = input.nextInt(); // read second integer
```

```
22
23         System.out.print( "Enter third integer: " ); // prompt for input
24         z = input.nextInt(); // read third integer
25
26         result = x * y * z; // calculate product of numbers
27
28         System.out.printf( "Product is %d\n", result );
29
30      } // end method main
31
32   } // end class Product
```

```
Enter first integer: 10
Enter second integer: 20
Enter third integer: 30
Product is 6000
```

Exercises

2.7   Write Java statements that accomplish each of the following tasks:
   a) Display the message "Enter an integer: ", leaving the cursor on the same line.
   b) Assign the product of variables b and c to variable a.
   c) State that a program performs a sample payroll calculation (i.e., use text that helps to document a program).

2.8   Assuming that x = 2 and y = 3, what does each of the following statements display?
   a) System.out.printf("x = %d\n", x);
   b) System.out.printf("Value of %d + %d is %d\n", x, x, (x + x));
   c) System.out.printf("x =");
   d) System.out.printf("%d = %d\n", (x + y), (y + x));

2.9   Given that $y = ax^3 + 7$, which of the following are correct Java statements for this equation?
   a) y = a * x * x * x + 7;
   b) y = a * x * x * (x + 7);
   c) y = (a * x) * x * (x + 7);
   d) y = (a * x) * x * x + 7;
   e) y = a * (x * x * x) + 7;
   f) y = a * x * (x * x + 7);

2.10   Write an application that displays the numbers 1 to 4 on the same line, with each pair of adjacent numbers separated by one space. Write the program using the following techniques:
   a) Use one System.out.println statement.
   b) Use four System.out.print statements.
   c) Use one System.out.printf statement.

2.11   Write an application that asks the user to enter two integers, obtains them from the user and prints their sum, product, difference and quotient (division). Use the techniques shown in Fig. 2.7.

2.12   Write an application that asks the user to enter two integers, obtains them from the user and displays the larger number followed by the words "is larger". If the numbers are equal, print the message "These numbers are equal". Use the techniques shown in Fig. 2.15.

2.13   Write an application that inputs three integers from the user and displays the sum, average, product, smallest and largest of the numbers. Use the techniques shown in Fig. 2.15. [*Note:* The calculation of the average in this exercise should result in an integer representation of the average. So if the sum of the values is 7, the average should be 2, not 2.3333….]

2.14 What does the following code print?

```
System.out.println( "*\n**\n***\n****\n*****" );
```

2.15 What does the following code print?

```
System.out.println( "*" );
System.out.println( "***" );
System.out.println( "*****" );
System.out.println( "****" );
System.out.println( "**" );
```

2.16 What does the following code print?

```
System.out.print( "*" );
System.out.print( "***" );
System.out.print( "*****" );
System.out.print( "****" );
System.out.println( "**" );
```

2.17 What does the following code print?

```
System.out.print( "*" );
System.out.println( "***" );
System.out.println( "*****" );
System.out.print( "****" );
System.out.println( "**" );
```

2.18 What does the following code print?

```
System.out.printf( "%s\n%s\n%s\n", "*", "***", "*****" );
```

2.19 Write an application that reads five integers, determines and prints the largest and smallest integers in the group. Use only the programming techniques you learned in this chapter.

2.20 Write an application that reads an integer and determines and prints whether it is odd or even. [*Hint:* Use the remainder operator. An even number is a multiple of 2. Any multiple of 2 leaves a remainder of 0 when divided by 2.]

2.21 Write an application that reads two integers, determines whether the first is a multiple of the second and prints the result. [*Hint:* Use the remainder operator.]

2.22 Here's a peek ahead. In this chapter, you have learned about integers and the type int. Java can also represent floating-point numbers that contain decimal points, such as 3.14159. Write an application that inputs from the user the radius of a circle as an integer and prints the circle's diameter, circumference and area using the floating-point value 3.14159 for π. Use the techniques shown in Fig. 2.7. [*Note:* You may also use the predefined constant Math.PI for the value of π. This constant is more precise than the value 3.14159. Class Math is defined in package java.lang. Classes in that package are imported automatically, so you do not need to import class Math to use it.] Use the following formulas (r is the radius):

$$diameter = 2r$$
$$circumference = 2\pi r$$
$$area = \pi r^2$$

Do not store the results of each calculation in a variable. Rather, specify each calculation as the value that will be output in a System.out.printf statement. Note that the values produced by the circumference and area calculations are floating-point numbers. Such values can be output with the format specifier %f in a System.out.printf statement. You will learn more about floating-point numbers in Chapter 3.

2.23   Write an application that inputs one number consisting of five digits from the user, separates the number into its individual digits and prints the digits separated from one another by three spaces each. For example, if the user types in the number 42339, the program should print

```
4   2   3   3   9
```

Assume that the user enters the correct number of digits. What happens when you execute the program and type a number with more than five digits? What happens when you execute the program and type a number with fewer than five digits? [*Hint:* It is possible to do this exercise with the techniques you learned in this chapter. You will need to use both division and remainder operations to "pick off" each digit.]

2.24   Using only the programming techniques you learned in this chapter, write an application that calculates the squares and cubes of the numbers from 0 to 10 and prints the resulting values in table format, as shown below. [*Note:* This program does not require any input from the user.]

```
number   square   cube
0        0        0
1        1        1
2        4        8
3        9        27
4        16       64
5        25       125
6        36       216
7        49       343
8        64       512
9        81       729
10       100      1000
```

2.25   Write a program that inputs five numbers and determines and prints the number of negative numbers input, the number of positive numbers input and the number of zeros input.

You will see something new.
Two things. And I call them
Thing One and Thing Two.
—Dr. Theodor Seuss Geisel

Nothing can have value
without being an object of
utility.
—Karl Marx

Your public servants serve
you right.
—Adlai E. Stevenson

Knowing how to answer one
who speaks,
To reply to one who sends a
message.
—Amenemope

3

Introduction to Classes and Objects

OBJECTIVES

In this chapter you will learn:

- What classes, objects, methods and instance variables are.

- How to declare a class and use it to create an object.

- How to declare methods in a class to implement the class's behaviors.

- How to declare instance variables in a class to implement the class's attributes.

- How to call an object's methods to make those methods perform their tasks.

- The differences between instance variables of a class and local variables of a method.

- How to use a constructor to ensure that an object's data is initialized when the object is created.

- The differences between primitive and reference types.

3.1 Introduction

We introduced the basic terminology and concepts of object-oriented programming in Section 1.16. In Chapter 2, you began to use those concepts to create simple applications that displayed messages to the user, obtained information from the user, performed calculations and made decisions. One common feature of every application in Chapter 2 was that all the statements that performed tasks were located in method main. Typically, the applications you develop in this book will consist of two or more classes, each containing one or more methods. If you become part of a development team in industry, you might work on applications that contain hundreds, or even thousands, of classes. In this chapter, we present a simple framework for organizing object-oriented applications in Java.

First, we motivate the notion of classes with a real-world example. Then we present five complete working applications to demonstrate creating and using your own classes. The first four of these examples begin our case study on developing a grade-book class that instructors can use to maintain student test scores. This case study is enhanced over the next several chapters, culminating with the version presented in Chapter 7, Arrays. The last example in the chapter introduces floating-point numbers—that is, numbers containing decimal points, such as 0.0345, –7.23 and 100.7—in the context of a bank account class that maintains a customer's balance.

3.2 Classes, Objects, Methods and Instance Variables

Let's begin with a simple analogy to help you understand classes and their contents. Suppose you want to drive a car and make it go faster by pressing down on its accelerator pedal. What must happen before you can do this? Well, before you can drive a car, someone has to design it. A car typically begins as engineering drawings, similar to the blueprints used to design a house. These engineering drawings include the design for an accelerator pedal to make the car go faster. The pedal "hides" from the driver the complex mechanisms that actually make the car go faster, just as the brake pedal "hides" the mechanisms that slow the car and the steering wheel "hides" the mechanisms that turn the car. This enables people with little or no knowledge of how engines work to drive a car easily.

Unfortunately, you cannot drive the engineering drawings of a car. Before you can drive a car, the car must be built from the engineering drawings that describe it. A completed car has an actual accelerator pedal to make the car go faster, but even that's not enough—the car won't accelerate on its own, so the driver must press the accelerator pedal.

Now let's use our car example to introduce the key programming concepts of this section. Performing a task in a program requires a method. The method describes the mechanisms that actually perform its tasks. The method hides from its user the complex tasks that it performs, just as the accelerator pedal of a car hides from the driver the complex mechanisms of making the car go faster. In Java, we begin by creating a program unit called a class to house a method, just as a car's engineering drawings house the design of an accelerator pedal. In a class, you provide one or more methods that are designed to perform the class's tasks. For example, a class that represents a bank account might contain one method to deposit money to an account, another to withdraw money from an account and a third to inquire what the current balance is.

Just as you cannot drive an engineering drawing of a car, you cannot "drive" a class. Just as someone has to build a car from its engineering drawings before you can actually drive a car, you must build an object of a class before you can get a program to perform the tasks the class describes how to do. That is one reason Java is known as an object-oriented programming language.

When you drive a car, pressing its gas pedal sends a message to the car to perform a task—that is, make the car go faster. Similarly, you send **messages** to an object—each message is known as a **method call** and tells a method of the object to perform its task.

Thus far, we've used the car analogy to introduce classes, objects and methods. In addition to a car's capabilities, a car also has many attributes, such as its color, the number of doors, the amount of gas in its tank, its current speed and its total miles driven (i.e., its odometer reading). Like the car's capabilities, these attributes are represented as part of a car's design in its engineering diagrams. As you drive a car, these attributes are always associated with the car. Every car maintains its own attributes. For example, each car knows how much gas is in its own gas tank, but not how much is in the tanks of other cars. Similarly, an object has attributes that are carried with the object as it is used in a program. These attributes are specified as part of the object's class. For example, a bank account object has a balance attribute that represents the amount of money in the account. Each bank account object knows the balance in the account it represents, but not the balances of the other accounts in the bank. Attributes are specified by the class's **instance variables**.

The remainder of this chapter presents examples that demonstrate the concepts we introduced in the context of the car analogy. The first four examples incrementally build a GradeBook class to demonstrate these concepts:

1. The first example presents a GradeBook class with one method that simply displays a welcome message when it is called. We then show how to create an object of that class and call the method so that it displays the welcome message.

2. The second example modifies the first by allowing the method to receive a course name as an argument and by displaying the name as part of the welcome message.

3. The third example shows how to store the course name in a GradeBook object. For this version of the class, we also show how to use methods to set the course name and obtain the course name.

4. The fourth example demonstrates how the data in a GradeBook object can be initialized when the object is created—the initialization is performed by the class's constructor.

The last example in the chapter presents an Account class that reinforces the concepts presented in the first four examples and introduces floating-point numbers. For this purpose, we present an Account class that represents a bank account and maintains its balance as a floating-point number. The class contains two methods—one that credits a deposit to the account, thus increasing the balance, and another that retrieves the balance. The class's constructor allows the balance of each Account object to be initialized as the object is created. We create two Account objects and make deposits into each to show that each object maintains its own balance. The example also demonstrates how to input and display floating-point numbers.

3.3 Declaring a Class with a Method and Instantiating an Object of a Class

We begin with an example that consists of classes GradeBook (Fig. 3.1) and GradeBook-Test (Fig. 3.2). Class GradeBook (declared in file GradeBook.java) will be used to display a message on the screen (Fig. 3.2) welcoming the instructor to the grade-book application. Class GradeBookTest (declared in file GradeBookTest.java) is an application class in which the main method will use class GradeBook. Each class declaration that begins with keyword public must be stored in a file that has the same name as the class and ends with the .java file-name extension. Thus, classes GradeBook and GradeBookTest must be declared in separate files, because each class is declared public.

 Common Programming Error 3.1

Declaring more than one public class in the same file is a compilation error.

Class **GradeBook**
The GradeBook class declaration (Fig. 3.1) contains a displayMessage method (lines 7–10) that displays a message on the screen. Line 9 of the class performs the work of displaying the message. Recall that a class is like a blueprint—we'll need to make an object of this class and call its method to get line 9 to execute and display its message.

```
1   // Fig. 3.1: GradeBook.java
2   // Class declaration with one method.
3
4   public class GradeBook
5   {
6      // display a welcome message to the GradeBook user
7      public void displayMessage()
8      {
9         System.out.println( "Welcome to the Grade Book!" );
10     } // end method displayMessage
11
12  } // end class GradeBook
```

Fig. 3.1 | Class declaration with one method.

The class declaration begins in line 4. The keyword `public` is an **access modifier**. For now, we will simply declare every class `public`. Every class declaration contains keyword `class` followed immediately by the class's name. Every class's body is enclosed in a pair of left and right braces ({ and }), as in lines 5 and 12 of class `GradeBook`.

In Chapter 2, each class we declared had one method named `main`. Class `GradeBook` also has one method—`displayMessage` (lines 7–10). Recall that `main` is a special method that is always called automatically by the Java Virtual Machine (JVM) when you execute an application. Most methods do not get called automatically. As you will soon see, you must call method `displayMessage` to tell it to perform its task.

The method declaration begins with keyword `public` to indicate that the method is "available to the public"—that is, it can be called from outside the class declaration's body by methods of other classes. Keyword `void` indicates that this method will perform a task but will not return (i.e., give back) any information to its **calling method** when it completes its task. You have already used methods that return information—for example, in Chapter 2 you used `Scanner` method `nextInt` to input an integer typed by the user at the keyboard. When `nextInt` inputs a value, it returns that value for use in the program.

The name of the method, `displayMessage`, follows the return type. By convention, method names begin with a lowercase first letter and all subsequent words in the name begin with a capital letter. The parentheses after the method name indicate that this is a method. An empty set of parentheses, as shown in line 7, indicates that this method does not require additional information to perform its task. Line 7 is commonly referred to as the **method header**. Every method's body is delimited by left and right braces ({ and }), as in lines 8 and 10.

The body of a method contains statement(s) that perform the method's task. In this case, the method contains one statement (line 9) that displays the message `"Welcome to the Grade Book!"` followed by a newline in the command window. After this statement executes, the method has completed its task.

Next, we'd like to use class `GradeBook` in an application. As you learned in Chapter 2, method `main` begins the execution of every application. A class that contains method `main` is a Java application. Such a class is special because the JVM can use `main` as an entry point to begin execution. Class `GradeBook` is not an application because it does not contain `main`. Therefore, if you try to execute `GradeBook` by typing `java GradeBook` in the command window, you will receive an error message like:

```
Exception in thread "main" java.lang.NoSuchMethodError: main
```

This was not a problem in Chapter 2, because every class you declared had a `main` method. To fix this problem for the `GradeBook`, we must either declare a separate class that contains a `main` method or place a `main` method in class `GradeBook`. To help you prepare for the larger programs you will encounter later in this book and in industry, we use a separate class (`GradeBookTest` in this example) containing method `main` to test each new class we create in this chapter.

Class *GradeBookTest*

The `GradeBookTest` class declaration (Fig. 3.2) contains the `main` method that will control our application's execution. Any class that contains `main` declared as shown in line 7 can be used to execute an application. The `GradeBookTest` class declaration begins in line 4

```
1   // Fig. 3.2: GradeBookTest.java
2   // Create a GradeBook object and call its displayMessage method.
3
4   public class GradeBookTest
5   {
6      // main method begins program execution
7      public static void main( String args[] )
8      {
9         // create a GradeBook object and assign it to myGradeBook
10        GradeBook myGradeBook = new GradeBook();
11
12        // call myGradeBook's displayMessage method
13        myGradeBook.displayMessage();
14     } // end main
15
16  } // end class GradeBookTest
```

```
Welcome to the Grade Book!
```

Fig. 3.2 | Creating an object of class GradeBook and calling its displayMessage method.

and ends in line 16. The class contains only a main method, which is typical of many class-es that begin an application's execution.

Lines 7–14 declare method main. Recall from Chapter 2 that the main header must appear as shown in line 7; otherwise, the application will not execute. A key part of enabling the JVM to locate and call method main to begin the application's execution is the static keyword (line 7), which indicates that main is a static method. A static method is special because it can be called without first creating an object of the class in which the method is declared. We thoroughly explain static methods in Chapter 6, Methods: A Deeper Look.

In this application, we'd like to call class GradeBook's displayMessage method to display the welcome message in the command window. Typically, you cannot call a method that belongs to another class until you create an object of that class, as shown in line 10. We begin by declaring variable myGradeBook. Note that the variable's type is GradeBook— the class we declared in Fig. 3.1. Each new class you create becomes a new type that can be used to declare variables and create objects. Programmers can declare new class types as needed; this is one reason why Java is known as an extensible language.

Variable myGradeBook is initialized with the result of the class instance creation expression new GradeBook(). Keyword new creates a new object of the class specified to the right of the keyword (i.e., GradeBook). The parentheses to the right of GradeBook are required. As you will learn in Section 3.7, those parentheses in combination with a class name represent a call to a constructor, which is similar to a method, but is used only at the time an object is created to initialize the object's data. In that section you will see that data can be placed in parentheses to specify initial values for the object's data. For now, we simply leave the parentheses empty.

Just as we can use object System.out to call methods print, printf and println, we can use object myGradeBook to call method displayMessage. Line 13 calls the method displayMessage (lines 7–10 of Fig. 3.1) using myGradeBook followed by a dot separator

(.), the method name displayMessage and an empty set of parentheses. This call causes the displayMessage method to perform its task. This method call differs from those in Chapter 2 that displayed information in a command window—each of those method calls provided arguments that specified the data to display. At the beginning of line 13, "myGradeBook." indicates that main should use the myGradeBook object that was created in line 10. Line 7 of Fig. 3.1 indicates that method displayMessage has an empty parameter list—that is, displayMessage does not require additional information to perform its task. For this reason, the method call (line 13 of Fig. 3.2) specifies an empty set of parentheses after the method name to indicate that no arguments are being passed to method displayMessage. When method displayMessage completes its task, method main continues executing in line 14. This is the end of method main, so the program terminates.

Compiling an Application with Multiple Classes

You must compile the classes in Fig. 3.1 and Fig. 3.2 before you can execute the application. First, change to the directory that contains the application's source-code files. Next, type the command

```
javac GradeBook.java GradeBookTest.java
```

to compile both classes at once. If the directory containing the application includes only this application's files, you can compile all the classes in the directory with the command

```
javac *.java
```

The asterisk (*) in *.java indicates that all files in the current directory that end with the file name extension ".java" should be compiled.

UML Class Diagram for Class GradeBook

Figure 3.3 presents a UML class diagram for class GradeBook of Fig. 3.1. Recall from Section 1.16 that the UML is a graphical language used by programmers to represent object-oriented systems in a standardized manner. In the UML, each class is modeled in a class diagram as a rectangle with three compartments. The top compartment contains the name of the class centered horizontally in boldface type. The middle compartment contains the class's attributes, which correspond to instance variables in Java. In Fig. 3.3, the middle compartment is empty because the version of class GradeBook in Fig. 3.1 does not have any attributes. The bottom compartment contains the class's operations, which correspond to methods in Java. The UML models operations by listing the operation name preceded by an access modifier and followed by a set of parentheses. Class GradeBook has one method, displayMessage, so the bottom compartment of Fig. 3.3 lists one operation with this name. Method displayMessage does not require additional information to per-

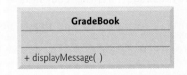

Fig. 3.3 | UML class diagram indicating that class GradeBook has a public displayMessage operation.

form its tasks, so the parentheses following the method name in the class diagram are empty, just as they were in the method's declaration in line 7 of Fig. 3.1. The plus sign (+) in front of the operation name indicates that displayMessage is a public operation in the UML (i.e., a public method in Java). We will often use UML class diagrams to summarize a class's attributes and operations.

3.4 Declaring a Method with a Parameter

In our car analogy from Section 3.2, we discussed the fact that pressing a car's gas pedal sends a message to the car to perform a task—make the car go faster. But how fast should the car accelerate? As you know, the farther down you press the pedal, the faster the car accelerates. So the message to the car actually includes the task to perform and additional information that helps the car perform the task. This additional information is known as a parameter—the value of the parameter helps the car determine how fast to accelerate. Similarly, a method can require one or more parameters that represent additional information it needs to perform its task. A method call supplies values—called arguments—for each of the method's parameters. For example, the method System.out.println requires an argument that specifies the data to output in a command window. Similarly, to make a deposit into a bank account, a deposit method specifies a parameter that represents the deposit amount. When the deposit method is called, an argument value representing the deposit amount is assigned to the method's parameter. The method then makes a deposit of that amount.

Our next example declares class GradeBook (Fig. 3.4) with a displayMessage method that displays the course name as part of the welcome message. (See the sample execution in Fig. 3.5.) The new displayMessage method requires a parameter that represents the course name to output.

Before discussing the new features of class GradeBook, let's see how the new class is used from the main method of class GradeBookTest (Fig. 3.5). Line 12 creates a Scanner named input for reading the course name from the user. Line 15 creates an object of class GradeBook and assigns it to variable myGradeBook. Line 18 prompts the user to enter a course name. Line 19 reads the name from the user and assigns it to the nameOfCourse variable, using Scanner method nextLine to perform the input. The user types the course name and presses *Enter* to submit the course name to the program. Note that pressing *Enter*

```
1   // Fig. 3.4: GradeBook.java
2   // Class declaration with a method that has a parameter.
3
4   public class GradeBook
5   {
6      // display a welcome message to the GradeBook user
7      public void displayMessage( String courseName )
8      {
9         System.out.printf( "Welcome to the grade book for\n%s!\n",
10           courseName );
11     } // end method displayMessage
12
13  } // end class GradeBook
```

Fig. 3.4 | Class declaration with one method that has a parameter.

```
 1   // Fig. 3.5: GradeBookTest.java
 2   // Create GradeBook object and pass a String to
 3   // its displayMessage method.
 4   import java.util.Scanner; // program uses Scanner
 5
 6   public class GradeBookTest
 7   {
 8      // main method begins program execution
 9      public static void main( String args[] )
10      {
11         // create Scanner to obtain input from command window
12         Scanner input = new Scanner( System.in );
13
14         // create a GradeBook object and assign it to myGradeBook
15         GradeBook myGradeBook = new GradeBook();
16
17         // prompt for and input course name
18         System.out.println( "Please enter the course name:" );
19         String nameOfCourse = input.nextLine(); // read a line of text
20         System.out.println(); // outputs a blank line
21
22         // call myGradeBook's displayMessage method
23         // and pass nameOfCourse as an argument
24         myGradeBook.displayMessage( nameOfCourse );
25      } // end main
26
27   } // end class GradeBookTest
```

```
Please enter the course name:
CS101 Introduction to Java Programming

Welcome to the grade book for
CS101 Introduction to Java Programming!
```

Fig. 3.5 | Creating a GradeBook object and passing a String to its displayMessage method.

inserts a newline character at the end of the characters typed by the user. Method nextLine reads characters typed by the user until the newline character is encountered, then returns a String containing the characters up to, but not including, the newline. The newline character is discarded. Class Scanner also provides a similar method—next—that reads individual words. When the user presses *Enter* after typing input, method next reads characters until a white-space character (such as a space, tab or newline) is encountered, then returns a String containing the characters up to, but not including, the white-space character (which is discarded). All information after the first white-space character is not lost— it can be read by other statements that call the Scanner's methods later in the program.

Line 24 calls myGradeBooks's displayMessage method. The variable nameOfCourse in parentheses is the argument that is passed to method displayMessage so that the method can perform its task. The value of variable nameOfCourse in main becomes the value of method displayMessage's parameter courseName in line 7 of Fig. 3.4. When you execute this application, notice that method displayMessage outputs the name you type as part of the welcome message (Fig. 3.5).

Software Engineering Observation 3.1

Normally, objects are created with new. One exception is a string literal that is contained in quotes, such as "hello". String literals are references to String objects that are implicitly created by Java.

More on Arguments and Parameters

When you declare a method, you must specify whether the method requires data to perform its task. To do so, you place additional information in the method's **parameter list**, which is located in the parentheses that follow the method name. The parameter list may contain any number of parameters, including none at all. Empty parentheses following the method name (as in Fig. 3.1, line 7) indicate that a method does not require any parameters. In Fig. 3.4, displayMessage's parameter list (line 7) declares that the method requires one parameter. Each parameter must specify a type and an identifier. In this case, the type String and the identifier courseName indicate that method displayMessage requires a String to perform its task. At the time the method is called, the argument value in the call is assigned to the corresponding parameter (in this case, courseName) in the method header. Then, the method body uses the parameter courseName to access the value. Lines 9–10 of Fig. 3.4 display parameter courseName's value, using the %s format specifier in printf's format string. Note that the parameter variable's name (Fig. 3.4, line 7) can be the same or different from the argument variable's name (Fig. 3.5, line 24).

A method can specify multiple parameters by separating each parameter from the next with a comma (we'll see an example of this in Chapter 6). The number of arguments in a method call must match the number of parameters in the parameter list of the called method's declaration. Also, the argument types in the method call must be "consistent with" the types of the corresponding parameters in the method's declaration. (As you will learn in subsequent chapters, an argument's type and its corresponding parameter's type are not always required to be identical.) In our example, the method call passes one argument of type String (nameOfCourse is declared as a String in line 19 of Fig. 3.5) and the method declaration specifies one parameter of type String (line 7 in Fig. 3.4). So in this example the type of the argument in the method call exactly matches the type of the parameter in the method header.

Common Programming Error 3.2

A compilation error occurs if the number of arguments in a method call does not match the number of parameters in the method declaration.

Common Programming Error 3.3

A compilation error occurs if the types of the arguments in a method call are not consistent with the types of the corresponding parameters in the method declaration.

Updated UML Class Diagram for Class **GradeBook**

The UML class diagram of Fig. 3.6 models class GradeBook of Fig. 3.4. Like Fig. 3.1, this GradeBook class contains public operation displayMessage. However, this version of displayMessage has a parameter. The UML models a parameter a bit differently from Java by listing the parameter name, followed by a colon and the parameter type in the parentheses following the operation name. The UML has its own data types similar to those of Java (but as you will see, not all the UML data types have the same names as the corresponding Java

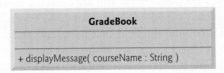

Fig. 3.6 | UML class diagram indicating that class GradeBook has a displayMessage operation with a courseName parameter of UML type String.

types). The UML type String does correspond to the Java type String. GradeBook method displayMessage (Fig. 3.4) has a String parameter named courseName, so Fig. 3.6 lists courseName : String between the parentheses following displayMessage.

*Notes on **import** Declarations*
Notice the import declaration in Fig. 3.5 (line 4). This indicates to the compiler that the program uses class Scanner. Why do we need to import class Scanner, but not classes System, String or GradeBook? Most classes you will use in Java programs must be imported. Classes System and String are in package java.lang, which is implicitly imported into every Java program, so all programs can use package java.lang's classes without explicitly importing them.

There is a special relationship between classes that are compiled in the same directory on disk, like classes GradeBook and GradeBookTest. By default, such classes are considered to be in the same package—known as the default package. Classes in the same package are implicitly imported into the source code files of other classes in the same package. Thus, an import declaration is not required when one class in a package uses another in the same package—such as when class GradeBookTest uses class GradeBook.

The import declaration in line 4 is not required if we always refer to class Scanner as java.util.Scanner, which includes the full package name and class name. This is known as the class's fully qualified class name. For example, line 12 could be written as

```
java.util.Scanner input = new java.util.Scanner( System.in );
```

 Software Engineering Observation 3.2

The Java compiler does not require import declarations in a Java source code file if the fully qualified class name is specified every time a class name is used in the source code. But most Java programmers consider using fully qualified names to be cumbersome, and instead prefer to use import declarations.

3.5 Instance Variables, *set* Methods and *get* Methods

In Chapter 2, we declared all of an application's variables in the application's main method. Variables declared in the body of a particular method are known as local variables and can be used only in that method. When that method terminates, the values of its local variables are lost. Recall from Section 3.2 that an object has attributes that are carried with the object as it is used in a program. Such attributes exist before a method is called on an object and after the method completes execution.

A class normally consists of one or more methods that manipulate the attributes that belong to a particular object of the class. Attributes are represented as variables in a class declaration. Such variables are called fields and are declared inside a class declaration but outside the bodies of the class's method declarations. When each object of a class maintains its own copy of an attribute, the field that represents the attribute is also known as an instance variable—each object (instance) of the class has a separate instance of the variable in memory. The example in this section demonstrates a GradeBook class that contains a courseName instance variable to represent a particular GradeBook object's course name.

GradeBook *Class with an Instance Variable, a* set *Method and a* get *Method*

In our next application (Fig. 3.7–Fig. 3.8), class GradeBook (Fig. 3.7) maintains the course name as an instance variable so that it can be used or modified at any time during an application's execution. The class contains three methods—setCourseName, getCourseName and displayMessage. Method setCourseName stores a course name in a GradeBook. Method getCourseName obtains a GradeBook's course name. Method displayMessage, which now specifies no parameters, still displays a welcome message that includes the course name; as you will see, the method now obtains the course name by calling another method in the same class—getCourseName.

```java
1   // Fig. 3.7: GradeBook.java
2   // GradeBook class that contains a courseName instance variable
3   // and methods to set and get its value.
4
5   public class GradeBook
6   {
7      private String courseName; // course name for this GradeBook
8
9      // method to set the course name
10     public void setCourseName( String name )
11     {
12        courseName = name; // store the course name
13     } // end method setCourseName
14
15     // method to retrieve the course name
16     public String getCourseName()
17     {
18        return courseName;
19     } // end method getCourseName
20
21     // display a welcome message to the GradeBook user
22     public void displayMessage()
23     {
24        // this statement calls getCourseName to get the
25        // name of the course this GradeBook represents
26        System.out.printf( "Welcome to the grade book for\n%s!\n",
27           getCourseName() );
28     } // end method displayMessage
29
30  } // end class GradeBook
```

Fig. 3.7 | GradeBook class that contains a courseName instance variable and methods to set and get its value.

A typical instructor teaches more than one course, each with its own course name. Line 7 declares that courseName is a variable of type String. Because the variable is declared in the body of the class but outside the bodies of the class's methods (lines 10–13, 16–19 and 22–28), line 7 is a declaration for an instance variable. Every instance (i.e., object) of class GradeBook contains one copy of each instance variable. For example, if there are two GradeBook objects, each object has its own copy of courseName (one per object). A benefit of making courseName an instance variable is that all the methods of the class (in this case, GradeBook) can manipulate any instance variables that appear in the class (in this case, courseName).

Access Modifiers *public* and *private*

Most instance variable declarations are preceded with the keyword private (as in line 7). Like public, keyword private is an access modifier. Variables or methods declared with access modifier private are accessible only to methods of the class in which they are declared. Thus, variable courseName can be used only in methods setCourseName, get-CourseName and displayMessage of (every object of) class GradeBook.

Software Engineering Observation 3.3

Precede every field and method declaration with an access modifier. As a rule of thumb, instance variables should be declared private and methods should be declared public. (We will see that it is appropriate to declare certain methods private, if they will be accessed only by other methods of the class.)

Good Programming Practice 3.1

We prefer to list the fields of a class first, so that, as you read the code, you see the names and types of the variables before you see them used in the methods of the class. It is possible to list the class's fields anywhere in the class outside its method declarations, but scattering them tends to lead to hard-to-read code.

Good Programming Practice 3.2

Place a blank line between method declarations to separate the methods and enhance program readability.

Declaring instance variables with access modifier private is known as data hiding. When a program creates (instantiates) an object of class GradeBook, variable courseName is encapsulated (hidden) in the object and can be accessed only by methods of the object's class. In class GradeBook, methods setCourseName and getCourseName manipulate the instance variable courseName.

Method setCourseName (lines 10–13) does not return any data when it completes its task, so its return type is void. The method receives one parameter—name—which represents the course name that will be passed to the method as an argument. Line 12 assigns name to instance variable courseName.

Method getCourseName (lines 16–19) returns a particular GradeBook object's courseName. The method has an empty parameter list, so it does not require additional information to perform its task. The method specifies that it returns a String—this is known as the method's return type. When a method that specifies a return type is called and completes its task, the method returns a result to its calling method. For example, when you go to an automated teller machine (ATM) and request your account balance, you expect the ATM to give you back a value that represents your balance. Similarly, when a statement calls method getCourseName on a GradeBook object, the statement expects to receive the GradeBook's course name (in this case, a String, as specified in the method declaration's return type). If you have a method square that returns the square of its argument, you would expect the statement

```
int result = square( 2 );
```

to return 4 from method square and assign 4 to the variable result. If you have a method maximum that returns the largest of three integer arguments, you would expect the following statement

```
int biggest = maximum( 27, 114, 51 );
```

to return 114 from method maximum and assign 114 to variable biggest.

Note that the statements in lines 12 and 18 each use courseName even though it was not declared in any of the methods. We can use courseName in the methods of class GradeBook because courseName is a field of the class. Also note that the order in which methods are declared in a class does not determine when they are called at execution time. So method getCourseName could be declared before method setCourseName.

Method displayMessage (lines 22–28) does not return any data when it completes its task, so its return type is void. The method does not receive parameters, so the parameter list is empty. Lines 26–27 output a welcome message that includes the value of instance variable courseName. Once again, we need to create an object of class GradeBook and call its methods before the welcome message can be displayed.

GradeBookTest *Class That Demonstrates Class* GradeBook

Class GradeBookTest (Fig. 3.8) creates one object of class GradeBook and demonstrates its methods. Line 11 creates a Scanner that will be used to obtain a course name from the user. Line 14 creates a GradeBook object and assigns it to local variable myGradeBook of type GradeBook. Lines 17–18 display the initial course name calling the object's getCourseName method. Note that the first line of the output shows the name "null." Unlike local variables, which are not automatically initialized, every field has a **default initial value**—a value provided by Java when the programmer does not specify the field's initial value. Thus, fields are not required to be explicitly initialized before they are used in a program—unless they must be initialized to values other than their default values. The default value for a field of type String (like courseName in this example) is null, which we say more about in Section 3.6.

Line 21 prompts the user to enter a course name. Local String variable theName (declared in line 22) is initialized with the course name entered by the user, which is returned by the call to the nextLine method of the Scanner object input. Line 23 calls object myGradeBook's setCourseName method and supplies theName as the method's argument. When the method is called, the argument's value is assigned to parameter name (line 10, Fig. 3.7) of method setCourseName (lines 10–13, Fig. 3.7). Then the parameter's value is assigned to instance variable courseName (line 12, Fig. 3.7). Line 24 (Fig. 3.8) skips a line in the output, then line 27 calls object myGradeBook's displayMessage method to display the welcome message containing the course name.

```
 1    // Fig. 3.8: GradeBookTest.java
 2    // Create and manipulate a GradeBook object.
 3    import java.util.Scanner; // program uses Scanner
 4
 5    public class GradeBookTest
 6    {
 7       // main method begins program execution
 8       public static void main( String args[] )
 9       {
10          // create Scanner to obtain input from command window
11          Scanner input = new Scanner( System.in );
12
13          // create a GradeBook object and assign it to myGradeBook
14          GradeBook myGradeBook = new GradeBook();
15
16          // display initial value of courseName
17          System.out.printf( "Initial course name is: %s\n\n",
18             myGradeBook.getCourseName() );
19
20          // prompt for and read course name
21          System.out.println( "Please enter the course name:" );
22          String theName = input.nextLine(); // read a line of text
23          myGradeBook.setCourseName( theName ); // set the course name
24          System.out.println(); // outputs a blank line
25
26          // display welcome message after specifying course name
27          myGradeBook.displayMessage();
28       } // end main
29
30    } // end class GradeBookTest
```

```
Initial course name is: null

Please enter the course name:
CS101 Introduction to Java Programming

Welcome to the grade book for
CS101 Introduction to Java Programming!
```

Fig. 3.8 | Creating and manipulating a GradeBook object.

set *and* get *Methods*

A class's private fields can be manipulated only by methods of that class. So a **client of an object**—that is, any class that calls the object's methods—calls the class's public methods to manipulate the private fields of an object of the class. This is why the statements in method main (Fig. 3.8) call the setCourseName, getCourseName and displayMessage methods on a GradeBook object. Classes often provide public methods to allow clients of the class to *set* (i.e., assign values to) or *get* (i.e., obtain the values of) private instance variables. The names of these methods need not begin with *set* or *get*, but this naming convention is highly recommended in Java and is required for special Java software components called JavaBeans that can simplify programming in many Java integrated development environments (IDEs). The method that *sets* instance variable courseName in this example is called setCourseName, and the method that *gets* the value of instance variable courseName is called getCourseName.

UML Class Diagram for class **GradeBook** *with an Instance Variable and* set *and* get *Methods*

Figure 3.9 contains an updated UML class diagram for the version of class GradeBook in Fig. 3.7. This diagram models class GradeBook's instance variable courseName as an attribute in the middle compartment of the class. The UML represents instance variables as attributes by listing the attribute name, followed by a colon and the attribute type. The UML type of attribute courseName is String. Instance variable courseName is private in Java, so the class diagram lists a minus sign (–) in front of the corresponding attribute's name. Class GradeBook contains three public methods, so the class diagram lists three operations in the third compartment. Recall that the plus (+) sign before each operation name indicates that the operation is public. Operation setCourseName has a String parameter called name. The UML indicates the return type of an operation by placing a colon and the return type after the parentheses following the operation name. Method getCourseName of class GradeBook (Fig. 3.7) has a String return type in Java, so the class diagram shows a String return type in the UML. Note that operations setCourseName and displayMessage do not return values (i.e., they return void in Java), so the UML class diagram does not specify a return type after the parentheses of these operations.

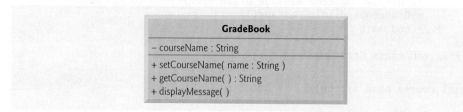

Fig. 3.9 | UML class diagram indicating that class GradeBook has a courseName attribute of UML type String and three operations—setCourseName (with a name parameter of UML type String), getCourseName (which returns UML type String) and displayMessage.

3.6 Primitive Types vs. Reference Types

Data types in Java are divided into two categories—primitive types and reference types (sometimes called nonprimitive types). The primitive types are boolean, byte, char, short, int, long, float and double. All nonprimitive types are reference types, so classes, which specify the types of objects, are reference types.

A primitive-type variable can store exactly one value of its declared type at a time. For example, an int variable can store one whole number (such as 7) at a time. When another value is assigned to that variable, its initial value is replaced. Primitive-type instance variables are initialized by default—variables of types byte, char, short, int, long, float and double are initialized to 0, and variables of type boolean are initialized to false. You can specify your own initial values for primitive-type variables. Recall that local variables are *not* initialized by default.

Error-Prevention Tip 3.1
Any attempt to use a local variable that has not been initialized results in a compilation error.

Programs use variables of reference types (normally called **references**) to store the locations of objects in the computer's memory. Such a variable is said to **refer to an object** in the program. Objects that are referenced may each contain many instance variables and methods. Line 14 of Fig. 3.8 creates an object of class `GradeBook`, and the variable `myGradeBook` contains a reference to that `GradeBook` object. Reference-type instance variables are initialized by default to the value `null`—a reserved word that represents a "reference to nothing." This is why the first call to `getCourseName` in line 18 of Fig. 3.8 returned `null`—the value of `courseName` had not been set, so the default initial value `null` was returned. The complete list of reserved words and keywords is listed in Appendix C, Keywords and Reserved Words.

A reference to an object is required to **invoke** (i.e., call) the object's methods. In the application of Fig. 3.8, the statements in method `main` use the variable `myGradeBook` to send messages to the `GradeBook` object. These messages are calls to methods (like `set-CourseName` and `getCourseName`) that enable the program to interact with the `GradeBook` object. For example, the statement in line 23 uses `myGradeBook` to send the `setCourse-Name` message to the `GradeBook` object. The message includes the argument that `set-CourseName` requires to perform its task. The `GradeBook` object uses this information to set the `courseName` instance variable. Note that primitive-type variables do not refer to objects, so such variables cannot be used to invoke methods.

Software Engineering Observation 3.4
A variable's declared type (e.g., `int`, `double` or `GradeBook`) indicates whether the variable is of a primitive or a reference type. If a variable's type is not one of the eight primitive types, then it is a reference type. For example, `Account account1` indicates that `account1` is a reference to an `Account` object).

3.7 Initializing Objects with Constructors

As mentioned in Section 3.5, when an object of class `GradeBook` (Fig. 3.7) is created, its instance variable `courseName` is initialized to `null` by default. What if you want to provide a course name when you create a `GradeBook` object? Each class you declare can provide a constructor that can be used to initialize an object of a class when the object is created. In fact, Java requires a constructor call for every object that is created. Keyword `new` calls the class's constructor to perform the initialization. The constructor call is indicated by the class name followed by parentheses—the constructor *must* have the same name as the class. For example, line 14 of Fig. 3.8 first uses `new` to create a `GradeBook` object. The empty parentheses after "`new GradeBook`" indicate a call to the class's constructor without arguments. By default, the compiler provides a **default constructor** with no parameters in any class that does not explicitly include a constructor. When a class has only the default constructor, its instance variables are initialized to their default values. Variables of types `char`, `byte`, `short`, `int`, `long`, `float` and `double` are initialized to 0, variables of type `boolean` are initialized to `false`, and reference-type variables are initialized to `null`.

When you declare a class, you can provide your own constructor to specify custom initialization for objects of your class. For example, a programmer might want to specify a course name for a GradeBook object when the object is created, as in

```
GradeBook myGradeBook =
    new GradeBook( "CS101 Introduction to Java Programming" );
```

In this case, the argument "CS101 Introduction to Java Programming" is passed to the GradeBook object's constructor and used to initialize the courseName. The preceding statement requires that the class provide a constructor with a String parameter. Figure 3.10 contains a modified GradeBook class with such a constructor.

Lines 9–12 declare the constructor for class GradeBook. A constructor must have the same name as its class. Like a method, a constructor specifies in its parameter list the data it requires to perform its task. When you create a new object (as we will do in Fig. 3.11),

```java
1   // Fig. 3.10: GradeBook.java
2   // GradeBook class with a constructor to initialize the course name.
3
4   public class GradeBook
5   {
6      private String courseName; // course name for this GradeBook
7
8      // constructor initializes courseName with String supplied as argument
9      public GradeBook( String name )
10     {
11        courseName = name; // initializes courseName
12     } // end constructor
13
14     // method to set the course name
15     public void setCourseName( String name )
16     {
17        courseName = name; // store the course name
18     } // end method setCourseName
19
20     // method to retrieve the course name
21     public String getCourseName()
22     {
23        return courseName;
24     } // end method getCourseName
25
26     // display a welcome message to the GradeBook user
27     public void displayMessage()
28     {
29        // this statement calls getCourseName to get the
30        // name of the course this GradeBook represents
31        System.out.printf( "Welcome to the grade book for\n%s!\n",
32           getCourseName() );
33     } // end method displayMessage
34
35  } // end class GradeBook
```

Fig. 3.10 | GradeBook class with a constructor to initialize the course name.

this data is placed in the parentheses that follow the class name. Line 9 indicates that class GradeBook's constructor has a String parameter called name. The name passed to the constructor is assigned to instance variable courseName in line 11 of the constructor's body.

Figure 3.11 demonstrates initializing GradeBook objects using the constructor. Lines 11–12 create and initialize the GradeBook object gradeBook1. The constructor of class GradeBook is called with the argument "CS101 Introduction to Java Programming" to initialize the course name. The class instance creation expression to the right of the = in lines 11–12 returns a reference to the new object, which is assigned to the variable gradeBook1. Lines 13–14 repeat this process for another GradeBook object gradeBook2, this time passing the argument "CS102 Data Structures in Java" to initialize the course name for gradeBook2. Lines 17–20 use each object's getCourseName method to obtain the course names and show that they were indeed initialized when the objects were created. In the introduction to Section 3.5, you learned that each instance (i.e., object) of a class contains its own copy of the class's instance variables. The output confirms that each Grade-Book maintains its own copy of instance variable courseName.

Like methods, constructors also can take arguments. However, an important difference between constructors and methods is that constructors cannot return values, so they cannot specify a return type (not even void). Normally, constructors are declared public. If a class does not include a constructor, the class's instance variables are initialized to their

```
 1   // Fig. 3.11: GradeBookTest.java
 2   // GradeBook constructor used to specify the course name at the
 3   // time each GradeBook object is created.
 4
 5   public class GradeBookTest
 6   {
 7      // main method begins program execution
 8      public static void main( String args[] )
 9      {
10         // create GradeBook object
11         GradeBook gradeBook1 = new GradeBook(
12            "CS101 Introduction to Java Programming" );
13         GradeBook gradeBook2 = new GradeBook(
14            "CS102 Data Structures in Java" );
15
16         // display initial value of courseName for each GradeBook
17         System.out.printf( "gradeBook1 course name is: %s\n",
18            gradeBook1.getCourseName() );
19         System.out.printf( "gradeBook2 course name is: %s\n",
20            gradeBook2.getCourseName() );
21      } // end main
22
23   } // end class GradeBookTest
```

```
gradeBook1 course name is: CS101 Introduction to Java Programming
gradeBook2 course name is: CS102 Data Structures in Java
```

Fig. 3.11 | GradeBook constructor used to specify the course name at the time each GradeBook object is created.

default values. If a programmer declares any constructors for a class, the Java compiler will not create a default constructor for that class.

Error-Prevention Tip 3.2

Unless default initialization of your class's instance variables is acceptable, provide a constructor to ensure that your class's instance variables are properly initialized with meaningful values when each new object of your class is created.

Adding the Constructor to Class **GradeBook**'s UML Class Diagram

The UML class diagram of Fig. 3.12 models class GradeBook of Fig. 3.10, which has a constructor that has a name parameter of type String. Like operations, the UML models constructors in the third compartment of a class in a class diagram. To distinguish a constructor from a class's operations, the UML requires that the word "constructor" be placed between guillemets (« and ») before the constructor's name. It is customary to list constructors before other operations in the third compartment.

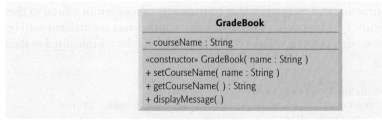

Fig. 3.12 | UML class diagram indicating that class GradeBook has a constructor that has a name parameter of UML type String.

3.8 Floating-Point Numbers and Type double

In our next application, we depart temporarily from our GradeBook case study to declare a class called Account that maintains the balance of a bank account. Most account balances are not whole numbers (e.g., 0, –22 and 1024). For this reason, class Account represents the account balance as a **floating-point number** (i.e., a number with a decimal point, such as 7.33, 0.0975 or 1000.12345). Java provides two primitive types for storing floating-point numbers in memory—float and double. The primary difference between them is that double variables can store numbers with larger magnitude and finer detail (i.e., more digits to the right of the decimal point—also known as the number's **precision**) than float variables.

Floating-Point Number Precision and Memory Requirements

Variables of type float represent **single-precision floating-point numbers** and have seven significant digits. Variables of type double represent **double-precision floating-point numbers**. These require twice as much memory as float variables and provide 15 significant digits—approximately double the precision of float variables. For the range of values required by most programs, variables of type float should suffice, but you can use double to "play it safe." In some applications, even variables of type double will be inadequate—such applications are beyond the scope of this book. Most programmers represent floating-point numbers with type double. In fact, Java treats all floating-point numbers you type in a program's source code (such as 7.33 and 0.0975) as double values by default. Such values in the source code are known as **floating-point literals**. See Appendix D, Primitive Types, for the ranges of values for floats and doubles.

Although floating-point numbers are not always 100% precise, they have numerous applications. For example, when we speak of a "normal" body temperature of 98.6, we do not need to be precise to a large number of digits. When we read the temperature on a thermometer as 98.6, it may actually be 98.5999473210643. Calling this number simply 98.6 is fine for most applications involving body temperatures. Due to the imprecise nature of floating-point numbers, type double is preferred over type float because double variables can represent floating-point numbers more accurately. For this reason, we use type double throughout the book.

Floating-point numbers also arise as a result of division. In conventional arithmetic, when we divide 10 by 3, the result is 3.3333333…, with the sequence of 3s repeating infinitely. The computer allocates only a fixed amount of space to hold such a value, so clearly the stored floating-point value can be only an approximation.

Common Programming Error 3.4

Using floating-point numbers in a manner that assumes they are represented precisely can lead to logic errors.

Account *Class with an Instance Variable of Type* double

Our next application (Figs. 3.13–3.14) contains a class named Account (Fig. 3.13) that maintains the balance of a bank account. A typical bank services many accounts, each with its own balance, so line 7 declares an instance variable named balance of type double. Variable balance is an instance variable because it is declared in the body of the class but outside the class's method declarations (lines 10–16, 19–22 and 25–28). Every instance (i.e., object) of class Account contains its own copy of balance.

```
 1   // Fig. 3.13: Account.java
 2   // Account class with a constructor to
 3   // initialize instance variable balance.
 4
 5   public class Account
 6   {
 7      private double balance; // instance variable that stores the balance
 8
 9      // constructor
10      public Account( double initialBalance )
11      {
12         // validate that initialBalance is greater than 0.0;
13         // if it is not, balance is initialized to the default value 0.0
14         if ( initialBalance > 0.0 )
15            balance = initialBalance;
16      } // end Account constructor
17
```

Fig. 3.13 | Account class with an instance variable of type double. (Part 1 of 2.)

```
18      // credit (add) an amount to the account
19      public void credit( double amount )
20      {
21          balance = balance + amount; // add amount to balance
22      } // end method credit
23
24      // return the account balance
25      public double getBalance()
26      {
27          return balance; // gives the value of balance to the calling method
28      } // end method getBalance
29
30  } // end class Account
```

Fig. 3.13 | Account class with an instance variable of type double. (Part 2 of 2.)

Class Account contains a constructor and two methods. Since it is common for someone opening an account to place money in the account immediately, the constructor (lines 10–16) receives a parameter initialBalance of type double that represents the account's starting balance. Lines 14–15 ensure that initialBalance is greater than 0.0. If so, initialBalance's value is assigned to instance variable balance. Otherwise, balance remains at 0.0—its default initial value.

Method credit (lines 19–22) does not return any data when it completes its task, so its return type is void. The method receives one parameter named amount—a double value that will be added to the balance. Line 21 adds amount to the current value of balance, then assigns the result to balance (thus replacing the prior balance amount).

Method getBalance (lines 25–28) allows clients of the class (i.e., other classes that use this class) to obtain the value of a particular Account object's balance. The method specifies return type double and an empty parameter list.

Once again, note that the statements in lines 15, 21 and 27 use instance variable balance even though it was not declared in any of the methods. We can use balance in these methods because it is an instance variable of the class.

AccountTest Class to Use Class Account

Class AccountTest (Fig. 3.14) creates two Account objects (lines 10–11) and initializes them with 50.00 and -7.53, respectively. Lines 14–17 output the balance in each Account by calling the Account's getBalance method. When method getBalance is called for account1 from line 15, the value of account1's balance is returned from line 27 of Fig. 3.13 and displayed by the System.out.printf statement (Fig. 3.14, lines 14–15). Similarly, when method getBalance is called for account2 from line 17, the value of the account2's balance is returned from line 27 of Fig. 3.13 and displayed by the System.out.printf statement (Fig. 3.14, lines 16–17). Note that the balance of account2 is 0.00 because the constructor ensured that the account could not begin with a negative balance. The value is output by printf with the format specifier %.2f. The format specifier %f is used to output values of type float or double. The .2 between % and f represents the number of decimal places (2) that should be output to the right of the decimal point in the floating-point number—also known as the number's **precision**. Any floating-point value output with `%.2f` will be rounded to the hundredths position—for example, 123.457 would be rounded to 123.46, and 27.333 would be rounded to 27.33.

```java
1   // Fig. 3.14: AccountTest.java
2   // Inputting and outputting floating-point numbers with Account objects.
3   import java.util.Scanner;
4
5   public class AccountTest
6   {
7      // main method begins execution of Java application
8      public static void main( String args[] )
9      {
10        Account account1 = new Account( 50.00 ); // create Account object
11        Account account2 = new Account( -7.53 ); // create Account object
12
13        // display initial balance of each object
14        System.out.printf( "account1 balance: $%.2f\n",
15           account1.getBalance() );
16        System.out.printf( "account2 balance: $%.2f\n\n",
17           account2.getBalance() );
18
19        // create Scanner to obtain input from command window
20        Scanner input = new Scanner( System.in );
21        double depositAmount; // deposit amount read from user
22
23        System.out.print( "Enter deposit amount for account1: " ); // prompt
24        depositAmount = input.nextDouble(); // obtain user input
25        System.out.printf( "\nadding %.2f to account1 balance\n\n",
26           depositAmount );
27        account1.credit( depositAmount ); // add to account1 balance
28
29        // display balances
30        System.out.printf( "account1 balance: $%.2f\n",
31           account1.getBalance() );
32        System.out.printf( "account2 balance: $%.2f\n\n",
33           account2.getBalance() );
34
35        System.out.print( "Enter deposit amount for account2: " ); // prompt
36        depositAmount = input.nextDouble(); // obtain user input
37        System.out.printf( "\nadding %.2f to account2 balance\n\n",
38           depositAmount );
39        account2.credit( depositAmount ); // add to account2 balance
40
41        // display balances
42        System.out.printf( "account1 balance: $%.2f\n",
43           account1.getBalance() );
44        System.out.printf( "account2 balance: $%.2f\n",
45           account2.getBalance() );
46     } // end main
47
48  } // end class AccountTest
```

Fig. 3.14 | Inputting and outputting floating-point numbers with Account objects. (Part 1 of 2.)

```
account1 balance: $50.00
account2 balance: $0.00

Enter deposit amount for account1: 25.53

adding 25.53 to account1 balance

account1 balance: $75.53
account2 balance: $0.00

Enter deposit amount for account2: 123.45

adding 123.45 to account2 balance

account1 balance: $75.53
account2 balance: $123.45
```

Fig. 3.14 | Inputting and outputting floating-point numbers with Account objects. (Part 2 of 2.)

Line 20 creates a Scanner that will be used to obtain deposit amounts from a user. Line 21 declares local variable depositAmount to store each deposit amount entered by the user. Unlike the instance variable balance in class Account, local variable depositAmount in main is not initialized to 0.0 by default. However, this variable does not need to be initialized here because its value will be determined by the user's input.

Line 23 prompts the user to enter a deposit amount for account1. Line 24 obtains the input from the user by calling Scanner object input's nextDouble method, which returns a double value entered by the user. Lines 25–26 display the deposit amount. Line 27 calls object account1's credit method and supplies depositAmount as the method's argument. When the method is called, the argument's value is assigned to parameter amount (line 19 of Fig. 3.13) of method credit (lines 19–22 of Fig. 3.13), then method credit adds that value to the balance (line 21 of Fig. 3.13). Lines 30–33 (Fig. 3.14) output the balances of both Accounts again to show that only account1's balance changed.

Line 35 prompts the user to enter a deposit amount for account2. Line 36 obtains the input from the user by calling Scanner object input's nextDouble method. Lines 37–38 display the deposit amount. Line 39 calls object account2's credit method and supplies depositAmount as the method's argument, then method credit adds that value to the balance. Finally, lines 42–45 output the balances of both Accounts again to show that only account2's balance changed.

UML Class Diagram for Class Account

The UML class diagram in Fig. 3.15 models class Account of Fig. 3.13. The diagram models the private attribute balance with UML type Double to correspond to the class's instance variable balance of Java type double. The diagram models class Account's constructor with a parameter initialBalance of UML type Double in the third compartment of the class. The class's two public methods are modeled as operations in the third compartment as well. The diagram models operation credit with an amount parameter of UML type Double (because the corresponding method has an amount parameter of Java type double) and operation getBalance with a return type of Double (because the corresponding Java method returns a double value).

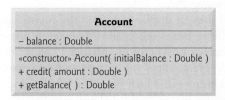

Fig. 3.15 | UML class diagram indicating that class `Account` has a `private balance` attribute of UML type `Double`, a constructor (with a parameter of UML type `Double`) and two `public` operations—`credit` (with an `amount` parameter of UML type `Double`) and `getBalance` (returns UML type `Double`).

3.9 (Optional) GUI and Graphics Case Study: Using Dialog Boxes

This optional case study is designed for those who want to begin learning Java's powerful capabilities for creating graphical user interfaces (GUIs) and graphics earlier in the book than the main discussions of these topics in Chapter 11, GUI Components: Part 1, Chapter 12, Graphics and Java 2D™, and Chapter 22, GUI Components: Part 2.

The GUI and Graphics Case Study appears in 10 brief sections (Fig. 3.16). Each section introduces a few basic concepts and provides visual, graphical examples. In the first few sections, you create your first graphical applications. In the subsequent sections, you use the object-oriented programming concepts presented through Chapter 10 to create a drawing application that draws a variety of shapes. When we formally introduce GUIs in Chapter 11, we use the mouse to choose exactly which shapes to draw and where to draw them. In Chapter 12, we add capabilities of the Java 2D graphics API to draw the shapes with different line thicknesses and fills. We hope you find this case study informative and entertaining.

Location	Title—Exercise(s)
Section 3.9	Using Dialog Boxes—Basic input and output with dialog boxes
Section 4.14	Creating Simple Drawings—Displaying and drawing lines on the screen
Section 5.10	Drawing Rectangles and Ovals—Using shapes to represent data
Section 6.13	Colors and Filled Shapes—Drawing a bull's-eye and random graphics
Section 7.13	Drawing Arcs—Drawing spirals with arcs
Section 8.18	Using Objects with Graphics—Storing shapes as objects
Section 9.8	Displaying Text and Images Using Labels—Providing status information
Section 10.8	Drawing with Polymorphism—Identifying the similarities between shapes
Exercise 11.18	Expanding the Interface—Using GUI components and event handling
Exercise 12.31	Adding Java 2D—Using the Java 2D API to enhance drawings

Fig. 3.16 | Summary of the GUI and Graphics Case Study in each chapter.

Displaying Text in a Dialog Box

The programs presented thus far display output in the command window. Many applications use windows or **dialog boxes** (also called **dialogs**) to display output. For example, web browsers such as Firefox or Microsoft Internet Explorer display web pages in their own windows. E-mail programs allow you to type and read messages in a window. Typically, dialog boxes are windows in which programs display important messages to users. Class `JOptionPane` provides prepackaged dialog boxes that enable programs to display windows containing messages—such windows are called **message dialogs**. Figure 3.17 displays the `String` "Welcome\nto\nJava" in a message dialog.

Line 3 indicates that the program uses class `JOptionPane` from package `javax.swing`. This package contains many classes that help you create **graphical user interfaces (GUIs)** for applications. **GUI components** facilitate data entry by a program's user, and presenting data outputs to the user. Line 10 calls `JOptionPane` method `showMessageDialog` to display a dialog box containing a message. The method requires two arguments. The first argument helps the Java application determine where to position the dialog box. When the first argument is `null`, the dialog box appears in the center of the computer screen. The second argument is the `String` to display in the dialog box.

Method `showMessageDialog` is **static** method of class `JOptionPane`. `static` methods often define frequently used tasks that do not explicitly require creating an object. For example, many programs display dialog boxes. Rather than require you to create code that performs this task, the designers of Java's `JOptionPane` class declared a `static` method that performs this task for you. A `static` method typically is called by using its class name followed by a dot (`.`) and the method name, as in

ClassName.*methodName*(*arguments*)

Chapter 6, Methods: A Deeper Look, discusses `static` methods in detail.

```
1   // Fig. 3.17: Dialog1.java
2   // Printing multiple lines in dialog box.
3   import javax.swing.JOptionPane; // import class JOptionPane
4
5   public class Dialog1
6   {
7      public static void main( String args[] )
8      {
9         // display a dialog with a message
10         JOptionPane.showMessageDialog( null, "Welcome\nto\nJava" );
11      } // end main
12   } // end class Dialog1
```

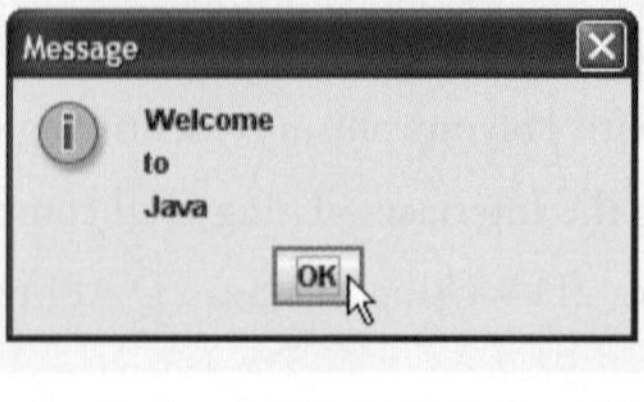

Fig. 3.17 | Using `JOptionPane` to display multiple lines in a dialog box.

Entering Text in a Dialog Box

The application of Fig. 3.18 uses another predefined JOptionPane dialog box called an **input dialog** that allows the user to enter data into the program. The program asks for the user's name, and responds with a message dialog containing a greeting and the name entered by the user.

Lines 10–11 use JOptionPane method `showInputDialog` to display an input dialog containing a prompt and a field (known as a **text field**) in which the user can enter text. Method showInputDialog's argument is the prompt that indicates what the user should enter. The user types characters in the text field, then clicks the **OK** button or presses the *Enter* key to return the String to the program. Method showInputDialog (line 11) returns a String containing the characters typed by the user. We store the String in variable name (line 10). [*Note:* If you press the **Cancel** button in the dialog, the method returns null and the program displays the word "null" as the name.]

Lines 14–15 use static String method `format` to return a String containing a greeting with the user's name. Method format is similar to method System.out.printf, except that format returns the formatted String rather than displaying it in a command window. Line 18 displays the greeting in a message dialog.

```java
1   // Fig. 3.18: NameDialog.java
2   // Basic input with a dialog box.
3   import javax.swing.JOptionPane;
4
5   public class NameDialog
6   {
7      public static void main( String args[] )
8      {
9         // prompt user to enter name
10        String name =
11           JOptionPane.showInputDialog( "What is your name?" );
12
13        // create the message
14        String message =
15           String.format( "Welcome, %s, to Java Programming!", name );
16
17        // display the message to welcome the user by name
18        JOptionPane.showMessageDialog( null, message );
19     } // end main
20  } // end class NameDialog
```

Fig. 3.18 | Obtaining user input from a dialog.

GUI and Graphics Case Study Exercise

3.1   Modify the addition program in Fig. 2.7 to use dialog-based input and output with the methods of class JOptionPane. Since method showInputDialog returns a String, you must convert the String the user enters to an int for use in calculations. The method

```
Integer.parseInt( String s )
```

takes a String argument representing an integer (e.g., the result of JOptionPane.showInputDialog) and returns the value as an int. Method parseInt is a static method of class Integer (from package java.lang). Note that if the String does not contain a valid integer, the program will terminate with an error.

3.10 (Optional) Software Engineering Case Study: Identifying the Classes in a Requirements Document

Now we begin designing the ATM system that we introduced in Chapter 2. In this section, we identify the classes that are needed to build the ATM system by analyzing the nouns and noun phrases that appear in the requirements document. We introduce UML class diagrams to model the relationships between these classes. This is an important first step in defining the structure of our system.

Identifying the Classes in a System

We begin our OOD process by identifying the classes required to build the ATM system. We will eventually describe these classes using UML class diagrams and implement these classes in Java. First, we review the requirements document of Section 2.9 and identify key nouns and noun phrases to help us identify classes that comprise the ATM system. We may decide that some of these nouns and noun phrases are attributes of other classes in the system. We may also conclude that some of the nouns do not correspond to parts of the system and thus should not be modeled at all. Additional classes may become apparent to us as we proceed through the design process.

Figure 3.19 lists the nouns and noun phrases found in the requirements document of Section 2.9. We list them from left to right in the order in which we first encounter them in the requirements document. We list only the singular form of each noun or noun phrase.

Nouns and noun phrases in the ATM requirements document		
bank	money / funds	account number
ATM	screen	PIN
user	keypad	bank database
customer	cash dispenser	balance inquiry
transaction	$20 bill / cash	withdrawal
account	deposit slot	deposit
balance	deposit envelope	

Fig. 3.19 | Nouns and noun phrases in the ATM requirements document.

We create classes only for the nouns and noun phrases that have significance in the ATM system. We don't model "bank" as a class, because the bank is not a part of the ATM system—the bank simply wants us to build the ATM. "Customer" and "user" also represent outside entities—they are important because they interact with our ATM system, but we do not need to model them as classes in the ATM software. Recall that we modeled an ATM user (i.e., a bank customer) as the actor in the use case diagram of Fig. 2.20.

We do not model "$20 bill" or "deposit envelope" as classes. These are physical objects in the real world, but they are not part of what is being automated. We can adequately represent the presence of bills in the system using an attribute of the class that models the cash dispenser. (We assign attributes to the ATM system's classes in Section 4.15.) For example, the cash dispenser maintains a count of the number of bills it contains. The requirements document does not say anything about what the system should do with deposit envelopes after it receives them. We can assume that simply acknowledging the receipt of an envelope—an operation performed by the class that models the deposit slot—is sufficient to represent the presence of an envelope in the system. (We assign operations to the ATM system's classes in Section 6.14.)

In our simplified ATM system, representing various amounts of "money," including an account's "balance," as attributes of classes seems most appropriate. Likewise, the nouns "account number" and "PIN" represent significant pieces of information in the ATM system. They are important attributes of a bank account. They do not, however, exhibit behaviors. Thus, we can most appropriately model them as attributes of an account class.

Though the requirements document frequently describes a "transaction" in a general sense, we do not model the broad notion of a financial transaction at this time. Instead, we model the three types of transactions (i.e., "balance inquiry," "withdrawal" and "deposit") as individual classes. These classes possess specific attributes needed for executing the transactions they represent. For example, a withdrawal needs to know the amount of money the user wants to withdraw. A balance inquiry, however, does not require any additional data. Furthermore, the three transaction classes exhibit unique behaviors. A withdrawal includes dispensing cash to the user, whereas a deposit involves receiving deposit envelopes from the user. [*Note:* In Section 10.9, we "factor out" common features of all transactions into a general "transaction" class using the object-oriented concept of inheritance.]

We determine the classes for our system based on the remaining nouns and noun phrases from Fig. 3.19. Each of these refers to one or more of the following:

- ATM
- screen
- keypad
- cash dispenser
- deposit slot
- account
- bank database
- balance inquiry
- withdrawal
- deposit

The elements of this list are likely to be classes we will need to implement our system.

We can now model the classes in our system based on the list we've created. We capitalize class names in the design process—a UML convention—as we'll do when we write the actual Java code that implements our design. If the name of a class contains more than one word, we run the words together and capitalize each word (e.g., MultipleWordName). Using this convention, we create classes ATM, Screen, Keypad, CashDispenser, DepositSlot, Account, BankDatabase, BalanceInquiry, Withdrawal and Deposit. We construct our system using these classes as building blocks. Before we begin building the system, however, we must gain a better understanding of how the classes relate to one another.

Modeling Classes

The UML enables us to model, via class diagrams, the classes in the ATM system and their interrelationships. Figure 3.20 represents class ATM. In the UML, each class is modeled as a rectangle with three compartments. The top compartment contains the name of the class centered horizontally in boldface. The middle compartment contains the class's attributes. (We discuss attributes in Section 4.15 and Section 5.11.) The bottom compartment contains the class's operations (discussed in Section 6.14). In Fig. 3.20, the middle and bottom compartments are empty because we have not yet determined this class's attributes and operations.

Class diagrams also show the relationships between the classes of the system. Figure 3.21 shows how our classes ATM and Withdrawal relate to one another. For the moment, we choose to model only this subset of classes for simplicity. We present a more complete class diagram later in this section. Notice that the rectangles representing classes in this diagram are not subdivided into compartments. The UML allows the suppression of class attributes and operations in this manner to create more readable diagrams, when appropriate. Such a diagram is said to be an elided diagram—one in which some information, such as the contents of the second and third compartments, is not modeled. We will place information in these compartments in Section 4.15 and Section 6.14.

In Fig. 3.21, the solid line that connects the two classes represents an association—a relationship between classes. The numbers near each end of the line are multiplicity values, which indicate how many objects of each class participate in the association. In this case, following the line from one end to the other reveals that, at any given moment, one ATM object participates in an association with either zero or one Withdrawal objects—zero if the current user is not currently performing a transaction or has requested a different type of transaction, and one if the user has requested a withdrawal. The UML can model many types of multiplicity. Figure 3.22 lists and explains the multiplicity types.

An association can be named. For example, the word Executes above the line connecting classes ATM and Withdrawal in Fig. 3.21 indicates the name of that association. This part of the diagram reads "one object of class ATM executes zero or one objects of class

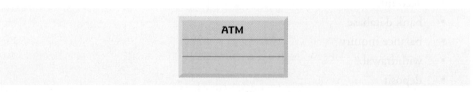

Fig. 3.20 | Representing a class in the UML using a class diagram.

Fig. 3.21 | Class diagram showing an association among classes.

Symbol	Meaning
0	None
1	One
m	An integer value
0..1	Zero or one
m, n	m or n
$m..n$	At least m, but not more than n
*	Any non-negative integer (zero or more)
0..*	Zero or more (identical to *)
1..*	One or more

Fig. 3.22 | Multiplicity types.

Withdrawal." Note that association names are directional, as indicated by the filled arrowhead—so it would be improper, for example, to read the preceding association from right to left as "zero or one objects of class Withdrawal execute one object of class ATM."

The word currentTransaction at the Withdrawal end of the association line in Fig. 3.21 is a **role name**, which identifies the role the Withdrawal object plays in its relationship with the ATM. A role name adds meaning to an association between classes by identifying the role a class plays in the context of an association. A class can play several roles in the same system. For example, in a school personnel system, a person may play the role of "professor" when relating to students. The same person may take on the role of "colleague" when participating in an association with another professor, and "coach" when coaching student athletes. In Fig. 3.21, the role name currentTransaction indicates that the Withdrawal object participating in the Executes association with an object of class ATM represents the transaction currently being processed by the ATM. In other contexts, a Withdrawal object may take on other roles (e.g., the previous transaction). Notice that we do not specify a role name for the ATM end of the Executes association. Role names in class diagrams are often omitted when the meaning of an association is clear without them.

In addition to indicating simple relationships, associations can specify more complex relationships, such as objects of one class being composed of objects of other classes. Consider a real-world automated teller machine. What "pieces" does a manufacturer put together to build a working ATM? Our requirements document tells us that the ATM is composed of a screen, a keypad, a cash dispenser and a deposit slot.

In Fig. 3.23, the **solid diamonds** attached to the association lines of class ATM indicate that class ATM has a **composition** relationship with classes Screen, Keypad, CashDispenser

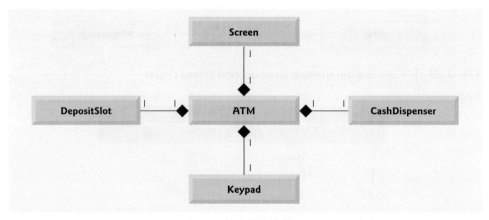

Fig. 3.23 | Class diagram showing composition relationships.

and DepositSlot. Composition implies a whole/part relationship. The class that has the composition symbol (the solid diamond) on its end of the association line is the whole (in this case, ATM), and the classes on the other end of the association lines are the parts—in this case, classes Screen, Keypad, CashDispenser and DepositSlot. The compositions in Fig. 3.23 indicate that an object of class ATM is formed from one object of class Screen, one object of class CashDispenser, one object of class Keypad and one object of class Deposit-Slot. The ATM "has a" screen, a keypad, a cash dispenser and a deposit slot. The *has-a* relationship defines composition. (We will see in the Software Engineering Case Study section in Chapter 10 that the *is-a* relationship defines inheritance.)

According to the UML specification (www.uml.org), composition relationships have the following properties:

1. Only one class in the relationship can represent the whole (i.e., the diamond can be placed on only one end of the association line). For example, either the screen is part of the ATM or the ATM is part of the screen, but the screen and the ATM cannot both represent the whole in the relationship.

2. The parts in the composition relationship exist only as long as the whole, and the whole is responsible for the creation and destruction of its parts. For example, the act of constructing an ATM includes manufacturing its parts. Also, if the ATM is destroyed, its screen, keypad, cash dispenser and deposit slot are also destroyed.

3. A part may belong to only one whole at a time, although the part may be removed and attached to another whole, which then assumes responsibility for the part.

The solid diamonds in our class diagrams indicate composition relationships that fulfill these three properties. If a *has-a* relationship does not satisfy one or more of these criteria, the UML specifies that hollow diamonds be attached to the ends of association lines to indicate aggregation—a weaker form of composition. For example, a personal computer and a computer monitor participate in an aggregation relationship—the computer "has a" monitor, but the two parts can exist independently, and the same monitor can be attached to multiple computers at once, thus violating the second and third properties of composition.

Figure 3.24 shows a class diagram for the ATM system. This diagram models most of the classes that we identified earlier in this section, as well as the associations between them that we can infer from the requirements document. [*Note:* Classes `BalanceInquiry` and `Deposit` participate in associations similar to those of class `Withdrawal`, so we have chosen to omit them from this diagram to keep the diagram simple. In Chapter 10, we expand our class diagram to include all the classes in the ATM system.]

Figure 3.24 presents a graphical model of the structure of the ATM system. This class diagram includes classes `BankDatabase` and `Account`, and several associations that were not present in either Fig. 3.21 or Fig. 3.23. The class diagram shows that class `ATM` has a one-to-one relationship with class `BankDatabase`—one `ATM` object authenticates users against one `BankDatabase` object. In Fig. 3.24, we also model the fact that the bank's database contains information about many accounts—one object of class `BankDatabase` participates in a composition relationship with zero or more objects of class `Account`. Recall from Fig. 3.22 that the multiplicity value 0..* at the `Account` end of the association between class `BankDatabase` and class `Account` indicates that zero or more objects of class `Account` take part in the association. Class `BankDatabase` has a one-to-many relationship with class `Account`—the `BankDatabase` stores many `Accounts`. Similarly, class `Account` has a many-to-one relationship with class `BankDatabase`—there can be many `Accounts` stored in the `BankDatabase`. [*Note:* Recall from Fig. 3.22 that the multiplicity value * is identical to 0..*. We include 0..* in our class diagrams for clarity.]

Figure 3.24 also indicates that if the user is performing a withdrawal, "one object of class `Withdrawal` accesses/modifies an account balance through one object of class `BankDatabase`." We could have created an association directly between class `Withdrawal` and class `Account`. The requirements document, however, states that the "ATM must interact with the bank's account information database" to perform transactions. A bank account contains sensitive information, and systems engineers must always consider the security of personal data when designing a system. Thus, only the `BankDatabase` can access and manipulate an account directly. All other parts of the system must interact with the database to retrieve or update account information (e.g., an account balance).

The class diagram in Fig. 3.24 also models associations between class `Withdrawal` and classes `Screen`, `CashDispenser` and `Keypad`. A withdrawal transaction includes prompting the user to choose a withdrawal amount and receiving numeric input. These actions require the use of the screen and the keypad, respectively. Furthermore, dispensing cash to the user requires access to the cash dispenser.

Classes `BalanceInquiry` and `Deposit`, though not shown in Fig. 3.24, take part in several associations with the other classes of the ATM system. Like class `Withdrawal`, each of these classes associates with classes `ATM` and `BankDatabase`. An object of class `BalanceInquiry` also associates with an object of class `Screen` to display the balance of an account to the user. Class `Deposit` associates with classes `Screen`, `Keypad` and `DepositSlot`. Like withdrawals, deposit transactions require use of the screen and the keypad to display prompts and receive input, respectively. To receive deposit envelopes, an object of class `Deposit` accesses the deposit slot.

We have now identified the classes in our ATM system (although we may discover others as we proceed with the design and implementation). In Section 4.15, we determine the attributes for each of these classes, and in Section 5.11, we use these attributes to examine how the system changes over time.

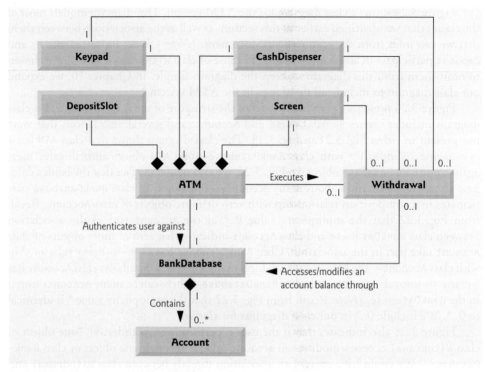

Fig. 3.24 | Class diagram for the ATM system model.

Software Engineering Case Study Self-Review Exercises

3.1 Suppose we have a class Car that represents a car. Think of some of the different pieces that a manufacturer would put together to produce a whole car. Create a class diagram (similar to Fig. 3.23) that models some of the composition relationships of class Car.

3.2 Suppose we have a class File that represents an electronic document in a standalone, non-networked computer represented by class Computer. What sort of association exists between class Computer and class File?

    a) Class Computer has a one-to-one relationship with class File.
    b) Class Computer has a many-to-one relationship with class File.
    c) Class Computer has a one-to-many relationship with class File.
    d) Class Computer has a many-to-many relationship with class File.

3.3 State whether the following statement is *true* or *false*, and if *false*, explain why: A UML diagram in which a class's second and third compartments are not modeled is said to be an elided diagram.

3.4 Modify the class diagram of Fig. 3.24 to include class Deposit instead of class Withdrawal.

Answers to Software Engineering Case Study Self-Review Exercises

3.1 [*Note:* Student answers may vary.] Figure 3.25 presents a class diagram that shows some of the composition relationships of a class Car.

3.2 c. [*Note:* In a computer network, this relationship could be many-to-many.]

3.3   True.

3.4   Figure 3.26 presents a class diagram for the ATM including class Deposit instead of class Withdrawal (as in Fig. 3.24). Note that Deposit does not access CashDispenser, but does access DepositSlot.

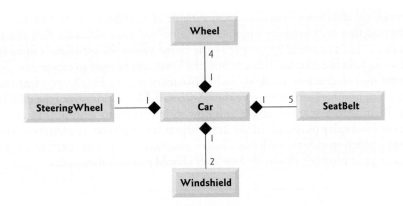

Fig. 3.25 | Class diagram showing composition relationships of a class Car.

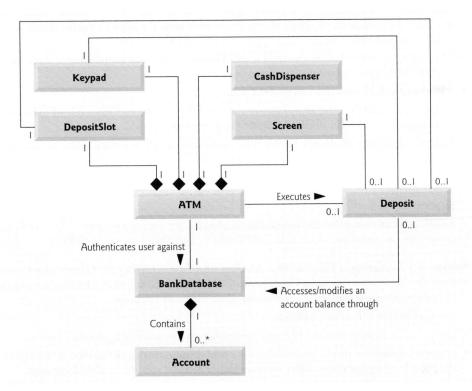

Fig. 3.26 | Class diagram for the ATM system model including class Deposit.

3.11 Wrap-Up

In this chapter, you learned the basic concepts of classes, objects, methods and instance variables—these will be used in most Java applications you create. In particular, you learned how to declare instance variables of a class to maintain data for each object of the class, and how to declare methods that operate on that data. You learned how to call a method to tell it to perform its task and how to pass information to methods as arguments. You learned the difference between a local variable of a method and an instance variable of a class and that only instance variables are initialized automatically. You also learned how to use a class's constructor to specify the initial values for an object's instance variables. Throughout the chapter, you saw how the UML can be used to create class diagrams that model the constructors, methods and attributes of classes. Finally, you learned about floating-point numbers—how to store them with variables of primitive type `double`, how to input them with a `Scanner` object and how to format them with `printf` and format specifier `%f` for display purposes. In the next chapter we begin our introduction to control statements, which specify the order in which a program's actions are performed. You will use these in your methods to specify how they should perform their tasks.

Summary

Section 3.2 Classes, Objects, Methods and Instance Variables

- Performing a task in a program requires a method. Inside the method you put the mechanisms that make the method do its tasks—that is, the method hides the implementation details of the tasks that it performs.

- The program unit that houses a method is called a class. A class may contain one or more methods that are designed to perform the class's tasks.

- A method can perform a task and return a result.

- A class can be used to create an instance of the class called an object. This is one of the reasons Java is known as an object-oriented programming language.

- Each message sent to an object is known as a method call and tells a method of the object to perform its task.

- Each method can specify parameters that represent additional information the method requires to perform its task correctly. A method call supplies values—called arguments—for the method's parameters.

- An object has attributes that are carried with the object as it is used in a program. These attributes are specified as part of the object's class. Attributes are specified in classes by fields.

Section 3.3 Declaring a Class with a Method and Instantiating an Object of a Class

- Each class declaration that begins with keyword `public` must be stored in a file that has exactly the same name as the class and ends with the `.java` file-name extension.

- Keyword `public` is an access modifier.

- Every class declaration contains keyword `class` followed immediately by the class's name.

- A method declaration that begins with keyword `public` indicates that the method is "available to the public"—that is, it can be called by other classes declared outside the class declaration.

- Keyword void indicates that a method will perform a task but will not return any information when it completes its task.
- By convention, method names begin with a lowercase first letter and all subsequent words in the name begin with a capital first letter.
- Empty parentheses following a method name indicate that the method does not require any parameters to perform its task.
- Every method's body is delimited by left and right braces ({ and }).
- The body of a method contains statements that perform the method's task. After the statements execute, the method has completed its task.
- When you attempt to execute a class, Java looks for the class's main method to begin execution.
- Any class that contains public static void main(String args[]) can be used to execute an application.
- Typically, you cannot call a method that belongs to another class until you create an object of that class.
- Class instance creation expressions beginning with keyword new create new objects.
- To call a method of an object, follow the variable name with a dot separator (.), the method name and a set of parentheses containing the method's arguments.
- In the UML, each class is modeled in a class diagram as a rectangle with three compartments. The top compartment contains the name of the class centered horizontally in boldface. The middle compartment contains the class's attributes, which correspond to fields in Java. The bottom compartment contains the class's operations, which correspond to methods and constructors in Java.
- The UML models operations by listing the operation name followed by a set of parentheses. A plus sign (+) in front of the operation name indicates that the operation is a public operation in the UML (i.e., a public method in Java).

Section 3.4 Declaring a Method with a Parameter
- Methods often require additional information to perform their tasks. Such additional information is provided to methods via arguments in method calls.
- Scanner method nextLine reads characters until a newline character is encountered, then returns the characters as a String.
- Scanner method next reads characters until any white-space character is encountered, then returns the characters as a String.
- A method that requires data to perform its task must specify this in its declaration by placing additional information in the method's parameter list.
- Each parameter must specify both a type and an identifier.
- At the time a method is called, its arguments are assigned to its parameters. Then the method body uses the parameter variables to access the argument values.
- A method can specify multiple parameters by separating each parameter from the next with a comma.
- The number of arguments in the method call must match the number of parameters in the method declaration's parameter list. Also, the argument types in the method call must be consistent with the types of the corresponding parameters in the method's declaration.
- Class String is in package java.lang, which is imported implicitly into all source-code files.

- There is a special relationship between classes that are compiled in the same directory on disk. By default, such classes are considered to be in the same package—known as the default package. Classes in the same package are implicitly imported into the source code files of other classes in the same package. Thus, an `import` declaration is not required when one class in a package uses another in the same package.

- An `import` declaration is not required if you always refer to a class with its fully qualified class name.

- The UML models a parameter of an operation by listing the parameter name, followed by a colon and the parameter type between the parentheses following the operation name.

- The UML has its own data types similar to those of Java. Not all the UML data types have the same names as the corresponding Java types.

- The UML type `String` corresponds to the Java type `String`.

Section 3.5 Instance Variables, set Methods and get Methods

- Variables declared in the body of a particular method are known as local variables and can be used only in that method.

- A class normally consists of one or more methods that manipulate the attributes (data) that belong to a particular object of the class. Attributes are represented as fields in a class declaration. Such variables are called fields and are declared inside a class declaration but outside the bodies of the class's method declarations.

- When each object of a class maintains its own copy of an attribute, the field that represents the attribute is also known as an instance variable. Each object (instance) of the class has a separate instance of the variable in memory.

- Most instance variable declarations are preceded with the `private` access modifier. Variables or methods declared with access modifier `private` are accessible only to methods of the class in which they are declared.

- Declaring instance variables with access modifier `private` is known as data hiding.

- A benefit of fields is that all the methods of the class can use the fields. Another distinction between a field and a local variable is that a field has a default initial value provided by Java when the programmer does not specify the field's initial value, but a local variable does not.

- The default value for a field of type `String` is `null`.

- When a method that specifies a return type is called and completes its task, the method returns a result to its calling method.

- Classes often provide `public` methods to allow clients of the class to *set* or *get* `private` instance variables. The names of these methods need not begin with *set* or *get*, but this naming convention is highly recommended in Java and is required for special Java software components called Java-Beans.

- The UML represents instance variables as attributes by listing the attribute name, followed by a colon and the attribute type.

- Private attributes are preceded by a minus sign (–) in the UML.

- The UML indicates the return type of an operation by placing a colon and the return type after the parentheses following the operation name.

- UML class diagrams do not specify return types for operations that do not return values.

Section 3.6 Primitive Types vs. Reference Types

- Types in Java are divided into two categories—primitive types and reference types (sometimes called nonprimitive types). The primitive types are boolean, byte, char, short, int, long, float and double. All other types are reference types, so classes, which specify the types of objects, are reference types.

- A primitive-type variable can store exactly one value of its declared type at a time.

- Primitive-type instance variables are initialized by default. Variables of types byte, char, short, int, long, float and double are initialized to 0. Variables of type boolean are initialized to false.

- Programs use variables of reference types (called references) to store the location of an object in the computer's memory. Such variables refer to objects in the program. The object that is referenced may contain many instance variables and methods.

- Reference-type fields are initialized by default to the value null.

- A reference to an object is required to invoke an object's instance methods. A primitive-type variable does not refer to an object and therefore cannot be used to invoke a method.

Section 3.7 Initializing Objects with Constructors

- A constructor can be used to initialize an object of a class when the object is created.

- Constructors can specify parameters but cannot specify return types.

- If no constructor is provided for a class, the compiler provides a default constructor with no parameters.

- When a class has only the default constructor, its instance variables are initialized to their default values. Variables of types char, byte, short, int, long, float and double are initialized to 0, variables of type boolean are initialized to false, and reference-type variables are initialized to null.

- Like operations, the UML models constructors in the third compartment of a class diagram. To distinguish a constructor from a class's operations, the UML places the word "constructor" between guillemets (« and ») before the constructor's name.

Section 3.8 Floating-Point Numbers and Type `double`

- A floating-point number is a number with a decimal point, such as 7.33, 0.0975 or 1000.12345. Java provides two primitive types for storing floating-point numbers in memory—float and double. The primary difference between these types is that double variables can store numbers with larger magnitude and finer detail (known as the number's precision) than float variables.

- Variables of type float represent single-precision floating-point numbers and have seven significant digits. Variables of type double represent double-precision floating-point numbers. These require twice as much memory as float variables and provide 15 significant digits—approximately double the precision of float variables.

- Floating-point values that appear in source code are known as floating-point literals and are type double by default.

- Scanner method nextDouble returns a double value.

- The format specifier %f is used to output values of type float or double. A precision can be specified between % and f to represent the number of decimal places that should be output to the right of the decimal point in the floating-point number.

- The default value for a field of type double is 0.0, and the default value for a field of type int is 0.

Terminology

%f format specifier	JOptionPane class (GUI)
access modifier	local variable
aggregation (UML)	many-to-many relationship (UML)
attribute (UML)	many-to-one relationship (UML)
calling method	message
class	message dialog (GUI)
class declaration	method
class instance	method call
class keyword	method header
class instance creation expression	multiplicity (UML)
client of an object or a class	new keyword
compartment in a class diagram (UML)	next method of class Scanner
composition (UML)	nextDouble method of class Scanner
constructor	nextLine method of class Scanner
create an object	nonprimitive types
data hiding	null reserved word
declare a method	object (or instance)
default constructor	one-to-many relationship (UML)
default initial value	operation (UML)
default package	parameter
default value	parameter list
dialog (GUI)	precision of a floating-point value
dialog box (GUI)	precision of a formatted floating-point number
dot (.) separator	private access modifier
double-precision floating-point number	public access modifier
double primitive type	public method
elided diagram (UML)	refer to an object
extensible language	reference
field	reference type
float primitive type	return type of a method
floating-point literal	role name (UML)
floating-point number	send a message
get method	set method
graphical user interface (GUI)	showInputDialog method of class JOptionPane
graphical user interface (GUI) component	(GUI)
guillemets, « and » (UML)	showMessageDialog method of class JOption-
has-a relationship	Pane (GUI)
input dialog (GUI)	single-precision floating-point number
instance of a class (object)	solid diamond (UML)
instance variable	text field (GUI)
instantiate (or create) an object	UML class diagram
invoke a method	void keyword

Self-Review Exercises

3.1 Fill in the blanks in each of the following:
   a) A house is to a blueprint as a(n) _____ is to a class.
   b) Each class declaration that begins with keyword _____ must be stored in a file that has exactly the same name as the class and ends with the .java file-name extension.

c) Every class declaration contains keyword _____ followed immediately by the class's name.

d) Keyword _____ creates an object of the class specified to the right of the keyword.

e) Each parameter must specify both a(n) _____ and a(n) _____.

f) By default, classes that are compiled in the same directory are considered to be in the same package, known as the _____.

g) When each object of a class maintains its own copy of an attribute, the field that represents the attribute is also known as a(n) _____.

h) Java provides two primitive types for storing floating-point numbers in memory: _____ and _____.

i) Variables of type `double` represent _____ floating-point numbers.

j) `Scanner` method _____ returns a `double` value.

k) Keyword `public` is a(n) _____.

l) Return type _____ indicates that a method will perform a task but will not return any information when it completes its task.

m) `Scanner` method _____ reads characters until a newline character is encountered, then returns those characters as a `String`.

n) Class `String` is in package _____.

o) A(n) _____ is not required if you always refer to a class with its fully qualified class name.

p) A(n) _____ is a number with a decimal point, such as 7.33, 0.0975 or 1000.12345.

q) Variables of type `float` represent _____ floating-point numbers.

r) The format specifier _____ is used to output values of type `float` or `double`.

s) Types in Java are divided into two categories—_____ types and _____ types.

3.2 State whether each of the following is *true* or *false*. If *false*, explain why.

a) By convention, method names begin with an uppercase first letter and all subsequent words in the name begin with a capital first letter.

b) An `import` declaration is not required when one class in a package uses another in the same package.

c) Empty parentheses following a method name in a method declaration indicate that the method does not require any parameters to perform its task.

d) Variables or methods declared with access modifier `private` are accessible only to methods of the class in which they are declared.

e) A primitive-type variable can be used to invoke a method.

f) Variables declared in the body of a particular method are known as instance variables and can be used in all methods of the class.

g) Every method's body is delimited by left and right braces (`{` and `}`).

h) Primitive-type local variables are initialized by default.

i) Reference-type instance variables are initialized by default to the value `null`.

j) Any class that contains `public static void main( String args[] )` can be used to execute an application.

k) The number of arguments in the method call must match the number of parameters in the method declaration's parameter list.

l) Floating-point values that appear in source code are known as floating-point literals and are type `float` by default.

3.3 What is the difference between a local variable and a field?

3.4 Explain the purpose of a method parameter. What is the difference between a parameter and an argument?

Answers to Self-Review Exercises

3.1 a) object. b) `public`. c) `class`. d) `new`. e) type, name. f) default package. g) instance variable. h) `float`, `double`. i) double-precision. j) `nextDouble`. k) access modifier. l) `void`. m) `nextLine`. n) `java.lang`. o) `import` declaration. p) floating-point number. q) single-precision. r) `%f`. s) primitive, reference.

3.2 a) False. By convention, method names begin with a lowercase first letter and all subsequent words in the name begin with a capital first letter. b) True. c) True. d) True. e) False. A primitive-type variable cannot be used to invoke a method—a reference to an object is required to invoke the object's methods. f) False. Such variables are called local variables and can be used only in the method in which they are declared. g) True. h) False. Primitive-type instance variables are initialized by default. Each local variable must explicitly be assigned a value. i) True. j) True. k) True. l) False. Such literals are of type `double` by default.

3.3 A local variable is declared in the body of a method and can be used only from the point at which it is declared through the end of the method declaration. A field is declared in a class, but not in the body of any of the class's methods. Every object (instance) of a class has a separate copy of the class's fields. Also, fields are accessible to all methods of the class. (We will see an exception to this in Chapter 8, Classes and Objects: A Deeper Look.)

3.4 A parameter represents additional information that a method requires to perform its task. Each parameter required by a method is specified in the method's declaration. An argument is the actual value for a method parameter. When a method is called, the argument values are passed to the method so that it can perform its task.

Exercises

3.5 What is a default constructor? How are an object's instance variables initialized if a class has only a default constructor?

3.6 Most classes need to be imported before they can be used in an application. Why is every application allowed to use classes `System` and `String` without first importing them?

3.7 Explain why a class might provide a *set* method and a *get* method for an instance variable.

3.8 Modify class `GradeBook` (Fig. 3.10) as follows:
  a) Include a second `String` instance variable that represents the name of the course's instructor.
  b) Provide a *set* method to change the instructor's name and a *get* method to retrieve it.
  c) Modify the constructor to specify two parameters—one for the course name and one for the instructor's name.
  d) Modify method `displayMessage` such that it first outputs the welcome message and course name, then outputs "This course is presented by: " followed by the instructor's name.

Use your modified class in a test application that demonstrates the class's new capabilities.

3.9 Modify class `Account` (Fig. 3.13) to provide a method called `debit` that withdraws money from an `Account`. Ensure that the debit amount does not exceed the `Account`'s balance. If it does, the balance should be left unchanged and the method should print a message indicating "Debit amount exceeded account balance." Modify class `AccountTest` (Fig. 3.14) to test method `debit`.

3.10 Create a class called `Employee` that includes three pieces of information as instance variables—a first name (type `String`), a last name (type `String`) and a monthly salary (`double`). Your class should have a constructor that initializes the three instance variables. Provide a *set* and a *get* method for each instance variable. If the monthly salary is not positive, set it to `0.0`. Write a test application named EmployeeTest that demonstrates class Employee's capabilities. Create two Employee objects and display each object's *yearly* salary. Then give each Employee a 10% raise and display each Employee's yearly salary again.

4

Control Statements: Part 1

OBJECTIVES

In this chapter you will learn:

- To use basic problem-solving techniques.
- To develop algorithms through the process of top-down, stepwise refinement using pseudocode.
- To use the `if` and `if...else` selection statements to choose among alternative actions.
- To use the `while` repetition statement to execute statements in a program repeatedly.
- To use counter-controlled repetition and sentinel-controlled repetition.
- To use the compound assignment, increment and decrement operators.
- The primitive data types.

4.1 Introduction

Before writing a program to solve a problem, you must have a thorough understanding of the problem and a carefully planned approach to solving it. When writing a program, you also must understand the types of building blocks that are available and employ proven program-construction techniques. In this chapter and in Chapter 5, Control Statements: Part 2, we discuss these issues in our presentation of the theory and principles of structured programming. The concepts presented here are crucial in building classes and manipulating objects.

In this chapter, we introduce Java's `if...else` and `while` statements, three of the building blocks that allow programmers to specify the logic required for methods to perform their tasks. We devote a portion of this chapter (and Chapters 5 and 7) to further developing the `GradeBook` class introduced in Chapter 3. In particular, we add a method to the `GradeBook` class that uses control statements to calculate the average of a set of student grades. Another example demonstrates additional ways to combine control statements to solve a similar problem. We introduce Java's compound assignment operators and explore Java's increment and decrement operators. These additional operators abbreviate and simplify many program statements. Finally, we present an overview of the primitive data types available to programmers.

4.2 Algorithms

Any computing problem can be solved by executing a series of actions in a specific order. A procedure for solving a problem in terms of

1. the actions to execute and
2. the order in which these actions execute

is called an algorithm. The following example demonstrates that correctly specifying the order in which the actions execute is important.

Consider the "rise-and-shine algorithm" followed by one executive for getting out of bed and going to work: (1) Get out of bed; (2) take off pajamas; (3) take a shower; (4) get dressed; (5) eat breakfast; (6) carpool to work. This routine gets the executive to work well prepared to make critical decisions. Suppose that the same steps are performed in a slightly different order: (1) Get out of bed; (2) take off pajamas; (3) get dressed; (4) take a shower; (5) eat breakfast; (6) carpool to work. In this case, our executive shows up for work soaking wet.

Specifying the order in which statements (actions) execute in a program is called program control. This chapter investigates program control using Java's control statements.

4.3 Pseudocode

Pseudocode is an informal language that helps programmers develop algorithms without having to worry about the strict details of Java language syntax. The pseudocode we present is particularly useful for developing algorithms that will be converted to structured portions of Java programs. Pseudocode is similar to everyday English—it is convenient and user friendly, but it is not an actual computer programming language. We begin using pseudocode in Section 4.5, and a sample pseudocode program appears in Fig. 4.5.

Pseudocode does not execute on computers. Rather, it helps the programmer "think out" a program before attempting to write it in a programming language, such as Java. This chapter provides several examples of how to use pseudocode to develop Java programs.

The style of pseudocode we present consists purely of characters, so programmers can type pseudocode conveniently, using any text-editor program. A carefully prepared pseudocode program can easily be converted to a corresponding Java program. In many cases, this simply requires replacing pseudocode statements with Java equivalents.

Pseudocode normally describes only statements representing the actions that occur after a programmer converts a program from pseudocode to Java and the program is run on a computer. Such actions might include input, output or a calculation. We typically do not include variable declarations in our pseudocode, but some programmers choose to list variables and mention their purposes at the beginning of their pseudocode.

4.4 Control Structures

Normally, statements in a program are executed one after the other in the order in which they are written. This process is called sequential execution. Various Java statements, which we will soon discuss, enable the programmer to specify that the next statement to execute is not necessarily the next one in sequence. This is called transfer of control.

During the 1960s, it became clear that the indiscriminate use of transfers of control was the root of much difficulty experienced by software development groups. The blame was pointed at the goto statement (used in most programming languages of the time), which allows the programmer to specify a transfer of control to one of a very wide range of possible destinations in a program. The notion of so-called structured programming became almost synonymous with "goto elimination." [*Note:* Java does not have a goto statement; however, the word `goto` is reserved by Java and should not be used as an identifier in programs.]

The research of Bohm and Jacopini[1] had demonstrated that programs could be written without any `goto` statements. The challenge of the era for programmers was to shift their styles to "goto-less programming." Not until the 1970s did programmers start taking structured programming seriously. The results were impressive. Software development groups reported shorter development times, more frequent on-time delivery of systems and more frequent within-budget completion of software projects. The key to these successes was that structured programs were clearer, easier to debug and modify, and more likely to be bug free in the first place.

Bohm and Jacopini's work demonstrated that all programs could be written in terms of only three control structures—the **sequence structure**, the **selection structure** and the **repetition structure**. The term "control structures" comes from the field of computer science. When we introduce Java's implementations of control structures, we will refer to them in the terminology of the *Java Language Specification* as "control statements."

Sequence Structure in Java

The sequence structure is built into Java. Unless directed otherwise, the computer executes Java statements one after the other in the order in which they are written—that is, in sequence. The **activity diagram** in Fig. 4.1 illustrates a typical sequence structure in which two calculations are performed in order. Java lets us have as many actions as we want in a sequence structure. As we will soon see, anywhere a single action may be placed, we may place several actions in sequence.

Activity diagrams are part of the UML. An activity diagram models the **workflow** (also called the **activity**) of a portion of a software system. Such workflows may include a portion of an algorithm, such as the sequence structure in Fig. 4.1. Activity diagrams are composed of special-purpose symbols, such as **action-state symbols** (rectangles with their left and right sides replaced with arcs curving outward), **diamonds** and **small circles**. These symbols are connected by **transition arrows**, which represent the flow of the activity—that is, the order in which the actions should occur.

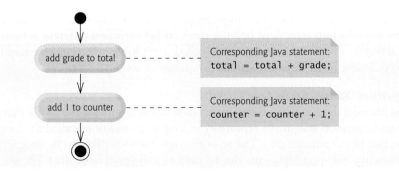

Fig. 4.1 | Sequence structure activity diagram.

---

1. Bohm, C., and G. Jacopini, "Flow Diagrams, Turing Machines, and Languages with Only Two Formation Rules," *Communications of the ACM*, Vol. 9, No. 5, May 1966, pp. 336–371.

Like pseudocode, activity diagrams help programmers develop and represent algorithms, although many programmers prefer pseudocode. Activity diagrams clearly show how control structures operate.

Consider the activity diagram for the sequence structure in Fig. 4.1. It contains two **action states** that represent actions to perform. Each action state contains an **action expression**—for example, "add grade to total" or "add 1 to counter"—that specifies a particular action to perform. Other actions might include calculations or input/output operations. The arrows in the activity diagram represent **transitions**, which indicate the order in which the actions represented by the action states occur. The program that implements the activities illustrated by the diagram in Fig. 4.1 first adds `grade` to `total`, then adds 1 to `counter`.

The **solid circle** located at the top of the activity diagram represents the activity's **initial state**—the beginning of the workflow before the program performs the modeled actions. The **solid circle surrounded by a hollow circle** that appears at the bottom of the diagram represents the **final state**—the end of the workflow after the program performs its actions.

Figure 4.1 also includes rectangles with the upper-right corners folded over. These are UML **notes** (like comments in Java)—explanatory remarks that describe the purpose of symbols in the diagram. Figure 4.1 uses UML notes to show the Java code associated with each action state in the activity diagram. A **dotted line** connects each note with the element that the note describes. Activity diagrams normally do not show the Java code that implements the activity. We use notes for this purpose here to illustrate how the diagram relates to Java code. For more information on the UML, see our optional case study, which appears in the Software Engineering Case Study sections at the ends of Chapters 1–8 and 10, or visit www.uml.org.

Selection Statements in Java

Java has three types of **selection statements** (discussed in this chapter and Chapter 5). The `if` statement either performs (selects) an action, if a condition is true, or skips it, if the condition is false. The `if...else` statement performs an action if a condition is true and performs a different action if the condition is false. The `switch` statement (Chapter 5) performs one of many different actions, depending on the value of an expression.

The `if` statement is a **single-selection statement** because it selects or ignores a single action (or, as we will soon see, a single group of actions). The `if...else` statement is called a **double-selection statement** because it selects between two different actions (or groups of actions). The `switch` statement is called a **multiple-selection statement** because it selects among many different actions (or groups of actions).

Repetition Statements in Java

Java provides three repetition statements (also called **looping statements**) that enable programs to perform statements repeatedly as long as a condition (called the **loop-continuation condition**) remains true. The repetition statements are the `while`, `do...while` and `for` statements. (Chapter 5 presents the `do...while` and `for` statements.) The `while` and `for` statements perform the action (or group of actions) in their bodies zero or more times—if the loop-continuation condition is initially false, the action (or group of actions) will not execute. The `do...while` statement performs the action (or group of actions) in its body one or more times.

The words if, else, switch, while, do and for are Java keywords. Recall that keywords are used to implement various Java features, such as control statements. Keywords cannot be used as identifiers, such as variable names. A complete list of Java keywords appears in Appendix C.

Summary of Control Statements in Java

Java has only three kinds of control structures, which from this point forward we refer to as control statements: the sequence statement, selection statements (three types) and repetition statements (three types). Every program is formed by combining as many sequence, selection and repetition statements as is appropriate for the algorithm the program implements. As with the sequence statement in Fig. 4.1, we can model each control statement as an activity diagram. Each diagram contains an initial state and a final state that represent a control statement's entry point and exit point, respectively. Single-entry/single-exit control statements make it easy to build programs—we "attached" the control statements to one another by connecting the exit point of one to the entry point of the next. This procedure is similar to the way in which a child stacks building blocks, so we call it control-statement stacking. We will learn that there is only one other way in which control statements may be connected—control-statement nesting—in which one control statement appears inside another. Thus, algorithms in Java programs are constructed from only three kinds of control statements, combined in only two ways. This is the essence of simplicity.

4.5 if Single-Selection Statement

Programs use selection statements to choose among alternative courses of action. For example, suppose that the passing grade on an exam is 60. The pseudocode statement

> *If student's grade is greater than or equal to 60*
> *Print "Passed"*

determines whether the condition "student's grade is greater than or equal to 60" is true or false. If it is true, "Passed" is printed, and the next pseudocode statement in order is "performed." (Remember that pseudocode is not a real programming language.) If the condition is false, the *Print* statement is ignored, and the next pseudocode statement in order is performed. The indentation of the second line of this selection statement is optional, but recommended, because it emphasizes the inherent structure of structured programs.

The preceding pseudocode *If* statement may be written in Java as

```
if ( studentGrade >= 60 )
    System.out.println( "Passed" );
```

Note that the Java code corresponds closely to the pseudocode. This is one of the properties of pseudocode that makes it such a useful program development tool.

Figure 4.2 illustrates the single-selection if statement. This figure contains what is perhaps the most important symbol in an activity diagram—the diamond, or decision symbol, which indicates that a decision is to be made. The workflow will continue along a path determined by the symbol's associated guard conditions, which can be true or false. Each transition arrow emerging from a decision symbol has a guard condition (specified in square brackets next to the transition arrow). If a guard condition is true, the workflow enters the action state to which the transition arrow points. In Fig. 4.2, if the grade is

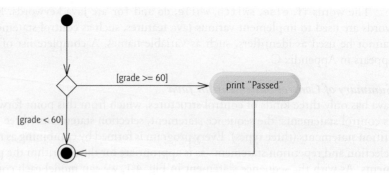

Fig. 4.2 | if single-selection statement UML activity diagram.

greater than or equal to 60, the program prints "Passed," then transitions to the final state of this activity. If the grade is less than 60, the program immediately transitions to the final state without displaying a message.

The if statement is a single-entry/single-exit control statement. We will see that the activity diagrams for the remaining control statements also contain initial states, transition arrows, action states that indicate actions to perform, decision symbols (with associated guard conditions) that indicate decisions to be made and final states. This is consistent with the **action/decision model of programming** we have been emphasizing.

Envision seven bins, each containing only one type of Java control statement. The control statements are all empty. Your task is to assemble a program from as many of each type of control statement as the algorithm demands, combining them in only two possible ways (stacking or nesting), then filling in the action states and decisions with action expressions and guard conditions appropriate for the algorithm. We will discuss the variety of ways in which actions and decisions can be written.

4.6 if...else Double-Selection Statement

The if single-selection statement performs an indicated action only when the condition is true; otherwise, the action is skipped. The if...else double-selection statement allows the programmer to specify an action to perform when the condition is true and a different action when the condition is false. For example, the pseudocode statement

> *If student's grade is greater than or equal to 60*
> > *Print "Passed"*
> *Else*
> > *Print "Failed"*

prints "Passed" if the student's grade is greater than or equal to 60, but prints "Failed" if it is less than 60. In either case, after printing occurs, the next pseudocode statement in sequence is "performed."

The preceding *If...Else* pseudocode statement can be written in Java as

```
if ( grade >= 60 )
    System.out.println( "Passed" );
else
    System.out.println( "Failed" );
```

Note that the body of the else is also indented. Whatever indentation convention you choose should be applied consistently throughout your programs. It is difficult to read programs that do not obey uniform spacing conventions.

Good Programming Practice 4.1

Indent both body statements of an if...else statement.

Good Programming Practice 4.2

If there are several levels of indentation, each level should be indented the same additional amount of space.

Figure 4.3 illustrates the flow of control in the if...else statement. Once again, the symbols in the UML activity diagram (besides the initial state, transition arrows and final state) represent action states and decisions. We continue to emphasize this action/decision model of computing. Imagine again a deep bin containing as many empty if...else statements as might be needed to build any Java program. Your job is to assemble these if...else statements (by stacking and nesting) with any other control statements required by the algorithm. You fill in the action states and decision symbols with action expressions and guard conditions appropriate to the algorithm you are developing.

Conditional Operator (?:)

Java provides the conditional operator (?:) that can be used in place of an if...else statement. This is Java's only ternary operator—this means that it takes three operands. Together, the operands and the ?: symbol form a conditional expression. The first operand (to the left of the ?) is a boolean expression (i.e., a condition that evaluates to a boolean value—true or false), the second operand (between the ? and :) is the value of the conditional expression if the boolean expression is true and the third operand (to the right of the :) is the value of the conditional expression if the boolean expression evaluates to false. For example, the statement

```
System.out.println( studentGrade >= 60 ? "Passed" : "Failed" );
```

prints the value of println's conditional-expression argument. The conditional expression in this statement evaluates to the string "Passed" if the boolean expression studentGrade >= 60 is true and evaluates to the string "Failed" if the boolean expression is false.

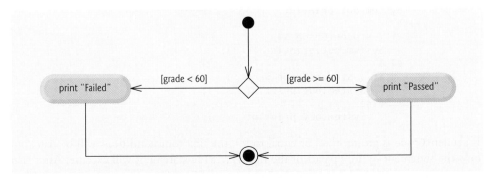

Fig. 4.3 | if...else double-selection statement UML activity diagram.

Thus, this statement with the conditional operator performs essentially the same function as the if...else statement shown earlier in this section. The precedence of the conditional operator is low, so the entire conditional expression is normally placed in parentheses. We will see that conditional expressions can be used in some situations where if...else statements cannot.

 Good Programming Practice 4.3

Conditional expressions are more difficult to read than if...else statements and should be used to replace only simple if...else statements that choose between two values.

Nested if...else Statements

A program can test multiple cases by placing if...else statements inside other if...else statements to create nested if...else statements. For example, the following pseudocode represents a nested if...else that prints A for exam grades greater than or equal to 90, B for grades in the range 80 to 89, C for grades in the range 70 to 79, D for grades in the range 60 to 69 and F for all other grades:

> *If student's grade is greater than or equal to 90*
>> *Print "A"*
> *else*
>> *If student's grade is greater than or equal to 80*
>>> *Print "B"*
>> *else*
>>> *If student's grade is greater than or equal to 70*
>>>> *Print "C"*
>>> *else*
>>>> *If student's grade is greater than or equal to 60*
>>>>> *Print "D"*
>>>> *else*
>>>>> *Print "F"*

This pseudocode may be written in Java as

```java
if ( studentGrade >= 90 )
    System.out.println( "A" );
else
    if ( studentGrade >= 80 )
        System.out.println( "B" );
    else
        if ( studentGrade >= 70 )
            System.out.println( "C" );
        else
            if ( studentGrade >= 60 )
                System.out.println( "D" );
            else
                System.out.println( "F" );
```

If studentGrade is greater than or equal to 90, the first four conditions will be true, but only the statement in the if-part of the first if...else statement will execute. After that statement executes, the else-part of the "outermost" if...else statement is skipped. Most Java programmers prefer to write the preceding if...else statement as

```
if ( studentGrade >= 90 )
   System.out.println( "A" );
else if ( studentGrade >= 80 )
   System.out.println( "B" );
else if ( studentGrade >= 70 )
   System.out.println( "C" );
else if ( studentGrade >= 60 )
   System.out.println( "D" );
else
   System.out.println( "F" );
```

The two forms are identical except for the spacing and indentation, which the compiler ignores. The latter form is popular because it avoids deep indentation of the code to the right. Such indentation often leaves little room on a line of code, forcing lines to be split and decreasing program readability.

Dangling-else Problem

The Java compiler always associates an else with the immediately preceding if unless told to do otherwise by the placement of braces ({ and }). This behavior can lead to what is referred to as the **dangling-else problem**. For example,

```
if ( x > 5 )
   if ( y > 5 )
      System.out.println( "x and y are > 5" );
else
   System.out.println( "x is <= 5" );
```

appears to indicate that if x is greater than 5, the nested if statement determines whether y is also greater than 5. If so, the string "x and y are > 5" is output. Otherwise, it appears that if x is not greater than 5, the else part of the if...else outputs the string "x is <= 5".

Beware! This nested if...else statement does not execute as it appears. The compiler actually interprets the statement as

```
if ( x > 5 )
   if ( y > 5 )
      System.out.println( "x and y are > 5" );
   else
      System.out.println( "x is <= 5" );
```

in which the body of the first if is a nested if...else. The outer if statement tests whether x is greater than 5. If so, execution continues by testing whether y is also greater than 5. If the second condition is true, the proper string—"x and y are > 5"—is displayed. However, if the second condition is false, the string "x is <= 5" is displayed, even though we know that x is greater than 5. Equally bad, if the outer if statement's condition is false, the inner if...else is skipped and nothing is displayed.

To force the nested if...else statement to execute as it was originally intended, we must write it as follows:

```
if ( x > 5 )
{
   if ( y > 5 )
      System.out.println( "x and y are > 5" );
}
else
   System.out.println( "x is <= 5" );
```

The braces ({}) indicate to the compiler that the second if statement is in the body of the first if and that the else is associated with the *first* if. Exercises 4.24–4.25 investigate the dangling-else problem further.

Blocks

The if statement normally expects only one statement in its body. To include several statements in the body of an if (or the body of an else for an if...else statement), enclose the statements in braces ({ and }). A set of statements contained within a pair of braces is called a block. A block can be placed anywhere in a program that a single statement can be placed.

The following example includes a block in the else-part of an if...else statement:

```
if ( grade >= 60 )
    System.out.println( "Passed" );
else
{
    System.out.println( "Failed" );
    System.out.println( "You must take this course again." );
}
```

In this case, if grade is less than 60, the program executes both statements in the body of the else and prints

```
Failed.
You must take this course again.
```

Note the braces surrounding the two statements in the else clause. These braces are important. Without the braces, the statement

```
System.out.println( "You must take this course again." );
```

would be outside the body of the else-part of the if...else statement and would execute regardless of whether the grade was less than 60.

Syntax errors (e.g., when one brace in a block is left out of the program) are caught by the compiler. A logic error (e.g., when both braces in a block are left out of the program) has its effect at execution time. A fatal logic error causes a program to fail and terminate prematurely. A nonfatal logic error allows a program to continue executing, but causes the program to produce incorrect results.

Common Programming Error 4.1

Forgetting one or both of the braces that delimit a block can lead to syntax errors or logic errors in a program.

Good Programming Practice 4.4

Always using braces in an if...else (or other) statement helps prevent their accidental omission, especially when adding statements to the if-part or the else-part at a later time. To avoid omitting one or both of the braces, some programmers type the beginning and ending braces of blocks before typing the individual statements within the braces.

Just as a block can be placed anywhere a single statement can be placed, it is also possible to have an empty statement. Recall from Section 2.8 that the empty statement is represented by placing a semicolon (;) where a statement would normally be.

Common Programming Error 4.2

Placing a semicolon after the condition in an if or if...else statement leads to a logic error in single-selection if statements and a syntax error in double-selection if...else statements (when the if-part contains an actual body statement).

4.7 while Repetition Statement

A repetition statement (also called a looping statement or a loop) allows the programmer to specify that a program should repeat an action while some condition remains true. The pseudocode statement

> *While there are more items on my shopping list*
> *Purchase next item and cross it off my list*

describes the repetition that occurs during a shopping trip. The condition "there are more items on my shopping list" may be true or false. If it is true, then the action "Purchase next item and cross it off my list" is performed. This action will be performed repeatedly while the condition remains true. The statement(s) contained in the *While* repetition statement constitute its body, which may be a single statement or a block. Eventually, the condition will become false (when the last item on the shopping list has been purchased and crossed off). At this point, the repetition terminates, and the first statement after the repetition statement executes.

As an example of Java's while repetition statement, consider a program segment designed to find the first power of 3 larger than 100. Suppose that the int variable product is initialized to 3. When the following while statement finishes executing, product contains the result:

```
int product = 3;

while ( product <= 100 )
    product = 3 * product;
```

When this while statement begins execution, the value of variable product is 3. Each iteration of the while statement multiplies product by 3, so product takes on the values 9, 27, 81 and 243 successively. When variable product becomes 243, the while statement condition—product <= 100—becomes false. This terminates the repetition, so the final value of product is 243. At this point, program execution continues with the next statement after the while statement.

Common Programming Error 4.3

Not providing, in the body of a while statement, an action that eventually causes the condition in the while to become false normally results in a logic error called an infinite loop, in which the loop never terminates.

The UML activity diagram in Fig. 4.4 illustrates the flow of control that corresponds to the preceding while statement. Once again, the symbols in the diagram (besides the initial state, transition arrows, a final state and three notes) represent an action state and a decision. This diagram also introduces the UML's merge symbol. The UML represents both the merge symbol and the decision symbol as diamonds. The merge symbol joins two flows of activity into one. In this diagram, the merge symbol joins the transitions from the initial state and from the action state, so they both flow into the decision that determines

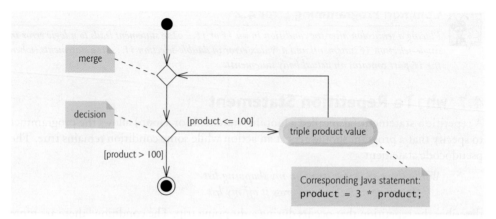

Fig. 4.4 | `while` repetition statement UML activity diagram.

whether the loop should begin (or continue) executing. The decision and merge symbols can be distinguished by the number of "incoming" and "outgoing" transition arrows. A decision symbol has one transition arrow pointing to the diamond and two or more transition arrows pointing out from the diamond to indicate possible transitions from that point. In addition, each transition arrow pointing out of a decision symbol has a guard condition next to it. A merge symbol has two or more transition arrows pointing to the diamond and only one transition arrow pointing from the diamond, to indicate multiple activity flows merging to continue the activity. None of the transition arrows associated with a merge symbol has a guard condition.

Figure 4.4 clearly shows the repetition of the `while` statement discussed earlier in this section. The transition arrow emerging from the action state points back to the merge, from which program flow transitions back to the decision that is tested at the beginning of each iteration of the loop. The loop continues to execute until the guard condition `product > 100` becomes true. Then the `while` statement exits (reaches its final state), and control passes to the next statement in sequence in the program.

4.8 Formulating Algorithms: Counter-Controlled Repetition

To illustrate how algorithms are developed, we modify the `GradeBook` class of Chapter 3 to solve two variations of a problem that averages student grades. Consider the following problem statement:

> *A class of ten students took a quiz. The grades (integers in the range 0 to 100) for this quiz are available to you. Determine the class average on the quiz.*

The class average is equal to the sum of the grades divided by the number of students. The algorithm for solving this problem on a computer must input each grade, keep track of the total of all grades input, perform the averaging calculation and print the result.

Pseudocode Algorithm with Counter-Controlled Repetition

Let's use pseudocode to list the actions to execute and specify the order in which they should execute. We use counter-controlled repetition to input the grades one at a time.

This technique uses a variable called a counter (or control variable) to control the number of times a set of statements will execute. Counter-controlled repetition is often called definite repetition, because the number of repetitions is known before the loop begins executing. In this example, repetition terminates when the counter exceeds 10. This section presents a fully developed pseudocode algorithm (Fig. 4.5) and a version of class Grade-Book (Fig. 4.6) that implements the algorithm in a Java method. We then present an application (Fig. 4.7) that demonstrates the algorithm in action. In Section 4.9, we demonstrate how to use pseudocode to develop such an algorithm from scratch.

> ### Software Engineering Observation 4.1
> *Experience has shown that the most difficult part of solving a problem on a computer is developing the algorithm for the solution. Once a correct algorithm has been specified, the process of producing a working Java program from the algorithm is usually straightforward.*

Note the references in the algorithm of Fig. 4.5 to a total and a counter. A total is a variable used to accumulate the sum of several values. A counter is a variable used to count—in this case, the grade counter indicates which of the 10 grades is about to be entered by the user. Variables used to store totals are normally initialized to zero before being used in a program.

Implementing Counter-Controlled Repetition in Class *GradeBook*
Class GradeBook (Fig. 4.6) contains a constructor (lines 11–14) that assigns a value to the class's instance variable courseName (declared in line 8). Lines 17–20, 23–26 and 29–34 declare methods setCourseName, getCourseName and displayMessage, respectively. Lines 37–66 declare method determineClassAverage, which implements the class-averaging algorithm described by the pseudocode in Fig. 4.5.

Line 40 declares and initializes Scanner variable input, which is used to read values entered by the user. Lines 42–45 declare local variables total, gradeCounter, grade and average to be of type int. Variable grade stores the user input.

Note that the declarations (in lines 42–45) appear in the body of method determine-ClassAverage. Recall that variables declared in a method body are local variables and can be used only from the line of their declaration in the method to the closing right brace (})

1 *Set total to zero*
2 *Set grade counter to one*
3
4 *While grade counter is less than or equal to ten*
5   *Prompt the user to enter the next grade*
6   *Input the next grade*
7   *Add the grade into the total*
8   *Add one to the grade counter*
9
10 *Set the class average to the total divided by ten*
11 *Print the class average*

Fig. 4.5 | Pseudocode algorithm that uses counter-controlled repetition to solve the class-average problem.

```java
1   // Fig. 4.6: GradeBook.java
2   // GradeBook class that solves class-average problem using
3   // counter-controlled repetition.
4   import java.util.Scanner; // program uses class Scanner
5
6   public class GradeBook
7   {
8      private String courseName; // name of course this GradeBook represents
9
10     // constructor initializes courseName
11     public GradeBook( String name )
12     {
13        courseName = name; // initializes courseName
14     } // end constructor
15
16     // method to set the course name
17     public void setCourseName( String name )
18     {
19        courseName = name; // store the course name
20     } // end method setCourseName
21
22     // method to retrieve the course name
23     public String getCourseName()
24     {
25        return courseName;
26     } // end method getCourseName
27
28     // display a welcome message to the GradeBook user
29     public void displayMessage()
30     {
31        // getCourseName gets the name of the course
32        System.out.printf( "Welcome to the grade book for\n%s!\n\n",
33           getCourseName() );
34     } // end method displayMessage
35
36     // determine class average based on 10 grades entered by user
37     public void determineClassAverage()
38     {
39        // create Scanner to obtain input from command window
40        Scanner input = new Scanner( System.in );
41
42        int total; // sum of grades entered by user
43        int gradeCounter; // number of the grade to be entered next
44        int grade; // grade value entered by user
45        int average; // average of grades
46
47        // initialization phase
48        total = 0; // initialize total
49        gradeCounter = 1; // initialize loop counter
50
51        // processing phase
52        while ( gradeCounter <= 10 ) // loop 10 times
53        {
```

Fig. 4.6 | Counter-controlled repetition: Class-average problem. (Part 1 of 2.)

```
54          System.out.print( "Enter grade: " ); // prompt
55          grade = input.nextInt(); // input next grade
56          total = total + grade; // add grade to total
57          gradeCounter = gradeCounter + 1; // increment counter by 1
58       } // end while
59
60       // termination phase
61       average = total / 10; // integer division yields integer result
62
63       // display total and average of grades
64       System.out.printf( "\nTotal of all 10 grades is %d\n", total );
65       System.out.printf( "Class average is %d\n", average );
66    } // end method determineClassAverage
67
68 } // end class GradeBook
```

Fig. 4.6 | Counter-controlled repetition: Class-average problem. (Part 2 of 2.)

of the method declaration. A local variable's declaration must appear before the variable is used in that method. A local variable cannot be accessed outside the method in which it is declared.

In the versions of class GradeBook in this chapter, we simply read and process a set of grades. The averaging calculation is performed in method determineClassAverage using local variables—we do not preserve any information about student grades in instance variables of the class. In later versions of the class (in Chapter 7, Arrays), we maintain the grades in memory using an instance variable that refers to a data structure known as an array. This allows a GradeBook object to perform various calculations on the same set of grades without requiring the user to enter the grades multiple times.

Good Programming Practice 4.5

Separate declarations from other statements in methods with a blank line for readability.

The assignments (in lines 48–49) initialize total to 0 and gradeCounter to 1. Note that these initializations occur before the variables are used in calculations. Variables grade and average (for the user input and calculated average, respectively) need not be initialized here—their values will be assigned as they are input or calculated later in the method.

Common Programming Error 4.4

Reading the value of a local variable before it is initialized results in a compilation error. All local variables must be initialized before their values are read in expressions.

Error-Prevention Tip 4.1

Initialize each counter and total, either in its declaration or in an assignment statement. Totals are normally initialized to 0. Counters are normally initialized to 0 or 1, depending on how they are used (we will show examples of when to use 0 and when to use 1).

Line 52 indicates that the while statement should continue looping (also called iterating) as long as the value of gradeCounter is less than or equal to 10. While this condition remains true, the while statement repeatedly executes the statements between the braces that delimit its body (lines 54–57).

Line 54 displays the prompt "Enter grade: ". Line 55 reads the grade entered by the user and assigns it to variable grade. Then line 56 adds the new grade entered by the user to the total and assigns the result to total, which replaces its previous value.

Line 57 adds 1 to gradeCounter to indicate that the program has processed a grade and is ready to input the next grade from the user. Incrementing gradeCounter eventually causes gradeCounter to exceed 10. At that point the while loop terminates because its condition (line 52) becomes false.

When the loop terminates, line 61 performs the averaging calculation and assigns its result to the variable average. Line 64 uses System.out's printf method to display the text "Total of all 10 grades is " followed by variable total's value. Line 65 then uses printf to display the text "Class average is " followed by variable average's value. After reaching line 66, method determineClassAverage returns control to the calling method (i.e., main in GradeBookTest of Fig. 4.7).

Class *GradeBookTest*

Class GradeBookTest (Fig. 4.7) creates an object of class GradeBook (Fig. 4.6) and demonstrates its capabilities. Lines 10–11 of Fig. 4.7 create a new GradeBook object and assign it to variable myGradeBook. The String in line 11 is passed to the GradeBook constructor (lines 11–14 of Fig. 4.6). Line 13 calls myGradeBook's displayMessage method to display a welcome message to the user. Line 14 then calls myGradeBook's determineClassAverage method to allow the user to enter 10 grades, for which the method then calculates and prints the average—the method performs the algorithm shown in Fig. 4.5.

Notes on Integer Division and Truncation

The averaging calculation performed by method determineClassAverage in response to the method call at line 14 in Fig. 4.7 produces an integer result. The program's output

```
 1   // Fig. 4.7: GradeBookTest.java
 2   // Create GradeBook object and invoke its determineClassAverage method.
 3
 4   public class GradeBookTest
 5   {
 6      public static void main( String args[] )
 7      {
 8         // create GradeBook object myGradeBook and
 9         // pass course name to constructor
10         GradeBook myGradeBook = new GradeBook(
11            "CS101 Introduction to Java Programming" );
12
13         myGradeBook.displayMessage(); // display welcome message
14         myGradeBook.determineClassAverage(); // find average of 10 grades
15      } // end main
16
17   } // end class GradeBookTest
```

Fig. 4.7 | GradeBookTest class creates an object of class GradeBook (Fig. 4.6) and invokes its determineClassAverage method. (Part 1 of 2.)

```
Welcome to the grade book for
CS101 Introduction to Java Programming!

Enter grade: 67
Enter grade: 78
Enter grade: 89
Enter grade: 67
Enter grade: 87
Enter grade: 98
Enter grade: 93
Enter grade: 85
Enter grade: 82
Enter grade: 100

Total of all 10 grades is 846
Class average is 84
```

Fig. 4.7 | GradeBookTest class creates an object of class GradeBook (Fig. 4.6) and invokes its determineClassAverage method. (Part 2 of 2.)

indicates that the sum of the grade values in the sample execution is 846, which, when divided by 10, should yield the floating-point number 84.6. However, the result of the calculation total / 10 (line 61 of Fig. 4.6) is the integer 84, because total and 10 are both integers. Dividing two integers results in integer division—any fractional part of the calculation is lost (i.e., truncated). We will see how to obtain a floating-point result from the averaging calculation in the next section.

Common Programming Error 4.5

Assuming that integer division rounds (rather than truncates) can lead to incorrect results. For example, 7 ÷ 4, which yields 1.75 in conventional arithmetic, truncates to 1 in integer arithmetic, rather than rounding to 2.

4.9 Formulating Algorithms: Sentinel-Controlled Repetition

Let us generalize Section 4.8's class-average problem. Consider the following problem:

> *Develop a class-averaging program that processes grades for an arbitrary number of students each time it is run.*

In the previous class-average example, the problem statement specified the number of students, so the number of grades (10) was known in advance. In this example, no indication is given of how many grades the user will enter during the program's execution. The program must process an arbitrary number of grades. How can it determine when to stop the input of grades? How will it know when to calculate and print the class average?

One way to solve this problem is to use a special value called a sentinel value (also called a signal value, a dummy value or a flag value) to indicate "end of data entry." The user enters grades until all legitimate grades have been entered. The user then types the sentinel value to indicate that no more grades will be entered. Sentinel-controlled repetition is often called indefinite repetition because the number of repetitions is not known before the loop begins executing.

Clearly, a sentinel value must be chosen that cannot be confused with an acceptable input value. Grades on a quiz are nonnegative integers, so –1 is an acceptable sentinel value for this problem. Thus, a run of the class-average program might process a stream of inputs such as 95, 96, 75, 74, 89 and –1. The program would then compute and print the class average for the grades 95, 96, 75, 74 and 89; since –1 is the sentinel value, it should not enter into the averaging calculation.

Common Programming Error 4.6

Choosing a sentinel value that is also a legitimate data value is a logic error.

Developing the Pseudocode Algorithm with Top-Down, Stepwise Refinement: The Top and First Refinement

We approach this class-average program with a technique called top-down, stepwise refinement, which is essential to the development of well-structured programs. We begin with a pseudocode representation of the top—a single statement that conveys the overall function of the program:

> *Determine the class average for the quiz*

The top is, in effect, a *complete* representation of a program. Unfortunately, the top rarely conveys sufficient detail from which to write a Java program. So we now begin the refinement process. We divide the top into a series of smaller tasks and list these in the order in which they will be performed. This results in the following first refinement:

> *Initialize variables*
> *Input, sum and count the quiz grades*
> *Calculate and print the class average*

This refinement uses only the sequence structure—the steps listed should execute in order, one after the other.

Software Engineering Observation 4.2

Each refinement, as well as the top itself, is a complete specification of the algorithm—only the level of detail varies.

Software Engineering Observation 4.3

Many programs can be divided logically into three phases: an initialization phase that initializes the variables; a processing phase that inputs data values and adjusts program variables (e.g., counters and totals) accordingly; and a termination phase that calculates and outputs the final results.

Prosceeding to the Second Refinement

The preceding Software Engineering Observation is often all you need for the first refinement in the top-down process. To proceed to the next level of refinement—that is, the second refinement—we commit to specific variables. In this example, we need a running total of the numbers, a count of how many numbers have been processed, a variable to receive the value of each grade as it is input by the user and a variable to hold the calculated average. The pseudocode statement

> *Initialize variables*

can be refined as follows:

> *Initialize total to zero*
> *Initialize counter to zero*

Only the variables *total* and *counter* need to be initialized before they are used. The variables *average* and *grade* (for the calculated average and the user input, respectively) need not be initialized, because their values will be replaced as they are calculated or input.

The pseudocode statement

> *Input, sum and count the quiz grades*

requires a repetition structure (i.e., a loop) that successively inputs each grade. We do not know in advance how many grades are to be processed, so we will use sentinel-controlled repetition. The user enters grades one at a time. After entering the last grade, the user enters the sentinel value. The program tests for the sentinel value after each grade is input and terminates the loop when the user enters the sentinel value. The second refinement of the preceding pseudocode statement is then

> *Prompt the user to enter the first grade*
> *Input the first grade (possibly the sentinel)*
>
> *While the user has not yet entered the sentinel*
>   *Add this grade into the running total*
>   *Add one to the grade counter*
>   *Prompt the user to enter the next grade*
>   *Input the next grade (possibly the sentinel)*

In pseudocode, we do not use braces around the statements that form the body of the *While* structure. We simply indent the statements under the *While* to show that they belong to the *While*. Again, pseudocode is only an informal program development aid.

The pseudocode statement

> *Calculate and print the class average*

can be refined as follows:

> *If the counter is not equal to zero*
>   *Set the average to the total divided by the counter*
>   *Print the average*
> *else*
>   *Print "No grades were entered"*

We are careful here to test for the possibility of division by zero—normally a logic error that, if undetected, would cause the program to fail or produce invalid output. The complete second refinement of the pseudocode for the class-average problem is shown in Fig. 4.8.

Error-Prevention Tip 4.2

When performing division by an expression whose value could be zero, explicitly test for this possibility and handle it appropriately in your program (e.g., by printing an error message) rather than allow the error to occur.

```
 1    Initialize total to zero
 2    Initialize counter to zero
 3
 4    Prompt the user to enter the first grade
 5    Input the first grade (possibly the sentinel)
 6
 7    While the user has not yet entered the sentinel
 8        Add this grade into the running total
 9        Add one to the grade counter
10        Prompt the user to enter the next grade
11        Input the next grade (possibly the sentinel)
12
13    If the counter is not equal to zero
14        Set the average to the total divided by the counter
15        Print the average
16    else
17        Print "No grades were entered"
```

Fig. 4.8 | Class-average problem pseudocode algorithm with sentinel-controlled repetition.

In Fig. 4.5 and Fig. 4.8, we included some blank lines and indentation in the pseudocode to make it more readable. The blank lines separate the pseudocode algorithms into their various phases and set off control statements; the indentation emphasizes the bodies of the control statements.

The pseudocode algorithm in Fig. 4.8 solves the more general class-averaging problem. This algorithm was developed after only two refinements. Sometimes more refinements are necessary.

Software Engineering Observation 4.4

Terminate the top-down, stepwise refinement process when you have specified the pseudocode algorithm in sufficient detail for you to convert the pseudocode to Java. Normally, implementing the Java program is then straightforward.

Software Engineering Observation 4.5

Some experienced programmers write programs without using program development tools like pseudocode. They feel that their ultimate goal is to solve the problem on a computer and that writing pseudocode merely delays the production of final outputs. Although this may work for simple and familiar problems, it can lead to serious errors and delays in large, complex projects.

Implementing Sentinel-Controlled Repetition in Class *GradeBook*

Figure 4.9 shows the Java class GradeBook containing method determineClassAverage that implements the pseudocode algorithm of Fig. 4.8. Although each grade is an integer, the averaging calculation is likely to produce a number with a decimal point—in other words, a real (i.e., floating-point) number. The type int cannot represent such a number, so this class uses type double to do so.

In this example, we see that control statements may be stacked on top of one another (in sequence) just as a child stacks building blocks. The while statement (lines 57–65) is followed in sequence by an if...else statement (lines 69–80). Much of the code in this program is identical to that in Fig. 4.6, so we concentrate on the new concepts.

```java
1   // Fig. 4.9: GradeBook.java
2   // GradeBook class that solves class-average program using
3   // sentinel-controlled repetition.
4   import java.util.Scanner; // program uses class Scanner
5
6   public class GradeBook
7   {
8      private String courseName; // name of course this GradeBook represents
9
10     // constructor initializes courseName
11     public GradeBook( String name )
12     {
13        courseName = name; // initializes courseName
14     } // end constructor
15
16     // method to set the course name
17     public void setCourseName( String name )
18     {
19        courseName = name; // store the course name
20     } // end method setCourseName
21
22     // method to retrieve the course name
23     public String getCourseName()
24     {
25        return courseName;
26     } // end method getCourseName
27
28     // display a welcome message to the GradeBook user
29     public void displayMessage()
30     {
31        // getCourseName gets the name of the course
32        System.out.printf( "Welcome to the grade book for\n%s!\n\n",
33           getCourseName() );
34     } // end method displayMessage
35
36     // determine the average of an arbitrary number of grades
37     public void determineClassAverage()
38     {
39        // create Scanner to obtain input from command window
40        Scanner input = new Scanner( System.in );
41
42        int total; // sum of grades
43        int gradeCounter; // number of grades entered
44        int grade; // grade value
45        double average; // number with decimal point for average
46
47        // initialization phase
48        total = 0; // initialize total
49        gradeCounter = 0; // initialize loop counter
```

Fig. 4.9 | Sentinel-controlled repetition: Class-average problem. (Part 1 of 2.)

```
50
51        // processing phase
52        // prompt for input and read grade from user
53        System.out.print( "Enter grade or -1 to quit: " );
54        grade = input.nextInt();
55
56        // loop until sentinel value read from user
57        while ( grade != -1 )
58        {
59            total = total + grade; // add grade to total
60            gradeCounter = gradeCounter + 1; // increment counter
61
62            // prompt for input and read next grade from user
63            System.out.print( "Enter grade or -1 to quit: " );
64            grade = input.nextInt();
65        } // end while
66
67        // termination phase
68        // if user entered at least one grade...
69        if ( gradeCounter != 0 )
70        {
71            // calculate average of all grades entered
72            average = (double) total / gradeCounter;
73
74            // display total and average (with two digits of precision)
75            System.out.printf( "\nTotal of the %d grades entered is %d\n",
76                gradeCounter, total );
77            System.out.printf( "Class average is %.2f\n", average );
78        } // end if
79        else // no grades were entered, so output appropriate message
80            System.out.println( "No grades were entered" );
81    } // end method determineClassAverage
82
83 } // end class GradeBook
```

Fig. 4.9 | Sentinel-controlled repetition: Class-average problem. (Part 2 of 2.)

Line 45 declares double variable average, which allows us to store the calculated class average as a floating-point number. Line 49 initializes gradeCounter to 0, because no grades have been entered yet. Remember that this program uses sentinel-controlled repetition to input the grades from the user. To keep an accurate record of the number of grades entered, the program increments gradeCounter only when the user enters a valid grade value.

Program Logic for Sentinel-Controlled Repetition vs. Counter-Controlled Repetition
Compare the program logic for sentinel-controlled repetition in this application with that for counter-controlled repetition in Fig. 4.6. In counter-controlled repetition, each iteration of the while statement (e.g., lines 52–58 of Fig. 4.6) reads a value from the user, for the specified number of iterations. In sentinel-controlled repetition, the program reads the first value (lines 53–54 of Fig. 4.9) before reaching the while. This value determines whether the program's flow of control should enter the body of the while. If the condition of the while is false, the user entered the sentinel value, so the body of the while does not

execute (i.e., no grades were entered). If, on the other hand, the condition is true, the body begins execution, and the loop adds the grade value to the total (line 59). Then lines 63–64 in the loop body input the next value from the user. Next, program control reaches the closing right brace (}) of the loop body at line 65, so execution continues with the test of the while's condition (line 57). The condition uses the most recent grade input by the user to determine whether the loop body should execute again. Note that the value of variable grade is always input from the user immediately before the program tests the while condition. This allows the program to determine whether the value just input is the sentinel value *before* the program processes that value (i.e., adds it to the total). If the sentinel value is input, the loop terminates, and the program does not add –1 to the total.

Good Programming Practice 4.6

In a sentinel-controlled loop, the prompts requesting data entry should explicitly remind the user of the sentinel value.

After the loop terminates, the if...else statement at lines 69–80 executes. The condition at line 69 determines whether any grades were input. If none were input, the else part (lines 79–80) of the if...else statement executes and displays the message "No grades were entered" and the method returns control to the calling method.

Notice the while statement's block in Fig. 4.9 (lines 58–65). Without the braces, the loop would consider its body to be only the first statement, which adds the grade to the total. The last three statements in the block would fall outside the loop body, causing the computer to interpret the code incorrectly as follows:

```
while ( grade != -1 )
   total = total + grade; // add grade to total
gradeCounter = gradeCounter + 1; // increment counter

// prompt for input and read next grade from user
System.out.print( "Enter grade or -1 to quit: " );
grade = input.nextInt();
```

The preceding code would cause an infinite loop in the program if the user did not input the sentinel -1 at line 54 (before the while statement).

Common Programming Error 4.7

Omitting the braces that delimit a block can lead to logic errors, such as infinite loops. To prevent this problem, some programmers enclose the body of every control statement in braces, even if the body contains only a single statement.

Explicitly and Implicitly Converting Between Primitive Types

If at least one grade was entered, line 72 of Fig. 4.9 calculates the average of the grades. Recall from Fig. 4.6 that integer division yields an integer result. Even though variable average is declared as a double (line 45), the calculation

```
average = total / gradeCounter;
```

loses the fractional part of the quotient before the result of the division is assigned to average. This occurs because total and gradeCounter are both integers, and integer division yields an integer result. To perform a floating-point calculation with integer values, we must temporarily treat these values as floating-point numbers for use in the calculation.

Java provides the **unary cast operator** to accomplish this task. Line 72 uses the **(double)** cast operator—a unary operator—to create a *temporary* floating-point copy of its operand `total` (which appears to the right of the operator). Using a cast operator in this manner is called **explicit conversion**. The value stored in `total` is still an integer.

The calculation now consists of a floating-point value (the temporary `double` version of `total`) divided by the integer `gradeCounter`. Java knows how to evaluate only arithmetic expressions in which the operands' types are identical. To ensure that the operands are of the same type, Java performs an operation called **promotion** (or **implicit conversion**) on selected operands. For example, in an expression containing values of the types `int` and `double`, the `int` values are **promoted** to `double` values for use in the expression. In this example, the value of `gradeCounter` is promoted to type `double`, then the floating-point division is performed and the result of the calculation is assigned to `average`. As long as the `(double)` cast operator is applied to any variable in the calculation, the calculation will yield a `double` result. Later in this chapter, we discuss all the primitive types. You will learn more about the promotion rules in Section 6.7.

Common Programming Error 4.8

The cast operator can be used to convert between primitive numeric types, such as `int` and `double`, and between related reference types (as we discuss in Chapter 10, Object-Oriented Programming: Polymorphism). Casting to the wrong type may cause compilation errors or runtime errors.

Cast operators are available for any type. The cast operator is formed by placing parentheses around the name of a type. The operator is a **unary operator** (i.e., an operator that takes only one operand). In Chapter 2, we studied the binary arithmetic operators. Java also supports unary versions of the plus (+) and minus (−) operators, so the programmer can write expressions like -7 or +5. Cast operators associate from right to left and have the same precedence as other unary operators, such as unary + and unary -. This precedence is one level higher than that of the **multiplicative operators** *, / and %. (See the operator precedence chart in Appendix A.) We indicate the cast operator with the notation (*type*) in our precedence charts, to indicate that any type name can be used to form a cast operator.

Line 77 outputs the class average using `System.out`'s `printf` method. In this example, we display the class average rounded to the nearest hundredth. The format specifier `%.2f` in `printf`'s format control string (line 77) indicates that variable `average`'s value should be displayed with two digits of precision to the right of the decimal point—indicated by `.2` in the format specifier. The three grades entered during the sample execution of class `GradeBookTest` (Fig. 4.10) total 257, which yields the average 85.666666.... Method `printf` uses the precision in the format specifier to round the value to the specified

```
1   // Fig. 4.10: GradeBookTest.java
2   // Create GradeBook object and invoke its determineClassAverage method.
3
4   public class GradeBookTest
5   {
6      public static void main( String args[] )
7      {
```

Fig. 4.10 | `GradeBookTest` class creates an object of class `GradeBook` (Fig. 4.9) and invokes its `determineClassAverage` method. (Part 1 of 2.)

```
 8          // create GradeBook object myGradeBook and
 9          // pass course name to constructor
10          GradeBook myGradeBook = new GradeBook(
11             "CS101 Introduction to Java Programming" );
12
13          myGradeBook.displayMessage(); // display welcome message
14          myGradeBook.determineClassAverage(); // find average of grades
15       } // end main
16
17    } // end class GradeBookTest
```

```
Welcome to the grade book for
CS101 Introduction to Java Programming!

Enter grade or -1 to quit: 97
Enter grade or -1 to quit: 88
Enter grade or -1 to quit: 72
Enter grade or -1 to quit: -1

Total of the 3 grades entered is 257
Class average is 85.67
```

Fig. 4.10 | GradeBookTest class creates an object of class GradeBook (Fig. 4.9) and invokes its determineClassAverage method. (Part 2 of 2.)

number of digits. In this program, the average is rounded to the hundredths position and the average is displayed as 85.67.

4.10 Formulating Algorithms: Nested Control Statements

For the next example, we once again formulate an algorithm by using pseudocode and top-down, stepwise refinement, and write a corresponding Java program. We have seen that control statements can be stacked on top of one another (in sequence). In this case study, we examine the only other structured way control statements can be connected, namely, by **nesting** one control statement within another.

Consider the following problem statement:

A college offers a course that prepares students for the state licensing exam for real estate brokers. Last year, ten of the students who completed this course took the exam. The college wants to know how well its students did on the exam. You have been asked to write a program to summarize the results. You have been given a list of these 10 students. Next to each name is written a 1 if the student passed the exam or a 2 if the student failed.

Your program should analyze the results of the exam as follows:

1. *Input each test result (i.e., a 1 or a 2). Display the message "Enter result" on the screen each time the program requests another test result.*

2. *Count the number of test results of each type.*

3. *Display a summary of the test results indicating the number of students who passed and the number who failed.*

4. *If more than eight students passed the exam, print the message "Raise tuition."*

After reading the problem statement carefully, we make the following observations:

1. The program must process test results for 10 students. A counter-controlled loop can be used because the number of test results is known in advance.

2. Each test result has a numeric value—either a 1 or a 2. Each time the program reads a test result, the program must determine whether the number is a 1 or a 2. We test for a 1 in our algorithm. If the number is not a 1, we assume that it is a 2. (Exercise 4.23 considers the consequences of this assumption.)

3. Two counters are used to keep track of the exam results—one to count the number of students who passed the exam and one to count the number of students who failed the exam.

4. After the program has processed all the results, it must decide whether more than eight students passed the exam.

Let us proceed with top-down, stepwise refinement. We begin with a pseudocode representation of the top:

Analyze exam results and decide whether tuition should be raised

Once again, the top is a *complete* representation of the program, but several refinements are likely to be needed before the pseudocode can evolve naturally into a Java program.

Our first refinement is

Initialize variables
Input the 10 exam results, and count passes and failures
Print a summary of the exam results and decide whether tuition should be raised

Here, too, even though we have a complete representation of the entire program, further refinement is necessary. We now commit to specific variables. Counters are needed to record the passes and failures, a counter will be used to control the looping process and a variable is needed to store the user input. The variable in which the user input will be stored is not initialized at the start of the algorithm, because its value is read from the user during each iteration of the loop.

The pseudocode statement

Initialize variables

can be refined as follows:

Initialize passes to zero
Initialize failures to zero
Initialize student counter to one

Notice that only the counters are initialized at the start of the algorithm.

The pseudocode statement

Input the 10 exam results, and count passes and failures

requires a loop that successively inputs the result of each exam. We know in advance that there are precisely 10 exam results, so counter-controlled looping is appropriate. Inside the loop (i.e., nested within the loop), a double-selection structure will determine whether each exam result is a pass or a failure and will increment the appropriate counter. The refinement of the preceding pseudocode statement is then

> *While student counter is less than or equal to 10*
>> *Prompt the user to enter the next exam result*
>> *Input the next exam result*
>
>> *If the student passed*
>>> *Add one to passes*
>> *Else*
>>> *Add one to failures*
>
>> *Add one to student counter*

We use blank lines to isolate the *If…Else* control structure, which improves readability. The pseudocode statement

> *Print a summary of the exam results and decide whether tuition should be raised*

can be refined as follows:

> *Print the number of passes*
> *Print the number of failures*
>
> *If more than eight students passed*
>> *Print "Raise tuition"*

Complete Second Refinement of Pseudocode and Conversion to Class `Analysis`

The complete second refinement appears in Fig. 4.11. Notice that blank lines are also used to set off the *While* structure for program readability. This pseudocode is now sufficiently refined for conversion to Java. The Java class that implements the pseudocode algorithm is shown in Fig. 4.12, and two sample executions appear in Fig. 4.13.

```
 1   Initialize passes to zero
 2   Initialize failures to zero
 3   Initialize student counter to one
 4
 5   While student counter is less than or equal to 10
 6       Prompt the user to enter the next exam result
 7       Input the next exam result
 8
 9       If the student passed
10           Add one to passes
11       Else
12           Add one to failures
13
14       Add one to student counter
15
16   Print the number of passes
17   Print the number of failures
18
19   If more than eight students passed
20       Print "Raise tuition"
```

Fig. 4.11 | Pseudocode for examination-results problem.

```java
1   // Fig. 4.12: Analysis.java
2   // Analysis of examination results.
3   import java.util.Scanner; // class uses class Scanner
4
5   public class Analysis
6   {
7      public void processExamResults()
8      {
9         // create Scanner to obtain input from command window
10        Scanner input = new Scanner( System.in );
11
12        // initializing variables in declarations
13        int passes = 0; // number of passes
14        int failures = 0; // number of failures
15        int studentCounter = 1; // student counter
16        int result; // one exam result (obtains value from user)
17
18        // process 10 students using counter-controlled loop
19        while ( studentCounter <= 10 )
20        {
21           // prompt user for input and obtain value from user
22           System.out.print( "Enter result (1 = pass, 2 = fail): " );
23           result = input.nextInt();
24
25           // if...else nested in while
26           if ( result == 1 )          // if result 1,
27              passes = passes + 1;     // increment passes;
28           else                        // else result is not 1, so
29              failures = failures + 1; // increment failures
30
31           // increment studentCounter so loop eventually terminates
32           studentCounter = studentCounter + 1;
33        } // end while
34
35        // termination phase; prepare and display results
36        System.out.printf( "Passed: %d\nFailed: %d\n", passes, failures );
37
38        // determine whether more than 8 students passed
39        if ( passes > 8 )
40           System.out.println( "Raise Tuition" );
41     } // end method processExamResults
42
43  } // end class Analysis
```

Fig. 4.12 | Nested control structures: Examination-results problem.

Lines 13–16 of Fig. 4.12 declare the variables that method processExamResults of class Analysis uses to process the examination results. Several of these declarations use Java's ability to incorporate variable initialization into declarations (passes is assigned 0, failures is assigned 0 and studentCounter is assigned 1). Looping programs may require initialization at the beginning of each repetition—such reinitialization would normally be performed by assignment statements rather than in declarations.

The while statement (lines 19–33) loops 10 times. During each iteration, the loop inputs and processes one exam result. Notice that the if...else statement (lines 26–29) for processing each result is nested in the while statement. If the result is 1, the if...else statement increments passes; otherwise, it assumes the result is 2 and increments failures. Line 32 increments studentCounter before the loop condition is tested again at line 19. After 10 values have been input, the loop terminates and line 36 displays the number of passes and failures. The if statement at lines 39–40 determines whether more than eight students passed the exam and, if so, outputs the message "Raise Tuition".

Error-Prevention Tip 4.3

Initializing local variables when they are declared helps the programmer avoid any compilation errors that might arise from attempts to use uninitialized data. While Java does not require that local variable initializations be incorporated into declarations, it does require that local variables be initialized before their values are used in an expression.

AnalysisTest Class That Demonstrates Class Analysis

Class AnalysisTest (Fig. 4.13) creates an Analysis object (line 8) and invokes the object's processExamResults method (line 9) to process a set of exam results entered by the user. Figure 4.13 shows the input and output from two sample executions of the program. During the first sample execution, the condition at line 39 of method processExamResults in Fig. 4.12 is true—more than eight students passed the exam, so the program outputs a message indicating that the tuition should be raised.

```java
1   // Fig. 4.13: AnalysisTest.java
2   // Test program for class Analysis.
3
4   public class AnalysisTest
5   {
6      public static void main( String args[] )
7      {
8         Analysis application = new Analysis(); // create Analysis object
9         application.processExamResults(); // call method to process results
10     } // end main
11
12  } // end class AnalysisTest
```

```
Enter result (1 = pass, 2 = fail): 1
Enter result (1 = pass, 2 = fail): 2
Enter result (1 = pass, 2 = fail): 1
Enter result (1 = pass, 2 = fail): 1
Enter result (1 = pass, 2 = fail): 1
Enter result (1 = pass, 2 = fail): 1
Enter result (1 = pass, 2 = fail): 1
Enter result (1 = pass, 2 = fail): 1
Enter result (1 = pass, 2 = fail): 1
Enter result (1 = pass, 2 = fail): 1
Passed: 9
Failed: 1
Raise Tuition
```

Fig. 4.13 | Test program for class Analysis (Fig. 4.12). (Part 1 of 2.)

```
Enter result (1 = pass, 2 = fail): 1
Enter result (1 = pass, 2 = fail): 2
Enter result (1 = pass, 2 = fail): 1
Enter result (1 = pass, 2 = fail): 2
Enter result (1 = pass, 2 = fail): 1
Enter result (1 = pass, 2 = fail): 2
Enter result (1 = pass, 2 = fail): 2
Enter result (1 = pass, 2 = fail): 1
Enter result (1 = pass, 2 = fail): 1
Enter result (1 = pass, 2 = fail): 1
Passed: 6
Failed: 4
```

Fig. 4.13 | Test program for class `Analysis` (Fig. 4.12). (Part 2 of 2.)

4.11 Compound Assignment Operators

Java provides several compound assignment operators for abbreviating assignment expressions. Any statement of the form

variable = *variable operator expression*;

where *operator* is one of the binary operators +, -, *, / or % (or others we discuss later in the text) can be written in the form

variable operator= expression;

For example, you can abbreviate the statement

c = c + 3;

with the addition compound assignment operator, +=, as

c += 3;

The += operator adds the value of the expression on the right of the operator to the value of the variable on the left of the operator and stores the result in the variable on the left of the operator. Thus, the assignment expression c += 3 adds 3 to c. Figure 4.14 shows the arithmetic compound assignment operators, sample expressions using the operators and explanations of what the operators do.

Assignment operator	Sample expression	Explanation	Assigns
Assume: int c = 3, d = 5, e = 4, f = 6, g = 12;			
+=	c += 7	c = c + 7	10 to c
-=	d -= 4	d = d - 4	1 to d
*=	e *= 5	e = e * 5	20 to e

Fig. 4.14 | Arithmetic compound assignment operators. (Part 1 of 2.)

Assignment operator	Sample expression	Explanation	Assigns
/=	f /= 3	f = f / 3	2 to f
%=	g %= 9	g = g % 9	3 to g

Fig. 4.14 | Arithmetic compound assignment operators. (Part 2 of 2.)

4.12 Increment and Decrement Operators

Java provides two unary operators for adding 1 to or subtracting 1 from the value of a numeric variable. These are the unary increment operator, ++, and the unary decrement operator, --, which are summarized in Fig. 4.15. A program can increment by 1 the value of a variable called c using the increment operator, ++, rather than the expression c = c + 1 or c += 1. An increment or decrement operator that is prefixed to (placed before) a variable is referred to as the prefix increment or prefix decrement operator, respectively. An increment or decrement operator that is postfixed to (placed after) a variable is referred to as the postfix increment or postfix decrement operator, respectively.

Using the prefix increment (or decrement) operator to add (or subtract) 1 from a variable is known as preincrementing (or predecrementing) the variable. Preincrementing (or predecrementing) a variable causes the variable to be incremented (decremented) by 1, and then the new value of the variable is used in the expression in which it appears. Using the postfix increment (or decrement) operator to add (or subtract) 1 from a variable is known as postincrementing (or postdecrementing) the variable. Postincrementing (or postdecrementing) the variable causes the current value of the variable to be used in the expression in which it appears, and then the variable's value is incremented (decremented) by 1.

Good Programming Practice 4.7

Unlike binary operators, the unary increment and decrement operators should be placed next to their operands, with no intervening spaces.

Operator	Operator name	Sample expression	Explanation
++	prefix increment	++a	Increment a by 1, then use the new value of a in the expression in which a resides.
++	postfix increment	a++	Use the current value of a in the expression in which a resides, then increment a by 1.
--	prefix decrement	--b	Decrement b by 1, then use the new value of b in the expression in which b resides.
--	postfix decrement	b--	Use the current value of b in the expression in which b resides, then decrement b by 1.

Fig. 4.15 | Increment and decrement operators.

Figure 4.16 demonstrates the difference between the prefix increment and postfix increment versions of the ++ increment operator. The decrement operator (--) works similarly. Note that this example contains only one class, with method main performing all the class's work. In this chapter and in Chapter 3, you have seen examples consisting of two classes—one class containing methods that perform useful tasks and one containing method main, which creates an object of the other class and calls its methods. In this example, we simply want to show the mechanics of the ++ operator, so we use only one class declaration containing method main. Occasionally, when it does not make sense to try to create a reusable class to demonstrate a simple concept, we will use a "mechanical" example contained entirely within the main method of a single class.

Line 11 initializes the variable c to 5, and line 12 outputs c's initial value. Line 13 outputs the value of the expression c++. This expression postincrements the variable c, so c's original value (5) is output, then c's value is incremented (to 6). Thus, line 13 outputs c's

```java
 1   // Fig. 4.16: Increment.java
 2   // Prefix increment and postfix increment operators.
 3
 4   public class Increment
 5   {
 6      public static void main( String args[] )
 7      {
 8         int c;
 9
10         // demonstrate postfix increment operator
11         c = 5; // assign 5 to c
12         System.out.println( c );    // prints 5
13         System.out.println( c++ ); // prints 5 then postincrements
14         System.out.println( c );    // prints 6
15
16         System.out.println(); // skip a line
17
18         // demonstrate prefix increment operator
19         c = 5; // assign 5 to c
20         System.out.println( c );    // prints 5
21         System.out.println( ++c ); // preincrements then prints 6
22         System.out.println( c );    // prints 6
23
24      } // end main
25
26   } // end class Increment
```

```
5
5
6

5
6
6
```

Fig. 4.16 | Preincrementing and postincrementing.

initial value (5) again. Line 14 outputs c's new value (6) to prove that the variable's value was indeed incremented in line 13.

Line 19 resets c's value to 5, and line 20 outputs c's value. Line 21 outputs the value of the expression ++c. This expression preincrements c, so its value is incremented, then the new value (6) is output. Line 22 outputs c's value again to show that the value of c is still 6 after line 21 executes.

The arithmetic compound assignment operators and the increment and decrement operators can be used to simplify program statements. For example, the three assignment statements in Fig. 4.12 (lines 27, 29 and 32)

```
passes = passes + 1;
failures = failures + 1;
studentCounter = studentCounter + 1;
```

can be written more concisely with compound assignment operators as

```
passes += 1;
failures += 1;
studentCounter += 1;
```

with prefix increment operators as

```
++passes;
++failures;
++studentCounter;
```

or with postfix increment operators as

```
passes++;
failures++;
studentCounter++;
```

When incrementing or decrementing a variable in a statement by itself, the prefix increment and postfix increment forms have the same effect, and the prefix decrement and postfix decrement forms have the same effect. It is only when a variable appears in the context of a larger expression that preincrementing and postincrementing the variable have different effects (and similarly for predecrementing and postdecrementing).

Common Programming Error 4.9

Attempting to use the increment or decrement operator on an expression other than one to which a value can be assigned is a syntax error. For example, writing ++(x + 1) is a syntax error because (x + 1) is not a variable.

Figure 4.17 shows the precedence and associativity of the operators we have introduced to this point. The operators are shown from top to bottom in decreasing order of precedence. The second column describes the associativity of the operators at each level of precedence. The conditional operator (?:); the unary operators increment (++), decrement (--), plus (+) and minus (-); the cast operators and the assignment operators =, +=, -=, *=, /= and %= associate from right to left. All the other operators in the operator precedence chart in Fig. 4.17 associate from left to right. The third column lists the type of each group of operators.

Operators						Associativity	Type
++	--					right to left	unary postfix
++	--	+	-	(*type*)		right to left	unary prefix
*	/	%				left to right	multiplicative
+	-					left to right	additive
<	<=	>	>=			left to right	relational
==	!=					left to right	equality
?:						right to left	conditional
=	+=	-=	*=	/=	%=	right to left	assignment

Fig. 4.17 | Precedence and associativity of the operators discussed so far.

4.13 Primitive Types

The table in Appendix D, Primitive Types, lists the eight primitive types in Java. Like its predecessor languages C and C++, Java requires all variables to have a type. For this reason, Java is referred to as a strongly typed language.

In C and C++, programmers frequently have to write separate versions of programs to support different computer platforms, because the primitive types are not guaranteed to be identical from computer to computer. For example, an int value on one machine might be represented by 16 bits (2 bytes) of memory, and on another machine by 32 bits (4 bytes) of memory. In Java, int values are always 32 bits (4 bytes).

Portability Tip 4.1

Unlike C and C++, the primitive types in Java are portable across all computer platforms that support Java.

Each type in Appendix D is listed with its size in bits (there are eight bits to a byte) and its range of values. Because the designers of Java want it to be maximally portable, they use internationally recognized standards for both character formats (Unicode; for more information, visit www.unicode.org) and floating-point numbers (IEEE 754; for more information, visit grouper.ieee.org/groups/754/).

Recall from Section 3.5 that variables of primitive types declared outside of a method as fields of a class are automatically assigned default values unless explicitly initialized. Instance variables of types char, byte, short, int, long, float and double are all given the value 0 by default. Instance variables of type boolean are given the value false by default. Reference-type instance variables are initialized by default to the value null.

4.14 (Optional) GUI and Graphics Case Study: Creating Simple Drawings

One of Java's appealing features is its graphics support that enables programmers to visually enhance their applications. This section introduces one of Java's graphical capabilities—drawing lines. It also covers the basics of creating a window to display a drawing on the computer screen.

To draw in Java, you must understand Java's coordinate system (Fig. 4.18), a scheme for identifying every point on the screen. By default, the upper-left corner of a GUI component has the coordinates (0, 0). A coordinate pair is composed of an *x*-coordinate (the horizontal coordinate) and a *y*-coordinate (the vertical coordinate). The *x*-coordinate is the horizontal location moving from left to right. The *y*-coordinate is the vertical location moving top to bottom. The *x*-axis describes every horizontal coordinate, and the *y*-axis every vertical coordinate.

Coordinates indicate where graphics should be displayed on a screen. Coordinate units are measured in pixels. A pixel is a display monitor's smallest unit of resolution. (The term pixel stands for "picture element.")

Our first drawing application simply draws two lines. Class DrawPanel (Fig. 4.19) performs the actual drawing, while class DrawPanelTest (Fig. 4.20) creates a window to display the drawing. In class DrawPanel, the import statements in lines 3–4 allow us to use class Graphics (from package java.awt), which provides various methods for drawing text and shapes onto the screen, and class JPanel (from package javax.swing), which provides an area on which we can draw.

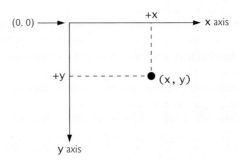

Fig. 4.18 | Java coordinate system. Units are measured in pixels.

```
1   // Fig. 4.19: DrawPanel.java
2   // Using drawLine to connect the corners of a panel.
3   import java.awt.Graphics;
4   import javax.swing.JPanel;
5
6   public class DrawPanel extends JPanel
7   {
8      // draws an X from the corners of the panel
9      public void paintComponent( Graphics g )
10     {
11        // call paintComponent to ensure the panel displays correctly
12        super.paintComponent( g );
13
```

Fig. 4.19 | Using drawLine to connect the corners of a panel. (Part 1 of 2.)

```
14          int width = getWidth(); // total width
15          int height = getHeight(); // total height
16
17          // draw a line from the upper-left to the lower-right
18          g.drawLine( 0, 0, width, height );
19
20          // draw a line from the lower-left to the upper-right
21          g.drawLine( 0, height, width, 0 );
22      } // end method paintComponent
23   } // end class DrawPanel
```

Fig. 4.19 | Using drawLine to connect the corners of a panel. (Part 2 of 2.)

Line 6 uses the keyword **extends** to indicate that class DrawPanel is an enhanced type of JPanel. The keyword extends represents a so-called inheritance relationship in which our new class DrawPanel begins with the existing members (data and methods) from class JPanel. The class from which DrawPanel inherits, JPanel, appears to the right of keyword extends. In this inheritance relationship, JPanel is called the superclass and DrawPanel is called the subclass. This results in a DrawPanel class that has the attributes (data) and behaviors (methods) of class JPanel as well as the new features we are adding in our Draw-Panel class declaration—specifically, the ability to draw two lines along the diagonals of the panel. Inheritance is explained in detail in Chapter 9.

Every JPanel, including our DrawPanel, has a **paintComponent** method (lines 9–22), which the system automatically calls every time it needs to display the JPanel. Method paintComponent must be declared as shown in line 9—otherwise, the system will not call the method. This method is called when a JPanel is first displayed on the screen, when it is covered then uncovered by a window on the screen and when the window in which it appears is resized. Method paintComponent requires one argument, a Graphics object, that is provided for you by the system when it calls paintComponent.

The first statement in every paintComponent method you create should always be

```
super.paintComponent( g );
```

which ensures that the panel is properly rendered on the screen before we begin drawing on it. Next, lines 14 and 15 call two methods that class DrawPanel inherits from class JPanel. Because DrawPanel extends JPanel, DrawPanel can use any public methods that are declared in JPanel. Methods **getWidth** and **getHeight** return the width and the height of the JPanel respectively. Lines 14–15 store these values in the local variables width and height. Finally, lines 18 and 21 use the Graphics reference g to call method **drawLine** to draw the two lines. Method drawLine draws a line between two points represented by its four arguments. The first two arguments are the x- and y-coordinates for one endpoint of the line, and the last two arguments are the coordinates for the other endpoint. If you re-size the window, the lines will scale accordingly, because the arguments are based on the width and height of the panel. Resizing the window in this application causes the system to call paintComponent to redraw the DrawPanel's contents.

To display the DrawPanel on the screen, we must place it in a window. You create a window with an object of class JFrame. In DrawPanelTest.java (Fig. 4.20), line 3 imports class JFrame from package javax.swing. Line 10 in the main method of class Draw-PanelTest creates an instance of class DrawPanel, which contains our drawing, and line

```
1    // Fig. 4.20: DrawPanelTest.java
2    // Application to display a DrawPanel.
3    import javax.swing.JFrame;
4
5    public class DrawPanelTest
6    {
7       public static void main( String args[] )
8       {
9          // create a panel that contains our drawing
10         DrawPanel panel = new DrawPanel();
11
12         // create a new frame to hold the panel
13         JFrame application = new JFrame();
14
15         // set the frame to exit when it is closed
16         application.setDefaultCloseOperation( JFrame.EXIT_ON_CLOSE );
17
18         application.add( panel ); // add the panel to the frame
19         application.setSize( 250, 250 ); // set the size of the frame
20         application.setVisible( true ); // make the frame visible
21      } // end main
22   } // end class DrawPanelTest
```

 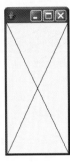

Fig. 4.20 | Creating JFrame to display DrawPanel.

13 creates a new JFrame that can hold and display our panel. Line 16 calls method **set-DefaultCloseOperation** with the argument JFrame.EXIT_ON_CLOSE to indicate that the application should terminate when the user closes the window. Line 18 uses JFrame's **add** method to attach the DrawPanel containing our drawing to the JFrame. Line 19 sets the size of the JFrame. Method **setSize** takes two parameters—the width of the JFrame, and the height. Finally, line 20 displays the JFrame. When the JFrame is displayed, the Draw-Panel's paintComponent method (lines 9–22 of Fig. 4.19) is called, and the two lines are drawn (see the sample outputs in Fig. 4.20). Try resizing the window to see that the lines always draw based on the window's current width and height.

GUI and Graphics Case Study Exercises

4.1   Using loops and control statements to draw lines can lead to many interesting designs.
    a) Create the design in the left screen capture of Fig. 4.21. This design draws lines from the top-left corner, fanning out the lines until they cover the upper-left half of the panel. One approach is to divide the width and height into an equal number of steps (we found

15 steps worked well). The first endpoint of a line will always be in the top-left corner (0, 0). The second endpoint can be found by starting at the bottom-left corner and moving up one vertical step and right one horizontal step. Draw a line between the two endpoints. Continue moving up and to the right one step to find each successive endpoint. The figure should scale accordingly as you resize the window.

b) Modify your answer in part (a) to have lines fan out from all four corners, as shown in the right screen capture of Fig. 4.21. Lines from opposite corners should intersect along the middle.

4.2 Figure 4.22 displays two additional designs created using `while` loops and `drawLine`.

a) Create the design in the left screen capture of Fig. 4.22. Begin by dividing each edge into an equal number of increments (we chose 15 again). The first line starts in the top-left corner and ends one step right on the bottom edge. For each successive line, move down one increment on the left edge and right one increment on the bottom edge. Continue drawing lines until you reach the bottom-right corner. The figure should scale as you resize the window so that the endpoints always touch the edges.

b) Modify your answer in part (a) to mirror the design in all four corners, as shown in the right screen capture of Fig. 4.22.

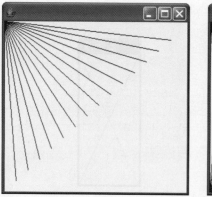
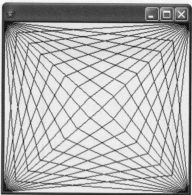

Fig. 4.21 | Lines fanning from a corner.

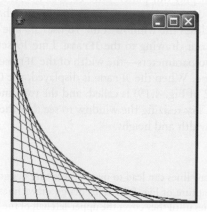
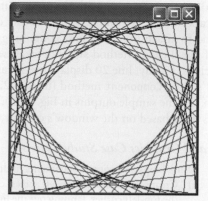

Fig. 4.22 | Line art with loops and `drawLine`.

4.15 (Optional) Software Engineering Case Study: Identifying Class Attributes

In Section 3.10, we began the first stage of an object-oriented design (OOD) for our ATM system—analyzing the requirements document and identifying the classes needed to implement the system. We listed the nouns and noun phrases in the requirements document and identified a separate class for each one that plays a significant role in the ATM system. We then modeled the classes and their relationships in a UML class diagram (Fig. 3.24). Classes have attributes (data) and operations (behaviors). Class attributes are implemented in Java programs as fields, and class operations are implemented as methods. In this section, we determine many of the attributes needed in the ATM system. In Chapter 5, we examine how these attributes represent an object's state. In Chapter 6, we determine class operations.

Identifying Attributes

Consider the attributes of some real-world objects: A person's attributes include height, weight and whether the person is left-handed, right-handed or ambidextrous. A radio's attributes include its station setting, its volume setting and its AM or FM setting. A car's attributes include its speedometer and odometer readings, the amount of gas in its tank and what gear it is in. A personal computer's attributes include its manufacturer (e.g., Dell, Sun, Apple or IBM), type of screen (e.g., LCD or CRT), main memory size and hard disk size.

We can identify many attributes of the classes in our system by looking for descriptive words and phrases in the requirements document. For each one we find that plays a significant role in the ATM system, we create an attribute and assign it to one or more of the classes identified in Section 3.10. We also create attributes to represent any additional data that a class may need, as such needs become clear throughout the design process.

Figure 4.23 lists the words or phrases from the requirements document that describe each class. We formed this list by reading the requirements document and identifying any words or phrases that refer to characteristics of the classes in the system. For example, the requirements document describes the steps taken to obtain a "withdrawal amount," so we list "amount" next to class `Withdrawal`.

Class	Descriptive words and phrases
`ATM`	user is authenticated
`BalanceInquiry`	account number
`Withdrawal`	account number amount
`Deposit`	account number amount
`BankDatabase`	[no descriptive words or phrases]

Fig. 4.23 | Descriptive words and phrases from the ATM requirements. (Part 1 of 2.)

Class	Descriptive words and phrases
Account	account number PIN balance
Screen	[no descriptive words or phrases]
Keypad	[no descriptive words or phrases]
CashDispenser	begins each day loaded with 500 $20 bills
DepositSlot	[no descriptive words or phrases]

Fig. 4.23 | Descriptive words and phrases from the ATM requirements. (Part 2 of 2.)

Figure 4.23 leads us to create one attribute of class ATM. Class ATM maintains information about the state of the ATM. The phrase "user is authenticated" describes a state of the ATM (we introduce states in Section 5.11), so we include userAuthenticated as a **Boolean attribute** (i.e., an attribute that has a value of either true or false) in class ATM. Note that the Boolean attribute type in the UML is equivalent to the boolean type in Java. This attribute indicates whether the ATM has successfully authenticated the current user—userAuthenticated must be true for the system to allow the user to perform transactions and access account information. This attribute helps ensure the security of the data in the system.

Classes BalanceInquiry, Withdrawal and Deposit share one attribute. Each transaction involves an "account number" that corresponds to the account of the user making the transaction. We assign an integer attribute accountNumber to each transaction class to identify the account to which an object of the class applies.

Descriptive words and phrases in the requirements document also suggest some differences in the attributes required by each transaction class. The requirements document indicates that to withdraw cash or deposit funds, users must input a specific "amount" of money to be withdrawn or deposited, respectively. Thus, we assign to classes Withdrawal and Deposit an attribute amount to store the value supplied by the user. The amounts of money related to a withdrawal and a deposit are defining characteristics of these transactions that the system requires for these transactions to take place. Class BalanceInquiry, however, needs no additional data to perform its task—it requires only an account number to indicate the account whose balance should be retrieved.

Class Account has several attributes. The requirements document states that each bank account has an "account number" and "PIN," which the system uses for identifying accounts and authenticating users. We assign to class Account two integer attributes: accountNumber and pin. The requirements document also specifies that an account maintains a "balance" of the amount of money in the account and that money the user deposits does not become available for a withdrawal until the bank verifies the amount of cash in the deposit envelope, and any checks in the envelope clear. An account must still record the amount of money that a user deposits, however. Therefore, we decide that an account should represent a balance using two attributes: availableBalance and totalBalance.

Attribute `availableBalance` tracks the amount of money that a user can withdraw from the account. Attribute `totalBalance` refers to the total amount of money that the user has "on deposit" (i.e., the amount of money available, plus the amount waiting to be verified or cleared). For example, suppose an ATM user deposits $50.00 into an empty account. The `totalBalance` attribute would increase to $50.00 to record the deposit, but the `availableBalance` would remain at $0. [*Note:* We assume that the bank updates the `availableBalance` attribute of an `Account` some length of time after the ATM transaction occurs, in response to confirming that $50 worth of cash or checks was found in the deposit envelope. We assume that this update occurs through a transaction that a bank employee performs using some piece of bank software other than the ATM. Thus, we do not discuss this transaction in our case study.]

Class `CashDispenser` has one attribute. The requirements document states that the cash dispenser "begins each day loaded with 500 $20 bills." The cash dispenser must keep track of the number of bills it contains to determine whether enough cash is on hand to satisfy withdrawal requests. We assign to class `CashDispenser` an integer attribute `count`, which is initially set to 500.

For real problems in industry, there is no guarantee that requirements documents will be rich enough and precise enough for the object-oriented systems designer to determine all the attributes or even all the classes. The need for additional classes, attributes and behaviors may become clear as the design process proceeds. As we progress through this case study, we too will continue to add, modify and delete information about the classes in our system.

Modeling Attributes

The class diagram in Fig. 4.24 lists some of the attributes for the classes in our system—the descriptive words and phrases in Fig. 4.23 lead us to identify these attributes. For simplicity, Fig. 4.24 does not show the associations among classes—we showed these in Fig. 3.24. This is a common practice of systems designers when designs are being developed. Recall from Section 3.10 that in the UML, a class's attributes are placed in the middle compartment of the class's rectangle. We list each attribute's name and type separated by a colon (:), followed in some cases by an equal sign (=) and an initial value.

Consider the `userAuthenticated` attribute of class `ATM`:

```
userAuthenticated : Boolean = false
```

This attribute declaration contains three pieces of information about the attribute. The **attribute name** is `userAuthenticated`. The **attribute type** is `Boolean`. In Java, an attribute can be represented by a primitive type, such as `boolean`, `int` or `double`, or a reference type like a class—as discussed in Chapter 3. We have chosen to model only primitive-type attributes in Fig. 4.24—we discuss the reasoning behind this decision shortly. [*Note:* The attribute types in Fig. 4.24 are in UML notation. We will associate the types `Boolean`, `Integer` and `Double` in the UML diagram with the primitive types `boolean`, `int` and `double` in Java, respectively.]

We can also indicate an initial value for an attribute. The `userAuthenticated` attribute in class `ATM` has an initial value of `false`. This indicates that the system initially does not consider the user to be authenticated. If an attribute has no initial value specified, only its name and type (separated by a colon) are shown. For example, the `accountNumber` attribute of class `BalanceInquiry` is an integer. Here we show no initial value, because the value of this attribute is a number that we do not yet know. This number will be determined at execution time based on the account number entered by the current ATM user.

Figure 4.24 does not include any attributes for classes `Screen`, `Keypad` and `DepositSlot`. These are important components of our system, for which our design process simply has not yet revealed any attributes. We may still discover some, however, in the remaining phases of design or when we implement these classes in Java. This is perfectly normal.

Software Engineering Observation 4.6

At early stages in the design process, classes often lack attributes (and operations). Such classes should not be eliminated, however, because attributes (and operations) may become evident in the later phases of design and implementation.

Note that Fig. 4.24 also does not include attributes for class `BankDatabase`. Recall from Chapter 3 that in Java, attributes can be represented by either primitive types or reference types. We have chosen to include only primitive-type attributes in the class diagram in Fig. 4.24 (and in similar class diagrams throughout the case study). A reference-type attribute is modeled more clearly as an association (in particular, a composition) between the class holding the reference and the class of the object to which the reference points.

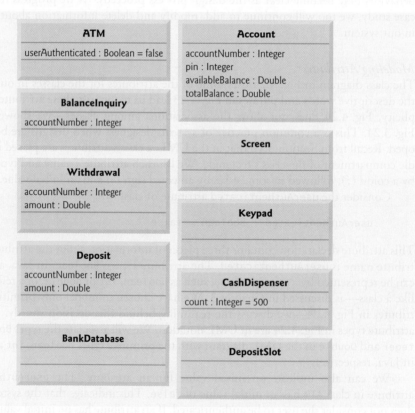

Fig. 4.24 | Classes with attributes.

For example, the class diagram in Fig. 3.24 indicates that class `BankDatabase` participates in a composition relationship with zero or more `Account` objects. From this composition, we can determine that when we implement the ATM system in Java, we will be required to create an attribute of class `BankDatabase` to hold references to zero or more `Account` objects. Similarly, we can determine reference-type attributes of class `ATM` that correspond to its composition relationships with classes `Screen`, `Keypad`, `CashDispenser` and `DepositSlot`. These composition-based attributes would be redundant if modeled in Fig. 4.24, because the compositions modeled in Fig. 3.24 already convey the fact that the database contains information about zero or more accounts and that an ATM is composed of a screen, keypad, cash dispenser and deposit slot. Software developers typically model these whole/part relationships as compositions rather than as attributes required to implement the relationships.

The class diagram in Fig. 4.24 provides a solid basis for the structure of our model, but the diagram is not complete. In Section 5.11, we identify the states and activities of the objects in the model, and in Section 6.14 we identify the operations that the objects perform. As we present more of the UML and object-oriented design, we will continue to strengthen the structure of our model.

Software Engineering Case Study Self-Review Exercises

4.1 We typically identify the attributes of the classes in our system by analyzing the _____ in the requirements document.
   a) nouns and noun phrases
   b) descriptive words and phrases
   c) verbs and verb phrases
   d) All of the above.

4.2 Which of the following is not an attribute of an airplane?
   a) length
   b) wingspan
   c) fly
   d) number of seats

4.3 Describe the meaning of the following attribute declaration of class `CashDispenser` in the class diagram in Fig. 4.24:

```
count : Integer = 500
```

Answers to Software Engineering Case Study Self-Review Exercises

4.1 b.

4.2 c. Fly is an operation or behavior of an airplane, not an attribute.

4.3 This indicates that `count` is an `Integer` with an initial value of 500. This attribute keeps track of the number of bills available in the `CashDispenser` at any given time.

4.16 Wrap-Up

This chapter presented basic problem-solving strategies that programmers use in building classes and developing methods for these classes. We demonstrated how to construct an algorithm (i.e., an approach to solving a problem), then how to refine the algorithm through several phases of pseudocode development, resulting in Java code that can be executed as part of a method. The chapter showed how to use top-down, stepwise refinement to plan out the specific actions that a method must perform and the order in which the method must perform these actions.

Only three types of control structures—sequence, selection and repetition—are needed to develop any problem-solving algorithm. Specifically, this chapter demonstrated the if single-selection statement, the if...else double-selection statement and the while repetition statement. These are some of the building blocks used to construct solutions to many problems. We used control-statement stacking to total and compute the average of a set of student grades with counter- and sentinel-controlled repetition, and we used control-statement nesting to analyze and make decisions based on a set of exam results. We introduced Java's compound assignment operators, and its increment and decrement operators. Finally, we discussed the primitive types available to Java programmers. In Chapter 5, Control Statements: Part 2, we continue our discussion of control statements, introducing the for, do...while and switch statements.

Summary

Section 4.1 Introduction
- Before writing a program to solve a problem, you must have a thorough understanding of the problem and a carefully planned approach to solving it. You must also understand the building blocks that are available and to employ proven program-construction techniques.

Section 4.2 Algorithms
- Any computing problem can be solved by executing a series of actions in a specific order.
- A procedure for solving a problem in terms of the actions to execute and the order in which they execute is called an algorithm.
- Specifying the order in which statements execute in a program is called program control.

Section 4.3 Pseudocode
- Pseudocode is an informal language that helps programmers develop algorithms without having to worry about the strict details of Java language syntax.
- Pseudocode is similar to everyday English—it is convenient and user friendly, but it is not an actual computer programming language.
- Pseudocode helps the programmer "think out" a program before attempting to write it in a programming language, such as Java.
- Carefully prepared pseudocode can easily be converted to a corresponding Java program.

Section 4.4 Control Structures
- Normally, statements in a program are executed one after the other in the order in which they are written. This process is called sequential execution.
- Various Java statements enable the programmer to specify that the next statement to execute is not necessarily the next one in sequence. This is called transfer of control.
- Bohm and Jacopini demonstrated that all programs could be written in terms of only three control structures—the sequence structure, the selection structure and the repetition structure.
- The term "control structures" comes from the field of computer science. The *Java Language Specification* refers to "control structures" as "control statements."

- The sequence structure is built into Java. Unless directed otherwise, the computer executes Java statements one after the other in the order in which they are written—that is, in sequence.

- Anywhere a single action may be placed, several actions may be placed in sequence.

- Activity diagrams are part of the UML. An activity diagram models the workflow (also called the activity) of a portion of a software system.

- Activity diagrams are composed of special-purpose symbols, such as action-state symbols, diamonds and small circles. These symbols are connected by transition arrows, which represent the flow of the activity.

- Action states represent actions to perform. Each action state contains an action expression that specifies a particular action to perform.

- The arrows in an activity diagram represent transitions, which indicate the order in which the actions represented by the action states occur.

- The solid circle located at the top of an activity diagram represents the activity's initial state— the beginning of the workflow before the program performs the modeled actions.

- The solid circle surrounded by a hollow circle that appears at the bottom of the diagram represents the final state—the end of the workflow after the program performs its actions.

- Rectangles with their upper-right corners folded over are UML notes—explanatory remarks that describe the purpose of symbols in the diagram.

- Java has three types of selection statements. The if statement either performs an action if a condition is true or skips the action if the condition is false. The if...else statement performs an action if a condition is true and a different action if the condition is false. The switch statement performs one of many different actions, depending on the value of an expression.

- The if statement is a single-selection statement because it selects or ignores a single action or a single group of actions.

- The if...else statement is called a double-selection statement because it selects between two different actions or groups of actions.

- The switch statement is called a multiple-selection statement because it selects among many different actions or groups of actions.

- Java provides the the while, do...while and for repetition (looping) statements that enable programs to perform statements repeatedly as long as a loop-continuation condition remains true.

- The while and for statements perform the action(s) in their bodies zero or more times—if the loop-continuation condition is initially false, the action(s) will not execute. The do...while statement performs the action(s) in its body one or more times.

- The words if, else, switch, while, do and for are Java keywords. Keywords cannot be used as identifiers, such as variable names.

- Every program is formed by combining as many sequence, selection and repetition statements as is appropriate for the algorithm the program implements.

- Single-entry/single-exit control statements make it easy to build programs—we "attach" the control statements to one another by connecting the exit point of one to the entry point of the next. This is known as control-statement stacking.

- There is only one other way in which control statements may be connected—control-statement nesting—in which a control statement appears inside another control statement.

Section 4.5 if Single-Selection Statement
- Programs use selection statements to choose among alternative courses of action.

- The activity diagram for the single-selection `if` statement contains the diamond, or decision symbol, which indicates that a decision is to be made. The workflow will continue along a path determined by the symbol's associated guard conditions, which can be true or false. Each transition arrow emerging from a decision symbol has a guard condition. If a guard condition is true, the workflow enters the action state to which the transition arrow points.
- The `if` statement is a single-entry/single-exit control statement.

Section 4.6 *`if...else` Double-Selection Statement*
- The `if` single-selection statement performs an indicated action only when the condition is `true`.
- The `if...else` double-selection statement performs one action when the condition is true and a different action when the condition is false.
- The conditional operator (`?:`) can be used in place of an `if...else` statement. This is Java's only ternary operator—it takes three operands. Together, the operands and the `?:` symbol form a conditional expression.
- A program can test multiple cases by placing `if...else` statements inside other `if...else` statements to create nested `if...else` statements.
- The Java compiler always associates an `else` with the immediately preceding `if` unless told to do otherwise by the placement of braces (`{` and `}`). This behavior can lead to what is referred to as the dangling-`else` problem.
- The `if` statement normally expects only one statement in its body. To include several statements in the body of an `if` (or the body of an `else` for an `if...else` statement), enclose the statements in braces (`{` and `}`).
- A set of statements contained within a pair of braces is called a block. A block can be placed anywhere in a program that a single statement can be placed.
- Syntax errors are caught by the compiler.
- A logic error has its effect at execution time. A fatal logic error causes a program to fail and terminate prematurely. A nonfatal logic error allows a program to continue executing, but causes the program to produce incorrect results.
- Just as a block can be placed anywhere a single statement can be placed, you can also use an empty statement, represented by placing a semicolon (`;`) where a statement would normally be.

Section 4.7 *`while` Repetition Statement*
- The `while` repetition statement allows the programmer to specify that a program should repeat an action while some condition remains true.
- The UML's merge symbol joins two flows of activity into one.
- The decision and merge symbols can be distinguished by the number of "incoming" and "outgoing" transition arrows. A decision symbol has one transition arrow pointing to the diamond and two or more transition arrows pointing out from the diamond to indicate possible transitions from that point. Each transition arrow pointing out of a decision symbol has a guard condition. A merge symbol has two or more transition arrows pointing to the diamond and only one transition arrow pointing from the diamond, to indicate multiple activity flows merging to continue the activity. None of the transition arrows associated with a merge symbol has a guard condition.

Section 4.8 *Formulating Algorithms: Counter-Controlled Repetition*
- Counter-controlled repetition uses a variable called a counter (or control variable) to control the number of times a set of statements execute.

- Counter-controlled repetition is often called definite repetition, because the number of repetitions is known before the loop begins executing.

- A total is a variable used to accumulate the sum of several values. Variables used to store totals are normally initialized to zero before being used in a program.

- A local variable's declaration must appear before the variable is used in that method. A local variable cannot be accessed outside the method in which it is declared.

- Dividing two integers results in integer division—the calculation's fractional part is truncated.

Section 4.9 Formulating Algorithms: Sentinel-Controlled Repetition

- In sentinel-controlled repetition, a special value called a sentinel value (also called a signal value, a dummy value or a flag value) is used to indicate "end of data entry."

- A sentinel value must be chosen that cannot be confused with an acceptable input value.

- Top-down, stepwise refinement is essential to the development of well-structured programs.

- Division by zero is normally a logic error that, if undetected, would cause the program to fail or produce invalid output.

- To perform a floating-point calculation with integer values, cast one of the integers to type `double`. Using a cast operator in this manner is called explicit conversion.

- Java knows how to evaluate only arithmetic expressions in which the operands' types are identical. To ensure that the operands are of the same type, Java performs an operation called promotion (or implicit conversion) on selected operands. In an expression containing values of the types `int` and `double`, the `int` values are promoted to `double` values for use in the expression.

- Cast operators are available for any type. The cast operator is formed by placing parentheses around the name of a type. The operator is a unary operator.

Section 4.11 Compound Assignment Operators

- Java provides several compound assignment operators for abbreviating assignment expressions. Any statement of the form

    variable = *variable*   *operator*   *expression*;

  where *operator* is one of the binary operators +, -, *, / or % can be written in the form

    variable   *operator*=   *expression*;

- The += operator adds the value of the expression on the right of the operator to the value of the variable on the left of the operator and stores the result in the variable on the left of the operator.

Section 4.12 Increment and Decrement Operators

- Java provides two unary operators for adding 1 to or subtracting 1 from the value of a numeric variable. These are the unary increment operator, ++, and the unary decrement operator, --.

- An increment or decrement operator that is prefixed to a variable is the prefix increment or prefix decrement operator, respectively. An increment or decrement operator that is postfixed to a variable is the postfix increment or postfix decrement operator, respectively.

- Using the prefix increment or decrement operator to add or subtract 1 is known as preincrementing or predecrementing, respectively.

- Preincrementing or predecrementing a variable causes the variable to be incremented or decremented by 1, and then the new value of the variable is used in the expression in which it appears.

- Using the postfix increment or decrement operator to add or subtract 1 is known as postincrementing or postdecrementing, respectively.

- Postincrementing or postdecrementing the variable causes the current value of the variable to be used in the expression in which it appears, and then the variable's value is incremented or decremented by 1.

- When incrementing or decrementing a variable in a statement by itself, the prefix and postfix increment forms have the same effect, and the prefix and postfix decrement forms have the same effect.

Section 4.13 Primitive Types

- Java requires all variables to have a type. Thus, Java is referred to as a strongly typed language.

- Because the designers of Java want it to be maximally portable, they use internationally recognized standards for both character formats (Unicode) and floating-point numbers (IEEE 754).

Section 4.14 (Optional) GUI and Graphics Case Study: Creating Simple Drawings

- Java's coordinate system provides a scheme for identifying every point on the screen. By default, the upper-left corner of a GUI component has the coordinates (0, 0).

- A coordinate pair is composed of an *x*-coordinate (the horizontal coordinate) and a *y*-coordinate (the vertical coordinate). The *x*-coordinate is the horizontal location moving from left to right. The *y*-coordinate is the vertical location moving top to bottom.

- The *x*-axis describes every horizontal coordinate, and the *y*-axis every vertical coordinate.

- Coordinate units are measured in pixels. A pixel is a display monitor's smallest unit of resolution.

- Class Graphics (from package java.awt) provides various methods for drawing text and shapes onto the screen.

- Class JPanel (from package javax.swing) provides an area on which a program can draw.

- The keyword extends indicates that a class inherits from another class. The new class begins with the existing members (data and methods) from the existing class.

- The class from which the new class inherits is called the superclass and the new class is called the subclass.

- Every JPanel has a paintComponent method, which the system automatically calls every time it needs to display the JPanel—when a JPanel is first displayed on the screen, when it is covered then uncovered by a window on the screen and when the window in which it appears is resized.

- Method paintComponent requires one argument, a Graphics object, that is provided for you by the system when it calls paintComponent.

- The first statement in every paintComponent method you create should always be

  ```
  super.paintComponent( g );
  ```

  This ensures that the panel is properly rendered on the screen before you begin drawing on it.

- JPanel methods getWidth and getHeight return the width and height of a JPanel, respectively.

- Graphics method drawLine draws a line between two points represented by its four arguments. The first two arguments are the *x*- and *y*-coordinates for one endpoint of the line, and the last two arguments are the coordinates for the other endpoint of the line.

- To display a JPanel on the screen, you must place it in a window. You create a window with an object of class JFrame from package javax.swing.

- JFrame method setDefaultCloseOperation with the argument JFrame.EXIT_ON_CLOSE indicates that the application should terminate when the user closes the window.

- `JFrame` method add attaches a GUI component to a `JFrame`.
- `JFrame` method `setSize` sets the width and height of the `JFrame`.

Terminology

++ operator
+= operator
-- operator
?: operator
action
action/decision model of programming
action expression (in the UML)
action state (in the UML)
action-state symbol (in the UML)
activity (in the UML)
activity diagram (in the UML)
add method of class `JFrame` (GUI)
addition compound assignment operator (+=)
algorithm
arithmetic compound assignment operators:
    +=, -=, *=, /= and %=
block
`boolean` expression
`boolean` primitive type
body of a loop
cast operator, (*type*)
compound assignment operator
conditional expression
conditional operator (?:)
control statement
control-statement nesting
control-statement stacking
control variable
coordinate system (GUI)
counter
counter-controlled repetition
dangling-`else` problem
decision
decision symbol (in the UML)
decrement operator (--)
definite repetition
diamond (in the UML)
dotted line (in the UML)
(`double`) cast operator
double-selection statement
`drawLine` method of class `Graphics` (GUI)
dummy value
explicit conversion
extends
`false`
fatal error

fatal logic error
final state (in the UML)
first refinement
flag value
`getHeight` method of class `JPanel` (GUI)
`getWidth` method of class `JPanel` (GUI)
goto statement
`Graphics` class (GUI)
guard condition (in the UML)
horizontal coordinate (GUI)
`if` single-selection statement
`if...else` double-selection statement
implicit conversion
increment operator (++)
indefinite repetition
infinite loop
inherit from an existing class
initial state (in the UML)
initialization
integer division
iteration
`JComponent` class (GUI)
`JFrame` class (GUI)
`JPanel` class (GUI)
logic error
loop
loop-continuation condition
loop counter
looping statement
merge symbol (in the UML)
multiple-selection statement
multiplicative operator
nested control statements
nested `if...else` statements
nonfatal logic error
note (in the UML)
order in which actions should execute
`paintComponent` method of class `JComponent`
    (GUI)
pixel (GUI)
postdecrement a variable
postfix decrement operator
postfix increment operator
postincrement a variable
predecrement a variable
prefix decrement operator

prefix increment operator
preincrement a variable
primitive types
procedure for solving a problem
program control
promotion
pseudocode
repetition
repetition statement
repetition structure
second refinement
selection statement
selection structure
sentinel-controlled repetition
sentinel value
sequence structure
sequential execution
setDefaultCloseOperation method of class
    JFrame (GUI)
setSize method of class JFrame (GUI)
signal value
single-entry/single-exit control statements
single-selection statement
small circle (in the UML)
solid circle (in the UML)

solid circle surrounded by a hollow circle
    (in the UML)
stacked control statements
strongly typed language
structured programming
syntax error
ternary operator
top-down stepwise refinement
top
total
transfer of control
transition (in the UML)
transition arrow (in the UML)
true
truncate the fractional part of a calculation
unary cast operator
unary operator
vertical coordinate (GUI)
while repetition statement
workflow
x-axis
x-coordinate
y-axis
y-coordinate

Self-Review Exercises

4.1 Fill in the blanks in each of the following statements:
a) All programs can be written in terms of three types of control structures: _____, _____ and _____.
b) The _____ statement is used to execute one action when a condition is true and another when that condition is false.
c) Repeating a set of instructions a specific number of times is called _____ repetition.
d) When it is not known in advance how many times a set of statements will be repeated, a(n) _____ value can be used to terminate the repetition.
e) The _____ structure is built into Java—by default, statements execute in the order they appear.
f) Instance variables of types char, byte, short, int, long, float and double are all given the value _____ by default.
g) Java is a(n) _____ language—it requires all variables to have a type.
h) If the increment operator is _____ to a variable, the variable is incremented by 1 first, then its new value is used in the expression.

4.2 State whether each of the following is *true* or *false*. If *false*, explain why.
a) An algorithm is a procedure for solving a problem in terms of the actions to execute and the order in which they execute.
b) A set of statements contained within a pair of parentheses is called a block.
c) A selection statement specifies that an action is to be repeated while some condition remains true.

    d) A nested control statement appears in the body of another control statement.

    e) Java provides the arithmetic compound assignment operators +=, -=, *=, /= and %= for abbreviating assignment expressions.

    f) The primitive types (boolean, char, byte, short, int, long, float and double) are portable across only Windows platforms.

    g) Specifying the order in which statements (actions) execute in a program is called program control.

    h) The unary cast operator (double) creates a temporary integer copy of its operand.

    i) Instance variables of type boolean are given the value true by default.

    j) Pseudocode helps a programmer think out a program before attempting to write it in a programming language.

4.3 Write four different Java statements that each add 1 to integer variable x.

4.4 Write Java statements to accomplish each of the following tasks:

    a) Assign the sum of x and y to z, and increment x by 1 after the calculation. Use only one statement.

    b) Test whether variable count is greater than 10. If it is, print "Count is greater than 10".

    c) Decrement the variable x by 1, then subtract it from the variable total. Use only one statement.

    d) Calculate the remainder after q is divided by divisor, and assign the result to q. Write this statement in two different ways.

4.5 Write a Java statement to accomplish each of the following tasks:

    a) Declare variables sum and x to be of type int.

    b) Assign 1 to variable x.

    c) Assign 0 to variable sum.

    d) Add variable x to variable sum, and assign the result to variable sum.

    e) Print "The sum is: ", followed by the value of variable sum.

4.6 Combine the statements that you wrote in Exercise 4.5 into a Java application that calculates and prints the sum of the integers from 1 to 10. Use a while statement to loop through the calculation and increment statements. The loop should terminate when the value of x becomes 11.

4.7 Determine the value of the variables in the following statement after the calculation is performed. Assume that when the statement begins executing, all variables are type int and have the value 5.

```
product *= x++;
```

4.8 Identify and correct the errors in each of the following sets of code:

    a)
```
while ( c <= 5 )
{
    product *= c;
    ++c;
```

    b)
```
if ( gender == 1 )
    System.out.println( "Woman" );
else;
    System.out.println( "Man" );
```

4.9 What is wrong with the following while statement?

```
while ( z >= 0 )
    sum += z;
```

Answers to Self-Review Exercises

4.1 a) sequence, selection, repetition. b) if...else. c) counter-controlled (or definite). d) sentinel, signal, flag or dummy. e) sequence. f) 0 (zero). g) strongly typed. h) prefixed.

4.2 a) True. b) False. A set of statements contained within a pair of braces ({ and }) is called a block. c) False. A repetition statement specifies that an action is to be repeated while some condition remains true. d) True. e) True. f) False. The primitive types (boolean, char, byte, short, int, long, float and double) are portable across all computer platforms that support Java. g) True. h) False. The unary cast operator (double) creates a temporary floating-point copy of its operand. i) False. Instance variables of type boolean are given the value false by default. j) True.

4.3
```
x = x + 1;
x += 1;
++x;
x++;
```

4.4
a) z = x++ + y;
b) if (count > 10)
       System.out.println("Count is greater than 10");
c) total -= --x;
d) q %= divisor;
   q = q % divisor;

4.5
a) int sum, x;
b) x = 1;
c) sum = 0;
d) sum += x; or sum = sum + x;
e) System.out.printf("The sum is: %d\n", sum);

4.6 The program is as follows:

```
1   // Calculate the sum of the integers from 1 to 10
2   public class Calculate
3   {
4      public static void main( String args[] )
5      {
6         int sum;
7         int x;
8
9         x = 1;   // initialize x to 1 for counting
10        sum = 0; // initialize sum to 0 for totaling
11
12        while ( x <= 10 ) // while x is less than or equal to 10
13        {
14           sum += x; // add x to sum
15           ++x; // increment x
16        } // end while
17
18        System.out.printf( "The sum is: %d\n", sum );
19     } // end main
20
21  } // end class Calculate
```

```
The sum is: 55
```

4.7   product = 25, x = 6

4.8   a) Error: The closing right brace of the `while` statement's body is missing.
Correction: Add a closing right brace after the statement `++c;`.
b) Error: The semicolon after `else` results in a logic error. The second output statement will always be executed.
Correction: Remove the semicolon after `else`.

4.9   The value of the variable z is never changed in the `while` statement. Therefore, if the loop-continuation condition (z >= 0) is true, an infinite loop is created. To prevent an infinite loop from occurring, z must be decremented so that it eventually becomes less than 0.

Exercises

4.10   Compare and contrast the `if` single-selection statement and the `while` repetition statement. How are these two statements similar? How are they different?

4.11   Explain what happens when a Java program attempts to divide one integer by another. What happens to the fractional part of the calculation? How can a programmer avoid that outcome?

4.12   Describe the two ways in which control statements can be combined.

4.13   What type of repetition would be appropriate for calculating the sum of the first 100 positive integers? What type of repetition would be appropriate for calculating the sum of an arbitrary number of positive integers? Briefly describe how each of these tasks could be performed.

4.14   What is the difference between preincrementing and postincrementing a variable?

4.15   What does the following program print?

```
1   public class Mystery
2   {
3      public static void main( String args[] )
4      {
5         int y;
6         int x = 1;
7         int total = 0;
8
9         while ( x <= 10 )
10        {
11           y = x * x;
12           System.out.println( y );
13           total += y;
14           ++x;
15        } // end while
16
17        System.out.printf( "Total is %d\n", total );
18     } // end main
19
20   } // end class Mystery
```

For Exercise 4.16 through Exercise 4.19, perform each of the following steps:
a) Read the problem statement.
b) Formulate the algorithm using pseudocode and top-down, stepwise refinement.
c) Write a Java program.
d) Test, debug and execute the Java program.

e) Process three complete sets of data.

4.16   Drivers are concerned with the mileage their automobiles get. One driver has kept track of several tankfuls of gasoline by recording the miles driven and gallons used for each tankful. Develop a Java application that will input the miles driven and gallons used (both as integers) for each tankful. The program should calculate and display the miles per gallon obtained for each tankful and print the combined miles per gallon obtained for all tankfuls up to this point. All averaging calculations should produce floating-point results. Use class Scanner and sentinel-controlled repetition to obtain the data from the user.

4.17   Develop a Java application that will determine whether any of several department-store customers has exceeded the credit limit on a charge account. For each customer, the following facts are available:

a) account number
b) balance at the beginning of the month
c) total of all items charged by the customer this month
d) total of all credits applied to the customer's account this month
e) allowed credit limit.

The program should input all these facts as integers, calculate the new balance (= *beginning balance + charges – credits*), display the new balance and determine whether the new balance exceeds the customer's credit limit. For those customers whose credit limit is exceeded, the program should display the message "Credit limit exceeded".

4.18   A large company pays its salespeople on a commission basis. The salespeople receive $200 per week plus 9% of their gross sales for that week. For example, a salesperson who sells $5000 worth of merchandise in a week receives $200 plus 9% of $5000, or a total of $650. You have been supplied with a list of the items sold by each salesperson. The values of these items are as follows:

```
Item    Value
1       239.99
2       129.75
3        99.95
4       350.89
```

Develop a Java application that inputs one salesperson's items sold for last week and calculates and displays that salesperson's earnings. There is no limit to the number of items that can be sold by a salesperson.

4.19   Develop a Java application that will determine the gross pay for each of three employees. The company pays straight time for the first 40 hours worked by each employee and time and a half for all hours worked in excess of 40 hours. You are given a list of the employees of the company, the number of hours each employee worked last week and the hourly rate of each employee. Your program should input this information for each employee and should determine and display the employee's gross pay. Use class Scanner to input the data.

4.20   The process of finding the largest value (i.e., the maximum of a group of values) is used frequently in computer applications. For example, a program that determines the winner of a sales contest would input the number of units sold by each salesperson. The salesperson who sells the most units wins the contest. Write a pseudocode program and then a Java application that inputs a series of 10 integers and determines and prints the largest integer. Your program should use at least the following three variables:

a) counter: A counter to count to 10 (i.e., to keep track of how many numbers have been input and to determine when all 10 numbers have been processed).
b) number: The integer most recently input by the user.
c) largest: The largest number found so far.

4.21   Write a Java application that uses looping to print the following table of values:

N	10*N	100*N	1000*N
1	10	100	1000
2	20	200	2000
3	30	300	3000
4	40	400	4000
5	50	500	5000

4.22   Using an approach similar to that for Exercise 4.20, find the *two* largest values of the 10 values entered. [*Note:* You may input each number only once.]

4.23   Modify the program in Fig. 4.12 to validate its inputs. For any input, if the value entered is other than 1 or 2, keep looping until the user enters a correct value.

4.24   (*Dangling-else Problem*) Determine the output for each of the given sets of code when x is 9 and y is 11 and when x is 11 and y is 9. Note that the compiler ignores the indentation in a Java program. Also, the Java compiler always associates an else with the immediately preceding if unless told to do otherwise by the placement of braces ({}). On first glance, the programmer may not be sure which if an else matches—this situation is referred to as the "dangling-else problem." We have eliminated the indentation from the following code to make the problem more challenging. [*Hint:* Apply the indentation conventions you have learned.]

a)
```
if ( x < 10 )
if ( y > 10 )
System.out.println( "*****" );
else
System.out.println( "#####" );
System.out.println( "$$$$$" );
```

b)
```
if ( x < 10 )
{
if ( y > 10 )
System.out.println( "*****" );
}
else
{
System.out.println( "#####" );
System.out.println( "$$$$$" );
}
```

4.25   (*Another Dangling-else Problem*) Modify the given code to produce the output shown in each part of the problem. Use proper indentation techniques. Make no changes other than inserting braces and changing the indentation of the code. The compiler ignores indentation in a Java program. We have eliminated the indentation from the given code to make the problem more challenging. [*Note:* It is possible that no modification is necessary for some of the parts.]

```
if ( y == 8 )
if ( x == 5 )
System.out.println( "@@@@@" );
else
System.out.println( "#####" );
System.out.println( "$$$$$" );
System.out.println( "&&&&&" );
```

a) Assuming that x = 5 and y = 8, the following output is produced:

```
@@@@@
$$$$$
&&&&&
```

b) Assuming that x = 5 and y = 8, the following output is produced:

```
@@@@@
```

c) Assuming that x = 5 and y = 8, the following output is produced:

```
@@@@@
&&&&&
```

d) Assuming that x = 5 and y = 7, the following output is produced. [*Note:* The last three output statements after the else are all part of a block.]

```
#####
$$$$$
&&&&&
```

4.26 Write an application that prompts the user to enter the size of the side of a square, then displays a hollow square of that size made of asterisks. Your program should work for squares of all side lengths between 1 and 20.

4.27 *(Palindromes)* A palindrome is a sequence of characters that reads the same backward as forward. For example, each of the following five-digit integers is a palindrome: 12321, 55555, 45554 and 11611. Write an application that reads in a five-digit integer and determines whether it is a palindrome. If the number is not five digits long, display an error message and allow the user to enter a new value.

4.28 Write an application that inputs an integer containing only 0s and 1s (i.e., a binary integer) and prints its decimal equivalent. [*Hint:* Use the remainder and division operators to pick off the binary number's digits one at a time, from right to left. In the decimal number system, the rightmost digit has a positional value of 1 and the next digit to the left has a positional value of 10, then 100, then 1000, and so on. The decimal number 234 can be interpreted as 4 * 1 + 3 * 10 + 2 * 100. In the binary number system, the rightmost digit has a positional value of 1, the next digit to the left has a positional value of 2, then 4, then 8, and so on. The decimal equivalent of binary 1101 is 1 * 1 + 0 * 2 + 1 * 4 + 1 * 8, or 1 + 0 + 4 + 8 or, 13.]

4.29 Write an application that uses only the output statements

```
System.out.print( "* " );
System.out.print( "  " );
System.out.println();
```

to display the checkerboard pattern that follows. Note that a System.out.println method call with no arguments causes the program to output a single newline character. [*Hint:* Repetition statements are required.]

```
*  *  *  *  *  *  *  *
 *  *  *  *  *  *  *  *
*  *  *  *  *  *  *  *
 *  *  *  *  *  *  *  *
*  *  *  *  *  *  *  *
 *  *  *  *  *  *  *  *
*  *  *  *  *  *  *  *
 *  *  *  *  *  *  *  *
```

4.30   Write an application that keeps displaying in the command window the multiples of the integer 2—namely, 2, 4, 8, 16, 32, 64, and so on. Your loop should not terminate (i.e., create an infinite loop). What happens when you run this program?

4.31   What is wrong with the following statement? Provide the correct statement to add one to the sum of x and y.

```
System.out.println( ++(x + y) );
```

4.32   Write an application that reads three nonzero values entered by the user and determines and prints whether they could represent the sides of a triangle.

4.33   Write an application that reads three nonzero integers and determines and prints whether they could represent the sides of a right triangle.

4.34   A company wants to transmit data over the telephone but is concerned that its phones may be tapped. It has asked you to write a program that will encrypt the data so that it may be transmitted more securely. All the data is transmitted as four-digit integers. Your application should read a four-digit integer entered by the user and encrypt it as follows: Replace each digit with the result of adding 7 to the digit and getting the remainder after dividing the new value by 10. Then swap the first digit with the third, and swap the second digit with the fourth. Then print the encrypted integer. Write a separate application that inputs an encrypted four-digit integer and decrypts it to form the original number.

5

Control Statements: Part 2

OBJECTIVES

In this chapter you will learn:

- The essentials of counter-controlled repetition.

- To use the **for** and **do…while** repetition statements to execute statements in a program repeatedly.

- To understand multiple selection using the **switch** selection statement.

- To use the **break** and **continue** program control statements to alter the flow of control.

- To use the logical operators to form complex conditional expressions in control statements.

5.1 Introduction

Chapter 4 began our introduction to the types of building blocks that are available for problem solving. We used those building blocks to employ proven program-construction techniques. This chapter continues our presentation of structured programming theory and principles by introducing Java's remaining control statements. The control statements we study here and in Chapter 4 are helpful in building and manipulating objects.

In this chapter, we demonstrate Java's `for`, `do...while` and `switch` statements. Through a series of short examples using `while` and `for`, we explore the essentials of counter-controlled repetition. We devote a portion of the chapter (and Chapter 7) to expanding the `GradeBook` class presented in Chapters 3–4. In particular, we create a version of class `GradeBook` that uses a `switch` statement to count the number of A, B, C, D and F grade equivalents in a set of numeric grades entered by the user. We introduce the `break` and `continue` program control statements. We discuss Java's logical operators, which enable you to use more complex conditional expressions in control statements. Finally, we summarize Java's control statements and the proven problem-solving techniques presented in this chapter and Chapter 4.

5.2 Essentials of Counter-Controlled Repetition

This section uses the `while` repetition statement introduced in Chapter 4 to formalize the elements required to perform counter-controlled repetition. Counter-controlled repetition requires

1. a control variable (or loop counter)

2. the initial value of the control variable

3. the increment (or decrement) by which the control variable is modified each time through the loop (also known as each iteration of the loop)

4. the loop-continuation condition that determines whether looping should continue.

To see these elements of counter-controlled repetition, consider the application of Fig. 5.1, which uses a loop to display the numbers from 1 through 10. Note that Fig. 5.1 contains only one method, main, which does all of the class's work. For most applications in Chapters 3–4 we have encouraged the use of two separate files—one that declares a reusable class (e.g., Account) and one that instantiates one or more objects of that class (e.g., AccountTest) and demonstrates its (their) functionality. Occasionally, however, it is more appropriate simply to create one class whose main method concisely illustrates a basic concept. Throughout this chapter, we use several one-class examples like Fig. 5.1 to demonstrate the mechanics of Java's control statements.

In Fig. 5.1, the elements of counter-controlled repetition are defined in lines 8, 10 and 13. Line 8 declares the control variable (counter) as an int, reserves space for it in memory and sets its initial value to 1. Variable counter could also have been declared and initialized with the following local-variable declaration and assignment statements:

```
int counter; // declare counter
counter = 1; // initialize counter to 1
```

Line 12 displays control variable counter's value during each iteration of the loop. Line 13 increments the control variable by 1 for each iteration of the loop. The loop-continuation condition in the while (line 10) tests whether the value of the control variable is less than or equal to 10 (the final value for which the condition is true). Note that the program performs the body of this while even when the control variable is 10. The loop terminates when the control variable exceeds 10 (i.e., counter becomes 11).

Common Programming Error 5.1

Because floating-point values may be approximate, controlling loops with floating-point variables may result in imprecise counter values and inaccurate termination tests.

```
1   // Fig. 5.1: WhileCounter.java
2   // Counter-controlled repetition with the while repetition statement.
3
4   public class WhileCounter
5   {
6      public static void main( String args[] )
7      {
8         int counter = 1; // declare and initialize control variable
9
10        while ( counter <= 10 ) // loop-continuation condition
11        {
12           System.out.printf( "%d  ", counter );
13           ++counter; // increment control variable by 1
14        } // end while
15
16        System.out.println(); // output a newline
17     } // end main
18  } // end class WhileCounter
```

```
1  2  3  4  5  6  7  8  9  10
```

Fig. 5.1 | Counter-controlled repetition with the while repetition statement.

Error-Prevention Tip 5.1

Control counting loops with integers.

Good Programming Practice 5.1

Place blank lines above and below repetition and selection control statements, and indent the statement bodies to enhance readability.

The program in Fig. 5.1 can be made more concise by initializing counter to 0 in line 8 and preincrementing counter in the while condition as follows:

```
while ( ++counter <= 10 ) // loop-continuation condition
    System.out.printf( "%d  ", counter );
```

This code saves a statement (and eliminates the need for braces around the loop's body), because the while condition performs the increment before testing the condition. (Recall from Section 4.12 that the precedence of ++ is higher than that of <=.) Coding in such a condensed fashion takes practice, might make code more difficult to read, debug, modify and maintain, and typically should be avoided.

Software Engineering Observation 5.1

"Keep it simple" is good advice for most of the code you will write.

5.3 for Repetition Statement

Section 5.2 presented the essentials of counter-controlled repetition. The while statement can be used to implement any counter-controlled loop. Java also provides the for repetition statement, which specifies the counter-controlled-repetition details in a single line of code. Figure 5.2 reimplements the application of Fig. 5.1 using for.

```
1   // Fig. 5.2: ForCounter.java
2   // Counter-controlled repetition with the for repetition statement.
3
4   public class ForCounter
5   {
6      public static void main( String args[] )
7      {
8         // for statement header includes initialization,
9         // loop-continuation condition and increment
10        for ( int counter = 1; counter <= 10; counter++ )
11           System.out.printf( "%d  ", counter );
12
13        System.out.println(); // output a newline
14     } // end main
15  } // end class ForCounter
```

```
1  2  3  4  5  6  7  8  9  10
```

Fig. 5.2 | Counter-controlled repetition with the for repetition statement.

The application's main method operates as follows: When the for statement (lines 10–11) begins executing, the control variable counter is declared and initialized to 1. (Recall from Section 5.2 that the first two elements of counter-controlled repetition are the control variable and its initial value.) Next, the program checks the loop-continuation condition, counter <= 10, which is between the two required semicolons. Because the initial value of counter is 1, the condition initially is true. Therefore, the body statement (line 11) displays control variable counter's value, namely 1. After executing the loop's body, the program increments counter in the expression counter++, which appears to the right of the second semicolon. Then the loop-continuation test is performed again to determine whether the program should continue with the next iteration of the loop. At this point, the control variable value is 2, so the condition is still true (the final value is not exceeded)—thus, the program performs the body statement again (i.e., the next iteration of the loop). This process continues until the numbers 1 through 10 have been displayed and the counter's value becomes 11, causing the loop-continuation test to fail and repetition to terminate (after 10 repetitions of the loop body at line 11). Then the program performs the first statement after the for—in this case, line 13.

Note that Fig. 5.2 uses (in line 10) the loop-continuation condition counter <= 10. If you incorrectly specified counter < 10 as the condition, the loop would iterate only nine times. This mistake is a common logic error called an off-by-one error.

Common Programming Error 5.2

Using an incorrect relational operator or an incorrect final value of a loop counter in the loop-continuation condition of a repetition statement can cause an off-by-one error.

Good Programming Practice 5.2

Using the final value in the condition of a while or for statement and using the <= relational operator helps avoid off-by-one errors. For a loop that prints the values 1 to 10, the loop-continuation condition should be counter <= 10 rather than counter < 10 (which causes an off-by-one error) or counter < 11 (which is correct). Many programmers prefer so-called zero-based counting, in which to count 10 times, counter would be initialized to zero and the loop-continuation test would be counter < 10.

Figure 5.3 takes a closer look at the for statement in Fig. 5.2. The for's first line (including the keyword for and everything in parentheses after for)—line 10 in Fig. 5.2—is sometimes called the for **statement header**, or simply the for **header**. Note

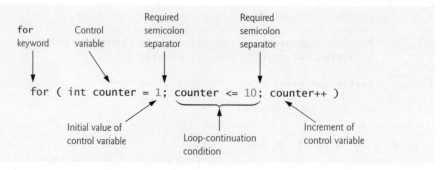

Fig. 5.3 | for statement header components.

that the for header "does it all"—it specifies each item needed for counter-controlled repetition with a control variable. If there is more than one statement in the body of the for, braces ({ and }) are required to define the body of the loop.

The general format of the for statement is

> for (*initialization*; *loopContinuationCondition*; *increment*)
>   *statement*

where the *initialization* expression names the loop's control variable and optionally provides its initial value, *loopContinuationCondition* is the condition that determines whether the loop should continue executing and *increment* modifies the control variable's value (possibly an increment or decrement), so that the loop-continuation condition eventually becomes false. The two semicolons in the for header are required.

Common Programming Error 5.3

Using commas instead of the two required semicolons in a for header is a syntax error.

In most cases, the for statement can be represented with an equivalent while statement as follows:

> *initialization*;
>
> while (*loopContinuationCondition*)
> {
>   *statement*
>   *increment*;
> }

In Section 5.7, we show a case in which a for statement cannot be represented with an equivalent while statement.

Typically, for statements are used for counter-controlled repetition and while statements for sentinel-controlled repetition. However, while and for can each be used for either repetition type.

If the *initialization* expression in the for header declares the control variable (i.e., the control variable's type is specified before the variable name, as in Fig. 5.2), the control variable can be used only in that for statement—it will not exist outside the for statement. This restricted use of the name of the control variable is known as the variable's scope. The scope of a variable defines where it can be used in a program. For example, a local variable can be used only in the method that declares the variable and only from the point of declaration through the end of the method. Scope is discussed in detail in Chapter 6, Methods: A Deeper Look.

Common Programming Error 5.4

When a for statement's control variable is declared in the initialization section of the for's header, using the control variable after the for's body is a compilation error.

All three expressions in a for header are optional. If the *loopContinuationCondition* is omitted, Java assumes that the loop-continuation condition is always true, thus creating an infinite loop. You might omit the *initialization* expression if the program initializes the control variable before the loop. You might omit the *increment* expression if the program calculates the increment with statements in the loop's body or if no increment is needed. The increment expression in a for acts as if it were a standalone statement at the end of the for's body. Therefore, the expressions

```
counter = counter + 1
counter += 1
++counter
counter++
```

are equivalent increment expressions in a for statement. Many programmers prefer counter++ because it is concise and because a for loop evaluates its increment expression after its body executes. Therefore, the postfix increment form seems more natural. In this case, the variable being incremented does not appear in a larger expression, so preincrementing and postincrementing actually have the same effect.

Performance Tip 5.1

There is a slight performance advantage to preincrementing, but if you choose to postincrement because it seems more natural (as in a for header), optimizing compilers will generate Java bytecode that uses the more efficient form anyway.

Good Programming Practice 5.3

In most cases, preincrementing and postincrementing are both used to add 1 to a variable in a statement by itself. In these cases, the effect is exactly the same, except that preincrementing has a slight performance advantage. Given that the compiler typically optimizes your code to help you get the best performance, use the idiom with which you feel most comfortable in these situations.

Common Programming Error 5.5

Placing a semicolon immediately to the right of the right parenthesis of a for header makes that for's body an empty statement. This is normally a logic error.

Error-Prevention Tip 5.2

Infinite loops occur when the loop-continuation condition in a repetition statement never becomes false. To prevent this situation in a counter-controlled loop, ensure that the control variable is incremented (or decremented) during each iteration of the loop. In a sentinel-controlled loop, ensure that the sentinel value is eventually input.

The initialization, loop-continuation condition and increment portions of a for statement can contain arithmetic expressions. For example, assume that x = 2 and y = 10. If x and y are not modified in the body of the loop, the statement

```
for ( int j = x; j <= 4 * x * y; j += y / x )
```

is equivalent to the statement

```
for ( int j = 2; j <= 80; j += 5 )
```

The increment of a for statement may also be negative, in which case it is really a decrement, and the loop counts downward.

If the loop-continuation condition is initially false, the program does not execute the for statement's body. Instead, execution proceeds with the statement following the for.

Programs frequently display the control variable value or use it in calculations in the loop body, but this use is not required. The control variable is commonly used to control repetition without mentioning the control variable in the body of the for.

Error-Prevention Tip 5.3

Although the value of the control variable can be changed in the body of a for loop, avoid doing so, because this practice can lead to subtle errors.

The for statement's UML activity diagram is similar to that of the while statement (Fig. 4.4). Figure 5.4 shows the activity diagram of the for statement in Fig. 5.2. The diagram makes it clear that initialization occurs once before the loop-continuation test is evaluated the first time, and that incrementing occurs each time through the loop after the body statement executes.

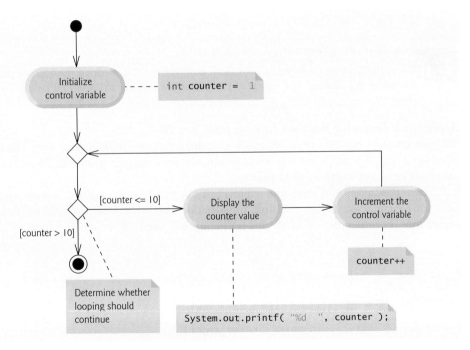

Fig. 5.4 | UML activity diagram for the for statement in Fig. 5.2.

5.4 Examples Using the for Statement

The following examples show techniques for varying the control variable in a for statement. In each case, we write the appropriate for header. Note the change in the relational operator for loops that decrement the control variable.

a) Vary the control variable from 1 to 100 in increments of 1.

```
for ( int i = 1; i <= 100; i++ )
```

b) Vary the control variable from 100 to 1 in decrements of 1.

```
for ( int i = 100; i >= 1; i-- )
```

c) Vary the control variable from 7 to 77 in increments of 7.

```
for ( int i = 7; i <= 77; i += 7 )
```

d) Vary the control variable from 20 to 2 in decrements of 2.

```
for ( int i = 20; i >= 2; i -= 2 )
```

e) Vary the control variable over the following sequence of values: 2, 5, 8, 11, 14, 17, 20.

```
for ( int i = 2; i <= 20; i += 3 )
```

f) Vary the control variable over the following sequence of values: 99, 88, 77, 66, 55, 44, 33, 22, 11, 0.

```
for ( int i = 99; i >= 0; i -= 11 )
```

 Common Programming Error 5.6

Not using the proper relational operator in the loop-continuation condition of a loop that counts downward (e.g., using i <= 1 instead of i >= 1 in a loop counting down to 1) is usually a logic error.

Application: Summing the Even Integers from 2 to 20

We now consider two sample applications that demonstrate simple uses of for. The application in Fig. 5.5 uses a for statement to sum the even integers from 2 to 20 and store the result in an int variable called total.

The *initialization* and *increment* expressions can be comma-separated lists of expressions that enable you to use multiple initialization expressions or multiple increment expressions. For example, although this is discouraged, the body of the for statement in

```
 1   // Fig. 5.5: Sum.java
 2   // Summing integers with the for statement.
 3
 4   public class Sum
 5   {
 6      public static void main( String args[] )
 7      {
 8         int total = 0; // initialize total
 9
10         // total even integers from 2 through 20
11         for ( int number = 2; number <= 20; number += 2 )
12            total += number;
13
14         System.out.printf( "Sum is %d\n", total ); // display results
15      } // end main
16   } // end class Sum
```

```
Sum is 110
```

Fig. 5.5 | Summing integers with the for statement.

lines 11–12 of Fig. 5.5 could be merged into the increment portion of the for header by using a comma as follows:

```
for ( int number = 2; number <= 20; total += number, number += 2 )
    ; // empty statement
```

Good Programming Practice 5.4

Limit the size of control statement headers to a single line if possible.

Application: Compound-Interest Calculations

The next application uses the for statement to compute compound interest. Consider the following problem:

A person invests $1000 in a savings account yielding 5% interest. Assuming that all the interest is left on deposit, calculate and print the amount of money in the account at the end of each year for 10 years. Use the following formula to determine the amounts:

$$a = p \, (1 + r)^n$$

where

> p is the original amount invested (i.e., the principal)
> r is the annual interest rate (e.g., use 0.05 for 5%)
> n is the number of years
> a is the amount on deposit at the end of the nth year.

This problem involves a loop that performs the indicated calculation for each of the 10 years the money remains on deposit. The solution is the application shown in Fig. 5.6. Lines 8–10 in method main declare double variables amount, principal and rate, and initialize principal to 1000.0 and rate to 0.05. Java treats floating-point constants like 1000.0 and 0.05 as type double. Similarly, Java treats whole-number constants like 7 and -22 as type int.

Line 13 outputs the headers for this application's two columns of output. The first column displays the year, and the second column the amount on deposit at the end of that year. Note that we use the format specifier %20s to output the String "Amount on Deposit". The integer 20 between the % and the conversion character s indicates that the value output should be displayed with a field width of 20—that is, printf displays the value with at least 20 character positions. If the value to be output is less than 20 character positions wide (17 characters in this example), the value is right justified in the field by default. If the year value to be output were more than four character positions wide, the field width would be extended to the right to accommodate the entire value—this would push the amount field to the right, upsetting the neat columns of our tabular output. To indicate that values should be output left justified, simply precede the field width with the minus sign (–) formatting flag.

The for statement (lines 16–23) executes its body 10 times, varying control variable year from 1 to 10 in increments of 1. This loop terminates when control variable year becomes 11. (Note that year represents n in the problem statement.)

Classes provide methods that perform common tasks on objects. In fact, most methods must be called on a specific object. For example, to output text in Fig. 5.6, line

```
 1   // Fig. 5.6: Interest.java
 2   // Compound-interest calculations with for.
 3
 4   public class Interest
 5   {
 6      public static void main( String args[] )
 7      {
 8         double amount; // amount on deposit at end of each year
 9         double principal = 1000.0; // initial amount before interest
10         double rate = 0.05; // interest rate
11
12         // display headers
13         System.out.printf( "%s%20s\n", "Year", "Amount on deposit" );
14
15         // calculate amount on deposit for each of ten years
16         for ( int year = 1; year <= 10; year++ )
17         {
18            // calculate new amount for specified year
19            amount = principal * Math.pow( 1.0 + rate, year );
20
21            // display the year and the amount
22            System.out.printf( "%4d%,20.2f\n", year, amount );
23         } // end for
24      } // end main
25   } // end class Interest
```

```
Year    Amount on deposit
   1            1,050.00
   2            1,102.50
   3            1,157.63
   4            1,215.51
   5            1,276.28
   6            1,340.10
   7            1,407.10
   8            1,477.46
   9            1,551.33
  10            1,628.89
```

Fig. 5.6 | Compound-interest calculations with `for`.

13 calls method `printf` on the `System.out` object. Many classes also provide methods that perform common tasks and do not require objects. Recall from Section 3.9 that these are called `static` methods. For example, Java does not include an exponentiation operator, so the designers of Java's `Math` class defined `static` method `pow` for raising a value to a power. You can call a `static` method by specifying the class name followed by a dot (.) and the method name, as in

>   *ClassName*.*methodName*(*arguments*)

In Chapter 6, you'll learn how to implement `static` methods in your own classes.

We use `static` method `pow` of class `Math` to perform the compound-interest calculation in Fig. 5.6. `Math.pow(x, y)` calculates the value of x raised to the yth power. The method receives two double arguments and returns a double value. Line 19 performs the calculation $a = p (1 + r)^n$, where a is amount, p is principal, r is rate and n is year.

After each calculation, line 22 outputs the year and the amount on deposit at the end of that year. The year is output in a field width of four characters (as specified by %4d). The amount is output as a floating-point number with the format specifier %,20.2f. The comma (,) formatting flag indicates that the floating-point value should be output with a grouping separator. The actual separator used is specific to the user's locale (i.e., country). For example, in the United States, the number will be output using commas to separate every three digits and a decimal point to separate the fractional part of the number, as in 1,234.45. The number 20 in the format specification indicates that the value should be output right justified in a field width of 20 characters. The .2 specifies the formatted number's precision—in this case, the number is rounded to the nearest hundredth and output with two digits to the right of the decimal point.

We declared variables amount, principal and rate to be of type double in this example. We are dealing with fractional parts of dollars and thus need a type that allows decimal points in its values. Unfortunately, floating-point numbers can cause trouble. Here is a simple explanation of what can go wrong when using double (or float) to represent dollar amounts (assuming that dollar amounts are displayed with two digits to the right of the decimal point): Two double dollar amounts stored in the machine could be 14.234 (which would normally be rounded to 14.23 for display purposes) and 18.673 (which would normally be rounded to 18.67 for display purposes). When these amounts are added, they produce the internal sum 32.907, which would normally be rounded to 32.91 for display purposes. Thus, your output could appear as

```
  14.23
+ 18.67
-------
  32.91
```

but a person adding the individual numbers as displayed would expect the sum to be 32.90. You have been warned!

Good Programming Practice 5.5

Do not use variables of type double (or float) to perform precise monetary calculations. The imprecision of floating-point numbers can cause errors. In the exercises, we use integers to perform monetary calculations.

Note that some third-party vendors provide for-sale class libraries that perform precise monetary calculations. In addition, the Java API provides class java.math.BigDecimal for performing calculations with arbitrary precision floating-point values.

Note that the body of the for statement contains the calculation 1.0 + rate, which appears as an argument to the Math.pow method. In fact, this calculation produces the same result each time through the loop, so repeating the calculation every iteration of the loop is wasteful.

Performance Tip 5.2

In loops, avoid calculations for which the result never changes—such calculations should typically be placed before the loop. [Note: Many of today's sophisticated optimizing compilers will place such calculations outside loops in the compiled code.]

5.5 do...while Repetition Statement

The do...while repetition statement is similar to the while statement. In the while, the program tests the loop-continuation condition at the beginning of the loop, before executing the loop's body; if the condition is false, the body never executes. The do...while statement tests the loop-continuation condition *after* executing the loop's body; therefore, the body always executes at least once. When a do...while statement terminates, execution continues with the next statement in sequence. Figure 5.7 uses a do...while (lines 10–14) to output the numbers 1–10.

Line 8 declares and initializes control variable counter. Upon entering the do...while statement, line 12 outputs counter's value and line 13 increments counter. Then the program evaluates the loop-continuation test at the bottom of the loop (line 14). If the condition is true, the loop continues from the first body statement in the do...while (line 12). If the condition is false, the loop terminates and the program continues with the next statement after the loop.

Figure 5.8 contains the UML activity diagram for the do...while statement. This diagram makes it clear that the loop-continuation condition is not evaluated until after the loop performs the action state at least once. Compare this activity diagram with that of the while statement (Fig. 4.4).

It is not necessary to use braces in the do...while repetition statement if there is only one statement in the body. However, most programmers include the braces, to avoid confusion between the while and do...while statements. For example,

```
while ( condition )
```

is normally the first line of a while statement. A do...while statement with no braces around a single-statement body appears as:

```
 1   // Fig. 5.7: DoWhileTest.java
 2   // do...while repetition statement.
 3
 4   public class DoWhileTest
 5   {
 6      public static void main( String args[] )
 7      {
 8         int counter = 1; // initialize counter
 9
10         do
11         {
12            System.out.printf( "%d  ", counter );
13            ++counter;
14         } while ( counter <= 10 ); // end do...while
15
16         System.out.println(); // outputs a newline
17      } // end main
18   } // end class DoWhileTest
```

```
1  2  3  4  5  6  7  8  9  10
```

Fig. 5.7 | do...while repetition statement.

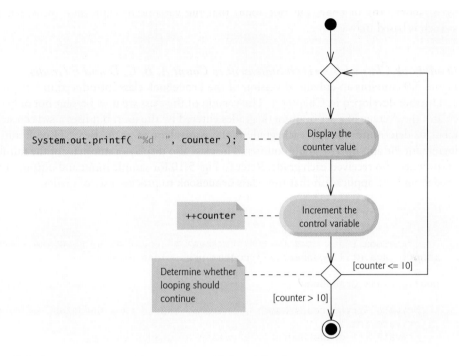

Fig. 5.8 | do...while repetition statement UML activity diagram.

```
do
    statement
while ( condition );
```

which can be confusing. A reader may misinterpret the last line—while(*condition*);—as a while statement containing an empty statement (the semicolon by itself). Thus, the do...while statement with one body statement is usually written as follows:

```
do
{
    statement
} while ( condition );
```

Good Programming Practice 5.6

Always include braces in a do...while statement, even if they are not necessary. This helps eliminate ambiguity between the while statement and a do...while statement containing only one statement.

5.6 switch Multiple-Selection Statement

We discussed the if single-selection statement and the if...else double-selection statement in Chapter 4. Java provides the switch multiple-selection statement to perform different actions based on the possible values of an integer variable or expression. Each action is associated with the value of a **constant integral expression** (i.e., a constant value of type byte, short, int or char, but not long) that the variable or expression on which the switch is based may assume.

GradeBook Class with switch Statement to Count A, B, C, D and F Grades

Figure 5.9 contains an enhanced version of the GradeBook class introduced in Chapter 3 and further developed in Chapter 4. The version of the class we now present not only calculates the average of a set of numeric grades entered by the user, but uses a switch statement to determine whether each grade is the equivalent of an A, B, C, D or F and to increment the appropriate grade counter. The class also displays a summary of the number of students who received each grade. Refer to Fig. 5.10 for sample input and output of the GradeBookTest application that uses class GradeBook to process a set of grades.

```java
1   // Fig. 5.9: GradeBook.java
2   // GradeBook class uses switch statement to count A, B, C, D and F grades.
3   import java.util.Scanner; // program uses class Scanner
4
5   public class GradeBook
6   {
7      private String courseName; // name of course this GradeBook represents
8      private int total; // sum of grades
9      private int gradeCounter; // number of grades entered
10     private int aCount; // count of A grades
11     private int bCount; // count of B grades
12     private int cCount; // count of C grades
13     private int dCount; // count of D grades
14     private int fCount; // count of F grades
15
16     // constructor initializes courseName;
17     // int instance variables are initialized to 0 by default
18     public GradeBook( String name )
19     {
20        courseName = name; // initializes courseName
21     } // end constructor
22
23     // method to set the course name
24     public void setCourseName( String name )
25     {
26        courseName = name; // store the course name
27     } // end method setCourseName
28
29     // method to retrieve the course name
30     public String getCourseName()
31     {
32        return courseName;
33     } // end method getCourseName
34
35     // display a welcome message to the GradeBook user
36     public void displayMessage()
37     {
```

Fig. 5.9 | GradeBook class uses switch statement to count A, B, C, D and F grades. (Part 1 of 3.)

```
38          // getCourseName gets the name of the course
39          System.out.printf( "Welcome to the grade book for\n%s!\n\n",
40             getCourseName() );
41       } // end method displayMessage
42
43       // input arbitrary number of grades from user
44       public void inputGrades()
45       {
46          Scanner input = new Scanner( System.in );
47
48          int grade; // grade entered by user
49
50          System.out.printf( "%s\n%s\n   %s\n   %s\n",
51             "Enter the integer grades in the range 0-100.",
52             "Type the end-of-file indicator to terminate input:",
53             "On UNIX/Linux/Mac OS X type <ctrl> d then press Enter",
54             "On Windows type <ctrl> z then press Enter" );
55
56          // loop until user enters the end-of-file indicator
57          while ( input.hasNext() )
58          {
59             grade = input.nextInt(); // read grade
60             total += grade; // add grade to total
61             ++gradeCounter; // increment number of grades
62
63             // call method to increment appropriate counter
64             incrementLetterGradeCounter( grade );
65          } // end while
66       } // end method inputGrades
67
68       // add 1 to appropriate counter for specified grade
69       public void incrementLetterGradeCounter( int Grade )
70       {
71          // determine which grade was entered
72          switch ( grade / 10 )
73          {
74             case 9:  // grade was between 90
75             case 10: // and 100
76                ++aCount; // increment aCount
77                break; // necessary to exit switch
78
79             case 8: // grade was between 80 and 89
80                ++bCount; // increment bCount
81                break; // exit switch
82
83             case 7: // grade was between 70 and 79
84                ++cCount; // increment cCount
85                break; // exit switch
86
87             case 6: // grade was between 60 and 69
88                ++dCount; // increment dCount
89                break; // exit switch
90
```

Fig. 5.9 | GradeBook class uses switch statement to count A, B, C, D and F grades. (Part 2 of 3.)

```
91              default: // grade was less than 60
92                 ++fCount; // increment fCount
93                 break; // optional; will exit switch anyway
94          } // end switch
95      } // end method incrementLetterGradeCounter
96
97      // display a report based on the grades entered by user
98      public void displayGradeReport()
99      {
100         System.out.println( "\nGrade Report:" );
101
102         // if user entered at least one grade...
103         if ( gradeCounter != 0 )
104         {
105             // calculate average of all grades entered
106             double average = (double) total / gradeCounter;
107
108             // output summary of results
109             System.out.printf( "Total of the %d grades entered is %d\n",
110                 gradeCounter, total );
111             System.out.printf( "Class average is %.2f\n", average );
112             System.out.printf( "%s\n%s%d\n%s%d\n%s%d\n%s%d\n%s%d\n",
113                 "Number of students who received each grade:",
114                 "A: ", aCount,    // display number of A grades
115                 "B: ", bCount,    // display number of B grades
116                 "C: ", cCount,    // display number of C grades
117                 "D: ", dCount,    // display number of D grades
118                 "F: ", fCount );  // display number of F grades
119         } // end if
120         else // no grades were entered, so output appropriate message
121             System.out.println( "No grades were entered" );
122     } // end method displayGradeReport
123 } // end class GradeBook
```

Fig. 5.9 | GradeBook class uses switch statement to count A, B, C, D and F grades. (Part 3 of 3.)

Like earlier versions of the class, class GradeBook (Fig. 5.9) declares instance variable courseName (line 7) and contains methods setCourseName (lines 24–27), getCourseName (lines 30–33) and displayMessage (lines 36–41), which set the course name, store the course name and display a welcome message to the user, respectively. The class also contains a constructor (lines 18–21) that initializes the course name.

Class GradeBook also declares instance variables total (line 8) and gradeCounter (line 9), which keep track of the sum of the grades entered by the user and the number of grades entered, respectively. Lines 10–14 declare counter variables for each grade category. Class GradeBook maintains total, gradeCounter and the five letter-grade counters as instance variables so that these variables can be used or modified in any of the class's methods. Note that the class's constructor (lines 18–21) sets only the course name, because the remaining seven instance variables are ints and are initialized to 0 by default.

Class GradeBook (Fig. 5.9) contains three additional methods—inputGrades, incrementLetterGradeCounter and displayGradeReport. Method inputGrades (lines 44–66) reads an arbitrary number of integer grades from the user using sentinel-controlled repetition and updates instance variables `total` and `gradeCounter`. Method `inputGrades` calls method `incrementLetterGradeCounter` (lines 69–95) to update the appropriate letter-grade counter for each grade entered. Class `GradeBook` also contains method `display-GradeReport` (lines 98–122), which outputs a report containing the total of all grades entered, the average of the grades and the number of students who received each letter grade. Let's examine these methods in more detail.

Line 48 in method `inputGrades` declares variable `grade`, which will store the user's input. Lines 50–54 prompt the user to enter integer grades and to type the end-of-file indicator to terminate the input. The **end-of-file indicator** is a system-dependent keystroke combination which the user enters to indicate that there is no more data to input. In Chapter 14, Files and Streams, we will see how the end-of-file indicator is used when a program reads its input from a file.

On UNIX/Linux/Mac OS X systems, end-of-file is entered by typing the sequence

    <ctrl> d

on a line by itself. This notation means to simultaneously press both the *ctrl* key and the *d* key. On Windows systems, end-of-file can be entered by typing

    <ctrl> z

[*Note:* On some systems, you must press *Enter* after typing the end-of-file key sequence. Also, Windows typically displays the characters ^Z on the screen when the end-of-file indicator is typed, as is shown in the output of Fig. 5.10.]

Portability Tip 5.1

The keystroke combinations for entering end-of-file are system dependent.

The `while` statement (lines 57–65) obtains the user input. The condition at line 57 calls `Scanner` method **hasNext** to determine whether there is more data to input. This method returns the `boolean` value `true` if there is more data; otherwise, it returns `false`. The returned value is then used as the value of the condition in the `while` statement. As long as the end-of-file indicator has not been typed, method `hasNext` will return `true`.

Line 59 inputs a grade value from the user. Line 60 uses the += operator to add `grade` to `total`. Line 61 increments `gradeCounter`. The class's `displayGradeReport` method uses these variables to compute the average of the grades. Line 64 calls the class's `incrementLetterGradeCounter` method (declared in lines 69–95) to increment the appropriate letter-grade counter based on the numeric grade entered.

Method `incrementLetterGradeCounter` contains a `switch` statement (lines 72–94) that determines which counter to increment. In this example, we assume that the user enters a valid grade in the range 0–100. A grade in the range 90–100 represents A, 80–89 represents B, 70–79 represents C, 60–69 represents D and 0–59 represents F. The `switch` statement consists of a block that contains a sequence of **case** labels and an optional **default** case. These are used in this example to determine which counter to increment based on the grade.

When the flow of control reaches the `switch`, the program evaluates the expression in the parentheses (`grade / 10`) following keyword `switch`. This is called the **controlling expression** of the `switch`. The program compares the value of the controlling expression (which must evaluate to an integral value of type byte, char, short or int) with each case label. The controlling expression in line 72 performs integer division, which truncates the fractional part of the result. Thus, when we divide any value for 0–100 by 10, the result is always a value from 0 to 10. We use several of these values in our case labels. For example, if the user enters the integer 85, the controlling expression evaluates to the int value 8. The switch compares 8 with each case label. If a match occurs (case 8: at line 79), the program executes the statements for that case. For the integer 8, line 80 increments bCount, because a grade in the 80s is a B. The break statement (line 81) causes program control to proceed with the first statement after the switch—in this program, we reach the end of method incrementLetterGradeCounter's body, so control returns to line 65 in method input-Grades (the first line after the call to incrementLetterGradeCounter). This line marks the end of the body of the while loop that inputs grades (lines 57–65), so control flows to the while's condition (line 57) to determine whether the loop should continue executing.

The cases in our switch explicitly test for the values 10, 9, 8, 7 and 6. Note the cases at lines 74–75 that test for the values 9 and 10 (both of which represent the grade A). Listing cases consecutively in this manner with no statements between them enables the cases to perform the same set of statements—when the controlling expression evaluates to 9 or 10, the statements in lines 76–77 will execute. The switch statement does not provide a mechanism for testing ranges of values, so every value that must be tested should be listed in a separate case label. Note that each case can have multiple statements. The switch statement differs from other control statements in that it does not require braces around multiple statements in a case.

Without break statements, each time a match occurs in the switch, the statements for that case and subsequent cases execute until a break statement or the end of the switch is encountered. This is often referred to as "falling through" to the statements in subsequent cases. (This feature is perfect for writing a concise program that displays the iterative song "The Twelve Days of Christmas" in Exercise 5.24.)

Common Programming Error 5.7

Forgetting a break statement when one is needed in a switch is a logic error.

If no match occurs between the controlling expression's value and a case label, the default case (lines 91–93) executes. We use the default case in this example to process all controlling-expression values that are less than 6—that is, all failing grades. If no match occurs and the switch does not contain a default case, program control simply continues with the first statement after the switch.

GradeBookTest Class That Demonstrates Class GradeBook

Class GradeBookTest (Fig. 5.10) creates a GradeBook object (lines 10–11). Line 13 invokes the object's displayMessage method to output a welcome message to the user. Line 14 invokes the object's inputGrades method to read a set of grades from the user and keep track of the sum of all the grades entered and the number of grades. Recall that method inputGrades also calls method incrementLetterGradeCounter to keep track of the number of students who received each letter grade. Line 15 invokes method displayGradeReport of class GradeBook, which outputs a report based on the grades entered (as in the input/output window in Fig. 5.10). Line 103 of class GradeBook (Fig. 5.9) determines whether the user entered at least one grade—this helps us avoid dividing by zero. If so, line 106 calculates the average of the grades. Lines 109–118 then output the total of all the grades, the class average and the number of students who received each letter grade. If no grades were entered, line 121 outputs an appropriate message. The output in Fig. 5.10 shows a sample grade report based on 10 grades.

```java
1   // Fig. 5.10: GradeBookTest.java
2   // Create GradeBook object, input grades and display grade report.
3
4   public class GradeBookTest
5   {
6      public static void main( String args[] )
7      {
8         // create GradeBook object myGradeBook and
9         // pass course name to constructor
10        GradeBook myGradeBook = new GradeBook(
11           "CS101 Introduction to Java Programming" );
12
13        myGradeBook.displayMessage(); // display welcome message
14        myGradeBook.inputGrades(); // read grades from user
15        myGradeBook.displayGradeReport(); // display report based on grades
16     } // end main
17  } // end class GradeBookTest
```

```
Welcome to the grade book for
CS101 Introduction to Java Programming!

Enter the integer grades in the range 0-100.
Type the end-of-file indicator to terminate input:
   On UNIX/Linux/Mac OS X type <ctrl> d then press Enter
   On Windows type <ctrl> z then press Enter
99
92
45
57
63
71
76
85
90
100
^Z

Grade Report:
Total of the 10 grades entered is 778
Class average is 77.80
Number of students who received each grade:
A: 4
B: 1
C: 2
D: 1
F: 2
```

Fig. 5.10 | GradeBookTest creates a GradeBook object and invokes its methods.

Note that class `GradeBookTest` (Fig. 5.10) does not directly call `GradeBook` method `incrementLetterGradeCounter` (lines 69–95 of Fig. 5.9). This method is used exclusively by method `inputGrades` of class `GradeBook` to update the appropriate letter-grade counter as each new grade is entered by the user. Method `incrementLetterGradeCounter` exists solely to support the operations of class `GradeBook`'s other methods and thus could be declared `private`. Recall from Chapter 3 that methods declared with access modifier `private` can be called only by other methods of the class in which the `private` methods are declared. Such methods are commonly referred to as **utility methods** or **helper methods** because they can be called only by other methods of that class and are used to support the operation of those methods.

switch Statement UML Activity Diagram

Figure 5.11 shows the UML activity diagram for the general `switch` statement. Most `switch` statements use a `break` in each `case` to terminate the `switch` statement after processing the `case`. Figure 5.11 emphasizes this by including `break` statements in the activity diagram. The diagram makes it clear that the `break` statement at the end of a `case` causes control to exit the `switch` statement immediately.

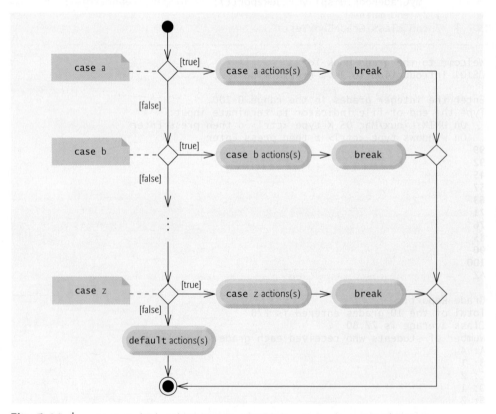

Fig. 5.11 | `switch` multiple-selection statement UML activity diagram with `break` statements.

The break statement is not required for the switch's last case (or the optional default case, when it appears last), because execution continues with the next statement after the switch.

Software Engineering Observation 5.2

Provide a default case in switch statements. Including a default case focuses you on the need to process exceptional conditions.

Good Programming Practice 5.7

Although each case and the default case in a switch can occur in any order, place the default case last. When the default case is listed last, the break for that case is not required. Some programmers include this break for clarity and symmetry with other cases.

When using the switch statement, remember that the expression after each case must be a constant integral expression—that is, any combination of integer constants that evaluates to a constant integer value (e.g., –7, 0 or 221). An integer constant is simply an integer value. In addition, you can use character constants—specific characters in single quotes, such as 'A', '7' or '$'—which represent the integer values of characters. (Appendix B, ASCII Character Set, shows the integer values of the characters in the ASCII character set, which is a subset of the Unicode character set used by Java.)

The expression in each case also can be a constant variable—a variable that contains a value which does not change for the entire program. Such a variable is declared with keyword final (discussed in Chapter 6, Methods: A Deeper Look). Java has a feature called enumerations, which we also present in Chapter 6. Enumeration constants can also be used in case labels. In Chapter 10, Object-Oriented Programming: Polymorphism, we present a more elegant way to implement switch logic—we use a technique called polymorphism to create programs that are often clearer, easier to maintain and easier to extend than programs using switch logic.

5.7 break and continue Statements

In addition to selection and repetition statements, Java provides statements break and continue (presented in this section and Appendix N, Labeled break and continue Statements) to alter the flow of control. The preceding section showed how break can be used to terminate a switch statement's execution. This section discusses how to use break in repetition statements.

Java also provides the labeled break and continue statements for use in cases in which you need to conveniently alter the flow of control in nested control statements. We discuss the labeled break and continue statements in Appendix N.

break Statement

The break statement, when executed in a while, for, do...while or switch, causes immediate exit from that statement. Execution continues with the first statement after the control statement. Common uses of the break statement are to escape early from a loop or to skip the remainder of a switch (as in Fig. 5.9). Figure 5.12 demonstrates a break statement exiting a for.

```
1   // Fig. 5.12: BreakTest.java
2   // break statement exiting a for statement.
3   public class BreakTest
4   {
5      public static void main( String args[] )
6      {
7         int count; // control variable also used after loop terminates
8
9         for ( count = 1; count <= 10; count++ ) // loop 10 times
10        {
11           if ( count == 5 ) // if count is 5,
12              break;          // terminate loop
13
14           System.out.printf( "%d ", count );
15        } // end for
16
17        System.out.printf( "\nBroke out of loop at count = %d\n", count );
18     } // end main
19  } // end class BreakTest
```

```
1 2 3 4
Broke out of loop at count = 5
```

Fig. 5.12 | break statement exiting a for statement.

When the if statement nested at line 11 in the for statement (lines 9–15) detects that count is 5, the break statement at line 12 executes. This terminates the for statement, and the program proceeds to line 17 (immediately after the for statement), which displays a message indicating the value of the control variable when the loop terminated. The loop fully executes its body only four times instead of 10.

continue Statement

The continue statement, when executed in a while, for or do…while, skips the remaining statements in the loop body and proceeds with the next iteration of the loop. In while and do…while statements, the program evaluates the loop-continuation test immediately after the continue statement executes. In a for statement, the increment expression executes, then the program evaluates the loop-continuation test.

Figure 5.13 uses the continue statement in a for to skip the statement at line 12 when the nested if (line 9) determines that the value of count is 5. When the continue statement executes, program control continues with the increment of the control variable in the for statement (line 7).

In Section 5.3, we stated that while could be used in most cases in place of for. The one exception occurs when the increment expression in the while follows a continue statement. In this case, the increment does not execute before the program evaluates the repetition-continuation condition, so the while does not execute in the same manner as the for.

Software Engineering Observation 5.3

Some programmers feel that break and continue violate structured programming. Since the same effects are achievable with structured programming techniques, these programmers do not use break or continue.

```
 1   // Fig. 5.13: ContinueTest.java
 2   // continue statement terminating an iteration of a for statement.
 3   public class ContinueTest
 4   {
 5      public static void main( String args[] )
 6      {
 7         for ( int count = 1; count <= 10; count++ ) // loop 10 times
 8         {
 9            if ( count == 5 ) // if count is 5,
10               continue; // skip remaining code in loop
11
12            System.out.printf( "%d ", count );
13         } // end for
14
15         System.out.println( "\nUsed continue to skip printing 5" );
16      } // end main
17   } // end class ContinueTest
```

```
1 2 3 4 6 7 8 9 10
Used continue to skip printing 5
```

Fig. 5.13 | `continue` statement terminating an iteration of a `for` statement.

Software Engineering Observation 5.4

There is a tension between achieving quality software engineering and achieving the best-performing software. Often, one of these goals is achieved at the expense of the other. For all but the most performance-intensive situations, apply the following rule of thumb: First, make your code simple and correct; then make it fast and small, but only if necessary.

5.8 Logical Operators

The `if`, `if...else`, `while`, `do...while` and `for` statements each require a condition to determine how to continue a program's flow of control. So far, we have studied only simple conditions, such as `count <= 10`, `number != sentinelValue` and `total > 1000`. Simple conditions are expressed in terms of the relational operators `>`, `<`, `>=` and `<=` and the equality operators `==` and `!=`, and each expression tests only one condition. To test multiple conditions in the process of making a decision, we performed these tests in separate statements or in nested `if` or `if...else` statements. Sometimes, control statements require more complex conditions to determine a program's flow of control.

Java provides logical operators to enable you to form more complex conditions by combining simple conditions. The logical operators are `&&` (conditional AND), `||` (conditional OR), `&` (boolean logical AND), `|` (boolean logical inclusive OR), `^` (boolean logical exclusive OR) and `!` (logical NOT).

Conditional AND (&&) Operator

Suppose that we wish to ensure at some point in a program that two conditions are *both* true before we choose a certain path of execution. In this case, we can use the `&&` (conditional AND) operator, as follows:

```
if ( gender == FEMALE && age >= 65 )
   ++seniorFemales;
```

This if statement contains two simple conditions. The condition gender == FEMALE compares variable gender to the constant FEMALE. This might be evaluated, for example, to determine whether a person is female. The condition age >= 65 might be evaluated to determine whether a person is a senior citizen. The if statement considers the combined condition

```
gender == FEMALE && age >= 65
```

which is true if and only if both simple conditions are true. If the combined condition is true, the if statement's body increments seniorFemales by 1. If either or both of the simple conditions are false, the program skips the increment. Some programmers find that the preceding combined condition is more readable when redundant parentheses are added, as in:

```
( gender == FEMALE ) && ( age >= 65 )
```

The table in Fig. 5.14 summarizes the && operator. The table shows all four possible combinations of false and true values for *expression1* and *expression2*. Such tables are called truth tables. Java evaluates to false or true all expressions that include relational operators, equality operators or logical operators.

Conditional OR (||) Operator
Now suppose that we wish to ensure that either *or* both of two conditions are true before we choose a certain path of execution. In this case, we use the || (conditional OR) operator, as in the following program segment:

```
if ( ( semesterAverage >= 90 ) || ( finalExam >= 90 ) )
   System.out.println ( "Student grade is A" );
```

This statement also contains two simple conditions. The condition semesterAverage >= 90 evaluates to determine whether the student deserves an A in the course because of a solid performance throughout the semester. The condition finalExam >= 90 evaluates to determine whether the student deserves an A in the course because of an outstanding performance on the final exam. The if statement then considers the combined condition

```
( semesterAverage >= 90 ) || ( finalExam >= 90 )
```

expression1	expression2	expression1 && expression2
false	false	false
false	true	false
true	false	false
true	true	true

Fig. 5.14 | && (conditional AND) operator truth table.

and awards the student an A if either or both of the simple conditions are true. The only time the message "Student grade is A" is *not* printed is when both of the simple conditions are false. Figure 5.15 is a truth table for operator conditional OR (||). Operator && has a higher precedence than operator ||. Both operators associate from left to right.

Short-Circuit Evaluation of Complex Conditions

The parts of an expression containing && or || operators are evaluated only until it is known whether the condition is true or false. Thus, evaluation of the expression

        (gender == FEMALE) && (age >= 65)

stops immediately if gender is not equal to FEMALE (i.e., the entire expression is false) and continues if gender *is* equal to FEMALE (i.e., the entire expression could still be true if the condition age >= 65 is true). This feature of conditional AND and conditional OR expressions is called short-circuit evaluation.

 Common Programming Error 5.8

In expressions using operator &&, a condition—we will call this the dependent condition—may require another condition to be true for the evaluation of the dependent condition to be meaningful. In this case, the dependent condition should be placed after the other condition, or an error might occur. For example, in the expression (i != 0) && (10 / i == 2), the second condition must appear after the first condition, or a divide-by-zero error might occur.

Boolean Logical AND (&) and Boolean Logical Inclusive OR (|) Operators

The boolean logical AND (&) and boolean logical inclusive OR (|) operators work identically to the && (conditional AND) and || (conditional OR) operators, with one exception: The boolean logical operators always evaluate both of their operands (i.e., they do not perform short-circuit evaluation). Therefore, the expression

        (gender == 1) & (age >= 65)

evaluates age >= 65 regardless of whether gender is equal to 1. This is useful if the right operand of the boolean logical AND or boolean logical inclusive OR operator has a required side effect—a modification of a variable's value. For example, the expression

        (birthday == true) | (++age >= 65)

guarantees that the condition ++age >= 65 will be evaluated. Thus, the variable age is incremented in the preceding expression, regardless of whether the overall expression is true or false.

expression1	expression2	expression1 || expression2
false	false	false
false	true	true
true	false	true
true	true	true

Fig. 5.15 | || (conditional OR) operator truth table.

Error-Prevention Tip 5.4

For clarity, avoid expressions with side effects in conditions. The side effects may look clever, but they can make it harder to understand code and can lead to subtle logic errors.

Boolean Logical Exclusive OR (^)

A simple condition containing the boolean logical exclusive OR (^) operator is `true` *if and only if one of its operands is* `true` *and the other is* `false`. If both operands are `true` or both are `false`, the entire condition is `false`. Figure 5.16 is a truth table for the boolean logical exclusive OR operator (^). This operator is also guaranteed to evaluate both of its operands.

Logical Negation (!) Operator

The `!` (logical NOT, also called logical negation or logical complement) operator "reverses" the meaning of a condition. Unlike the logical operators `&&`, `||`, `&`, `|` and `^`, which are binary operators that combine two conditions, the logical negation operator is a unary operator that has only a single condition as an operand. The logical negation operator is placed before a condition to choose a path of execution if the original condition (without the logical negation operator) is `false`, as in the program segment

```
if ( ! ( grade == sentinelValue ) )
    System.out.printf( "The next grade is %d\n", grade );
```

which executes the `printf` call only if `grade` is not equal to `sentinelValue`. The parentheses around the condition `grade == sentinelValue` are needed because the logical negation operator has a higher precedence than the equality operator.

In most cases, you can avoid using logical negation by expressing the condition differently with an appropriate relational or equality operator. For example, the previous statement may also be written as follows:

```
if ( grade != sentinelValue )
    System.out.printf( "The next grade is %d\n", grade );
```

This flexibility can help you express a condition in a more convenient manner. Figure 5.17 is a truth table for the logical negation operator.

expression1	expression2	expression1 ^ expression2
false	false	false
false	true	true
true	false	true
true	true	false

Fig. 5.16 | ^ (boolean logical exclusive OR) operator truth table.

expression	!expression
false	true
true	false

Fig. 5.17 | ! (logical negation, or logical NOT) operator truth table.

Logical Operators Example

Figure 5.18 demonstrates the logical operators and boolean logical operators by producing their truth tables. The output shows the expression that was evaluated and the boolean result of that expression. The values of the boolean expressions are displayed with printf using the %b format specifier, which outputs the word "true" or the word "false" based on the expression's value. Lines 9–13 produce the truth table for &&. Lines 16–20 produce the truth table for ||. Lines 23–27 produce the truth table for &. Lines 30–35 produce the truth table for |. Lines 38–43 produce the truth table for ^. Lines 46–47 produce the truth table for !.

```java
 1   // Fig. 5.18: LogicalOperators.java
 2   // Logical operators.
 3
 4   public class LogicalOperators
 5   {
 6      public static void main( String args[] )
 7      {
 8         // create truth table for && (conditional AND) operator
 9         System.out.printf( "%s\n%s: %b\n%s: %b\n%s: %b\n%s: %b\n\n",
10            "Conditional AND (&&)", "false && false", ( false && false ),
11            "false && true", ( false && true ),
12            "true && false", ( true && false ),
13            "true && true", ( true && true ) );
14
15         // create truth table for || (conditional OR) operator
16         System.out.printf( "%s\n%s: %b\n%s: %b\n%s: %b\n%s: %b\n\n",
17            "Conditional OR (||)", "false || false", ( false || false ),
18            "false || true", ( false || true ),
19            "true || false", ( true || false ),
20            "true || true", ( true || true ) );
21
22         // create truth table for & (boolean logical AND) operator
23         System.out.printf( "%s\n%s: %b\n%s: %b\n%s: %b\n%s: %b\n\n",
24            "Boolean logical AND (&)", "false & false", ( false & false ),
25            "false & true", ( false & true ),
26            "true & false", ( true & false ),
27            "true & true", ( true & true ) );
28
```

Fig. 5.18 | Logical operators. (Part 1 of 2.)

```
29          // create truth table for | (boolean logical inclusive OR) operator
30          System.out.printf( "%s\n%s: %b\n%s: %b\n%s: %b\n%s: %b\n\n",
31              "Boolean logical inclusive OR (|)",
32              "false | false", ( false | false ),
33              "false | true", ( false | true ),
34              "true | false", ( true | false ),
35              "true | true", ( true | true ) );
36
37          // create truth table for ^ (boolean logical exclusive OR) operator
38          System.out.printf( "%s\n%s: %b\n%s: %b\n%s: %b\n%s: %b\n\n",
39              "Boolean logical exclusive OR (^)",
40              "false ^ false", ( false ^ false ),
41              "false ^ true", ( false ^ true ),
42              "true ^ false", ( true ^ false ),
43              "true ^ true", ( true ^ true ) );
44
45          // create truth table for ! (logical negation) operator
46          System.out.printf( "%s\n%s: %b\n%s: %b\n", "Logical NOT (!)",
47              "!false", ( !false ), "!true", ( !true ) );
48      } // end main
49  } // end class LogicalOperators
```

```
Conditional AND (&&)
false && false: false
false && true: false
true && false: false
true && true: true

Conditional OR (||)
false || false: false
false || true: true
true || false: true
true || true: true

Boolean logical AND (&)
false & false: false
false & true: false
true & false: false
true & true: true

Boolean logical inclusive OR (|)
false | false: false
false | true: true
true | false: true
true | true: true

Boolean logical exclusive OR (^)
false ^ false: false
false ^ true: true
true ^ false: true
true ^ true: false

Logical NOT (!)
!false: true
!true: false
```

Fig. 5.18 | Logical operators. (Part 2 of 2.)

Figure 5.19 shows the precedence and associativity of the Java operators introduced so far. The operators are shown from top to bottom in decreasing order of precedence.

Operators						Associativity	Type
++	--					right to left	unary postfix
++	-	+	-	!	*(type)*	right to left	unary prefix
*	/	%				left to right	multiplicative
+	-					left to right	additive
<	<=	>	>=			left to right	relational
==	!=					left to right	equality
&						left to right	boolean logical AND
^						left to right	boolean logical exclusive OR
|						left to right	boolean logical inclusive OR
&&						left to right	conditional AND
||						left to right	conditional OR
?:						right to left	conditional
=	+=	-=	*=	/=	%=	right to left	assignment

Fig. 5.19 | Precedence/associativity of the operators discussed so far.

5.9 Structured Programming Summary

Just as architects design buildings by employing the collective wisdom of their profession, so should programmers design programs. Our field is much younger than architecture, and our collective wisdom is considerably sparser. We have learned that structured programming produces programs that are easier than unstructured programs to understand, test, debug, modify and even prove correct in a mathematical sense.

Figure 5.20 uses UML activity diagrams to summarize Java's control statements. The initial and final states indicate the single entry point and the single exit point of each control statement. Arbitrarily connecting individual symbols in an activity diagram can lead to unstructured programs. Therefore, the programming profession has chosen a limited set of control statements that can be combined in only two simple ways to build structured programs.

For simplicity, only single-entry/single-exit control statements are used—there is only one way to enter and only one way to exit each control statement. Connecting control statements in sequence to form structured programs is simple. The final state of one control statement is connected to the initial state of the next control statement—that is, the control statements are placed one after another in a program in sequence. We call this "control-statement stacking." The rules for forming structured programs also allow for control statements to be nested.

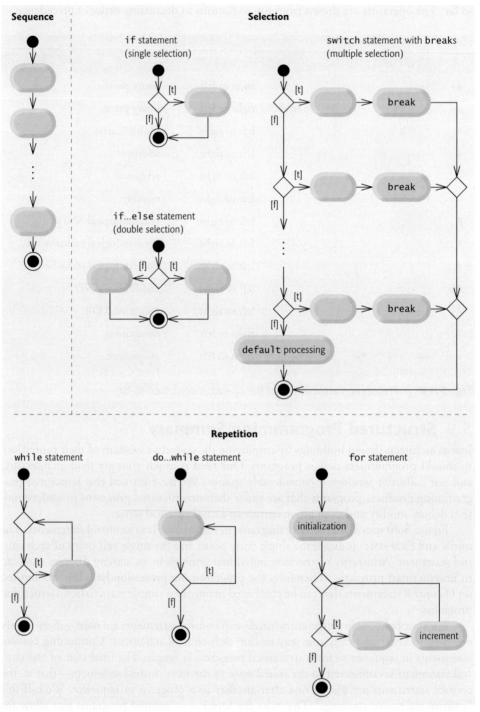

Fig. 5.20 | Java's single-entry/single-exit sequence, selection and repetition statements.

Rules for forming structured programs
1 Begin with the simplest activity diagram (Fig. 5.22).
2 Any action state can be replaced by two action states in sequence.
3 Any action state can be replaced by any control statement (sequence of action states, `if`, `if...else`, `switch`, `while`, `do...while` or `for`).
4 Rules 2 and 3 can be applied as often as you like and in any order.

Fig. 5.21 | Rules for forming structured programs.

Figure 5.21 shows the rules for forming structured programs. The rules assume that action states may be used to indicate any action. The rules also assume that we begin with the simplest activity diagram (Fig. 5.22) consisting of only an initial state, an action state, a final state and transition arrows.

Applying the rules in Fig. 5.21 always results in a properly structured activity diagram with a neat, building-block appearance. For example, repeatedly applying rule 2 to the simplest activity diagram results in an activity diagram containing many action states in sequence (Fig. 5.23). Rule 2 generates a stack of control statements, so let us call rule 2 the stacking rule. [*Note:* The vertical dashed lines in Fig. 5.23 are not part of the UML. We use them to separate the four activity diagrams that demonstrate rule 2 of Fig. 5.21 being applied.]

Rule 3 is called the **nesting rule**. Repeatedly applying rule 3 to the simplest activity diagram results in an activity diagram with neatly nested control statements. For example, in Fig. 5.24, the action state in the simplest activity diagram is replaced with a double-selection (`if...else`) statement. Then rule 3 is applied again to the action states in the double-selection statement, replacing each with a double-selection statement. The dashed action-state symbol around each double-selection statement represents the action state that was replaced. [*Note:* The dashed arrows and dashed action-state symbols shown in Fig. 5.24 are not part of the UML. They are used here to illustrate that any action state can be replaced with a control statement.]

Rule 4 generates larger, more involved and more deeply nested statements. The diagrams that emerge from applying the rules in Fig. 5.21 constitute the set of all possible

Fig. 5.22 | Simplest activity diagram.

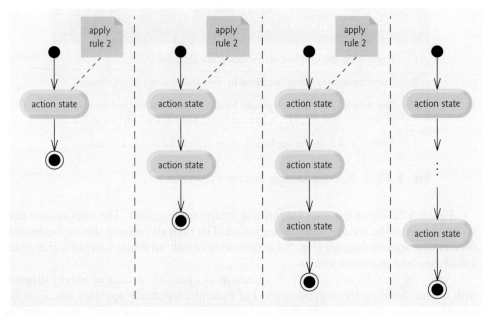

Fig. 5.23 | Repeatedly applying the stacking rule (rule 2) of Fig. 5.21 to the simplest activity diagram.

structured activity diagrams and hence the set of all possible structured programs. The beauty of the structured approach is that we use only seven simple single-entry/single-exit control statements and assemble them in only two simple ways.

If the rules in Fig. 5.21 are followed, an "unstructured' activity diagram (like the one in Fig. 5.25) cannot be created. If you are uncertain about whether a particular diagram is structured, apply the rules of Fig. 5.21 in reverse to reduce the diagram to the simplest activity diagram. If you can reduce it, the original diagram is structured; otherwise, it is not.

Structured programming promotes simplicity. Bohm and Jacopini have given us the result that only three forms of control are needed to implement an algorithm:

- Sequence
- Selection
- Repetition

The sequence structure is trivial. Simply list the statements to execute in the order in which they should execute. Selection is implemented in one of three ways:

- `if` statement (single selection)
- `if...else` statement (double selection)
- `switch` statement (multiple selection)

In fact, it is straightforward to prove that the simple `if` statement is sufficient to provide any form of selection—everything that can be done with the `if...else` statement and the `switch` statement can be implemented by combining `if` statements (although perhaps not as clearly and efficiently).

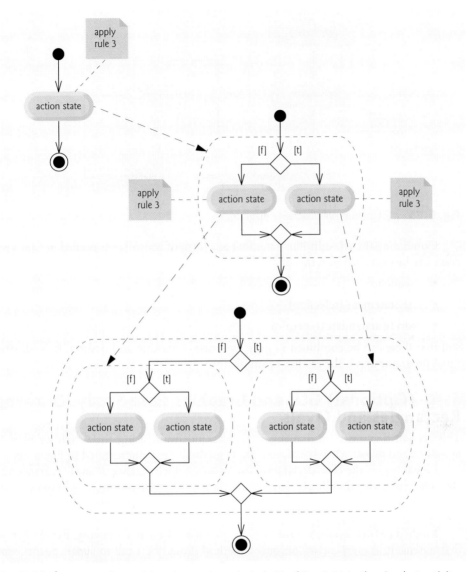

Fig. 5.24 | Repeatedly applying the nesting rule (rule 3) of Fig. 5.21 to the simplest activity diagram.

Repetition is implemented in one of three ways:

- `while` statement
- `do...while` statement
- `for` statement

It is straightforward to prove that the `while` statement is sufficient to provide any form of repetition. Everything that can be done with the `do...while` statement and the `for` statement can be done with the `while` statement (although perhaps not as conveniently).

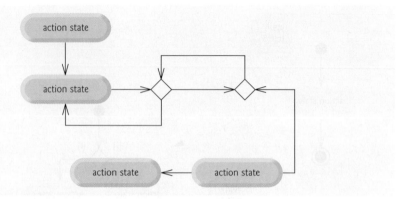

Fig. 5.25 | "Unstructured" activity diagram.

Combining these results illustrates that any form of control ever needed in a Java program can be expressed in terms of

- sequence
- `if` statement (selection)
- `while` statement (repetition)

and that these can be combined in only two ways—stacking and nesting. Indeed, structured programming is the essence of simplicity.

5.10 (Optional) GUI and Graphics Case Study: Drawing Rectangles and Ovals

This section demonstrates drawing rectangles and ovals, using the `Graphics` methods `drawRect` and `drawOval`, respectively. These methods are demonstrated in Fig. 5.26.

Line 6 begins the class declaration for `Shapes`, which extends `JPanel`. Instance variable, `choice`, declared in line 8, determines whether `paintComponent` should draw rectangles or ovals. The `Shapes` constructor at lines 11–14 initializes `choice` with the value passed in parameter `userChoice`.

Method `paintComponent` (lines 17–36) performs the actual drawing. Remember, the first statement in every `paintComponent` method should be a call to `super.paintComponent`, as in line 19. Lines 21–35 loop 10 times to draw 10 shapes. The `switch` statement (Lines 24–34) chooses between drawing rectangles and drawing ovals.

If `choice` is 1, then the program draws a rectangle. Lines 27–28 call `Graphics` method `drawRect`. Method `drawRect` requires four arguments. The first two represent the *x*- and *y*-coordinates of the upper-left corner of the rectangle; the next two represent the width and the height of the rectangle. In this example, we start at a position 10 pixels down and 10 pixels right of the top-left corner, and every iteration of the loop moves the upper-left corner another 10 pixels down and to the right. The width and the height of the rectangle start at 50 pixels and increase by 10 pixels in each iteration.

If `choice` is 2, the program draws an oval. When drawing an oval, an imaginary rectangle called a **bounding rectangle** is created, and an oval that touches the midpoints of all four sides of the bounding rectangle is placed inside. Method `drawOval` (lines 31–32)

```
1   // Fig. 5.26: Shapes.java
2   // Demonstrates drawing different shapes.
3   import java.awt.Graphics;
4   import javax.swing.JPanel;
5
6   public class Shapes extends JPanel
7   {
8      private int choice; // user's choice of which shape to draw
9
10     // constructor sets the user's choice
11     public Shapes( int userChoice )
12     {
13        choice = userChoice;
14     } // end Shapes constructor
15
16     // draws a cascade of shapes starting from the top-left corner
17     public void paintComponent( Graphics g )
18     {
19        super.paintComponent( g );
20
21        for ( int i = 0; i < 10; i++ )
22        {
23           // pick the shape based on the user's choice
24           switch ( choice )
25           {
26              case 1: // draw rectangles
27                 g.drawRect( 10 + i * 10, 10 + i * 10,
28                    50 + i * 10, 50 + i * 10 );
29                 break;
30              case 2: // draw ovals
31                 g.drawOval( 10 + i * 10, 10 + i * 10,
32                    50 + i * 10, 50 + i * 10 );
33                 break;
34           } // end switch
35        } // end for
36     } // end method paintComponent
37  } // end class Shapes
```

Fig. 5.26 | Drawing a cascade of shapes based on the user's choice.

requires the same four arguments as method drawRect. The arguments specify the position and size of the bounding rectangle for the oval. The values passed to drawOval in this example are exactly the same as the values passed to drawRect in lines 27–28. Since the width and height of the bounding rectangle are identical in this example, lines 27–28 draw a circle. You may modify the program to draw both rectangles and ovals to see how drawOval and drawRect are related.

Figure 5.27 is responsible for handling input from the user and creating a window to display the appropriate drawing based on the user's response. Line 3 imports JFrame to handle the display, and Line 4 imports JOptionPane to handle the input.

Lines 11–13 prompt the user with an input dialog and store the user's response in variable input. Line 15 uses Integer method parseInt to convert the String entered by the user to an int and stores the result in variable choice. An instance of class Shapes is

```
1   // Fig. 5.27: ShapesTest.java
2   // Test application that displays class Shapes.
3   import javax.swing.JFrame;
4   import javax.swing.JOptionPane;
5
6   public class ShapesTest
7   {
8      public static void main( String args[] )
9      {
10        // obtain user's choice
11        String input = JOptionPane.showInputDialog(
12           "Enter 1 to draw rectangles\n" +
13           "Enter 2 to draw ovals" );
14
15        int choice = Integer.parseInt( input ); // convert input to int
16
17        // create the panel with the user's input
18        Shapes panel = new Shapes( choice );
19
20        JFrame application = new JFrame(); // creates a new JFrame
21
22        application.setDefaultCloseOperation( JFrame.EXIT_ON_CLOSE );
23        application.add( panel ); // add the panel to the frame
24        application.setSize( 300, 300 ); // set the desired size
25        application.setVisible( true ); // show the frame
26     } // end main
27  } // end class ShapesTest
```

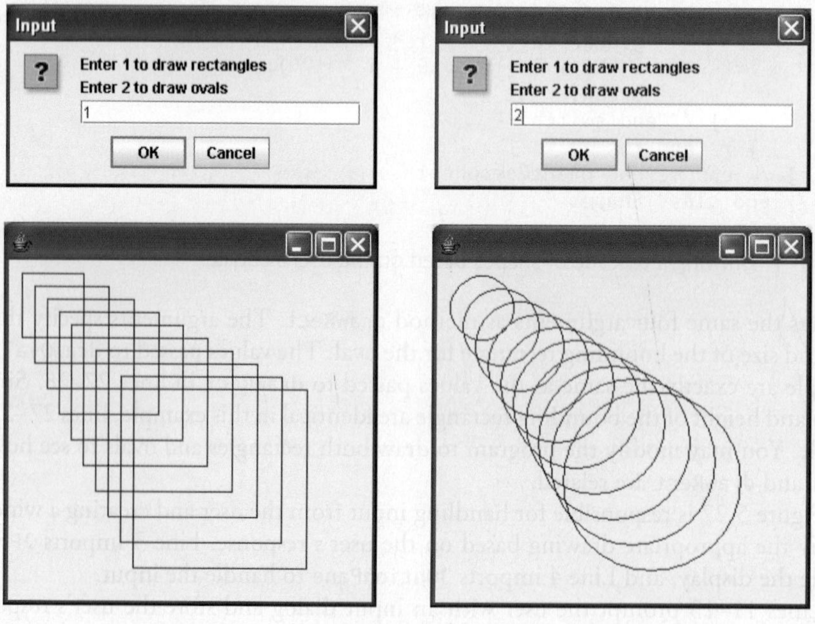

Fig. 5.27 | Obtaining user input and creating a JFrame to display Shapes.

created at line 18, with the user's choice passed to the constructor. Lines 20–25 perform the standard operations for creating and setting up a window—creating a frame, setting it to exit the application when closed, adding the drawing to the frame, setting the frame size and making it visible.

GUI and Graphics Case Study Exercises

5.1 Draw 12 concentric circles in the center of a JPanel (Fig. 5.28). The innermost circle should have a radius of 10 pixels, and each successive circle should have a radius 10 pixels larger than the previous one. Begin by finding the center of the JPanel. To get the upper-left corner of a circle, move up one radius and to the left one radius from the center. The width and height of the bounding rectangle is the diameter of the circle (twice the radius).

5.2 Modify Exercise 5.15 from the end-of-chapter exercises to read input using dialogs and to display the bar chart using rectangles of varying lengths.

Fig. 5.28 | Drawing concentric circles.

5.11 (Optional) Software Engineering Case Study: Identifying Objects' States and Activities

In Section 4.15, we identified many of the class attributes needed to implement the ATM system and added them to the class diagram in Fig. 4.24. In this section, we show how these attributes represent an object's state. We identify some key states that our objects may occupy and discuss how objects change state in response to various events occurring in the system. We also discuss the workflow, or activities, that objects perform in the ATM system. We present the activities of BalanceInquiry and Withdrawal transaction objects in this section.

State Machine Diagrams

Each object in a system goes through a series of states. An object's current state is indicated by the values of the object's attributes at a given time. State machine diagrams (commonly called state diagrams) model several states of an object and show under what circumstances the object changes state. Unlike the class diagrams presented in earlier case study sections, which focused primarily on the structure of the system, state diagrams model some of the behavior of the system.

Figure 5.29 is a simple state diagram that models some of the states of an object of class ATM. The UML represents each state in a state diagram as a rounded rectangle with the name of the state placed inside it. A solid circle with an attached stick arrowhead designates the initial state. Recall that we modeled this state information as the Boolean attribute userAuthenticated in the class diagram of Fig. 4.24. This attribute is initialized to false, or the "User not authenticated" state, according to the state diagram.

The arrows with stick arrowheads indicate transitions between states. An object can transition from one state to another in response to various events that occur in the system. The name or description of the event that causes a transition is written near the line that corresponds to the transition. For example, the ATM object changes from the "User not authenticated" to the "User authenticated" state after the database authenticates the user. Recall from the requirements document that the database authenticates a user by comparing the account number and PIN entered by the user with those of an account in the database. If the database indicates that the user has entered a valid account number and the correct PIN, the ATM object transitions to the "User authenticated" state and changes its userAuthenticated attribute to a value of true. When the user exits the system by choosing the "exit" option from the main menu, the ATM object returns to the "User not authenticated" state.

> ### Software Engineering Observation 5.5
>
> *Software designers do not generally create state diagrams showing every possible state and state transition for all attributes—there are simply too many of them. State diagrams typically show only key states and state transitions.*

Activity Diagrams

Like a state diagram, an activity diagram models aspects of system behavior. Unlike a state diagram, an activity diagram models an object's workflow (sequence of events) during program execution. An activity diagram models the actions the object will perform and in what order. The activity diagram in Fig. 5.30 models the actions involved in executing a balance-inquiry transaction. We assume that a BalanceInquiry object has already been initialized and assigned a valid account number (that of the current user), so the object knows which balance to retrieve. The diagram includes the actions that occur after the user selects a balance inquiry from the main menu and before the ATM returns the user to the main menu—a BalanceInquiry object does not perform or initiate these actions, so we do not model them here. The diagram begins with retrieving the balance of the account from the database. Next, the BalanceInquiry displays the balance on the screen. This action completes the execution of the transaction. Recall that we have chosen to represent an account balance as both the availableBalance and totalBalance attributes of class Account, so the actions modeled in Fig. 5.30 refer to the retrieval and display of both balance attributes.

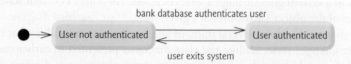

bank database authenticates user

User not authenticated   User authenticated

user exits system

Fig. 5.29 | State diagram for the ATM object.

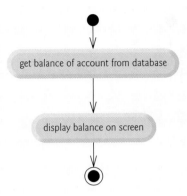

Fig. 5.30 | Activity diagram for a `BalanceInquiry` object.

The UML represents an action in an activity diagram as an action state modeled by a rectangle with its left and right sides replaced by arcs curving outward. Each action state contains an action expression—for example, "get balance of account from database"—that specifies an action to be performed. An arrow with a stick arrowhead connects two action states, indicating the order in which the actions represented by the action states occur. The solid circle (at the top of Fig. 5.30) represents the activity's initial state—the beginning of the workflow before the object performs the modeled actions. In this case, the transaction first executes the "get balance of account from database" action expression. The transaction then displays both balances on the screen. The solid circle enclosed in an open circle (at the bottom of Fig. 5.30) represents the final state—the end of the workflow after the object performs the modeled actions. We used UML activity diagrams to illustrate the flow of control for the control statements presented in Chapters 4–5.

Figure 5.31 shows an activity diagram for a withdrawal transaction. We assume that a `Withdrawal` object has been assigned a valid account number. We do not model the user selecting a withdrawal from the main menu or the ATM returning the user to the main menu because these are not actions performed by a `Withdrawal` object. The transaction first displays a menu of standard withdrawal amounts (shown in Fig. 2.19) and an option to cancel the transaction. The transaction then receives a menu selection from the user. The activity flow now arrives at a decision (a fork indicated by the small diamond symbol). [*Note:* A decision was known as a branch in earlier versions of the UML.] This point determines the next action based on the associated guard condition (in square brackets next to the transition), which states that the transition occurs if this guard condition is met. If the user cancels the transaction by choosing the "cancel" option from the menu, the activity flow immediately skips to the final state. Note the merge (indicated by the small diamond symbol) where the cancellation flow of activity joins the main flow of activity before reaching the activity's final state. If the user selects a withdrawal amount from the menu, `Withdrawal` sets `amount` (an attribute originally modeled in Fig. 4.24) to the value chosen by the user.

After setting the withdrawal amount, the transaction retrieves the available balance of the user's account (i.e., the `availableBalance` attribute of the user's `Account` object) from the database. The activity flow then arrives at another decision. If the requested withdrawal amount exceeds the user's available balance, the system displays an appropriate

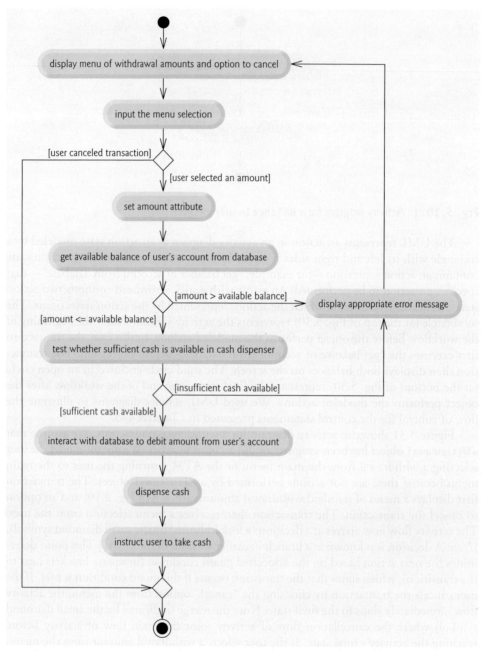

Fig. 5.31 | Activity diagram for a withdrawal transaction.

error message informing the user of the problem, then returns to the beginning of the activity diagram and prompts the user to input a new amount. If the requested withdrawal amount is less than or equal to the user's available balance, the transaction proceeds. The transaction next tests whether the cash dispenser has enough cash remaining to satisfy the withdrawal request. If it does not, the transaction displays an appropriate error message, then returns to the beginning of the activity diagram and prompts the user to choose a new amount. If sufficient cash is available, the transaction interacts with the database to debit the withdrawal amount from the user's account (i.e., subtract the amount from both the availableBalance and totalBalance attributes of the user's Account object). The transaction then dispenses the desired amount of cash and instructs the user to take the cash that is dispensed. Finally, the main flow of activity merges with the cancellation flow of activity before reaching the final state.

We have taken the first steps in modeling the behavior of the ATM system and have shown how an object's attributes participate in performing the object's activities. In Section 6.14, we investigate the behaviors for all classes to give a more accurate interpretation of the system behavior by "filling in" the third compartments of the classes in our class diagram.

Software Engineering Case Study Self-Review Exercises

5.1 State whether the following statement is *true* or *false*, and if *false*, explain why: State diagrams model structural aspects of a system.

5.2 An activity diagram models the _____ that an object performs and the order in which it performs them.
  a) actions
  b) attributes
  c) states
  d) state transitions

5.3 Based on the requirements document, create an activity diagram for a deposit transaction.

Answers to Software Engineering Case Study Self-Review Exercises

5.1 False. State diagrams model some of the behavior of a system.

5.2 a.

5.3 Figure 5.32 presents an activity diagram for a deposit transaction. The diagram models the actions that occur after the user chooses the deposit option from the main menu and before the ATM returns the user to the main menu. Recall that part of receiving a deposit amount from the user involves converting an integer number of cents to a dollar amount. Also recall that crediting a deposit amount to an account involves increasing only the totalBalance attribute of the user's Account object. The bank updates the availableBalance attribute of the user's Account object only after confirming the amount of cash in the deposit envelope and after the enclosed checks clear—this occurs independently of the ATM system.

5.12 Wrap-Up

In this chapter, we completed our introduction to Java's control statements, which enable you to control the flow of execution in methods. Chapter 4 discussed Java's if, if...else and while statements. The current chapter demonstrated Java's remaining control statements—for, do...while and switch. We showed that any algorithm can be developed using combinations of the sequence structure (i.e., statements listed in the order in which they should execute), the three types of selection statements—if, if...else and switch—and the three types of repetition statements—while, do...while and for. In this chapter and Chapter 4, we discussed how you can combine these building blocks to utilize proven

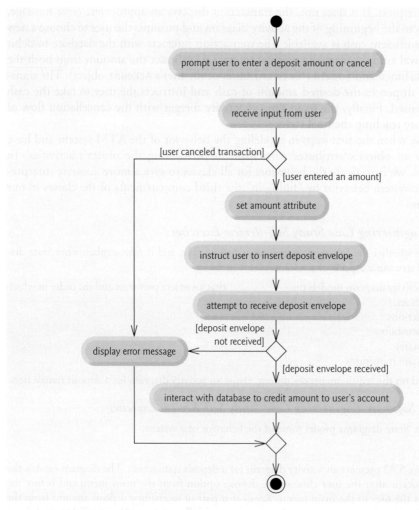

Fig. 5.32 | Activity diagram for a deposit transaction.

program-construction and problem-solving techniques. This chapter also introduced Java's logical operators, which enable you to use more complex conditional expressions in control statements.

In Chapter 3, we introduced the basic concepts of objects, classes and methods. Chapter 4 and Chapter 5 introduced the types of control statements that you can use to specify program logic in methods. In Chapter 6, we examine methods in greater depth.

Summary

Section 5.2 Essentials of Counter-Controlled Repetition

- Counter-controlled repetition requires a control variable (or loop counter), the initial value of the control variable, the increment (or decrement) by which the control variable is modified each time through the loop (also known as each iteration of the loop) and the loop-continuation condition that determines whether looping should continue.

- You can declare a variable and initialize it in the same statement.

Section 5.3 **for** *Repetition Statement*
- The `while` statement can be used to implement any counter-controlled loop.
- The `for` repetition statement specifies the details of counter-controlled-repetition in a single line of code.
- When the `for` statement begins executing, its control variable is declared and initialized. Next, the program checks the loop-continuation condition. If the condition is initially true, the body executes. After executing the loop's body, the increment expression executes. Then the loop-continuation test is performed again to determine whether the program should continue with the next iteration of the loop.
- The general format of the `for` statement is

      for (*initialization*; *loopContinuationCondition*; *increment*)
          statement

  where the *initialization* expression names the loop's control variable and optionally provides its initial value, *loopContinuationCondition* is the condition that determines whether the loop should continue executing and *increment* modifies the control variable's value (possibly an increment or decrement), so that the loop-continuation condition eventually becomes false. The two semicolons in the `for` header are required.
- In most cases, the `for` statement can be represented with an equivalent `while` statement as follows:

      initialization;

      while (*loopContinuationCondition*)
      {
          statement
          increment;
      }

- Typically, `for` statements are used for counter-controlled repetition and `while` statements for sentinel-controlled repetition.
- If the *initialization* expression in the `for` header declares the control variable, the control variable can be used only in that `for` statement—it will not exist outside the `for` statement.
- All three expressions in a `for` header are optional. If the *loopContinuationCondition* is omitted, Java assumes that the loop-continuation condition is always true, thus creating an infinite loop. You might omit the *initialization* expression if the program initializes the control variable before the loop. You might omit the *increment* expression if the program calculates the increment with statements in the loop's body or if no increment is needed.
- The increment expression in a `for` acts as if it were a standalone statement at the end of the `for`'s body.
- The increment of a `for` statement may also be negative, in which case it is really a decrement, and the loop counts downward.
- If the loop-continuation condition is initially `false`, the program does not execute the `for` statement's body. Instead, execution proceeds with the statement following the `for`.

Section 5.4 Examples Using the **for** Statement
- Java treats floating-point constants like `1000.0` and `0.05` as type `double`. Similarly, Java treats whole number constants like `7` and `-22` as type `int`.

- The format specifier %20s indicates that the String output should be displayed with a field width of 20—that is, printf displays the value with at least 20 character positions. If the value to be output is less than 20 character positions wide, the value is right justified in the field by default.
- Math.pow(x, y) calculates the value of x raised to the yth power. The method receives two double arguments and returns a double value.
- The comma (,) formatting flag in a format specifier (e.g., %,20.2f) indicates that a floating-point value should be output with a grouping separator. The actual separator used is specific to the user's locale (i.e., country). For example, in the United States, the number will be output using commas to separate every three digits and a decimal point to separate the fractional part of the number, as in 1,234.45.
- The .2 specifies in a format specifier (e.g., %,20.2f) indicates a formatted number's precision—in this case, the number is rounded to the nearest hundredth and output with two digits to the right of the decimal point.

Section 5.5 do...while *Repetition Statement*
- The do...while repetition statement is similar to the while statement. In the while, the program tests the loop-continuation condition at the beginning of the loop, before executing the loop's body; if the condition is false, the body never executes. The do...while statement tests the loop-continuation condition *after* executing the loop's body; therefore, the body always executes at least once. When a do...while statement terminates, execution continues with the next statement in sequence.
- It is not necessary to use braces in the do...while repetition statement if there is only one statement in the body. However, most programmers include the braces, to avoid confusion between the while and do...while statements.

Section 5.6 switch *Multiple-Selection Statement*
- The switch multiple-selection statement performs different actions based on the possible values of an integer variable or expression. Each action is associated with the value of a constant integral expression (i.e., a constant value of type byte, short, int or char, but not long) that the variable or expression on which the switch is based may assume.
- The end-of-file indicator is a system-dependent keystroke combination which the user enters to indicate that there is no more data to input. On UNIX/Linux/Mac OS X systems, end-of-file is entered by typing the sequence *<ctrl> d* on a line by itself. This notation means to simultaneously press both the *ctrl* key and the *d* key. On Windows systems, end-of-file can be entered by typing *<ctrl> z*.
- Scanner method hasNext determines whether there is more data to input. This method returns the boolean value true if there is more data; otherwise, it returns false. As long as the end-of-file indicator has not been typed, method hasNext will return true.
- The switch statement consists of a block that contains a sequence of case labels and an optional default case.
- When the flow of control reaches the switch, the program evaluates the controlling expression of the switch. The program compares the value of the controlling expression (which must evaluate to an integral value of type byte, char, short or int) with each case label. If a match occurs, the program executes the statements for that case.
- Listing cases consecutively with no statements between them enables the cases to perform the same set of statements.
- The switch statement does not provide a mechanism for testing ranges of values, so every value that must be tested should be listed in a separate case label.

- Each case can have multiple statements. The switch statement differs from other control statements in that it does not require braces around multiple statements in a case.

- Without break statements, each time a match occurs in the switch, the statements for that case and subsequent cases execute until a break statement or the end of the switch is encountered. This is often referred to as "falling through" to the statements in subsequent cases.

- If no match occurs between the controlling expression's value and a case label, the optional default case executes. If no match occurs and the switch does not contain a default case, program control simply continues with the first statement after the switch.

- The break statement is not required for the switch's last case (or the optional default case, when it appears last), because execution continues with the next statement after the switch.

Section 5.7 *break and* cont inue *Statements*
- In addition to selection and repetition statements, Java provides statements break and continue (presented in this section and Appendix N, Labeled break and continue Statements) to alter the flow of control. The preceding section showed how break can be used to terminate a switch statement's execution. This section discusses how to use break in repetition statements.

- The break statement, when executed in a while, for, do...while or switch, causes immediate exit from that statement. Execution continues with the first statement after the control statement.

- The continue statement, when executed in a while, for or do...while, skips the remaining statements in the loop body and proceeds with the next iteration of the loop. In while and do...while statements, the program evaluates the loop-continuation test immediately after the continue statement executes. In a for statement, the increment expression executes, then the program evaluates the loop-continuation test.

Section 5.8 *Logical Operators*
- Simple conditions are expressed in terms of the relational operators >, <, >= and <= and the equality operators == and !=, and each expression tests only one condition.

- Logical operators to enable you to form more complex conditions by combining simple conditions. The logical operators are && (conditional AND), || (conditional OR), & (boolean logical AND), | (boolean logical inclusive OR), ∧ (boolean logical exclusive OR) and ! (logical NOT).

- To ensure that two conditions are *both* true before choosing a certain path of execution, use the && (conditional AND) operator. This operator yields true if and only if both of its simple conditions are true. If either or both of the simple conditions are false, the entire expression is false.

- To ensure that either *or* both of two conditions are true before choosing a certain path of execution, use the || (conditional OR) operator, which evaluates to true if either or both of its simple conditions are true.

- The parts of an expression containing && or || operators are evaluated only until it is known whether the condition is true or false. This feature of conditional AND and conditional OR expressions is called short-circuit evaluation.

- The boolean logical AND (&) and boolean logical inclusive OR (|) operators work identically to the && (conditional AND) and || (conditional OR) operators, with one exception: The boolean logical operators always evaluate both of their operands (i.e., they do not perform short-circuit evaluation).

- A simple condition containing the boolean logical exclusive OR (∧) operator is true *if and only if one of its operands is* true *and the other is* false. If both operands are true or both are false, the entire condition is false. This operator is also guaranteed to evaluate both of its operands.

- The ! (logical NOT, also called logical negation or logical complement) operator "reverses" the meaning of a condition. The logical negation operator is a unary operator that has only a single condition as an operand. The logical negation operator is placed before a condition to choose a path of execution if the original condition (without the logical negation operator) is false.

- In most cases, you can avoid using logical negation by expressing the condition differently with an appropriate relational or equality operator.

Section 5.10 (Optional) GUI and Graphics Case Study: Drawing Rectangles and Ovals

- Graphics methods drawRect and drawOval draw rectangles and ovals, respectively.

- Graphics method drawRect requires four arguments. The first two represent the *x*- and *y*-coordinates of the upper-left corner of the rectangle; the next two represent the width and the height of the rectangle.

- When drawing an oval, an imaginary rectangle called a bounding rectangle is created, and an oval that touches the midpoints of all four sides of the bounding rectangle is placed inside. Method drawOval requires the same four arguments as method drawRect. The arguments specify the position and size of the bounding rectangle for the oval.

Terminology

!, logical not operator	final keyword
%b format specifier	for header
&, boolean logical AND operator	for repetition statement
&&, conditional AND operator	for statement header
- (minus) format flag	hasNext method of class Scanner
, (comma) format flag	helper method
|, boolean logical OR operator	increment a control variable
||, conditional OR operator	initial value
^, boolean logical exclusive OR operator	iteration of a loop
boolean logical AND (&)	left justify
boolean logical exclusive OR (^)	logical complement (!)
boolean logical inclusive OR (|)	logical negation (!)
bounding rectangle of an oval (GUI)	logical operators
break statement	loop-continuation condition
case label	multiple selection
character constant	nested control statements
conditional AND (&&)	nesting rule
conditional OR (||)	off-by-one error
constant integral expression	repetition statement
constant variable	right justify
continue statement	scope of a variable
control variable	short-circuit evaluation
controlling expression of a switch	side effect
decrement a control variable	simple condition
default case in switch	single-entry/single-exit control statements
do...while repetition statement	stacked control statements
drawOval method of class Graphics (GUI)	stacking rule
drawRect method of class Graphics (GUI)	static method
end-of-file indicator	switch selection statement
field width	truth table

Self-Review Exercises

5.1 Fill in the blanks in each of the following statements:
  a) Typically, _____ statements are used for counter-controlled repetition and _____ statements are used for sentinel-controlled repetition.
  b) The do...while statement tests the loop-continuation condition _____ executing the loop's body; therefore, the body always executes at least once.
  c) The _____ statement selects among multiple actions based on the possible values of an integer variable or expression.
  d) The _____ statement, when executed in a repetition statement, skips the remaining statements in the loop body and proceeds with the next iteration of the loop.
  e) The _____ operator can be used to ensure that two conditions are *both* true before choosing a certain path of execution.
  f) If the loop-continuation condition in a for header is initially _____, the program does not execute the for statement's body.
  g) Methods that perform common tasks and do not require objects are called _____ methods.

5.2 State whether each of the following is *true* or *false*. If *false*, explain why.
  a) The default case is required in the switch selection statement.
  b) The break statement is required in the last case of a switch selection statement.
  c) The expression ((x > y) && (a < b)) is true if either x > y is true or a < b is true.
  d) An expression containing the || operator is true if either or both of its operands are true.
  e) The comma (,) formatting flag in a format specifier (e.g., %,20.2f) indicates that a value should be output with a thousands separator.
  f) To test for a range of values in a switch statement, use a hyphen (–) between the start and end values of the range in a case label.
  g) Listing cases consecutively with no statements between them enables the cases to perform the same set of statements.

5.3 Write a Java statement or a set of Java statements to accomplish each of the following tasks:
  a) Sum the odd integers between 1 and 99, using a for statement. Assume that the integer variables sum and count have been declared.
  b) Calculate the value of 2.5 raised to the power of 3, using the pow method.
  c) Print the integers from 1 to 20, using a while loop and the counter variable i. Assume that the variable i has been declared, but not initialized. Print only five integers per line. [*Hint:* Use the calculation i % 5. When the value of this expression is 0, print a newline character; otherwise, print a tab character. Assume that this code is an application. Use the System.out.println() method to output the newline character, and use the System.out.print('\t') method to output the tab character.]
  d) Repeat part (c), using a for statement.

5.4 Find the error in each of the following code segments, and explain how to correct it:
  a)
```
i = 1;

while ( i <= 10 );
    i++;

}
```
  b)
```
for ( k = 0.1; k != 1.0; k += 0.1 )
    System.out.println( k );
```

```
c)  switch ( n )
    {
        case 1:
            System.out.println( "The number is 1" );
        case 2:
            System.out.println( "The number is 2" );
            break;
        default:
            System.out.println( "The number is not 1 or 2" );
            break;
    }
```

d) The following code should print the values 1 to 10:

```
n = 1;
while ( n < 10 )
    System.out.println( n++ );
```

Answers to Self-Review Exercises

5.1   a) `for`, `while`. b) after. c) `switch`. d) `continue`. e) `&&` (conditional AND). f) `false`.
g) `static`.

5.2   a) False. The `default` case is optional. If no default action is needed, then there is no need
for a `default` case. b) False. The `break` statement is used to exit the `switch` statement. The `break`
statement is not required for the last case in a `switch` statement. c) False. Both of the relational expressions must be true for the entire expression to be true when using the `&&` operator. d) True.
e) True. f) False. The `switch` statement does not provide a mechanism for testing ranges of values,
so every value that must be tested should be listed in a separate case label. g) True.

5.3   a)
```
    sum = 0;
    for ( count = 1; count <= 99; count += 2 )
        sum += count;
```
        b) `double result = Math.pow( 2.5, 3 );`
        c) `i = 1;`

```
        while ( i <= 20 )
        {
            System.out.print( i );

            if ( i % 5 == 0 )
                System.out.println();
            else
                System.out.print( '\t' );

            ++i;
        }
```
        d)
```
    for ( i = 1; i <= 20; i++ )
    {
        System.out.print( i );

        if ( i % 5 == 0 )
            System.out.println();
        else
            System.out.print( '\t' );
    }
```

5.4   a)   Error: The semicolon after the `while` header causes an infinite loop, and there is a missing left brace.

Correction: Replace the semicolon by a {, or remove both the ; and the }.

b)   Error: Using a floating-point number to control a `for` statement may not work, because floating-point numbers are represented only approximately by most computers.

Correction: Use an integer, and perform the proper calculation in order to get the values you desire:

```
for ( k = 1; k != 10; k++ )
    System.out.println( (double) k / 10 );
```

c)   Error: The missing code is the break statement in the statements for the first case.

Correction: Add a break statement at the end of the statements for the first case. Note that this omission is not necessarily an error if you want the statement of `case 2:` to execute every time the `case 1:` statement executes.

d)   Error: An improper relational operator is used in the `while` repetition-continuation condition.

Correction: Use <= rather than <, or change 10 to 11.

Exercises

5.5   Describe the four basic elements of counter-controlled repetition.

5.6   Compare and contrast the `while` and `for` repetition statements.

5.7   Discuss a situation in which it would be more appropriate to use a do...while statement than a `while` statement. Explain why.

5.8   Compare and contrast the `break` and `continue` statements.

5.9   What does the following program do?

```
1   public class Printing
2   {
3      public static void main( String args[] )
4      {
5         for ( int i = 1; i <= 10; i++ )
6         {
7            for ( int j = 1; j <= 5; j++ )
8               System.out.print( '@' );
9
10           System.out.println();
11        } // end outer for
12     } // end main
13  } // end class Printing
```

5.10   Write an application that finds the smallest of several integers. Assume that the first value read specifies the number of values to input from the user.

5.11   Write an application that calculates the product of the odd integers from 1 to 15.

5.12 *Factorials* are used frequently in probability problems. The factorial of a positive integer *n* (written *n*! and pronounced "*n* factorial") is equal to the product of the positive integers from 1 to *n*. Write an application that evaluates the factorials of the integers from 1 to 5. Display the results in tabular format. What difficulty might prevent you from calculating the factorial of 20?

5.13 Modify the compound-interest application of Fig. 5.6 to repeat its steps for interest rates of 5%, 6%, 7%, 8%, 9% and 10%. Use a for loop to vary the interest rate.

5.14 Write an application that displays the following patterns separately, one below the other. Use for loops to generate the patterns. All asterisks (*) should be printed by a single statement of the form System.out.print('*'); which causes the asterisks to print side by side. A statement of the form System.out.println(); can be used to move to the next line. A statement of the form System.out.print(' '); can be used to display a space for the last two patterns. There should be no other output statements in the program. [*Hint:* The last two patterns require that each line begin with an appropriate number of blank spaces.]

```
    (a)            (b)            (c)            (d)
    *          **********     **********              *
    **          *********      *********             **
    ***          ********       ********            ***
    ****          *******        *******           ****
    *****          ******         ******          *****
    ******          *****          *****         ******
    *******          ****           ****        *******
    ********          ***            ***       ********
    *********          **             **      *********
    **********          *              *     **********
```

5.15 One interesting application of computers is to display graphs and bar charts. Write an application that reads five numbers between 1 and 30. For each number that is read, your program should display the same number of adjacent asterisks. For example, if your program reads the number 7, it should display *******.

5.16 A mail-order house sells five products whose retail prices are as follows: Product 1, $2.98; product 2, $4.50; product 3, $9.98; product 4, $4.49 and product 5, $6.87. Write an application that reads a series of pairs of numbers as follows:
   a) product number
   b) quantity sold

Your program should use a switch statement to determine the retail price for each product. It should calculate and display the total retail value of all products sold. Use a sentinel-controlled loop to determine when the program should stop looping and display the final results.

5.17 Modify the application in Fig. 5.6 to use only integers to calculate the compound interest. [*Hint:* Treat all monetary amounts as integral numbers of pennies. Then break the result into its dollars and cents portions by using the division and remainder operations, respectively. Insert a period between the dollars and the cents portions.]

5.18 Assume that i = 1, j = 2, k = 3 and m = 2. What does each of the following statements print?
   a) System.out.println(i == 1);
   b) System.out.println(j == 3);
   c) System.out.println((i >= 1) && (j < 4));
   d) System.out.println((m <= 99) & (k < m));
   e) System.out.println((j >= i) || (k == m));
   f) System.out.println((k + m < j) | (3 - j >= k));
   g) System.out.println(!(k > m));

5.19   Calculate the value of π from the infinite series

$$\pi = 4 - \frac{4}{3} + \frac{4}{5} - \frac{4}{7} + \frac{4}{9} - \frac{4}{11} + \cdots$$

Print a table that shows the value of π approximated by computing one term of this series, by two terms, by three terms, and so on. How many terms of this series do you have to use before you first get 3.14? 3.141? 3.1415? 3.14159?

5.20   Modify Exercise 5.14 to combine your code from the four separate triangles of asterisks such that all four patterns print side by side. [*Hint:* Make clever use of nested for loops.]

5.21   Write an application that prints the following diamond shape. You may use output statements that print a single asterisk (*), a single space or a single newline character. Maximize your use of repetition (with nested for statements), and minimize the number of output statements.

```
    *
   ***
  *****
 *******
*********
 *******
  *****
   ***
    *
```

5.22   Modify the application you wrote in Exercise 5.21 to read an odd number in the range 1 to 19 to specify the number of rows in the diamond. Your program should then display a diamond of the appropriate size.

5.23   Describe in general how you would remove any continue statement from a loop in a program and replace it with some structured equivalent. Use the technique you develop here to remove the continue statement from the program in Fig. 5.13.

5.24   (*"The Twelve Days of Christmas" Song*) Write an application that uses repetition and switch statements to print the song "The Twelve Days of Christmas." One switch statement should be used to print the day ("first," "second," and so on). A separate switch statement should be used to print the remainder of each verse. Visit the website en.wikipedia.org/wiki/Twelvetide for the complete lyrics of the song.

6

Methods:
A Deeper Look

OBJECTIVES

In this chapter you will learn:

- How `static` methods and fields are associated with an entire class rather than specific instances of the class.

- To use common `Math` methods available in the Java API.

- To understand the mechanisms for passing information between methods.

- How the method call/return mechanism is supported by the method-call stack and activation records.

- How packages group related classes.

- How to use random-number generation to implement game-playing applications.

- How the visibility of declarations is limited to specific regions of programs.

- What method overloading is and how to create overloaded methods.

6.1 Introduction

Most computer programs that solve real-world problems are much larger than the programs presented in the first few chapters of this book. Experience has shown that the best way to develop and maintain a large program is to construct it from small, simple pieces, or modules. This technique is called divide and conquer. We introduced methods in Chapter 3. In Chapter 6, we study methods in more depth. We emphasize how to declare and use methods to facilitate the design, implementation, operation and maintenance of large programs.

You'll see that it is possible for certain methods, called static methods, to be called without the need for an object of the class to exist. You'll learn how to declare a method with more than one parameter. You'll also learn how Java is able to keep track of which method is currently executing, how local variables of methods are maintained in memory and how a method knows where to return after it completes execution.

We will take a brief diversion into simulation techniques with random-number generation and develop a version of the casino dice game called craps that uses most of the programming techniques you've used to this point in the book. In addition, you'll learn how to declare values that cannot change (i.e., constants) in your programs.

Many of the classes you'll use or create while developing applications will have more than one method of the same name. This technique, called overloading, is used to implement methods that perform similar tasks for arguments of different types or for different numbers of arguments.

We continue our discussion of methods in Chapter 15, Recursion. Recursion provides an entirely different way of thinking about methods and algorithms.

6.2 Program Modules in Java

Three kinds of modules exist in Java—methods, classes and packages. Java programs are written by combining new methods and classes that you write with predefined methods and classes available in the Java Application Programming Interface (also referred to as the Java API or Java class library) and in various other class libraries. Related classes are typically grouped into packages so that they can be imported into programs and reused. You'll learn how to group your own classes into packages in Chapter 8. The Java API provides a rich collection of predefined classes that contain methods for performing common mathematical calculations, string manipulations, character manipulations, input/output operations, database operations, networking operations, file processing, error checking and many other useful operations.

Good Programming Practice 6.1

Familiarize yourself with the rich collection of classes and methods provided by the Java API (java.sun.com/javase/6/docs/api/). In Section 6.8, we present an overview of several common packages. In Appendix J, we explain how to navigate the Java API documentation.

Software Engineering Observation 6.1

Don't try to reinvent the wheel. When possible, reuse Java API classes and methods. This reduces program development time and avoids introducing programming errors.

Methods (called functions or procedures in other languages) allow you to modularize a program by separating its tasks into self-contained units. You've declared methods in every program you have written—these methods are sometimes referred to as programmer-declared methods. The statements in the method bodies are written only once, are reused from perhaps several locations in a program and are hidden from other methods.

One motivation for modularizing a program into methods is the divide-and-conquer approach, which makes program development more manageable by constructing programs from small, simple pieces. Another is software reusability—using existing methods as building blocks to create new programs. Often, you can create programs mostly from standardized methods rather than by building customized code. For example, in earlier programs, we did not have to define how to read data values from the keyboard—Java provides these capabilities in class Scanner. A third motivation is to avoid repeating code. Dividing a program into meaningful methods makes the program easier to debug and maintain.

Software Engineering Observation 6.2

To promote software reusability, every method should be limited to performing a single, well-defined task, and the name of the method should express that task effectively. Such methods make programs easier to write, debug, maintain and modify.

Error-Prevention Tip 6.1

A small method that performs one task is easier to test and debug than a larger method that performs many tasks.

Software Engineering Observation 6.3

If you cannot choose a concise name that expresses a method's task, your method might be attempting to perform too many diverse tasks. It is usually best to break such a method into several smaller method declarations.

As you know, a method is invoked by a method call, and when the called method completes its task, it returns either a result or simply control to the caller. An analogy to this program structure is the hierarchical form of management (Figure 6.1). A boss (the caller) asks a worker (the called method) to perform a task and report back (return) the results after completing the task. The boss method does not know how the worker method performs its designated tasks. The worker may also call other worker methods, unbeknown to the boss. This "hiding" of implementation details promotes good software engineering. Figure 6.1 shows the boss method communicating with several worker methods in a hierarchical manner. The boss method divides its responsibilities among the various worker methods. Note that worker1 acts as a "boss method" to worker4 and worker5.

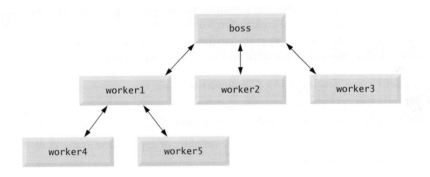

Fig. 6.1 | Hierarchical boss-method/worker-method relationship.

6.3 static Methods, static Fields and Class Math

As you know, every class provides methods that perform common tasks on objects of the class. For example, to input data from the keyboard, you have called methods on a Scanner object that was initialized in its constructor to obtain input from the standard input stream (System.in). As you'll learn in Chapter 14, Files and Streams, you can initialize a Scanner to obtain input from other sources, such as a file on disk. One program could have a Scanner object that inputs information from the standard input stream and a second Scanner that inputs information from a file. Each input method called on the standard input stream Scanner would obtain input from the keyboard, and each input method called on the file Scanner would obtain input from the specified file on disk.

Although most methods execute in response to method calls on specific objects, this is not always the case. Sometimes a method performs a task that does not depend on the contents of any object. Such a method applies to the class in which it is declared as a whole and is known as a static method or a **class method**. It is common for classes to contain convenient static methods to perform common tasks. For example, recall that we used static method pow of class Math to raise a value to a power in Fig. 5.6. To declare a method as static, place the keyword static before the return type in the method's declaration. You can call any static method by specifying the name of the class in which the method is declared, followed by a dot (.) and the method name, as in

ClassName.*methodName*(*arguments*)

We use various `Math` class methods here to present the concept of `static` methods. Class `Math` provides a collection of methods that enable you to perform common mathematical calculations. For example, you can calculate the square root of 900.0 with the `static` method call

```
Math.sqrt( 900.0 )
```

The preceding expression evaluates to 30.0. Method `sqrt` takes an argument of type `double` and returns a result of type `double`. To output the value of the preceding method call in the command window, you might write the statement

```
System.out.println( Math.sqrt( 900.0 ) );
```

In this statement, the value that `sqrt` returns becomes the argument to method `println`. Note that there was no need to create a `Math` object before calling method `sqrt`. Also note that *all* `Math` class methods are `static`—therefore, each is called by preceding the name of the method with the class name `Math` and the dot (.) separator.

 Software Engineering Observation 6.4

Class `Math` is part of the `java.lang` package, which is implicitly imported by the compiler, so it is not necessary to import class `Math` to use its methods.

Method arguments may be constants, variables or expressions. If c = 13.0, d = 3.0 and f = 4.0, then the statement

```
System.out.println( Math.sqrt( c + d * f ) );
```

calculates and prints the square root of 13.0 + 3.0 * 4.0 = 25.0—namely, 5.0. Figure 6.2 summarizes several `Math` class methods. In the figure, *x* and *y* are of type `double`.

Method	Description	Example
abs(*x*)	absolute value of *x*	abs(23.7) is 23.7 abs(0.0) is 0.0 abs(-23.7) is 23.7
ceil(*x*)	rounds *x* to the smallest integer not less than *x*	ceil(9.2) is 10.0 ceil(-9.8) is -9.0
cos(*x*)	trigonometric cosine of *x* (*x* in radians)	cos(0.0) is 1.0
exp(*x*)	exponential method e^x	exp(1.0) is 2.71828 exp(2.0) is 7.38906
floor(*x*)	rounds *x* to the largest integer not greater than *x*	floor(9.2) is 9.0 floor(-9.8) is -10.0
log(*x*)	natural logarithm of *x* (base *e*)	log(Math.E) is 1.0 log(Math.E * Math.E) is 2.0

Fig. 6.2 | Math class methods. (Part 1 of 2.)

Method	Description	Example
max(x, y)	larger value of x and y	max(2.3, 12.7) is 12.7 max(-2.3, -12.7) is -2.3
min(x, y)	smaller value of x and y	min(2.3, 12.7) is 2.3 min(-2.3, -12.7) is -12.7
pow(x, y)	x raised to the power y (i.e., x^y)	pow(2.0, 7.0) is 128.0 pow(9.0, 0.5) is 3.0
sin(x)	trigonometric sine of x (x in radians)	sin(0.0) is 0.0
sqrt(x)	square root of x	sqrt(900.0) is 30.0
tan(x)	trigonometric tangent of x (x in radians)	tan(0.0) is 0.0

Fig. 6.2 | Math class methods. (Part 2 of 2.)

Math Class Constants PI and E

Class Math also declares two fields that represent commonly used mathematical constants: Math.PI and Math.E. The constant Math.PI (3.14159265358979323846) is the ratio of a circle's circumference to its diameter. The constant Math.E (2.7182818284590452354) is the base value for natural logarithms (calculated with static Math method log). These fields are declared in class Math with the modifiers public, final and static. Making them public allows other programmers to use these fields in their own classes. Any field declared with keyword final is constant—its value cannot be changed after the field is initialized. Both PI and E are declared final because their values never change. Making these fields static allows them to be accessed via the class name Math and a dot (.) separator, just like class Math's methods. Recall from Section 3.5 that when each object of a class maintains its own copy of an attribute, the field that represents the attribute is also known as an instance variable—each object (instance) of the class has a separate instance of the variable in memory. There are fields for which each object of a class does not have a separate instance of the field. That is the case with static fields, which are also known as class variables. When objects of a class containing static fields are created, all the objects of that class share one copy of the class's static fields. Together the class variables (i.e., static variables) and instance variables represent the fields of a class. You'll learn more about static fields in Section 8.11.

Why Is Method main Declared static?

Why must main be declared static? When you execute the Java Virtual Machine (JVM) with the java command, the JVM attempts to invoke the main method of the class you specify—when no objects of the class have been created. Declaring main as static allows the JVM to invoke main without creating an instance of the class. Method main is declared with the header:

```
public static void main( String args[] )
```

When you execute your application, you specify its class name as an argument to the command java, as in java *ClassName argument1 argument2* ...

The JVM loads the class specified by *ClassName* and uses that class name to invoke method main. In the preceding command, *ClassName* is a **command-line argument** to the JVM that tells it which class to execute. Following the *ClassName*, you can also specify a list of Strings (separated by spaces) as command-line arguments that the JVM will pass to your application. Such arguments might be used to specify options (e.g., a file name) to run the application. As you'll learn in Chapter 7, Arrays, your application can access those command-line arguments and use them to customize the application.

Additional Comments about Method main

In earlier chapters, every application had one class that contained only main and possibly a second class that was used by main to create and manipulate objects. Actually, any class can contain a main method. In fact, each of our two-class examples could have been implemented as one class. For example, in the application in Fig. 5.9 and Fig. 5.10, method main (lines 6–16 of Fig. 5.10) could have been taken as is and placed in class GradeBook (Fig. 5.9). You would then execute the application by typing the command java Grade-Book in the command window—the application results would be identical to those of the two-class version. You can place a main method in every class you declare. The JVM invokes the main method only in the class used to execute the application. Some programmers take advantage of this to build a small test program into each class they declare.

6.4 Declaring Methods with Multiple Parameters

Chapters 3–5 presented classes containing simple methods that had at most one parameter. Methods often require more than one piece of information to perform their tasks. We now show how to write methods with multiple parameters.

The application in Fig. 6.3 and Fig. 6.4 uses a programmer-declared method called maximum to determine and return the largest of three double values that are input by the user. When the application begins execution, class MaximumFinderTest's main method (lines 7–11 of Fig. 6.4) creates one object of class MaximumFinder (line 9) and calls the object's determineMaximum method (line 10) to produce the program's output. In class MaximumFinder (Fig. 6.3), lines 14–18 of method determineMaximum prompt the user to enter three double values, then read them from the user. Line 21 calls method maximum (declared in lines 28–41) to determine the largest of the three double values passed as arguments to the method. When method maximum returns the result to line 21, the program assigns maximum's return value to local variable result. Then line 24 outputs the maximum value. At the end of this section, we'll discuss the use of operator + in line 24.

```
1   // Fig. 6.3: MaximumFinder.java
2   // Programmer-declared method maximum.
3   import java.util.Scanner;
4
5   public class MaximumFinder
6   {
```

Fig. 6.3 | Programmer-declared method maximum that has three double parameters. (Part 1 of 2.)

```
7     // obtain three floating-point values and locate the maximum value
8     public void determineMaximum()
9     {
10       // create Scanner for input from command window
11       Scanner input = new Scanner( System.in );
12
13       // obtain user input
14       System.out.print(
15          "Enter three floating-point values separated by spaces: " );
16       double number1 = input.nextDouble(); // read first double
17       double number2 = input.nextDouble(); // read second double
18       double number3 = input.nextDouble(); // read third double
19
20       // determine the maximum value
21       double result = maximum( number1, number2, number3 );
22
23       // display maximum value
24       System.out.println( "Maximum is: " + result );
25    } // end method determineMaximum
26
27    // returns the maximum of its three double parameters
28    public double maximum( double x, double y, double z )
29    {
30       double maximumValue = x; // assume x is the largest to start
31
32       // determine whether y is greater than maximumValue
33       if ( y > maximumValue )
34          maximumValue = y;
35
36       // determine whether z is greater than maximumValue
37       if ( z > maximumValue )
38          maximumValue = z;
39
40       return maximumValue;
41    } // end method maximum
42 } // end class MaximumFinder
```

Fig. 6.3 | Programmer-declared method `maximum` that has three `double` parameters. (Part 2 of 2.)

```
1  // Fig. 6.4: MaximumFinderTest.java
2  // Application to test class MaximumFinder.
3
4  public class MaximumFinderTest
5  {
6     // application starting point
7     public static void main( String args[] )
8     {
9        MaximumFinder maximumFinder = new MaximumFinder();
10       maximumFinder.determineMaximum();
11    } // end main
12 } // end class MaximumFinderTest
```

Fig. 6.4 | Application to test class `MaximumFinder`. (Part 1 of 2.)

```
Enter three floating-point values separated by spaces: 9.35 2.74 5.1
Maximum is: 9.35
```

```
Enter three floating-point values separated by spaces: 5.8 12.45 8.32
Maximum is: 12.45
```

```
Enter three floating-point values separated by spaces: 6.46 4.12 10.54
Maximum is: 10.54
```

Fig. 6.4 | Application to test class `MaximumFinder`. (Part 2 of 2.)

Consider the declaration of method `maximum` (lines 28–41). Line 28 indicates that the method returns a `double` value, that the method's name is `maximum` and that the method requires three `double` parameters (x, y and z) to accomplish its task. When a method has more than one parameter, the parameters are specified as a comma-separated list. When maximum is called from line 21, the parameter x is initialized with the value of the argument `number1`, the parameter y is initialized with the value of the argument `number2` and the parameter z is initialized with the value of the argument `number3`. There must be one argument in the method call for each parameter (sometimes called a formal parameter) in the method declaration. Also, each argument must be consistent with the type of the corresponding parameter. For example, a parameter of type `double` can receive values like 7.35, 22 or –0.03456, but not `String`s like "hello" nor the `boolean` values `true` or `false`. Section 6.7 discusses the argument types that can be provided in a method call for each parameter of a primitive type.

To determine the maximum value, we begin with the assumption that parameter x contains the largest value, so line 30 declares local variable `maximumValue` and initializes it with the value of parameter x. Of course, it is possible that parameter y or z contains the actual largest value, so we must compare each of these values with `maximumValue`. The `if` statement at lines 33–34 determines whether y is greater than `maximumValue`. If so, line 34 assigns y to `maximumValue`. The `if` statement at lines 37–38 determines whether z is greater than `maximumValue`. If so, line 38 assigns z to `maximumValue`. At this point the largest of the three values resides in `maximumValue`, so line 40 returns that value to line 21. When program control returns to the point in the program where maximum was called, maximum's parameters x, y and z no longer exist in memory. Note that methods can return at most one value, but the returned value could be a reference to an object that contains many values.

Note that `result` is a local variable in `determineMaximum` because it is declared in the block that represents the method's body. Variables should be declared as fields of a class only if they are required for use in more than one method of the class or if the program should save their values between calls to the class's methods.

Common Programming Error 6.1

Declaring method parameters of the same type as float x, y *instead of* float x, float y *is a syntax error—a type is required for each parameter in the parameter list.*

Software Engineering Observation 6.5

A method that has many parameters may be performing too many tasks. Consider dividing the method into smaller methods that perform the separate tasks. As a guideline, try to fit the method header on one line if possible.

Implementing Method `maximum` by Reusing Method `Math.max`

Recall from Fig. 6.2 that class `Math` has a `max` method that can determine the larger of two values. The entire body of our maximum method could also be implemented with two calls to `Math.max`, as follows:

```
return Math.max( x, Math.max( y, z ) );
```

The first call to `Math.max` specifies arguments x and `Math.max( y, z )`. Before any method can be called, its arguments must be evaluated to determine their values. If an argument is a method call, the method call must be performed to determine its return value. So, in the preceding statement, `Math.max( y, z )` is evaluated first to determine the maximum of y and z. Then the result is passed as the second argument to the other call to `Math.max`, which returns the larger of its two arguments. This is a good example of software reuse—we find the largest of three values by reusing `Math.max`, which finds the largest of two values. Note how concise this code is compared to lines 30–40 of Fig. 6.3.

Assembling Strings with String Concatenation

Java allows `String` objects to be created by assembling smaller strings into larger strings using operator + (or the compound assignment operator +=). This is known as **string concatenation**. When both operands of operator + are `String` objects, operator + creates a new `String` object in which the characters of the right operand are placed at the end of those in the left operand. For example, the expression `"hello "` + `"there"` creates the `String` `"hello there"`.

In line 24 of Fig. 6.3, the expression `"Maximum is: "` + `result` uses operator + with operands of types `String` and `double`. Every primitive value and object in Java has a `String` representation. When one of the + operator's operands is a `String`, the other is converted to a `String`, then the two are concatenated. In line 24, the `double` value is converted to its `String` representation and placed at the end of the `String` `"Maximum is: "`. If there are any trailing zeros in a `double` value, these will be discarded when the number is converted to a `String`. Thus, the number 9.3500 would be represented as 9.35 in the resulting `String`.

For primitive values used in string concatenation, the primitive values are converted to `Strings`. If a `boolean` is concatenated with a `String`, the `boolean` is converted to the `String` `"true"` or `"false"`. All objects have a method named `toString` that returns a `String` representation of the object. When an object is concatenated with a `String`, the object's `toString` method is implicitly called to obtain the `String` representation of the object. You will learn more about the method `toString` in Chapter 7, Arrays.

When a large `String` literal is typed into a program's source code, programmers sometimes prefer to break that `String` into several smaller `Strings` and place them on multiple lines of code for readability. In this case, the `Strings` can be reassembled using concatenation. We discuss the details of `Strings` in Chapter 30, Strings, Characters and Regular Expressions.

Common Programming Error 6.2

It is a syntax error to break a String literal across multiple lines in a program. If a String does not fit on one line, split the String into several smaller Strings and use concatenation to form the desired String.

Common Programming Error 6.3

Confusing the + operator used for string concatenation with the + operator used for addition can lead to strange results. Java evaluates the operands of an operator from left to right. For example, if integer variable y has the value 5, the expression "y + 2 = " + y + 2 results in the string "y + 2 = 52", not "y + 2 = 7", because first the value of y (5) is concatenated with the string "y + 2 = ", then the value 2 is concatenated with the new larger string "y + 2 = 5". The expression "y + 2 = " + (y + 2) produces the desired result "y + 2 = 7".

6.5 Notes on Declaring and Using Methods

There are three ways to call a method:

1. Using a method name by itself to call another method of the same class—such as maximum(number1, number2, number3) in line 21 of Fig. 6.3.

2. Using a variable that contains a reference to an object, followed by a dot (.) and the method name to call a method of the referenced object—such as the method call in line 10 of Fig. 6.4, maximumFinder.determineMaximum(), which calls a method of class MaximumFinder from the main method of MaximumFinderTest.

3. Using the class name and a dot (.) to call a static method of a class—such as Math.sqrt(900.0) in Section 6.3.

Note that a static method can call only other static methods of the same class directly (i.e., using the method name by itself) and can manipulate only static fields in the same class directly. To access the class's non-static members, a static method must use a reference to an object of the class. Recall that static methods relate to a class as a whole, whereas non-static methods are associated with a specific instance (object) of the class and may manipulate the instance variables of that object. Many objects of a class, each with its own copies of the instance variables, may exist at the same time. Suppose a static method were to invoke a non-static method directly. How would the method know which object's instance variables to manipulate? What would happen if no objects of the class existed at the time the non-static method was invoked? Clearly, such a situation would be problematic. Thus, Java does not allow a static method to access non-static members of the same class directly.

There are three ways to return control to the statement that calls a method. If the method does not return a result, control returns when the program flow reaches the method-ending right brace or when the statement

```
return;
```

is executed. If the method returns a result, the statement

```
return expression;
```

evaluates the *expression*, then returns the result to the caller.

Common Programming Error 6.4

Declaring a method outside the body of a class declaration or inside the body of another method is a syntax error.

Common Programming Error 6.5

Omitting the return-value-type *in a method declaration is a syntax error.*

Common Programming Error 6.6

Placing a semicolon after the right parenthesis enclosing the parameter list of a method declaration is a syntax error.

Common Programming Error 6.7

Redeclaring a method parameter as a local variable in the method's body is a compilation error.

Common Programming Error 6.8

Forgetting to return a value from a method that should return a value is a compilation error. If a return-value-type *other than* void *is specified, the method must contain a* return *statement that returns a value consistent with the method's* return-value-type. *Returning a value from a method whose return type has been declared* void *is a compilation error.*

6.6 **Method-Call Stack and Activation Records**

To understand how Java performs method calls, we first need to consider a data structure (i.e., collection of related data items) known as a **stack**. Students can think of a stack as analogous to a pile of dishes. When a dish is placed on the pile, it is normally placed at the top (referred to as **pushing** the dish onto the stack). Similarly, when a dish is removed from the pile, it is always removed from the top (referred to as **popping** the dish off the stack). Stacks are known as **last-in, first-out (LIFO) data structures**—the last item pushed (inserted) on the stack is the first item popped (removed) from the stack.

When a program calls a method, the called method must know how to return to its caller, so the return address of the calling method is pushed onto the **program execution stack** (sometimes referred to as the **method-call stack**). If a series of method calls occurs, the successive return addresses are pushed onto the stack in last-in, first-out order so that each method can return to its caller.

The program execution stack also contains the memory for the local variables used in each invocation of a method during a program's execution. This data, stored as a portion of the program execution stack, is known as the **activation record** or **stack frame** of the method call. When a method call is made, the activation record for that method call is pushed onto the program execution stack. When the method returns to its caller, the activation record for this method call is popped off the stack and those local variables are no longer known to the program. If a local variable holding a reference to an object is the only variable in the program with a reference to that object, when the activation record containing that local variable is popped off the stack, the object can no longer be accessed by the program and will eventually be deleted from memory by the JVM during "garbage collection." We'll discuss garbage collection in Section 8.10.

Of course, the amount of memory in a computer is finite, so only a certain amount of memory can be used to store activation records on the program execution stack. If more method calls occur than can have their activation records stored on the program execution stack, an error known as a **stack overflow** occurs.

6.7 Argument Promotion and Casting

Another important feature of method calls is **argument promotion**—converting an argument's value to the type that the method expects to receive in its corresponding parameter. For example, a program can call Math method sqrt with an integer argument even though the method expects to receive a double argument (but, as we will soon see, not vice versa). The statement

```
System.out.println( Math.sqrt( 4 ) );
```

correctly evaluates Math.sqrt(4) and prints the value 2.0. The method declaration's parameter list causes Java to convert the int value 4 to the double value 4.0 before passing the value to sqrt. Attempting these conversions may lead to compilation errors if Java's **promotion rules** are not satisfied. The promotion rules specify which conversions are allowed—that is, which conversions can be performed without losing data. In the sqrt example above, an int is converted to a double without changing its value. However, converting a double to an int truncates the fractional part of the double value—thus, part of the value is lost. Converting large integer types to small integer types (e.g., long to int) may also result in changed values.

The promotion rules apply to expressions containing values of two or more primitive types and to primitive-type values passed as arguments to methods. Each value is promoted to the "highest" type in the expression. (Actually, the expression uses a temporary copy of each value—the types of the original values remain unchanged.) Figure 6.5 lists the primitive types and the types to which each can be promoted. Note that the valid promotions for a given type are always to a type higher in the table. For example, an int can be promoted to the higher types long, float and double.

Type	Valid promotions
double	None
float	double
long	float or double
int	long, float or double
char	int, long, float or double
short	int, long, float or double (but not char)
byte	short, int, long, float or double (but not char)
boolean	None (boolean values are not considered to be numbers in Java)

Fig. 6.5 | Promotions allowed for primitive types.

Converting values to types lower in the table of Fig. 6.5 will result in different values if the lower type cannot represent the value of the higher type (e.g., the int value 2000000 cannot be represented as a short, and any floating-point number with digits after its decimal point cannot be represented in an integer type such as long, int or short). Therefore, in cases where information may be lost due to conversion, the Java compiler requires you to use a cast operator (introduced in Section 4.9) to explicitly force the conversion to occur—otherwise a compilation error occurs. This enables you to "take control" from the compiler. You essentially say, "I know this conversion might cause loss of information, but for my purposes here, that's fine." Suppose method square calculates the square of an integer and thus requires an int argument. To call square with a double argument named doubleValue, we would be required to write the method call as

```
square( (int) doubleValue )
```

This method call explicitly casts (converts) the value of doubleValue to an integer for use in method square. Thus, if doubleValue's value is 4.5, the method receives the value 4 and returns 16, not 20.25.

 Common Programming Error 6.9

Converting a primitive-type value to another primitive type may change the value if the new type is not a valid promotion. For example, converting a floating-point value to an integral value may introduce truncation errors (loss of the fractional part) into the result.

6.8 Java API Packages

As we have seen, Java contains many predefined classes that are grouped into categories of related classes called packages. Together, we refer to these packages as the Java Application Programming Interface (Java API), or the Java class library.

Throughout the text, import declarations specify the classes required to compile a Java program. For example, a program includes the declaration

```
import java.util.Scanner;
```

to specify that the program uses class Scanner from the java.util package. This allows you to use the simple class name Scanner, rather than the fully qualified class name java.util.Scanner, in the code. A great strength of Java is the large number of classes in the packages of the Java API. Some key Java API packages are described in Fig. 6.6, which represents only a small portion of the reusable components in the Java API. When learning Java, spend a portion of your time browsing the packages and classes in the Java API documentation (java.sun.com/javase/6/docs/api/).

The set of packages available in Java SE 6 is quite large. In addition to the packages summarized in Fig. 6.6, Java SE 6 includes packages for complex graphics, advanced graphical user interfaces, printing, advanced networking, security, database processing, multimedia, accessibility (for people with disabilities) and many other capabilities. For an overview of the packages in Java SE 6, visit

```
java.sun.com/javase/6/docs/api/overview-summary.html
```

Many other packages are also available for download at java.sun.com.

Package	Description
`java.applet`	The Java Applet Package contains a class and several interfaces required to create Java applets—programs that execute in Web browsers. (Applets are discussed in Chapter 20, Introduction to Java Applets; interfaces are discussed in Chapter 10, Object-Oriented Programming: Polymorphism.)
`java.awt`	The Java Abstract Window Toolkit Package contains the classes and interfaces required to create and manipulate GUIs in Java 1.0 and 1.1. In current versions of Java, the Swing GUI components of the `javax.swing` packages are often used instead. (Some elements of the `java.awt` package are discussed in Chapter 11, GUI Components: Part 1, Chapter 12, Graphics and Java 2D™, and Chapter 22, GUI Components: Part 2.)
`java.awt.event`	The Java Abstract Window Toolkit Event Package contains classes and interfaces that enable event handling for GUI components in both the `java.awt` and `javax.swing` packages. (You'll learn more about this package in Chapter 11, GUI Components: Part 1 and Chapter 22, GUI Components: Part 2.)
`java.io`	The Java Input/Output Package contains classes and interfaces that enable programs to input and output data. (You will learn more about this package in Chapter 14, Files and Streams.)
`java.lang`	The Java Language Package contains classes and interfaces (discussed throughout this text) that are required by many Java programs. This package is imported by the compiler into all programs, so you do not need to do so.
`java.net`	The Java Networking Package contains classes and interfaces that enable programs to communicate via computer networks like the Internet. (You will learn more about this in Chapter 24, Networking.)
`java.text`	The Java Text Package contains classes and interfaces that enable programs to manipulate numbers, dates, characters and strings. The package provides internationalization capabilities that enable a program to be customized to a specific locale (e.g., a program may display strings in different languages, based on the user's country).
`java.util`	The Java Utilities Package contains utility classes and interfaces that enable such actions as date and time manipulations, random-number processing (class `Random`), the storing and processing of large amounts of data and the breaking of strings into smaller pieces called tokens (class `StringTokenizer`). (You will learn more about the features of this package in Chapter 19, Collections.)

Fig. 6.6 | Java API packages (a subset). (Part 1 of 2.)

Package	Description
`javax.swing`	The Java Swing GUI Components Package contains classes and interfaces for Java's Swing GUI components that provide support for portable GUIs. (You will learn more about this package in Chapter 11, GUI Components: Part 1 and Chapter 22, GUI Components: Part 2.)
`javax.swing.event`	The Java Swing Event Package contains classes and interfaces that enable event handling (e.g., responding to button clicks) for GUI components in package `javax.swing`. (You will learn more about this package in Chapter 11, GUI Components: Part 1 and Chapter 22, GUI Components: Part 2.)

Fig. 6.6 | Java API packages (a subset). (Part 2 of 2.)

You can locate additional information about a predefined Java class's methods in the Java API documentation at java.sun.com/javase/6/docs/api/. When you visit this site, click the **Index** link to see an alphabetical listing of all the classes and methods in the Java API. Locate the class name and click its link to see the online description of the class. Click the **METHOD** link to see a table of the class's methods. Each `static` method will be listed with the word `"static"` preceding the method's return type. For a more detailed overview of navigating the Java API documentation, see Appendix J, Using the Java API Documentation.

Good Programming Practice 6.2

The online Java API documentation is easy to search and provides many details about each class. As you learn a class in this book, you should get in the habit of looking at the class in the online documentation for additional information.

6.9 Case Study: Random-Number Generation

We now take a brief and, hopefully, entertaining diversion into a popular type of programming application—simulation and game playing. In this and the next section, we develop a nicely structured game-playing program with multiple methods. The program uses most of the control statements presented thus far in the book and introduces several new programming concepts.

There is something in the air of a casino that invigorates people—from the high rollers at the plush mahogany-and-felt craps tables to the quarter poppers at the one-armed bandits. It is the element of chance, the possibility that luck will convert a pocketful of money into a mountain of wealth. The element of chance can be introduced in a program via an object of class Random (package java.util) or via the `static` method random of class Math. Objects of class Random can produce random `boolean`, `byte`, `float`, `double`, `int`, `long` and Gaussian values, whereas Math method random can produce only `double` values in the range $0.0 \leq x < 1.0$, where x is the value returned by method random. In the next several examples, we use objects of class Random to produce random values.

A new random-number generator object can be created as follows:

```
Random randomNumbers = new Random();
```

The random-number generator object can then be used to generate random boolean, byte, float, double, int, long and Gaussian values—we discuss only random int values here. For more information on the Random class, see java.sun.com/javase/6/docs/api/java/util/Random.html.

Consider the following statement:

```
int randomValue = randomNumbers.nextInt();
```

Method nextInt of class Random generates a random int value from –2,147,483,648 to +2,147,483,647. If the nextInt method truly produces values at random, then every value in that range should have an equal chance (or probability) of being chosen each time method nextInt is called. The values returned by nextInt are actually **pseudorandom** numbers—a sequence of values produced by a complex mathematical calculation. The calculation uses the current time of day (which, of course, changes constantly) to **seed** the random-number generator such that each execution of a program yields a different sequence of random values.

The range of values produced directly by method nextInt often differs from the range of values required in a particular Java application. For example, a program that simulates coin tossing might require only 0 for "heads" and 1 for "tails." A program that simulates the rolling of a six-sided die might require random integers in the range 1–6. A program that randomly predicts the next type of spaceship (out of four possibilities) that will fly across the horizon in a video game might require random integers in the range 1–4. For cases like these, class Random provides another version of method nextInt that receives an int argument and returns a value from 0 up to, but not including, the argument's value. For example, to simulate coin tossing, you might use the statement

```
int randomValue = randomNumbers.nextInt( 2 );
```

which returns 0 or 1.

Rolling a Six-Sided Die

To demonstrate random numbers, let us develop a program that simulates 20 rolls of a six-sided die and displays the value of each roll. We begin by using nextInt to produce random values in the range 0–5, as follows:

```
face = randomNumbers.nextInt( 6 );
```

The argument 6—called the **scaling** factor—represents the number of unique values that nextInt should produce (in this case six—0, 1, 2, 3, 4 and 5). This manipulation is called **scaling** the range of values produced by Random method nextInt.

A six-sided die has the numbers 1–6 on its faces, not 0–5. So we **shift** the range of numbers produced by adding a **shifting value**—in this case 1—to our previous result, as in

```
face = 1 + randomNumbers.nextInt( 6 );
```

The shifting value (1) specifies the first value in the desired set of random integers. The preceding statement assigns face a random integer in the range 1–6.

Figure 6.7 shows two sample outputs which confirm that the results of the preceding calculation are integers in the range 1–6, and that each run of the program can produce a different sequence of random numbers. Line 3 imports class Random from the java.util package. Line 9 creates the Random object randomNumbers to produce random values. Line 16 executes 20 times in a loop to roll the die. The if statement (lines 21–22) in the loop starts a new line of output after every five numbers.

Rolling a Six-Sided Die 6000 Times

To show that the numbers produced by nextInt occur with approximately equal likelihood, let us simulate 6000 rolls of a die with the application in Fig. 6.8. Each integer from 1 to 6 should appear approximately 1000 times.

```
1   // Fig. 6.7: RandomIntegers.java
2   // Shifted and scaled random integers.
3   import java.util.Random; // program uses class Random
4
5   public class RandomIntegers
6   {
7       public static void main( String args[] )
8       {
9           Random randomNumbers = new Random(); // random number generator
10          int face; // stores each random integer generated
11
12          // loop 20 times
13          for ( int counter = 1; counter <= 20; counter++ )
14          {
15              // pick random integer from 1 to 6
16              face = 1 + randomNumbers.nextInt( 6 );
17
18              System.out.printf( "%d  ", face ); // display generated value
19
20              // if counter is divisible by 5, start a new line of output
21              if ( counter % 5 == 0 )
22                  System.out.println();
23          } // end for
24      } // end main
25  } // end class RandomIntegers
```

```
1  5  3  6  2
5  2  6  5  2
4  4  4  2  6
3  1  6  2  2
```

```
6  5  4  2  6
1  2  5  1  3
6  3  2  2  1
6  4  2  6  4
```

Fig. 6.7 | Shifted and scaled random integers.

As the two sample outputs show, scaling and shifting the values produced by method `nextInt` enables the program to realistically simulate rolling a six-sided die. The application uses nested control statements (the `switch` is nested inside the `for`) to determine the number of times each side of the die occurred. The `for` statement (lines 21–47) iterates 6000 times. During each iteration, line 23 produces a random value from 1 to 6. That value is then used as the controlling expression (line 26) of the `switch` statement (lines 26–46). Based on the `face` value, the `switch` statement increments one of the six counter variables during each iteration of the loop. When we study arrays in Chapter 7, we will show an elegant way to replace the entire `switch` statement in this program with a single statement! Note that the `switch` statement has no `default` case, because we have a `case` for every possible die value that the expression in line 23 could produce. Run the program several times, and observe the results. As you will see, every time you execute this program, it produces different results.

```java
1   // Fig. 6.8: RollDie.java
2   // Roll a six-sided die 6000 times.
3   import java.util.Random;
4
5   public class RollDie
6   {
7      public static void main( String args[] )
8      {
9         Random randomNumbers = new Random(); // random number generator
10
11        int frequency1 = 0; // maintains count of 1s rolled
12        int frequency2 = 0; // count of 2s rolled
13        int frequency3 = 0; // count of 3s rolled
14        int frequency4 = 0; // count of 4s rolled
15        int frequency5 = 0; // count of 5s rolled
16        int frequency6 = 0; // count of 6s rolled
17
18        int face; // stores most recently rolled value
19
20        // summarize results of 6000 rolls of a die
21        for ( int roll = 1; roll <= 6000; roll++ )
22        {
23           face = 1 + randomNumbers.nextInt( 6 ); // number from 1 to 6
24
25           // determine roll value 1-6 and increment appropriate counter
26           switch ( face )
27           {
28              case 1:
29                 ++frequency1; // increment the 1s counter
30                 break;
31              case 2:
32                 ++frequency2; // increment the 2s counter
33                 break;
34              case 3:
35                 ++frequency3; // increment the 3s counter
36                 break;
```

Fig. 6.8 | Rolling a six-sided die 6000 times. (Part 1 of 2.)

```
37                    case 4:
38                        ++frequency4; // increment the 4s counter
39                        break;
40                    case 5:
41                        ++frequency5; // increment the 5s counter
42                        break;
43                    case 6:
44                        ++frequency6; // increment the 6s counter
45                        break; // optional at end of switch
46                } // end switch
47            } // end for
48
49        System.out.println( "Face\tFrequency" ); // output headers
50        System.out.printf( "1\t%d\n2\t%d\n3\t%d\n4\t%d\n5\t%d\n6\t%d\n",
51            frequency1, frequency2, frequency3, frequency4,
52            frequency5, frequency6 );
53    } // end main
54 } // end class RollDie
```

Face	Frequency
1	982
2	1001
3	1015
4	1005
5	1009
6	988

Face	Frequency
1	1029
2	994
3	1017
4	1007
5	972
6	981

Fig. 6.8 | Rolling a six-sided die 6000 times. (Part 2 of 2.)

6.9.1 Generalized Scaling and Shifting of Random Numbers

Previously, we demonstrated the statement

```
face = 1 + randomNumbers.nextInt( 6 );
```

which simulates the rolling of a six-sided die. This statement always assigns to variable face an integer in the range 1 ≤ face ≤ 6. The width of this range (i.e., the number of consecutive integers in the range) is 6, and the starting number in the range is 1. Referring to the preceding statement, we see that the width of the range is determined by the number 6 that is passed as an argument to Random method nextInt, and the starting number of the range is the number 1 that is added to randomNumberGenerator.nextInt(6). We can generalize this result as

```
number = shiftingValue + randomNumbers.nextInt( scalingFactor );
```

where *shiftingValue* specifies the first number in the desired range of consecutive integers and *scalingFactor* specifies how many numbers are in the range.

It is also possible to choose integers at random from sets of values other than ranges of consecutive integers. For example, to obtain a random value from the sequence 2, 5, 8, 11 and 14, you could use the statement

```
number = 2 + 3 * randomNumbers.nextInt( 5 );
```

In this case, `randomNumberGenerator.nextInt( 5 )` produces values in the range 0–4. Each value produced is multiplied by 3 to produce a number in the sequence 0, 3, 6, 9 and 12. We then add 2 to that value to shift the range of values and obtain a value from the sequence 2, 5, 8, 11 and 14. We can generalize this result as

```
number = shiftingValue +
         differenceBetweenValues * randomNumbers.nextInt( scalingFactor );
```

where *shiftingValue* specifies the first number in the desired range of values, *differenceBetweenValues* represents the difference between consecutive numbers in the sequence and *scalingFactor* specifies how many numbers are in the range.

6.9.2 Random-Number Repeatability for Testing and Debugging

As we mentioned earlier in Section 6.9, the methods of class `Random` actually generate pseudorandom numbers based on complex mathematical calculations. Repeatedly calling any of `Random`'s methods produces a sequence of numbers that appears to be random. The calculation that produces the pseudorandom numbers uses the time of day as a seed value to change the sequence's starting point. Each new `Random` object seeds itself with a value based on the computer system's clock at the time the object is created, enabling each execution of a program to produce a different sequence of random numbers.

When debugging an application, it is sometimes useful to repeat the exact same sequence of pseudorandom numbers during each execution of the program. This repeatability enables you to prove that your application is working for a specific sequence of random numbers before you test the program with different sequences of random numbers. When repeatability is important, you can create a `Random` object as follows:

```
Random randomNumbers = new Random( seedValue );
```

The `seedValue` argument (of type `long`) seeds the random-number calculation. If the same `seedValue` is used every time, the `Random` object produces the same sequence of random numbers. You can set a `Random` object's seed at any time during program execution by calling the object's `setSeed` method, as in

```
randomNumbers.setSeed( seedValue );
```

Error-Prevention Tip 6.2

While a program is under development, create the `Random` object with a specific seed value to produce a repeatable sequence of random numbers each time the program executes. If a logic error occurs, fix the error and test the program again with the same seed value—this allows you to reconstruct the same sequence of random numbers that caused the error. Once the logic errors have been removed, create the `Random` object without using a seed value, causing the `Random` object to generate a new sequence of random numbers each time the program executes.

6.10 Case Study: A Game of Chance (Introducing Enumerations)

A popular game of chance is a dice game known as craps, which is played in casinos and back alleys throughout the world. The rules of the game are straightforward:

> *You roll two dice. Each die has six faces, which contain one, two, three, four, five and six spots, respectively. After the dice have come to rest, the sum of the spots on the two upward faces is calculated. If the sum is 7 or 11 on the first throw, you win. If the sum is 2, 3 or 12 on the first throw (called "craps"), you lose (i.e., the "house" wins). If the sum is 4, 5, 6, 8, 9 or 10 on the first throw, that sum becomes your "point." To win, you must continue rolling the dice until you "make your point" (i.e., roll that same point value). You lose by rolling a 7 before making the point.*

The application in Fig. 6.9 and Fig. 6.10 simulates the game of craps, using methods to define the logic of the game. In the main method of class CrapsTest (Fig. 6.10), line 8 creates an object of class Craps (Fig. 6.9) and line 9 calls its play method to start the game. The play method (Fig. 6.9, lines 21–65) calls the rollDice method (Fig. 6.9, lines 68–81) as necessary to roll the two dice and compute their sum. Four sample outputs in Fig. 6.10 show winning on the first roll, losing on the first roll, winning on a subsequent roll and losing on a subsequent roll, respectively.

```java
 1   // Fig. 6.9: Craps.java
 2   // Craps class simulates the dice game craps.
 3   import java.util.Random;
 4
 5   public class Craps
 6   {
 7      // create random number generator for use in method rollDice
 8      private Random randomNumbers = new Random();
 9
10      // enumeration with constants that represent the game status
11      private enum Status { CONTINUE, WON, LOST };
12
13      // constants that represent common rolls of the dice
14      private final static int SNAKE_EYES = 2;
15      private final static int TREY = 3;
16      private final static int SEVEN = 7;
17      private final static int YO_LEVEN = 11;
18      private final static int BOX_CARS = 12;
19
20      // plays one game of craps
21      public void play()
22      {
23         int myPoint = 0; // point if no win or loss on first roll
24         Status gameStatus; // can contain CONTINUE, WON or LOST
25
26         int sumOfDice = rollDice(); // first roll of the dice
27
28         // determine game status and point based on first roll
29         switch ( sumOfDice )
30         {
```

Fig. 6.9 | Craps class simulates the dice game craps. (Part 1 of 2.)

```
31          case SEVEN: // win with 7 on first roll
32          case YO_LEVEN: // win with 11 on first roll
33             gameStatus = Status.WON;
34             break;
35          case SNAKE_EYES: // lose with 2 on first roll
36          case TREY: // lose with 3 on first roll
37          case BOX_CARS: // lose with 12 on first roll
38             gameStatus = Status.LOST;
39             break;
40          default: // did not win or lose, so remember point
41             gameStatus = Status.CONTINUE; // game is not over
42             myPoint = sumOfDice; // remember the point
43             System.out.printf( "Point is %d\n", myPoint );
44             break; // optional at end of switch
45       } // end switch
46
47       // while game is not complete
48       while ( gameStatus == Status.CONTINUE ) // not WON or LOST
49       {
50          sumOfDice = rollDice(); // roll dice again
51
52          // determine game status
53          if ( sumOfDice == myPoint ) // win by making point
54             gameStatus = Status.WON;
55          else
56             if ( sumOfDice == SEVEN ) // lose by rolling 7 before point
57                gameStatus = Status.LOST;
58       } // end while
59
60       // display won or lost message
61       if ( gameStatus == Status.WON )
62          System.out.println( "Player wins" );
63       else
64          System.out.println( "Player loses" );
65    } // end method play
66
67    // roll dice, calculate sum and display results
68    public int rollDice()
69    {
70       // pick random die values
71       int die1 = 1 + randomNumbers.nextInt( 6 ); // first die roll
72       int die2 = 1 + randomNumbers.nextInt( 6 ); // second die roll
73
74       int sum = die1 + die2; // sum of die values
75
76       // display results of this roll
77       System.out.printf( "Player rolled %d + %d = %d\n",
78          die1, die2, sum );
79
80       return sum; // return sum of dice
81    } // end method rollDice
82 } // end class Craps
```

Fig. 6.9 | Craps class simulates the dice game craps. (Part 2 of 2.)

```
1   // Fig. 6.10: CrapsTest.java
2   // Application to test class Craps.
3
4   public class CrapsTest
5   {
6      public static void main( String args[] )
7      {
8         Craps game = new Craps();
9         game.play(); // play one game of craps
10      } // end main
11   } // end class CrapsTest
```

```
Player rolled 5 + 6 = 11
Player wins
```

```
Player rolled 1 + 2 = 3
Player loses
```

```
Player rolled 5 + 4 = 9
Point is 9
Player rolled 2 + 2 = 4
Player rolled 2 + 6 = 8
Player rolled 4 + 2 = 6
Player rolled 3 + 6 = 9
Player wins
```

```
Player rolled 2 + 6 = 8
Point is 8
Player rolled 5 + 1 = 6
Player rolled 2 + 1 = 3
Player rolled 1 + 6 = 7
Player loses
```

Fig. 6.10 | Application to test class Craps.

Let's discuss the declaration of class Craps in Fig. 6.9. In the rules of the game, the player must roll two dice on the first roll, and must do the same on all subsequent rolls. We declare method rollDice (lines 68–81) to roll the dice and compute and print their sum. Method rollDice is declared once, but it is called from two places (lines 26 and 50) in method play, which contains the logic for one complete game of craps. Method roll-Dice takes no arguments, so it has an empty parameter list. Each time it is called, rollDice returns the sum of the dice, so the return type int is indicated in the method header (line 68). Although lines 71 and 72 look the same (except for the die names), they do not necessarily produce the same result. Each of these statements produces a random value in the range 1–6. Note that randomNumbers (used in lines 71–72) is not declared in the method. Rather it is declared as a private instance variable of the class and initialized in line 8. This enables us to create one Random object that is reused in each call to rollDice.

The game is reasonably involved. The player may win or lose on the first roll, or may win or lose on any subsequent roll. Method play (lines 21–65) uses local variable myPoint (line 23) to store the "point" if the player does not win or lose on the first roll, local variable gameStatus (line 24) to keep track of the overall game status and local variable sumOfDice (line 26) to hold the sum of the dice for the most recent roll. Note that myPoint is initialized to 0 to ensure that the application will compile. If you do not initialize myPoint, the compiler issues an error, because myPoint is not assigned a value in every case of the switch statement, and thus the program could try to use myPoint before it is assigned a value. By contrast, gameStatus does not require initialization because it *is* assigned a value in every case of the switch statement—thus, it is guaranteed to be initialized before it is used.

Note that local variable gameStatus (line 24) is declared to be of a new type called Status, which we declared at line 11. Type Status is declared as a private member of class Craps, because Status will be used only in that class. Status is a programmer-declared type called an **enumeration**, which, in its simplest form, declares a set of constants represented by identifiers. An enumeration is a special kind of class that is introduced by the keyword enum and a type name (in this case, Status). As with any class, braces ({ and }) delimit the body of an enum declaration. Inside the braces is a comma-separated list of **enumeration constants**, each representing a unique value. The identifiers in an enum must be unique. (You will learn more about enumerations in Chapter 8.)

Good Programming Practice 6.3

Use only uppercase letters in the names of enumeration constants. This makes the constants stand out and reminds you that enumeration constants are not variables.

Variables of type Status can be assigned only one of the three constants declared in the enumeration (line 11) or a compilation error will occur. When the game is won, the program sets local variable gameStatus to Status.WON (lines 33 and 54). When the game is lost, the program sets local variable gameStatus to Status.LOST (lines 38 and 57). Otherwise, the program sets local variable gameStatus to Status.CONTINUE (line 41) to indicate that the game is not over and the dice must be rolled again.

Good Programming Practice 6.4

Using enumeration constants (like Status.WON, Status.LOST and Status.CONTINUE) rather than literal integer values (such as 0, 1 and 2) can make programs easier to read and maintain.

Line 26 in method play calls rollDice, which picks two random values from 1 to 6, displays the value of the first die, the value of the second die and the sum of the dice, and returns the sum of the dice. Method play next enters the switch statement at lines 29–45, which uses the sumOfDice value from line 26 to determine whether the game has been won or lost, or whether it should continue with another roll. The sums of the dice that would result in a win or loss on the first roll are declared as public final static int constants in lines 14–18. These are used in the cases of the switch statement. The identifier names use casino parlance for these sums. Note that these constants, like enum constants, are declared with all capital letters by convention, to make them stand out in the program. Lines 31–34 determine whether the player won on the first roll with SEVEN (7) or YO_LEVEN (11). Lines 35–39 determine whether the player lost on the first roll with SNAKE_EYES (2), TREY (3), or BOX_CARS (12). After the first roll, if the game is not over, the default case (lines 40–44) sets gameStatus to Status.CONTINUE, saves sumOfDice in myPoint and displays the point.

If we are still trying to "make our point" (i.e., the game is continuing from a prior roll), the loop in lines 48–58 executes. Line 50 rolls the dice again. In line 53, if sumOfDice matches myPoint, line 54 sets gameStatus to Status.WON, then the loop terminates because the game is complete. In line 56, if sumOfDice is equal to SEVEN (7), line 57 sets gameStatus to Status.LOST, and the loop terminates because the game is complete. When the game completes, lines 61–64 display a message indicating whether the player won or lost, and the program terminates.

Note the use of the various program-control mechanisms we have discussed. The Craps class in concert with class CrapsTest uses two methods—main, play (called from main) and rollDice (called twice from play)—and the switch, while, if...else and nested if control statements. Note also the use of multiple case labels in the switch statement to execute the same statements for sums of SEVEN and YO_LEVEN (lines 31–32) and for sums of SNAKE_EYES, TREY and BOX_CARS (lines 35–37).

You might be wondering why we declared the sums of the dice as public final static int constants rather than as enum constants. The answer lies in the fact that the program must compare the int variable sumOfDice (line 26) to these constants to determine the outcome of each roll. Suppose we were to declare enum Sum containing constants (e.g., Sum.SNAKE_EYES) representing the five sums used in the game, then use these constants in the cases of the switch statement (lines 29–45). Doing so would prevent us from using sumOfDice as the switch statement's controlling expression, because Java does not allow an int to be compared to an enumeration constant. To achieve the same functionality as the current program, we would have to use a variable currentSum of type Sum as the switch's controlling expression. Unfortunately, Java does not provide an easy way to convert an int value to a particular enum constant. Translating an int into an enum constant could be done with a separate switch statement. Clearly this would be cumbersome and not improve the readability of the program (thus defeating the purpose of using an enum).

6.11 **Scope of Declarations**

You have seen declarations of various Java entities, such as classes, methods, variables and parameters. Declarations introduce names that can be used to refer to such Java entities. The scope of a declaration is the portion of the program that can refer to the declared entity by its name. Such an entity is said to be "in scope" for that portion of the program. This section introduces several important scope issues. (For more scope information, see the *Java Language Specification, Section 6.3: Scope of a Declaration*, at java.sun.com/docs/books/jls/second_edition/html/names.doc.html#103228.)

The basic scope rules are as follows:

1. The scope of a parameter declaration is the body of the method in which the declaration appears.

2. The scope of a local-variable declaration is from the point at which the declaration appears to the end of that block.

3. The scope of a local-variable declaration that appears in the initialization section of a for statement's header is the body of the for statement and the other expressions in the header.

4. The scope of a method or field of a class is the entire body of the class. This enables non-static methods of a class to use the class's fields and other methods.

Any block may contain variable declarations. If a local variable or parameter in a method has the same name as a field, the field is "hidden" until the block terminates execution—this is called shadowing. In Chapter 8, we discuss how to access shadowed fields.

Common Programming Error 6.10

A compilation error occurs when a local variable is declared more than once in a method.

Error-Prevention Tip 6.3

Use different names for fields and local variables to help prevent subtle logic errors that occur when a method is called and a local variable of the method shadows a field of the same name in the class.

The application in Fig. 6.11 and Fig. 6.12 demonstrates scoping issues with fields and local variables. When the application begins execution, class ScopeTest's main method (Fig. 6.12, lines 7–11) creates an object of class Scope (line 9) and calls the object's begin method (line 10) to produce the program's output (shown in Fig. 6.12).

```java
 1  // Fig. 6.11: Scope.java
 2  // Scope class demonstrates field and local variable scopes.
 3
 4  public class Scope
 5  {
 6     // field that is accessible to all methods of this class
 7     private int x = 1;
 8
 9     // method begin creates and initializes local variable x
10     // and calls methods useLocalVariable and useField
11     public void begin()
12     {
13        int x = 5; // method's local variable x shadows field x
14
15        System.out.printf( "local x in method begin is %d\n", x );
16
17        useLocalVariable(); // useLocalVariable has local x
18        useField(); // useField uses class Scope's field x
19        useLocalVariable(); // useLocalVariable reinitializes local x
20        useField(); // class Scope's field x retains its value
21
22        System.out.printf( "\nlocal x in method begin is %d\n", x );
23     } // end method begin
24
25     // create and initialize local variable x during each call
26     public void useLocalVariable()
27     {
28        int x = 25; // initialized each time useLocalVariable is called
29
30        System.out.printf(
31           "\nlocal x on entering method useLocalVariable is %d\n", x );
32        ++x; // modifies this method's local variable x
```

Fig. 6.11 | Scope class demonstrating scopes of a field and local variables. (Part 1 of 2.)

```
33          System.out.printf(
34              "local x before exiting method useLocalVariable is %d\n", x );
35      } // end method useLocalVariable
36
37      // modify class Scope's field x during each call
38      public void useField()
39      {
40          System.out.printf(
41              "\nfield x on entering method useField is %d\n", x );
42          x *= 10; // modifies class Scope's field x
43          System.out.printf(
44              "field x before exiting method useField is %d\n", x );
45      } // end method useField
46  } // end class Scope
```

Fig. 6.11 | Scope class demonstrating scopes of a field and local variables. (Part 2 of 2.)

```
1   // Fig. 6.12: ScopeTest.java
2   // Application to test class Scope.
3
4   public class ScopeTest
5   {
6       // application starting point
7       public static void main( String args[] )
8       {
9           Scope testScope = new Scope();
10          testScope.begin();
11      } // end main
12  } // end class ScopeTest
```

```
local x in method begin is 5

local x on entering method useLocalVariable is 25
local x before exiting method useLocalVariable is 26

field x on entering method useField is 1
field x before exiting method useField is 10

local x on entering method useLocalVariable is 25
local x before exiting method useLocalVariable is 26

field x on entering method useField is 10
field x before exiting method useField is 100

local x in method begin is 5
```

Fig. 6.12 | Application to test class Scope.

In class Scope, line 7 declares and initializes the field x to 1. This field is shadowed (hidden) in any block (or method) that declares a local variable named x. Method begin (lines 11–23) declares a local variable x (line 13) and initializes it to 5. This local variable's value is output to show that the field x (whose value is 1) is shadowed in method begin. The program declares two other methods—useLocalVariable (lines 26–35) and use-Field (lines 38–45)—that each take no arguments and do not return results. Method begin calls each method twice (lines 17–20). Method useLocalVariable declares local variable x (line 28). When useLocalVariable is first called (line 17), it creates local variable x and initializes it to 25 (line 28), outputs the value of x (lines 30–31), increments x (line 32) and outputs the value of x again (lines 33–34). When useLocalVariable is called a second time (line 19), it re-creates local variable x and re-initializes it to 25, so the output of each useLocalVariable call is identical.

Method useField does not declare any local variables. Therefore, when it refers to x, field x (line 7) of the class is used. When method useField is first called (line 18), it outputs the value (1) of field x (lines 40–41), multiplies the field x by 10 (line 42) and outputs the value (10) of field x again (lines 43–44) before returning. The next time method use-Field is called (line 20), the field has its modified value, 10, so the method outputs 10, then 100. Finally, in method begin, the program outputs the value of local variable x again (line 22) to show that none of the method calls modified begin's local variable x, because the methods all referred to variables named x in other scopes.

6.12 Method Overloading

Methods of the same name can be declared in the same class, as long as they have different sets of parameters (determined by the number, types and order of the parameters)—this is called method overloading. When an overloaded method is called, the Java compiler selects the appropriate method by examining the number, types and order of the arguments in the call. Method overloading is commonly used to create several methods with the same name that perform the same or similar tasks, but on different types or different numbers of arguments. For example, Math methods abs, min and max (summarized in Section 6.3) are overloaded with four versions each:

1. One with two double parameters.
2. One with two float parameters.
3. One with two int parameters.
4. One with two long parameters.

Our next example demonstrates declaring and invoking overloaded methods. We present examples of overloaded constructors in Chapter 8.

Declaring Overloaded Methods

In our class MethodOverload (Fig. 6.13), we include two overloaded versions of a method called square—one that calculates the square of an int (and returns an int) and one that calculates the square of a double (and returns a double). Although these methods have the same name and similar parameter lists and bodies, you can think of them simply as *different* methods. It may help to think of the method names as "square of int" and "square of double," respectively. When the application begins execution, class MethodOver-loadTest's main method (Fig. 6.14, lines 6–10) creates an object of class MethodOverload (line 8) and calls the object's method testOverloadedMethods (line 9) to produce the program's output (Fig. 6.14).

```
1   // Fig. 6.13: MethodOverload.java
2   // Overloaded method declarations.
3
4   public class MethodOverload
5   {
6      // test overloaded square methods
7      public void testOverloadedMethods()
8      {
9         System.out.printf( "Square of integer 7 is %d\n", square( 7 ) );
10        System.out.printf( "Square of double 7.5 is %f\n", square( 7.5 ) );
11     } // end method testOverloadedMethods
12
13     // square method with int argument
14     public int square( int intValue )
15     {
16        System.out.printf( "\nCalled square with int argument: %d\n",
17           intValue );
18        return intValue * intValue;
19     } // end method square with int argument
20
21     // square method with double argument
22     public double square( double doubleValue )
23     {
24        System.out.printf( "\nCalled square with double argument: %f\n",
25           doubleValue );
26        return doubleValue * doubleValue;
27     } // end method square with double argument
28  } // end class MethodOverload
```

Fig. 6.13 | Overloaded method declarations.

```
1   // Fig. 6.14: MethodOverloadTest.java
2   // Application to test class MethodOverload.
3
4   public class MethodOverloadTest
5   {
6      public static void main( String args[] )
7      {
8         MethodOverload methodOverload = new MethodOverload();
9         methodOverload.testOverloadedMethods();
10     } // end main
11  } // end class MethodOverloadTest
```

```
Called square with int argument: 7
Square of integer 7 is 49

Called square with double argument: 7.500000
Square of double 7.5 is 56.250000
```

Fig. 6.14 | Application to test class MethodOverload.

In Fig. 6.13, line 9 invokes method `square` with the argument 7. Literal integer values are treated as type `int`, so the method call in line 9 invokes the version of `square` at lines 14–19 that specifies an `int` parameter. Similarly, line 10 invokes method `square` with the argument 7.5. Literal floating-point values are treated as type `double`, so the method call in line 10 invokes the version of `square` at lines 22–27 that specifies a `double` parameter. Each method first outputs a line of text to prove that the proper method was called in each case. Note that the values in lines 10 and 24 are displayed with the format specifier %f and that we did not specify a precision in either case. By default, floating-point values are displayed with six digits of precision if the precision is not specified in the format specifier.

Distinguishing Between Overloaded Methods

The compiler distinguishes overloaded methods by their signature—a combination of the method's name and the number, types and order of its parameters. If the compiler looked only at method names during compilation, the code in Fig. 6.13 would be ambiguous— the compiler would not know how to distinguish between the two `square` methods (lines 14–19 and 22–27). Internally, the compiler uses longer method names that include the original method name, the types of each parameter and the exact order of the parameters to determine whether the methods in a class are unique in that class.

For example, in Fig. 6.13, the compiler might use the logical name "square of int" for the `square` method that specifies an `int` parameter and "square of double" for the `square` method that specifies a `double` parameter (the actual names the compiler uses are messier). If `method1`'s declaration begins as

```
void method1( int a, float b )
```

then the compiler might use the logical name "`method1` of `int` and `float`." If the parameters are specified as

```
void method1( float a, int b )
```

then the compiler might use the logical name "`method1` of `float` and `int`." Note that the order of the parameter types is important—the compiler considers the preceding two `method1` headers to be distinct.

Return Types of Overloaded Methods

In discussing the logical names of methods used by the compiler, we did not mention the return types of the methods. This is because method *calls* cannot be distinguished by return type. The program in Fig. 6.15 illustrates the compiler errors generated when two methods have the same signature and different return types. Overloaded methods can have different return types if the methods have different parameter lists. Also, overloaded methods need not have the same number of parameters.

```
1   // Fig. 6.15: MethodOverloadError.java
2   // Overloaded methods with identical signatures
3   // cause compilation errors, even if return types are different.
```

Fig. 6.15 | Overloaded method declarations with identical signatures cause compilation errors, even if the return types are different. (Part 1 of 2.)

```
4
5    public class MethodOverloadError
6    {
7        // declaration of method square with int argument
8        public int square( int x )
9        {
10           return x * x;
11       }
12
13       // second declaration of method square with int argument
14       // causes compilation error even though return types are different
15       public double square( int y )
16       {
17           return y * y;
18       }
19   } // end class MethodOverloadError
```

```
MethodOverloadError.java:15: square(int) is already defined in
MethodOverloadError
    public double square( int y )
                  ^
1 error
```

Fig. 6.15 | Overloaded method declarations with identical signatures cause compilation errors, even if the return types are different. (Part 2 of 2.)

Common Programming Error 6.11

Declaring overloaded methods with identical parameter lists is a compilation error regardless of whether the return types are different.

6.13 (Optional) GUI and Graphics Case Study: Colors and Filled Shapes

Although you can create many interesting designs with just lines and basic shapes, class Graphics provides many more capabilities. The next two features we introduce are colors and filled shapes. Adding color brings another dimension to the drawings a user sees on the computer screen. Filled shapes fill entire regions with solid colors, rather than just drawing outlines.

Colors displayed on computer screens are defined by their red, green, and blue components. These components, called RGB values, have integer values from 0 to 255. The higher the value of a particular component, the richer the particular shade will be in the final color. Java uses class Color in package java.awt to represent colors using their RGB values. For convenience, the Color object contains 13 predefined static Color objects—Color.BLACK, Color.BLUE, Color.CYAN, Color.DARK_GRAY, Color.GRAY, Color.GREEN, Color.LIGHT_GRAY,   Color.MAGENTA,   Color.ORANGE,   Color.PINK,   Color.RED, Color.WHITE and Color.YELLOW. Class Color also contains a constructor of the form:

```
public Color( int r, int g, int b )
```

so you can create custom colors by specifying values for the individual red, green and blue components of a color.

Filled rectangles and filled ovals are drawn using Graphics methods fillRect and fillOval, respectively. These two methods have the same parameters as their unfilled counterparts drawRect and drawOval; the first two parameters are the coordinates for the upper-left corner of the shape, while the next two parameters determine its width and height. The example in Fig. 6.16 and Fig. 6.17 demonstrates colors and filled shapes by drawing and displaying a yellow smiley face on the screen.

```java
 1    // Fig. 6.16: DrawSmiley.java
 2    // Demonstrates filled shapes.
 3    import java.awt.Color;
 4    import java.awt.Graphics;
 5    import javax.swing.JPanel;
 6
 7    public class DrawSmiley extends JPanel
 8    {
 9       public void paintComponent( Graphics g )
10       {
11          super.paintComponent( g );
12
13          // draw the face
14          g.setColor( Color.YELLOW );
15          g.fillOval( 10, 10, 200, 200 );
16
17          // draw the eyes
18          g.setColor( Color.BLACK );
19          g.fillOval( 55, 65, 30, 30 );
20          g.fillOval( 135, 65, 30, 30 );
21
22          // draw the mouth
23          g.fillOval( 50, 110, 120, 60 );
24
25          // "touch up" the mouth into a smile
26          g.setColor( Color.YELLOW );
27          g.fillRect( 50, 110, 120, 30 );
28          g.fillOval( 50, 120, 120, 40 );
29       } // end method paintComponent
30    } // end class DrawSmiley
```

Fig. 6.16 | Drawing a smiley face using colors and filled shapes.

```java
 1    // Fig. 6.17: DrawSmileyTest.java
 2    // Test application that displays a smiley face.
 3    import javax.swing.JFrame;
 4
 5    public class DrawSmileyTest
 6    {
 7       public static void main( String args[] )
 8       {
```

Fig. 6.17 | Creating JFrame to display a smiley face. (Part 1 of 2.)

```
 9          DrawSmiley panel = new DrawSmiley();
10          JFrame application = new JFrame();
11
12          application.setDefaultCloseOperation( JFrame.EXIT_ON_CLOSE );
13          application.add( panel );
14          application.setSize( 230, 250 );
15          application.setVisible( true );
16       } // end main
17    } // end class DrawSmileyTest
```

Fig. 6.17 | Creating JFrame to display a smiley face. (Part 2 of 2.)

The import statements in lines 3–5 of Fig. 6.16 import classes Color, Graphics and JPanel. Class DrawSmiley (lines 7–30) uses class Color to specify drawing colors, and uses class Graphics to draw. Class JPanel again provides the area in which we draw. Line 14 in method paintComponent uses Graphics method **setColor** to set the current drawing color to Color.YELLOW. Method setColor requires one argument, the Color to set as the drawing color. In this case, we use the predefined object Color.YELLOW. Line 15 draws a circle with diameter 200 to represent the face—when the width and height arguments are identical, method fillOval draws a circle. Next, line 18 sets the color to Color.Black, and lines 19–20 draw the eyes. Line 23 draws the mouth as an oval, but this is not quite what we want. To create a happy face, we will "touch up" the mouth. Line 26 sets the color to Color.YELLOW, so any shapes we draw will blend in with the face. Line 27 draws a rectangle that is half the mouth's height. This "erases" the top half of the mouth, leaving just the bottom half. To create a better smile, line 28 draws another oval to slightly cover the upper portion of the mouth. Class DrawSmileyTest (Fig. 6.17) creates and displays a JFrame containing the drawing. When the JFrame is displayed, the system calls method paintComponent to draw the smiley face.

GUI and Graphics Case Study Exercises

6.1   Using method fillOval, draw a bull's-eye that alternates between two random colors, as in Fig. 6.18. Use the constructor Color(int r, int g, int b) with random arguments to generate random colors.

6.2   Create a program that draws 10 random filled shapes in random colors, positions and sizes (Fig. 6.19). Method paintComponent should contain a loop that iterates 10 times. In each iteration, the loop should determine whether to draw a filled rectangle or an oval, create a random color and choose coordinates and dimensions at random. The coordinates should be chosen based on the panel's width and height. Lengths of sides should be limited to half the width or height of the window.

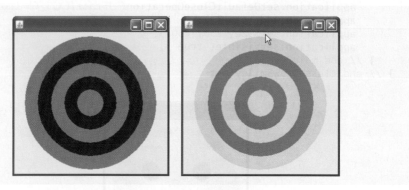

Fig. 6.18 | A bull's-eye with two alternating, random colors.

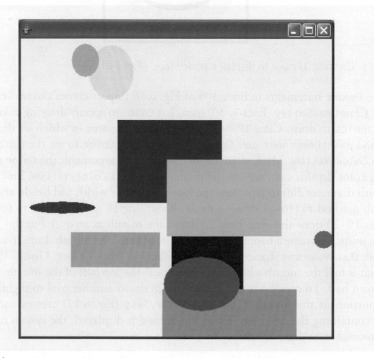

Fig. 6.19 | Randomly generated shapes.

6.14 (Optional) Software Engineering Case Study: Identifying Class Operations

In the Software Engineering Case Study sections at the ends of Chapters 3–5, we performed the first few steps in the object-oriented design of our ATM system. In Chapter 3, we identified the classes that we'll need to implement and created our first class diagram.

In Chapter 4, we described some attributes of our classes. In Chapter 5, we examined objects' states and modeled objects' state transitions and activities. In this section, we determine some of the class operations (or behaviors) needed to implement the ATM system.

Identifying Operations

An operation is a service that objects of a class provide to clients (users) of the class. Consider the operations of some real-world objects. A radio's operations include setting its station and volume (typically invoked by a person adjusting the radio's controls). A car's operations include accelerating (invoked by the driver pressing the accelerator pedal), decelerating (invoked by the driver pressing the brake pedal or releasing the gas pedal), turning and shifting gears. Software objects can offer operations as well—for example, a software graphics object might offer operations for drawing a circle, drawing a line, drawing a square and the like. A spreadsheet software object might offer operations like printing the spreadsheet, totaling the elements in a row or column and graphing information in the spreadsheet as a bar chart or pie chart.

We can derive many of the operations of each class by examining the key verbs and verb phrases in the requirements document. We then relate each of these to particular classes in our system (Fig. 6.20). The verb phrases in Fig. 6.20 help us determine the operations of each class.

Modeling Operations

To identify operations, we examine the verb phrases listed for each class in Fig. 6.20. The "executes financial transactions" phrase associated with class ATM implies that class ATM instructs transactions to execute. Therefore, classes BalanceInquiry, Withdrawal and

Class	Verbs and verb phrases
ATM	executes financial transactions
BalanceInquiry	[none in the requirements document]
Withdrawal	[none in the requirements document]
Deposit	[none in the requirements document]
BankDatabase	authenticates a user, retrieves an account balance, credits a deposit amount to an account, debits a withdrawal amount from an account
Account	retrieves an account balance, credits a deposit amount to an account, debits a withdrawal amount from an account
Screen	displays a message to the user
Keypad	receives numeric input from the user
CashDispenser	dispenses cash, indicates whether it contains enough cash to satisfy a withdrawal request
DepositSlot	receives a deposit envelope

Fig. 6.20 | Verbs and verb phrases for each class in the ATM system.

Deposit each need an operation to provide this service to the ATM. We place this operation (which we have named `execute`) in the third compartment of the three transaction classes in the updated class diagram of Fig. 6.21. During an ATM session, the ATM object will invoke these transaction operations as necessary.

The UML represents operations (which are implemented as methods in Java) by listing the operation name, followed by a comma-separated list of parameters in parentheses, a colon and the return type:

operationName(*parameter1*, *parameter2*, …, *parameterN*) : *return type*

Each parameter in the comma-separated parameter list consists of a parameter name, followed by a colon and the parameter type:

parameterName : *parameterType*

For the moment, we do not list the parameters of our operations—we will identify and model the parameters of some of the operations shortly. For some of the operations,

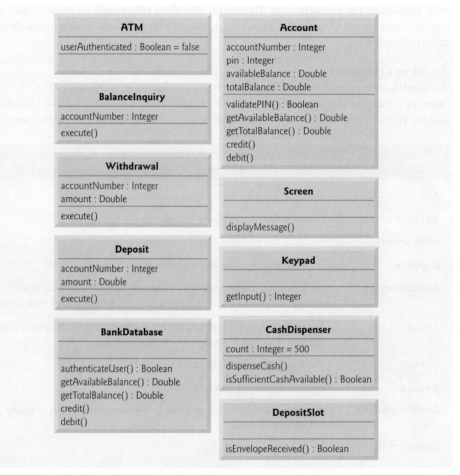

Fig. 6.21 | Classes in the ATM system with attributes and operations.

we do not yet know the return types, so we also omit them from the diagram. These omissions are perfectly normal at this point. As our design and implementation proceed, we will add the remaining return types.

Figure 6.20 lists the phrase "authenticates a user" next to class BankDatabase—the database is the object that contains the account information necessary to determine whether the account number and PIN entered by a user match those of an account held at the bank. Therefore, class BankDatabase needs an operation that provides an authentication service to the ATM. We place the operation authenticateUser in the third compartment of class BankDatabase (Fig. 6.21). However, an object of class Account, not class BankDatabase, stores the account number and PIN that must be accessed to authenticate a user, so class Account must provide a service to validate a PIN obtained through user input against a PIN stored in an Account object. Therefore, we add a validatePIN operation to class Account. Note that we specify a return type of Boolean for the authenticateUser and validatePIN operations. Each operation returns a value indicating either that the operation was successful in performing its task (i.e., a return value of true) or that it was not (i.e., a return value of false).

Figure 6.20 lists several additional verb phrases for class BankDatabase: "retrieves an account balance," "credits a deposit amount to an account" and "debits a withdrawal amount from an account." Like "authenticates a user," these remaining phrases refer to services that the database must provide to the ATM, because the database holds all the account data used to authenticate a user and perform ATM transactions. However, objects of class Account actually perform the operations to which these phrases refer. Thus, we assign an operation to both class BankDatabase and class Account to correspond to each of these phrases. Recall from Section 3.10 that, because a bank account contains sensitive information, we do not allow the ATM to access accounts directly. The database acts as an intermediary between the ATM and the account data, thus preventing unauthorized access. As we will see in Section 7.14, class ATM invokes the operations of class BankDatabase, each of which in turn invokes the operation with the same name in class Account.

The phrase "retrieves an account balance" suggests that classes BankDatabase and Account each need a getBalance operation. However, recall that we created two attributes in class Account to represent a balance—availableBalance and totalBalance. A balance inquiry requires access to both balance attributes so that it can display them to the user, but a withdrawal needs to check only the value of availableBalance. To allow objects in the system to obtain each balance attribute individually, we add operations getAvailableBalance and getTotalBalance to the third compartment of classes Bank-Database and Account (Fig. 6.21). We specify a return type of Double for these operations because the balance attributes which they retrieve are of type Double.

The phrases "credits a deposit amount to an account" and "debits a withdrawal amount from an account" indicate that classes BankDatabase and Account must perform operations to update an account during a deposit and withdrawal, respectively. We therefore assign credit and debit operations to classes BankDatabase and Account. You may recall that crediting an account (as in a deposit) adds an amount only to the totalBalance attribute. Debiting an account (as in a withdrawal), on the other hand, subtracts the amount from both balance attributes. We hide these implementation details inside class Account. This is a good example of encapsulation and information hiding.

If this were a real ATM system, classes BankDatabase and Account would also provide a set of operations to allow another banking system to update a user's account balance after either confirming or rejecting all or part of a deposit. Operation confirmDepositAmount, for example, would add an amount to the availableBalance attribute, thus making deposited funds available for withdrawal. Operation rejectDepositAmount would subtract an amount from the totalBalance attribute to indicate that a specified amount, which had recently been deposited through the ATM and added to the totalBalance, was not found in the deposit envelope. The bank would invoke this operation after determining either that the user failed to include the correct amount of cash or that any checks did not clear (i.e., they "bounced"). While adding these operations would make our system more complete, we do not include them in our class diagrams or our implementation because they are beyond the scope of the case study.

Class Screen "displays a message to the user" at various times in an ATM session. All visual output occurs through the screen of the ATM. The requirements document describes many types of messages (e.g., a welcome message, an error message, a thank you message) that the screen displays to the user. The requirements document also indicates that the screen displays prompts and menus to the user. However, a prompt is really just a message describing what the user should input next, and a menu is essentially a type of prompt consisting of a series of messages (i.e., menu options) displayed consecutively. Therefore, rather than assign class Screen an individual operation to display each type of message, prompt and menu, we simply create one operation that can display any message specified by a parameter. We place this operation (displayMessage) in the third compartment of class Screen in our class diagram (Fig. 6.21). Note that we do not worry about the parameter of this operation at this time—we model the parameter later in this section.

From the phrase "receives numeric input from the user" listed by class Keypad in Fig. 6.20, we conclude that class Keypad should perform a getInput operation. Because the ATM's keypad, unlike a computer keyboard, contains only the numbers 0–9, we specify that this operation returns an integer value. Recall from the requirements document that in different situations the user may be required to enter a different type of number (e.g., an account number, a PIN, the number of a menu option, a deposit amount as a number of cents). Class Keypad simply obtains a numeric value for a client of the class—it does not determine whether the value meets any specific criteria. Any class that uses this operation must verify that the user entered an appropriate number in a given situation, then respond accordingly (i.e., display an error message via class Screen). [*Note:* When we implement the system, we simulate the ATM's keypad with a computer keyboard, and for simplicity we assume that the user does not enter non-numeric input using keys on the computer keyboard that do not appear on the ATM's keypad.]

Figure 6.20 lists "dispenses cash" for class CashDispenser. Therefore, we create operation dispenseCash and list it under class CashDispenser in Fig. 6.21. Class CashDispenser also "indicates whether it contains enough cash to satisfy a withdrawal request." Thus, we include isSufficientCashAvailable, an operation that returns a value of UML type Boolean, in class CashDispenser. Figure 6.20 also lists "receives a deposit envelope" for class DepositSlot. The deposit slot must indicate whether it received an envelope, so we place an operation isEnvelopeReceived, which returns a Boolean value, in the third compartment of class DepositSlot. [*Note:* A real hardware deposit slot would most likely send the ATM a signal to indicate that an envelope was received. We simulate this behavior, however, with an operation in class DepositSlot that class ATM can invoke to find out whether the deposit slot received an envelope.]

We do not list any operations for class ATM at this time. We are not yet aware of any services that class ATM provides to other classes in the system. When we implement the system with Java code, however, operations of this class, and additional operations of the other classes in the system, may emerge.

Identifying and Modeling Operation Parameters

So far, we have not been concerned with the parameters of our operations—we have attempted to gain only a basic understanding of the operations of each class. Let's now take a closer look at some operation parameters. We identify an operation's parameters by examining what data the operation requires to perform its assigned task.

Consider the authenticateUser operation of class BankDatabase. To authenticate a user, this operation must know the account number and PIN supplied by the user. Thus we specify that operation authenticateUser takes integer parameters userAccountNumber and userPIN, which the operation must compare to the account number and PIN of an Account object in the database. We prefix these parameter names with "user" to avoid confusion between the operation's parameter names and the attribute names that belong to class Account. We list these parameters in the class diagram in Fig. 6.22 that models only class BankDatabase. [*Note:* It is perfectly normal to model only one class in a class diagram. In this case, we are most concerned with examining the parameters of this one class in particular, so we omit the other classes. In class diagrams later in the case study, in which parameters are no longer the focus of our attention, we omit these parameters to save space. Remember, however, that the operations listed in these diagrams still have parameters.]

Recall that the UML models each parameter in an operation's comma-separated parameter list by listing the parameter name, followed by a colon and the parameter type (in UML notation). Figure 6.22 thus specifies that operation authenticateUser takes two parameters—userAccountNumber and userPIN, both of type Integer. When we implement the system in Java, we will represent these parameters with int values.

Class BankDatabase operations getAvailableBalance, getTotalBalance, credit and debit also each require a userAccountNumber parameter to identify the account to which the database must apply the operations, so we include these parameters in the class diagram of Fig. 6.22. In addition, operations credit and debit each require a Double parameter amount to specify the amount of money to be credited or debited, respectively.

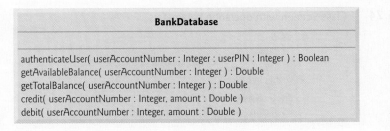

Fig. 6.22 | Class BankDatabase with operation parameters.

The class diagram in Fig. 6.23 models the parameters of class Account's operations. Operation validatePIN requires only a userPIN parameter, which contains the user-specified PIN to be compared with the PIN associated with the account. Like their counterparts in class BankDatabase, operations credit and debit in class Account each require a Double parameter amount that indicates the amount of money involved in the operation. Operations getAvailableBalance and getTotalBalance in class Account require no additional data to perform their tasks. Note that class Account's operations do not require an account number parameter to distinguish between Accounts, because these operations can be invoked only on a specific Account object.

Figure 6.24 models class Screen with a parameter specified for operation displayMessage. This operation requires only a String parameter message that indicates the text to be displayed. Recall that the parameter types listed in our class diagrams are in UML notation, so the String type listed in Fig. 6.24 refers to the UML type. When we implement the system in Java, we will in fact use the Java class String to represent this parameter.

The class diagram in Fig. 6.25 specifies that operation dispenseCash of class CashDispenser takes a Double parameter amount to indicate the amount of cash (in dollars) to be dispensed. Operation isSufficientCashAvailable also takes a Double parameter amount to indicate the amount of cash in question.

Account
accountNumber : Integer
pin : Integer
availableBalance : Double
totalBalance : Double
validatePIN(userPIN: Integer) : Boolean
getAvailableBalance() : Double
getTotalBalance() : Double
credit(amount : Double)
debit(amount : Double)

Fig. 6.23 | Class Account with operation parameters.

Screen
displayMessage(message : String)

Fig. 6.24 | Class Screen with operation parameters.

CashDispenser
count : Integer = 500
dispenseCash(amount : Double)
isSufficientCashAvailable(amount : Double) : Boolean

Fig. 6.25 | Class CashDispenser with operation parameters.

Note that we do not discuss parameters for operation execute of classes BalanceInquiry, Withdrawal and Deposit, operation getInput of class Keypad and operation isEnvelopeReceived of class DepositSlot. At this point in our design process, we cannot determine whether these operations require additional data to perform their tasks, so we leave their parameter lists empty. As we progress through the case study, we may decide to add parameters to these operations.

In this section, we have determined many of the operations performed by the classes in the ATM system. We have identified the parameters and return types of some of the operations. As we continue our design process, the number of operations belonging to each class may vary—we might find that new operations are needed or that some current operations are unnecessary—and we might determine that some of our class operations need additional parameters and different return types.

Software Engineering Case Study Self-Review Exercises

6.1   Which of the following is not a behavior?
a) reading data from a file
b) printing output
c) text output
d) obtaining input from the user

6.2   If you were to add to the ATM system an operation that returns the amount attribute of class Withdrawal, how and where would you specify this operation in the class diagram of Fig. 6.21?

6.3   Describe the meaning of the following operation listing that might appear in a class diagram for an object-oriented design of a calculator:

```
add( x : Integer, y : Integer ) : Integer
```

Answers to Software Engineering Case Study Self-Review Exercises

6.1   c.

6.2   To specify an operation that retrieves the amount attribute of class Withdrawal, the following operation listing would be placed in the operation (i.e., third) compartment of class Withdrawal:

```
getAmount( ) : Double
```

6.3   This operation listing indicates an operation named add that takes integers x and y as parameters and returns an integer value.

6.15 **Wrap-Up**

In this chapter, you learned more about the details of method declarations. You also learned the difference between non-static and static methods and how to call static methods by preceding the method name with the name of the class in which it appears and the dot (.) separator. You learned how to use operator + to perform string concatenations. You learned how to declare named constants using both enum types and public final static variables. You saw how to use class Random to generate sets of random numbers that can be used for simulations. You also learned about the scope of fields and local variables in a class. Finally, you learned that multiple methods in one class can be overloaded by providing methods with the same name and different signatures. Such methods can be used to perform the same or similar tasks using different types or different numbers of parameters.

In Chapter 7, you will learn how to maintain lists and tables of data in arrays. You will see a more elegant implementation of the application that rolls a die 6000 times and two enhanced versions of our GradeBook case study that you studied in Chapters 3–5. You will also learn how to access an application's command-line arguments that are passed to method main when an application begins execution.

Summary

Section 6.1 Introduction
- Experience has shown that the best way to develop and maintain a large program is to construct it from small, simple pieces, or modules. This technique is called divide and conquer.

Section 6.2 Program Modules in Java
- There are three kinds of modules in Java—methods, classes and packages. Methods are declared within classes. Classes are typically grouped into packages so that they can be imported into programs and reused.

- Methods allow you to modularize a program by separating its tasks into self-contained units. The statements in a method are written only once and hidden from other methods.

- Using existing methods as building blocks to create new programs is a form of software reusability that allows you to avoid repeating code within a program.

Section 6.3 static Methods, static Fields and Class Math
- A method call specifies the name of the method to call and provides the arguments that the called method requires to perform its task. When the method call completes, the method returns either a result or simply control to its caller.

- A class may contain static methods to perform common tasks that do not require an object of the class. Any data a static method might require to perform its tasks can be sent to the method as arguments in a method call. A static method is called by specifying the name of the class in which the method is declared followed by a dot (.) and the method name, as in

      ClassName.*methodName*(*arguments*)

- Method arguments may be constants, variables or expressions.

- Class Math provides static methods for performing common mathematical calculations. Class Math declares two fields that represent commonly used mathematical constants: Math.PI and Math.E. The constant Math.PI (3.14159265358979323846) is the ratio of a circle's circumference to its diameter. The constant Math.E (2.7182818284590452354) is the base value for natural logarithms (calculated with static Math method log).

- Math.PI and Math.E are declared with the modifiers public, final and static. Making them public allows other programmers to use these fields in their own classes. Any field declared with keyword final is constant—its value cannot be changed after the field is initialized. Both PI and E are declared final because their values never change. Making these fields static allows them to be accessed via the class name Math and a dot (.) separator, just like class Math's methods.

- When objects of a class containing static fields (class variables) are created, all the objects of that class share one copy of the class's static fields. Together the class variables and instance variables represent the fields of a class. You will learn more about static fields in Section 8.11.

- When you execute the Java Virtual Machine (JVM) with the java command, the JVM attempts to invoke the main method of the class you specify. The JVM loads the class specified by *Class-*

Name and uses that class name to invoke method `main`. You can specify an optional list of `String`s (separated by spaces) as command-line arguments that the JVM will pass to your application.

- You can place a `main` method in every class you declare—only the `main` method in the class you use to execute the application will be called. Some programmers take advantage of this to build a small test program into each class they declare.

Section 6.4 Declaring Methods with Multiple Parameters

- When a method is called, the program makes a copy of the method's argument values and assigns them to the method's corresponding parameters, which are created and initialized when the method is called. When program control returns to the point in the program where the method was called, the method's parameters are removed from memory.

- A method can return at most one value, but the returned value could be a reference to an object that contains many values.

- Variables should be declared as fields of a class only if they are required for use in more than one method of the class or if the program should save their values between calls to the class's methods.

Section 6.5 Notes on Declaring and Using Methods

- There are three ways to call a method—using a method name by itself to call another method of the same class; using a variable that contains a reference to an object, followed by a dot (.) and the method name to call a method of the referenced object; and using the class name and a dot (.) to call a `static` method of a class.

- There are three ways to return control to a statement that calls a method. If the method does not return a result, control returns when the program flow reaches the method-ending right brace or when the statement

    ```
    return;
    ```

    is executed. If the method returns a result, the statement

    ```
    return expression;
    ```

    evaluates the *expression*, then immediately returns the resulting value to the caller.

- When a method has more than one parameter, the parameters are specified as a comma-separated list. There must be one argument in the method call for each parameter in the method declaration. Also, each argument must be consistent with the type of the corresponding parameter. If a method does not accept arguments, the parameter list is empty.

- `String`s can be concatenated using operator +, which places the characters of the right operand at the end of those in the left operand.

- Every primitive value and object in Java has a `String` representation. When an object is concatenated with a `String`, the object is converted to a `String`, then the two `String`s are concatenated.

- For primitive values used in string concatenation, the JVM handles the conversion of the primitive values to `String`s. If a `boolean` is concatenated with a `String`, the word `"true"` or the word `"false"` is used to represent the `boolean` value. If there are any trailing zeros in a floating-point value, these will be discarded when the number is concatenated to a `String`.

- All objects in Java have a special method named `toString` that returns a `String` representation of the object's contents. When an object is concatenated with a `String`, the JVM implicitly calls the object's `toString` method to obtain the string representation of the object.

- When a large `String` literal is typed into a program's source code, programmers sometimes break that `String` into several smaller `String`s and place them on multiple lines of code for readability, then reassemble the `String`s using concatenation.

Section 6.6 Method-Call Stack and Activation Records

- Stacks are known as last-in, first-out (LIFO) data structures—the last item pushed (inserted) on the stack is the first item popped (removed) from the stack.

- A called method must know how to return to its caller, so the return address of the calling method is pushed onto the program execution stack when the method is called. If a series of method calls occurs, the successive return addresses are pushed onto the stack in last-in, first-out order so that the last method to execute will be the first to return to its caller.

- The program execution stack contains the memory for the local variables used in each invocation of a method during a program's execution. This data is known as the activation record or stack frame of the method call. When a method call is made, the activation record for that method call is pushed onto the program execution stack. When the method returns to its caller, the activation record for this method call is popped off the stack and those local variables are no longer known to the program. If a local variable holding a reference to an object is the only variable in the program with a reference to that object, when the activation record containing that local variable is popped off the stack, the object can no longer be accessed by the program and will eventually be deleted from memory by the JVM during "garbage collection."

- The amount of memory in a computer is finite, so only a certain amount of memory can be used to store activation records on the program execution stack. If there are more method calls than can have their activation records stored on the program execution stack, an error known as a stack overflow occurs. The application will compile correctly, but its execution causes a stack overflow.

Section 6.7 Argument Promotion and Casting

- An important feature of method calls is argument promotion—converting an argument's value to the type that the method expects to receive in its corresponding parameter.

- A set of promotion rules apply to expressions containing values of two or more primitive types and to primitive-type values passed as arguments to methods. Each value is promoted to the "highest" type in the expression. In cases where information may be lost due to conversion, the Java compiler requires you to use a cast operator to explicitly force the conversion to occur.

Section 6.9 Case Study: Random-Number Generation

- Objects of class Random (package java.util) can produce random int, long, float or double values. Math method random can produce double values in the range $0.0 \leq x < 1.0$, where x is the value returned by method random.

- Random method nextInt generates a random int value in the range −2,147,483,648 to +2,147,483,647. The values returned by nextInt are actually pseudorandom numbers—a sequence of values produced by a complex mathematical calculation. That calculation uses the current time of day to seed the random-number generator such that each execution of a program yields a different sequence of random values.

- Class Random provides another version of method nextInt that receives an int argument and returns a value from 0 up to, but not including, the argument's value.

- Random numbers in a range can be generated with

      number = *shiftingValue* + randomNumbers.nextInt(*scalingFactor*);

  where *shiftingValue* specifies the first number in the desired range of consecutive integers, and *scalingFactor* specifies how many numbers are in the range.

- Random numbers can be chosen from nonconsecutive integer ranges, as in

      number = *shiftingValue* +
          differenceBetweenValues * randomNumbers.nextInt(*scalingFactor*);

where *shiftingValue* specifies the first number in the range of values, *differenceBetweenValues* represents the difference between consecutive numbers in the sequence and *scalingFactor* specifies how many numbers are in the range.

- For debugging, it is sometimes useful to repeat the same sequence of pseudorandom numbers during each program execution to prove that your application is working for a specific sequence of random numbers before testing the program with different sequences of random numbers. When repeatability is important, you can create a Random object by passing a long integer value to the constructor. If the same seed is used every time the program executes, the Random object produces the same sequence of random numbers. You can also set a Random object's seed at any time by calling the object's setSeed method.

Section 6.10 Case Study: A Game of Chance (Introducing Enumerations)
- An enumeration is introduced by the keyword enum and a type name. As with any class, braces ({ and }) delimit the body of an enum declaration. Inside the braces is a comma-separated list of enumeration constants, each representing a unique value. The identifiers in an enum must be unique. Variables of an enum type can be assigned only constants of that enum type.
- Constants can also be declared as public final static variables. Such constants are declared with all capital letters by convention to make them stand out in the program.

Section 6.11 Scope of Declarations
- Scope is the portion of the program in which an entity, such as a variable or a method, can be referred to by its name. Such an entity is said to be "in scope" for that portion of the program.
- The scope of a parameter declaration is the body of the method in which the declaration appears.
- The scope of a local-variable declaration is from the point at which the declaration appears to the end of that block.
- The scope of a label in a labeled break or continue statement is the labeled statement's body.
- The scope of a local-variable declaration that appears in the initialization section of a for statement's header is the body of the for statement and the other expressions in the header.
- The scope of a method or field of a class is the entire body of the class. This enables a class's methods to use simple names to call the class's other methods and to access the class's fields.
- Any block may contain variable declarations. If a local variable or parameter in a method has the same name as a field, the field is shadowed until the block terminates execution.

Section 6.12 Method Overloading
- Java allows several methods of the same name to be declared in a class, as long as the methods have different sets of parameters (determined by the number, order and types of the parameters). This technique is called method overloading.
- Overloaded methods are distinguished by their signatures—combinations of the methods' names and the number, types and order of their parameters. Methods cannot be distinguished by return type.

Terminology

activation record	Color class
application programming interface (API)	comma-separated list of parameters
argument promotion	command-line argument
block	divide-and-conquer approach
class method	element of chance
class variable	enum keyword

enumeration
enumeration constant
fillOval method of class Graphics
fillRect method of class Graphics
final keyword
formal parameter
function
"hidden" fields
hide implementation details
hierarchical boss-method/worker-method
    relationship
invoke a method
Java API documentation
Java Application Programming Interface (API)
last-in, first-out (LIFO) data structure
local variable
method call
method-call stack
method declaration
method overloading
modularizing a program with methods
module
nextInt method of class Random
overload a method
package
parameter
parameter list
popping (from a stack)

primitive-type promotions
procedure
program execution stack
programmer-declared method
promotion rules
pseudorandom number
pushing (onto a stack)
Random class
random of class Math
random numbers
return keyword
reusable software components
RGB values
scaling factor (random numbers)
scope of a declaration
seed value (random numbers)
setColor method of class Graphics
setSeed method of class Random
shadow a field
shift a range (random numbers)
shifting value (random numbers)
signature of a method
simulation
software reuse
stack
stack frame
stack overflow
string concatenation

Self-Review Exercises

6.1 Fill in the blanks in each of the following statements:
    a) A method is invoked with a(n) _____.
    b) A variable known only within the method in which it is declared is called a(n) _____.
    c) The _____ statement in a called method can be used to pass the value of an expression back to the calling method.
    d) The keyword _____ indicates that a method does not return a value.
    e) Data can be added or removed only from the _____ of a stack.
    f) Stacks are known as _____ data structures—the last item pushed (inserted) on the stack is the first item popped (removed) from the stack.
    g) The three ways to return control from a called method to a caller are _____, _____ and _____.
    h) An object of class _____ produces random numbers.
    i) The program execution stack contains the memory for local variables on each invocation of a method during a program's execution. This data, stored as a portion of the program execution stack, is known as the _____ or _____ of the method call.
    j) If there are more method calls than can be stored on the program execution stack, an error known as a(n) _____ occurs.
    k) The _____ of a declaration is the portion of a program that can refer to the entity in the declaration by name.

l) In Java, it is possible to have several methods with the same name that each operate on different types or numbers of arguments. This feature is called method _____.

m) The program execution stack is also referred to as the _____ stack.

6.2 For the class Craps in Fig. 6.9, state the scope of each of the following entities:
a) the variable randomNumbers.
b) the variable die1.
c) the method rollDice.
d) the method play.
e) the variable sumOfDice.

6.3 Write an application that tests whether the examples of the Math class method calls shown in Fig. 6.2 actually produce the indicated results.

6.4 Give the method header for each of the following methods:
a) Method hypotenuse, which takes two double-precision, floating-point arguments side1 and side2 and returns a double-precision, floating-point result.
b) Method smallest, which takes three integers x, y and z and returns an integer.
c) Method instructions, which does not take any arguments and does not return a value. [*Note:* Such methods are commonly used to display instructions to a user.]
d) Method intToFloat, which takes an integer argument number and returns a floating-point result.

6.5 Find the error in each of the following program segments. Explain how to correct the error.

a)
```java
int g()
{
    System.out.println( "Inside method g" );

    int h()
    {
        System.out.println( "Inside method h" );
    }
}
```

b)
```java
int sum( int x, int y )
{
    int result;
    result = x + y;
}
```

c)
```java
void f( float a );
{
    float a;
    System.out.println( a );
}
```

d)
```java
void product()
{
    int a = 6, b = 5, c = 4, result;
    result = a * b * c;
    System.out.printf( "Result is %d\n", result );
    return result;
}
```

6.6 Write a complete Java application to prompt the user for the double radius of a sphere, and call method sphereVolume to calculate and display the volume of the sphere. Use the following statement to calculate the volume:

```java
double volume = ( 4.0 / 3.0 ) * Math.PI * Math.pow( radius, 3 )
```

Answers to Self-Review Exercises

6.1 a) method call. b) local variable. c) return. d) void. e) top. f) last-in, first-out (LIFO). g) return; or return *expression*; or encountering the closing right brace of a method. h) Random. i) activation record, stack frame. j) stack overflow. k) scope. l) method overloading. m) method call.

6.2 a) class body. b) block that defines method rollDice's body. c) class body. d) class body. e) block that defines method play's body.

6.3 The following solution demonstrates the Math class methods in Fig. 6.2:

```
1   // Exercise 6.3: MathTest.java
2   // Testing the Math class methods.
3
4   public class MathTest
5   {
6      public static void main( String args[] )
7      {
8         System.out.printf( "Math.abs( 23.7 ) = %f\n", Math.abs( 23.7 ) );
9         System.out.printf( "Math.abs( 0.0 ) = %f\n", Math.abs( 0.0 ) );
10        System.out.printf( "Math.abs( -23.7 ) = %f\n", Math.abs( -23.7 ) );
11        System.out.printf( "Math.ceil( 9.2 ) = %f\n", Math.ceil( 9.2 ) );
12        System.out.printf( "Math.ceil( -9.8 ) = %f\n", Math.ceil( -9.8 ) );
13        System.out.printf( "Math.cos( 0.0 ) = %f\n", Math.cos( 0.0 ) );
14        System.out.printf( "Math.exp( 1.0 ) = %f\n", Math.exp( 1.0 ) );
15        System.out.printf( "Math.exp( 2.0 ) = %f\n", Math.exp( 2.0 ) );
16        System.out.printf( "Math.floor( 9.2 ) = %f\n", Math.floor( 9.2 ) );
17        System.out.printf( "Math.floor( -9.8 ) = %f\n",
18           Math.floor( -9.8 ) );
19        System.out.printf( "Math.log( Math.E ) = %f\n",
20           Math.log( Math.E ) );
21        System.out.printf( "Math.log( Math.E * Math.E ) = %f\n",
22           Math.log( Math.E * Math.E ) );
23        System.out.printf( "Math.max( 2.3, 12.7 ) = %f\n",
24           Math.max( 2.3, 12.7 ) );
25        System.out.printf( "Math.max( -2.3, -12.7 ) = %f\n",
26           Math.max( -2.3, -12.7 ) );
27        System.out.printf( "Math.min( 2.3, 12.7 ) = %f\n",
28           Math.min( 2.3, 12.7 ) );
29        System.out.printf( "Math.min( -2.3, -12.7 ) = %f\n",
30           Math.min( -2.3, -12.7 ) );
31        System.out.printf( "Math.pow( 2.0, 7.0 ) = %f\n",
32           Math.pow( 2.0, 7.0 ) );
33        System.out.printf( "Math.pow( 9.0, 0.5 ) = %f\n",
34           Math.pow( 9.0, 0.5 ) );
35        System.out.printf( "Math.sin( 0.0 ) = %f\n", Math.sin( 0.0 ) );
36        System.out.printf( "Math.sqrt( 900.0 ) = %f\n",
37           Math.sqrt( 900.0 ) );
38        System.out.printf( "Math.sqrt( 9.0 ) = %f\n", Math.sqrt( 9.0 ) );
39        System.out.printf( "Math.tan( 0.0 ) = %f\n", Math.tan( 0.0 ) );
40     } // end main
41  } // end class MathTest
```

```
Math.abs( 23.7 ) = 23.700000
Math.abs( 0.0 ) = 0.000000
Math.abs( -23.7 ) = 23.700000
Math.ceil( 9.2 ) = 10.000000
Math.ceil( -9.8 ) = -9.000000
Math.cos( 0.0 ) = 1.000000
Math.exp( 1.0 ) = 2.718282
Math.exp( 2.0 ) = 7.389056
Math.floor( 9.2 ) = 9.000000
Math.floor( -9.8 ) = -10.000000
Math.log( Math.E ) = 1.000000
Math.log( Math.E * Math.E ) = 2.000000
Math.max( 2.3, 12.7 ) = 12.700000
Math.max( -2.3, -12.7 ) = -2.300000
Math.min( 2.3, 12.7 ) = 2.300000
Math.min( -2.3, -12.7 ) = -12.700000
Math.pow( 2.0, 7.0 ) = 128.000000
Math.pow( 9.0, 0.5 ) = 3.000000
Math.sin( 0.0 ) = 0.000000
Math.sqrt( 900.0 ) = 30.000000
Math.sqrt( 9.0 ) = 3.000000
Math.tan( 0.0 ) = 0.000000
```

6.4 a) `double hypotenuse( double side1, double side2 )`
      b) `int smallest( int x, int y, int z )`
      c) `void instructions()`
      d) `float intToFloat( int number )`

6.5 a) Error: Method h is declared within method g.
          Correction: Move the declaration of h outside the declaration of g.
      b) Error: The method is supposed to return an integer, but does not.
          Correction: Delete the variable result, and place the statement

              `return x + y;`

          in the method, or add the following statement at the end of the method body:

              `return result;`

      c) Error: The semicolon after the right parenthesis of the parameter list is incorrect, and
          the parameter a should not be redeclared in the method.
          Correction: Delete the semicolon after the right parenthesis of the parameter list, and
          delete the declaration `float a;`.
      d) Error: The method returns a value when it is not supposed to.
          Correction: Change the return type from `void` to `int`.

6.6 The following solution calculates the volume of a sphere, using the radius entered by the user:

```
1   // Exercise 6.6: Sphere.java
2   // Calculate the volume of a sphere.
3   import java.util.Scanner;
4
5   public class Sphere
6   {
7      // obtain radius from user and display volume of sphere
8      public void determineSphereVolume()
9      {
```

```
10          Scanner input = new Scanner( System.in );
11
12          System.out.print( "Enter radius of sphere: " );
13          double radius = input.nextDouble();
14
15          System.out.printf( "Volume is %f\n", sphereVolume( radius ) );
16      } // end method determineSphereVolume
17
18      // calculate and return sphere volume
19      public double sphereVolume( double radius )
20      {
21          double volume = ( 4.0 / 3.0 ) * Math.PI * Math.pow( radius, 3 );
22          return volume;
23      } // end method sphereVolume
24  } // end class Sphere
```

```
1   // Exercise 6.6: SphereTest.java
2   // Calculate the volume of a sphere.
3
4   public class SphereTest
5   {
6      // application starting point
7      public static void main( String args[] )
8      {
9          Sphere mySphere = new Sphere();
10         mySphere.determineSphereVolume();
11     } // end main
12  } // end class SphereTest
```

```
Enter radius of sphere: 4
Volume is 268.082573
```

Exercises

6.7   What is the value of x after each of the following statements is executed?

   a) x = Math.abs(7.5);
   b) x = Math.floor(7.5);
   c) x = Math.abs(0.0);
   d) x = Math.ceil(0.0);
   e) x = Math.abs(-6.4);
   f) x = Math.ceil(-6.4);
   g) x = Math.ceil(-Math.abs(-8 + Math.floor(-5.5)));

6.8   A parking garage charges a $2.00 minimum fee to park for up to three hours. The garage charges an additional $0.50 per hour for each hour *or part thereof* in excess of three hours. The maximum charge for any given 24-hour period is $10.00. Assume that no car parks for longer than 24 hours at a time. Write an application that calculates and displays the parking charges for each customer who parked in the garage yesterday. You should enter the hours parked for each customer. The program should display the charge for the current customer and should calculate and display the running total of yesterday's receipts. The program should use the method calculateCharges to determine the charge for each customer.

6.9   An application of method `Math.floor` is rounding a value to the nearest integer. The statement

```
y = Math.floor( x + 0.5 );
```

will round the number x to the nearest integer and assign the result to y. Write an application that reads `double` values and uses the preceding statement to round each of the numbers to the nearest integer. For each number processed, display both the original number and the rounded number.

6.10   Answer each of the following questions:
a) What does it mean to choose numbers "at random?"
b) Why is the `nextInt` method of class `Random` useful for simulating games of chance?
c) Why is it often necessary to scale or shift the values produced by a `Random` object?
d) Why is computerized simulation of real-world situations a useful technique?

6.11   Write statements that assign random integers to the variable n in the following ranges:
a) $1 \le n \le 2$.
b) $1 \le n \le 100$.
c) $0 \le n \le 9$.
d) $1000 \le n \le 1112$.
e) $-1 \le n \le 1$.
f) $-3 \le n \le 11$.

6.12   For each of the following sets of integers, write a single statement that will display a number at random from the set:
a) 2, 4, 6, 8, 10.
b) 3, 5, 7, 9, 11.
c) 6, 10, 14, 18, 22.

6.13   Write a method `integerPower( base, exponent )` that returns the value of

$$base^{\,exponent}$$

For example, `integerPower( 3, 4 )` calculates 3^4 (or 3 * 3 * 3 * 3). Assume that exponent is a positive, nonzero integer and that base is an integer. Method `integerPower` should use a `for` or `while` statement to control the calculation. Do not use any math library methods. Incorporate this method into an application that reads integer values for base and exponent and performs the calculation with the `integerPower` method.

6.14   Write a method `multiple` that determines, for a pair of integers, whether the second integer is a multiple of the first. The method should take two integer arguments and return `true` if the second is a multiple of the first and `false` otherwise. [*Hint:* Use the remainder operator.] Incorporate this method into an application that inputs a series of pairs of integers (one pair at a time) and determines whether the second value in each pair is a multiple of the first.

6.15   Write a method `isEven` that uses the remainder operator (%) to determine whether an integer is even. The method should take an integer argument and return `true` if the integer is even and `false` otherwise. Incorporate this method into an application that inputs a sequence of integers (one at a time) and determines whether each is even or odd.

6.16   Write a method `squareOfAsterisks` that displays a solid square (the same number of rows and columns) of asterisks whose side is specified in integer parameter `side`. For example, if `side` is 4, the method should display

```
****
****
****
****
```

Incorporate this method into an application that reads an integer value for side from the user and outputs the asterisks with the squareOfAsterisks method.

6.17   Modify the method created in Exercise 6.16 to form the square out of whatever character is contained in character parameter fillCharacter. Thus, if side is 5 and fillCharacter is "#", the method should display

```
#####
#####
#####
#####
#####
```

6.18   Write an application that prompts the user for the radius of a circle and uses a method called circleArea to calculate the area of the circle.

6.19   Write program segments that accomplish each of the following tasks:
   a) Calculate the integer part of the quotient when integer a is divided by integer b.
   b) Calculate the integer remainder when integer a is divided by integer b.
   c) Use the program pieces developed in parts (a) and (b) to write a method displayDigits that receives an integer between 1 and 99999 and displays it as a sequence of digits, separating each pair of digits by two spaces. For example, the integer 4562 should appear as

       4   5   6   2

   d) Incorporate the method developed in part (c) into an application that inputs an integer and calls displayDigits by passing the method the integer entered. Display the results.

6.20   Implement the following integer methods:
   a) Method celsius returns the Celsius equivalent of a Fahrenheit temperature, using the calculation

   ```
   celsius = 5.0 / 9.0 * ( fahrenheit - 32 );
   ```

   b) Method fahrenheit returns the Fahrenheit equivalent of a Celsius temperature, using the calculation

   ```
   fahrenheit = 9.0 / 5.0 * celsius + 32;
   ```

   c) Use the methods from parts (a) and (b) to write an application that enables the user either to enter a Fahrenheit temperature and display the Celsius equivalent or to enter a Celsius temperature and display the Fahrenheit equivalent.

6.21   Write a method minimum3 that returns the smallest of three floating-point numbers. Use the Math.min method to implement minimum3. Incorporate the method into an application that reads three values from the user, determines the smallest value and displays the result.

6.22   An integer number is said to be a *perfect number* if its factors, including 1 (but not the number itself), sum to the number. For example, 6 is a perfect number, because 6 = 1 + 2 + 3. Write a method perfect that determines whether parameter number is a perfect number. Use this method in an application that determines and displays all the perfect numbers between 1 and 1000. Display the factors of each perfect number to confirm that the number is indeed perfect. Challenge the computing power of your computer by testing numbers much larger than 1000. Display the results.

6.23   Write a method that takes an integer value and returns the number with its digits reversed. For example, given the number 7631, the method should return 1367. Incorporate the method into an application that reads a value from the user and displays the result.

6.24   The *greatest common divisor* (*GCD*) of two integers is the largest integer that evenly divides each of the two numbers. Write a method gcd that returns the greatest common divisor of two integers. [*Hint:* You might want to use Euclid's Algorithm. You can find information about the algorithm at en.wikipedia.org/wiki/Euclidean_algorithm.] Incorporate the method into an application that reads two values from the user and displays the result.

6.25   Write a method qualityPoints that inputs a student's average and returns 4 if the student's average is 90–100, 3 if the average is 80–89, 2 if the average is 70–79, 1 if the average is 60–69 and 0 if the average is lower than 60. Incorporate the method into an application that reads a value from the user and displays the result.

6.26   Write an application that simulates coin tossing. Let the program toss a coin each time the user chooses the "Toss Coin" menu option. Count the number of times each side of the coin appears. Display the results. The program should call a separate method flip that takes no arguments and returns false for tails and true for heads. [*Note:* If the program realistically simulates coin tossing, each side of the coin should appear approximately half the time.]

6.27   Computers are playing an increasing role in education. Write a program that will help an elementary school student learn multiplication. Use a Random object to produce two positive one-digit integers. The program should then prompt the user with a question, such as

        How much is 6 times 7?

The student then inputs the answer. Next, the program checks the student's answer. If it is correct, display the message "Very good!" and ask another multiplication question. If the answer is wrong, display the message "No. Please try again." and let the student try the same question repeatedly until the student finally gets it right. A separate method should be used to generate each new question. This method should be called once when the application begins execution and each time the user answers the question correctly.

6.28   The use of computers in education is referred to as *computer-assisted instruction* (*CAI*). One problem that develops in CAI environments is student fatigue. This problem can be eliminated by varying the computer's responses to hold the student's attention. Modify the program of Exercise 6.27 so that the various comments are displayed for each correct answer and each incorrect answer as follows:

Responses to a correct answer:

        Very good!
        Excellent!
        Nice work!
        Keep up the good work!

Responses to an incorrect answer:

        No. Please try again.
        Wrong. Try once more.
        Don't give up!
        No. Keep trying.

Use random-number generation to choose a number from 1 to 4 that will be used to select an appropriate response to each answer. Use a switch statement to issue the responses.

6.29   More sophisticated computer-assisted instruction systems monitor the student's performance over a period of time. The decision to begin a new topic is often based on the student's success with previous topics. Modify the program of Exercise 6.28 to count the number of correct and incorrect responses typed by the student. After the student types 10 answers, your program should calculate the percentage of correct responses. If the percentage is lower than 75%, display Please ask your instructor for extra help and reset the program so another student can try it.

6.30 Write an application that plays "guess the number" as follows: Your program chooses the number to be guessed by selecting a random integer in the range 1 to 1000. The application displays the prompt Guess a number between 1 and 1000. The player inputs a first guess. If the player's guess is incorrect, your program should display Too high. Try again. or Too low. Try again. to help the player "zero in" on the correct answer. The program should prompt the user for the next guess. When the user enters the correct answer, display Congratulations. You guessed the number!, and allow the user to choose whether to play again. [*Note:* The guessing technique employed in this problem is similar to a binary search, which is discussed in Chapter 16, Searching and Sorting.]

6.31 Modify the program of Exercise 6.30 to count the number of guesses the player makes. If the number is 10 or fewer, display Either you know the secret or you got lucky! If the player guesses the number in 10 tries, display Aha! You know the secret! If the player makes more than 10 guesses, display You should be able to do better! Why should it take no more than 10 guesses? Well, with each "good guess," the player should be able to eliminate half of the numbers, then half of the remaining numbers, and so on.

6.32 Exercise 6.27 through Exercise 6.29 developed a computer-assisted instruction program to teach an elementary school student multiplication. Perform the following enhancements:

a) Modify the program to allow the user to enter a school grade-level capability. A grade level of 1 means that the program should use only single-digit numbers in the problems, a grade level of 2 means that the program should use numbers as large as two digits, and so on.

b) Modify the program to allow the user to pick the type of arithmetic problems he or she wishes to study. An option of 1 means addition problems only, 2 means subtraction problems only, 3 means multiplication problems only, 4 means division problems only and 5 means a random mixture of problems of all these types.

6.33 Write method distance to calculate the distance between two points ($x1$, $y1$) and ($x2$, $y2$). All numbers and return values should be of type double. Incorporate this method into an application that enables the user to enter the coordinates of the points.

6.34 Write an application that displays a table of the binary, octal, and hexadecimal equivalents of the decimal numbers in the range 1 through 256. If you are not familiar with these number systems, read Appendix E first.

7

Arrays

OBJECTIVES

In this chapter you will learn:

- What arrays are.

- To use arrays to store data in and retrieve data from lists and tables of values.

- To declare arrays, initialize arrays and refer to individual elements of arrays.

- To use the enhanced **for** statement to iterate through arrays.

- To pass arrays to methods.

- To declare and manipulate multidimensional arrays.

- To write methods that use variable-length argument lists.

- To read command-line arguments into a program.

7.1 **Introduction**

This chapter introduces **data structures**—collections of related data items. **Arrays** are data structures consisting of related data items of the same type. Arrays are fixed-length entities—they remain the same length once they are created, although an array variable may be reassigned such that it refers to a new array of a different length. We study data structures in depth in Chapters 17–19.

After discussing how arrays are declared, created and initialized, we present a series of practical examples that demonstrate several common array manipulations. We also present a case study that examines how arrays can help simulate the shuffling and dealing of playing cards for use in an application that implements a card game. The chapter then introduces Java's enhanced **for** statement, which allows a program to access the data in an array more easily than does the counter-controlled **for** statement presented in Section 5.3. Two sections of the chapter enhance the case study of class **GradeBook** in Chapters 3–5. In particular, we use arrays to enable the class to maintain a set of grades in memory and analyze student grades from multiple exams in a semester—two capabilities that were absent from previous versions of the class. These and other chapter examples demonstrate the ways in which arrays allow programmers to organize and manipulate data.

7.2 **Arrays**

An array is a group of variables (called **elements** or **components**) containing values that all have the same type. Recall that types are divided into two categories—primitive types and reference types. Arrays are objects, so they are considered reference types. As you will soon see, what we typically think of as an array is actually a reference to an array object in memory. The elements of an array can be either primitive types or reference types (including arrays, as we will see in Section 7.9). To refer to a particular element in an array, we specify the name of the reference to the array and the position number of the element in the array. The position number of the element is called the element's index or subscript.

Figure 7.1 shows a logical representation of an integer array called c. This array contains 12 elements. A program refers to any one of these elements with an array-access expression that includes the name of the array followed by the index of the particular element in square brackets ([]). The first element in every array has index zero and is sometimes called the zeroth element. Thus, the elements of array c are c[0], c[1], c[2] and so on. The highest index in array c is 11, which is 1 less than 12—the number of elements in the array. Array names follow the same conventions as other variable names.

An index must be a nonnegative integer. A program can use an expression as an index. For example, if we assume that variable a is 5 and variable b is 6, then the statement

```
c[ a + b ] += 2;
```

adds 2 to array element c[11]. Note that an indexed array name is an array-access expression. Such expressions can be used on the left side of an assignment to place a new value into an array element.

Common Programming Error 7.1

Using a value of type long *as an array index results in a compilation error. An index must be an* int *value or a value of a type that can be promoted to* int—*namely,* byte, short *or* char, *but not* long.

Let us examine array c in Fig. 7.1 more closely. The name of the array is c. Every array object knows its own length and maintains this information in a length field. The expression c.length accesses array c's length field to determine the length of the array. Note that, even though the length member of an array is public, it cannot be changed because

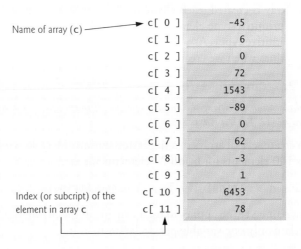

Name of array (c) →	c[0]	-45
	c[1]	6
	c[2]	0
	c[3]	72
	c[4]	1543
	c[5]	-89
	c[6]	0
	c[7]	62
	c[8]	-3
	c[9]	1
Index (or subcript) of the	c[10]	6453
element in array c	c[11]	78

Fig. 7.1 | A 12-element array.

it is a final variable. This array's 12 elements are referred to as c[0], c[1], c[2], ...,
c[11]. The value of c[0] is –45, the value of c[1] is 6, the value of c[2] is 0, the value
of c[7] is 62 and the value of c[11] is 78. To calculate the sum of the values contained
in the first three elements of array c and store the result in variable sum, we would write

```
sum = c[ 0 ] + c[ 1 ] + c[ 2 ];
```

To divide the value of c[6] by 2 and assign the result to the variable x, we would write

```
x = c[ 6 ] / 2;
```

7.3 Declaring and Creating Arrays

Array objects occupy space in memory. Like other objects, arrays are created with keyword
new. To create an array object, the programmer specifies the type of the array elements and
the number of elements as part of an array-creation expression that uses keyword new.
Such an expression returns a reference that can be stored in an array variable. The following declaration and array-creation expression create an array object containing 12 int elements and store the array's reference in variable c:

```
int c[] = new int[ 12 ];
```

This expression can be used to create the array shown in Fig. 7.1. This task also can be
performed in two steps as follows:

```
int c[];             // declare the array variable
c = new int[ 12 ];   // create the array; assign to array variable
```

In the declaration, the square brackets following the variable name c indicate that c is a
variable that will refer to an array (i.e., the variable will store an array reference). In the
assignment statement, the array variable c receives the reference to a new array of 12 int
elements. When an array is created, each element of the array receives a default value—
zero for the numeric primitive-type elements, false for boolean elements and null for
references (any nonprimitive type). As we will soon see, we can provide specific, nonde-
fault initial element values when we create an array.

 Common Programming Error 7.2

*In an array declaration, specifying the number of elements in the square brackets of the declara-
tion (e.g., int c[12];) is a syntax error.*

A program can create several arrays in a single declaration. The following String array
declaration reserves 100 elements for b and 27 elements for x:

```
String b[] = new String[ 100 ], x[] = new String[ 27 ];
```

In this case, the class name String applies to each variable in the declaration. For readability, we prefer to declare only one variable per declaration, as in:

```
String b[] = new String[ 100 ]; // create array b
String x[] = new String[ 27 ]; // create array x
```

Good Programming Practice 7.1

For readability, declare only one variable per declaration. Keep each declaration on a separate line, and include a comment describing the variable being declared.

When an array is declared, the type of the array and the square brackets can be combined at the beginning of the declaration to indicate that all the identifiers in the declaration are array variables. For example, the declaration

```
double[] array1, array2;
```

indicates that `array1` and `array2` are each "array of `double`" variables. The preceding declaration is equivalent to:

```
double array1[];
double array2[];
```

or

```
double[] array1;
double[] array2;
```

The preceding pairs of declarations are equivalent—when only one variable is declared in each declaration, the square brackets can be placed either after the type or after the array variable name.

Common Programming Error 7.3

Declaring multiple array variables in a single declaration can lead to subtle errors. Consider the declaration `int[] a, b, c;`. If a, b and c should be declared as array variables, then this declaration is correct—placing square brackets directly following the type indicates that all the identifiers in the declaration are array variables. However, if only a is intended to be an array variable, and b and c are intended to be individual `int` variables, then this declaration is incorrect—the declaration `int a[], b, c;` would achieve the desired result.

A program can declare arrays of any type. Every element of a primitive-type array contains a value of the array's declared type. Similarly, in an array of a reference type, every element is a reference to an object of the array's declared type. For example, every element of an `int` array is an `int` value, and every element of a `String` array is a reference to a `String` object.

7.4 Examples Using Arrays

This section presents several examples that demonstrate declaring arrays, creating arrays, initializing arrays and manipulating array elements.

Creating and Initializing an Array

The application of Fig. 7.2 uses keyword `new` to create an array of 10 `int` elements, which are initially zero (the default for `int` variables).

Line 8 declares `array`—a reference capable of referring to an array of `int` elements. Line 10 creates the array object and assigns its reference to variable `array`. Line 12 outputs the column headings. The first column contains the index (0–9) of each array element, and the second column contains the default value (0) of each array element.

```
1    // Fig. 7.2: InitArray.java
2    // Creating an array.
3
4    public class InitArray
5    {
6       public static void main( String args[] )
7       {
8          int array[]; // declare array named array
9
10         array = new int[ 10 ]; // create the space for array
11
12         System.out.printf( "%s%8s\n", "Index", "Value" ); // column headings
13
14         // output each array element's value
15         for ( int counter = 0; counter < array.length; counter++ )
16            System.out.printf( "%5d%8d\n", counter, array[ counter ] );
17      } // end main
18   } // end class InitArray
```

```
Index    Value
   0         0
   1         0
   2         0
   3         0
   4         0
   5         0
   6         0
   7         0
   8         0
   9         0
```

Fig. 7.2 | Initializing the elements of an array to default values of zero.

The for statement in lines 15–16 outputs the index number (represented by counter) and the value of each array element (represented by array[counter]). Note that the loop control variable counter is initially 0—index values start at 0, so using zero-based counting allows the loop to access every element of the array. The for's loop-continuation condition uses the expression array.length (line 15) to determine the length of the array. In this example, the length of the array is 10, so the loop continues executing as long as the value of control variable counter is less than 10. The highest index value of a 10-element array is 9, so using the less-than operator in the loop-continuation condition guarantees that the loop does not attempt to access an element beyond the end of the array (i.e., during the final iteration of the loop, counter is 9). We will soon see what Java does when it encounters such an out-of-range index at execution time.

Using an Array Initializer
A program can create an array and initialize its elements with an **array initializer**, which is a comma-separated list of expressions (called an **initializer list**) enclosed in braces ({ and }); the array length is determined by the number of elements in the initializer list. For example, the declaration

```
int n[] = { 10, 20, 30, 40, 50 };
```

creates a five-element array with index values 0, 1, 2, 3 and 4. Element n[0] is initialized to 10, n[1] is initialized to 20, and so on. This declaration does not require new to create the array object. When the compiler encounters an array declaration that includes an initializer list, it counts the number of initializers in the list to determine the size of the array, then sets up the appropriate new operation "behind the scenes."

The application in Fig. 7.3 initializes an integer array with 10 values (line 9) and displays the array in tabular format. The code for displaying the array elements (lines 14–15) is identical to that in Fig. 7.2 (lines 15–16).

Calculating the Values to Store in an Array

The application in Fig. 7.4 creates a 10-element array and assigns to each element one of the even integers from 2 to 20 (2, 4, 6, ..., 20). Then the application displays the array in tabular format. The for statement at lines 12–13 calculates an array element's value by multiplying the current value of the control variable counter by 2, then adding 2.

Line 8 uses the modifier final to declare the **constant variable** ARRAY_LENGTH with the value 10. Constant variables (also known as final variables) must be initialized before they are used and cannot be modified thereafter. If you attempt to modify a final variable after it is initialized in its declaration (as in line 8), the compiler issues the error message

        cannot assign a value to final variable *variableName*

```
1   // Fig. 7.3: InitArray.java
2   // Initializing the elements of an array with an array initializer.
3
4   public class InitArray
5   {
6      public static void main( String args[] )
7      {
8         // initializer list specifies the value for each element
9         int array[] = { 32, 27, 64, 18, 95, 14, 90, 70, 60, 37 };
10
11        System.out.printf( "%s%8s\n", "Index", "Value" ); // column headings
12
13        // output each array element's value
14        for ( int counter = 0; counter < array.length; counter++ )
15           System.out.printf( "%5d%8d\n", counter, array[ counter ] );
16     } // end main
17  } // end class InitArray
```

```
Index   Value
    0      32
    1      27
    2      64
    3      18
    4      95
    5      14
    6      90
    7      70
    8      60
    9      37
```

Fig. 7.3 | Initializing the elements of an array with an array initializer.

```
1    // Fig. 7.4: InitArray.java
2    // Calculating values to be placed into elements of an array.
3
4    public class InitArray
5    {
6       public static void main( String args[] )
7       {
8          final int ARRAY_LENGTH = 10; // declare constant
9          int array[] = new int[ ARRAY_LENGTH ]; // create array
10
11         // calculate value for each array element
12         for ( int counter = 0; counter < array.length; counter++ )
13            array[ counter ] = 2 + 2 * counter;
14
15         System.out.printf( "%s%8s\n", "Index", "Value" ); // column headings
16
17         // output each array element's value
18         for ( int counter = 0; counter < array.length; counter++ )
19            System.out.printf( "%5d%8d\n", counter, array[ counter ] );
20      } // end main
21   } // end class InitArray
```

```
Index   Value
    0       2
    1       4
    2       6
    3       8
    4      10
    5      12
    6      14
    7      16
    8      18
    9      20
```

Fig. 7.4 | Calculating the values to be placed into the elements of an array.

If an attempt is made to access the value of a final variable before it is initialized, the compiler issues the error message

variable *variableName* might not have been initialized

Good Programming Practice 7.2

Constant variables also are called named constants or read-only variables. Such variables often make programs more readable than programs that use literal values (e.g., 10)—a named constant such as ARRAY_LENGTH clearly indicates its purpose, whereas a literal value could have different meanings based on the context in which it is used.

Common Programming Error 7.4

Assigning a value to a constant after the variable has been initialized is a compilation error.

Common Programming Error 7.5

Attempting to use a constant before it is initialized is a compilation error.

Summing the Elements of an Array
Often, the elements of an array represent a series of values to be used in a calculation. For example, if the elements of an array represent exam grades, a professor may wish to total the elements of the array and use that sum to calculate the class average for the exam. The examples using class GradeBook later in the chapter, namely Fig. 7.14 and Fig. 7.18, use this technique.

The application in Fig. 7.5 sums the values contained in a 10-element integer array. The program declares, creates and initializes the array at line 8. The for statement performs the calculations. [*Note:* The values supplied as array initializers are often read into a program rather than specified in an initializer list. For example, an application could input the values from a user or from a file on disk (as discussed in Chapter 14, Files and Streams). Reading the data into a program makes the program more reusable, because it can be used with different sets of data.]

Using Bar Charts to Display Array Data Graphically
Many programs present data to users in a graphical manner. For example, numeric values are often displayed as bars in a bar chart. In such a chart, longer bars represent proportionally larger numeric values. One simple way to display numeric data graphically is with a bar chart that shows each numeric value as a bar of asterisks (*).

Professors often like to examine the distribution of grades on an exam. A professor might graph the number of grades in each of several categories to visualize the grade distribution. Suppose the grades on an exam were 87, 68, 94, 100, 83, 78, 85, 91, 76 and 87. Note that there was one grade of 100, two grades in the 90s, four grades in the 80s, two grades in the 70s, one grade in the 60s and no grades below 60. Our next application (Fig. 7.6) stores this grade distribution data in an array of 11 elements, each corresponding to a category of grades. For example, array[0] indicates the number of grades in the

```java
1    // Fig. 7.5: SumArray.java
2    // Computing the sum of the elements of an array.
3
4    public class SumArray
5    {
6       public static void main( String args[] )
7       {
8          int array[] = { 87, 68, 94, 100, 83, 78, 85, 91, 76, 87 };
9          int total = 0;
10
11         // add each element's value to total
12         for ( int counter = 0; counter < array.length; counter++ )
13            total += array[ counter ];
14
15         System.out.printf( "Total of array elements: %d\n", total );
16      } // end main
17   } // end class SumArray
```

```
Total of array elements: 849
```

Fig. 7.5 | Computing the sum of the elements of an array.

```
1    // Fig. 7.6: BarChart.java
2    // Bar chart printing program.
3
4    public class BarChart
5    {
6       public static void main( String args[] )
7       {
8          int array[] = { 0, 0, 0, 0, 0, 0, 1, 2, 4, 2, 1 };
9
10         System.out.println( "Grade distribution:" );
11
12         // for each array element, output a bar of the chart
13         for ( int counter = 0; counter < array.length; counter++ )
14         {
15            // output bar label ( "00-09: ", ..., "90-99: ", "100: " )
16            if ( counter == 10 )
17               System.out.printf( "%5d: ", 100 );
18            else
19               System.out.printf( "%02d-%02d: ",
20                  counter * 10, counter * 10 + 9 );
21
22            // print bar of asterisks
23            for ( int stars = 0; stars < array[ counter ]; stars++ )
24               System.out.print( "*" );
25
26            System.out.println(); // start a new line of output
27         } // end outer for
28      } // end main
29   } // end class BarChart
```

```
Grade distribution:
00-09:
10-19:
20-29:
30-39:
40-49:
50-59:
60-69: *
70-79: **
80-89: ****
90-99: **
  100: *
```

Fig. 7.6 | Bar chart printing program.

range 0–9, array[7] indicates the number of grades in the range 70–79 and array[10] indicates the number of 100 grades. The two versions of class GradeBook later in the chapter (Fig. 7.14 and Fig. 7.18) contain code that calculates these grade frequencies based on a set of grades. For now, we manually create the array by looking at the set of grades.

The application reads the numbers from the array and graphs the information as a bar chart. The program displays each grade range followed by a bar of asterisks indicating the number of grades in that range. To label each bar, lines 16–20 output a grade range (e.g.,

"70-79: ") based on the current value of counter. When counter is 10, line 17 outputs 100 with a field width of 5, followed by a colon and a space, to align the label "100: " with the other bar labels. The nested for statement (lines 23–24) outputs the bars. Note the loop-continuation condition at line 23 (stars < array[counter]). Each time the program reaches the inner for, the loop counts from 0 up to array[counter], thus using a value in array to determine the number of asterisks to display. In this example, array[0]– array[5] contain zeroes because no students received a grade below 60. Thus, the program displays no asterisks next to the first six grade ranges. Note that line 19 uses the format specifier %02d to output the numbers in a grade range. This specifier indicates that an int value should be formatted as a field of two digits. The **0 flag** in the format specifier indicates that values with fewer digits than the field width (2) should begin with a leading 0.

Using the Elements of an Array as Counters

Sometimes, programs use counter variables to summarize data, such as the results of a survey. In Fig. 6.8, we used separate counters in our die-rolling program to track the number of occurrences of each side of a die as the program rolled the die 6000 times. An array version of the application in Fig. 6.8 is shown in Fig. 7.7.

```java
1   // Fig. 7.7: RollDie.java
2   // Roll a six-sided die 6000 times.
3   import java.util.Random;
4
5   public class RollDie
6   {
7      public static void main( String args[] )
8      {
9         Random randomNumbers = new Random(); // random number generator
10        int frequency[] = new int[ 7 ]; // array of frequency counters
11
12        // roll die 6000 times; use die value as frequency index
13        for ( int roll = 1; roll <= 6000; roll++ )
14           ++frequency[ 1 + randomNumbers.nextInt( 6 ) ];
15
16        System.out.printf( "%s%10s\n", "Face", "Frequency" );
17
18        // output each array element's value
19        for ( int face = 1; face < frequency.length; face++ )
20           System.out.printf( "%4d%10d\n", face, frequency[ face ] );
21     } // end main
22  } // end class RollDie
```

```
Face Frequency
   1       988
   2       963
   3      1018
   4      1041
   5       978
   6      1012
```

Fig. 7.7 | Die-rolling program using arrays instead of switch.

Fig. 7.7 uses the array `frequency` (line 10) to count the occurrences of each side of the die. *The single statement in line 14 of this program replaces lines 23–46 of Fig. 6.8.* Line 14 uses the random value to determine which `frequency` element to increment during each iteration of the loop. The calculation in line 14 produces random numbers from 1 to 6, so the array `frequency` must be large enough to store six counters. However, we use a seven-element array in which we ignore `frequency[ 0 ]`—it is more logical to have the face value 1 increment `frequency[ 1 ]` than `frequency[ 0 ]`. Thus, each face value is used as an index for array `frequency`. We also replaced lines 50–52 from Fig. 6.8 by looping through array `frequency` to output the results (lines 19–20).

Using Arrays to Analyze Survey Results

Our next example uses arrays to summarize the results of data collected in a survey:

> *Forty students were asked to rate the quality of the food in the student cafeteria on a scale of 1 to 10 (where 1 means awful and 10 means excellent). Place the 40 responses in an integer array, and summarize the results of the poll.*

This is a typical array-processing application (see Fig. 7.8). We wish to summarize the number of responses of each type (i.e., 1 through 10). The array `responses` (lines 9–11) is a 40-element integer array of the students' responses to the survey. We use an 11-element array `frequency` (line 12) to count the number of occurrences of each response. Each element of the array is used as a counter for one of the survey responses and is initialized to zero by default. As in Fig. 7.7, we ignore `frequency[ 0 ]`.

```java
1   // Fig. 7.8: StudentPoll.java
2   // Poll analysis program.
3
4   public class StudentPoll
5   {
6      public static void main( String args[] )
7      {
8         // array of survey responses
9         int responses[] = { 1, 2, 6, 4, 8, 5, 9, 7, 8, 10, 1, 6, 3, 8, 6,
10           10, 3, 8, 2, 7, 6, 5, 7, 6, 8, 6, 7, 5, 6, 6, 5, 6, 7, 5, 6,
11           4, 8, 6, 8, 10 };
12        int frequency[] = new int[ 11 ]; // array of frequency counters
13
14        // for each answer, select responses element and use that value
15        // as frequency index to determine element to increment
16        for ( int answer = 0; answer < responses.length; answer++ )
17           ++frequency[ responses[ answer ] ];
18
19        System.out.printf( "%s%10s", "Rating", "Frequency" );
20
21        // output each array element's value
22        for ( int rating = 1; rating < frequency.length; rating++ )
23           System.out.printf( "%d%10d", rating, frequency[ rating ] );
24     } // end main
25  } // end class StudentPoll
```

Fig. 7.8 | Poll analysis program. (Part I of 2.)

```
Rating Frequency
    1        2
    2        2
    3        2
    4        2
    5        5
    6       11
    7        5
    8        7
    9        1
   10        3
```

Fig. 7.8 | Poll analysis program. (Part 2 of 2.)

The for loop at lines 16–17 takes the responses one at a time from array responses and increments one of the 10 counters in the frequency array (frequency[1] to frequency[10]). The key statement in the loop is line 17, which increments the appropriate frequency counter, depending on the value of responses[answer].

Let's consider several iterations of the for loop. When control variable answer is 0, the value of responses[answer] is the value of responses[0] (i.e., 1), so the program interprets ++frequency[responses[answer]] as

++frequency[1]

which increments the value in array element 1. To evaluate the expression, start with the value in the innermost set of square brackets (answer). Once you know answer's value (which is the value of the loop control variable in line 16), plug it into the expression and evaluate the next outer set of square brackets (i.e., responses[answer], which is a value selected from the responses array in lines 9–11). Then use the resulting value as the index for the frequency array to specify which counter to increment.

When answer is 1, responses[answer] is the value of responses[1] (2), so the program interprets ++frequency[responses[answer]] as

++frequency[2]

which increments array element 2.

When answer is 2, responses[answer] is the value of responses[2] (6), so the program interprets ++frequency[responses[answer]] as

++frequency[6]

which increments array element 6, and so on. Regardless of the number of responses processed in the survey, the program requires only an 11-element array (ignoring element zero) to summarize the results, because all the response values are between 1 and 10 and the index values for an 11-element array are 0 through 10.

If the data in the responses array had contained invalid values, such as 13, the program would have attempted to add 1 to frequency[13], which is outside the bounds of the array. Java disallows this. When a Java program executes, the JVM checks array indices to ensure that they are valid (i.e., they must be greater than or equal to 0 and less than the length of the array). If a program uses an invalid index, Java generates a so-called exception to indicate that an error occurred in the program at execution time. A control statement can be used to prevent such an "out-of-bounds" error from occurring. For example, the condition in a control statement could determine whether an index is valid before allowing it to be used in an array-access expression.

Error-Prevention Tip 7.1

An exception indicates that an error has occurred in a program. A programmer often can write code to recover from an exception and continue program execution, rather than abnormally terminating the program. When a program attempts to access an element outside the array bounds, an `ArrayIndexOutOfBoundsException` occurs. Exception handling is discussed in Chapter 13.

Error-Prevention Tip 7.2

When writing code to loop through an array, ensure that the array index is always greater than or equal to 0 and less than the length of the array. The loop-continuation condition should prevent the accessing of elements outside this range.

7.5 Case Study: Card Shuffling and Dealing Simulation

The examples in the chapter thus far have used arrays containing elements of primitive types. Recall from Section 7.2 that the elements of an array can be either primitive types or reference types. This section uses random number generation and an array of reference-type elements, namely objects representing playing cards, to develop a class that simulates card shuffling and dealing. This class can then be used to implement applications that play specific card games. The exercises at the end of the chapter use the classes developed here to build a simple poker application.

We first develop class Card (Fig. 7.9), which represents a playing card that has a face (e.g., "Ace", "Deuce", "Three", …, "Jack", "Queen", "King") and a suit (e.g., "Hearts", "Diamonds", "Clubs", "Spades"). Next, we develop the DeckOfCards class (Fig. 7.10), which creates a deck of 52 playing cards in which each element is a Card object. We then build a test application (Fig. 7.11) that demonstrates class DeckOfCards's card shuffling and dealing capabilities.

Class *Card*
Class Card (Fig. 7.9) contains two String instance variables—face and suit—that are used to store references to the face name and suit name for a specific Card. The constructor for the class (lines 10–14) receives two Strings that it uses to initialize face and suit. Method toString (lines 17–20) creates a String consisting of the face of the card, the String " of " and the suit of the card. Recall from Chapter 6 that the + operator can be used to concatenate (i.e., combine) several Strings to form one larger String. Card's toString method can be invoked explicitly to obtain a string representation of a Card object (e.g., "Ace of Spades"). The toString method of an object is called implicitly when the object is used where a String is expected (e.g., when printf outputs the object as a String using the %s format specifier or when the object is concatenated to a String using the + operator). For this behavior to occur, toString must be declared with the header shown in Fig. 7.9.

Class *DeckOfCards*
Class DeckOfCards (Fig. 7.10) declares an instance variable array named deck of Card objects (line 7). Like primitive-type array declarations, the declaration of an array of objects

```
1   // Fig. 7.9: Card.java
2   // Card class represents a playing card.
3
4   public class Card
5   {
6      private String face; // face of card ("Ace", "Deuce", ...)
7      private String suit; // suit of card ("Hearts", "Diamonds", ...)
8
9      // two-argument constructor initializes card's face and suit
10     public Card( String cardFace, String cardSuit )
11     {
12        face = cardFace; // initialize face of card
13        suit = cardSuit; // initialize suit of card
14     } // end two-argument Card constructor
15
16     // return String representation of Card
17     public String toString()
18     {
19        return face + " of " + suit;
20     } // end method toString
21  } // end class Card
```

Fig. 7.9 | Card class represents a playing card.

includes the type of the elements in the array, followed by the name of the array variable and square brackets (e.g., Card deck[]). Class DeckOfCards also declares an integer instance variable currentCard (line 8) representing the next Card to be dealt from the deck array and a named constant NUMBER_OF_CARDS (line 9) indicating the number of Cards in the deck (52).

```
1   // Fig. 7.10: DeckOfCards.java
2   // DeckOfCards class represents a deck of playing cards.
3   import java.util.Random;
4
5   public class DeckOfCards
6   {
7      private Card deck[]; // array of Card objects
8      private int currentCard; // index of next Card to be dealt
9      private final int NUMBER_OF_CARDS = 52; // constant number of Cards
10     private Random randomNumbers; // random number generator
11
12     // constructor fills deck of Cards
13     public DeckOfCards()
14     {
15        String faces[] = { "Ace", "Deuce", "Three", "Four", "Five", "Six",
16           "Seven", "Eight", "Nine", "Ten", "Jack", "Queen", "King" };
17        String suits[] = { "Hearts", "Diamonds", "Clubs", "Spades" };
18
19        deck = new Card[ NUMBER_OF_CARDS ]; // create array of Card objects
```

Fig. 7.10 | DeckOfCards class represents a deck of playing cards that can be shuffled and dealt one at a time. (Part 1 of 2.)

```
20        currentCard = 0; // set currentCard so first Card dealt is deck[ 0 ]
21        randomNumbers = new Random(); // create random number generator
22
23        // populate deck with Card objects
24        for ( int count = 0; count < deck.length; count++ )
25           deck[ count ] =
26              new Card( faces[ count % 13 ], suits[ count / 13 ] );
27     } // end DeckOfCards constructor
28
29     // shuffle deck of Cards with one-pass algorithm
30     public void shuffle()
31     {
32        // after shuffling, dealing should start at deck[ 0 ] again
33        currentCard = 0; // reinitialize currentCard
34
35        // for each Card, pick another random Card and swap them
36        for ( int first = 0; first < deck.length; first++ )
37        {
38           // select a random number between 0 and 51
39           int second =  randomNumbers.nextInt( NUMBER_OF_CARDS );
40
41           // swap current Card with randomly selected Card
42           Card temp = deck[ first ];
43           deck[ first ] = deck[ second ];
44           deck[ second ] = temp;
45        } // end for
46     } // end method shuffle
47
48     // deal one Card
49     public Card dealCard()
50     {
51        // determine whether Cards remain to be dealt
52        if ( currentCard < deck.length )
53           return deck[ currentCard++ ]; // return current Card in array
54        else
55           return null; // return null to indicate that all Cards were dealt
56     } // end method dealCard
57  } // end class DeckOfCards
```

Fig. 7.10 | DeckOfCards class represents a deck of playing cards that can be shuffled and dealt one at a time. (Part 2 of 2.)

The class's constructor instantiates the deck array (line 19) to be of size NUMBER_OF_CARDS. When first created, the elements of the deck array are null by default, so the constructor uses a for statement (lines 24–26) to fill the deck array with Cards. The for statement initializes control variable count to 0 and loops while count is less than deck.length, causing count to take on each integer value from 0 to 51 (the indices of the deck array). Each Card is instantiated and initialized with two Strings—one from the faces array (which contains the Strings "Ace" through "King") and one from the suits array (which contains the Strings "Hearts", "Diamonds", "Clubs" and "Spades"). The calculation count % 13 always results in a value from 0 to 12 (the 13 indices of the faces array in lines 15–16), and the calculation count / 13 always results in a value from 0 to 3 (the four indices of the suits array in line 17). When the deck array is initialized, it contains the Cards with faces "Ace" through "King" in order for each suit ("Hearts" then "Diamonds" then "Clubs" then "Spades").

Method shuffle (lines 30–46) shuffles the Cards in the deck. The method loops through all 52 Cards (array indices 0 to 51). For each Card, a number between 0 and 51 is picked randomly to select another Card. Next, the current Card object and the randomly selected Card object are swapped in the array. This exchange is performed by the three assignments in lines 42–44. The extra variable temp temporarily stores one of the two Card objects being swapped. The swap cannot be performed with only the two statements

```
deck[ first ] = deck[ second ];
deck[ second ] = deck[ first ];
```

If deck[first] is the "Ace" of "Spades" and deck[second] is the "Queen" of "Hearts", after the first assignment, both array elements contain the "Queen" of "Hearts" and the "Ace" of "Spades" is lost—hence, the extra variable temp is needed. After the for loop terminates, the Card objects are randomly ordered. A total of only 52 swaps are made in a single pass of the entire array, and the array of Card objects is shuffled!

Method dealCard (lines 49–56) deals one Card in the array. Recall that currentCard indicates the index of the next Card to be dealt (i.e., the Card at the top of the deck). Thus, line 52 compares currentCard to the length of the deck array. If the deck is not empty (i.e., currentCard is less than 52), line 53 returns the "top" Card and postincrements currentCard to prepare for the next call to dealCard—otherwise, null is returned. Recall from Chapter 3 that null represents a "reference to nothing."

Shuffling and Dealing Cards

The application of Fig. 7.11 demonstrates the card dealing and shuffling capabilities of class DeckOfCards (Fig. 7.10). Line 9 creates a DeckOfCards object named myDeckOfCards. Recall that the DeckOfCards constructor creates the deck with the 52 Card objects in order by suit and face. Line 10 invokes myDeckOfCards's shuffle method to rearrange the Card objects. The for statement in lines 13–19 deals all 52 Cards in the deck and prints them in four columns of 13 Cards each. Lines 16–18 deal and print four Card objects, each obtained by invoking myDeckOfCards's dealCard method. When printf outputs a Card with the %-20s format specifier, the Card's toString method (declared in lines 17–20 of Fig. 7.9) is implicitly invoked, and the result is output left justified in a field of width 20.

```
1   // Fig. 7.11: DeckOfCardsTest.java
2   // Card shuffling and dealing application.
3
4   public class DeckOfCardsTest
5   {
6      // execute application
7      public static void main( String args[] )
8      {
9         DeckOfCards myDeckOfCards = new DeckOfCards();
10        myDeckOfCards.shuffle(); // place Cards in random order
```

Fig. 7.11 | Card shuffling and dealing. (Part 1 of 2.)

```
11
12          // print all 52 Cards in the order in which they are dealt
13          for ( int i = 0; i < 13; i++ )
14          {
15              // deal and print 4 Cards
16              System.out.printf( "%-20s%-20s%-20s%-20s\n",
17                  myDeckOfCards.dealCard(), myDeckOfCards.dealCard(),
18                  myDeckOfCards.dealCard(), myDeckOfCards.dealCard() );
19          } // end for
20      } // end main
21  } // end class DeckOfCardsTest
```

Six of Spades	Eight of Spades	Six of Clubs	Nine of Hearts
Queen of Hearts	Seven of Clubs	Nine of Spades	King of Hearts
Three of Diamonds	Deuce of Clubs	Ace of Hearts	Ten of Spades
Four of Spades	Ace of Clubs	Seven of Diamonds	Four of Hearts
Three of Clubs	Deuce of Hearts	Five of Spades	Jack of Diamonds
King of Clubs	Ten of Hearts	Three of Hearts	Six of Diamonds
Queen of Clubs	Eight of Diamonds	Deuce of Diamonds	Ten of Diamonds
Three of Spades	King of Diamonds	Nine of Clubs	Six of Hearts
Ace of Spades	Four of Diamonds	Seven of Hearts	Eight of Clubs
Deuce of Spades	Eight of Hearts	Five of Hearts	Queen of Spades
Jack of Hearts	Seven of Spades	Four of Clubs	Nine of Diamonds
Ace of Diamonds	Queen of Diamonds	Five of Clubs	King of Spades
Five of Diamonds	Ten of Clubs	Jack of Spades	Jack of Clubs

Fig. 7.11 | Card shuffling and dealing. (Part 2 of 2.)

7.6 **Enhanced for Statement**

In previous examples, we demonstrated how to use counter-controlled for statements to iterate through the elements of an array. In this section, we introduce the **enhanced for statement**, which iterates through the elements of an array or a collection without using a counter (thus avoiding the possibility of "stepping outside" the array). This section discusses how to use the enhanced for statement to loop through an array. We show how to use the enhanced for statement with collections in Chapter 19, Collections. The syntax of an enhanced for statement is:

> for (*parameter* : *arrayName*)
>   *statement*

where *parameter* has two parts—a type and an identifier (e.g., int number)—and *arrayName* is the array through which to iterate. The type of the parameter must be consistent with the type of the elements in the array. As the next example illustrates, the identifier represents successive values in the array on successive iterations of the enhanced for statement.

Figure 7.12 uses the enhanced for statement (lines 12–13) to sum the integers in an array of student grades. The type specified in the parameter to the enhanced for is int, because array contains int values—the loop selects one int value from the array during each iteration. The enhanced for statement iterates through successive values in the array one by one. The enhanced for header can be read as "for each iteration, assign the next element of array to int variable number, then execute the following statement." Thus, for

```
 1   // Fig. 7.12: EnhancedForTest.java
 2   // Using enhanced for statement to total integers in an array.
 3
 4   public class EnhancedForTest
 5   {
 6      public static void main( String args[] )
 7      {
 8         int array[] = { 87, 68, 94, 100, 83, 78, 85, 91, 76, 87 };
 9         int total = 0;
10
11         // add each element's value to total
12         for ( int number : array )
13            total += number;
14
15         System.out.printf( "Total of array elements: %d\n", total );
16      } // end main
17   } // end class EnhancedForTest
```

```
Total of array elements: 849
```

Fig. 7.12 | Using the enhanced for statement to total integers in an array.

each iteration, identifier number represents an int value in array. Lines 12–13 are equivalent to the following counter-controlled repetition used in lines 12–13 of Fig. 7.5 to total the integers in array:

```
for ( int counter = 0; counter < array.length; counter++ )
   total += array[ counter ];
```

The enhanced for statement simplifies the code for iterating through an array. Note, however, that the enhanced for statement can be used only to obtain array elements—it cannot be used to modify elements. If your program needs to modify elements, use the traditional counter-controlled for statement.

The enhanced for statement can be used in place of the counter-controlled for statement whenever code looping through an array does not require access to the counter indicating the index of the current array element. For example, totaling the integers in an array requires access only to the element values—the index of each element is irrelevant. However, if a program must use a counter for some reason other than simply to loop through an array (e.g., to print an index number next to each array element value, as in the examples earlier in this chapter), use the counter-controlled for statement.

7.7 Passing Arrays to Methods

This section demonstrates how to pass arrays and individual array elements as arguments to methods. At the end of the section, we discuss how all types of arguments are passed to methods. To pass an array argument to a method, specify the name of the array without any brackets. For example, if array hourlyTemperatures is declared as

```
double hourlyTemperatures[] = new double[ 24 ];
```

then the method call

```
modifyArray( hourlyTemperatures );
```

passes the reference of array hourlyTemperatures to method modifyArray. Every array object "knows" its own length (via its length field). Thus, when we pass an array object's reference into a method, we need not pass the array length as an additional argument.

For a method to receive an array reference through a method call, the method's parameter list must specify an array parameter. For example, the method header for method modifyArray might be written as

```
void modifyArray( int b[] )
```

indicating that modifyArray receives the reference of an integer array in parameter b. The method call passes array hourlyTemperature's reference, so when the called method uses the array variable b, it refers to the same array object as hourlyTemperatures in the caller.

When an argument to a method is an entire array or an individual array element of a reference type, the called method receives a copy of the reference. However, when an argument to a method is an individual array element of a primitive type, the called method receives a copy of the element's value. Such primitive values are called scalars or scalar quantities. To pass an individual array element to a method, use the indexed name of the array element as an argument in the method call.

Figure 7.13 demonstrates the difference between passing an entire array and passing a primitive-type array element to a method. The enhanced for statement at lines 16–17 outputs the five elements of array (an array of int values). Line 19 invokes method modifyArray, passing array as an argument. Method modifyArray (lines 36–40) receives a copy of array's reference and uses the reference to multiply each of array's elements by 2. To prove that array's elements were modified, the for statement at lines 23–24 outputs the five elements of array again. As the output shows, method modifyArray doubled the value of each element. Note that we could not use the enhanced for statement in lines 38–39 because we are modifying the array's elements.

```java
 1   // Fig. 7.13: PassArray.java
 2   // Passing arrays and individual array elements to methods.
 3
 4   public class PassArray
 5   {
 6      // main creates array and calls modifyArray and modifyElement
 7      public static void main( String args[] )
 8      {
 9         int array[] = { 1, 2, 3, 4, 5 };
10
11         System.out.println(
12            "Effects of passing reference to entire array:\n" +
13            "The values of the original array are:" );
14
15         // output original array elements
16         for ( int value : array )
17            System.out.printf( "   %d", value );
```

Fig. 7.13 | Passing arrays and individual array elements to methods. (Part 1 of 2.)

```
18
19          modifyArray( array ); // pass array reference
20          System.out.println( "\n\nThe values of the modified array are:" );
21
22          // output modified array elements
23          for ( int value : array )
24             System.out.printf( "   %d", value );
25
26          System.out.printf(
27             "\n\nEffects of passing array element value:\n" +
28             "array[3] before modifyElement: %d\n", array[ 3 ] );
29
30          modifyElement( array[ 3 ] ); // attempt to modify array[ 3 ]
31          System.out.printf(
32             "array[3] after modifyElement: %d\n", array[ 3 ] );
33       } // end main
34
35       // multiply each element of an array by 2
36       public static void modifyArray( int array2[] )
37       {
38          for ( int counter = 0; counter < array2.length; counter++ )
39             array2[ counter ] *= 2;
40       } // end method modifyArray
41
42       // multiply argument by 2
43       public static void modifyElement( int element )
44       {
45          element *= 2;
46          System.out.printf(
47             "Value of element in modifyElement: %d\n", element );
48       } // end method modifyElement
49    } // end class PassArray
```

```
Effects of passing reference to entire array:
The values of the original array are:
   1   2   3   4   5

The values of the modified array are:
   2   4   6   8   10

Effects of passing array element value:
array[3] before modifyElement: 8
Value of element in modifyElement: 16
array[3] after modifyElement: 8
```

Fig. 7.13 | Passing arrays and individual array elements to methods. (Part 2 of 2.)

Figure 7.13 next demonstrates that when a copy of an individual primitive-type array element is passed to a method, modifying the copy in the called method does not affect the original value of that element in the calling method's array. Lines 26–28 output the value of array[3] (8) before invoking method modifyElement. Line 30 calls method modifyElement and passes array[3] as an argument. Remember that array[3] is actually one int value (8) in array. Therefore, the program passes a copy of the value of array[3]. Method modifyElement (lines 43–48) multiplies the value received as an argument by 2, stores the result in its parameter element, then outputs the value of element (16). Since method parameters, like local variables, cease to exist when the method in which they are declared completes execution, the method parameter element is destroyed when method modifyElement terminates. Thus, when the program returns control to main, lines 31–32 output the unmodified value of array[3] (i.e., 8).

Notes on Passing Arguments to Methods

The preceding example demonstrated the different ways that arrays and primitive-type array elements are passed as arguments to methods. We now take a closer look at how arguments in general are passed to methods. Two ways to pass arguments in method calls in many programming languages are pass-by-value and pass-by-reference (also called call-by-value and call-by-reference). When an argument is passed by value, a copy of the argument's value is passed to the called method. The called method works exclusively with the copy. Changes to the called method's copy do not affect the original variable's value in the caller.

When an argument is passed by reference, the called method can access the argument's value in the caller directly and modify that data, if necessary. Pass-by-reference improves performance by eliminating the need to copy possibly large amounts of data.

Unlike some other languages, Java does not allow programmers to choose pass-by-value or pass-by-reference—all arguments are passed by value. A method call can pass two types of values to a method—copies of primitive values (e.g., values of type int and double) and copies of references to objects (including references to arrays). Objects themselves cannot be passed to methods. When a method modifies a primitive-type parameter, changes to the parameter have no effect on the original argument value in the calling method. For example, when line 30 in main of Fig. 7.13 passes array[3] to method modifyElement, the statement in line 45 that doubles the value of parameter element has no effect on the value of array[3] in main. This is also true for reference-type parameters. If you modify a reference-type parameter by assigning it the reference of another object, the parameter refers to the new object, but the reference stored in the caller's variable still refers to the original object.

Although an object's reference is passed by value, a method can still interact with the referenced object by calling its public methods using the copy of the object's reference. Since the reference stored in the parameter is a copy of the reference that was passed as an argument, the parameter in the called method and the argument in the calling method refer to the same object in memory. For example, in Fig. 7.13, both parameter array2 in method modifyArray and variable array in main refer to the same array object in memory. Any changes made using the parameter array2 are carried out on the same object that is referenced by the variable that was passed as an argument in the calling method. In Fig. 7.13, the changes made in modifyArray using array2 affect the contents of the array object referenced by array in main. Thus, with a reference to an object, the called method can manipulate the caller's object directly.

Performance Tip 7.1

Passing arrays by reference makes sense for performance reasons. If arrays were passed by value, a copy of each element would be passed. For large, frequently passed arrays, this would waste time and consume considerable storage for the copies of the arrays.

7.8 Case Study: Class GradeBook Using an Array to Store Grades

This section further evolves class GradeBook, introduced in Chapter 3 and expanded in Chapters 4–5. Recall that this class represents a grade book used by a professor to store and analyze a set of student grades. Previous versions of the class process a set of grades entered by the user, but do not maintain the individual grade values in instance variables of the class. Thus, repeat calculations require the user to reenter the same grades. One way to solve this problem would be to store each grade entered in an individual instance of the class. For example, we could create instance variables grade1, grade2, …, grade10 in class GradeBook to store 10 student grades. However, the code to total the grades and determine the class average would be cumbersome, and the class would not be able to process any more than 10 grades at a time. In this section, we solve this problem by storing grades in an array.

Storing Student Grades in an Array in Class *GradeBook*

The version of class GradeBook (Fig. 7.14) presented here uses an array of integers to store the grades of several students on a single exam. This eliminates the need to repeatedly input the same set of grades. Array grades is declared as an instance variable in line 7—therefore, each GradeBook object maintains its own set of grades. The class's constructor (lines 10–14) has two parameters—the name of the course and an array of grades. When an application (e.g., class GradeBookTest in Fig. 7.15) creates a GradeBook object, the application passes an existing int array to the constructor, which assigns the array's reference to instance variable grades (line 13). The size of the array grades is determined by the class that passes the array to the constructor. Thus, a GradeBook object can process a variable number of grades. The grade values in the passed array could have been input from a user or read from a file on disk (as discussed in Chapter 14). In our test application, we simply initialize an array with a set of grade values (Fig. 7.15, line 10). Once the grades are stored in instance variable grades of class GradeBook, all the class's methods can access the elements of grades as often as needed to perform various calculations.

```java
1   // Fig. 7.14: GradeBook.java
2   // Grade book using an array to store test grades.
3
4   public class GradeBook
5   {
6      private String courseName; // name of course this GradeBook represents
7      private int grades[]; // array of student grades
8
9      // two-argument constructor initializes courseName and grades array
10     public GradeBook( String name, int gradesArray[] )
11     {
12        courseName = name; // initialize courseName
13        grades = gradesArray; // store grades
14     } // end two-argument GradeBook constructor
15
```

Fig. 7.14 | GradeBook class using an array to store test grades. (Part 1 of 4.)

```
16      // method to set the course name
17      public void setCourseName( String name )
18      {
19          courseName = name; // store the course name
20      } // end method setCourseName
21
22      // method to retrieve the course name
23      public String getCourseName()
24      {
25          return courseName;
26      } // end method getCourseName
27
28      // display a welcome message to the GradeBook user
29      public void displayMessage()
30      {
31          // getCourseName gets the name of the course
32          System.out.printf( "Welcome to the grade book for\n%s!\n\n",
33              getCourseName() );
34      } // end method displayMessage
35
36      // perform various operations on the data
37      public void processGrades()
38      {
39          // output grades array
40          outputGrades();
41
42          // call method getAverage to calculate the average grade
43          System.out.printf( "\nClass average is %.2f\n", getAverage() );
44
45          // call methods getMinimum and getMaximum
46          System.out.printf( "Lowest grade is %d\nHighest grade is %d\n\n",
47              getMinimum(), getMaximum() );
48
49          // call outputBarChart to print grade distribution chart
50          outputBarChart();
51      } // end method processGrades
52
53      // find minimum grade
54      public int getMinimum()
55      {
56          int lowGrade = grades[ 0 ]; // assume grades[ 0 ] is smallest
57
58          // loop through grades array
59          for ( int grade : grades )
60          {
61              // if grade lower than lowGrade, assign it to lowGrade
62              if ( grade < lowGrade )
63                  lowGrade = grade; // new lowest grade
64          } // end for
65
66          return lowGrade; // return lowest grade
67      } // end method getMinimum
```

Fig. 7.14 | GradeBook class using an array to store test grades. (Part 2 of 4.)

```
68
69      // find maximum grade
70      public int getMaximum()
71      {
72         int highGrade = grades[ 0 ]; // assume grades[ 0 ] is largest
73
74         // loop through grades array
75         for ( int grade : grades )
76         {
77            // if grade greater than highGrade, assign it to highGrade
78            if ( grade > highGrade )
79               highGrade = grade; // new highest grade
80         } // end for
81
82         return highGrade; // return highest grade
83      } // end method getMaximum
84
85      // determine average grade for test
86      public double getAverage()
87      {
88         int total = 0; // initialize total
89
90         // sum grades for one student
91         for ( int grade : grades )
92            total += grade;
93
94         // return average of grades
95         return (double) total / grades.length;
96      } // end method getAverage
97
98      // output bar chart displaying grade distribution
99      public void outputBarChart()
100     {
101        System.out.println( "Grade distribution:" );
102
103        // stores frequency of grades in each range of 10 grades
104        int frequency[] = new int[ 11 ];
105
106        // for each grade, increment the appropriate frequency
107        for ( int grade : grades )
108           ++frequency[ grade / 10 ];
109
110        // for each grade frequency, print bar in chart
111        for ( int count = 0; count < frequency.length; count++ )
112        {
113           // output bar label ( "00-09: ", ..., "90-99: ", "100: " )
114           if ( count == 10 )
115              System.out.printf( "%5d: ", 100 );
116           else
117              System.out.printf( "%02d-%02d: ",
118                 count * 10, count * 10 + 9  );
119
```

Fig. 7.14 | GradeBook class using an array to store test grades. (Part 3 of 4.)

```
120            // print bar of asterisks
121            for ( int stars = 0; stars < frequency[ count ]; stars++ )
122                System.out.print( "*" );
123
124            System.out.println(); // start a new line of output
125         } // end outer for
126      } // end method outputBarChart
127
128      // output the contents of the grades array
129      public void outputGrades()
130      {
131         System.out.println( "The grades are:\n" );
132
133         // output each student's grade
134         for ( int student = 0; student < grades.length; student++ )
135            System.out.printf( "Student %2d: %3d\n",
136               student + 1, grades[ student ] );
137      } // end method outputGrades
138   } // end class GradeBook
```

Fig. 7.14 | GradeBook class using an array to store test grades. (Part 4 of 4.)

Method processGrades (lines 37–51) contains a series of method calls that output a report summarizing the grades. Line 40 calls method outputGrades to print the contents of the array grades. Lines 134–136 in method outputGrades use a for statement to output the students' grades. A counter-controlled for must be used in this case, because lines 135–136 use counter variable student's value to output each grade next to a particular student number (see Fig. 7.15). Although array indices start at 0, a professor would typically number students starting at 1. Thus, lines 135–136 output student + 1 as the student number to produce grade labels "Student 1: ", "Student 2: ", and so on.

Method processGrades next calls method getAverage (line 43) to obtain the average of the grades in the array. Method getAverage (lines 86–96) uses an enhanced for statement to total the values in array grades before calculating the average. The parameter in the enhanced for's header (e.g., int grade) indicates that for each iteration, the int variable grade takes on a value in the array grades. Note that the averaging calculation in line 95 uses grades.length to determine the number of grades being averaged.

Lines 46–47 in method processGrades calls methods getMinimum and getMaximum to determine the lowest and highest grades of any student on the exam, respectively. Each of these methods uses an enhanced for statement to loop through array grades. Lines 59–64 in method getMinimum loop through the array. Lines 62–63 compare each grade to lowGrade; if a grade is less than lowGrade, lowGrade is set to that grade. When line 66 executes, lowGrade contains the lowest grade in the array. Method getMaximum (lines 70–83) works similarly to method getMinimum.

Finally, line 50 in method processGrades calls method outputBarChart to print a distribution chart of the grade data using a technique similar to that in Fig. 7.6. In that example, we manually calculated the number of grades in each category (i.e., 0–9, 10–19, ..., 90–99 and 100) by simply looking at a set of grades. In this example, lines 107–108 use a technique similar to that in Fig. 7.7 and Fig. 7.8 to calculate the frequency of grades in each category. Line 104 declares and creates array frequency of 11 ints to store the frequency of grades in each grade category. For each grade in array grades, lines 107–108 increment the appropriate element of the frequency array. To determine which element to increment, line 108 divides the current grade by 10 using integer division. For example, if grade is 85, line 108 increments frequency[8] to update the count of grades in the range 80–89. Lines 111–125 next print the bar chart (see Fig. 7.15) based on the values in array frequency. Like lines 23–24 of Fig. 7.6, lines 121–122 of Fig. 7.14 use a value in array frequency to determine the number of asterisks to display in each bar.

Class *GradeBookTest* That Demonstrates Class *GradeBook*

The application of Fig. 7.15 creates an object of class GradeBook (Fig. 7.14) using the int array gradesArray (declared and initialized in line 10). Lines 12–13 pass a course name and gradesArray to the GradeBook constructor. Line 14 displays a welcome message, and

```
1   // Fig. 7.15: GradeBookTest.java
2   // Creates GradeBook object using an array of grades.
3
4   public class GradeBookTest
5   {
6      // main method begins program execution
7      public static void main( String args[] )
8      {
9         // array of student grades
10        int gradesArray[] = { 87, 68, 94, 100, 83, 78, 85, 91, 76, 87 };
11
12        GradeBook myGradeBook = new GradeBook(
13           "CS101 Introduction to Java Programming", gradesArray );
14        myGradeBook.displayMessage();
15        myGradeBook.processGrades();
16     } // end main
17  } // end class GradeBookTest
```

```
Welcome to the grade book for
CS101 Introduction to Java Programming!

The grades are:

Student  1:  87
Student  2:  68
Student  3:  94
Student  4: 100
Student  5:  83
Student  6:  78
Student  7:  85
Student  8:  91
Student  9:  76
Student 10:  87
```

(continued…)

Fig. 7.15 | GradeBookTest creates a GradeBook object using an array of grades, then invokes method processGrades to analyze them. (Part 1 of 2.)

```
Class average is 84.90
Lowest grade is 68
Highest grade is 100

Grade distribution:
00-09:
10-19:
20-29:
30-39:
40-49:
50-59:
60-69: *
70-79: **
80-89: ****
90-99: **
  100: *
```

Fig. 7.15 | GradeBookTest creates a GradeBook object using an array of grades, then invokes method processGrades to analyze them. (Part 2 of 2.)

line 15 invokes the GradeBook object's processGrades method. The output summarizes the 10 grades in myGradeBook.

Software Engineering Observation 7.1

A test harness (or test application) is responsible for creating an object of the class being tested and providing it with data. This data could come from any of several sources. Test data can be placed directly into an array with an array initializer, it can come from the user at the keyboard, it can come from a file (as you will see in Chapter 14), or it can come from a network (as you will see in Chapter 24). After passing this data to the class's constructor to instantiate the object, the test harness should call upon the object to test its methods and manipulate its data. Gathering data in the test harness like this allows the class to manipulate data from several sources.

7.9 Multidimensional Arrays

Multidimensional arrays with two dimensions are often used to represent tables of values consisting of information arranged in rows and columns. To identify a particular table element, we must specify two indices. By convention, the first identifies the element's row and the second its column. Arrays that require two indices to identify a particular element are called two-dimensional arrays. (Multidimensional arrays can have more than two dimensions.) Java does not support multidimensional arrays directly, but it does allow the programmer to specify one-dimensional arrays whose elements are also one-dimensional arrays, thus achieving the same effect. Figure 7.16 illustrates a two-dimensional array a that contains three rows and four columns (i.e., a three-by-four array). In general, an array with m rows and n columns is called an m-by-n array.

Every element in array a is identified in Fig. 7.16 by an array-access expression of the form a[row][column]; a is the name of the array, and row and column are the indices that uniquely identify each element in array a by row and column number. Note that the names of the elements in row 0 all have a first index of 0, and the names of the elements in column 3 all have a second index of 3.

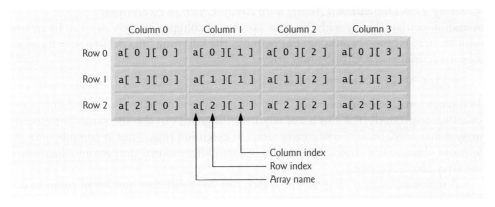

Fig. 7.16 | Two-dimensional array with three rows and four columns.

Arrays of One-Dimensional Arrays

Like one-dimensional arrays, multidimensional arrays can be initialized with array initializers in declarations. A two-dimensional array b with two rows and two columns could be declared and initialized with **nested array initializers** as follows:

```
int b[][] = { { 1, 2 }, { 3, 4 } };
```

The initializer values are grouped by row in braces. So 1 and 2 initialize b[0][0] and b[0][1], respectively, and 3 and 4 initialize b[1][0] and b[1][1], respectively. The compiler counts the number of nested array initializers (represented by sets of braces within the outer braces) in the array declaration to determine the number of rows in array b. The compiler counts the initializer values in the nested array initializer for a row to determine the number of columns in that row. As we will see momentarily, this means that rows can have different lengths.

Multidimensional arrays are maintained as arrays of one-dimensional arrays. Therefore array b in the preceding declaration is actually composed of two separate one-dimensional arrays—one containing the values in the first nested initializer list { 1, 2 } and one containing the values in the second nested initializer list { 3, 4 }. Thus, array b itself is an array of two elements, each a one-dimensional array of int values.

Two-Dimensional Arrays with Rows of Different Lengths

The manner in which multidimensional arrays are represented makes them quite flexible. In fact, the lengths of the rows in array b are not required to be the same. For example,

```
int b[][] = { { 1, 2 }, { 3, 4, 5 } };
```

creates integer array b with two elements (determined by the number of nested array initializers) that represent the rows of the two-dimensional array. Each element of b is a reference to a one-dimensional array of int variables. The int array for row 0 is a one-dimensional array with two elements (1 and 2), and the int array for row 1 is a one-dimensional array with three elements (3, 4 and 5).

Creating Two-Dimensional Arrays with Array-Creation Expressions

A multidimensional array with the same number of columns in every row can be created with an array-creation expression. For example, the following lines declare array b and assign it a reference to a three-by-four array:

```
int b[][] = new int[ 3 ][ 4 ];
```

In this case, we use the literal values 3 and 4 to specify the number of rows and number of columns, respectively, but this is not required. Programs can also use variables to specify array dimensions, because new creates arrays at execution time—not at compile time. As with one-dimensional arrays, the elements of a multidimensional array are initialized when the array object is created.

A multidimensional array in which each row has a different number of columns can be created as follows:

```
int b[][] = new int[ 2 ][ ];    // create 2 rows
b[ 0 ] = new int[ 5 ]; // create 5 columns for row 0
b[ 1 ] = new int[ 3 ]; // create 3 columns for row 1
```

The preceding statements create a two-dimensional array with two rows. Row 0 has five columns, and row 1 has three columns.

Two-Dimensional Array Example: Displaying Element Values

Figure 7.17 demonstrates initializing two-dimensional arrays with array initializers and using nested for loops to traverse the arrays (i.e., manipulate every element of each array).

Class InitArray's main declares two arrays. The declaration of array1 (line 9) uses nested array initializers to initialize the first row of the array to the values 1, 2 and 3, and the second row to the values 4, 5 and 6. The declaration of array2 (line 10) uses nested initializers of different lengths. In this case, the first row is initialized to have two elements with the values 1 and 2, respectively. The second row is initialized to have one element with the value 3. The third row is initialized to have three elements with the values 4, 5 and 6, respectively.

```
 1    // Fig. 7.17: InitArray.java
 2    // Initializing two-dimensional arrays.
 3
 4    public class InitArray
 5    {
 6       // create and output two-dimensional arrays
 7       public static void main( String args[] )
 8       {
 9          int array1[][] = { { 1, 2, 3 }, { 4, 5, 6 } };
10          int array2[][] = { { 1, 2 }, { 3 }, { 4, 5, 6 } };
11
12          System.out.println( "Values in array1 by row are" );
13          outputArray( array1 ); // displays array1 by row
14
15          System.out.println( "\nValues in array2 by row are" );
16          outputArray( array2 ); // displays array2 by row
17       } // end main
```

Fig. 7.17 | Initializing two-dimensional arrays. (Part 1 of 2.)

```
18
19      // output rows and columns of a two-dimensional array
20      public static void outputArray( int array[][] )
21      {
22         // loop through array's rows
23         for ( int row = 0; row < array.length; row++ )
24         {
25            // loop through columns of current row
26            for ( int column = 0; column < array[ row ].length; column++ )
27               System.out.printf( "%d  ", array[ row ][ column ] );
28
29            System.out.println(); // start new line of output
30         } // end outer for
31      } // end method outputArray
32   } // end class InitArray
```

```
Values in array1 by row are
1  2  3
4  5  6

Values in array2 by row are
1  2
3
4  5  6
```

Fig. 7.17 | Initializing two-dimensional arrays. (Part 2 of 2.)

Lines 13 and 16 call method `outputArray` (lines 20–31) to output the elements of `array1` and `array2`, respectively. Method `outputArray` specifies the array parameter as `int array[][]` to indicate that the method receives a two-dimensional array. The `for` statement (lines 23–30) outputs the rows of a two-dimensional array. In the loop-continuation condition of the outer `for` statement, the expression `array.length` determines the number of rows in the array. In the inner `for` statement, the expression `array[ row ].length` determines the number of columns in the current row of the array. This condition enables the loop to determine the exact number of columns in each row.

Common Multidimensional-Array Manipulations Performed with for Statements

Many common array manipulations use `for` statements. As an example, the following `for` statement sets all the elements in row 2 of array a in Fig. 7.16 to zero:

```
for ( int column = 0; column < a[ 2 ].length; column++)
   a[ 2 ][ column ] = 0;
```

We specified row 2; therefore, we know that the first index is always 2 (0 is the first row, and 1 is the second row). This `for` loop varies only the second index (i.e., the column index). If row 2 of array a contains four elements, then the preceding `for` statement is equivalent to the assignment statements

```
a[ 2 ][ 0 ] = 0;
a[ 2 ][ 1 ] = 0;
a[ 2 ][ 2 ] = 0;
a[ 2 ][ 3 ] = 0;
```

The following nested `for` statement totals the values of all the elements in array a:

```
int total = 0;

for ( int row = 0; row < a.length; row++ )
{
   for ( int column = 0; column < a[ row ].length; column++ )
      total += a[ row ][ column ];
} // end outer for
```

This nested `for` statements total the array elements one row at a time. The outer `for` statement begins by setting the row index to 0 so that the first row's elements can be totaled by the inner `for` statement. The outer `for` then increments row to 1 so that the second row can be totaled. Then, the outer `for` increments row to 2 so that the third row can be totaled. The variable `total` can be displayed when the outer `for` statement terminates. In the next example, we show how to process a two-dimensional array in a similar manner using nested enhanced `for` statements.

7.10 Case Study: Class GradeBook Using a Two-Dimensional Array

In Section 7.8, we presented class `GradeBook` (Fig. 7.14), which used a one-dimensional array to store student grades on a single exam. In most semesters, students take several exams. Professors are likely to want to analyze grades across the entire semester, both for a single student and for the class as a whole.

Storing Student Grades in a Two-Dimensional Array in Class **GradeBook**

Figure 7.18 contains a version of class `GradeBook` that uses a two-dimensional array grades to store the grades of a number of students on multiple exams. Each row of the array represents a single student's grades for the entire course, and each column represents a grade on one of the exams the students took during the course. An application such as `Grade-BookTest` (Fig. 7.19) passes the array as an argument to the `GradeBook` constructor. In this example, we use a ten-by-three array containing ten students' grades on three exams. Five methods perform array manipulations to process the grades. Each method is similar to its counterpart in the earlier one-dimensional array version of class `GradeBook` (Fig. 7.14). Method `getMinimum` (lines 52–70) determines the lowest grade of any student for the semester. Method `getMaximum` (lines 73–91) determines the highest grade of any student for the semester. Method `getAverage` (lines 94–104) determines a particular student's semester average. Method `outputBarChart` (lines 107–137) outputs a bar chart of the distribution of all student grades for the semester. Method `outputGrades` (lines 140–164) outputs the two-dimensional array in a tabular format, along with each student's semester average.

Methods `getMinimum`, `getMaximum`, `outputBarChart` and `outputGrades` each loop through array grades by using nested `for` statements—for example, the nested enhanced `for` statement from the declaration of method `getMinimum` (lines 58–67). The outer enhanced `for` statement iterates through the two-dimensional array grades, assigning successive rows to parameter `studentGrades` on successive iterations. The square brackets following the parameter name indicate that `studentGrades` refers to a one-dimensional `int` array—namely, a row in array grades containing one student's grades. To find the lowest overall grade, the inner `for` statement compares the elements of the current one-dimen-

```
1   // Fig. 7.18: GradeBook.java
2   // Grade book using a two-dimensional array to store grades.
3
4   public class GradeBook
5   {
6      private String courseName; // name of course this grade book represents
7      private int grades[][]; // two-dimensional array of student grades
8
9      // two-argument constructor initializes courseName and grades array
10     public GradeBook( String name, int gradesArray[][] )
11     {
12        courseName = name; // initialize courseName
13        grades = gradesArray; // store grades
14     } // end two-argument GradeBook constructor
15
16     // method to set the course name
17     public void setCourseName( String name )
18     {
19        courseName = name; // store the course name
20     } // end method setCourseName
21
22     // method to retrieve the course name
23     public String getCourseName()
24     {
25        return courseName;
26     } // end method getCourseName
27
28     // display a welcome message to the GradeBook user
29     public void displayMessage()
30     {
31        // getCourseName gets the name of the course
32        System.out.printf( "Welcome to the grade book for\n%s!\n\n",
33           getCourseName() );
34     } // end method displayMessage
35
36     // perform various operations on the data
37     public void processGrades()
38     {
39        // output grades array
40        outputGrades();
41
42        // call methods getMinimum and getMaximum
43        System.out.printf( "\n%s %d\n%s %d\n\n",
44           "Lowest grade in the grade book is", getMinimum(),
45           "Highest grade in the grade book is", getMaximum() );
46
47        // output grade distribution chart of all grades on all tests
48        outputBarChart();
49     } // end method processGrades
50
51     // find minimum grade
52     public int getMinimum()
53     {
```

Fig. 7.18 | GradeBook class using a two-dimensional array to store grades. (Part 1 of 4.)

```
54          // assume first element of grades array is smallest
55          int lowGrade = grades[ 0 ][ 0 ];
56
57          // loop through rows of grades array
58          for ( int studentGrades[] : grades )
59          {
60             // loop through columns of current row
61             for ( int grade : studentGrades )
62             {
63                // if grade less than lowGrade, assign it to lowGrade
64                if ( grade < lowGrade )
65                   lowGrade = grade;
66             } // end inner for
67          } // end outer for
68
69          return lowGrade; // return lowest grade
70       } // end method getMinimum
71
72       // find maximum grade
73       public int getMaximum()
74       {
75          // assume first element of grades array is largest
76          int highGrade = grades[ 0 ][ 0 ];
77
78          // loop through rows of grades array
79          for ( int studentGrades[] : grades )
80          {
81             // loop through columns of current row
82             for ( int grade : studentGrades )
83             {
84                // if grade greater than highGrade, assign it to highGrade
85                if ( grade > highGrade )
86                   highGrade = grade;
87             } // end inner for
88          } // end outer for
89
90          return highGrade; // return highest grade
91       } // end method getMaximum
92
93       // determine average grade for particular set of grades
94       public double getAverage( int setOfGrades[] )
95       {
96          int total = 0; // initialize total
97
98          // sum grades for one student
99          for ( int grade : setOfGrades )
100            total += grade;
101
102         // return average of grades
103         return (double) total / setOfGrades.length;
104      } // end method getAverage
105
```

Fig. 7.18 | GradeBook class using a two-dimensional array to store grades. (Part 2 of 4.)

```
106     // output bar chart displaying overall grade distribution
107     public void outputBarChart()
108     {
109        System.out.println( "Overall grade distribution:" );
110
111        // stores frequency of grades in each range of 10 grades
112        int frequency[] = new int[ 11 ];
113
114        // for each grade in GradeBook, increment the appropriate frequency
115        for ( int studentGrades[] : grades )
116        {
117           for ( int grade : studentGrades )
118              ++frequency[ grade / 10 ];
119        } // end outer for
120
121        // for each grade frequency, print bar in chart
122        for ( int count = 0; count < frequency.length; count++ )
123        {
124           // output bar label ( "00-09: ", ..., "90-99: ", "100: " )
125           if ( count == 10 )
126              System.out.printf( "%5d: ", 100 );
127           else
128              System.out.printf( "%02d-%02d: ",
129                 count * 10, count * 10 + 9  );
130
131           // print bar of asterisks
132           for ( int stars = 0; stars < frequency[ count ]; stars++ )
133              System.out.print( "*" );
134
135           System.out.println(); // start a new line of output
136        } // end outer for
137     } // end method outputBarChart
138
139     // output the contents of the grades array
140     public void outputGrades()
141     {
142        System.out.println( "The grades are:\n" );
143        System.out.print( "                " ); // align column heads
144
145        // create a column heading for each of the tests
146        for ( int test = 0; test < grades[ 0 ].length; test++ )
147           System.out.printf( "Test %d  ", test + 1 );
148
149        System.out.println( "Average" ); // student average column heading
150
151        // create rows/columns of text representing array grades
152        for ( int student = 0; student < grades.length; student++ )
153        {
154           System.out.printf( "Student %2d", student + 1 );
155
156           for ( int test : grades[ student ] ) // output student's grades
157              System.out.printf( "%8d", test );
```

Fig. 7.18 | GradeBook class using a two-dimensional array to store grades. (Part 3 of 4.)

```
158
159          // call method getAverage to calculate student's average grade;
160          // pass row of grades as the argument to getAverage
161          double average = getAverage( grades[ student ] );
162          System.out.printf( "%9.2f\n", average );
163       } // end outer for
164    } // end method outputGrades
165 } // end class GradeBook
```

Fig. 7.18 | GradeBook class using a two-dimensional array to store grades. (Part 4 of 4.)

sional array studentGrades to variable lowGrade. For example, on the first iteration of the outer for, row 0 of grades is assigned to parameter studentGrades. The inner enhanced for statement then loops through studentGrades and compares each grade value with lowGrade. If a grade is less than lowGrade, lowGrade is set to that grade. On the second iteration of the outer enhanced for statement, row 1 of grades is assigned to student-Grades, and the elements of this row are compared with variable lowGrade. This repeats until all rows of grades have been traversed. When execution of the nested statement is complete, lowGrade contains the lowest grade in the two-dimensional array. Method get-Maximum works similarly to method getMinimum.

Method outputBarChart in Fig. 7.18 is nearly identical to the one in Fig. 7.14. However, to output the overall grade distribution for a whole semester, the method here uses a nested enhanced for statement (lines 115–119) to create the one-dimensional array frequency based on all the grades in the two-dimensional array. The rest of the code in each of the two outputBarChart methods that displays the chart is identical.

Method outputGrades (lines 140–164) also uses nested for statements to output values of the array grades and each student's semester average. The output in Fig. 7.19 shows the result, which resembles the tabular format of a professor's physical grade book. Lines 146–147 print the column headings for each test. We use a counter-controlled for statement here so that we can identify each test with a number. Similarly, the for statement in lines 152–163 first outputs a row label using a counter variable to identify each student (line 154). Although array indices start at 0, note that lines 147 and 154 output test + 1 and student + 1, respectively, to produce test and student numbers starting at 1 (see Fig. 7.19). The inner for statement in lines 156–157 uses the outer for statement's counter variable student to loop through a specific row of array grades and output each student's test grade. Note that an enhanced for statement can be nested in a counter-controlled for statement, and vice versa. Finally, line 161 obtains each student's semester average by passing the current row of grades (i.e., grades[student]) to method getAverage.

Method getAverage (lines 94–104) takes one argument—a one-dimensional array of test results for a particular student. When line 161 calls getAverage, the argument is grades[student], which specifies that a particular row of the two-dimensional array grades should be passed to getAverage. For example, based on the array created in Fig. 7.19, the argument grades[1] represents the three values (a one-dimensional array of grades) stored in row 1 of the two-dimensional array grades. Recall that a two-dimensional array is an array whose elements are one-dimensional arrays. Method getAverage calculates the sum of the array elements, divides the total by the number of test results and returns the floating-point result as a double value (line 103).

*Class **GradeBookTest** That Demonstrates Class **GradeBook***
The application in Fig. 7.19 creates an object of class GradeBook (Fig. 7.18) using the two-dimensional array of ints named gradesArray (declared and initialized in lines 10–19). Lines 21–22 pass a course name and gradesArray to the GradeBook constructor. Lines 23–24 then invoke myGradeBook's displayMessage and processGrades methods to display a welcome message and obtain a report summarizing the students' grades for the semester, respectively.

```
1    // Fig. 7.19: GradeBookTest.java
2    // Creates GradeBook object using a two-dimensional array of grades.
3
4    public class GradeBookTest
5    {
6       // main method begins program execution
7       public static void main( String args[] )
8       {
9          // two-dimensional array of student grades
10         int gradesArray[][] = { { 87, 96, 70 },
11                                 { 68, 87, 90 },
12                                 { 94, 100, 90 },
13                                 { 100, 81, 82 },
14                                 { 83, 65, 85 },
15                                 { 78, 87, 65 },
16                                 { 85, 75, 83 },
17                                 { 91, 94, 100 },
18                                 { 76, 72, 84 },
19                                 { 87, 93, 73 } };
20
21         GradeBook myGradeBook = new GradeBook(
22            "CS101 Introduction to Java Programming", gradesArray );
23         myGradeBook.displayMessage();
24         myGradeBook.processGrades();
25      } // end main
26   } // end class GradeBookTest
```

```
Welcome to the grade book for
CS101 Introduction to Java Programming!

The grades are:

              Test 1   Test 2   Test 3   Average
Student  1       87       96       70     84.33
Student  2       68       87       90     81.67
Student  3       94      100       90     94.67
Student  4      100       81       82     87.67
Student  5       83       65       85     77.67
Student  6       78       87       65     76.67
Student  7       85       75       83     81.00
Student  8       91       94      100     95.00
Student  9       76       72       84     77.33
Student 10       87       93       73     84.33
```
(continued...)

Fig. 7.19 | Creates GradeBook object using a two-dimensional array of grades, then invokes method processGrades to analyze them. (Part 1 of 2.)

```
Lowest grade in the grade book is 65
Highest grade in the grade book is 100

Overall grade distribution:
00-09:
10-19:
20-29:
30-39:
40-49:
50-59:
60-69: ***
70-79: ******
80-89: ***********
90-99: *******
  100: ***
```

Fig. 7.19 | Creates GradeBook object using a two-dimensional array of grades, then invokes method processGrades to analyze them. (Part 2 of 2.)

7.11 Variable-Length Argument Lists

With **variable-length argument lists**, you can create methods that receive an unspecified number of arguments. An argument type followed by an **ellipsis (. . .) in a method's parameter list** indicates that the method receives a variable number of arguments of that particular type. This use of the ellipsis can occur only once in a parameter list, and the ellipsis, together with its type, must be placed at the end of the parameter list. While programmers can use method overloading and array passing to accomplish much of what is accomplished with "varargs," or variable-length argument lists, using an ellipsis in a method's parameter list is more concise.

Figure 7.20 demonstrates method average (lines 7–16), which receives a variable-length sequence of doubles. Java treats the variable-length argument list as an array whose elements are all of the same type. Hence, the method body can manipulate the parameter numbers as an array of doubles. Lines 12–13 use the enhanced for loop to walk through the array and calculate the total of the doubles in the array. Line 15 accesses numbers.length to obtain the size of the numbers array for use in the averaging calculation. Lines 29, 31 and 33 in main call method average with two, three and four arguments, respectively. Method average has a variable-length argument list (line 7), so it can average as many double arguments as the caller passes. The output shows that each call to method average returns the correct value.

```
1   // Fig. 7.20: VarargsTest.java
2   // Using variable-length argument lists.
3
4   public class VarargsTest
5   {
6      // calculate average
7      public static double average( double... numbers )
8      {
```

Fig. 7.20 | Using variable-length argument lists. (Part 1 of 2.)

```
 9            double total = 0.0; // initialize total
10
11            // calculate total using the enhanced for statement
12            for ( double d : numbers )
13               total += d;
14
15            return total / numbers.length;
16         } // end method average
17
18         public static void main( String args[] )
19         {
20            double d1 = 10.0;
21            double d2 = 20.0;
22            double d3 = 30.0;
23            double d4 = 40.0;
24
25            System.out.printf( "d1 = %.1f\nd2 = %.1f\nd3 = %.1f\nd4 = %.1f\n\n",
26               d1, d2, d3, d4 );
27
28            System.out.printf( "Average of d1 and d2 is %.1f\n",
29               average( d1, d2 ) );
30            System.out.printf( "Average of d1, d2 and d3 is %.1f\n",
31               average( d1, d2, d3 ) );
32            System.out.printf( "Average of d1, d2, d3 and d4 is %.1f\n",
33               average( d1, d2, d3, d4 ) );
34         } // end main
35      } // end class VarargsTest
```

```
d1 = 10.0
d2 = 20.0
d3 = 30.0
d4 = 40.0

Average of d1 and d2 is 15.0
Average of d1, d2 and d3 is 20.0
Average of d1, d2, d3 and d4 is 25.0
```

Fig. 7.20 | Using variable-length argument lists. (Part 2 of 2.)

 Common Programming Error 7.6

Placing an ellipsis indicating a variable-length argument list in the middle of a method parameter list is a syntax error. An ellipsis may be placed only at the end of the parameter list.

7.12 Using Command-Line Arguments

On many systems it is possible to pass arguments from the command line (these are known as **command-line arguments**) to an application by including a parameter of type String[] (i.e., an array of Strings) in the parameter list of main, exactly as we have done in every application in the book. By convention, this parameter is named args. When an application is executed using the java command, Java passes the command-line arguments that appear after the class name in the java command to the application's main method as Strings in the array args. The number of arguments passed in from the command line is obtained by accessing the array's length attribute. For example, the command "java MyClass a b" passes two command-line arguments, a and b, to application MyClass. Note that command-line arguments are separated by white space, not commas. When this command executes, MyClass's main method receives the two-element array args (i.e., args.length is 2) in which args[0] contains the String "a" and args[1] contains the String "b". Common uses of command-line arguments include passing options and file names to applications.

Figure 7.21 uses three command-line arguments to initialize an array. When the program executes, if args.length is not 3, the program prints an error message and terminates (lines 9–12). Otherwise, lines 14–32 initialize and display the array based on the values of the command-line arguments.

The command-line arguments become available to main as Strings in args. Line 16 gets args[0]—a String that specifies the array size—and converts it to an int value that the program uses to create the array in line 17. The static method parseInt of class Integer converts its String argument to an int.

```
 1   // Fig. 7.21: InitArray.java
 2   // Using command-line arguments to initialize an array.
 3
 4   public class InitArray
 5   {
 6      public static void main( String args[] )
 7      {
 8         // check number of command-line arguments
 9         if ( args.length != 3 )
10            System.out.println(
11               "Error: Please re-enter the entire command, including\n" +
12               "an array size, initial value and increment." );
13         else
14         {
15            // get array size from first command-line argument
16            int arrayLength = Integer.parseInt( args[ 0 ] );
17            int array[] = new int[ arrayLength ]; // create array
18
19            // get initial value and increment from command-line arguments
20            int initialValue = Integer.parseInt( args[ 1 ] );
21            int increment = Integer.parseInt( args[ 2 ] );
22
23            // calculate value for each array element
24            for ( int counter = 0; counter < array.length; counter++ )
25               array[ counter ] = initialValue + increment * counter;
26
27            System.out.printf( "%s%8s\n", "Index", "Value" );
28
29            // display array index and value
30            for ( int counter = 0; counter < array.length; counter++ )
31               System.out.printf( "%5d%8d\n", counter, array[ counter ] );
32         } // end else
33      } // end main
34   } // end class InitArray
```

Fig. 7.21 | Initializing an array using command-line arguments. (Part 1 of 2.)

```
java InitArray
Error: Please re-enter the entire command, including
an array size, initial value and increment.
```

```
java InitArray 5 0 4
Index    Value
    0        0
    1        4
    2        8
    3       12
    4       16
```

```
java InitArray 10 1 2
Index    Value
    0        1
    1        3
    2        5
    3        7
    4        9
    5       11
    6       13
    7       15
    8       17
    9       19
```

Fig. 7.21 | Initializing an array using command-line arguments. (Part 2 of 2.)

Lines 20–21 convert the args[1] and args[2] command-line arguments to int values and store them in initialValue and increment, respectively. Lines 24–25 calculate the value for each array element.

The output of the first execution shows that the application received an insufficient number of command-line arguments. The second execution uses command-line arguments 5, 0 and 4 to specify the size of the array (5), the value of the first element (0) and the increment of each value in the array (4), respectively. The corresponding output shows that these values create an array containing the integers 0, 4, 8, 12 and 16. The output from the third execution shows that the command-line arguments 10, 1 and 2 produce an array whose 10 elements are the nonnegative odd integers from 1 to 19.

7.13 (Optional) GUI and Graphics Case Study: Drawing Arcs

Using Java's graphics features, we can create complex drawings that would be more tedious to code line by line. In Fig. 7.22 and Fig. 7.23, we use arrays and repetition statements to draw a rainbow by using Graphics method fillArc. Drawing arcs in Java is similar to drawing ovals—an arc is simply a section of an oval.

Figure 7.22 begins with the usual import statements for creating drawings (lines 3–5). Lines 9–10 declare and create two new colors—VIOLET and INDIGO. As you may know, the colors of a rainbow are red, orange, yellow, green, blue, indigo and violet. Java has pre-

```
 1   // Fig. 7.22: DrawRainbow.java
 2   // Demonstrates using colors in an array.
 3   import java.awt.Color;
 4   import java.awt.Graphics;
 5   import javax.swing.JPanel;
 6
 7   public class DrawRainbow extends JPanel
 8   {
 9      // Define indigo and violet
10      final Color VIOLET = new Color( 128, 0, 128 );
11      final Color INDIGO = new Color( 75, 0, 130 );
12
13      // colors to use in the rainbow, starting from the innermost
14      // The two white entries result in an empty arc in the center
15      private Color colors[] =
16         { Color.WHITE, Color.WHITE, VIOLET, INDIGO, Color.BLUE,
17           Color.GREEN, Color.YELLOW, Color.ORANGE, Color.RED };
18
19      // constructor
20      public DrawRainbow()
21      {
22         setBackground( Color.WHITE ); // set the background to white
23      } // end DrawRainbow constructor
24
25      // draws a rainbow using concentric circles
26      public void paintComponent( Graphics g )
27      {
28         super.paintComponent( g );
29
30         int radius = 20; // radius of an arc
31
32         // draw the rainbow near the bottom-center
33         int centerX = getWidth() / 2;
34         int centerY = getHeight() - 10;
35
36         // draws filled arcs starting with the outermost
37         for ( int counter = colors.length; counter > 0; counter-- )
38         {
39            // set the color for the current arc
40            g.setColor( colors[ counter - 1 ] );
41
42            // fill the arc from 0 to 180 degrees
43            g.fillArc( centerX - counter * radius,
44               centerY - counter * radius,
45               counter * radius * 2, counter * radius * 2, 0, 180 );
46         } // end for
47      } // end method paintComponent
48   } // end class DrawRainbow
```

Fig. 7.22 | Drawing a rainbow using arcs and an array of colors.

defined constants only for the first five colors. Lines 15–17 initialize an array with the colors of the rainbow, starting with the innermost arcs first. The array begins with two Color.WHITE elements, which, as you will soon see, are for drawing the empty arcs at the center of the rainbow. Note that the instance variables can be initialized when they are declared, as shown in lines 10–17. The constructor (lines 20–23) contains a single statement that calls method `setBackground` (which is inherited from class JPanel) with the parameter Color.WHITE. Method `setBackground` takes a single Color argument and sets the background of the component to that color.

Line 30 in `paintComponent` declares local variable radius, which determines the radius of each arc. Local variables centerX and centerY (lines 33–34) determine the location of the midpoint on the base of the rainbow. The loop at lines 37–46 uses control variable counter to count backward from the end of the array, drawing the largest arcs first and placing each successive smaller arc on top of the previous one. Line 40 sets the color to draw the current arc from the array. The reason we have Color.WHITE entries at the beginning of the array is to create the empty arc in the center. Otherwise, the center of the rainbow would just be a solid violet semicircle. [*Note:* You can change the individual colors and the number of entries in the array to create new designs.]

The `fillArc` method call at lines 43–45 draws a filled semicircle. Method `fillArc` requires six parameters. The first four represent the bounding rectangle in which the arc will be drawn. The first two of these specify the coordinates for the upper-left corner of

```
1   // Fig. 7.23: DrawRainbowTest.java
2   // Test application to display a rainbow.
3   import javax.swing.JFrame;
4
5   public class DrawRainbowTest
6   {
7      public static void main( String args[] )
8      {
9         DrawRainbow panel = new DrawRainbow();
10        JFrame application = new JFrame();
11
12        application.setDefaultCloseOperation( JFrame.EXIT_ON_CLOSE );
13        application.add( panel );
14        application.setSize( 400, 250 );
15        application.setVisible( true );
16     } // end main
17  } // end class DrawRainbowTest
```

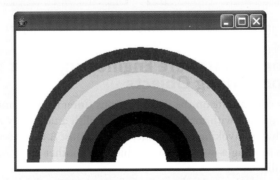

Fig. 7.23 | Creating JFrame to display a rainbow.

the bounding rectangle, and the next two specify its width and height. The fifth parameter is the starting angle on the oval, and the sixth specifies the sweep, or the amount of arc to cover. The starting angle and sweep are measured in degrees, with zero degrees pointing right. A positive sweep draws the arc counterclockwise, while a negative sweep draws the arc clockwise. A method similar to fillArc is drawArc—it requires the same parameters as fillArc, but draws the edge of the arc rather than filling it.

Class DrawRainbowTest (Fig. 7.23) creates and sets up a JFrame to display the rainbow. Once the program makes the JFrame visible, the system calls the paintComponent method in class DrawRainbow to draw the rainbow on the screen.

GUI and Graphics Case Study Exercise

7.1   (*Drawing Spirals*) In this exercise, you will draw spirals with methods drawLine and drawArc.

a) Draw a square-shaped spiral (as in the left screen capture of Fig. 7.24), centered on the panel, using method drawLine. One technique is to use a loop that increases the line length after drawing every second line. The direction in which to draw the next line should follow a distinct pattern, such as down, left, up, right.

b) Draw a circular spiral (as in the right screen capture of Fig. 7.24), using method drawArc to draw one semicircle at a time. Each successive semicircle should have a larger radius (as specified by the bounding rectangle's width) and should continue drawing where the previous semicircle finished.

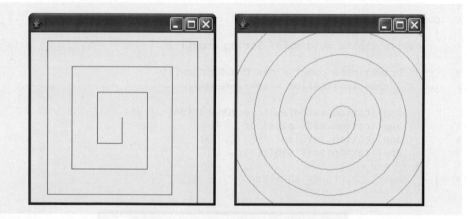

Fig. 7.24 | Drawing a spiral using drawLine (left) and drawArc (right).

7.14 (Optional) Software Engineering Case Study: Collaboration Among Objects

In this section, we concentrate on the collaborations (interactions) among objects. When two objects communicate with each other to accomplish a task, they are said to collaborate—objects do this by invoking one another's operations. A collaboration consists of an object of one class sending a message to an object of another class. Messages are sent in Java via method calls.

In Section 6.14, we determined many of the operations of the classes in our system. In this section, we concentrate on the messages that invoke these operations. To identify the collaborations in the system, we return to the requirements document in Section 2.9. Recall that this document specifies the range of activities that occur during an ATM session (e.g., authenticating a user, performing transactions). The steps used to describe how the system must perform each of these tasks are our first indication of the collaborations in our system. As we proceed through this and the remaining Software Engineering Case Study sections, we may discover additional collaborations.

Identifying the Collaborations in a System

We identify the collaborations in the system by carefully reading the sections of the requirements document that specify what the ATM should do to authenticate a user and to perform each transaction type. For each action or step described in the requirements document, we decide which objects in our system must interact to achieve the desired result. We identify one object as the sending object and another as the receiving object. We then select one of the receiving object's operations (identified in Section 6.14) that must be invoked by the sending object to produce the proper behavior. For example, the ATM displays a welcome message when idle. We know that an object of class Screen displays a message to the user via its displayMessage operation. Thus, we decide that the system can display a welcome message by employing a collaboration between the ATM and the Screen in which the ATM sends a displayMessage message to the Screen by invoking the displayMessage operation of class Screen. [*Note:* To avoid repeating the phrase "an object of class...," we refer to an object by using its class name preceded by an article (e.g., "a," "an" or "the")—for example, "the ATM" refers to an object of class ATM.]

Figure 7.25 lists the collaborations that can be derived from the requirements document. For each sending object, we list the collaborations in the order in which they first occur during an ATM session (i.e., the order in which they are discussed in the require-

An object of class...	sends the message...	to an object of class...
ATM	displayMessage	Screen
	getInput	Keypad
	authenticateUser	BankDatabase
	execute	BalanceInquiry
	execute	Withdrawal
	execute	Deposit
BalanceInquiry	getAvailableBalance	BankDatabase
	getTotalBalance	BankDatabase
	displayMessage	Screen
Withdrawal	displayMessage	Screen
	getInput	Keypad
	getAvailableBalance	BankDatabase
	isSufficientCashAvailable	CashDispenser
	debit	BankDatabase
	dispenseCash	CashDispenser

Fig. 7.25 | Collaborations in the ATM system. (Part I of 2.)

An object of class...	sends the message...	to an object of class...
Deposit	displayMessage	Screen
	getInput	Keypad
	isEnvelopeReceived	DepositSlot
	credit	BankDatabase
BankDatabase	validatePIN	Account
	getAvailableBalance	Account
	getTotalBalance	Account
	debit	Account
	credit	Account

Fig. 7.25 | Collaborations in the ATM system. (Part 2 of 2.)

ments document). We list each collaboration involving a unique sender, message and recipient only once, even though the collaborations may occur at several different times throughout an ATM session. For example, the first row in Fig. 7.25 indicates that the ATM collaborates with the Screen whenever the ATM needs to display a message to the user.

Let's consider the collaborations in Fig. 7.25. Before allowing a user to perform any transactions, the ATM must prompt the user to enter an account number, then to enter a PIN. It accomplishes each of these tasks by sending a displayMessage message to the Screen. Both of these actions refer to the same collaboration between the ATM and the Screen, which is already listed in Fig. 7.25. The ATM obtains input in response to a prompt by sending a getInput message to the Keypad. Next, the ATM must determine whether the user-specified account number and PIN match those of an account in the database. It does so by sending an authenticateUser message to the BankDatabase. Recall that the BankDatabase cannot authenticate a user directly—only the user's Account (i.e., the Account that contains the account number specified by the user) can access the user's PIN on record to authenticate the user. Figure 7.25 therefore lists a collaboration in which the BankDatabase sends a validatePIN message to an Account.

After the user is authenticated, the ATM displays the main menu by sending a series of displayMessage messages to the Screen and obtains input containing a menu selection by sending a getInput message to the Keypad. We have already accounted for these collaborations, so we do not add anything to Fig. 7.25. After the user chooses a type of transaction to perform, the ATM executes the transaction by sending an execute message to an object of the appropriate transaction class (i.e., a BalanceInquiry, a Withdrawal or a Deposit). For example, if the user chooses to perform a balance inquiry, the ATM sends an execute message to a BalanceInquiry.

Further examination of the requirements document reveals the collaborations involved in executing each transaction type. A BalanceInquiry retrieves the amount of money available in the user's account by sending a getAvailableBalance message to the BankDatabase, which responds by sending a getAvailableBalance message to the user's Account. Similarly, the BalanceInquiry retrieves the amount of money on deposit by sending a getTotalBalance message to the BankDatabase, which sends the same message to the user's Account. To display both measures of the user's balance at the same time, the BalanceInquiry sends a displayMessage message to the Screen.

A Withdrawal sends a series of displayMessage messages to the Screen to display a menu of standard withdrawal amounts (i.e., $20, $40, $60, $100, $200). The Withdrawal sends a getInput message to the Keypad to obtain the user's menu selection. Next, the Withdrawal determines whether the requested withdrawal amount is less than or equal to the user's account balance. The Withdrawal can obtain the amount of money available in the user's account by sending a getAvailableBalance message to the BankDatabase. The Withdrawal then tests whether the cash dispenser contains enough cash by sending an isSufficientCashAvailable message to the CashDispenser. A Withdrawal sends a debit message to the BankDatabase to decrease the user's account balance. The BankDatabase in turn sends the same message to the appropriate Account. Recall that debiting funds from an Account decreases both the totalBalance and the availableBalance. To dispense the requested amount of cash, the Withdrawal sends a dispenseCash message to the CashDispenser. Finally, the Withdrawal sends a displayMessage message to the Screen, instructing the user to take the cash.

A Deposit responds to an execute message first by sending a displayMessage message to the Screen to prompt the user for a deposit amount. The Deposit sends a getInput message to the Keypad to obtain the user's input. The Deposit then sends a displayMessage message to the Screen to tell the user to insert a deposit envelope. To determine whether the deposit slot received an incoming deposit envelope, the Deposit sends an isEnvelopeReceived message to the DepositSlot. The Deposit updates the user's account by sending a credit message to the BankDatabase, which subsequently sends a credit message to the user's Account. Recall that crediting funds to an Account increases the totalBalance but not the availableBalance.

Interaction Diagrams

Now that we have identified a set of possible collaborations between the objects in our ATM system, let us graphically model these interactions using the UML. The UML provides several types of interaction diagrams that model the behavior of a system by modeling how objects interact. The communication diagram emphasizes *which objects* participate in collaborations. [*Note:* Communication diagrams were called collaboration diagrams in earlier versions of the UML.] Like the communication diagram, the sequence diagram shows collaborations among objects, but it emphasizes *when* messages are sent between objects *over time.*

Communication Diagrams

Figure 7.26 shows a communication diagram that models the ATM executing a BalanceInquiry. Objects are modeled in the UML as rectangles containing names in the form objectName : ClassName. In this example, which involves only one object of each type, we disregard the object name and list only a colon followed by the class name. [*Note:* Specifying the name of each object in a communication diagram is recommended when modeling multiple objects of the same type.] Communicating objects are connected with solid lines, and messages are passed between objects along these lines in the direction shown by arrows. The name of the message, which appears next to the arrow, is the name of an operation (i.e., a method in Java) belonging to the receiving object—think of the name as a "service" that the receiving object provides to sending objects (its "clients").

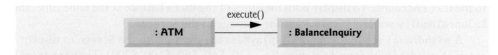

Fig. 7.26 | Communication diagram of the ATM executing a balance inquiry.

The solid filled arrow in Fig. 7.26 represents a message—or **synchronous call**—in the UML and a method call in Java. This arrow indicates that the flow of control is from the sending object (the ATM) to the receiving object (a BalanceInquiry). Since this is a synchronous call, the sending object may not send another message, or do anything at all, until the receiving object processes the message and returns control to the sending object. The sender just waits. For example, in Fig. 7.26, the ATM calls method execute of a BalanceInquiry and may not send another message until execute has finished and returns control to the ATM. [*Note:* If this were an **asynchronous call**, represented by a stick arrowhead, the sending object would not have to wait for the receiving object to return control—it would continue sending additional messages immediately following the asynchronous call. Asynchronous calls are implemented in Java using a technique called multithreading, which is discussed in Chapter 23, Multithreading.]

Sequence of Messages in a Communication Diagram
Figure 7.27 shows a communication diagram that models the interactions among objects in the system when an object of class BalanceInquiry executes. We assume that the object's accountNumber attribute contains the account number of the current user. The collaborations in Fig. 7.27 begin after the ATM sends an execute message to a BalanceInquiry (i.e., the interaction modeled in Fig. 7.26). The number to the left of a message name indicates the order in which the message is passed. The **sequence of messages** in a communication diagram progresses in numerical order from least to greatest. In this diagram, the numbering starts with message 1 and ends with message 3. The BalanceInquiry first sends a getAvailableBalance message to the BankDatabase (message 1), then sends a getTotalBalance message to the BankDatabase (message 2). Within the parentheses following a message name, we can specify a comma-separated list of the names of the parameters sent with the message (i.e., arguments in a Java method call)—the BalanceInquiry passes attribute accountNumber with its messages to the BankDatabase to indicate which Account's balance information to retrieve. Recall from Fig. 6.22 that operations getAvailableBalance and getTotalBalance of class BankDatabase each require a parameter to identify an account. The BalanceInquiry next displays the availableBalance and the totalBalance to the user by passing a displayMessage message to the Screen (message 3) that includes a parameter indicating the message to be displayed.

Note that Fig. 7.27 models two additional messages passing from the BankDatabase to an Account (message 1.1 and message 2.1). To provide the ATM with the two balances of the user's Account (as requested by messages 1 and 2), the BankDatabase must pass a getAvailableBalance and a getTotalBalance message to the user's Account. Such messages passed within the handling of another message are called **nested messages**. The UML recommends using a decimal numbering scheme to indicate nested messages. For example, message 1.1 is the first message nested in message 1—the BankDatabase passes a getAvailableBalance message during BankDatabase's processing of a message by the same name. [*Note:* If the BankDatabase needed to pass a second nested message while pro-

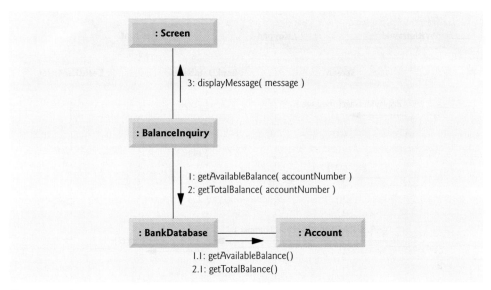

Fig. 7.27 | Communication diagram for executing a balance inquiry.

cessing message 1, the second message would be numbered 1.2.] A message may be passed only when all the nested messages from the previous message have been passed. For example, the BalanceInquiry passes message 3 only after messages 2 and 2.1 have been passed, in that order.

The nested numbering scheme used in communication diagrams helps clarify precisely when and in what context each message is passed. For example, if we numbered the messages in Fig. 7.27 using a flat numbering scheme (i.e., 1, 2, 3, 4, 5), someone looking at the diagram might not be able to determine that BankDatabase passes the getAvailableBalance message (message 1.1) to an Account *during* the BankDatabase's processing of message 1, as opposed to *after* completing the processing of message 1. The nested decimal numbers make it clear that the second getAvailableBalance message (message 1.1) is passed to an Account within the handling of the first getAvailableBalance message (message 1) by the BankDatabase.

Sequence Diagrams

Communication diagrams emphasize the participants in collaborations, but model their timing a bit awkwardly. A sequence diagram helps model the timing of collaborations more clearly. Figure 7.28 shows a sequence diagram modeling the sequence of interactions that occur when a Withdrawal executes. The dotted line extending down from an object's rectangle is that object's **lifeline**, which represents the progression of time. Actions occur along an object's lifeline in chronological order from top to bottom—an action near the top happens before one near the bottom.

Message passing in sequence diagrams is similar to message passing in communication diagrams. A solid arrow with a filled arrowhead extending from the sending object to the receiving object represents a message between two objects. The arrowhead points to an activation on the receiving object's lifeline. An **activation**, shown as a thin vertical rectangle, indicates that an object is executing. When an object returns control, a return mes-

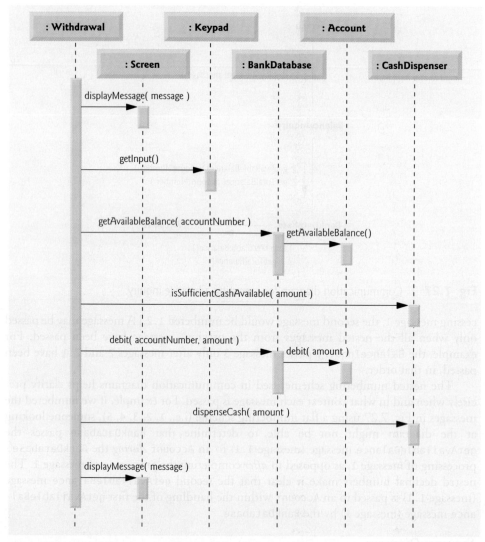

Fig. 7.28 | Sequence diagram that models a `Withdrawal` executing.

sage, represented as a dashed line with a stick arrowhead, extends from the activation of the object returning control to the activation of the object that initially sent the message. To eliminate clutter, we omit the return-message arrows—the UML allows this practice to make diagrams more readable. Like communication diagrams, sequence diagrams can indicate message parameters between the parentheses following a message name.

The sequence of messages in Fig. 7.28 begins when a `Withdrawal` prompts the user to choose a withdrawal amount by sending a `displayMessage` message to the `Screen`. The `Withdrawal` then sends a `getInput` message to the `Keypad`, which obtains input from the user. We have already modeled the control logic involved in a `Withdrawal` in the activity diagram of Fig. 5.31, so we do not show this logic in the sequence diagram of Fig. 7.28.

Instead, we model the best-case scenario in which the balance of the user's account is greater than or equal to the chosen withdrawal amount, and the cash dispenser contains a sufficient amount of cash to satisfy the request. For information on how to model control logic in a sequence diagram, please refer to the web resources and recommended readings listed at the end of Section 2.9.

After obtaining a withdrawal amount, the Withdrawal sends a getAvailableBalance message to the BankDatabase, which in turn sends a getAvailableBalance message to the user's Account. Assuming that the user's account has enough money available to permit the transaction, the Withdrawal next sends an isSufficientCashAvailable message to the CashDispenser. Assuming that there is enough cash available, the Withdrawal decreases the balance of the user's account (i.e., both the totalBalance and the availableBalance) by sending a debit message to the BankDatabase. The BankDatabase responds by sending a debit message to the user's Account. Finally, the Withdrawal sends a dispenseCash message to the CashDispenser and a displayMessage message to the Screen, telling the user to remove the cash from the machine.

We have identified the collaborations among objects in the ATM system and modeled some of these collaborations using UML interaction diagrams—both communication diagrams and sequence diagrams. In the next Software Engineering Case Study section (Section 8.19), we enhance the structure of our model to complete a preliminary object-oriented design, then we begin implementing the ATM system in Java.

Software Engineering Case Study Self-Review Exercises

7.1 A(n) _____ consists of an object of one class sending a message to an object of another class.
   a) association
   b) aggregation
   c) collaboration
   d) composition

7.2 Which form of interaction diagram emphasizes *what* collaborations occur? Which form emphasizes *when* collaborations occur?

7.3 Create a sequence diagram that models the interactions among objects in the ATM system that occur when a Deposit executes successfully, and explain the sequence of messages modeled by the diagram.

Answers to Software Engineering Case Study Self-Review Exercises

7.1 c.

7.2 Communication diagrams emphasize *what* collaborations occur. Sequence diagrams emphasize *when* collaborations occur.

7.3 Figure 7.29 presents a sequence diagram that models the interactions between objects in the ATM system that occur when a Deposit executes successfully. Figure 7.29 indicates that a Deposit first sends a displayMessage message to the Screen to ask the user to enter a deposit amount. Next the Deposit sends a getInput message to the Keypad to receive input from the user. The Deposit then instructs the user to enter a deposit envelope by sending a displayMessage message to the Screen. The Deposit next sends an isEnvelopeReceived message to the DepositSlot to confirm that the deposit envelope has been received by the ATM. Finally, the Deposit increases the totalBalance attribute (but not the availableBalance attribute) of the user's Account by sending a credit message to the BankDatabase. The BankDatabase responds by sending the same message to the user's Account.

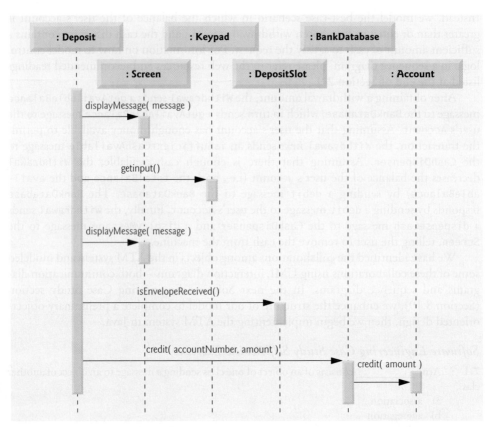

Fig. 7.29 | Sequence diagram that models a `Deposit` executing.

7.15 Wrap-Up

This chapter began our introduction to data structures, exploring the use of arrays to store data in and retrieve data from lists and tables of values. The chapter examples demonstrated how to declare an array, initialize an array and refer to individual elements of an array. The chapter introduced the enhanced `for` statement to iterate through arrays. We also illustrated how to pass arrays to methods and how to declare and manipulate multidimensional arrays. Finally, the chapter showed how to write methods that use variable-length argument lists and how to read arguments passed to a program from the command line.

We continue our coverage of data structures in Chapter 17, Data Structures, which introduces dynamic data structures, such as lists, queues, stacks and trees, that can grow and shrink as programs execute. Chapter 18, Generics, presents the topic of generics, which provide the means to create general models of methods and classes that can be declared once, but used with many different data types. Chapter 19, Collections, introduces the Java Collections Framework, which uses generics to allow programmers to specify the exact types of objects that a particular data structure will store. Chapter 19 also introduces Java's predefined data structures, which programmers can use instead of building their own. Chapter 19 discusses many data structures classes, including `Vector` and `ArrayList`, which are array-like data structures that can grow and shrink in response to a program's changing storage requirements. The Collections API also provides class `Arrays`, which contains utility methods for array manipulation. Chapter 19 uses several `static` methods of class `Arrays` to perform such manipulations as sorting and searching the data in an array. You will be able to use some of the `Arrays` methods discussed in Chapter 19 after reading the current chapter, but some of the `Arrays` methods require knowledge of concepts presented later in the book.

We have now introduced the basic concepts of classes, objects, control statements, methods and arrays. In Chapter 8, we take a deeper look at classes and objects.

Summary

Section 7.1, Introduction

- Arrays are data structures consisting of related data items of the same type. Arrays are fixed-length entities—they remain the same length once they are created, although an array variable may be reassigned the reference of a new array of a different length.

Section 7.2, Arrays

- An array is a group of variables (called elements or components) containing values that all have the same type. Arrays are objects, so they are considered reference types. The elements of an array can be either primitive types or reference types (including arrays).

- To refer to a particular element in an array, we specify the name of the reference to the array and the index (subscript) of the element in the array.

- A program refers to any one of an array's elements with an array-access expression that includes the name of the array followed by the index of the particular element in square brackets (`[]`).

- The first element in every array has index zero and is sometimes called the zeroth element.

- An index must be a nonnegative integer. A program can use an expression as an index.

- Every array object knows its own length and maintains this information in a `length` field. The expression *array*.`length` accesses *array*'s `length` field to determine the length of the array.

Section 7.3, Declaring and Creating Arrays

- To create an array object, the programmer specifies the type of the array elements and the number of elements as part of an array-creation expression that uses keyword `new`. The following array-creation expression creates an array of 100 `int` values:

    ```
    int b[] = new int[ 100 ];
    ```

- When an array is created, each element of the array receives a default value—zero for numeric primitive-type elements, `false` for boolean elements and `null` for references (any nonprimitive type).

- When an array is declared, the type of the array and the square brackets can be combined at the beginning of the declaration to indicate that all the identifiers in the declaration are array variables, as in

    ```
    double[] array1, array2;
    ```

- A program can declare arrays of any type. Every element of a primitive-type array contains a variable of the array's declared type. Similarly, in an array of a reference type, every element is a reference to an object of the array's declared type.

Section 7.4, Examples Using Arrays

- A program can create an array and initialize its elements with an array initializer (i.e., an initializer list enclosed in braces).
- Constant variables (also called named constants or read-only variables) must be initialized before they are used and cannot be modified thereafter.
- When a Java program executes, the JVM checks array indices to ensure that they are valid (i.e., they must be greater than or equal to 0 and less than the length of the array). If a program uses an invalid index, Java generates a so-called exception to indicate that an error occurred in the program at execution time.

*Section 7.6, Enhanced **for** Statement*

- The enhanced for statement allows programmers to iterate through the elements of an array or a collection without using a counter. The syntax of an enhanced for statement is:

      for (*parameter* : *arrayName*)
          statement

  where *parameter* has two parts—a type and an identifier (e.g., int number), and *arrayName* is the array through which to iterate.
- The enhanced for statement cannot be used to modify elements in an array. If a program needs to modify elements, use the traditional counter-controlled for statement.

Section 7.7, Passing Arrays to Methods

- When an argument is passed by value, a copy of the argument's value is made and passed to the called method. The called method works exclusively with the copy.
- When an argument is passed by reference, the called method can access the argument's value in the caller directly and possibly modify it.
- Java does not allow programmers to choose between pass-by-value and pass-by-reference—all arguments are passed by value. A method call can pass two types of values to a method—copies of primitive values (e.g., values of type int and double) and copies of references to objects. Although an object's reference is passed by value, a method can still interact with the referenced object by calling its public methods using the copy of the object's reference.
- To pass an object reference to a method, simply specify in the method call the name of the variable that refers to the object.
- When an argument to a method is an entire array or an individual array element of a reference type, the called method receives a copy of the array or element's reference. When an argument to a method is an individual array element of a primitive type, the called method receives a copy of the element's value.
- To pass an individual array element to a method, use the indexed name of the array as an argument in the method call.

Section 7.9, Multidimensional Arrays

- Multidimensional arrays with two dimensions are often used to represent tables of values consisting of information arranged in rows and columns.
- Arrays that require two indices to identify a particular element are called two-dimensional arrays. An array with *m* rows and *n* columns is called an *m*-by-*n* array. A two-dimensional array can be initialized with an array initializer of the form

      arrayType *arrayName*[][] = { { *row1 initializer* }, { *row2 initializer* }, ... };

- Multidimensional arrays are maintained as arrays of separate one-dimensional arrays. As a result, the lengths of the rows in a two-dimensional array are not required to be the same.
- A multidimensional array with the same number of columns in every row can be created with an array-creation expression of the form

  arrayType arrayName[][] = new *arrayType*[*numRows*][*numColumns*];

- An argument type followed by an ellipsis (...) in a method's parameter list indicates that the method receives a variable number of arguments of that particular type. The ellipsis can occur only once in a method's parameter list, and it must be at the end of the parameter list.

Section 7.11, Variable-Length Argument Lists
- A variable-length argument list is treated as an array within the method body. The number of arguments in the array can be obtained using the array's length field.

Section 7.12, Using Command-Line Arguments
- Passing arguments to main in a Java application from the command line is achieved by including a parameter of type String[] in the parameter list of main. By convention, main's parameter is named args.
- Java passes the command-line arguments that appear after the class name in the java command to the application's main method as Strings in the array args. The number of arguments passed in from the command line is obtained by accessing the array's length attribute.

Terminology

0 flag (in a format specifier)	length field of an array
a[i]	*m*-by-*n* array
a[i][j]	multidimensional array
array	name of an array
array-access expression	named constant
array-creation expression	nested array initializers
array initializer	off-by-one error
bounds checking	one-dimensional array
call-by-reference	parseInt method of class Integer
call-by-value	pass-by-reference
column index	pass-by-value
column of a two-dimensional array	passing arrays to methods
command-line arguments	position number
component of an array	read-only variable
constant variable	row index
data structure	row of a two-dimensional array
declare a constant variable	scalar
declare an array	scalar quantity
element of an array	square brackets, []
ellipsis (...) in a method's parameter list	subscript
enhanced for statement	table of values
final keyword	tabular format
index	traverse an array
index zero	two-dimensional array
initialize an array	value of an element
initializer list	variable-length argument list

Self-Review Exercises

7.1   Fill in the blank(s) in each of the following statements:
a) Lists and tables of values can be stored in _____.
b) An array is a group of _____ (called elements or components) containing values that all have the same _____.
c) The _____ allows programmers to iterate through the elements in an array without using a counter.
d) The number used to refer to a particular element of an array is called the element's _____.
e) An array that uses two indices is referred to as a(n) _____ array.
f) Use the enhanced for statement _____ to walk through double array numbers.
g) Command-line arguments are stored in _____.
h) Use the expression _____ to receive the total number of arguments in a command line. Assume that command-line arguments are stored in String args[].
i) Given the command java MyClass test, the first command-line argument is _____.
j) A(n) _____ in the parameter list of a method indicates that the method can receive a variable number of arguments.

7.2   Determine whether each of the following is *true* or *false*. If *false*, explain why.
a) An array can store many different types of values.
b) An array index should normally be of type float.
c) An individual array element that is passed to a method and modified in that method will contain the modified value when the called method completes execution.
d) Command-line arguments are separated by commas.

7.3   Perform the following tasks for an array called fractions:
a) Declare a constant ARRAY_SIZE that is initialized to 10.
b) Declare an array with ARRAY_SIZE elements of type double, and initialize the elements to 0.
c) Refer to array element 4.
d) Assign the value 1.667 to array element 9.
e) Assign the value 3.333 to array element 6.
f) Sum all the elements of the array, using a for statement. Declare the integer variable x as a control variable for the loop.

7.4   Perform the following tasks for an array called table:
a) Declare and create the array as an integer array that has three rows and three columns. Assume that the constant ARRAY_SIZE has been declared to be 3.
b) How many elements does the array contain?
c) Use a for statement to initialize each element of the array to the sum of its indices. Assume that the integer variables x and y are declared as control variables.

7.5   Find and correct the error in each of the following program segments:
a) ```
final int ARRAY_SIZE = 5;
ARRAY_SIZE = 10;
```
b) ```
Assume int b[] = new int[ 10 ];
for ( int i = 0; i <= b.length; i++ )
    b[ i ] = 1;
```
c) ```
Assume int a[][] = { { 1, 2 }, { 3, 4 } };
    a[1, 1] = 5;
```
```

Answers to Self-Review Exercises

7.1   a) arrays. b) variables, type. c) enhanced for statement. d) index (or subscript or position number). e) two-dimensional. f) for (double d : numbers). g) an array of Strings, called args by convention. h) args.length. i) test. j) ellipsis (...).

7.2   a) False. An array can store only values of the same type.
   b) False. An array index must be an integer or an integer expression.
   c) For individual primitive-type elements of an array: False. A called method receives and manipulates a copy of the value of such an element, so modifications do not affect the original value. If the reference of an array is passed to a method, however, modifications to the array elements made in the called method are indeed reflected in the original. For individual elements of a nonprimitive type: True. A called method receives a copy of the reference of such an element, and changes to the referenced object will be reflected in the original array element.
   d) False. Command-line arguments are separated by white space.

7.3   a) `final int ARRAY_SIZE = 10;`
   b) `double fractions[] = new double[ ARRAY_SIZE ];`
   c) `fractions[ 4 ]`
   d) `fractions[ 9 ] = 1.667;`
   e) `fractions[ 6 ] = 3.333;`
   f) `double total = 0.0;`
       `for ( int x = 0; x < fractions.length; x++ )`
          `total += fractions[ x ];`

7.4   a) `int table[][] = new int[ ARRAY_SIZE ][ ARRAY_SIZE ];`
   b) Nine.
   c) `for ( int x = 0; x < table.length; x++ )`
          `for ( int y = 0; y < table[ x ].length; y++ )`
             `table[ x ][ y ] = x + y;`

7.5   a) Error: Assigning a value to a constant after it has been initialized.
       Correction: Assign the correct value to the constant in a `final int ARRAY_SIZE` declaration or declare another variable.
   b) Error: Referencing an array element outside the bounds of the array (b[10]).
       Correction: Change the <= operator to <.
   c) Error: Array indexing is performed incorrectly.
       Correction: Change the statement to `a[ 1 ][ 1 ] = 5;`.

Exercises

7.6   Fill in the blanks in each of the following statements:
   a) One-dimensional array p contains four elements. The names of those elements are _____, _____, _____ and _____.
   b) Naming an array, stating its type and specifying the number of dimensions in the array is called _____ the array.
   c) In a two-dimensional array, the first index identifies the _____ of an element and the second index identifies the _____ of an element.
   d) An *m*-by-*n* array contains _____ rows, _____ columns and _____ elements.
   e) The name of the element in row 3 and column 5 of array d is _____.

7.7   Consider a two-by-three integer array t.
   a) Write a statement that declares and creates t.
   b) How many rows does t have?
   c) How many columns does t have?
   d) How many elements does t have?
   e) Write access expressions for all the elements in row 1 of t.
   f) Write access expressions for all the elements in column 2 of t.
   g) Write a single statement that sets the element of t in row 0 and column 1 to zero.
   h) Write a series of statements that initializes each element of t to zero. Do not use a rep-
       etition statement.
   i) Write a nested for statement that initializes each element of t to zero.
   j) Write a nested for statement that inputs the values for the elements of t from the user.
   k) Write a series of statements that determines and displays the smallest value in t.
   l) Write a printf statement that displays the elements of the first row of t. Do not use
       repetition.
   m) Write a statement that totals the elements of the third column of t. Do not use repeti-
       tion.
   n) Write a series of statements that displays the contents of t in tabular format. List the
       column indices as headings across the top, and list the row indices at the left of each row.

7.8   (*Sales Commissions*) Use a one-dimensional array to solve the following problem: A company pays its salespeople on a commission basis. The salespeople receive $200 per week plus 9% of
their gross sales for that week. For example, a salesperson who grosses $5000 in sales in a week re-
ceives $200 plus 9% of $5000, or a total of $650. Write an application (using an array of counters)
that determines how many of the salespeople earned salaries in each of the following ranges (assume
that each salesperson's salary is truncated to an integer amount):
   a) $200–299
   b) $300–399
   c) $400–499
   d) $500–599
   e) $600–699
   f) $700–799
   g) $800–899
   h) $900–999
   i) $1000 and over
Summarize the results in tabular format.

7.9   Write statements that perform the following one-dimensional-array operations:
   a) Set the 10 elements of integer array counts to zero.
   b) Add one to each of the 15 elements of integer array bonus.
   c) Display the five values of integer array bestScores in column format.

7.10   (*Duplicate Elimination*) Use a one-dimensional array to solve the following problem: Write
an application that inputs five numbers, each between 10 and 100, inclusive. As each number is
read, display it only if it is not a duplicate of a number already read. Provide for the "worst case," in
which all five numbers are different. Use the smallest possible array to solve this problem. Display
the complete set of unique values input after the user enters each new value.

7.11   Write an application that calculates the product of a series of integers that are passed to
method product using a variable-length argument list. Test your method with several calls, each
with a different number of arguments.

7.12   Rewrite Fig. 7.2 so that the size of the array is specified by the first command-line argument. If no command-line argument is supplied, use 10 as the default size of the array.

7.13   Write an application that uses an enhanced for statement to sum the double values passed by the command-line arguments. [*Hint:* Use the static method parseDouble of class Double to convert a String to a double value.]

7.14   (*Airline Reservations System*) A small airline has just purchased a computer for its new automated reservations system. You have been asked to develop the new system. You are to write an application to assign seats on each flight of the airline's only plane (capacity: 10 seats).

Your application should display the following alternatives: Please type 1 for First Class and Please type 2 for Economy. If the user types 1, your application should assign a seat in the first-class section (seats 1–5). If the user types 2, your application should assign a seat in the economy section (seats 6–10). Your application should then display a boarding pass indicating the person's seat number and whether it is in the first-class or economy section of the plane.

Use a one-dimensional array of primitive type boolean to represent the seating chart of the plane. Initialize all the elements of the array to false to indicate that all the seats are empty. As each seat is assigned, set the corresponding elements of the array to true to indicate that the seat is no longer available.

Your application should never assign a seat that has already been assigned. When the economy section is full, your application should ask the person if it is acceptable to be placed in the first-class section (and vice versa). If yes, make the appropriate seat assignment. If no, display the message "Next flight leaves in 3 hours."

7.15   (*Total Sales*) Use a two-dimensional array to solve the following problem: A company has four salespeople (1 to 4) who sell five different products (1 to 5). Once a day, each salesperson passes in a slip for each type of product sold. Each slip contains the following:

a)   The salesperson number
b)   The product number
c)   The total dollar value of that product sold that day

Thus, each salesperson passes in between 0 and 5 sales slips per day. Assume that the information from all the slips for last month is available. Write an application that will read all this information for last month's sales and summarize the total sales by salesperson and by product. All totals should be stored in the two-dimensional array sales. After processing all the information for last month, display the results in tabular format, with each column representing a particular salesperson and each row representing a particular product. Cross-total each row to get the total sales of each product for last month. Cross-total each column to get the total sales by salesperson for last month. Your tabular output should include these cross-totals to the right of the totaled rows and to the bottom of the totaled columns.

7.16   (*Turtle Graphics*) The Logo language made the concept of *turtle graphics* famous. Imagine a mechanical turtle that walks around the room under the control of a Java application. The turtle holds a pen in one of two positions, up or down. While the pen is down, the turtle traces out shapes as it moves, and while the pen is up, the turtle moves about freely without writing anything. In this problem, you will simulate the operation of the turtle and create a computerized sketchpad.

Use a 20-by-20 array floor that is initialized to zeros. Read commands from an array that contains them. Keep track of the current position of the turtle at all times and whether the pen is currently up or down. Assume that the turtle always starts at position (0, 0) of the floor with its pen up. The set of turtle commands your application must process are shown in Fig. 7.30.

Suppose that the turtle is somewhere near the center of the floor. The following "program" would draw and display a 12-by-12 square, leaving the pen in the up position:

```
2
5,12
```

```
3
5,12
3
5,12
3
5,12
1
6
9
```

As the turtle moves with the pen down, set the appropriate elements of array floor to 1s. When the 6 command (display the array) is given, wherever there is a 1 in the array, display an asterisk or any character you choose. Wherever there is a 0, display a blank.

Write an application to implement the turtle graphics capabilities discussed here. Write several turtle graphics programs to draw interesting shapes. Add other commands to increase the power of your turtle graphics language.

7.17 (*Knight's Tour*) One of the more interesting puzzlers for chess buffs is the Knight's Tour problem, originally proposed by the mathematician Euler. Can the chess piece called the knight move around an empty chessboard and touch each of the 64 squares once and only once? We study this intriguing problem in depth here.

The knight makes only L-shaped moves (two spaces in one direction and one space in a perpendicular direction). Thus, as shown in Fig. 7.31, from a square near the middle of an empty chessboard, the knight (labeled K) can make eight different moves (numbered 0 through 7).

a) Draw an eight-by-eight chessboard on a sheet of paper, and attempt a Knight's Tour by hand. Put a 1 in the starting square, a 2 in the second square, a 3 in the third, and so on. Before starting the tour, estimate how far you think you will get, remembering that a full tour consists of 64 moves. How far did you get? Was this close to your estimate?

Command	Meaning
1	Pen up
2	Pen down
3	Turn right
4	Turn left
5,10	Move forward 10 spaces (replace 10 for a different number of spaces)
6	Display the 20-by-20 array
9	End of data (sentinel)

Fig. 7.30 | Turtle graphics commands.

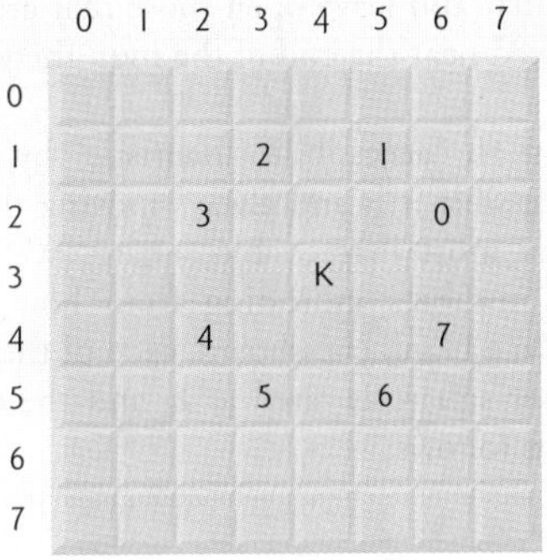

Fig. 7.31 | The eight possible moves of the knight.

b) Now let us develop an application that will move the knight around a chessboard. The board is represented by an eight-by-eight two-dimensional array board. Each square is initialized to zero. We describe each of the eight possible moves in terms of its horizontal and vertical components. For example, a move of type 0, as shown in Fig. 7.31, consists of moving two squares horizontally to the right and one square vertically upward. A move of type 2 consists of moving one square horizontally to the left and two squares vertically upward. Horizontal moves to the left and vertical moves upward are indicated with negative numbers. The eight moves may be described by two one-dimensional arrays, horizontal and vertical, as follows:

```
horizontal[ 0 ] = 2          vertical[ 0 ] = -1
horizontal[ 1 ] = 1          vertical[ 1 ] = -2
horizontal[ 2 ] = -1         vertical[ 2 ] = -2
horizontal[ 3 ] = -2         vertical[ 3 ] = -1
horizontal[ 4 ] = -2         vertical[ 4 ] = 1
horizontal[ 5 ] = -1         vertical[ 5 ] = 2
horizontal[ 6 ] = 1          vertical[ 6 ] = 2
horizontal[ 7 ] = 2          vertical[ 7 ] = 1
```

Let the variables currentRow and currentColumn indicate the row and column, respectively, of the knight's current position. To make a move of type moveNumber, where moveNumber is between 0 and 7, your application should use the statements

```
currentRow += vertical[ moveNumber ];
currentColumn += horizontal[ moveNumber ];
```

Write an application to move the knight around the chessboard. Keep a counter that varies from 1 to 64. Record the latest count in each square the knight moves to. Test each potential move to see if the knight has already visited that square. Test every potential move to ensure that the knight does not land off the chessboard. Run the application. How many moves did the knight make?

c) After attempting to write and run a Knight's Tour application, you have probably developed some valuable insights. We will use these insights to develop a *heuristic* (or "rule of thumb") for moving the knight. Heuristics do not guarantee success, but a carefully developed heuristic greatly improves the chance of success. You may have observed that the outer squares are more troublesome than the squares nearer the center of the board. In fact, the most troublesome or inaccessible squares are the four corners.

Intuition may suggest that you should attempt to move the knight to the most troublesome squares first and leave open those that are easiest to get to, so that when the board gets congested near the end of the tour, there will be a greater chance of success.

We could develop an "accessibility heuristic" by classifying each of the squares according to how accessible it is and always moving the knight (using the knight's L-shaped moves) to the most inaccessible square. We label a two-dimensional array accessibility with numbers indicating from how many squares each particular square is accessible. On a blank chessboard, each of the 16 squares nearest the center is rated as 8, each corner square is rated as 2, and the other squares have accessibility numbers of 3, 4 or 6 as follows:

```
2   3   4   4   4   4   3   2
3   4   6   6   6   6   4   3
4   6   8   8   8   8   6   4
4   6   8   8   8   8   6   4
4   6   8   8   8   8   6   4
4   6   8   8   8   8   6   4
3   4   6   6   6   6   4   3
2   3   4   4   4   4   3   2
```

Write a new version of the Knight's Tour, using the accessibility heuristic. The knight should always move to the square with the lowest accessibility number. In case of a tie, the knight may move to any of the tied squares. Therefore, the tour may begin in any of the four corners. [*Note:* As the knight moves around the chessboard, your application should reduce the accessibility numbers as more squares become occupied. In this way, at any given time during the tour, each available square's accessibility number will remain equal to precisely the number of squares from which that square may be reached.] Run this version of your application. Did you get a full tour? Modify the application to run 64 tours, one starting from each square of the chessboard. How many full tours did you get?

d) Write a version of the Knight's Tour application that, when encountering a tie between two or more squares, decides what square to choose by looking ahead to those squares reachable from the "tied" squares. Your application should move to the tied square for which the next move would arrive at a square with the lowest accessibility number.

7.18 (*Knight's Tour: Brute-Force Approaches*) In part (c) of Exercise 7.17, we developed a solution to the Knight's Tour problem. The approach used, called the "accessibility heuristic," generates many solutions and executes efficiently.

As computers continue to increase in power, we will be able to solve more problems with sheer computer power and relatively unsophisticated algorithms. Let us call this approach "brute-force" problem solving.

a) Use random-number generation to enable the knight to walk around the chessboard (in its legitimate L-shaped moves) at random. Your application should run one tour and display the final chessboard. How far did the knight get?

b) Most likely, the application in part (a) produced a relatively short tour. Now modify your application to attempt 1000 tours. Use a one-dimensional array to keep track of the number of tours of each length. When your application finishes attempting the 1000 tours, it should display this information in neat tabular format. What was the best result?

c) Most likely, the application in part (b) gave you some "respectable" tours, but no full tours. Now let your application run until it produces a full tour. [*Caution:* This version of the application could run for hours on a powerful computer.] Once again, keep a table of the number of tours of each length, and display this table when the first full tour is found. How many tours did your application attempt before producing a full tour? How much time did it take?

   d) Compare the brute-force version of the Knight's Tour with the accessibility-heuristic version. Which required a more careful study of the problem? Which algorithm was more difficult to develop? Which required more computer power? Could we be certain (in advance) of obtaining a full tour with the accessibility-heuristic approach? Could we be certain (in advance) of obtaining a full tour with the brute-force approach? Argue the pros and cons of brute-force problem solving in general.

7.19 (*Eight Queens*) Another puzzler for chess buffs is the Eight Queens problem, which asks the following: Is it possible to place eight queens on an empty chessboard so that no queen is "attacking" any other (i.e., no two queens are in the same row, in the same column or along the same diagonal)? Use the thinking developed in Exercise 7.17 to formulate a heuristic for solving the Eight Queens problem. Run your application. [*Hint:* It is possible to assign a value to each square of the chessboard to indicate how many squares of an empty chessboard are "eliminated" if a queen is placed in that square. Each of the corners would be assigned the value 22, as demonstrated by Fig. 7.32. Once these "elimination numbers" are placed in all 64 squares, an appropriate heuristic might be as follows: Place the next queen in the square with the smallest elimination number. Why is this strategy intuitively appealing?]

7.20 (*Eight Queens: Brute-Force Approaches*) In this exercise, you will develop several brute-force approaches to solving the Eight Queens problem introduced in Exercise 7.19.

   a) Use the random brute-force technique developed in Exercise 7.18 to solve the Eight Queens problem.

   b) Use an exhaustive technique (i.e., try all possible combinations of eight queens on the chessboard) to solve the Eight Queens problem.

   c) Why might the exhaustive brute-force approach not be appropriate for solving the Knight's Tour problem?

   d) Compare and contrast the random brute-force and exhaustive brute-force approaches.

7.21 (*Knight's Tour: Closed-Tour Test*) In the Knight's Tour (Exercise 7.17), a full tour occurs when the knight makes 64 moves, touching each square of the chessboard once and only once. A closed tour occurs when the 64th move is one move away from the square in which the knight started the tour. Modify the application you wrote in Exercise 7.17 to test for a closed tour if a full tour has occurred.

Fig. 7.32 | The 22 squares eliminated by placing a queen in the upper left corner.

7.22 (*Sieve of Eratosthenes*) A prime number is any integer greater than 1 that is evenly divisible only by itself and 1. The Sieve of Eratosthenes is a method of finding prime numbers. It operates as follows:

   a) Create a primitive type `boolean` array with all elements initialized to `true`. Array elements with prime indices will remain `true`. All other array elements will eventually be set to `false`.

   b) Starting with array index 2, determine whether a given element is `true`. If so, loop through the remainder of the array and set to `false` every element whose index is a multiple of the index for the element with value `true`. Then continue the process with the next element with value `true`. For array index 2, all elements beyond element 2 in the array that have indices which are multiples of 2 (indices 4, 6, 8, 10, etc.) will be set to `false`; for array index 3, all elements beyond element 3 in the array that have indices which are multiples of 3 (indices 6, 9, 12, 15, etc.) will be set to `false`; and so on.

When this process completes, the array elements that are still `true` indicate that the index is a prime number. These indices can be displayed. Write an application that uses an array of 1000 elements to determine and display the prime numbers between 2 and 999. Ignore array elements 0 and 1.

7.23 (*Simulation: The Tortoise and the Hare*) In this problem, you will re-create the classic race of the tortoise and the hare. You will use random-number generation to develop a simulation of this memorable event.

Our contenders begin the race at square 1 of 70 squares. Each square represents a possible position along the race course. The finish line is at square 70. The first contender to reach or pass square 70 is rewarded with a pail of fresh carrots and lettuce. The course weaves its way up the side of a slippery mountain, so occasionally the contenders lose ground.

A clock ticks once per second. With each tick of the clock, your application should adjust the position of the animals according to the rules in Fig. 7.33. Use variables to keep track of the positions of the animals (i.e., position numbers are 1–70). Start each animal at position 1 (the "starting gate"). If an animal slips left before square 1, move it back to square 1.

Generate the percentages in Fig. 7.33 by producing a random integer i in the range $1 \leq i \leq 10$. For the tortoise, perform a "fast plod" when $1 \leq i \leq 5$, a "slip" when $6 \leq i \leq 7$ or a "slow plod" when $8 \leq i \leq 10$. Use a similar technique to move the hare.

Animal	Move type	Percentage of the time	Actual move
Tortoise	Fast plod	50%	3 squares to the right
	Slip	20%	6 squares to the left
	Slow plod	30%	1 square to the right
Hare	Sleep	20%	No move at all
	Big hop	20%	9 squares to the right
	Big slip	10%	12 squares to the left
	Small hop	30%	1 square to the right
	Small slip	20%	2 squares to the left

Fig. 7.33 | Rules for adjusting the positions of the tortoise and the hare.

Begin the race by displaying

```
BANG !!!!!
AND THEY'RE OFF !!!!!
```

Then, for each tick of the clock (i.e., each repetition of a loop), display a 70-position line showing the letter T in the position of the tortoise and the letter H in the position of the hare. Occasionally, the contenders will land on the same square. In this case, the tortoise bites the hare, and your application should display OUCH!!! beginning at that position. All output positions other than the T, the H or the OUCH!!! (in case of a tie) should be blank.

After each line is displayed, test for whether either animal has reached or passed square 70. If so, display the winner and terminate the simulation. If the tortoise wins, display TORTOISE WINS!!! YAY!!! If the hare wins, display Hare wins. Yuch. If both animals win on the same tick of the clock, you may want to favor the tortoise (the "underdog"), or you may want to display It's a tie. If neither animal wins, perform the loop again to simulate the next tick of the clock. When you are ready to run your application, assemble a group of fans to watch the race. You'll be amazed at how involved your audience gets!

Later in the book, we introduce a number of Java capabilities, such as graphics, images, animation, sound and multithreading. As you study those features, you might enjoy enhancing your tortoise-and-hare contest simulation.

7.24 *(Fibonacci Series)* The Fibonacci series

0, 1, 1, 2, 3, 5, 8, 13, 21, …

begins with the terms 0 and 1 and has the property that each succeeding term is the sum of the two preceding terms.
   a) Write a method fibonacci(n) that calculates the nth Fibonacci number. Incorporate this method into an application that enables the user to enter the value of n.
   b) Determine the largest Fibonacci number that can be displayed on your system.
   c) Modify the application you wrote in part (a) to use double instead of int to calculate and return Fibonacci numbers, and use this modified application to repeat part (b).

Exercises 7.25—7.28 are reasonably challenging. Once you have done these problems, you ought to be able to implement most popular card games easily.

7.25 *(Card Shuffling and Dealing)* Modify the application of Fig. 7.11 to deal a five-card poker hand. Then modify class DeckOfCards of Fig. 7.10 to include methods that determine whether a hand contains
   a) a pair
   b) two pairs
   c) three of a kind (e.g., three jacks)
   d) four of a kind (e.g., four aces)
   e) a flush (i.e., all five cards of the same suit)
   f) a straight (i.e., five cards of consecutive face values)
   g) a full house (i.e., two cards of one face value and three cards of another face value)

[*Hint:* Add methods getFace and getSuit to class Card of Fig. 7.9.]

7.26 *(Card Shuffling and Dealing)* Use the methods developed in Exercise 7.25 to write an application that deals two five-card poker hands, evaluates each hand and determines which is better.

7.27 *(Card Shuffling and Dealing)* Modify the application developed in Exercise 7.26 so that it can simulate the dealer. The dealer's five-card hand is dealt "face down," so the player cannot see it. The application should then evaluate the dealer's hand, and, based on the quality of the hand, the dealer should draw one, two or three more cards to replace the corresponding number of unneeded cards in the original hand. The application should then reevaluate the dealer's hand. [*Caution:* This is a difficult problem!]

7.28 (*Card Shuffling and Dealing*) Modify the application developed in Exercise 7.27 so that it can handle the dealer's hand automatically, but the player is allowed to decide which cards of the player's hand to replace. The application should then evaluate both hands and determine who wins. Now use this new application to play 20 games against the computer. Who wins more games, you or the computer? Have a friend play 20 games against the computer. Who wins more games? Based on the results of these games, refine your poker-playing application. (This, too, is a difficult problem.) Play 20 more games. Does your modified application play a better game?

Special Section: Building Your Own Computer

In the next several problems, we take a temporary diversion from the world of high-level language programming to "peel open" a computer and look at its internal structure. We introduce machine-language programming and write several machine-language programs. To make this an especially valuable experience, we then build a computer (through the technique of software-based *simulation*) on which you can execute your machine-language programs.

7.29 (*Machine-Language Programming*) Let us create a computer called the Simpletron. As its name implies, it is a simple, but powerful, machine. The Simpletron runs programs written in the only language it directly understands: Simpletron Machine Language (SML).

The Simpletron contains an *accumulator*—a special register in which information is put before the Simpletron uses that information in calculations or examines it in various ways. All the information in the Simpletron is handled in terms of *words*. A word is a signed four-digit decimal number, such as +3364, -1293, +0007 and -0001. The Simpletron is equipped with a 100-word memory, and these words are referenced by their location numbers 00, 01, ..., 99.

Before running an SML program, we must *load*, or place, the program into memory. The first instruction (or statement) of every SML program is always placed in location 00. The simulator will start executing at this location.

Each instruction written in SML occupies one word of the Simpletron's memory (and hence instructions are signed four-digit decimal numbers). We shall assume that the sign of an SML instruction is always plus, but the sign of a data word may be either plus or minus. Each location in the Simpletron's memory may contain an instruction, a data value used by a program or an unused (and hence undefined) area of memory. The first two digits of each SML instruction are the *operation code* specifying the operation to be performed. SML operation codes are summarized in Fig. 7.34.

Operation code	Meaning
Input/output operations:	
`final int READ = 10;`	Read a word from the keyboard into a specific location in memory.
`final int WRITE = 11;`	Write a word from a specific location in memory to the screen.

Fig. 7.34 | Simpletron Machine Language (SML) operation codes. (Part I of 2.)

Operation code	Meaning
Load/store operations:	
`final int LOAD = 20;`	Load a word from a specific location in memory into the accumulator.
`final int STORE = 21;`	Store a word from the accumulator into a specific location in memory.
Arithmetic operations:	
`final int ADD = 30;`	Add a word from a specific location in memory to the word in the accumulator (leave the result in the accumulator).
`final int SUBTRACT = 31;`	Subtract a word from a specific location in memory from the word in the accumulator (leave the result in the accumulator).
`final int DIVIDE = 32;`	Divide a word from a specific location in memory into the word in the accumulator (leave result in the accumulator).
`final int MULTIPLY = 33;`	Multiply a word from a specific location in memory by the word in the accumulator (leave the result in the accumulator).
Transfer-of-control operations:	
`final int BRANCH = 40;`	Branch to a specific location in memory.
`final int BRANCHNEG = 41;`	Branch to a specific location in memory if the accumulator is negative.
`final int BRANCHZERO = 42;`	Branch to a specific location in memory if the accumulator is zero.
`final int HALT = 43;`	Halt. The program has completed its task.

Fig. 7.34 | Simpletron Machine Language (SML) operation codes. (Part 2 of 2.)

The last two digits of an SML instruction are the *operand*—the address of the memory location containing the word to which the operation applies. Let's consider several simple SML programs.

The first SML program (Fig. 7.35) reads two numbers from the keyboard and computes and displays their sum. The instruction +1007 reads the first number from the keyboard and places it into location 07 (which has been initialized to 0). Then instruction +1008 reads the next number into location 08. The *load* instruction, +2007, puts the first number into the accumulator, and the *add* instruction, +3008, adds the second number to the number in the accumulator. *All SML arithmetic instructions leave their results in the accumulator.* The *store* instruction, +2109, places the result back into memory location 09, from which the *write* instruction, +1109, takes the number and displays it (as a signed four-digit decimal number). The *halt* instruction, +4300, terminates execution.

Location	Number	Instruction
00	+1007	(Read A)
01	+1008	(Read B)
02	+2007	(Load A)
03	+3008	(Add B)
04	+2109	(Store C)
05	+1109	(Write C)
06	+4300	(Halt)
07	+0000	(Variable A)
08	+0000	(Variable B)
09	+0000	(Result C)

Fig. 7.35 | SML program that reads two integers and computes their sum.

The second SML program (Fig. 7.36) reads two numbers from the keyboard and determines and displays the larger value. Note the use of the instruction +4107 as a conditional transfer of control, much the same as Java's if statement.

Location	Number	Instruction
00	+1009	(Read A)
01	+1010	(Read B)
02	+2009	(Load A)
03	+3110	(Subtract B)
04	+4107	(Branch negative to 07)
05	+1109	(Write A)
06	+4300	(Halt)
07	+1110	(Write B)
08	+4300	(Halt)
09	+0000	(Variable A)
10	+0000	(Variable B)

Fig. 7.36 | SML program that reads two integers and determines the larger.

Now write SML programs to accomplish each of the following tasks:

a) Use a sentinel-controlled loop to read 10 positive numbers. Compute and display their sum.

b) Use a counter-controlled loop to read seven numbers, some positive and some negative, and compute and display their average.

c) Read a series of numbers, and determine and display the largest number. The first number read indicates how many numbers should be processed.

7.30 (*Computer Simulator*) In this problem, you are going to build your own computer. No, you will not be soldering components together. Rather, you will use the powerful technique of *software-based simulation* to create an object-oriented *software model* of the Simpletron of Exercise 7.29. Your Simpletron simulator will turn the computer you are using into a Simpletron, and you will actually be able to run, test and debug the SML programs you wrote in Exercise 7.29.

When you run your Simpletron simulator, it should begin by displaying:

```
*** Welcome to Simpletron! ***
*** Please enter your program one instruction  ***
*** (or data word) at a time into the input    ***
*** text field. I will display the location    ***
*** number and a question mark (?). You then   ***
*** type the word for that location. Press the ***
*** Done button to stop entering your program. ***
```

Your application should simulate the memory of the Simpletron with a one-dimensional array memory that has 100 elements. Now assume that the simulator is running, and let us examine the dialog as we enter the program of Fig. 7.36 (Exercise 7.29):

```
00 ? +1009
01 ? +1010
02 ? +2009
03 ? +3110
04 ? +4107
05 ? +1109
06 ? +4300
07 ? +1110
08 ? +4300
09 ? +0000
10 ? +0000
11 ? -99999
```

Your program should display the memory location followed by a question mark. Each value to the right of a question mark is input by the user. When the sentinel value -99999 is input, the program should display the following:

```
*** Program loading completed ***
*** Program execution begins   ***
```

The SML program has now been placed (or loaded) in array memory. Now the Simpletron executes the SML program. Execution begins with the instruction in location 00 and, as in Java, continues sequentially, unless directed to some other part of the program by a transfer of control.

Use the variable accumulator to represent the accumulator register. Use the variable instructionCounter to keep track of the location in memory that contains the instruction being performed. Use the variable operationCode to indicate the operation currently being performed (i.e., the left two digits of the instruction word). Use the variable operand to indicate the memory location on which the current instruction operates. Thus, operand is the rightmost two digits of the instruction currently being performed. Do not execute instructions directly from memory. Rather, transfer the next instruction to be performed from memory to a variable called `instructionRegis-ter`. Then "pick off" the left two digits and place them in `operationCode`, and "pick off" the right two digits and place them in `operand`. When the Simpletron begins execution, the special registers are all initialized to zero.

Now, let us "walk through" execution of the first SML instruction, +1009 in memory location 00. This procedure is called an *instruction execution cycle*.

The `instructionCounter` tells us the location of the next instruction to be performed. We *fetch* the contents of that location from `memory` by using the Java statement

```
instructionRegister = memory[ instructionCounter ];
```

The operation code and the operand are extracted from the instruction register by the statements

```
operationCode = instructionRegister / 100;
operand = instructionRegister % 100;
```

Now the Simpletron must determine that the operation code is actually a *read* (versus a *write*, a *load*, and so on). A `switch` differentiates among the 12 operations of SML. In the `switch` statement, the behavior of various SML instructions is simulated as shown in Fig. 7.37. We discuss branch instructions shortly and leave the others to you.

When the SML program completes execution, the name and contents of each register as well as the complete contents of memory should be displayed. Such a printout is often called a computer dump (no, a computer dump is not a place where old computers go). To help you program your dump method, a sample dump format is shown in Fig. 7.38. Note that a dump after executing a Simpletron program would show the actual values of instructions and data values at the moment execution terminated.

Let us proceed with the execution of our program's first instruction—namely, the +1009 in location 00. As we have indicated, the `switch` statement simulates this task by prompting the user to enter a value, reading the value and storing it in memory location `memory[ operand ]`. The value is then read into location 09.

At this point, simulation of the first instruction is completed. All that remains is to prepare the Simpletron to execute the next instruction. Since the instruction just performed was not a transfer of control, we need merely increment the instruction-counter register as follows:

```
instructionCounter++;
```

This action completes the simulated execution of the first instruction. The entire process (i.e., the instruction execution cycle) begins anew with the fetch of the next instruction to execute.

Instruction	Description
read:	Display the prompt `"Enter an integer"`, then input the integer and store it in location `memory[ operand ]`.
load:	`accumulator = memory[ operand ];`
add:	`accumulator += memory[ operand ];`
halt:	This instruction displays the message `*** Simpletron execution terminated ***`

Fig. 7.37 | Behavior of several SML instructions in the Simpletron.

```
REGISTERS:
accumulator            +0000
instructionCounter        00
instructionRegister    +0000
operationCode             00
operand                   00

MEMORY:
         0     1     2     3     4     5     6     7     8     9
 0   +0000 +0000 +0000 +0000 +0000 +0000 +0000 +0000 +0000 +0000
10   +0000 +0000 +0000 +0000 +0000 +0000 +0000 +0000 +0000 +0000
20   +0000 +0000 +0000 +0000 +0000 +0000 +0000 +0000 +0000 +0000
30   +0000 +0000 +0000 +0000 +0000 +0000 +0000 +0000 +0000 +0000
40   +0000 +0000 +0000 +0000 +0000 +0000 +0000 +0000 +0000 +0000
50   +0000 +0000 +0000 +0000 +0000 +0000 +0000 +0000 +0000 +0000
60   +0000 +0000 +0000 +0000 +0000 +0000 +0000 +0000 +0000 +0000
70   +0000 +0000 +0000 +0000 +0000 +0000 +0000 +0000 +0000 +0000
80   +0000 +0000 +0000 +0000 +0000 +0000 +0000 +0000 +0000 +0000
90   +0000 +0000 +0000 +0000 +0000 +0000 +0000 +0000 +0000 +0000
```

Fig. 7.38 | A sample dump.

Now let us consider how the branching instructions—the transfers of control—are simulated. All we need to do is adjust the value in the instruction counter appropriately. Therefore, the unconditional branch instruction (40) is simulated within the switch as

```
instructionCounter = operand;
```

The conditional "branch if accumulator is zero" instruction is simulated as

```
if ( accumulator == 0 )
    instructionCounter = operand;
```

At this point, you should implement your Simpletron simulator and run each of the SML programs you wrote in Exercise 7.29. If you desire, you may embellish SML with additional features and provide for these features in your simulator.

Your simulator should check for various types of errors. During the program-loading phase, for example, each number the user types into the Simpletron's memory must be in the range -9999 to +9999. Your simulator should test that each number entered is in this range and, if not, keep prompting the user to reenter the number until the user enters a correct number.

During the execution phase, your simulator should check for various serious errors, such as attempts to divide by zero, attempts to execute invalid operation codes, and accumulator overflows (i.e., arithmetic operations resulting in values larger than +9999 or smaller than -9999). Such serious errors are called *fatal errors*. When a fatal error is detected, your simulator should display an error message, such as

```
*** Attempt to divide by zero ***
*** Simpletron execution abnormally terminated ***
```

and should display a full computer dump in the format we discussed previously. This treatment will help the user locate the error in the program.

7.31   (*Simpletron Simulator Modifications*) In Exercise 7.30, you wrote a software simulation of a computer that executes programs written in Simpletron Machine Language (SML). In this exercise, we propose several modifications and enhancements to the Simpletron Simulator. In Exercises 17.26–17.27, we propose building a compiler that converts programs written in a high-level programming language (a variation of Basic) to Simpletron Machine Language. Some of the following modifications and enhancements may be required to execute the programs produced by the compiler:

a) Extend the Simpletron Simulator's memory to contain 1000 memory locations to enable the Simpletron to handle larger programs.

b) Allow the simulator to perform remainder calculations. This modification requires an additional SML instruction.

c) Allow the simulator to perform exponentiation calculations. This modification requires an additional SML instruction.

d) Modify the simulator to use hexadecimal values rather than integer values to represent SML instructions.

e) Modify the simulator to allow output of a newline. This modification requires an additional SML instruction.

f) Modify the simulator to process floating-point values in addition to integer values.

g) Modify the simulator to handle string input. [*Hint:* Each Simpletron word can be divided into two groups, each holding a two-digit integer. Each two-digit integer represents the ASCII (see Appendix B) decimal equivalent of a character. Add a machine-language instruction that will input a string and store the string, beginning at a specific Simpletron memory location. The first half of the word at that location will be a count of the number of characters in the string (i.e., the length of the string). Each succeeding half-word contains one ASCII character expressed as two decimal digits. The machine-language instruction converts each character into its ASCII equivalent and assigns it to a half-word.]

h) Modify the simulator to handle output of strings stored in the format of part (g). [*Hint:* Add a machine-language instruction that will display a string, beginning at a certain Simpletron memory location. The first half of the word at that location is a count of the number of characters in the string (i.e., the length of the string). Each succeeding half-word contains one ASCII character expressed as two decimal digits. The machine-language instruction checks the length and displays the string by translating each two-digit number into its equivalent character.]

Classes and Objects: A Deeper Look

OBJECTIVES

In this chapter you will learn:

- Encapsulation and data hiding.
- The notions of data abstraction and abstract data types (ADTs).
- To use keyword **this**.
- To use **static** variables and methods.
- To import **static** members of a class.
- To use the **enum** type to create sets of constants with unique identifiers.
- To declare **enum** constants with parameters.
- To organize classes in packages to promote reuse.

8.1 Introduction

In our discussions of object-oriented programs in the preceding chapters, we introduced many basic concepts and terminology that relate to Java object-oriented programming (OOP). We also discussed our program development methodology: We selected appropriate variables and methods for each program and specified the manner in which an object of our class collaborated with objects of Java API classes to accomplish the program's overall goals.

In this chapter, we take a deeper look at building classes, controlling access to members of a class and creating constructors. We discuss composition—a capability that allows a class to have references to objects of other classes as members. We reexamine the use of *set* and *get* methods and further explore the class type enum (introduced in Section 6.10) that enables programmers to declare and manipulate sets of unique identifiers that represent constant values. In Section 6.10, we introduced the basic enum type, which appeared within another class and simply declared a set of constants. In this chapter, we discuss the relationship between enum types and classes, demonstrating that an enum, like a class, can be declared in its own file with constructors, methods and fields. The chapter also discusses static class members and final instance variables in detail. We investigate issues such as software reusability, data abstraction and encapsulation. Finally, we explain how to organize classes in packages to help manage large applications and promote reuse, then show a special relationship between classes in the same package.

Chapter 9, Object-Oriented Programming: Inheritance, and Chapter 10, Object-Oriented Programming: Polymorphism, introduce two additional key object-oriented programming technologies.

8.2 Time Class Case Study

Time1 Class Declaration

Our first example consists of two classes—Time1 (Fig. 8.1) and Time1Test (Fig. 8.2). Class Time1 represents the time of day. Class Time1Test is an application class in which the main method creates one object of class Time1 and invokes its methods. These classes must be declared in separate files because they are both public classes. The output of this program appears in Fig. 8.2.

Class Time1 contains three private instance variables of type int (Fig. 8.1, lines 6–8)—hour, minute and second—that represent the time in universal-time format (24-hour clock format in which hours are in the range 0–23). Class Time1 contains public methods setTime (lines 12–17), toUniversalString (lines 20–23) and toString (lines 26–31). These methods are also called the **public** services or the **public** interface that the class provides to its clients.

In this example, class Time1 does not declare a constructor, so the class has a default constructor that is supplied by the compiler. Each instance variable implicitly receives the default value 0 for an int. Note that instance variables also can be initialized when they are declared in the class body using the same initialization syntax as with a local variable.

```java
 1   // Fig. 8.1: Time1.java
 2   // Time1 class declaration maintains the time in 24-hour format.
 3
 4   public class Time1
 5   {
 6      private int hour;   // 0 - 23
 7      private int minute; // 0 - 59
 8      private int second; // 0 - 59
 9
10      // set a new time value using universal time; ensure that
11      // the data remains consistent by setting invalid values to zero
12      public void setTime( int h, int m, int s )
13      {
14         hour = ( ( h >= 0 && h < 24 ) ? h : 0 );   // validate hour
15         minute = ( ( m >= 0 && m < 60 ) ? m : 0 ); // validate minute
16         second = ( ( s >= 0 && s < 60 ) ? s : 0 ); // validate second
17      } // end method setTime
18
19      // convert to String in universal-time format (HH:MM:SS)
20      public String toUniversalString()
21      {
22         return String.format( "%02d:%02d:%02d", hour, minute, second );
23      } // end method toUniversalString
```

Fig. 8.1 | Time1 class declaration maintains the time in 24-hour format. (Part 1 of 2.)

```
24
25      // convert to String in standard-time format (H:MM:SS AM or PM)
26      public String toString()
27      {
28         return String.format( "%d:%02d:%02d %s",
29            ( ( hour == 0 || hour == 12 ) ? 12 : hour % 12 ),
30            minute, second, ( hour < 12 ? "AM" : "PM" ) );
31      } // end method toString
32   } // end class Time1
```

Fig. 8.1 | `Time1` class declaration maintains the time in 24-hour format. (Part 2 of 2.)

Method `setTime` (lines 12–17) is a `public` method that declares three `int` parameters and uses them to set the time. A conditional expression tests each argument to determine whether the value is in a specified range. For example, the `hour` value (line 14) must be greater than or equal to 0 and less than 24, because universal-time format represents hours as integers from 0 to 23 (e.g., 1 PM is hour 13 and 11 PM is hour 23; midnight is hour 0 and noon is hour 12). Similarly, both `minute` and `second` values (lines 15 and 16) must be greater than or equal to 0 and less than 60. Any values outside these ranges are set to zero to ensure that a `Time1` object always contains *consistent data*—that is, the object's data values are always kept in range, even if the values provided as arguments to method `setTime` were *incorrect*. In this example, zero is a consistent value for `hour`, `minute` and `second`.

A value passed to `setTime` is a correct value if it is in the allowed range for the member it is initializing. So, any number in the range 0–23 would be a correct value for the `hour`. A correct value is always a consistent value. However, a consistent value is not necessarily a correct value. If `setTime` sets `hour` to 0 because the argument received was out of range, then `setTime` is taking an incorrect value and making it consistent, so the object remains in a consistent state at all times. The *correct* time of day could actually be 11 AM, but because the person may have accidentally entered an out-of-range (incorrect) time, we choose to set the `hour` to the consistent value of zero. In this case, you might want to indicate that the object is incorrect. In Chapter 13, Exception Handling, you will learn elegant techniques that enable your classes to indicate when incorrect values are received.

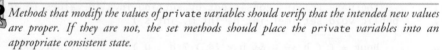

Software Engineering Observation 8.1

Methods that modify the values of `private` variables should verify that the intended new values are proper. If they are not, the set methods should place the `private` variables into an appropriate consistent state.

Method `toUniversalString` (lines 20–23) takes no arguments and returns a `String` in universal-time format, consisting of six digits—two for the hour, two for the minute and two for the second. For example, if the time were 1:30:07 PM, method `toUniversal-String` would return 13:30:07. The return statement (line 22) uses `static` method `format` of class `String` to return a `String` containing the formatted `hour`, `minute` and `second` values, each with two digits and possibly a leading 0 (specified with the 0 flag). Method `format` is similar to method `System.out.printf` except that `format` returns a formatted `String` rather than displaying it in a command window. The formatted `String` is returned by method `toUniversalString`.

Method toString (lines 26–31) takes no arguments and returns a String in standard-time format, consisting of the hour, minute and second values separated by colons and followed by an AM or PM indicator (e.g., 1:27:06 PM). Like method toUniversal-String, method toString uses static String method format to format the minute and second as two-digit values with leading zeros if necessary. Line 29 uses a conditional operator (?:) to determine the value for hour in the string—if the hour is 0 or 12 (AM or PM), it appears as 12—otherwise, the hour appears as a value from 1 to 11. The conditional operator in line 30 determines whether AM or PM will be returned as part of the String.

Recall from Section 6.4 that all objects in Java have a toString method that returns a String representation of the object. We chose to return a String containing the time in standard-time format. Method toString can be called implicitly whenever a Time1 object appears in the code where a String is needed, such as the value to output with a %s format specifier in a call to System.out.printf.

Using Class *Time1*

As you learned in Chapter 3, each class you declare represents a new type in Java. Therefore, after declaring class Time1, we can use it as a type in declarations such as

```
Time1 sunset; // sunset can hold a reference to a Time1 object
```

The Time1Test application class (Fig. 8.2) uses class Time1. Line 9 declares and creates a Time1 object and assigns it to local variable time. Note that new implicitly invokes class Time1's default constructor, since Time1 does not declare any constructors. Lines 12–16 output the time first in universal-time format (by invoking time's toUniversalString method in line 13), then in standard-time format (by explicitly invoking time's toString method in line 15) to confirm that the Time1 object was initialized properly.

```java
 1   // Fig. 8.2: Time1Test.java
 2   // Time1 object used in an application.
 3
 4   public class Time1Test
 5   {
 6      public static void main( String args[] )
 7      {
 8         // create and initialize a Time1 object
 9         Time1 time = new Time1(); // invokes Time1 constructor
10
11         // output string representations of the time
12         System.out.print( "The initial universal time is: " );
13         System.out.println( time.toUniversalString() );
14         System.out.print( "The initial standard time is: " );
15         System.out.println( time.toString() );
16         System.out.println(); // output a blank line
17
18         // change time and output updated time
19         time.setTime( 13, 27, 6 );
20         System.out.print( "Universal time after setTime is: " );
21         System.out.println( time.toUniversalString() );
22         System.out.print( "Standard time after setTime is: " );
```

Fig. 8.2 | Time1 object used in an application. (Part 1 of 2.)

```
23          System.out.println( time.toString() );
24          System.out.println(); // output a blank line
25
26          // set time with invalid values; output updated time
27          time.setTime( 99, 99, 99 );
28          System.out.println( "After attempting invalid settings:" );
29          System.out.print( "Universal time: " );
30          System.out.println( time.toUniversalString() );
31          System.out.print( "Standard time: " );
32          System.out.println( time.toString() );
33       } // end main
34    } // end class Time1Test
```

```
The initial universal time is: 00:00:00
The initial standard time is: 12:00:00 AM

Universal time after setTime is: 13:27:06
Standard time after setTime is: 1:27:06 PM

After attempting invalid settings:
Universal time: 00:00:00
Standard time: 12:00:00 AM
```

Fig. 8.2 | Time1 object used in an application. (Part 2 of 2.)

Line 19 invokes method setTime of the time object to change the time. Then lines 20–24 output the time again in both formats to confirm that the time was set correctly.

To illustrate that method setTime maintains the object in a consistent state, line 27 calls method setTime with arguments of 99 for the hour, minute and second. Lines 28–32 output the time again in both formats to confirm that setTime maintained the object's consistent state, then the program terminates. The last two lines of the application's output show that the time is reset to midnight—the initial value of a Time1 object—after an attempt to set the time with three out-of-range values.

Notes on the Time1 Class Declaration
Consider several issues of class design with respect to class Time1. The instance variables hour, minute and second are each declared private. The actual data representation used within the class is of no concern to the class's clients. For example, it would be perfectly reasonable for Time1 to represent the time internally as the number of seconds since midnight or the number of minutes and seconds since midnight. Clients could use the same public methods and get the same results without being aware of this. (Exercise 8.5 asks you to represent the time in class Time1 as the number of seconds since midnight and show that there is indeed no change visible to the clients of the class.)

Software Engineering Observation 8.2

Classes simplify programming, because the client can use only the public methods exposed by the class. Such methods are usually client oriented rather than implementation oriented. Clients are neither aware of, nor involved in, a class's implementation. Clients generally care about what *the class does but not* how *the class does it.*

Software Engineering Observation 8.3

Interfaces change less frequently than implementations. When an implementation changes, implementation-dependent code must change accordingly. Hiding the implementation reduces the possibility that other program parts will become dependent on class implementation details.

8.3 Controlling Access to Members

The access modifiers public and private control access to a class's variables and methods. (In Chapter 9, we will introduce the additional access modifier protected.) As we stated in Section 8.2, the primary purpose of public methods is to present to the class's clients a view of the services the class provides (the class's public interface). Clients of the class need not be concerned with how the class accomplishes its tasks. For this reason, the private variables and private methods of a class (i.e., the class's implementation details) are not directly accessible to the class's clients.

Figure 8.3 demonstrates that private class members are not directly accessible outside the class. Lines 9–11 attempt to access directly the private instance variables hour, minute and second of the Time1 object time. When this program is compiled, the compiler generates error messages stating that these private members are not accessible. [*Note:* This program assumes that the Time1 class from Fig. 8.1 is used.]

Common Programming Error 8.1

An attempt by a method that is not a member of a class to access a private member of that class is a compilation error.

```
1   // Fig. 8.3: MemberAccessTest.java
2   // Private members of class Time1 are not accessible.
3   public class MemberAccessTest
4   {
5      public static void main( String args[] )
6      {
7         Time1 time = new Time1(); // create and initialize Time1 object
8
9         time.hour = 7;    // error: hour has private access in Time1
10        time.minute = 15; // error: minute has private access in Time1
11        time.second = 30; // error: second has private access in Time1
12     } // end main
13  } // end class MemberAccessTest
```

```
MemberAccessTest.java:9: hour has private access in Time1
      time.hour = 7;    // error: hour has private access in Time1
          ^
MemberAccessTest.java:10: minute has private access in Time1
      time.minute = 15; // error: minute has private access in Time1
          ^
MemberAccessTest.java:11: second has private access in Time1
      time.second = 30; // error: second has private access in Time1
          ^
3 errors
```

Fig. 8.3 | Private members of class Time1 are not accessible.

8.4 Referring to the Current Object's Members with the this Reference

Every object can access a reference to itself with keyword this (sometimes called the this reference). When a non-static method is called for a particular object, the method's body implicitly uses keyword this to refer to the object's instance variables and other methods. As you will see in Fig. 8.4, you can also use keyword this explicitly in a non-static method's body. Section 8.5 shows another interesting use of keyword this. Section 8.11 explains why keyword this cannot be used in a static method.

We now demonstrate implicit and explicit use of the this reference to enable class ThisTest's main method to display the private data of a class SimpleTime object (Fig. 8.4). Note that this example is the first in which we declare two classes in one file—class ThisTest is declared in lines 4–11, and class SimpleTime is declared in lines 14–47. We did this to demonstrate that when you compile a .java file that contains more than one class, the compiler produces a separate class file with the .class extension for every compiled class. In this case two separate files are produced—SimpleTime.class and ThisTest.class. When one source-code (.java) file contains multiple class declarations, the class files for those classes are both placed in the same directory by the compiler. Also, note that only class ThisTest is declared public in Fig. 8.4. A source-code file can contain only one public class—otherwise, a compilation error occurs.

```java
1   // Fig. 8.4: ThisTest.java
2   // this used implicitly and explicitly to refer to members of an object.
3
4   public class ThisTest
5   {
6      public static void main( String args[] )
7      {
8         SimpleTime time = new SimpleTime( 15, 30, 19 );
9         System.out.println( time.buildString() );
10      } // end main
11   } // end class ThisTest
12
13   // class SimpleTime demonstrates the "this" reference
14   class SimpleTime
15   {
16      private int hour;   // 0-23
17      private int minute; // 0-59
18      private int second; // 0-59
19
20      // if the constructor uses parameter names identical to
21      // instance variable names the "this" reference is
22      // required to distinguish between names
23      public SimpleTime( int hour, int minute, int second )
24      {
25         this.hour = hour;     // set "this" object's hour
26         this.minute = minute; // set "this" object's minute
27         this.second = second; // set "this" object's second
28      } // end SimpleTime constructor
```

Fig. 8.4 | this used implicitly and explicitly to refer to members of an object. (Part 1 of 2.)

```
29
30      // use explicit and implicit "this" to call toUniversalString
31      public String buildString()
32      {
33         return String.format( "%24s: %s\n%24s: %s",
34            "this.toUniversalString()", this.toUniversalString(),
35            "toUniversalString()", toUniversalString() );
36      } // end method buildString
37
38      // convert to String in universal-time format (HH:MM:SS)
39      public String toUniversalString()
40      {
41         // "this" is not required here to access instance variables,
42         // because method does not have local variables with same
43         // names as instance variables
44         return String.format( "%02d:%02d:%02d",
45            this.hour, this.minute, this.second );
46      } // end method toUniversalString
47   } // end class SimpleTime
```

```
this.toUniversalString(): 15:30:19
    toUniversalString(): 15:30:19
```

Fig. 8.4 | this used implicitly and explicitly to refer to members of an object. (Part 2 of 2.)

Class SimpleTime (lines 14–47) declares three private instance variables—hour, minute and second (lines 16–18). The constructor (lines 23–28) receives three int arguments to initialize a SimpleTime object. Note that we used parameter names for the constructor (line 23) that are identical to the class's instance variable names (lines 16–18). We don't recommend this practice, but we did it here to shadow (hide) the corresponding instance variables so that we could illustrate explicit use of the this reference. If a method contains a local variable with the same name as a field, that method will refer to the local variable rather than the field. In this case, the local variable shadows the field in the method's scope. However, the method can use the this reference to refer to the shadowed field explicitly, as shown in lines 25–27 for SimpleTime's shadowed instance variables.

Method buildString (lines 31–36) returns a String created by a statement that uses the this reference explicitly and implicitly. Line 34 uses the this reference explicitly to call method toUniversalString. Line 35 uses the this reference implicitly to call the same method. Note that both lines perform the same task. Programmers typically do not use this explicitly to reference other methods within the current object. Also, note that line 45 in method toUniversalString explicitly uses the this reference to access each instance variable. This is not necessary here, because the method does not have any local variables that shadow the instance variables of the class.

Common Programming Error 8.2

It is often a logic error when a method contains a parameter or local variable that has the same name as a field of the class. In this case, use reference this if you wish to access the field of the class—otherwise, the method parameter or local variable will be referenced.

Error-Prevention Tip 8.1

Avoid method parameter names or local variable names that conflict with field names. This helps prevent subtle, hard-to-locate bugs.

Application class `ThisTest` (lines 4–11) demonstrates class `SimpleTime`. Line 8 creates an instance of class `SimpleTime` and invokes its constructor. Line 9 invokes the object's `buildString` method, then displays the results.

Performance Tip 8.1

Java conserves storage by maintaining only one copy of each method per class—this method is invoked by every object of the class. Each object, on the other hand, has its own copy of the class's instance variables (i.e., non-static fields). Each method of the class implicitly uses this to determine the specific object of the class to manipulate.

8.5 Time Class Case Study: Overloaded Constructors

As you know, you can declare your own constructor to specify how objects of a class should be initialized. Next, we demonstrate a class with several **overloaded constructors** that enable objects of that class to be initialized in different ways. To overload constructors, simply provide multiple constructor declarations with different signatures. Recall from Section 6.12 that the compiler differentiates signatures by the number of parameters, the types of the parameters and the order of the parameter types in each signature.

Class *Time2 with Overloaded Constructors*

The default constructor for class `Time1` (Fig. 8.1) initialized hour, `minute` and `second` to their default 0 values (which is midnight in universal time). The default constructor does not enable the class's clients to initialize the time with specific nonzero values. Class `Time2` (Fig. 8.5) contains five overloaded constructors that provide convenient ways to initialize objects of the new class `Time2`. Each constructor initializes the object to begin in a consistent state. In this program, four of the constructors invoke a fifth, which in turn calls method `setTime` to ensure that the value supplied for hour is in the range 0 to 23, and the values for `minute` and `second` are each in the range 0 to 59. If a value is out of range, it is set to zero by `setTime` (once again ensuring that each instance variable remains in a consistent state). The compiler invokes the appropriate constructor by matching the number, types and order of the types of the arguments specified in the constructor call with the number, types and order of the types of the parameters specified in each constructor declaration. Note that class `Time2` also provides *set* and *get* methods for each instance variable.

```
1   // Fig. 8.5: Time2.java
2   // Time2 class declaration with overloaded constructors.
3
4   public class Time2
5   {
6       private int hour;   // 0 - 23
7       private int minute; // 0 - 59
8       private int second; // 0 - 59
9
```

Fig. 8.5 | `Time2` class with overloaded constructors. (Part 1 of 3.)

```
10      // Time2 no-argument constructor: initializes each instance variable
11      // to zero; ensures that Time2 objects start in a consistent state
12      public Time2()
13      {
14         this( 0, 0, 0 ); // invoke Time2 constructor with three arguments
15      } // end Time2 no-argument constructor
16
17      // Time2 constructor: hour supplied, minute and second defaulted to 0
18      public Time2( int h )
19      {
20         this( h, 0, 0 ); // invoke Time2 constructor with three arguments
21      } // end Time2 one-argument constructor
22
23      // Time2 constructor: hour and minute supplied, second defaulted to 0
24      public Time2( int h, int m )
25      {
26         this( h, m, 0 ); // invoke Time2 constructor with three arguments
27      } // end Time2 two-argument constructor
28
29      // Time2 constructor: hour, minute and second supplied
30      public Time2( int h, int m, int s )
31      {
32         setTime( h, m, s ); // invoke setTime to validate time
33      } // end Time2 three-argument constructor
34
35      // Time2 constructor: another Time2 object supplied
36      public Time2( Time2 time )
37      {
38         // invoke Time2 three-argument constructor
39         this( time.getHour(), time.getMinute(), time.getSecond() );
40      } // end Time2 constructor with a Time2 object argument
41
42      // Set Methods
43      // set a new time value using universal time; ensure that
44      // the data remains consistent by setting invalid values to zero
45      public void setTime( int h, int m, int s )
46      {
47         setHour( h );   // set the hour
48         setMinute( m ); // set the minute
49         setSecond( s ); // set the second
50      } // end method setTime
51
52      // validate and set hour
53      public void setHour( int h )
54      {
55         hour = ( ( h >= 0 && h < 24 ) ? h : 0 );
56      } // end method setHour
57
58      // validate and set minute
59      public void setMinute( int m )
60      {
61         minute = ( ( m >= 0 && m < 60 ) ? m : 0 );
62      } // end method setMinute
```

Fig. 8.5 | Time2 class with overloaded constructors. (Part 2 of 3.)

```
63
64      // validate and set second
65      public void setSecond( int s )
66      {
67         second = ( ( s >= 0 && s < 60 ) ? s : 0 );
68      } // end method setSecond
69
70      // Get Methods
71      // get hour value
72      public int getHour()
73      {
74         return hour;
75      } // end method getHour
76
77      // get minute value
78      public int getMinute()
79      {
80         return minute;
81      } // end method getMinute
82
83      // get second value
84      public int getSecond()
85      {
86         return second;
87      } // end method getSecond
88
89      // convert to String in universal-time format (HH:MM:SS)
90      public String toUniversalString()
91      {
92         return String.format(
93            "%02d:%02d:%02d", getHour(), getMinute(), getSecond() );
94      } // end method toUniversalString
95
96      // convert to String in standard-time format (H:MM:SS AM or PM)
97      public String toString()
98      {
99         return String.format( "%d:%02d:%02d %s",
100           ( (getHour() == 0 || getHour() == 12) ? 12 : getHour() % 12 ),
101           getMinute(), getSecond(), ( getHour() < 12 ? "AM" : "PM" ) );
102     } // end method toString
103  } // end class Time2
```

Fig. 8.5 | Time2 class with overloaded constructors. (Part 3 of 3.)

Class *Time2*'s Constructors

Lines 12–15 declare a so-called **no-argument constructor**—that is, a constructor invoked without arguments. Such a constructor simply initializes the object as specified in the constructor's body. In the body, we introduce a use of the this reference that is allowed only as the first statement in a constructor's body. Line 14 uses this in method-call syntax to invoke the Time2 constructor that takes three arguments (lines 30–33). The no-argument constructor passes values of 0 for the hour, minute and second to the constructor with three parameters. Using the this reference as shown here is a popular way to reuse initialization code provided by another of the class's constructors rather than defining similar code in the no-argument constructor's body. We use this syntax in four of the five Time2 constructors to make the class easier to maintain and modify. If we need to change how objects of class Time2 are initialized, only the constructor that the class's other constructors call will need to be modified. In fact, even that constructor might not need modification in this example. That constructor simply calls the setTime method to perform the actual initialization, so it is possible that the changes the class might require would be localized to the *set* methods.

Common Programming Error 8.3

It is a syntax error when this is used in a constructor's body to call another constructor of the same class if that call is not the first statement in the constructor. It is also a syntax error when a method attempts to invoke a constructor directly via this.

Lines 18–21 declare a Time2 constructor with a single int parameter representing the hour, which is passed with 0 for the minute and second to the constructor at lines 30–33. Lines 24–27 declare a Time2 constructor that receives two int parameters representing the hour and minute, which are passed with 0 for the second to the constructor at lines 30–33. Like the no-argument constructor, each of these constructors invokes the constructor at lines 30–33 to minimize code duplication. Lines 30–33 declare the Time2 constructor that receives three int parameters representing the hour, minute and second. This constructor calls setTime to initialize the instance variables to consistent values.

Common Programming Error 8.4

A constructor can call methods of the class. Be aware that the instance variables might not yet be in a consistent state, because the constructor is in the process of initializing the object. Using instance variables before they have been initialized properly is a logic error.

Lines 36–40 declare a Time2 constructor that receives a Time2 reference to another Time2 object. In this case, the values from the Time2 argument are passed to the three-argument constructor at lines 30–33 to initialize the hour, minute and second. Note that line 39 could have directly accessed the hour, minute and second values of the constructor's argument time with the expressions time.hour, time.minute and time.second—even though hour, minute and second are declared as private variables of class Time2. This is due to a special relationship between objects of the same class. We'll see in a moment why it's preferable to use the *get* methods.

Software Engineering Observation 8.4

When one object of a class has a reference to another object of the same class, the first object can access all the second object's data and methods (including those that are private).

Notes Regarding Class Time2's Set and Get Methods and Constructors
Note that Time2's *set* and *get* methods are called throughout the body of the class. In particular, method setTime calls methods setHour, setMinute and setSecond in lines 47–49, and methods toUniversalString and toString call methods getHour, getMinute and getSecond in line 93 and lines 100–101, respectively. In each case, these methods could have accessed the class's private data directly without calling the *set* and *get* methods. However, consider changing the representation of the time from three int values (requiring 12 bytes of memory) to a single int value representing the total number of seconds that have

elapsed since midnight (requiring only 4 bytes of memory). If we made such a change, only the bodies of the methods that access the private data directly would need to change—in particular, the individual *set* and *get* methods for the hour, minute and second. There would be no need to modify the bodies of methods setTime, toUniversalString or toString because they do not access the data directly. Designing the class in this manner reduces the likelihood of programming errors when altering the class's implementation.

Similarly, each Time2 constructor could be written to include a copy of the appropriate statements from methods setHour, setMinute and setSecond. Doing so may be slightly more efficient, because the extra constructor call and call to setTime are eliminated. However, duplicating statements in multiple methods or constructors makes changing the class's internal data representation more difficult. Having the Time2 constructors call the constructor with three arguments (or even call setTime directly) requires any changes to the implementation of setTime to be made only once.

Software Engineering Observation 8.5

When implementing a method of a class, use the class's set *and* get *methods to access the class's* private *data. This simplifies code maintenance and reduces the likelihood of errors.*

Using Class *Time2's Overloaded Constructors*

Class Time2Test (Fig. 8.6) creates six Time2 objects (lines 8–13) to invoke the overloaded Time2 constructors. Line 8 shows that the no-argument constructor (lines 12–15 of Fig. 8.5) is invoked by placing an empty set of parentheses after the class name when allocating a Time2 object with new. Lines 9–13 of the program demonstrate passing arguments to the other Time2 constructors. Line 9 invokes the constructor at lines 18–21 of Fig. 8.5. Line 10 invokes the constructor at lines 24–27 of Fig. 8.5. Lines 11–12 invoke the constructor at lines 30–33 of Fig. 8.5. Line 13 invokes the constructor at lines 36–40 of Fig. 8.5. The application displays the String representation of each initialized Time2 object to confirm that it was initialized properly.

```java
1   // Fig. 8.6: Time2Test.java
2   // Overloaded constructors used to initialize Time2 objects.
3
4   public class Time2Test
5   {
6      public static void main( String args[] )
7      {
8         Time2 t1 = new Time2();              // 00:00:00
9         Time2 t2 = new Time2( 2 );           // 02:00:00
10        Time2 t3 = new Time2( 21, 34 );      // 21:34:00
11        Time2 t4 = new Time2( 12, 25, 42 );  // 12:25:42
12        Time2 t5 = new Time2( 27, 74, 99 );  // 00:00:00
13        Time2 t6 = new Time2( t4 );          // 12:25:42
14
15        System.out.println( "Constructed with:" );
16        System.out.println( "t1: all arguments defaulted" );
17        System.out.printf( "   %s\n", t1.toUniversalString() );
18        System.out.printf( "   %s\n", t1.toString() );
```

Fig. 8.6 | Overloaded constructors used to initialize Time2 objects. (Part 1 of 2.)

```
19        System.out.println(
20           "t2: hour specified; minute and second defaulted" );
21        System.out.printf( "   %s\n", t2.toUniversalString() );
22        System.out.printf( "   %s\n", t2.toString() );
23
24        System.out.println(
25           "t3: hour and minute specified; second defaulted" );
26        System.out.printf( "   %s\n", t3.toUniversalString() );
27        System.out.printf( "   %s\n", t3.toString() );
28
29        System.out.println( "t4: hour, minute and second specified" );
30        System.out.printf( "   %s\n", t4.toUniversalString() );
31        System.out.printf( "   %s\n", t4.toString() );
32
33        System.out.println( "t5: all invalid values specified" );
34        System.out.printf( "   %s\n", t5.toUniversalString() );
35        System.out.printf( "   %s\n", t5.toString() );
36
37        System.out.println( "t6: Time2 object t4 specified" );
38        System.out.printf( "   %s\n", t6.toUniversalString() );
39        System.out.printf( "   %s\n", t6.toString() );
40     } // end main
41  } // end class Time2Test
```

```
t1: all arguments defaulted
   00:00:00
   12:00:00 AM
t2: hour specified; minute and second defaulted
   02:00:00
   2:00:00 AM
t3: hour and minute specified; second defaulted
   21:34:00
   9:34:00 PM
t4: hour, minute and second specified
   12:25:42
   12:25:42 PM
t5: all invalid values specified
   00:00:00
   12:00:00 AM
t6: Time2 object t4 specified
   12:25:42
   12:25:42 PM
```

Fig. 8.6 | Overloaded constructors used to initialize Time2 objects. (Part 2 of 2.)

8.6 Default and No-Argument Constructors

Every class must have at least one constructor. Recall from Section 3.7, that if you do not provide any constructors in a class's declaration, the compiler creates a default constructor that takes no arguments when it is invoked. The default constructor initializes the instance variables to the initial values specified in their declarations or to their default values (zero for primitive numeric types, false for boolean values and null for references). In Section 9.4.1, you'll learn that the default constructor performs another task in addition to initializing each instance variable to its default value.

If your class declares constructors, the compiler will not create a default constructor. In this case, to specify the default initialization for objects of your class, you must declare a no-argument constructor—as in lines 12–15 of Fig. 8.5. Like a default constructor, a no-argument constructor is invoked with empty parentheses. Note that the Time2 no-argument constructor explicitly initializes a Time2 object by passing to the three-argument constructor 0 for each parameter. Since 0 is the default value for int instance variables, the no-argument constructor in this example could actually be declared with an empty body. In this case, each instance variable would receive its default value when the no-argument constructor was called. If we omit the no-argument constructor, clients of this class would not be able to create a Time2 object with the expression new Time2().

Common Programming Error 8.5

If a class has constructors, but none of the public constructors are no-argument constructors, and a program attempts to call a no-argument constructor to initialize an object of the class, a compilation error occurs. A constructor can be called with no arguments only if the class does not have any constructors (in which case the default constructor is called) or if the class has a public no-argument constructor.

Software Engineering Observation 8.6

Java allows other methods of the class besides its constructors to have the same name as the class and to specify return types. Such methods are not constructors and will not be called when an object of the class is instantiated. Java determines which methods are constructors by locating the methods that have the same name as the class and do not specify a return type.

8.7 Notes on *Set* and *Get* Methods

As you know, a class's private fields can be manipulated only by methods of that class. A typical manipulation might be the adjustment of a customer's bank balance (e.g., a private instance variable of a class BankAccount) by a method computeInterest. Classes often provide public methods to allow clients of the class to *set* (i.e., assign values to) or *get* (i.e., obtain the values of) private instance variables.

As a naming example, a method that sets instance variable interestRate would typically be named setInterestRate and a method that gets the interestRate would typically be called getInterestRate. *Set* methods are also commonly called **mutator methods**, because they typically change a value. *Get* methods are also commonly called **accessor methods** or **query methods**.

Set *and* Get *Methods vs.* public *Data*

It would seem that providing *set* and *get* capabilities is essentially the same as making the instance variables public. This is a subtlety of Java that makes the language so desirable for software engineering. A public instance variable can be read or written by any method that has a reference to an object that contains the instance variable. If an instance variable is declared private, a public *get* method certainly allows other methods to access the variable, but the *get* method can control how the client can access the variable. For example, a *get* method might control the format of the data it returns and thus shield the client code from the actual data representation. A public *set* method can—and should—carefully scrutinize attempts to modify the variable's value to ensure that the new value is appropriate for that data item. For example, an attempt to *set* the day of the month to 37 would be rejected, an attempt to *set* a person's weight to a negative value would be rejected, and so on. Thus, although *set* and *get* methods provide access to `private` data, the access is restricted by the programmer's implementation of the methods. This helps promote good software engineering.

Validity Checking in Set *Methods*

The benefits of data integrity are not automatic simply because instance variables are declared `private`—the programmer must provide validity checking. Java enables programmers to design better programs in a convenient manner. A class's *set* methods can return values indicating that attempts were made to assign invalid data to objects of the class. A client of the class can test the return value of a *set* method to determine whether the client's attempt to modify the object was successful and to take appropriate action.

Software Engineering Observation 8.7

When necessary, provide `public` methods to change and retrieve the values of `private` instance variables. This architecture helps hide the implementation of a class from its clients, which improves program modifiability.

Software Engineering Observation 8.8

Class designers need not provide set or get methods for each `private` field. These capabilities should be provided only when it makes sense.

Predicate Methods

Another common use for accessor methods is to test whether a condition is true or false—such methods are often called **predicate methods**. An example would be an `isEmpty` method for a **container class**—a class capable of holding many objects, such as a linked list, a stack or a queue. (These data structures are discussed in depth in Chapters 17 and 19.) A program might test `isEmpty` before attempting to read another item from a container object. A program might test `isFull` before attempting to insert another item into a container object.

Using Set *and* Get *Methods to Create a Class That Is Easier to Debug and Maintain*

If only one method performs a particular task, such as setting the hour in a `Time2` object, it is easier to debug and maintain the class. If the hour is not being set properly, the code that actually modifies instance variable `hour` is localized to one method's body—`setHour`. Thus, your debugging efforts can be focused on method `setHour`.

8.8 Composition

A class can have references to objects of other classes as members. Such a capability is called **composition** and is sometimes referred to as a *has-a* relationship. For example, an object of class `AlarmClock` needs to know the current time and the time when it is supposed to sound its alarm, so it is reasonable to include two references to `Time` objects as members of the `AlarmClock` object.

Software Engineering Observation 8.9

One form of software reuse is composition, in which a class has as members references to objects of other classes.

Our example of composition contains three classes—Date (Fig. 8.7), Employee (Fig. 8.8) and EmployeeTest (Fig. 8.9). Class Date (Fig. 8.7) declares instance variables month, day and year (lines 6–8) to represent a date. The constructor receives three int parameters. Line 14 invokes utility method checkMonth (lines 23–33) to validate the month—an out-of-range value is set to 1 to maintain a consistent state. Line 15 assumes that the value for year is correct and does not validate it. Line 16 invokes utility method checkDay (lines 36–52) to validate the value for day based on the current month and year. Lines 42–43 determine whether the day is correct based on the number of days in the particular month. If the day is not correct, lines 46–47 determine whether the month is February, the day is 29 and the year is a leap year. If lines 42–48 do not return a correct value for day, line 51 returns 1 to maintain the Date in a consistent state. Note that lines 18–19 in the constructor output the this reference as a String. Since this is a reference to the current Date object, the object's toString method (lines 55–58) is called implicitly to obtain the object's String representation.

```
1   // Fig. 8.7: Date.java
2   // Date class declaration.
3
4   public class Date
5   {
6      private int month; // 1-12
7      private int day;   // 1-31 based on month
8      private int year;  // any year
9
10     // constructor: call checkMonth to confirm proper value for month;
11     // call checkDay to confirm proper value for day
12     public Date( int theMonth, int theDay, int theYear )
13     {
14        month = checkMonth( theMonth ); // validate month
15        year = theYear; // could validate year
16        day = checkDay( theDay ); // validate day
17
18        System.out.printf(
19           "Date object constructor for date %s\n", this );
20     } // end Date constructor
21
22     // utility method to confirm proper month value
23     private int checkMonth( int testMonth )
24     {
25        if ( testMonth > 0 && testMonth <= 12 ) // validate month
26           return testMonth;
27        else // month is invalid
28        {
29           System.out.printf(
30              "Invalid month (%d) set to 1.", testMonth );
31           return 1; // maintain object in consistent state
32        } // end else
33     } // end method checkMonth
34
```

Fig. 8.7 | Date class declaration. (Part 1 of 2.)

```
35        // utility method to confirm proper day value based on month and year
36        private int checkDay( int testDay )
37        {
38           int daysPerMonth[] =
39              { 0, 31, 28, 31, 30, 31, 30, 31, 31, 30, 31, 30, 31 };
40
41           // check if day in range for month
42           if ( testDay > 0 && testDay <= daysPerMonth[ month ] )
43              return testDay;
44
45           // check for leap year
46           if ( month == 2 && testDay == 29 && ( year % 400 == 0 ||
47              ( year % 4 == 0 && year % 100 != 0 ) ) )
48              return testDay;
49
50           System.out.printf( "Invalid day (%d) set to 1.", testDay );
51           return 1;   // maintain object in consistent state
52        } // end method checkDay
53
54        // return a String of the form month/day/year
55        public String toString()
56        {
57           return String.format( "%d/%d/%d", month, day, year );
58        } // end method toString
59     } // end class Date
```

Fig. 8.7 | Date class declaration. (Part 2 of 2.)

Class Employee (Fig. 8.8) has instance variables firstName, lastName, birthDate and hireDate. Members birthDate and hireDate (lines 8–9) are references to Date objects. This demonstrates that a class can have as instance variables references to objects of other classes. The Employee constructor (lines 12–19) takes four parameters—first, last, dateOfBirth and dateOfHire. The objects referenced by the parameters dateOfBirth and dateOfHire are assigned to the Employee object's birthDate and hireDate instance variables, respectively. Note that when class Employee's toString method is called, it returns a String containing the String representations of the two Date objects. Each of these Strings is obtained with an implicit call to the Date class's toString method.

```
1     // Fig. 8.8: Employee.java
2     // Employee class with references to other objects.
3
4     public class Employee
5     {
6        private String firstName;
7        private String lastName;
8        private Date birthDate;
9        private Date hireDate;
10
```

Fig. 8.8 | Employee class with references to other objects. (Part 1 of 2.)

```
11        // constructor to initialize name, birth date and hire date
12        public Employee( String first, String last, Date dateOfBirth,
13           Date dateOfHire )
14        {
15           firstName = first;
16           lastName = last;
17           birthDate = dateOfBirth;
18           hireDate = dateOfHire;
19        } // end Employee constructor
20
21        // convert Employee to String format
22        public String toString()
23        {
24           return String.format( "%s, %s  Hired: %s  Birthday: %s",
25              lastName, firstName, hireDate, birthDate );
26        } // end method toString
27     } // end class Employee
```

Fig. 8.8 | Employee class with references to other objects. (Part 2 of 2.)

Class EmployeeTest (Fig. 8.9) creates two Date objects (lines 8–9) to represent an Employee's birthday and hire date, respectively. Line 10 creates an Employee and initializes its instance variables by passing to the constructor two Strings (representing the Employee's first and last names) and two Date objects (representing the birthday and hire date). Line 12 implicitly invokes the Employee's toString method to display the values of its instance variables and demonstrate that the object was initialized properly.

```
1     // Fig. 8.9: EmployeeTest.java
2     // Composition demonstration.
3
4     public class EmployeeTest
5     {
6        public static void main( String args[] )
7        {
8           Date birth = new Date( 7, 24, 1949 );
9           Date hire = new Date( 3, 12, 1988 );
10          Employee employee = new Employee( "Bob", "Blue", birth, hire );
11
12          System.out.println( employee );
13       } // end main
14    } // end class EmployeeTest
```

```
Date object constructor for date 7/24/1949
Date object constructor for date 3/12/1988
Blue, Bob  Hired: 3/12/1988  Birthday: 7/24/1949
```

Fig. 8.9 | Composition demonstration.

8.9 Enumerations

In Fig. 6.9 (Craps.java), we introduced the basic enum type which defines a set of constants that are represented as unique identifiers. In that program, the enum constants represented the game's status. In this section, we discuss the relationship between enum types and classes. Like classes, all enum types are reference types. An enum type is declared with an **enum** declaration, which is a comma-separated list of enum constants—the declaration may optionally include other components of traditional classes, such as constructors, fields and methods. Each enum declaration declares an enum class with the following restrictions:

1. enum types are implicitly `final`, because they declare constants that should not be modified.

2. enum constants are implicitly `static`.

3. Any attempt to create an object of an enum type with operator `new` results in a compilation error.

The enum constants can be used anywhere constants can be used, such as in the `case` labels of `switch` statements and to control enhanced `for` statements.

Figure 8.10 illustrates how to declare instance variables, a constructor and methods in an enum type. The enum declaration (lines 5–37) contains two parts—the enum constants and the other members of the enum type. The first part (lines 8–13) declares six enum constants. Each enum constant is optionally followed by arguments which are passed to the **enum constructor** (lines 20–24). Like the constructors you have seen in classes, an enum constructor can specify any number of parameters and can be overloaded. In this example, the enum constructor has two `String` parameters, hence each enum constant is followed by parentheses containing two `String` arguments. The second part (lines 16–36) declares the other members of the enum type—two instance variables (lines 16–17), a constructor (lines 20–24) and two methods (lines 27–30 and 33–36).

```
 1   // Fig. 8.10: Book.java
 2   // Declaring an enum type with constructor and explicit instance fields
 3   // and accessors for these fields
 4
 5   public enum Book
 6   {
 7      // declare constants of enum type
 8      JHTP6( "Java How to Program 6e", "2005" ),
 9      CHTP4( "C How to Program 4e", "2004" ),
10      IW3HTP3( "Internet & World Wide Web How to Program 3e", "2004" ),
11      CPPHTP4( "C++ How to Program 4e", "2003" ),
12      VBHTP2( "Visual Basic .NET How to Program 2e", "2002" ),
13      CSHARPHTP( "C# How to Program", "2002" );
14
15      // instance fields
16      private final String title; // book title
17      private final String copyrightYear; // copyright year
18
19      // enum constructor
20      Book( String bookTitle, String year )
21      {
22         title = bookTitle;
23         copyrightYear = year;
24      } // end enum Book constructor
```

Fig. 8.10 | Declaring **enum** type with instance fields, constructor and methods. (Part 1 of 2.)

```
25
26      // accessor for field title
27      public String getTitle()
28      {
29         return title;
30      } // end method getTitle
31
32      // accessor for field copyrightYear
33      public String getCopyrightYear()
34      {
35         return copyrightYear;
36      } // end method getCopyrightYear
37   } // end enum Book
```

Fig. 8.10 | Declaring enum type with instance fields, constructor and methods. (Part 2 of 2.)

Lines 16–17 declare the instance variables title and copyrightYear. Each enum constant in Book is actually an object of type Book that has its own copy of instance variables title and copyrightYear. The constructor (lines 20–24) takes two String parameters, one that specifies the book title and one that specifies the copyright year of the book. Lines 22–23 assign these parameters to the instance variables. Lines 27–36 declare two methods, which return the book title and copyright year, respectively.

Figure 8.11 tests the enum type declared in Fig. 8.10 and illustrates how to iterate through a range of enum constants. For every enum, the compiler generates the static method **values** (called in line 12) that returns an array of the enum's constants in the order they were declared. Recall from Section 7.6 that the enhanced for statement can be used

```
1    // Fig. 8.11: EnumTest.java
2    // Testing enum type Book.
3    import java.util.EnumSet;
4
5    public class EnumTest
6    {
7       public static void main( String args[] )
8       {
9          System.out.println( "All books:\n" );
10
11         // print all books in enum Book
12         for ( Book book : Book.values() )
13            System.out.printf( "%-10s%-45s%s\n", book,
14               book.getTitle(), book.getCopyrightYear() );
15
16         System.out.println( "\nDisplay a range of enum constants:\n" );
17
18         // print first four books
19         for ( Book book : EnumSet.range( Book.JHTP6, Book.CPPHTP4 ) )
20            System.out.printf( "%-10s%-45s%s\n", book,
21               book.getTitle(), book.getCopyrightYear() );
22      } // end main
23   } // end class EnumTest
```

Fig. 8.11 | Testing an enum type. (Part 1 of 2.)

```
All books:

JHTP6      Java How to Program 6e                        2005
CHTP4      C How to Program 4e                           2004
IW3HTP3    Internet & World Wide Web How to Program 3e   2004
CPPHTP4    C++ How to Program 4e                         2003
VBHTP2     Visual Basic .NET How to Program 2e           2002
CSHARPHTP  C# How to Program                             2002

Display a range of enum constants:

JHTP6      Java How to Program 6e                        2005
CHTP4      C How to Program 4e                           2004
IW3HTP3    Internet & World Wide Web How to Program 3e   2004
CPPHTP4    C++ How to Program 4e                         2003
```

Fig. 8.11 | Testing an enum type. (Part 2 of 2.)

to iterate through an array. Lines 12–14 use the enhanced `for` statement to display all the constants declared in the enum Book. Line 14 invokes the enum Book's `getTitle` and `get-CopyrightYear` methods to get the title and copyright year associated with the constant. Note that when an enum constant is converted to a `String` (e.g., book in line 13), the constant's identifier is used as the `String` representation (e.g., JHTP6 for the first enum constant).

Lines 19–21 use the `static` method **range** of class `EnumSet` (declared in package `java.util`) to display a range of the enum Book's constants. Method range takes two parameters—the first and the last enum constants in the range—and returns an `EnumSet` that contains all the constants between these two constants, inclusive. For example, the expression `EnumSet.range( Book.JHTP6, Book.CPPHTP4 )` returns an `EnumSet` containing `Book.JHTP6`, `Book.CHTP4`, `Book.IW3HTP3` and `Book.CPPHTP4`. The enhanced `for` statement can be used with an `EnumSet` just as it can with an array, so lines 19–21 use the enhanced `for` statement to display the title and copyright year of every book in the `EnumSet`. Class `EnumSet` provides several other `static` methods for creating sets of enum constants from the same enum type. For more details of class `EnumSet`, visit `java.sun.com/javase/6/docs/api/java/util/EnumSet.html`.

Common Programming Error 8.6

In an enum declaration, it is a syntax error to declare enum constants after the enum type's constructors, fields and methods in the enum declaration.

8.10 Garbage Collection and Method `finalize`

Every class in Java has the methods of class `Object` (package `java.lang`), one of which is the **`finalize` method**. This method is rarely used. In fact, we searched over 6500 source-code files for the Java API classes and found fewer than 50 declarations of the `finalize` method. Nevertheless, because `finalize` is part of every class, we discuss it here to help you understand its intended purpose in case you encounter it in your studies or in industry. The complete details of the `finalize` method are beyond the scope of this book, and most programmers should not use it—you'll soon see why. You will learn more about class `Object` in Chapter 9, Object-Oriented Programming: Inheritance.

Every object you create uses various system resources, such as memory. To avoid "resource leaks," we need a disciplined way to give resources back to the system when they are no longer needed. The Java Virtual Machine (JVM) performs automatic garbage collection to reclaim the memory occupied by objects that are no longer in use. When there are no more references to an object, the object is marked for garbage collection by the JVM. The memory for such an object can be reclaimed when the JVM executes its garbage collector, which is responsible for retrieving the memory of objects that are no longer used so it can be used for other objects. Therefore, memory leaks that are common in other languages like C and C++ (because memory is not automatically reclaimed in those languages) are less likely in Java (but some can still happen in subtle ways). Other types of resource leaks can occur. For example, an application could open a file on disk to modify the file's contents. If the application does not close the file, no other application can use it until the application that opened the file completes.

The finalize method is called by the garbage collector to perform termination housekeeping on an object just before the garbage collector reclaims the object's memory. Method finalize does not take parameters and has return type void. A problem with method finalize is that the garbage collector is not guaranteed to execute at a specified time. In fact, the garbage collector may never execute before a program terminates. Thus, it is unclear if, or when, method finalize will be called. For this reason, most programmers should avoid method finalize. In Section 8.11, we demonstrate a situation in which method finalize is called by the garbage collector.

Software Engineering Observation 8.10

A class that uses system resources, such as files on disk, should provide a method to eventually release the resources. Many Java API classes provide close or dispose methods for this purpose. For example, class Scanner (java.sun.com/javase/6/docs/api/java/util/Scanner.html) has a close method.

8.11 static Class Members

Every object has its own copy of all the instance variables of the class. In certain cases, only one copy of a particular variable should be shared by all objects of a class. A static field—called a class variable—is used in such cases. A static variable represents classwide information—all objects of the class share the same piece of data. The declaration of a static variable begins with the keyword static.

Let's motivate static data with an example. Suppose that we have a video game with Martians and other space creatures. Each Martian tends to be brave and willing to attack other space creatures when the Martian is aware that at least four other Martians are present. If fewer than five Martians are present, each of them becomes cowardly. Thus each Martian needs to know the martianCount. We could endow class Martian with martianCount as an instance variable. If we do this, then every Martian will have a separate copy of the instance variable, and every time we create a new Martian, we'll have to update the instance variable martianCount in every Martian. This wastes space with the redundant copies, wastes time in updating the separate copies and is error prone. Instead, we declare martianCount to be static, making martianCount classwide data. Every Martian can see the martianCount as if it were an instance variable of class Martian, but only one copy of the static martianCount is maintained. This saves space. We save time by having the Martian constructor increment the static martianCount—there is only one copy, so we do not have to increment separate copies of martianCount for each Martian object.

Software Engineering Observation 8.11

Use a static variable when all objects of a class must use the same copy of the variable.

Static variables have class scope. A class's public static members can be accessed through a reference to any object of the class, or by qualifying the member name with the class name and a dot (.), as in Math.random(). A class's private static class members can be accessed only through methods of the class. Actually, static class members exist even when no objects of the class exist—they are available as soon as the class is loaded into memory at execution time. To access a public static member when no objects of the class exist (and even when they do), prefix the class name and a dot (.) to the static member, as in Math.PI. To access a private static member when no objects of the class exist, a public static method must be provided and the method must be called by qualifying its name with the class name and a dot.

Software Engineering Observation 8.12

Static class variables and methods exist, and can be used, even if no objects of that class have been instantiated.

Our next program declares two classes—Employee (Fig. 8.12) and EmployeeTest (Fig. 8.13). Class Employee declares private static variable count (Fig. 8.12, line 9), and public static method getCount (lines 46–49). The static variable count is initialized to zero in line 9. If a static variable is not initialized, the compiler assigns a default value to the variable—in this case 0, the default value for type int. Variable count maintains a count of the number of objects of class Employee that currently reside in memory. This includes objects that have already been marked for garbage collection by the JVM but have not yet been reclaimed by the garbage collector.

```
1   // Fig. 8.12: Employee.java
2   // Static variable used to maintain a count of the number of
3   // Employee objects in memory.
4
5   public class Employee
6   {
7      private String firstName;
8      private String lastName;
9      private static int count = 0; // number of objects in memory
10
11     // initialize employee, add 1 to static count and
12     // output String indicating that constructor was called
13     public Employee( String first, String last )
14     {
15        firstName = first;
16        lastName = last;
```

Fig. 8.12 | static variable used to maintain a count of the number of Employee objects in memory. (Part 1 of 2.)

```
17
18        count++;  // increment static count of employees
19        System.out.printf( "Employee constructor: %s %s; count = %d\n",
20           firstName, lastName, count );
21     } // end Employee constructor
22
23     // subtract 1 from static count when garbage
24     // collector calls finalize to clean up object;
25     // confirm that finalize was called
26     protected void finalize()
27     {
28        count--; // decrement static count of employees
29        System.out.printf( "Employee finalizer: %s %s; count = %d\n",
30           firstName, lastName, count );
31     } // end method finalize
32
33     // get first name
34     public String getFirstName()
35     {
36        return firstName;
37     } // end method getFirstName
38
39     // get last name
40     public String getLastName()
41     {
42        return lastName;
43     } // end method getLastName
44
45     // static method to get static count value
46     public static int getCount()
47     {
48        return count;
49     } // end method getCount
50  } // end class Employee
```

Fig. 8.12 | static variable used to maintain a count of the number of Employee objects in memory. (Part 2 of 2.)

When Employee objects exist, member count can be used in any method of an Employee object—this example increments count in the constructor (line 18) and decrements it in the finalize method (line 28). When no objects of class Employee exist, member count can still be referenced, but only through a call to public static method getCount (lines 46–49), as in Employee.getCount(), which returns the number of Employee objects currently in memory. When objects exist, method getCount can also be called through any reference to an Employee object, as in the call e1.getCount().

Good Programming Practice 8.1

Invoke every static method by using the class name and a dot (.) to emphasize that the method being called is a static method.

Note that the Employee class has a finalize method (lines 26–31). This method is included only to show when the garbage collector executes in this program. Method finalize is normally declared protected, so it is not part of the public services of a class. We will discuss the protected member access modifier in detail in Chapter 9.

EmployeeTest method main (Fig. 8.13) instantiates two Employee objects (lines 13–14). When each Employee object's constructor is invoked, lines 15–16 of Fig. 8.12 assign the Employee's first name and last name to instance variables firstName and lastName. Note that these two statements do not make copies of the original String arguments. Actually, String objects in Java are immutable—they cannot be modified after they are created. Therefore, it is safe to have many references to one String object. This is not normally the case for objects of most other classes in Java. If String objects are immutable, you might wonder why are we able to use operators + and += to concatenate String objects. String concatenation operations actually result in a new Strings object containing the concatenated values. The original String objects are not modified.

When main has finished using the two Employee objects, the references e1 and e2 are set to null at lines 31–32. At this point, references e1 and e2 no longer refer to the objects that were instantiated in lines 13–14. This "marks the objects for garbage collection" because there are no more references to the objects in the program.

```java
1   // Fig. 8.13: EmployeeTest.java
2   // Static member demonstration.
3
4   public class EmployeeTest
5   {
6      public static void main( String args[] )
7      {
8         // show that count is 0 before creating Employees
9         System.out.printf( "Employees before instantiation: %d\n",
10            Employee.getCount() );
11
12         // create two Employees; count should be 2
13         Employee e1 = new Employee( "Susan", "Baker" );
14         Employee e2 = new Employee( "Bob", "Blue" );
15
16         // show that count is 2 after creating two Employees
17         System.out.println( "\nEmployees after instantiation: " );
18         System.out.printf( "via e1.getCount(): %d\n", e1.getCount() );
19         System.out.printf( "via e2.getCount(): %d\n", e2.getCount() );
20         System.out.printf( "via Employee.getCount(): %d\n",
21            Employee.getCount() );
22
23         // get names of Employees
24         System.out.printf( "\nEmployee 1: %s %s\nEmployee 2: %s %s\n\n",
25            e1.getFirstName(), e1.getLastName(),
26            e2.getFirstName(), e2.getLastName() );
27
28         // in this example, there is only one reference to each Employee,
29         // so the following two statements cause the JVM to mark each
30         // Employee object for garbage collection
31         e1 = null;
32         e2 = null;
```

Fig. 8.13 | static member demonstration. (Part 1 of 2.)

```
33
34            System.gc(); // ask for garbage collection to occur now
35
36            // show Employee count after calling garbage collector; count
37            // displayed may be 0, 1 or 2 based on whether garbage collector
38            // executes immediately and number of Employee objects collected
39            System.out.printf( "\nEmployees after System.gc(): %d\n",
40               Employee.getCount() );
41         } // end main
42    } // end class EmployeeTest
```

```
Employees before instantiation: 0
Employee constructor: Susan Baker; count = 1
Employee constructor: Bob Blue; count = 2

Employees after instantiation:
via e1.getCount(): 2
via e2.getCount(): 2
via Employee.getCount(): 2

Employee 1: Susan Baker
Employee 2: Bob Blue

Employee finalizer: Bob Blue; count = 1
Employee finalizer: Susan Baker; count = 0

Employees after System.gc(): 0
```

Fig. 8.13 | static member demonstration. (Part 2 of 2.)

Eventually, the garbage collector might reclaim the memory for these objects (or the operating system surely will reclaim the memory when the program terminates). The JVM does not guarantee when the garbage collector will execute (or even whether it will execute), so this program explicitly calls the garbage collector in line 34 (Fig. 8.13) using static method gc of class System (package java.lang) to indicate that the garbage collector should make a best-effort attempt to reclaim objects that are eligible for garbage collection. This is just a best effort—it is possible that no objects or only a subset of the eligible objects will be collected. In Fig. 8.13's sample output, the garbage collector did execute before lines 39–40 displayed current Employee count. The last output line indicates that the number of Employee objects in memory is 0 after the call to System.gc(). The third- and second-to-last lines of the output show that the Employee object for Bob Blue was finalized before the Employee object for Susan Baker. The output on your system may differ, because the garbage collector is not guaranteed to execute when System.gc() is called, nor is it guaranteed to collect objects in a specific order.

[*Note:* A method declared static cannot access non-static class members, because a static method can be called even when no objects of the class have been instantiated. For the same reason, the this reference cannot be used in a static method—it must refer to a specific object of the class, and when a static method is called, there might not be any objects of its class in memory. The this reference is required to allow a method of a class to access other non-static members of the same class.]

Common Programming Error 8.7

A compilation error occurs if a static method calls an instance (non-static) method in the same class by using only the method name. Similarly, a compilation error occurs if a static method attempts to access an instance variable in the same class by using only the variable name.

Common Programming Error 8.8

Referring to this in a static method is a syntax error.

8.12 static Import

In Section 6.3, you learned about the static fields and methods of class Math. We invoked class Math's static fields and methods by preceding each with the class name Math and a dot (.). A static import declaration enables you to refer to imported static members as if they were declared in the class that uses them—the class name and a dot (.) are not required to use an imported static member.

A static import declaration has two forms—one that imports a particular static member (which is known as **single static import**) and one that imports all static members of a class (which is known as **static import on demand**). The following syntax imports a particular static member:

```
import static packageName.ClassName.staticMemberName;
```

where *packageName* is the package of the class (e.g., java.lang), *ClassName* is the name of the class (e.g., Math) and *staticMemberName* is the name of the static field or method (e.g., PI or abs). The following syntax imports all static members of a class:

```
import static packageName.ClassName.*;
```

where *packageName* is the package of the class (e.g., java.lang) and *ClassName* is the name of the class (e.g., Math). The asterisk (*) indicates that *all* static members of the specified class should be available for use in the class(es) declared in the file. Note that static import declarations import only static class members. Regular import statements should be used to specify the classes used in a program.

Figure 8.14 demonstrates a static import. Line 3 is a static import declaration, which imports all static fields and methods of class Math from package java.lang. Lines 9–12 access the Math class's static field E (line 11) and the static methods sqrt (line 9),

```
1   // Fig. 8.14: StaticImportTest.java
2   // Using static import to import static methods of class Math.
3   import static java.lang.Math.*;
4
5   public class StaticImportTest
6   {
7      public static void main( String args[] )
8      {
9         System.out.printf( "sqrt( 900.0 ) = %.1f\n", sqrt( 900.0 ) );
10        System.out.printf( "ceil( -9.8 ) = %.1f\n", ceil( -9.8 ) );
```

Fig. 8.14 | Static import Math methods. (Part 1 of 2.)

```
11          System.out.printf( "log( E ) = %.1f\n", log( E ) );
12          System.out.printf( "cos( 0.0 ) = %.1f\n", cos( 0.0 ) );
13      } // end main
14  } // end class StaticImportTest
```

```
sqrt( 900.0 ) = 30.0
ceil( -9.8 ) = -9.0
log( E ) = 1.0
cos( 0.0 ) = 1.0
```

Fig. 8.14 | Static import `Math` methods. (Part 2 of 2.)

`ceil` (line 10), `log` (line 11) and `cos` (line 12) without preceding the field name or method names with class name `Math` and a dot.

Common Programming Error 8.9

A compilation error occurs if a program attempts to import `static` methods that have the same signature or `static` fields that have the same name from two or more classes.

8.13 `final` Instance Variables

The **principle of least privilege** is fundamental to good software engineering. In the context of an application, the principle states that code should be granted only the amount of privilege and access that it needs to accomplish its designated task, but no more. Let us see how this principle applies to instance variables.

Some instance variables need to be modifiable and some do not. You can use the keyword `final` to specify that a variable is not modifiable (i.e., it is a constant) and that any attempt to modify it is an error. For example,

```
private final int INCREMENT;
```

declares a `final` (constant) instance variable `INCREMENT` of type `int`. Although constants can be initialized when they are declared, this is not required. Constants can be initialized by each of the class's constructors.

Software Engineering Observation 8.13

Declaring an instance variable as `final` helps enforce the principle of least privilege. If an instance variable should not be modified, declare it to be `final` to prevent modification.

Our next example contains two classes—class `Increment` (Fig. 8.15) and class `IncrementTest` (Fig. 8.16). Class `Increment` contains a `final` instance variable of type `int` named `INCREMENT` (Fig. 8.15, line 7). Note that the `final` variable is not initialized in its declaration, so it must be initialized by the class's constructor (lines 9–13). If the class provided multiple constructors, every constructor would be required to initialize the `final` variable. The constructor receives `int` parameter `incrementValue` and assigns its value to `INCREMENT` (line 12). A `final` variable cannot be modified by assignment after it is initialized. Application class `IncrementTest` creates an object of class `Increment` (Fig. 8.16, line 8) and provides as the argument to the constructor the value 5 to be assigned to the constant `INCREMENT`.

```
1   // Fig. 8.15: Increment.java
2   // final instance variable in a class.
3
4   public class Increment
5   {
6      private int total = 0; // total of all increments
7      private final int INCREMENT; // constant variable (uninitialized)
8
9      // constructor initializes final instance variable INCREMENT
10     public Increment( int incrementValue )
11     {
12        INCREMENT = incrementValue; // initialize constant variable (once)
13     } // end Increment constructor
14
15     // add INCREMENT to total
16     public void addIncrementToTotal()
17     {
18        total += INCREMENT;
19     } // end method addIncrementToTotal
20
21     // return String representation of an Increment object's data
22     public String toString()
23     {
24        return String.format( "total = %d", total );
25     } // end method toIncrementString
26  } // end class Increment
```

Fig. 8.15 | final instance variable in a class.

```
1   // Fig. 8.16: IncrementTest.java
2   // final variable initialized with a constructor argument.
3
4   public class IncrementTest
5   {
6      public static void main( String args[] )
7      {
8         Increment value = new Increment( 5 );
9
10        System.out.printf( "Before incrementing: %s\n\n", value );
11
12        for ( int i = 1; i <= 3; i++ )
13        {
14           value.addIncrementToTotal();
15           System.out.printf( "After increment %d: %s\n", i, value );
16        } // end for
17     } // end main
18  } // end class IncrementTest
```

```
Before incrementing: total = 0

After increment 1: total = 5
After increment 2: total = 10
After increment 3: total = 15
```

Fig. 8.16 | final variable initialized with a constructor argument.

Common Programming Error 8.10

Attempting to modify a final *instance variable after it is initialized is a compilation error.*

Error-Prevention Tip 8.2

Attempts to modify a final *instance variable are caught at compilation time rather than causing execution-time errors. It is always preferable to get bugs out at compilation time, if possible, rather than allow them to slip through to execution time (where studies have found that repair is often many times more expensive).*

Software Engineering Observation 8.14

A final *field should also be declared* static *if it is initialized in its declaration. Once a* final *field is initialized in its declaration, its value can never change. Therefore, it is not necessary to have a separate copy of the field for every object of the class. Making the field* static *enables all objects of the class to share the* final *field.*

If a final variable is not initialized, a compilation error occurs. To demonstrate this, we placed line 12 of Fig. 8.15 in a comment and recompiled the class. Figure 8.17 shows the error message produced by the compiler.

Common Programming Error 8.11

Not initializing a final *instance variable in its declaration or in every constructor of the class yields a compilation error indicating that the variable might not have been initialized. The same error occurs if the class initializes the variable in some, but not all, of the class's constructors.*

```
Increment.java:13: variable INCREMENT might not have been initialized
   } // end Increment constructor
   ^
1 error
```

Fig. 8.17 | final variable INCREMENT must be initialized.

8.14 Software Reusability

Java programmers concentrate on crafting new classes and reusing existing classes. Many class libraries exist, and others are being developed worldwide. Software is then constructed from existing, well-defined, carefully tested, well-documented, portable, widely available components. This kind of software reusability speeds the development of powerful, high-quality software. **Rapid application development (RAD)** is of great interest today.

There are thousands of classes in the Java API from which to choose to help you implement Java programs. Indeed, Java is not just a programming language. It is a framework in which Java developers can work to achieve true reusability and rapid application development. Java programmers can focus on the task at hand when developing their programs and leave the lower-level details to the classes of the Java API. For example, to write a program that draws graphics, a Java programmer does not require knowledge of graphics on every computer platform where the program will execute. Instead, the programmer can concentrate on learning Java's graphics capabilities (which are quite substantial and growing) and write a Java program that draws the graphics, using Java's API classes, such as `Graphics`. When the program executes on a given computer, it is the job of the JVM to translate Java commands into commands that the local computer can understand.

The Java API classes enable Java programmers to bring new applications to market faster by using preexisting, tested components. Not only does this reduce development time, it also improves the programmer's ability to debug and maintain applications. To take advantage of Java's many capabilities, it is essential that you familiarize yourself with the variety of packages and classes in the Java API. There are many Web-based resources at `java.sun.com` to help you with this task. The primary resource for learning about the Java API is the Java API documentation, which can be found at

> `java.sun.com/javase/6/docs/api/`

We overview how to use the documentation in Appendix J, Using the Java API Documentation. You can download the API documentation from

> `java.sun.com/javase/downloads/ea.jsp`

In addition, `java.sun.com` provides many other resources, including tutorials, articles and sites specific to individual Java topics.

Good Programming Practice 8.2

Avoid reinventing the wheel. Study the capabilities of the Java API. If the API contains a class that meets your program's requirements, use that class rather than create your own.

To realize the full potential of software reusability, we need to improve cataloging schemes, licensing schemes, protection mechanisms which ensure that master copies of classes are not corrupted, description schemes that system designers use to determine whether existing objects meet their needs, browsing mechanisms that determine what classes are available and how closely they meet software developer requirements, and the like. Many interesting research and development problems have been solved and many more need to be solved. These problems will likely be solved because the potential value of increased software reuse is enormous.

8.15 Data Abstraction and Encapsulation

Classes normally hide the details of their implementation from their clients. This is called **information hiding**. As an example, let us consider the **stack** data structure introduced in Section 6.6. Recall that a stack is a **last-in, first-out (LIFO)** data structure—the last item pushed (inserted) on the stack is the first item popped (removed) from the stack.

Stacks can be implemented with arrays and with other data structures, such as linked lists. (We discuss stacks and linked lists in Chapter 17, Data Structures, and in Chapter 19, Collections.) A client of a stack class need not be concerned with the stack's implementation. The client knows only that when data items are placed in the stack, they will be recalled in last-in, first-out order. The client cares about what functionality a stack offers, not about how that functionality is implemented. This concept is referred to as **data abstraction**. Although programmers might know the details of a class's implementation, they should not write code that depends on these details. This enables a particular class (such as one that implements a stack and its operations, *push* and *pop*) to be replaced with another version without affecting the rest of the system. As long as the `public` services of the class do not change (i.e., every original method still has the same name, return type and parameter list in the new class declaration), the rest of the system is not affected.

Most programming languages emphasize actions. In these languages, data exists to support the actions that programs must take. Data is "less interesting" than actions. Data is "crude." Only a few primitive types exist, and it is difficult for programmers to create their own types. Java and the object-oriented style of programming elevate the importance of data. The primary activities of object-oriented programming in Java are the creation of types (e.g., classes) and the expression of the interactions among objects of those types. To create languages that emphasize data, the programming-languages community needed to formalize some notions about data. The formalization we consider here is the notion of abstract data types (ADTs), which improve the program-development process.

Consider primitive type int, which most people would associate with an integer in mathematics. Rather, an int is an abstract representation of an integer. Unlike mathematical integers, computer ints are fixed in size. For example, type int in Java is limited to the range –2,147,483,648 to +2,147,483,647. If the result of a calculation falls outside this range, an error occurs, and the computer responds in some machine-dependent manner. It might, for example, "quietly" produce an incorrect result, such as a value too large to fit in an int variable (commonly called arithmetic overflow). Mathematical integers do not have this problem. Therefore, the notion of a computer int is only an approximation of the notion of a real-world integer. The same is true of float and other built-in types.

We have taken the notion of int for granted until this point, but we now consider it from a new perspective. Types like int, float, and char are all examples of abstract data types. They are representations of real-world notions to some satisfactory level of precision within a computer system.

An ADT actually captures two notions: a data representation and the operations that can be performed on that data. For example, in Java, an int contains an integer value (data) and provides addition, subtraction, multiplication, division and remainder operations—division by zero is undefined. Java programmers use classes to implement abstract data types.

Software Engineering Observation 8.15

Programmers create types through the class mechanism. New types can be designed to be convenient to use as the built-in types. This marks Java as an extensible language. Although the language is easy to extend via new types, you cannot alter the base language itself.

Another abstract data type we discuss is a queue, which is similar to a "waiting line." Computer systems use many queues internally. A queue offers well-understood behavior to its clients: Clients place items in a queue one at a time via an *enqueue* operation, then get them back one at a time via a *dequeue* operation. A queue returns items in first-in, first-out (FIFO) order, which means that the first item inserted in a queue is the first item removed from the queue. Conceptually, a queue can become infinitely long, but real queues are finite.

The queue hides an internal data representation that keeps track of the items currently waiting in line, and it offers operations to its clients (*enqueue* and *dequeue*). The clients are not concerned about the implementation of the queue—they simply depend on the queue to operate "as advertised." When a client enqueues an item, the queue should accept that item and place it in some kind of internal FIFO data structure. Similarly, when the client wants the next item from the front of the queue, the queue should remove the item from its internal representation and deliver it in FIFO order (i.e., the item that has been in the queue the longest should be the next one returned by the next dequeue operation).

The queue ADT guarantees the integrity of its internal data structure. Clients cannot manipulate this data structure directly—only the queue ADT has access to its internal data. Clients are able to perform only allowable operations on the data representation—the ADT rejects operations that its public interface does not provide.

8.16 Time Class Case Study: Creating Packages

We have seen in almost every example in the text that classes from preexisting libraries, such as the Java API, can be imported into a Java program. Each class in the Java API belongs to a package that contains a group of related classes. As applications become more complex, packages help programmers manage the complexity of application components. Packages also facilitate software reuse by enabling programs to import classes from other packages (as we have done in most examples). Another benefit of packages is that they provide a convention for unique class names, which helps prevent class-name conflicts (discussed later in this section). This section introduces how to create your own packages.

Steps for Declaring a Reusable Class

Before a class can be imported into multiple applications, it must be placed in a package to make it reusable. Figure 8.18 shows how to specify the package in which a class should be placed. Figure 8.19 shows how to import our packaged class so that it can be used in an application. The steps for creating a reusable class are:

1. Declare a public class. If the class is not public, it can be used only by other classes in the same package.

2. Choose a unique package name and add a **package declaration** to the source-code file for the reusable class declaration. There can be only one package declaration in each Java source-code file, and it must precede all other declarations and statements in the file. Note that comments are not statements, so comments can be placed before a package statement in a file.

3. Compile the class so that it is placed in the appropriate package directory structure.

4. Import the reusable class into a program and use the class.

Steps 1 and 2: Creating a **public** Class and Adding the **package** Statement

For *Step 1*, we modify the public class Time1 declared in Fig. 8.1. The new version is shown in Fig. 8.18. No modifications have been made to the implementation of the class, so we will not discuss its implementation details again here.

```
1   // Fig. 8.18: Time1.java
2   // Time1 class declaration maintains the time in 24-hour format.
3   package com.deitel.jhtp7.ch08;
4
```

Fig. 8.18 | Packaging class Time1 for reuse. (Part 1 of 2.)

```
5    public class Time1
6    {
7       private int hour;    // 0 - 23
8       private int minute;  // 0 - 59
9       private int second;  // 0 - 59
10
11      // set a new time value using universal time; perform
12      // validity checks on the data; set invalid values to zero
13      public void setTime( int h, int m, int s )
14      {
15         hour = ( ( h >= 0 && h < 24 ) ? h : 0 );    // validate hour
16         minute = ( ( m >= 0 && m < 60 ) ? m : 0 ); // validate minute
17         second = ( ( s >= 0 && s < 60 ) ? s : 0 ); // validate second
18      } // end method setTime
19
20      // convert to String in universal-time format (HH:MM:SS)
21      public String toUniversalString()
22      {
23         return String.format( "%02d:%02d:%02d", hour, minute, second );
24      } // end method toUniversalString
25
26      // convert to String in standard-time format (H:MM:SS AM or PM)
27      public String toString()
28      {
29         return String.format( "%d:%02d:%02d %s",
30            ( ( hour == 0 || hour == 12 ) ? 12 : hour % 12 ),
31            minute, second, ( hour < 12 ? "AM" : "PM" ) );
32      } // end method toString
33   } // end class Time1
```

Fig. 8.18 | Packaging class Time1 for reuse. (Part 2 of 2.)

For *Step 2*, we add a package declaration (line 3) that declares a package named com.deitel.jhtp7.ch08. Placing a package declaration at the beginning of a Java source file indicates that the class declared in the file is part of the specified package. Only package declarations, import declarations and comments can appear outside the braces of a class declaration. A Java source-code file must have the following order:

1. a package declaration (if any),

2. import declarations (if any), then

3. class declarations.

Only one of the class declarations in a particular file can be public. Other classes in the file are placed in the package and can be used only by the other classes in the package. Non-public classes are in a package to support the reusable classes in the package.

In an effort to provide unique names for every package, Sun Microsystems specifies a convention for package naming that all Java programmers should follow. Every package name should start with your Internet domain name in reverse order. For example, our domain name is deitel.com, so our package names begin with com.deitel. For the domain name *yourcollege*.edu, the package name should begin with edu.*yourcollege*. After the domain name is reversed, you can choose any other names you want for your package.

If you are part of a company with many divisions or a university with many schools, you may want to use the name of your division or school as the next name in the package. We chose to use jhtp7 as the next name in our package name to indicate that this class is from *Java How to Program, Seventh Edition*. The last name in our package name specifies that this package is for Chapter 8 (ch08).

Step 3: Compiling the Packaged Class

Step 3 is to compile the class so that it is stored in the appropriate package. When a Java file containing a package declaration is compiled, the resulting class file is placed in the directory specified by the package declaration. The package declaration in Fig. 8.18 indicates that class Time1 should be placed in the directory

```
com
    deitel
        jhtp7
            ch08
```

The directory names in the package declaration specify the exact location of the classes in the package.

When compiling a class in a package, the javac command-line option -d causes the javac compiler to create appropriate directories based on the class's package declaration. The option also specifies where the directories should be stored. For example, in a command window, we used the compilation command

```
javac -d . Time1.java
```

to specify that the first directory in our package name should be placed in the current directory. The period (.) after -d in the preceding command represents the current directory on the Windows, UNIX and Linux operating systems (and several others as well). After executing the compilation command, the current directory contains a directory called com, com contains a directory called deitel, deitel contains a directory called jhtp7 and jhtp7 contains a directory called ch08. In the ch08 directory, you can find the file Time1.class. [*Note:* If you do not use the -d option, then you must copy or move the class file to the appropriate package directory after compiling it.]

The package name is part of the fully qualified class name, so the name of class Time1 is actually com.deitel.jhtp7.ch08.Time1. You can use this fully qualified name in your programs, or you can import the class and use its **simple name** (the class name by itself—Time1) in the program. If another package also contains a Time1 class, the fully qualified class names can be used to distinguish between the classes in the program and prevent a **name conflict** (also called a **name collision**).

Step 4: Importing the Reusable Class

Once the class is compiled and stored in its package, the class can be imported into programs (*Step 4*). In the Time1PackageTest application of Fig. 8.19, line 3 specifies that class Time1 should be imported for use in class Time1PackageTest. Class Time1PackageTest is in the default package because the class's .java file does not contain a package declaration. Since the two classes are in different packages, the import at line 3 is required so that class Time1PackageTest can use class Time1.

```
 1   // Fig. 8.19: Time1PackageTest.java
 2   // Time1 object used in an application.
 3   import com.deitel.jhtp7.ch08.Time1; // import class Time1
 4
 5   public class Time1PackageTest
 6   {
 7      public static void main( String args[] )
 8      {
 9         // create and initialize a Time1 object
10         Time1 time = new Time1(); // calls Time1 constructor
11
12         // output string representations of the time
13         System.out.print( "The initial universal time is: " );
14         System.out.println( time.toUniversalString() );
15         System.out.print( "The initial standard time is: " );
16         System.out.println( time.toString() );
17         System.out.println(); // output a blank line
18
19         // change time and output updated time
20         time.setTime( 13, 27, 6 );
21         System.out.print( "Universal time after setTime is: " );
22         System.out.println( time.toUniversalString() );
23         System.out.print( "Standard time after setTime is: " );
24         System.out.println( time.toString() );
25         System.out.println(); // output a blank line
26
27         // set time with invalid values; output updated time
28         time.setTime( 99, 99, 99 );
29         System.out.println( "After attempting invalid settings:" );
30         System.out.print( "Universal time: " );
31         System.out.println( time.toUniversalString() );
32         System.out.print( "Standard time: " );
33         System.out.println( time.toString() );
34      } // end main
35   } // end class Time1PackageTest
```

```
The initial universal time is: 00:00:00
The initial standard time is: 12:00:00 AM

Universal time after setTime is: 13:27:06
Standard time after setTime is: 1:27:06 PM

After attempting invalid settings:
Universal time: 00:00:00
Standard time: 12:00:00 AM
```

Fig. 8.19 | Time1 object used in an application.

Line 3 is known as a **single-type-import declaration**—that is, the import declaration specifies one class to import. When your program uses multiple classes from the same package, you can import those classes with a single import declaration. For example, the import declaration

```
import java.util.*; // import classes from package java.util
```

uses an asterisk (*) at the end of the `import` declaration to inform the compiler that all classes from the `java.util` package are available for use in the program. This is known as a type-import-on-demand declaration. Only the classes from package `java.util` that are used in the program are loaded by the JVM. The preceding `import` allows you to use the simple name of any class from the `java.util` package in the program. Throughout this book, we use single-type-import declarations for clarity.

Common Programming Error 8.12

Using the `import` *declaration* `import java.*;` *causes a compilation error. You must specify the exact name of the package from which you want to import classes.*

Specifying the Classpath During Compilation

When compiling `Time1PackageTest`, `javac` must locate the `.class` file for `Time1` to ensure that class `Time1PackageTest` uses class `Time1` correctly. The compiler uses a special object called a class loader to locate the classes it needs. The class loader begins by searching the standard Java classes that are bundled with the JDK. Then it searches for optional packages. Java provides an extension mechanism that enables new (optional) packages to be added to Java for development and execution purposes. [*Note:* The extension mechanism is beyond the scope of this book. For more information, visit `java.sun.com/javase/6/docs/technotes/guides/extensions/`.] If the class is not found in the standard Java classes or in the extension classes, the class loader searches the classpath, which contains a list of locations in which classes are stored. The classpath consists of a list of directories or archive files, each separated by a directory separator—a semicolon (;) on Windows or a colon (:) on UNIX/Linux/Mac OS X. Archive files are individual files that contain directories of other files, typically in a compressed format. For example, the standard classes used by your programs are contained in the archive file `rt.jar`, which is installed with the JDK. Archive files normally end with the `.jar` or `.zip` file-name extensions. The directories and archive files specified in the classpath contain the classes you wish to make available to the Java compiler and the JVM.

By default, the classpath consists only of the current directory. However, the classpath can be modified by

1. providing the `-classpath` option to the `javac` compiler or

2. setting the `CLASSPATH` environment variable (a special variable that you define and the operating system maintains so that applications can search for classes in the specified locations).

For more information on the classpath, visit `java.sun.com/javase/6/docs/technotes/tools/index.html`. The section entitled "General Information" contains information on setting the classpath for UNIX/Linux and Windows.

Common Programming Error 8.13

Specifying an explicit classpath eliminates the current directory from the classpath. This prevents classes in the current directory (including packages in the current directory) from loading properly. If classes must be loaded from the current directory, include a dot (.) in the classpath to specify the current directory.

Software Engineering Observation 8.16

In general, it is a better practice to use the -classpath option of the compiler, rather than the CLASSPATH environment variable, to specify the classpath for a program. This enables each application to have its own classpath.

Error-Prevention Tip 8.3

Specifying the classpath with the CLASSPATH environment variable can cause subtle and difficult-to-locate errors in programs that use different versions of the same package.

For the example of Fig. 8.18 and Fig. 8.19, we did not specify an explicit classpath. Thus, to locate the classes in the com.deitel.jhtp7.ch08 package from this example, the class loader looks in the current directory for the first name in the package—com. Next, the class loader navigates the directory structure. Directory com contains the subdirectory deitel. Directory deitel contains the subdirectory jhtp7. Finally, directory jhtp7 contains subdirectory ch08. In the ch08 directory is the file Time1.class, which is loaded by the class loader to ensure that the class is used properly in our program.

Specifying the Classpath When Executing an Application

When you execute an application, the JVM must be able to locate the classes used in that application. Like the compiler, the java command uses a class loader that searches the standard classes and extension classes first, then searches the classpath (the current directory by default). The classpath for the JVM can be specified explicitly by using either of the techniques discussed for the compiler. As with the compiler, it is better to specify an individual program's classpath via command-line options to the JVM. You can specify the classpath in the java command via the -classpath or -cp command-line options, followed by a list of directories or archive files separated by semicolons (;) on Microsoft Windows or by colons (:) on UNIX/Linux/Mac OS X. Again, if classes must be loaded from the current directory, be sure to include a dot (.) in the classpath to specify the current directory.

8.17 Package Access

If no access modifier (public, protected or private—protected is discussed in Chapter 9) is specified for a method or variable when it is declared in a class, the method or variable is considered to have **package access**. In a program that consists of one class declaration, this has no specific effect. However, if a program uses multiple classes from the same package (i.e., a group of related classes), these classes can access each other's package-access members directly through references to objects of the appropriate classes.

The application in Fig. 8.20 demonstrates package access. The application contains two classes in one source-code file—the PackageDataTest application class (lines 5–21) and the PackageData class (lines 24–41). When you compile this program, the compiler produces two separate .class files—PackageDataTest.class and PackageData.class. The compiler places the two .class files in the same directory, so the classes are considered to be part of the same package. Since they are part of the same package, class PackageDataTest is allowed to modify the package-access data of PackageData objects.

In the PackageData class declaration, lines 26–27 declare the instance variables number and string with no access modifiers—therefore, these are package-access instance variables. The PackageDataTest application's main method creates an instance of the PackageData class (line 9) to demonstrate the ability to modify the PackageData instance variables directly (as shown in lines 15–16). The results of the modification can be seen in the output window.

```java
1   // Fig. 8.20: PackageDataTest.java
2   // Package-access members of a class are accessible by other classes
3   // in the same package.
4
5   public class PackageDataTest
6   {
7      public static void main( String args[] )
8      {
9         PackageData packageData = new PackageData();
10
11        // output String representation of packageData
12        System.out.printf( "After instantiation:\n%s\n", packageData );
13
14        // change package access data in packageData object
15        packageData.number = 77;
16        packageData.string = "Goodbye";
17
18        // output String representation of packageData
19        System.out.printf( "\nAfter changing values:\n%s\n", packageData );
20     } // end main
21  } // end class PackageDataTest
22
23  // class with package access instance variables
24  class PackageData
25  {
26     int number; // package-access instance variable
27     String string; // package-access instance variable
28
29     // constructor
30     public PackageData()
31     {
32        number = 0;
33        string = "Hello";
34     } // end PackageData constructor
35
36     // return PackageData object String representation
37     public String toString()
38     {
39        return String.format( "number: %d; string: %s", number, string );
40     } // end method toString
41  } // end class PackageData
```

```
After instantiation:
number: 0; string: Hello

After changing values:
number: 77; string: Goodbye
```

Fig. 8.20 | Package-access members of a class are accessible by other classes in the same package.

8.18 (Optional) GUI and Graphics Case Study: Using Objects with Graphics

Most of the graphics you have seen to this point did not vary each time you executed the program. However, Exercise 6.2 asked you to create a program that generated shapes and colors at random. In that exercise, the drawing changed every time the system called paintComponent to redraw the panel. To create a more consistent drawing that remains the same each time it is drawn, we must store information about the displayed shapes so that we can reproduce them exactly each time the system calls paintComponent.

To do this, we will create a set of shape classes that store information about each shape. We will make these classes "smart" by allowing objects of these classes to draw themselves if provided with a Graphics object. Figure 8.21 declares class MyLine, which has all these capabilities.

Class MyLine imports Color and Graphics (lines 3–4). Lines 8–11 declare instance variables for the coordinates needed to draw a line, and line 12 declares the instance variable that stores the color of the line. The constructor at lines 15–22 takes five parameters, one for each instance variable that it initializes. Method draw at lines 25–29 requires a Graphics object and uses it to draw the line in the proper color and at the proper coordinates.

```java
1   // Fig. 8.21: MyLine.java
2   // Declaration of class MyLine.
3   import java.awt.Color;
4   import java.awt.Graphics;
5
6   public class MyLine
7   {
8      private int x1; // x-coordinate of first endpoint
9      private int y1; // y-coordinate of first endpoint
10     private int x2; // x-coordinate of second endpoint
11     private int y2; // y-coordinate of second endpoint
12     private Color myColor; // color of this shape
13
14     // constructor with input values
15     public MyLine( int x1, int y1, int x2, int y2, Color color )
16     {
17        this.x1 = x1; // set x-coordinate of first endpoint
18        this.y1 = y1; // set y-coordinate of first endpoint
19        this.x2 = x2; // set x-coordinate of second endpoint
20        this.y2 = y2; // set y-coordinate of second endpoint
21        myColor = color; // set the color
22     } // end MyLine constructor
23
24     // Draw the line in the specified color
25     public void draw( Graphics g )
26     {
27        g.setColor( myColor );
28        g.drawLine( x1, y1, x2, y2 );
29     } // end method draw
30  } // end class MyLine
```

Fig. 8.21 | MyLine class represents a line.

In Fig. 8.22, we declare class DrawPanel, which will generate random objects of class MyLine. Line 12 declares a MyLine array to store the lines to draw. Inside the constructor (lines 15–37), line 17 sets the background color to Color.WHITE. Line 19 creates the array with a random length between 5 and 9. The loop at lines 22–36 creates a new MyLine for every element in the array. Lines 25–28 generate random coordinates for each line's endpoints, and lines 31–32 generate a random color for the line. Line 35 creates a new MyLine object with the randomly generated values and stores it in the array.

```java
 1   // Fig. 8.22: DrawPanel.java
 2   // Program that uses class MyLine
 3   // to draw random lines.
 4   import java.awt.Color;
 5   import java.awt.Graphics;
 6   import java.util.Random;
 7   import javax.swing.JPanel;
 8
 9   public class DrawPanel extends JPanel
10   {
11      private Random randomNumbers = new Random();
12      private MyLine lines[]; // array of lines
13
14      // constructor, creates a panel with random shapes
15      public DrawPanel()
16      {
17         setBackground( Color.WHITE );
18
19         lines = new MyLine[ 5 + randomNumbers.nextInt( 5 ) ];
20
21         // create lines
22         for ( int count = 0; count < lines.length; count++ )
23         {
24            // generate random coordinates
25            int x1 = randomNumbers.nextInt( 300 );
26            int y1 = randomNumbers.nextInt( 300 );
27            int x2 = randomNumbers.nextInt( 300 );
28            int y2 = randomNumbers.nextInt( 300 );
29
30            // generate a random color
31            Color color = new Color( randomNumbers.nextInt( 256 ),
32               randomNumbers.nextInt( 256 ), randomNumbers.nextInt( 256 ) );
33
34            // add the line to the list of lines to be displayed
35            lines[ count ] = new MyLine( x1, y1, x2, y2, color );
36         } // end for
37      } // end DrawPanel constructor
38
39      // for each shape array, draw the individual shapes
40      public void paintComponent( Graphics g )
41      {
42         super.paintComponent( g );
43
```

Fig. 8.22 | Creating random MyLine objects. (Part 1 of 2.)

```
44          // draw the lines
45          for ( MyLine line : lines )
46              line.draw( g );
47       } // end method paintComponent
48   } // end class DrawPanel
```

Fig. 8.22 | Creating random MyLine objects. (Part 2 of 2.)

Method paintComponent iterates through the MyLine objects in array lines using an enhanced for statement (lines 45–46). Each iteration calls the draw method of the current MyLine object and passes it the Graphics object for drawing on the panel. Class TestDraw in Fig. 8.23 sets up a new window to display our drawing. Since we are setting the coordinates for the lines only once in the constructor, the drawing does not change if paintComponent is called to refresh the drawing on the screen.

```
 1   // Fig. 8.23: TestDraw.java
 2   // Test application to display a DrawPanel.
 3   import javax.swing.JFrame;
 4
 5   public class TestDraw
 6   {
 7      public static void main( String args[] )
 8      {
 9         DrawPanel panel = new DrawPanel();
10         JFrame application = new JFrame();
11
12         application.setDefaultCloseOperation( JFrame.EXIT_ON_CLOSE );
13         application.add( panel );
14         application.setSize( 300, 300 );
15         application.setVisible( true );
16      } // end main
17   } // end class TestDraw
```

Fig. 8.23 | Creating JFrame to display DrawPanel.

GUI and Graphics Case Study Exercise

8.1   Extend the program in Figs. 8.21–8.23 to randomly draw rectangles and ovals. Create classes MyRectangle and MyOval. Both of these classes should include *x1*, *y1*, *x2*, *y2* coordinates, a color and a boolean flag to determine whether the shape is a filled shape. Declare a constructor in each class with arguments for initializing all the instance variables. To help draw rectangles and ovals, each class should provide methods getUpperLeftX, getUpperLeftY, getWidth and getHeight that calculate the upper-left *x*-coordinate, upper-left *y*-coordinate, width and height, respectively. The upper-left *x*-coordinate is the smaller of the two *x*-coordinate values, the upper-left *y*-coordinate is the smaller of the two *y*-coordinate values, the width is the absolute value of the difference between the two *x*-coordinate values, and the height is the absolute value of the difference between the two *y*-coordinate values.

Class DrawPanel, which extends JPanel and handles the creation of the shapes, should declare three arrays, one for each shape type. The length of each array should be a random number between 1 and 5. The constructor of class DrawPanel will fill each of the arrays with shapes of random position, size, color and fill.

In addition, modify all three shape classes to include the following:

    a) A constructor with no arguments that sets all the coordinates of the shape to 0, the color of the shape to Color.BLACK, and the filled property to false (MyRect and MyOval only).

    b) *Set* methods for the instance variables in each class. The methods that set a coordinate value should verify that the argument is greater than or equal to zero before setting the coordinate—if it is not, they should set the coordinate to zero. The constructor should call the *set* methods rather than initialize the local variables directly.

    c) *Get* methods for the instance variables in each class. Method draw should reference the coordinates by the *get* methods rather than access them directly.

8.19 (Optional) Software Engineering Case Study: Starting to Program the Classes of the ATM System

In the Software Engineering Case Study sections in Chapters 1–7, we introduced the fundamentals of object orientation and developed an object-oriented design for our ATM system. Earlier in this chapter, we discussed many of the details of programming with classes. We now begin implementing our object-oriented design in Java. At the end of this section, we show how to convert class diagrams to Java code. In the final Software Engineering Case Study section (Section 10.9), we modify the code to incorporate the object-oriented concept of inheritance. We present the full Java code implementation in Appendix M.

Visibility

We now apply access modifiers to the members of our classes. In Chapter 3, we introduced access modifiers public and private. Access modifiers determine the **visibility** or accessibility of an object's attributes and methods to other objects. Before we can begin implementing our design, we must consider which attributes and methods of our classes should be public and which should be private.

In Chapter 3, we observed that attributes normally should be private and that methods invoked by clients of a given class should be public. Methods that are called only by other methods of the class as "utility methods," however, normally should be private. The UML employs **visibility markers** for modeling the visibility of attributes and operations. Public visibility is indicated by placing a plus sign (+) before an operation or an attribute, whereas a minus sign (–) indicates private visibility. Figure 8.24 shows our updated class diagram with visibility markers included. [*Note:* We do not include any operation parameters in Fig. 8.24—this is perfectly normal. Adding visibility markers does not affect the parameters already modeled in the class diagrams of Figs. 6.22–6.25.]

Navigability

Before we begin implementing our design in Java, we introduce an additional UML notation. The class diagram in Fig. 8.25 further refines the relationships among classes in the ATM system by adding navigability arrows to the association lines. Navigability arrows (represented as arrows with stick arrowheads in the class diagram) indicate in which direction an association can be traversed. When implementing a system designed using the UML, programmers use navigability arrows to help determine which objects need references to other objects. For example, the navigability arrow pointing from class ATM to class BankDatabase indicates that we can navigate from the former to the latter, thereby enabling the ATM to invoke the BankDatabase's operations. However, since Fig. 8.25 does not contain a navigability arrow pointing from class BankDatabase to class ATM, the BankData-

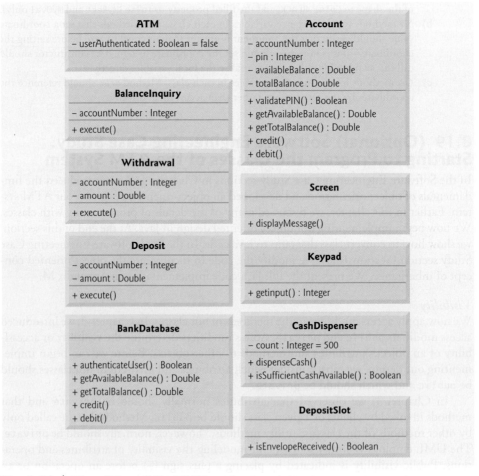

Fig. 8.24 | Class diagram with visibility markers.

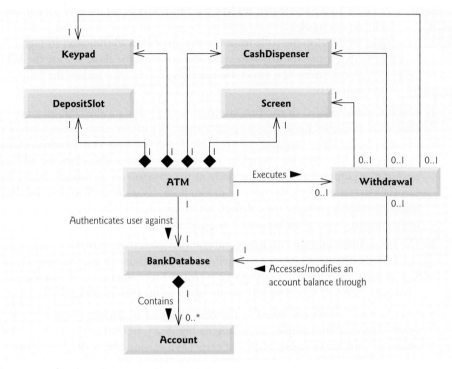

Fig. 8.25 | Class diagram with navigability arrows.

base cannot access the ATM's operations. Note that associations in a class diagram that have navigability arrows at both ends or do not have navigability arrows at all indicate bidirectional navigability—navigation can proceed in either direction across the association.

Like the class diagram of Fig. 3.24, the class diagram of Fig. 8.25 omits classes BalanceInquiry and Deposit to keep the diagram simple. The navigability of the associations in which these classes participate closely parallels the navigability of class Withdrawal. Recall from Section 3.10 that BalanceInquiry has an association with class Screen. We can navigate from class BalanceInquiry to class Screen along this association, but we cannot navigate from class Screen to class BalanceInquiry. Thus, if we were to model class BalanceInquiry in Fig. 8.25, we would place a navigability arrow at class Screen's end of this association. Also recall that class Deposit associates with classes Screen, Keypad and DepositSlot. We can navigate from class Deposit to each of these classes, but not vice versa. We therefore would place navigability arrows at the Screen, Keypad and DepositSlot ends of these associations. [*Note:* We model these additional classes and associations in our final class diagram in Section 10.9, after we have simplified the structure of our system by incorporating the object-oriented concept of inheritance.]

Implementing the ATM System from Its UML Design
We are now ready to begin implementing the ATM system. We first convert the classes in the diagrams of Fig. 8.24 and Fig. 8.25 into Java code. The code will represent the "skeleton" of the system. In Chapter 10, we modify the code to incorporate the object-oriented

concept of inheritance. In Appendix M, ATM Case Study Code, we present the complete working Java code for our model.

As an example, we develop the code from our design of class `Withdrawal` in Fig. 8.24. We use this figure to determine the attributes and operations of the class. We use the UML model in Fig. 8.25 to determine the associations among classes. We follow the following four guidelines for each class:

1. Use the name located in the first compartment to declare the class as a `public` class with an empty no-argument constructor. We include this constructor simply as a placeholder to remind us that most classes will indeed need constructors. In Appendix M, when we complete a working version of this class, we add any necessary arguments and code the body of the constructor as needed. For example, class `Withdrawal` yields the code in Fig. 8.26. [*Note:* If we find that the class's instance variables require only default initialization, then we remove the empty no-argument constructor because it is unnecessary.]

2. Use the attributes located in the second compartment to declare the instance variables. For example, the `private` attributes `accountNumber` and `amount` of class `Withdrawal` yield the code in Fig. 8.27. [*Note:* The constructor of the complete working version of this class will assign values to these attributes.]

3. Use the associations described in the class diagram to declare the references to other objects. For example, according to Fig. 8.25, `Withdrawal` can access one object of class `Screen`, one object of class `Keypad`, one object of class `CashDispenser` and one object of class `BankDatabase`. This yields the code in Fig. 8.28.

```
1    // Class Withdrawal represents an ATM withdrawal transaction
2    public class Withdrawal
3    {
4       // no-argument constructor
5       public Withdrawal()
6       {
7       } // end no-argument Withdrawal constructor
8    } // end class Withdrawal
```

Fig. 8.26 | Java code for class `Withdrawal` based on Fig. 8.24 and Fig. 8.25.

```
1    // Class Withdrawal represents an ATM withdrawal transaction
2    public class Withdrawal
3    {
4       // attributes
5       private int accountNumber; // account to withdraw funds from
6       private double amount; // amount to withdraw
7
8       // no-argument constructor
9       public Withdrawal()
10      {
11      } // end no-argument Withdrawal constructor
12   } // end class Withdrawal
```

Fig. 8.27 | Java code for class `Withdrawal` based on Fig. 8.24 and Fig. 8.25.

```
 1   // Class Withdrawal represents an ATM withdrawal transaction
 2   public class Withdrawal
 3   {
 4      // attributes
 5      private int accountNumber; // account to withdraw funds from
 6      private double amount; // amount to withdraw
 7
 8      // references to associated objects
 9      private Screen screen; // ATM's screen
10      private Keypad keypad; // ATM's keypad
11      private CashDispenser cashDispenser; // ATM's cash dispenser
12      private BankDatabase bankDatabase; // account info database
13
14      // no-argument constructor
15      public Withdrawal()
16      {
17      } // end no-argument Withdrawal constructor
18   } // end class Withdrawal
```

Fig. 8.28 | Java code for class `Withdrawal` based on Fig. 8.24 and Fig. 8.25.

[*Note:* The constructor of the complete working version of this class will initialize these instance variables with references to actual objects.]

4. Use the operations located in the third compartment of Fig. 8.24 to declare the shells of the methods. If we have not yet specified a return type for an operation, we declare the method with return type `void`. Refer to the class diagrams of Figs. 6.22–6.25 to declare any necessary parameters. For example, adding the `public` operation `execute` in class `Withdrawal`, which has an empty parameter list, yields the code in Fig. 8.29. [*Note:* We code the bodies of methods when we implement the complete system in Appendix M.]

```
 1   // Class Withdrawal represents an ATM withdrawal transaction
 2   public class Withdrawal
 3   {
 4      // attributes
 5      private int accountNumber; // account to withdraw funds from
 6      private double amount; // amount to withdraw
 7
 8      // references to associated objects
 9      private Screen screen; // ATM's screen
10      private Keypad keypad; // ATM's keypad
11      private CashDispenser cashDispenser; // ATM's cash dispenser
12      private BankDatabase bankDatabase; // account info database
13
14      // no-argument constructor
15      public Withdrawal()
16      {
17      } // end no-argument Withdrawal constructor
18
```

Fig. 8.29 | Java code for class `Withdrawal` based on Fig. 8.24 and Fig. 8.25. (Part 1 of 2.)

```
19      // operations
20      public void execute()
21      {
22      } // end method execute
23   } // end class Withdrawal
```

Fig. 8.29 | Java code for class `Withdrawal` based on Fig. 8.24 and Fig. 8.25. (Part 2 of 2.)

This concludes our discussion of the basics of generating classes from UML diagrams.

Software Engineering Case Study Self-Review Exercises

8.1 State whether the following statement is *true* or *false*, and if *false*, explain why: If an attribute of a class is marked with a minus sign (-) in a class diagram, the attribute is not directly accessible outside of the class.

8.2 In Fig. 8.25, the association between the ATM and the Screen indicates that:
  a) we can navigate from the Screen to the ATM
  b) we can navigate from the ATM to the Screen
  c) Both (a) and (b); the association is bidirectional
  d) None of the above

8.3 Write Java code to begin implementing the design for class `Keypad`.

Answers to Software Engineering Case Study Self-Review Exercises

8.1 True. The minus sign (-) indicates private visibility.

8.2 b.

8.3 The design for class `Keypad` yields the code in Fig. 8.30. Recall that class `Keypad` has no attributes for the moment, but attributes may become apparent as we continue the implementation. Also note that if we were designing a real ATM, method `getInput` would need to interact with the ATM's keypad hardware. We will actually do input from the keyboard of a personal computer when we write the complete Java code in Appendix M.

```
1    // Class Keypad represents an ATM's keypad
2    public class Keypad
3    {
4       // no attributes have been specified yet
5
6       // no-argument constructor
7       public Keypad()
8       {
9       } // end no-argument Keypad constructor
10
11      // operations
12      public int getInput()
13      {
14      } // end method getInput
15   } // end class Keypad
```

Fig. 8.30 | Java code for class `Keypad` based on Fig. 8.24 and Fig. 8.25.

8.20 Wrap-Up

In this chapter, we presented additional class concepts. The Time class case study presented a complete class declaration consisting of private data, overloaded public constructors for initialization flexibility, *set* and *get* methods for manipulating the class's data, and methods that returned String representations of a Time object in two different formats. You also learned that every class can declare a toString method that returns a String representation of an object of the class and that method toString can be called implicitly whenever an object of a class appears in the code where a String is expected.

You learned that the this reference is used implicitly in a class's non-static methods to access the class's instance variables and other non-static methods. You also saw explicit uses of the this reference to access the class's members (including shadowed fields) and how to use keyword this in a constructor to call another constructor of the class.

We discussed the differences between default constructors provided by the compiler and no-argument constructors provided by the programmer. You learned that a class can have references to objects of other classes as members—a concept known as composition. You saw the enum class type and learned how it can be used to create a set of constants for use in a program. You learned about Java's garbage collection capability and how it reclaims the memory of objects that are no longer used. The chapter explained the motivation for static fields in a class and demonstrated how to declare and use static fields and methods in your own classes. You also learned how to declare and initialize final variables.

You learned how to package your own classes for reuse and how to import those classes into an application. Finally, you learned that fields declared without an access modifier are given package access by default. You saw the relationship between classes in the same package that allows each class in a package to access the package-access members of other classes in the package.

In the next chapter, you will learn about an important aspect of object-oriented programming in Java—inheritance. You will see that all classes in Java are related directly or indirectly to the class called Object. You will also begin to understand how the relationships between classes enable you to build more powerful applications.

Summary

Section 8.2 *Time Class Case Study*
- Every class you declare represents a new type in Java.
- The public methods of a class are also known as the class's public services or public interface. The primary purpose of public methods is to present to the class's clients a view of the services the class provides. Clients of the class need not be concerned with how the class accomplishes its tasks. For this reason, private class members are not directly accessible to the class's clients.
- An object that contains consistent data has data values that are always kept in range.
- A value passed to a method to modify an instance variable is a correct value if that value is in the instance variable's allowed range. A correct value is always a consistent value, but a consistent value is not correct if a method receives an out-of-range value and sets it to a consistent value to maintain the object in a consistent state.
- String class static method format is similar to method System.out.printf except that format returns a formatted String rather than displaying it in a command window.

- All objects in Java have a toString method that returns a String representation of the object. Method toString is called implicitly when an object appears in code where a String is needed.

Section 8.4 Referring to the Current Object's Members with the **this** Reference
- A non-static method of an object implicitly uses keyword this to refer to the object's instance variables and other methods. Keyword this can also be used explicitly.
- The compiler produces a separate file with the .class extension for every compiled class.
- If a method contains a local variable with the same name as one of its class's fields, the local variable shadows the field in the method's scope. The method can use the this reference to refer to the shadowed field explicitly.

Section 8.5 **Time** Class Case Study: Overloaded Constructors
- Overloaded constructors enable objects of a class to be initialized in different ways. The compiler differentiates overloaded constructors by their signatures.

Section 8.6 Default and No-Argument Constructors
- Every class must have at least one constructor. If none are provided, the compiler creates a default constructor that initializes the instance variables to the initial values specified in their declarations or to their default values.
- If a class declares constructors, the compiler will not create a default constructor. To specify the default initialization for objects of a class with multiple constructors, the programmer must declare a no-argument constructor.

Section 8.7 Notes on **Set** and **Get** Methods
- *Set* methods are commonly called mutator methods because they typically change a value. *Get* methods are commonly called accessor methods or query methods. A predicate method tests whether a condition is true or false.

Section 8.8 Composition
- A class can have references to objects of other classes as members. Such a capability is called composition and is sometimes referred to as a *has-a* relationship.

Section 8.9 Enumerations
- All enum types are reference types. An enum type is declared with an enum declaration, which is a comma-separated list of enum constants. The declaration may optionally include other components of traditional classes, such as constructors, fields and methods.
- enum types are implicitly final, because they declare constants that should not be modified.
- enum constants are implicitly static.
- Any attempt to create an object of an enum type with operator new results in a compilation error.
- enum constants can be used anywhere constants can be used, such as in the case labels of switch statements and to control enhanced for statements.
- Each enum constant in an enum declaration is optionally followed by arguments which are passed to the enum constructor.
- For every enum, the compiler generates a static method called values that returns an array of the enum's constants in the order in which they were declared.
- EnumSet static method range takes two parameters—the first enum constant in a range and the last enum constant in a range—and returns an EnumSet that contains all the constants between these two constants, inclusive.

Section 8.10 Garbage Collection and Method `finalize`

- Every class in Java has the methods of class `Object`, one of which is the `finalize` method.

- The Java Virtual Machine (JVM) performs automatic garbage collection to reclaim the memory occupied by objects that are no longer in use. When there are no more references to an object, the object is marked for garbage collection by the JVM. The memory for such an object can be reclaimed when the JVM executes its garbage collector.

- The `finalize` method is called by the garbage collector just before it reclaims the object's memory. Method `finalize` does not take parameters and has return type `void`.

- The garbage collector may never execute before a program terminates. Thus, it is unclear whether, or when, method `finalize` will be called.

Section 8.11 `static` Class Members

- A `static` variable represents classwide information that is shared among all objects of the class.

- Static variables have class scope. A class's `public static` members can be accessed through a reference to any object of the class, or they can be accessed by qualifying the member name with the class name and a dot (`.`). A class's `private static` class members can be accessed only through methods of the class.

- `static` class members exist even when no objects of the class exist—they are available as soon as the class is loaded into memory at execution time. To access a `private static` member when no objects of the class exist, a `public static` method must be provided.

- `System` class `static` method `gc` indicates that the garbage collector should make a best-effort attempt to reclaim objects that are eligible for garbage collection.

- A method declared `static` cannot access non-static class members, because a `static` method can be called even when no objects of the class have been instantiated.

- The `this` reference cannot be used in a `static` method.

Section 8.12 `static` Import

- A `static` import declaration enables programmers to refer to imported `static` members without the class name and a dot (`.`). A single `static` import declaration imports one `static` member, and a `static` import on demand imports all `static` members of a class.

Section 8.13 `final` Instance Variables

- In the context of an application, the principle of least privilege states that code should be granted only the amount of privilege and access that the code needs to accomplish its designated task.

- Keyword `final` specifies that a variable is not modifiable—in other words, it is constant. Constants can be initialized when they are declared or by each of a class's constructors. If a `final` variable is not initialized, a compilation error occurs.

Section 8.14 Software Reusability

- Software is constructed from existing, well-defined, carefully tested, well-documented, portable, widely available components. Software reusability speeds the development of powerful, high-quality software. Rapid application development (RAD) is of great interest today.

- Java programmers now have thousands of classes in the Java API from which to choose to help them implement Java programs. The Java API classes enable Java programmers to bring new applications to market faster by using preexisting, tested components.

Section 8.15 Data Abstraction and Encapsulation

- The client of a class cares about the functionality the class offers, but not about how the functionality is implemented. This is referred to as data abstraction. Although programmers may know the details of a class's implementation, they should not write code that depends on these details. This enables a class to be replaced with another version without affecting the rest of the system.

- An abstract data type (ADT) consists of a data representation and the operations that can be performed on that data.

Section 8.16 Time Class Case Study: Creating Packages

- Each class in the Java API belongs to a package that contains a group of related classes. Packages help manage the complexity of application components and facilitate software reuse.

- Packages provide a convention for unique class names that helps prevent class name conflicts.

- Before a class can be imported into multiple applications, the class must be placed in a package. There can be only one package declaration in each Java source-code file, and it must precede all other declarations and statements in the file.

- Every package name should start with your Internet domain name in reverse order. After the domain name is reversed, you can choose any other names you want for your package.

- When compiling a class in a package, the javac command-line option -d specifies where to store the package and causes the compiler to create the package's directories if they do not exist.

- The package name is part of the fully qualified class name. This helps prevent name conflicts.

- A single-type-import declaration specifies one class to import. A type-import-on-demand declaration imports only the classes that the program uses from a particular package.

- The compiler uses a class loader to locate the classes it needs in the classpath. The classpath consists of a list of directories or archive files, each separated by a directory separator.

- The classpath for the compiler and JVM can be specified by providing the -classpath option to the javac or java command, or by setting the CLASSPATH environment variable. The classpath for the JVM can also be specified via the -cp command-line option. If classes must be loaded from the current directory, include a dot (.) in the classpath.

Section 8.17 Package Access

- If no access modifier is specified for a method or variable when it is declared in a class, the method or variable is considered to have package access.

Terminology

abstract data type (ADT)	constant variable
access modifier	-d command-line argument to javac
accessor method	data abstraction
archive file	data representation
arithmetic overflow	default constructor
attribute	directory separator
behavior	enum keyword
class library	enum constant
class loader	EnumSet class
class scope	extensible language
class variable	extensions mechanism
classpath	finalize method
-classpath command-line argument to javac	first-in, first-out (FIFO)
CLASSPATH environment variable	format method of class String
classwide information	garbage collector
composition	gc method of class System
container class	*has-a* relationship

last-in, first-out (LIFO)
mark an object for garbage collection
memory leak
mutator method
name collision
name conflict
no-argument constructor
optional package
overloaded constructors
package access
package declaration
predicate method
principle of least privilege
private access modifier
protected access modifier
public access modifier
public interface
public service

query method
range method of EnumSet
rapid application development (RAD)
resource leak
service of a class
simple name of a class, field or method
single static import
single-type-import declaration
stack
static field (class variable)
static import
static import on demand
termination housekeeping
this keyword
type-import-on-demand declaration
validity checking
values method of an enum
variable is not modifiable

Self-Review Exercise

8.1   Fill in the blanks in each of the following statements:

a) When compiling a class in a package, the javac command-line option _____ specifies where to store the package and causes the compiler to create the package's directories if they do not exist.

b) String class static method _____ is similar to method System.out.printf, but returns a formatted String rather than displaying a String in a command window.

c) If a method contains a local variable with the same name as one of its class's fields, the local variable _____ the field in that method's scope.

d) The _____ method is called by the garbage collector just before it reclaims an object's memory.

e) A(n) _____ declaration specifies one class to import.

f) If a class declares constructors, the compiler will not create a(n) _____.

g) An object's _____ method is called implicitly when an object appears in code where a String is needed.

h) *Get* methods are commonly called _____ or _____.

i) A(n) _____ method tests whether a condition is true or false.

j) For every enum, the compiler generates a static method called _____ that returns an array of the enum's constants in the order in which they were declared.

k) Composition is sometimes referred to as a(n) _____ relationship.

l) A(n) _____ declaration contains a comma-separated list of constants.

m) A(n) _____ variable represents classwide information that is shared by all the objects of the class.

n) A(n) _____ declaration imports one static member.

o) The _____ states that code should be granted only the amount of privilege and access that the code needs to accomplish its designated task.

p) Keyword _____ specifies that a variable is not modifiable.

q) A(n) _____ consists of a data representation and the operations that can be performed on the data.

r) There can be only one _____ in a Java source-code file, and it must precede all other declarations and statements in the file.

s) A(n) _____ declaration imports only the classes that the program uses from a particular package.

t) The compiler uses a(n) _____ to locate the classes it needs in the classpath.

u) The classpath for the compiler and JVM can be specified with the _____ option to the javac or java command, or by setting the _____ environment variable.

v) *Set* methods are commonly called _____ because they typically change a value.

w) A(n) _____ imports all static members of a class.

x) The public methods of a class are also known as the class's _____ or _____.

y) System class static method _____ indicates that the garbage collector should make a best-effort attempt to reclaim objects that are eligible for garbage collection.

z) An object that contains _____ has data values that are always kept in range.

Answers to Self-Review Exercise

8.1   a) -d. b) format. c) shadows. d) finalize. e) single-type-import. f) default constructor. g) toString. h) accessor methods, query methods. i) predicate. j) values. k) *has-a*. l) enum. m) static. n) single static import. o) principle of least privilege. p) final. q) abstract data type (ADT). r) package declaration. s) type-import-on-demand. t) class loader. u) -classpath, CLASSPATH. v) mutator methods. w) static import on demand. x) public services, public interface. y) gc. z) consistent data.

Exercises

8.2   Explain the notion of package access in Java. Explain the negative aspects of package access.

8.3   What happens when a return type, even void, is specified for a constructor?

8.4   *(Rectangle Class)* Create a class Rectangle. The class has attributes length and width, each of which defaults to 1. It has methods that calculate the perimeter and the area of the rectangle. It has *set* and *get* methods for both length and width. The *set* methods should verify that length and width are each floating-point numbers larger than 0.0 and less than 20.0. Write a program to test class Rectangle.

8.5   *(Modifying the Internal Data Representation of a Class)* It would be perfectly reasonable for the Time2 class of Fig. 8.5 to represent the time internally as the number of seconds since midnight rather than the three integer values hour, minute and second. Clients could use the same public methods and get the same results. Modify the Time2 class of Fig. 8.5 to implement the Time2 as the number of seconds since midnight and show that no change is visible to the clients of the class.

8.6   *(Enhancing Class Time2)* Modify class Time2 of Fig. 8.5 to include a tick method that increments the time stored in a Time2 object by one second. Provide method incrementMinute to increment the minute and method incrementHour to increment the hour. The Time2 object should always remain in a consistent state. Write a program that tests the tick method, the increment-Minute method and the incrementHour method to ensure that they work correctly. Be sure to test the following cases:

a) incrementing into the next minute,

b) incrementing into the next hour and

c) incrementing into the next day (i.e., 11:59:59 PM to 12:00:00 AM).

8.7   *(Enhancing Class Date)* Modify class Date of Fig. 8.7 to perform error checking on the initializer values for instance variables month, day and year (currently it validates only the month and day). Provide a method nextDay to increment the day by one. The Date object should always remain in a consistent state. Write a program that tests the nextDay method in a loop that prints the date during each iteration of the loop to illustrate that the nextDay method works correctly. Test the following cases:

a) incrementing into the next month and

b) incrementing into the next year.

8.8 *(Returning Error Indicators from Methods)* Modify the *set* methods in class Time2 of Fig. 8.5 to return appropriate error values if an attempt is made to set one of the instance variables hour, minute or second of an object of class Time to an invalid value. [*Hint:* Use boolean return types on each method.] Write a program that tests these new *set* methods and outputs error messages when incorrect values are supplied.

8.9 Write an enum type TrafficLight, whose constants (RED, GREEN, YELLOW) take one parameter—the duration of the light. Write a program to test the TrafficLight enum so that it displays the enum constants and their durations.

8.10 *(Complex Numbers)* Create a class called Complex for performing arithmetic with complex numbers. Complex numbers have the form

   realPart + *imaginaryPart* * *i*

where *i* is

$$\sqrt{-1}$$

Write a program to test your class. Use floating-point variables to represent the private data of the class. Provide a constructor that enables an object of this class to be initialized when it is declared. Provide a no-argument constructor with default values in case no initializers are provided. Provide public methods that perform the following operations:

a) Add two Complex numbers: The real parts are added together and the imaginary parts are added together.

b) Subtract two Complex numbers: The real part of the right operand is subtracted from the real part of the left operand, and the imaginary part of the right operand is subtracted from the imaginary part of the left operand.

c) Print Complex numbers in the form (a, b), where a is the real part and b is the imaginary part.

8.11 *(Date and Time Class)* Create class DateAndTime that combines the modified Time2 class of Exercise 8.6 and the modified Date class of Exercise 8.7. Modify method incrementHour to call method nextDay if the time is incremented into the next day. Modify methods toStandardString and toUniversalString to output the date in addition to the time. Write a program to test the new class DateAndTime. Specifically, test incrementing the time to the next day.

8.12 *(Enhanced Rectangle Class)* Create a more sophisticated Rectangle class than the one you created in Exercise 8.4. This class stores only the Cartesian coordinates of the four corners of the rectangle. The constructor calls a *set* method that accepts four sets of coordinates and verifies that each of these is in the first quadrant with no single *x*- or *y*-coordinate larger than 20.0. The *set* method also verifies that the supplied coordinates specify a rectangle. Provide methods to calculate the length, width, perimeter and area. The length is the larger of the two dimensions. Include a predicate method isSquare which determines whether the rectangle is a square. Write a program to test class Rectangle.

8.13 *(Set of Integers)* Create class IntegerSet. Each IntegerSet object can hold integers in the range 0–100. The set is represented by an array of booleans. Array element a[i] is true if integer *i* is in the set. Array element a[j] is false if integer *j* is not in the set. The no-argument constructor initializes the Java array to the "empty set" (i.e., a set whose array representation contains all false values).

Provide the following methods: Method `union` creates a third set that is the set-theoretic union of two existing sets (i.e., an element of the third set's array is set to `true` if that element is true in either or both of the existing sets—otherwise, the element of the third set is set to `false`). Method `intersection` creates a third set which is the set-theoretic intersection of two existing sets (i.e., an element of the third set's array is set to `false` if that element is `false` in either or both of the existing sets—otherwise, the element of the third set is set to `true`). Method `insertElement` inserts a new integer k into a set (by setting a[k] to `true`). Method `deleteElement` deletes integer m (by setting a[m] to `false`). Method `toSetString` returns a string containing a set as a list of numbers separated by spaces. Include only those elements that are present in the set. Use `---` to represent an empty set. Method `isEqualTo` determines whether two sets are equal. Write a program to test class `IntegerSet`. Instantiate several `IntegerSet` objects. Test that all your methods work properly.

8.14   *(Date Class)* Create class `Date` with the following capabilities:
a) Output the date in multiple formats, such as

```
MM/DD/YYYY
June 14, 1992
DDD YYYY
```

b) Use overloaded constructors to create `Date` objects initialized with dates of the formats in part (a). In the first case the constructor should receive three integer values. In the second case it should receive a `String` and two integer values. In the third case it should receive two integer values, the first of which represents the day number in the year. [*Hint:* To convert the string representation of the month to a numeric value, compare strings using the `equals` method. For example, if s1 and s2 are strings, the method call s1.equals(s2) returns `true` if the strings are identical and otherwise returns `false`.]

8.15   *(Huge Integer Class)* Create a class `HugeInteger` which uses a 40-element array of digits to store integers as large as 40 digits each. Provide methods `input`, `output`, `add` and `subtract`. For comparing `HugeInteger` objects, provide the following methods: `isEqualTo`, `isNotEqualTo`, `isGreaterThan`, `isLessThan`, `isGreaterThanOrEqualTo` and `isLessThanOrEqualTo`. Each of these is a predicate method that returns `true` if the relationship holds between the two `HugeInteger` objects and returns `false` if the relationship does not hold. Provide a predicate method `isZero`. If you feel ambitious, also provide methods `multiply`, `divide` and `remainder`. [*Note:* Primitive boolean values can be output as the word "true" or the word "false" with format specifier %b.]

9

Object-Oriented Programming: Inheritance

*Say not you know
another entirely,
till you have divided an
inheritance with him.*
—Johann Kasper Lavater

*This method is to define as
the number of a class the
class of all classes similar to
the given class.*
—Bertrand Russell

*Good as it is to inherit
a library, it is better to
collect one.*
—Augustine Birrell

*Save base authority from
others' books.*
—William Shakespeare

OBJECTIVES

In this chapter you will learn:

- How inheritance promotes software reusability.

- The notions of superclasses and subclasses.

- To use keyword **extends** to create a class that inherits attributes and behaviors from another class.

- To use access modifier **protected** to give subclass methods access to superclass members.

- To access superclass members with **super**.

- How constructors are used in inheritance hierarchies.

- The methods of class **Object**, the direct or indirect superclass of all classes in Java.

9.1 Introduction

This chapter continues our discussion of object-oriented programming (OOP) by introducing one of its primary features—inheritance, which is a form of software reuse in which a new class is created by absorbing an existing class's members and embellishing them with new or modified capabilities. With inheritance, programmers save time during program development by reusing proven and debugged high-quality software. This also increases the likelihood that a system will be implemented effectively.

When creating a class, rather than declaring completely new members, you can designate that the new class should inherit the members of an existing class. The existing class is called the superclass, and the new class is the subclass. (The C++ programming language refers to the superclass as the base class and the subclass as the derived class.) Each subclass can become the superclass for future subclasses.

A subclass normally adds its own fields and methods. Therefore, a subclass is more specific than its superclass and represents a more specialized group of objects. Typically, the subclass exhibits the behaviors of its superclass and additional behaviors that are specific to the subclass. This is why inheritance is sometimes referred to as specialization.

The direct superclass is the superclass from which the subclass explicitly inherits. An indirect superclass is any class above the direct superclass in the class hierarchy, which defines the inheritance relationships between classes. In Java, the class hierarchy begins with class Object (in package java.lang), which *every* class in Java directly or indirectly extends (or "inherits from"). Section 9.7 lists the methods of class Object, which every other class inherits. In the case of single inheritance, a class is derived from one direct superclass. Java, unlike C++, does not support multiple inheritance (which occurs when a class is derived from more than one direct superclass). In Chapter 10, Object-Oriented Programming: Polymorphism, we explain how Java programmers can use interfaces to realize many of the benefits of multiple inheritance while avoiding the associated problems.

Experience in building software systems indicates that significant amounts of code deal with closely related special cases. When you are preoccupied with special cases, the details can obscure the big picture. With object-oriented programming, you focus on the commonalities among objects in the system rather than on the special cases.

We distinguish between the *is-a* relationship and the *has-a* relationship. *Is-a* represents inheritance. In an *is-a* relationship, an object of a subclass can also be treated as an object of its superclass. For example, a car *is a* vehicle. By contrast, *has-a* represents composition (see Chapter 8). In a *has-a* relationship, an object contains as members references to other objects. For example, a car *has a* steering wheel (and a car object has a reference to a steering wheel object).

New classes can inherit from classes in class libraries. Organizations develop their own class libraries and can take advantage of others available worldwide. Some day, most new software likely will be constructed from standardized reusable components, just as automobiles and most computer hardware are constructed today. This will facilitate the development of more powerful, abundant and economical software.

9.2 Superclasses and Subclasses

Often, an object of one class *is an* object of another class as well. For example, in geometry, a rectangle *is a* quadrilateral (as are squares, parallelograms and trapezoids). Thus, in Java, class Rectangle can be said to inherit from class Quadrilateral. In this context, class Quadrilateral is a superclass and class Rectangle is a subclass. A rectangle *is a* specific type of quadrilateral, but it is incorrect to claim that every quadrilateral *is a* rectangle—the quadrilateral could be a parallelogram or some other shape. Figure 9.1 lists several simple examples of superclasses and subclasses—note that superclasses tend to be "more general" and subclasses "more specific."

Because every subclass object *is an* object of its superclass, and one superclass can have many subclasses, the set of objects represented by a superclass is typically larger than the set of objects represented by any of its subclasses. For example, the superclass Vehicle represents all vehicles, including cars, trucks, boats, bicycles and so on. By contrast, subclass Car represents a smaller, more specific subset of vehicles.

Superclass	Subclasses
Student	GraduateStudent, UndergraduateStudent
Shape	Circle, Triangle, Rectangle
Loan	CarLoan, HomeImprovementLoan, MortgageLoan
Employee	Faculty, Staff
BankAccount	CheckingAccount, SavingsAccount

Fig. 9.1 | Inheritance examples.

Inheritance relationships form tree-like hierarchical structures. A superclass exists in a hierarchical relationship with its subclasses. When classes participate in inheritance relationships, they become "affiliated" with other classes. A class becomes either a superclass, supplying members to other classes, or a subclass, inheriting its members from other classes. In some cases, a class is both a superclass and a subclass.

Let's develop a sample class hierarchy (Fig. 9.2), also called an inheritance hierarchy. A university community has thousands of members, including employees, students and alumni. Employees are either faculty or staff members. Faculty members are either administrators (e.g., deans and department chairpersons) or teachers. Note that the hierarchy could contain many other classes. For example, students can be graduate or undergraduate students. Undergraduate students can be freshmen, sophomores, juniors or seniors.

Each arrow in the hierarchy represents an *is a* relationship. As we follow the arrows in this class hierarchy, we can state, for instance, that "an Employee *is a* CommunityMember" and "a Teacher *is a* Faculty member." CommunityMember is the direct superclass of Employee, Student and Alumnus, and is an indirect superclass of all the other classes in the diagram. Starting from the bottom of the diagram, the reader can follow the arrows and apply the *is a* relationship up to the topmost superclass. For example, an Administrator *is a* Faculty member, *is an* Employee and *is a* CommunityMember.

Now consider the Shape inheritance hierarchy in Fig. 9.3. This hierarchy begins with superclass Shape, which is extended by subclasses TwoDimensionalShape and ThreeDimensionalShape—Shapes are either TwoDimensionalShapes or ThreeDimensionalShapes. The third level of this hierarchy contains some more specific types of TwoDimensionalShapes and ThreeDimensionalShapes. As in Fig. 9.2, we can follow the arrows from the bottom of the diagram to the topmost superclass in this class hierarchy to identify several *is a* relationships. For instance, a Triangle *is a* TwoDimensionalShape and *is a* Shape, while a Sphere *is a* ThreeDimensionalShape and *is a* Shape. Note that this hierarchy could contain many other classes. For example, ellipses and trapezoids are TwoDimensionalShapes.

Not every class relationship is an inheritance relationship. In Chapter 8, we discussed the *has-a* relationship, in which classes have members that are references to objects of other classes. Such relationships create classes by composition of existing classes. For example,

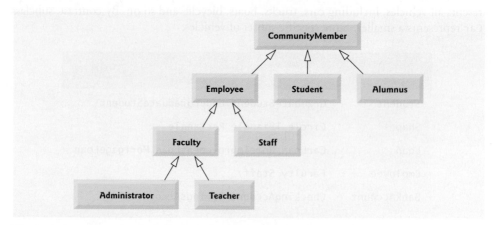

Fig. 9.2 | Inheritance hierarchy for university CommunityMembers.

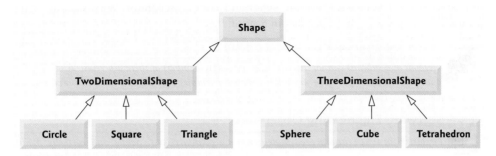

Fig. 9.3 | Inheritance hierarchy for Shapes.

given the classes Employee, BirthDate and TelephoneNumber, it is improper to say that an Employee *is a* BirthDate or that an Employee *is a* TelephoneNumber. However, an Employee *has a* BirthDate, and an Employee *has a* TelephoneNumber.

It is possible to treat superclass objects and subclass objects similarly—their commonalities are expressed in the members of the superclass. Objects of all classes that extend a common superclass can be treated as objects of that superclass (i.e., such objects have an *is a* relationship with the superclass). However, superclass objects cannot be treated as objects of their subclasses. For example, all cars are vehicles, but not all vehicles are cars (the other vehicles could be trucks, planes or bicycles, for example). Later in this chapter and in Chapter 10, Object-Oriented Programming: Polymorphism, we consider many examples that take advantage of the *is a* relationship.

One problem with inheritance is that a subclass can inherit methods that it does not need or should not have. Even when a superclass method is appropriate for a subclass, that subclass often needs a customized version of the method. In such cases, the subclass can override (redefine) the superclass method with an appropriate implementation, as we will see often in the chapter's code examples.

9.3 protected Members

Chapter 8 discussed access modifiers public and private. A class's public members are accessible wherever the program has a reference to an object of that class or one of its subclasses. A class's private members are accessible only from within the class itself. A superclass's private members are not inherited by its subclasses. In this section, we introduce access modifier protected. Using protected access offers an intermediate level of access between public and private. A superclass's protected members can be accessed by members of that superclass, by members of its subclasses and by members of other classes in the same package (i.e., protected members also have package access).

All public and protected superclass members retain their original access modifier when they become members of the subclass (i.e., public members of the superclass become public members of the subclass, and protected members of the superclass become protected members of the subclass).

Subclass methods can refer to public and protected members inherited from the superclass simply by using the member names. When a subclass method overrides a superclass method, the superclass method can be accessed from the subclass by preceding the superclass method name with keyword super and a dot (.) separator. We discuss accessing overridden members of the superclass in Section 9.4.

Software Engineering Observation 9.1

Methods of a subclass cannot directly access private members of their superclass. A subclass can change the state of private superclass instance variables only through non-private methods provided in the superclass and inherited by the subclass.

Software Engineering Observation 9.2

Declaring private instance variables helps programmers test, debug and correctly modify systems. If a subclass could access its superclass's private instance variables, classes that inherit from that subclass could access the instance variables as well. This would propagate access to what should be private instance variables, and the benefits of information hiding would be lost.

9.4 Relationship between Superclasses and Subclasses

In this section, we use an inheritance hierarchy containing types of employees in a company's payroll application to discuss the relationship between a superclass and its subclass. In this company, commission employees (who will be represented as objects of a superclass) are paid a percentage of their sales, while base-salaried commission employees (who will be represented as objects of a subclass) receive a base salary plus a percentage of their sales.

We divide our discussion of the relationship between commission employees and base-salaried commission employees into five examples. The first example declares class CommissionEmployee, which directly inherits from class Object and declares as private instance variables a first name, last name, social security number, commission rate and gross (i.e., total) sales amount.

The second example declares class BasePlusCommissionEmployee, which also directly inherits from class Object and declares as private instance variables a first name, last name, social security number, commission rate, gross sales amount and base salary. We create the latter class by writing every line of code the class requires—we will soon see that it is much more efficient to create this class by inheriting from class CommissionEmployee.

The third example declares a separate BasePlusCommissionEmployee2 class that extends class CommissionEmployee (i.e., a BasePlusCommissionEmployee2 *is a* CommissionEmployee who also has a base salary) and attempts to access class CommissionEmployee's private members—this results in compilation errors, because the subclass cannot access the superclass's private instance variables.

The fourth example shows that if CommissionEmployee's instance variables are declared as protected, a BasePlusCommissionEmployee3 class that extends class CommissionEmployee2 can access that data directly. For this purpose, we declare class CommissionEmployee2 with protected instance variables. Both of the BasePlusCommissionEmployee classes contain identical functionality, but we show how the class BasePlusCommissionEmployee3 is easier to create and manage.

After we discuss the convenience of using protected instance variables, we create the fifth example, which sets the CommissionEmployee instance variables back to private in class CommissionEmployee3 to enforce good software engineering. Then we show how a separate BasePlusCommissionEmployee4 class, which extends class CommissionEmployee3, can use CommissionEmployee3's public methods to manipulate CommissionEmployee3's private instance variables.

9.4.1 Creating and Using a CommissionEmployee Class

We begin by declaring class CommissionEmployee (Fig. 9.4). Line 4 begins the class declaration and indicates that class CommissionEmployee **extends** (i.e., inherits from) class Object (from package java.lang). Java programmers use inheritance to create classes from existing classes. In fact, every class in Java (except Object) extends an existing class. Because class CommissionEmployee extends class Object, class CommissionEmployee inherits the methods of class Object—class Object does not have any fields. In fact, every Java class directly or indirectly inherits Object's methods. If a class does not specify that it extends another class, the new class implicitly extends Object. For this reason, programmers typically do not include "extends Object" in their code—we do so in this example only for demonstration purposes.

Software Engineering Observation 9.3

The Java compiler sets the superclass of a class to Object when the class declaration does not explicitly extend a superclass.

```
 1   // Fig. 9.4: CommissionEmployee.java
 2   // CommissionEmployee class represents a commission employee.
 3
 4   public class CommissionEmployee extends Object
 5   {
 6      private String firstName;
 7      private String lastName;
 8      private String socialSecurityNumber;
 9      private double grossSales; // gross weekly sales
10      private double commissionRate; // commission percentage
11
12      // five-argument constructor
13      public CommissionEmployee( String first, String last, String ssn,
14         double sales, double rate )
15      {
16         // implicit call to Object constructor occurs here
17         firstName = first;
18         lastName = last;
19         socialSecurityNumber = ssn;
20         setGrossSales( sales ); // validate and store gross sales
21         setCommissionRate( rate ); // validate and store commission rate
22      } // end five-argument CommissionEmployee constructor
23
24      // set first name
25      public void setFirstName( String first )
26      {
27         firstName = first;
28      } // end method setFirstName
29
30      // return first name
31      public String getFirstName()
32      {
```

Fig. 9.4 | CommissionEmployee class represents an employee paid a percentage of gross sales. (Part 1 of 3.)

```
33           return firstName;
34     } // end method getFirstName
35
36     // set last name
37     public void setLastName( String last )
38     {
39         lastName = last;
40     } // end method setLastName
41
42     // return last name
43     public String getLastName()
44     {
45         return lastName;
46     } // end method getLastName
47
48     // set social security number
49     public void setSocialSecurityNumber( String ssn )
50     {
51         socialSecurityNumber = ssn; // should validate
52     } // end method setSocialSecurityNumber
53
54     // return social security number
55     public String getSocialSecurityNumber()
56     {
57         return socialSecurityNumber;
58     } // end method getSocialSecurityNumber
59
60     // set gross sales amount
61     public void setGrossSales( double sales )
62     {
63         grossSales = ( sales < 0.0 ) ? 0.0 : sales;
64     } // end method setGrossSales
65
66     // return gross sales amount
67     public double getGrossSales()
68     {
69         return grossSales;
70     } // end method getGrossSales
71
72     // set commission rate
73     public void setCommissionRate( double rate )
74     {
75         commissionRate = ( rate > 0.0 && rate < 1.0 ) ? rate : 0.0;
76     } // end method setCommissionRate
77
78     // return commission rate
79     public double getCommissionRate()
80     {
81         return commissionRate;
82     } // end method getCommissionRate
83
```

Fig. 9.4 | CommissionEmployee class represents an employee paid a percentage of gross sales. (Part 2 of 3.)

```
84        // calculate earnings
85        public double earnings()
86        {
87           return commissionRate * grossSales;
88        } // end method earnings
89
90        // return String representation of CommissionEmployee object
91        public String toString()
92        {
93           return String.format( "%s: %s %s\n%s: %s\n%s: %.2f\n%s: %.2f",
94              "commission employee", firstName, lastName,
95              "social security number", socialSecurityNumber,
96              "gross sales", grossSales,
97              "commission rate", commissionRate );
98        } // end method toString
99     } // end class CommissionEmployee
```

Fig. 9.4 | CommissionEmployee class represents an employee paid a percentage of gross sales. (Part 3 of 3.)

The public services of class CommissionEmployee include a constructor (lines 13–22) and methods earnings (lines 85–88) and toString (lines 91–98). Lines 25–82 declare public *get* and *set* methods for manipulating the class's instance variables (declared in lines 6–10) firstName, lastName, socialSecurityNumber, grossSales and commissionRate. Class CommissionEmployee declares each of its instance variables as private, so objects of other classes cannot directly access these variables. Declaring instance variables as private and providing *get* and *set* methods to manipulate and validate the instance variables helps enforce good software engineering. Methods setGrossSales and setCommissionRate, for example, validate their arguments before assigning the values to instance variables gross-Sales and commissionRate, respectively.

Constructors are not inherited, so class CommissionEmployee does not inherit class Object's constructor. However, class CommissionEmployee's constructor calls class Object's constructor implicitly. In fact, the first task of any subclass constructor is to call its direct superclass's constructor, either explicitly or implicitly (if no constructor call is specified), to ensure that the instance variables inherited from the superclass are initialized properly. The syntax for calling a superclass constructor explicitly is discussed in Section 9.4.3. If the code does not include an explicit call to the superclass constructor, Java implicitly calls the superclass's default or no-argument constructor. The comment in line 16 of Fig. 9.4 indicates where the implicit call to the superclass Object's default constructor is made (the programmer does not write the code for this call). Object's default (empty) constructor does nothing. Note that even if a class does not have constructors, the default constructor that the compiler implicitly declares for the class will call the superclass's default or no-argument constructor.

After the implicit call to Object's constructor occurs, lines 17–21 of CommissionEmployee's constructor assign values to the class's instance variables. Note that we do not validate the values of arguments first, last and ssn before assigning them to the corresponding instance variables. We could validate the first and last names—perhaps by ensuring that they are of a reasonable length. Similarly, a social security number could be validated to ensure that it contains nine digits, with or without dashes (e.g., 123-45-6789 or 123456789).

Method earnings (lines 85–88) calculates a CommissionEmployee's earnings. Line 87 multiplies the commissionRate by the grossSales and returns the result.

Method toString (lines 91–98) is special—it is one of the methods that every class inherits directly or indirectly from class Object, which is the root of the Java class hierarchy. Section 9.7 summarizes class Object's methods. Method toString returns a String representing an object. This method is called implicitly by a program whenever an object must be converted to a string representation, such as when an object is output by printf or String method format using the %s format specifier. Class Object's toString method returns a String that includes the name of the object's class. It is primarily a placeholder that can be overridden by a subclass to specify an appropriate string representation of the data in a subclass object. Method toString of class CommissionEmployee overrides (redefines) class Object's toString method. When invoked, CommissionEmployee's toString method uses String method format to return a String containing information about the CommissionEmployee. To override a superclass method, a subclass must declare a method with the same signature (method name, number of parameters, parameter types and order of parameter types) as the superclass method—Object's toString method takes no parameters, so CommissionEmployee declares toString with no parameters.

Common Programming Error 9.1

It is a syntax error to override a method with a more restricted access modifier—a public method of the superclass cannot become a protected or private method in the subclass; a protected method of the superclass cannot become a private method in the subclass. Doing so would break the is a relationship in which it is required that all subclass objects be able to respond to method calls that are made to public methods declared in the superclass. If a public method could be overridden as a protected or private method, the subclass objects would not be able to respond to the same method calls as superclass objects. Once a method is declared public in a superclass, the method remains public for all that class's direct and indirect subclasses.

Figure 9.5 tests class CommissionEmployee. Lines 9–10 instantiate a CommissionEmployee object and invoke CommissionEmployee's constructor (lines 13–22 of Fig. 9.4) to initialize it with "Sue" as the first name, "Jones" as the last name, "222-22-2222" as the social security number, 10000 as the gross sales amount and .06 as the commission rate. Lines 15–24 use CommissionEmployee's *get* methods to retrieve the object's instance vari-

```
1   // Fig. 9.5: CommissionEmployeeTest.java
2   // Testing class CommissionEmployee.
3
4   public class CommissionEmployeeTest
5   {
6      public static void main( String args[] )
7      {
8         // instantiate CommissionEmployee object
9         CommissionEmployee employee = new CommissionEmployee(
10           "Sue", "Jones", "222-22-2222", 10000, .06 );
11
```

Fig. 9.5 | CommissionEmployee class test program. (Part 1 of 2.)

```
12          // get commission employee data
13          System.out.println(
14             "Employee information obtained by get methods: \n" );
15          System.out.printf( "%s %s\n", "First name is",
16             employee.getFirstName() );
17          System.out.printf( "%s %s\n", "Last name is",
18             employee.getLastName() );
19          System.out.printf( "%s %s\n", "Social security number is",
20             employee.getSocialSecurityNumber() );
21          System.out.printf( "%s %.2f\n", "Gross sales is",
22             employee.getGrossSales() );
23          System.out.printf( "%s %.2f\n", "Commission rate is",
24             employee.getCommissionRate() );
25
26          employee.setGrossSales( 500 ); // set gross sales
27          employee.setCommissionRate( .1 ); // set commission rate
28
29          System.out.printf( "\n%s:\n\n%s\n",
30             "Updated employee information obtained by toString", employee );
31       } // end main
32    } // end class CommissionEmployeeTest
```

```
Employee information obtained by get methods:

First name is Sue
Last name is Jones
Social security number is 222-22-2222
Gross sales is 10000.00
Commission rate is 0.06

Updated employee information obtained by toString:

commission employee: Sue Jones
social security number: 222-22-2222
gross sales: 500.00
commission rate: 0.10
```

Fig. 9.5 | CommissionEmployee class test program. (Part 2 of 2.)

able values for output. Lines 26–27 invoke the object's methods setGrossSales and set-CommissionRate to change the values of instance variables grossSales and commissionRate. Lines 29–30 output the string representation of the updated CommissionEmployee. Note that when an object is output using the %s format specifier, the object's toString method is invoked implicitly to obtain the object's string representation.

9.4.2 Creating a BasePlusCommissionEmployee Class without Using Inheritance

We now discuss the second part of our introduction to inheritance by declaring and testing (a completely new and independent) class BasePlusCommissionEmployee (Fig. 9.6), which contains a first name, last name, social security number, gross sales amount, commission rate and base salary. Class BasePlusCommissionEmployee's public services include a BasePlusCommissionEmployee constructor (lines 15–25) and methods earnings

```
1    // Fig. 9.6: BasePlusCommissionEmployee.java
2    // BasePlusCommissionEmployee class represents an employee that receives
3    // a base salary in addition to commission.
4
5    public class BasePlusCommissionEmployee
6    {
7       private String firstName;
8       private String lastName;
9       private String socialSecurityNumber;
10      private double grossSales; // gross weekly sales
11      private double commissionRate; // commission percentage
12      private double baseSalary; // base salary per week
13
14      // six-argument constructor
15      public BasePlusCommissionEmployee( String first, String last,
16         String ssn, double sales, double rate, double salary )
17      {
18         // implicit call to Object constructor occurs here
19         firstName = first;
20         lastName = last;
21         socialSecurityNumber = ssn;
22         setGrossSales( sales ); // validate and store gross sales
23         setCommissionRate( rate ); // validate and store commission rate
24         setBaseSalary( salary ); // validate and store base salary
25      } // end six-argument BasePlusCommissionEmployee constructor
26
27      // set first name
28      public void setFirstName( String first )
29      {
30         firstName = first;
31      } // end method setFirstName
32
33      // return first name
34      public String getFirstName()
35      {
36         return firstName;
37      } // end method getFirstName
38
39      // set last name
40      public void setLastName( String last )
41      {
42         lastName = last;
43      } // end method setLastName
44
45      // return last name
46      public String getLastName()
47      {
48         return lastName;
49      } // end method getLastName
50
```

Fig. 9.6 | BasePlusCommissionEmployee class represents an employee who receives a base salary in addition to a commission. (Part 1 of 3.)

```
51    // set social security number
52    public void setSocialSecurityNumber( String ssn )
53    {
54       socialSecurityNumber = ssn; // should validate
55    } // end method setSocialSecurityNumber
56
57    // return social security number
58    public String getSocialSecurityNumber()
59    {
60       return socialSecurityNumber;
61    } // end method getSocialSecurityNumber
62
63    // set gross sales amount
64    public void setGrossSales( double sales )
65    {
66       grossSales = ( sales < 0.0 ) ? 0.0 : sales;
67    } // end method setGrossSales
68
69    // return gross sales amount
70    public double getGrossSales()
71    {
72       return grossSales;
73    } // end method getGrossSales
74
75    // set commission rate
76    public void setCommissionRate( double rate )
77    {
78       commissionRate = ( rate > 0.0 && rate < 1.0 ) ? rate : 0.0;
79    } // end method setCommissionRate
80
81    // return commission rate
82    public double getCommissionRate()
83    {
84       return commissionRate;
85    } // end method getCommissionRate
86
87    // set base salary
88    public void setBaseSalary( double salary )
89    {
90       baseSalary = ( salary < 0.0 ) ? 0.0 : salary;
91    } // end method setBaseSalary
92
93    // return base salary
94    public double getBaseSalary()
95    {
96       return baseSalary;
97    } // end method getBaseSalary
98
99    // calculate earnings
100   public double earnings()
101   {
```

Fig. 9.6 | `BasePlusCommissionEmployee` class represents an employee who receives a base salary in addition to a commission. (Part 2 of 3.)

```
102          return baseSalary + ( commissionRate * grossSales );
103       } // end method earnings
104
105       // return String representation of BasePlusCommissionEmployee
106       public String toString()
107       {
108          return String.format(
109             "%s: %s %s\n%s: %s\n%s: %.2f\n%s: %.2f\n%s: %.2f",
110             "base-salaried commission employee", firstName, lastName,
111             "social security number", socialSecurityNumber,
112             "gross sales", grossSales, "commission rate", commissionRate,
113             "base salary", baseSalary );
114       } // end method toString
115    } // end class BasePlusCommissionEmployee
```

Fig. 9.6 | `BasePlusCommissionEmployee` class represents an employee who receives a base salary in addition to a commission. (Part 3 of 3.)

(lines 100–103) and `toString` (lines 106–114). Lines 28–97 declare `public` *get* and *set* methods for the class's `private` instance variables (declared in lines 7–12) `firstName`, `lastName`, `socialSecurityNumber`, `grossSales`, `commissionRate` and `baseSalary`. These variables and methods encapsulate all the necessary features of a base-salaried commission employee. Note the similarity between this class and class `CommissionEmployee` (Fig. 9.4)—in this example, we will not yet exploit that similarity.

Note that class `BasePlusCommissionEmployee` does not specify "extends Object" in line 5, so the class implicitly extends `Object`. Also note that, like class `CommissionEmployee`'s constructor (lines 13–22 of Fig. 9.4), class `BasePlusCommissionEmployee`'s constructor invokes class `Object`'s default constructor implicitly, as noted in the comment in line 18.

Class `BasePlusCommissionEmployee`'s `earnings` method (lines 100–103) computes the earnings of a base-salaried commission employee. Line 102 returns the result of adding the employee's base salary to the product of the commission rate and the employee's gross sales.

Class `BasePlusCommissionEmployee` overrides `Object` method `toString` to return a `String` containing the `BasePlusCommissionEmployee`'s information. Once again, we use format specifier `%.2f` to format the gross sales, commission rate and base salary with two digits of precision to the right of the decimal point (line 109).

Figure 9.7 tests class `BasePlusCommissionEmployee`. Lines 9–11 instantiate a `BasePlusCommissionEmployee` object and pass "Bob", "Lewis", "333-33-3333", 5000, .04 and 300 to the constructor as the first name, last name, social security number, gross sales, commission rate and base salary, respectively. Lines 16–27 use `BasePlusCommissionEmployee`'s *get* methods to retrieve the values of the object's instance variables for output. Line 29 invokes the object's `setBaseSalary` method to change the base salary. Method `setBaseSalary` (Fig. 9.6, lines 88–91) ensures that instance variable `baseSalary` is not assigned a negative value, because an employee's base salary cannot be negative. Lines 31–33 of Fig. 9.7 invoke the object's `toString` method explicitly to get the object's string representation.

```
1   // Fig. 9.7: BasePlusCommissionEmployeeTest.java
2   // Testing class BasePlusCommissionEmployee.
3
4   public class BasePlusCommissionEmployeeTest
5   {
6      public static void main( String args[] )
7      {
8         // instantiate BasePlusCommissionEmployee object
9         BasePlusCommissionEmployee employee =
10           new BasePlusCommissionEmployee(
11           "Bob", "Lewis", "333-33-3333", 5000, .04, 300 );
12
13        // get base-salaried commission employee data
14        System.out.println(
15           "Employee information obtained by get methods: \n" );
16        System.out.printf( "%s %s\n", "First name is",
17           employee.getFirstName() );
18        System.out.printf( "%s %s\n", "Last name is",
19           employee.getLastName() );
20        System.out.printf( "%s %s\n", "Social security number is",
21           employee.getSocialSecurityNumber() );
22        System.out.printf( "%s %.2f\n", "Gross sales is",
23           employee.getGrossSales() );
24        System.out.printf( "%s %.2f\n", "Commission rate is",
25           employee.getCommissionRate() );
26        System.out.printf( "%s %.2f\n", "Base salary is",
27           employee.getBaseSalary() );
28
29        employee.setBaseSalary( 1000 ); // set base salary
30
31        System.out.printf( "\n%s:\n\n%s\n",
32           "Updated employee information obtained by toString",
33            employee.toString() );
34     } // end main
35  } // end class BasePlusCommissionEmployeeTest
```

```
Employee information obtained by get methods:

First name is Bob
Last name is Lewis
Social security number is 333-33-3333
Gross sales is 5000.00
Commission rate is 0.04
Base salary is 300.00

Updated employee information obtained by toString:

base-salaried commission employee: Bob Lewis
social security number: 333-33-3333
gross sales: 5000.00
commission rate: 0.04
base salary: 1000.00
```

Fig. 9.7 │ BasePlusCommissionEmployee test program.

Much of class `BasePlusCommissionEmployee`'s code (Fig. 9.6) is similar, if not identical, to that of class `CommissionEmployee` (Fig. 9.4). For example, in class `BasePlusCommissionEmployee`, private instance variables `firstName` and `lastName` and methods `setFirstName`, `getFirstName`, `setLastName` and `getLastName` are identical to those of class `CommissionEmployee`. Classes `CommissionEmployee` and `BasePlusCommissionEmployee` also both contain private instance variables `socialSecurityNumber`, `commissionRate` and `grossSales`, as well as *get* and *set* methods to manipulate these variables. In addition, the `BasePlusCommissionEmployee` constructor is almost identical to that of class `CommissionEmployee`, except that `BasePlusCommissionEmployee`'s constructor also sets the `baseSalary`. The other additions to class `BasePlusCommissionEmployee` are private instance variable `baseSalary` and methods `setBaseSalary` and `getBaseSalary`. Class `BasePlusCommissionEmployee`'s `toString` method is nearly identical to that of class `CommissionEmployee` except that `BasePlusCommissionEmployee`'s `toString` also outputs instance variable `baseSalary` with two digits of precision to the right of the decimal point.

We literally copied code from class `CommissionEmployee` and pasted it into class `BasePlusCommissionEmployee`, then modified class `BasePlusCommissionEmployee` to include a base salary and methods that manipulate the base salary. This "copy-and-paste" approach is often error prone and time consuming. Worse yet, it can spread many physical copies of the same code throughout a system, creating a code-maintenance nightmare. Is there a way to "absorb" the instance variables and methods of one class in a way that makes them part of other classes without duplicating code? In the next several examples, we answer this question, using a more elegant approach to building classes that emphasizes the benefits of inheritance.

Software Engineering Observation 9.4

Copying and pasting code from one class to another can spread errors across multiple source-code files. To avoid duplicating code (and possibly errors), use inheritance or, in some cases, composition, rather than the "copy-and-paste" approach, in situations where you want one class to "absorb" the instance variables and methods of another class.

Software Engineering Observation 9.5

With inheritance, the common instance variables and methods of all the classes in the hierarchy are declared in a superclass. When changes are required for these common features, software developers need only to make the changes in the superclass—subclasses then inherit the changes. Without inheritance, changes would need to be made to all the source-code files that contain a copy of the code in question.

9.4.3 Creating a CommissionEmployee–BasePlusCommissionEmployee Inheritance Hierarchy

Now we declare class `BasePlusCommissionEmployee2` (Fig. 9.8), which extends class `CommissionEmployee` (Fig. 9.4). A `BasePlusCommissionEmployee2` object *is a* `CommissionEmployee` (because inheritance passes on the capabilities of class `CommissionEmployee`), but class `BasePlusCommissionEmployee2` also has instance variable `baseSalary` (Fig. 9.8, line 6). Keyword `extends` in line 4 of the class declaration indicates inheritance. As a subclass, `BasePlusCommissionEmployee2` inherits the `public` and `protected` instance variables and methods of class `CommissionEmployee`. The constructor of class `CommissionEmployee` is not inherited. Thus, the `public` services of `BasePlusCommissionEmployee2` include its constructor (lines 9–16), `public` methods inherited from class `CommissionEmployee`, method `setBaseSalary` (lines 19–22), method `getBaseSalary` (lines 25–28), method `earnings` (lines 31–35) and method `toString` (lines 38–47).

```
1   // Fig. 9.8: BasePlusCommissionEmployee2.java
2   // BasePlusCommissionEmployee2 inherits from class CommissionEmployee.
3
4   public class BasePlusCommissionEmployee2 extends CommissionEmployee
5   {
6      private double baseSalary; // base salary per week
7
8      // six-argument constructor
9      public BasePlusCommissionEmployee2( String first, String last,
10        String ssn, double sales, double rate, double salary )
11     {
12        // explicit call to superclass CommissionEmployee constructor
13        super( first, last, ssn, sales, rate );
14
15        setBaseSalary( salary ); // validate and store base salary
16     } // end six-argument BasePlusCommissionEmployee2 constructor
17
18     // set base salary
19     public void setBaseSalary( double salary )
20     {
21        baseSalary = ( salary < 0.0 ) ? 0.0 : salary;
22     } // end method setBaseSalary
23
24     // return base salary
25     public double getBaseSalary()
26     {
27        return baseSalary;
28     } // end method getBaseSalary
29
30     // calculate earnings
31     public double earnings()
32     {
33        // not allowed: commissionRate and grossSales private in superclass
34        return baseSalary + ( commissionRate * grossSales );
35     } // end method earnings
36
37     // return String representation of BasePlusCommissionEmployee2
38     public String toString()
39     {
40        // not allowed: attempts to access private superclass members
41        return String.format(
42           "%s: %s %s\n%s: %s\n%s: %.2f\n%s: %.2f\n%s: %.2f",
43           "base-salaried commission employee", firstName, lastName,
44           "social security number", socialSecurityNumber,
45           "gross sales", grossSales, "commission rate", commissionRate,
46           "base salary", baseSalary );
47     } // end method toString
48  } // end class BasePlusCommissionEmployee2
```

Fig. 9.8 | `private` superclass members cannot be accessed in a subclass. (Part 1 of 2.)

```
BasePlusCommissionEmployee2.java:34: commissionRate has private access in
CommissionEmployee
      return baseSalary + ( commissionRate * grossSales );
                             ^
BasePlusCommissionEmployee2.java:34: grossSales has private access in
CommissionEmployee
      return baseSalary + ( commissionRate * grossSales );
                                              ^
BasePlusCommissionEmployee2.java:43: firstName has private access in
CommissionEmployee
         "base-salaried commission employee", firstName, lastName,
                                               ^
BasePlusCommissionEmployee2.java:43: lastName has private access in
CommissionEmployee
         "base-salaried commission employee", firstName, lastName,
                                                          ^
BasePlusCommissionEmployee2.java:44: socialSecurityNumber has private access
in CommissionEmployee
         "social security number", socialSecurityNumber,
                                   ^
BasePlusCommissionEmployee2.java:45: grossSales has private access in
CommissionEmployee
         "gross sales", grossSales, "commission rate", commissionRate,
                        ^
BasePlusCommissionEmployee2.java:45: commissionRate has private access in
CommissionEmployee
         "gross sales", grossSales, "commission rate", commissionRate,
                                                        ^
7 errors
```

Fig. 9.8 | private superclass members cannot be accessed in a subclass. (Part 2 of 2.)

Each subclass constructor must implicitly or explicitly call its superclass constructor to ensure that the instance variables inherited from the superclass are initialized properly. BasePlusCommissionEmployee2's six-argument constructor (lines 9–16) explicitly calls class CommissionEmployee's five-argument constructor to initialize the superclass portion of a BasePlusCommissionEmployee2 object (i.e., variables firstName, lastName, social-SecurityNumber, grossSales and commissionRate). Line 13 in BasePlusCommission-Employee2's six-argument constructor invokes the CommissionEmployee's five-argument constructor (declared at lines 13–22 of Fig. 9.4) by using the superclass constructor call syntax—keyword super, followed by a set of parentheses containing the superclass constructor arguments. The arguments first, last, ssn, sales and rate are used to initialize superclass members firstName, lastName, socialSecurityNumber, grossSales and commissionRate, respectively. If BasePlusCommissionEmployee2's constructor did not invoke CommissionEmployee's constructor explicitly, Java would attempt to invoke class CommissionEmployee's no-argument or default constructor—but the class does not have such a constructor, so the compiler would issue an error. The explicit superclass constructor call in line 13 of Fig. 9.8 must be the first statement in the subclass constructor's body. Also, when a superclass contains a no-argument constructor, you can use super() to call that constructor explicitly, but this is rarely done.

Common Programming Error 9.2

A compilation error occurs if a subclass constructor calls one of its superclass constructors with arguments that do not match exactly the number and types of parameters specified in one of the superclass constructor declarations.

The compiler generates errors for line 34 of Fig. 9.8 because superclass Commission-Employee's instance variables commissionRate and grossSales are private—subclass BasePlusCommissionEmployee2's methods are not allowed to access superclass CommissionEmployee's private instance variables. Note that we used red text in Fig. 9.8 to indicate erroneous code. The compiler issues additional errors at lines 43–45 of BasePlusCommissionEmployee2's toString method for the same reason. The errors in BasePlusCommissionEmployee2 could have been prevented by using the *get* methods inherited from class CommissionEmployee. For example, line 34 could have used getCommissionRate and getGrossSales to access CommissionEmployee's private instance variables commissionRate and grossSales, respectively. Lines 43–45 also could have used appropriate *get* methods to retrieve the values of the superclass's instance variables.

9.4.4 CommissionEmployee–BasePlusCommissionEmployee Inheritance Hierarchy Using protected Instance Variables

To enable class BasePlusCommissionEmployee to directly access superclass instance variables firstName, lastName, socialSecurityNumber, grossSales and commissionRate, we can declare those members as protected in the superclass. As we discussed in Section 9.3, a superclass's protected members *are* inherited by all subclasses of that superclass. Class CommissionEmployee2 (Fig. 9.9) is a modification of class CommissionEmployee (Fig. 9.4) that declares instance variables firstName, lastName, socialSecurityNumber, grossSales and commissionRate as protected (Fig. 9.9, lines 6–10) rather than private. Other than the change in the class name (and thus the change in the constructor name) to CommissionEmployee2, the rest of the class declaration in Fig. 9.9 is identical to that of Fig. 9.4.

```java
// Fig. 9.9: CommissionEmployee2.java
// CommissionEmployee2 class represents a commission employee.

public class CommissionEmployee2
{
   protected String firstName;
   protected String lastName;
   protected String socialSecurityNumber;
   protected double grossSales; // gross weekly sales
   protected double commissionRate; // commission percentage

   // five-argument constructor
   public CommissionEmployee2( String first, String last, String ssn,
      double sales, double rate )
   {
      // implicit call to Object constructor occurs here
      firstName = first;
```

Fig. 9.9 | CommissionEmployee2 with protected instance variables. (Part 1 of 3.)

```
18              lastName = last;
19              socialSecurityNumber = ssn;
20              setGrossSales( sales ); // validate and store gross sales
21              setCommissionRate( rate ); // validate and store commission rate
22          } // end five-argument CommissionEmployee2 constructor
23
24          // set first name
25          public void setFirstName( String first )
26          {
27              firstName = first;
28          } // end method setFirstName
29
30          // return first name
31          public String getFirstName()
32          {
33              return firstName;
34          } // end method getFirstName
35
36          // set last name
37          public void setLastName( String last )
38          {
39              lastName = last;
40          } // end method setLastName
41
42          // return last name
43          public String getLastName()
44          {
45              return lastName;
46          } // end method getLastName
47
48          // set social security number
49          public void setSocialSecurityNumber( String ssn )
50          {
51              socialSecurityNumber = ssn; // should validate
52          } // end method setSocialSecurityNumber
53
54          // return social security number
55          public String getSocialSecurityNumber()
56          {
57              return socialSecurityNumber;
58          } // end method getSocialSecurityNumber
59
60          // set gross sales amount
61          public void setGrossSales( double sales )
62          {
63              grossSales = ( sales < 0.0 ) ? 0.0 : sales;
64          } // end method setGrossSales
65
66          // return gross sales amount
67          public double getGrossSales()
68          {
69              return grossSales;
70          } // end method getGrossSales
```

Fig. 9.9 | CommissionEmployee2 with protected instance variables. (Part 2 of 3.)

```
71
72        // set commission rate
73        public void setCommissionRate( double rate )
74        {
75           commissionRate = ( rate > 0.0 && rate < 1.0 ) ? rate : 0.0;
76        } // end method setCommissionRate
77
78        // return commission rate
79        public double getCommissionRate()
80        {
81           return commissionRate;
82        } // end method getCommissionRate
83
84        // calculate earnings
85        public double earnings()
86        {
87           return commissionRate * grossSales;
88        } // end method earnings
89
90        // return String representation of CommissionEmployee2 object
91        public String toString()
92        {
93           return String.format( "%s: %s %s\n%s: %s\n%s: %.2f\n%s: %.2f",
94              "commission employee", firstName, lastName,
95              "social security number", socialSecurityNumber,
96              "gross sales", grossSales,
97              "commission rate", commissionRate );
98        } // end method toString
99     } // end class CommissionEmployee2
```

Fig. 9.9 | CommissionEmployee2 with protected instance variables. (Part 3 of 3.)

We could have declared the superclass CommissionEmployee2's instance variables firstName, lastName, socialSecurityNumber, grossSales and commissionRate as public to enable subclass BasePlusCommissionEmployee2 to access the superclass instance variables. However, declaring public instance variables is poor software engineering because it allows unrestricted access to the instance variables, greatly increasing the chance of errors. With protected instance variables, the subclass gets access to the instance variables, but classes that are not subclasses and classes that are not in the same package cannot access these variables directly—recall that protected class members are also visible to other classes in the same package.

Class BasePlusCommissionEmployee3 (Fig. 9.10) is a modification of class BasePlusCommissionEmployee2 (Fig. 9.8) that extends CommissionEmployee2 (line 5) rather than class CommissionEmployee. Objects of class BasePlusCommissionEmployee3 inherit CommissionEmployee2's protected instance variables firstName, lastName, socialSecurityNumber, grossSales and commissionRate—all these variables are now protected members of BasePlusCommissionEmployee3. As a result, the compiler does not generate errors when compiling line 32 of method earnings and lines 40–42 of method toString. If another class extends BasePlusCommissionEmployee3, the new subclass also inherits the protected members.

```java
1   // Fig. 9.10: BasePlusCommissionEmployee3.java
2   // BasePlusCommissionEmployee3 inherits from CommissionEmployee2 and has
3   // access to CommissionEmployee2's protected members.
4
5   public class BasePlusCommissionEmployee3 extends CommissionEmployee2
6   {
7      private double baseSalary; // base salary per week
8
9      // six-argument constructor
10     public BasePlusCommissionEmployee3( String first, String last,
11        String ssn, double sales, double rate, double salary )
12     {
13        super( first, last, ssn, sales, rate );
14        setBaseSalary( salary ); // validate and store base salary
15     } // end six-argument BasePlusCommissionEmployee3 constructor
16
17     // set base salary
18     public void setBaseSalary( double salary )
19     {
20        baseSalary = ( salary < 0.0 ) ? 0.0 : salary;
21     } // end method setBaseSalary
22
23     // return base salary
24     public double getBaseSalary()
25     {
26        return baseSalary;
27     } // end method getBaseSalary
28
29     // calculate earnings
30     public double earnings()
31     {
32        return baseSalary + ( commissionRate * grossSales );
33     } // end method earnings
34
35     // return String representation of BasePlusCommissionEmployee3
36     public String toString()
37     {
38        return String.format(
39           "%s: %s %s\n%s: %s\n%s: %.2f\n%s: %.2f\n%s: %.2f",
40           "base-salaried commission employee", firstName, lastName,
41           "social security number", socialSecurityNumber,
42           "gross sales", grossSales, "commission rate", commissionRate,
43           "base salary", baseSalary );
44     } // end method toString
45  } // end class BasePlusCommissionEmployee3
```

Fig. 9.10 | BasePlusCommissionEmployee3 inherits protected instance variables from CommissionEmployee2.

Class BasePlusCommissionEmployee3 does not inherit class CommissionEmployee2's constructor. However, class BasePlusCommissionEmployee3's six-argument constructor (lines 10–15) calls class CommissionEmployee2's five-argument constructor explicitly. BasePlusCommissionEmployee3's six-argument constructor must explicitly call the five-argument constructor of class CommissionEmployee2, because CommissionEmployee2 does not provide a no-argument constructor that could be invoked implicitly.

Figure 9.11 uses a BasePlusCommissionEmployee3 object to perform the same tasks that Fig. 9.7 performed on a BasePlusCommissionEmployee object (Fig. 9.6). Note that the outputs of the two programs are identical. Although we declared class BasePlusCommissionEmployee without using inheritance and declared class BasePlusCommissionEmployee3 using inheritance, both classes provide the same functionality. The source code for class BasePlusCommissionEmployee3, which is 45 lines, is considerably shorter than that for class BasePlusCommissionEmployee, which is 115 lines, because class BasePlusCommissionEmployee3 inherits most of its functionality from CommissionEmployee2, whereas class BasePlusCommissionEmployee inherits only class Object's functionality. Also, there is now only one copy of the commission employee functionality

```java
1   // Fig. 9.11: BasePlusCommissionEmployeeTest3.java
2   // Testing class BasePlusCommissionEmployee3.
3
4   public class BasePlusCommissionEmployeeTest3
5   {
6      public static void main( String args[] )
7      {
8         // instantiate BasePlusCommissionEmployee3 object
9         BasePlusCommissionEmployee3 employee =
10           new BasePlusCommissionEmployee3(
11           "Bob", "Lewis", "333-33-3333", 5000, .04, 300 );
12
13        // get base-salaried commission employee data
14        System.out.println(
15           "Employee information obtained by get methods: \n" );
16        System.out.printf( "%s %s\n", "First name is",
17           employee.getFirstName() );
18        System.out.printf( "%s %s\n", "Last name is",
19           employee.getLastName() );
20        System.out.printf( "%s %s\n", "Social security number is",
21           employee.getSocialSecurityNumber() );
22        System.out.printf( "%s %.2f\n", "Gross sales is",
23           employee.getGrossSales() );
24        System.out.printf( "%s %.2f\n", "Commission rate is",
25           employee.getCommissionRate() );
26        System.out.printf( "%s %.2f\n", "Base salary is",
27           employee.getBaseSalary() );
28
29        employee.setBaseSalary( 1000 ); // set base salary
30
31        System.out.printf( "\n%s:\n\n%s\n",
32           "Updated employee information obtained by toString",
33           employee.toString() );
34     } // end main
35  } // end class BasePlusCommissionEmployeeTest3
```

Fig. 9.11 | protected superclass members inherited into subclass BasePlusCommissionEmployee3. (Part I of 2.)

```
Employee information obtained by get methods:

First name is Bob
Last name is Lewis
Social security number is 333-33-3333
Gross sales is 5000.00
Commission rate is 0.04
Base salary is 300.00

Updated employee information obtained by toString:

base-salaried commission employee: Bob Lewis
social security number: 333-33-3333
gross sales: 5000.00
commission rate: 0.04
base salary: 1000.00
```

Fig. 9.11 | protected superclass members inherited into subclass BasePlusCommission-Employee3. (Part 2 of 2.)

declared in class CommissionEmployee2. This makes the code easier to maintain, modify and debug, because the code related to a commission employee exists only in class CommissionEmployee2.

In this example, we declared superclass instance variables as protected so that subclasses could inherit them. Inheriting protected instance variables slightly increases performance, because we can directly access the variables in the subclass without incurring the overhead of a *set* or *get* method call. In most cases, however, it is better to use private instance variables to encourage proper software engineering, and leave code optimization issues to the compiler. Your code will be easier to maintain, modify and debug.

Using protected instance variables creates several potential problems. First, the subclass object can set an inherited variable's value directly without using a *set* method. Therefore, a subclass object can assign an invalid value to the variable, thus leaving the object in an inconsistent state. For example, if we were to declare CommissionEmployee3's instance variable grossSales as protected, a subclass object (e.g., BasePlusCommissionEmployee) could then assign a negative value to grossSales. The second problem with using protected instance variables is that subclass methods are more likely to be written so that they depend on the superclass's data implementation. In practice, subclasses should depend only on the superclass services (i.e., non-private methods) and not on the superclass data implementation. With protected instance variables in the superclass, we may need to modify all the subclasses of the superclass if the superclass implementation changes. For example, if for some reason we were to change the names of instance variables firstName and lastName to first and last, then we would have to do so for all occurrences in which a subclass directly references superclass instance variables firstName and lastName. In such a case, the software is said to be fragile or brittle, because a small change in the superclass can "break" subclass implementation. The programmer should be able to change the superclass implementation while still providing the same services to the subclasses. (Of course, if the superclass services change, we must reimplement our subclasses.) A third problem is that a class's protected members are visible to all classes in the same package as the class containing the protected members—this is not always desirable.

Software Engineering Observation 9.6

Use the protected access modifier when a superclass should provide a method only to its subclasses and other classes in the same package, but not to other clients.

Software Engineering Observation 9.7

Declaring superclass instance variables private (as opposed to protected) enables the superclass implementation of these instance variables to change without affecting subclass implementations.

Error-Prevention Tip 9.1

When possible, do not include protected instance variables in a superclass. Instead, include non-private methods that access private instance variables. This will ensure that objects of the class maintain consistent states.

9.4.5 CommissionEmployee-BasePlusCommissionEmployee Inheritance Hierarchy Using private Instance Variables

We now reexamine our hierarchy once more, this time using the best software engineering practices. Class CommissionEmployee3 (Fig. 9.12) declares instance variables firstName, lastName, socialSecurityNumber, grossSales and commissionRate as private (lines 6–10) and provides public methods setFirstName, getFirstName, setLastName, getLast-Name, setSocialSecurityNumber, getSocialSecurityNumber, setGrossSales, get-GrossSales, setCommissionRate, getCommissionRate, earnings and toString for manipulating these values. Note that methods earnings (lines 85–88) and toString (lines 91–98) use the class's *get* methods to obtain the values of its instance variables. If we decide to change the instance variable names, the earnings and toString declarations will not require modification—only the bodies of the *get* and *set* methods that directly manipulate the instance variables will need to change. Note that these changes occur solely within the

```
 1   // Fig. 9.12: CommissionEmployee3.java
 2   // CommissionEmployee3 class represents a commission employee.
 3
 4   public class CommissionEmployee3
 5   {
 6      private String firstName;
 7      private String lastName;
 8      private String socialSecurityNumber;
 9      private double grossSales; // gross weekly sales
10      private double commissionRate; // commission percentage
11
12      // five-argument constructor
13      public CommissionEmployee3( String first, String last, String ssn,
14         double sales, double rate )
15      {
16         // implicit call to Object constructor occurs here
17         firstName = first;
18         lastName = last;
19         socialSecurityNumber = ssn;
```

Fig. 9.12 | CommissionEmployee3 class uses methods to manipulate its private instance variables. (Part 1 of 3.)

```
20          setGrossSales( sales ); // validate and store gross sales
21          setCommissionRate( rate ); // validate and store commission rate
22      } // end five-argument CommissionEmployee3 constructor
23
24      // set first name
25      public void setFirstName( String first )
26      {
27          firstName = first;
28      } // end method setFirstName
29
30      // return first name
31      public String getFirstName()
32      {
33          return firstName;
34      } // end method getFirstName
35
36      // set last name
37      public void setLastName( String last )
38      {
39          lastName = last;
40      } // end method setLastName
41
42      // return last name
43      public String getLastName()
44      {
45          return lastName;
46      } // end method getLastName
47
48      // set social security number
49      public void setSocialSecurityNumber( String ssn )
50      {
51          socialSecurityNumber = ssn; // should validate
52      } // end method setSocialSecurityNumber
53
54      // return social security number
55      public String getSocialSecurityNumber()
56      {
57          return socialSecurityNumber;
58      } // end method getSocialSecurityNumber
59
60      // set gross sales amount
61      public void setGrossSales( double sales )
62      {
63          grossSales = ( sales < 0.0 ) ? 0.0 : sales;
64      } // end method setGrossSales
65
66      // return gross sales amount
67      public double getGrossSales()
68      {
69          return grossSales;
70      } // end method getGrossSales
```

Fig. 9.12 | CommissionEmployee3 class uses methods to manipulate its private instance variables. (Part 2 of 3.)

```
71
72      // set commission rate
73      public void setCommissionRate( double rate )
74      {
75         commissionRate = ( rate > 0.0 && rate < 1.0 ) ? rate : 0.0;
76      } // end method setCommissionRate
77
78      // return commission rate
79      public double getCommissionRate()
80      {
81         return commissionRate;
82      } // end method getCommissionRate
83
84      // calculate earnings
85      public double earnings()
86      {
87         return getCommissionRate() * getGrossSales();
88      } // end method earnings
89
90      // return String representation of CommissionEmployee3 object
91      public String toString()
92      {
93         return String.format( "%s: %s %s\n%s: %s\n%s: %.2f\n%s: %.2f",
94            "commission employee", getFirstName(), getLastName(),
95            "social security number", getSocialSecurityNumber(),
96            "gross sales", getGrossSales(),
97            "commission rate", getCommissionRate() );
98      } // end method toString
99   } // end class CommissionEmployee3
```

Fig. 9.12 | CommissionEmployee3 class uses methods to manipulate its private instance variables. (Part 3 of 3.)

superclass—no changes to the subclass are needed. Localizing the effects of changes like this is a good software engineering practice. Subclass BasePlusCommissionEmployee4 (Fig. 9.13) inherits CommissionEmployee3's non-private methods and can access the private superclass members via those methods.

Class BasePlusCommissionEmployee4 (Fig. 9.13) has several changes to its method implementations that distinguish it from class BasePlusCommissionEmployee3 (Fig. 9.10). Methods earnings (Fig. 9.13, lines 31–34) and toString (lines 37–41) each invoke method getBaseSalary to obtain the base salary value, rather than accessing baseSalary directly. If we decide to rename instance variable baseSalary, only the bodies of method setBaseSalary and getBaseSalary will need to change.

Class BasePlusCommissionEmployee4's earnings method (Fig. 9.13, lines 31–34) overrides class CommissionEmployee3's earnings method (Fig. 9.12, lines 85–88) to calculate the earnings of a base-salaried commission employee. The new version obtains the portion of the employee's earnings based on commission alone by calling CommissionEmployee3's earnings method with the expression super.earnings() (Fig. 9.13, line 33). BasePlusCommissionEmployee4's earnings method then adds the base salary to this value to calculate the total earnings of the employee. Note the syntax used to invoke an overridden superclass method from a subclass—place the keyword

```
1   // Fig. 9.13: BasePlusCommissionEmployee4.java
2   // BasePlusCommissionEmployee4 class inherits from CommissionEmployee3 and
3   // accesses CommissionEmployee3's private data via CommissionEmployee3's
4   // public methods.
5
6   public class BasePlusCommissionEmployee4 extends CommissionEmployee3
7   {
8      private double baseSalary; // base salary per week
9
10     // six-argument constructor
11     public BasePlusCommissionEmployee4( String first, String last,
12        String ssn, double sales, double rate, double salary )
13     {
14        super( first, last, ssn, sales, rate );
15        setBaseSalary( salary ); // validate and store base salary
16     } // end six-argument BasePlusCommissionEmployee4 constructor
17
18     // set base salary
19     public void setBaseSalary( double salary )
20     {
21        baseSalary = ( salary < 0.0 ) ? 0.0 : salary;
22     } // end method setBaseSalary
23
24     // return base salary
25     public double getBaseSalary()
26     {
27        return baseSalary;
28     } // end method getBaseSalary
29
30     // calculate earnings
31     public double earnings()
32     {
33        return getBaseSalary() + super.earnings();
34     } // end method earnings
35
36     // return String representation of BasePlusCommissionEmployee4
37     public String toString()
38     {
39        return String.format( "%s %s\n%s: %.2f", "base-salaried",
40           super.toString(), "base salary", getBaseSalary() );
41     } // end method toString
42  } // end class BasePlusCommissionEmployee4
```

Fig. 9.13 | BasePlusCommissionEmployee4 class extends CommissionEmployee3, which provides only private instance variables.

super and a dot (.) separator before the superclass method name. This method invocation is a good software engineering practice: Recall from *Software Engineering Observation 8.5* that if a method performs all or some of the actions needed by another method, call that method rather than duplicate its code. By having BasePlusCommissionEmployee4's earnings method invoke CommissionEmployee3's earnings method to calculate part of a BasePlusCommissionEmployee4 object's earnings, we avoid duplicating the code and reduce code-maintenance problems.

Common Programming Error 9.3

When a superclass method is overridden in a subclass, the subclass version often calls the superclass version to do a portion of the work. Failure to prefix the superclass method name with the keyword super and a dot (.) separator when referencing the superclass's method causes the subclass method to call itself, potentially creating an error called infinite recursion. Recursion, used correctly, is a powerful capability discussed in Chapter 15, Recursion.

Similarly, `BasePlusCommissionEmployee4`'s `toString` method (Fig. 9.13, lines 37–41) overrides class `CommissionEmployee3`'s `toString` method (Fig. 9.12, lines 91–98) to return a string representation that is appropriate for a base-salaried commission employee. The new version creates part of a `BasePlusCommissionEmployee4` object's string representation (i.e., the string `"commission employee"` and the values of class `CommissionEmployee3`'s private instance variables) by calling `CommissionEmployee3`'s `toString` method with the expression `super.toString()` (Fig. 9.13, line 40). `BasePlusCommissionEmployee4`'s `toString` method then outputs the remainder of a `BasePlusCommissionEmployee4` object's string representation (i.e., the value of class `BasePlusCommissionEmployee4`'s base salary).

Figure 9.14 performs the same manipulations on a `BasePlusCommissionEmployee4` object as did Fig. 9.7 and Fig. 9.11 on objects of classes `BasePlusCommissionEmployee` and `BasePlusCommissionEmployee3`, respectively. Although each "base-salaried commission employee" class behaves identically, class `BasePlusCommissionEmployee4` is the best engineered. By using inheritance and by calling methods that hide the data and ensure consistency, we have efficiently and effectively constructed a well-engineered class.

```
1   // Fig. 9.14: BasePlusCommissionEmployeeTest4.java
2   // Testing class BasePlusCommissionEmployee4.
3
4   public class BasePlusCommissionEmployeeTest4
5   {
6      public static void main( String args[] )
7      {
8         // instantiate BasePlusCommissionEmployee4 object
9         BasePlusCommissionEmployee4 employee =
10           new BasePlusCommissionEmployee4(
11           "Bob", "Lewis", "333-33-3333", 5000, .04, 300 );
12
13        // get base-salaried commission employee data
14        System.out.println(
15           "Employee information obtained by get methods: \n" );
16        System.out.printf( "%s %s\n", "First name is",
17           employee.getFirstName() );
18        System.out.printf( "%s %s\n", "Last name is",
19           employee.getLastName() );
20        System.out.printf( "%s %s\n", "Social security number is",
21           employee.getSocialSecurityNumber() );
22        System.out.printf( "%s %.2f\n", "Gross sales is",
23           employee.getGrossSales() );
```

Fig. 9.14 | Superclass `private` instance variables are accessible to a subclass via `public` or `protected` methods inherited by the subclass. (Part 1 of 2.)

```
24        System.out.printf( "%s %.2f\n", "Commission rate is",
25            employee.getCommissionRate() );
26        System.out.printf( "%s %.2f\n", "Base salary is",
27            employee.getBaseSalary() );
28
29        employee.setBaseSalary( 1000 ); // set base salary
30
31        System.out.printf( "\n%s:\n\n%s\n",
32            "Updated employee information obtained by toString",
33            employee.toString() );
34    } // end main
35 } // end class BasePlusCommissionEmployeeTest4
```

```
Employee information obtained by get methods:

First name is Bob
Last name is Lewis
Social security number is 333-33-3333
Gross sales is 5000.00
Commission rate is 0.04
Base salary is 300.00

Updated employee information obtained by toString:

base-salaried commission employee: Bob Lewis
social security number: 333-33-3333
gross sales: 5000.00
commission rate: 0.04
base salary: 1000.00
```

Fig. 9.14 | Superclass `private` instance variables are accessible to a subclass via `public` or `protected` methods inherited by the subclass. (Part 2 of 2.)

In this section, you saw an evolutionary set of examples that was designed to teach key capabilities for good software engineering with inheritance. You learned how to use the keyword `extends` to create a subclass using inheritance, how to use `protected` superclass members to enable a subclass to access inherited superclass instance variables and how to override superclass methods to provide versions that are more appropriate for subclass objects. In addition, you learned how to apply software engineering techniques from Chapter 8 and this chapter to create classes that are easy to maintain, modify and debug.

9.5 Constructors in Subclasses

As we explained in the preceding section, instantiating a subclass object begins a chain of constructor calls in which the subclass constructor, before performing its own tasks, invokes its direct superclass's constructor either explicitly (via the `super` reference) or implicitly (calling the superclass's default constructor or no-argument constructor). Similarly, if the superclass is derived from another class (as is, of course, every class except `Object`), the superclass constructor invokes the constructor of the next class up in the hierarchy, and so on. The last constructor called in the chain is always the constructor for class `Object`. The original subclass constructor's body finishes executing last. Each superclass's constructor manipulates the superclass instance variables that the subclass object inherits. For example, consider again the

CommissionEmployee3–BasePlusCommissionEmployee4 hierarchy from Fig. 9.12 and
Fig. 9.13. When a program creates a BasePlusCommissionEmployee4 object, the BasePlus-
CommissionEmployee4 constructor is called. That constructor calls CommissionEmployee3's
constructor, which in turn calls Object's constructor. Class Object's constructor has an
empty body, so it immediately returns control to CommissionEmployee3's constructor,
which then initializes the private instance variables of CommissionEmployee3 that are part
of the BasePlusCommissionEmployee4 object. When CommissionEmployee3's constructor
completes execution, it returns control to BasePlusCommissionEmployee4's constructor,
which initializes the BasePlusCommissionEmployee4 object's baseSalary.

Software Engineering Observation 9.8

*When a program creates a subclass object, the subclass constructor immediately calls the superclass
constructor (explicitly, via super, or implicitly). The superclass constructor's body executes to
initialize the superclass's instance variables that are part of the subclass object, then the subclass
constructor's body executes to initialize the subclass-only instance variables. Java ensures that
even if a constructor does not assign a value to an instance variable, the variable is still initialized
to its default value (e.g., 0 for primitive numeric types, false for booleans, null for references).*

Our next example revisits the commission employee hierarchy by declaring a
CommissionEmployee4 class (Fig. 9.15) and a BasePlusCommissionEmployee5 class
(Fig. 9.16). Each class's constructor prints a message when invoked, enabling us to observe
the order in which the constructors in the hierarchy execute.

```java
 1   // Fig. 9.15: CommissionEmployee4.java
 2   // CommissionEmployee4 class represents a commission employee.
 3
 4   public class CommissionEmployee4
 5   {
 6      private String firstName;
 7      private String lastName;
 8      private String socialSecurityNumber;
 9      private double grossSales; // gross weekly sales
10      private double commissionRate; // commission percentage
11
12      // five-argument constructor
13      public CommissionEmployee4( String first, String last, String ssn,
14         double sales, double rate )
15      {
16         // implicit call to Object constructor occurs here
17         firstName = first;
18         lastName = last;
19         socialSecurityNumber = ssn;
20         setGrossSales( sales ); // validate and store gross sales
21         setCommissionRate( rate ); // validate and store commission rate
22
23         System.out.printf(
24            "\nCommissionEmployee4 constructor:\n%s\n", this );
25      } // end five-argument CommissionEmployee4 constructor
26
```

Fig. 9.15 | CommissionEmployee4's constructor outputs text. (Part 1 of 3.)

```
27      // set first name
28      public void setFirstName( String first )
29      {
30         firstName = first;
31      } // end method setFirstName
32
33      // return first name
34      public String getFirstName()
35      {
36         return firstName;
37      } // end method getFirstName
38
39      // set last name
40      public void setLastName( String last )
41      {
42         lastName = last;
43      } // end method setLastName
44
45      // return last name
46      public String getLastName()
47      {
48         return lastName;
49      } // end method getLastName
50
51      // set social security number
52      public void setSocialSecurityNumber( String ssn )
53      {
54         socialSecurityNumber = ssn; // should validate
55      } // end method setSocialSecurityNumber
56
57      // return social security number
58      public String getSocialSecurityNumber()
59      {
60         return socialSecurityNumber;
61      } // end method getSocialSecurityNumber
62
63      // set gross sales amount
64      public void setGrossSales( double sales )
65      {
66         grossSales = ( sales < 0.0 ) ? 0.0 : sales;
67      } // end method setGrossSales
68
69      // return gross sales amount
70      public double getGrossSales()
71      {
72         return grossSales;
73      } // end method getGrossSales
74
75      // set commission rate
76      public void setCommissionRate( double rate )
77      {
78         commissionRate = ( rate > 0.0 && rate < 1.0 ) ? rate : 0.0;
79      } // end method setCommissionRate
```

Fig. 9.15 | CommissionEmployee4's constructor outputs text. (Part 2 of 3.)

```
80
81     // return commission rate
82     public double getCommissionRate()
83     {
84        return commissionRate;
85     } // end method getCommissionRate
86
87     // calculate earnings
88     public double earnings()
89     {
90        return getCommissionRate() * getGrossSales();
91     } // end method earnings
92
93     // return String representation of CommissionEmployee4 object
94     public String toString()
95     {
96        return String.format( "%s: %s %s\n%s: %s\n%s: %.2f\n%s: %.2f",
97           "commission employee", getFirstName(), getLastName(),
98           "social security number", getSocialSecurityNumber(),
99           "gross sales", getGrossSales(),
100          "commission rate", getCommissionRate() );
101    } // end method toString
102 } // end class CommissionEmployee4
```

Fig. 9.15 | CommissionEmployee4's constructor outputs text. (Part 3 of 3.)

Class CommissionEmployee4 (Fig. 9.15) contains the same features as the version of the class shown in Fig. 9.4. We modified the constructor (lines 13–25) to output text upon its invocation. Note that outputting this with the %s format specifier (lines 23–24) implicitly invokes the toString method of the object being constructed to obtain the object's string representation.

Class BasePlusCommissionEmployee5 (Fig. 9.16) is almost identical to BasePlusCommissionEmployee4 (Fig. 9.13), except that BasePlusCommissionEmployee5's constructor also outputs text when invoked. As in CommissionEmployee4 (Fig. 9.15), we output this using the %s format specifier (line 16) to get the object's string representation.

```
1    // Fig. 9.16: BasePlusCommissionEmployee5.java
2    // BasePlusCommissionEmployee5 class declaration.
3
4    public class BasePlusCommissionEmployee5 extends CommissionEmployee4
5    {
6       private double baseSalary; // base salary per week
7
8       // six-argument constructor
9       public BasePlusCommissionEmployee5( String first, String last,
10          String ssn, double sales, double rate, double salary )
11       {
12          super( first, last, ssn, sales, rate );
13          setBaseSalary( salary ); // validate and store base salary
14
```

Fig. 9.16 | BasePlusCommissionEmployee5's constructor outputs text. (Part 1 of 2.)

```
15          System.out.printf(
16             "\nBasePlusCommissionEmployee5 constructor:\n%s\n", this );
17       } // end six-argument BasePlusCommissionEmployee5 constructor
18
19       // set base salary
20       public void setBaseSalary( double salary )
21       {
22          baseSalary = ( salary < 0.0 ) ? 0.0 : salary;
23       } // end method setBaseSalary
24
25       // return base salary
26       public double getBaseSalary()
27       {
28          return baseSalary;
29       } // end method getBaseSalary
30
31       // calculate earnings
32       public double earnings()
33       {
34          return getBaseSalary() + super.earnings();
35       } // end method earnings
36
37       // return String representation of BasePlusCommissionEmployee5
38       public String toString()
39       {
40          return String.format( "%s %s\n%s: %.2f", "base-salaried",
41             super.toString(), "base salary", getBaseSalary() );
42       } // end method toString
43    } // end class BasePlusCommissionEmployee5
```

Fig. 9.16 | BasePlusCommissionEmployee5's constructor outputs text. (Part 2 of 2.)

Figure 9.17 demonstrates the order in which constructors are called for objects of classes that are part of an inheritance hierarchy. Method main begins by instantiating CommissionEmployee4 object employee1 (lines 8–9). Next, lines 12–14 instantiate

```
1    // Fig. 9.17: ConstructorTest.java
2    // Display order in which superclass and subclass constructors are called.
3
4    public class ConstructorTest
5    {
6       public static void main( String args[] )
7       {
8          CommissionEmployee4 employee1 = new CommissionEmployee4(
9             "Bob", "Lewis", "333-33-3333", 5000, .04 );
10
11         System.out.println();
12         BasePlusCommissionEmployee5 employee2 =
13            new BasePlusCommissionEmployee5(
14            "Lisa", "Jones", "555-55-5555", 2000, .06, 800 );
15
```

Fig. 9.17 | Constructor call order. (Part I of 2.)

```
16              System.out.println();
17              BasePlusCommissionEmployee5 employee3 =
18                 new BasePlusCommissionEmployee5(
19                 "Mark", "Sands", "888-88-8888", 8000, .15, 2000 );
20       } // end main
21    } // end class ConstructorTest
```

```
CommissionEmployee4 constructor:
commission employee: Bob Lewis
social security number: 333-33-3333
gross sales: 5000.00
commission rate: 0.04


CommissionEmployee4 constructor:
base-salaried commission employee: Lisa Jones
social security number: 555-55-5555
gross sales: 2000.00
commission rate: 0.06
base salary: 0.00

BasePlusCommissionEmployee5 constructor:
base-salaried commission employee: Lisa Jones
social security number: 555-55-5555
gross sales: 2000.00
commission rate: 0.06
base salary: 800.00


CommissionEmployee4 constructor:
base-salaried commission employee: Mark Sands
social security number: 888-88-8888
gross sales: 8000.00
commission rate: 0.15
base salary: 0.00

BasePlusCommissionEmployee5 constructor:
base-salaried commission employee: Mark Sands
social security number: 888-88-8888
gross sales: 8000.00
commission rate: 0.15
base salary: 2000.00
```

Fig. 9.17 | Constructor call order. (Part 2 of 2.)

BasePlusCommissionEmployee5 object employee2. This invokes the CommissionEmployee4 constructor, which prints output with the values passed from the BasePlusCommissionEmployee5 constructor, then performs the output specified in the BasePlusCommissionEmployee5 constructor. Lines 17–19 then instantiate BasePlusCommissionEmployee5 object employee3. Again, the CommissionEmployee4 and BasePlusCommissionEmployee5 constructors are both called. In each case, the body of the CommissionEmployee4 constructor executes before the body of the BasePlusCommissionEmployee5 constructor executes. Note that employee2 is constructed completely before construction of employee3 begins.

9.6 Software Engineering with Inheritance

This section discusses customizing existing software with inheritance. When a new class extends an existing class, the new class inherits the non-`private` members of the existing class. We can customize the new class to meet our needs by including additional members and by overriding superclass members. Doing this does not require the subclass programmer to change the superclass's source code. Java simply requires access to the superclass's `.class` file so it can compile and execute any program that uses or extends the superclass. This powerful capability is attractive to independent software vendors (ISVs), who can develop proprietary classes for sale or license and make them available to users in bytecode format. Users then can derive new classes from these library classes rapidly and without accessing the ISVs' proprietary source code.

> **Software Engineering Observation 9.9**
>
> *Although inheriting from a class does not require access to the class's source code, developers often insist on seeing the source code to understand how the class is implemented. Developers in industry want to ensure that they are extending a solid class—for example, a class that performs well and is implemented securely.*

Sometimes, students have difficulty appreciating the scope of the problems faced by designers who work on large-scale software projects in industry. People experienced with such projects say that effective software reuse improves the software-development process. Object-oriented programming facilitates software reuse, potentially shortening development time.

The availability of substantial and useful class libraries delivers the maximum benefits of software reuse through inheritance. Application designers build their applications with these libraries, and library designers are rewarded by having their libraries included with the applications. The standard Java class libraries that are shipped with Java SE 6 tend to be rather general purpose. Many special-purpose class libraries exist and more are being created.

> **Software Engineering Observation 9.10**
>
> *At the design stage in an object-oriented system, the designer often finds that certain classes are closely related. The designer should "factor out" common instance variables and methods and place them in a superclass. Then the designer should use inheritance to develop subclasses, specializing them with capabilities beyond those inherited from the superclass.*

> **Software Engineering Observation 9.11**
>
> *Declaring a subclass does not affect its superclass's source code. Inheritance preserves the integrity of the superclass.*

> **Software Engineering Observation 9.12**
>
> *Just as designers of non-object-oriented systems should avoid method proliferation, designers of object-oriented systems should avoid class proliferation. Such proliferation creates management problems and can hinder software reusability, because in a huge class library it becomes difficult for a client to locate the most appropriate classes. The alternative is to create fewer classes that provide more substantial functionality, but such classes might prove cumbersome.*

Performance Tip 9.1

If subclasses are larger than they need to be (i.e., contain too much functionality), memory and processing resources might be wasted. Extend the superclass that contains the functionality that is closest to what is needed.

Reading subclass declarations can be confusing, because inherited members are not declared explicitly in the subclasses, but are nevertheless present in them. A similar problem exists in documenting subclass members.

9.7 Object Class

As we discussed earlier in this chapter, all classes in Java inherit directly or indirectly from the Object class (package java.lang), so its 11 methods are inherited by all other classes. Figure 9.18 summarizes Object's methods.

Method	Description
clone	This protected method, which takes no arguments and returns an Object reference, makes a copy of the object on which it is called. When cloning is required for objects of a class, the class should override method clone as a public method and should implement interface Cloneable (package java.lang). The default implementation of this method performs a so-called shallow copy—instance variable values in one object are copied into another object of the same type. For reference types, only the references are copied. A typical overridden clone method's implementation would perform a deep copy that creates a new object for each reference-type instance variable. There are many subtleties to overriding method clone. You can learn more about cloning in the following article: java.sun.com/developer/JDCTechTips/2001/tt0306.html
equals	This method compares two objects for equality and returns true if they are equal and false otherwise. The method takes any Object as an argument. When objects of a particular class must be compared for equality, the class should override method equals to compare the contents of the two objects. The method's implementation should meet the following requirements: • It should return false if the argument is null. • It should return true if an object is compared to itself, as in object1.equals(object1). • It should return true only if both object1.equals(object2) and object2.equals(object1) would return true. • For three objects, if object1.equals(object2) returns true and object2.equals(object3) returns true, then object1.equals(object3) should also return true. • If equals is called multiple times with the two objects and the objects do not change, the method should consistently return true if the objects are equal and false otherwise.

Fig. 9.18 | Object methods that are inherited directly or indirectly by all classes. (Part 1 of 2.)

Method	Description
equals (continued)	A class that overrides equals should also override hashCode to ensure that equal objects have identical hashcodes. The default equals implementation uses operator == to determine whether two references *refer to the same object in memory*. Section 30.3.3 demonstrates class String's equals method and differentiates between comparing String objects with == and with equals.
finalize	This protected method (introduced in Section 8.10 and Section 8.11) is called by the garbage collector to perform termination housekeeping on an object just before the garbage collector reclaims the object's memory. It is not guaranteed that the garbage collector will reclaim an object, so it cannot be guaranteed that the object's finalize method will execute. The method must specify an empty parameter list and must return void. The default implementation of this method serves as a placeholder that does nothing.
getClass	Every object in Java knows its own type at execution time. Method getClass (used in Section 10.5 and Section 21.3) returns an object of class Class (package java.lang) that contains information about the object's type, such as its class name (returned by Class method getName). You can learn more about class Class in the online API documentation at java.sun.com/javase/6/docs/api/java/lang/Class.html.
hashCode	A hashtable is a data structure (discussed in Section 19.10) that relates one object, called the key, to another object, called the value. When initially inserting a value into a hashtable, the key's hashCode method is called. The hashcode value returned is used by the hashtable to determine the location at which to insert the corresponding value. The key's hashcode is also used by the hashtable to locate the key's corresponding value.
notify, notifyAll, wait	Methods notify, notifyAll and the three overloaded versions of wait are related to multithreading, which is discussed in Chapter 23. In recent versions of Java, the multithreading model has changed substantially, but these features continue to be supported.
toString	This method (introduced in Section 9.4.1) returns a String representation of an object. The default implementation of this method returns the package name and class name of the object's class followed by a hexadecimal representation of the value returned by the object's hashCode method.

Fig. 9.18 | Object methods that are inherited directly or indirectly by all classes. (Part 2 of 2.)

We discuss several of Object methods throughout this book (as indicated in Fig. 9.18). You can learn more about Object's methods in Object's online API documentation and in *The Java Tutorial* at the following sites:

```
java.sun.com/javase/6/docs/api/java/lang/Object.html
java.sun.com/docs/books/tutorial/java/IandI/objectclass.html
```

Recall from Chapter 7 that arrays are objects. As a result, like all other objects, an array inherits the members of class Object. Note that every array has an overridden clone method that copies the array. However, if the array stores references to objects, the objects are not copied. For more information about the relationship between arrays and class Object, please see *Java Language Specification, Chapter 10*, at

java.sun.com/docs/books/jls/second_edition/html/arrays.doc.html

9.8 (Optional) GUI and Graphics Case Study: Displaying Text and Images Using Labels

Programs often use labels when they need to display information or instructions to the user in a graphical user interface. Labels are a convenient way of identifying GUI components on the screen and keeping the user informed about the current state of the program. In Java, an object of class JLabel (from package javax.swing) can display a single line of text, an image or both. The example in Fig. 9.19 demonstrates several JLabel features.

```java
1   // Fig 9.19: LabelDemo.java
2   // Demonstrates the use of labels.
3   import java.awt.BorderLayout;
4   import javax.swing.ImageIcon;
5   import javax.swing.JLabel;
6   import javax.swing.JFrame;
7
8   public class LabelDemo
9   {
10     public static void main( String args[] )
11     {
12        // Create a label with plain text
13        JLabel northLabel = new JLabel( "North" );
14
15        // create an icon from an image so we can put it on a JLabel
16        ImageIcon labelIcon = new ImageIcon( "GUItip.gif" );
17
18        // create a label with an Icon instead of text
19        JLabel centerLabel = new JLabel( labelIcon );
20
21        // create another label with an Icon
22        JLabel southLabel = new JLabel( labelIcon );
23
24        // set the label to display text (as well as an icon)
25        southLabel.setText( "South" );
26
27        // create a frame to hold the labels
28        JFrame application = new JFrame();
29
30        application.setDefaultCloseOperation( JFrame.EXIT_ON_CLOSE );
31
32        // add the labels to the frame; the second argument specifies
33        // where on the frame to add the label
34        application.add( northLabel, BorderLayout.NORTH );
35        application.add( centerLabel, BorderLayout.CENTER );
36        application.add( southLabel, BorderLayout.SOUTH );
```

Fig. 9.19 | JLabel with text and with images. (Part 1 of 2.)

```
37
38          application.setSize( 300, 300 ); // set the size of the frame
39          application.setVisible( true ); // show the frame
40      } // end main
41  } // end class LabelDemo
```

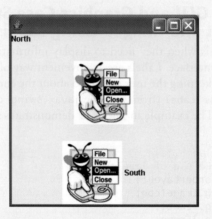

Fig. 9.19 | JLabel with text and with images. (Part 2 of 2.)

Lines 3–6 import the classes we need to display JLabels. BorderLayout from package java.awt contains constants that specify where we can place GUI components in the JFrame. Class **ImageIcon** represents an image that can be displayed on a JLabel, and class JFrame represents the window that will contain all the labels.

Line 13 creates a JLabel that displays its constructor argument—the string "North". Line 16 declares local variable labelIcon and assigns it a new ImageIcon. The constructor for ImageIcon receives a String that specifies the path to the image. Since we specify only a file name, Java assumes that it is in the same directory as class LabelDemo. ImageIcon can load images in GIF, JPEG and PNG image formats. Line 19 declares and initializes local variable centerLabel with a JLabel that displays the labelIcon. Line 22 declares and initializes local variable southLabel with a JLabel similar to the one in line 19. However, line 25 calls method **setText** to change the text the label displays. Method setText can be called on any JLabel to change its text. This JLabel displays both the icon and the text.

Line 28 creates the JFrame that displays the JLabels, and line 30 indicates that the program should terminate when the JFrame is closed. We attach the labels to the JFrame in lines 34–36 by calling an overloaded version of method add that takes two parameters. The first parameter is the component we want to attach, and the second is the region in which it should be placed. Each JFrame has an associated layout that helps the JFrame position the GUI components that are attached to it. The default layout for a JFrame is known as a **BorderLayout** and has five regions—NORTH (top), SOUTH (bottom), EAST (right side), WEST (left side) and CENTER. Each of these is declared as a constant in class Border-Layout. When calling method add with one argument, the JFrame places the component in the CENTER automatically. If a position already contains a component, then the new component takes its place. Lines 38 and 39 set the size of the JFrame and make it visible on screen.

GUI and Graphics Case Study Exercise

9.1 Modify Exercise 8.1 to include a JLabel as a status bar that displays counts representing the number of each shape displayed. Class DrawPanel should declare a method that returns a String containing the status text. In main, first create the DrawPanel, then create the JLabel with the status text as an argument to the JLabel's constructor. Attach the JLabel to the SOUTH region of the JFrame, as shown in Fig. 9.20.

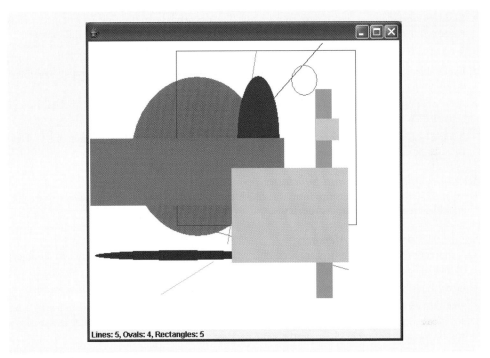

Fig. 9.20 | JLabel displaying shape statistics.

9.9 Wrap-Up

This chapter introduced inheritance—the ability to create classes by absorbing an existing class's members and embellishing them with new capabilities. You learned the notions of superclasses and subclasses and used keyword extends to create a subclass that inherits members from a superclass. The chapter introduced the access modifier protected; subclass methods can access protected superclass members. You learned how to access superclass members with super. You also saw how constructors are used in inheritance hierarchies. Finally, you learned about the methods of class Object, the direct or indirect superclass of all classes in Java.

In Chapter 10, Object-Oriented Programming: Polymorphism, we build on our discussion of inheritance by introducing polymorphism—an object-oriented concept that enables us to write programs that conveniently handle, in a more general manner, objects of a wide variety of classes related by inheritance. After studying Chapter 10, you will be familiar with classes, objects, encapsulation, inheritance and polymorphism—the key technologies of object-oriented programming.

Summary

Section 9.1 Introduction
- Software reuse reduces program-development time.
- The direct superclass of a subclass (specified by the keyword extends in the first line of a class declaration) is the superclass from which the subclass inherits. An indirect superclass of a subclass is two or more levels up the class hierarchy from that subclass.
- In single inheritance, a class is derived from one direct superclass. In multiple inheritance, a class is derived from more than one direct superclass. Java does not support multiple inheritance.
- A subclass is more specific than its superclass and represents a smaller group of objects.
- Every object of a subclass is also an object of that class's superclass. However, a superclass object is not an object of its class's subclasses.
- An *is a* relationship represents inheritance. In an *is a* relationship, an object of a subclass also can be treated as an object of its superclass.
- A *has-a* relationship represents composition. In a *has-a* relationship, a class object contains references to objects of other classes.

Section 9.2 Superclasses and Subclasses
- Single-inheritance relationships form tree-like hierarchical structures—a superclass exists in a hierarchical relationship with its subclasses.

Section 9.3 **protected** Members
- A superclass's public members are accessible wherever the program has a reference to an object of that superclass or one of its subclasses.
- A superclass's private members are accessible only within the declaration of that superclass.
- A superclass's protected members have an intermediate level of protection between public and private access. They can be accessed by members of the superclass, by members of its subclasses and by members of other classes in the same package.
- When a subclass method overrides a superclass method, the superclass method can be accessed from the subclass if the superclass method name is preceded by the keyword super and a dot (.) separator.

Section 9.4 Relationship between Superclasses and Subclasses
- A subclass cannot access or inherit the private members of its superclass—allowing this would violate the encapsulation of the superclass. A subclass can, however, inherit the non-private members of its superclass.
- A superclass method can be overridden in a subclass to declare an appropriate implementation for the subclass.
- Method toString takes no arguments and returns a String. The Object class's toString method is normally overridden by a subclass.
- When an object is output using the %s format specifier, the object's toString method is called implicitly to obtain its string representation.

Section 9.5 Constructors in Subclasses
- The first task of any subclass constructor is to call its direct superclass's constructor, either explicitly or implicitly, to ensure that the instance variables inherited from the superclass are initialized properly.

- A subclass can explicitly invoke a constructor of its superclass by using the superclass constructor call syntax—keyword super, followed by a set of parentheses containing the superclass constructor arguments.

Section 9.6 Software Engineering with Inheritance
- Declaring instance variables private, while providing non-private methods to manipulate and perform validation, helps enforce good software engineering.

Terminology

base class	invoke a superclass method
brittle software	*is a* relationship
class hierarchy	Object class
class library	object of a subclass
clone method of class Object	object of a superclass
composition	override (redefine) a superclass method
derived class	private superclass member
direct superclass	protected keyword
equals method of class Object	protected superclass member
extends keyword	public superclass member
fragile software	single inheritance
getClass method of class Object	software reusability
has-a relationship	specialization
hashCode method of class Object	standardized reusable components
hierarchical relationship	subclass
hierarchy diagram	subclass constructor
indirect superclass	super keyword
inheritance	superclass
inheritance hierarchy	superclass constructor
inherited member	superclass constructor call syntax
inherited method	superclass no-argument constructor
invoke a superclass constructor	toString method of class Object

Self-Review Exercises

9.1 Fill in the blanks in each of the following statements:
   a) _____ is a form of software reusability in which new classes acquire the members of existing classes and embellish those classes with new capabilities.
   b) A superclass's _____ members can be accessed in the superclass declaration and in subclass declarations.
   c) In a(n) _____ relationship, an object of a subclass can also be treated as an object of its superclass.
   d) In a(n) _____ relationship, a class object has references to objects of other classes as members.
   e) In single inheritance, a class exists in a(n) _____ relationship with its subclasses.
   f) A superclass's _____ members are accessible anywhere that the program has a reference to an object of that superclass or to an object of one of its subclasses.
   g) When an object of a subclass is instantiated, a superclass _____ is called implicitly or explicitly.
   h) Subclass constructors can call superclass constructors via the _____ keyword.

9.2   State whether each of the following is *true* or *false*. If a statement is *false*, explain why.
 a) Superclass constructors are not inherited by subclasses.
 b) A *has-a* relationship is implemented via inheritance.
 c) A Car class has an *is a* relationship with the SteeringWheel and Brakes classes.
 d) Inheritance encourages the reuse of proven high-quality software.
 e) When a subclass redefines a superclass method by using the same signature, the subclass is said to overload that superclass method.

Answers to Self-Review Exercises

9.1   a) Inheritance. b) public and protected. c) *is a* or inheritance. d) *has-a* or composition. e) hierarchical. f) public. g) constructor. h) super.

9.2   a) True. b) False. A *has-a* relationship is implemented via composition. An *is a* relationship is implemented via inheritance. c) False. This is an example of a *has-a* relationship. Class Car has an *is a* relationship with class Vehicle. d) True. e) False. This is known as overriding, not overloading—an overloaded method has the same name, but a different signature.

Exercises

9.3   Many programs written with inheritance could be written with composition instead, and vice versa. Rewrite class BasePlusCommissionEmployee4 (Fig. 9.13) of the CommissionEmployee3– BasePlusCommissionEmployee4 hierarchy to use composition rather than inheritance. After you do this, assess the relative merits of the two approaches for the CommissionEmployee3 and BasePlusCommissionEmployee4 problems, as well as for object-oriented programs in general. Which approach is more natural? Why?

9.4   Discuss the ways in which inheritance promotes software reuse, saves time during program development and helps prevent errors.

9.5   The world of shapes is much richer than the shapes included in the inheritance hierarchy of Fig. 9.3. Write down all the shapes you can think of—both two-dimensional and three-dimensional—and form them into a more complete Shape hierarchy with as many levels as possible. Your hierarchy should have class Shape at the top. Class TwoDimensionalShape and class ThreeDimensionalShape should extend Shape. Add additional subclasses, such as Quadrilateral and Sphere, at their correct locations in the hierarchy as necessary.

9.6   Some programmers prefer not to use protected access, because they believe it breaks the encapsulation of the superclass. Discuss the relative merits of using protected access vs. using private access in superclasses.

9.7   Write an inheritance hierarchy for classes Quadrilateral, Trapezoid, Parallelogram, Rectangle and Square. Use Quadrilateral as the superclass of the hierarchy. Make the hierarchy as deep (i.e., as many levels) as possible. Specify the instance variables and methods for each class. The private instance variables of Quadrilateral should be the *x-y* coordinate pairs for the four endpoints of the Quadrilateral. Write a program that instantiates objects of your classes and outputs each object's area (except Quadrilateral).

10

Object-Oriented Programming: Polymorphism

OBJECTIVES

In this chapter you will learn:

- The concept of polymorphism.
- To use overridden methods to effect polymorphism.
- To distinguish between abstract and concrete classes.
- To declare abstract methods to create abstract classes.
- How polymorphism makes systems extensible and maintainable.
- To determine an object's type at execution time.
- To declare and implement interfaces.

10.1 Introduction

We now continue our study of object-oriented programming by explaining and demonstrating **polymorphism** with inheritance hierarchies. Polymorphism enables us to "program in the general" rather than "program in the specific." In particular, polymorphism enables us to write programs that process objects that share the same superclass in a class hierarchy as if they are all objects of the superclass; this can simplify programming.

Consider the following example of polymorphism. Suppose we create a program that simulates the movement of several types of animals for a biological study. Classes Fish, Frog and Bird represent the three types of animals under investigation. Imagine that each of these classes extends superclass Animal, which contains a method move and maintains an animal's current location as *x-y* coordinates. Each subclass implements method move. Our program maintains an array of references to objects of the various Animal subclasses. To simulate the animals' movements, the program sends each object the same message once per second—namely, move. However, each specific type of Animal responds to a move message in a unique way—a Fish might swim three feet, a Frog might jump five feet and a Bird might fly ten feet. The program issues the same message (i.e., move) to each animal object generically, but each object knows how to modify its *x-y* coordinates appropriately for its specific type of movement. Relying on each object to know how to "do the right thing" (i.e., do what is appropriate for that type of object) in response to the same method call is the key concept of polymorphism. The same message (in this case, move) sent to a variety of objects has "many forms" of results—hence the term polymorphism.

With polymorphism, we can design and implement systems that are easily extensible—new classes can be added with little or no modification to the general portions of the program, as long as the new classes are part of the inheritance hierarchy that the program processes generically. The only parts of a program that must be altered to accommodate new classes are those that require direct knowledge of the new classes that the programmer adds to the hierarchy. For example, if we extend class Animal to create class Tortoise (which might respond to a move message by crawling one inch), we need to write only the Tortoise class and the part of the simulation that instantiates a Tortoise object. The portions of the simulation that process each Animal generically can remain the same.

This chapter has several parts. First, we discuss common examples of polymorphism. We then provide an example demonstrating polymorphic behavior. We'll use superclass references to manipulate both superclass objects and subclass objects polymorphically.

We then present a case study that revisits the employee hierarchy of Section 9.4.5. We develop a simple payroll application that polymorphically calculates the weekly pay of several different types of employees using each employee's earnings method. Though the earnings of each type of employee are calculated in a specific way, polymorphism allows us to process the employees "in the general." In the case study, we enlarge the hierarchy to include two new classes—SalariedEmployee (for people paid a fixed weekly salary) and HourlyEmployee (for people paid an hourly salary and so-called time-and-a-half for overtime). We declare a common set of functionality for all the classes in the updated hierarchy in a so-called abstract class, Employee, from which classes SalariedEmployee, HourlyEmployee and CommissionEmployee inherit directly and class BasePlusCommissionEmployee4 inherits indirectly. As you'll soon see, when we invoke each employee's earnings method off a superclass Employee reference, the correct earnings calculation is performed due to Java's polymorphic capabilities.

Occasionally, when performing polymorphic processing, we need to program "in the specific." Our Employee case study demonstrates that a program can determine the type of an object at execution time and act on that object accordingly. In the case study, we use these capabilities to determine whether a particular employee object *is a* BasePlusCommissionEmployee. If so, we increase that employee's base salary by 10%.

The chapter continues with an introduction to Java interfaces. An interface describes a set of methods that can be called on an object, but does not provide concrete implementations for the methods. Programmers can declare classes that *implement* (i.e., provide concrete implementations for the methods of) one or more interfaces. Each interface method must be declared in all the classes that implement the interface. Once a class implements an interface, all objects of that class have an *is-a* relationship with the interface type, and all objects of the class are guaranteed to provide the functionality described by the interface. This is true of all subclasses of that class as well.

Interfaces are particularly useful for assigning common functionality to possibly unrelated classes. This allows objects of unrelated classes to be processed polymorphically—objects of classes that implement the same interface can respond to the same method calls. To demonstrate creating and using interfaces, we modify our payroll application to create a general accounts payable application that can calculate payments due for company employees and invoice amounts to be billed for purchased goods. As you'll see, interfaces enable polymorphic capabilities similar to those possible with inheritance.

10.2 Polymorphism Examples

We now consider several additional examples of polymorphism. If class Rectangle is derived from class Quadrilateral, then a Rectangle object is a more specific version of a Quadrilateral object. Any operation (e.g., calculating the perimeter or the area) that can be performed on a Quadrilateral object can also be performed on a Rectangle object. These operations can also be performed on other Quadrilaterals, such as Squares, Parallelograms and Trapezoids. The polymorphism occurs when a program invokes a method through a superclass variable—at execution time, the correct subclass version of the method is called, based on the type of the reference stored in the superclass variable. You will see a simple code example that illustrates this process in Section 10.3.

As another example, suppose we design a video game that manipulates objects of classes Martian, Venusian, Plutonian, SpaceShip and LaserBeam. Imagine that each class inherits from the common superclass called SpaceObject, which contains method draw. Each subclass implements this method. A screen-manager program maintains a collection (e.g., a SpaceObject array) of references to objects of the various classes. To refresh the screen, the screen manager periodically sends each object the same message—namely, draw. However, each object responds in a unique way. For example, a Martian object might draw itself in red with green eyes and the appropriate number of antennae. A SpaceShip object might draw itself as a bright silver flying saucer. A LaserBeam object might draw itself as a bright red beam across the screen. Again, the same message (in this case, draw) sent to a variety of objects has "many forms" of results.

A polymorphic screen manager might use polymorphism to facilitate adding new classes to a system with minimal modifications to the system's code. Suppose that we want to add Mercurian objects to our video game. To do so, we must build a class Mercurian that extends SpaceObject and provides its own draw method implementation. When objects of class Mercurian appear in the SpaceObject collection, the screen manager code invokes method draw, exactly as it does for every other object in the collection, regardless of its type. So the new Mercurian objects simply "plug right in" without any modification of the screen manager code by the programmer. Thus, without modifying the system (other than to build new classes and modify the code that creates new objects), programmers can use polymorphism to conveniently include additional types that were not envisioned when the system was created.

With polymorphism, the same method name and signature can be used to cause different actions to occur, depending on the type of object on which the method is invoked. This gives the programmer tremendous expressive capability.

Software Engineering Observation 10.1

Polymorphism enables programmers to deal in generalities and let the execution-time environment handle the specifics. Programmers can command objects to behave in manners appropriate to those objects, without knowing the types of the objects (as long as the objects belong to the same inheritance hierarchy).

Software Engineering Observation 10.2

Polymorphism promotes extensibility: Software that invokes polymorphic behavior is independent of the object types to which messages are sent. New object types that can respond to existing method calls can be incorporated into a system without requiring modification of the base system. Only client code that instantiates new objects must be modified to accommodate new types.

10.3 Demonstrating Polymorphic Behavior

Section 9.4 created a commission employee class hierarchy, in which class BasePlusCommissionEmployee inherited from class CommissionEmployee. The examples in that section manipulated CommissionEmployee and BasePlusCommissionEmployee objects by using references to them to invoke their methods—we aimed superclass references at superclass objects and subclass references at subclass objects. These assignments are natural and straightforward—superclass references are intended to refer to superclass objects, and subclass references are intended to refer to subclass objects. However, as you will soon see, other assignments are possible.

In the next example, we aim a superclass reference at a subclass object. We then show how invoking a method on a subclass object via a superclass reference invokes the subclass functionality—the type of the *actual referenced object*, not the type of the *reference*, determines which method is called. This example demonstrates the key concept that an object of a subclass can be treated as an object of its superclass. This enables various interesting manipulations. A program can create an array of superclass references that refer to objects of many subclass types. This is allowed because each subclass object *is an* object of its superclass. For instance, we can assign the reference of a BasePlusCommissionEmployee object to a superclass CommissionEmployee variable because a BasePlusCommissionEmployee *is a* CommissionEmployee—we can treat a BasePlusCommissionEmployee as a CommissionEmployee.

As you'll learn later in the chapter, we cannot treat a superclass object as a subclass object because a superclass object is not an object of any of its subclasses. For example, we cannot assign the reference of a CommissionEmployee object to a subclass BasePlusCommissionEmployee variable because a CommissionEmployee is not a BasePlusCommissionEmployee—a CommissionEmployee does not have a baseSalary instance variable and does not have methods setBaseSalary and getBaseSalary. The *is-a* relationship applies only from a subclass to its direct (and indirect) superclasses, and not vice versa.

The Java compiler does allow the assignment of a superclass reference to a subclass variable if we explicitly cast the superclass reference to the subclass type—a technique we discuss in detail in Section 10.5. Why would we ever want to perform such an assignment? A superclass reference can be used to invoke only the methods declared in the superclass—attempting to invoke subclass-only methods through a superclass reference results in compilation errors. If a program needs to perform a subclass-specific operation on a subclass object referenced by a superclass variable, the program must first cast the superclass reference to a subclass reference through a technique known as **downcasting**. This enables the program to invoke subclass methods that are not in the superclass. We show a concrete example of downcasting in Section 10.5.

The example in Fig. 10.1 demonstrates three ways to use superclass and subclass variables to store references to superclass and subclass objects. The first two are straightforward—as in Section 9.4, we assign a superclass reference to a superclass variable, and we assign a subclass reference to a subclass variable. Then we demonstrate the relationship between subclasses and superclasses (i.e., the *is-a* relationship) by assigning a subclass reference to a superclass variable. [*Note:* This program uses classes CommissionEmployee3 and BasePlusCommissionEmployee4 from Fig. 9.12 and Fig. 9.13, respectively.]

```java
 1    // Fig. 10.1: PolymorphismTest.java
 2    // Assigning superclass and subclass references to superclass and
 3    // subclass variables.
 4
 5    public class PolymorphismTest
 6    {
 7       public static void main( String args[] )
 8       {
 9          // assign superclass reference to superclass variable
10          CommissionEmployee3 commissionEmployee = new CommissionEmployee3(
11             "Sue", "Jones", "222-22-2222", 10000, .06 );
12
13          // assign subclass reference to subclass variable
14          BasePlusCommissionEmployee4 basePlusCommissionEmployee =
15             new BasePlusCommissionEmployee4(
16             "Bob", "Lewis", "333-33-3333", 5000, .04, 300 );
17
18          // invoke toString on superclass object using superclass variable
19          System.out.printf( "%s %s:\n\n%s\n\n",
20             "Call CommissionEmployee3's toString with superclass reference ",
21             "to superclass object", commissionEmployee.toString() );
22
23          // invoke toString on subclass object using subclass variable
24          System.out.printf( "%s %s:\n\n%s\n\n",
25             "Call BasePlusCommissionEmployee4's toString with subclass",
26             "reference to subclass object",
27             basePlusCommissionEmployee.toString() );
28
29          // invoke toString on subclass object using superclass variable
30          CommissionEmployee3 commissionEmployee2 =
31             basePlusCommissionEmployee;
32          System.out.printf( "%s %s:\n\n%s\n",
33             "Call BasePlusCommissionEmployee4's toString with superclass",
34             "reference to subclass object", commissionEmployee2.toString() );
35       } // end main
36    } // end class PolymorphismTest
```

Fig. 10.1 | Assigning superclass and subclass references to superclass and subclass variables. (Part 1 of 2.)

```
Call CommissionEmployee3's toString with superclass reference to superclass
object:

commission employee: Sue Jones
social security number: 222-22-2222
gross sales: 10000.00
commission rate: 0.06

Call BasePlusCommissionEmployee4's toString with subclass reference to
subclass object:

base-salaried commission employee: Bob Lewis
social security number: 333-33-3333
gross sales: 5000.00
commission rate: 0.04
base salary: 300.00

Call BasePlusCommissionEmployee4's toString with superclass reference to
subclass object:

base-salaried commission employee: Bob Lewis
social security number: 333-33-3333
gross sales: 5000.00
commission rate: 0.04
base salary: 300.00
```

Fig. 10.1 | Assigning superclass and subclass references to superclass and subclass variables. (Part 2 of 2.)

In Fig. 10.1, lines 10–11 create a CommissionEmployee3 object and assign its reference to a CommissionEmployee3 variable. Lines 14–16 create a BasePlusCommission-Employee4 object and assign its reference to a BasePlusCommissionEmployee4 variable. These assignments are natural—for example, a CommissionEmployee3 variable's primary purpose is to hold a reference to a CommissionEmployee3 object. Lines 19–21 use reference commissionEmployee to invoke toString explicitly. Because commissionEmployee refers to a CommissionEmployee3 object, superclass CommissionEmployee3's version of toString is called. Similarly, lines 24–27 use basePlusCommissionEmployee to invoke toString explicitly on the BasePlusCommissionEmployee4 object. This invokes subclass BasePlus-CommissionEmployee4's version of toString.

Lines 30–31 then assign the reference to subclass object basePlusCommissionEm-ployee to a superclass CommissionEmployee3 variable, which lines 32–34 use to invoke method toString. When a superclass variable contains a reference to a subclass object, and that reference is used to call a method, the subclass version of the method is called. Hence, commissionEmployee2.toString() in line 34 actually calls class BasePlusCommission-Employee4's toString method. The Java compiler allows this "crossover" because an object of a subclass *is an* object of its superclass (but not vice versa). When the compiler encounters a method call made through a variable, the compiler determines if the method can be called by checking the variable's class type. If that class contains the proper method declaration (or inherits one), the call is compiled. At execution time, the type of the object to which the variable refers determines the actual method to use.

10.4 Abstract Classes and Methods

When we think of a class type, we assume that programs will create objects of that type. In some cases, however, it is useful to declare classes for which the programmer never intends to instantiate objects. Such classes are called abstract classes. Because they are used only as superclasses in inheritance hierarchies, we refer to them as abstract superclasses. These classes cannot be used to instantiate objects, because, as we will soon see, abstract classes are incomplete. Subclasses must declare the "missing pieces." We demonstrate abstract classes in Section 10.5.

An abstract class's purpose is to provide an appropriate superclass from which other classes can inherit and thus share a common design. In the Shape hierarchy of Fig. 9.3, for example, subclasses inherit the notion of what it means to be a Shape—common attributes such as location, color and borderThickness, and behaviors such as draw, move, resize and changeColor. Classes that can be used to instantiate objects are called concrete classes. Such classes provide implementations of every method they declare (some of the implementations can be inherited). For example, we could derive concrete classes Circle, Square and Triangle from abstract superclass TwoDimensionalShape. Similarly, we could derive concrete classes Sphere, Cube and Tetrahedron from abstract superclass ThreeDimensionalShape. Abstract superclasses are too general to create real objects—they specify only what is common among subclasses. We need to be more specific before we can create objects. For example, if you send the draw message to abstract class TwoDimensionalShape, it knows that two-dimensional shapes should be drawable, but it does not know what specific shape to draw, so it cannot implement a real draw method. Concrete classes provide the specifics that make it reasonable to instantiate objects.

Not all inheritance hierarchies contain abstract classes. However, programmers often write client code that uses only abstract superclass types to reduce client code's dependencies on a range of specific subclass types. For example, a programmer can write a method with a parameter of an abstract superclass type. When called, such a method can be passed an object of any concrete class that directly or indirectly extends the superclass specified as the parameter's type.

Abstract classes sometimes constitute several levels of the hierarchy. For example, the Shape hierarchy of Fig. 9.3 begins with abstract class Shape. On the next level of the hierarchy are two more abstract classes, TwoDimensionalShape and ThreeDimensionalShape. The next level of the hierarchy declares concrete classes for TwoDimensionalShapes (Circle, Square and Triangle) and for ThreeDimensionalShapes (Sphere, Cube and Tetrahedron).

You make a class abstract by declaring it with keyword **abstract**. An abstract class normally contains one or more **abstract methods**. An abstract method is one with keyword abstract in its declaration, as in

```
public abstract void draw(); // abstract method
```

Abstract methods do not provide implementations. A class that contains any abstract methods must be declared as an abstract class even if that class contains some concrete (nonabstract) methods. Each concrete subclass of an abstract superclass also must provide concrete implementations of each of the superclass's abstract methods. Constructors and static methods cannot be declared abstract. Constructors are not inherited, so an abstract constructor could never be implemented. Though static methods are inherited, they are not associated with particular objects of the classes that declare the static methods. Since abstract methods are meant to be overridden so they can process objects based on their types, it would not make sense to declare a static method as abstract.

Software Engineering Observation 10.3

An abstract class declares common attributes and behaviors of the various classes in a class hierarchy. An abstract class typically contains one or more abstract methods that subclasses must override if the subclasses are to be concrete. The instance variables and concrete methods of an abstract class are subject to the normal rules of inheritance.

Common Programming Error 10.1

Attempting to instantiate an object of an abstract class is a compilation error.

Common Programming Error 10.2

Failure to implement a superclass's abstract methods in a subclass is a compilation error unless the subclass is also declared abstract.

Although we cannot instantiate objects of abstract superclasses, you will soon see that we *can* use abstract superclasses to declare variables that can hold references to objects of any concrete class derived from those abstract superclasses. Programs typically use such variables to manipulate subclass objects polymorphically. We also can use abstract superclass names to invoke static methods declared in those abstract superclasses.

Consider another application of polymorphism. A drawing program needs to display many shapes, including new shape types that the programmer will add to the system after writing the drawing program. The drawing program might need to display shapes, such as Circles, Triangles, Rectangles or others, that derive from abstract superclass Shape. The drawing program uses Shape variables to manage the objects that are displayed. To draw any object in this inheritance hierarchy, the drawing program uses a superclass Shape variable containing a reference to the subclass object to invoke the object's draw method. This method is declared abstract in superclass Shape, so each concrete subclass *must* implement method draw in a manner specific to that shape. Each object in the Shape inheritance hierarchy knows how to draw itself. The drawing program does not have to worry about the type of each object or whether the drawing program has ever encountered objects of that type.

Polymorphism is particularly effective for implementing so-called layered software systems. In operating systems, for example, each type of physical device could operate quite differently from the others. Even so, commands to read or write data from and to devices may have a certain uniformity. For each device, the operating system uses a piece of software called a device driver to control all communication between the system and the device. The write message sent to a device-driver object needs to be interpreted specifically in the context of that driver and how it manipulates devices of a specific type. However, the write call itself really is no different from the write to any other device in the system: Place some number of bytes from memory onto that device. An object-oriented operating system might use an abstract superclass to provide an "interface" appropriate for all device drivers. Then, through inheritance from that abstract superclass, subclasses are formed that all behave similarly. The device-driver methods are declared as abstract methods in the abstract superclass. The implementations of these abstract methods are provided in the subclasses that correspond to the specific types of device drivers. New devices are always being developed, and often long after the operating system has been released. When you buy a new device, it comes with a device driver provided by the device vendor. The device is immediately operational after you connect it to your computer and install the driver. This is another elegant example of how polymorphism makes systems extensible.

It is common in object-oriented programming to declare an iterator class that can traverse all the objects in a collection, such as an array (Chapter 7) or an ArrayList (Chapter 19, Collections). For example, a program can print an ArrayList of objects by creating an iterator object and using it to obtain the next list element each time the iterator is called. Iterators often are used in polymorphic programming to traverse a collection that contains references to objects from various levels of a hierarchy. (Chapter 19 presents a thorough treatment of ArrayList, iterators and "generics" capabilities.) An ArrayList of objects of class TwoDimensionalShape, for example, could contain objects from subclasses Square, Circle, Triangle and so on. Calling method draw for each TwoDimensionalShape object off a TwoDimensionalShape variable would polymorphically draw each object correctly on the screen.

10.5 Case Study: Payroll System Using Polymorphism

This section reexamines the CommissionEmployee-BasePlusCommissionEmployee hierarchy that we explored throughout Section 9.4. Now we use an abstract method and polymorphism to perform payroll calculations based on the type of employee. We create an enhanced employee hierarchy to solve the following problem:

> *A company pays its employees on a weekly basis. The employees are of four types: Salaried employees are paid a fixed weekly salary regardless of the number of hours worked, hourly employees are paid by the hour and receive overtime pay for all hours worked in excess of 40 hours, commission employees are paid a percentage of their sales and salaried-commission employees receive a base salary plus a percentage of their sales. For the current pay period, the company has decided to reward salaried-commission employees by adding 10% to their base salaries. The company wants to implement a Java application that performs its payroll calculations polymorphically.*

We use abstract class Employee to represent the general concept of an employee. The classes that extend Employee are SalariedEmployee, CommissionEmployee and HourlyEmployee. Class BasePlusCommissionEmployee—which extends CommissionEmployee—represents the last employee type. The UML class diagram in Fig. 10.2 shows the inheritance hierarchy for our polymorphic employee-payroll application. Note that abstract class Employee is italicized, as per the convention of the UML.

Abstract superclass Employee declares the "interface" to the hierarchy—that is, the set of methods that a program can invoke on all Employee objects. We use the term "interface" here in a general sense to refer to the various ways programs can communicate with objects of any Employee subclass. Be careful not to confuse the general notion of an "interface" to something with the formal notion of a Java interface, the subject of Section 10.7. Each employee, regardless of the way his or her earnings are calculated, has a first name, a last name and a social security number, so private instance variables firstName, lastName and socialSecurityNumber appear in abstract superclass Employee.

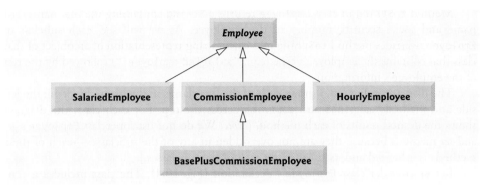

Fig. 10.2 | `Employee` hierarchy UML class diagram.

> **Software Engineering Observation 10.4**
>
> *A subclass can inherit "interface" or "implementation" from a superclass. Hierarchies designed for **implementation inheritance** tend to have their functionality high in the hierarchy—each new subclass inherits one or more methods that were implemented in a superclass, and the subclass uses the superclass implementations. Hierarchies designed for **interface inheritance** tend to have their functionality lower in the hierarchy—a superclass specifies one or more abstract methods that must be declared for each concrete class in the hierarchy, and the individual subclasses override these methods to provide subclass-specific implementations.*

The following sections implement the `Employee` class hierarchy. Each of the first four sections implements one of the concrete classes. The last section implements a test program that builds objects of all these classes and processes those objects polymorphically.

10.5.1 Creating Abstract Superclass `Employee`

Class `Employee` (Fig. 10.4) provides methods `earnings` and `toString`, in addition to the *get* and *set* methods that manipulate `Employee`'s instance variables. An `earnings` method certainly applies generically to all employees. But each earnings calculation depends on the employee's class. So we declare `earnings` as `abstract` in superclass `Employee` because a default implementation does not make sense for that method—there is not enough information to determine what amount `earnings` should return. Each subclass overrides `earnings` with an appropriate implementation. To calculate an employee's earnings, the program assigns a reference to the employee's object to a superclass `Employee` variable, then invokes the `earnings` method on that variable. We maintain an array of `Employee` variables, each of which holds a reference to an `Employee` object (of course, there cannot be `Employee` objects because `Employee` is an abstract class—because of inheritance, however, all objects of all subclasses of `Employee` may nevertheless be thought of as `Employee` objects). The program iterates through the array and calls method `earnings` for each `Employee` object. Java processes these method calls polymorphically. Including `earnings` as an abstract method in `Employee` forces every direct subclass of `Employee` to override `earnings` in order to become a concrete class. This enables the designer of the class hierarchy to demand that each concrete subclass provide an appropriate pay calculation.

Method `toString` in class `Employee` returns a `String` containing the first name, last name and social security number of the employee. As we will see, each subclass of `Employee` overrides method `toString` to create a string representation of an object of that class that contains the employee's type (e.g., `"salaried employee:"`) followed by the rest of the employee's information.

The diagram in Fig. 10.3 shows each of the five classes in the hierarchy down the left side and methods `earnings` and `toString` across the top. For each class, the diagram shows the desired results of each method. [*Note:* We do not list superclass `Employee`'s *get* and *set* methods because they are not overridden in any of the subclasses—each of these methods is inherited and used "as is" by each of the subclasses.]

Let us consider class `Employee`'s declaration (Fig. 10.4). The class includes a constructor that takes the first name, last name and social security number as arguments (lines 11–16); *get* methods that return the first name, last name and social security number (lines 25–28, 37–40 and 49–52, respectively); *set* methods that set the first name, last name and social security number (lines 19–22, 31–34 and 43–46, respectively); method `toString` (lines 55–59), which returns the string representation of `Employee`; and abstract method `earnings` (line 62), which will be implemented by subclasses. Note that the `Employee` constructor does not validate the social security number in this example. Normally, such validation should be provided.

	earnings	toString
Employee	abstract	*firstName lastName* `social security number:` *SSN*
Salaried- Employee	`weeklySalary`	`salaried employee:` *firstName lastName* `social security number:` *SSN* `weekly salary:` *weeklysalary*

Hourly-
Employee
	`if hours <= 40`
	  `wage * hours`
	`else if hours > 40`
	  `40 * wage +`
	  `( hours - 40 ) *`
	  `wage * 1.5`
		`hourly employee:` *firstName lastName*
		`social security number:` *SSN*
		`hourly wage:` *wage*`; hours worked:` *hours*

Commission- Employee	`commissionRate *` `grossSales`	`commission employee:` *firstName lastName* `social security number:` *SSN* `gross sales:` *grossSales*`;` `commission rate:` *commissionRate*

BasePlus-
Commission-
Employee
	`( commissionRate *`
	`grossSales ) +`
	`baseSalary`
		`base salaried commission employee:`
		  firstName lastName
		`social security number:` *SSN*
		`gross sales:` *grossSales*`;`
		`commission rate:` *commissionRate*`;`
		`base salary:` *baseSalary*

Fig. 10.3 | Polymorphic interface for the `Employee` hierarchy classes.

```java
1   // Fig. 10.4: Employee.java
2   // Employee abstract superclass.
3
4   public abstract class Employee
5   {
6      private String firstName;
7      private String lastName;
8      private String socialSecurityNumber;
9
10     // three-argument constructor
11     public Employee( String first, String last, String ssn )
12     {
13        firstName = first;
14        lastName = last;
15        socialSecurityNumber = ssn;
16     } // end three-argument Employee constructor
17
18     // set first name
19     public void setFirstName( String first )
20     {
21        firstName = first;
22     } // end method setFirstName
23
24     // return first name
25     public String getFirstName()
26     {
27        return firstName;
28     } // end method getFirstName
29
30     // set last name
31     public void setLastName( String last )
32     {
33        lastName = last;
34     } // end method setLastName
35
36     // return last name
37     public String getLastName()
38     {
39        return lastName;
40     } // end method getLastName
41
42     // set social security number
43     public void setSocialSecurityNumber( String ssn )
44     {
45        socialSecurityNumber = ssn; // should validate
46     } // end method setSocialSecurityNumber
47
48     // return social security number
49     public String getSocialSecurityNumber()
50     {
51        return socialSecurityNumber;
52     } // end method getSocialSecurityNumber
53
```

Fig. 10.4 | Employee abstract superclass. (Part 1 of 2.)

```
54        // return String representation of Employee object
55        public String toString()
56        {
57           return String.format( "%s %s\nsocial security number: %s",
58              getFirstName(), getLastName(), getSocialSecurityNumber() );
59        } // end method toString
60
61        // abstract method overridden by subclasses
62        public abstract double earnings(); // no implementation here
63     } // end abstract class Employee
```

Fig. 10.4 | Employee abstract superclass. (Part 2 of 2.)

Why did we decide to declare earnings as an abstract method? It simply does not make sense to provide an implementation of this method in class Employee. We cannot calculate the earnings for a general Employee—we first must know the specific Employee type to determine the appropriate earnings calculation. By declaring this method abstract, we indicate that each concrete subclass *must* provide an appropriate earnings implementation and that a program will be able to use superclass Employee variables to invoke method earnings polymorphically for any type of Employee.

10.5.2 Creating Concrete Subclass SalariedEmployee

Class SalariedEmployee (Fig. 10.5) extends class Employee (line 4) and overrides earnings (lines 29–32), which makes SalariedEmployee a concrete class. The class includes a constructor (lines 9–14) that takes a first name, a last name, a social security number and a weekly salary as arguments; a *set* method to assign a new nonnegative value to instance variable weeklySalary (lines 17–20); a *get* method to return weeklySalary's value (lines 23–26); a method earnings (lines 29–32) to calculate a SalariedEmployee's earnings; and a method toString (lines 35–39), which returns a String including the employee's type, namely, "salaried employee: " followed by employee-specific information produced by superclass Employee's toString method and SalariedEmployee's getWeeklySalary method. Class SalariedEmployee's constructor passes the first name, last name and social security number to the Employee constructor (line 12) to initialize the private instance variables not inherited from the superclass. Method earnings overrides abstract method earnings in Employee to provide a concrete implementation that returns the SalariedEmployee's weekly salary. If we do not implement earnings, class SalariedEmployee must be declared abstract—otherwise, a compilation error occurs (and, of course, we want SalariedEmployee here to be a concrete class).

Method toString (lines 35–39) of class SalariedEmployee overrides Employee method toString. If class SalariedEmployee did not override toString, SalariedEmployee would have inherited the Employee version of toString. In that case, SalariedEmployee's toString method would simply return the employee's full name and social security number, which does not adequately represent a SalariedEmployee. To produce a complete string representation of a SalariedEmployee, the subclass's toString method returns "salaried employee: " followed by the superclass Employee-specific information (i.e., first name, last name and social security number) obtained by invoking the superclass's toString method (line 38)—this is a nice example of code reuse. The string repre-

```java
1  // Fig. 10.5: SalariedEmployee.java
2  // SalariedEmployee class extends Employee.
3
4  public class SalariedEmployee extends Employee
5  {
6     private double weeklySalary;
7
8     // four-argument constructor
9     public SalariedEmployee( String first, String last, String ssn,
10       double salary )
11    {
12       super( first, last, ssn ); // pass to Employee constructor
13       setWeeklySalary( salary ); // validate and store salary
14    } // end four-argument SalariedEmployee constructor
15
16    // set salary
17    public void setWeeklySalary( double salary )
18    {
19       weeklySalary = salary < 0.0 ? 0.0 : salary;
20    } // end method setWeeklySalary
21
22    // return salary
23    public double getWeeklySalary()
24    {
25       return weeklySalary;
26    } // end method getWeeklySalary
27
28    // calculate earnings; override abstract method earnings in Employee
29    public double earnings()
30    {
31       return getWeeklySalary();
32    } // end method earnings
33
34    // return String representation of SalariedEmployee object
35    public String toString()
36    {
37       return String.format( "salaried employee: %s\n%s: $%,.2f",
38          super.toString(), "weekly salary", getWeeklySalary() );
39    } // end method toString
40  } // end class SalariedEmployee
```

Fig. 10.5 | `SalariedEmployee` class derived from `Employee`.

sentation of a `SalariedEmployee` also contains the employee's weekly salary obtained by invoking the class's `getWeeklySalary` method.

10.5.3 Creating Concrete Subclass HourlyEmployee

Class `HourlyEmployee` (Fig. 10.6) also extends `Employee` (line 4). The class includes a constructor (lines 10–16) that takes as arguments a first name, a last name, a social security number, an hourly wage and the number of hours worked. Lines 19–22 and 31–35 declare *set* methods that assign new values to instance variables wage and hours, respectively. Method `setWage` (lines 19–22) ensures that wage is nonnegative, and method `setHours`

```
 1   // Fig. 10.6: HourlyEmployee.java
 2   // HourlyEmployee class extends Employee.
 3
 4   public class HourlyEmployee extends Employee
 5   {
 6      private double wage; // wage per hour
 7      private double hours; // hours worked for week
 8
 9      // five-argument constructor
10      public HourlyEmployee( String first, String last, String ssn,
11         double hourlyWage, double hoursWorked )
12      {
13         super( first, last, ssn );
14         setWage( hourlyWage ); // validate hourly wage
15         setHours( hoursWorked ); // validate hours worked
16      } // end five-argument HourlyEmployee constructor
17
18      // set wage
19      public void setWage( double hourlyWage )
20      {
21         wage = ( hourlyWage < 0.0 ) ? 0.0 : hourlyWage;
22      } // end method setWage
23
24      // return wage
25      public double getWage()
26      {
27         return wage;
28      } // end method getWage
29
30      // set hours worked
31      public void setHours( double hoursWorked )
32      {
33         hours = ( ( hoursWorked >= 0.0 ) && ( hoursWorked <= 168.0 ) ) ?
34            hoursWorked : 0.0;
35      } // end method setHours
36
37      // return hours worked
38      public double getHours()
39      {
40         return hours;
41      } // end method getHours
42
43      // calculate earnings; override abstract method earnings in Employee
44      public double earnings()
45      {
46         if ( getHours() <= 40 ) // no overtime
47            return getWage() * getHours();
48         else
49            return 40 * getWage() + ( gethours() - 40 ) * getWage() * 1.5;
50      } // end method earnings
51
```

Fig. 10.6 | HourlyEmployee class derived from Employee. (Part 1 of 2.)

```
52        // return String representation of HourlyEmployee object
53        public String toString()
54        {
55           return String.format( "hourly employee: %s\n%s: $%,.2f; %s: %,.2f",
56              super.toString(), "hourly wage", getWage(),
57              "hours worked", getHours() );
58        } // end method toString
59     } // end class HourlyEmployee
```

Fig. 10.6 | HourlyEmployee class derived from Employee. (Part 2 of 2.)

(lines 31–35) ensures that hours is between 0 and 168 (the total number of hours in a week) inclusive. Class HourlyEmployee also includes *get* methods (lines 25–28 and 38–41) to return the values of wage and hours, respectively; a method earnings (lines 44–50) to calculate an HourlyEmployee's earnings; and a method toString (lines 53–58), which returns the employee's type, namely, "hourly employee: " and Employee-specific information. Note that the HourlyEmployee constructor, like the SalariedEmployee constructor, passes the first name, last name and social security number to the superclass Employee constructor (line 13) to initialize the private instance variables. In addition, method toString calls superclass method toString (line 56) to obtain the Employee-specific information (i.e., first name, last name and social security number)—this is another nice example of code reuse.

10.5.4 Creating Concrete Subclass CommissionEmployee

Class CommissionEmployee (Fig. 10.7) extends class Employee (line 4). The class includes a constructor (lines 10–16) that takes a first name, a last name, a social security number, a sales amount and a commission rate; *set* methods (lines 19–22 and 31–34) to assign new values to instance variables commissionRate and grossSales, respectively; *get* methods (lines 25–28 and 37–40) that retrieve the values of these instance variables; method earnings (lines 43–46) to calculate a CommissionEmployee's earnings; and method toString (lines 49–55), which returns the employee's type, namely, "commission employee: " and Employee-specific information. The constructor also passes the first name, last name and social security number to Employee's constructor (line 13) to initialize Employee's private instance variables. Method toString calls superclass method toString (line 52) to obtain the Employee-specific information (i.e., first name, last name and social security number).

```
 1   // Fig. 10.7: CommissionEmployee.java
 2   // CommissionEmployee class extends Employee.
 3
 4   public class CommissionEmployee extends Employee
 5   {
 6      private double grossSales; // gross weekly sales
 7      private double commissionRate; // commission percentage
 8
 9      // five-argument constructor
10      public CommissionEmployee( String first, String last, String ssn,
11         double sales, double rate )
12      {
```

Fig. 10.7 | CommissionEmployee class derived from Employee. (Part 1 of 2.)

```
13          super( first, last, ssn );
14          setGrossSales( sales );
15          setCommissionRate( rate );
16      } // end five-argument CommissionEmployee constructor
17
18      // set commission rate
19      public void setCommissionRate( double rate )
20      {
21          commissionRate = ( rate > 0.0 && rate < 1.0 ) ? rate : 0.0;
22      } // end method setCommissionRate
23
24      // return commission rate
25      public double getCommissionRate()
26      {
27          return commissionRate;
28      } // end method getCommissionRate
29
30      // set gross sales amount
31      public void setGrossSales( double sales )
32      {
33          grossSales = ( sales < 0.0 ) ? 0.0 : sales;
34      } // end method setGrossSales
35
36      // return gross sales amount
37      public double getGrossSales()
38      {
39          return grossSales;
40      } // end method getGrossSales
41
42      // calculate earnings; override abstract method earnings in Employee
43      public double earnings()
44      {
45          return getCommissionRate() * getGrossSales();
46      } // end method earnings
47
48      // return String representation of CommissionEmployee object
49      public String toString()
50      {
51          return String.format( "%s: %s\n%s: $%,.2f; %s: %.2f",
52              "commission employee", super.toString(),
53              "gross sales", getGrossSales(),
54              "commission rate", getCommissionRate() );
55      } // end method toString
56  } // end class CommissionEmployee
```

Fig. 10.7 | CommissionEmployee class derived from Employee. (Part 2 of 2.)

10.5.5 Creating Indirect Concrete Subclass BasePlusCommissionEmployee

Class BasePlusCommissionEmployee (Fig. 10.8) extends class CommissionEmployee (line 4) and therefore is an indirect subclass of class Employee. Class BasePlusCommission-Employee has a constructor (lines 9–14) that takes as arguments a first name, a last name, a social security number, a sales amount, a commission rate and a base salary. It then passes the first name, last name, social security number, sales amount and commission rate to the CommissionEmployee constructor (line 12) to initialize the inherited members. BasePlus-CommissionEmployee also contains a *set* method (lines 17–20) to assign a new value to instance variable baseSalary and a *get* method (lines 23–26) to return baseSalary's value. Method earnings (lines 29–32) calculates a BasePlusCommissionEmployee's earnings. Note that line 31 in method earnings calls superclass CommissionEmployee's earnings method to calculate the commission-based portion of the employee's earnings. This is a nice example of code reuse. BasePlusCommissionEmployee's toString method (lines 35–40) creates a string representation of a BasePlusCommissionEmployee that contains "base-salaried", followed by the String obtained by invoking superclass Commission-Employee's toString method (another example of code reuse), then the base salary. The result is a String beginning with "base-salaried commission employee" followed by the rest of the BasePlusCommissionEmployee's information. Recall that CommissionEmployee's toString obtains the employee's first name, last name and social security number by invoking the toString method of its superclass (i.e., Employee)—yet another example of code reuse. Note that BasePlusCommissionEmployee's toString initiates a chain of method calls that span all three levels of the Employee hierarchy.

```java
1   // Fig. 10.8: BasePlusCommissionEmployee.java
2   // BasePlusCommissionEmployee class extends CommissionEmployee.
3
4   public class BasePlusCommissionEmployee extends CommissionEmployee
5   {
6      private double baseSalary; // base salary per week
7
8      // six-argument constructor
9      public BasePlusCommissionEmployee( String first, String last,
10        String ssn, double sales, double rate, double salary )
11     {
12        super( first, last, ssn, sales, rate );
13        setBaseSalary( salary ); // validate and store base salary
14     } // end six-argument BasePlusCommissionEmployee constructor
15
16     // set base salary
17     public void setBaseSalary( double salary )
18     {
19        baseSalary = ( salary < 0.0 ) ? 0.0 : salary; // non-negative
20     } // end method setBaseSalary
21
22     // return base salary
23     public double getBaseSalary()
24     {
25        return baseSalary;
26     } // end method getBaseSalary
27
28     // calculate earnings; override method earnings in CommissionEmployee
29     public double earnings()
30     {
```

Fig. 10.8 | BasePlusCommissionEmployee class derived from CommissionEmployee. (Part 1 of 2.)

```
31          return getBaseSalary() + super.earnings();
32       } // end method earnings
33
34       // return String representation of BasePlusCommissionEmployee object
35       public String toString()
36       {
37          return String.format( "%s %s; %s: $%,.2f",
38             "base-salaried", super.toString(),
39             "base salary", getBaseSalary() );
40       } // end method toString
41    } // end class BasePlusCommissionEmployee
```

Fig. 10.8 | BasePlusCommissionEmployee class derived from CommissionEmployee. (Part 2 of 2.)

10.5.6 Demonstrating Polymorphic Processing, Operator instanceof and Downcasting

To test our Employee hierarchy, the application in Fig. 10.9 creates an object of each of the four concrete classes SalariedEmployee, HourlyEmployee, CommissionEmployee and BasePlusCommissionEmployee. The program manipulates these objects, first via variables of each object's own type, then polymorphically, using an array of Employee variables. While processing the objects polymorphically, the program increases the base salary of each BasePlusCommissionEmployee by 10% (this, of course, requires determining the object's type at execution time). Finally, the program polymorphically determines and outputs the type of each object in the Employee array. Lines 9–18 create objects of each of the four concrete Employee subclasses. Lines 22–30 output the string representation and earnings of each of these objects. Note that each object's toString method is called implicitly by printf when the object is output as a String with the %s format specifier.

```
 1   // Fig. 10.9: PayrollSystemTest.java
 2   // Employee hierarchy test program.
 3
 4   public class PayrollSystemTest
 5   {
 6      public static void main( String args[] )
 7      {
 8         // create subclass objects
 9         SalariedEmployee salariedEmployee =
10            new SalariedEmployee( "John", "Smith", "111-11-1111", 800.00 );
11         HourlyEmployee hourlyEmployee =
12            new HourlyEmployee( "Karen", "Price", "222-22-2222", 16.75, 40 );
13         CommissionEmployee commissionEmployee =
14            new CommissionEmployee(
15            "Sue", "Jones", "333-33-3333", 10000, .06 );
16         BasePlusCommissionEmployee basePlusCommissionEmployee =
17            new BasePlusCommissionEmployee(
18            "Bob", "Lewis", "444-44-4444", 5000, .04, 300 );
19
```

Fig. 10.9 | Employee class hierarchy test program. (Part 1 of 3.)

```
20          System.out.println( "Employees processed individually:\n" );
21
22          System.out.printf( "%s\n%s: $%,.2f\n\n",
23             salariedEmployee, "earned", salariedEmployee.earnings() );
24          System.out.printf( "%s\n%s: $%,.2f\n\n",
25             hourlyEmployee, "earned", hourlyEmployee.earnings() );
26          System.out.printf( "%s\n%s: $%,.2f\n\n",
27             commissionEmployee, "earned", commissionEmployee.earnings() );
28          System.out.printf( "%s\n%s: $%,.2f\n\n",
29             basePlusCommissionEmployee,
30             "earned", basePlusCommissionEmployee.earnings() );
31
32          // create four-element Employee array
33          Employee employees[] = new Employee[ 4 ];
34
35          // initialize array with Employees
36          employees[ 0 ] = salariedEmployee;
37          employees[ 1 ] = hourlyEmployee;
38          employees[ 2 ] = commissionEmployee;
39          employees[ 3 ] = basePlusCommissionEmployee;
40
41          System.out.println( "Employees processed polymorphically:\n" );
42
43          // generically process each element in array employees
44          for ( Employee currentEmployee : employees )
45          {
46             System.out.println( currentEmployee ); // invokes toString
47
48             // determine whether element is a BasePlusCommissionEmployee
49             if ( currentEmployee instanceof BasePlusCommissionEmployee )
50             {
51                // downcast Employee reference to
52                // BasePlusCommissionEmployee reference
53                BasePlusCommissionEmployee employee =
54                   ( BasePlusCommissionEmployee ) currentEmployee;
55
56                double oldBaseSalary = employee.getBaseSalary();
57                employee.setBaseSalary( 1.10 * oldBaseSalary );
58                System.out.printf(
59                   "new base salary with 10%% increase is: $%,.2f\n",
60                   employee.getBaseSalary() );
61             } // end if
62
63             System.out.printf(
64                "earned $%,.2f\n\n", currentEmployee.earnings() );
65          } // end for
66
67          // get type name of each object in employees array
68          for ( int j = 0; j < employees.length; j++ )
69             System.out.printf( "Employee %d is a %s\n", j,
70                employees[ j ].getClass().getName() );
71       } // end main
72    } // end class PayrollSystemTest
```

Fig. 10.9 | Employee class hierarchy test program. (Part 2 of 3.)

```
Employees processed individually:

salaried employee: John Smith
social security number: 111-11-1111
weekly salary: $800.00
earned: $800.00

hourly employee: Karen Price
social security number: 222-22-2222
hourly wage: $16.75; hours worked: 40.00
earned: $670.00

commission employee: Sue Jones
social security number: 333-33-3333
gross sales: $10,000.00; commission rate: 0.06
earned: $600.00

base-salaried commission employee: Bob Lewis
social security number: 444-44-4444
gross sales: $5,000.00; commission rate: 0.04; base salary: $300.00
earned: $500.00

Employees processed polymorphically:

salaried employee: John Smith
social security number: 111-11-1111
weekly salary: $800.00
earned $800.00

hourly employee: Karen Price
social security number: 222-22-2222
hourly wage: $16.75; hours worked: 40.00
earned $670.00

commission employee: Sue Jones
social security number: 333-33-3333
gross sales: $10,000.00; commission rate: 0.06
earned $600.00

base-salaried commission employee: Bob Lewis
social security number: 444-44-4444
gross sales: $5,000.00; commission rate: 0.04; base salary: $300.00
new base salary with 10% increase is: $330.00
earned $530.00

Employee 0 is a SalariedEmployee
Employee 1 is a HourlyEmployee
Employee 2 is a CommissionEmployee
Employee 3 is a BasePlusCommissionEmployee
```

Fig. 10.9 | Employee class hierarchy test program. (Part 3 of 3.)

Line 33 declares employees and assigns it an array of four Employee variables. Line 36 assigns the reference to a SalariedEmployee object to employees[0]. Line 37 assigns the reference to an HourlyEmployee object to employees[1]. Line 38 assigns the reference to a CommissionEmployee object to employees[2]. Line 39 assigns the reference to a BasePlusCommissionEmployee object to employee[3]. Each assignment is allowed, because a SalariedEmployee *is an* Employee, an HourlyEmployee *is an* Employee, a CommissionEmployee *is an* Employee and a BasePlusCommissionEmployee *is an* Employee. Therefore, we can assign the references of SalariedEmployee, HourlyEmployee, CommissionEmployee and BasePlusCommissionEmployee objects to superclass Employee variables, even though Employee is an abstract class.

Lines 44–65 iterate through array employees and invoke methods toString and earnings with Employee variable currentEmployee, which is assigned the reference to a different Employee in the array during each iteration. The output illustrates that the appropriate methods for each class are indeed invoked. All calls to method toString and earnings are resolved at execution time, based on the type of the object to which currentEmployee refers. This process is known as **dynamic binding** or **late binding**. For example, line 46 implicitly invokes method toString of the object to which currentEmployee refers. As a result of dynamic binding, Java decides which class's toString method to call at execution time rather than at compile time. Note that only the methods of class Employee can be called via an Employee variable (and Employee, of course, includes the methods of class Object). (Section 9.7 discusses the set of methods that all classes inherit from class Object.) A superclass reference can be used to invoke only methods of the superclass (and the superclass can invoke overridden versions of these in the subclass).

We perform special processing on BasePlusCommissionEmployee objects—as we encounter these objects, we increase their base salary by 10%. When processing objects polymorphically, we typically do not need to worry about the "specifics," but to adjust the base salary, we do have to determine the specific type of Employee object at execution time. Line 49 uses the **instanceof** operator to determine whether a particular Employee object's type is BasePlusCommissionEmployee. The condition in line 49 is true if the object referenced by currentEmployee *is a* BasePlusCommissionEmployee. This would also be true for any object of a BasePlusCommissionEmployee subclass because of the *is-a* relationship a subclass has with its superclass. Lines 53–54 downcast currentEmployee from type Employee to type BasePlusCommissionEmployee—this cast is allowed only if the object has an *is-a* relationship with BasePlusCommissionEmployee. The condition at line 49 ensures that this is the case. This cast is required if we are to invoke subclass BasePlusCommissionEmployee methods getBaseSalary and setBaseSalary on the current Employee object—as you'll see momentarily, attempting to invoke a subclass-only method directly on a superclass reference is a compilation error.

Common Programming Error 10.3

Assigning a superclass variable to a subclass variable (without an explicit cast) is a compilation error.

Software Engineering Observation 10.5

If at execution time the reference of a subclass object has been assigned to a variable of one of its direct or indirect superclasses, it is acceptable to cast the reference stored in that superclass variable back to a reference of the subclass type. Before performing such a cast, use the instanceof operator to ensure that the object is indeed an object of an appropriate subclass type.

Common Programming Error 10.4

When downcasting an object, a ClassCastException occurs if at execution time the object does not have an is-a relationship with the type specified in the cast operator. An object can be cast only to its own type or to the type of one of its superclasses.

If the instanceof expression in line 49 is true, the body of the if statement (lines 49–61) performs the special processing required for the BasePlusCommissionEmployee object. Using BasePlusCommissionEmployee variable employee, lines 56 and 57 invoke subclass-only methods getBaseSalary and setBaseSalary to retrieve and update the employee's base salary with the 10% raise.

Lines 63–64 invoke method earnings on currentEmployee, which calls the appropriate subclass object's earnings method polymorphically. As you can see, obtaining the earnings of the SalariedEmployee, HourlyEmployee and CommissionEmployee polymorphically in lines 63–64 produces the same result as obtaining these employees' earnings individually in lines 22–27. However, the earnings amount obtained for the BasePlusCommissionEmployee in lines 63–64 is higher than that obtained in lines 28–30, due to the 10% increase in its base salary.

Lines 68–70 display each employee's type as a string. Every object in Java knows its own class and can access this information through the **getClass** method, which all classes inherit from class Object. The getClass method returns an object of type **Class** (from package java.lang), which contains information about the object's type, including its class name. Line 70 invokes the getClass method on the object to get its runtime class (i.e., a Class object that represents the object's type). Then method **getName** is invoked on the object returned by getClass to get the class's name. To learn more about class Class, see its online documentation at java.sun.com/javase/6/docs/api/java/lang/Class.html.

In the previous example, we avoided several compilation errors by downcasting an Employee variable to a BasePlusCommissionEmployee variable in lines 53–54. If you remove the cast operator (BasePlusCommissionEmployee) from line 54 and attempt to assign Employee variable currentEmployee directly to BasePlusCommissionEmployee variable employee, you will receive an "incompatible types" compilation error. This error indicates that the attempt to assign the reference of superclass object commissionEmployee to subclass variable basePlusCommissionEmployee is not allowed. The compiler prevents this assignment because a CommissionEmployee is not a BasePlusCommissionEmployee—the *is-a* relationship applies only between the subclass and its superclasses, not vice versa.

Similarly, if lines 56, 57 and 60 used superclass variable currentEmployee, rather than subclass variable employee, to invoke subclass-only methods getBaseSalary and setBaseSalary, we would receive a "cannot find symbol" compilation error on each of these lines. Attempting to invoke subclass-only methods on a superclass reference is not allowed. While lines 56, 57 and 60 execute only if instanceof in line 49 returns true to indicate that currentEmployee has been assigned a reference to a BasePlusCommissionEmployee object, we cannot attempt to invoke subclass BasePlusCommissionEmployee methods getBaseSalary and setBaseSalary on superclass Employee reference currentEmployee. The compiler would generate errors in lines 56, 57 and 60, because getBaseSalary and setBaseSalary are not superclass methods and cannot be invoked on a superclass variable. Although the actual method that is called depends on the object's type at execution time, a variable can be used to invoke only those methods that are members of that variable's type, which the compiler verifies. Using a superclass Employee variable, we can invoke only methods found in class Employee—earnings, toString and Employee's *get* and *set* methods.

10.5.7 Summary of the Allowed Assignments Between Superclass and Subclass Variables

Now that you have seen a complete application that processes diverse subclass objects polymorphically, we summarize what you can and cannot do with superclass and subclass objects and variables. Although a subclass object also *is a* superclass object, the two objects are nevertheless different. As discussed previously, subclass objects can be treated as if they are superclass objects. But because the subclass can have additional subclass-only members, assigning a superclass reference to a subclass variable is not allowed without an explicit cast—such an assignment would leave the subclass members undefined for the superclass object.

In the current section and in Section 10.3 and Chapter 9, we have discussed four ways to assign superclass and subclass references to variables of superclass and subclass types:

1. Assigning a superclass reference to a superclass variable is straightforward.

2. Assigning a subclass reference to a subclass variable is straightforward.

3. Assigning a subclass reference to a superclass variable is safe, because the subclass object *is an* object of its superclass. However, this reference can be used to refer only to superclass members. If this code refers to subclass-only members through the superclass variable, the compiler reports errors.

4. Attempting to assign a superclass reference to a subclass variable is a compilation error. To avoid this error, the superclass reference must be cast to a subclass type explicitly. At execution time, if the object to which the reference refers is not a subclass object, an exception will occur. (For more on exception handling, see Chapter 13, Exception Handling.) The instanceof operator can be used to ensure that such a cast is performed only if the object is a subclass object.

10.6 final Methods and Classes

We saw in Section 6.10 that variables can be declared final to indicate that they cannot be modified after they are initialized—such variables represent constant values. It is also possible to declare methods, method parameters and classes with the final modifier.

A method that is declared final in a superclass cannot be overridden in a subclass. Methods that are declared private are implicitly final, because it is impossible to override them in a subclass. Methods that are declared static are also implicitly final. A final method's declaration can never change, so all subclasses use the same method implementation, and calls to final methods are resolved at compile time—this is known as static binding. Since the compiler knows that final methods cannot be overridden, it can optimize programs by removing calls to final methods and replacing them with the expanded code of their declarations at each method call location—a technique known as inlining the code.

Performance Tip 10.1

The compiler can decide to inline a final method call and will do so for small, simple final methods. Inlining does not violate encapsulation or information hiding, but does improve performance because it eliminates the overhead of making a method call.

A class that is declared final cannot be a superclass (i.e., a class cannot extend a final class). All methods in a final class are implicitly final. Class String is an example of a final class. This class cannot be extended, so programs that use Strings can rely on the functionality of String objects as specified in the Java API. Making the class final also prevents programmers from creating subclasses that might bypass security restrictions. For more information on final classes and methods, visit java.sun.com/docs/books/tutorial/java/IandI/final.html. This site contains additional insights into using final classes to improve the security of a system.

Common Programming Error 10.5

Attempting to declare a subclass of a final class is a compilation error.

Software Engineering Observation 10.6

In the Java API, the vast majority of classes are not declared final. This enables inheritance and polymorphism—the fundamental capabilities of object-oriented programming. However, in some cases, it is important to declare classes final—typically for security reasons.

10.7 Case Study: Creating and Using Interfaces

Our next example (Figs. 10.11–10.13) reexamines the payroll system of Section 10.5. Suppose that the company involved wishes to perform several accounting operations in a single accounts payable application—in addition to calculating the earnings that must be paid to each employee, the company must also calculate the payment due on each of several invoices (i.e., bills for goods purchased). Though applied to unrelated things (i.e., employees and invoices), both operations have to do with obtaining some kind of payment amount. For an employee, the payment refers to the employee's earnings. For an invoice, the payment refers to the total cost of the goods listed on the invoice. Can we calculate such different things as the payments due for employees and invoices in a single application polymorphically? Does Java offer a capability that requires that unrelated classes implement a set of common methods (e.g., a method that calculates a payment amount)? Java interfaces offer exactly this capability.

Interfaces define and standardize the ways in which things such as people and systems can interact with one another. For example, the controls on a radio serve as an interface between radio users and a radio's internal components. The controls allow users to perform only a limited set of operations (e.g., changing the station, adjusting the volume, choosing between AM and FM), and different radios may implement the controls in different ways (e.g., using push buttons, dials, voice commands). The interface specifies *what* operations a radio must permit users to perform but does not specify *how* the operations are performed. Similarly, the interface between a driver and a car with a manual transmission includes the steering wheel, the gear shift, the clutch pedal, the gas pedal and the brake pedal. This same interface is found in nearly all manual transmission cars, enabling someone who knows how to drive one particular manual transmission car to drive just about any manual transmission car. The components of each individual car may look different, but their general purpose is the same—to allow people to drive the car.

Software objects also communicate via interfaces. A Java interface describes a set of methods that can be called on an object, to tell the object to perform some task or return some piece of information, for example. The next example introduces an interface named Payable to describe the functionality of any object that must be capable of being paid and thus must offer a method to determine the proper payment amount due. An **interface declaration** begins with the keyword `interface` and contains only constants and abstract methods. Unlike classes, all interface members must be `public`, and interfaces may not specify any implementation details, such as concrete method declarations and instance variables. So all methods declared in an interface are implicitly `public abstract` methods and all fields are implicitly `public`, `static` and `final`.

Good Programming Practice 10.1

According to Chapter 9 of the Java Language Specification, *it is proper style to declare an interface's methods without keywords* `public` *and* `abstract` *because they are redundant in interface method declarations. Similarly, constants should be declared without keywords* `public`, `static` *and* `final` *because they, too, are redundant.*

To use an interface, a concrete class must specify that it `implements` the interface and must declare each method in the interface with the signature specified in the interface declaration. A class that does not implement all the methods of the interface is an abstract class and must be declared `abstract`. Implementing an interface is like signing a contract with the compiler that states, "I will declare all the methods specified by the interface or I will declare my class `abstract`."

Common Programming Error 10.6

Failing to implement any method of an interface in a concrete class that `implements` *the interface results in a compilation error indicating that the class must be declared* `abstract`.

An interface is typically used when disparate (i.e., unrelated) classes need to share common methods and constants. This allows objects of unrelated classes to be processed polymorphically—objects of classes that implement the same interface can respond to the same method calls. You can create an interface that describes the desired functionality, then implement this interface in any classes that require that functionality. For example, in the accounts payable application developed in this section, we implement interface Payable in any class that must be able to calculate a payment amount (e.g., Employee, Invoice).

An interface is often used in place of an `abstract` class when there is no default implementation to inherit—that is, no fields and no default method implementations. Like `public abstract` classes, interfaces are typically `public` types, so they are normally declared in files by themselves with the same name as the interface and the `.java` file-name extension.

10.7.1 Developing a Payable Hierarchy

To build an application that can determine payments for employees and invoices alike, we first create interface Payable, which contains method getPaymentAmount that returns a double amount that must be paid for an object of any class that implements the interface. Method getPaymentAmount is a general purpose version of method earnings of the Employee hierarchy—method earnings calculates a payment amount specifically for an Employee, while getPaymentAmount can be applied to a broad range of unrelated objects. After declaring interface Payable, we introduce class Invoice, which implements interface Payable. We then modify class Employee such that it also implements interface Payable. Finally, we update `Employee` subclass `SalariedEmployee` to "fit" into the `Payable` hierarchy (i.e., we rename `SalariedEmployee` method `earnings` as `getPaymentAmount`).

Good Programming Practice 10.2

When declaring a method in an interface, choose a method name that describes the method's purpose in a general manner, because the method may be implemented by many unrelated classes.

Classes `Invoice` and `Employee` both represent things for which the company must be able to calculate a payment amount. Both classes implement `Payable`, so a program can invoke method `getPaymentAmount` on `Invoice` objects and `Employee` objects alike. As we will soon see, this enables the polymorphic processing of `Invoices` and `Employees` required for our company's accounts payable application.

The UML class diagram in Fig. 10.10 shows the hierarchy used in our accounts payable application. The hierarchy begins with interface `Payable`. The UML distinguishes an interface from other classes by placing the word "interface" in guillemets (« and ») above the interface name. The UML expresses the relationship between a class and an interface through a relationship known as a **realization**. A class is said to "realize," or implement, the methods of an interface. A class diagram models a realization as a dashed arrow with a hollow arrowhead pointing from the implementing class to the interface. The diagram in Fig. 10.10 indicates that classes `Invoice` and `Employee` each realize (i.e., implement) interface `Payable`. Note that, as in the class diagram of Fig. 10.2, class `Employee` appears in italics, indicating that it is an abstract class. Concrete class `SalariedEmployee` extends `Employee` and inherits its superclass's realization relationship with interface `Payable`.

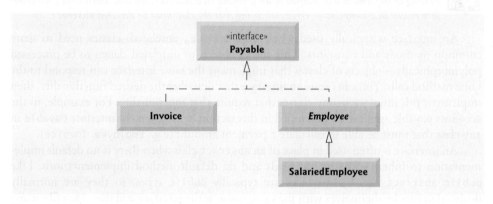

Fig. 10.10 | `Payable` interface hierarchy UML class diagram.

10.7.2 Declaring Interface `Payable`

The declaration of interface `Payable` begins in Fig. 10.11 at line 4. Interface `Payable` contains public abstract method `getPaymentAmount` (line 6). Note that the method is not explicitly declared `public` or `abstract`. Interface methods must be `public` and `abstract`, so they do not need to be declared as such. Interface `Payable` has only one method—interfaces can have any number of methods. (We will see later in the book the notion of "tagging interfaces"—these actually have *no* methods. In fact, a tagging interface contains no constant values, either—it simply contains an empty interface declaration.) In addition, method `getPaymentAmount` has no parameters, but interface methods can have parameters.

```
 1   // Fig. 10.11: Payable.java
 2   // Payable interface declaration.
 3
 4   public interface Payable
 5   {
 6      double getPaymentAmount(); // calculate payment; no implementation
 7   } // end interface Payable
```

Fig. 10.11 | Payable interface declaration.

10.7.3 Creating Class Invoice

We now create class Invoice (Fig. 10.12) to represent a simple invoice that contains billing information for only one kind of part. The class declares private instance variables partNumber, partDescription, quantity and pricePerItem (in lines 6–9) that indicate the part number, a description of the part, the quantity of the part ordered and the price per item. Class Invoice also contains a constructor (lines 12–19), *get* and *set* methods (lines 22–67) that manipulate the class's instance variables and a toString method (lines 70–75) that returns a string representation of an Invoice object. Note that methods set-Quantity (lines 46–49) and setPricePerItem (lines 58–61) ensure that quantity and pricePerItem obtain only nonnegative values.

Line 4 of Fig. 10.12 indicates that class Invoice implements interface Payable. Like all classes, class Invoice also implicitly extends Object. Java does not allow subclasses to inherit from more than one superclass, but it does allow a class to inherit from a superclass and implement more than one interface. In fact, a class can implement as many interfaces as it needs, in addition to extending one other class. To implement more than one interface, use a comma-separated list of interface names after keyword implements in the class declaration, as in:

> public class *ClassName* extends *SuperclassName* implements *FirstInterface*, *SecondInterface*, ...

All objects of a class that implement multiple interfaces have the *is-a* relationship with each implemented interface type.

```
 1   // Fig. 10.12: Invoice.java
 2   // Invoice class implements Payable.
 3
 4   public class Invoice implements Payable
 5   {
 6      private String partNumber;
 7      private String partDescription;
 8      private int quantity;
 9      private double pricePerItem;
10
11      // four-argument constructor
12      public Invoice( String part, String description, int count,
13         double price )
14      {
```

Fig. 10.12 | Invoice class that implements Payable. (Part 1 of 3.)

```
15         partNumber = part;
16         partDescription = description;
17         setQuantity( count ); // validate and store quantity
18         setPricePerItem( price ); // validate and store price per item
19      } // end four-argument Invoice constructor
20
21      // set part number
22      public void setPartNumber( String part )
23      {
24         partNumber = part;
25      } // end method setPartNumber
26
27      // get part number
28      public String getPartNumber()
29      {
30         return partNumber;
31      } // end method getPartNumber
32
33      // set description
34      public void setPartDescription( String description )
35      {
36         partDescription = description;
37      } // end method setPartDescription
38
39      // get description
40      public String getPartDescription()
41      {
42         return partDescription;
43      } // end method getPartDescription
44
45      // set quantity
46      public void setQuantity( int count )
47      {
48         quantity = ( count < 0 ) ? 0 : count; // quantity cannot be negative
49      } // end method setQuantity
50
51      // get quantity
52      public int getQuantity()
53      {
54         return quantity;
55      } // end method getQuantity
56
57      // set price per item
58      public void setPricePerItem( double price )
59      {
60         pricePerItem = ( price < 0.0 ) ? 0.0 : price; // validate price
61      } // end method setPricePerItem
62
63      // get price per item
64      public double getPricePerItem()
65      {
66         return pricePerItem;
67      } // end method getPricePerItem
```

Fig. 10.12 | Invoice class that implements Payable. (Part 2 of 3.)

```
68
69        // return String representation of Invoice object
70        public String toString()
71        {
72           return String.format( "%s: \n%s: %s (%s) \n%s: %d \n%s: $%,.2f",
73              "invoice", "part number", getPartNumber(), getPartDescription(),
74              "quantity", getQuantity(), "price per item", getPricePerItem() );
75        } // end method toString
76
77        // method required to carry out contract with interface Payable
78        public double getPaymentAmount()
79        {
80           return getQuantity() * getPricePerItem(); // calculate total cost
81        } // end method getPaymentAmount
82     } // end class Invoice
```

Fig. 10.12 | `Invoice` class that implements `Payable`. (Part 3 of 3.)

Class `Invoice` implements the one method in interface `Payable`. Method `getPaymentAmount` is declared in lines 78–81. The method calculates the total payment required to pay the invoice. The method multiplies the values of `quantity` and `pricePerItem` (obtained through the appropriate *get* methods) and returns the result (line 80). This method satisfies the implementation requirement for this method in interface `Payable`—we have fulfilled the interface contract with the compiler.

10.7.4 Modifying Class `Employee` to Implement Interface `Payable`

We now modify class `Employee` such that it implements interface `Payable`. Figure 10.13 contains the modified `Employee` class. This class declaration is identical to that of Fig. 10.4 with only two exceptions. First, line 4 of Fig. 10.13 indicates that class `Employee` now implements interface `Payable`. Second, since `Employee` now implements interface `Payable`, we must rename `earnings` to `getPaymentAmount` throughout the `Employee` hierarchy. As with method `earnings` in the version of class `Employee` in Fig. 10.4, however, it does not make sense to implement method `getPaymentAmount` in class `Employee` because we cannot calculate the earnings payment owed to a general `Employee`—first we must know the specific type of `Employee`. In Fig. 10.4, we declared method `earnings` as `abstract` for this reason, and as a result class `Employee` had to be declared `abstract`. This forced each `Employee` subclass to override `earnings` with a concrete implementation.

```
1   // Fig. 10.13: Employee.java
2   // Employee abstract superclass implements Payable.
3
4   public abstract class Employee implements Payable
5   {
6      private String firstName;
7      private String lastName;
8      private String socialSecurityNumber;
9
10     // three-argument constructor
```

Fig. 10.13 | `Employee` class that implements `Payable`. (Part 1 of 2.)

```
11      public Employee( String first, String last, String ssn )
12      {
13         firstName = first;
14         lastName = last;
15         socialSecurityNumber = ssn;
16      } // end three-argument Employee constructor
17
18      // set first name
19      public void setFirstName( String first )
20      {
21         firstName = first;
22      } // end method setFirstName
23
24      // return first name
25      public String getFirstName()
26      {
27         return firstName;
28      } // end method getFirstName
29
30      // set last name
31      public void setLastName( String last )
32      {
33         lastName = last;
34      } // end method setLastName
35
36      // return last name
37      public String getLastName()
38      {
39         return lastName;
40      } // end method getLastName
41
42      // set social security number
43      public void setSocialSecurityNumber( String ssn )
44      {
45         socialSecurityNumber = ssn; // should validate
46      } // end method setSocialSecurityNumber
47
48      // return social security number
49      public String getSocialSecurityNumber()
50      {
51         return socialSecurityNumber;
52      } // end method getSocialSecurityNumber
53
54      // return String representation of Employee object
55      public String toString()
56      {
57         return String.format( "%s %s\nsocial security number: %s",
58            getFirstName(), getLastName(), getSocialSecurityNumber() );
59      } // end method toString
60
61      // Note: We do not implement Payable method getPaymentAmount here so
62      // this class must be declared abstract to avoid a compilation error.
63   } // end abstract class Employee
```

Fig. 10.13 | `Employee` class that implements `Payable`. (Part 2 of 2.)

In Fig. 10.13, we handle this situation differently. Recall that when a class implements an interface, the class makes a contract with the compiler stating either that the class will implement each of the methods in the interface or that the class will be declared `abstract`. If the latter option is chosen, we do not need to declare the interface methods as `abstract` in the abstract class—they are already implicitly declared as such in the interface. Any concrete subclass of the abstract class must implement the interface methods to fulfill the superclass's contract with the compiler. If the subclass does not do so, it too must be declared `abstract`. As indicated by the comments in lines 61–62, class `Employee` of Fig. 10.13 does not implement method `getPaymentAmount`, so the class is declared `abstract`. Each direct `Employee` subclass inherits the superclass's contract to implement method `getPaymentAmount` and thus must implement this method to become a concrete class for which objects can be instantiated. A class that extends one of `Employee`'s concrete subclasses will inherit an implementation of `getPaymentAmount` and thus will also be a concrete class.

10.7.5 Modifying Class `SalariedEmployee` for Use in the `Payable` Hierarchy

Figure 10.14 contains a modified version of class `SalariedEmployee` that extends `Employee` and fulfills superclass `Employee`'s contract to implement method `getPaymentAmount` of interface `Payable`. This version of `SalariedEmployee` is identical to that of Fig. 10.5 with the exception that the version here implements method `getPaymentAmount` (lines 30–33) instead of method `earnings`. The two methods contain the same functionality but have different names. Recall that the `Payable` version of the method has a more general name to be applicable to possibly disparate classes. The remaining `Employee` subclasses (e.g., `HourlyEmployee`, `CommissionEmployee` and `BasePlusCommissionEmployee`) also must be modified to contain method `getPaymentAmount` in place of `earnings` to reflect the fact that `Employee` now implements `Payable`. We leave these modifications as an exercise and use only `SalariedEmployee` in our test program in this section.

```
1   // Fig. 10.14: SalariedEmployee.java
2   // SalariedEmployee class extends Employee, which implements Payable.
3
4   public class SalariedEmployee extends Employee
5   {
6      private double weeklySalary;
7
8      // four-argument constructor
9      public SalariedEmployee( String first, String last, String ssn,
10         double salary )
11     {
12        super( first, last, ssn ); // pass to Employee constructor
13        setWeeklySalary( salary ); // validate and store salary
14     } // end four-argument SalariedEmployee constructor
15
16     // set salary
17     public void setWeeklySalary( double salary )
18     {
```

Fig. 10.14 | `SalariedEmployee` class that implements interface `Payable` method `getPaymentAmount`. (Part 1 of 2.)

```
19          weeklySalary = salary < 0.0 ? 0.0 : salary;
20     } // end method setWeeklySalary
21
22     // return salary
23     public double getWeeklySalary()
24     {
25          return weeklySalary;
26     } // end method getWeeklySalary
27
28     // calculate earnings; implement interface Payable method that was
29     // abstract in superclass Employee
30     public double getPaymentAmount()
31     {
32          return getWeeklySalary();
33     } // end method getPaymentAmount
34
35     // return String representation of SalariedEmployee object
36     public String toString()
37     {
38          return String.format( "salaried employee: %s\n%s: $%,.2f",
39               super.toString(), "weekly salary", getWeeklySalary() );
40     } // end method toString
41 } // end class SalariedEmployee
```

Fig. 10.14 | SalariedEmployee class that implements interface Payable method getPaymentAmount. (Part 2 of 2.)

When a class implements an interface, the same *is-a* relationship provided by inheritance applies. For example, class Employee implements Payable, so we can say that an Employee *is a* Payable. In fact, objects of any classes that extend Employee are also Payable objects. SalariedEmployee objects, for instance, are Payable objects. As with inheritance relationships, an object of a class that implements an interface may be thought of as an object of the interface type. Objects of any subclasses of the class that implements the interface can also be thought of as objects of the interface type. Thus, just as we can assign the reference of a SalariedEmployee object to a superclass Employee variable, we can assign the reference of a SalariedEmployee object to an interface Payable variable. Invoice implements Payable, so an Invoice object also *is a* Payable object, and we can assign the reference of an Invoice object to a Payable variable.

Software Engineering Observation 10.7

Inheritance and interfaces are similar in their implementation of the is-a *relationship. An object of a class that implements an interface may be thought of as an object of that interface type. An object of any subclasses of a class that implements an interface also can be thought of as an object of the interface type.*

Software Engineering Observation 10.8

The is-a *relationship that exists between superclasses and subclasses, and between interfaces and the classes that implement them, holds when passing an object to a method. When a method parameter receives a variable of a superclass or interface type, the method processes the object received as an argument polymorphically.*

> **Software Engineering Observation 10.9**
>
> *Using a superclass reference, we can polymorphically invoke any method specified in the superclass declaration (and in class Object). Using an interface reference, we can polymorphically invoke any method specified in the interface declaration (and in class Object— because a variable of an interface type must refer to an object to call methods, and all objects contain the methods of class Object).*

10.7.6 Using Interface Payable to Process Invoices and Employees Polymorphically

PayableInterfaceTest (Fig. 10.15) illustrates that interface Payable can be used to process a set of Invoices and Employees polymorphically in a single application. Line 9 declares payableObjects and assigns it an array of four Payable variables. Lines 12–13 assign the references of Invoice objects to the first two elements of payableObjects. Lines 14–17 then assign the references of SalariedEmployee objects to the remaining two elements of payableObjects. These assignments are allowed because an Invoice *is a* Payable, a SalariedEmployee *is an* Employee and an Employee *is a* Payable. Lines 23–29 use the enhanced for statement to polymorphically process each Payable object in payableObjects, printing the object as a String, along with the payment amount due. Note that line 27 invokes method toString off a Payable interface reference, even though toString is not declared in interface Payable—all references (including those of interface types) refer to objects that extend Object and therefore have a toString method. (Note that toString also can be invoked implicitly here.) Line 28 invokes Payable method getPaymentAmount to obtain the payment amount for each object in payableObjects, regardless of the actual type of the object. The output reveals that the method calls in lines 27–28 invoke the appropriate class's implementation of methods toString and getPaymentAmount. For instance, when currentEmployee refers to an Invoice during the first iteration of the for loop, class Invoice's toString and getPaymentAmount execute.

```
1   // Fig. 10.15: PayableInterfaceTest.java
2   // Tests interface Payable.
3
4   public class PayableInterfaceTest
5   {
6      public static void main( String args[] )
7      {
8         // create four-element Payable array
9         Payable payableObjects[] = new Payable[ 4 ];
10
11        // populate array with objects that implement Payable
12        payableObjects[ 0 ] = new Invoice( "01234", "seat", 2, 375.00 );
13        payableObjects[ 1 ] = new Invoice( "56789", "tire", 4, 79.95 );
14        payableObjects[ 2 ] =
15           new SalariedEmployee( "John", "Smith", "111-11-1111", 800.00 );
16        payableObjects[ 3 ] =
17           new SalariedEmployee( "Lisa", "Barnes", "888-88-8888", 1200.00 );
```

Fig. 10.15 | Payable interface test program processing Invoices and Employees polymorphically. (Part 1 of 2.)

```
18
19          System.out.println(
20              "Invoices and Employees processed polymorphically:\n" );
21
22          // generically process each element in array payableObjects
23          for ( Payable currentPayable : payableObjects )
24          {
25              // output currentPayable and its appropriate payment amount
26              System.out.printf( "%s \n%s: $%,.2f\n\n",
27                  currentPayable.toString(),
28                  "payment due", currentPayable.getPaymentAmount() );
29          } // end for
30      } // end main
31  } // end class PayableInterfaceTest
```

```
Invoices and Employees processed polymorphically:

invoice:
part number: 01234 (seat)
quantity: 2
price per item: $375.00
payment due: $750.00

invoice:
part number: 56789 (tire)
quantity: 4
price per item: $79.95
payment due: $319.80

salaried employee: John Smith
social security number: 111-11-1111
weekly salary: $800.00
payment due: $800.00

salaried employee: Lisa Barnes
social security number: 888-88-8888
weekly salary: $1,200.00
payment due: $1,200.00
```

Fig. 10.15 | Payable interface test program processing Invoices and Employees polymorphically. (Part 2 of 2.)

Software Engineering Observation 10.10

All methods of class Object can be called by using a reference of an interface type. A reference refers to an object, and all objects inherit the methods of class Object.

10.7.7 Declaring Constants with Interfaces

As we mentioned in Section 10.7, an interface can declare constants. The constants are implicitly public, static and final—again, these keywords are not required in the interface declaration. One popular use of an interface is to declare a set of constants that can be used in many class declarations. Consider interface Constants:

```
public interface Constants
{
    int ONE = 1;
    int TWO = 2;
    int THREE = 3;
}
```

A class can use these constants by importing the interface, then referring to each constant as `Constants.ONE`, `Constants.TWO` and `Constants.THREE`. Note that a class can refer to the imported constants with just their names (i.e., `ONE`, `TWO` and `THREE`) if it uses a `static import` declaration (presented in Section 8.12) to import the interface.

Software Engineering Observation 10.11

As of Java SE 5.0, it became a better programming practice to create sets of constants as enumerations with keyword enum. *See Section 6.10 for an introduction to* enum *and Section 8.9 for additional* enum *details.*

10.7.8 Common Interfaces of the Java API

In this section, we overview several common interfaces found in the Java API. The power and flexibility of interfaces is used frequently throughout the Java API. These interfaces are implemented and used in the same manner as the interfaces you create (e.g., interface `Payable` in Section 10.7.2). As you'll see throughout this book, the Java API's interfaces enable you to use your own classes within the frameworks provided by Java, such as comparing objects of your own types and creating tasks that can execute concurrently with other tasks in the same program. Figure 10.16 presents a brief overview of a few of the more popular interfaces of the Java API that we use in *Java How to Program, Seventh Edition*.

Interface	Description
Comparable	As you learned in Chapter 2, Java contains several comparison operators (e.g., <, <=, >, >=, ==, !=) that allow you to compare primitive values. However, these operators cannot be used to compare the contents of objects. Interface Comparable is used to allow objects of a class that implements the interface to be compared to one another. The interface contains one method, compareTo, that compares the object that calls the method to the object passed as an argument to the method. Classes must implement compareTo such that it returns a value indicating whether the object on which it is invoked is less than (negative integer return value), equal to (0 return value) or greater than (positive integer return value) the object passed as an argument, using any criteria specified by the programmer. For example, if class Employee implements Comparable, its compareTo method could compare Employee objects by their earnings amounts. Interface Comparable is commonly used for ordering objects in a collection such as an array. We use Comparable in Chapter 18, Generics, and Chapter 19, Collections.

Fig. 10.16 | Common interfaces of the Java API. (Part 1 of 2.)

Interface	Description
Serializable	An interface used to identify classes whose objects can be written to (i.e., serialized) or read from (i.e., deserialized) some type of storage (e.g., file on disk, database field) or transmitted across a network. We use Serializable in Chapter 14, Files and Streams, and Chapter 24, Networking.
Runnable	Implemented by any class for which objects of that class should be able to execute in parallel using a technique called multithreading (discussed in Chapter 23, Multithreading). The interface contains one method, run, which describes the behavior of an object when executed.
GUI event-listener interfaces	You work with graphical user interfaces (GUIs) every day. For example, in your web browser, you might type in a text field the address of a website to visit, or you might click a button to return to the previous site you visited. When you type a website address or click a button in the web browser, the browser must respond to your interaction and perform the desired task for you. Your interaction is known as an event, and the code that the browser uses to respond to an event is known as an event handler. In Chapter 11, GUI Components: Part 1, and Chapter 22, GUI Components: Part 2, you will learn how to build Java GUIs and how to build event handlers to respond to user interactions. The event handlers are declared in classes that implement an appropriate event-listener interface. Each event-listener interface specifies one or more methods that must be implemented to respond to user interactions.
SwingConstants	Contains a set of constants used in GUI programming to position GUI elements on the screen. We explore GUI programming in Chapters 11 and 22.

Fig. 10.16 | Common interfaces of the Java API. (Part 2 of 2.)

10.8 (Optional) GUI and Graphics Case Study: Drawing with Polymorphism

You may have noticed in the drawing program created in Exercise 8.1 (and modified in Exercise 9.1) that there are many similarities between the shape classes. Using inheritance, we can "factor out" the common features from all three classes and place them in a single shape superclass. We can then manipulate objects of all three shape types polymorphically using variables of the superclass type. Removing the redundancy in the code will result in a smaller, more flexible program that is easier to maintain.

GUI and Graphics Case Study Exercises

10.1 Modify the MyLine, MyOval and MyRectangle classes of Exercise 8.1 and Exercise 9.1 to create the class hierarchy in Fig. 10.17. Classes of the MyShape hierarchy should be "smart" shape classes that know how to draw themselves (if provided with a Graphics object that tells them where to draw). Once the program creates an object from this hierarchy, it can manipulate it polymorphically for the rest of its lifetime as a MyShape.

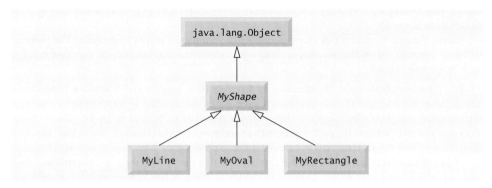

Fig. 10.17 | MyShape hierarchy.

In your solution, class MyShape in Fig. 10.17 *must* be abstract. Since MyShape represents any shape in general, you cannot implement a draw method without knowing exactly what shape it is. The data representing the coordinates and color of the shapes in the hierarchy should be declared as private members of class MyShape. In addition to the common data, class MyShape should declare the following methods:

a) A no-argument constructor that sets all the coordinates of the shape to 0 and the color to Color.BLACK.

b) A constructor that initializes the coordinates and color to the values of the arguments supplied.

c) *Set* methods for the individual coordinates and color that allow the programmer to set any piece of data independently for a shape in the hierarchy.

d) *Get* methods for the individual coordinates and color that allow the programmer to retrieve any piece of data independently for a shape in the hierarchy.

e) The abstract method

```
public abstract void draw( Graphics g );
```

which will be called from the program's paintComponent method to draw a shape on the screen.

To ensure proper encapsulation, all data in class MyShape must be private. This requires declaring proper *set* and *get* methods to manipulate the data. Class MyLine should provide a no-argument constructor and a constructor with arguments for the coordinates and color. Classes MyOval and MyRect should provide a no-argument constructor and a constructor with arguments for the coordinates, color and determining whether the shape is filled. The no-argument constructor should, in addition to setting the default values, set the shape to be an unfilled shape.

You can draw lines, rectangles and ovals if you know two points in space. Lines require $x1$, $y1$, $x2$ and $y2$ coordinates. The drawLine method of the Graphics class will connect the two points supplied with a line. If you have the same four coordinate values ($x1$, $y1$, $x2$ and $y2$) for ovals and rectangles, you can calculate the four arguments needed to draw them. Each requires an upper-left x-coordinate value (the smaller of the two x-coordinate values), an upper-left y-coordinate value (the smaller of the two y-coordinate values), a *width* (the absolute value of the difference between the two x-coordinate values) and a *height* (the absolute value of the difference between the two y-coordinate values). Rectangles and ovals should also have a filled flag that determines whether to draw the shape as a filled shape.

There should be no MyLine, MyOval or MyRectangle variables in the program—only MyShape variables that contain references to MyLine, MyOval and MyRectangle objects. The program should generate random shapes and store them in an array of type MyShape. Method paintComponent should walk through the MyShape array and draw every shape (i.e., polymorphically calling every shape's draw method).

Allow the user to specify (via an input dialog) the number of shapes to generate. The program will then generate and display the shapes along with a status bar that informs the user how many of each shape were created.

10.2 *(Drawing Application Modification)* In Exercise 10.1, you created a MyShape hierarchy in which classes MyLine, MyOval and MyRectangle extend MyShape directly. If your hierarchy was properly designed, you should be able to see the similarities between the MyOval and MyRectangle classes. Redesign and reimplement the code for the MyOval and MyRectangle classes to "factor out" the common features into the abstract class MyBoundedShape to produce the hierarchy in Fig. 10.18.

Class MyBoundedShape should declare two constructors that mimic those of class MyShape, only with an added parameter to set whether the shape is filled. Class MyBoundedShape should also declare *get* and *set* methods for manipulating the filled flag and methods that calculate the upper-left *x*-coordinate, upper-left *y*-coordinate, width and height. Remember, the values needed to draw an oval or a rectangle can be calculated from two *(x, y)* coordinates. If designed properly, the new MyOval and MyRectangle classes should each have two constructors and a draw method.

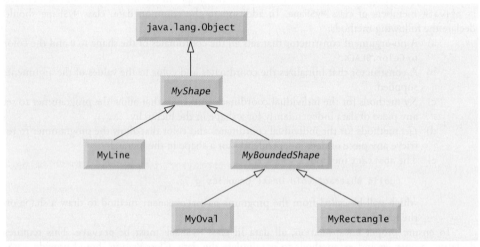

Fig. 10.18 | MyShape hierarchy with MyBoundedShape.

10.9 (Optional) Software Engineering Case Study: Incorporating Inheritance into the ATM System

We now revisit our ATM system design to see how it might benefit from inheritance. To apply inheritance, we first look for commonality among classes in the system. We create an inheritance hierarchy to model similar (yet not identical) classes in a more elegant and efficient manner. We then modify our class diagram to incorporate the new inheritance relationships. Finally, we demonstrate how our updated design is translated into Java code.

In Section 3.10, we encountered the problem of representing a financial transaction in the system. Rather than create one class to represent all transaction types, we decided to create three individual transaction classes—BalanceInquiry, Withdrawal and Deposit—to represent the transactions that the ATM system can perform. Figure 10.19 shows the attributes and operations of classes BalanceInquiry, Withdrawal and Deposit. Note that

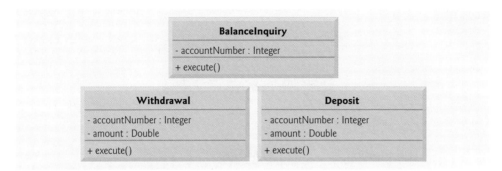

Fig. 10.19 | Attributes and operations of classes `BalanceInquiry`, `Withdrawal` and `Deposit`.

these classes have one attribute (`accountNumber`) and one operation (`execute`) in common. Each class requires attribute `accountNumber` to specify the account to which the transaction applies. Each class contains operation `execute`, which the ATM invokes to perform the transaction. Clearly, `BalanceInquiry`, `Withdrawal` and `Deposit` represent *types of* transactions. Figure 10.19 reveals commonality among the transaction classes, so using inheritance to factor out the common features seems appropriate for designing classes `BalanceInquiry`, `Withdrawal` and `Deposit`. We place the common functionality in a superclass, `Transaction`, that classes `BalanceInquiry`, `Withdrawal` and `Deposit` extend.

The UML specifies a relationship called a generalization to model inheritance. Figure 10.20 is the class diagram that models the generalization of superclass `Transaction` and subclasses `BalanceInquiry`, `Withdrawal` and `Deposit`. The arrows with triangular hollow arrowheads indicate that classes `BalanceInquiry`, `Withdrawal` and `Deposit` extend class `Transaction`. Class `Transaction` is said to be a generalization of classes `BalanceInquiry`, `Withdrawal` and `Deposit`. Class `BalanceInquiry`, `Withdrawal` and `Deposit` are said to be specializations of class `Transaction`.

Classes `BalanceInquiry`, `Withdrawal` and `Deposit` share integer attribute `accountNumber`, so we factor out this common attribute and place it in superclass `Transaction`. We no longer list `accountNumber` in the second compartment of each subclass, because the three subclasses inherit this attribute from `Transaction`. Recall, however, that subclasses cannot access `private` attributes of a superclass. We therefore include `public` method `getAccountNumber` in class `Transaction`. Each subclass will inherit this method, enabling the subclass to access its `accountNumber` as needed to execute a transaction.

According to Fig. 10.19, classes `BalanceInquiry`, `Withdrawal` and `Deposit` also share operation `execute`, so we decided that superclass `Transaction` should contain `public` method `execute`. However, it does not make sense to implement `execute` in class `Transaction`, because the functionality that this method provides depends on the type of the actual transaction. We therefore declare method `execute` as `abstract` in superclass `Transaction`. Any class that contains at least one abstract method must also be declared abstract. This forces any subclass of `Transaction` that must be a concrete class (i.e., `BalanceInquiry`, `Withdrawal` and `Deposit`) to implement method `execute`. The UML requires that we place abstract class names (and abstract methods) in italics, so `Transaction` and its method `execute` appear in italics in Fig. 10.20. Note that method `execute`

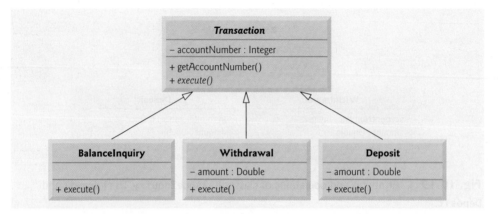

Fig. 10.20 | Class diagram modeling generalization of superclass `Transaction` and subclasses `BalanceInquiry`, `Withdrawal` and `Deposit`. Note that abstract class names (e.g., `Transaction`) and method names (e.g., `execute` in class `Transaction`) appear in italics.

is not italicized in subclasses `BalanceInquiry`, `Withdrawal` and `Deposit`. Each subclass overrides superclass `Transaction`'s execute method with a concrete implementation that performs the steps appropriate for completing that type of transaction. Note that Fig. 10.20 includes operation execute in the third compartment of classes `BalanceInquiry`, `Withdrawal` and `Deposit`, because each class has a different concrete implementation of the overridden method.

Incorporating inheritance provides the ATM with an elegant way to execute all transactions "in the general." For example, suppose a user chooses to perform a balance inquiry. The ATM sets a `Transaction` reference to a new object of class `BalanceInquiry`. When the ATM uses its `Transaction` reference to invoke method execute, `BalanceInquiry`'s version of execute is called.

This polymorphic approach also makes the system easily extensible. Should we wish to create a new transaction type (e.g., funds transfer or bill payment), we would just create an additional `Transaction` subclass that overrides the execute method with a version of the method appropriate for executing the new transaction type. We would need to make only minimal changes to the system code to allow users to choose the new transaction type from the main menu and for the ATM to instantiate and execute objects of the new subclass. The ATM could execute transactions of the new type using the current code, because it executes all transactions polymorphically using a general `Transaction` reference.

As you learned earlier in the chapter, an abstract class like `Transaction` is one for which the programmer never intends to instantiate objects. An abstract class simply declares common attributes and behaviors of its subclasses in an inheritance hierarchy. Class `Transaction` defines the concept of what it means to be a transaction that has an account number and executes. You may wonder why we bother to include abstract method execute in class `Transaction` if it lacks a concrete implementation. Conceptually, we include this method because it corresponds to the defining behavior of all transactions—executing. Technically, we must include method execute in superclass Transaction so that the ATM (or any other class) can polymorphically invoke each subclass's overridden version of this method through a Transaction reference. Also, from a software engineering perspective, including an abstract method in a superclass forces the implementor of the subclasses to override that method with concrete implementations in the subclasses, or else the subclasses, too, will be abstract, preventing objects of those subclasses from being instantiated.

Subclasses BalanceInquiry, Withdrawal and Deposit inherit attribute account-Number from superclass Transaction, but classes Withdrawal and Deposit contain the additional attribute amount that distinguishes them from class BalanceInquiry. Classes Withdrawal and Deposit require this additional attribute to store the amount of money that the user wishes to withdraw or deposit. Class BalanceInquiry has no need for such an attribute and requires only an account number to execute. Even though two of the three Transaction subclasses share this attribute, we do not place it in superclass Transaction—we place only features common to all the subclasses in the superclass, otherwise subclasses could inherit attributes (and methods) that they do not need and should not have.

Figure 10.21 presents an updated class diagram of our model that incorporates inheritance and introduces class Transaction. We model an association between class ATM and

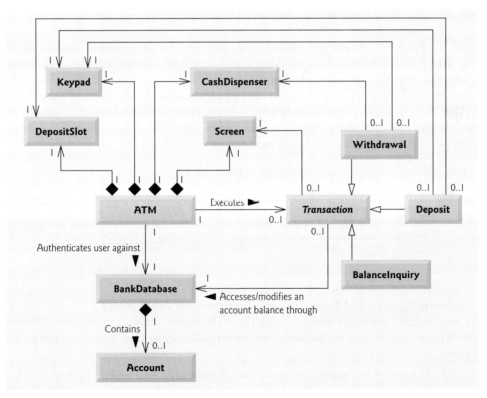

Fig. 10.21 | Class diagram of the ATM system (incorporating inheritance). Note that abstract class names (e.g., Transaction) appear in italics.

class Transaction to show that the ATM, at any given moment is either executing a transaction or it is not (i.e., zero or one objects of type Transaction exist in the system at a time). Because a Withdrawal is a type of Transaction, we no longer draw an association line directly between class ATM and class Withdrawal. Subclass Withdrawal inherits superclass Transaction's association with class ATM. Subclasses BalanceInquiry and Deposit inherit this association, too, so the previously omitted associations between ATM and classes BalanceInquiry and Deposit no longer exist either.

We also add an association between class Transaction and the BankDatabase (Fig. 10.21). All Transactions require a reference to the BankDatabase so they can access and modify account information. Because each Transaction subclass inherits this reference, we no longer model the association between class Withdrawal and the BankDatabase. Similarly, the previously omitted associations between the BankDatabase and classes BalanceInquiry and Deposit no longer exist.

We show an association between class Transaction and the Screen. All Transactions display output to the user via the Screen. Thus, we no longer include the association previously modeled between Withdrawal and the Screen, although Withdrawal still participates in associations with the CashDispenser and the Keypad. Our class diagram incorporating inheritance also models Deposit and BalanceInquiry. We show associations between Deposit and both the DepositSlot and the Keypad. Note that class BalanceInquiry takes part in no associations other than those inherited from class Transaction—a BalanceInquiry needs to interact only with the BankDatabase and with the Screen.

The class diagram of Fig. 8.24 showed attributes and operations with visibility markers. Now we present a modified class diagram that incorporates inheritance in Fig. 10.22. This abbreviated diagram does not show inheritance relationships, but instead shows the attributes and methods after we have employed inheritance in our system. To save space, as we did in Fig. 4.24, we do not include those attributes shown by associations in Fig. 10.21—we do, however, include them in the Java implementation in Appendix M. We also omit all operation parameters, as we did in Fig. 8.24—incorporating inheritance does not affect the parameters already modeled in Figs. 6.22–6.25.

> **Software Engineering Observation 10.12**
>
> *A complete class diagram shows all the associations among classes and all the attributes and operations for each class. When the number of class attributes, methods and associations is substantial (as in Figs. 10.21 and 10.22), a good practice that promotes readability is to divide this information between two class diagrams—one focusing on associations and the other on attributes and methods.*

Implementing the ATM System Design (Incorporating Inheritance)

In Section 8.19, we began implementing the ATM system design in Java code. We now modify our implementation to incorporate inheritance, using class Withdrawal as an example.

1. If a class A is a generalization of class B, then class B extends class A in the class declaration. For example, abstract superclass Transaction is a generalization of class Withdrawal. Figure 10.23 contains the shell of class Withdrawal containing the appropriate class declaration.

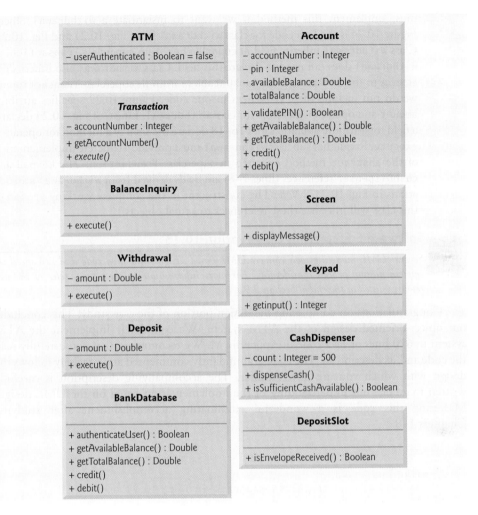

Fig. 10.22 | Class diagram with attributes and operations (incorporating inheritance). Note that abstract class names (e.g., `Transaction`) and method names (e.g., `execute` in class `Transaction`) appear in italics.

```
1   // Class Withdrawal represents an ATM withdrawal transaction
2   public class Withdrawal extends Transaction
3   {
4   } // end class Withdrawal
```

Fig. 10.23 | Java code for shell of class `Withdrawal`.

2. If class A is an abstract class and class B is a subclass of class A, then class B must implement the abstract methods of class A if class B is to be a concrete class. For example, class `Transaction` contains abstract method `execute`, so class `Withdrawal`

must implement this method if we want to instantiate a `Withdrawal` object. Figure 10.24 is the Java code for class `Withdrawal` from Fig. 10.21 and Fig. 10.22. Class `Withdrawal` inherits field `accountNumber` from superclass `Transaction`, so `Withdrawal` does not need to declare this field. Class `Withdrawal` also inherits references to the `Screen` and the `BankDatabase` from its superclass `Transaction`, so we do not include these references in our code. Figure 10.22 specifies attribute `amount` and operation `execute` for class `Withdrawal`. Line 6 of Fig. 10.24 declares a field for attribute `amount`. Lines 16–18 declare the shell of a method for operation `execute`. Recall that subclass `Withdrawal` must provide a concrete implementation of the `abstract` method `execute` in superclass `Transaction`. The keypad and `cashDispenser` references (lines 7–8) are fields derived from `Withdrawal`'s associations in Fig. 10.21. [*Note:* The constructor in the complete working version of this class will initialize these references to actual objects.]

Software Engineering Observation 10.13

Several UML modeling tools convert UML-based designs into Java code and can speed the implementation process considerably. For more information on these tools, refer to the web resources listed at the end of Section 2.9.

Congratulations on completing the design portion of the case study! This concludes our object-oriented design of the ATM system. We completely implement the ATM system in 670 lines of Java code in Appendix M. We recommend that you carefully read the code and its description. The code is abundantly commented and precisely follows the design with which you are now familiar. The accompanying description is carefully written to guide your understanding of the implementation based on the UML design. Mastering this code is a wonderful culminating accomplishment after studying Chapters 1–8.

```java
1   // Withdrawal.java
2   // Generated using the class diagrams in Fig. 10.21 and Fig. 10.22
3   public class Withdrawal extends Transaction
4   {
5      // attributes
6      private double amount; // amount to withdraw
7      private Keypad keypad; // reference to keypad
8      private CashDispenser cashDispenser; // reference to cash dispenser
9
10     // no-argument constructor
11     public Withdrawal()
12     {
13     } // end no-argument Withdrawal constructor
14
15     // method overriding execute
16     public void execute()
17     {
18     } // end method execute
19  } // end class Withdrawal
```

Fig. 10.24 | Java code for class `Withdrawal` based on Figs. 10.21 and 10.22.

Software Engineering Case Study Self-Review Exercises

10.1 The UML uses an arrow with a _____ to indicate a generalization relationship.
a) solid filled arrowhead
b) triangular hollow arrowhead
c) diamond-shaped hollow arrowhead
d) stick arrowhead

10.2 State whether the following statement is *true* or *false*, and if *false*, explain why: The UML requires that we underline abstract class names and method names.

10.3 Write Java code to begin implementing the design for class Transaction specified in Figs. 10.21 and 10.22. Be sure to include private reference-type attributes based on class Transaction's associations. Also be sure to include public *get* methods that provide access to any of these private attributes that the subclasses require to perform their tasks.

Answers to Software Engineering Case Study Self-Review Exercises

10.1 b.

10.2 False. The UML requires that we italicize abstract class names and method names.

10.3 The design for class Transaction yields the code in Fig. 10.25. The bodies of the class constructor and methods will be completed in Appendix M. When fully implemented, methods getScreen and getBankDatabase will return superclass Transaction's private reference attributes screen and bankDatabase, respectively. These methods allow the Transaction subclasses to access the ATM's screen and interact with the bank's database.

```
1   // Abstract class Transaction represents an ATM transaction
2   public abstract class Transaction
3   {
4      // attributes
5      private int accountNumber; // indicates account involved
6      private Screen screen; // ATM's screen
7      private BankDatabase bankDatabase; // account info database
8
9      // no-argument constructor invoked by subclasses using super()
10     public Transaction()
11     {
12     } // end no-argument Transaction constructor
13
14     // return account number
15     public int getAccountNumber()
16     {
17     } // end method getAccountNumber
18
19     // return reference to screen
20     public Screen getScreen()
21     {
22     } // end method getScreen
23
24     // return reference to bank database
25     public BankDatabase getBankDatabase()
26     {
27     } // end method getBankDatabase
```

Fig. 10.25 | Java code for class Transaction based on Figs. 10.21 and 10.22. (Part 1 of 2.)

```
28
29      // abstract method overridden by subclasses
30      public abstract void execute();
31   } // end class Transaction
```

Fig. 10.25 | Java code for class `Transaction` based on Figs. 10.21 and 10.22. (Part 2 of 2.)

10.10 Wrap-Up

This chapter introduced polymorphism—the ability to process objects that share the same superclass in a class hierarchy as if they are all objects of the superclass. The chapter discussed how polymorphism makes systems extensible and maintainable, then demonstrated how to use overridden methods to effect polymorphic behavior. We introduced abstract classes, which allow programmers to provide an appropriate superclass from which other classes can inherit. You learned that an abstract class can declare abstract methods that each subclass must implement to become a concrete class and that a program can use variables of an abstract class to invoke the subclasses' implementations of abstract methods polymorphically. You also learned how to determine an object's type at execution time. Finally, the chapter discussed declaring and implementing an interface as another way to achieve polymorphic behavior.

You should now be familiar with classes, objects, encapsulation, inheritance, interfaces and polymorphism—the most essential aspects of object-oriented programming. In the next chapter, we take a deeper look at graphical user interfaces (GUIs).

Summary

Section 10.1 Introduction

- Polymorphism enables us to write programs that process objects that share the same superclass in a class hierarchy as if they are all objects of the superclass; this can simplify programming.
- With polymorphism, we can design and implement systems that are easily extensible—new classes can be added with little or no modification to the general portions of the program, as long as the new classes are part of the inheritance hierarchy that the program processes generically. The only parts of a program that must be altered to accommodate new classes are those that require direct knowledge of the new classes that the programmer adds to the hierarchy.

Section 10.3 Demonstrating Polymorphic Behavior

- When the compiler encounters a method call made through a variable, the compiler determines if the method can be called by checking the variable's class type. If that class contains the proper method declaration (or inherits one), the call is compiled. At execution time, the type of the object to which the variable refers determines the actual method to use.

Section 10.4 Abstract Classes and Methods

- In some cases, it is useful to declare classes for which you never intend to instantiate objects. Such classes are called abstract classes. Because they are used only as superclasses in inheritance hierarchies, we refer to them as abstract superclasses. These classes cannot be used to instantiate objects, because they are incomplete.
- The purpose of an abstract class is primarily to provide an appropriate superclass from which other classes can inherit and thus share a common design.

- Classes that can be used to instantiate objects are called concrete classes. Such classes provide implementations of every method they declare (some of the implementations can be inherited).

- Not all inheritance hierarchies contain abstract classes. However, programmers often write client code that uses only abstract superclass types to reduce client code's dependencies on a range of specific subclass types.

- Abstract classes sometimes constitute several levels of the hierarchy.

- You make a class abstract by declaring it with keyword abstract. An abstract class normally contains one or more abstract methods.

- Abstract methods do not provide implementations.

- A class that contains any abstract methods must be declared as an abstract class even if that class contains some concrete (nonabstract) methods. Each concrete subclass of an abstract superclass also must provide concrete implementations of each of the superclass's abstract methods.

- Constructors and static methods cannot be declared abstract.

- Although you cannot instantiate objects of abstract superclasses, you *can* use abstract superclasses to declare variables that can hold references to objects of any concrete class derived from those abstract superclasses. Programs typically use such variables to manipulate subclass objects polymorphically.

- Polymorphism is particularly effective for implementing layered software systems.

Section 10.5 Case Study: Payroll System Using Polymorphism
- Including an abstract method in a superclass forces every direct subclass of the superclass to override the abstract method in order to become a concrete class. This enables the designer of the class hierarchy to demand that each concrete subclass provide an appropriate method implementation.

- Most method calls are resolved at execution time, based on the type of the object being manipulated. This process is known as dynamic binding or late binding.

- A superclass reference can be used to invoke only methods of the superclass (and the superclass can invoke overridden versions of these in the subclass).

- The instanceof operator can be used to determine whether a particular object's type has the *is-a* relationship with a specific type.

- Every object in Java knows its own class and can access this information through method getClass, which all classes inherit from class Object. Method getClass returns an object of type Class (package java.lang), which contains information about the object's type, including its class name.

- The *is-a* relationship applies only between the subclass and its superclasses, not vice versa.

- Attempting to invoke subclass-only methods on a superclass reference is not allowed. Although the actual method that is called depends on the object's type at execution time, a variable can be used to invoke only those methods that are members of that variable's type, which the compiler verifies.

Section 10.6 final Methods and Classes
- A method that is declared final in a superclass cannot be overridden in a subclass.

- Methods that are declared private are implicitly final, because it is impossible to override them in a subclass.

- Methods that are declared static are implicitly final.

- A final method's declaration can never change, so all subclasses use the same method implementation, and calls to final methods are resolved at compile time—this is known as static binding.

- Since the compiler knows that `final` methods cannot be overridden, it can optimize programs by removing calls to `final` methods and replacing them with the expanded code of their declarations at each method-call location—a technique known as inlining the code.

- A class that is declared `final` cannot be a superclass (i.e., a class cannot extend a `final` class).

- All methods in a `final` class are implicitly `final`.

Section 10.7 Case Study: Creating and Using Interfaces

- Interfaces define and standardize the ways in which things such as people and systems can interact with one another.

- An interface specifies *what* operations are allowed but does not specify *how* the operations are performed.

- A Java interface describes a set of methods that can be called on an object.

- An interface declaration begins with the keyword `interface` and contains only constants and abstract methods.

- All interface members must be `public`, and interfaces may not specify any implementation details, such as concrete method declarations and instance variables.

- All methods declared in an interface are implicitly `public abstract` methods and all fields are implicitly `public`, `static` and `final`.

- To use an interface, a concrete class must specify that it `implements` the interface and must declare each interface method with the signature specified in the interface declaration. A class that does not implement all the interface's methods is an abstract class and must be declared `abstract`.

- Implementing an interface is like signing a contract with the compiler that states, "I will declare all the methods specified by the interface or I will declare my class `abstract`."

- An interface is typically used when disparate (i.e., unrelated) classes need to share common methods and constants. This allows objects of unrelated classes to be processed polymorphically—objects of classes that implement the same interface can respond to the same method calls.

- You can create an interface that describes the desired functionality, then implement the interface in any classes that require that functionality.

- An interface is often used in place of an `abstract` class when there is no default implementation to inherit—that is, no fields and no default method implementations.

- Like `public abstract` classes, interfaces are typically `public` types, so they are normally declared in files by themselves with the same name as the interface and the `.java` file-name extension.

- Java does not allow subclasses to inherit from more than one superclass, but it does allow a class to inherit from a superclass and implement more than one interface. To implement more than one interface, use a comma-separated list of interface names after keyword `implements` in the class declaration.

- All objects of a class that implement multiple interfaces have the *is-a* relationship with each implemented interface type.

- An interface can declare constants. The constants are implicitly `public`, `static` and `final`.

Terminology

abstract class	concrete class
abstract keyword	constants declared in an interface
abstract method	downcasting
abstract superclass	dynamic binding
Class class	final class

final method   interface inheritance
generalization in the UML   interface keyword
getClass method of Object   iterator class
getName method of Class   late binding
implement an interface   polymorphism
implementation inheritance   realization in the UML
implements keyword   specialization in the UML
inlining method calls   static binding
instanceof operator   subclass reference
interface declaration   superclass reference

Self-Review Exercises

10.1 Fill in the blanks in each of the following statements:
   a) Polymorphism helps eliminate _____ logic.
   b) If a class contains at least one abstract method, it is a(n) _____ class.
   c) Classes from which objects can be instantiated are called _____ classes.
   d) _____ involves using a superclass variable to invoke methods on superclass and sub-class objects, enabling you to "program in the general."
   e) Methods that are not interface methods and that do not provide implementations must be declared using keyword _____.
   f) Casting a reference stored in a superclass variable to a subclass type is called _____.

10.2 State whether each of the statements that follows is *true* or *false*. If *false*, explain why.
   a) It is possible to treat superclass objects and subclass objects similarly.
   b) All methods in an abstract class must be declared as abstract methods.
   c) It is dangerous to try to invoke a subclass-only method through a subclass variable.
   d) If a superclass declares an abstract method, a subclass must implement that method.
   e) An object of a class that implements an interface may be thought of as an object of that interface type.

Answers to Self-Review Exercises

10.1 a) switch. b) abstract. c) concrete. d) Polymorphism. e) abstract. f) downcasting.

10.2 a) True. b) False. An abstract class can include methods with implementations and abstract methods. c) False. Trying to invoke a subclass-only method with a superclass variable is dangerous. d) False. Only a concrete subclass must implement the method. e) True.

Exercises

10.3 How does polymorphism enable you to program "in the general" rather than "in the specific"? Discuss the key advantages of programming "in the general."

10.4 What are abstract methods? Describe the circumstances in which an abstract method would be appropriate.

10.5 Discuss four ways in which you can assign superclass and subclass references to variables of superclass and subclass types.

10.6 Compare and contrast abstract classes and interfaces. Why would you use an abstract class? Why would you use an interface?

10.7 *(Payroll System Modification)* Modify the payroll system of Figs. 10.4–10.9 to include private instance variable birthDate in class Employee. Use class Date of Fig. 8.7 to represent an employee's birthday. Add *get* methods to class Date and replace method toDateString with method toString. Assume that payroll is processed once per month. Create an array of Employee variables to store references to the various employee objects. In a loop, calculate the payroll for each Employee (polymorphically), and add a $100.00 bonus to the person's payroll amount if the current month is the one in which the Employee's birthday occurs.

10.8 *(Payroll System Modification)* Modify the payroll system of Figs. 10.4–10.9 to include an additional Employee subclass PieceWorker that represents an employee whose pay is based on the number of pieces of merchandise produced. Class PieceWorker should contain private instance variables wage (to store the employee's wage per piece) and pieces (to store the number of pieces produced). Provide a concrete implementation of method earnings in class PieceWorker that calculates the employee's earnings by multiplying the number of pieces produced by the wage per piece. Create an array of Employee variables to store references to objects of each concrete class in the new Employee hierarchy. For each Employee, display its string representation and earnings.

10.9 *(Accounts Payable System Modification)* In this exercise, we modify the accounts payable application of Figs. 10.11–10.15 to include the complete functionality of the payroll application of Figs. 10.4–10.9. The application should still process two Invoice objects, but now should process one object of each of the four Employee subclasses. If the object currently being processed is a BasePlusCommissionEmployee, the application should increase the BasePlusCommissionEmployee's base salary by 10%. Finally, the application should output the payment amount for each object. Complete the following steps to create the new application:

a) Modify classes HourlyEmployee (Fig. 10.6) and CommissionEmployee (Fig. 10.7) to place them in the Payable hierarchy as subclasses of the version of Employee (Fig. 10.13) that implements Payable. [*Hint:* Change the name of method earnings to getPaymentAmount in each subclass so that the class satisfies its inherited contract with interface Payable.]

b) Modify class BasePlusCommissionEmployee (Fig. 10.8) such that it extends the version of class CommissionEmployee created in Part *a*.

c) Modify PayableInterfaceTest (Fig. 10.15) to polymorphically process two Invoices, one SalariedEmployee, one HourlyEmployee, one CommissionEmployee and one BasePlusCommissionEmployee. First output a string representation of each Payable object. Next, if an object is a BasePlusCommissionEmployee, increase its base salary by 10%. Finally, output the payment amount for each Payable object.

11

*Do you think I can listen all
day to such stuff?*
—Lewis Carroll

*Even a minor event in the
life of a child is an event of
that child's world and thus a
world event.*
—Gaston Bachelard

*You pays your money and
you takes your choice.*
—Punch

*Guess if you can, choose if
you dare.*
—Pierre Corneille

GUI
Components:
Part I

OBJECTIVES

In this chapter you will learn:

■ The design principles of graphical user interfaces (GUIs).

■ To build GUIs and handle events generated by user interactions with GUIs.

■ To understand the packages containing GUI components, event-handling classes and interfaces.

■ To create and manipulate buttons, labels, lists, text fields and panels.

■ To handle mouse events and keyboard events.

■ To use layout managers to arrange GUI components

11.1 Introduction

A graphical user interface (GUI) presents a user-friendly mechanism for interacting with an application. A GUI (pronounced "GOO-ee") gives an application a distinctive "look" and "feel." Providing different applications with consistent, intuitive user interface components allows users to be somewhat familiar with an application, so that they can learn it more quickly and use it more productively.

Look-and-Feel Observation 11.1

Consistent user interfaces enable a user to learn new applications faster.

As an example of a GUI, Fig. 11.1 contains an Internet Explorer web-browser window with some of its GUI components labeled. At the top is a title bar that contains the window's title. Below that is a menu bar containing menus (File, Edit, View, etc.).

button   menus   title bar   menu bar   combo box   scroll bars

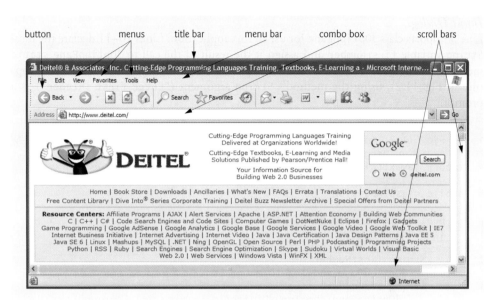

Fig. 11.1 | Internet Explorer window with GUI components.

Below the menu bar is a set of **buttons** that the user can click to perform tasks in Internet Explorer. Below the buttons is a **combo box**; the user can type into it the name of a website to visit or can click the down arrow at the right side of the box to select from a list of sites previously visited. The menus, buttons and combo box are part of Internet Explorer's GUI. They enable you to interact with Internet Explorer.

GUIs are built from **GUI components**. These are sometimes called **controls** or **widgets**—short for **window gadgets**—in other languages. A GUI component is an object with which the user interacts via the mouse, the keyboard or another form of input, such as voice recognition. In this chapter and Chapter 22, GUI Components: Part 2, you will learn about many of Java's GUI components. [*Note:* Several concepts covered in this chapter have already been covered in the optional GUI and Graphics Case Study of Chapters 3–10. So, some material will be repetitive if you read the case study. You do not need to read the case study to understand this chapter.]

11.2 Simple GUI-Based Input/Output with JOptionPane

The applications in Chapters 2–10 display text at the command window and obtain input from the command window. Most applications you use on a daily basis use windows or **dialog boxes** (also called **dialogs**) to interact with the user. For example, e-mail programs allow you to type and read messages in a window provided by the e-mail program. Typically, dialog boxes are windows in which programs display important messages to the user or obtain information from the user. Java's JOptionPane class (package javax.swing) provides prepackaged dialog boxes for both input and output. These dialogs are displayed by invoking static JOptionPane methods. Figure 11.2 presents a simple addition application that uses two **input dialogs** to obtain integers from the user and a **message dialog** to display the sum of the integers the user enters.

Input Dialogs

Line 3 imports class JOptionPane for use in this application. Lines 10–11 declare the local String variable firstNumber and assign it the result of the call to JOptionPane static method **showInputDialog**. This method displays an input dialog (see the first screen capture in Fig. 11.2), using the method's String argument ("Enter first integer") as a prompt.

```
 1   // Fig. 11.2: Addition.java
 2   // Addition program that uses JOptionPane for input and output.
 3   import javax.swing.JOptionPane; // program uses JOptionPane
 4
 5   public class Addition
 6   {
 7      public static void main( String args[] )
 8      {
 9         // obtain user input from JOptionPane input dialogs
10         String firstNumber =
11            JOptionPane.showInputDialog( "Enter first integer" );
12         String secondNumber =
13            JOptionPane.showInputDialog( "Enter second integer" );
14
15         // convert String inputs to int values for use in a calculation
16         int number1 = Integer.parseInt( firstNumber );
17         int number2 = Integer.parseInt( secondNumber );
18
19         int sum = number1 + number2; // add numbers
20
21         // display result in a JOptionPane message dialog
22         JOptionPane.showMessageDialog( null, "The sum is " + sum,
23            "Sum of Two Integers", JOptionPane.PLAIN_MESSAGE );
24      } // end method main
25   } // end class Addition
```

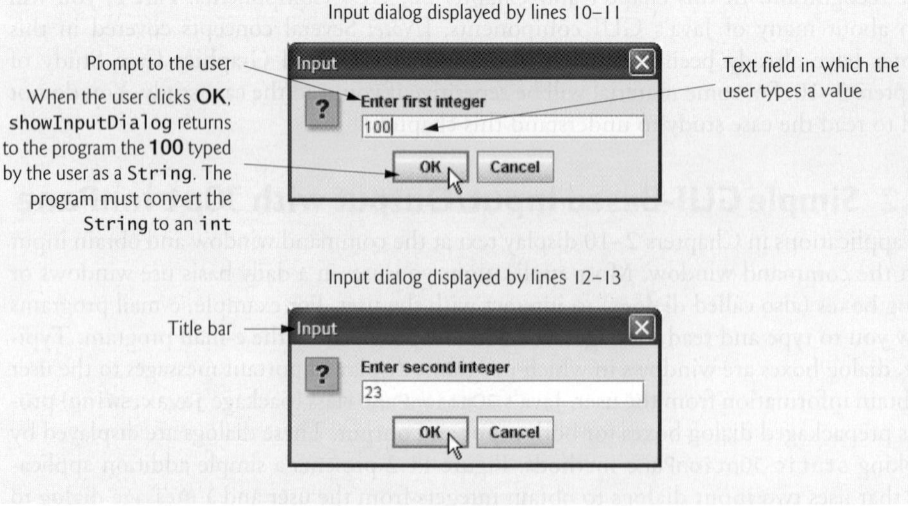

Input dialog displayed by lines 10–11

Prompt to the user

When the user clicks **OK**, showInputDialog returns to the program the **100** typed by the user as a String. The program must convert the String to an int

Text field in which the user types a value

Input dialog displayed by lines 12–13

Title bar

Fig. 11.2 | Addition program that uses JOptionPane for input and output. (Part 1 of 2.)

Message dialog displayed by lines 22–23

When the user clicks **OK**, the message dialog is dismissed (removed from the screen).

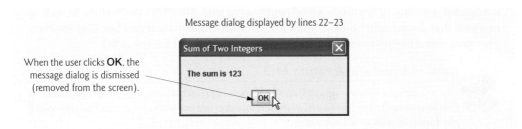

Fig. 11.2 | Addition program that uses JOptionPane for input and output. (Part 2 of 2.)

 Look-and-Feel Observation 11.2

The prompt in an input dialog typically uses sentence-style capitalization—a style that capitalizes only the first letter of the first word in the text unless the word is a proper noun (for example, Deitel).

The user types characters in the text field, then clicks the **OK** button or presses the *Enter* key to submit the String to the program. Clicking **OK** also dismisses (hides) the dialog. [*Note:* If you type in the text field and nothing appears, activate the text field by clicking it with the mouse.] Unlike Scanner, which can be used to input values of several types from the user at the keyboard, an input dialog can input only input Strings. This is typical of most GUI components. Technically, the user can type anything in the input dialog's text field. Our program assumes that the user enters a valid integer value. If the user clicks the **Cancel** button, showInputDialog returns null. If the user either types a noninteger value or clicks the **Cancel** button in the input dialog, a runtime logic error will occur in this program and it will not operate correctly. Chapter 13, Exception Handling, discusses how to handle such errors. Lines 12–13 display another input dialog that prompts the user to enter the second integer.

*Converting **Strings** to **int** Values*
To perform the calculation in this application, we must convert the Strings that the user entered to int values. Recall from Section 7.12 that the Integer class's static method parseInt converts its String argument to an int value. Lines 16–17 assign the converted values to local variables number1 and number2. Then, line 19 sums these values and assigns the result to local variable sum.

Message Dialogs
Lines 22–23 use JOptionPane static method showMessageDialog to display a message dialog (the last screen capture of Fig. 11.2) containing the sum. The first argument helps the Java application determine where to position the dialog box. The value null indicates that the dialog should appear in the center of the computer screen. The first argument can also be used to specify that the dialog should appear centered over a particular window, which we will demonstrate later in Section 11.8. The second argument is the message to display—in this case, the result of concatenating the String "The sum is " and the value of sum. The third argument—"Sum of Two Integers"—represents the string that should appear in the dialog's title bar at the top of the dialog. The fourth argument—JOption-Pane.PLAIN_MESSAGE—is the type of message dialog to display. A PLAIN_MESSAGE dialog does not display an icon to the left of the message. Class JOptionPane provides several

overloaded versions of methods `showInputDialog` and `showMessageDialog`, as well as methods that display other dialog types. For complete information on class `JOptionPane`, visit `java.sun.com/javase/6/docs/api/javax/swing/JOptionPane.html`.

Look-and-Feel Observation 11.3

*The title bar of a window typically uses **book-title capitalization**—a style that capitalizes the first letter of each significant word in the text and does not end with any punctuation (for example, Capitalization in a Book Title).*

JOptionPane Message Dialog Constants

The constants that represent the message dialog types are shown in Fig. 11.3. All message dialog types except `PLAIN_MESSAGE` display an icon to the left of the message. These icons provide a visual indication of the message's importance to the user. Note that a `QUESTION_MESSAGE` icon is the default icon for an input dialog box (see Fig. 11.2).

Message dialog type	Icon	Description
ERROR_MESSAGE	 x	A dialog that indicates an error to the user.
INFORMATION_MESSAGE	 i	A dialog with an informational message to the user.
WARNING_MESSAGE	 !	A dialog warning the user of a potential problem.
QUESTION_MESSAGE	 ?	A dialog that poses a question to the user. This dialog normally requires a response, such as clicking a **Yes** or a **No** button.
PLAIN_MESSAGE	no icon	A dialog that contains a message, but no icon.

Fig. 11.3 | `JOptionPane` static constants for message dialogs.

11.3 Overview of Swing Components

Though it is possible to perform input and output using the `JOptionPane` dialogs presented in Section 11.2, most GUI applications require more elaborate, customized user interfaces. The remainder of this chapter discusses many GUI components that enable application developers to create robust GUIs. Figure 11.4 lists several Swing GUI components from package `javax.swing` that are used to build Java GUIs. Most Swing components are pure Java components—they are written, manipulated and displayed completely in Java. They are part of the Java Foundation Classes (JFC)—Java's libraries for cross-platform GUI development. Visit `java.sun.com/products/jfc` for more information on JFC.

Swing vs. AWT

There are actually two sets of GUI components in Java. Before Swing was introduced in Java SE 1.2, Java GUIs were built with components from the Abstract Window Toolkit

Component	Description
JLabel	Displays uneditable text or icons.
JTextField	Enables user to enter data from the keyboard. Can also be used to display editable or uneditable text.
JButton	Triggers an event when clicked with the mouse.
JCheckBox	Specifies an option that can be selected or not selected.
JComboBox	Provides a drop-down list of items from which the user can make a selection by clicking an item or possibly by typing into the box.
JList	Provides a list of items from which the user can make a selection by clicking on any item in the list. Multiple elements can be selected.
JPanel	Provides an area in which components can be placed and organized. Can also be used as a drawing area for graphics.

Fig. 11.4 | Some basic GUI components.

(AWT) in package `java.awt`. When a Java application with an AWT GUI executes on different Java platforms, the application's GUI components display differently on each platform. Consider an application that displays an object of type `Button` (package `java.awt`). On a computer running the Microsoft Windows operating system, the `Button` will have the same appearance as the buttons in other Windows applications. Similarly, on a computer running the Apple Mac OS X operating system, the `Button` will have the same look and feel as the buttons in other Macintosh applications. Sometimes, the manner in which a user can interact with a particular AWT component differs between platforms.

Together, the appearance and the way in which the user interacts with the application are known as that application's look-and-feel. Swing GUI components allow you to specify a uniform look-and-feel for your application across all platforms or to use each platform's custom look-and-feel. An application can even change the look-and-feel during execution to enable users to choose their own preferred look-and-feel.

Portability Tip 11.1

Swing components are implemented in Java, so they are more portable and flexible than the original Java GUI components from package `java.awt`, which were based on the GUI components of the underlying platform. For this reason, Swing GUI components are generally preferred.

Lightweight vs. Heavyweight GUI Components

Most Swing components are not tied to actual GUI components supported by the underlying platform on which an application executes. Such GUI components are known as lightweight components. AWT components (many of which parallel the Swing components) are tied to the local platform and are called heavyweight components, because they rely on the local platform's windowing system to determine their functionality and their look-and-feel.

Several Swing components are heavyweight components. Like AWT components, heavyweight Swing GUI components require direct interaction with the local windowing system, which may restrict their appearance and functionality, making them less flexible than lightweight components.

Look-and-Feel Observation 11.4

The look-and-feel of a GUI defined with heavyweight GUI components from package java.awt may vary across platforms. Because heavyweight components are tied to the local-platform GUI, the look-and-feel varies from platform to platform.

Superclasses of Swing's Lightweight GUI Components

The UML class diagram of Fig. 11.5 shows an inheritance hierarchy containing classes from which lightweight Swing components inherit their common attributes and behaviors. As discussed in Chapter 9, class Object is the superclass of the Java class hierarchy.

Software Engineering Observation 11.1

Study the attributes and behaviors of the classes in the class hierarchy of Fig. 11.5. These classes declare the features that are common to most Swing components.

Class Component (package java.awt) is a subclass of Object that declares many of the attributes and behaviors common to the GUI components in packages java.awt and javax.swing. Most GUI components extend class Component directly or indirectly. Visit java.sun.com/javase/6/docs/api/java/awt/Component.html for a complete list of these common features.

Class Container (package java.awt) is a subclass of Component. As you will soon see, Components are attached to Containers (such as windows) so the Components can be organized and displayed on the screen. Any object that *is a* Container can be used to organize other Components in a GUI. Because a Container *is a* Component, you can attach Containers to other Containers to help organize a GUI. Visit java.sun.com/javase/6/docs/api/java/awt/Container.html for a complete list of the Container features that are common to Swing lightweight components.

Class JComponent (package javax.swing) is a subclass of Container. JComponent is the superclass of all lightweight Swing components and declares their common attributes

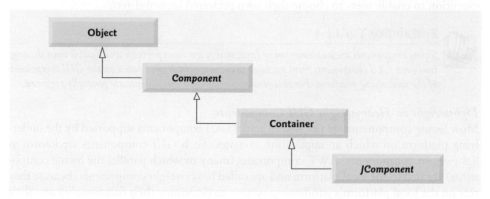

Fig. 11.5 | Common superclasses of many of the Swing components.

and behaviors. Because `JComponent` is a subclass of `Container`, all lightweight Swing components are also `Containers`. Some common lightweight component features supported by `JComponent` include:

1. A pluggable look-and-feel that can be used to customize the appearance of components (e.g., for use on particular platforms). You will see an example of this in Section 22.6.

2. Shortcut keys (called mnemonics) for direct access to GUI components through the keyboard. You will see an example of this in Section 22.4.

3. Common event-handling capabilities for cases where several GUI components initiate the same actions in an application.

4. Brief descriptions of a GUI component's purpose (called tool tips) that are displayed when the mouse cursor is positioned over the component for a short time. You will see an example of this in the next section.

5. Support for assistive technologies, such as braille screen readers for the visually impaired.

6. Support for user-interface localization—that is, customizing the user interface to display in different languages and use local cultural conventions.

These are just some of the many features of the Swing components. Visit `java.sun.com/javase/6/docs/api/javax/swing/JComponent.html` for more details of the common lightweight component features.

11.4 Displaying Text and Images in a Window

Our next example introduces a framework for building GUI applications. This framework uses several concepts that you will see in many of our GUI applications. This is our first example in which the application appears in its own window. Most windows you will create are an instance of class `JFrame` or a subclass of `JFrame`. `JFrame` provides the basic attributes and behaviors of a window—a title bar at the top of the window, and buttons to minimize, maximize and close the window. Since an application's GUI is typically specific to the application, most of our examples will consist of two classes—a subclass of `JFrame` that helps us demonstrate new GUI concepts and an application class in which `main` creates and displays the application's primary window.

Labeling GUI Components

A typical GUI consists of many components. In a large GUI, it can be difficult to identify the purpose of every component unless the GUI designer provides text instructions or information stating the purpose of each component. Such text is known as a label and is created with class `JLabel`—a subclass of `JComponent`. A `JLabel` displays a single line of read-only text, an image, or both text and an image. Applications rarely change a label's contents after creating it.

 Look-and-Feel Observation 11.5

Text in a `JLabel` *normally uses sentence-style capitalization.*

The application of Figs. 11.6–11.7 demonstrates several JLabel features and presents the framework we use in most of our GUI examples. We did not highlight the code in this example, since most of it is new. [*Note:* There are many more features for each GUI component than we can cover in our examples. To learn the complete details of each GUI component, visit its page in the online documentation. For class JLabel, visit java.sun.com/javase/6/docs/api/javax/swing/JLabel.html.]

Class LabelFrame (Fig. 11.6) is a subclass of JFrame. We will use an instance of class LabelFrame to display a window containing three JLabels. Lines 3–8 import the classes used in class LabelFrame. The class extends JFrame to inherit the features of a window. Lines 12–14 declare the three JLabel instance variables, each of which is instantiated in the LabelFrame constructor (lines 17–41). Typically, the JFrame subclass's constructor builds the GUI that is displayed in the window when the application executes. Line 19 invokes superclass JFrame's constructor with the argument "Testing JLabel". JFrame's constructor uses this String as the text in the window's title bar.

```java
1   // Fig. 11.6: LabelFrame.java
2   // Demonstrating the JLabel class.
3   import java.awt.FlowLayout; // specifies how components are arranged
4   import javax.swing.JFrame; // provides basic window features
5   import javax.swing.JLabel; // displays text and images
6   import javax.swing.SwingConstants; // common constants used with Swing
7   import javax.swing.Icon; // interface used to manipulate images
8   import javax.swing.ImageIcon; // loads images
9
10  public class LabelFrame extends JFrame
11  {
12     private JLabel label1; // JLabel with just text
13     private JLabel label2; // JLabel constructed with text and icon
14     private JLabel label3; // JLabel with added text and icon
15
16     // LabelFrame constructor adds JLabels to JFrame
17     public LabelFrame()
18     {
19        super( "Testing JLabel" );
20        setLayout( new FlowLayout() ); // set frame layout
21
22        // JLabel constructor with a string argument
23        label1 = new JLabel( "Label with text" );
24        label1.setToolTipText( "This is label1" );
25        add( label1 ); // add label1 to JFrame
26
27        // JLabel constructor with string, Icon and alignment arguments
28        Icon bug = new ImageIcon( getClass().getResource( "bug1.gif" ) );
29        label2 = new JLabel( "Label with text and icon", bug,
30           SwingConstants.LEFT );
31        label2.setToolTipText( "This is label2" );
32        add( label2 ); // add label2 to JFrame
33
34        label3 = new JLabel(); // JLabel constructor no arguments
35        label3.setText( "Label with icon and text at bottom" );
```

Fig. 11.6 | JLabels with text and icons. (Part 1 of 2.)

```
36          label3.setIcon( bug ); // add icon to JLabel
37          label3.setHorizontalTextPosition( SwingConstants.CENTER );
38          label3.setVerticalTextPosition( SwingConstants.BOTTOM );
39          label3.setToolTipText( "This is label3" );
40          add( label3 ); // add label3 to JFrame
41       } // end LabelFrame constructor
42    } // end class LabelFrame
```

Fig. 11.6 | `JLabels` with text and icons. (Part 2 of 2.)

```
 1    // Fig. 11.7: LabelTest.java
 2    // Testing LabelFrame.
 3    import javax.swing.JFrame;
 4
 5    public class LabelTest
 6    {
 7       public static void main( String args[] )
 8       {
 9          LabelFrame labelFrame = new LabelFrame(); // create LabelFrame
10          labelFrame.setDefaultCloseOperation( JFrame.EXIT_ON_CLOSE );
11          labelFrame.setSize( 275, 180 ); // set frame size
12          labelFrame.setVisible( true ); // display frame
13       } // end main
14    } // end class LabelTest
```

Fig. 11.7 | Test class for `LabelFrame`.

Specifying the Layout

When building a GUI, each GUI component must be attached to a container, such as a window created with a JFrame. Also, you typically must decide where to position each GUI component. This is known as specifying the layout of the GUI components. As you will learn at the end of this chapter and in Chapter 22, GUI Components: Part 2, Java provides several **layout managers** that can help you position components.

Many integrated development environments provide GUI design tools in which you can specify the exact size and location of a component in a visual manner by using the mouse, then the IDE will generate the GUI code for you. Though such IDEs can greatly simplify GUI creation, they are each different in capability.

To ensure that the code in this book can be used with any IDE, we did not use an IDE to create the GUI code in most of our examples. For this reason, we use Java's layout managers in our GUI examples. One such layout manager is `FlowLayout`, in which GUI components are placed on a container from left to right in the order in which the program attaches them to the container. When there is no more room to fit components left to right, components continue to display left to right on the next line. If the container is resized, a `FlowLayout` reflows (i.e., rearranges) the components to accommodate the new width of the container, possibly with fewer or more rows of GUI components. Line 20 specifies that the layout of the `LabelFrame` should be a `FlowLayout`. Method `setLayout` is inherited into class `LabelFrame` indirectly from class `Container`. The argument to the method must be an object of a class that implements the `LayoutManager` interface (e.g., `FlowLayout`). Line 20 creates a new `FlowLayout` object and pass its reference as the argument to `setLayout`.

Creating and Attaching `label1`
Now that we have specified the window's layout, we can begin creating and attaching GUI components to the window. Line 23 creates a `JLabel` object and passes `"Label with text"` to the constructor. The `JLabel` displays this text on the screen as part of the application's GUI. Line 24 uses method `setToolTipText` (inherited by `JLabel` from `JComponent`) to specify the tool tip that is displayed when the user positions the mouse cursor over the `JLabel` in the GUI. You can see a sample tool tip in the second screen capture of Fig. 11.7. When you execute this application, try positioning the mouse over each `JLabel` to see its tool tip. Line 25 attaches `label1` to the `LabelFrame` by passing `label1` to the **add** method, which is inherited indirectly from class `Container`.

Common Programming Error 11.1

If you do not explicitly add a GUI component to a container, the GUI component will not be displayed when the container appears on the screen.

Look-and-Feel Observation 11.6

Use tool tips to add descriptive text to your GUI components. This text helps the user determine the GUI component's purpose in the user interface.

Creating and Attaching `label2`
Icons are a popular way to enhance the look-and-feel of an application and are also commonly used to indicate functionality. For examples, most of today's VCRs and DVD players use the same icon to play a tape or DVD. Several Swing components can display images. An icon is normally specified with an `Icon` argument to a constructor or to the component's `setIcon` method. An `Icon` is an object of any class that implements interface `Icon` (package `javax.swing`). One such class is `ImageIcon` (package `javax.swing`), which supports several image formats, including Graphics Interchange Format (GIF), Portable Network Graphics (PNG) and Joint Photographic Experts Group (JPEG). File names for each of these types end with `.gif`, `.png` or `.jpg` (or `.jpeg`), respectively. We discuss images in more detail in Chapter 21, Multimedia: Applets and Applications.

Line 28 declares an `ImageIcon` object. The file `bug1.gif` contains the image to load and store in the `ImageIcon` object. (This image is included in the directory for this example on the CD that accompanies this book.) The `ImageIcon` object is assigned to `Icon` reference `bug`. Remember, class `ImageIcon` implements interface `Icon`; an `ImageIcon` *is an* `Icon`.

In line 28, the expression getClass().getResource("bug1.gif") invokes method getClass (inherited from class Object) to retrieve a reference to the Class object that represents the LabelFrame class declaration. That reference is then used to invoke Class method getResource, which returns the location of the image as a URL. The ImageIcon constructor uses the URL to locate the image, then loads it into memory. As we discussed in Chapter 1, the JVM loads class declarations into memory, using a class loader. The class loader knows where each class it loads is located on disk. Method getResource uses the Class object's class loader to determine the location of a resource, such as an image file. In this example, the image file is stored in the same location as the LabelFrame.class file. The techniques described here enable an application to load image files from locations that are relative to LabelFrame's .class file on disk.

A JLabel can display an Icon. Lines 29–30 use another JLabel constructor to create a JLabel that displays the text "Label with text and icon" and the Icon bug created in line 28. The last constructor argument indicates that the label's contents are left justified, or left aligned (i.e., the icon and text are at the left side of the label's area on the screen). Interface SwingConstants (package javax.swing) declares a set of common integer constants (such as SwingConstants.LEFT) that are used with many Swing components. By default, the text appears to the right of the image when a label contains both text and an image. Note that the horizontal and vertical alignments of a JLabel can be set with methods setHorizontalAlignment and setVerticalAlignment, respectively. Line 31 specifies the tool-tip text for label2, and line 32 adds label2 to the JFrame.

Creating and Attaching label3

Class JLabel provides many methods to change a label's appearance after the label has been instantiated. Line 34 creates a JLabel and invokes its no-argument constructor. Such a label initially has no text or Icon. Line 35 uses JLabel method setText to set the text displayed on the label. The corresponding method getText retrieves the current text displayed on a label. Line 36 uses JLabel method setIcon to specify the Icon to display on the label. The corresponding method getIcon retrieves the current Icon displayed on a label. Lines 37–38 use JLabel methods setHorizontalTextPosition and setVerticalTextPosition to specify the text position in the label. In this case, the text will be centered horizontally and will appear at the bottom of the label. Thus, the Icon will appear above the text. The horizontal-position constants in SwingConstants are LEFT, CENTER and RIGHT (Fig. 11.8). The vertical-position constants in SwingConstants are TOP, CENTER and BOTTOM (Fig. 11.8). Line 39 sets the tool-tip text for label3. Line 40 adds label3 to the JFrame.

Constant	Description
Horizontal-position constants	
SwingConstants.LEFT	Place text on the left.
SwingConstants.CENTER	Place text in the center.
SwingConstants.RIGHT	Place text on the right.

Fig. 11.8 | Some basic GUI components. (Part 1 of 2.)

Constant	Description
Vertical-position constants	
SwingConstants.TOP	Place text at the top.
SwingConstants.CENTER	Place text in the center.
SwingConstants.BOTTOM	Place text at the bottom.

Fig. 11.8 | Some basic GUI components. (Part 2 of 2.)

Creating and Displaying a LabelFrame Window

Class LabelTest (Fig. 11.7) creates an object of class LabelFrame (line 9), then specifies the default close operation for the window. By default, closing a window simply hides the window. However, when the user closes the LabelFrame window, we would like the application to terminate. Line 10 invokes LabelFrame's setDefaultCloseOperation method (inherited from class JFrame) with constant JFrame.EXIT_ON_CLOSE as the argument to indicate that the program should terminate when the window is closed by the user. This line is important. Without it the application will not terminate when the user closes the window. Next, line 11 invokes LabelFrame's setSize method to specify the width and height of the window. Finally, line 12 invokes LabelFrame's setVisible method with the argument true to display the window on the screen. Try resizing the window to see how the FlowLayout changes the JLabel positions as the window width changes.

11.5 Text Fields and an Introduction to Event Handling with Nested Classes

Normally, a user interacts with an application's GUI to indicate the tasks that the application should perform. For example, when you write an e-mail in an e-mail application, clicking the **Send** button tells the application to send the e-mail to the specified e-mail addresses. GUIs are event driven. When the user interacts with a GUI component, the interaction—known as an event—drives the program to perform a task. Some common events (user interactions) that might cause an application to perform a task include clicking a button, typing in a text field, selecting an item from a menu, closing a window and moving the mouse. The code that performs a task in response to an event is called an event handler and the overall process of responding to events is known as event handling.

In this section, we introduce two new GUI components that can generate events—JTextFields and JPasswordFields (package javax.swing). Class JTextField extends class JTextComponent (package javax.swing.text), which provides many features common to Swing's text-based components. Class JPasswordField extends JTextField and adds several methods that are specific to processing passwords. Each of these components is a single-line area in which the user can enter text via the keyboard. Applications can also display text in a JTextField (see the output of Fig. 11.10). A JPasswordField shows that characters are being typed as the user enters them, but hides the actual characters with an echo character, assuming that they represent a password that should remain known only to the user.

When the user types data into a JTextField or a JPasswordField, then presses *Enter*, an event occurs. Our next example demonstrates how a program can perform a task in response to that event. The techniques shown here are applicable to all GUI components that generate events.

The application of Figs. 11.9–11.10 uses classes JTextField and JPasswordField to create and manipulate four text fields. When the user types in one of the text fields, then presses *Enter*, the application displays a message dialog box containing the text the user typed. You can only type in the text field that is "in **focus.**" A component receives the focus when the user clicks the component. This is important, because the text field with the focus is the one that generates an event when the user presses *Enter*. In this example, when the user presses *Enter* in the JPasswordField, the password is revealed. We begin by discussing the setup of the GUI, then discuss the event-handling code.

```java
 1   // Fig. 11.9: TextFieldFrame.java
 2   // Demonstrating the JTextField class.
 3   import java.awt.FlowLayout;
 4   import java.awt.event.ActionListener;
 5   import java.awt.event.ActionEvent;
 6   import javax.swing.JFrame;
 7   import javax.swing.JTextField;
 8   import javax.swing.JPasswordField;
 9   import javax.swing.JOptionPane;
10
11   public class TextFieldFrame extends JFrame
12   {
13      private JTextField textField1; // text field with set size
14      private JTextField textField2; // text field constructed with text
15      private JTextField textField3; // text field with text and size
16      private JPasswordField passwordField; // password field with text
17
18      // TextFieldFrame constructor adds JTextFields to JFrame
19      public TextFieldFrame()
20      {
21         super( "Testing JTextField and JPasswordField" );
22         setLayout( new FlowLayout() ); // set frame layout
23
24         // construct textfield with 10 columns
25         textField1 = new JTextField( 10 );
26         add( textField1 ); // add textField1 to JFrame
27
28         // construct textfield with default text
29         textField2 = new JTextField( "Enter text here" );
30         add( textField2 ); // add textField2 to JFrame
31
32         // construct textfield with default text and 21 columns
33         textField3 = new JTextField( "Uneditable text field", 21 );
34         textField3.setEditable( false ); // disable editing
35         add( textField3 ); // add textField3 to JFrame
36
```

Fig. 11.9 | JTextFields and JPasswordFields. (Part 1 of 2.)

```
37        // construct passwordfield with default text
38        passwordField = new JPasswordField( "Hidden text" );
39        add( passwordField ); // add passwordField to JFrame
40
41        // register event handlers
42        TextFieldHandler handler = new TextFieldHandler();
43        textField1.addActionListener( handler );
44        textField2.addActionListener( handler );
45        textField3.addActionListener( handler );
46        passwordField.addActionListener( handler );
47     } // end TextFieldFrame constructor
48
49     // private inner class for event handling
50     private class TextFieldHandler implements ActionListener
51     {
52        // process text field events
53        public void actionPerformed( ActionEvent event )
54        {
55           String string = ""; // declare string to display
56
57           // user pressed Enter in JTextField textField1
58           if ( event.getSource() == textField1 )
59              string = String.format( "textField1: %s",
60                 event.getActionCommand() );
61
62           // user pressed Enter in JTextField textField2
63           else if ( event.getSource() == textField2 )
64              string = String.format( "textField2: %s",
65                 event.getActionCommand() );
66
67           // user pressed Enter in JTextField textField3
68           else if ( event.getSource() == textField3 )
69              string = String.format( "textField3: %s",
70                 event.getActionCommand() );
71
72           // user pressed Enter in JTextField passwordField
73           else if ( event.getSource() == passwordField )
74              string = String.format( "passwordField: %s",
75                 new String( passwordField.getPassword() ) );
76
77           // display JTextField content
78           JOptionPane.showMessageDialog( null, string );
79        } // end method actionPerformed
80     } // end private inner class TextFieldHandler
81  } // end class TextFieldFrame
```

Fig. 11.9 | JTextFields and JPasswordFields. (Part 2 of 2.)

Lines 3–9 import the classes and interfaces we use in this example. Class TextField-Frame extends JFrame and declares three JTextField variables and a JPasswordField variable (lines 13–16). Each of the corresponding text fields is instantiated and attached to the TextFieldFrame in the constructor (lines 19–47).

```
1   // Fig. 11.10: TextFieldTest.java
2   // Testing TextFieldFrame.
3   import javax.swing.JFrame;
4
5   public class TextFieldTest
6   {
7      public static void main( String args[] )
8      {
9         TextFieldFrame textFieldFrame = new TextFieldFrame();
10        textFieldFrame.setDefaultCloseOperation( JFrame.EXIT_ON_CLOSE );
11        textFieldFrame.setSize( 350, 100 ); // set frame size
12        textFieldFrame.setVisible( true ); // display frame
13     } // end main
14  } // end class TextFieldTest
```

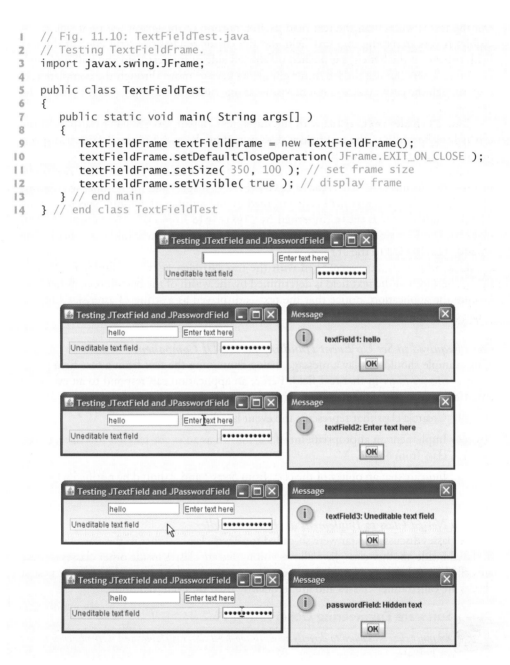

Fig. 11.10 | Test class for `TextFieldFrame`.

Creating the GUI

Line 22 sets the layout of the `TextFieldFrame` to `FlowLayout`. Line 25 creates `textField1` with 10 columns of text. The width in pixels of a text column is determined by the average width of a character in the text field's current font. When text is displayed in a text field and the text is wider than the text field itself, a portion of the text at the right side is not visible. If you are typing in a text field and the cursor reaches the right edge of the text field, the text at the left edge is pushed off the left side of the text field and will no longer be visible. Users can use the left and right arrow keys to move through the complete text even though the entire text will not be visible at one time. Line 26 adds textField1 to the JFrame.

Line 29 creates textField2 with the initial text "Enter text here" to display in the text field. The width of the text field is determined by the width of the default text specified in the constructor. Line 30 adds textField2 to the JFrame.

Line 33 creates textField3 and calls the JTextField constructor with two arguments—the default text "Uneditable text field" to display and the number of columns (21). The width of the text field is determined by the number of columns specified. Line 34 uses method setEditable (inherited by JTextField from class JTextComponent) to make the text field uneditable—i.e., the user cannot modify the text in the text field. Line 35 adds textField3 to the JFrame.

Line 38 creates passwordField with the text "Hidden text" to display in the text field. The width of the text field is determined by the width of the default text. When you execute the application, notice that the text is displayed as a string of asterisks. Line 39 adds passwordField to the JFrame.

Steps Required to Set Up Event Handling for a GUI Component
This example should display a message dialog containing the text from a text field when the user presses *Enter* in that text field. Before an application can respond to an event for a particular GUI component, you must perform several coding steps:

1. Create a class that represents the event handler.

2. Implement an appropriate interface, known as an event-listener interface, in the class from *Step 1*.

3. Indicate that an object of the class from *Steps 1* and *2* should be notified when the event occurs. This is known as registering the event handler.

Using a Nested Class to Implement an Event Handler
All the classes discussed so far were so-called top-level classes—that is, the classes were not declared inside another class. Java allows you to declare classes inside other classes—these are called nested classes. Nested classes can be static or non-static. Non-static nested classes are called inner classes and are frequently used for event handling.

 Software Engineering Observation 11.2

An inner class is allowed to directly access its top-level class's variables and methods, even if they are private.

Before an object of an inner class can be created, there must first be an object of the top-level class that contains the inner class. This is required because an inner-class object implicitly has a reference to an object of its top-level class. There is also a special relationship between these objects—the inner-class object is allowed to directly access all the instance variables and methods of the outer class. A nested class that is static does not require an object of its top-level class and does not implicitly have a reference to an object of the top-level class. As you will see in Chapter 12, Graphics and Java 2D™, the Java 2D graphics API uses static nested classes extensively.

The event handling in this example is performed by an object of the private inner class TextFieldHandler (lines 50–80). This class is private because it will be used only to create event handlers for the text fields in top-level class TextFieldFrame. As with other members of a class, inner classes can be declared public, protected or private.

GUI components can generate a variety of events in response to user interactions. Each event is represented by a class and can be processed only by the appropriate type of event handler. In most cases, the events a GUI component supports are described in the Java API documentation for that component's class and its superclasses. When the user presses *Enter* in a JTextField or JPasswordField, the GUI component generates an ActionEvent (package java.awt.event). Such an event is processed by an object that implements the interface ActionListener (package java.awt.event). The information discussed here is available in the Java API documentation for classes JTextField and ActionEvent. Since JPasswordField is a subclass of JTextField, JPasswordField supports the same events.

To prepare to handle the events in this example, inner class TextFieldHandler implements interface ActionListener and declares the only method in that interface—actionPerformed (lines 53–79). This method specifies the tasks to perform when an ActionEvent occurs. So inner class TextFieldHandler satisfies *Steps 1* and *2* listed earlier in this section. We'll discuss the details of method actionPerformed shortly.

Registering the Event Handler for Each Text Field

In the TextFieldFrame constructor, line 42 creates a TextFieldHandler object and assigns it to variable handler. This object's actionPerformed method will be called automatically when the user presses *Enter* in any of the GUI's text fields. However, before this can occur, the program must register this object as the event handler for each text field. Lines 43–46 are the event-registration statements that specify handler as the event handler for the three JTextFields and the JPasswordField. The application calls JTextField method addActionListener to register the event handler for each component. This method receives as its argument an ActionListener object, which can be an object of any class that implements ActionListener. The object handler *is an* ActionListener, because class TextFieldHandler implements ActionListener. After lines 43–46 execute, the object handler listens for events. Now, when the user presses *Enter* in any of these four text fields, method actionPerformed (line 53–79) in class TextFieldHandler is called to handle the event. If an event handler is not registered for a particular text field, the event that occurs when the user presses *Enter* in that text field is consumed—i.e., it is simply ignored by the application.

Software Engineering Observation 11.3

The event listener for an event must implement the appropriate event-listener interface.

Common Programming Error 11.2

Forgetting to register an event-handler object for a particular GUI component's event type causes events of that type to be ignored.

Details of Class `TextFieldHandler`'s `actionPerformed` *Method*

In this example, we are using one event-handling object's `actionPerformed` method (lines 53–79) to handle the events generated by four text fields. Since we'd like to output the name of each text field's instance variable for demonstration purposes, we must determine which text field generated the event each time `actionPerformed` is called. The GUI component with which the user interacts is the event source. In this example, the event source is one of the text fields or the password field. When the user presses *Enter* while one of these GUI components has the focus, the system creates a unique `ActionEvent` object that contains information about the event that just occurred, such as the event source and the text in the text field. The system then passes this `ActionEvent` object in a method call to the event listener's `actionPerformed` method. In this example, we display some of that information in a message dialog. Line 55 declares the `String` that will be displayed. The variable is initialized with the empty string—a string containing no characters. The compiler requires this in case none of the branches of the nested `if` in lines 58–75 executes.

ActionEvent method `getSource` (called in lines 58, 63, 68 and 73) returns a reference to the event source. The condition in line 58 asks, "Is the event source `textField1`?" This condition compares the references on either side of the `==` operator to determine whether they refer to the same object. If they both refer to `textField1`, then the program knows that the user pressed *Enter* in `textField1`. In this case, lines 59–60 create a `String` containing the message that line 78 will display in a message dialog. Line 60 uses `ActionEvent` method `getActionCommand` to obtain the text the user typed in the text field that generated the event.

If the user interacted with the `JPasswordField`, lines 74–75 use `JPasswordField` method `getPassword` to obtain the password and create the `String` to display. This method returns the password as an array of type `char` that is used as an argument to a `String` constructor to create a string containing the characters in the array.

Class `TextFieldTest`

Class `TextFieldTest` (Fig. 11.10) contains the `main` method that executes this application and displays an object of class `TextFieldFrame`. When you execute the application, note that even the uneditable `JTextField` (`textField3`) can generate an `ActionEvent`. To test this, click the text field to give it the focus, then press *Enter*. Also note that the actual text of the password is displayed when you press *Enter* in the `JPasswordField`. Of course, you would normally not display the password!

This application used a single object of class `TextFieldHandler` as the event listener for four text fields. Starting in Section 11.9, you will see that it is possible to declare several event-listener objects of the same type and register each individual object for a separate GUI component's event. This technique enables us to eliminate the `if...else` logic used in this example's event handler by providing separate event handlers for each component's events.

11.6 Common GUI Event Types and Listener Interfaces

In Section 11.5, you learned that information about the event that occurs when the user presses *Enter* in a text field is stored in an `ActionEvent` object. Many different types of events can occur when the user interacts with a GUI. The information about any GUI event that occurs is stored in an object of a class that extends `AWTEvent`. Figure 11.11 illustrates a hierarchy containing many event classes from the package `java.awt.event`. Some of these are discussed in this chapter and Chapter 22. These event types are used with both AWT and Swing components. Additional event types that are specific to Swing GUI components are declared in package `javax.swing.event`.

Let's summarize the three parts to the event-handling mechanism that you saw in Section 11.5—the event source, the event object and the event listener. The event source is the particular GUI component with which the user interacts. The event object encapsulates information about the event that occurred, such as a reference to the event source and any event-specific information that may be required by the event listener for it to handle the event. The event listener is an object that is notified by the event source when an event occurs; in effect, it "listens" for an event, and one of its methods executes in response to the event. A method of the event listener receives an event object when the event listener is notified of the event. The event listener then uses the event object to respond to the event. The event-handling model described here is known as the delegation event model—an event's processing is delegated to a particular object (the event listener) in the application.

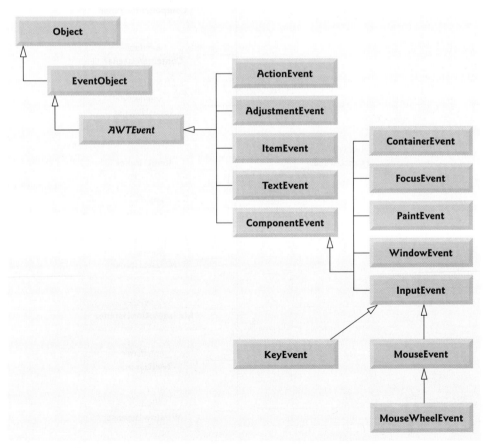

Fig. 11.11 | Some event classes of package `java.awt.event`.

For each event-object type, there is typically a corresponding event-listener interface. An event listener for a GUI event is an object of a class that implements one or more of the event-listener interfaces from packages java.awt.event and javax.swing.event. Many of the event-listener types are common to both Swing and AWT components. Such types are declared in package java.awt.event, and some of them are shown in Fig. 11.12. Additional event-listener types that are specific to Swing components are declared in package javax.swing.event.

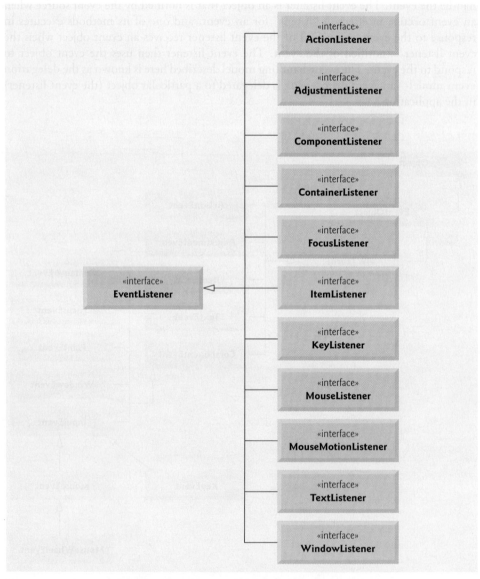

Fig. 11.12 | Some common event-listener interfaces of package java.awt.event.

Each event-listener interface specifies one or more event-handling methods that must be declared in the class that implements the interface. Recall from Section 10.7 that any class which implements an interface must declare all the abstract methods of that interface; otherwise, the class is an abstract class and cannot be used to create objects.

When an event occurs, the GUI component with which the user interacted notifies its registered listeners by calling each listener's appropriate event-handling method. For example, when the user presses the *Enter* key in a JTextField, the registered listener's actionPerformed method is called. How did the event handler get registered? How does the GUI component know to call actionPerformed rather than another event-handling method? We answer these questions and diagram the interaction in the next section.

11.7 How Event Handling Works

Let us illustrate how the event-handling mechanism works, using textField1 from the example of Fig. 11.9. We have two remaining open questions from Section 11.5:

1. How did the event handler get registered?
2. How does the GUI component know to call actionPerformed rather than some other event-handling method?

The first question is answered by the event registration performed in lines 43–46 of the application. Figure 11.13 diagrams JTextField variable textField1, TextFieldHandler variable handler and the objects to which they refer.

Registering Events

Every JComponent has an instance variable called listenerList that refers to an object of class EventListenerList (package javax.swing.event). Each object of a JComponent subclass maintains a references to all its registered listeners in the listenerList. For simplicity, we have diagramed listenerList as an array below the JTextField object in Fig. 11.13.

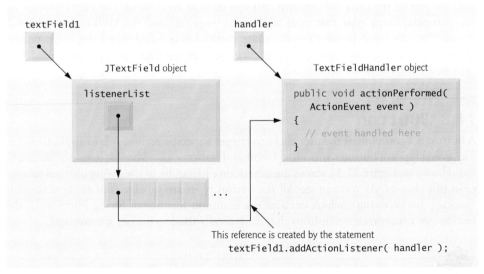

Fig. 11.13 | Event registration for JTextField textField1.

When line 43 of Fig. 11.9

```
textField1.addActionListener( handler );
```

executes, a new entry containing a reference to the TextFieldHandler object is placed in textField1's listenerList. Although not shown in the diagram, this new entry also includes the listener's type (in this case, ActionListener). Using this mechanism, each light-weight Swing GUI component maintains its own list of listeners that were registered to handle the component's events.

Event-Handler Invocation

The event-listener type is important in answering the second question: How does the GUI component know to call actionPerformed rather than another method? Every GUI component supports several event types, including mouse events, key events and others. When an event occurs, the event is dispatched to only the event listeners of the appropriate type. Dispatching is simply the process by which the GUI component calls an event-handling method on each of its listeners that are registered for the particular event type that occurred.

Each event type has one or more corresponding event-listener interfaces. For example, ActionEvents are handled by ActionListeners, MouseEvents are handled by MouseListeners and MouseMotionListeners, and KeyEvents are handled by KeyListeners. When an event occurs, the GUI component receives (from the JVM) a unique event ID specifying the event type. The GUI component uses the event ID to decide the listener type to which the event should be dispatched and to decide which method to call on each listener object. For an ActionEvent, the event is dispatched to every registered ActionListener's actionPerformed method (the only method in interface ActionListener). For a MouseEvent, the event is dispatched to every registered MouseListener or MouseMotionListener, depending on the mouse event that occurs. The MouseEvent's event ID determines which of the several mouse event-handling methods are called. All these decisions are handled for you by the GUI components. All you need to do is register an event handler for the particular event type that your application requires, and the GUI component will ensure that the event handler's appropriate method gets called when the event occurs. [*Note:* We discuss other event types and event-listener interfaces as they are needed with each new component we introduce.]

11.8 JButton

A button is a component the user clicks to trigger a specific action. A Java application can use several types of buttons, including command buttons, checkboxes, toggle buttons and radio buttons. Figure 11.14 shows the inheritance hierarchy of the Swing buttons we cover in this chapter. As you can see, all the button types are subclasses of AbstractButton (package javax.swing), which declares the common features of Swing buttons. In this section, we concentrate on buttons that are typically used to initiate a command.

 Look-and-Feel Observation 11.7

Buttons typically use book-title capitalization.

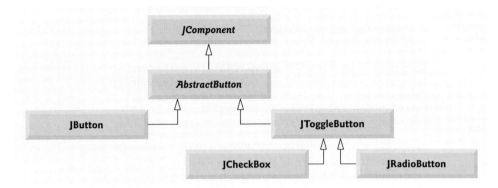

Fig. 11.14 | Swing button hierarchy.

A command button (see the output of Fig. 11.15) generates an ActionEvent when the user clicks the button. Command buttons are created with class JButton. The text on the face of a JButton is called a button label. A GUI can have many JButtons, but each button label typically should be unique in the portion of the GUI that is currently displayed.

Look-and-Feel Observation 11.8

Having more than one JButton with the same label makes the JButtons ambiguous to the user. Provide a unique label for each button.

The application of Figs. 11.15 and 11.16 creates two JButtons and demonstrates that JButtons support the display of Icons. Event handling for the buttons is performed by a single instance of inner class ButtonHandler (lines 39–47).

```
 1  // Fig. 11.15: ButtonFrame.java
 2  // Creating JButtons.
 3  import java.awt.FlowLayout;
 4  import java.awt.event.ActionListener;
 5  import java.awt.event.ActionEvent;
 6  import javax.swing.JFrame;
 7  import javax.swing.JButton;
 8  import javax.swing.Icon;
 9  import javax.swing.ImageIcon;
10  import javax.swing.JOptionPane;
11
12  public class ButtonFrame extends JFrame
13  {
14     private JButton plainJButton; // button with just text
15     private JButton fancyJButton; // button with icons
16
17     // ButtonFrame adds JButtons to JFrame
18     public ButtonFrame()
19     {
20        super( "Testing Buttons" );
21        setLayout( new FlowLayout() ); // set frame layout
```

Fig. 11.15 | Command buttons and action events. (Part 1 of 2.)

```
22
23        plainJButton = new JButton( "Plain Button" ); // button with text
24        add( plainJButton ); // add plainJButton to JFrame
25
26        Icon bug1 = new ImageIcon( getClass().getResource( "bug1.gif" ) );
27        Icon bug2 = new ImageIcon( getClass().getResource( "bug2.gif" ) );
28        fancyJButton = new JButton( "Fancy Button", bug1 ); // set image
29        fancyJButton.setRolloverIcon( bug2 ); // set rollover image
30        add( fancyJButton ); // add fancyJButton to JFrame
31
32        // create new ButtonHandler for button event handling
33        ButtonHandler handler = new ButtonHandler();
34        fancyJButton.addActionListener( handler );
35        plainJButton.addActionListener( handler );
36     } // end ButtonFrame constructor
37
38     // inner class for button event handling
39     private class ButtonHandler implements ActionListener
40     {
41        // handle button event
42        public void actionPerformed( ActionEvent event )
43        {
44           JOptionPane.showMessageDialog( ButtonFrame.this, String.format(
45              "You pressed: %s", event.getActionCommand() ) );
46        } // end method actionPerformed
47     } // end private inner class ButtonHandler
48  } // end class ButtonFrame
```

Fig. 11.15 | Command buttons and action events. (Part 2 of 2.)

```
1   // Fig. 11.16: ButtonTest.java
2   // Testing ButtonFrame.
3   import javax.swing.JFrame;
4
5   public class ButtonTest
6   {
7      public static void main( String args[] )
8      {
9         ButtonFrame buttonFrame = new ButtonFrame(); // create ButtonFrame
10        buttonFrame.setDefaultCloseOperation( JFrame.EXIT_ON_CLOSE );
11        buttonFrame.setSize( 275, 110 ); // set frame size
12        buttonFrame.setVisible( true ); // display frame
13     } // end main
14  } // end class ButtonTest
```

Fig. 11.16 | Test class for ButtonFrame. (Part 1 of 2.)

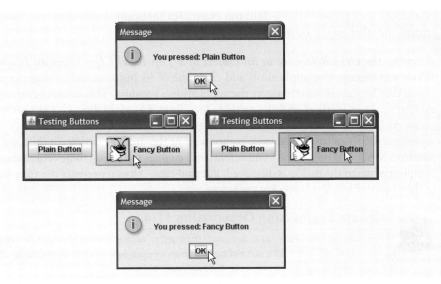

Fig. 11.16 | Test class for `ButtonFrame`. (Part 2 of 2.)

Lines 14–15 declare `JButton` variables `plainButton` and `fancyButton`. The corresponding objects are instantiated in the constructor. Line 23 creates `plainButton` with the button label `"Plain Button"`. Line 24 adds the button to the `JFrame`.

A `JButton` can display an `Icon`. To provide the user with an extra level of visual interaction with the GUI, a `JButton` can also have a rollover `Icon`—an `Icon` that is displayed when the user positions the mouse over the button. The icon on the button changes as the mouse moves in and out of the button's area on the screen. Lines 26–27 create two `ImageIcon` objects that represent the default `Icon` and rollover `Icon` for the `JButton` created at line 28. Both statements assume that the image files are stored in the same directory as the application (which is commonly the case for applications that use images). These image files have been provided for you.

Line 28 creates `fancyButton` with the text `"Fancy Button"` and the icon `bug1`. By default, the text is displayed to the right of the icon. Line 29 uses `setRolloverIcon` (inherited from class `AbstractButton`) to specify the image displayed on the button when the user positions the mouse over it. Line 30 adds the button to the `JFrame`.

Look-and-Feel Observation 11.9

Because class `AbstractButton` supports displaying text and images on a button, all subclasses of `AbstractButton` also support displaying text and images.

Look-and-Feel Observation 11.10

Using rollover icons for `JButton`s provides users with visual feedback indicating that when they click the mouse while the cursor is positioned over the button, an action will occur.

`JButton`s, like `JTextField`s, generate `ActionEvent`s that can be processed by any `ActionListener` object. Lines 33–35 create an object of `private` inner class `ButtonHandler` and register it as the event handler for each `JButton`. Class `ButtonHandler` (lines 39–47) declares `actionPerformed` to display a message dialog box containing the label for the button the user pressed. For a JButton event, ActionEvent method getActionCommand returns the label on the button.

Accessing the this Reference in an Object of a Top-Level Class From an Inner Class
When you execute this application and click one of its buttons, notice that the message dialog that appears is centered over the application's window. This occurs because the call to JOptionPane method showMessageDialog (lines 44–45 of Fig. 11.15) uses Button-Frame.this rather than null as the first argument. When this argument is not null, it represents the so-called parent GUI component of the message dialog (in this case the application window is the parent component) and enables the dialog to be centered over that component when the dialog is displayed. ButtonFrame.this represents the this reference of the object of top-level class ButtonFrame.

> **Software Engineering Observation 11.4**
>
> *When used in an inner class, keyword this refers to the current inner-class object being manipulated. An inner-class method can use its outer-class object's this by preceding this with the outer-class name and a dot, as in ButtonFrame.this.*

11.9 Buttons That Maintain State

The Swing GUI components contain three types of state buttons—JToggleButton, JCheckBox and JRadioButton—that have on/off or true/false values. Classes JCheckBox and JRadioButton are subclasses of JToggleButton (Fig. 11.14). A JRadioButton is different from a JCheckBox in that normally several JRadioButtons are grouped together, and are mutually exclusive—only one in the group can be selected at any time, just like the buttons on a car radio. We first discuss class JCheckBox. The next two subsections also demonstrate that an inner class can access the members of its top-level class.

11.9.1 JCheckBox

The application of Figs. 11.17–11.18 uses two JCheckBox objects to select the desired font style of the text displayed in a JTextField. When selected, one applies a bold style and the other an italic style. If both are selected, the style of the font is bold and italic. When the application initially executes, neither JCheckBox is checked (i.e., they are both false), so the font is plain. Class CheckBoxTest (Fig. 11.18) contains the main method that executes this application.

```
1   // Fig. 11.17: CheckBoxFrame.java
2   // Creating JCheckBox buttons.
3   import java.awt.FlowLayout;
4   import java.awt.Font;
5   import java.awt.event.ItemListener;
6   import java.awt.event.ItemEvent;
7   import javax.swing.JFrame;
8   import javax.swing.JTextField;
9   import javax.swing.JCheckBox;
10
```

Fig. 11.17 | JCheckBox buttons and item events. (Part 1 of 2.)

```
11   public class CheckBoxFrame extends JFrame
12   {
13      private JTextField textField; // displays text in changing fonts
14      private JCheckBox boldJCheckBox; // to select/deselect bold
15      private JCheckBox italicJCheckBox; // to select/deselect italic
16
17      // CheckBoxFrame constructor adds JCheckBoxes to JFrame
18      public CheckBoxFrame()
19      {
20         super( "JCheckBox Test" );
21         setLayout( new FlowLayout() ); // set frame layout
22
23         // set up JTextField and set its font
24         textField = new JTextField( "Watch the font style change", 20 );
25         textField.setFont( new Font( "Serif", Font.PLAIN, 14 ) );
26         add( textField ); // add textField to JFrame
27
28         boldJCheckBox = new JCheckBox( "Bold" ); // create bold checkbox
29         italicJCheckBox = new JCheckBox( "Italic" ); // create italic
30         add( boldJCheckBox ); // add bold checkbox to JFrame
31         add( italicJCheckBox ); // add italic checkbox to JFrame
32
33         // register listeners for JCheckBoxes
34         CheckBoxHandler handler = new CheckBoxHandler();
35         boldJCheckBox.addItemListener( handler );
36         italicJCheckBox.addItemListener( handler );
37      } // end CheckBoxFrame constructor
38
39      // private inner class for ItemListener event handling
40      private class CheckBoxHandler implements ItemListener
41      {
42         private int valBold = Font.PLAIN; // controls bold font style
43         private int valItalic = Font.PLAIN; // controls italic font style
44
45         // respond to checkbox events
46         public void itemStateChanged( ItemEvent event )
47         {
48            // process bold checkbox events
49            if ( event.getSource() == boldJCheckBox )
50               valBold =
51                  boldJCheckBox.isSelected() ? Font.BOLD : Font.PLAIN;
52
53            // process italic checkbox events
54            if ( event.getSource() == italicJCheckBox )
55               valItalic =
56                  italicJCheckBox.isSelected() ? Font.ITALIC : Font.PLAIN;
57
58            // set text field font
59            textField.setFont(
60               new Font( "Serif", valBold + valItalic, 14 ) );
61         } // end method itemStateChanged
62      } // end private inner class CheckBoxHandler
63   } // end class CheckBoxFrame
```

Fig. 11.17 | JCheckBox buttons and item events. (Part 2 of 2.)

```
 1   // Fig. 11.18: CheckBoxTest.java
 2   // Testing CheckBoxFrame.
 3   import javax.swing.JFrame;
 4
 5   public class CheckBoxTest
 6   {
 7      public static void main( String args[] )
 8      {
 9         CheckBoxFrame checkBoxFrame = new CheckBoxFrame();
10         checkBoxFrame.setDefaultCloseOperation( JFrame.EXIT_ON_CLOSE );
11         checkBoxFrame.setSize( 275, 100 ); // set frame size
12         checkBoxFrame.setVisible( true ); // display frame
13      } // end main
14   } // end class CheckBoxTest
```

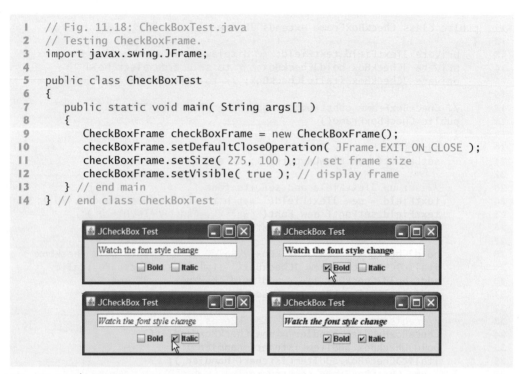

Fig. 11.18 | Test class for `CheckBoxFrame`.

After the `JTextField` is created and initialized (Fig. 11.17, line 24), line 25 uses method `setFont` (inherited by `JTextField` indirectly from class `Component`) to set the font of the `JTextField` to a new object of class `Font` (package `java.awt`). The new `Font` is initialized with `"Serif"` (a generic font name representing a font such as Times and is supported on all Java platforms), `Font.PLAIN` style and 14-point size. Next, lines 28–29 create two `JCheckBox` objects. The string passed to the `JCheckBox` constructor is the checkbox label that appears to the right of the `JCheckBox` by default.

When the user clicks a `JCheckBox`, an `ItemEvent` occurs. This event can be handled by an `ItemListener` object, which must implement method `itemStateChanged`. In this example, the event handling is performed by an instance of `private` inner class `CheckBox-Handler` (lines 40–62). Lines 34–36 create an instance of class `CheckBoxHandler` and register it with method `addItemListener` as the listener for both the `JCheckBox` objects.

Lines 42–43 declare instance variables for the inner class `CheckBoxHandler`. Together, these variables represent the font style for the text displayed in the `JTextField`. Initially both are `Font.PLAIN` to indicate that the font is not bold and is not italic. Method `item-StateChanged` (lines 46–61) is called when the user clicks the `bold` or the `italic` `JCheckBox`. The method uses `event.getSource()` to determine which `JCheckBox` the user clicked. If it was the `boldJCheckBox`, line 51 uses `JCheckBox` method `isSelected` to determine if the `JCheckBox` is selected (i.e., it is checked). If the checkbox is selected, local variable `valBold` is assigned `Font.BOLD`; otherwise, it is assigned `Font.PLAIN`. A similar statement executes if the user clicks the `italicJCheckBox`. If the `italicJCheckBox` is selected, local variable `valItalic` is assigned `Font.ITALIC`; otherwise, it is assigned

Font.PLAIN. Lines 59–60 change the font of the JTextField, using the same font name and point size. The sum of valBold and valItalic represents the JTextField's new font style. Each of the Font constants represents a unique value. Font.PLAIN has the value 0, so if both valBold and valItalic are set to Font.PLAIN, the font will have the plain style. If one of the values is Font.BOLD or Font.ITALIC, the font will be bold or italic accordingly. If one is BOLD and the other is ITALIC, the font will be both bold and italic.

Relationship Between an Inner Class and Its Top-Level Class

You may have noticed that class CheckBoxHandler used variables boldJCheckBox (Fig. 11.17, lines 49 and 51), italicJCheckBox (lines 54 and 56) and textField (line 59) even though these variables are not declared in the inner class. An inner class has a special relationship with its top-level class—the inner class is allowed to access directly all the instance variables and methods of the top-level class. Method itemStateChanged (line 46–61) of class CheckBoxHandler uses this relationship to determine which JCheckBox is the event source, to determine the state of a JCheckBox and to set the font on the JTextField. Notice that none of the code in inner class CheckBoxHandler requires a reference to the top-level class object.

11.9.2 JRadioButton

Radio buttons (declared with class **JRadioButton**) are similar to checkboxes in that they have two states—selected and not selected (also called deselected). However, radio buttons normally appear as a group in which only one button can be selected at a time (see the output of Fig. 11.20). Selecting a different radio button forces all others to be deselected. Radio buttons are used to represent mutually exclusive options (i.e., multiple options in the group cannot be selected at the same time). The logical relationship between radio buttons is maintained by a **ButtonGroup** object (package javax.swing), which itself is not a GUI component. A ButtonGroup object organizes a group of buttons and is not itself displayed in a user interface. Rather, the individual JRadioButton objects from the group are displayed in the GUI.

Common Programming Error 11.3

Adding a ButtonGroup object (or an object of any other class that does not derive from Component) to a container results in a compilation error.

The application of Figs. 11.19–11.20 is similar to that of Figs. 11.17–11.18. The user can alter the font style of a JTextField's text. The application uses radio buttons that permit only a single font style in the group to be selected at a time. Class RadioButtonTest (Fig. 11.20) contains the main method that executes this application.

```
1   // Fig. 11.19: RadioButtonFrame.java
2   // Creating radio buttons using ButtonGroup and JRadioButton.
3   import java.awt.FlowLayout;
4   import java.awt.Font;
5   import java.awt.event.ItemListener;
6   import java.awt.event.ItemEvent;
7   import javax.swing.JFrame;
```

Fig. 11.19 | JRadioButtons and ButtonGroups. (Part 1 of 3.)

```
 8   import javax.swing.JTextField;
 9   import javax.swing.JRadioButton;
10   import javax.swing.ButtonGroup;
11
12   public class RadioButtonFrame extends JFrame
13   {
14      private JTextField textField; // used to display font changes
15      private Font plainFont; // font for plain text
16      private Font boldFont; // font for bold text
17      private Font italicFont; // font for italic text
18      private Font boldItalicFont; // font for bold and italic text
19      private JRadioButton plainJRadioButton; // selects plain text
20      private JRadioButton boldJRadioButton; // selects bold text
21      private JRadioButton italicJRadioButton; // selects italic text
22      private JRadioButton boldItalicJRadioButton; // bold and italic
23      private ButtonGroup radioGroup; // buttongroup to hold radio buttons
24
25      // RadioButtonFrame constructor adds JRadioButtons to JFrame
26      public RadioButtonFrame()
27      {
28         super( "RadioButton Test" );
29         setLayout( new FlowLayout() ); // set frame layout
30
31         textField = new JTextField( "Watch the font style change", 25 );
32         add( textField ); // add textField to JFrame
33
34         // create radio buttons
35         plainJRadioButton = new JRadioButton( "Plain", true );
36         boldJRadioButton = new JRadioButton( "Bold", false );
37         italicJRadioButton = new JRadioButton( "Italic", false );
38         boldItalicJRadioButton = new JRadioButton( "Bold/Italic", false );
39         add( plainJRadioButton ); // add plain button to JFrame
40         add( boldJRadioButton ); // add bold button to JFrame
41         add( italicJRadioButton ); // add italic button to JFrame
42         add( boldItalicJRadioButton ); // add bold and italic button
43
44         // create logical relationship between JRadioButtons
45         radioGroup = new ButtonGroup(); // create ButtonGroup
46         radioGroup.add( plainJRadioButton ); // add plain to group
47         radioGroup.add( boldJRadioButton ); // add bold to group
48         radioGroup.add( italicJRadioButton ); // add italic to group
49         radioGroup.add( boldItalicJRadioButton ); // add bold and italic
50
51         // create font objects
52         plainFont = new Font( "Serif", Font.PLAIN, 14 );
53         boldFont = new Font( "Serif", Font.BOLD, 14 );
54         italicFont = new Font( "Serif", Font.ITALIC, 14 );
55         boldItalicFont = new Font( "Serif", Font.BOLD + Font.ITALIC, 14 );
56         textField.setFont( plainFont ); // set initial font to plain
57
58         // register events for JRadioButtons
59         plainJRadioButton.addItemListener(
60            new RadioButtonHandler( plainFont ) );
```

Fig. 11.19 | JRadioButtons and ButtonGroups. (Part 2 of 3.)

```
61          boldJRadioButton.addItemListener(
62             new RadioButtonHandler( boldFont ) );
63          italicJRadioButton.addItemListener(
64             new RadioButtonHandler( italicFont ) );
65          boldItalicJRadioButton.addItemListener(
66             new RadioButtonHandler( boldItalicFont ) );
67       } // end RadioButtonFrame constructor
68
69       // private inner class to handle radio button events
70       private class RadioButtonHandler implements ItemListener
71       {
72          private Font font; // font associated with this listener
73
74          public RadioButtonHandler( Font f )
75          {
76             font = f; // set the font of this listener
77          } // end constructor RadioButtonHandler
78
79          // handle radio button events
80          public void itemStateChanged( ItemEvent event )
81          {
82             textField.setFont( font ); // set font of textField
83          } // end method itemStateChanged
84       } // end private inner class RadioButtonHandler
85    } // end class RadioButtonFrame
```

Fig. 11.19 | JRadioButtons and ButtonGroups. (Part 3 of 3.)

```
 1   // Fig. 11.20: RadioButtonTest.java
 2   // Testing RadioButtonFrame.
 3   import javax.swing.JFrame;
 4
 5   public class RadioButtonTest
 6   {
 7      public static void main( String args[] )
 8      {
 9         RadioButtonFrame radioButtonFrame = new RadioButtonFrame();
10         radioButtonFrame.setDefaultCloseOperation( JFrame.EXIT_ON_CLOSE );
11         radioButtonFrame.setSize( 300, 100 ); // set frame size
12         radioButtonFrame.setVisible( true ); // display frame
13      } // end main
14   } // end class RadioButtonTest
```

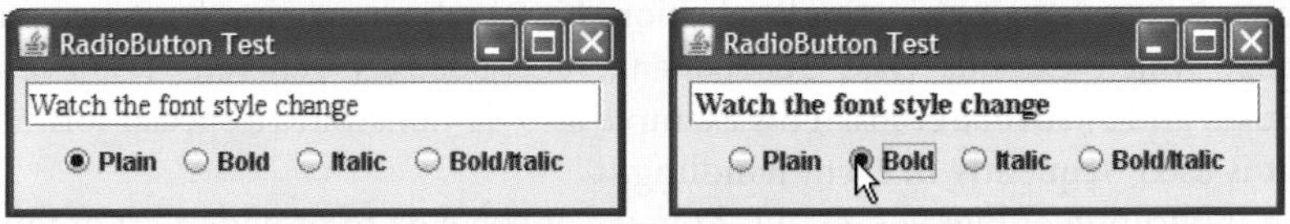

Fig. 11.20 | Test class for RadioButtonFrame. (Part 1 of 2.)

Fig. 11.20 | Test class for `RadioButtonFrame`. (Part 2 of 2.)

Lines 35–42 in the constructor (Fig. 11.19) create four `JRadioButton` objects and add them to the `JFrame`. Each `JRadioButton` is created with a constructor call like that in line 35. This constructor specifies the label that appears to the right of the `JRadioButton` by default and the initial state of the `JRadioButton`. A `true` second argument indicates that the `JRadioButton` should appear selected when it is displayed.

Line 45 instantiates `ButtonGroup` object `radioGroup`. This object is the "glue" that forms the logical relationship between the four `JRadioButton` objects and allows only one of the four to be selected at a time. It is possible that no `JRadioButtons` in a `ButtonGroup` are selected, but this can occur only if no preselected `JRadioButtons` are added to the `But-tonGroup` and the user has not selected a `JRadioButton` yet. Lines 46–49 use `ButtonGroup` method **add** to associate each of the `JRadioButtons` with `radioGroup`. If more than one selected `JRadioButton` object is added to the group, the selected one that was added first will be selected when the GUI is displayed.

`JRadioButtons`, like `JCheckBoxes`, generate `ItemEvents` when they are clicked. Lines 59–66 create four instances of inner class `RadioButtonHandler` (declared at lines 70–84). In this example, each event-listener object is registered to handle the `ItemEvent` generated when the user clicks a particular `JRadioButton`. Notice that each `RadioButtonHandler` object is initialized with a particular `Font` object (created in lines 52–55).

Class `RadioButtonHandler` (line 70–84) implements interface `ItemListener` so it can handle `ItemEvents` generated by the `JRadioButtons`. The constructor stores the `Font` object it receives as an argument in the event-listener object's instance variable `font` (declared at line 72). When the user clicks a `JRadioButton`, `radioGroup` turns off the previously selected `JRadioButton` and method `itemStateChanged` (line 80–83) sets the font in the `JTextField` to the `Font` stored in the `JRadioButton`'s corresponding event-listener object. Notice that line 82 of inner class `RadioButtonHandler` uses the top-level class's `textField` instance variable to set the font.

11.10 JComboBox and Using an Anonymous Inner Class for Event Handling

A combo box (sometimes called a drop-down list) provides a list of items (Fig. 11.22) from which the user can make a single selection. Combo boxes are implemented with class `JComboBox`, which extends class `JComponent`. `JComboBoxes` generate `ItemEvents` like `JCheckBoxes` and `JRadioButtons`. This example also demonstrates a special form of inner class that is used frequently in event handling.

The application of Figs. 11.21–11.22 uses a `JComboBox` to provide a list of four image file names from which the user can select one image to display. When the user selects a name, the application displays the corresponding image as an `Icon` on a `JLabel`. Class `ComboBoxTest` (Fig. 11.22) contains the `main` method that executes this application. The screen captures for this application show the JComboBox list after the selection was made to illustrate which image file name was selected.

```
1   // Fig. 11.21: ComboBoxFrame.java
2   // Using a JComboBox to select an image to display.
3   import java.awt.FlowLayout;
4   import java.awt.event.ItemListener;
5   import java.awt.event.ItemEvent;
6   import javax.swing.JFrame;
7   import javax.swing.JLabel;
8   import javax.swing.JComboBox;
9   import javax.swing.Icon;
10  import javax.swing.ImageIcon;
11
12  public class ComboBoxFrame extends JFrame
13  {
14     private JComboBox imagesJComboBox; // combobox to hold names of icons
15     private JLabel label; // label to display selected icon
16
17     private String names[] =
18        { "bug1.gif", "bug2.gif",  "travelbug.gif", "buganim.gif" };
19     private Icon icons[] = {
20        new ImageIcon( getClass().getResource( names[ 0 ] ) ),
21        new ImageIcon( getClass().getResource( names[ 1 ] ) ),
22        new ImageIcon( getClass().getResource( names[ 2 ] ) ),
23        new ImageIcon( getClass().getResource( names[ 3 ] ) ) };
24
25     // ComboBoxFrame constructor adds JComboBox to JFrame
26     public ComboBoxFrame()
27     {
28        super( "Testing JComboBox" );
29        setLayout( new FlowLayout() ); // set frame layout
30
31        imagesJComboBox = new JComboBox( names ); // set up JComboBox
32        imagesJComboBox.setMaximumRowCount( 3 ); // display three rows
33
34        imagesJComboBox.addItemListener(
35           new ItemListener() // anonymous inner class
36           {
37              // handle JComboBox event
38              public void itemStateChanged( ItemEvent event )
39              {
40                 // determine whether checkbox selected
41                 if ( event.getStateChange() == ItemEvent.SELECTED )
42                    label.setIcon( icons[
43                       imagesJComboBox.getSelectedIndex() ] );
44              } // end method itemStateChanged
45           } // end anonymous inner class
46        ); // end call to addItemListener
47
48        add( imagesJComboBox ); // add combobox to JFrame
49        label = new JLabel( icons[ 0 ] ); // display first icon
```

Fig. 11.21 | JComboBox that displays a list of image names. (Part 1 of 2.)

```
50          add( label ); // add label to JFrame
51       } // end ComboBoxFrame constructor
52    } // end class ComboBoxFrame
```

Fig. 11.21 | JComboBox that displays a list of image names. (Part 2 of 2.)

```
1    // Fig. 11.22: ComboBoxTest.java
2    // Testing ComboBoxFrame.
3    import javax.swing.JFrame;
4
5    public class ComboBoxTest
6    {
7       public static void main( String args[] )
8       {
9          ComboBoxFrame comboBoxFrame = new ComboBoxFrame();
10         comboBoxFrame.setDefaultCloseOperation( JFrame.EXIT_ON_CLOSE );
11         comboBoxFrame.setSize( 350, 150 ); // set frame size
12         comboBoxFrame.setVisible( true ); // display frame
13      } // end main
14   } // end class ComboBoxTest
```

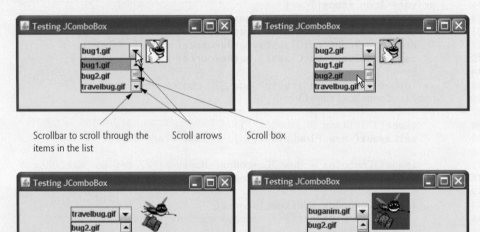

Fig. 11.22 | Test class for ComboBoxFrame.

Lines 19–23 (Fig. 11.21) declare and initialize array icons with four new ImageIcon objects. String array names (lines 17–18) contains the names of the four image files that are stored in the same directory as the application.

At line 31, the constructor creates a JComboBox object, using the Strings in array names as the elements in the list. Each item in the list has an index. The first item is added at index 0, the next at index 1 and so forth. The first item added to a JComboBox appears as the currently selected item when the JComboBox is displayed. Other items are selected by clicking the JComboBox, which expands into a list from which the user can make a selection.

Line 32 uses JComboBox method setMaximumRowCount to set the maximum number of elements that are displayed when the user clicks the JComboBox. If there are additional items, the JComboBox provides a scrollbar (see the first screen capture) that allows the user to scroll through all the elements in the list. The user can click the scroll arrows at the top and bottom of the scrollbar to move up and down through the list one element at a time, or else drag the scroll box in the middle of the scrollbar up and down. To drag the scroll box, position the mouse cursor on it, hold the mouse button down and move the mouse.

Look-and-Feel Observation 11.11

Set the maximum row count for a JComboBox to a number of rows that prevents the list from expanding outside the bounds of the window in which it is used. This configuration will ensure that the list displays correctly when it is expanded by the user.

Line 48 attaches the JComboBox to the ComboBoxFrame's FlowLayout (set in line 29). Line 49 creates the JLabel that displays ImageIcons and initializes it with the first Image-Icon in array icons. Line 50 attaches the JLabel to the ComboBoxFrame's FlowLayout.

Using an Anonymous Inner Class for Event Handling

Lines 34–46 are one statement that declares the event listener's class, creates an object of that class and registers that object as the listener for imagesJComboBox's ItemEvents. In this example, the event-listener object is an instance of an anonymous inner class—a special form of inner class that is declared without a name and typically appears inside a method declaration. As with other inner classes, an anonymous inner class can access its top-level class's members. However, an anonymous inner class has limited access to the local variables of the method in which it is declared. Since an anonymous inner class has no name, one object of the anonymous inner class must be created at the point where the class is declared (starting at line 35).

Software Engineering Observation 11.5

An anonymous inner class declared in a method can access the instance variables and methods of the top-level class object that declared it, as well as the method's final local variables, but cannot access the method's non-final local variables.

Lines 34–46 are a call to imagesJComboBox's addItemListener method. The argument to this method must be an object that *is an* ItemListener (i.e., any object of a class that implements ItemListener). Lines 35–45 are a class-instance creation expression that declares an anonymous inner class and creates one object of that class. A reference to that object is then passed as the argument to addItemListener. The syntax ItemListener() after new begins the declaration of an anonymous inner class that implements interface ItemListener. This is similar to beginning a class declaration with

```
public class MyHandler implements ItemListener
```

The parentheses after ItemListener indicate a call to the default constructor of the anonymous inner class.

The opening left brace ({) at 36 and the closing right brace (}) at line 45 delimit the body of the anonymous inner class. Lines 38–44 declare the ItemListener's itemState-Changed method. When the user makes a selection from imagesJComboBox, this method sets label's Icon. The Icon is selected from array icons by determining the index of the selected item in the JComboBox with method `getSelectedIndex` in line 43. Note that for each item selected from a JComboBox, another item is first deselected—so two ItemEvents occur when an item is selected. We wish to display only the icon for the item the user just selected. For this reason, line 41 determines whether ItemEvent method `getStateChange` returns ItemEvent.SELECTED. If so, lines 42–43 set label's icon.

Software Engineering Observation 11.6

Like any other class, when an anonymous inner class implements an interface, the class must implement every method in the interface.

The syntax shown in lines 35–45 for creating an event handler with an anonymous inner class is similar to the code that would be generated by a Java integrated development environment (IDE). Typically, an IDE enables the programmer to design a GUI visually, then the IDE generates code that implements the GUI. The programmer simply inserts statements in the event-handling methods that declare how to handle each event.

11.11 JList

A *list* displays a series of items from which the user may select one or more items (see the output of Fig. 11.23). Lists are created with class JList, which directly extends class JComponent. Class JList supports single-selection lists (which allow only one item to be selected at a time) and multiple-selection lists (which allow any number of items to be selected). In this section, we discuss single-selection lists.

The application of Figs. 11.23–11.24 creates a JList containing 13 color names. When a color name is clicked in the JList, a `ListSelectionEvent` occurs and the application changes the background color of the application window to the selected color. Class ListTest (Fig. 11.24) contains the main method that executes this application.

```
 1    // Fig. 11.23: ListFrame.java
 2    // Selecting colors from a JList.
 3    import java.awt.FlowLayout;
 4    import java.awt.Color;
 5    import javax.swing.JFrame;
 6    import javax.swing.JList;
 7    import javax.swing.JScrollPane;
 8    import javax.swing.event.ListSelectionListener;
 9    import javax.swing.event.ListSelectionEvent;
10    import javax.swing.ListSelectionModel;
11
12    public class ListFrame extends JFrame
13    {
14       private JList colorJList; // list to display colors
15       private final String colorNames[] = { "Black", "Blue", "Cyan",
16          "Dark Gray", "Gray", "Green", "Light Gray", "Magenta",
17          "Orange", "Pink", "Red", "White", "Yellow" };
18       private final Color colors[] = { Color.BLACK, Color.BLUE, Color.CYAN,
19          Color.DARK_GRAY, Color.GRAY, Color.GREEN, Color.LIGHT_GRAY,
20          Color.MAGENTA, Color.ORANGE, Color.PINK, Color.RED, Color.WHITE,
21          Color.YELLOW };
```

Fig. 11.23 | JList that displays a list of colors. (Part 1 of 2.)

```
22
23      // ListFrame constructor add JScrollPane containing JList to JFrame
24      public ListFrame()
25      {
26         super( "List Test" );
27         setLayout( new FlowLayout() ); // set frame layout
28
29         colorJList = new JList( colorNames ); // create with colorNames
30         colorJList.setVisibleRowCount( 5 ); // display five rows at once
31
32         // do not allow multiple selections
33         colorJList.setSelectionMode( ListSelectionModel.SINGLE_SELECTION );
34
35         // add a JScrollPane containing JList to frame
36         add( new JScrollPane( colorJList ) );
37
38         colorJList.addListSelectionListener(
39            new ListSelectionListener() // anonymous inner class
40            {
41               // handle list selection events
42               public void valueChanged( ListSelectionEvent event )
43               {
44                  getContentPane().setBackground(
45                     colors[ colorJList.getSelectedIndex() ] );
46               } // end method valueChanged
47            } // end anonymous inner class
48         ); // end call to addListSelectionListener
49      } // end ListFrame constructor
50   } // end class ListFrame
```

Fig. 11.23 | JList that displays a list of colors. (Part 2 of 2.)

Line 29 (Fig. 11.23) creates JList object colorList. The argument to the JList constructor is the array of Objects (in this case Strings) to display in the list. Line 30 uses JList method **setVisibleRowCount** to determine the number of items that are visible in the list.

Line 33 uses JList method **setSelectionMode** to specify the list's selection mode. Class **ListSelectionModel** (of package javax.swing) declares three constants that specify a JList's selection mode—**SINGLE_SELECTION** (which allows only one item to be selected at a time), **SINGLE_INTERVAL_SELECTION** (for a multiple-selection list that allows selection of several contiguous items) and **MULTIPLE_INTERVAL_SELECTION** (for a multiple-selection list that does not restrict the items that can be selected).

Unlike a JComboBox, a JList *does not* provide a scrollbar if there are more items in the list than the number of visible rows. In this case, a **JScrollPane** object is used to provide the scrolling capability. Line 36 adds a new instance of class JScrollPane to the JFrame. The JScrollPane constructor receives as its argument the JComponent that needs scrolling functionality (in this case, colorList). Notice in the screen captures that a scrollbar created by the JScrollPane appears at the right side of the JList. By default, the scrollbar appears only when the number of items in the JList exceeds the number of visible items.

Lines 38–48 use JList method **addListSelectionListener** to register an object that implements **ListSelectionListener** (package javax.swing.event) as the listener for the

```
1   // Fig. 11.24: ListTest.java
2   // Selecting colors from a JList.
3   import javax.swing.JFrame;
4
5   public class ListTest
6   {
7      public static void main( String args[] )
8      {
9         ListFrame listFrame = new ListFrame(); // create ListFrame
10        listFrame.setDefaultCloseOperation( JFrame.EXIT_ON_CLOSE );
11        listFrame.setSize( 350, 150 ); // set frame size
12        listFrame.setVisible( true ); // display frame
13     } // end main
14  } // end class ListTest
```

Fig. 11.24 | Test class for ListFrame.

JList's selection events. Once again, we use an instance of an anonymous inner class (lines 39–47) as the listener. In this example, when the user makes a selection from colorList, method **valueChanged** (line 42–46) should change the background color of the List-Frame to the selected color. This is accomplished in lines 44–45. Note the use of JFrame method **getContentPane** in line 44. Each JFrame actually consists of three layers—the background, the content pane and the glass pane. The content pane appears in front of the background and is where the GUI components in the JFrame are displayed. The glass pane is used to display tool tips and other items that should appear in front of the GUI components on the screen. The content pane completely hides the background of the JFrame; thus, to change the background color behind the GUI components, you must change the content pane's background color. Method getContentPane returns a reference to the JFrame's content pane (an object of class Container). In line 44, we then use that reference to call method **setBackground**, which sets the content pane's background color to an element in the colors array. The color is selected from the array by using the selected item's index. JList method **getSelectedIndex** returns the selected item's index. As with arrays and JComboBoxes, JList indexing is zero based.

11.12 Multiple-Selection Lists

A multiple-selection list enables the user to select many items from a JList (see the output of Fig. 11.26). A SINGLE_INTERVAL_SELECTION list allows selecting a contiguous range of items. To do so, click the first item, then press and hold the *Shift* key while clicking the last item in the range. A MULTIPLE_INTERVAL_SELECTION list allows continuous range selection as described for a SINGLE_INTERVAL_SELECTION list. Such a list allows miscellaneous items to be selected by pressing and holding the *Ctrl* key (sometimes called the

Control key) while clicking each item to select. To deselect an item, press and hold the *Ctrl* key while clicking the item a second time.

The application of Figs. 11.25–11.26 uses multiple-selection lists to copy items from one JList to another. One list is a MULTIPLE_INTERVAL_SELECTION list and the other is a SINGLE_INTERVAL_SELECTION list. When you execute the application, try using the selection techniques described previously to select items in both lists.

```java
1   // Fig. 11.25: MultipleSelectionFrame.java
2   // Copying items from one List to another.
3   import java.awt.FlowLayout;
4   import java.awt.event.ActionListener;
5   import java.awt.event.ActionEvent;
6   import javax.swing.JFrame;
7   import javax.swing.JList;
8   import javax.swing.JButton;
9   import javax.swing.JScrollPane;
10  import javax.swing.ListSelectionModel;
11
12  public class MultipleSelectionFrame extends JFrame
13  {
14     private JList colorJList; // list to hold color names
15     private JList copyJList; // list to copy color names into
16     private JButton copyJButton; // button to copy selected names
17     private final String colorNames[] = { "Black", "Blue", "Cyan",
18        "Dark Gray", "Gray", "Green", "Light Gray", "Magenta", "Orange",
19        "Pink", "Red", "White", "Yellow" };
20
21     // MultipleSelectionFrame constructor
22     public MultipleSelectionFrame()
23     {
24        super( "Multiple Selection Lists" );
25        setLayout( new FlowLayout() ); // set frame layout
26
27        colorJList = new JList( colorNames ); // holds names of all colors
28        colorJList.setVisibleRowCount( 5 ); // show five rows
29        colorJList.setSelectionMode(
30           ListSelectionModel.MULTIPLE_INTERVAL_SELECTION );
31        add( new JScrollPane( colorJList ) ); // add list with scrollpane
32
33        copyJButton = new JButton( "Copy >>>" ); // create copy button
34        copyJButton.addActionListener(
35
36           new ActionListener() // anonymous inner class
37           {
38              // handle button event
39              public void actionPerformed( ActionEvent event )
40              {
41                 // place selected values in copyJList
42                 copyJList.setListData( colorJList.getSelectedValues() );
43              } // end method actionPerformed
44           } // end anonymous inner class
45        ); // end call to addActionListener
```

Fig. 11.25 | JList that allows multiple selections. (Part 1 of 2.)

```
46
47         add( copyJButton ); // add copy button to JFrame
48
49         copyJList = new JList(); // create list to hold copied color names
50         copyJList.setVisibleRowCount( 5 ); // show 5 rows
51         copyJList.setFixedCellWidth( 100 ); // set width
52         copyJList.setFixedCellHeight( 15 ); // set height
53         copyJList.setSelectionMode(
54             ListSelectionModel.SINGLE_INTERVAL_SELECTION );
55         add( new JScrollPane( copyJList ) ); // add list with scrollpane
56     } // end MultipleSelectionFrame constructor
57 } // end class MultipleSelectionFrame
```

Fig. 11.25 | JList that allows multiple selections. (Part 2 of 2.)

```
1   // Fig. 11.26: MultipleSelectionTest.java
2   // Testing MultipleSelectionFrame.
3   import javax.swing.JFrame;
4
5   public class MultipleSelectionTest
6   {
7      public static void main( String args[] )
8      {
9         MultipleSelectionFrame multipleSelectionFrame =
10            new MultipleSelectionFrame();
11        multipleSelectionFrame.setDefaultCloseOperation(
12            JFrame.EXIT_ON_CLOSE );
13        multipleSelectionFrame.setSize( 350, 140 ); // set frame size
14        multipleSelectionFrame.setVisible( true ); // display frame
15     } // end main
16 } // end class MultipleSelectionTest
```

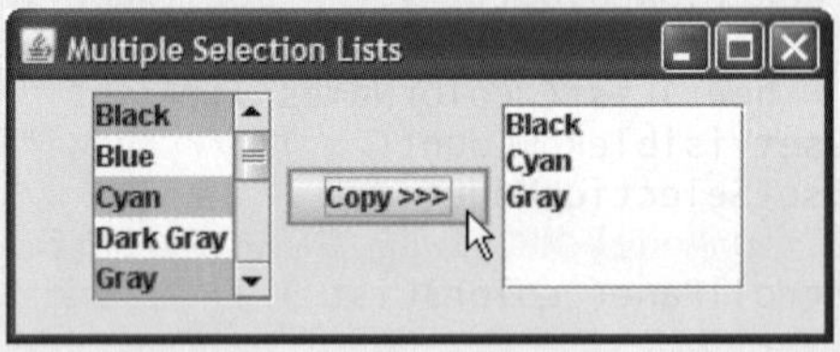

Fig. 11.26 | Test class for MultipleSelectionFrame.

Line 27 of Fig. 11.25 creates JList colorJList and initializes it with the strings in the array colorNames. Line 28 sets the number of visible rows in colorJList to 5. Lines 29–30 specify that colorList is a MULTIPLE_INTERVAL_SELECTION list. Line 31 adds a new JScrollPane containing colorJList to the JFrame. Lines 49–55 perform similar tasks for copyJList, which is declared as a SINGLE_INTERVAL_SELECTION list. Line 51 uses JList method **setFixedCellWidth** to set copyJList's width to 100 pixels. Line 52 uses JList method **setFixedCellHeight** to set the height of each item in the JList to 15 pixels.

There are no events to indicate that a user has made multiple selections in a multiple-selection list. Normally, an event generated by another GUI component (known as an external event) specifies when the multiple selections in a JList should be processed. In this example, the user clicks the JButton called copyJButton to trigger the event that copies the selected items in colorJList to copyJList.

Lines 39–45 declare, create and register an ActionListener for the copyButton. When the user clicks copyJButton, method actionPerformed (lines 39–43) uses JList method **setListData** to set the items displayed in copyJList. Line 42 calls colorJList's method **getSelectedValues**, which returns an array of Objects representing the selected items in colorJList. In this example, the returned array is passed as the argument to copyJList's setListData method.

You might be wondering why copyJList can be used in line 42 even though the application does not create the object to which it refers until line 49. Remember that method actionPerformed (lines 39–43) does not execute until the user presses the copy-JButton, which cannot occur until after the constructor completes execution and the application displays the GUI. At that point in the application's execution, copyJList is already initialized with a new JList object.

11.13 Mouse Event Handling

This section presents the **MouseListener** and **MouseMotionListener** event-listener interfaces for handling mouse events. Mouse events can be trapped for any GUI component that derives from java.awt.Component. The methods of interfaces MouseListener and MouseMotionListener are summarized in Figure 11.27. Package javax.swing.event contains interface **MouseInputListener**, which extends interfaces MouseListener and MouseMotionListener to create a single interface containing all the MouseListener and MouseMotionListener methods. The MouseListener and MouseMotionListener methods are called when the mouse interacts with a Component if appropriate event-listener objects are registered for that Component.

MouseListener and MouseMotionListener interface methods

Methods of interface MouseListener

public void mousePressed(MouseEvent event)

    Called when a mouse button is pressed while the mouse cursor is on a component.

public void mouseClicked(MouseEvent event)

    Called when a mouse button is pressed and released while the mouse cursor remains stationary on a component. This event is always preceded by a call to mousePressed.

public void mouseReleased(MouseEvent event)

    Called when a mouse button is released after being pressed. This event is always preceded by a call to mousePressed and one or more calls to mouseDragged.

public void mouseEntered(MouseEvent event)

    Called when the mouse cursor enters the bounds of a component.

Fig. 11.27 | MouseListener and MouseMotionListener interface methods. (Part 1 of 2.)

> ### MouseListener and MouseMotionListener interface methods
>
> ```
> public void mouseExited( MouseEvent event )
> ```
>
> Called when the mouse cursor leaves the bounds of a component.
>
> *Methods of interface MouseMotionListener*
>
> ```
> public void mouseDragged( MouseEvent event )
> ```
>
> Called when the mouse button is pressed while the mouse cursor is on a component and the mouse is moved while the mouse button remains pressed. This event is always preceded by a call to mousePressed. All drag events are sent to the component on which the user began to drag the mouse.
>
> ```
> public void mouseMoved( MouseEvent event )
> ```
>
> Called when the mouse is moved when the mouse cursor is on a component. All move events are sent to the component over which the mouse is currently positioned.

Fig. 11.27 | MouseListener and MouseMotionListener interface methods. (Part 1 of 2.)

Each of the mouse event-handling methods takes a **MouseEvent** object as its argument. A MouseEvent object contains information about the mouse event that occurred, including the *x*- and *y*-coordinates of the location where the event occurred. These coordinates are measured from the upper-left corner of the GUI component on which the event occurred. The *x*-coordinates start at 0 and increase from left to right. The *y*-coordinates start at 0 and increase from top to bottom. In addition, the methods and constants of class **InputEvent** (MouseEvent's superclass) enable an application to determine which mouse button the user clicked.

Look-and-Feel Observation 11.12

Method calls to mouseDragged and mouseReleased are sent to the MouseMotionListener for the Component on which a mouse drag operation started. Similarly, the mouseReleased method call at the end of a drag operation is sent to the MouseListener for the Component on which the drag operation started.

Java also provides interface **MouseWheelListener** to enable applications to respond to the rotation of a mouse wheel. This interface declares method **mouseWheelMoved**, which receives a **MouseWheelEvent** as its argument. Class MouseWheelEvent (a subclass of Mouse-Event) contains methods that enable the event handler to obtain information about the amount of wheel rotation.

Tracking Mouse Events on a JPanel

The MouseTracker application (Figs. 11.28–11.29) demonstrates the MouseListener and MouseMotionListener interface methods. The application class implements both interfaces so it can listen for its own mouse events. Note that all seven methods from these two interfaces must be declared by the programmer when a class implements both interfaces. Each mouse event in this example displays a string in the JLabel called statusBar at the bottom of the window.

```java
 1   // Fig. 11.28: MouseTrackerFrame.java
 2   // Demonstrating mouse events.
 3   import java.awt.Color;
 4   import java.awt.BorderLayout;
 5   import java.awt.event.MouseListener;
 6   import java.awt.event.MouseMotionListener;
 7   import java.awt.event.MouseEvent;
 8   import javax.swing.JFrame;
 9   import javax.swing.JLabel;
10   import javax.swing.JPanel;
11
12   public class MouseTrackerFrame extends JFrame
13   {
14      private JPanel mousePanel; // panel in which mouse events will occur
15      private JLabel statusBar; // label that displays event information
16
17      // MouseTrackerFrame constructor sets up GUI and
18      // registers mouse event handlers
19      public MouseTrackerFrame()
20      {
21         super( "Demonstrating Mouse Events" );
22
23         mousePanel = new JPanel(); // create panel
24         mousePanel.setBackground( Color.WHITE ); // set background color
25         add( mousePanel, BorderLayout.CENTER ); // add panel to JFrame
26
27         statusBar = new JLabel( "Mouse outside JPanel" );
28         add( statusBar, BorderLayout.SOUTH ); // add label to JFrame
29
30         // create and register listener for mouse and mouse motion events
31         MouseHandler handler = new MouseHandler();
32         mousePanel.addMouseListener( handler );
33         mousePanel.addMouseMotionListener( handler );
34      } // end MouseTrackerFrame constructor
35
36      private class MouseHandler implements MouseListener,
37         MouseMotionListener
38      {
39         // MouseListener event handlers
40         // handle event when mouse released immediately after press
41         public void mouseClicked( MouseEvent event )
42         {
43            statusBar.setText( String.format( "Clicked at [%d, %d]",
44               event.getX(), event.getY() ) );
45         } // end method mouseClicked
46
47         // handle event when mouse pressed
48         public void mousePressed( MouseEvent event )
49         {
50            statusBar.setText( String.format( "Pressed at [%d, %d]",
51               event.getX(), event.getY() ) );
52         } // end method mousePressed
53
```

Fig. 11.28 | Mouse event handling. (Part 1 of 2.)

```
54        // handle event when mouse released after dragging
55        public void mouseReleased( MouseEvent event )
56        {
57           statusBar.setText( String.format( "Released at [%d, %d]",
58              event.getX(), event.getY() ) );
59        } // end method mouseReleased
60
61        // handle event when mouse enters area
62        public void mouseEntered( MouseEvent event )
63        {
64           statusBar.setText( String.format( "Mouse entered at [%d, %d]",
65              event.getX(), event.getY() ) );
66           mousePanel.setBackground( Color.GREEN );
67        } // end method mouseEntered
68
69        // handle event when mouse exits area
70        public void mouseExited( MouseEvent event )
71        {
72           statusBar.setText( "Mouse outside JPanel" );
73           mousePanel.setBackground( Color.WHITE );
74        } // end method mouseExited
75
76        // MouseMotionListener event handlers
77        // handle event when user drags mouse with button pressed
78        public void mouseDragged( MouseEvent event )
79        {
80           statusBar.setText( String.format( "Dragged at [%d, %d]",
81              event.getX(), event.getY() ) );
82        } // end method mouseDragged
83
84        // handle event when user moves mouse
85        public void mouseMoved( MouseEvent event )
86        {
87           statusBar.setText( String.format( "Moved at [%d, %d]",
88              event.getX(), event.getY() ) );
89        } // end method mouseMoved
90     } // end inner class MouseHandler
91  } // end class MouseTrackerFrame
```

Fig. 11.28 | Mouse event handling. (Part 2 of 2.)

```
1   // Fig. 11.29: MouseTrackerFrame.java
2   // Testing MouseTrackerFrame.
3   import javax.swing.JFrame;
4
5   public class MouseTracker
6   {
7      public static void main( String args[] )
8      {
9         MouseTrackerFrame mouseTrackerFrame = new MouseTrackerFrame();
10        mouseTrackerFrame.setDefaultCloseOperation( JFrame.EXIT_ON_CLOSE );
```

Fig. 11.29 | Test class for MouseTrackerFrame. (Part 1 of 2.)

```
11          mouseTrackerFrame.setSize( 300, 100 ); // set frame size
12          mouseTrackerFrame.setVisible( true ); // display frame
13      } // end main
14   } // end class MouseTracker
```

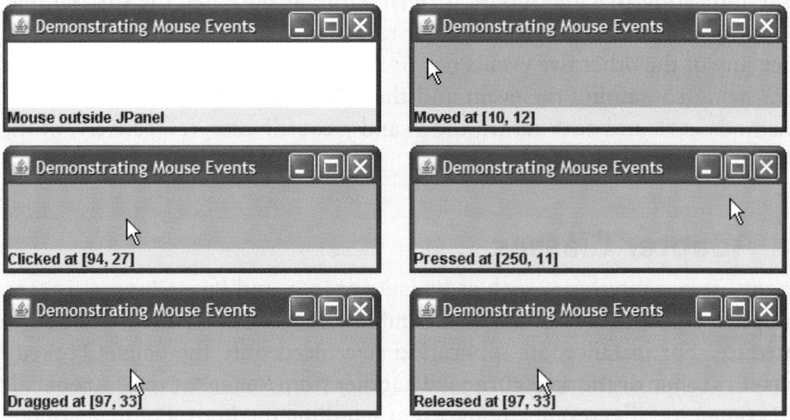

Fig. 11.29 | Test class for MouseTrackerFrame. (Part 2 of 2.)

Line 23 in Fig. 11.28 creates JPanel mousePanel. This JPanel's mouse events will be tracked by the application. Line 24 sets mousePanel's background color to white. When the user moves the mouse into the mousePanel, the application will change mousePanel's background color to green. When the user moves the mouse out of the mousePanel, the application will change the background color back to white. Line 25 attaches mousePanel to the JFrame. As you learned in Section 11.4, you typically must specify the layout of the GUI components in a JFrame. In that section, we introduced the layout manager Flow-Layout. Here we use the default layout of a JFrame's content pane—**BorderLayout**. This layout manager arranges components into five regions: NORTH, SOUTH, EAST, WEST and CENTER. NORTH corresponds to the top of the container. This example uses the CENTER and SOUTH regions. Line 25 uses a two-argument version of method add to place mousePanel in the CENTER region. The BorderLayout automatically sizes the component in the CENTER to use all the space in the JFrame that is not occupied by components in the other regions. Section 11.17.2 discusses BorderLayout in more detail.

Lines 27–28 in the constructor declare JLabel statusBar and attach it to the JFrame's SOUTH region. This JLabel occupies the width of the JFrame. The region's height is determined by the JLabel.

Line 31 creates an instance of inner class MouseHandler (lines 36–90) called handler that responds to mouse events. Lines 32–33 register handler as the listener for mouse-Panel's mouse events. Methods **addMouseListener** and **addMouseMotionListener** are inherited indirectly from class Component and can be used to register MouseListeners and MouseMotionListeners, respectively. A MouseHandler object is both a MouseListener and a MouseMotionListener because the class implements both interfaces. [*Note:* In this example, we chose to implement both interfaces to demonstrate a class that implements more than one interface. However, we also could have implemented interface MouseIn-putListener here.]

When the mouse enters and exits mousePanel's area, methods mouseEntered (lines 62–67) and mouseExited (lines 70–74) are called, respectively. Method mouseEntered displays a message in the statusBar indicating that the mouse entered the JPanel and changes the background color to green. Method mouseExited displays a message in the statusBar indicating that the mouse is outside the JPanel (see the first sample output window) and changes the background color to white.

When any of the other five events occurs, it displays a message in the statusBar that includes a string containing the event and the coordinates at which it occurred. Mouse-Event methods getX and getY return the *x*- and *y*-coordinates, respectively, of the mouse at the time the event occurred.

11.14 Adapter Classes

Many event-listener interfaces, such as MouseListener and MouseMotionListener, contain multiple methods. It is not always desirable to declare every method in an event-listener interface. For instance, an application may need only the mouseClicked handler from MouseListener or the mouseDragged handler from MouseMotionListener. Interface WindowListener specifies seven window event-handling methods. For many of the listener interfaces that have multiple methods, packages java.awt.event and javax.swing.event provide event-listener adapter classes. An adapter class implements an interface and provides a default implementation (with an empty method body) of each method in the interface. Figure 11.30 shows several java.awt.event adapter classes and the interfaces they implement. You can extend an adapter class to inherit the default implementation of every method and subsequently override only the method(s) you need for event handling.

> **Software Engineering Observation 11.7**
>
> *When a class implements an interface, the class has an is-a relationship with that interface. All direct and indirect subclasses of that class inherit this interface. Thus, an object of a class that extends an event-adapter class is an object of the corresponding event-listener type (e.g., an object of a subclass of MouseAdapter is a MouseListener).*

Event-adapter class in java.awt.event	Implements interface
ComponentAdapter	ComponentListener
ContainerAdapter	ContainerListener
FocusAdapter	FocusListener
KeyAdapter	KeyListener
MouseAdapter	MouseListener
MouseMotionAdapter	MouseMotionListener
WindowAdapter	WindowListener

Fig. 11.30 | Event-adapter classes and the interfaces they implement in package java.awt.event.

Extending *MouseAdapter*

The application of Figs. 11.31–11.32 demonstrates how to determine the number of mouse clicks (i.e., the click count) and how to distinguish between the different mouse buttons. The event listener in this application is an object of inner class `MouseClickHandler` (lines 26–46) that extends `MouseAdapter`, so we can declare just the `mouseClicked` method we need in this example.

 Common Programming Error 11.4

If you extend an adapter class and misspell the name of the method you are overriding, your method simply becomes another method in the class. This is a logic error that is difficult to detect, since the program will call the empty version of the method inherited from the adapter class.

```java
1   // Fig. 11.31: MouseDetailsFrame.java
2   // Demonstrating mouse clicks and distinguishing between mouse buttons.
3   import java.awt.BorderLayout;
4   import java.awt.Graphics;
5   import java.awt.event.MouseAdapter;
6   import java.awt.event.MouseEvent;
7   import javax.swing.JFrame;
8   import javax.swing.JLabel;
9
10  public class MouseDetailsFrame extends JFrame
11  {
12     private String details; // String representing
13     private JLabel statusBar; // JLabel that appears at bottom of window
14
15     // constructor sets title bar String and register mouse listener
16     public MouseDetailsFrame()
17     {
18        super( "Mouse clicks and buttons" );
19
20        statusBar = new JLabel( "Click the mouse" );
21        add( statusBar, BorderLayout.SOUTH );
22        addMouseListener( new MouseClickHandler() ); // add handler
23     } // end MouseDetailsFrame constructor
24
25     // inner class to handle mouse events
26     private class MouseClickHandler extends MouseAdapter
27     {
28        // handle mouse-click event and determine which button was pressed
29        public void mouseClicked( MouseEvent event )
30        {
31           int xPos = event.getX(); // get x-position of mouse
32           int yPos = event.getY(); // get y-position of mouse
33
34           details = String.format( "Clicked %d time(s)",
35              event.getClickCount() );
36
37           if ( event.isMetaDown() ) // right mouse button
38              details += " with right mouse button";
```

Fig. 11.31 | Left, center and right mouse-button clicks. (Part 1 of 2.)

```
39            else if ( event.isAltDown() ) // middle mouse button
40                details += " with center mouse button";
41            else // left mouse button
42                details += " with left mouse button";
43
44            statusBar.setText( details ); // display message in statusBar
45         } // end method mouseClicked
46      } // end private inner class MouseClickHandler
47   } // end class MouseDetailsFrame
```

Fig. 11.31 | Left, center and right mouse-button clicks. (Part 2 of 2.)

```
1  // Fig. 11.32: MouseDetails.java
2  // Testing MouseDetailsFrame.
3  import javax.swing.JFrame;
4
5  public class MouseDetails
6  {
7     public static void main( String args[] )
8     {
9        MouseDetailsFrame mouseDetailsFrame = new MouseDetailsFrame();
10       mouseDetailsFrame.setDefaultCloseOperation( JFrame.EXIT_ON_CLOSE );
11       mouseDetailsFrame.setSize( 400, 150 ); // set frame size
12       mouseDetailsFrame.setVisible( true ); // display frame
13    } // end main
14 } // end class MouseDetails
```

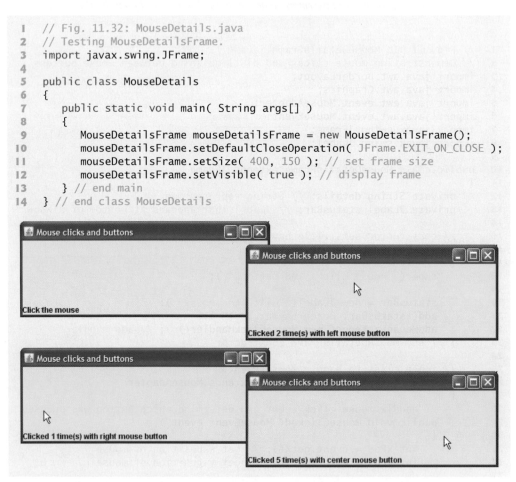

Fig. 11.32 | Test class for MouseDetailsFrame.

A user of a Java application may be on a system with a one-, two- or three-button mouse. Java provides a mechanism to distinguish among mouse buttons. Class Mouse-Event inherits several methods from class InputEvent that can distinguish among mouse buttons on a multi-button mouse or can mimic a multi-button mouse with a combined keystroke and mouse-button click. Figure 11.33 shows the InputEvent methods used to distinguish among mouse-button clicks. Java assumes that every mouse contains a left mouse button. Thus, it is simple to test for a left-mouse-button click. However, users with a one- or two-button mouse must use a combination of keystrokes and mouse-button clicks at the same time to simulate the missing buttons on the mouse. In the case of a one- or two-button mouse, a Java application assumes that the center mouse button is clicked if the user holds down the *Alt* key and clicks the left mouse button on a two-button mouse or the only mouse button on a one-button mouse. In the case of a one-button mouse, a Java application assumes that the right mouse button is clicked if the user holds down the *Meta* key and clicks the mouse button.

Line 22 of Fig. 11.31 registers a MouseListener for the MouseDetailsFrame. The event listener is an object of class MouseClickHandler, which extends MouseAdapter. This enables us to declare only method mouseClicked (lines 29–45). This method first captures the coordinates where the event occurred and stores them in local variables xPos and yPos (lines 31–32). Lines 34–35 create a String called details containing the number of mouse clicks, which is returned by MouseEvent method getClickCount at line 35. Lines 37–42 use methods isMetaDown and isAltDown to determine which mouse button the user clicked and append an appropriate String to details in each case. The resulting String is displayed in the statusBar. Class MouseDetails (Fig. 11.32) contains the main method that executes the application. Try clicking with each of your mouse's buttons repeatedly to see the click count increment.

InputEvent method	Description
isMetaDown()	Returns true when the user clicks the right mouse button on a mouse with two or three buttons. To simulate a right-mouse-button click on a one-button mouse, the user can hold down the *Meta* key on the keyboard and click the mouse button.
isAltDown()	Returns true when the user clicks the middle mouse button on a mouse with three buttons. To simulate a middle-mouse-button click on a one- or two-button mouse, the user can press the *Alt* key on the keyboard and click the only or left mouse button, respectively.

Fig. 11.33 | InputEvent methods that help distinguish among left-, center- and right-mouse-button clicks.

11.15 JPanel Subclass for Drawing with the Mouse

Section 11.13 showed how to track mouse events in a JPanel. In this section, we use a JPanel as a dedicated drawing area in which the user can draw by dragging the mouse. In addition, this section demonstrates an event listener that extends an adapter class.

Method *paintComponent*

Lightweight Swing components that extend class JComponent (such as JPanel) contain method paintComponent, which is called when a lightweight Swing component is displayed. By overriding this method, you can specify how to draw shapes using Java's graphics capabilities. When customizing a JPanel for use as a dedicated drawing area, the subclass should override method paintComponent and call the superclass version of paint-Component as the first statement in the body of the overridden method to ensure that the component displays correctly. The reason for this is that subclasses of JComponent support transparency. To display a component correctly, the program must determine whether the component is transparent. The code that determines this is in superclass JComponent's paintComponent implementation. When a component is transparent, paintComponent will not clear its background when the program displays the component. When a component is opaque, paintComponent clears the component's background before the component is displayed. If the superclass version of paintComponent is not called, an opaque GUI component typically will not display correctly on the user interface. Also, if the superclass version is called after performing the customized drawing statements, the results typically will be erased. The transparency of a Swing lightweight component can be set with method setOpaque (a false argument indicates that the component is transparent).

Look-and-Feel Observation 11.13

Most Swing GUI components can be transparent or opaque. If a Swing GUI component is opaque, its background will be cleared when its paintComponent method is called. Only opaque components can display a customized background color. JPanel objects are opaque by default.

Error-Prevention Tip 11.1

In a JComponent subclass's paintComponent method, the first statement should always be a call to the superclass's paintComponent method to ensure that an object of the subclass displays correctly.

Common Programming Error 11.5

If an overridden paintComponent method does not call the superclass's version, the subclass component may not display properly. If an overridden paintComponent method calls the superclass's version after other drawing is performed, the drawing will be erased.

Defining the Custom Drawing Area

The Painter application of Figs. 11.34–11.35 demonstrates a customized subclass of JPanel that is used to create a dedicated drawing area. The application uses the mouse-Dragged event handler to create a simple drawing application. The user can draw pictures by dragging the mouse on the JPanel. This example does not use method mouseMoved, so our event-listener class (the anonymous inner class at lines 22-34) extends Mouse-MotionAdapter. Since this class already declares both mouseMoved and mouseDragged, we can simply override mouseDragged to provide the event handling this application requires.

Class PaintPanel (Fig. 11.34) extends JPanel to create the dedicated drawing area. Lines 3–7 import the classes used in class PaintPanel. Class **Point** (package java.awt) represents an *x-y* coordinate. We use objects of this class to store the coordinates of each mouse drag event. Class **Graphics** is used to draw.

In this example, we use an array of 10,000 Points (line 14) to store the location at which each mouse-drag event occurs. As you will see, method paintComponent uses these Points to draw. Instance variable pointCount (line 11) maintains the total number of Points captured from mouse drag events so far.

```
 1   // Fig. 11.34: PaintPanel.java
 2   // Using class MouseMotionAdapter.
 3   import java.awt.Point;
 4   import java.awt.Graphics;
 5   import java.awt.event.MouseEvent;
 6   import java.awt.event.MouseMotionAdapter;
 7   import javax.swing.JPanel;
 8
 9   public class PaintPanel extends JPanel
10   {
11      private int pointCount = 0; // count number of points
12
13      // array of 10000 java.awt.Point references
14      private Point points[] = new Point[ 10000 ];
15
16      // set up GUI and register mouse event handler
17      public PaintPanel()
18      {
19         // handle frame mouse motion event
20         addMouseMotionListener(
21
22            new MouseMotionAdapter() // anonymous inner class
23               {
24                  // store drag coordinates and repaint
25                  public void mouseDragged( MouseEvent event )
26                  {
27                     if ( pointCount < points.length )
28                     {
29                        points[ pointCount ] = event.getPoint(); // find point
30                        pointCount++; // increment number of points in array
31                        repaint(); // repaint JFrame
32                     } // end if
33                  } // end method mouseDragged
34               } // end anonymous inner class
35         ); // end call to addMouseMotionListener
36      } // end PaintPanel constructor
37
38      // draw oval in a 4-by-4 bounding box at specified location on window
39      public void paintComponent( Graphics g )
40      {
41         super.paintComponent( g ); // clears drawing area
42
43         // draw all points in array
44         for ( int i = 0; i < pointCount; i++ )
45            g.fillOval( points[ i ].x, points[ i ].y, 4, 4 );
46      } // end method paintComponent
47   } // end class PaintPanel
```

Fig. 11.34 | Adapter classes used to implement event handlers.

Lines 20–35 register a MouseMotionListener to listen for the PaintPanel's mouse-motion events. Lines 22–34 create an object of an anonymous inner class that extends the adapter class MouseMotionAdapter. Recall that MouseMotionAdapter implements Mouse-MotionListener, so the anonymous inner class object is a MouseMotionListener. The

```
 1   // Fig. 11.35: Painter.java
 2   // Testing PaintPanel.
 3   import java.awt.BorderLayout;
 4   import javax.swing.JFrame;
 5   import javax.swing.JLabel;
 6
 7   public class Painter
 8   {
 9      public static void main( String args[] )
10      {
11         // create JFrame
12         JFrame application = new JFrame( "A simple paint program" );
13
14         PaintPanel paintPanel = new PaintPanel(); // create paint panel
15         application.add( paintPanel, BorderLayout.CENTER ); // in center
16
17         // create a label and place it in SOUTH of BorderLayout
18         application.add( new JLabel( "Drag the mouse to draw" ),
19            BorderLayout.SOUTH );
20
21         application.setDefaultCloseOperation( JFrame.EXIT_ON_CLOSE );
22         application.setSize( 400, 200 ); // set frame size
23         application.setVisible( true ); // display frame
24      } // end main
25   } // end class Painter
```

Fig. 11.35 | Test class for `PaintFrame`.

anonymous inner class inherits a default implementation of methods mouseMoved and mouseDragged, so it already satisfies the requirement that all methods of the interface must be implemented. However, the default methods do nothing when they are called. So, we override method mouseDragged at lines 25–33 to capture the coordinates of a mouse-dragged event and store them as a Point object. Line 27 ensures that we store the event's coordinates only if there are still empty elements in the array. If so, line 29 invokes the MouseEvent's **getPoint** method to obtain the Point where the event occurred and stores it in the array at index pointCount. Line 30 increments the pointCount, and line 31 calls method **repaint** (inherited indirectly from class Component) to indicate that the Paint-Panel should be refreshed on the screen as soon as possible with a call to the PaintPanel's paintComponent method.

Method paintComponent (lines 39–46), which receives a Graphics parameter, is called automatically any time the PaintPanel needs to be displayed on the screen (such as when the GUI is first displayed) or refreshed on the screen (such as when method repaint is called or when the GUI component was hidden by another window on the screen and subsequently becomes visible again).

> **Look-and-Feel Observation 11.14**
>
> *Calling* repaint *for a Swing GUI component indicates that the component should be refreshed on the screen as soon as possible. The background of the GUI component is cleared only if the component is opaque.* JComponent *method* setOpaque *can be passed a* boolean *argument indicating whether the component is opaque (*true*) or transparent (*false*).*

Line 41 invokes the superclass version of paintComponent to clear the PaintPanel's background (JPanels are opaque by default). Lines 44–45 draw an oval at the location specified by each Point in the array (up to the pointCount). Graphics method fillOval draws a solid oval. The method's four parameters represent a rectangular area (called the bounding box) in which the oval is displayed. The first two parameters are the upper-left *x*-coordinate and the upper-left *y*-coordinate of the rectangular area. The last two coordinates represent the rectangular area's width and height. Method fillOval draws the oval so it touches the middle of each side of the rectangular area. In line 45, the first two arguments are specified by using class Point's two public instance variables—x and y. The loop terminates either when a null reference is encountered in the array or when the end of the array is reached. You will learn more Graphics features in Chapter 12.

> **Look-and-Feel Observation 11.15**
>
> *Drawing on any GUI component is performed with coordinates that are measured from the upper-left corner (0, 0) of that GUI component, not the upper-left corner of the screen.*

Using the Custom JPanel in an Application
Class Painter (Fig. 11.35) contains the main method that executes this application. Line 14 creates a PaintPanel object on which the user can drag the mouse to draw. Line 15 attaches the PaintPanel to the JFrame.

11.16 Key-Event Handling

This section presents the **KeyListener** interface for handling key events. Key events are generated when keys on the keyboard are pressed and released. A class that implements KeyListener must provide declarations for methods **keyPressed**, **keyReleased** and **keyTyped**, each of which receives a **KeyEvent** as its argument. Class KeyEvent is a subclass of InputEvent. Method keyPressed is called in response to pressing any key. Method keyTyped is called in response to pressing any key that is not an **action key**. (The action keys are any arrow key, *Home, End, Page Up, Page Down*, any function key, *Num Lock, Print Screen, Scroll Lock, Caps Lock* and *Pause*.) Method keyReleased is called when the key is released after any keyPressed or keyTyped event.

The application of Figs. 11.36–11.37 demonstrates the KeyListener methods. Class KeyDemo implements the KeyListener interface, so all three methods are declared in the application.

The constructor (Fig. 11.36, lines 17–28) registers the application to handle its own key events by using method **addKeyListener** at line 27. Method addKeyListener is declared in class Component, so every subclass of Component can notify KeyListener objects of key events for that Component.

```java
 1   // Fig. 11.36: KeyDemoFrame.java
 2   // Demonstrating keystroke events.
 3   import java.awt.Color;
 4   import java.awt.event.KeyListener;
 5   import java.awt.event.KeyEvent;
 6   import javax.swing.JFrame;
 7   import javax.swing.JTextArea;
 8
 9   public class KeyDemoFrame extends JFrame implements KeyListener
10   {
11      private String line1 = ""; // first line of textarea
12      private String line2 = ""; // second line of textarea
13      private String line3 = ""; // third line of textarea
14      private JTextArea textArea; // textarea to display output
15
16      // KeyDemoFrame constructor
17      public KeyDemoFrame()
18      {
19         super( "Demonstrating Keystroke Events" );
20
21         textArea = new JTextArea( 10, 15 ); // set up JTextArea
22         textArea.setText( "Press any key on the keyboard..." );
23         textArea.setEnabled( false ); // disable textarea
24         textArea.setDisabledTextColor( Color.BLACK ); // set text color
25         add( textArea ); // add textarea to JFrame
26
27         addKeyListener( this ); // allow frame to process key events
28      } // end KeyDemoFrame constructor
29
30      // handle press of any key
31      public void keyPressed( KeyEvent event )
32      {
33         line1 = String.format( "Key pressed: %s",
34            event.getKeyText( event.getKeyCode() ) ); // output pressed key
35         setLines2and3( event ); // set output lines two and three
36      } // end method keyPressed
37
38      // handle release of any key
39      public void keyReleased( KeyEvent event )
40      {
41         line1 = String.format( "Key released: %s",
42            event.getKeyText( event.getKeyCode() ) ); // output released key
43         setLines2and3( event ); // set output lines two and three
44      } // end method keyReleased
45
46      // handle press of an action key
47      public void keyTyped( KeyEvent event )
48      {
49         line1 = String.format( "Key typed: %s", event.getKeyChar() );
50         setLines2and3( event ); // set output lines two and three
51      } // end method keyTyped
52
```

Fig. 11.36 | Key event handling. (Part 1 of 2.)

```
53      // set second and third lines of output
54      private void setLines2and3( KeyEvent event )
55      {
56         line2 = String.format( "This key is %san action key",
57            ( event.isActionKey() ? "" : "not " ) );
58
59         String temp = event.getKeyModifiersText( event.getModifiers() );
60
61         line3 = String.format( "Modifier keys pressed: %s",
62            ( temp.equals( "" ) ? "none" : temp ) ); // output modifiers
63
64         textArea.setText( String.format( "%s\n%s\n%s\n",
65            line1, line2, line3 ) ); // output three lines of text
66      } // end method setLines2and3
67   } // end class KeyDemoFrame
```

Fig. 11.36 | Key event handling. (Part 2 of 2.)

```
1   // Fig. 11.37: KeyDemo.java
2   // Testing KeyDemoFrame.
3   import javax.swing.JFrame;
4
5   public class KeyDemo
6   {
7      public static void main( String args[] )
8      {
9         KeyDemoFrame keyDemoFrame = new KeyDemoFrame();
10        keyDemoFrame.setDefaultCloseOperation( JFrame.EXIT_ON_CLOSE );
11        keyDemoFrame.setSize( 350, 100 ); // set frame size
12        keyDemoFrame.setVisible( true ); // display frame
13     } // end main
14  } // end class KeyDemo
```

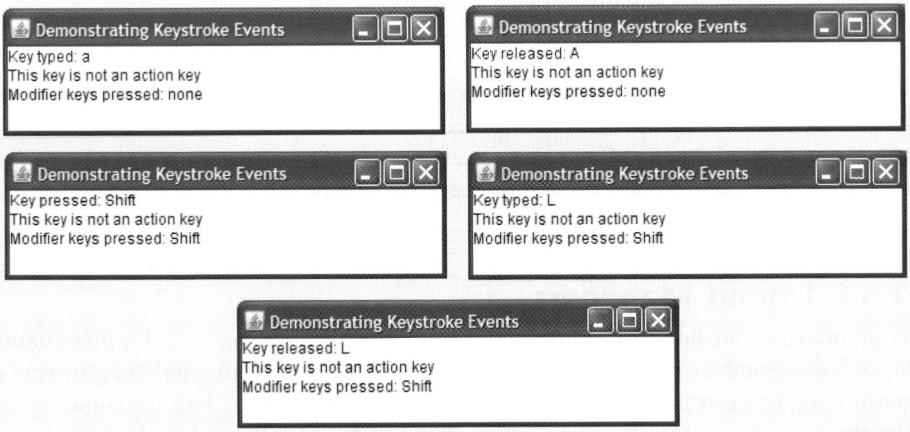

Fig. 11.37 | Test class for KeyDemoFrame. (Part 1 of 2.)

Fig. 11.37 | Test class for `KeyDemoFrame`. (Part 2 of 2.)

At line 25, the constructor adds `JTextArea textArea` (where the application's output is displayed) to the `JFrame`. Notice in the screen captures that `textArea` occupies the entire window. This is due to the `JFrame`'s default `BorderLayout` (discussed in Section 11.17.2 and demonstrated in Fig. 11.41). When a single `Component` is added to a `BorderLayout`, the `Component` occupies the entire `Container`. Note that line 24 uses method `setDisabledTextColor` to change the color of the text in the textarea to black.

Methods `keyPressed` (lines 31–36) and `keyReleased` (lines 39–44) use `KeyEvent` method **getKeyCode** to get the virtual key code of the key that was pressed. Class `KeyEvent` maintains a set of constants—the virtual key-code constants—that represents every key on the keyboard. These constants can be compared with the return value of `getKeyCode` to test for individual keys on the keyboard. The value returned by `getKeyCode` is passed to `KeyEvent` method **getKeyText**, which returns a string containing the name of the key that was pressed. For a complete list of virtual key constants, see the on-line documentation for class `KeyEvent` (package `java.awt.event`). Method `keyTyped` (lines 47–51) uses `KeyEvent` method **getKeyChar** to get the Unicode value of the character typed.

All three event-handling methods finish by calling method `setLines2and3` (lines 54–66) and passing it the `KeyEvent` object. This method uses `KeyEvent` method **isActionKey** (line 57) to determine whether the key in the event was an action key. Also, `InputEvent` method **getModifiers** is called (line 59) to determine whether any modifier keys (such as *Shift*, *Alt* and *Ctrl*) were pressed when the key event occurred. The result of this method is passed to `KeyEvent` method **getKeyModifiersText**, which produces a string containing the names of the pressed modifier keys.

[*Note:* If you need to test for a specific key on the keyboard, class `KeyEvent` provides a key constant for every key on the keyboard. These constants can be used from the key event handlers to determine whether a particular key was pressed. Also, to determine whether the *Alt*, *Ctrl*, *Meta* and *Shift* keys are pressed individually, `InputEvent` methods `isAltDown`, `isControlDown`, `isMetaDown` and `isShiftDown` each return a `boolean` indicating if the particular key was pressed during the key event.]

11.17 Layout Managers

Layout managers are provided to arrange GUI components in a container for presentation purposes. Programmers can use the layout managers for basic layout capabilities instead of determining the exact position and size of every GUI component. This functionality enables the programmer to concentrate on the basic look-and-feel and lets the layout managers process most of the layout details. All layout managers implement the interface `LayoutManager` (in package `java.awt`). Class `Container`'s `setLayout` method takes an object that implements the `LayoutManager` interface as an argument. There are basically three ways for you to arrange components in a GUI:

1. Absolute positioning: This provides the greatest level of control over a GUI's appearance. By setting a `Container`'s layout to `null`, you can specify the absolute position of each GUI component with respect to the upper-left corner of the `Container`. If you do this, you also must specify each GUI component's size. Programming a GUI with absolute positioning can be tedious, unless you have an integrated development environment (IDE) that can generate the code for you.

2. Layout managers: Using layout managers to position elements can be simpler and faster than creating a GUI with absolute positioning, but you lose some control over the size and the precise positioning of GUI components.

3. Visual programming in an IDE: IDEs provide tools that make it easy to create GUIs. Each IDE typically provides a GUI design tool that allows you to drag and drop GUI components from a tool box onto a design area. You can then position, size and align GUI components as you like. The IDE generates the Java code that creates the GUI. In addition, you can typically add event-handling code for a particular component by double-clicking the component. Some design tools also allow you to use the layout managers described in this chapter and in Chapter 22.

Look-and-Feel Observation 11.16

Most Java programming environments provide GUI design tools that help a programmer graphically design a GUI; the design tools then write the Java code to create the GUI. Such tools often provide greater control over the size, position and alignment of GUI components than do the built-in layout managers.

Look-and-Feel Observation 11.17

It is possible to set a `Container`'s layout to `null`, which indicates that no layout manager should be used. In a `Container` without a layout manager, the programmer must position and size the components in the given container and take care that, on resize events, all components are repositioned as necessary. A component's resize events can be processed by a `ComponentListener`.

Figure 11.38 summarizes the layout managers presented in this chapter. Other layout managers are discussed in Chapter 22.

Layout manager	Description
`FlowLayout`	Default for `javax.swing.JPanel`. Places components sequentially (left to right) in the order they were added. It is also possible to specify the order of the components by using the `Container` method add, which takes a `Component` and an integer index position as arguments.
`BorderLayout`	Default for `JFrames` (and other windows). Arranges the components into five areas: NORTH, SOUTH, EAST, WEST and CENTER.
`GridLayout`	Arranges the components into rows and columns.

Fig. 11.38 | Layout managers.

11.17.1 FlowLayout

FlowLayout is the simplest layout manager. GUI components are placed on a container from left to right in the order in which they are added to the container. When the edge of the container is reached, components continue to display on the next line. Class FlowLayout allows GUI components to be left aligned, centered (the default) and right aligned.

The application of Figs. 11.39–11.40 creates three JButton objects and adds them to the application, using a FlowLayout layout manager. The components are center aligned by default. When the user clicks **Left**, the alignment for the layout manager is changed to a left-aligned FlowLayout. When the user clicks **Right**, the alignment for the layout manager is changed to a right-aligned FlowLayout. When the user clicks **Center**, the alignment for the layout manager is changed to a center-aligned FlowLayout. Each button has its own event handler that is declared with an inner class that implements ActionListener. The sample output windows show each of the FlowLayout alignments. Also, the last sample output window shows the centered alignment after the window has been resized to a smaller width. Notice that the button **Right** flows onto a new line.

```java
 1   // Fig. 11.39: FlowLayoutFrame.java
 2   // Demonstrating FlowLayout alignments.
 3   import java.awt.FlowLayout;
 4   import java.awt.Container;
 5   import java.awt.event.ActionListener;
 6   import java.awt.event.ActionEvent;
 7   import javax.swing.JFrame;
 8   import javax.swing.JButton;
 9
10   public class FlowLayoutFrame extends JFrame
11   {
12      private JButton leftJButton; // button to set alignment left
13      private JButton centerJButton; // button to set alignment center
14      private JButton rightJButton; // button to set alignment right
15      private FlowLayout layout; // layout object
16      private Container container; // container to set layout
17
18      // set up GUI and register button listeners
19      public FlowLayoutFrame()
20      {
21         super( "FlowLayout Demo" );
22
23         layout = new FlowLayout(); // create FlowLayout
24         container = getContentPane(); // get container to layout
25         setLayout( layout ); // set frame layout
26
27         // set up leftJButton and register listener
28         leftJButton = new JButton( "Left" ); // create Left button
29         add( leftJButton ); // add Left button to frame
30         leftJButton.addActionListener(
31
32            new ActionListener() // anonymous inner class
33            {
```

Fig. 11.39 | FlowLayout allows components to flow over multiple lines. (Part 1 of 2.)

```
34              // process leftJButton event
35              public void actionPerformed( ActionEvent event )
36              {
37                 layout.setAlignment( FlowLayout.LEFT );
38
39                 // realign attached components
40                 layout.layoutContainer( container );
41              } // end method actionPerformed
42           } // end anonymous inner class
43        ); // end call to addActionListener
44
45        // set up centerJButton and register listener
46        centerJButton = new JButton( "Center" ); // create Center button
47        add( centerJButton ); // add Center button to frame
48        centerJButton.addActionListener(
49
50           new ActionListener() // anonymous inner class
51           {
52              // process centerJButton event
53              public void actionPerformed( ActionEvent event )
54              {
55                 layout.setAlignment( FlowLayout.CENTER );
56
57                 // realign attached components
58                 layout.layoutContainer( container );
59              } // end method actionPerformed
60           } // end anonymous inner class
61        ); // end call to addActionListener
62
63        // set up rightJButton and register listener
64        rightJButton = new JButton( "Right" ); // create Right button
65        add( rightJButton ); // add Right button to frame
66        rightJButton.addActionListener(
67
68           new ActionListener() // anonymous inner class
69           {
70              // process rightJButton event
71              public void actionPerformed( ActionEvent event )
72              {
73                 layout.setAlignment( FlowLayout.RIGHT );
74
75                 // realign attached components
76                 layout.layoutContainer( container );
77              } // end method actionPerformed
78           } // end anonymous inner class
79        ); // end call to addActionListener
80     } // end FlowLayoutFrame constructor
81  } // end class FlowLayoutFrame
```

Fig. 11.39 | FlowLayout allows components to flow over multiple lines. (Part 2 of 2.)

As seen previously, a container's layout is set with method setLayout of class Container. Line 25 sets the layout manager to the FlowLayout declared at line 23. Normally, the layout is set before any GUI components are added to a container.

```
1   // Fig. 11.40: FlowLayoutDemo.java
2   // Testing FlowLayoutFrame.
3   import javax.swing.JFrame;
4
5   public class FlowLayoutDemo
6   {
7      public static void main( String args[] )
8      {
9         FlowLayoutFrame flowLayoutFrame = new FlowLayoutFrame();
10        flowLayoutFrame.setDefaultCloseOperation( JFrame.EXIT_ON_CLOSE );
11        flowLayoutFrame.setSize( 300, 75 ); // set frame size
12        flowLayoutFrame.setVisible( true ); // display frame
13     } // end main
14  } // end class FlowLayoutDemo
```

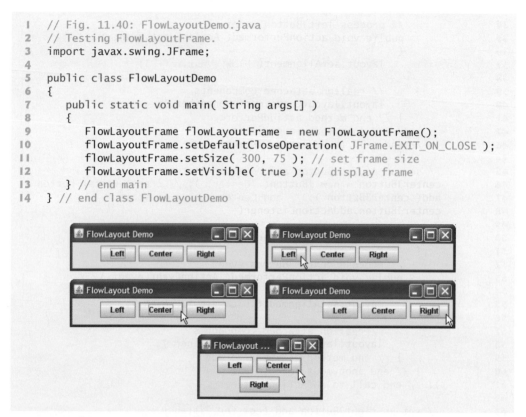

Fig. 11.40 | Test class for FlowLayoutFrame.

Look-and-Feel Observation 11.18

Each container can have only one layout manager. Separate containers in the same application can use different layout managers.

Note in this example that each button's event handler is specified with a separate anonymous inner-class object (lines 30–43, 48–61 and 66–71, respectively). Each button's actionPerformed event handler executes two statements. For example, line 37 in method actionPerformed for button left uses FlowLayout method **setAlignment** to change the alignment for the FlowLayout to a left-aligned (FlowLayout.LEFT) FlowLayout. Line 40 uses LayoutManager interface method **layoutContainer** (which is inherited by all layout managers) to specify that the JFrame should be rearranged based on the adjusted layout. According to which button was clicked, the actionPerformed method for each button sets the FlowLayout's alignment to FlowLayout.LEFT (line 37), FlowLayout.CENTER (line 55) or FlowLayout.RIGHT (line 73).

11.17.2 BorderLayout

The BorderLayout layout manager (the default layout manager for a JFrame) arranges components into five regions: NORTH, SOUTH, EAST, WEST and CENTER. NORTH corresponds to the top of the container. Class BorderLayout extends Object and implements interface

LayoutManager2 (a subinterface of LayoutManager that adds several methods for enhanced layout processing).

A BorderLayout limits a Container to containing at most five components—one in each region. The component placed in each region can be a container to which other components are attached. The components placed in the NORTH and SOUTH regions extend horizontally to the sides of the container and are as tall as the components placed in those regions. The EAST and WEST regions expand vertically between the NORTH and SOUTH regions and are as wide as the components placed in those regions. The component placed in the CENTER region expands to fill all remaining space in the layout (which is the reason the JTextArea in Fig. 11.36 occupies the entire window). If all five regions are occupied, the entire container's space is covered by GUI components. If the NORTH or SOUTH region is not occupied, the GUI components in the EAST, CENTER and WEST regions expand vertically to fill the remaining space. If the EAST or WEST region is not occupied, the GUI component in the CENTER region expands horizontally to fill the remaining space. If the CENTER region is not occupied, the area is left empty—the other GUI components do not expand to fill the remaining space. The application of Figs. 11.41–11.42 demonstrates the BorderLayout layout manager by using five JButtons.

```java
1   // Fig. 11.41: BorderLayoutFrame.java
2   // Demonstrating BorderLayout.
3   import java.awt.BorderLayout;
4   import java.awt.event.ActionListener;
5   import java.awt.event.ActionEvent;
6   import javax.swing.JFrame;
7   import javax.swing.JButton;
8
9   public class BorderLayoutFrame extends JFrame implements ActionListener
10  {
11     private JButton buttons[]; // array of buttons to hide portions
12     private final String names[] = { "Hide North", "Hide South",
13        "Hide East", "Hide West", "Hide Center" };
14     private BorderLayout layout; // borderlayout object
15
16     // set up GUI and event handling
17     public BorderLayoutFrame()
18     {
19        super( "BorderLayout Demo" );
20
21        layout = new BorderLayout( 5, 5 ); // 5 pixel gaps
22        setLayout( layout ); // set frame layout
23        buttons = new JButton[ names.length ]; // set size of array
24
25        // create JButtons and register listeners for them
26        for ( int count = 0; count < names.length; count++ )
27        {
28           buttons[ count ] = new JButton( names[ count ] );
29           buttons[ count ].addActionListener( this );
30        } // end for
31
```

Fig. 11.41 | BorderLayout containing five buttons. (Part 1 of 2.)

```
32          add( buttons[ 0 ], BorderLayout.NORTH );  // add button to north
33          add( buttons[ 1 ], BorderLayout.SOUTH );  // add button to south
34          add( buttons[ 2 ], BorderLayout.EAST );   // add button to east
35          add( buttons[ 3 ], BorderLayout.WEST );   // add button to west
36          add( buttons[ 4 ], BorderLayout.CENTER ); // add button to center
37       } // end BorderLayoutFrame constructor
38
39       // handle button events
40       public void actionPerformed( ActionEvent event )
41       {
42          // check event source and lay out content pane correspondingly
43          for ( JButton button : buttons )
44          {
45             if ( event.getSource() == button )
46                button.setVisible( false ); // hide button clicked
47             else
48                button.setVisible( true );  // show other buttons
49          } // end for
50
51          layout.layoutContainer( getContentPane() ); // lay out content pane
52       } // end method actionPerformed
53    } // end class BorderLayoutFrame
```

Fig. 11.41 | BorderLayout containing five buttons. (Part 2 of 2.)

```
1    // Fig. 11.42: BorderLayoutDemo.java
2    // Testing BorderLayoutFrame.
3    import javax.swing.JFrame;
4
5    public class BorderLayoutDemo
6    {
7       public static void main( String args[] )
8       {
9          BorderLayoutFrame borderLayoutFrame = new BorderLayoutFrame();
10         borderLayoutFrame.setDefaultCloseOperation( JFrame.EXIT_ON_CLOSE );
11         borderLayoutFrame.setSize( 300, 200 ); // set frame size
12         borderLayoutFrame.setVisible( true ); // display frame
13      } // end main
14   } // end class BorderLayoutDemo
```

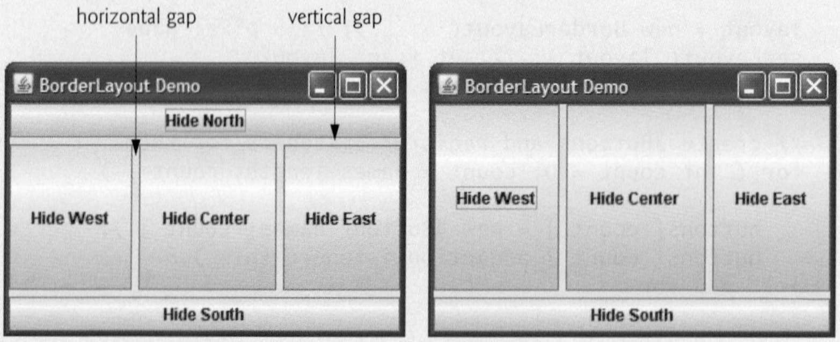

Fig. 11.42 | Test class for BorderLayoutFrame. (Part 1 of 2.)

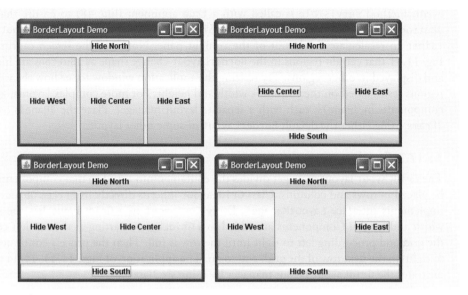

Fig. 11.42 | Test class for BorderLayoutFrame. (Part 2 of 2.)

Line 21 of Fig. 11.41 creates a BorderLayout. The constructor arguments specify the number of pixels between components that are arranged horizontally (horizontal gap space) and between components that are arranged vertically (vertical gap space), respectively. The default is one pixel of gap space horizontally and vertically. Line 22 uses method setLayout to set the content pane's layout to layout.

We add Components to a BorderLayout with another version of Container method add that takes two arguments—the Component to add and the region in which the Component should appear. For example, line 32 specifies that buttons[0] should appear in the NORTH region. The components can be added in any order, but only one component should be added to each region.

Look-and-Feel Observation 11.19

If no region is specified when adding a Component to a BorderLayout, the layout manager assumes that the Component should be added to region BorderLayout.CENTER.

Common Programming Error 11.6

When more than one component is added to a region in a BorderLayout, only the last component added to that region will be displayed. There is no error that indicates this problem.

Note that class BorderLayoutFrame implements ActionListener directly in this example, so the BorderLayoutFrame will handle the events of the JButtons. For this reason, line 29 passes the this reference to the addActionListener method of each JButton. When the user clicks a particular JButton in the layout, method action-Performed (lines 40–52) executes. The enhanced for statement at lines 43–49 uses an if...else to hide the particular JButton that generated the event. Method **setVisible** (inherited into JButton from class Component) is called with a false argument (line 46) to hide the JButton. If the current JButton in the array is not the one that generated the event, method setVisible is called with a true argument (line 48) to ensure that the JButton is displayed on the screen. Line 51 uses LayoutManager method layoutContainer to recalculate the layout of the content pane. Notice in the screen captures of Fig. 11.41 that certain regions in the BorderLayout change shape as JButtons are hidden and displayed in other regions. Try resizing the application window to see how the various regions resize based on the window's width and height. For more complex layouts, group components in JPanels, each with a separate layout manager. Place the JPanels on the JFrame using either the default BorderLayout or some other layout.

11.17.3 GridLayout

The **GridLayout** layout manager divides the container into a grid so that components can be placed in rows and columns. Class GridLayout inherits directly from class Object and implements interface LayoutManager. Every Component in a GridLayout has the same width and height. Components are added to a GridLayout starting at the top-left cell of the grid and proceeding left to right until the row is full. Then the process continues left to right on the next row of the grid, and so on. The application of Figs. 11.43–11.44 demonstrates the GridLayout layout manager by using six JButtons.

```
1   // Fig. 11.43: GridLayoutFrame.java
2   // Demonstrating GridLayout.
3   import java.awt.GridLayout;
4   import java.awt.Container;
5   import java.awt.event.ActionListener;
6   import java.awt.event.ActionEvent;
7   import javax.swing.JFrame;
8   import javax.swing.JButton;
9
10  public class GridLayoutFrame extends JFrame implements ActionListener
11  {
12     private JButton buttons[]; // array of buttons
13     private final String names[] =
14        { "one", "two", "three", "four", "five", "six" };
15     private boolean toggle = true; // toggle between two layouts
16     private Container container; // frame container
17     private GridLayout gridLayout1; // first gridlayout
18     private GridLayout gridLayout2; // second gridlayout
19
20     // no-argument constructor
21     public GridLayoutFrame()
22     {
23        super( "GridLayout Demo" );
24        gridLayout1 = new GridLayout( 2, 3, 5, 5 ); // 2 by 3; gaps of 5
25        gridLayout2 = new GridLayout( 3, 2 ); // 3 by 2; no gaps
26        container = getContentPane(); // get content pane
27        setLayout( gridLayout1 ); // set JFrame layout
28        buttons = new JButton[ names.length ]; // create array of JButtons
29
30        for ( int count = 0; count < names.length; count++ )
31        {
```

Fig. 11.43 | GridLayout containing six buttons. (Part 1 of 2.)

```
32          buttons[ count ] = new JButton( names[ count ] );
33          buttons[ count ].addActionListener( this ); // register listener
34          add( buttons[ count ] ); // add button to JFrame
35       } // end for
36    } // end GridLayoutFrame constructor
37
38    // handle button events by toggling between layouts
39    public void actionPerformed( ActionEvent event )
40    {
41       if ( toggle )
42          container.setLayout( gridLayout2 ); // set layout to second
43       else
44          container.setLayout( gridLayout1 ); // set layout to first
45
46       toggle = !toggle; // set toggle to opposite value
47       container.validate(); // re-lay out container
48    } // end method actionPerformed
49 } // end class GridLayoutFrame
```

Fig. 11.43 | GridLayout containing six buttons. (Part 2 of 2.)

```
1  // Fig. 11.44: GridLayoutDemo.java
2  // Testing GridLayoutFrame.
3  import javax.swing.JFrame;
4
5  public class GridLayoutDemo
6  {
7     public static void main( String args[] )
8     {
9        GridLayoutFrame gridLayoutFrame = new GridLayoutFrame();
10       gridLayoutFrame.setDefaultCloseOperation( JFrame.EXIT_ON_CLOSE );
11       gridLayoutFrame.setSize( 300, 200 ); // set frame size
12       gridLayoutFrame.setVisible( true ); // display frame
13    } // end main
14 } // end class GridLayoutDemo
```

Fig. 11.44 | Test class for GridLayoutFrame.

Lines 24–25 create two GridLayout objects. The GridLayout constructor used at line 24 specifies a GridLayout with 2 rows, 3 columns, 5 pixels of horizontal-gap space between Components in the grid and 5 pixels of vertical-gap space between Components in the grid. The GridLayout constructor used at line 25 specifies a GridLayout with 3 rows and 2 columns that uses the default gap space (1 pixel).

The JButton objects in this example initially are arranged using gridLayout1 (set for the content pane at line 27 with method setLayout). The first component is added to the first column of the first row. The next component is added to the second column of the first row, and so on. When a JButton is pressed, method actionPerformed (lines 39–48) is called. Every call to actionPerformed toggles the layout between gridLayout2 and gridLayout1, using boolean variable toggle to determine the next layout to set.

Line 47 shows another way to reformat a container for which the layout has changed. Container method validate recomputes the container's layout based on the current layout manager for the Container and the current set of displayed GUI components.

11.18 Using Panels to Manage More Complex Layouts

Complex GUIs (like Fig. 11.1) require that each component be placed in an exact location. They often consist of multiple panels, with each panel's components arranged in a specific layout. Class JPanel extends JComponent and JComponent extends class Container, so every JPanel is a Container. Thus, every JPanel may have components, including other panels, attached to it with Container method add. The application of Figs. 11.45–11.46 demonstrates how a JPanel can be used to create a more complex layout in which several JButtons are placed in the SOUTH region of a BorderLayout.

After JPanel buttonPanel is declared in line 11 and created at line 19, line 20 sets buttonPanel's layout to a GridLayout of one row and five columns (there are five JButtons in array buttons). Lines 23–27 add the five JButtons in array buttons to the JPanel in the loop. Line 26 adds the buttons directly to the JPanel—class JPanel does not have a content pane, unlike a JFrame. Line 29 uses the default BorderLayout to add buttonPanel to the SOUTH region. Note that the SOUTH region is as tall as the buttons on buttonPanel. A JPanel is sized to the components it contains. As more components are added, the JPanel grows (according to the restrictions of its layout manager) to accommodate the components. Resize the window to see how the layout manager affects the size of the JButtons.

```
1   // Fig. 11.45: PanelFrame.java
2   // Using a JPanel to help lay out components.
3   import java.awt.GridLayout;
4   import java.awt.BorderLayout;
5   import javax.swing.JFrame;
6   import javax.swing.JPanel;
7   import javax.swing.JButton;
8
9   public class PanelFrame extends JFrame
10  {
11     private JPanel buttonJPanel; // panel to hold buttons
12     private JButton buttons[]; // array of buttons
13
14     // no-argument constructor
15     public PanelFrame()
16     {
17        super( "Panel Demo" );
```

Fig. 11.45 | JPanel with five JButtons in a GridLayout attached to the SOUTH region of a BorderLayout. (Part 1 of 2.)

```
18              buttons = new JButton[ 5 ]; // create buttons array
19              buttonJPanel = new JPanel(); // set up panel
20              buttonJPanel.setLayout( new GridLayout( 1, buttons.length ) );
21
22              // create and add buttons
23              for ( int count = 0; count < buttons.length; count++ )
24              {
25                  buttons[ count ] = new JButton( "Button " + ( count + 1 ) );
26                  buttonJPanel.add( buttons[ count ] ); // add button to panel
27              } // end for
28
29              add( buttonJPanel, BorderLayout.SOUTH ); // add panel to JFrame
30          } // end PanelFrame constructor
31      } // end class PanelFrame
```

Fig. 11.45 | JPanel with five JButtons in a GridLayout attached to the SOUTH region of a BorderLayout. (Part 2 of 2.)

```
1   // Fig. 11.46: PanelDemo.java
2   // Testing PanelFrame.
3   import javax.swing.JFrame;
4
5   public class PanelDemo extends JFrame
6   {
7       public static void main( String args[] )
8       {
9           PanelFrame panelFrame = new PanelFrame();
10          panelFrame.setDefaultCloseOperation( JFrame.EXIT_ON_CLOSE );
11          panelFrame.setSize( 450, 200 ); // set frame size
12          panelFrame.setVisible( true ); // display frame
13      } // end main
14  } // end class PanelDemo
```

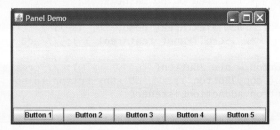

Fig. 11.46 | Test class for PanelFrame.

11.19 JTextArea

A JTextArea provides an area for manipulating multiple lines of text. Like class JText-Field, JTextArea is a subclass of JTextComponent, which declares common methods for JTextFields, JTextAreas and several other text-based GUI components.

The application in Figs. 11.47–11.48 demonstrates JTextAreas. One JTextArea displays text that the user can select. The other JTextArea is uneditable and is used to display the text the user selected in the first JTextArea. Unlike JTextFields, JTextAreas do not have action events. As with multiple-selection JLists (Section 11.12), an external event from another GUI component indicates when to process the text in a JTextArea. For example, when typing an e-mail message, you normally click a **Send** button to send the text of the message to the recipient. Similarly, when editing a document in a word processor, you normally save the file by selecting a **Save** or **Save As...** menu item. In this program, the button **Copy >>>** generates the external event that copies the selected text in the left JTextArea and displays it in the right JTextArea.

```java
 1   // Fig. 11.47: TextAreaFrame.java
 2   // Copying selected text from one textarea to another.
 3   import java.awt.event.ActionListener;
 4   import java.awt.event.ActionEvent;
 5   import javax.swing.Box;
 6   import javax.swing.JFrame;
 7   import javax.swing.JTextArea;
 8   import javax.swing.JButton;
 9   import javax.swing.JScrollPane;
10
11   public class TextAreaFrame extends JFrame
12   {
13      private JTextArea textArea1; // displays demo string
14      private JTextArea textArea2; // highlighted text is copied here
15      private JButton copyJButton; // initiates copying of text
16
17      // no-argument constructor
18      public TextAreaFrame()
19      {
20         super( "TextArea Demo" );
21         Box box = Box.createHorizontalBox(); // create box
22         String demo = "This is a demo string to\n" +
23            "illustrate copying text\nfrom one textarea to \n" +
24            "another textarea using an\nexternal event\n";
25
26         textArea1 = new JTextArea( demo, 10, 15 ); // create textarea1
27         box.add( new JScrollPane( textArea1 ) ); // add scrollpane
28
29         copyJButton = new JButton( "Copy >>>" ); // create copy button
30         box.add( copyJButton ); // add copy button to box
31         copyJButton.addActionListener(
32
33            new ActionListener() // anonymous inner class
34            {
35               // set text in textArea2 to selected text from textArea1
36               public void actionPerformed( ActionEvent event )
37               {
38                  textArea2.setText( textArea1.getSelectedText() );
39               } // end method actionPerformed
40            } // end anonymous inner class
41         ); // end call to addActionListener
42
```

Fig. 11.47 | Copying selected text from one JTextArea to another. (Part 1 of 2.)

```
43            textArea2 = new JTextArea( 10, 15 ); // create second textarea
44            textArea2.setEditable( false ); // disable editing
45            box.add( new JScrollPane( textArea2 ) ); // add scrollpane
46
47            add( box ); // add box to frame
48         } // end TextAreaFrame constructor
49      } // end class TextAreaFrame
```

Fig. 11.47 | Copying selected text from one JTextArea to another. (Part 2 of 2.)

```
1    // Fig. 11.48: TextAreaDemo.java
2    // Copying selected text from one textarea to another.
3    import javax.swing.JFrame;
4
5    public class TextAreaDemo
6    {
7       public static void main( String args[] )
8       {
9          TextAreaFrame textAreaFrame = new TextAreaFrame();
10         textAreaFrame.setDefaultCloseOperation( JFrame.EXIT_ON_CLOSE );
11         textAreaFrame.setSize( 425, 200 ); // set frame size
12         textAreaFrame.setVisible( true ); // display frame
13      } // end main
14   } // end class TextAreaDemo
```

Fig. 11.48 | Test class for TextAreaFrame.

In the constructor (lines 18–48), line 21 creates a **Box** container (package javax.swing) to organize the GUI components. Box is a subclass of Container that uses a **BoxLayout** layout manager (discussed in detail in Section 22.9) to arrange the GUI components either horizontally or vertically. Box's static method **createHorizontalBox** creates a Box that arranges components from left to right in the order that they are attached.

Lines 26 and 43 create JTextAreas textArea1 and textArea2. Line 26 uses JTextArea's three-argument constructor, which takes a String representing the initial text and two ints specifying that the JTextArea has 10 rows and 15 columns. Line 43 uses JTextArea's two-argument constructor, specifying that the JTextArea has 10 rows and 15 columns. Line 26 specifies that demo should be displayed as the default JTextArea content. A JTextArea does not provide scrollbars if it cannot display its complete contents. So, line 27 creates a **JScrollPane** object, initializes it with textArea1 and attaches it to container box. By default, horizontal and vertical scrollbars will appear as necessary in a JScrollPane.

Lines 29–41 create JButton object copyButton with the label "Copy >>>", add copy-Button to container box and register the event handler for copyButton's ActionEvent. This button provides the external event that determines when the program should copy the selected text in textArea1 to textArea2. When the user clicks copyButton, line 38 in actionPerformed indicates that method **getSelectedText** (inherited into JTextArea from JTextComponent) should return the selected text from textArea1. The user selects text by dragging the mouse over the desired text to highlight it. Method setText changes the text in textArea2 to the string returned by getSelectedText.

Lines 43–45 create textArea2, set its editable property to false and add it to container box. Line 47 adds box to the JFrame. Recall from Section 11.17 that the default layout of a JFrame is a BorderLayout and that the add method by default attaches its argument to the CENTER of the BorderLayout.

It is sometimes desirable, when text reaches the right side of a JTextArea, to have the text wrap to the next line. This is referred to as line wrapping. By default, JTextArea does not wrap lines.

Look-and-Feel Observation 11.20

To provide line wrapping functionality for a JTextArea, invoke JTextArea method setLine-Wrap with a true argument.

JScrollPane *Scrollbar Policies*

This example uses a JScrollPane to provide scrolling for a JTextArea. By default, JScrollPane displays scrollbars only if they are required. You can set the horizontal and vertical scrollbar policies of a JScrollPane when it is constructed. If a program has a reference to a JScrollPane, the program can use JScrollPane methods **setHorizontal-ScrollBarPolicy** and **setVerticalScrollBarPolicy** to change the scrollbar policies at any time. Class JScrollPane declares the constants

```
JScrollPane.VERTICAL_SCROLLBAR_ALWAYS
JScrollPane.HORIZONTAL_SCROLLBAR_ALWAYS
```

to indicate that a scrollbar should always appear, constants

```
JScrollPane.VERTICAL_SCROLLBAR_AS_NEEDED
JScrollPane.HORIZONTAL_SCROLLBAR_AS_NEEDED
```

to indicate that a scrollbar should appear only if necessary (the defaults) and constants

```
JScrollPane.VERTICAL_SCROLLBAR_NEVER
JScrollPane.HORIZONTAL_SCROLLBAR_NEVER
```

to indicate that a scrollbar should never appear. If the horizontal scrollbar policy is set to JScrollPane.HORIZONTAL_SCROLLBAR_NEVER, a JTextArea attached to the JScrollPane will automatically wrap lines.

11.20 Wrap-Up

In this chapter, you learned many GUI components and how to implement event handling. You also learned about nested classes, inner classes and anonymous inner classes. You saw the special relationship between an inner-class object and an object of its top-level class. You learned how to use JOptionPane dialogs to obtain text input from the user and how to display messages to the user. You also learned how to create applications that execute in their own windows. We discussed class JFrame and components that enable a user to interact with an application. We also showed you how to display text and images to the user. You learned how to customize JPanels to create custom drawing areas, which you will use extensively in the next chapter. You saw how to organize components on a window using layout managers and how to creating more complex GUIs by using JPanels to organize components. Finally, you learned about the JTextArea component in which a user can enter text and an application can display text. In Chapter 22, GUI Components: Part 2, you will learn about more advanced GUI components, such as sliders, menus and more complex layout managers. In the next chapter, you will learn how to add graphics to your GUI application. Graphics allow you to draw shapes and text with colors and styles.

Summary

Section 11.1 Introduction
- A graphical user interface (GUI) presents a user-friendly mechanism for interacting with an application. A GUI gives an application a distinctive "look" and "feel."
- Providing different applications with consistent, intuitive user interface components allows users to be somewhat familiar with an application, so that they can learn it more quickly.
- GUIs are built from GUI components—sometimes called controls or widgets.

Section 11.2 Simple GUI-Based Input/Output with *JOptionPane*
- Most applications use windows or dialog boxes (also called dialogs) to interact with the user.
- Class JOptionPane (package javax.swing) provides prepackaged dialog boxes for both input and output. JOptionPane static method showInputDialog displays an input dialog.
- A prompt typically uses sentence-style capitalization—a style that capitalizes only the first letter of the first word in the text unless the word is a proper noun.
- An input dialog can input only input Strings. This is typical of most GUI components.
- JOptionPane static method showMessageDialog displays a message dialog.

Section 11.3 Overview of Swing Components
- Most Swing GUI components are located in package javax.swing. They are part of the Java Foundation Classes (JFC)—Java's libraries for cross-platform GUI development.
- Together, the appearance and the way in which the user interacts with the application are known as that application's look-and-feel. Swing GUI components allow you to specify a uniform look-and-feel for your application across all platforms or to use each platform's custom look-and-feel.
- Lightweight Swing components are not tied to actual GUI components supported by the underlying platform on which an application executes.
- Several Swing components are heavyweight components that require direct interaction with the local windowing system, which may restrict their appearance and functionality.
- Class Component (package java.awt) declares many of the attributes and behaviors common to the GUI components in packages java.awt and javax.swing.
- Class Container (package java.awt) is a subclass of Component. Components are attached to Containers so the Components can be organized and displayed on the screen.

- Class JComponent (package javax.swing) is a subclass of Container. JComponent is the superclass of all lightweight Swing components and declares their common attributes and behaviors.
- Some common JComponent features include a pluggable look-and-feel, shortcut keys called mnemonics, tool tips, support for assistive technologies and support for user interface localization.

Section 11.4 Displaying Text and Images in a Window
- Most windows are instances of class JFrame or a subclass of JFrame. JFrame provides the basic attributes and behaviors of a window.
- A JLabel displays a single line of read-only text, an image, or both text and an image. Text in a JLabel normally uses sentence-style capitalization.
- When building a GUI, each GUI component must be attached to a container, such as a window created with a JFrame.
- Many IDEs provide GUI design tools in which you can specify the exact size and location of a component by using the mouse, then the IDE will generate the GUI code for you.
- JComponent method setToolTipText specifies the tool tip that is displayed when the user positions the mouse cursor over a lightweight component.
- Container method add attaches a GUI component to a Container.
- Class ImageIcon (package javax.swing) supports several image formats, including GIF, PNG and JPEG.
- Method getClass (of class Object) retrieves a reference to the Class object that represents the the class declaration for the object on which the method is called.
- Class method getResource returns the location of its argument as a URL. Method getResource uses the Class object's class loader to determine the location of the resource.
- Interface SwingConstants (package javax.swing) declares a set of common integer constants that are used with many Swing components.
- The horizontal and vertical alignments of a JLabel can be set with methods setHorizontalAlignment and setVerticalAlignment, respectively.
- JLabel method setText sets the text displayed on a label. The corresponding method getText retrieves the current text displayed on a label.
- JLabel method setIcon specifies the Icon to display on a label. The corresponding method getIcon retrieves the current Icon displayed on a label.
- JLabel methods setHorizontalTextPosition and setVerticalTextPosition specify the text position in the label.
- JFrame method setDefaultCloseOperation with constant JFrame.EXIT_ON_CLOSE as the argument indicates that the program should terminate when the window is closed by the user.
- Component method setSize specifies the width and height of a component.
- Component method setVisible with the argument true displays a JFrame on the screen.

Section 11.5 Text Fields and an Introduction to Event Handling with Nested Classes
- GUIs are event driven—when the user interacts with a GUI component, events drive the program to perform tasks.
- The code that performs a task in response to an event is called an event handler and the overall process of responding to events is known as event handling.
- Class JTextField extends class JTextComponent (package javax.swing.text), which provides many features common to Swing's text-based components. Class JPasswordField extends JTextField and adds several methods that are specific to processing passwords.

- A JPasswordField shows that characters are being typed as the user enters them, but hides the actual characters with echo characters.
- A component receives the focus when the user clicks the component.
- JTextComponent method setEditable can be used to make a text field uneditable.
- Before an application can respond to an event for a particular GUI component, you must perform several coding steps: 1) Create a class that represents the event handler. 2) Implement an appropriate interface, known as an event-listener interface, in the class from *Step 1*. 3) Indicate that an object of the class from *Steps 1* and *2* should be notified when the event occurs. This is known as registering the event handler.
- Nested classes can be static or non-static. Non-static nested classes are called inner classes and are frequently used for event handling.
- Before an object of an inner class can be created, there must first be an object of the top-level class that contains the inner class, because an inner-class object implicitly has a reference to an object of its top-level class.
- An inner-class object is allowed to directly access all the instance variables and methods of its top-level class.
- A nested class that is static does not require an object of its top-level class and does not implicitly have a reference to an object of the top-level class.
- When the user presses *Enter* in a JTextField or JPasswordField, the GUI component generates an ActionEvent (package java.awt.event). Such an event is processed by an object that implements the interface ActionListener (package java.awt.event).
- JTextField method addActionListener registers the event handler for a component text field. This method receives as its argument an ActionListener object.
- The GUI component with which the user interacts is the event source.
- An ActionEvent object contains information about the event that just occurred, such as the event source and the text in the text field.
- ActionEvent method getSource returns a reference to the event source. ActionEvent method getActionCommand returns the text the user typed in a text field or the label on a JButton.
- JPasswordField method getPassword returns the password the user typed.

Section 11.6 Common GUI Event Types and Listener Interfaces
- For each event-object type, there is typically a corresponding event-listener interface. Each event-listener interface specifies one or more event-handling methods that must be declared in the class that implements the interface.

Section 11.7 How Event Handling Works
- When an event occurs, the GUI component with which the user interacted notifies its registered listeners by calling each listener's appropriate event-handling method.
- Every JComponent has an instance variable called listenerList that refers to an object of class EventListenerList (package javax.swing.event). Each object of a JComponent subclass maintains references to all of its registered listeners in the listenerList.
- Every GUI component supports several event types, including mouse events, key events and others. When an event occurs, the event is dispatched only to the event listeners of the appropriate type. The GUI component receives a unique event ID specifying the event type, which it uses to decide the listener type to which the event should be dispatched and which method to call on each listener object.

Section 11.8 *JButton*

- A button is a component the user clicks to trigger a specific action. All the button types are subclasses of `AbstractButton` (package `javax.swing`), which declares the common features of Swing buttons. Button labels typically use book-title capitalization—a style that capitalizes the first letter of each significant word in the text and does not end with any punctuation.

- Command buttons are created with class `JButton`.

- A `JButton` can display an `Icon`. To provide the user with an extra level of visual interaction with the GUI, a `JButton` can also have a rollover `Icon`—an `Icon` that is displayed when the user positions the mouse over the button.

- Method `setRolloverIcon` (of class `AbstractButton`) specifies the image displayed on a button when the user positions the mouse over it.

Section 11.9 *Buttons That Maintain State*

- The Swing GUI components contain three types of state buttons—`JToggleButton`, `JCheckBox` and `JRadioButton`.

- Classes `JCheckBox` and `JRadioButton` are subclasses of `JToggleButton`. A `JRadioButton` is different from a `JCheckBox` in that normally several `JRadioButtons` are grouped together, and only one in the group can be selected at any time.

- Method `setFont` (of class `Component`) sets the font of a component to a new object of class `Font` (package `java.awt`).

- When the user clicks a `JCheckBox`, an `ItemEvent` occurs. This event can be handled by an `ItemListener` object, which must implement method `itemStateChanged`. Method `addItemListener` registers the listener for a `JCheckBox` or `JRadioButton` object.

- `JCheckBox` method `isSelected` determines whether a `JCheckBox` is selected.

- `JRadioButtons` are similar to `JCheckBoxes` in that they have two states—selected and not selected. However, radio buttons normally appear as a group in which only one button can be selected at a time. Selecting a different radio button forces all others to be deselected.

- `JRadioButtons` are used to represent mutually exclusive options.

- The logical relationship between `JRadioButtons` is maintained by a `ButtonGroup` object (package `javax.swing`).

- `ButtonGroup` method `add` associates each a `JRadioButton` with a `ButtonGroup`. If more than one selected `JRadioButton` object is added to a group, the selected one that was added first will be selected when the GUI is displayed.

- `JRadioButtons` generate `ItemEvents` when they are clicked.

Section 11.10 *JComboBox and Using an Anonymous Inner Class for Event Handling*

- A `JComboBox` provides a list of items from which the user can make a single selection. `JComboBoxes` generate `ItemEvents`.

- Each item in a `JComboBox` has an index. The first item added to a `JComboBox` appears as the currently selected item when the `JComboBox` is displayed. Other items are selected by clicking the `JComboBox`, which expands into a list from which the user can make a selection.

- `JComboBox` method `setMaximumRowCount` sets the maximum number of elements that are displayed when the user clicks the `JComboBox`. If there are additional items, the `JComboBox` provides a scrollbar that allows the user to scroll through all the elements in the list.

- An anonymous inner class is a special form of inner class that is declared without a name and typically appears inside a method declaration. Since an anonymous inner class has no name, one object of the anonymous inner class must be created at the point where the class is declared.

- `JComboBox` method `getSelectedIndex` returns the index of the selected item.

Section 11.11 `JList`

- A `JList` displays a series of items from which the user may select one or more items. Class `JList` supports single-selection lists and multiple-selection lists.
- When the user clicks an item in a `JList`, a `ListSelectionEvent` occurs. `JList` method `addListSelectionListener` registers a `ListSelectionListener` for a `JList`'s selection events. A `ListSelectionListener` (package `javax.swing.event`) must implement method `valueChanged`.
- `JList` method `setVisibleRowCount` specifies the number of items that are visible in the list.
- `JList` method `setSelectionMode` specifies a list's selection mode.
- A `JList` does not provide a scrollbar if there are more items in the list than the number of visible rows. In this case, a `JScrollPane` object can be used to provide the scrolling capability.
- `JFrame` method `getContentPane` returns a reference to the `JFrame`'s content pane where GUI components are displayed.
- `JList` method `getSelectedIndex` returns the selected item's index.

Section 11.12 Multiple-Selection Lists

- A multiple-selection list enables the user to select many items from a `JList`.
- `JList` method `setFixedCellWidth` sets a `JList`'s width. Method `setFixedCellHeight` sets the height of each item in a `JList`.
- There are no events to indicate that a user has made multiple selections in a multiple-selection list. Normally, an external event generated by another GUI component specifies when the multiple selections in a `JList` should be processed.
- `JList` method `setListData` sets the items displayed in a `JList`. `JList` method `getSelectedValues` returns an array of `Object`s representing the selected items in a `JList`.

Section 11.13 Mouse Event Handling

- The `MouseListener` and `MouseMotionListener` event-listener interfaces are used to handle mouse events. Mouse events can be trapped for any GUI component that extends `Component`.
- Interface `MouseInputListener` (package `javax.swing.event`) extends interfaces `MouseListener` and `MouseMotionListener` to create a single interface containing all their methods.
- Each of the mouse event-handling methods takes a `MouseEvent` object as its argument. A `MouseEvent` object contains information about the mouse event that occurred, including the *x*- and *y*-coordinates of the location where the event occurred. These coordinates are measured from the upper-left corner of the GUI component on which the event occurred.
- The methods and constants of class `InputEvent` (`MouseEvent`'s superclass) enable an application to determine which mouse button the user clicked.
- Interface `MouseWheelListener` enables applications to respond to the rotation of a mouse wheel.
- GUI components inherit methods `addMouseListener` and `addMouseMotionListener` from class `Component`.

Section 11.14 Adapter Classes

- Many event-listener interfaces contain multiple methods. For many of these interfaces, packages `java.awt.event` and `javax.swing.event` provide event-listener adapter classes. An adapter class implements an interface and provides a default implementation of each method in the interface. You can extend an adapter class to inherit the default implementation of every method and subsequently override only the method(s) you need for event handling.

- MouseEvent method getClickCount returns the number of mouse button clicks. Methods is-MetaDown and isAltDown determine which mouse button the user clicked.

Section 11.15 JPanel Subclass for Drawing with the Mouse

- Lightweight Swing components that extend class JComponent contain method paintComponent, which is called when a lightweight Swing component is displayed. By overriding this method, you can specify how to draw shapes using Java's graphics capabilities.
- When customizing a JPanel for use as a dedicated drawing area, the subclass should override method paintComponent and call the superclass version of paintComponent as the first statement in the body of the overridden method.
- Subclasses of JComponent support transparency. When a component is opaque, paintComponent clears the component's background before the component is displayed.
- The transparency of a Swing lightweight component can be set with method setOpaque (a false argument indicates that the component is transparent).
- Class Point (package java.awt) represents an *x-y* coordinate.
- Class Graphics is used to draw.
- MouseEvent method getPoint obtains the Point where a mouse event occurred.
- Method repaint (inherited indirectly from class Component) indicates that a component should be refreshed on the screen as soon as possible.
- Method paintComponent receives a Graphics parameter and is called automatically any time a lightweight component needs to be displayed on the screen.
- Graphics method fillOval draws a solid oval. The method's four parameters represent the bounding box in which the oval is displayed. The first two parameters are the upper-left *x*-coordinate and the upper-left *y*-coordinate of the rectangular area. The last two coordinates represent the rectangular area's width and height.

Section 11.16 Key-Event Handling

- Interface KeyListener is used to handle key events that are generated when keys on the keyboard are pressed and released. Method addKeyListener of class Component registers a KeyListener for a component.
- KeyEvent method getKeyCode gets the virtual key code of the key that was pressed. Class KeyEvent maintains a set of virtual key-code constants that represent every key on the keyboard.
- KeyEvent method getKeyText returns a string containing the name of the key that was pressed.
- KeyEvent method getKeyChar gets the Unicode value of the character typed.
- KeyEvent method isActionKey determines whether the key in an event was an action key.
- InputEvent method getModifiers determines whether any modifier keys (such as *Shift*, *Alt* and *Ctrl*) were pressed when the key event occurred.
- KeyEvent method getKeyModifiersText produces a string containing the names of the pressed modifier keys.

Section 11.17 Layout Managers

- Layout managers arrange GUI components in a container for presentation purposes.
- All layout managers implement the interface LayoutManager (package java.awt).
- Container method setLayout specifies the layout of a container.
- FlowLayout is the simplest layout manager. GUI components are placed on a container from left to right in the order in which they are added to the container. When the edge of the container is

reached, components continue to display on the next line. Class `FlowLayout` allows GUI components to be left aligned, centered (the default) and right aligned.

- `FlowLayout` method `setAlignment` changes the alignment for a `FlowLayout`.
- The `BorderLayout` layout manager (the default for a `JFrame`) arranges components into five regions: `NORTH`, `SOUTH`, `EAST`, `WEST` and `CENTER`. `NORTH` corresponds to the top of the container.
- A `BorderLayout` limits a `Container` to containing at most five components—one in each region.
- The `GridLayout` layout manager divides the container into a grid so that components can be placed in rows and columns.
- `Container` method `validate` recomputes a container's layout based on the current layout manager for the `Container` and the current set of displayed GUI components.

Section 11.19 *JTextArea*

- A `JTextArea` provides an area for manipulating multiple lines of text. `JTextArea` is a subclass of `JTextComponent`, which declares common methods for `JTextFields`, `JTextAreas` and several other text-based GUI components.
- Class `Box` is a subclass of `Container` that uses a `BoxLayout` layout manager to arrange the GUI components either horizontally or vertically.
- `Box` static method `createHorizontalBox` creates a `Box` that arranges components from left to right in the order that they are attached.
- Method `getSelectedText` (inherited into `JTextArea` from `JTextComponent`) returns the selected text from a `JTextArea`.
- You can set the horizontal and vertical scrollbar policies of a `JScrollPane` when it is constructed. `JScrollPane` methods `setHorizontalScrollBarPolicy`, and `setVerticalScrollBarPolicy` can be used change the scrollbar policies at any time.

Terminology

AbstractButton class
ActionEvent class
ActionListener interface
actionPerformed method of ActionListener
adapter class
add method of class ButtonGroup
add method of Container
addActionListener method of class JTextField
addItemListener method of class
    AbstractButton
addKeyListener method of class Component
addListSelectionListener method of
    class JList
addMouseListener method of class Component
addMouseMotionListener method of class
    Component
addWindowListener method of class JFrame
anonymous inner class
AWTEvent class
book-title capitalization
BorderLayout class
Box class

BoxLayout class
ButtonGroup class
Class class
Component class
Container class
content pane
createHorizontalBox method of class Box
dedicated drawing area
default constructor of an anonymous inner class
delegation event model
dialog box
dispatch an event
event
event driven
event handler
event handling
event listener
event-listener adapter class
event-listener interface
event object
event registration
event source

MouseWheelListener interface

mouseWheelMoved method of
     MouseWheelListener

nested class

paintComponent method of JComponent

Point class

registering an event handler

repaint method of Component

rollover Icon

setAlignment method of FlowLayout

setBackground method of Component

setDefaultCloseOperation method of JFrame

setEditable method of JTextComponent

setFixedCellHeight method of JList

setFixedCellWidth method of JList

setFont method of Component

setHorizontalAlignment method of JLabel

setHorizontalScrollBarPolicy method of
     JScrollPane

setHorizontalTextPosition method of JLabel

setIcon method of JLabel

setLayout method of Container

setLineWrap method of JTextArea

setListData method of JList

setMaximumRowCount method of JComboBox

setOpaque method of JComponent

setRolloverIcon method of AbstractButton

setSelectionMode method of JList

setSize method of JFrame

setText method of JLabel

setText method of JTextComponent

setToolTipText method of JComponent

setVerticalAlignment method of JLabel

setVerticalScrollBarPolicy method of
     JSlider

setVerticalTextPosition method of JLabel

setVisible method of Component

setVisible method of JFrame

setVisibleRowCount method of JList

showInputDialog method of JOptionPane

showMessageDialog method of JOptionPane

static nested class

Swing GUI components

SwingConstants interface

tool tip

top-level class

transparency of a JComponent

typing in a text field

validate method of Container

valueChanged method of
     ListSelectionListener

WindowAdapter class

windowClosing method of WindowListener

WindowListener interface

Self-Review Exercises

11.1 Fill in the blanks in each of the following statements:
   a) Method _____ is called when the mouse is moved with no buttons pressed and an event listener is registered to handle the event.
   b) Text that cannot be modified by the user is called _____ text.
   c) A(n) _____ arranges GUI components in a Container.
   d) The add method for attaching GUI components is a method of class _____.
   e) GUI is an acronym for _____.
   f) Method _____ is used to specify the layout manager for a container.
   g) A mouseDragged method call is preceded by a(n) _____ method call and followed by a(n) _____ method call.
   h) Class _____ contains methods that display message dialogs and input dialogs.
   i) An input dialog capable of receiving input from the user is displayed with method _____ of class _____.
   j) A dialog capable of displaying a message to the user is displayed with method _____ of class _____.
   k) Both JTextFields and JTextAreas directly extend class _____.

11.2 Determine whether each statement is *true* or *false*. If *false*, explain why.
   a) BorderLayout is the default layout manager for a JFrame's content pane.
   b) When the mouse cursor is moved into the bounds of a GUI component, method mouseOver is called.
   c) A JPanel cannot be added to another JPanel.

d) In a BorderLayout, two buttons added to the NORTH region will be placed side by side.

e) When one is using BorderLayout, a maximum of five components can be displayed.

f) Inner classes are not allowed to access the members of the enclosing class.

g) A JTextArea's text is always read-only.

h) Class JTextArea is a direct subclass of class Component.

11.3 Find the error(s) in each of the following statements, and explain how to correct it (them):

a) ```
buttonName = JButton("Caption");
```

b) ```
JLabel aLabel, JLabel;    // create references
```

c) ```
txtField = new JTextField(50, "Default Text");
```

d) ```
Container container = getContentPane();
setLayout( new BorderLayout() );
button1 = new JButton( "North Star" );
button2 = new JButton( "South Pole" );
container.add( button1 );
container.add( button2 );
```

Answers to Self-Review Exercises

11.1 a) mouseMoved. b) uneditable (read-only). c) layout manager. d) Container. e) graphical user interface. f) setLayout. g) mousePressed, mouseReleased. h) JOptionPane. i) showInputDialog, JOptionPane. j) showMessageDialog, JOptionPane. k) JTextComponent.

11.2 a) True.

b) False. Method mouseEntered is called.

c) False. A JPanel can be added to another JPanel, because JPanel is an indirect subclass of Component. So, a JPanel is a Component. Any Component can be added to a Container.

d) False. Only the last button added will be displayed. Remember that only one component should be added to each region in a BorderLayout.

e) True.

f) False. Inner classes have access to all members of the enclosing class declaration.

g) False. JTextAreas are editable by default.

h) False. JTextArea derives from class JTextComponent.

11.3 a) new is needed to create an object.

b) JLabel is a class name and cannot be used as a variable name.

c) The arguments passed to the constructor are reversed. The String must be passed first.

d) BorderLayout has been set, and components are being added without specifying the region, so both are added to the center region. Proper add statements might be

```
container.add( button1, BorderLayout.NORTH );
container.add( button2, BorderLayout.SOUTH );
```

Exercises

11.4 Determine whether each statement is *true* or *false*. If *false*, explain why.

a) Only one layout manager can be used per Container.

b) GUI components can be added to a Container in any order in a BorderLayout.

c) JRadioButtons provide a series of mutually exclusive options (i.e., only one can be true at a time).

d) Graphics method setFont is used to set the font for text fields.

e) A JList displays a scrollbar if there are more items in the list than can be displayed.

f) A Mouse object has a method called mouseDragged.

11.5 Find any errors in each of the following lines of code, and explain how to correct them.

a) `import javax.swing.JFrame`
b) `panelObject.GridLayout( 8, 8 ); // set GridLayout`
c) `container.setLayout( new FlowLayout( FlowLayout.DEFAULT ) );`
d) `container.add( eastButton, EAST );   // BorderLayout`

11.6   Create the following GUI. You do not have to provide any functionality.

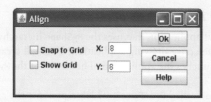

11.7   Create the following GUI. You do not have to provide any functionality.

11.8   Write a temperature conversion application that converts from Fahrenheit to Celsius. The Fahrenheit temperature should be entered from the keyboard (via a `JTextField`). A `JLabel` should be used to display the converted temperature. Use the following formula for the conversion:

$$Celsius = \frac{5}{9} \times (\ Fahrenheit - 32\ )$$

11.9   Enhance the temperature conversion application of Exercise 11.8 by adding the Kelvin temperature scale. The application should also allow the user to make conversions between any two scales. Use the following formula for the conversion between Kelvin and Celsius (in addition to the formula in Exercise 11.8):

$$Kelvin = Celsius + 273.15$$

11.10   Write an application that plays "guess the number" as follows: Your application chooses the number to be guessed by selecting an integer at random in the range 1–1000. The application then displays the following in a label:

```
I have a number between 1 and 1000. Can you guess my number?
Please enter your first guess.
```

A `JTextField` should be used to input the guess. As each guess is input, the background color should change to either red or blue. Red indicates that the user is getting "warmer," and blue indicates that the user is getting "colder." A `JLabel` should display either `"Too High"` or `"Too Low"` to help the user zero in on the correct answer. When the user gets the correct answer, `"Correct!"` should be displayed, and the `JTextField` used for input should be changed to be uneditable. A `JButton` should be provided to allow the user to play the game again. When the `JButton` is clicked, a new random number should be generated and the input `JTextField` changed to be editable.

11.11   Modify the application of Section 6.10 to provide a GUI that enables the user to click a JButton to roll the dice. The application should also display four JLabels and four JTextFields, with one JLabel for each JTextField. The JTextFields should be used to display the values of each die and the sum of the dice after each roll. The point should be displayed in the fourth JTextField when the user does not win or lose on the first roll and should continue to be displayed until the game is lost.

(Optional) GUI and Graphics Case Study Exercise: Expanding the Interface

11.12   In this exercise, you will implement a GUI application that uses the MyShape hierarchy from the GUI case study Exercise 10.2 to create an interactive drawing application. You will create two classes for the GUI and provide a test class that launches the application. The classes of the MyShape hierarchy require no additional changes.

The first class to create is a subclass of JPanel called DrawPanel, which represents the area on which the user draws the shapes. Class DrawPanel should have the following instance variables:

a) An array shapes of type MyShape that will store all the shapes the user draws.
b) An integer shapeCount that counts the number of shapes in the array.
c) An integer shapeType that determines the type of shape to draw.
d) A MyShape currentShape that represents the current shape the user is drawing.
e) A Color currentColor that represents the current drawing color.
f) A boolean filledShape that determines whether to draw a filled shape.
g) A JLabel statusLabel that represents the status bar. The status bar will display the coordinates of the current mouse position.

Class DrawPanel should also declare the following methods:

a) Overridden method paintComponent that draws the shapes in the array. Use instance variable shapeCount to determine how many shapes to draw. Method paintComponent should also call currentShape's draw method, provided that currentShape is not null.
b) Set methods for the shapeType, currentColor and filledShape.
c) Method clearLastShape should clear the last shape drawn by decrementing instance variable shapeCount. Ensure that shapeCount is never less than zero.
d) Method clearDrawing should remove all the shapes in the current drawing by setting shapeCount to zero.

Methods clearLastShape and clearDrawing should call method repaint (inherited from JPanel) to refresh the drawing on the DrawPanel by indicating that the system should call method paintComponent.

Class DrawPanel should also provide event handling to enable the user to draw with the mouse. Create a single inner class that both extends MouseAdapter and implements MouseMotionListener to handle all mouse events in one class.

In the inner class, override method mousePressed so that it assigns currentShape a new shape of the type specified by shapeType and initializes both points to the mouse position. Next, override method mouseReleased to finish drawing the current shape and place it in the array. Set the second point of currentShape to the current mouse position and add currentShape to the array. Instance variable shapeCount determines the insertion index. Set currentShape to null and call method repaint to update the drawing with the new shape.

Override method mouseMoved to set the text of the statusLabel so that it displays the mouse coordinates—this will update the label with the coordinates every time the user moves (but does not drag) the mouse within the DrawPanel. Next, override method mouseDragged so that it sets the second point of the currentShape to the current mouse position and calls method repaint. This will allow the user to see the shape while dragging the mouse. Also, update the JLabel in mouseDragged with the current position of the mouse.

Create a constructor for DrawPanel that has a single JLabel parameter. In the constructor, initialize statusLabel with the value passed to the parameter. Also initialize array shapes with 100 entries, shapeCount to 0, shapeType to the value that represents a line, currentShape to null and currentColor to Color.BLACK. The constructor should then set the background color of the Draw-Panel to Color.WHITE and register the MouseListener and MouseMotionListener so the JPanel properly handles mouse events.

Next, create a JFrame subclass called DrawFrame that provides a GUI that enables the user to control various aspects of drawing. For the layout of the DrawFrame, we recommend a BorderLayout, with the components in the NORTH region, the main drawing panel in the CENTER region, and a status bar in the SOUTH region, as in Fig. 11.49. In the top panel, create the components listed below. Each component's event handler should call the appropriate method in class DrawPanel.

 a) A button to undo the last shape drawn.
 b) A button to clear all shapes from the drawing.
 c) A combo box for selecting the color from the 13 predefined colors.
 d) A combo box for selecting the shape to draw.
 e) A checkbox that specifies whether a shape should be filled or unfilled.

Declare and create the interface components in DrawFrame's constructor. You will need to create the status bar JLabel before you create the DrawPanel, so you can pass the JLabel as an argument to DrawPanel's constructor. Finally, create a test class that initializes and displays the DrawFrame to execute the application.

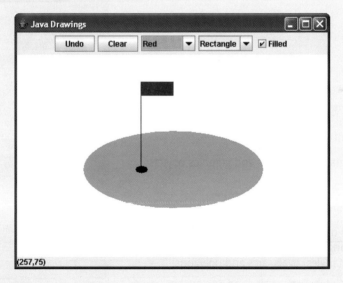

Fig. 11.49 | Interface for drawing shapes.

12

Graphics and Java 2D™

OBJECTIVES

In this chapter you will learn:

- To understand graphics contexts and graphics objects.

- To manipulate colors.

- To manipulate fonts.

- To use methods of class **Graphics** to draw lines, rectangles, rectangles with rounded corners, three-dimensional rectangles, ovals, arcs and polygons.

- To use methods of class **Graphics2D** from the **Java 2D** API to draw lines, rectangles, rectangles with rounded corners, ellipses, arcs and general paths.

- To specify **Paint** and **Stroke** characteristics of shapes displayed with **Graphics2D**.

12.1 Introduction

In this chapter, we overview several of Java's capabilities for drawing two-dimensional shapes, controlling colors and controlling fonts. One of Java's initial appeals was its support for graphics that enabled programmers to visually enhance their applications. Java now contains many more sophisticated drawing capabilities as part of the Java 2D™ API. This chapter begins with an introduction to many of Java's original drawing capabilities. Next we present several of the more powerful Java 2D capabilities, such as controlling the style of lines used to draw shapes and the way shapes are filled with color and patterns. [*Note:* Several concepts covered in this chapter have already been covered in the optional GUI and Graphics Case Study of Chapters 3–10. So, some material will be repetitive if you read the case study. You do not need to read the case study to understand this chapter.]

Figure 12.1 shows a portion of the Java class hierarchy that includes several of the basic graphics classes and Java 2D API classes and interfaces covered in this chapter. Class `Color` contains methods and constants for manipulating colors. Class `JComponent` contains method `paintComponent`, which is used to draw graphics on a component. Class `Font` contains methods and constants for manipulating fonts. Class `FontMetrics` contains methods for obtaining font information. Class `Graphics` contains methods for drawing strings, lines, rectangles and other shapes. Class `Graphics2D`, which extends class `Graphics`, is used for drawing with the Java 2D API. Class `Polygon` contains methods for creating polygons. The bottom half of the figure lists several classes and interfaces from the Java 2D API. Class `BasicStroke` helps specify the drawing characteristics of lines. Classes `GradientPaint` and `TexturePaint` help specify the characteristics for filling shapes with colors or patterns. Classes `GeneralPath`, `Line2D`, `Arc2D`, `Ellipse2D`, `Rectangle2D` and `RoundRectangle2D` represent several Java 2D shapes. [*Note:* We begin the chapter by discussing Java's original graphics capabilities, then move on to the Java 2D API. Now, the classes that were part of Java's original graphics capabilities are considered to be part of the Java 2D API.]

To begin drawing in Java, we must first understand Java's coordinate system (Fig. 12.2), which is a scheme for identifying every point on the screen. By default, the upper-left corner of a GUI component (e.g., a window) has the coordinates (0, 0). A coordinate pair is composed of an *x*-coordinate (the horizontal coordinate) and a *y*-coordinate (the vertical coordinate). The *x*-coordinate is the horizontal distance moving right from the left of the screen. The *y*-coordinate is the vertical distance moving down from the top

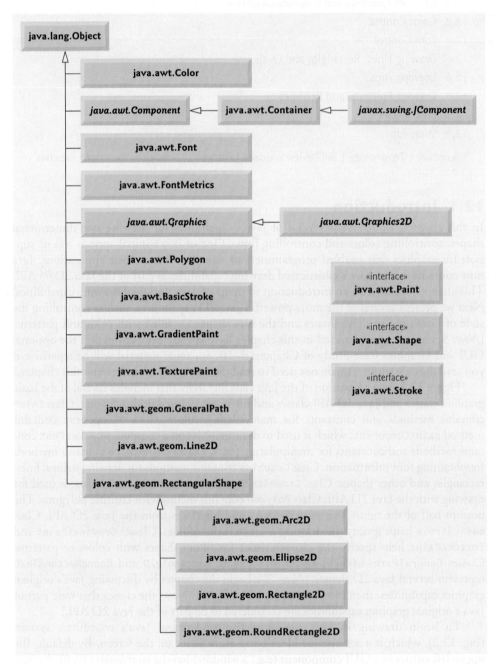

Fig. 12.1 | Classes and interfaces used in this chapter from Java's original graphics capabilities and from the Java 2D API. [*Note:* Class Object appears here because it is the superclass of the Java class hierarchy. Also, abstract classes appear in italics.]

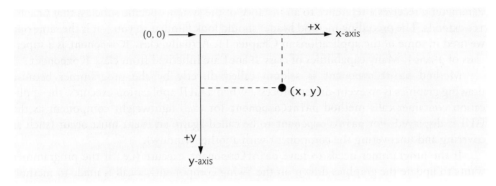

Fig. 12.2 | Java coordinate system. Units are measured in pixels.

of the screen. The *x*-axis describes every horizontal coordinate, and the *y*-axis every vertical coordinate. The coordinates are used to indicate where graphics should be displayed on a screen. Coordinate units are measured in pixels (which stands for "picture element"). A pixel is a display monitor's smallest unit of resolution.

Portability Tip 12.1

Different display monitors have different resolutions (i.e., the density of the pixels varies). This can cause graphics to appear in different sizes on different monitors or on the same monitor with different settings.

12.2 Graphics Contexts and Graphics Objects

A **graphics context** enables drawing on the screen. A Graphics object manages a graphics context and draws pixels on the screen that represent text and other graphical objects (e.g., lines, ellipses, rectangles and other polygons). Graphics objects contain methods for drawing, font manipulation, color manipulation and the like.

Class Graphics is an abstract class (i.e., Graphics objects cannot be instantiated). This contributes to Java's portability. Because drawing is performed differently on every platform that supports Java, there cannot be only one implementation of the drawing capabilities across all systems. For example, the graphics capabilities that enable a PC running Microsoft Windows to draw a rectangle are different from those that enable a Linux workstation to draw a rectangle—and they are both different from the graphics capabilities that enable a Macintosh to draw a rectangle. When Java is implemented on each platform, a subclass of Graphics is created that implements the drawing capabilities. This implementation is hidden by class Graphics, which supplies the interface that enables us to use graphics in a platform-independent manner.

Class Component is the superclass for many of the classes in the java.awt package. (We introduced class Component in Chapter 11.) Class JComponent, which inherits indirectly from class Component, contains a paintComponent method that can be used to draw graphics. Method paintComponent takes a Graphics object as an argument. This object is passed to the paintComponent method by the system when a lightweight Swing component needs to be repainted. The header for the paintComponent method is

```
public void paintComponent( Graphics g )
```

Parameter g receives a reference to an instance of the system-specific subclass that Graphics extends. The preceding method header should look familiar to you—it is the same one we used in some of the applications in Chapter 11. Actually, class JComponent is a superclass of JPanel. Many capabilities of class JPanel are inherited from class JComponent.

Method paintComponent is seldom called directly by the programmer because drawing graphics is an event-driven process. When a GUI application executes, the application container calls method paintComponent for each lightweight component as the GUI is displayed. For paintComponent to be called again, an event must occur (such as covering and uncovering the component with another window).

If the programmer needs to have paintComponent execute (i.e., if the programmer wants to update the graphics drawn on the Swing component), a call is made to method repaint, which is inherited by all JComponents indirectly from class Component (package java.awt). Method repaint is frequently called to request a call to method paintComponent. The header for repaint is

```
public void repaint()
```

12.3 Color Control

Class Color declares methods and constants for manipulating colors in a Java program. The predeclared color constants are summarized in Fig. 12.3, and several color methods and constructors are summarized in Fig. 12.4. Note that two of the methods in Fig. 12.4 are Graphics methods that are specific to colors.

Color constant	RGB value
public final static Color RED	255, 0, 0
public final static Color GREEN	0, 255, 0
public final static Color BLUE	0, 0, 255
public final static Color ORANGE	255, 200, 0
public final static Color PINK	255, 175, 175
public final static Color CYAN	0, 255, 255
public final static Color MAGENTA	255, 0, 255
public final static Color YELLOW	255, 255, 0
public final static Color BLACK	0, 0, 0
public final static Color WHITE	255, 255, 255
public final static Color GRAY	128, 128, 128
public final static Color LIGHT_GRAY	192, 192, 192
public final static Color DARK_GRAY	64, 64, 64

Fig. 12.3 | Color constants and their RGB values.

Method	Description
Color constructors and methods	
`public Color( int r, int g, int b )`	
	Creates a color based on red, green and blue components expressed as integers from 0 to 255.
`public Color( float r, float g, float b )`	
	Creates a color based on red, green and blue components expressed as floating-point values from 0.0 to 1.0.
`public int getRed()`	
	Returns a value between 0 and 255 representing the red content.
`public int getGreen()`	
	Returns a value between 0 and 255 representing the green content.
`public int getBlue()`	
	Returns a value between 0 and 255 representing the blue content.
Graphics methods for manipulating Colors	
`public Color getColor()`	
	Returns `Color` object representing current color for the graphics context.
`public void setColor( Color c )`	
	Sets the current color for drawing with the graphics context.

Fig. 12.4 | `Color` methods and color-related `Graphics` methods .

Every color is created from a red, a green and a blue component. Together these components are called **RGB values**. All three RGB components can be integers in the range from 0 to 255, or they can be floating-point values in the range 0.0 to 1.0. The first RGB component specifies the amount of red, the second the amount of green and the third the amount of blue. The larger the RGB value, the greater the amount of that particular color. Java enables the programmer to choose from $256 \times 256 \times 256$ (approximately 16.7 million) colors. Not all computers are capable of displaying all these colors. The computer will display the closest color it can.

Two of class `Color`'s constructors are shown in Fig. 12.4—one that takes three `int` arguments and one that takes three `float` arguments, with each argument specifying the amount of red, green and blue. The `int` values must be in the range 0–255 and the `float` values must be in the range 0.0–1.0. The new `Color` object will have the specified amounts of red, green and blue. `Color` methods `getRed`, `getGreen` and `getBlue` return integer values from 0 to 255 representing the amount of red, green and blue, respectively. `Graphics` method `getColor` returns a `Color` object representing the current drawing color. `Graphics` method `setColor` sets the current drawing color.

Figures 12.5–12.6 demonstrates several methods from Fig. 12.4 by drawing filled rectangles and strings in several different colors. When the application begins execution, class `ColorJPanel`'s `paintComponent` method (lines 10–37 of Fig. 12.5) is called to paint the window. Line 17 uses `Graphics` method `setColor` to set the drawing color. Method setColor receives a Color object. The expression new Color(255, 0, 0) creates a new Color object that represents red (red value 255, and 0 for the green and blue values). Line 18 uses Graphics method **fillRect** to draw a filled rectangle in the current color. Method fillRect draws a rectangle based on its four arguments. The first two integer values represent the upper-left *x*-coordinate and upper-left *y*-coordinate, where the Graphics object begins drawing the rectangle. The third and fourth arguments are nonnegative integers that represent the width and the height of the rectangle in pixels, respectively. A rectangle drawn using method fillRect is filled by the current color of the Graphics object.

Line 19 uses Graphics method **drawString** to draw a String in the current color. The expression g.getColor() retrieves the current color from the Graphics object. The returned Color object is concatenated with string "Current RGB: ", resulting in an

```java
1   // Fig. 12.5: ColorJPanel.java
2   // Demonstrating Colors.
3   import java.awt.Graphics;
4   import java.awt.Color;
5   import javax.swing.JPanel;
6
7   public class ColorJPanel extends JPanel
8   {
9      // draw rectangles and Strings in different colors
10     public void paintComponent( Graphics g )
11     {
12        super.paintComponent( g ); // call superclass's paintComponent
13
14        this.setBackground( Color.WHITE );
15
16        // set new drawing color using integers
17        g.setColor( new Color( 255, 0, 0 ) );
18        g.fillRect( 15, 25, 100, 20 );
19        g.drawString( "Current RGB: " + g.getColor(), 130, 40 );
20
21        // set new drawing color using floats
22        g.setColor( new Color( 0.50f, 0.75f, 0.0f ) );
23        g.fillRect( 15, 50, 100, 20 );
24        g.drawString( "Current RGB: " + g.getColor(), 130, 65 );
25
26        // set new drawing color using static Color objects
27        g.setColor( Color.BLUE );
28        g.fillRect( 15, 75, 100, 20 );
29        g.drawString( "Current RGB: " + g.getColor(), 130, 90 );
30
31        // display individual RGB values
32        Color color = Color.MAGENTA;
33        g.setColor( color );
34        g.fillRect( 15, 100, 100, 20 );
35        g.drawString( "RGB values: " + color.getRed() + ", " +
36           color.getGreen() + ", " + color.getBlue(), 130, 115 );
37     } // end method paintComponent
38  } // end class ColorJPanel
```

Fig. 12.5 | Color changed for drawing.

```
 1    // Fig. 12.6: ShowColors.java
 2    // Demonstrating Colors.
 3    import javax.swing.JFrame;
 4
 5    public class ShowColors
 6    {
 7       // execute application
 8       public static void main( String args[] )
 9       {
10          // create frame for ColorJPanel
11          JFrame frame = new JFrame( "Using colors" );
12          frame.setDefaultCloseOperation( JFrame.EXIT_ON_CLOSE );
13
14          ColorJPanel colorJPanel = new ColorJPanel(); // create ColorJPanel
15          frame.add( colorJPanel ); // add colorJPanel to frame
16          frame.setSize( 400, 180 ); // set frame size
17          frame.setVisible( true ); // display frame
18       } // end main
19    } // end class ShowColors
```

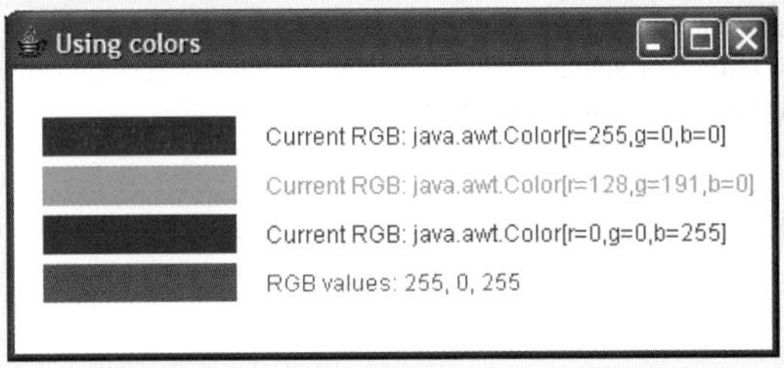

Fig. 12.6 | Creating JFrame to display colors on JPanel.

implicit call to class Color's toString method. The String representation of a Color contains the class name and package (java.awt.Color), and the red, green and blue values.

Look-and-Feel Observation 12.1

Everyone perceives colors differently. Choose your colors carefully to ensure that your application is readable, both for people who can perceive color and for people who are color blind. Try to avoid using many different colors in close proximity.

Lines 22–24 and lines 27–29 perform the same tasks again. Line 22 uses the Color constructor with three float arguments to create a dark green color (0.50f for red, 0.75f for green and 0.0f for blue). Note the syntax of the values. The letter f appended to a floating-point literal indicates that the literal should be treated as type float. Recall that by default, floating-point literals are treated as type double.

Line 27 sets the current drawing color to one of the predeclared Color constants (Color.BLUE). The Color constants are static, so they are created when class Color is loaded into memory at execution time.

The statement in lines 35–36 makes calls to Color methods getRed, getGreen and getBlue on the predeclared Color.MAGENTA constant. Method main of class ShowColors (lines 8–18 of Fig. 12.6) creates the JFrame that will contain a ColorJPanel object where the colors will be displayed.

 Software Engineering Observation 12.1

To change the color, you must create a new Color object (or use one of the predeclared Color constants). Like String objects, Color objects are immutable (not modifiable).

Package javax.swing provides the JColorChooser GUI component that enables application users to select colors. The application of Figs. 12.7–12.8 demonstrates a JColorChooser dialog. When you click the **Change Color** button, a JColorChooser dialog appears. When you select a color and press the dialog's **OK** button, the background color of the application window changes.

```java
1   // Fig. 12.7: ShowColors2JFrame.java
2   // Choosing colors with JColorChooser.
3   import java.awt.BorderLayout;
4   import java.awt.Color;
5   import java.awt.event.ActionEvent;
6   import java.awt.event.ActionListener;
7   import javax.swing.JButton;
8   import javax.swing.JFrame;
9   import javax.swing.JColorChooser;
10  import javax.swing.JPanel;
11
12  public class ShowColors2JFrame extends JFrame
13  {
14     private JButton changeColorJButton;
15     private Color color = Color.LIGHT_GRAY;
16     private JPanel colorJPanel;
17
18     // set up GUI
19     public ShowColors2JFrame()
20     {
21        super( "Using JColorChooser" );
22
23        // create JPanel for display color
24        colorJPanel = new JPanel();
25        colorJPanel.setBackground( color );
26
27        // set up changeColorJButton and register its event handler
28        changeColorJButton = new JButton( "Change Color" );
29        changeColorJButton.addActionListener(
30
31           new ActionListener() // anonymous inner class
32           {
33              // display JColorChooser when user clicks button
34              public void actionPerformed( ActionEvent event )
35              {
36                 color = JColorChooser.showDialog(
37                    ShowColors2JFrame.this, "Choose a color", color );
38
```

Fig. 12.7 | JColorChooser dialog. (Part 1 of 2.)

```
39                    // set default color, if no color is returned
40                    if ( color == null )
41                        color = Color.LIGHT_GRAY;
42
43                    // change content pane's background color
44                    colorJPanel.setBackground( color );
45                } // end method actionPerformed
46            } // end anonymous inner class
47        ); // end call to addActionListener
48
49        add( colorJPanel, BorderLayout.CENTER ); // add colorJPanel
50        add( changeColorJButton, BorderLayout.SOUTH ); // add button
51
52        setSize( 400, 130 ); // set frame size
53        setVisible( true ); // display frame
54    } // end ShowColor2JFrame constructor
55 } // end class ShowColors2JFrame
```

Fig. 12.7 | JColorChooser dialog. (Part 2 of 2.)

Class JColorChooser provides static method showDialog, which creates a JColor-Chooser object, attaches it to a dialog box and displays the dialog. Lines 36–37 of Fig. 12.7 invoke this method to display the color chooser dialog. Method showDialog returns the selected Color object, or null if the user presses **Cancel** or closes the dialog without pressing **OK**. The method takes three arguments—a reference to its parent Component, a String to display in the title bar of the dialog and the initial selected Color for the dialog. The parent component is a reference to the window from which the dialog is displayed (in this case the JFrame, with the reference name frame). The dialog will be centered on the parent. If the parent is null, the dialog is centered on the screen. While the color chooser dialog is on the screen, the user cannot interact with the parent component. This type of dialog is called a **modal dialog** (discussed in Chapter 22, GUI Components: Part 2).

After the user selects a color, lines 40–41 determine whether color is null, and, if so, set color to Color.LIGHT_GRAY. Line 44 invokes method setBackground to change the background color of the JPanel. Method setBackground is one of the many Component

```
1   // Fig. 12.8: ShowColors2.java
2   // Choosing colors with JColorChooser.
3   import javax.swing.JFrame;
4
5   public class ShowColors2
6   {
7       // execute application
8       public static void main( String args[] )
9       {
10          ShowColors2JFrame application = new ShowColors2JFrame();
11          application.setDefaultCloseOperation( JFrame.EXIT_ON_CLOSE );
12      } // end main
13  } // end class ShowColors2
```

Fig. 12.8 | Choosing colors with JColorChooser. (Part 1 of 2.)

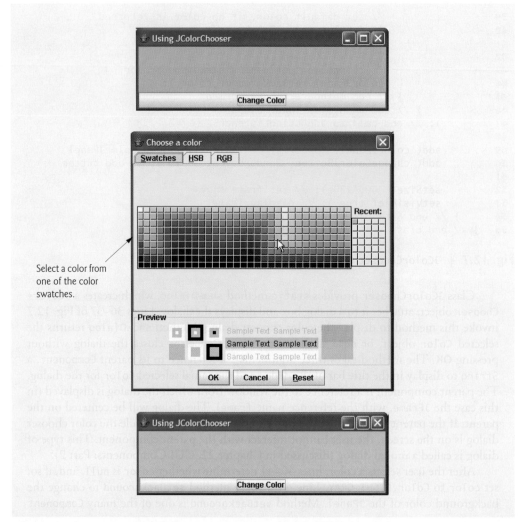

Fig. 12.8 | Choosing colors with `JColorChooser`. (Part 2 of 2.)

methods that can be used on most GUI components. Note that the user can continue to use the **Change Color** button to change the background color of the application. Figure 12.8 contains method `main`, which executes the program.

The second screen capture of Fig. 12.8 demonstrates the default `JColorChooser` dialog that allows the user to select a color from a variety of color swatches. Note that there are actually three tabs across the top of the dialog—**Swatches**, **HSB** and **RGB**. These represent three different ways to select a color. The **HSB** tab allows you to select a color based on hue, saturation and brightness—values that are used to define the amount of light in a color. We do not discuss HSB values. For more information on hue, saturation and brightness, visit whatis.techtarget.com/definition/0,,sid9_gci212262,00.html. The **RGB** tab allows you to select a color by using sliders to select the red, green and blue components. The **HSB** and **RGB** tabs are shown in Fig. 12.9.

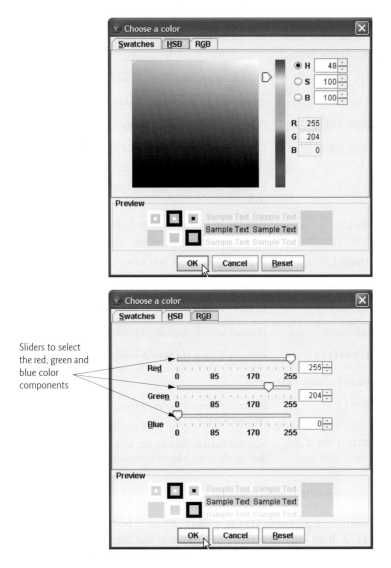

Fig. 12.9 | **HSB** and **RGB** tabs of the `JColorChooser` dialog.

12.4 **Font Control**

This section introduces methods and constants for font control. Most font methods and font constants are part of class `Font`. Some methods of class `Font` and class `Graphics` are summarized in Fig. 12.10.

Class `Font`'s constructor takes three arguments—the font name, font style and font size. The font name is any font currently supported by the system on which the program is running, such as standard Java fonts `Monospaced`, `SansSerif` and `Serif`. The font style is `Font.PLAIN`, `Font.ITALIC` or `Font.BOLD` (each is a `static` field of class `Font`). Font styles

Method or constant	Description
Font constants, constructors and methods	
`public final static int PLAIN`	A constant representing a plain font style.
`public final static int BOLD`	A constant representing a bold font style.
`public final static int ITALIC`	A constant representing an italic font style.
`public Font( String name, int style, int size )`	Creates a Font object with the specified font name, style and size.
`public int getStyle()`	Returns an integer value indicating the current font style.
`public int getSize()`	Returns an integer value indicating the current font size.
`public String getName()`	Returns the current font name as a string.
`public String getFamily()`	Returns the font's family name as a string.
`public boolean isPlain()`	Returns true if the font is plain, else false.
`public boolean isBold()`	Returns true if the font is bold, else false.
`public boolean isItalic()`	Returns true if the font is italic, else false.
Graphics methods for manipulating Fonts	
`public Font getFont()`	Returns a Font object reference representing the current font.
`public void setFont( Font f )`	Sets the current font to the font, style and size specified by the Font object reference f.

Fig. 12.10 | Font-related methods and constants.

can be used in combination (e.g., Font.ITALIC + Font.BOLD). The font size is measured in points. A **point** is 1/72 of an inch. Graphics method **setFont** sets the current drawing font—the font in which text will be displayed—to its Font argument.

Portability Tip 12.2

The number of fonts varies greatly across systems. Java provides five font names—Serif, Monospaced, SansSerif, Dialog and DialogInput—that can be used on all Java platforms. The Java runtime environment (JRE) on each platform maps these logical font names to actual fonts installed on the platform. The actual fonts used may vary by platform.

The application of Figs. 12.11–12.12 displays text in four different fonts, with each font in a different size. Figure 12.11 uses the Font constructor to initialize Font objects (in lines 16, 20, 24 and 29) that are each passed to Graphics method setFont to change the drawing font. Each call to the Font constructor passes a font name (Serif, Monospaced or SansSerif) as a string, a font style (Font.PLAIN, Font.ITALIC or Font.BOLD) and a font

```
 1   // Fig. 12.11: FontJPanel.java
 2   // Display strings in different fonts and colors.
 3   import java.awt.Font;
 4   import java.awt.Color;
 5   import java.awt.Graphics;
 6   import javax.swing.JPanel;
 7
 8   public class FontJPanel extends JPanel
 9   {
10      // display Strings in different fonts and colors
11      public void paintComponent( Graphics g )
12      {
13         super.paintComponent( g ); // call superclass's paintComponent
14
15         // set font to Serif (Times), bold, 12pt and draw a string
16         g.setFont( new Font( "Serif", Font.BOLD, 12 ) );
17         g.drawString( "Serif 12 point bold.", 20, 50 );
18
19         // set font to Monospaced (Courier), italic, 24pt and draw a string
20         g.setFont( new Font( "Monospaced", Font.ITALIC, 24 ) );
21         g.drawString( "Monospaced 24 point italic.", 20, 70 );
22
23         // set font to SansSerif (Helvetica), plain, 14pt and draw a string
24         g.setFont( new Font( "SansSerif", Font.PLAIN, 14 ) );
25         g.drawString( "SansSerif 14 point plain.", 20, 90 );
26
27         // set font to Serif (Times), bold/italic, 18pt and draw a string
28         g.setColor( Color.RED );
29         g.setFont( new Font( "Serif", Font.BOLD + Font.ITALIC, 18 ) );
30         g.drawString( g.getFont().getName() + " " + g.getFont().getSize() +
31            " point bold italic.", 20, 110 );
32      } // end method paintComponent
33   } // end class FontJPanel
```

Fig. 12.11 | Graphics method setFont changes the drawing font.

```
 1   // Fig. 12.12: Fonts.java
 2   // Using fonts.
 3   import javax.swing.JFrame;
 4
 5   public class Fonts
 6   {
 7      // execute application
 8      public static void main( String args[] )
 9      {
10         // create frame for FontJPanel
11         JFrame frame = new JFrame( "Using fonts" );
12         frame.setDefaultCloseOperation( JFrame.EXIT_ON_CLOSE );
13
14         FontJPanel fontJPanel = new FontJPanel(); // create FontJPanel
15         frame.add( fontJPanel ); // add fontJPanel to frame
```

Fig. 12.12 | Creating a JFrame to display fonts. (Part 1 of 2.)

```
16          frame.setSize( 420, 170 ); // set frame size
17          frame.setVisible( true ); // display frame
18      } // end main
19  } // end class Fonts
```

Fig. 12.12 | Creating a JFrame to display fonts. (Part 2 of 2.)

size. Once Graphics method setFont is invoked, all text displayed following the call will appear in the new font until the font is changed. Each font's information is displayed in lines 17, 21, 25 and 30–31 using method drawString. Note that the coordinate passed to drawString corresponds to the lower-left corner of the baseline of the font. Line 28 changes the drawing color to red, so the next string displayed appears in red. Lines 30–31 display information about the final Font object. Method getFont of class Graphics returns a Font object representing the current font. Method getName returns the current font name as a string. Method getSize returns the font size in points.

Figure 12.12 contains method main, which creates a JFrame. We add a FontJPanel object to this JFrame (line 15), which displays the graphics created in Fig. 12.11.

Software Engineering Observation 12.2

To change the font, you must create a new Font object. Font objects are immutable—class Font has no set methods to change the characteristics of the current font.

Font Metrics

Sometimes it is necessary to get information about the current drawing font, such as its name, style and size. Several Font methods used to get font information are summarized in Fig. 12.10. Method getStyle returns an integer value representing the current style. The integer value returned is either Font.PLAIN, Font.ITALIC, Font.BOLD or the combination of Font.ITALIC and Font.BOLD. Method getFamily returns the name of the font family to which the current font belongs. The name of the font family is platform specific. Font methods are also available to test the style of the current font, and these too are summarized in Fig. 12.10. Methods isPlain, isBold and isItalic return true if the current font style is plain, bold or italic, respectively.

Sometimes precise information about a font's metrics must be known—such as height, descent (the amount a character dips below the baseline), ascent (the amount a character rises above the baseline) and leading (the difference between the descent of one line of text and the ascent of the line of text below it—that is, the interline spacing). Figure 12.13 illustrates some of the common font metrics.

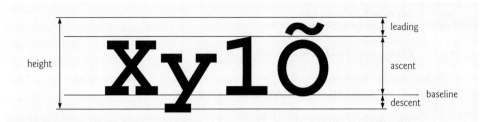

Fig. 12.13 | Font metrics.

Class `FontMetrics` declares several methods for obtaining font metrics. These methods and `Graphics` method `getFontMetrics` are summarized in Fig. 12.14. The application of Figs. 12.15–12.16 uses the methods of Fig. 12.14 to obtain font metric information for two fonts.

Method	Description
FontMetrics methods	
`public int getAscent()`	
	Returns the ascent of a font in points.
`public int getDescent()`	
	Returns the descent of a font in points.
`public int getLeading()`	
	Returns the leading of a font in points.
`public int getHeight()`	
	Returns the height of a font in points.
Graphics methods for getting a Font's FontMetrics	
`public FontMetrics getFontMetrics()`	
	Returns the `FontMetrics` object for the current drawing `Font`.
`public FontMetrics getFontMetrics( Font f )`	
	Returns the `FontMetrics` object for the specified `Font` argument.

Fig. 12.14 | `FontMetrics` and `Graphics` methods for obtaining font metrics.

```
1   // Fig. 12.15: MetricsJPanel.java
2   // FontMetrics and Graphics methods useful for obtaining font metrics.
3   import java.awt.Font;
4   import java.awt.FontMetrics;
```

Fig. 12.15 | Font metrics. (Part 1 of 2.)

```
5   import java.awt.Graphics;
6   import javax.swing.JPanel;
7
8   public class MetricsJPanel extends JPanel
9   {
10     // display font metrics
11     public void paintComponent( Graphics g )
12     {
13        super.paintComponent( g ); // call superclass's paintComponent
14
15        g.setFont( new Font( "SansSerif", Font.BOLD, 12 ) );
16        FontMetrics metrics = g.getFontMetrics();
17        g.drawString( "Current font: " + g.getFont(), 10, 40 );
18        g.drawString( "Ascent: " + metrics.getAscent(), 10, 55 );
19        g.drawString( "Descent: " + metrics.getDescent(), 10, 70 );
20        g.drawString( "Height: " + metrics.getHeight(), 10, 85 );
21        g.drawString( "Leading: " + metrics.getLeading(), 10, 100 );
22
23        Font font = new Font( "Serif", Font.ITALIC, 14 );
24        metrics = g.getFontMetrics( font );
25        g.setFont( font );
26        g.drawString( "Current font: " + font, 10, 130 );
27        g.drawString( "Ascent: " + metrics.getAscent(), 10, 145 );
28        g.drawString( "Descent: " + metrics.getDescent(), 10, 160 );
29        g.drawString( "Height: " + metrics.getHeight(), 10, 175 );
30        g.drawString( "Leading: " + metrics.getLeading(), 10, 190 );
31     } // end method paintComponent
32   } // end class MetricsJPanel
```

Fig. 12.15 | Font metrics. (Part 2 of 2.)

```
1   // Fig. 12.16: Metrics.java
2   // Displaying font metrics.
3   import javax.swing.JFrame;
4
5   public class Metrics
6   {
7     // execute application
8     public static void main( String args[] )
9     {
10        // create frame for MetricsJPanel
11        JFrame frame = new JFrame( "Demonstrating FontMetrics" );
12        frame.setDefaultCloseOperation( JFrame.EXIT_ON_CLOSE );
13
14        MetricsJPanel metricsJPanel = new MetricsJPanel();
15        frame.add( metricsJPanel ); // add metricsJPanel to frame
16        frame.setSize( 510, 250 ); // set frame size
17        frame.setVisible( true ); // display frame
18     } // end main
19   } // end class Metrics
```

Fig. 12.16 | Creating JFrame to display font metric information. (Part 1 of 2.)

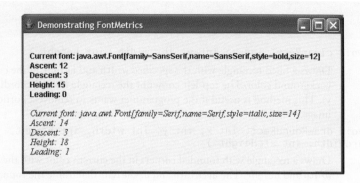

Fig. 12.16 | Creating JFrame to display font metric information. (Part 1 of 2.)

Line 15 of Fig. 12.15 creates and sets the current drawing font to a SansSerif, bold, 12-point font. Line 16 uses Graphics method getFontMetrics to obtain the FontMetrics object for the current font. Line 17 outputs the String representation of the Font returned by g.getFont(). Lines 18–21 use FontMetric methods to obtain the ascent, descent, height and leading for the font.

Line 23 creates a new Serif, italic, 14-point font. Line 24 uses a second version of Graphics method getFontMetrics, which accepts a Font argument and returns a corresponding FontMetrics object. Lines 27–30 obtain the ascent, descent, height and leading for the font. Note that the font metrics are slightly different for the two fonts.

12.5 Drawing Lines, Rectangles and Ovals

This section presents Graphics methods for drawing lines, rectangles and ovals. The methods and their parameters are summarized in Fig. 12.17. For each drawing method that requires a width and height parameter, the width and height must be nonnegative values. Otherwise, the shape will not display.

Method	Description
public void drawLine(int x1, int y1, int x2, int y2)	Draws a line between the point (x1, y1) and the point (x2, y2).
public void drawRect(int x, int y, int width, int height)	Draws a rectangle of the specified width and height. The top-left corner of the rectangle has the coordinates (x, y). Only the outline of the rectangle is drawn using the Graphics object's color—the body of the rectangle is not filled with this color.
public void fillRect(int x, int y, int width, int height)	Draws a filled rectangle with the specified width and height. The top-left corner of the rectangle has the coordinates (x, y). The rectangle is filled with the Graphics object's color.

Fig. 12.17 | Graphics methods that draw lines, rectangles and ovals. (Part 1 of 2.)

Method	Description
public void clearRect(int x, int y, int width, int height)	
	Draws a filled rectangle with the specified width and height in the current background color. The top-left corner of the rectangle has the coordinates (x, y). This method is useful if the programmer wants to remove a portion of an image.
public void drawRoundRect(int x, int y, int width, int height, int arcWidth, int arcHeight)	
	Draws a rectangle with rounded corners in the current color with the specified width and height. The arcWidth and arcHeight determine the rounding of the corners (see Fig. 12.20). Only the outline of the shape is drawn.
public void fillRoundRect(int x, int y, int width, int height, int arcWidth, int arcHeight)	
	Draws a filled rectangle with rounded corners in the current color with the specified width and height. The arcWidth and arcHeight determine the rounding of the corners (see Fig. 12.20).
public void draw3DRect(int x, int y, int width, int height, boolean b)	
	Draws a three-dimensional rectangle in the current color with the specified width and height. The top-left corner of the rectangle has the coordinates (x, y). The rectangle appears raised when b is true and lowered when b is false. Only the outline of the shape is drawn.
public void fill3DRect(int x, int y, int width, int height, boolean b)	
	Draws a filled three-dimensional rectangle in the current color with the specified width and height. The top-left corner of the rectangle has the coordinates (x, y). The rectangle appears raised when b is true and lowered when b is false.
public void drawOval(int x, int y, int width, int height)	
	Draws an oval in the current color with the specified width and height. The bounding rectangle's top-left corner is at the coordinates (x, y). The oval touches all four sides of the bounding rectangle at the center of each side (see Fig. 12.21). Only the outline of the shape is drawn.
public void fillOval(int x, int y, int width, int height)	
	Draws a filled oval in the current color with the specified width and height. The bounding rectangle's top-left corner is at the coordinates (x, y). The oval touches all four sides of the bounding rectangle at the center of each side (see Fig. 12.21).

Fig. 12.17 | Graphics methods that draw lines, rectangles and ovals. (Part 2 of 2.)

The application of Figs. 12.18–12.19 demonstrates drawing a variety of lines, rectangles, three-dimensional rectangles, rounded rectangles and ovals.

In Fig. 12.18, line 17 draws a red line, line 20 draws an empty blue rectangle and line 21 draws a filled blue rectangle. Methods **fillRoundRect** (line 24) and **drawRoundRect** (line 25) draw rectangles with rounded corners. Their first two arguments specify the coordinates of the upper-left corner of the bounding rectangle—the area in which the rounded rectangle will be drawn. Note that the upper-left corner coordinates are not the edge of

```
1   // Fig. 12.18: LinesRectsOvalsJPanel.java
2   // Drawing lines, rectangles and ovals.
3   import java.awt.Color;
4   import java.awt.Graphics;
5   import javax.swing.JPanel;
6
7   public class LinesRectsOvalsJPanel extends JPanel
8   {
9      // display various lines, rectangles and ovals
10     public void paintComponent( Graphics g )
11     {
12        super.paintComponent( g ); // call superclass's paint method
13
14        this.setBackground( Color.WHITE );
15
16        g.setColor( Color.RED );
17        g.drawLine( 5, 30, 380, 30 );
18
19        g.setColor( Color.BLUE );
20        g.drawRect( 5, 40, 90, 55 );
21        g.fillRect( 100, 40, 90, 55 );
22
23        g.setColor( Color.CYAN );
24        g.fillRoundRect( 195, 40, 90, 55, 50, 50 );
25        g.drawRoundRect( 290, 40, 90, 55, 20, 20 );
26
27        g.setColor( Color.YELLOW );
28        g.draw3DRect( 5, 100, 90, 55, true );
29        g.fill3DRect( 100, 100, 90, 55, false );
30
31        g.setColor( Color.MAGENTA );
32        g.drawOval( 195, 100, 90, 55 );
33        g.fillOval( 290, 100, 90, 55 );
34     } // end method paintComponent
35  } // end class LinesRectsOvalsJPanel
```

Fig. 12.18 | Drawing lines, rectangles and ovals.

```
1   // Fig. 12.19: LinesRectsOvals.java
2   // Drawing lines, rectangles and ovals.
3   import java.awt.Color;
4   import javax.swing.JFrame;
5
6   public class LinesRectsOvals
7   {
8      // execute application
9      public static void main( String args[] )
10     {
11        // create frame for LinesRectsOvalsJPanel
12        JFrame frame =
13           new JFrame( "Drawing lines, rectangles and ovals" );
14        frame.setDefaultCloseOperation( JFrame.EXIT_ON_CLOSE );
```

Fig. 12.19 | Creating JFrame to display lines, rectangles and ovals. (Part 1 of 2.)

```
15
16          LinesRectsOvalsJPanel linesRectsOvalsJPanel =
17             new LinesRectsOvalsJPanel();
18          linesRectsOvalsJPanel.setBackground( Color.WHITE );
19          frame.add( linesRectsOvalsJPanel ); // add panel to frame
20          frame.setSize( 400, 210 ); // set frame size
21          frame.setVisible( true ); // display frame
22       } // end main
23    } // end class LinesRectsOvals
```

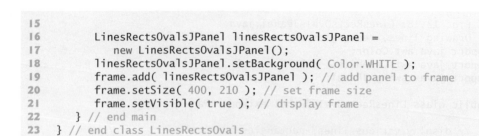

Fig. 12.19 | Creating JFrame to display lines, rectangles and ovals. (Part 2 of 2.)

the rounded rectangle, but the coordinates where the edge would be if the rectangle had square corners. The third and fourth arguments specify the width and height of the rectangle. The last two arguments determine the horizontal and vertical diameters of the arc (i.e., the arc width and arc height) used to represent the corners.

Figure 12.20 labels the arc width, arc height, width and height of a rounded rectangle. Using the same value for the arc width and arc height produces a quarter-circle at each corner. When the arc width, arc height, width and height have the same values, the result is a circle. If the values for width and height are the same and the values of arcWidth and arcHeight are 0, the result is a square.

Methods **draw3DRect** (line 28) and **fill3DRect** (line 29) take the same arguments. The first two arguments specify the top-left corner of the rectangle. The next two arguments specify the width and height of the rectangle, respectively. The last argument deter-

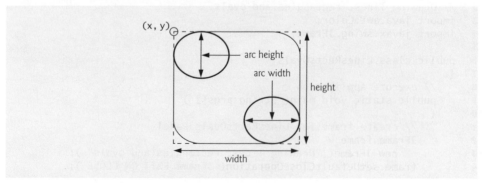

Fig. 12.20 | Arc width and arc height for rounded rectangles.

mines whether the rectangle is raised (true) or lowered (false). The three-dimensional effect of draw3DRect appears as two edges of the rectangle in the original color and two edges in a slightly darker color. The three-dimensional effect of fill3DRect appears as two edges of the rectangle in the original drawing color and the fill and other two edges in a slightly darker color. Raised rectangles have the original drawing color edges at the top and left of the rectangle. Lowered rectangles have the original drawing color edges at the bottom and right of the rectangle. The three-dimensional effect is difficult to see in some colors.

Methods drawOval and fillOval (lines 32–33) take the same four arguments. The first two arguments specify the top-left coordinate of the bounding rectangle that contains the oval. The last two arguments specify the width and height of the bounding rectangle, respectively. Figure 12.21 shows an oval bounded by a rectangle. Note that the oval touches the center of all four sides of the bounding rectangle. (The bounding rectangle is not displayed on the screen.)

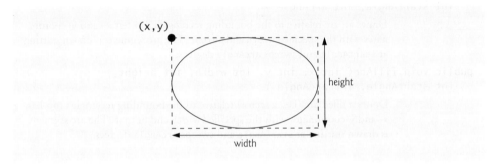

Fig. 12.21 | Oval bounded by a rectangle.

12.6 Drawing Arcs

An arc is drawn as a portion of an oval. Arc angles are measured in degrees. Arcs sweep (i.e., move along a curve) from a starting angle by the number of degrees specified by their arc angle. The starting angle indicates in degrees where the arc begins. The arc angle specifies the total number of degrees through which the arc sweeps. Figure 12.22 illustrates two arcs. The left set of axes shows an arc sweeping from zero degrees to approximately 110 degrees. Arcs that sweep in a counterclockwise direction are measured in positive

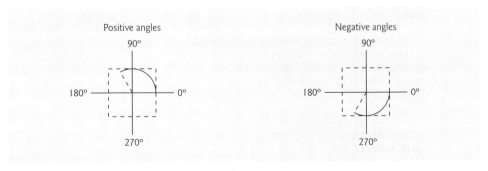

Fig. 12.22 | Positive and negative arc angles.

degrees. The set of axes on the right shows an arc sweeping from zero degrees to approximately −110 degrees. Arcs that sweep in a clockwise direction are measured in negative degrees. Note the dashed boxes around the arcs in Fig. 12.22. When drawing an arc, we specify a bounding rectangle for an oval. The arc will sweep along part of the oval. Graphics methods `drawArc` and `fillArc` for drawing arcs are summarized in Fig. 12.23.

The application of Fig. 12.24–Fig. 12.25 demonstrates the arc methods of Fig. 12.23. The application draws six arcs (three unfilled and three filled). To illustrate the bounding rectangle that helps determine where the arc appears, the first three arcs are displayed inside a red rectangle that has the same x, y, `width` and `height` arguments as the arcs.

Method	Description
`public void drawArc( int x, int y, int width, int height,` `    int startAngle, int arcAngle )`	
	Draws an arc relative to the bounding rectangle's top-left x- and y-coordinates with the specified `width` and `height`. The arc segment is drawn starting at `startAngle` and sweeps `arcAngle` degrees.
`public void fillArc( int x, int y, int width, int height,` `    int startAngle, int arcAngle )`	
	Draws a filled arc (i.e., a sector) relative to the bounding rectangle's top-left x- and y-coordinates with the specified `width` and `height`. The arc segment is drawn starting at `startAngle` and sweeps `arcAngle` degrees.

Fig. 12.23 | `Graphics` methods for drawing arcs.

```
1   // Fig. 12.24: ArcsJPanel.java
2   // Drawing arcs.
3   import java.awt.Color;
4   import java.awt.Graphics;
5   import javax.swing.JPanel;
6
7   public class ArcsJPanel extends JPanel
8   {
9      // draw rectangles and arcs
10     public void paintComponent( Graphics g )
11     {
12        super.paintComponent( g ); // call superclass's paintComponent
13
14        // start at 0 and sweep 360 degrees
15        g.setColor( Color.RED );
16        g.drawRect( 15, 35, 80, 80 );
17        g.setColor( Color.BLACK );
18        g.drawArc( 15, 35, 80, 80, 0, 360 );
19
20        // start at 0 and sweep 110 degrees
21        g.setColor( Color.RED );
22        g.drawRect( 100, 35, 80, 80 );
```

Fig. 12.24 | Arcs displayed with `drawArc` and `fillArc`. (Part 1 of 2.)

```
23          g.setColor( Color.BLACK );
24          g.drawArc( 100, 35, 80, 80, 0, 110 );
25
26          // start at 0 and sweep -270 degrees
27          g.setColor( Color.RED );
28          g.drawRect( 185, 35, 80, 80 );
29          g.setColor( Color.BLACK );
30          g.drawArc( 185, 35, 80, 80, 0, -270 );
31
32          // start at 0 and sweep 360 degrees
33          g.fillArc( 15, 120, 80, 40, 0, 360 );
34
35          // start at 270 and sweep -90 degrees
36          g.fillArc( 100, 120, 80, 40, 270, -90 );
37
38          // start at 0 and sweep -270 degrees
39          g.fillArc( 185, 120, 80, 40, 0, -270 );
40       } // end method paintComponent
41    } // end class ArcsJPanel
```

Fig. 12.24 | Arcs displayed with `drawArc` and `fillArc`. (Part 2 of 2.)

```
1     // Fig. 12.25: DrawArcs.java
2     // Drawing arcs.
3     import javax.swing.JFrame;
4
5     public class DrawArcs
6     {
7        // execute application
8        public static void main( String args[] )
9        {
10          // create frame for ArcsJPanel
11          JFrame frame = new JFrame( "Drawing Arcs" );
12          frame.setDefaultCloseOperation( JFrame.EXIT_ON_CLOSE );
13
14          ArcsJPanel arcsJPanel = new ArcsJPanel(); // create ArcsJPanel
15          frame.add( arcsJPanel ); // add arcsJPanel to frame
16          frame.setSize( 300, 210 ); // set frame size
17          frame.setVisible( true ); // display frame
18       } // end main
19    } // end class DrawArcs
```

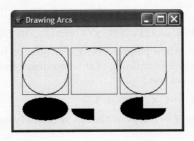

Fig. 12.25 | Creating `JFrame` to display arcs.

12.7 Drawing Polygons and Polylines

Polygons are closed multisided shapes composed of straight-line segments. Polylines are sequences of connected points. Figure 12.26 discusses methods for drawing polygons and polylines. Note that some methods require a `Polygon` object (package java.awt). Class Polygon's constructors are also described in Fig. 12.26. The application of Figs. 12.27–12.28 draws polygons and polylines.

Method	Description
Graphics methods for drawing polygons	
`public void drawPolygon( int xPoints[], int yPoints[], int points )`	
	Draws a polygon. The *x*-coordinate of each point is specified in the xPoints array, and the *y*-coordinate of each point in the yPoints array. The last argument specifies the number of points. This method draws a closed polygon. If the last point is different from the first, the polygon is closed by a line that connects the last point to the first.
`public void drawPolyline( int xPoints[], int yPoints[], int points )`	
	Draws a sequence of connected lines. The *x*-coordinate of each point is specified in the xPoints array, and the *y*-coordinate of each point in the yPoints array. The last argument specifies the number of points. If the last point is different from the first, the polyline is not closed.
`public void drawPolygon( Polygon p )`	
	Draws the specified polygon.
`public void fillPolygon( int xPoints[], int yPoints[], int points )`	
	Draws a filled polygon. The *x*-coordinate of each point is specified in the xPoints array, and the *y*-coordinate of each point in the yPoints array. The last argument specifies the number of points. This method draws a closed polygon. If the last point is different from the first, the polygon is closed by a line that connects the last point to the first.
`public void fillPolygon( Polygon p )`	
	Draws the specified filled polygon. The polygon is closed.
Polygon constructors and methods	
`public Polygon()`	
	Constructs a new polygon object. The polygon does not contain any points.
`public Polygon( int xValues[], int yValues[], int numberOfPoints )`	
	Constructs a new polygon object. The polygon has numberOfPoints sides, with each point consisting of an *x*-coordinate from xValues and a *y*-coordinate from yValues.
`public void addPoint( int x, int y )`	
	Adds pairs of *x*- and *y*-coordinates to the Polygon.

Fig. 12.26 | Graphics methods for polygons and class Polygon methods.

```
1   // Fig. 12.27: PolygonsJPanel.java
2   // Drawing polygons.
3   import java.awt.Graphics;
4   import java.awt.Polygon;
5   import javax.swing.JPanel;
6
7   public class PolygonsJPanel extends JPanel
8   {
9      // draw polygons and polylines
10     public void paintComponent( Graphics g )
11     {
12        super.paintComponent( g ); // call superclass's paintComponent
13
14        // draw polygon with Polygon object
15        int xValues[] = { 20, 40, 50, 30, 20, 15 };
16        int yValues[] = { 50, 50, 60, 80, 80, 60 };
17        Polygon polygon1 = new Polygon( xValues, yValues, 6 );
18        g.drawPolygon( polygon1 );
19
20        // draw polylines with two arrays
21        int xValues2[] = { 70, 90, 100, 80, 70, 65, 60 };
22        int yValues2[] = { 100, 100, 110, 110, 130, 110, 90 };
23        g.drawPolyline( xValues2, yValues2, 7 );
24
25        // fill polygon with two arrays
26        int xValues3[] = { 120, 140, 150, 190 };
27        int yValues3[] = { 40, 70, 80, 60 };
28        g.fillPolygon( xValues3, yValues3, 4 );
29
30        // draw filled polygon with Polygon object
31        Polygon polygon2 = new Polygon();
32        polygon2.addPoint( 165, 135 );
33        polygon2.addPoint( 175, 150 );
34        polygon2.addPoint( 270, 200 );
35        polygon2.addPoint( 200, 220 );
36        polygon2.addPoint( 130, 180 );
37        g.fillPolygon( polygon2 );
38     } // end method paintComponent
39  } // end class PolygonsJPanel
```

Fig. 12.27 | Polygons displayed with drawPolygon and fillPolygon.

```
1   // Fig. 12.28: DrawPolygons.java
2   // Drawing polygons.
3   import javax.swing.JFrame;
4
5   public class DrawPolygons
6   {
7      // execute application
8      public static void main( String args[] )
9      {
```

Fig. 12.28 | Creating JFrame to display polygons. (Part 1 of 2.)

```
10        // create frame for PolygonsJPanel
11        JFrame frame = new JFrame( "Drawing Polygons" );
12        frame.setDefaultCloseOperation( JFrame.EXIT_ON_CLOSE );
13
14        PolygonsJPanel polygonsJPanel = new PolygonsJPanel();
15        frame.add( polygonsJPanel ); // add polygonsJPanel to frame
16        frame.setSize( 280, 270 ); // set frame size
17        frame.setVisible( true ); // display frame
18     } // end main
19   } // end class DrawPolygons
```

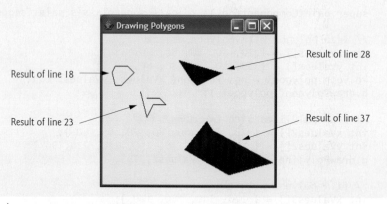

Fig. 12.28 | Creating JFrame to display polygons. (Part 2 of 2.)

Lines 15–16 of Fig. 12.27 create two int arrays and use them to specify the points for Polygon polygon1. The Polygon constructor call in line 17 receives array xValues, which contains the *x*-coordinate of each point; array yValues, which contains the *y*-coordinate of each point and 6 (the number of points in the polygon). Line 18 displays polygon1 by passing it as an argument to Graphics method **drawPolygon**.

Lines 21–22 create two int arrays and use them to specify the points for a series of connected lines. Array xValues2 contains the *x*-coordinate of each point and array yValues2 the *y*-coordinate of each point. Line 23 uses Graphics method **drawPolyline** to display the series of connected lines specified with the arguments xValues2, yValues2 and 7 (the number of points).

Lines 26–27 create two int arrays and use them to specify the points of a polygon. Array xValues3 contains the *x*-coordinate of each point and array yValues3 the *y*-coordinate of each point. Line 28 displays a polygon by passing to Graphics method **fillPolygon** the two arrays (xValues3 and yValues3) and the number of points to draw (4).

Common Programming Error 12.1

An ArrayIndexOutOfBoundsException is thrown if the number of points specified in the third argument to method drawPolygon or method fillPolygon is greater than the number of elements in the arrays of coordinates that specify the polygon to display.

Line 31 creates Polygon polygon2 with no points. Lines 32–36 use Polygon method **addPoint** to add pairs of *x*- and *y*-coordinates to the Polygon. Line 37 displays Polygon polygon2 by passing it to Graphics method fillPolygon.

12.8 Java 2D API

The Java 2D API provides advanced two-dimensional graphics capabilities for programmers who require detailed and complex graphical manipulations. The API includes features for processing line art, text and images in packages java.awt, java.awt.image, java.awt.color, java.awt.font, java.awt.geom, java.awt.print and java.awt.image.renderable. The capabilities of the API are far too broad to cover in this textbook. For an overview of the capabilities, see the Java 2D demo (discussed in Chapter 20, Introduction to Java Applets) or visit java.sun.com/products/java-media/2D/index.html. In this section, we overview several Java 2D capabilities.

Drawing with the Java 2D API is accomplished with a `Graphics2D` reference (package java.awt). `Graphics2D` is an abstract subclass of class `Graphics`, so it has all the graphics capabilities demonstrated earlier in this chapter. In fact, the actual object used to draw in every `paintComponent` method is an instance of a subclass of `Graphics2D` that is passed to method `paintComponent` and accessed via the superclass `Graphics`. To access `Graphics2D` capabilities, we must cast the `Graphics` reference (g) passed to `paintComponent` into a `Graphics2D` reference with a statement such as

```
Graphics2D g2d = ( Graphics2D ) g;
```

The next two examples use this technique.

Lines, Rectangles, Round Rectangles, Arcs and Ellipses

The next example demonstrates several Java 2D shapes from package java.awt.geom, including `Line2D.Double`, `Rectangle2D.Double`, `RoundRectangle2D.Double`, `Arc2D.Double` and `Ellipse2D.Double`. Note the syntax of each class name. Each of these classes represents a shape with dimensions specified as double-precision floating-point values. There is a separate version of each represented with single-precision floating-point values (e.g., `Ellipse2D.Float`). In each case, `Double` is a static nested class of the class specified to the left of the dot (e.g., `Ellipse2D`). To use the static nested class, we simply qualify its name with the outer class name.

In Figs. 12.29–12.30, we draw Java 2D shapes and modify their drawing characteristics, such as changing line thickness, filling shapes with patterns and drawing dashed lines. These are just a few of the many capabilities provided by Java 2D.

```
1   // Fig. 12.29: ShapesJPanel.java
2   // Demonstrating some Java 2D shapes.
3   import java.awt.Color;
4   import java.awt.Graphics;
5   import java.awt.BasicStroke;
6   import java.awt.GradientPaint;
7   import java.awt.TexturePaint;
8   import java.awt.Rectangle;
9   import java.awt.Graphics2D;
10  import java.awt.geom.Ellipse2D;
11  import java.awt.geom.Rectangle2D;
12  import java.awt.geom.RoundRectangle2D;
13  import java.awt.geom.Arc2D;
```

Fig. 12.29 | Java 2D shapes. (Part 1 of 3.)

```
14   import java.awt.geom.Line2D;
15   import java.awt.image.BufferedImage;
16   import javax.swing.JPanel;
17
18   public class ShapesJPanel extends JPanel
19   {
20      // draw shapes with Java 2D API
21      public void paintComponent( Graphics g )
22      {
23         super.paintComponent( g ); // call superclass's paintComponent
24
25         Graphics2D g2d = ( Graphics2D ) g; // cast g to Graphics2D
26
27         // draw 2D ellipse filled with a blue-yellow gradient
28         g2d.setPaint( new GradientPaint( 5, 30, Color.BLUE, 35, 100,
29            Color.YELLOW, true ) );
30         g2d.fill( new Ellipse2D.Double( 5, 30, 65, 100 ) );
31
32         // draw 2D rectangle in red
33         g2d.setPaint( Color.RED );
34         g2d.setStroke( new BasicStroke( 10.0f ) );
35         g2d.draw( new Rectangle2D.Double( 80, 30, 65, 100 ) );
36
37         // draw 2D rounded rectangle with a buffered background
38         BufferedImage buffImage = new BufferedImage( 10, 10,
39            BufferedImage.TYPE_INT_RGB );
40
41         // obtain Graphics2D from buffImage and draw on it
42         Graphics2D gg = buffImage.createGraphics();
43         gg.setColor( Color.YELLOW ); // draw in yellow
44         gg.fillRect( 0, 0, 10, 10 ); // draw a filled rectangle
45         gg.setColor( Color.BLACK );  // draw in black
46         gg.drawRect( 1, 1, 6, 6 ); // draw a rectangle
47         gg.setColor( Color.BLUE ); // draw in blue
48         gg.fillRect( 1, 1, 3, 3 ); // draw a filled rectangle
49         gg.setColor( Color.RED ); // draw in red
50         gg.fillRect( 4, 4, 3, 3 ); // draw a filled rectangle
51
52         // paint buffImage onto the JFrame
53         g2d.setPaint( new TexturePaint( buffImage,
54            new Rectangle( 10, 10 ) ) );
55         g2d.fill(
56            new RoundRectangle2D.Double( 155, 30, 75, 100, 50, 50 ) );
57
58         // draw 2D pie-shaped arc in white
59         g2d.setPaint( Color.WHITE );
60         g2d.setStroke( new BasicStroke( 6.0f ) );
61         g2d.draw(
62            new Arc2D.Double( 240, 30, 75, 100, 0, 270, Arc2D.PIE ) );
63
64         // draw 2D lines in green and yellow
65         g2d.setPaint( Color.GREEN );
66         g2d.draw( new Line2D.Double( 395, 30, 320, 150 ) );
```

Fig. 12.29 | Java 2D shapes. (Part 2 of 3.)

```
67
68          // draw 2D line using stroke
69          float dashes[] = { 10 }; // specify dash pattern
70          g2d.setPaint( Color.YELLOW );
71          g2d.setStroke( new BasicStroke( 4, BasicStroke.CAP_ROUND,
72             BasicStroke.JOIN_ROUND, 10, dashes, 0 ) );
73          g2d.draw( new Line2D.Double( 320, 30, 395, 150 ) );
74       } // end method paintComponent
75    } // end class ShapesJPanel
```

Fig. 12.29 | Java 2D shapes. (Part 3 of 3.)

```
 1    // Fig. 12.30: Shapes.java
 2    // Demonstrating some Java 2D shapes.
 3    import javax.swing.JFrame;
 4
 5    public class Shapes
 6    {
 7       // execute application
 8       public static void main( String args[] )
 9       {
10          // create frame for ShapesJPanel
11          JFrame frame = new JFrame( "Drawing 2D shapes" );
12          frame.setDefaultCloseOperation( JFrame.EXIT_ON_CLOSE );
13
14          // create ShapesJPanel
15          ShapesJPanel shapesJPanel = new ShapesJPanel();
16
17          frame.add( shapesJPanel ); // add shapesJPanel to frame
18          frame.setSize( 425, 200 ); // set frame size
19          frame.setVisible( true ); // display frame
20       } // end main
21    } // end class Shapes
```

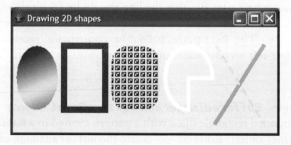

Fig. 12.30 | Creating JFrame to display shapes.

Line 25 of Fig. 12.29 casts the Graphics reference received by paintComponent to a Graphics2D reference and assigns it to g2d to allow access to the Java 2D features.

Ovals, Gradient Fills and *Paint* Objects

The first shape we draw is an oval filled with gradually changing colors. Lines 28–29 invoke Graphics2D method **setPaint** to set the **Paint** object that determines the color for the shape to display. A Paint object implements interface java.awt.Paint. It can be something as simple as one of the predeclared Color objects introduced in Section 12.3 (class Color implements Paint), or it can be an instance of the Java 2D API's Gradient-Paint, SystemColor, TexturePaint, LinearGradientPaint or RadialGradientPaint classes. In this case, we use a GradientPaint object.

Class GradientPaint helps draw a shape in gradually changing colors—called a gradient. The GradientPaint constructor used here requires seven arguments. The first two specify the starting coordinate for the gradient. The third specifies the starting Color for the gradient. The fourth and fifth specify the ending coordinate for the gradient. The sixth specifies the ending Color for the gradient. The last argument specifies whether the gradient is cyclic (true) or acyclic (false). The two sets of coordinates determine the direction of the gradient. Because the second coordinate (35, 100) is down and to the right of the first coordinate (5, 30), the gradient goes down and to the right at an angle. Because this gradient is cyclic (true), the color starts with blue, gradually becomes yellow, then gradually returns to blue. If the gradient is acyclic, the color transitions from the first color specified (e.g., blue) to the second color (e.g., yellow).

Line 30 uses Graphics2D method fill to draw a filled Shape object—an object that implements interface Shape (package java.awt). In this case, we display an Ellipse2D.Double object. The Ellipse2D.Double constructor receives four arguments specifying the bounding rectangle for the ellipse to display.

Rectangles, Strokes

Next we draw a red rectangle with a thick border. Line 33 invokes setPaint to set the Paint object to Color.RED. Line 34 uses Graphics2D method setStroke to set the characteristics of the rectangle's border (or the lines for any other shape). Method setStroke requires as its argument an object that implements interface Stroke (package java.awt). In this case, we use an instance of class BasicStroke. Class BasicStroke provides several constructors to specify the width of the line, how the line ends (called the end caps), how lines join together (called line joins) and the dash attributes of the line (if it is a dashed line). The constructor here specifies that the line should be 10 pixels wide.

Line 35 uses Graphics2D method draw to draw a Shape object—in this case, a Rectangle2D.Double. The Rectangle2D.Double constructor receives four arguments specifying the upper-left x-coordinate, upper-left y-coordinate, width and height of the rectangle.

Rounded Rectangles, BufferedImages and TexturePaint Objects

Next we draw a rounded rectangle filled with a pattern created in a BufferedImage (package java.awt.image) object. Lines 38–39 create the BufferedImage object. Class BufferedImage can be used to produce images in color and grayscale. This particular BufferedImage is 10 pixels wide and 10 pixels tall (as specified by the first two arguments of the constructor). The third argument BufferedImage.TYPE_INT_RGB indicates that the image is stored in color using the RGB color scheme.

To create the rounded rectangle's fill pattern, we must first draw into the BufferedImage. Line 42 creates a Graphics2D object (with a call to BufferedImage method createGraphics) that can be used to draw into the BufferedImage. Lines 43–50 use methods setColor, fillRect and drawRect (discussed earlier in this chapter) to create the pattern.

Lines 53–54 set the Paint object to a new TexturePaint (package java.awt) object. A TexturePaint object uses the image stored in its associated BufferedImage (the first constructor argument) as the fill texture for a filled-in shape. The second argument specifies the Rectangle area from the BufferedImage that will be replicated through the texture. In this case, the Rectangle is the same size as the BufferedImage. However, a smaller portion of the BufferedImage can be used.

Lines 55–56 use Graphics2D method fill to draw a filled Shape object—in this case, a RoundRectangle2D.Double. The constructor for class RoundRectangle2D.Double receives six arguments specifying the rectangle dimensions and the arc width and arc height used to determine the rounding of the corners.

Arcs

Next we draw a pie-shaped arc with a thick white line. Line 59 sets the Paint object to Color.WHITE. Line 60 sets the Stroke object to a new BasicStroke for a line 6 pixels wide. Lines 61–62 use Graphics2D method draw to draw a Shape object—in this case, an Arc2D.Double. The Arc2D.Double constructor's first four arguments specify the upper-left *x*-coordinate, upper-left *y*-coordinate, width and height of the bounding rectangle for the arc. The fifth argument specifies the start angle. The sixth argument specifies the arc angle. The last argument specifies how the arc is closed. Constant Arc2D.PIE indicates that the arc is closed by drawing two lines—one line from the arc's starting point to the center of the bounding rectangle and one line from the center of the bounding rectangle to the ending point. Class Arc2D provides two other static constants for specifying how the arc is closed. Constant Arc2D.CHORD draws a line from the starting point to the ending point. Constant Arc2D.OPEN specifies that the arc should not be closed.

Lines

Finally, we draw two lines using Line2D objects—one solid and one dashed. Line 65 sets the Paint object to Color.GREEN. Line 66 uses Graphics2D method draw to draw a Shape object—in this case, an instance of class Line2D.Double. The Line2D.Double constructor's arguments specify the starting coordinates and ending coordinates of the line.

Line 69 declares a one-element float array containing the value 10. This array will be used to describe the dashes in the dashed line. In this case, each dash will be 10 pixels long. To create dashes of different lengths in a pattern, simply provide the length of each dash as an element in the array. Line 70 sets the Paint object to Color.YELLOW. Lines 71–72 set the Stroke object to a new BasicStroke. The line will be 4 pixels wide and will have rounded ends (BasicStroke.CAP_ROUND). If lines join together (as in a rectangle at the corners), their joining will be rounded (BasicStroke.JOIN_ROUND). The dashes argument specifies the dash lengths for the line. The last argument indicates the starting index in the dashes array for the first dash in the pattern. Line 73 then draws a line with the current Stroke.

Creating Your Own Shapes with General Paths

Next we present a general path—a shape constructed from straight lines and complex curves. A general path is represented with an object of class GeneralPath (package java.awt.geom). The application of Figs. 12.31 and 12.32 demonstrates drawing a general path in the shape of a five-pointed star.

```
 1   // Fig. 12.31: Shapes2JPanel.java
 2   // Demonstrating a general path.
 3   import java.awt.Color;
 4   import java.awt.Graphics;
 5   import java.awt.Graphics2D;
 6   import java.awt.geom.GeneralPath;
 7   import java.util.Random;
 8   import javax.swing.JPanel;
 9
10   public class Shapes2JPanel extends JPanel
11   {
12      // draw general paths
13      public void paintComponent( Graphics g )
14      {
15         super.paintComponent( g ); // call superclass's paintComponent
16         Random random = new Random(); // get random number generator
17
18         int xPoints[] = { 55, 67, 109, 73, 83, 55, 27, 37, 1, 43 };
19         int yPoints[] = { 0, 36, 36, 54, 96, 72, 96, 54, 36, 36 };
20
21         Graphics2D g2d = ( Graphics2D ) g;
22         GeneralPath star = new GeneralPath(); // create GeneralPath object
23
24         // set the initial coordinate of the General Path
25         star.moveTo( xPoints[ 0 ], yPoints[ 0 ] );
26
27         // create the star--this does not draw the star
28         for ( int count = 1; count < xPoints.length; count++ )
29            star.lineTo( xPoints[ count ], yPoints[ count ] );
30
31         star.closePath(); // close the shape
32
33         g2d.translate( 200, 200 ); // translate the origin to (200, 200)
34
35         // rotate around origin and draw stars in random colors
36         for ( int count = 1; count <= 20; count++ )
37         {
38            g2d.rotate( Math.PI / 10.0 ); // rotate coordinate system
39
40            // set random drawing color
41            g2d.setColor( new Color( random.nextInt( 256 ),
42               random.nextInt( 256 ), random.nextInt( 256 ) ) );
43
44            g2d.fill( star ); // draw filled star
45         } // end for
46      } // end method paintComponent
47   } // end class Shapes2JPanel
```

Fig. 12.31 | Java 2D general paths.

Lines 18–19 declare two int arrays representing the *x*- and *y*-coordinates of the points in the star. Line 22 creates GeneralPath object star. Line 25 uses GeneralPath method moveTo to specify the first point in the star. The for statement in lines 28–29 uses GeneralPath method lineTo to draw a line to the next point in the star. Each new call to

```
1   // Fig. 12.32: Shapes2.java
2   // Demonstrating a general path.
3   import java.awt.Color;
4   import javax.swing.JFrame;
5
6   public class Shapes2
7   {
8       // execute application
9       public static void main( String args[] )
10      {
11          // create frame for Shapes2JPanel
12          JFrame frame = new JFrame( "Drawing 2D Shapes" );
13          frame.setDefaultCloseOperation( JFrame.EXIT_ON_CLOSE );
14
15          Shapes2JPanel shapes2JPanel = new Shapes2JPanel();
16          frame.add( shapes2JPanel ); // add shapes2JPanel to frame
17          frame.setBackground( Color.WHITE ); // set frame background color
18          frame.setSize( 400, 400 ); // set frame size
19          frame.setVisible( true ); // display frame
20      } // end main
21  } // end class Shapes2
```

Fig. 12.32 | Creating JFrame to display stars.

lineTo draws a line from the previous point to the current point. Line 31 uses General-Path method **closePath** to draw a line from the last point to the point specified in the last call to moveTo. This completes the general path.

Line 33 uses Graphics2D method **translate** to move the drawing origin to location (200, 200). All drawing operations now use location (200, 200) as (0, 0).

The for statement in lines 36–45 draws the star 20 times by rotating it around the new origin point. Line 38 uses Graphics2D method **rotate** to rotate the next displayed shape. The argument specifies the rotation angle in radians (with 360° = 2π radians). Line 44 uses Graphics2D method fill to draw a filled version of the star.

12.9 Wrap-Up

In this chapter, you learned how to use Java's graphics capabilities to produce colorful drawings. You learned how to specify the location of an object using Java's coordinate system, and how to draw on a window using the paintComponent method. You were introduced to class Color, and learned how to use this class to specify different colors using their RGB components. You used the JColorChooser dialog to allow users to select colors in a program. You then learned how to work with fonts when drawing text on a window. You learned how to create a Font object from a font name, style and size, as well as how to access the metrics of a font. From there, you learned how to draw various shapes on a window, such as rectangles (regular, rounded and 3D), ovals and polygons, as well as lines and arcs. You then used the Java 2D API to create more complex shapes and to fill them with gradients or patterns. The chapter concluded with a discussion of general paths, used to construct shapes from straight lines and complex curves. In the next chapter, you will learn about exceptions, useful for handling errors during a program's execution. Handling errors in this way provides for more robust programs.

Summary

Section 12.1 Introduction
- Java's coordinate system is a scheme for identifying every point on the screen.
- A coordinate pair is composed of an *x*-coordinate (the horizontal coordinate) and a *y*-coordinate (the vertical coordinate).
- Text and shapes are displayed on the screen by specifying coordinates. The coordinates are used to indicate where graphics should be displayed on a screen.
- Coordinate units are measured in pixels. A pixel is a display monitor's smallest unit of resolution.

Section 12.2 Graphics Contexts and Graphics Objects
- A Java graphics context enables drawing on the screen.
- Class Graphics contains methods for drawing strings, lines, rectangles and other shapes. Methods are also included for font manipulation and color manipulation.
- A Graphics object manages a graphics context and draws pixels on the screen that represent text and other graphical object (e.g., lines, ellipses, rectangles and other polygons).
- Class Graphics is an abstract class. This contributes to Java's portability—when Java is implemented on a platform, a subclass of Graphics is created that implements the drawing capabilities. This implementation is hidden from us by class Graphics, which supplies the interface that enables us to use graphics in a platform-independent manner.
- Class JComponent contains a paintComponent method that can be used to draw graphics in a Swing component.
- Method paintComponent takes as an argument a Graphics object that is passed to the paintComponent method by the system when a lightweight Swing component needs to be repainted.
- Method paintComponent is seldom called directly by the programmer because drawing graphics is an event-driven process. When an application executes, the application container calls method paintComponent. For paintComponent to be called again, an event must occur.
- When a JComponent is displayed, its paintComponent method is called.
- Programmers call method repaint to update the graphics drawn on the Swing component.

Section 12.3 Color Control

- Class `Color` declares methods and constants for manipulating colors in a Java program.

- Every color is created from a red, a green and a blue component. Together these components are called RGB values.

- The RGB components specify the amount of red, green and blue in a color, respectively. The larger the RGB value, the greater the amount of that particular color.

- `Color` methods `getRed`, `getGreen` and `getBlue` return integer values from 0 to 255 representing the amount of red, green and blue, respectively.

- `Graphics` method `getColor` returns a `Color` object representing the current drawing color.

- `Graphics` method `setColor` sets the current drawing color.

- `Graphics` method `fillRect` draws a rectangle filled by the current color of the `Graphics` object.

- `Graphics` method `drawString` draws a `String` in the current color.

- The `JColorChooser` GUI component enables application users to select colors.

- Class `JColorChooser` provides the `static` convenience method `showDialog` that creates a `JColorChooser` object, attaches it to a dialog box and displays the dialog.

- While the color chooser dialog is on the screen, the user cannot interact with the parent component. This type of dialog is called a modal dialog.

Section 12.4 Font Control

- Class `Font` contains methods and constants for manipulating fonts.

- Class `Font`'s constructor takes three arguments—the font name, font style and font size.

- A `Font`'s font style can be `Font.PLAIN`, `Font.ITALIC` or `Font.BOLD` (each is a `static` field of class `Font`). Font styles can be used in combination (e.g., `Font.ITALIC + Font.BOLD`).

- The font size is measured in points. A point is 1/72 of an inch.

- `Graphics` method `setFont` sets the drawing font in which text will be displayed.

- `Font` method `getStyle` returns an integer value representing the current `Font`'s style.

- `Font` method `getSize` returns the font size in points.

- `Font` method `getName` returns the current font name as a string.

- `Font` method `getFamily` returns the name of the font family to which the current font belongs. The name of the font family is platform specific.

- Class `FontMetrics` contains methods for obtaining font information.

- Font metrics include height, descent (the amount a character dips below the baseline), ascent (the amount a character rises above the baseline) and leading (the difference between the descent of one line of text and the ascent of the line of text below it—that is, the interline spacing).

Section 12.5 Drawing Lines, Rectangles and Ovals

- `Graphics` methods `fillRoundRect` and `drawRoundRect` draw rectangles with rounded corners.

- `Graphics` methods `draw3DRect` and `fill3DRect` draw three-dimensional rectangles.

- `Graphics` methods `drawOval` and `fillOval` draw ovals.

Section 12.6 Drawing Arcs

- An arc is drawn as a portion of an oval.

- Arcs sweep from a starting angle by the number of degrees specified by their arc angle.

- `Graphics` methods `drawArc` and `fillArc` are used for drawing arcs.

Section 12.7 Drawing Polygons and Polylines

- Class `Polygon` contains methods for creating polygons.

- Polygons are closed multisided shapes composed of straight-line segments.

- Polylines are a sequence of connected points.

- `Graphics` method `drawPolyline` displays a series of connected lines.

- `Graphics` methods `drawPolygon` and `fillPolygon` are used to draw polygons.

- `Polygon` method `addPoint` of class `Polygon` adds pairs of *x*- and *y*-coordinates to the `Polygon`.

Section 12.8 Java 2D API

- The Java 2D API provides advanced two-dimensional graphics capabilities for programmers who require detailed and complex graphical manipulations.

- Class `Graphics2D`, which extends class `Graphics`, is used for drawing with the Java 2D API.

- The Java 2D API contains several classes for drawing shapes, including `Line2D.Double`, `Rectangle2D.Double`, `RoundRectangle2D.Double`, `Arc2D.Double` and `Ellipse2D.Double`.

- Class `GradientPaint` helps draw a shape in gradually changing colors—called a gradient.

- `Graphics2D` method `fill` draws a filled `Shape` object—an object that implements interface `Shape`.

- Class `BasicStroke` helps specify the drawing characteristics of lines.

- `Graphics2D` method `draw` is used to draw a `Shape` object.

- Classes `GradientPaint` and `TexturePaint` help specify the characteristics for filling shapes with colors or patterns.

- A general path is a shape constructed from straight lines and complex curves.

- A general path is represented with an object of class `GeneralPath`.

- `GeneralPath` method `moveTo` specifies the first point in a general path.

- `GeneralPath` method `lineTo` draws a line to the next point in the path. Each new call to `lineTo` draws a line from the previous point to the current point.

- `GeneralPath` method `closePath` draws a line from the last point to the point specified in the last call to `moveTo`. This completes the general path.

- `Graphics2D` method `translate` is used to move the drawing origin to a new location.

- `Graphics2D` method `rotate` is used to rotate the next displayed shape.

Terminology

acyclic gradient	color manipulation
addPoint method of class Polygon	color swatches
arc	complex curve
arc angle	connected lines
ascent (font metrics)	coordinate system
baseline (font metrics)	createGraphics method of class BufferedImage
BasicStroke class	cyclic gradient
BOLD constant of class Font	dashed lines
bounding rectangle	descent (font metrics)
CAP_ROUND constant of class BasicStroke	draw method of class Graphics2D
clearRect method of class Graphics	draw3DRect method of class Graphics
closed polygons	drawArc method of class Graphics
closePath method of class GeneralPath	drawLine method of class Graphics
Color class	drawOval method of class Graphics

drawPolygon method of class Graphics
drawPolyline method of class Graphics
drawRect method of class Graphics
drawRoundRect method of class Graphics
drawString method of class Graphics
fill method of class Graphics2D
fill pattern
fill3DRect method of class Graphics
fillArc method of class Graphics
fillOval method of class Graphics
fillPolygon method of class Graphics
fillRect method of class Graphics
fillRoundRect method of class Graphics
Font class
font metric
FontMetrics class
general path
GeneralPath class
getAscent method of class FontMetrics
getBlue method of class Color
getColor method of class Graphics
getDescent method of class FontMetrics
getFamily method of class Font
getFont method of class Graphics
getFontMetrics method of class Graphics
getGreen method of class Color
getHeight method of class FontMetrics
getLeading method of class FontMetrics
getName method of class Font
getRed method of class Color
getSize method of class Font
getStyle method of class Font
gradient
GradientPaint class
Graphics class
graphics context
Graphics2D class
height (font metrics)
horizontal coordinate
isBold method of class Font
isItalic method of class Font
isPlain method of class Font
ITALIC constant of class Font
Java 2D API
JColorChooser class

JOIN_ROUND constant of class BasicStroke
leading (font metrics)
line join
LinearGradientPaint class
lineTo method of class GeneralPath
modal dialog
moveTo method of class GeneralPath
oval
oval bounded by a rectangle
Paint object
paintComponent method of class JComponent
pixel ("picture element")
PLAIN constant of class Font
point (font size)
polygon
Polygon class
polylines
raised rectangle
RadialGradientPaint class
repaint method of class JComponent
RGB value
rotate method of class Graphics2D
rounded rectangle
setBackground method of class Component
setColor method of class Graphics
setFont method of class Graphics
setPaint method of class Graphics2D
setStroke method of class Graphics2D
showDialog method of class JColorChooser
starting angle
Stroke object
sweep
TexturePaint class
three-dimensional rectangle
translate method of class Graphics2D
two-dimensional graphics
two-dimensional shapes
upper-left corner of a GUI component
upper-left x-coordinate
upper-left y-coordinate
vertical coordinate
x-axis
x-coordinate
y-axis
y-coordinate

Self-Review Exercises

12.1   Fill in the blanks in each of the following statements:
    a) In Java 2D, method _____ of class _____ sets the characteristics of a line used to
       draw a shape.

    b) Class _____ helps specify the fill for a shape such that the fill gradually changes from one color to another.

    c) The _____ method of class `Graphics` draws a line between two points.

    d) RGB is short for _____, _____ and _____.

    e) Font sizes are measured in units called _____.

    f) Class _____ helps specify the fill for a shape using a pattern drawn in a `Buffered-Image`.

12.2 State whether each of the following is *true* or *false*. If *false*, explain why.

    a) The first two arguments of `Graphics` method `drawOval` specify the center coordinate of the oval.

    b) In the Java coordinate system, *x*-values increase from left to right.

    c) `Graphics` method `fillPolygon` draws a filled polygon in the current color.

    d) `Graphics` method `drawArc` allows negative angles.

    e) `Graphics` method `getSize` returns the size of the current font in centimeters.

    f) Pixel coordinate (0, 0) is located at the exact center of the monitor.

12.3 Find the error(s) in each of the following and explain how to correct the error(s). Assume that g is a `Graphics` object.

```
a) g.setFont( "SansSerif" );
b) g.erase( x, y, w, h );     // clear rectangle at (x, y)
c) Font f = new Font( "Serif", Font.BOLDITALIC, 12 );
d) g.setColor( 255, 255, 0 ); // change color to yellow
```

Answers to Self-Review Exercises

12.1 a) `setStroke`, `Graphics2D`. b) `GradientPaint`. c) `drawLine`. d) red, green, blue. e) points. f) `TexturePaint`.

12.2 a) False. The first two arguments specify the upper-left corner of the bounding rectangle.

    b) True.

    c) True.

    d) True.

    e) False. Font sizes are measured in points.

    f) False. The coordinate (0,0) corresponds to the upper-left corner of a GUI component on which drawing occurs.

12.3 a) The `setFont` method takes a `Font` object as an argument—not a `String`.

    b) The `Graphics` class does not have an erase method. The `clearRect` method should be used.

    c) `Font.BOLDITALIC` is not a valid font style. To get a bold italic font, use `Font.BOLD` + `Font.ITALIC`.

    d) Method `setColor` takes a `Color` object as an argument, not three integers.

Exercises

12.4 *(Concentric Circles Using Method drawArc)* Write an application that draws a series of eight concentric circles. The circles should be separated by 10 pixels. Use `Graphics` method `drawArc`.

12.5 *(Concentric Circles Using Class Ellipse2D.Double)* Modify your solution to Exercise 12.4 to draw the ovals by using class `Ellipse2D.Double` and method draw of class `Graphics2D`.

12.6 *(Random Lines Using Class Line2D.Double)* Modify your solution to Exercise 12.5 to draw random lines, in random colors and random line thicknesses. Use class `Line2D.Double` and method draw of class `Graphics2D` to draw the lines.

12.7 *(Grid Using Method drawLine)* Write an application that draws an 8-by-8 grid. Use Graphics method drawLine.

12.8 *(Grid Using Class Line2D.Double)* Modify your solution to Exercise 12.7 to draw the grid using instances of class Line2D.Double and method draw of class Graphics2D.

12.9 *(Grid Using Method drawRect)* Write an application that draws a 10-by-10 grid. Use the Graphics method drawRect.

12.10 *(Grid Using Class Rectangle2D.Double)* Modify your solution to Exercise 12.9 to draw the grid by using class Rectangle2D.Double and method draw of class Graphics2D.

12.11 *(Drawing Cubes)* Write an application that draws a cube. Use class GeneralPath and method draw of class Graphics2D.

12.12 *(Circles Using Class Ellipse2D.Double)* Write an application that asks the user to input the radius of a circle as a floating-point number and draws the circle, as well as the values of the circle's diameter, circumference and area. Use the value 3.14159 for π. [*Note:* You may also use the predefined constant Math.PI for the value of π. This constant is more precise than the value 3.14159. Class Math is declared in the java.lang package, so you do not need to import it.] Use the following formulas (*r* is the radius):

$$diameter = 2r$$
$$circumference = 2\pi r$$
$$area = \pi r^2$$

The user should also be prompted for a set of coordinates in addition to the radius. Then draw the circle, and display the circle's diameter, circumference and area, using an Ellipse2D.Double object to represent the circle and method draw of class Graphics2D to display the circle.

12.13 *(Screen Saver)* Write an application that simulates a screen saver. The application should randomly draw lines using method drawLine of class Graphics. After drawing 100 lines, the application should clear itself and start drawing lines again. To allow the program to draw continuously, place a call to repaint as the last line in method paintComponent. Do you notice any problems with this on your system?

12.14 *(Screen Saver Using Timer)* Package javax.swing contains a class called Timer that is capable of calling method actionPerformed of interface ActionListener at a fixed time interval (specified in milliseconds). Modify your solution to Exercise 12.13 to remove the call to repaint from method paintComponent. Declare your class to implement ActionListener. (The actionPerformed method should simply call repaint.) Declare an instance variable of type Timer called timer in your class. In the constructor for your class, write the following statements:

```
timer = new Timer( 1000, this );
timer.start();
```

This creates an instance of class Timer that will call this object's actionPerformed method every 1000 milliseconds (i.e., every second).

12.15 *(Turtle Graphics)* Modify your solution to Exercise 7.21—*Turtle Graphics*—to add a graphical user interface using JTextFields and JButtons. Draw lines rather than asterisks (*). When the turtle graphics program specifies a move, translate the number of positions into a number of pixels on the screen by multiplying the number of positions by 10 (or any value you choose). Implement the drawing with Java 2D API features.

12.16 *(Knight's Tour)* Produce a graphical version of the Knight's Tour problem (Exercise 7.22, Exercise 7.23 and Exercise 7.26). As each move is made, the appropriate cell of the chessboard should be updated with the proper move number. If the result of the program is a *full tour* or a *closed* *tour*, the program should display an appropriate message. If you like, use class Timer (see Exercise 12.14) to help animate the Knight's Tour.

12.17 *(Drawing Spirals)* Write an application that uses Graphics method drawPolyline to draw a spiral similar to the one shown in Fig. 12.33.

12.18 *(Selecting Shapes)* Write an application that allows the user to select a shape from a JCombo-Box and draws it 20 times with random locations and dimensions in method paintComponent. The first item in the JComboBox should be the default shape that is displayed the first time paintComponent is called.

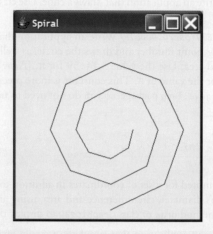

Fig. 12.33 | Spiral drawn using method drawPolyline.

12.19 *(Random Colors)* Modify Exercise 12.18 to draw each of the 20 randomly sized shapes in a randomly selected color. Use all 13 predefined Color objects in an array of Colors.

12.20 *(JColorChooser Dialog)* Modify Exercise 12.18 to allow the user to select the color in which shapes should be drawn from a JColorChooser dialog.

(Optional) GUI and Graphics Case Study: Adding Java2D

12.21 Java2D introduces many new capabilities for creating unique and impressive graphics. We will add a small subset of these features to the drawing application you created in Exercise 11.18. In this version of the drawing application, you will enable the user to specify gradients for filling shapes and to change stroke characteristics for drawing lines and outlines of shapes. The user will be able to choose which colors compose the gradient and set the width and dash length of the stroke.

First, you must update the MyShape hierarchy to support Java2D functionality. Make the following changes in class MyShape:

a) Change abstract method draw's parameter type from Graphics to Graphics2D.

b) Change all variables of type Color to type Paint to enable support for gradients. [*Note:* Recall that class Color implements interface Paint.]

c) Add an instance variable of type Stroke in class MyShape and a Stroke parameter in the constructor to initialize the new instance variable. The default stroke should be an instance of class BasicStroke.

Classes MyLine, MyBoundedShape, MyOval and MyRect should each add a Stroke parameter to their constructors. In the draw methods, each shape should set the Paint and the Stroke before drawing or filling a shape. Since Graphics2D is a subclass of Graphics, we can continue to use Graphics methods drawLine, drawOval, fillOval, and so on. to draw the shapes. When these methods are called, they will draw the appropriate shape using the specified Paint and Stroke settings.

Next, you will update the DrawPanel to handle the Java2D features. Change all Color variables to Paint variables. Declare an instance variable currentStroke of type Stroke and provide a *set* method for it. Update the calls to the individual shape constructors to include the Paint and Stroke arguments. In method paintComponent, cast the Graphics reference to type Graphics2D and use the Graphics2D reference in each call to MyShape method draw.

Next, make the new Java2D features accessible from the GUI. Create a JPanel of GUI components for setting the Java2D options. Add these components at the top of the DrawFrame below the panel that currently contains the standard shape controls (see Fig. 12.34). These GUI components should include:

a) A check box to specify whether to paint using a gradient

b) Two JButtons that each show a JColorChooser dialog to allow the user to choose the first and second color in the gradient. (These will replace the JComboBox used for choosing the color in Exercise 11.18.)

c) A text field for entering the Stroke width

d) A text field for entering the Stroke dash length

e) A check box for selecting whether to draw a dashed or solid line

If the user selects to draw with a gradient, set the Paint on the DrawPanel to be a gradient of the two colors chosen by the user. The expression

```
new GradientPaint( 0, 0, color1, 50, 50, color2, true ) )
```

creates a GradientPaint that cycles diagonally from the upper-left to the bottom-right every 50 pixels. Variables color1 and color2 represent the colors chosen by the user. If the user does not select to use a gradient, then simply set the Paint on the DrawPanel to be the first Color chosen by the user.

For strokes, if the user chooses a solid line, then create the Stroke with the expression

```
new BasicStroke( width, BasicStroke.CAP_ROUND, BasicStroke.JOIN_ROUND )
```

where variable width is the width specified by the user in the line-width text field. If the user chooses a dashed line, then create the Stroke with the expression

```
new BasicStroke( width, BasicStroke.CAP_ROUND, BasicStroke.JOIN_ROUND,
    10, dashes, 0 )
```

where width again is the width in the line-width field, and dashes is an array with one element whose value is the length specified in the dash-length field. The Panel and Stroke objects should be passed to the shape object's constructor when the shape is created in DrawPanel.

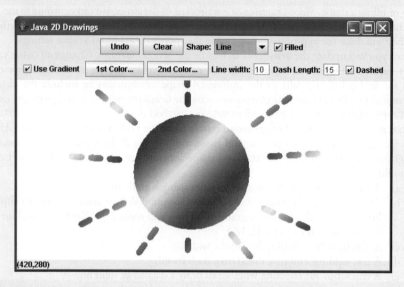

Fig. 12.34 | Drawing with Java2D.

13

Exception Handling

It is common sense to take a method and try it. If it fails, admit it frankly and try another. But above all, try something.

—Franklin Delano Roosevelt

*O! throw away the worser part of it,
And live the purer with the other half.*

—William Shakespeare

If they're running and they don't look where they're going I have to come out from somewhere and catch them.

—Jerome David Salinger

O infinite virtue! com'st thou smiling from the world's great snare uncaught?

—William Shakespeare

OBJECTIVES

In this chapter you will learn:

- How exception and error handling works.

- To use **try**, **throw** and **catch** to detect, indicate and handle exceptions, respectively.

- To use the **finally** block to release resources.

- How stack unwinding enables exceptions not caught in one scope to be caught in another scope.

- How stack traces help in debugging.

- How exceptions are arranged in an exception-class hierarchy.

- To declare new exception classes.

- To create chained exceptions that maintain complete stack-trace information.

13.1 Introduction

In this chapter, we introduce exception handling. An exception is an indication of a problem that occurs during a program's execution. The name "exception" implies that the problem occurs infrequently—if the "rule" is that a statement normally executes correctly, then the "exception to the rule" is that a problem occurs. Exception handling enables you to create applications that can resolve (or handle) exceptions. In many cases, handling an exception allows a program to continue executing as if no problem had been encountered. A more severe problem could prevent a program from continuing normal execution, instead requiring it to notify the user of the problem before terminating in a controlled manner. The features presented in this chapter enable programmers to write robust and fault-tolerant programs (i.e., programs that are able to deal with problems that may arise and continue executing). The style and details of Java exception handling are based in part on Andrew Koenig's and Bjarne Stroustrup's paper, "Exception Handling for C++ (revised)."[1]

 Error-Prevention Tip 13.1

Exception handling helps improve a program's fault tolerance.

You have already been briefly introduced to exceptions in earlier chapters. In Chapter 7 you learned that an `ArrayIndexOutOfBoundsException` occurs when an attempt is made to access an element past the end of an array. Such a problem may occur if there is an "off-by-one" error in a `for` statement that manipulates an array. In Chapter 10, we introduced the `ClassCastException`, which occurs when an attempt is made to cast an object that does not have an *is-a* relationship with the type specified in the cast operator. Chapter 11

---

1. Koenig, A., and B. Stroustrup. "Exception Handling for C++ (revised)," *Proceedings of the Usenix C++ Conference*, pp. 149–176, San Francisco, April 1990.

briefly mentioned the `NullPointerException`, which occurs whenever a `null` reference is used where an object is expected (for example, when an attempt is made to attach a GUI component to a `Container`, but the GUI component has not yet been created). Throughout this text you have also used class `Scanner`—which, as you will see in this chapter, also may cause exceptions.

The chapter begins with an overview of exception-handling concepts, then demonstrates basic exception-handling techniques. We show these techniques in action by handling an exception that occurs when a method attempts to divide an integer by zero. Next, we introduce several classes at the top of Java's class hierarchy for exception handling. As you will see, only classes that extend `Throwable` (package `java.lang`) directly or indirectly can be used with exception handling. We then discuss the chained exception feature that allows programmers to wrap information about an exception that occurred in another exception object to provide more detailed information about a problem in a program. Next, we discuss additional exception-handling issues, such as how to handle exceptions that occur in a constructor. We introduce preconditions and postconditions, which must be true when your methods are called and when those methods return, respectively. Finally, we present assertions, which programmers use at development time to help debug their code.

13.2 Exception-Handling Overview

Programs frequently test conditions to determine how program execution should proceed. Consider the following pseudocode:

> *Perform a task*
>
> *If the preceding task did not execute correctly*
> *Perform error processing*
>
> *Perform next task*
>
> *If the preceding task did not execute correctly*
> *Perform error processing*
>
> *...*

In this pseudocode, we begin by performing a task; then we test whether that task executed correctly. If not, we perform error processing. Otherwise, we continue with the next task. Although this form of error handling works, intermixing program logic with error-handling logic can make programs difficult to read, modify, maintain and debug—especially in large applications.

Performance Tip 13.1

If the potential problems occur infrequently, intermixing program and error-handling logic can degrade a program's performance, because the program must perform (potentially frequent) tests to determine whether the task executed correctly and the next task can be performed.

Exception handling enables programmers to remove error-handling code from the "main line" of the program's execution, improving program clarity and enhancing modifiability. You can decide to handle any exceptions you choose—all exceptions, all exceptions of a certain type or all exceptions of a group of related types (i.e., exception types that are related through an inheritance hierarchy). Such flexibility reduces the likelihood that errors will be overlooked, thus making programs more robust.

With programming languages that do not support exception handling, programmers often delay writing error-processing code or sometimes forget to include it. This results in less robust software products. Java enables programmers to deal with exception handling easily from the inception of a project.

13.3 Example: Divide by Zero without Exception Handling

First we demonstrate what happens when errors arise in an application that does not use exception handling. Figure 13.1 prompts the user for two integers and passes them to method quotient, which calculates the quotient and returns an int result. In this example, we'll see that exceptions are thrown (i.e., the exception occurs) when a method detects a problem and is unable to handle it.

The first of the three sample executions in Fig. 13.1 shows a successful division. In the second sample execution, the user enters the value 0 as the denominator. Notice that sev-

```java
1   // Fig. 13.1: DivideByZeroNoExceptionHandling.java
2   // An application that attempts to divide by zero.
3   import java.util.Scanner;
4
5   public class DivideByZeroNoExceptionHandling
6   {
7      // demonstrates throwing an exception when a divide-by-zero occurs
8      public static int quotient( int numerator, int denominator )
9      {
10        return numerator / denominator; // possible division by zero
11     } // end method quotient
12
13     public static void main( String args[] )
14     {
15        Scanner scanner = new Scanner( System.in ); // scanner for input
16
17        System.out.print( "Please enter an integer numerator: " );
18        int numerator = scanner.nextInt();
19        System.out.print( "Please enter an integer denominator: " );
20        int denominator = scanner.nextInt();
21
22        int result = quotient( numerator, denominator );
23        System.out.printf(
24           "\nResult: %d / %d = %d\n", numerator, denominator, result );
25     } // end main
26  } // end class DivideByZeroNoExceptionHandling
```

```
Please enter an integer numerator: 100
Please enter an integer denominator: 7

Result: 100 / 7 = 14
```

Fig. 13.1 | Integer division without exception handling. (Part 1 of 2.)

```
Please enter an integer numerator: 100
Please enter an integer denominator: 0
Exception in thread "main" java.lang.ArithmeticException: / by zero
        at DivideByZeroNoExceptionHandling.quotient(
            DivideByZeroNoExceptionHandling.java:10)
        at DivideByZeroNoExceptionHandling.main(
            DivideByZeroNoExceptionHandling.java:22)
```

```
Please enter an integer numerator: 100
Please enter an integer denominator: hello
Exception in thread "main" java.util.InputMismatchException
        at java.util.Scanner.throwFor(Unknown Source)
        at java.util.Scanner.next(Unknown Source)
        at java.util.Scanner.nextInt(Unknown Source)
        at java.util.Scanner.nextInt(Unknown Source)
        at DivideByZeroNoExceptionHandling.main(
           DivideByZeroNoExceptionHandling.java:20)
```

Fig. 13.1 | Integer division without exception handling. (Part 2 of 2.)

eral lines of information are displayed in response to this invalid input. This information is known as the stack trace, which includes the name of the exception (java.lang.ArithmeticException) in a descriptive message that indicates the problem that occurred and the complete method-call stack (i.e., the call chain) at the time the exception occurred. The stack trace includes the path of execution that led to the exception method by method. This information helps in debugging a program. The first line specifies that an ArithmeticException has occurred. The text after the name of the exception ("/ by zero") indicates that this exception occurred as a result of an attempt to divide by zero. Java does not allow division by zero in integer arithmetic. [*Note:* Java *does* allow division by zero with floating-point values. Such a calculation results in the value infinity, which is represented in Java as a floating-point value (but actually displays as the string Infinity).] When division by zero in integer arithmetic occurs, Java throws an ArithmeticException. ArithmeticExceptions can arise from a number of different problems in arithmetic, so the extra data ("/ by zero") gives us more information about this specific exception.

Starting from the last line of the stack trace, we see that the exception was detected in line 22 of method main. Each line of the stack trace contains the class name and method (DivideByZeroNoExceptionHandling.main) followed by the file name and line number (DivideByZeroNoExceptionHandling.java:22). Moving up the stack trace, we see that the exception occurs in line 10, in method quotient. The top row of the call chain indicates the throw point—the initial point at which the exception occurs. The throw point of this exception is in line 10 of method quotient.

In the third execution, the user enters the string "hello" as the denominator. Notice again that a stack trace is displayed. This informs us that an InputMismatchException has occurred (package java.util). Our prior examples that read numeric values from the user assumed that the user would input a proper integer value. However, users sometimes make mistakes and input noninteger values. An InputMismatchException occurs when Scanner method nextInt receives a string that does not represent a valid integer. Starting from the end of the stack trace, we see that the exception was detected in line 20 of method main.

Moving up the stack trace, we see that the exception occurs in method `nextInt`. Notice that in place of the file name and line number, we are provided with the text `Unknown Source`. This means that the JVM does not have access to the source code for where the exception occurred.

Notice that in the sample executions of Fig. 13.1 when exceptions occur and stack traces are displayed, the program also exits. This does not always occur in Java—sometimes a program may continue even though an exception has occurred and a stack trace has been printed. In such cases, the application may produce unexpected results. The next section demonstrates how to handle these exceptions and keep the program running successfully.

In Fig. 13.1 both types of exceptions were detected in method `main`. In the next example, we will see how to handle these exceptions to enable the program to run to normal completion.

13.4 Example: Handling ArithmeticExceptions and InputMismatchExceptions

The application in Fig. 13.2, which is based on Fig. 13.1, uses exception handling to process any `ArithmeticExceptions` and `InputMistmatchExceptions` that arise. The application still prompts the user for two integers and passes them to method `quotient`, which calculates the quotient and returns an `int` result. This version of the application uses exception handling so that if the user makes a mistake, the program catches and handles (i.e., deals with) the exception—in this case, allowing the user to try to enter the input again.

The first sample execution in Fig. 13.2 shows a successful execution that does not encounter any problems. In the second execution, the user enters a zero denominator and an `ArithmeticException` exception occurs. In the third execution, the user enters the string `"hello"` as the denominator, and an `InputMismatchException` occurs. For each exception, the user is informed of the mistake and asked to try again, then is prompted for two new integers. In each sample execution, the program runs successfully to completion.

```
1   // Fig. 13.2: DivideByZeroWithExceptionHandling.java
2   // An exception-handling example that checks for divide-by-zero.
3   import java.util.InputMismatchException;
4   import java.util.Scanner;
5
6   public class DivideByZeroWithExceptionHandling
7   {
8      // demonstrates throwing an exception when a divide-by-zero occurs
9      public static int quotient( int numerator, int denominator )
10         throws ArithmeticException
11     {
12        return numerator / denominator; // possible division by zero
13     } // end method quotient
14
15     public static void main( String args[] )
16     {
```

Fig. 13.2 | Handling `ArithmeticExceptions` and `InputMismatchExceptions`. (Part 1 of 3.)

```
17          Scanner scanner = new Scanner( System.in ); // scanner for input
18          boolean continueLoop = true; // determines if more input is needed
19
20          do
21          {
22             try // read two numbers and calculate quotient
23             {
24                System.out.print( "Please enter an integer numerator: " );
25                int numerator = scanner.nextInt();
26                System.out.print( "Please enter an integer denominator: " );
27                int denominator = scanner.nextInt();
28
29                int result = quotient( numerator, denominator );
30                System.out.printf( "\nResult: %d / %d = %d\n", numerator,
31                   denominator, result );
32                continueLoop = false; // input successful; end looping
33             } // end try
34             catch ( InputMismatchException inputMismatchException )
35             {
36                System.err.printf( "\nException: %s\n",
37                   inputMismatchException );
38                scanner.nextLine(); // discard input so user can try again
39                System.out.println(
40                   "You must enter integers. Please try again.\n" );
41             } // end catch
42             catch ( ArithmeticException arithmeticException )
43             {
44                System.err.printf( "\nException: %s\n", arithmeticException );
45                System.out.println(
46                   "Zero is an invalid denominator. Please try again.\n" );
47             } // end catch
48          } while ( continueLoop ); // end do...while
49       } // end main
50    } // end class DivideByZeroWithExceptionHandling
```

```
Please enter an integer numerator: 100
Please enter an integer denominator: 7

Result: 100 / 7 = 14
```

```
Please enter an integer numerator: 100
Please enter an integer denominator: 0

Exception: java.lang.ArithmeticException: / by zero
Zero is an invalid denominator. Please try again.

Please enter an integer numerator: 100
Please enter an integer denominator: 7

Result: 100 / 7 = 14
```

Fig. 13.2 | Handling ArithmeticExceptions and InputMismatchExceptions. (Part 2 of 3.)

```
Please enter an integer numerator: 100
Please enter an integer denominator: hello

Exception: java.util.InputMismatchException
You must enter integers. Please try again.

Please enter an integer numerator: 100
Please enter an integer denominator: 7

Result: 100 / 7 = 14
```

Fig. 13.2 | Handling `ArithmeticExceptions` and `InputMismatchExceptions`. (Part 3 of 3.)

Class `InputMismatchException` is imported in line 3. Class `ArithmeticException` does not need to be imported because it is located in package `java.lang`. Method `main` (lines 15–49) creates a `Scanner` object at line 17. Line 18 creates the `boolean` variable continueLoop, which is true if the user has not yet entered valid input. Lines 20–48 repeatedly ask users for input until a valid input is received.

Enclosing Code in a *try* Block

Lines 22–33 contain a try block, which encloses the code that might `throw` an exception and the code that should not execute if an exception occurs (i.e., if an exception occurs, the remaining code in the try block will be skipped). A try block consists of the keyword try followed by a block of code enclosed in curly braces ({}). [*Note:* The term "try block" sometimes refers only to the block of code that follows the try keyword (not including the try keyword itself). For simplicity, we use the term "try block" to refer to the block of code that follows the try keyword, as well as the try keyword.] The statements that read the integers from the keyboard (lines 25 and 27) each use method nextInt to read an int value. Method nextInt throws an `InputMismatchException` if the value read in is not a valid integer.

The division that can cause an `ArithmeticException` is not performed in the try block. Rather, the call to method quotient (line 29) invokes the code that attempts the division (line 12); the JVM throws an `ArithmeticException` object when the denominator is zero.

Software Engineering Observation 13.1

Exceptions may surface through explicitly mentioned code in a try block, through calls to other methods, through deeply nested method calls initiated by code in a try block or from the Java Virtual Machine as it executes Java bytecodes.

Catching Exceptions

The try block in this example is followed by two catch blocks—one that handles an InputMismatchException (lines 34–41) and one that handles an `ArithmeticException` (lines 42–47). A catch block (also called a catch clause or exception handler) catches (i.e., receives) and handles an exception. A catch block begins with the keyword catch and is followed by a parameter in parentheses (called the exception parameter, discussed shortly) and a block of code enclosed in curly braces. [*Note:* The term "catch clause" is sometimes used to refer to the keyword catch followed by a block of code, where the term "catch block" refers to only the block of code following the `catch` keyword, but not including it. For simplicity, we use the term "catch block" to refer to the block of code following the `catch` keyword, as well as the keyword itself.]

At least one `catch` block or a **`finally` block** (discussed in Section 13.7) must immediately follow the `try` block. Each `catch` block specifies in parentheses an **exception parameter** that identifies the exception type the handler can process. When an exception occurs in a `try` block, the `catch` block that executes is the one whose type matches the type of the exception that occurred (i.e., the type in the `catch` block matches the thrown exception type exactly or is a superclass of it). The exception parameter's name enables the `catch` block to interact with a caught exception object—e.g., to implicitly invoke the caught exception's `toString` method (as in lines 37 and 44), which displays basic information about the exception. Line 38 of the first `catch` block calls `Scanner` method `nextLine`. Because an `InputMismatchException` occurred, the call to method `nextInt` never successfully read in the user's data—so we read that input with a call to method `nextLine`. We do not do anything with the input at this point, because we know that it is invalid. Each `catch` block displays an error message and asks the user to try again. After either `catch` block terminates, the user is prompted for input. We will soon take a deeper look at how this flow of control works in exception handling.

Common Programming Error 13.1

It is a syntax error to place code between a `try` block and its corresponding `catch` blocks.

Common Programming Error 13.2

Each `catch` block can have only a single parameter—specifying a comma-separated list of exception parameters is a syntax error.

An **uncaught exception** is an exception that occurs for which there are no matching `catch` blocks. You saw uncaught exceptions in the second and third outputs of Fig. 13.1. Recall that when exceptions occurred in that example, the application terminated early (after displaying the exception's stack trace). This does not always occur as a result of uncaught exceptions. As you will learn in Chapter 23, Multithreading, Java uses a multithreaded model of program execution. Each **thread** is a parallel activity. One program can have many threads. If a program has only one thread, an uncaught exception will cause the program to terminate. If a program has multiple threads, an uncaught exception will terminate only the thread where the exception occurred. In such programs, however, certain threads may rely on others and if one thread terminates due to an uncaught exception, there may be adverse effects to the rest of the program.

Termination Model of Exception Handling

If an exception occurs in a `try` block (such as an `InputMismatchException` being thrown as a result of the code at line 25 of Fig. 13.2), the `try` block terminates immediately and program control transfers to the first of the following `catch` blocks in which the exception parameter's type matches the thrown exception's type. In Fig. 13.2, the first `catch` block catches `InputMismatchExceptions` (which occur if invalid input is entered) and the second `catch` block catches `ArithmeticExceptions` (which occur if an attempt is made to divide by zero). After the exception is handled, program control does not return to the throw point because the `try` block has expired (and its local variables have been lost). Rather, control resumes after the last catch block. This is known as the **termination model of exception handling**. [*Note:* Some languages use the **resumption model of exception handling**, in which, after an exception is handled, control resumes just after the throw point.]

Common Programming Error 13.3

Logic errors can occur if you assume that after an exception is handled, control will return to the first statement after the throw point.

Error-Prevention Tip 13.2

With exception handling, a program can continue executing (rather than terminating) after dealing with a problem. This helps ensure the kind of robust applications that contribute to what is called mission-critical computing or business-critical computing.

Notice that we name our exception parameters (inputMismatchException and arithmeticException) based on their type. Java programmers often simply use the letter e as the name of their exception parameters.

Good Programming Practice 13.1

Using an exception parameter name that reflects the parameter's type promotes clarity by reminding the programmer of the type of exception being handled.

After executing a catch block, this program's flow of control proceeds to the first statement after the last catch block (line 48 in this case). The condition in the do...while statement is true (variable continueLoop contains its initial value of true), so control returns to the beginning of the loop and the user is once again prompted for input. This control statement will loop until valid input is entered. At that point, program control reaches line 32, which assigns false to variable continueLoop. The try block then terminates. If no exceptions are thrown in the try block, the catch blocks are skipped and control continues with the first statement after the catch blocks (we'll learn about another possibility when we discuss the finally block in Section 13.7). Now the condition for the do...while loop is false, and method main ends.

The try block and its corresponding catch and/or finally blocks together form a **try statement**. It is important not to confuse the terms "try block" and "try statement"—the term "try block" refers to the keyword try followed by a block of code, while "try statement" includes the try block as well as the following catch blocks and/or finally block.

As with any other block of code, when a try block terminates, local variables declared in the block are destroyed. When a catch block terminates, local variables declared within the catch block (including the exception parameter of that catch block) also go out of scope and are destroyed. Any remaining catch blocks in the try statement are ignored, and execution resumes at the first line of code after the try...catch sequence—this will be a finally block, if one is present.

Using the *throws Clause*

Now let us examine method quotient (Fig. 13.2; lines 9–13). The portion of the method declaration located at line 10 is known as a **throws clause**. A throws clause specifies the exceptions the method throws. This clause appears after the method's parameter list and before the method's body. It contains a comma-separated list of the exceptions that the method will throw if a problem occurs. Such exceptions may be thrown by statements in the method's body or by methods called from the body. A method can throw exceptions of the classes listed in its throws clause or of their subclasses. We have added the throws clause to this application to indicate to the rest of the program that this method may throw an ArithmeticException. Clients of method quotient are thus informed that the method may throw an ArithmeticException. You will learn more about the throws clause in Section 13.6.

Error-Prevention Tip 13.3

If you know that a method might throw an exception, include appropriate exception-handling code in your program to make it more robust.

Error-Prevention Tip 13.4

Read the online API documentation for a method before using that method in a program. The documentation specifies the exceptions thrown by the method (if any) and indicates reasons why such exceptions may occur. Then provide for handling those exceptions in your program.

Error-Prevention Tip 13.5

Read the online API documentation for an exception class before writing exception-handling code for that type of exception. The documentation for an exception class typically contains potential reasons that such exceptions occur during program execution.

When line 12 executes, if the denominator is zero, the JVM throws an ArithmeticException object. This object will be caught by the catch block at lines 42–47, which displays basic information about the exception by implicitly invoking the exception's toString method, then asks the user to try again.

If the denominator is not zero, method quotient performs the division and returns the result to the point of invocation of method quotient in the try block (line 29). Lines 30–31 display the result of the calculation and line 32 sets continueLoop to false. In this case, the try block completes successfully, so the program skips the catch blocks and fails the condition at line 48, and method main completes execution normally.

Note that when quotient throws an ArithmeticException, quotient terminates and does not return a value, and quotient's local variables go out of scope (and the variables are destroyed). If quotient contained local variables that were references to objects and there were no other references to those objects, the objects would be marked for garbage collection. Also, when an exception occurs, the try block from which quotient was called terminates before lines 30–32 can execute. Here, too, if local variables were created in the try block prior to the exception being thrown, these variables would go out of scope.

If an InputMismatchException is generated by lines 25 or 27, the try block terminates and execution continues with the catch block at lines 34–41. In this case, method quotient is not called. Then method main continues after the last catch block (line 48).

13.5 When to Use Exception Handling

Exception handling is designed to process synchronous errors, which occur when a statement executes. Common examples we will see throughout the book are out-of-range array indices, arithmetic overflow (i.e., a value outside the representable range of values), division by zero, invalid method parameters, thread interruption and unsuccessful memory allocation (due to lack of memory). Exception handling is not designed to process problems associated with asynchronous events (e.g., disk I/O completions, network message arrivals, mouse clicks and keystrokes), which occur in parallel with, and independent of, the program's flow of control.

Software Engineering Observation 13.2

Incorporate your exception-handling strategy into your system from the inception of the design process. Including effective exception handling after a system has been implemented can be difficult.

Software Engineering Observation 13.3

Exception handling provides a single, uniform technique for processing problems. This helps programmers working on large projects understand each other's error-processing code.

Software Engineering Observation 13.4

Avoid using exception handling as an alternate form of flow of control. These "additional" exceptions can "get in the way" of genuine error-type exceptions.

Software Engineering Observation 13.5

Exception handling simplifies combining software components and enables them to work together effectively by enabling predefined components to communicate problems to application-specific components, which can then process the problems in an application-specific manner.

13.6 Java Exception Hierarchy

All Java exception classes inherit, either directly or indirectly, from class `Exception`, forming an inheritance hierarchy. Programmers can extend this hierarchy to create their own exception classes.

Figure 13.3 shows a small portion of the inheritance hierarchy for class `Throwable` (a subclass of `Object`), which is the superclass of class `Exception`. Only `Throwable` objects can be used with the exception-handling mechanism. Class `Throwable` has two subclasses: `Exception` and `Error`. Class `Exception` and its subclasses—for instance, `RuntimeException` (package `java.lang`) and `IOException` (package `java.io`)—represent exceptional situations that can occur in a Java program and that can be caught by the application. Class `Error` and its subclasses (e.g., `OutOfMemoryError`) represent abnormal situations that could happen in the JVM. Errors happen infrequently and should not be caught by applications—it is usually not possible for applications to recover from Errors. [*Note:* The Java exception hierarchy contains hundreds of classes. Information about Java's exception classes can be found throughout the Java API. The documentation for class `Throwable` can be found at `java.sun.com/javase/6/docs/api/java/lang/Throwable.html`. From there, you can look at this class's subclasses to get more information about Java's Exceptions and Errors.]

Java distinguishes between two categories of exceptions: checked exceptions and unchecked exceptions. This distinction is important, because the Java compiler enforces a catch-or-declare requirement for checked exceptions. An exception's type determines whether the exception is checked or unchecked. All exception types that are direct or indirect subclasses of class `RuntimeException` (package `java.lang`) are unchecked exceptions.

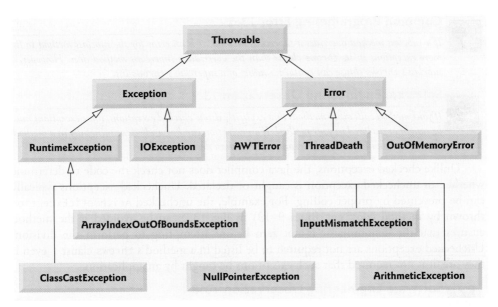

Fig. 13.3 | Portion of class `Throwable`'s inheritance hierarchy.

This includes exceptions you have seen already, such as `ArrayIndexOutOfBoundsExceptions` and `ArithmeticExceptions` (shown in Fig. 13.3). All classes that inherit from class `Exception` but not class `RuntimeException` are considered to be checked exceptions. Classes that inherit from class `Error` are considered to be unchecked. The compiler *checks* each method call and method declaration to determine whether the method throws checked exceptions. If so, the compiler ensures that the checked exception is caught or is declared in a `throws` clause. Recall from Section 13.4 that the `throws` clause specifies the exceptions a method throws. Such exceptions are not caught in the method's body. To satisfy the *catch* part of the catch-or-declare requirement, the code that generates the exception must be wrapped in a `try` block and must provide a `catch` handler for the checked-exception type (or one of its superclass types). To satisfy the *declare* part of the catch-or-declare requirement, the method containing the code that generates the exception must provide a `throws` clause containing the checked-exception type after its parameter list and before its method body. If the catch-or-declare requirement is not satisfied, the compiler will issue an error message indicating that the exception must be caught or declared. This forces programmers to think about the problems that may occur when a method that throws checked exceptions is called. Exception classes are defined to be checked when they are considered important enough to catch or declare.

Software Engineering Observation 13.6

Programmers are forced to deal with checked exceptions. This results in more robust code than would be created if programmers were able to simply ignore the exceptions.

Common Programming Error 13.4

A compilation error occurs if a method explicitly attempts to throw a checked exception (or calls another method that throws a checked exception) and that exception is not listed in that method's throws clause.

Common Programming Error 13.5

If a subclass method overrides a superclass method, it is an error for the subclass method to list more exceptions in its throws clause than the overridden superclass method does. However, a subclass's throws clause can contain a subset of a superclass's throws list.

Software Engineering Observation 13.7

If your method calls other methods that explicitly throw checked exceptions, those exceptions must be caught or declared in your method. If an exception can be handled meaningfully in a method, the method should catch the exception rather than declare it.

Unlike checked exceptions, the Java compiler does not check the code to determine whether an unchecked exception is caught or declared. Unchecked exceptions typically can be prevented by proper coding. For example, the unchecked ArithmeticException thrown by method quotient (lines 9–13) in Fig. 13.2 can be avoided if the method ensures that the denominator is not zero before attempting to perform the division. Unchecked exceptions are not required to be listed in a method's throws clause—even if they are, it is not required that such exceptions be caught by an application.

Software Engineering Observation 13.8

Although the compiler does not enforce the catch-or-declare requirement for unchecked exceptions, provide appropriate exception-handling code when it is known that such exceptions might occur. For example, a program should process the NumberFormatException from Integer method parseInt, even though NumberFormatException (a subclass of RuntimeException) is an unchecked exception type. This makes your programs more robust.

Exception classes can be derived from a common superclass. If a catch handler is written to catch superclass-type exception objects, it can also catch all objects of that class's subclasses. This enables catch to handle related errors with a concise notation and allows for polymorphic processing of related exceptions. You can certainly catch each subclass type individually if those exceptions require different processing. Catching related exceptions in one catch block makes sense only if the handling behavior is the same for all subclasses.

If there are multiple catch blocks that match a particular exception type, only the first matching catch block executes when an exception of that type occurs. It is a compilation error to catch the exact same type in two different catch blocks associated with a particular try block. However, there may be several catch blocks that match an exception—i.e., several catch blocks whose types are the same as the exception type or a superclass of that type. For instance, we could follow a catch block for type ArithmeticException with a catch block for type Exception—both would match ArithmeticExceptions, but only the first matching catch block would execute.

Error-Prevention Tip 13.6

Catching subclass types individually is subject to error if you forget to test for one or more of the subclass types explicitly; catching the superclass guarantees that objects of all subclasses will be caught. Positioning a catch block for the superclass type after all other subclass catch blocks for subclasses of that superclass ensures that all subclass exceptions are eventually caught.

Common Programming Error 13.6

Placing a catch block for a superclass exception type before other catch blocks that catch subclass exception types prevents those catch blocks from executing, so a compilation error occurs.

13.7 finally Block

Programs that obtain certain types of resources must return them to the system explicitly to avoid so-called resource leaks. In programming languages such as C and C++, the most common kind of resource leak is a memory leak. Java performs automatic garbage collection of memory no longer used by programs, thus avoiding most memory leaks. However, other types of resource leaks can occur. For example, files, database connections and network connections that are not closed properly might not be available for use in other programs.

Error-Prevention Tip 13.7

A subtle issue is that Java does not entirely eliminate memory leaks. Java will not garbage-collect an object until there are no remaining references to it. Thus, if programmers erroneously keep references to unwanted objects, memory leaks can occur.

The finally block (which consists of the finally keyword, followed by code enclosed in curly braces) is optional, and is sometimes referred to as the finally clause. If it is present, it is placed after the last catch block, as in Fig. 13.4.

Java guarantees that a finally block (if one is present in a try statement) will execute whether or not an exception is thrown in the corresponding try block or any of its corresponding catch blocks. Java also guarantees that a finally block (if one is present) will execute if a try block exits by using a return, break or continue statement, or simply by reaching the try block's closing right brace. The finally block will *not* execute if the application exits early from a try block by calling method System.exit. This method, which we demonstrate in the next chapter, immediately terminates an application.

Because a finally block almost always executes, it typically contains resource-release code. Suppose a resource is allocated in a try block. If no exception occurs, the catch

```
try
{
    statements
    resource-acquisition statements
} // end try
catch ( AKindOfException exception1 )
{
    exception-handling statements
} // end catch
  .
  .
  .
catch ( AnotherKindOfException exception2 )
{
    exception-handling statements
} // end catch
finally
{
    statements
    resource-release statements
} // end finally
```

Fig. 13.4 | A try statement with a finally block.

blocks are skipped and control proceeds to the finally block, which frees the resource. Control then proceeds to the first statement after the finally block. If an exception does occur in the try block, the program skips the rest of the try block. If the program catches the exception in one of the catch blocks, the program processes the exception, then the finally block releases the resource, and control proceeds to the first statement after the finally block.

Performance Tip 13.2

Always release each resource explicitly and at the earliest possible moment at which it is no longer needed. This makes resources immediately available to be reused by your program or other programs, thus improving resource utilization.

Error-Prevention Tip 13.8

Because the finally block is guaranteed to execute whether or not an exception occurs in the corresponding try block, this block is an ideal place to release resources acquired in a try block. This is also an effective way to eliminate resource leaks. For example, the finally block should close any files opened in the try block.

If an exception that occurs in a try block cannot be caught by one of that try block's catch handlers, the program skips the rest of the try block and control proceeds to the finally block. Then the program passes the exception to the next outer try block—normally in the calling method—where an associated catch block might catch it. This process can occur through many levels of try blocks. It is also possible that the exception could go uncaught.

If a catch block throws an exception, the finally block still executes. Then the exception is passed to the next outer try block—again, normally in the calling method.

Figure 13.5 demonstrates that the finally block executes even if an exception is not thrown in the corresponding try block. The program contains static methods main (lines 7–19), throwException (lines 22–45) and doesNotThrowException (lines 48–65). Methods throwException and doesNotThrowException are declared static, so main can call them directly without instantiating a UsingExceptions object.

```
1   // Fig. 13.5: UsingExceptions.java
2   // Demonstration of the try...catch...finally exception handling
3   // mechanism.
4
5   public class UsingExceptions
6   {
7      public static void main( String args[] )
8      {
9         try
10        {
11           throwException(); // call method throwException
12        } // end try
13        catch ( Exception exception ) // exception thrown by throwException
14        {
```

Fig. 13.5 | try...catch...finally exception-handling mechanism. (Part 1 of 3.)

```
15          System.err.println( "Exception handled in main" );
16       } // end catch
17
18       doesNotThrowException();
19    } // end main
20
21    // demonstrate try...catch...finally
22    public static void throwException() throws Exception
23    {
24       try // throw an exception and immediately catch it
25       {
26          System.out.println( "Method throwException" );
27          throw new Exception(); // generate exception
28       } // end try
29       catch ( Exception exception ) // catch exception thrown in try
30       {
31          System.err.println(
32             "Exception handled in method throwException" );
33          throw exception; // rethrow for further processing
34
35          // any code here would not be reached
36
37       } // end catch
38       finally // executes regardless of what occurs in try...catch
39       {
40          System.err.println( "Finally executed in throwException" );
41       } // end finally
42
43       // any code here would not be reached, exception rethrown in catch
44
45    } // end method throwException
46
47    // demonstrate finally when no exception occurs
48    public static void doesNotThrowException()
49    {
50       try // try block does not throw an exception
51       {
52          System.out.println( "Method doesNotThrowException" );
53       } // end try
54       catch ( Exception exception ) // does not execute
55       {
56          System.err.println( exception );
57       } // end catch
58       finally // executes regardless of what occurs in try...catch
59       {
60          System.err.println(
61             "Finally executed in doesNotThrowException" );
62       } // end finally
63
64       System.out.println( "End of method doesNotThrowException" );
65    } // end method doesNotThrowException
66 } // end class UsingExceptions
```

Fig. 13.5 | try...catch...finally exception-handling mechanism. (Part 2 of 3.)

```
Method throwException
Exception handled in method throwException
Finally executed in throwException
Exception handled in main
Method doesNotThrowException
Finally executed in doesNotThrowException
End of method doesNotThrowException
```

Fig. 13.5 | `try...catch...finally` exception-handling mechanism. (Part 3 of 3.)

Note the use of the `System.err` to output data (lines 15, 31–32, 40, 56 and 60–61). By default, `System.err.println`, like `System.out.println`, displays data to the command prompt.

Both `System.out` and `System.err` are streams—a sequence of bytes. While `System.out` (known as the standard output stream) is used to display a program's output, `System.err` (known as the standard error stream) is used to display a program's errors. Output from these streams can be redirected (i.e., sent somewhere other than the command prompt, such as to a file). Using two different streams enables the programmer to easily separate error messages from other output. For instance, data output from `System.err` could be sent to a log file, while data output from `System.out` can be displayed on the screen. For simplicity, this chapter will not redirect output from `System.err`, but will display such messages to the command prompt. You will learn more about streams in Chapter 14, Files and Streams.

Throwing Exceptions Using the **throw** Statement

Method `main` (Fig. 13.5) begins executing, enters its `try` block and immediately calls method `throwException` (line 11). Method `throwException` throws an `Exception`. The statement at line 27 is known as a **throw statement**. The `throw` statement is executed to indicate that an exception has occurred. So far, you have only caught exceptions thrown by called methods. Programmers can throw exceptions by using the `throw` statement. Just as with exceptions thrown by the Java API's methods, this indicates to client applications that an error has occurred. A `throw` statement specifies an object to be thrown. The operand of a `throw` can be of any class derived from class `Throwable`.

Software Engineering Observation 13.9

When toString is invoked on any Throwable object, its resulting string includes the descriptive string that was supplied to the constructor, or simply the class name if no string was supplied.

Software Engineering Observation 13.10

An object can be thrown without containing information about the problem that occurred. In this case, simple knowledge that an exception of a particular type occurred may provide sufficient information for the handler to process the problem correctly.

Software Engineering Observation 13.11

Exceptions can be thrown from constructors. When an error is detected in a constructor, an exception should be thrown rather than creating an improperly formed object.

Rethrowing Exceptions

Line 33 of Fig. 13.5 rethrows the exception. Exceptions are rethrown when a catch block, upon receiving an exception, decides either that it cannot process that exception or that it can only partially process it. Rethrowing an exception defers the exception handling (or perhaps a portion of it) to another catch block associated with an outer try statement. An exception is rethrown by using the **throw keyword**, followed by a reference to the exception object that was just caught. Note that exceptions cannot be rethrown from a finally block, as the exception parameter from the catch block has expired.

When a rethrow occurs, the next enclosing try block detects the rethrown exception, and that try block's catch blocks attempt to handle the exception. In this case, the next enclosing try block is found at lines 9–12 in method main. Before the rethrown exception is handled, however, the finally block (lines 38–41) executes. Then method main detects the rethrown exception in the try block and handles it in the catch block (lines 13–16).

Next, main calls method doesNotThrowException (line 18). No exception is thrown in doesNotThrowException's try block (lines 50–53), so the program skips the catch block (lines 54–57), but the finally block (lines 58–62) nevertheless executes. Control proceeds to the statement after the finally block (line 64). Then control returns to main and the program terminates.

Common Programming Error 13.7

If an exception has not been caught when control enters a finally block and the finally block throws an exception that is not caught in the finally block, the first exception will be lost and the exception from the finally block will be returned to the calling method.

Error-Prevention Tip 13.9

Avoid placing code that can throw an exception in a finally block. If such code is required, enclose the code in a try...catch within the finally block.

Common Programming Error 13.8

Assuming that an exception thrown from a catch block will be processed by that catch block or any other catch block associated with the same try statement can lead to logic errors.

Good Programming Practice 13.2

Java's exception-handling mechanism is intended to remove error-processing code from the main line of a program's code to improve program clarity. Do not place try...catch...finally around every statement that may throw an exception. This makes programs difficult to read. Rather, place one try block around a significant portion of your code, follow that try block with catch blocks that handle each possible exception and follow the catch blocks with a single finally block (if one is required).

13.8 **Stack Unwinding**

When an exception is thrown but not caught in a particular scope, the method-call stack is "unwound," and an attempt is made to catch the exception in the next outer try block. This process is called **stack unwinding**. Unwinding the method-call stack means that the method in which the exception was not caught terminates, all local variables in that method are destroyed and control returns to the statement that originally invoked that method. If a try block encloses that statement, an attempt is made to catch the exception. If a try block does not enclose that statement, stack unwinding occurs again. If no catch block ever catches this exception and the exception is checked (as in the following example), compiling the program will result in an error. The program of Fig. 13.6 demonstrates stack unwinding.

When method main executes, line 10 in the try block calls method throwException (lines 19–35). In the try block of method throwException (lines 21–25), line 24 throws an Exception. This terminates the try block immediately, and control skips the catch block at line 26, because the type being caught (RuntimeException) is not an exact match with the thrown type (Exception) and is not a superclass of it. Method throwException

```java
1   // Fig. 13.6: UsingExceptions.java
2   // Demonstration of stack unwinding.
3
4   public class UsingExceptions
5   {
6      public static void main( String args[] )
7      {
8         try // call throwException to demonstrate stack unwinding
9         {
10            throwException();
11         } // end try
12         catch ( Exception exception ) // exception thrown in throwException
13         {
14            System.err.println( "Exception handled in main" );
15         } // end catch
16      } // end main
17
18      // throwException throws exception that is not caught in this method
19      public static void throwException() throws Exception
20      {
21         try // throw an exception and catch it in main
22         {
23            System.out.println( "Method throwException" );
24            throw new Exception(); // generate exception
25         } // end try
26         catch ( RuntimeException runtimeException ) // catch incorrect type
27         {
28            System.err.println(
29               "Exception handled in method throwException" );
30         } // end catch
31         finally // finally block always executes
32         {
33            System.err.println( "Finally is always executed" );
34         } // end finally
35      } // end method throwException
36   } // end class UsingExceptions
```

```
Method throwException
Finally is always executed
Exception handled in main
```

Fig. 13.6 | Stack unwinding.

terminates (but not until its `finally` block executes) and returns control to line 10—the point from which it was called in the program. Line 10 is in an enclosing `try` block. The exception has not yet been handled, so the `try` block terminates and an attempt is made to catch the exception at line 12. The type being caught (`Exception`) does match the thrown type. Consequently, the `catch` block processes the exception, and the program terminates at the end of `main`. If there were no matching `catch` blocks, a compilation error would occur. Remember that this is not always the case—for unchecked exceptions, the application will compile, but will run with unexpected results.

13.9 printStackTrace, getStackTrace and getMessage

Recall from Section 13.6 that exceptions derive from class `Throwable`. Class `Throwable` offers a **printStackTrace** method that outputs to the standard error stream the stack trace (discussed in Section 13.3). Often, this is helpful in testing and debugging. Class `Throwable` also provides a **getStackTrace** method that retrieves stack-trace information that might be printed by `printStackTrace`. Class `Throwable`'s **getMessage** method returns the descriptive string stored in an exception. The example in this section demonstrates these three methods.

Error-Prevention Tip 13.10

An exception that is not caught in an application causes Java's default exception handler to run. This displays the name of the exception, a descriptive message that indicates the problem that occurred and a complete execution stack trace. In an application with a single thread of execution, the application terminates. In an application with multiple threads, the thread that caused the exception terminates.

Error-Prevention Tip 13.11

`Throwable` method `toString` (inherited by all `Throwable` subclasses) returns a string containing the name of the exception's class and a descriptive message.

Figure 13.7 demonstrates `getMessage`, `printStackTrace` and `getStackTrace`. If we wanted to output the stack-trace information to streams other than the standard error stream, we could use the information returned from `getStackTrace`, and output this data to another stream. Sending data to other streams is discussed in Chapter 14, Files and Streams.

In `main`, the `try` block (lines 8–11) calls `method1` (declared at lines 35–38). Next, `method1` calls `method2` (declared at lines 41–44), which in turn calls `method3` (declared at lines 47–50). Line 49 of `method3` throws an `Exception` object—this is the throw point. Because the `throw` statement at line 49 is not enclosed in a `try` block, stack unwinding occurs—`method3` terminates at line 49, then returns control to the statement in `method2` that invoked `method3` (i.e., line 43). Because no `try` block encloses line 43, stack unwinding occurs again—`method2` terminates at line 43 and returns control to the statement in `method1` that invoked `method2` (i.e., line 37). Because no `try` block encloses line 37, stack unwinding occurs one more time—`method1` terminates at line 37 and returns control to the statement in `main` that invoked `method1` (i.e., line 10). The `try` block at lines 8–11 encloses this statement. The exception has not been handled, so the `try` block terminates and the first matching `catch` block (lines 12–31) catches and processes the exception.

```
 1   // Fig. 13.7: UsingExceptions.java
 2   // Demonstrating getMessage and printStackTrace from class Exception.
 3
 4   public class UsingExceptions
 5   {
 6      public static void main( String args[] )
 7      {
 8         try
 9         {
10            method1(); // call method1
11         } // end try
12         catch ( Exception exception ) // catch exception thrown in method1
13         {
14            System.err.printf( "%s\n\n", exception.getMessage() );
15            exception.printStackTrace(); // print exception stack trace
16
17            // obtain the stack-trace information
18            StackTraceElement[] traceElements = exception.getStackTrace();
19
20            System.out.println( "\nStack trace from getStackTrace:" );
21            System.out.println( "Class\t\tFile\t\t\tLine\tMethod" );
22
23            // loop through traceElements to get exception description
24            for ( StackTraceElement element : traceElements )
25            {
26               System.out.printf( "%s\t", element.getClassName() );
27               System.out.printf( "%s\t", element.getFileName() );
28               System.out.printf( "%s\t", element.getLineNumber() );
29               System.out.printf( "%s\n", element.getMethodName() );
30            } // end for
31         } // end catch
32      } // end main
33
34      // call method2; throw exceptions back to main
35      public static void method1() throws Exception
36      {
37         method2();
38      } // end method method1
39
40      // call method3; throw exceptions back to method1
41      public static void method2() throws Exception
42      {
43         method3();
44      } // end method method2
45
46      // throw Exception back to method2
47      public static void method3() throws Exception
48      {
49         throw new Exception( "Exception thrown in method3" );
50      } // end method method3
51   } // end class UsingExceptions
```

Fig. 13.7 | Throwable methods getMessage, getStackTrace and printStackTrace. (Part 1 of 2.)

```
Exception thrown in method3

java.lang.Exception: Exception thrown in method3
        at UsingExceptions.method3(UsingExceptions.java:49)
        at UsingExceptions.method2(UsingExceptions.java:43)
        at UsingExceptions.method1(UsingExceptions.java:37)
        at UsingExceptions.main(UsingExceptions.java:10)

Stack trace from getStackTrace:
Class            File                  Line    Method
UsingExceptions  UsingExceptions.java  49      method3
UsingExceptions  UsingExceptions.java  43      method2
UsingExceptions  UsingExceptions.java  37      method1
UsingExceptions  UsingExceptions.java  10      main
```

Fig. 13.7 | `Throwable` methods `getMessage`, `getStackTrace` and `printStackTrace`. (Part 2 of 2.)

Line 14 invokes the exception's `getMessage` method to get the exception description. Line 15 invokes the exception's `printStackTrace` method to output the stack trace that indicates where the exception occurred. Line 18 invokes the exception's `getStackTrace` method to obtain the stack-trace information as an array of `StackTraceElement` objects. Lines 24–30 get each `StackTraceElement` in the array and invoke its methods `getClass-Name`, `getFileName`, `getLineNumber` and `getMethodName` to get the class name, file name, line number and method name, respectively, for that `StackTraceElement`. Each `StackTraceElement` represents one method call on the method-call stack.

The output in Fig. 13.7 shows that the stack-trace information printed by `printStackTrace` follows the pattern: *className.methodName(fileName:lineNumber)*, where *className*, *methodName* and *fileName* indicate the names of the class, method and file in which the exception occurred, respectively, and the *lineNumber* indicates where in the file the exception occurred. You saw this in the output for Fig. 13.1. Method `getStackTrace` enables custom processing of the exception information. Compare the output of `printStackTrace` with the output created from the `StackTraceElement`s to see that both contain the same stack-trace information.

Software Engineering Observation 13.12

Never ignore an exception you catch. At least use `printStackTrace` to output an error message. This will inform users that a problem exists, so that they can take appropriate actions.

13.10 Chained Exceptions

Sometimes a `catch` block catches one exception type, then throws a new exception of a different type to indicate that a program-specific exception occurred. In earlier Java versions, there was no mechanism to wrap the original exception information with the new exception's information to provide a complete stack trace showing where the original problem occurred in the program. This made debugging such problems particularly difficult. Chained exceptions enable an exception object to maintain the complete stack-trace information. Figure 13.8 demonstrates chained exceptions.

The program consists of four methods—main (lines 6–16), method1 (lines 19–29), method2 (lines 32–42) and method3 (lines 45–48). Line 10 in method main's try block calls method1. Line 23 in method1's try block calls method2. Line 36 in method2's try block calls method3. In method3, line 47 throws a new Exception. Because this statement

```
1    // Fig. 13.8: UsingChainedExceptions.java
2    // Demonstrating chained exceptions.
3
4    public class UsingChainedExceptions
5    {
6       public static void main( String args[] )
7       {
8          try
9          {
10            method1(); // call method1
11         } // end try
12         catch ( Exception exception ) // exceptions thrown from method1
13         {
14            exception.printStackTrace();
15         } // end catch
16      } // end main
17
18      // call method2; throw exceptions back to main
19      public static void method1() throws Exception
20      {
21         try
22         {
23            method2(); // call method2
24         } // end try
25         catch ( Exception exception ) // exception thrown from method2
26         {
27            throw new Exception( "Exception thrown in method1", exception );
28         } // end try
29      } // end method method1
30
31      // call method3; throw exceptions back to method1
32      public static void method2() throws Exception
33      {
34         try
35         {
36            method3(); // call method3
37         } // end try
38         catch ( Exception exception ) // exception thrown from method3
39         {
40            throw new Exception( "Exception thrown in method2", exception );
41         } // end catch
42      } // end method method2
43
44      // throw Exception back to method2
45      public static void method3() throws Exception
46      {
47         throw new Exception( "Exception thrown in method3" );
48      } // end method method3
49   } // end class UsingChainedExceptions
```

Fig. 13.8 | Chained exceptions. (Part 1 of 2.)

```
java.lang.Exception: Exception thrown in method1
        at UsingChainedExceptions.method1(UsingChainedExceptions.java:27)
        at UsingChainedExceptions.main(UsingChainedExceptions.java:10)
Caused by: java.lang.Exception: Exception thrown in method2
        at UsingChainedExceptions.method2(UsingChainedExceptions.java:40)
        at UsingChainedExceptions.method1(UsingChainedExceptions.java:23)
        ... 1 more
Caused by: java.lang.Exception: Exception thrown in method3
        at UsingChainedExceptions.method3(UsingChainedExceptions.java:47)
        at UsingChainedExceptions.method2(UsingChainedExceptions.java:36)
        ... 2 more
```

Fig. 13.8 | Chained exceptions. (Part 2 of 2.)

is not in a `try` block, `method3` terminates, and the exception is returned to the calling method (`method2`) at line 36. This statement *is* in a `try` block; therefore, the `try` block terminates and the exception is caught at lines 38–41. Line 40 in the `catch` block throws a new exception. In this case, the `Exception` constructor with two arguments is called. The second argument represents the exception that was the original cause of the problem. In this program, that exception occurred at line 47. Because an exception is thrown from the `catch` block, `method2` terminates and returns the new exception to the calling method (`method1`) at line 23. Once again, this statement is in a `try` block, so the `try` block terminates and the exception is caught at lines 25–28. Line 27 in the `catch` block throws a new exception and uses the exception that was caught as the second argument to the `Exception` constructor. Because an exception is thrown from the `catch` block, `method1` terminates and returns the new exception to the calling method (`main`) at line 10. The `try` block in `main` terminates, and the exception is caught at lines 12–15. Line 14 prints a stack trace.

Notice in the program output that the first three lines show the most recent exception that was thrown (i.e., the one from `method1` at line 23). The next four lines indicate the exception that was thrown from `method2` at line 40. Finally, the last four lines represent the exception that was thrown from `method3` at line 47. Also notice that, as you read the output in reverse, it shows how many more chained exceptions remain.

13.11 Declaring New Exception Types

Most Java programmers use existing classes from the Java API, third-party vendors and freely available class libraries (usually downloadable from the Internet) to build Java applications. The methods of those classes typically are declared to throw appropriate exceptions when problems occur. Programmers write code that processes these existing exceptions to make programs more robust.

If you build classes that other programmers will use, you might find it useful to declare your own exception classes that are specific to the problems that can occur when another programmer uses your reusable classes.

Software Engineering Observation 13.13

If possible, indicate exceptions from your methods by using existing exception classes, rather than creating new exception classes. The Java API contains many exception classes that might be suitable for the type of problem your method needs to indicate.

A new exception class must extend an existing exception class to ensure that the class can be used with the exception-handling mechanism. Like any other class, an exception class can contains fields and methods. However, a typical new exception class contains only two constructors—one that takes no arguments and passes a default exception message to the superclass constructor, and one that receives a customized exception message as a string and passes it to the superclass constructor.

Good Programming Practice 13.3

Associating each type of serious execution-time malfunction with an appropriately named Exception class improves program clarity.

Software Engineering Observation 13.14

When defining your own exception type, study the existing exception classes in the Java API and try to extend a related exception class. For example, if you are creating a new class to represent when a method attempts a division by zero, you might extend class ArithmeticException because division by zero occurs during arithmetic. If the existing classes are not appropriate superclasses for your new exception class, decide whether your new class should be a checked or an unchecked exception class. The new exception class should be a checked exception (i.e., extend Exception but not RuntimeException) if possible clients should be required to handle the exception. The client application should be able to reasonably recover from such an exception. The new exception class should extend RuntimeException if the client code should be able to ignore the exception (i.e., the exception is an unchecked exception).

In Chapter 17, Data Structures, we provide an example of a custom exception class. We declare a reusable class called List that is capable of storing a list of references to objects. Some operations typically performed on a List are not allowed if the List is empty, such as removing an item from the front or back of the list (i.e., no items can be removed, as the List does not currently contain any items). For this reason, some List methods throw exceptions of exception class EmptyListException.

Good Programming Practice 13.4

By convention, all exception-class names should end with the word Exception.

13.12 Preconditions and Postconditions

Programmers spend significant portions of their time maintaining and debugging code. To facilitate these tasks and to improve the overall design, they generally specify the expected states before and after a method's execution. These states are called preconditions and postconditions, respectively.

A **precondition** must be true when a method is invoked. Preconditions describe constraints on method parameters and any other expectations the method has about the current state of a program. If the preconditions are not met, then the method's behavior is undefined—it may throw an exception, proceed with an illegal value or attempt to recover from the error. However, you should never rely on or expect consistent behavior if the preconditions are not satisfied.

A **postcondition** is true after the method successfully returns. Postconditions describe constraints on the return value and any other side effects the method may have. When calling a method, you may assume that a method fulfills all of its postconditions. If you are writing your own method, you should document all postconditions so others know what to expect when they call your method, and you should make certain that your method honors all its postconditions if its preconditions are indeed met.

When their preconditions or postconditions are not met, methods typically throw exceptions. As an example, examine `String` method `charAt`, which has one `int` parameter—an index in the `String`. For a precondition, method `charAt` assumes that `index` is greater than or equal to zero and less than the length of the `String`. If the precondition is met, the postcondition states the method will return the character at the position in the `String` specified by the parameter `index`. Otherwise, the method throws an `IndexOutOfBoundsException`. We trust that method `charAt` satisfies its postcondition, provided that we meet the precondition. We do not need to be concerned with the details of how the method actually retrieves the character at the index.

Some programmers state the preconditions and postconditions informally as part of the general method specification, while others prefer a more formal approach by explicitly defining them. When designing your own methods, you should state the preconditions and postconditions in a comment before the method declaration in whichever manner you prefer. Stating the preconditions and postconditions before writing a method will also help guide you as you implement the method.

13.13 Assertions

When implementing and debugging a class, it is sometimes useful to state conditions that should be true at a particular point in a method. These conditions, called assertions, help ensure a program's validity by catching potential bugs and identifying possible logic errors during development. Preconditions and postconditions are two types of assertions. Preconditions are assertions about a program's state when a method is invoked, and postconditions are assertions about a program's state after a method finishes.

While assertions can be stated as comments to guide the programmer during development, Java includes two versions of the `assert` statement for validating assertions programatically. The `assert` statement evaluates a `boolean` expression and determines whether it is true or false. The first form of the `assert` statement is

```
assert expression;
```

This statement evaluates *expression* and throws an `AssertionError` if the expression is `false`. The second form is

```
assert expression1 : expression2;
```

This statement evaluates *expression1* and throws an `AssertionError` with *expression2* as the error message if *expression1* is `false`.

You can use assertions to programmatically implement preconditions and postconditions or to verify any other intermediate states that help you ensure your code is working correctly. The example in Fig. 13.9 demonstrates the functionality of the `assert` statement. Line 11 prompts the user to enter a number between 0 and 10, then line 12 reads the number from the command line. The `assert` statement at line 15 determines whether the user entered a number within the valid range. If the number is out of range, then the program reports an error; otherwise, the program proceeds normally.

```
 1    // Fig. 13.9: AssertTest.java
 2    // Demonstrates the assert statement
 3    import java.util.Scanner;
 4
 5    public class AssertTest
 6    {
 7       public static void main( String args[] )
 8       {
 9          Scanner input = new Scanner( System.in );
10
11          System.out.print( "Enter a number between 0 and 10: " );
12          int number = input.nextInt();
13
14          // assert that the absolute value is >= 0
15          assert ( number >= 0 && number <= 10 ) : "bad number: " + number;
16
17          System.out.printf( "You entered %d\n", number );
18       } // end main
19    } // end class AssertTest
```

```
Enter a number between 0 and 10: 5
You entered 5
```

```
Enter a number between 0 and 10: 50
Exception in thread "main" java.lang.AssertionError: bad number: 50
        at AssertTest.main(AssertTest.java:15)
```

Fig. 13.9 | Checking with assert that a value is within range.

Assertions are primarily used by the programmer for debugging and identifying logic errors in an application. By default, assertions are disabled when executing a program because they reduce performance and are unnecessary for the program's user. To enable assertions at runtime, use the java command's -ea command-line option. To execute the program in Fig. 13.9 with assertions enabled, type

        java -ea AssertTest

You should not encounter any AssertionErrors through normal execution of a properly written program. Such errors should only indicate bugs in the implementation. As a result, you should never catch an AssertionError. Rather, you should allow the program to terminate when the error occurs, so you can see the error message; then you should locate and fix the source of the problem. Since application users can choose not to enable assertions at runtime, you should not use the assert statement to indicate runtime problems in production code. Rather, you should use the exception mechanism for this purpose.

13.14 Wrap-Up

In this chapter, you learned how to use exception handling to deal with errors in an application. You learned that exception handling enables programmers to remove error-handling code from the "main line" of the program's execution. You saw exception handling in the context of a divide-by-zero example. You learned how to use `try` blocks to enclose code that may throw an exception, and how to use `catch` blocks to deal with exceptions that may arise. You learned about the termination model of exception handling, which dictates that after an exception is handled, program control does not return to the throw point. You learned the difference between checked and unchecked exceptions, and how to specify with the `throws` clause that specific exceptions occurring in a method will be thrown by that method to its caller. You learned how to use the `finally` block to release resources whether or not an exception occurs. You also learned how to throw and rethrow exceptions. You then learned how to obtain information about an exception using methods `printStackTrace`, `getStackTrace` and `getMessage`. The chapter continued with a discussion of chained exceptions, which allow programmers to wrap original exception information with new exception information. Next, we overviewed how to create your own exception classes. We then introduced preconditions and postconditions to help programmers using your methods understand conditions that must be true with the method is called and when it returns. When preconditions and postconditions are not met, methods typically throw exceptions. Finally, we discussed the `assert` statement and how it can be used to help you debug your programs. In particular, these can be used to ensure that preconditions and postconditions are met. In the next chapter, you will learn about file processing, including how persistent data is stored and how to manipulate it.

Summary

Section 13.1 Introduction

- An exception is an indication of a problem that occurs during a program's execution.
- Exception handling enables programmers to create applications that can resolve exceptions.

Section 13.2 Exception-Handling Overview

- Exception handling enables programmers to remove error-handling code from the "main line" of the program's execution, improving program clarity and enhancing modifiability.

Section 13.3 Example: Divide by Zero without Exception Handling

- Exceptions are thrown when a method detects a problem and is unable to handle it.
- An exception's stack trace includes the name of the exception in a descriptive message that indicates the problem that occurred and the complete method-call stack (i.e., the call chain) at the time the exception occurred.
- The point in the program at which an exception occurs is called the throw point.

Section 13.4 Example: Handling `ArithmeticExceptions` and `InputMismatchExceptions`

- A `try` block encloses the code that might `throw` an exception and the code that should not execute if that exception occurs.
- Exceptions may surface through explicitly mentioned code in a `try` block, through calls to other methods or even through deeply nested method calls initiated by code in the `try` block.
- A `catch` block begins with the keyword `catch` and an exception parameter followed by a block of code that catches (i.e., receives) and handles the exception. This code executes when the `try` block detects the exception.

- An uncaught exception is an exception that occurs for which there are no matching catch blocks.
- An uncaught exception will cause a program to terminate early if that program contains only one thread. If the program contains more than one thread, only the thread where the exception occurred will terminate. The rest of the program will run but may yield adverse effects.
- At least one catch block or a finally block must immediately follow the try block.
- Each catch block specifies in parentheses an exception parameter that identifies the exception type the handler can process. The exception parameter's name enables the catch block to interact with a caught exception object.
- If an exception occurs in a try block, the try block terminates immediately and program control transfers to the first of the following catch blocks whose exception parameter type matches the type of the thrown exception.
- After an exception is handled, program control does not return to the throw point, because the try block has expired. This is known as the termination model of exception handling.
- If there are multiple matching catch blocks when an exception occurs, only the first is executed.
- After executing a catch block, the program's flow of control proceeds to the first statement after the last catch block.
- A throws clause specifies the exceptions the method throws, and appears after the method's parameter list and before the method body.
- The throws clause contains a comma-separated list of exceptions that the method will throw if a problem occurs when the method executes.

Section 13.5 When to Use Exception Handling
- Exception handling is designed to process synchronous errors, which occur when a statement executes.
- Exception handling is not designed to process problems associated with asynchronous events, which occur in parallel with, and independent of, the program's flow of control.

Section 13.6 Java Exception Hierarchy
- All Java exception classes inherit, either directly or indirectly, from class Exception. Because of this fact, Java's exception classes form a hierarchy. Programmers can extend this hierarchy to create their own exception classes.
- Class Throwable is the superclass of class Exception, and is therefore also the superclass of all exceptions. Only Throwable objects can be used with the exception-handling mechanism.
- Class Throwable has two subclasses: Exception and Error.
- Class Exception and its subclasses represent exceptional situations that could occur in a Java program and be caught by the application.
- Class Error and its subclasses represent exceptional situations that could happen in the Java runtime system. Errors happen infrequently, and typically should not be caught by an application.
- Java distinguishes between two categories of exceptions: checked and unchecked.
- Unlike checked exceptions, the Java compiler does not check the code to determine whether an unchecked exception is caught or declared. Unchecked exceptions typically can be prevented by proper coding.
- An exception's type determines whether the exception is checked or unchecked. All exception types that are direct or indirect subclasses of class RuntimeException are unchecked exceptions. All exception types that inherit from class Exception but not from RuntimeException are checked.

- Various exception classes can be derived from a common superclass. If a catch block is written to catch exception objects of a superclass type, it can also catch all objects of that class's subclasses. This allows for polymorphic processing of related exceptions.

Section 13.7 `finally` block

- Programs that obtain certain types of resources must return them to the system explicitly to avoid so-called resource leaks. Resource-release code typically is placed in a `finally` block.
- The `finally` block is optional. If it is present, it is placed after the last catch block.
- Java guarantees that a provided `finally` block will execute whether or not an exception is thrown in the corresponding try block or any of its corresponding catch blocks. Java also guarantees that a `finally` block executes if a try block exits by using a return, break or continue statement.
- If an exception that occurs in the try block cannot be caught by one of that try block's associated catch handlers, the program skips the rest of the try block and control proceeds to the `finally` block, which releases the resource. Then the program passes to the next outer try block—normally in the calling method.
- If a catch block throws an exception, the `finally` block still executes. Then the exception is passed to the next outer try block—normally in the calling method.
- Programmers can throw exceptions by using the throw statement.
- A throw statement specifies an object to be thrown. The operand of a throw can be of any class derived from class Throwable.

Section 13.8 Stack Unwinding

- Exceptions are rethrown when a catch block, upon receiving an exception, decides either that it cannot process that exception or that it can only partially process it. Rethrowing an exception defers the exception handling (or perhaps a portion of it) to another catch block.
- When a rethrow occurs, the next enclosing try block detects the rethrown exception, and that try block's catch blocks attempt to handle the exception.
- When an exception is thrown but not caught in a particular scope, the method-call stack is unwound, and an attempt is made to catch the exception in the next outer try statement. This process is called stack unwinding.

Section 13.9 printStackTrace, getStackTrace and getMessage

- Class Throwable offers a printStackTrace method that prints the method-call stack. Often, this is helpful in testing and debugging.
- Class Throwable also provides a getStackTrace method that obtains stack-trace information printed by printStackTrace.
- Class Throwable's getMessage method returns the descriptive string stored in an exception.
- Method getStackTrace obtains the stack-trace information as an array of StackTraceElement objects. Each StackTraceElement represents one method call on the method-call stack.
- StackTraceElement methods getClassName, getFileName, getLineNumber and getMethodName get the class name, file name, line number and method name, respectively.

Section 13.10 Chained Exceptions

- Chained exceptions enable an exception object to maintain the complete stack-trace information, including information about previous exceptions that caused the current exception.

Section 13.11 Declaring New Exception Types

- A new exception class must extend an existing exception class to ensure that the class can be used with the exception-handling mechanism.

Section 13.12 Preconditions and Postconditions

- A method's precondition is a condition that must be true when the method is invoked.

- A method's postcondition is a condition that is true after the method successfully returns.

- When designing your own methods, you should state the preconditions and postconditions in a comment before the method declaration.

Section 13.13 Assertions

- Within an application, programmers may state conditions that they assumed to be true at a particular point. These conditions, called assertions, help ensure a program's validity by catching potential bugs and indentifying possible logic errors.

- Java includes two versions of an `assert` statement for validating assertions programatically.

- To enable assertions at runtime, use the `-ea` switch when running the `java` command.

Terminology

`ArithmeticException` class	`getStackTrace` method of class `Throwable`
`assert` statement	`InputMismatchException` class
assertion	postcondition
asynchronous event	precondition
catch an exception	`printStackTrace` method of class `Throwable`
catch block	release a resource
catch clause	resource leak
catch-or-declare requirement	resumption model of exception handling
chained exception	rethrowing an exception
checked exception	`RuntimeException` class
constructor failure	stack trace
enclosing try block	`StackTraceElement` class
`Error` class	stack unwinding
exception	standard error stream
`Exception` class	standard output stream
exception handler	synchronous error
exception handling	`System.err` stream
exception parameter	termination model of exception handling
fault-tolerant program	throw an exception
`finally` block	throw keyword
`finally` clause	throw point
`getClassName` method of class	throw statement
`StackTraceElement`	`Throwable` class
`getFileName` method of class	throws clause
`StackTraceElement`	try block
`getLineNumber` method of class	try statement
`StackTraceElement`	`try...catch...finally` exception-handling
`getMessage` method of class `Throwable`	mechanism
`getMethodName` method of class	uncaught exception
`StackTraceElement`	unchecked exceptions

Self-Review Exercises

13.1 List five common examples of exceptions.

13.2 Give several reasons why exception-handling techniques should not be used for conventional program control.

13.3   Why are exceptions particularly appropriate for dealing with errors produced by methods of classes in the Java API?

13.4   What is a "resource leak"?

13.5   If no exceptions are thrown in a try block, where does control proceed to, when the try block completes execution?

13.6   Give a key advantage of using catch(Exception *exceptionName*).

13.7   Should a conventional application catch Error objects? Explain.

13.8   What happens if no catch handler matches the type of a thrown object?

13.9   What happens if several catch blocks match the type of the thrown object?

13.10   Why would a programmer specify a superclass type as the type in a catch block?

13.11   What is the key reason for using finally blocks?

13.12   What happens when a catch block throws an Exception?

13.13   What does the statement throw *exceptionReference* do?

13.14   What happens to a local reference in a try block when that block throws an Exception?

Answers to Self-Review Exercises

13.1   Memory exhaustion, array index out of bounds, arithmetic overflow, division by zero, invalid method parameters.

13.2   (a) Exception handling is designed to handle infrequently occurring situations that often result in program termination, not situations that arise all the time. (b) Flow of control with conventional control structures is generally clearer and more efficient than with exceptions. (c) The "additional" exceptions can get in the way of genuine error-type exceptions. It becomes more difficult for the programmer to keep track of the larger number of exception cases.

13.3   It is unlikely that methods of classes in the Java API could perform error processing that would meet the unique needs of all users.

13.4   A "resource leak" occurs when an executing program does not properly release a resource when it is no longer needed.

13.5   The catch blocks for that try statement are skipped, and the program resumes execution after the last catch block. If there is a finally block, it is executed first; then the program resumes execution after the finally block.

13.6   The form catch(Exception *exceptionName*) catches any type of exception thrown in a try block. An advantage is that no thrown Exception can slip by without being caught. The programmer can then decide to handle the exception or possibly rethrow it.

13.7   Errors are usually serious problems with the underlying Java system; most programs will not want to catch Errors because the program will not be able to recover from such problems.

13.8   This causes the search for a match to continue in the next enclosing try statement. If there is a finally block, it will be executed before the exception goes to the next enclosing try statement. If there are no enclosing try statements for which there are matching catch blocks, and the exception is *checked*, a compilation error occurs. If there are no enclosing try statements for which there are matching catch blocks and the exception is *unchecked*, a stack trace is printed and the current thread terminates early.

13.9   The first matching catch block after the try block is executed.

13.10 This enables a program to catch related types of exceptions and process them in a uniform manner. However, it is often useful to process the subclass types individually for more precise exception handling.

13.11 The `finally` block is the preferred means for releasing resources to prevent resource leaks.

13.12 First, control passes to the `finally` block if there is one. Then the exception will be processed by a `catch` block (if one exists) associated with an enclosing `try` block (if one exists).

13.13 It rethrows the exception for processing by an exception handler of an enclosing `try` statement, after the `finally` block of the current `try` statement executes.

13.14 The reference goes out of scope, and the reference count for the object is decremented. If the reference count becomes zero, the object is marked for garbage collection.

Exercises

13.15 List the various exceptional conditions that have occurred in programs throughout this text so far. List as many additional exceptional conditions as you can. For each of these, describe briefly how a program typically would handle the exception by using the exception-handling techniques discussed in this chapter. Some typical exceptions are division by zero, arithmetic overflow, and array index out of bounds.

13.16 *(Catching Exceptions with Superclasses)* Use inheritance to create an exception superclass (called `ExceptionA`) and exception subclasses `ExceptionB` and `ExceptionC`, where `ExceptionB` inherits from `ExceptionA` and `ExceptionC` inherits from `ExceptionB`. Write a program to demonstrate that the catch block for type `ExceptionA` catches exceptions of types `ExceptionB` and `ExceptionC`.

13.17 *(Order of catch Blocks)* Write a program that shows that the order of `catch` blocks is important. If you try to catch a superclass exception type before a subclass type, the compiler should generate errors.

13.18 *(Rethrowing Exceptions)* Write a program that illustrates rethrowing an exception. Define methods `someMethod` and `someMethod2`. Method `someMethod2` should initially throw an exception. Method `someMethod` should call `someMethod2`, catch the exception and rethrow it. Call `someMethod` from method `main`, and catch the rethrown exception. Print the stack trace of this exception.

13.19 *(Catching Exceptions Using Outer Scopes)* Write a program showing that a method with its own `try` block does not have to catch every possible error generated within the `try`. Some exceptions can slip through to, and be handled in, other scopes.

Files and Streams

OBJECTIVES

In this chapter you will learn:

- To create, read, write and update files.
- To use class **File** to retrieve information about files and directories.
- The Java input/output stream class hierarchy.
- The differences between text files and binary files.
- Sequential-access file processing.
- To use classes **Scanner** and **Formatter** to process text files.
- To use the **FileInputStream** and **FileOutputStream** classes.
- To use a **JFileChooser** dialog.
- To use the **ObjectInputStream** and **ObjectOutputStream** classes.

14.1 Introduction

Storage of data in variables and arrays is temporary—the data is lost when a local variable goes out of scope or when the program terminates. Computers use files for long-term retention of large amounts of data, even after the programs that created the data terminate. You use files every day for tasks such as writing an essay or creating a spreadsheet. We refer to data maintained in files as **persistent data** because it exists beyond the duration of program execution. Computers store files on **secondary storage devices** such as hard disks, optical disks and magnetic tapes. In this chapter, we explain how Java programs create, update and process files.

File processing is one of the most important capabilities a language must have to support commercial applications, which typically store and process massive amounts of persistent data. In this chapter, we discuss Java's powerful file-processing and stream input/output features. The term "stream" refers to ordered data that is read from or written to a file. We discuss streams in more detail in Section 14.3. File processing is a subset of Java's stream-processing capabilities, which enable a program to read and write data in memory, in files and over network connections. We have two goals in this chapter—to introduce file-processing concepts (making the reader more comfortable with using files programmatically) and to provide the reader with sufficient stream-processing capabilities to support the networking features introduced in Chapter 24, Networking. Java provides substantial stream-processing capabilities—far more than we can cover in one chapter. We discuss two forms of file processing here—text-file processing and object serialization.

We begin by discussing the hierarchy of data contained in files. We then cover Java's architecture for handling files programmatically by discussing several classes in package java.io. Next we explain that data can be stored in two different types of files—text files and binary files—and cover the differences between them. We demonstrate retrieving information about a file or directory using class `File` and then devote several sections to the different mechanisms for writing data to and reading data from files. First we demonstrate creating and manipulating sequential-access text files. Working with text files allows the reader to quickly and easily start manipulating files. As you will learn, however, it is difficult to read data from text files back into object form. Fortunately, many object-oriented languages (including Java) provide ways to write objects to and read objects from files (known as object serialization and deserialization). To demonstrate this, we recreate some of the sequential-access programs that used text files, this time by storing objects in binary files.

14.2 Data Hierarchy

Ultimately, a computer processes all data items as combinations of zeros and ones, because it is simple and economical for engineers to build electronic devices that can assume two stable states—one representing 0 and the other representing 1. It is remarkable that the impressive functions performed by computers involve only the most fundamental manipulations of 0s and 1s.

The smallest data item in a computer can assume the value 0 or the value 1. Such a data item is called a **bit** (short for "binary digit"—a digit that can assume one of two values). Computer circuitry performs various simple bit manipulations, such as examining the value of a bit, setting the value of a bit and reversing the value of a bit (from 1 to 0 or from 0 to 1).

It is cumbersome for programmers to work with data in the low-level form of bits. Instead, they prefer to work with data in such forms as **decimal digits** (0–9), **letters** (A–Z and a–z), and **special symbols** (e.g., $, @, %, &, *, (,), –, +, ", :, ? and /). Digits, letters and special symbols are known as **characters**. The computer's **character set** is the set of all the characters used to write programs and represent data items. Computers process only 1s and 0s, so a computer's character set represents every character as a pattern of 1s and 0s. Characters in Java are **Unicode** characters composed of two **bytes**, each composed of eight bits. Java contains a data type, `byte`, that can be used to represent byte data. The Unicode character set contains characters for many of the world's languages. See Appendix I for more information on this character set. See Appendix B, ASCII Character Set, for more information on the ASCII (American Standard Code for Information Interchange) character set, a subset of the Unicode character set that represents uppercase and lowercase letters, digits and various common special characters.

Just as characters are composed of bits, **fields** are composed of characters or bytes. A field is a group of characters or bytes that conveys meaning. For example, a field consisting of uppercase and lowercase letters can be used to represent a person's name.

Data items processed by computers form a **data hierarchy** that becomes larger and more complex in structure as we progress from bits to characters to fields, and so on.

Typically, several fields compose a **record** (implemented as a `class` in Java). In a payroll system, for example, the record for an employee might consist of the following fields (possible types for these fields are shown in parentheses):

- Employee identification number (`int`)
- Name (`String`)
- Address (`String`)

- Hourly pay rate (`double`)
- Number of exemptions claimed (`int`)
- Year-to-date earnings (`int` or `double`)
- Amount of taxes withheld (`int` or `double`)

Thus, a record is a group of related fields. In the preceding example, all the fields belong to the same employee. Of course, a company might have many employees and thus have a payroll record for each employee. A **file** is a group of related records. [*Note:* More generally, a file contains arbitrary data in arbitrary formats. In some operating systems, a file is viewed as nothing more than a collection of bytes—any organization of the bytes in a file (e.g., organizing the data into records) is a view created by the applications programmer.] A company's payroll file normally contains one record for each employee. Thus, a payroll file for a small company might contain only 22 records, whereas one for a large company might contain 100,000 records. It is not unusual for a company to have many files, some containing billions, or even trillions, of characters of information. Figure 14.1 illustrates a portion of the data hierarchy.

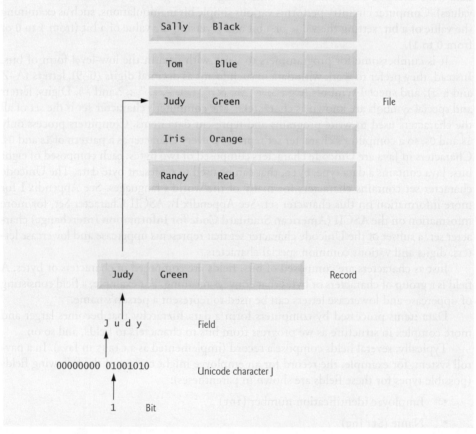

Fig. 14.1 | Data hierarchy.

To facilitate the retrieval of specific records from a file, at least one field in each record is chosen as a record key. A record key identifies a record as belonging to a particular person or entity and is unique to each record. This field typically is used to search and sort records. In the payroll record described previously, the employee identification number normally would be chosen as the record key.

There are many ways to organize records in a file. The most common is called a sequential file, in which records are stored in order by the record-key field. In a payroll file, records are placed in ascending order by employee identification number.

Most businesses store data in many different files. For example, companies might have payroll files, accounts receivable files (listing money due from clients), accounts payable files (listing money due to suppliers), inventory files (listing facts about all the items handled by the business) and many others. Often, a group of related files is called a database. A collection of programs designed to create and manage databases is called a database management system (DBMS). We discuss this topic in Chapter 25, Accessing Databases with JDBC.

14.3 Files and Streams

Java views each file as a sequential stream of bytes (Fig. 14.2). Every operating system provides a mechanism to determine the end of a file, such as an end-of-file marker or a count of the total bytes in the file that is recorded in a system-maintained administrative data structure. A Java program processing a stream of bytes simply receives an indication from the operating system when it reaches the end of the stream—the program does not need to know how the underlying platform represents files or streams. In some cases, the end-of-file indication occurs as an exception. In other cases, the indication is a return value from a method invoked on a stream-processing object.

File streams can be used to input and output data as either characters or bytes. Streams that input and output bytes to files are known as byte-based streams, storing data in its binary format. Streams that input and output characters to files are known as character-based streams, storing data as a sequence of characters. For instance, if the value 5 were being stored using a byte-based stream, it would be stored in the binary format of the numeric value 5, or 101. If the value 5 were being stored using a character-based stream, it would be stored in the binary format of the character 5, or 00000000 00110101 (this is the binary for the numeric value 53, which indicates the character 5 in the Unicode character set). The difference between the numeric value 5 and the character 5 is that the numeric value can be used as an integer in calculations, whereas the character 5 is simply a character that can be used in a string of text, as in "Sarah Miller is 15 years old". Files that are created using byte-based streams are referred to as binary files, while files created using character-based streams are referred to as text files. Text files can be read by text editors, while binary files are read by a program that converts the data to a human-readable format.

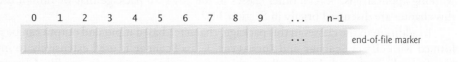

Fig. 14.2 | Java's view of a file of *n* bytes.

A Java program opens a file by creating an object and associating a stream of bytes or characters with it. The classes used to create these objects are discussed shortly. Java can also associate streams with different devices. In fact, Java creates three stream objects that are associated with devices when a Java program begins executing—System.in, System.out and System.err. Object System.in (the standard input stream object) normally enables a program to input bytes from the keyboard; object System.out (the standard output stream object) normally enables a program to output data to the screen; and object System.err (the standard error stream object) normally enables a program to output error messages to the screen. Each of these streams can be redirected. For System.in, this capability enables the program to read bytes from a different source. For System.out and System.err, this capability enables the output to be sent to a different location, such as a file on disk. Class System provides methods setIn, setOut and setErr to redirect the standard input, output and error streams, respectively.

Java programs perform file processing by using classes from package java.io. This package includes definitions for stream classes, such as FileInputStream (for byte-based input from a file), FileOutputStream (for byte-based output to a file), FileReader (for character-based input from a file) and FileWriter (for character-based output to a file). Files are opened by creating objects of these stream classes, which inherit from classes InputStream, OutputStream, Reader and Writer, respectively (these classes will be discussed later in this chapter). Thus, the methods of these stream classes can all be applied to file streams as well.

Java contains classes that enable the programmer to perform input and output of objects or variables of primitive data types. The data will still be stored as bytes or characters behind the scenes, allowing the programmer to read or write data in the form of integers, strings, or other data types without having to worry about the details of converting such values to byte format. To perform such input and output, objects of classes ObjectInputStream and ObjectOutputStream can be used together with the byte-based file stream classes FileInputStream and FileOutputStream (these classes will be discussed in more detail shortly). The complete hierarchy of classes in package java.io can be viewed in the online documentation at

> java.sun.com/javase/6/docs/api/java/io/package-tree.html

Each indentation level in the hierarchy indicates that the indented class extends the class under which it is indented. For example, class InputStream is a subclass of Object. Click a class's name in the hierarchy to view the details of the class.

As you can see in the hierarchy, Java offers many classes for performing input/output operations. We use several of these classes in this chapter to implement file-processing programs that create and manipulate sequential-access files. We also include a detailed example on class File, which is useful for obtaining information about files and directories. In Chapter 24, Networking, we use stream classes extensively to implement networking applications. Several other classes in the java.io package that we do not use in this chapter are discussed briefly in Section 14.7.

In addition to the classes in this package, character-based input and output can be performed with classes Scanner and Formatter. Class Scanner is used extensively to input data from the keyboard. As we will see, this class can also read data from a file. Class Formatter enables formatted data to be output to the screen or to a file in a manner similar to `System.out.printf`. Chapter 29, Formatted Output, presents the details of formatted output with `System.out.printf`. All these features can be used to format text files as well.

14.4 **Class `File`**

This section presents class `File`, which is particularly useful for retrieving information about files or directories from disk. Objects of class `File` do not open files or provide any file-processing capabilities. However, `File` objects are used frequently with objects of other `java.io` classes to specify files or directories to manipulate.

Creating *`File` Objects*
Class `File` provides four constructors. The constructor

```
public File( String name )
```

specifies the `name` of a file or directory to associate with the `File` object. The `name` can contain **path information** as well as a file or directory name. A file or directory's path specifies its location on disk. The path includes some or all of the directories leading to the file or directory. An **absolute path** contains all the directories, starting with the **root directory**, that lead to a specific file or directory. Every file or directory on a particular disk drive has the same root directory in its path. A **relative path** normally starts from the directory in which the application began executing, and is therefore a path that is "relative" to the current directory.

The constructor

```
public File( String pathToName, String name )
```

uses argument `pathToName` (an absolute or relative path) to locate the file or directory specified by `name`.

The constructor

```
public File( File directory, String name )
```

uses an existing `File` object `directory` (an absolute or relative path) to locate the file or directory specified by `name`. Figure 14.3 lists some common `File` methods. The complete list can be viewed at `java.sun.com/javase/6/docs/api/java/io/File.html`.

Method	Description
`boolean canRead()`	Returns `true` if a file is readable by the current application; `false` otherwise.
`boolean canWrite()`	Returns `true` if a file is writable by the current application; `false` otherwise.
`boolean exists()`	Returns `true` if the name specified as the argument to the `File` constructor is a file or directory in the specified path; `false` otherwise.

Fig. 14.3 | `File` methods. (Part 1 of 2.)

Method	Description
`boolean isFile()`	Returns true if the name specified as the argument to the File constructor is a file; false otherwise.
`boolean isDirectory()`	Returns true if the name specified as the argument to the File constructor is a directory; false otherwise.
`boolean isAbsolute()`	Returns true if the arguments specified to the File constructor indicate an absolute path to a file or directory; false otherwise.
`String getAbsolutePath()`	Returns a string with the absolute path of the file or directory.
`String getName()`	Returns a string with the name of the file or directory.
`String getPath()`	Returns a string with the path of the file or directory.
`String getParent()`	Returns a string with the parent directory of the file or directory (i.e., the directory in which the file or directory can be found).
`long length()`	Returns the length of the file, in bytes. If the File object represents a directory, 0 is returned.
`long lastModified()`	Returns a platform-dependent representation of the time at which the file or directory was last modified. The value returned is useful only for comparison with other values returned by this method.
`String[] list()`	Returns an array of strings representing the contents of a directory. Returns null if the File object does not represent a directory.

Fig. 14.3 | File methods. (Part 2 of 2.)

The constructor

```
public File( URI uri )
```

uses the given URI object to locate the file. A **Uniform Resource Identifier (URI)** is a more general form of the **Uniform Resource Locators (URLs)** that are used to locate websites. For example, `http://www.deitel.com/` is the URL for the Deitel & Associates' website. URIs for locating files vary across operating systems. On Windows platforms, the URI

```
file:/C:/data.txt
```

identifies the file data.txt stored in the root directory of the C: drive. On UNIX/Linux platforms, the URI

```
file:/home/student/data.txt
```

identifies the file data.txt stored in the home directory of the user student.

Error-Prevention Tip 14.1

Use `File` method `isFile` to determine whether a `File` object represents a file (not a directory) before attempting to open the file.

Demonstrating Class `File`

Figures 14.4–14.5 demonstrate class `File`. The application prompts the user to enter a file name or directory name, then outputs information about the file name or directory name input.

```java
1   // Fig. 14.4: FileDemonstration.java
2   // Demonstrating the File class.
3   import java.io.File;
4
5   public class FileDemonstration
6   {
7      // display information about file user specifies
8      public void analyzePath( String path )
9      {
10         // create File object based on user input
11         File name = new File( path );
12
13         if ( name.exists() ) // if name exists, output information about it
14         {
15            // display file (or directory) information
16            System.out.printf(
17               "%s%s\n%s\n%s\n%s%s\n%s%s\n%s%s\n%s%s\n%s%s",
18               name.getName(), " exists",
19               ( name.isFile() ? "is a file" : "is not a file" ),
20               ( name.isDirectory() ? "is a directory" :
21                  "is not a directory" ),
22               ( name.isAbsolute() ? "is absolute path" :
23                  "is not absolute path" ), "Last modified: ",
24               name.lastModified(), "Length: ", name.length(),
25               "Path: ", name.getPath(), "Absolute path: ",
26               name.getAbsolutePath(), "Parent: ", name.getParent() );
27
28            if ( name.isDirectory() ) // output directory listing
29            {
30               String directory[] = name.list();
31               System.out.println( "\n\nDirectory contents:\n" );
32
33               for ( String directoryName : directory )
34                  System.out.printf( "%s\n", directoryName );
35            } // end if
36         } // end outer if
37         else // not file or directory, output error message
38         {
39            System.out.printf( "%s %s", path, "does not exist." );
40         } // end else
41      } // end method analyzePath
42   } // end class FileDemonstration
```

Fig. 14.4 | `File` class used to obtain file and directory information.

```
 1   // Fig. 14.5: FileDemonstrationTest.java
 2   // Testing the FileDemonstration class.
 3   import java.util.Scanner;
 4
 5   public class FileDemonstrationTest
 6   {
 7      public static void main( String args[] )
 8      {
 9         Scanner input = new Scanner( System.in );
10         FileDemonstration application = new FileDemonstration();
11
12         System.out.print( "Enter file or directory name here: " );
13         application.analyzePath( input.nextLine() );
14      } // end main
15   } // end class FileDemonstrationTest
```

```
Enter file or directory name here: C:\Program Files\Java\jdk1.6.0\demo\jfc
jfc exists
is not a file
is a directory
is absolute path
Last modified: 1162570370359
Length: 0
Path: C:\Program Files\Java\jdk1.6.0\demo\jfc
Absolute path: C:\Program Files\Java\jdk1.6.0\demo\jfc
Parent: C:\Program Files\Java\jdk1.6.0\demo

Directory contents:

CodePointIM
FileChooserDemo
Font2DTest
Java2D
Metalworks
Notepad
SampleTree
Stylepad
SwingApplet
SwingSet2
TableExample
```

```
Enter file or directory name here: C:\Program
Files\Java\jdk1.6.0\demo\jfc\Java2D\readme.txt
readme.txt exists
is a file
is not a directory
is absolute path
Last modified: 1162570365875
Length: 7518
Path: C:\Program Files\Java\jdk1.6.0\demo\jfc\Java2D\readme.txt
Absolute path: C:\Program Files\Java\jdk1.6.0\demo\jfc\Java2D\readme.txt
Parent: C:\Program Files\Java\jdk1.6.0\demo\jfc\Java2D
```

Fig. 14.5 | Testing class FileDemonstration.

The program begins by prompting the user for a file or directory (line 12 of Fig. 14.5). Line 13 inputs the file name or directory name and passes it to method analyzePath (lines 8–41 of Fig. 14.4). The method creates a new File object (line 11) and assigns its reference to name. Line 13 invokes File method exists to determine whether the name input by the user exists (either as a file or as a directory) on the disk. If the name input by the user does not exist, control proceeds to lines 37–40 and displays a message to the screen containing the name the user typed, followed by "does not exist." Otherwise, the body of the if statement (lines 13–36) executes. The program outputs the name of the file or directory (line 18), followed by the results of testing the File object with isFile (line 19), isDirectory (line 20) and isAbsolute (line 22). Next, the program displays the values returned by lastModified (line 24), length (line 24), getPath (line 25), getAbsolutePath (line 26) and getParent (line 26). If the File object represents a directory (line 28), the program obtains a list of the directory's contents as an array of Strings by using File method list (line 30) and displays the list on the screen.

The first output of this program demonstrates a File object associated with the jfc directory from the Java 2 Software Development Kit. The second output demonstrates a File object associated with the readme.txt file from the Java 2D example that comes with the Java 2 Software Development Kit. In both cases, we specified an absolute path on our personal computer.

A *separator character* is used to separate directories and files in the path. On a Windows computer, the separator character is a backslash (\) character. On a UNIX workstation, it is a forward slash (/) character. Java processes both characters identically in a path name. For example, if we were to use the path

```
c:\Program Files\Java\jdk1.6.0\demo/jfc
```

which employs each separator character, Java would still process the path properly. When building strings that represent path information, use File.separator to obtain the local computer's proper separator character rather than explicitly using / or \. This constant returns a String consisting of one character—the proper separator for the system.

Common Programming Error 14.1

Using \ as a directory separator rather than \\ in a string literal is a logic error. A single \ indicates that the \ followed by the next character represents an escape sequence. Use \\ to insert a \ in a string literal.

14.5 Sequential-Access Text Files

In this section, we create and manipulate sequential-access files. As mentioned earlier, these are files in which records are stored in order by the record-key field. We first demonstrate sequential-access files using text files, allowing the reader to quickly create and edit human-readable files. In the subsections of this chapter we discuss creating, writing data to, reading data from and updating sequential-access text files. We also include a credit-inquiry program that retrieves specific data from a file.

14.5.1 Creating a Sequential-Access Text File

Java imposes no structure on a file—notions such as a record do not exist as part of the Java language. Therefore, the programmer must structure files to meet the requirements of the intended application. In the following example, we see how to impose a record structure on a file.

The program in Figs. 14.6–14.7 and Fig. 14.9 creates a simple sequential-access file that might be used in an accounts receivable system to help keep track of the amounts owed to a company by its credit clients. For each client, the program obtains from the user an account number, the client's name and the client's balance (i.e., the amount the client owes the company for goods and services received). The data obtained for each client constitutes a "record" for that client. The account number is used as the record key in this application—the file will be created and maintained in account-number order. The program assumes that the user enters the records in account-number order. In a comprehensive accounts receivable system (based on sequential-access files), a sorting capability would be provided so that the user could enter the records in any order. The records would then be sorted and written to the file.

Class AccountRecord (Fig. 14.6) encapsulates the client record information (i.e., account, first name, and so on) used by the examples in this chapter. The class Account-Record is declared in package com.deitel.jhtp7.ch14 (line 3), so that it can be imported into several examples. Class AccountRecord contains private data members account, firstName, lastName and balance (lines 7–10). This class also provides public *set* and *get* methods for accessing the private fields.

```java
1    // Fig. 14.6: AccountRecord.java
2    // A class that represents one record of information.
3    package com.deitel.jhtp7.ch14; // packaged for reuse
4
5    public class AccountRecord
6    {
7       private int account;
8       private String firstName;
9       private String lastName;
10      private double balance;
11
12      // no-argument constructor calls other constructor with default values
13      public AccountRecord()
14      {
15         this( 0, "", "", 0.0 ); // call four-argument constructor
16      } // end no-argument AccountRecord constructor
17
18      // initialize a record
19      public AccountRecord( int acct, String first, String last, double bal )
20      {
21         setAccount( acct );
22         setFirstName( first );
23         setLastName( last );
24         setBalance( bal );
25      } // end four-argument AccountRecord constructor
26
27      // set account number
28      public void setAccount( int acct )
29      {
```

Fig. 14.6 | AccountRecord maintains information for one account. (Part 1 of 2.)

```
30        account = acct;
31     } // end method setAccount
32
33     // get account number
34     public int getAccount()
35     {
36        return account;
37     } // end method getAccount
38
39     // set first name
40     public void setFirstName( String first )
41     {
42        firstName = first;
43     } // end method setFirstName
44
45     // get first name
46     public String getFirstName()
47     {
48        return firstName;
49     } // end method getFirstName
50
51     // set last name
52     public void setLastName( String last )
53     {
54        lastName = last;
55     } // end method setLastName
56
57     // get last name
58     public String getLastName()
59     {
60        return lastName;
61     } // end method getLastName
62
63     // set balance
64     public void setBalance( double bal )
65     {
66        balance = bal;
67     } // end method setBalance
68
69     // get balance
70     public double getBalance()
71     {
72        return balance;
73     } // end method getBalance
74  } // end class AccountRecord
```

Fig. 14.6 | AccountRecord maintains information for one account. (Part 2 of 2.)

Compile class AccountRecord as follows:

```
javac -d c:\examples\ch14 com\deitel\jhtp7\ch14\AccountRecord.java
```

This places AccountRecord.class in its package directory structure and places the package in c:\examples\ch14. When you compile class AccountRecord (or any other classes that will be reused in this chapter), you should place them in a common directory (e.g., c:\examples\ch14). When you compile or execute classes that use AccountRecord (e.g., CreateTextFile in Fig. 14.7), you must specify the command-line argument -classpath to both javac and java, as in

```
javac -classpath .;c:\examples\ch14 CreateTextFile.java
java -classpath .;c:\examples\ch14 CreateTextFile
```

Note that the current directory (specified with .) is included in the classpath. This ensures that the compiler can locate other classes in the same directory as the class being compiled. The path separator used in the preceding commands should be the one that is appropriate for your platform—for example, a semicolon (;) on Windows and a colon (:) on UNIX/ Linux/Mac OS X.

Now let us examine class CreateTextFile (Fig. 14.7). Line 14 declares Formatter variable output. As discussed in Section 14.3, a Formatter object outputs formatted strings, using the same formatting capabilities as method System.out.printf. A For-matter object can output to various locations, such as the screen or a file, as is done here. The Formatter object is instantiated in line 21 in method openFile (lines 17–34). The constructor used in line 21 takes one argument—a String containing the name of the file, including its path. If a path is not specified, as is the case here, the JVM assumes that the files is in the directory from which the program was executed. For text files, we use the .txt file extension. If the file does not exist, it will be created. If an existing file is opened, its contents are truncated—all the data in the file is discarded. At this point the file is open for writing, and the resulting Formatter object can be used to write data to the file. Lines 23–28 handle the SecurityException, which occurs if the user does not have permission to write data to the file. Lines 29–33 handle the FileNotFoundException, which occurs if the file does not exist and a new file cannot be created. This exception may also occur if there is an error opening the file. Note that in both exception handlers, we call static method System.exit, and pass the value 1. This method terminates the application. An argument of 0 to method exit indicates successful program termination. A nonzero value, such as 1 in this example, normally indicates that an error has occurred. This value is passed to the command window that executed the program. The argument is useful if the program is executed from a batch file on Windows systems or a shell script on UNIX/ Linux/Mac OS X systems. Batch files and shell scripts offer a convenient way of executing several programs in sequence. When the first program ends, the next program begins exe-cution. It is possible to use the argument to method exit in a batch file or shell script to determine whether other programs should execute. For more information on batch files or shell scripts, see your operating system's documentation.

```
 1   // Fig. 14.7: CreateTextFile.java
 2   // Writing data to a text file with class Formatter.
 3   import java.io.FileNotFoundException;
 4   import java.lang.SecurityException;
 5   import java.util.Formatter;
 6   import java.util.FormatterClosedException;
 7   import java.util.NoSuchElementException;
 8   import java.util.Scanner;
```

Fig. 14.7 | Creating a sequential text file. (Part 1 of 3.)

```
 9
10     import com.deitel.jhtp7.ch14.AccountRecord;
11
12     public class CreateTextFile
13     {
14        private Formatter output; // object used to output text to file
15
16        // enable user to open file
17        public void openFile()
18        {
19           try
20           {
21              output = new Formatter( "clients.txt" );
22           } // end try
23           catch ( SecurityException securityException )
24           {
25              System.err.println(
26                 "You do not have write access to this file." );
27              System.exit( 1 );
28           } // end catch
29           catch ( FileNotFoundException filesNotFoundException )
30           {
31              System.err.println( "Error creating file." );
32              System.exit( 1 );
33           } // end catch
34        } // end method openFile
35
36        // add records to file
37        public void addRecords()
38        {
39           // object to be written to file
40           AccountRecord record = new AccountRecord();
41
42           Scanner input = new Scanner( System.in );
43
44           System.out.printf( "%s\n%s\n%s\n%s\n\n",
45              "To terminate input, type the end-of-file indicator ",
46              "when you are prompted to enter input.",
47              "On UNIX/Linux/Mac OS X type <ctrl> d then press Enter",
48              "On Windows type <ctrl> z then press Enter" );
49
50           System.out.printf( "%s\n%s",
51              "Enter account number (> 0), first name, last name and balance.",
52              "? " );
53
54           while ( input.hasNext() ) // loop until end-of-file indicator
55           {
56              try // output values to file
57              {
58                 // retrieve data to be output
59                 record.setAccount( input.nextInt() ); // read account number
60                 record.setFirstName( input.next() ); // read first name
61                 record.setLastName( input.next() ); // read last name
```

Fig. 14.7 | Creating a sequential text file. (Part 2 of 3.)

```
62              record.setBalance( input.nextDouble() ); // read balance
63
64              if ( record.getAccount() > 0 )
65              {
66                 // write new record
67                 output.format( "%d %s %s %.2f\n", record.getAccount(),
68                    record.getFirstName(), record.getLastName(),
69                    record.getBalance() );
70              } // end if
71              else
72              {
73                 System.out.println(
74                    "Account number must be greater than 0." );
75              } // end else
76           } // end try
77           catch ( FormatterClosedException formatterClosedException )
78           {
79              System.err.println( "Error writing to file." );
80              return;
81           } // end catch
82           catch ( NoSuchElementException elementException )
83           {
84              System.err.println( "Invalid input. Please try again." );
85              input.nextLine(); // discard input so user can try again
86           } // end catch
87
88           System.out.printf( "%s %s\n%s", "Enter account number (>0),",
89              "first name, last name and balance.", "? " );
90        } // end while
91     } // end method addRecords
92
93     // close file
94     public void closeFile()
95     {
96        if ( output != null )
97           output.close();
98     } // end method closeFile
99  } // end class CreateTextFile
```

Fig. 14.7 | Creating a sequential text file. (Part 3 of 3.)

Method addRecords (lines 37–91) prompts the user to enter the various fields for each record or to enter the end-of-file key sequence when data entry is complete. Figure 14.8 lists the key combinations for entering end-of-file for various computer systems.

Line 40 creates an AccountRecord object, which will be used to store the values of the current record entered by the user. Line 42 creates a Scanner object to read input from the user at the keyboard. Lines 44–48 and 50–52 prompt the user for input.

Line 54 uses Scanner method hasNext to determine whether the end-of-file key combination has been entered. The loop executes until hasNext encounters the end-of-file indicators.

Lines 59–62 read data from the user, storing the record information in the AccountRecord object. Each statement throws a NoSuchElementException (handled in

Operating system	Key combination
UNIX/Linux/Mac OS X	*<Enter> <Ctrl> d*
Windows	*<Ctrl> z*

Fig. 14.8 | End-of-file key combinations for various popular operating systems.

lines 82–86) if the data is in the wrong format (e.g., a string when an int is expected) or if there is no more data to input. If the account number is greater than 0 (line 64), the record's information is written to clients.txt (lines 67–69) using method format. This method can perform identical formatting to the System.out.printf method used extensively in earlier chapters. This method outputs a formatted string to the output destination of the Formatter object, in this case the file clients.txt. The format string "%d %s %s %.2\n" indicates that the current record will be stored as an integer (the account number) followed by a string (the first name), another string (the last name) and a floating-point value (the balance). Each piece of information is separated from the next by a space, and the double value (the balance) is output with two digits to the right of the decimal point. The data in the text file can be viewed with a text editor, or retrieved later by a program designed to read the file (14.5.2). When lines 67–69 execute, if the Formatter object is closed, a FormatterClosedException will be thrown (handled in lines 77–81). [*Note:* You can also output data to a text file using class java.io.PrintWriter, which also provides method format for outputting formatted data.]

Lines 94–98 declare method closeFile, which closes the Formatter and the underlying output file. Line 97 closes the object by simply calling method **close**. If method close is not called explicitly, the operating system normally will close the file when program execution terminates—this is an example of operating system "housekeeping."

Figure 14.9 runs the program. Line 8 creates a CreateTextFile object, which is then used to open, add records to and close the file (lines 10–12). The sample data for this application is shown in Fig. 14.10. In the sample execution for this program, the user enters information for five accounts, then enters end-of-file to signal that data entry is complete. The sample execution does not show how the data records actually appear in the file. In the next section, to verify that the file has been created successfully, we present a program that reads the file and prints its contents. Because this is a text file, you can also verify the information by opening the file in a text editor.

```
 1   // Fig. 14.9: CreateTextFileTest.java
 2   // Testing the CreateTextFile class.
 3
 4   public class CreateTextFileTest
 5   {
 6      public static void main( String args[] )
 7      {
 8         CreateTextFile application = new CreateTextFile();
```

Fig. 14.9 | Testing the CreateTextFile class. (Part 1 of 2.)

```
 9
10          application.openFile();
11          application.addRecords();
12          application.closeFile();
13       } // end main
14    } // end class CreateTextFileTest
```

```
To terminate input, type the end-of-file indicator
when you are prompted to enter input.
On UNIX/Linux/Mac OS X type <ctrl> d then press Enter
On Windows type <ctrl> z then press Enter

Enter account number (> 0), first name, last name and balance.
? 100 Bob Jones 24.98
Enter account number (> 0), first name, last name and balance.
? 200 Steve Doe -345.67
Enter account number (> 0), first name, last name and balance.
? 300 Pam White 0.00
Enter account number (> 0), first name, last name and balance.
? 400 Sam Stone -42.16
Enter account number (> 0), first name, last name and balance.
? 500 Sue Rich 224.62
Enter account number (> 0), first name, last name and balance.
? ^Z
```

Fig. 14.9 | Testing the CreateTextFile class. (Part 2 of 2.)

Sample data			
100	Bob	Jones	24.98
200	Steve	Doe	-345.67
300	Pam	White	0.00
400	Sam	Stone	-42.16
500	Sue	Rich	224.62

Fig. 14.10 | Sample data for the program in Fig. 14.7.

14.5.2 Reading Data from a Sequential-Access Text File

Data is stored in files so that it may be retrieved for processing when needed. Section 14.5.1 demonstrated how to create a file for sequential access. This section shows how to read data sequentially from a text file. In this section, we demonstrate how class Scanner can be used to input data from a file rather than the keyboard.

The application in Figs. 14.11 and 14.12 reads records from the file "clients.txt" created by the application of Section 14.5.1 and displays the record contents. Line 13 of Fig. 14.11 declares a Scanner that will be used to retrieve input from the file.

Method openFile (lines 16–27) opens the file for reading by instantiating a Scanner object in line 20. We pass a File object to the constructor, which specifies that the

```
 1    // Fig. 14.11: ReadTextFile.java
 2    // This program reads a text file and displays each record.
 3    import java.io.File;
 4    import java.io.FileNotFoundException;
 5    import java.lang.IllegalStateException;
 6    import java.util.NoSuchElementException;
 7    import java.util.Scanner;
 8
 9    import com.deitel.jhtp7.ch14.AccountRecord;
10
11    public class ReadTextFile
12    {
13       private Scanner input;
14
15       // enable user to open file
16       public void openFile()
17       {
18          try
19          {
20             input = new Scanner( new File( "clients.txt" ) );
21          } // end try
22          catch ( FileNotFoundException fileNotFoundException )
23          {
24             System.err.println( "Error opening file." );
25             System.exit( 1 );
26          } // end catch
27       } // end method openFile
28
29       // read record from file
30       public void readRecords()
31       {
32          // object to be written to screen
33          AccountRecord record = new AccountRecord();
34
35          System.out.printf( "%-10s%-12s%-12s%10s\n", "Account",
36             "First Name", "Last Name", "Balance" );
37
38          try // read records from file using Scanner object
39          {
40             while ( input.hasNext() )
41             {
42                record.setAccount( input.nextInt() ); // read account number
43                record.setFirstName( input.next() ); // read first name
44                record.setLastName( input.next() ); // read last name
45                record.setBalance( input.nextDouble() ); // read balance
46
47                // display record contents
48                System.out.printf( "%-10d%-12s%-12s%10.2f\n",
49                   record.getAccount(), record.getFirstName(),
50                   record.getLastName(), record.getBalance() );
51             } // end while
52          } // end try
```

Fig. 14.11 | Sequential file reading using a Scanner. (Part 1 of 2.)

```
53          catch ( NoSuchElementException elementException )
54          {
55             System.err.println( "File improperly formed." );
56             input.close();
57             System.exit( 1 );
58          } // end catch
59          catch ( IllegalStateException stateException )
60          {
61             System.err.println( "Error reading from file." );
62             System.exit( 1 );
63          } // end catch
64       } // end method readRecords
65
66       // close file and terminate application
67       public void closeFile()
68       {
69          if ( input != null )
70             input.close(); // close file
71       } // end method closeFile
72    } // end class ReadTextFile
```

Fig. 14.11 | Sequential file reading using a Scanner. (Part 2 of 2.)

```
1    // Fig. 14.12: ReadTextFileTest.java
2    // This program test class ReadTextFile.
3
4    public class ReadTextFileTest
5    {
6       public static void main( String args[] )
7       {
8          ReadTextFile application = new ReadTextFile();
9
10         application.openFile();
11         application.readRecords();
12         application.closeFile();
13      } // end main
14   } // end class ReadTextFileTest
```

Account	First Name	Last Name	Balance
100	Bob	Jones	24.98
200	Steve	Doe	-345.67
300	Pam	White	0.00
400	Sam	Stone	-42.16
500	Sue	Rich	224.62

Fig. 14.12 | Testing the ReadTextFile class.

Scanner object will read from the file "clients.txt" located in the directory from which the application executes. If the file cannot be found, a FileNotFoundException occurs. The exception is handled in lines 22–26.

Method readRecords (lines 30–64) reads and displays records from the file. Line 33 creates AccountRecord object record to store the current record's information. Lines 35–

36 display headers for the columns in the application's output. Lines 40–51 read data from the file until the end-of-file marker is reached (in which case, method hasNext will return false at line 40). Lines 42–45 use Scanner methods nextInt, next and nextDouble to input an integer (the account number), two strings (the first and last names) and a double value (the balance). Each record is one line of data in the file. The values are stored in object record. If the information in the file is not properly formed (e.g., there is a last name where there should be a balance), a NoSuchElementException occurs when the record is input. This exception is handled in lines 53–58. If the Scanner was closed before the data was input, an IllegalStateException occurs (handled in lines 59–63). If no exceptions occur, the record's information is displayed on the screen (lines 48–50). Note in the format string in line 48 that the account number, first name and last name are left justified, while the balance is right justified and output with two digits of precision. Each iteration of the loop inputs one line of text from the text file, which represents one record.

Lines 67–71 define method closeFile, which closes the Scanner. Method main is defined in Fig. 14.12, in lines 6–13. Line 8 creates a ReadTextFile object, which is then used to open, add records to and close the file (lines 10–12).

14.5.3 Case Study: A Credit-Inquiry Program

To retrieve data sequentially from a file, programs normally start reading from the beginning of the file and read all the data consecutively until the desired information is found. It might be necessary to process the file sequentially several times (from the beginning of the file) during the execution of a program. Class Scanner does not provide the ability to reposition to the beginning of the file. If it is necessary to read the file again, the program must close the file and reopen it.

The program in Figs. 14.13–14.15 allows a credit manager to obtain lists of customers with zero balances (i.e., customers who do not owe any money), customers with credit balances (i.e., customers to whom the company owes money) and customers with debit balances (i.e., customers who owe the company money for goods and services received). A credit balance is a negative amount, and a debit balance is a positive amount.

We begin by creating an enum type (Fig. 14.13) to define the different menu options the user will have. The options and their values are listed in lines 7–10. Method getValue (lines 19–22) retrieves the value of a specific enum constant.

```
1   // Fig. 14.13: MenuOption.java
2   // Defines an enum type for the credit-inquiry program's options.
3
4   public enum MenuOption
5   {
6      // declare contents of enum type
7      ZERO_BALANCE( 1 ),
8      CREDIT_BALANCE( 2 ),
9      DEBIT_BALANCE( 3 ),
10     END( 4 );
11
12     private final int value; // current menu option
```

Fig. 14.13 | Enumeration for menu options. (Part 1 of 2.)

```
13
14      MenuOption( int valueOption )
15      {
16          value = valueOption;
17      } // end MenuOptions enum constructor
18
19      public int getValue()
20      {
21          return value;
22      } // end method getValue
23  } // end enum MenuOption
```

Fig. 14.13 | Enumeration for menu options. (Part 2 of 2.)

```
 1  // Fig. 14.14: CreditInquiry.java
 2  // This program reads a file sequentially and displays the
 3  // contents based on the type of account the user requests
 4  // (credit balance, debit balance or zero balance).
 5  import java.io.File;
 6  import java.io.FileNotFoundException;
 7  import java.lang.IllegalStateException;
 8  import java.util.NoSuchElementException;
 9  import java.util.Scanner;
10
11  import com.deitel.jhtp7.ch14.AccountRecord;
12
13  public class CreditInquiry
14  {
15      private MenuOption accountType;
16      private Scanner input;
17      private MenuOption choices[] = { MenuOption.ZERO_BALANCE,
18          MenuOption.CREDIT_BALANCE, MenuOption.DEBIT_BALANCE,
19          MenuOption.END };
20
21      // read records from file and display only records of appropriate type
22      private void readRecords()
23      {
24          // object to be written to file
25          AccountRecord record = new AccountRecord();
26
27          try // read records
28          {
29              // open file to read from beginning
30              input = new Scanner( new File( "clients.txt" ) );
31
32              while ( input.hasNext() ) // input the values from the file
33              {
34                  record.setAccount( input.nextInt() ); // read account number
35                  record.setFirstName( input.next() ); // read first name
36                  record.setLastName( input.next() ); // read last name
37                  record.setBalance( input.nextDouble() ); // read balance
```

Fig. 14.14 | Credit-inquiry program. (Part 1 of 3.)

```
38
39                // if proper acount type, display record
40                if ( shouldDisplay( record.getBalance() ) )
41                   System.out.printf( "%-10d%-12s%-12s%10.2f\n",
42                      record.getAccount(), record.getFirstName(),
43                      record.getLastName(), record.getBalance() );
44             } // end while
45          } // end try
46          catch ( NoSuchElementException elementException )
47          {
48             System.err.println( "File improperly formed." );
49             input.close();
50             System.exit( 1 );
51          } // end catch
52          catch ( IllegalStateException stateException )
53          {
54             System.err.println( "Error reading from file." );
55             System.exit( 1 );
56          } // end catch
57          catch ( FileNotFoundException fileNotFoundException )
58          {
59             System.err.println( "File cannot be found." );
60             System.exit( 1 );
61          } // end catch
62          finally
63          {
64             if ( input != null )
65                input.close(); // close the Scanner and the file
66          } // end finally
67       } // end method readRecords
68
69       // use record type to determine if record should be displayed
70       private boolean shouldDisplay( double balance )
71       {
72          if ( ( accountType == MenuOption.CREDIT_BALANCE )
73             && ( balance < 0 ) )
74             return true;
75
76          else if ( ( accountType == MenuOption.DEBIT_BALANCE )
77             && ( balance > 0 ) )
78             return true;
79
80          else if ( ( accountType == MenuOption.ZERO_BALANCE )
81             && ( balance == 0 ) )
82             return true;
83
84          return false;
85       } // end method shouldDisplay
86
87       // obtain request from user
88       private MenuOption getRequest()
89       {
```

Fig. 14.14 | Credit-inquiry program. (Part 2 of 3.)

```
 90          Scanner textIn = new Scanner( System.in );
 91          int request = 1;
 92
 93       // display request options
 94       System.out.printf( "\n%s\n%s\n%s\n%s\n%s\n",
 95          "Enter request", " 1 - List accounts with zero balances",
 96          " 2 - List accounts with credit balances",
 97          " 3 - List accounts with debit balances", " 4 - End of run" );
 98
 99       try // attempt to input menu choice
100       {
101          do // input user request
102          {
103             System.out.print( "\n? " );
104             request = textIn.nextInt();
105          } while ( ( request < 1 ) || ( request > 4 ) );
106       } // end try
107       catch ( NoSuchElementException elementException )
108       {
109          System.err.println( "Invalid input." );
110          System.exit( 1 );
111       } // end catch
112
113       return choices[ request - 1 ]; // return enum value for option
114    } // end method getRequest
115
116    public void processRequests()
117    {
118       // get user's request (e.g., zero, credit or debit balance)
119       accountType = getRequest();
120
121       while ( accountType != MenuOption.END )
122       {
123          switch ( accountType )
124          {
125             case ZERO_BALANCE:
126                System.out.println( "\nAccounts with zero balances:\n" );
127                break;
128             case CREDIT_BALANCE:
129                System.out.println( "\nAccounts with credit balances:\n" );
130                break;
131             case DEBIT_BALANCE:
132                System.out.println( "\nAccounts with debit balances:\n" );
133                break;
134          } // end switch
135
136          readRecords();
137          accountType = getRequest();
138       } // end while
139    } // end method processRequests
140 } // end class CreditInquiry
```

Fig. 14.14 | Credit-inquiry program. (Part 3 of 3.)

```
 1   // Fig. 14.15: CreditInquiryTest.java
 2   // This program tests class CreditInquiry.
 3
 4   public class CreditInquiryTest
 5   {
 6      public static void main( String args[] )
 7      {
 8         CreditInquiry application = new CreditInquiry();
 9         application.processRequests();
10      } // end main
11   } // end class CreditInquiryTest
```

Fig. 14.15 | Testing the CreditInquiry class.

Figure 14.14 contains the functionality for the credit-inquiry program, and Fig. 14.15 contains the main method that executes the program. The program displays a text menu and allows the credit manager to enter one of three options to obtain credit information. Option 1 (ZERO_BALANCE) produces a list of accounts with zero balances. Option 2 (CREDIT_BALANCE) produces a list of accounts with credit balances. Option 3 (DEBIT_BALANCE) produces a list of accounts with debit balances. Option 4 (END) terminates program execution. A sample output is shown in Fig. 14.16.

The record information is collected by reading through the entire file and determining whether each record satisfies the criteria for the account type selected by the credit manager. Method processRequests (lines 116–139 of Fig. 14.14) calls method getRequest to display the menu options (line 119) and stores the result in MenuOption variable accountType. Note that getRequest translates the number typed by the user into a Menu-Option by using the number to select a MenuOption from array choices. Lines 121–138 loop until the user specifies that the program should terminate. The switch statement in lines 123–134 displays a header for the current set of records to be output to the screen. Line 136 calls method readRecords (lines 22–67), which loops through the file and reads every record.

Line 30 of method readRecords opens the file for reading with a Scanner. Note that the file will be opened for reading with a new Scanner object each time this method is called, so that we can again read from the beginning of the file. Lines 34–37 read a record. Line 40 calls method shouldDisplay (lines 70–85) to determine whether the current record satisfies the account type requested. If shouldDisplay returns true, the program displays the account information. When the end-of-file marker is reached, the loop terminates and line 65 calls the Scanner's close method to close the Scanner and the file. Notice that this occurs in a finally block, which will execute whether or not the file was successfully read. Once all the records have been read, control returns to method process-Requests and getRequest is again called (line 137) to retrieve the user's next menu option. Figure 14.15 contains method main, and calls method processRequests in line 9.

14.5.4 Updating Sequential-Access Files

The data in many sequential files cannot be modified without the risk of destroying other data in the file. For example, if the name "White" needed to be changed to "Worthington," the old name cannot simply be overwritten because the new name requires more space. The record for White was written to the file as

```
Enter request
 1 - List accounts with zero balances
 2 - List accounts with credit balances
 3 - List accounts with debit balances
 4 - End of run

? 1

Accounts with zero balances:

300        Pam        White              0.00

Enter request
 1 - List accounts with zero balances
 2 - List accounts with credit balances
 3 - List accounts with debit balances
 4 - End of run

? 2

Accounts with credit balances:
200        Steve      Doe             -345.67
400        Sam        Stone            -42.16

Enter request
 1 - List accounts with zero balances
 2 - List accounts with credit balances
 3 - List accounts with debit balances
 4 - End of run

? 3

Accounts with debit balances:
100        Bob        Jones             24.98
500        Sue        Rich             224.62

? 4
```

Fig. 14.16 | Sample output of the credit-inquiry program in Fig. 14.15.

```
    300 Pam White 0.00
```

If the record is rewritten beginning at the same location in the file using the new name, the record will be

```
    300 Pam Worthington 0.00
```

The new record is larger (has more characters) than the original record. The characters beyond the second "o" in "Worthington" will overwrite the beginning of the next sequential record in the file. The problem here is that fields in a text file—and hence records—can vary in size. For example, 7, 14, –117, 2074 and 27383 are all ints stored in the same number of bytes (4) internally, but they are different-sized fields when displayed on the screen or written to a file as text.

Therefore, records in a sequential-access file are not usually updated in place. Instead, the entire file is usually rewritten. To make the preceding name change, the records before 300 Pam White 0.00 would be copied to a new file, the new record (which can be of a different size than the one it replaces) would be written and the records after 300 Pam White 0.00 would be copied to the new file. It is uneconomical to update just one record, but reasonable if a substantial portion of the records needs to be updated.

14.6 Object Serialization

In Section 14.5, we demonstrated how to write the individual fields of an AccountRecord object into a file as text, and how to read those fields from a file and place their values into an AccountRecord object in memory. In the examples, AccountRecord was used to aggregate the information for one record. When the instance variables for an AccountRecord were output to a disk file, certain information was lost, such as the type of each value. For instance, if the value "3" were read from a file, there is no way to tell whether the value came from an int, a String or a double. We have only data, not type information, on a disk. If the program that is going to read this data "knows" what object type the data corresponds to, then the data is simply read into objects of that type. For example, in Section 14.5.2, we know that we are inputting an int (the account number), followed by two Strings (the first and last name) and a double (the balance). We also know that these values are separated by spaces, with only one record on each line. Sometimes we will not know exactly how the data is stored in a file. In such cases, we would like to read or write an entire object from a file. Java provides such a mechanism, called object serialization. A so-called serialized object is an object represented as a sequence of bytes that includes the object's data as well as information about the object's type and the types of data stored in the object. After a serialized object has been written into a file, it can be read from the file and deserialized—that is, the type information and bytes that represent the object and its data can be used to recreate the object in memory.

Classes ObjectInputStream and ObjectOutputStream, which respectively implement the ObjectInput and ObjectOutput interfaces, enable entire objects to be read from or written to a stream (possibly a file). To use serialization with files, we initialize Object-InputStream and ObjectOutputStream objects with stream objects that read from and write to files—objects of classes FileInputStream and FileOutputStream, respectively. Initializing stream objects with other stream objects in this manner is sometimes called wrapping—the new stream object being created wraps the stream object specified as a constructor argument. To wrap a FileInputStream in an ObjectInputStream, for instance, we pass the FileInputStream object to the ObjectInputStream's constructor.

The ObjectOutput interface contains method **writeObject**, which takes an Object that implements interface Serializable (discussed shortly) as an argument and writes its information to an OutputStream. Correspondingly, the ObjectInput interface contains method **readObject**, which reads and returns a reference to an Object from an Input-Stream. After an object has been read, its reference can be cast to the object's actual type. As you will see in Chapter 24, Networking, applications that communicate via a network, such as the Internet, can also transmit entire objects across the network.

In this section, we create and manipulate sequential-access files using object serialization. Object serialization is performed with byte-based streams, so the sequential files created and manipulated will be binary files. Recall that binary files cannot be viewed in standard text editors. For this reason, we write a separate application that knows how to read and display serialized objects.

14.6.1 Creating a Sequential-Access File Using Object Serialization

We begin by creating and writing serialized objects to a sequential-access file. In this section, we reuse much of the code from Section 14.5, so we focus only on the new features.

Defining the AccountRecordSerializable Class

Let us begin by modifying our AccountRecord class so that objects of this class can be serialized. Class AccountRecordSerializable (Fig. 14.17) implements interface Serializable (line 7), which allows objects of AccountRecordSerializable to be serialized and deserialized with ObjectOutputStreams and ObjectInputStreams. Interface Serializable is a tagging interface. Such an interface does not contain methods. A class that implements Serializable is tagged as being a Serializable object. This is important because an ObjectOutputStream will not output an object unless it *is a* Serializable object, which is the case for any object of a class that implements Serializable.

In a class that implements Serializable, the programmer must ensure that every instance variable of the class is a Serializable type. Any instance variable that is not seri-

```
1   // Fig. 14.17: AccountRecordSerializable.java
2   // A class that represents one record of information.
3   package com.deitel.jhtp7.ch14; // packaged for reuse
4
5   import java.io.Serializable;
6
7   public class AccountRecordSerializable implements Serializable
8   {
9      private int account;
10     private String firstName;
11     private String lastName;
12     private double balance;
13
14     // no-argument constructor calls other constructor with default values
15     public AccountRecordSerializable()
16     {
17        this( 0, "", "", 0.0 );
18     } // end no-argument AccountRecordSerializable constructor
19
20     // four-argument constructor initializes a record
21     public AccountRecordSerializable(
22        int acct, String first, String last, double bal )
23     {
24        setAccount( acct );
25        setFirstName( first );
26        setLastName( last );
27        setBalance( bal );
28     } // end four-argument AccountRecordSerializable constructor
29
```

Fig. 14.17 | AccountRecordSerializable class for serializable objects. (Part I of 2.)

```
30      // set account number
31      public void setAccount( int acct )
32      {
33          account = acct;
34      } // end method setAccount
35
36      // get account number
37      public int getAccount()
38      {
39          return account;
40      } // end method getAccount
41
42      // set first name
43      public void setFirstName( String first )
44      {
45          firstName = first;
46      } // end method setFirstName
47
48      // get first name
49      public String getFirstName()
50      {
51          return firstName;
52      } // end method getFirstName
53
54      // set last name
55      public void setLastName( String last )
56      {
57          lastName = last;
58      } // end method setLastName
59
60      // get last name
61      public String getLastName()
62      {
63          return lastName;
64      } // end method getLastName
65
66      // set balance
67      public void setBalance( double bal )
68      {
69          balance = bal;
70      } // end method setBalance
71
72      // get balance
73      public double getBalance()
74      {
75          return balance;
76      } // end method getBalance
77  } // end class AccountRecordSerializable
```

Fig. 14.17 | AccountRecordSerializable class for serializable objects. (Part 2 of 2.)

alizable must be declared **transient** to indicate that it is not Serializable and should be ignored during the serialization process. By default, all primitive-type variables are serializable. For variables of reference types, you must check the definition of the class (and possibly its superclasses) to ensure that the type is Serializable. By default, array objects are serializable. However, if the array contains references to other objects, those objects may or may not be serializable.

Class AccountRecordSerializable contains private data members account, firstName, lastName and balance. This class also provides public *get* and *set* methods for accessing the private fields.

Now let us discuss the code that creates the sequential-access file (Figs. 14.18–14.19). We concentrate only on new concepts here. As stated in Section 14.3, a program can open a file by creating an object of stream class FileInputStream or FileOutputStream. In this example, the file is to be opened for output, so the program creates a FileOutputStream (line 21 of Fig. 14.18). The string argument that is passed to the FileOutputStream's constructor represents the name and path of the file to be opened. Existing files that are opened for output in this manner are truncated. Note that the .ser file extension is used—we use this file extension for binary files that contain serialized objects.

```
1   // Fig. 14.18: CreateSequentialFile.java
2   // Writing objects sequentially to a file with class ObjectOutputStream.
3   import java.io.FileOutputStream;
4   import java.io.IOException;
5   import java.io.ObjectOutputStream;
6   import java.util.NoSuchElementException;
7   import java.util.Scanner;
8
9   import com.deitel.jhtp7.ch14.AccountRecordSerializable;
10
11  public class CreateSequentialFile
12  {
13     private ObjectOutputStream output; // outputs data to file
14
15     // allow user to specify file name
16     public void openFile()
17     {
18        try // open file
19        {
20           output = new ObjectOutputStream(
21              new FileOutputStream( "clients.ser" ) );
22        } // end try
23        catch ( IOException ioException )
24        {
25           System.err.println( "Error opening file." );
26        } // end catch
27     } // end method openFile
28
29     // add records to file
30     public void addRecords()
31     {
32        AccountRecordSerializable record; // object to be written to file
33        int accountNumber = 0; // account number for record object
34        String firstName; // first name for record object
```

Fig. 14.18 | Sequential file created using ObjectOutputStream. (Part 1 of 3.)

```
35          String lastName; // last name for record object
36          double balance; // balance for record object
37
38          Scanner input = new Scanner( System.in );
39
40          System.out.printf( "%s\n%s\n%s\n%s\n\n",
41             "To terminate input, type the end-of-file indicator ",
42             "when you are prompted to enter input.",
43             "On UNIX/Linux/Mac OS X type <ctrl> d then press Enter",
44             "On Windows type <ctrl> z then press Enter" );
45
46          System.out.printf( "%s\n%s",
47             "Enter account number (> 0), first name, last name and balance.",
48             "? " );
49
50          while ( input.hasNext() ) // loop until end-of-file indicator
51          {
52             try // output values to file
53             {
54                accountNumber = input.nextInt(); // read account number
55                firstName = input.next(); // read first name
56                lastName = input.next(); // read last name
57                balance = input.nextDouble(); // read balance
58
59                if ( accountNumber > 0 )
60                {
61                   // create new record
62                   record = new AccountRecordSerializable( accountNumber,
63                      firstName, lastName, balance );
64                   output.writeObject( record ); // output record
65                } // end if
66                else
67                {
68                   System.out.println(
69                      "Account number must be greater than 0." );
70                } // end else
71             } // end try
72             catch ( IOException ioException )
73             {
74                System.err.println( "Error writing to file." );
75                return;
76             } // end catch
77             catch ( NoSuchElementException elementException )
78             {
79                System.err.println( "Invalid input. Please try again." );
80                input.nextLine(); // discard input so user can try again
81             } // end catch
82
83             System.out.printf( "%s %s\n%s", "Enter account number (>0),",
84                "first name, last name and balance.", "? " );
85          } // end while
86       } // end method addRecords
87
```

Fig. 14.18 | Sequential file created using `ObjectOutputStream`. (Part 2 of 3.)

```
88        // close file and terminate application
89        public void closeFile()
90        {
91           try // close file
92           {
93              if ( output != null )
94                 output.close();
95           } // end try
96           catch ( IOException ioException )
97           {
98              System.err.println( "Error closing file." );
99              System.exit( 1 );
100          } // end catch
101       } // end method closeFile
102    } // end class CreateSequentialFile
```

Fig. 14.18 | Sequential file created using `ObjectOutputStream`. (Part 3 of 3.)

```
1     // Fig. 14.19: CreateSequentialFileTest.java
2     // Testing class CreateSequentialFile.
3
4     public class CreateSequentialFileTest
5     {
6        public static void main( String args[] )
7        {
8           CreateSequentialFile application = new CreateSequentialFile();
9
10          application.openFile();
11          application.addRecords();
12          application.closeFile();
13       } // end main
14    } // end class CreateSequentialFileTest
```

```
To terminate input, type the end-of-file indicator
when you are prompted to enter input.
On UNIX/Linux/Mac OS X type <ctrl> d then press Enter
On Windows type <ctrl> z then press Enter

Enter account number (> 0), first name, last name and balance.
? 100 Bob Jones 24.98
Enter account number (> 0), first name, last name and balance.
? 200 Steve Doe -345.67
Enter account number (> 0), first name, last name and balance.
? 300 Pam White 0.00
Enter account number (> 0), first name, last name and balance.
? 400 Sam Stone -42.16
Enter account number (> 0), first name, last name and balance.
? 500 Sue Rich 224.62
Enter account number (> 0), first name, last name and balance.
? ^Z
```

Fig. 14.19 | Testing class `CreateSequentialFile`.

Common Programming Error 14.2

It is a logic error to open an existing file for output when, in fact, the user wishes to preserve the file.

Class `FileOutputStream` provides methods for writing `byte` arrays and individual bytes to a file. In this program we wish to write objects to a file—a capability not provided by `FileOutputStream`. For this reason, we wrap a `FileOutputStream` in an `ObjectOutputStream` by passing the new `FileOutputStream` object to the `ObjectOutputStream`'s constructor (lines 20–21). The `ObjectOutputStream` object uses the `FileOutputStream` object to write objects into the file. Lines 20–21 might throw an `IOException` if a problem occurs while opening the file (e.g., when a file is opened for writing on a drive with insufficient space or when a read-only file is opened for writing). If so, the program displays an error message (lines 23–26). If no exception occurs, the file is open and variable `output` can be used to write objects to the file.

This program assumes that data is input correctly and in the proper record-number order. Method `addRecords` (lines 30–86) performs the write operation. Lines 62–63 create an `AccountRecordSerializable` object from the data entered by the user. Line 64 calls `ObjectOutputStream` method `writeObject` to write the `record` object to the output file. Note that only one statement is required to write the entire object.

Method `closeFile` (lines 89–101) closes the file. Method `closeFile` calls `ObjectOutputStream` method **`close`** on `output` to close both the `ObjectOutputStream` and its underlying `FileOutputStream` (line 94). Note that the call to method `close` is contained in a `try` block. Method `close` throws an `IOException` if the file cannot be closed properly. In this case, it is important to notify the user that the information in the file might be corrupted. When using wrapped streams, closing the outermost stream also closes the underlying file.

In the sample execution for the program in Fig. 14.19, we entered information for five accounts—the same information shown in Fig. 14.10. The program does not show how the data records actually appear in the file. Remember that now we are using binary files, which are not humanly readable. To verify that the file has been created successfully, the next section presents a program to read the file's contents.

14.6.2 Reading and Deserializing Data from a Sequential-Access File

As discussed in Section 14.5.2, data is stored in files so that it may be retrieved for processing when needed. The preceding section showed how to create a file for sequential access using object serialization. In this section, we discuss how to read serialized data sequentially from a file.

The program in Figs. 14.20–14.21 reads records from a file created by the program in Section 14.6.1 and displays the contents. The program opens the file for input by creating a `FileInputStream` object (line 21). The name of the file to open is specified as an argument to the `FileInputStream` constructor. In Fig. 14.18, we wrote objects to the file, using an `ObjectOutputStream` object. Data must be read from the file in the same format in which it was written. Therefore, we use an `ObjectInputStream` wrapped around a `FileInputStream` in this program (lines 20–21). If no exceptions occur when opening the file, variable `input` can be used to read objects from the file.

```
1   // Fig. 14.20: ReadSequentialFile.java
2   // This program reads a file of objects sequentially
3   // and displays each record.
4   import java.io.EOFException;
5   import java.io.FileInputStream;
6   import java.io.IOException;
7   import java.io.ObjectInputStream;
8
9   import com.deitel.jhtp7.ch14.AccountRecordSerializable;
10
11  public class ReadSequentialFile
12  {
13     private ObjectInputStream input;
14
15     // enable user to select file to open
16     public void openFile()
17     {
18        try // open file
19        {
20           input = new ObjectInputStream(
21              new FileInputStream( "clients.ser" ) );
22        } // end try
23        catch ( IOException ioException )
24        {
25           System.err.println( "Error opening file." );
26        } // end catch
27     } // end method openFile
28
29     // read record from file
30     public void readRecords()
31     {
32        AccountRecordSerializable record;
33        System.out.printf( "%-10s%-12s%-12s%10s\n", "Account",
34           "First Name", "Last Name", "Balance" );
35
36        try // input the values from the file
37        {
38           while ( true )
39           {
40              record = ( AccountRecordSerializable ) input.readObject();
41
42              // display record contents
43              System.out.printf( "%-10d%-12s%-12s%10.2f\n",
44                 record.getAccount(), record.getFirstName(),
45                 record.getLastName(), record.getBalance() );
46           } // end while
47        } // end try
48        catch ( EOFException endOfFileException )
49        {
50           return; // end of file was reached
51        } // end catch
52        catch ( ClassNotFoundException classNotFoundException )
53        {
```

Fig. 14.20 | Sequential file read using an `ObjectInputStream`. (Part 1 of 2.)

```
54              System.err.println( "Unable to create object." );
55           } // end catch
56           catch ( IOException ioException )
57           {
58              System.err.println( "Error during read from file." );
59           } // end catch
60        } // end method readRecords
61
62        // close file and terminate application
63        public void closeFile()
64        {
65           try // close file and exit
66           {
67              if ( input != null )
68                 input.close();
69           } // end try
70           catch ( IOException ioException )
71           {
72              System.err.println( "Error closing file." );
73              System.exit( 1 );
74           } // end catch
75        } // end method closeFile
76     } // end class ReadSequentialFile
```

Fig. 14.20 | Sequential file read using an `ObjectInputStream`. (Part 2 of 2.)

```
1     // Fig. 14.21: ReadSequentialFileTest.java
2     // This program test class ReadSequentialFile.
3
4     public class ReadSequentialFileTest
5     {
6        public static void main( String args[] )
7        {
8           ReadSequentialFile application = new ReadSequentialFile();
9
10          application.openFile();
11          application.readRecords();
12          application.closeFile();
13       } // end main
14    } // end class ReadSequentialFileTest
```

Account	First Name	Last Name	Balance
100	Bob	Jones	24.98
200	Steve	Doe	-345.67
300	Pam	White	0.00
400	Sam	Stone	-42.16
500	Sue	Rich	224.62

Fig. 14.21 | Testing class `ReadSequentialFile`.

The program reads records from the file in method `readRecords` (lines 30–60). Line 40 calls `ObjectInputStream` method `readObject` to read an `Object` from the file. To use `AccountRecordSerializable`-specific methods, we downcast the returned `Object` to type

AccountRecordSerializable. Method readObject throws an EOFException (processed at lines 48–51) if an attempt is made to read beyond the end of the file. Method readObject throws a ClassNotFoundException if the class for the object being read cannot be located. This might occur if the file is accessed on a computer that does not have the class. Figure 14.21 contains method main (lines 6–13), which opens the file, calls method readRecords and closes the file.

14.7 Additional java.io Classes

We now introduce you to other useful classes in the java.io package. We overview additional interfaces and classes for byte-based input and output streams and character-based input and output streams.

Interfaces and Classes for Byte-Based Input and Output

InputStream and OutputStream (subclasses of Object) are abstract classes that declare methods for performing byte-based input and output, respectively. We used concrete classes FileInputStream (a subclass of InputStream) and FileOutputStream (a subclass of OutputStream) to manipulate files in this chapter.

Pipes are synchronized communication channels between threads. We discuss threads in Chapter 23, Multithreading. Java provides PipedOutputStream (a subclass of OutputStream) and PipedInputStream (a subclass of InputStream) to establish pipes between two threads in a program. One thread sends data to another by writing to a PipedOutputStream. The target thread reads information from the pipe via a PipedInputStream.

A FilterInputStream filters an InputStream, and a FilterOutputStream filters an OutputStream. Filtering means simply that the filter stream provides additional functionality, such as aggregating data bytes into meaningful primitive-type units. FilterInputStream and FilterOutputStream are abstract classes, so some of their filtering capabilities are provided by their concrete subclasses.

A PrintStream (a subclass of FilterOutputStream) performs text output to the specified stream. Actually, we have been using PrintStream output throughout the text to this point—System.out and System.err are PrintStream objects.

Reading data as raw bytes is fast, but crude. Usually, programs read data as aggregates of bytes that form ints, floats, doubles and so on. Java programs can use several classes to input and output data in aggregate form.

Interface DataInput describes methods for reading primitive types from an input stream. Classes DataInputStream and RandomAccessFile each implement this interface to read sets of bytes and view them as primitive-type values. Interface DataInput includes methods readLine (for byte arrays), readBoolean, readByte, readChar, readDouble, readFloat, readFully (for byte arrays), readInt, readLong, readShort, readUnsignedByte, readUnsignedShort, readUTF (for reading Unicode characters encoded by Java—we discuss UTF encoding in Appendix I, Unicode®) and skipBytes.

Interface DataOutput describes a set of methods for writing primitive types to an output stream. Classes DataOutputStream (a subclass of FilterOutputStream) and RandomAccessFile each implement this interface to write primitive-type values as bytes. Interface DataOutput includes overloaded versions of method write (for a byte or for a byte array) and methods `writeBoolean`, `writeByte`, `writeBytes`, `writeChar`, `writeChars` (for Unicode `Strings`), `writeDouble`, `writeFloat`, `writeInt`, `writeLong`, `writeShort` and `writeUTF` (to output text modified for Unicode).

Buffering is an I/O-performance-enhancement technique. With a `BufferedOutput-Stream` (a subclass of class `FilterOutputStream`), each output statement does not necessarily result in an actual physical transfer of data to the output device (which is a slow operation compared to processor and main memory speeds). Rather, each output operation is directed to a region in memory called a **buffer** that is large enough to hold the data of many output operations. Then, actual transfer to the output device is performed in one large **physical output operation** each time the buffer fills. The output operations directed to the output buffer in memory are often called **logical output operations**. With a `BufferedOutputStream`, a partially filled buffer can be forced out to the device at any time by invoking the stream object's `flush` method.

Using buffering can greatly increase the efficiency of an application. Typical I/O operations are extremely slow compared with the speed of accessing computer memory. Buffering reduces the number of I/O operations by first combining smaller outputs together in memory. The number of actual physical I/O operations is small compared with the number of I/O requests issued by the program. Thus, the program that is using buffering is more efficient.

Performance Tip 14.1

Buffered I/O can yield significant performance improvements over unbuffered I/O.

With a `BufferedInputStream` (a subclass of class `FilterInputStream`), many "logical" chunks of data from a file are read as one large **physical input operation** into a memory buffer. As a program requests each new chunk of data, it is taken from the buffer. (This procedure is sometimes referred to as a **logical input operation**.) When the buffer is empty, the next actual physical input operation from the input device is performed to read in the next group of "logical" chunks of data. Thus, the number of actual physical input operations is small compared with the number of read requests issued by the program.

Java stream I/O includes capabilities for inputting from byte arrays in memory and outputting to byte arrays in memory. A `ByteArrayInputStream` (a subclass of `InputStream`) reads from a byte array in memory. A `ByteArrayOutputStream` (a subclass of `OutputStream`) outputs to a byte array in memory. One use of byte-array I/O is data validation. A program can input an entire line at a time from the input stream into a byte array. Then a validation routine can scrutinize the contents of the byte array and correct the data if necessary. Finally, the program can proceed to input from the byte array, "knowing" that the input data is in the proper format. Outputting to a byte array is a nice way to take advantage of the powerful output-formatting capabilities of Java streams. For example, data can be stored in a byte array, using the same formatting that will be displayed at a later time, and the byte array can then be output to a disk file to preserve the screen image.

A `SequenceInputStream` (a subclass of `InputStream`) enables concatenation of several `InputStreams`, which means that the program sees the group as one continuous `InputStream`. When the program reaches the end of an input stream, that stream closes, and the next stream in the sequence opens.

Interfaces and Classes for Character-Based Input and Output

In addition to the byte-based streams, Java provides the `Reader` and `Writer` abstract classes, which are Unicode two-byte, character-based streams. Most of the byte-based streams have corresponding character-based concrete `Reader` or `Writer` classes.

Classes `BufferedReader` (a subclass of abstract class `Reader`) and `BufferedWriter` (a subclass of abstract class `Writer`) enable buffering for character-based streams. Remember that character-based streams use Unicode characters—such streams can process data in any language that the Unicode character set represents.

Classes `CharArrayReader` and `CharArrayWriter` read and write, respectively, a stream of characters to a character array. A `LineNumberReader` (a subclass of `BufferedReader`) is a buffered character stream that keeps track of the number of lines read (i.e., a newline, a return or a carriage-return–line-feed combination). Keeping track of line numbers can be useful if the program needs to inform the reader of an error on a specific line.

Class `FileReader` (a subclass of `InputStreamReader`) and class `FileWriter` (a subclass of `OutputStreamWriter`) read characters from and write characters to a file, respectively. Class `PipedReader` and class `PipedWriter` implement piped-character streams that can be used to transfer information between threads. Class `StringReader` and `StringWriter` read characters from and write characters to `String`s, respectively. A `PrintWriter` writes characters to a stream.

14.8 Opening Files with `JFileChooser`

Class `JFileChooser` displays a dialog (known as the `JFileChooser` dialog) that enables the user to easily select files or directories. To demonstrate the `JFileChooser` dialog, we enhance the example in Section 14.4, as shown in Figs. 14.22–14.23. The example now contains a graphical user interface, but still displays the same data as before. The constructor calls method `analyzePath` in line 34. This method then calls method `getFile` in line 68 to retrieve the `File` object.

```java
 1   // Fig. 14.22: FileDemonstration.java
 2   // Demonstrating the File class.
 3   import java.awt.BorderLayout;
 4   import java.awt.event.ActionEvent;
 5   import java.awt.event.ActionListener;
 6   import java.io.File;
 7   import javax.swing.JFileChooser;
 8   import javax.swing.JFrame;
 9   import javax.swing.JOptionPane;
10   import javax.swing.JScrollPane;
11   import javax.swing.JTextArea;
12   import javax.swing.JTextField;
13
14   public class FileDemonstration extends JFrame
15   {
16      private JTextArea outputArea; // used for output
17      private JScrollPane scrollPane; // used to provide scrolling to output
18
```

Fig. 14.22 | Demonstrating `JFileChooser`. (Part 1 of 3.)

```
19      // set up GUI
20      public FileDemonstration()
21      {
22         super( "Testing class File" );
23
24         outputArea = new JTextArea();
25
26         // add outputArea to scrollPane
27         scrollPane = new JScrollPane( outputArea );
28
29         add( scrollPane, BorderLayout.CENTER ); // add scrollPane to GUI
30
31         setSize( 400, 400 ); // set GUI size
32         setVisible( true ); // display GUI
33
34         analyzePath(); // create and analyze File object
35      } // end FileDemonstration constructor
36
37      // allow user to specify file name
38      private File getFile()
39      {
40         // display file dialog, so user can choose file to open
41         JFileChooser fileChooser = new JFileChooser();
42         fileChooser.setFileSelectionMode(
43            JFileChooser.FILES_AND_DIRECTORIES );
44
45         int result = fileChooser.showOpenDialog( this );
46
47         // if user clicked Cancel button on dialog, return
48         if ( result == JFileChooser.CANCEL_OPTION )
49            System.exit( 1 );
50
51         File fileName = fileChooser.getSelectedFile(); // get selected file
52
53         // display error if invalid
54         if ( ( fileName == null ) || ( fileName.getName().equals( "" ) ) )
55         {
56            JOptionPane.showMessageDialog( this, "Invalid File Name",
57               "Invalid File Name", JOptionPane.ERROR_MESSAGE );
58            System.exit( 1 );
59         } // end if
60
61         return fileName;
62      } // end method getFile
63
64      // display information about file user specifies
65      public void analyzePath()
66      {
67         // create File object based on user input
68         File name = getFile();
69
70         if ( name.exists() ) // if name exists, output information about it
71         {
```

Fig. 14.22 | Demonstrating `JFileChooser`. (Part 2 of 3.)

```
72          // display file (or directory) information
73          outputArea.setText( String.format(
74             "%s%s\n%s\n%s\n%s\n%s%s\n%s%s\n%s%s\n%s%s\n%s%s",
75             name.getName(), " exists",
76             ( name.isFile() ? "is a file" : "is not a file" ),
77             ( name.isDirectory() ? "is a directory" :
78                "is not a directory" ),
79             ( name.isAbsolute() ? "is absolute path" :
80                "is not absolute path" ), "Last modified: ",
81             name.lastModified(), "Length: ", name.length(),
82             "Path: ", name.getPath(), "Absolute path: ",
83             name.getAbsolutePath(), "Parent: ", name.getParent() ) );
84
85          if ( name.isDirectory() ) // output directory listing
86          {
87             String directory[] = name.list();
88             outputArea.append( "\n\nDirectory contents:\n" );
89
90             for ( String directoryName : directory )
91                outputArea.append( directoryName + "\n" );
92          } // end else
93       } // end outer if
94       else // not file or directory, output error message
95       {
96          JOptionPane.showMessageDialog( this, name +
97             " does not exist.", "ERROR", JOptionPane.ERROR_MESSAGE );
98       } // end else
99    } // end method analyzePath
100 } // end class FileDemonstration
```

Fig. 14.22 | Demonstrating JFileChooser. (Part 3 of 3.)

Method getFile is defined in lines 38–62 of Fig. 14.22. Line 41 creates a JFile-Chooser and assigns its reference to fileChooser. Lines 42–43 call method **setFileSelectionMode** to specify what the user can select from the fileChooser. For this program, we use JFileChooser static constant **FILES_AND_DIRECTORIES** to indicate that files and directories can be selected. Other static constants include **FILES_ONLY** and **DIRECTORIES_ONLY**.

```
1    // Fig. 14.23: FileDemonstrationTest.java
2    // Testing the FileDmonstration class.
3    import javax.swing.JFrame;
4
5    public class FileDemonstrationTest
6    {
7       public static void main( String args[] )
8       {
9          FileDemonstration application = new FileDemonstration();
10         application.setDefaultCloseOperation( JFrame.EXIT_ON_CLOSE );
11      } // end main
12   } // end class FileDemonstrationTest
```

Fig. 14.23 | Testing class FileDemonstration. (Part 1 of 2.)

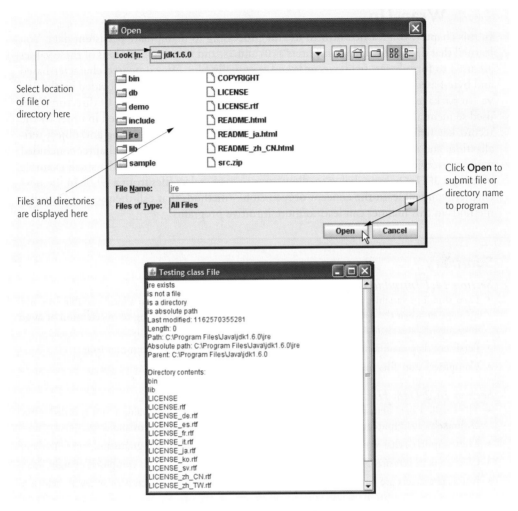

Fig. 14.23 | Testing class `FileDemonstration`. (Part 2 of 2.)

Line 45 calls method **showOpenDialog** to display the `JFileChooser` dialog titled **Open**. Argument `this` specifies the `JFileChooser` dialog's parent window, which determines the position of the dialog on the screen. If `null` is passed, the dialog is displayed in the center of the screen—otherwise, the dialog is centered over the application window (specified by the argument `this`). A `JFileChooser` dialog is a modal dialog that does not allow the user to interact with any other window in the program until the user closes the `JFileChooser` by clicking the **Open** or **Cancel** button. The user selects the drive, directory or file name, then clicks **Open**. Method `showOpenDialog` returns an integer specifying which button (**Open** or **Cancel**) the user clicked to close the dialog. Line 48 tests whether the user clicked **Cancel** by comparing the result with `static` constant `CANCEL_OPTION`. If they are equal, the program terminates. Line 51 retrieves the file the user selected by calling `JFileChooser` method **getSelectedFile**. The program then displays information about the selected file or directory.

14.9 Wrap-Up

In this chapter, you learned how to use file processing to manipulate persistent data. You learned that data is stored in computers as 0s and 1s, and that combinations of these values are used to form bytes, fields, records and eventually files. We compared character-based and byte-based streams, and introduced several file-processing classes provided by the java.io package. You used class File to retrieve information about a file or directory. You used sequential-access file processing to manipulate records that are stored in order by the record-key field. You learned the differences between text-file processing and object serialization, and used serialization to store and retrieve entire objects. The chapter concluded with an overview of other classes provided by the java.io package, and a small example of using a JFileChooser dialog to allow users to easily select files from a GUI. In the next chapter, you will learn the concept of recursion—methods that call themselves. Defining methods in this manner can lead to more intuitive programs.

Summary

Section 14.1 Introduction

- Data stored in variables and arrays is temporary—the data is lost when a local variable goes out of scope or when the program terminates. Computers use files for long-term retention of large amounts of data, even after the programs that created the data terminate.
- Persistent data maintained in files exists beyond the duration of program execution.
- Computers store files on secondary storage devices such as hard disks.

Section 14.2 Data Hierarchy

- The smallest data item in a computer can assume the value 0 or the value 1 and is called a bit. Ultimately, a computer processes all data items as combinations of zeros and ones.
- The computer's character set is the set of all characters used to write programs and represent data.
- Characters in Java are Unicode characters composed of two bytes, each composed of eight bits.
- Just as characters are composed of bits, fields are composed of characters or bytes. A field is a group of characters or bytes that conveys meaning.
- Data items processed by computers form a data hierarchy that becomes larger and more complex in structure as we progress from bits to characters to fields, and so on.
- Typically, several fields compose a record (implemented as a class in Java).
- A record is a group of related fields.
- A file is a group of related records.
- To facilitate the retrieval of specific records from a file, at least one field in each record is chosen as a record key. A record key identifies a record as belonging to a particular person or entity and is unique to each record.
- There are many ways to organize records in a file. The most common is called a sequential file, in which records are stored in order by the record-key field.
- A group of related files is often called a database. A collection of programs designed to create and manage databases is called a database management system (DBMS).

Section 14.3 Files and Streams

- Java views each file as a sequential stream of bytes.

- Every operating system provides a mechanism to determine the end of a file, such as an end-of-file marker or a count of the total bytes in the file that is recorded in a system-maintained administrative data structure.

- Byte-based streams represent data in binary format.

- Character-based streams represent data as sequences of characters.

- Files that are created using byte-based streams are binary files. Files created using character-based streams are text files. Text files can be read by text editors, whereas binary files are read by a program that converts the data to a human-readable format.

- Java also can associate streams with different devices. Three stream objects are associated with devices when a Java program begins executing—System.in, System.out and System.err.

- The java.io package includes definitions for stream classes, such as FileInputStream (for byte-based input from a file), FileOutputStream (for byte-based output to a file), FileReader (for character-based input from a file) and FileWriter (for character-based output to a file). Files are opened by creating objects of these stream classes.

Section 14.4 Class `File`

- Class File is used to obtain information about files and directories.

- Character-based input and output can be performed with classes Scanner and Formatter.

- Class Formatter enables formatted data to be output to the screen or to a file in a manner similar to System.out.printf.

- A file or directory's path specifies its location on disk.

- An absolute path contains all the directories, starting with the root directory, that lead to a specific file or directory. Every file or directory on a disk drive has the same root directory in its path.

- A relative path normally starts from the directory in which the application began executing.

- A separator character is used to separate directories and files in the path.

Section 14.5 Sequential-Access Text Files

- Java imposes no structure on a file—notions such as a record do not exist as part of the Java language. The programmer must structure files to meet an application's requirements.

- To retrieve data sequentially from a file, programs normally start reading from the beginning of the file and read all the data consecutively until the desired information is found.

- Data in many sequential files cannot be modified without the risk of destroying other data in the file. Therefore, records in a sequential-access file are not usually updated in place. Instead, the entire file is usually rewritten.

Section 14.6 Object Serialization

- Java provides a mechanism called object serialization that enables entire objects to be written to or read from a stream.

- A serialized object is an object represented as a sequence of bytes that includes the object's data as well as information about the object's type and the types of data stored in the object.

- After a serialized object has been written into a file, it can be read from the file and deserialized—that is, the type information and bytes that represent the object and its data can be used to re-create the object in memory.

- Classes ObjectInputStream and ObjectOutputStream, which respectively implement the ObjectInput and ObjectOutput interfaces, enable entire objects to be read from or written to a stream (possibly a file).

- Only classes that implement interface Serializable can be serialized and deserialized with ObjectOutputStreams and ObjectInputStreams.

Section 14.7 Additional **java.io** Classes

- The ObjectOutput interface contains method writeObject, which takes an Object that implements interface Serializable as an argument and writes its information to an OutputStream.

- The ObjectInput interface contains method readObject, which reads and returns a reference to an Object from an InputStream. After an object has been read, its reference can be cast to the object's actual type.

- Buffering is an I/O-performance-enhancement technique. With a BufferedOutputStream, each output statement does not necessarily result in an actual physical transfer of data to the output device. Rather, each output operation is directed to a region in memory called a buffer that is large enough to hold the data of many output operations. Actual transfer to the output device is then performed in one large physical output operation each time the buffer fills.

- With a BufferedInputStream, many "logical" chunks of data from a file are read as one large physical input operation into a memory buffer. As a program requests each new chunk of data, it is taken from the buffer. When the buffer is empty, the next actual physical input operation from the input device is performed to read in the next group of "logical" chunks of data.

Section 14.8 Opening Files with **JFileChooser**

- Class JFileChooser is used to display a dialog that enables users of a program to easily select files from a GUI.

Terminology

absolute path	deserialized object
ASCII (American Standard Code for Information Interchange) character set	direct-access application
	direct-access files
batch file	DIRECTORIES_ONLY constant of class JFileChooser
binary file	
bit (binary digit)	directory
buffer	directory name
byte-based stream	disk
byte data type	end-of-file marker
CANCEL_OPTION constant of class JFileChooser	EndOfFileException
canRead method of class File	exists method of class File
canWrite method of class File	exit method of class System
capacity	field
character-based stream	file
character set	File class
-classpath command-line argument to java	file-position pointer
-classpath command-line argument to javac	file processing
data hierarchy	FileInputStream class
database	FileOutputStream class
database management system (DBMS)	FileReader class
DataInput interface	FILES_AND_DIRECTORIES constant of class JFileChooser
DataInputStream class	
DataOutput interface	FILES_ONLY constant of class JFileChooser
DataOutputStream class	FileWriter class
decimal digit	fixed-length record

Formatter class
getAbsolutePath method of class File
getName method of class File
getParent method of class File
getPath method of class File
getSelectedFile method of class JFileChooser
InputStream class
IOException
isAbsolute method of class File
isDirectory method of class File
isFile method of class File
java.io package
JFileChooser class
JFileChooser dialog
lastModified method of class File
length method of class File
list method of class File
logical input operations
logical output operations
memory buffer
NoSuchElementException
object serialization
ObjectInputStream class
ObjectOutputStream class
optical disk
OutputStream class
parent directory
pathSeparator static field of class File
persistent data
physical input operation
physical output operation
PrintStream class
PrintWriter class
read-only file
Reader class
readLine method of class BufferedReader
readObject method of class ObjectInputStream
readObject method of interface ObjectInput
record
record key

relative path
root directory
secondary storage devices
sequential-access file
Serializable interface
serialized object
setErr method of class System
setIn method of class System
setOut method of class System
setSelectionMode of class JFileChooser
shell script
showOpenDialog of class JFileChooser
standard error stream object
stream object
stream of bytes
stream processing
System.err (standard error stream)
tagging interface
text file
transient keyword
truncated
Unicode character set
URI (Uniform Resource Identifier)
wrapped byte array
wrapping of stream objects
writeBoolean method of interface DataOutput
writeByte method of interface DataOutput
writeBytes method of interface DataOutput
writeChar method of interface DataOutput
writeChars method of interface DataOutput
writeDouble method of interface DataOutput
writeFloat method of interface DataOutput
writeInt method of interface DataOutput
writeLong method of interface DataOutput
writeObject method of class
    ObjectOutputStream
writeObject method of interface ObjectOutput
Writer class
writeShort method of interface DataOutput
writeUTF method of interface DataOutput

Self-Review Exercises

14.1   Fill in the blanks in each of the following statements:
a) Ultimately, all data items processed by a computer are reduced to combinations of _____ and _____.
b) The smallest data item a computer can process is called a(n) _____.
c) A(n) _____ can sometimes be viewed as a group of related records.
d) Digits, letters and special symbols are referred to as _____.
e) A database is a group of related _____.
f) Object _____ normally enables a program to output error messages to the screen.

14.2 Determine which of the following statements are *true* and which are *false*. If *false*, explain why.

a) The programmer must explicitly create the stream objects System.in, System.out and System.err.

b) When reading data from a file using class Scanner, if the programmer wishes to read data in the file multiple times, the file must be closed and reopened to read from the beginning of the file. This moves the file-position pointer back to the beginning of the file.

c) Method exists of class File returns true if the name specified as the argument to the File constructor is a file or directory in the specified path.

d) Binary files are human readable.

e) An absolute path contains all the directories, starting with the root directory, that lead to a specific file or directory.

f) Class Formatter contains method printf, which enables formatted data to be output to the screen or to a file.

14.3 Complete the following tasks, assuming that each applies to the same program:

a) Write a statement that opens file "oldmast.txt" for input—use Scanner variable in-OldMaster.

b) Write a statement that opens file "trans.txt" for input—use Scanner variable in-Transaction.

c) Write a statement that opens file "newmast.txt" for output (and creation)—use for-matter variable outNewMaster.

d) Write the statements needed to read a record from the file "oldmast.txt". The data read should be used to create an object of class AccountRecord—use Scanner variable inOldMaster. Assume that class AccountRecord is the same as the AccountRecord class in Fig. 14.6.

e) Write the statements needed to read a record from the file "trans.txt". The record is an object of class TransactionRecord—use Scanner variable inTransaction. Assume that class TransactionRecord contains method setAccount (which takes an int) to set the account number and method setAmount (which takes a double) to set the amount of the transaction.

f) Write a statement that outputs a record to the file "newmast.txt". The record is an object of type AccountRecord—use Formatter variable outNewMaster.

14.4 Complete the following tasks, assuming that each applies to the same program:

a) Write a statement that opens file "oldmast.ser" for input—use ObjectInputStream variable inOldMaster to wrap a FileInputStream object.

b) Write a statement that opens file "trans.ser" for input—use ObjectInputStream variable inTransaction to wrap a FileInputStream object.

c) Write a statement that opens file "newmast.ser" for output (and creation)—use Ob-jectOutputStream variable outNewMaster to wrap a FileOutputStream.

d) Write a statement that reads a record from the file "oldmast.ser". The record is an object of class AccountRecordSerializable—use ObjectInputStream variable inOld-Master. Assume class AccountRecordSerializable is the same as the AccountRecord-Serializable class in Fig. 14.17

e) Write a statement that reads a record from the file "trans.ser". The record is an object of class TransactionRecord—use ObjectInputStream variable inTransaction.

f) Write a statement that outputs a record to the file "newmast.ser". The record is an object of type AccountRecordSerializable—use ObjectOutputStream variable outNew-Master.

14.5 Find the error in each block of code and show how to correct it.

a) Assume that account, company and amount are declared.

```
ObjectOutputStream outputStream;

outputStream.writeInt( account );
outputStream.writeChars( company );
outputStream.writeDouble( amount );
```

b) The following statements should read a record from the file "payables.txt". The Scanner variable inPayable should be used to refer to this file.

```
Scanner inPayable = new Scanner( new File( "payables.txt" ) );
PayablesRecord record = ( PayablesRecord ) inPayable.readObject();
```

Answers to Self-Review Exercises

14.1 a) ones, zeros. b) bit. c) file. d) characters. e) files. f) System.err.

14.2 a) False. These three streams are created for the programmer when a Java application begins executing.

b) True.

c) True.

d) False. Text files are human readable.

e) True.

f) False. Class Formatter contains method format, which enables formatted data to be output to the screen or to a file.

14.3 a) Scanner inOldMaster = new Scanner(new File ("oldmast.txt"));

b) Scanner inTransaction = new Scanner(new File("trans.txt"));

c) Formatter outNewMaster = new Formatter("newmast.txt");

d) AccountRecord account = new AccountRecord();
```
    account.setAccount( inOldMaster.nextInt() );
    account.setFirstName( inOldMaster.next() );
    account.setLastName( inOldMaster.next() );
    account.setBalance( inOldMaster.nextDouble() );
```

e) TransactionRecord transaction = new Transaction();
```
    transaction.setAccount( inTransaction.nextInt() );
    transaction.setAmount( inTransaction.nextDouble() );
```

f) outNewMaster.format("%d %s %s %.2f\n",
```
    account.getAccount(), account.getFirstName(),
    account.getLastName(), account.getBalance() );
```

14.4 a) ObjectInputStream inOldMaster = new ObjectInputStream(
```
    new FileInputStream( "oldmast.ser" ) );
```

b) ObjectInputStream inTransaction = new ObjectInputStream(
```
    new FileInputStream( "trans.ser" ) );
```

c) ObjectOutputStream outNewMaster = new ObjectOutputStream(
```
    new FileOutputStream( "newmast.ser" ) );
```

d) accountRecord = (AccountRecordSerializable) inOldMaster.readObject();

e) transactionRecord = (TransactionRecord) inTransaction.readObject();

f) outNewMaster.writeObject(newAccountRecord);

14.5 a) Error: The file has not been opened before the attempt is made to output data to the stream.
Correction: Open a file for output by creating a new ObjectOutputStream object that wraps a FileOutputStream object.

b) Error: This example uses text files with a Scanner, there is no object serialization. As a result, method readObject cannot be used to read that data from the file. Each piece of data must be read separately, then used to create a PayablesRecord object.

Correction: Use methods of inPayable to read each piece of the PayablesRecord object.

Exercises

14.6 Fill in the blanks in each of the following statements:

a) Computers store large amounts of data on secondary storage devices as _____.

b) A(n) _____ is composed of several fields.

c) To facilitate the retrieval of specific records from a file, one field in each record is chosen as a(n) _____.

d) Files that are created using byte-based streams are referred to as _____ files, while files created using character-based streams are referred to as _____ files.

e) The standard stream objects are _____, _____ and _____.

14.7 *(File Matching)* Self-Review Exercise 14.3 asks the reader to write a series of single statements. Actually, these statements form the core of an important type of file-processing program, namely, a file-matching program. In commercial data processing, it is common to have several files in each application system. In an accounts receivable system, for example, there is generally a master file containing detailed information about each customer, such as the customer's name, address, telephone number, outstanding balance, credit limit, discount terms, contract arrangements and possibly a condensed history of recent purchases and cash payments.

As transactions occur (i.e., sales are made and payments arrive in the mail), information about them is entered into a file. At the end of each business period (a month for some companies, a week for others, and a day in some cases), the file of transactions (called "trans.txt") is applied to the master file (called "oldmast.txt") to update each account's purchase and payment record. During an update, the master file is rewritten as the file "newmast.txt", which is then used at the end of the next business period to begin the updating process again.

File-matching programs must deal with certain problems that do not arise in single-file programs. For example, a match does not always occur. If a customer on the master file has not made any purchases or cash payments in the current business period, no record for this customer will appear on the transaction file. Similarly, a customer who did make some purchases or cash payments could have just moved to this community, and if so, the company may not have had a chance to create a master record for this customer.

Write a complete file-matching accounts receivable program. Use the account number on each file as the record key for matching purposes. Assume that each file is a sequential text file with records stored in increasing account-number order.

a) Define class TransactionRecord. Objects of this class contain an account number and amount for the transaction. Provide methods to modify and retrieve these values.

b) Modify class AccountRecord in Fig. 14.6 to include method combine, which takes a TransactionRecord object and combines the balance of the AccountRecord object and the amount value of the TransactionRecord object.

c) Write a program to create data for testing the program. Use the sample account data in Figs. 14.24 and 14.25. Run the program to create the files trans.txt and oldmast.txt, to be used by your file-matching program.

d) Create class FileMatch to perform the file-matching functionality. The class should contain methods that read oldmast.txt and trans.txt. When a match occurs (i.e., records with the same account number appear in both the master file and the transaction file), add the dollar amount in the transaction record to the current balance in the master record, and write the "newmast.txt" record. (Assume that purchases are indicated by positive amounts in the transaction file and payments by negative amounts.) When there is a master record for a particular account, but no corresponding transaction record, merely write the master record to "newmast.txt". When there is a transaction record, but no corresponding master record, print to a log file the message "Unmatched transaction record for account number..." (fill in the account number from the transaction record). The log file should be a text file named "log.txt".

14.8 *(File Matching with Multiple Transactions)* It is possible (and actually common) to have several transaction records with the same record key. This situation occurs, for example, when a customer makes several purchases and cash payments during a business period. Rewrite your accounts receivable file-matching program from Exercise 14.7 to provide for the possibility of handling several transaction records with the same record key. Modify the test data of CreateData.java to include the additional transaction records in Fig. 14.26.

Master file account number	Name	Balance
100	Alan Jones	348.17
300	Mary Smith	27.19
500	Sam Sharp	0.00
700	Suzy Green	−14.22

Fig. 14.24 | Sample data for master file.

Transaction file account number	Transaction amount
100	27.14
300	62.11
400	100.56
900	82.17

Fig. 14.25 | Sample data for transaction file.

Account number	Dollar amount
300	83.89
700	80.78
700	1.53

Fig. 14.26 | Additional transaction records.

14.9 *(File Matching with Object Serialization)* Recreate your solution for Exercise 14.8 using object serialization. Use the statements from Exercise 14.4 as your basis for this program. You may want to create applications to read the data stored in the .ser files—the code in Section 14.6.2 can be modified for this purpose.

14.10 *(Student Poll)* Figure 7.8 contains an array of survey responses that is hard coded into the program. Suppose we wish to process survey results that are stored in a file. This exercise requires two separate programs. First, create an application that prompts the user for survey responses and outputs each response to a file. Use a Formatter to create a file called numbers.txt. Each integer should be written using method format. Then modify the program in Fig. 7.8 to read the survey responses from numbers.txt. The responses should be read from the file by using a Scanner. Method nextInt should be used to input one integer at a time from the file. The program should continue to read responses until it reaches the end of file. The results should be output to the text file "output.txt".

14.11 Modify Exercise 11.18 to allow the user to save a drawing into a file or load a prior drawing from a file using object serialization. Add buttons **Load** (to read objects from a file), **Save** (to write objects to a file) and **Generate Shapes** (to display a random set of shapes on the screen). Use an ObjectOutputStream to write to the file and an ObjectInputStream to read from the file. Write the array of MyShape objects using method writeObject (class ObjectOutputStream), and read the array using method readObject (ObjectInputStream). Note that the object-serialization mechanism can read or write entire arrays—it is not necessary to manipulate each element of the array of MyShape objects individually. It is simply required that all the shapes be Serializable. For both the **Load** and **Save** buttons, use a JFileChooser to allow the user to select the file in which the shapes will be stored or from which they will be read. When the user first runs the program, no shapes should be displayed on the screen. The user can display shapes by opening a previously saved file of shapes or by clicking the **Generate Shapes** button. When the **Generate Shapes** button is clicked, the application should generate a random number of shapes up to a total of 15. Once there are shapes on the screen, users can save them to a file using the **Save** button.

15

Recursion

OBJECTIVES

In this chapter you will learn:

- The concept of recursion.
- How to write and use recursive methods.
- How to determine the base case and recursion step in a recursive algorithm.
- How recursive method calls are handled by the system.
- The differences between recursion and iteration, and when it is appropriate to use each.
- What the geometric shapes called fractals are and how to draw them using recursion.
- What recursive backtracking is and why it is an effective problem-solving technique.

15.1 Introduction

The programs we have discussed so far are generally structured as methods that call one another in a disciplined, hierarchical manner. For some problems, however, it is useful to have a method call itself. Such a method is known as a recursive method. A recursive method can be called either directly or indirectly through another method. Recursion is an important topic discussed at length in upper-level computer science courses. In this chapter, we consider recursion conceptually, then present several programs containing recursive methods. Figure 15.1 summarizes the recursion examples and exercises in the book.

Chapter	Recursion examples and exercises in this book
15	Factorial Method (Figs. 15.3 and 15.4)
	Fibonacci Method (Figs. 15.5 and 15.6)
	Towers of Hanoi (Figs. 15.13 and 15.14)
	Fractals (Figs. 15.21 and 15.22)
	What Does This Code Do? (Exercise 15.7, Exercise 15.11 and Exercise 15.13)
	Find the Error in the Following Code (Exercise 15.8)
	Raising an Integer to an Integer Power (Exercise 15.9)
	Visualizing Recursion (Exercise 15.10)
	Greatest Common Divisor (Exercise 15.10)
	Determine Whether a String Is a Palindrome (Exercise 15.12)
	Eight Queens (Exercise 15.15)
	Print an Array (Exercise 15.13)
	Print an Array Backward (Exercise 15.14)
	Minimum Value in an Array (Exercise 15.15)
	Star Fractal (Exercise 15.16)
	Maze Traversal Using Recursive Backtracking (Exercise 15.17)
	Generating Mazes Randomly (Exercise 15.18)
	Mazes of Any Size (Exercise 15.19)
	Time Needed to Calculate a Fibonacci Number (Exercise 15.23)

Fig. 15.1 | Summary of the recursion examples and exercises in this text. (Part 1 of 2.)

Chapter	Recursion examples and exercises in this book
16	Merge Sort (Figs. 16.10 and 16.11)
	Linear Search (Exercise 16.8)
	Binary Search (Exercise 16.9)
	Quicksort (Exercise 16.10)
17	Binary-Tree Insert (Fig. 17.17)
	Preorder Traversal of a Binary Tree (Fig. 17.17)
	Inorder Traversal of a Binary Tree (Fig. 17.17)
	Postorder Traversal of a Binary Tree (Fig. 17.17)
	Print a Linked List Backward (Exercise 17.20)
	Search a Linked List (Exercise 17.21)

Fig. 15.1 | Summary of the recursion examples and exercises in this text. (Part 2 of 2.)

15.2 Recursion Concepts

Recursive problem-solving approaches have a number of elements in common. When a recursive method is called to solve a problem, the method actually is capable of solving only the simplest case(s), or base case(s). If the method is called with a base case, the method returns a result. If the method is called with a more complex problem, the method typically divides the problem into two conceptual pieces—a piece that the method knows how to do and a piece that it does not know how to do. To make recursion feasible, the latter piece must resemble the original problem, but be a slightly simpler or smaller version of it. Because this new problem looks like the original problem, the method calls a fresh copy of itself to work on the smaller problem—this is referred to as a recursive call and is also called the recursion step. The recursion step normally includes a return statement, because its result will be combined with the portion of the problem the method knew how to solve to form a result that will be passed back to the original caller. This concept of separating the problem into two smaller portions is a form of the divide-and-conquer approach introduced in Chapter 6.

The recursion step executes while the original call to the method is still active (i.e., while it has not finished executing). It can result in many more recursive calls as the method divides each new subproblem into two conceptual pieces. For the recursion to eventually terminate, each time the method calls itself with a simpler version of the original problem, the sequence of smaller and smaller problems must converge on a base case. At that point, the method recognizes the base case and returns a result to the previous copy of the method. A sequence of returns ensues until the original method call returns the final result to the caller.

A recursive method may call another method, which may in turn make a call back to the recursive method. Such a process is known as an indirect recursive call or indirect recursion. For example, method A calls method B, which makes a call back to method A. This is still considered recursion, because the second call to method A is made while the first call to method A is active—that is, the first call to method A has not yet finished executing (because it is waiting on method B to return a result to it) and has not returned to method A's original caller.

To better understand the concept of recursion, let us look at an example of recursion that is quite common to computer users—the recursive definition of a directory on a computer. A computer normally stores related files in a directory. A directory can be empty, can contain files and/or can contain other directories (usually referred to as subdirectories). Each of these subdirectories, in turn, may also contain both files and directories. If we want to list each file in a directory (including all the files in the directory's subdirectories), we need to create a method that first lists the initial directory's files, then makes recursive calls to list the files in each of that directory's subdirectories. The base case occurs when a directory is reached that does not contain any subdirectories. At this point, all the files in the original directory have been listed and no further recursion is necessary.

15.3 Example Using Recursion: Factorials

Let us write a recursive program to perform a popular mathematical calculation. Consider the factorial of a positive integer n, written $n!$ (and pronounced "n factorial"), which is the product

$$n \cdot (n-1) \cdot (n-2) \cdot \ldots \cdot 1$$

with 1! equal to 1 and 0! defined to be 1. For example, 5! is the product $5 \cdot 4 \cdot 3 \cdot 2 \cdot 1$, which is equal to 120.

The factorial of integer number (where number $\geq$ 0) can be calculated *iteratively* (non-recursively) using a for statement as follows:

```
factorial = 1;

for ( int counter = number; counter >= 1; counter-- )
    factorial *= counter;
```

A recursive declaration of the factorial method is arrived at by observing the following relationship:

$$n! = n \cdot (n-1)!$$

For example, 5! is clearly equal to $5 \cdot 4!$, as is shown by the following equations:

$$5! = 5 \cdot 4 \cdot 3 \cdot 2 \cdot 1$$
$$5! = 5 \cdot (4 \cdot 3 \cdot 2 \cdot 1)$$
$$5! = 5 \cdot (4!)$$

The evaluation of 5! would proceed as shown in Fig. 15.2. Figure 15.2(a) shows how the succession of recursive calls proceeds until 1! (the base case) is evaluated to be 1, which terminates the recursion. Figure 15.2(b) shows the values returned from each recursive call to its caller until the final value is calculated and returned.

Figure 15.3 uses recursion to calculate and print the factorials of the integers from 0–10. The recursive method factorial (lines 7–13) first tests to determine whether a terminating condition (line 9) is true. If number is less than or equal to 1 (the base case), factorial returns 1, no further recursion is necessary and the method returns. If number is greater than 1, line 12 expresses the problem as the product of number and a recursive call to factorial evaluating the factorial of number - 1, which is a slightly smaller problem than the original calculation, factorial(number).

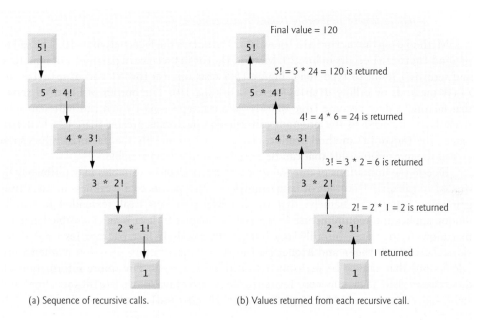

(a) Sequence of recursive calls.   (b) Values returned from each recursive call.

Fig. 15.2 | Recursive evaluation of 5!.

```
1   // Fig. 15.3: FactorialCalculator.java
2   // Recursive factorial method.
3
4   public class FactorialCalculator
5   {
6      // recursive method factorial
7      public long factorial( long number )
8      {
9         if ( number <= 1 ) // test for base case
10           return 1; // base cases: 0! = 1 and 1! = 1
11        else // recursion step
12           return number * factorial( number - 1 );
13     } // end method factorial
14
15     // output factorials for values 0-10
16     public void displayFactorials()
17     {
18        // calculate the factorials of 0 through 10
19        for ( int counter = 0; counter <= 10; counter++ )
20           System.out.printf( "%d! = %d\n", counter, factorial( counter ) );
21     } // end method displayFactorials
22  } // end class FactorialCalculator
```

Fig. 15.3 | Factorial calculations with a recursive method.

Common Programming Error 15.1

Either omitting the base case or writing the recursion step incorrectly so that it does not converge on the base case can cause a logic error known as infinite recursion, *where recursive calls are continuously made until memory has been exhausted. This error is analogous to the problem of an infinite loop in an iterative (nonrecursive) solution.*

Method `displayFactorials` (lines 16–21) displays the factorials of 0–10. The call to method `factorial` occurs in line 20. Method `factorial` receives a parameter of type `long` and returns a result of type `long`. Figure 15.4 tests our `factorial` and `displayFactorials` methods by calling `displayFactorials` (line 10). The output of Fig. 15.4 shows that factorial values become large quickly. We use type `long` (which can represent relatively large integers) so the program can calculate factorials greater than 12!. Unfortunately, the `factorial` method produces large values so quickly that factorial values soon exceed the maximum value that can be stored even in a `long` variable.

Due to the limitations of integral types, `float` or `double` variables may ultimately be needed to calculate factorials of larger numbers. This points to a weakness in most programming languages—namely, that the languages are not easily extended to handle unique application requirements. As we saw in Chapter 9, Java is an extensible language that allows us to create arbitrarily large integers if we wish. In fact, package `java.math` provides classes `BigInteger` and `BigDecimal` explicitly for arbitrary precision mathematical calculations that cannot be performed with primitive types. For more information on these classes visit, `java.sun.com/javase/6/docs/api/java/math/BigInteger.html` and `java.sun.com/javase/6/docs/api/java/math/BigDecimal.html`, respectively.

```java
1   // Fig. 15.4: FactorialTest.java
2   // Testing the recursive factorial method.
3
4   public class FactorialTest
5   {
6      // calculate factorials of 0-10
7      public static void main( String args[] )
8      {
9         FactorialCalculator factorialCalculator = new FactorialCalculator();
10        factorialCalculator.displayFactorials();
11     } // end main
12  } // end class FactorialTest
```

```
0! = 1
1! = 1
2! = 2
3! = 6
4! = 24
5! = 120
6! = 720
7! = 5040
8! = 40320
9! = 362880
10! = 3628800
```

Fig. 15.4 | Testing the `factorial` method.

15.4 Example Using Recursion: Fibonacci Series

The Fibonacci series,

  0, 1, 1, 2, 3, 5, 8, 13, 21, …

begins with 0 and 1 and has the property that each subsequent Fibonacci number is the sum of the previous two Fibonacci numbers. This series occurs in nature and describes a form of spiral. The ratio of successive Fibonacci numbers converges on a constant value of 1.618…, a number that has been called the golden ratio or the golden mean. Humans tend to find the golden mean aesthetically pleasing. Architects often design windows, rooms and buildings whose length and width are in the ratio of the golden mean. Postcards are often designed with a golden-mean length-to-width ratio.

The Fibonacci series may be defined recursively as follows:

  fibonacci(0) = 0
  fibonacci(1) = 1
  fibonacci(n) = fibonacci(n − 1) + fibonacci(n − 2)

Note that there are two base cases for the Fibonacci calculation: fibonacci(0) is defined to be 0, and fibonacci(1) is defined to be 1. The program in Fig. 15.5 calculates the *i*th Fibonacci number recursively, using method fibonacci (lines 7–13). Method display-Fibonacci (lines 15–20) tests fibonacci, displaying the Fibonacci values of 0–10. The variable counter created in the for header in line 17 indicates which Fibonacci number to calculate for each iteration of the for statement. Fibonacci numbers tend to become large quickly. Therefore, we use type long as the parameter type and the return type of method fibonacci. Line 9 of Fig. 15.6 calls method displayFibonacci (line 9) to calculate the Fibonacci values.

```java
1   // Fig. 15.5: FibonacciCalculator.java
2   // Recursive fibonacci method.
3
4   public class FibonacciCalculator
5   {
6      // recursive declaration of method fibonacci
7      public long fibonacci( long number )
8      {
9         if ( ( number == 0 ) || ( number == 1 ) ) // base cases
10            return number;
11         else // recursion step
12            return fibonacci( number - 1 ) + fibonacci( number - 2 );
13      } // end method fibonacci
14
15      public void displayFibonacci()
16      {
17         for ( int counter = 0; counter <= 10; counter++ )
18            System.out.printf( "Fibonacci of %d is: %d\n", counter,
19               fibonacci( counter ) );
20      } // end method displayFibonacci
21   } // end class FibonacciCalculator
```

Fig. 15.5 | Fibonacci numbers generated with a recursive method.

```
 I    // Fig. 15.6: FibonacciTest.java
 2    // Testing the recursive fibonacci method.
 3
 4    public class FibonacciTest
 5    {
 6       public static void main( String args[] )
 7       {
 8          FibonacciCalculator fibonacciCalculator = new FibonacciCalculator();
 9          fibonacciCalculator.displayFibonacci();
10       } // end main
II    } // end class FibonacciTest
```

```
Fibonacci of 0 is: 0
Fibonacci of 1 is: 1
Fibonacci of 2 is: 1
Fibonacci of 3 is: 2
Fibonacci of 4 is: 3
Fibonacci of 5 is: 5
Fibonacci of 6 is: 8
Fibonacci of 7 is: 13
Fibonacci of 8 is: 21
Fibonacci of 9 is: 34
Fibonacci of 10 is: 55
```

Fig. 15.6 | Testing the fibonacci method.

The call to method fibonacci (line 19 of Fig. 15.5) from displayFibonacci is not a recursive call, but all subsequent calls to fibonacci performed from the body of fibonacci (line 12 of Fig. 15.5) are recursive, because at that point the calls are initiated by method fibonacci itself. Each time fibonacci is called, it immediately tests for the base cases—number equal to 0 or number equal to 1 (line 9). If this condition is true, fibonacci simply returns number because fibonacci(0) is 0, and fibonacci(1) is 1. Interestingly, if number is greater than 1, the recursion step generates *two* recursive calls (line 12), each for a slightly smaller problem than the original call to fibonacci.

Figure 15.7 shows how method fibonacci evaluates fibonacci(3). Note that at the bottom of the figure, we are left with the values 1, 0 and 1—the results of evaluating the base cases. The first two return values (from left to right), 1 and 0, are returned as the values for the calls fibonacci(1) and fibonacci(0). The sum 1 plus 0 is returned as the value of fibonacci(2). This is added to the result (1) of the call to fibonacci(1), producing the value 2. This final value is then returned as the value of fibonacci(3).

Figure 15.7 raises some interesting issues about the order in which Java compilers evaluate the operands of operators. This order is different from the order in which operators are applied to their operands—namely, the order dictated by the rules of operator precedence. From Figure 15.7, it appears that while fibonacci(3) is being evaluated, two recursive calls will be made—fibonacci(2) and fibonacci(1). But in what order will these calls be made? The Java language specifies that the order of evaluation of the operands is from left to right. Thus, the call fibonacci(2) is made first and the call fibonacci(1) is made second.

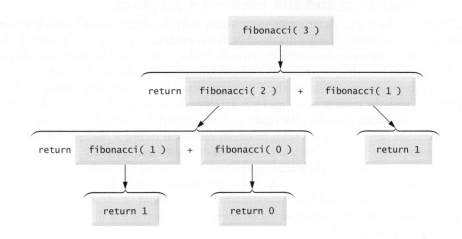

Fig. 15.7 | Set of recursive calls for `fibonacci( 3 )`.

A word of caution is in order about recursive programs like the one we use here to generate Fibonacci numbers. Each invocation of the `fibonacci` method that does not match one of the base cases (0 or 1) results in two more recursive calls to the `fibonacci` method. Hence, this set of recursive calls rapidly gets out of hand. Calculating the Fibonacci value of 20 with the program in Fig. 15.5 requires 21,891 calls to the `fibonacci` method; calculating the Fibonacci value of 30 requires 2,692,537 calls! As you try to calculate larger Fibonacci values, you will notice that each consecutive Fibonacci number you use the application to calculate results in a substantial increase in calculation time and in the number of calls to the `fibonacci` method. For example, the Fibonacci value of 31 requires 4,356,617 calls, and the Fibonacci value of 32 requires 7,049,155 calls! As you can see, the number of calls to `fibonacci` increases quickly—1,664,080 additional calls between Fibonacci values of 30 and 31 and 2,692,538 additional calls between Fibonacci values of 31 and 32! The difference in the number of calls made between Fibonacci values of 31 and 32 is more than 1.5 times the difference in the number of calls for Fibonacci values between 30 and 31. Problems of this nature can humble even the world's most powerful computers. [*Note:* In the field of complexity theory, computer scientists study how hard algorithms work to complete their tasks. Complexity issues are discussed in detail in the upper-level computer science curriculum course generally called "Algorithms." We introduce various complexity issues in Chapter 16, Searching and Sorting.] In the exercises, you will be asked to enhance the Fibonacci program of Fig. 15.5 such that it calculates the approximate amount of time required to perform the calculation. For this purpose, you will call static System method `currentTimeMillis`, which takes no arguments and returns the computer's current time in milliseconds.

Performance Tip 15.1

Avoid Fibonacci-style recursive programs, because they result in an exponential "explosion" of method calls.

15.5 Recursion and the Method-Call Stack

In Chapter 6, the stack data structure was introduced in the context of understanding how Java performs method calls. We discussed both the method-call stack (also known as the program execution stack) and activation records. In this section, we will use these concepts to demonstrate how the program execution stack handles recursive method calls.

Let's begin by returning to the Fibonacci example—specifically, calling method fibonacci with the value 3, as in Fig. 15.7. To show the order in which the method calls' activation records are placed on the stack, we have lettered the method calls in Fig. 15.8.

When the first method call (A) is made, an activation record is pushed onto the program execution stack which contains the value of the local variable number (3, in this case). The program execution stack, including the activation record for method call A, is illustrated in part (a) of Fig. 15.9. [*Note:* We use a simplified stack here. In an actual computer, the program execution stack and its activation records would be more complex than in Fig. 15.9, containing such information as where the method call is to return to when it has completed execution.]

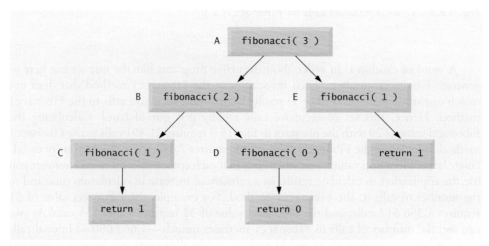

Fig. 15.8 | Method calls made within the call fibonacci(3).

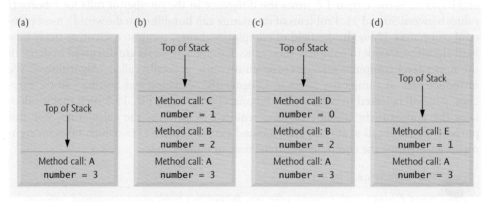

Fig. 15.9 | Method calls on the program execution stack.

Within method call A, method calls B and E are made. The original method call has not yet completed, so its activation record remains on the stack. The first method call to be made from within A is method call B, so the activation record for method call B is pushed onto the stack on top of the activation record for method call A. Method call B must execute and complete before method call E is made. Within method call B, method calls C and D will be made. Method call C is made first, and its activation record is pushed onto the stack [part (b) of Fig. 15.9]. Method call B has not yet finished, and its activation record is still on the method-call stack. When method call C executes, it does not make any further method calls, but simply returns the value 1. When this method returns, its activation record is popped off the top of the stack. The method call at the top of the stack is now B, which continues to execute by performing method call D. The activation record for method call D is pushed onto the stack [part (c) of Fig. 15.9]. Method call D completes without making any more method calls, and returns the value 0. The activation record for this method call is then popped off the stack. Now, both method calls made from within method call B have returned. Method call B continues to execute, returning the value 1. Method call B completes and its activation record is popped off the stack. At this point, the activation record for method call A is at the top of the stack and the method continues its execution. This method makes method call E, whose activation record is now pushed onto the stack [part (d) of Fig. 15.9]. Method call E completes and returns the value 1. The activation record for this method call is popped off the stack, and once again method call A continues to execute. At this point, method call A will not be making any other method calls and can finish its execution, returning the value 2 to A's caller (`fibonacci(3)` = 2). A's activation record is popped off the stack. Note that the executing method is always the one whose activation record is at the top of the stack, and the activation record for that method contains the values of its local variables.

15.6 Recursion vs. Iteration

In the preceding sections, we studied methods `factorial` and `fibonacci`, which can easily be implemented either recursively or iteratively. In this section, we compare the two approaches and discuss why the programmer might choose one approach over the other in a particular situation.

Both iteration and recursion are based on a control statement: Iteration uses a repetition statement (e.g., `for`, `while` or `do...while`), whereas recursion uses a selection statement (e.g., `if`, `if...else` or `switch`). Both iteration and recursion involve repetition: Iteration explicitly uses a repetition statement, whereas recursion achieves repetition through repeated method calls. Iteration and recursion each involve a termination test: Iteration terminates when the loop-continuation condition fails, whereas recursion terminates when a base case is reached. Iteration with counter-controlled repetition and recursion each gradually approach termination: Iteration keeps modifying a counter until the counter assumes a value that makes the loop-continuation condition fail, whereas recursion keeps producing smaller versions of the original problem until the base case is reached. Both iteration and recursion can occur infinitely: An infinite loop occurs with iteration if the loop-continuation test never becomes false, whereas infinite recursion occurs if the recursion step does not reduce the problem each time in a manner that converges on the base case, or if the base case is not tested.

To illustrate the differences between iteration and recursion, let us examine an iterative solution to the factorial problem (Figs. 15.10–15.11). Note that a repetition statement is used (lines 12–13 of Fig. 15.10) rather than the selection statement of the recursive solution (lines 9–12 of Fig. 15.3). Note that both solutions use a termination test. In the recursive solution, line 9 tests for the base case. In the iterative solution, line 12 tests the loop-continuation condition—if the test fails, the loop terminates. Finally, note that instead of producing smaller versions of the original problem, the iterative solution uses a counter that is modified until the loop-continuation condition becomes false.

```
1   // Fig. 15.10: FactorialCalculator.java
2   // Iterative factorial method.
3
4   public class FactorialCalculator
5   {
6      // recursive declaration of method factorial
7      public long factorial( long number )
8      {
9         long result = 1;
10
11         // iterative declaration of method factorial
12         for ( long i = number; i >= 1; i-- )
13            result *= i;
14
15         return result;
16      } // end method factorial
17
18      // output factorials for values 0-10
19      public void displayFactorials()
20      {
21         // calculate the factorials of 0 through 10
22         for ( int counter = 0; counter <= 10; counter++ )
23            System.out.printf( "%d! = %d\n", counter, factorial( counter ) );
24      } // end method displayFactorials
25   } // end class FactorialCalculator
```

Fig. 15.10 | Iterative factorial solution.

```
1   // Fig. 15.11: FactorialTest.java
2   // Testing the iterative factorial method.
3
4   public class FactorialTest
5   {
6      // calculate factorials of 0-10
7      public static void main( String args[] )
8      {
9         FactorialCalculator factorialCalculator = new FactorialCalculator();
10         factorialCalculator.displayFactorials();
11      } // end main
12   } // end class FactorialTest
```

Fig. 15.11 | Testing the iterative factorial solution. (Part 1 of 2.)

```
0!  = 1
1!  = 1
2!  = 2
3!  = 6
4!  = 24
5!  = 120
6!  = 720
7!  = 5040
8!  = 40320
9!  = 362880
10! = 3628800
```

Fig. 15.11 | Testing the iterative factorial solution. (Part 2 of 2.)

Recursion has many negatives. It repeatedly invokes the mechanism, and consequently the overhead, of method calls. This repetition can be expensive in terms of both processor time and memory space. Each recursive call causes another copy of the method (actually, only the method's variables, stored in the activation record) to be created—this set of copies can consume considerable memory space. Since iteration occurs within a method, repeated method calls and extra memory assignment are avoided. So why choose recursion?

Software Engineering Observation 15.1

Any problem that can be solved recursively can also be solved iteratively (nonrecursively). A recursive approach is normally preferred over an iterative approach when the recursive approach more naturally mirrors the problem and results in a program that is easier to understand and debug. A recursive approach can often be implemented with fewer lines of code. Another reason to choose a recursive approach is that an iterative one might not be apparent.

Performance Tip 15.2

Avoid using recursion in situations requiring high performance. Recursive calls take time and consume additional memory.

Common Programming Error 15.2

Accidentally having a nonrecursive method call itself either directly or indirectly through another method can cause infinite recursion.

15.7 Towers of Hanoi

In the preceding sections of this chapter, we studied methods that can be easily implemented both recursively and iteratively. In this section, we present a problem whose recursive solution demonstrates the elegance of recursion, and whose iterative solution may not be as apparent.

The Towers of Hanoi is one of the classic problems every budding computer scientist must grapple with. Legend has it that in a temple in the Far East, priests are attempting to move a stack of golden disks from one diamond peg to another (Fig. 15.12). The initial stack has 64 disks threaded onto one peg and arranged from bottom to top by decreasing size. The priests are attempting to move the stack from one peg to another under the constraints that exactly one disk is moved at a time and at no time may a larger disk be placed

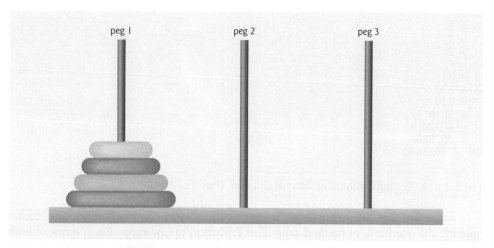

Fig. 15.12 | Towers of Hanoi for the case with four disks.

above a smaller disk. Three pegs are provided, one being used for temporarily holding disks. Supposedly, the world will end when the priests complete their task, so there is little incentive for us to facilitate their efforts.

Let's assume that the priests are attempting to move the disks from peg 1 to peg 3. We wish to develop an algorithm that prints the precise sequence of peg-to-peg disk transfers.

If we try to find an iterative solution, we will likely find ourselves hopelessly "knotted up" in managing the disks. Instead, attacking this problem recursively quickly yields a solution. Moving n disks can be viewed in terms of moving only n - 1 disks (hence the recursion) as follows:

1. Move $n - 1$ disks from peg 1 to peg 2, using peg 3 as a temporary holding area.

2. Move the last disk (the largest) from peg 1 to peg 3.

3. Move $n - 1$ disks from peg 2 to peg 3, using peg 1 as a temporary holding area.

The process ends when the last task involves moving $n = 1$ disk (i.e., the base case). This task is accomplished by simply moving the disk, without the need for a temporary holding area.

The program of Figs. 15.13–15.14 solves the Towers of Hanoi. In the constructor (lines 9–12), the number of disks to be moved (numDisks) is initialized. Method solveTowers (lines 15–34) solves the Towers of Hanoi puzzle, given the total number of disks (in this case 3), the starting peg, the ending peg, and the temporary holding peg as parameters. The base case (lines 19–23) occurs when only one disk needs to be moved from the starting peg to the ending peg. In the recursion step (lines 27–33), line 27 moves disks - 1 disks from the first peg (sourcePeg) to the temporary holding peg (tempPeg). When all but one of the disks have been moved to the temporary peg, line 30 moves the largest disk from the start peg to the destination peg. Line 33 finishes the rest of the moves by calling the method solveTowers to recursively move disks - 1 disks from the temporary peg (tempPeg) to the destination peg (destinationPeg), this time using the first peg (sourcePeg) as the temporary peg.

```
1    // Fig. 15.13: TowersOfHanoi.java
2    // Program solves the towers of Hanoi problem, and
3    // demonstrates recursion.
4
5    public class TowersOfHanoi
6    {
7       int numDisks; // number of disks to move
8
9       public TowersOfHanoi( int disks )
10      {
11         numDisks = disks;
12      } // end TowersOfHanoi constructor
13
14      // recursively move disks between towers
15      public void solveTowers( int disks, int sourcePeg, int destinationPeg,
16         int tempPeg )
17      {
18         // base case -- only one disk to move
19         if ( disks == 1 )
20         {
21            System.out.printf( "\n%d --> %d", sourcePeg, destinationPeg );
22            return;
23         } // end if
24
25         // recursion step -- move (disk - 1) disks from sourcePeg
26         // to tempPeg using destinationPeg
27         solveTowers( disks - 1, sourcePeg, tempPeg, destinationPeg );
28
29         // move last disk from sourcePeg to destinationPeg
30         System.out.printf( "\n%d --> %d", sourcePeg, destinationPeg );
31
32         // move ( disks - 1 ) disks from tempPeg to destinationPeg
33         solveTowers( disks - 1, tempPeg, destinationPeg, sourcePeg );
34      } // end method solveTowers
35   } // end class TowersOfHanoi
```

Fig. 15.13 | Towers of Hanoi solution with a recursive method.

Figure 15.14 tests our Towers of Hanoi solution. Line 12 creates a TowersOfHanoi object, passing as a parameter the total number of disks (in this case, 3) to be moved from one peg to another. Line 15 calls the recursive solveTowers method, which outputs the steps to the command prompt.

```
1    // Fig. 15.14: TowersOfHanoiTest.java
2    // Test the solution to the Towers of Hanoi problem.
3
4    public class TowersOfHanoiTest
5    {
6       public static void main( String args[] )
7       {
```

Fig. 15.14 | Testing the Towers of Hanoi solution. (Part 1 of 2.)

```
8          int startPeg = 1;   // value 1 used to indicate startPeg in output
9          int endPeg = 3;     // value 3 used to indicate endPeg in output
10         int tempPeg = 2;    // value 2 used to indicate tempPeg in output
11         int totalDisks = 3; // number of disks
12         TowersOfHanoi towersOfHanoi = new TowersOfHanoi( totalDisks );
13
14         // initial nonrecursive call: move all disks.
15         towersOfHanoi.solveTowers( totalDisks, startPeg, endPeg, tempPeg );
16      } // end main
17   } // end class TowersOfHanoiTest
```

```
1 --> 3
1 --> 2
3 --> 2
1 --> 3
2 --> 1
2 --> 3
1 --> 3
```

Fig. 15.14 | Testing the Towers of Hanoi solution. (Part 2 of 2.)

15.8 Fractals

A fractal is a geometric figure that can be generated from a pattern repeated recursively (Fig. 15.15). The figure is modified by applying the pattern to each segment of the original figure. We will look at a few such approximations in this section. [*Note:* We will refer to our geometric figures as fractals, even though they are approximations.] Although these figures had been studied before the 20th century, it was the Polish mathematician Benoit Mandelbrot who introduced the term "fractal" in the 1970s, along with the specifics of how a fractal is created and the practical applications of fractals. Mandelbrot's fractal geometry provides mathematical models for many complex forms found in nature, such as mountains, clouds and coastlines. Fractals have many uses in mathematics and science. Fractals can be used to better understand systems or patterns that appear in nature (e.g., ecosystems), in the human body (e.g., in the folds of the brain), or in the universe (e.g., galaxy clusters). Not all fractals resemble objects in nature. Drawing fractals has become a popular art form. Fractals have a self-similar property—when subdivided into parts, each resembles a reduced-size copy of the whole. Many fractals yield an exact copy of the original when a portion of the original image is magnified—such a fractal is said to be strictly self-similar. Links are provided in Section 15.11 for various websites that discuss and demonstrate fractals.

As an example, let us look at a popular strictly self-similar fractal known as the Koch Curve (Fig. 15.15). This fractal is formed by removing the middle third of each line in the drawing and replacing it with two lines that form a point, such that if the middle third of the original line remained, an equilateral triangle would be formed. Formulas for creating fractals often involve removing all or part of the previous fractal image. This pattern has already been determined for this fractal—in this section we focus not on how to determine what formulas are needed for a specific fractal, but how to use those formulas in a recursive solution.

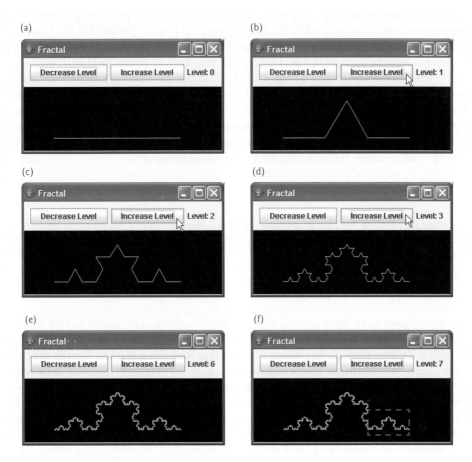

Fig. 15.15 | Koch Curve fractal.

We start with a straight line [Fig. 15.15, part (*a*)] and apply the pattern, creating a triangle from the middle third [Fig. 15.15, part (*b*)]. We then apply the pattern again to each straight line, resulting in Fig. 15.15, part (*c*). Each time the pattern is applied, we say that the fractal is at a new **level**, or **depth** (sometimes the term **order** is also used). Fractals can be displayed at many levels—for instance, a fractal at level 3 has had three iterations of the pattern applied [Fig. 15.15, part (*d*)]. After only a few iterations, this fractal begins to look like a portion of a snowflake [Fig. 15.15, parts (*e* and *f*)]. Since this is a strictly self-similar fractal, each portion of the fractal contains an exact copy of the fractal. In part (*f*) of Fig. 15.15, for example, we have highlighted a portion of the fractal with a dashed red box. If the image in this box were increased in size, it would look exactly like the entire fractal of part (*f*).

A similar fractal, the **Koch Snowflake**, is the same as the Koch Curve but begins with a triangle rather than a line. The same pattern is applied to each side of the triangle, resulting in an image that looks like an enclosed snowflake. We have chosen to focus on the Koch Curve for simplicity. To learn more about the Koch Curve and Koch Snowflake, see the links in Section 15.11.

We now demonstrate the use of recursion to draw fractals by writing a program to create a strictly self-similar fractal. We call this the "Lo fractal," named for Sin Han Lo, a Deitel & Associates colleague who created it. The fractal will eventually resemble one-half of a feather (see the outputs in Fig. 15.22). The base case, or fractal level of 0, begins as a line between two points, A and B (Fig. 15.16). To create the next higher level, we find the midpoint (C) of the line. To calculate the location of point C, use the following formula: [*Note:* The x and y to the left of each letter refer to the x-coordinate and y-coordinate of that point, respectively. For instance, xA refers to the x-coordinate of point A, while yC refers to the y-coordinate of point C. In our diagrams we denote the point by its letter, followed by two numbers representing the x- and y-coordinates.]

```
xC = (xA + xB) / 2;
yC = (yA + yB) / 2;
```

To create this fractal, we also must find a point D that lies left of segment AC and creates an isosceles right triangle ADC. To calculate the location of point D, use the following formulas:

```
xD = xA + (xC - xA) / 2 - (yC - yA) / 2;
yD = yA + (yC - yA) / 2 + (xC - xA) / 2;
```

We now move from level 0 to level 1 as follows: First, add points C and D (as in Fig. 15.17). Then, remove the original line and add segments DA, DC and DB. The remaining lines will curve at an angle, causing our fractal to look like a feather. For the next level of the fractal, this algorithm is repeated on each of the three lines in level 1. For each line, the formulas above are applied, where the former point D is now considered to be point A, while the other end of each line is considered to be point B. Figure 15.18 contains the line from level 0 (now a dashed line) and the three added lines from level 1. We have changed point D to be point A, and the original points A, C and B to B1, B2 and B3, respectively. The preceding formulas have been used to find the new points C and D on each line. These points are also numbered 1–3 to keep track of which point is associated with each line. The points C1 and D1, for instance, represent points C and D associated with the line formed

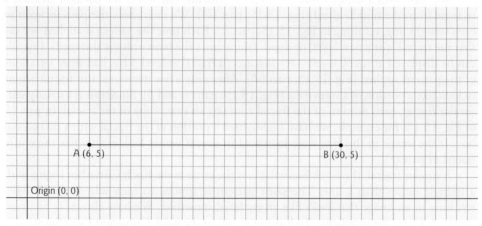

Fig. 15.16 | "Lo fractal" at level 0.

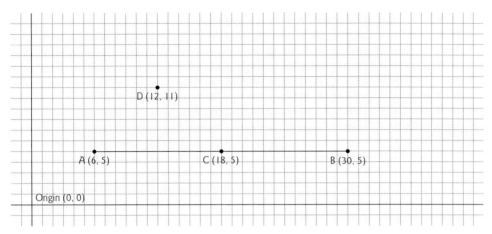

Fig. 15.17 | Determining points C and D for level 1 of the "Lo fractal."

from points A to B1. To achieve level 2, the three lines in Fig. 15.18 are removed and replaced with new lines from the C and D points just added. Figure 15.19 shows the new lines (the lines from level 2 are shown as dashed lines for your convenience). Figure 15.20 shows level 2 without the dashed lines from level 1. Once this process has been repeated several times, the fractal created will begin to look like one-half of a feather, as shown in the output of Fig. 15.22. We will present the code for this application shortly.

The application in Fig. 15.21 defines the user interface for drawing this fractal (shown at the end of Fig. 15.22). The interface consists of three buttons—one for the user to change the color of the fractal, one to increase the level of recursion and one to decrease the level of recursion. A JLabel keeps track of the current level of recursion, which is modified by calling method setLevel, to be discussed shortly. Lines 15–16 specify constants WIDTH and HEIGHT to be 400 and 480 respectively for the size of the JFrame. The default

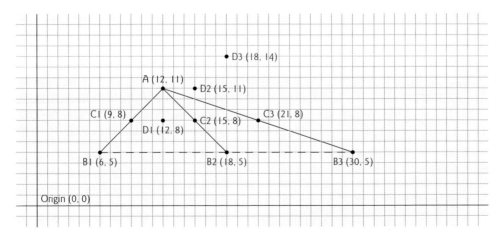

Fig. 15.18 | "Lo fractal" at level 1, with C and D points determined for level 2. [*Note:* The fractal at level 0 is included as a dashed line as a reminder of where the line was located in relation to the current fractal.]

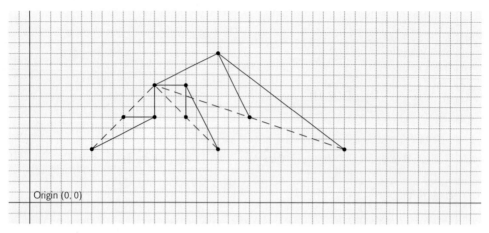

Fig. 15.19 | "Lo fractal" at level 2, with dashed lines from level 1 provided.

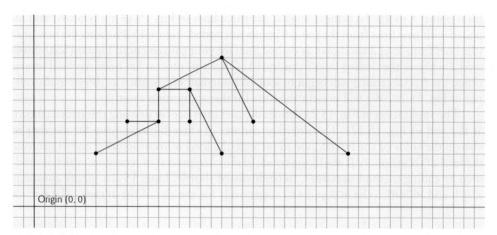

Fig. 15.20 | "Lo fractal" at level 2.

color to draw the fractal will be blue (line 18). The user triggers an ActionEvent by clicking the **Color** button. The event handler for this button is registered in lines 38–54. The method actionPerformed displays a JColorChooser. This dialog returns the selected Color object or blue (if the user presses **Cancel** or closes the dialog without pressing **OK**). Line 51 calls the setColor method in class FractalJPanel to update the color.

```
1   // Fig. 15.21: Fractal.java
2   // Demonstrates user interface for drawing a fractal.
3   import java.awt.Color;
4   import java.awt.FlowLayout;
5   import java.awt.event.ActionEvent;
6   import java.awt.event.ActionListener;
7   import javax.swing.JFrame;
```

Fig. 15.21 | Demonstrating the fractal user interface. (Part 1 of 4.)

```
 8   import javax.swing.JButton;
 9   import javax.swing.JLabel;
10   import javax.swing.JPanel;
11   import javax.swing.JColorChooser;
12
13   public class Fractal extends JFrame
14   {
15      private final int WIDTH = 400;  // define width of GUI
16      private final int HEIGHT = 480; // define height of GUI
17      private final int MIN_LEVEL = 0;
18      private Color color = Color.BLUE;
19
20      private JButton changeColorJButton, increaseLevelJButton,
21         decreaseLevelJButton;
22      private JLabel levelJLabel;
23      private FractalJPanel drawSpace;
24      private JPanel mainJPanel, controlJPanel;
25
26      // set up GUI
27      public Fractal()
28      {
29         super( "Fractal" );
30
31         // set up control panel
32         controlJPanel = new JPanel();
33         controlJPanel.setLayout( new FlowLayout() );
34
35         // set up color button and register listener
36         changeColorJButton = new JButton( "Color" );
37         controlJPanel.add( changeColorJButton );
38         changeColorJButton.addActionListener(
39            new ActionListener() // anonymous inner class
40            {
41               // process changeColorJButton event
42               public void actionPerformed( ActionEvent event )
43               {
44                  color = JColorChooser.showDialog(
45                     Fractal.this, "Choose a color", color );
46
47                  // set default color, if no color is returned
48                  if ( color == null )
49                     color = Color.BLUE;
50
51                  drawSpace.setColor( color );
52               } // end method actionPerformed
53            }  // end anonymous inner class
54         ); // end addActionListener
55
56         // set up decrease level button to add to control panel and
57         // register listener
58         decreaseLevelJButton = new JButton( "Decrease Level" );
59         controlJPanel.add( decreaseLevelJButton );
```

Fig. 15.21 | Demonstrating the fractal user interface. (Part 2 of 4.)

```
60        decreaseLevelJButton.addActionListener(
61           new ActionListener() // anonymous inner class
62           {
63              // process decreaseLevelJButton event
64              public void actionPerformed( ActionEvent event )
65              {
66                 int level = drawSpace.getLevel();
67                 level--; // decrease level by one
68
69                 // modify level if possible
70                 if ( level >= MIN_LEVEL )
71                 {
72                    levelJLabel.setText( "Level: " + level );
73                    drawSpace.setLevel( level );
74                    repaint();
75                 } // end if
76              } // end method actionPerformed
77           } // end anonymous inner class
78        ); // end addActionListener
79
80        // set up increase level button to add to control panel
81        // and register listener
82        increaseLevelJButton = new JButton( "Increase Level" );
83        controlJPanel.add( increaseLevelJButton );
84        increaseLevelJButton.addActionListener(
85           new ActionListener() // anonymous inner class
86           {
87              // process increaseLevelJButton event
88              public void actionPerformed( ActionEvent event )
89              {
90                 int level = drawSpace.getLevel();
91                 level++; // increase level by one
92
93                 // modify level if possible
94                 if ( level >= MIN_LEVEL )
95                 {
96                    levelJLabel.setText( "Level: " + level );
97                    drawSpace.setLevel( level );
98                    repaint();
99                 } // end if
100             } // end method actionPerformed
101          } // end anonymous inner class
102       ); // end addActionListener
103
104       // set up levelJLabel to add to controlJPanel
105       levelJLabel = new JLabel( "Level: 0" );
106       controlJPanel.add( levelJLabel );
107
108       drawSpace = new FractalJPanel( 0 );
109
110       // create mainJPanel to contain controlJPanel and drawSpace
111       mainJPanel = new JPanel();
112       mainJPanel.add( controlJPanel );
```

Fig. 15.21 | Demonstrating the fractal user interface. (Part 3 of 4.)

```
113          mainJPanel.add( drawSpace );
114
115          add( mainJPanel ); // add JPanel to JFrame
116
117          setSize( WIDTH, HEIGHT ); // set size of JFrame
118          setVisible( true ); // display JFrame
119       } // end Fractal constructor
120
121       public static void main( String args[] )
122       {
123          Fractal demo = new Fractal();
124          demo.setDefaultCloseOperation( JFrame.EXIT_ON_CLOSE );
125       } // end main
126   } // end class Fractal
```

Fig. 15.21 | Demonstrating the fractal user interface. (Part 4 of 4.)

The event handler for the **Decrease Level** button is registered in lines 60–78. In method actionPerformed, lines 66–67 retrieve the current level of recursion and decrement it by 1. Line 70 checks to make sure that the level is greater than or equal to 0 (MIN_LEVEL)—the fractal is not defined for any recursion level lower than 0. The program allows the user to go up to any desired level, but at a certain point (level 10 and higher in this example) the rendering of the fractal becomes increasingly slow, as there is a lot of detail to be drawn. Lines 72–74 reset the level label to reflect the change—the new level is set and the repaint method is called to update the image to show the fractal corresponding to the new level.

The **Increase Level** JButton works the same way as the **Decrease Level** JButton, except that the level is incremented rather than decremented to show more details of the fractal (lines 90–91). When the application is first executed, the level will be set to 0, which will display a blue line between two points that were specified in the FractalJPanel class.

The FractalJPanel class in Fig. 15.22 specifies the dimensions of the drawing JPanel to be 400 by 400 (lines 13–14). The FractalJPanel constructor (lines 18–24) takes the current level as a parameter and assigns it to its instance variable level. Instance variable color is set to the default color blue. Lines 22–23 change the background color of the JPanel to be white (for visibility of the colors used to draw the fractal), and set the new dimensions of the JPanel where the fractal will be drawn.

```
1    // Fig. 15.22: FractalJPanel.java
2    // FractalJPanel demonstrates recursive drawing of a fractal.
3    import java.awt.Graphics;
4    import java.awt.Color;
5    import java.awt.Dimension;
6    import javax.swing.JPanel;
7
8    public class FractalJPanel extends JPanel
9    {
10      private Color color; // stores color used to draw fractal
11      private int level;   // stores current level of fractal
```

Fig. 15.22 | Drawing the "Lo fractal" using recursion. (Part 1 of 4.)

```
12
13      private final int WIDTH = 400;  // defines width of JPanel
14      private final int HEIGHT = 400; // defines height of JPanel
15
16      // set the initial fractal level to the value specified
17      // and set up JPanel specifications
18      public FractalJPanel( int currentLevel )
19      {
20         color = Color.BLUE;  // initialize drawing color to blue
21         level = currentLevel; // set initial fractal level
22         setBackground( Color.WHITE );
23         setPreferredSize( new Dimension( WIDTH, HEIGHT ) );
24      } // end FractalJPanel constructor
25
26      // draw fractal recursively
27      public void drawFractal( int level, int xA, int yA, int xB,
28         int yB, Graphics g )
29      {
30         // base case: draw a line connecting two given points
31         if ( level == 0 )
32            g.drawLine( xA, yA, xB, yB );
33         else // recursion step: determine new points, draw next level
34         {
35            // calculate midpoint between (xA, yA) and (xB, yB)
36            int xC = ( xA + xB ) / 2;
37            int yC = ( yA + yB ) / 2;
38
39            // calculate the fourth point (xD, yD) which forms an
40            // isosceles right triangle between (xA, yA) and (xC, yC)
41            // where the right angle is at (xD, yD)
42            int xD = xA + ( xC - xA ) / 2 - ( yC - yA ) / 2;
43            int yD = yA + ( yC - yA ) / 2 + ( xC - xA ) / 2;
44
45            // recursively draw the Fractal
46            drawFractal( level - 1, xD, yD, xA, yA, g );
47            drawFractal( level - 1, xD, yD, xC, yC, g );
48            drawFractal( level - 1, xD, yD, xB, yB, g );
49         } // end else
50      } // end method drawFractal
51
52      // start drawing the fractal
53      public void paintComponent( Graphics g )
54      {
55         super.paintComponent( g );
56
57         // draw fractal pattern
58         g.setColor( color );
59         drawFractal( level, 100, 90, 290, 200, g );
60      } // end method paintComponent
61
62      // set the drawing color to c
63      public void setColor( Color c )
64      {
```

Fig. 15.22 | Drawing the "Lo fractal" using recursion. (Part 2 of 4.)

```
65          color = c;
66      } // end method setColor
67
68      // set the new level of recursion
69      public void setLevel( int currentLevel )
70      {
71          level = currentLevel;
72      } // end method setLevel
73
74      // returns level of recursion
75      public int getLevel()
76      {
77          return level;
78      } // end method getLevel
79  } // end class FractalJPanel
```

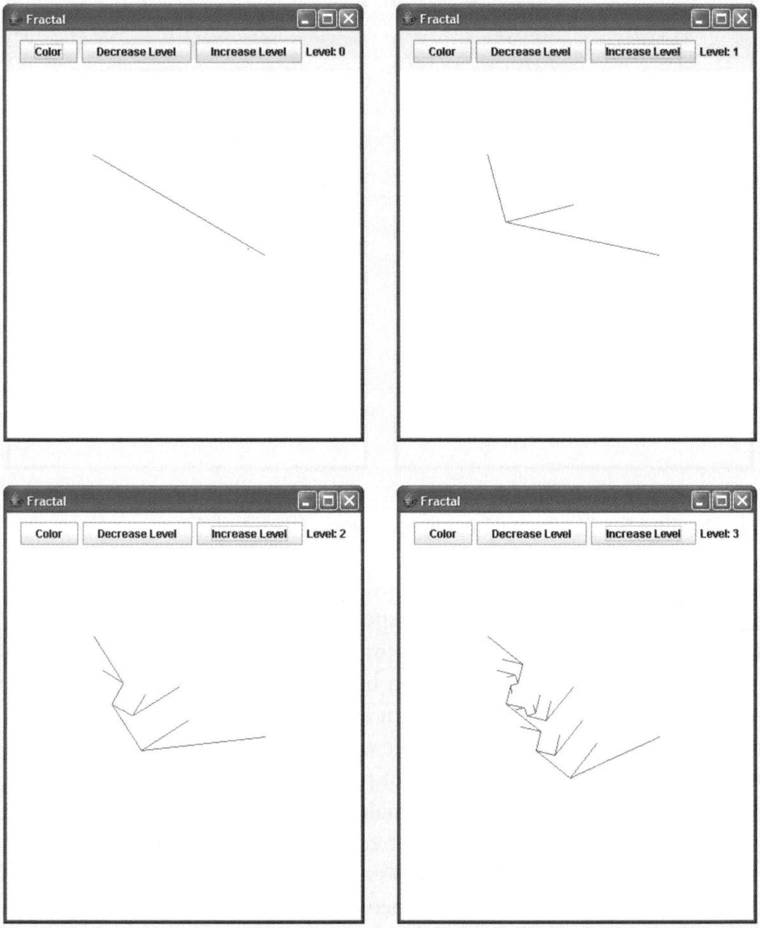

Fig. 15.22 | Drawing the "Lo fractal" using recursion. (Part 3 of 4.)

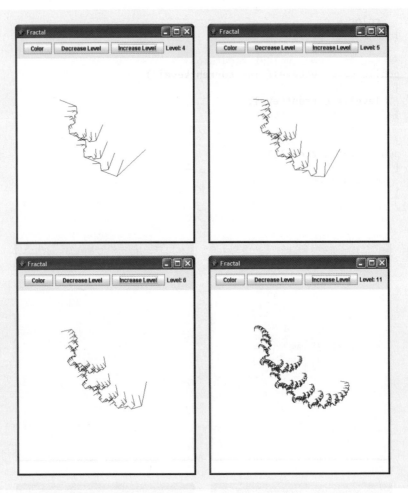

Fig. 15.22 | Drawing the "Lo fractal" using recursion. (Part 4 of 4.)

Lines 27–50 define the recursive method that creates the fractal. This method takes six parameters: the level, four integers that specify the *x*- and *y*-coordinates of two points, and the Graphics object g. The base case for this method (line 31) occurs when level equals 0, at which time a line will be drawn between the two points given as parameters. Lines 36–43 calculate (xC, yC), the midpoint between (xA, yA) and (xB, yB), and (xD, yD), the point that creates a right isosceles triangle with (xA, yA) and (xC, yC). Lines 46–48 make three recursive calls on three different sets of points.

In method paintComponent, line 59 makes the first call to method drawFractal to start the drawing. This method call is not recursive, but all subsequent calls to draw-Fractal performed from the body of drawFractal are. Since the lines will not be drawn until the base case is reached, the distance between two points decreases on each recursive call. As the level of recursion increases, the fractal becomes smoother and more detailed. The shape of this fractal stabilizes as the level approaches 11. Fractals will stabilize at different levels based on the shape and size of the fractal.

Figure 15.22 shows the development of the fractal from levels 0 to 6. The last image shows the defining shape of the fractal at level 11. If we focus on one of the arms of this fractal, it will be identical to the whole image. This property defines the fractal to be strictly self-similar. See Section 15.11 for further resources on fractals.

15.9 Recursive Backtracking

Our recursive methods all have a similar architecture—if the base case is reached, return a result; if not, make one or more recursive calls. In this section we will explore a more complex recursive method that finds a path through a maze, returning true if there is a possible solution to the maze. The solution involves moving through the maze one step at a time, where moves can be made by going down, right, up or left (diagonal moves are not permitted). From the current location in the maze (starting with the entry point), the following steps are taken: A direction is chosen, the move is made in that direction and a recursive call is made to solve the remainder of the maze from the new location. When a dead end is reached (i.e., we cannot take any more steps forward without hitting a wall), we back up to the previous location and try to go in a different direction. If no other direction can be taken, we back up again. This process continues until we find a point in the maze where a move can be made in another direction. Once such a location is found, we move in the new direction and continue with another recursive call to solve the rest of the maze.

To back up to the previous location in the maze, our recursive method simply returns false, moving up the method-call chain to the previous recursive call (which references the previous location in the maze). This process of using recursion to return to an earlier decision point is known as recursive backtracking. If one set of recursive calls does not result in a solution to the problem, the program backs up to the previous decision point and makes a different decision, often resulting in another set of recursive calls. In this example, the previous decision point is the previous location in the maze, and the decision to be made is the direction that the next move should take. One direction has led to a dead end, so the search continues with a different direction. Unlike our other recursive programs, which reached the base case and then returned all the way up the method-call chain to the original method call, the recursive backtracking solution to the maze problem uses recursion to return only partway up the method-call chain, then try a different direction. If the backtracking reaches the entry location of the maze and the paths in all directions have been attempted, the maze does not have a solution.

In the chapter exercises you are asked to implement recursive backtracking solutions to the maze problem (Exercise 15.17, Exercise 15.18 and Exercise 15.19) and the Eight Queens problem (Exercise 15.15), which attempts to find a way to place eight queens on an empty chessboard so that no queen is "attacking" any other (i.e., no two queens are in the same row, in the same column or along the same diagonal). See Section 15.11 for links to further information on recursive backtracking.

15.10 Wrap-Up

In this chapter, you learned how to create recursive methods—i.e., methods that call themselves. You learned that recursive methods typically divide a problem into two conceptual pieces—a piece that the method knows how to do (the base case) and a piece that the method does not know how to do (the recursion step). The recursion step is a slightly smaller version of the original problem and is performed by a recursive method call. You saw some popular recursion examples, including calculating factorials and producing values in the Fibonacci series. You then learned how recursion works "under the hood," including the order in which recursive method calls are pushed on or popped off the program execution stack. Next, you compared recursive and iterative (non-ecursive) approaches. You learned how to solve a more complex problem using recursion—displaying fractals. The chapter concluded with an introduction to recursive backtracking, a technique for solving problems that involves backing up through recursive calls to try different possible solutions. In the next chapter, you will learn numerous techniques for sorting lists of data and searching for an item in a list of data, and under what circumstances each searching and sorting technique should be used.

15.11 Internet and Web Resources

Recursion Concepts

en.wikipedia.org/wiki/Recursion
Article from Wikipedia provides the basics of recursion and several resources for students.

www.cafeaulait.org/javatutorial.html
Provides a brief introduction to recursion in Java, and also covers other Java topics.

Stacks

www.cs.auc.dk/~normark/eciu-recursion/html/recit-slide-implerec.html
Provides slides discussing the implementation of recursion using stacks.

faculty.juniata.edu/kruse/cs2java/recurimpl.htm
Provides a diagram of the program execution stack and discusses how the stack works.

Fractals

math.rice.edu/~lanius/frac/
Provides examples of other fractals, such as the Koch Snowflake, the Sierpinski gasket, and Jurassic Park fractals.

www.lifesmith.com/
Provides hundreds of colorful fractal images along with detailed explanation about the Mandelbrot and Julia sets, two common sets of fractals.

www.jracademy.com/~jtucek/math/fractals.html
Contains two AVI movies created by zooming in continuously on the fractals known as the Mandelbrot and Julia equation sets.

www.faqs.org/faqs/fractal-faq/
Provides answers to many questions about fractals.

spanky.triumf.ca/www/fractint/fractint.html
Contains links to download Fractint, a freeware program for generating fractals.

www.42explore.com/fractal.htm
Lists URLs on fractals and software tools that create fractals.

www.arcytech.org/java/fractals/koch.shtml
Provides a detailed introduction to the Koch Curve fractal and an applet demonstrating the fractal.

library.thinkquest.org/26688/koch.html
Displays a Koch Curve applet and provides the source code.

Recursive Backtracking

www.cs.sfu.ca/CourseCentral/201/havens/notes/Lecture14.pdf
Provides a brief introduction to recursive backtracking, including an example on planning a travel route.

www.cs.utexas.edu/users/scottm/cs307/handouts/Slides/
lec11RecursiveBacktracking-4Up.pdf
Demonstrates recursive backtracking and walks through several examples.

math.hws.edu/xJava/PentominosSolver
Provides a program that uses recursive backtracking to solve a problem known as the Pentominos puzzle (described at the site).

www.cs.rockhurst.edu/~burger/research/scramble/paper.pdf
Demonstrates using recursive backtracking to solve a scrambled squares puzzle.

Summary

Section 15.1 Introduction
- A recursive method calls itself directly or indirectly through another method.
- When a recursive method is called to solve a problem, the method actually is capable of solving only the simplest case(s), or base case(s). If it is called with a base case, the method returns a result.

Section 15.2 Recursion Concepts
- If a recursive method is called with a more complex problem than a base case, it typically divides the problem into two conceptual pieces—a piece that the method knows how to do and a piece that the method does not know how to do.
- To make recursion feasible, the piece that the method does not know how to do must resemble the original problem, but be a slightly simpler or smaller version of it. Because this new problem looks like the original problem, the method calls a fresh copy of itself to work on the smaller problem—this is called the recursion step.
- For recursion to eventually terminate, each time a method calls itself with a simpler version of the original problem, the sequence of smaller and smaller problems must converge on a base case. When, the method recognizes the base case, it returns a result to the previous copy of the method.
- A recursive call may be a call to another method, which in turn makes a call back to the original method. Such a process still results in a recursive call to the original method. This is known as an indirect recursive call or indirect recursion.

Section 15.3 Example Using Recursion: Factorials
- Either omitting the base case or writing the recursion step incorrectly so that it does not converge on the base case can cause infinite recursion, eventually exhausting memory. This error is analogous to the problem of an infinite loop in an iterative (nonrecursive) solution.

Section 15.4 Example Using Recursion: Fibonacci Series
- The Fibonacci series begins with 0 and 1 and has the property that each subsequent Fibonacci number is the sum of the preceding two.
- The ratio of successive Fibonacci numbers converges on a constant value of 1.618…, a number that has been called the golden ratio or the golden mean.
- Some recursive solutions, such as Fibonacci (which makes two calls per recursion step), result in an "explosion" of method calls.

Section 15.5 Recursion and the Method-Call Stack

- A stack is a data structure in which data can be added or removed only at the top.

- A stack is analogous to a pile of dishes. When a dish is placed on the pile, it is always placed at the top (referred to as pushing the dish onto the stack). Similarly, when a dish is removed from the pile, it is always removed from the top (referred to as popping the dish off the stack).

- Stacks are known as last-in, first-out (LIFO) data structures—the last item pushed (inserted) on the stack is the first item popped (removed) from the stack.

- Stacks have many interesting applications. For example, when a program calls a method, the called method must know how to return to its caller, so the return address of the calling method is pushed onto the program execution stack (sometimes referred to as the method-call stack).

- The program execution stack contains the memory for local variables on each invocation of a method during a program's execution. This data, stored as a portion of the program execution stack, is known as the activation record or stack frame of the method call.

- If there are more recursive or nested method calls than can be stored on the program execution stack, an error known as a stack overflow occurs.

Section 15.6 Recursion vs. Iteration

- Both iteration and recursion are based on a control statement: Iteration uses a repetition statement, recursion a selection statement.

- Both iteration and recursion involve repetition: Iteration explicitly uses a repetition statement, whereas recursion achieves repetition through repeated method calls.

- Iteration and recursion each involve a termination test: Iteration terminates when the loop-continuation condition fails, recursion when a base case is recognized.

- Iteration with counter-controlled repetition and recursion each gradually approach termination: Iteration keeps modifying a counter until the counter assumes a value that makes the loop-continuation condition fail, whereas recursion keeps producing simpler versions of the original problem until the base case is reached.

- Both iteration and recursion can occur infinitely: An infinite loop occurs with iteration if the loop-continuation test never becomes false, whereas infinite recursion occurs if the recursion step does not reduce the problem each time in a manner that converges on the base case.

- Recursion repeatedly invokes the mechanism, and consequently the overhead, of method calls.

- Any problem that can be solved recursively can also be solved iteratively.

- A recursive approach is normally preferred over an iterative approach when it more naturally mirrors the problem and results in a program that is easier to understand and debug.

- A recursive approach can often be implemented with few lines of code, but a corresponding iterative approach might take a large amount of code. Another reason to choose a recursive solution is that an iterative solution might not be apparent.

Section 15.8 Fractals

- A fractal is a geometric figure that is generated from a pattern repeated recursively an infinite number of times.

- Fractals have a self-similar property—subparts are reduced-size copies of the whole.

Section 15.9 Recursive Backtracking

- Using recursion to return to an earlier decision point is known as recursive backtracking. If one set of recursive calls does not result in a solution to the problem, the program backs up to the previous decision point and makes a different decision, often resulting in another set of recursive calls.

Terminology

activation record	last-in, first-out (LIFO) data structures
backtracking	level of a fractal
base case	maze traversal problem
complexity theory	method-call stack
converge on a base case	palindrome
Eight Queens problem	program execution stack
exhaustive recursion	recursion overhead
factorial	recursion step
Fibonacci series	recursive backtracking
fractal	recursive call
fractal depth	recursive evaluation
fractal level	recursive method
fractal order	self-similar fractal
golden mean	stack
golden ratio	stack frame
indirect recursion	stack overflow
infinite recursion	strictly self-similar fractal
Koch Curve fractal	termination test
Koch Snowflake fractal	Towers of Hanoi problem

Self-Review Exercises

15.1   State whether each of the following is *true* or *false*. If *false*, explain why.
   a) A method that calls itself indirectly is not an example of recursion.
   b) Recursion can be efficient in computation because of reduced memory-space usage.
   c) When a recursive method is called to solve a problem, it actually is capable of solving only the simplest case(s), or base case(s).
   d) To make recursion feasible, the recursion step in a recursive solution must resemble the original problem, but be a slightly larger version of it.

15.2   A _____ is needed to terminate recursion.
   a) recursion step
   b) break statement
   c) void return type
   d) base case

15.3   The first call to invoke a recursive method is _____.
   a) not recursive
   b) recursive
   c) the recursion step
   d) none of the above

15.4   Each time a fractal's pattern is applied, the fractal is said to be at a new _____.
   a) width
   b) height
   c) level
   d) volume

15.5   Iteration and recursion each involve a _____.
   a) repetition statement
   b) termination test

    c) counter variable

    d) none of the above

15.6 Fill in the blanks in each of the following statements:

    a) The ratio of successive Fibonacci numbers converges on a constant value of 1.618…, a number that has been called the _____ or the _____.

    b) Data can be added or removed only from the _____ of the stack.

    c) Stacks are known as _____ data structures—the last item pushed (inserted) on the stack is the first item popped (removed) from the stack.

    d) The program execution stack contains the memory for local variables on each invocation of a method during a program's execution. This data, stored as a portion of the program execution stack, is known as the _____ or _____ of the method call.

    e) If there are more recursive or nested method calls than can be stored on the program execution stack, an error known as a(n) _____ occurs.

    f) Iteration normally uses a repetition statement, whereas recursion normally uses a(n) _____ statement.

    g) Fractals have a(n) _____ property—when subdivided into parts, each is a reduced-size copy of the whole.

    h) The _____ of a string are all the different strings that can be created by rearranging the characters of the original string.

    i) The program execution stack is also referred to as the _____ stack.

Answers to Self-Review Exercises

15.1 a) False. A method that calls itself indirectly is an example of recursion—more specifically, an example of indirect recursion. b) False. Recursion can be inefficient in computation because of multiple method calls and memory-space usage. c) True. d) False. To make recursion feasible, the recursion step in a recursive solution must resemble the original problem, but be a slightly *smaller* version of it.

15.2 d

15.3 a

15.4 c

15.5 b

15.6 a) golden ratio, golden mean. b) top. c) last-in, first-out (LIFO). d) activation record, stack frame. e) stack overflow. f) selection. g) self-similar. h) permutations. i) method-call.

Exercises

15.7 What does the following code do?

```
1   public int mystery( int a, int b )
2   {
3       if ( b == 1 )
4           return a;
5       else
6           return a + mystery( a, b - 1 );
7   } // end method mystery
```

15.8 Find the error(s) in the following recursive method, and explain how to correct it (them). This method should find the sum of the values from 0 to n.

```
 I   public int sum( int n )
 2   {
 3      if ( n == 0 )
 4         return 0;
 5      else
 6         return n + sum( n );
 7   } // end method sum
```

15.9   (*Recursive power Method*) Write a recursive method power(base, exponent) that, when called, returns

    base ^{exponent}

For example, power(3,4) = 3 * 3 * 3 * 3. Assume that exponent is an integer greater than or equal to 1. [*Hint:* The recursion step should use the relationship

$$base^{exponent} = base \cdot base^{exponent - 1}$$

and the terminating condition occurs when exponent is equal to 1, because

$$base^1 = base$$

Incorporate this method into a program that enables the user to enter the base and exponent.]

15.10   (*Greatest Common Divisor*) The greatest common divisor of integers x and y is the largest integer that evenly divides into both x and y. Write a recursive method gcd that returns the greatest common divisor of x and y. The gcd of x and y is defined recursively as follows: If y is equal to 0, then gcd(x, y) is x; otherwise, gcd(x, y) is gcd(y, x % y), where % is the remainder operator. Use this method to replace the one you wrote in the application of Exercise 6.27.

15.11   What does the following program do?

```
 I   // Exercise 15.11 Solution: MysteryClass.java
 2
 3   public class MysteryClass
 4   {
 5      public int mystery( int array2[], int size )
 6      {
 7         if ( size == 1 )
 8            return array2[ 0 ];
 9         else
10            return array2[ size - 1 ] + mystery( array2, size - 1 );
11      } // end method mystery
12   } // end class MysteryClass
```

```
 I   // Exercise 15.11 Solution: MysteryTest.java
 2
 3   public class MysteryTest
 4   {
 5      public static void main( String args[] )
```

```
 6    {
 7        MysteryClass mysteryObject = new MysteryClass();
 8
 9        int array[] = { 1, 2, 3, 4, 5, 6, 7, 8, 9, 10 };
10
11        int result = mysteryObject.mystery( array, array.length );
12
13        System.out.printf( "Result is: %d\n", result );
14    } // end method main
15 } // end class MysteryTest
```

15.12 (*Palindromes*) A palindrome is a string that is spelled the same way forward and backward. Some examples of palindromes are "radar," "able was i ere i saw elba" and (if spaces are ignored) "a man a plan a canal panama." Write a recursive method testPalindrome that returns boolean value true if the string stored in the array is a palindrome and false otherwise. The method should ignore spaces and punctuation in the string.

15.13 (*Print an Array*) Write a recursive method printArray that displays all the elements in an array of integers, separated by spaces.

15.14 (*Print an Array Backward*) Write a recursive method stringReverse that takes a character array containing a string as an argument and prints the string backward. [*Hint:* Use String method toCharArray, which takes no arguments, to get a char array containing the characters in the String.]

15.15 (*Find the Minimum Value in an Array*) Write a recursive method recursiveMinimum that determines the smallest element in an array of integers. The method should return when it receives an array of one element.

15.16 (*Fractals*) Repeat the fractal pattern in Section 15.8 to form a star. Begin with five lines, instead of one, where each line is a different arm of the star. Apply the "Lo fractal" pattern to each arm of the star.

15.17 (*Maze Traversal Using Recursive Backtracking*) The grid of #s and dots (.) in Fig. 15.24 is a two-dimensional array representation of a maze. The #s represent the walls of the maze, and the dots represent locations in the possible paths through the maze. Moves can be made only to a location in the array that contains a dot.

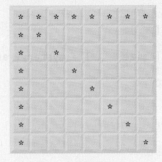

Fig. 15.23 | Squares eliminated by placing a queen in the upper-left corner of a chessboard.

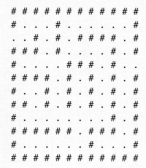

Fig. 15.24 | Two-dimensional array representation of a maze.

Write a recursive method (mazeTraversal) to walk through mazes like the one in Fig. 15.24. The method should receive as arguments a 12-by-12 character array representing the maze and the current location in the maze (the first time this method is called, the current location should be the entry point of the maze). As mazeTraversal attempts to locate the exit, it should place the character x in each square in the path. There is a simple algorithm for walking through a maze that guarantees finding the exit (assuming there is an exit). If there is no exit, you will arrive at the starting location again. The algorithm is as follows: From the current location in the maze, try to move one space in any of the possible directions (down, right, up or left). If it is possible to move in at least one direction, call mazeTraversal recursively, passing the new spot on the maze as the current spot. If it is not possible to go in any direction, "back up" to a previous location in the maze and try a new direction for that location. Program the method to display the maze after each move so the user can watch as the maze is solved. The final output of the maze should display only the path needed to solve the maze—if going in a particular direction results in a dead end, the x's going in that direction should not be displayed. [*Hint:* To display only the final path, it may be helpful to mark off spots that result in a dead end with another character (such as '0').]

15.18 (*Generating Mazes Randomly*) Write a method mazeGenerator that takes as an argument a two-dimensional 12-by-12 character array and randomly produces a maze. The method should also provide the starting and ending locations of the maze. Test your method mazeTraversal from Exercise 15.17, using several randomly generated mazes.

15.19 (*Mazes of Any Size*) Generalize methods mazeTraversal and mazeGenerator of Exercise 15.17 and Exercise 15.18 to process mazes of any width and height.

16

Searching and Sorting

OBJECTIVES

In this chapter you will learn:

- To search for a given value in an array using linear search and binary search.

- To sort arrays using the iterative selection and insertion sort algorithms.

- To sort arrays using the recursive merge sort algorithm.

- To determine the efficiency of searching and sorting algorithms.

- To use loop invariants to help ensure the correctness of your programs.

16.1 Introduction

Searching data involves determining whether a value (referred to as the search key) is present in the data and, if so, finding its location. Two popular search algorithms are the simple linear search and the faster but more complex binary search. Sorting places data in ascending or descending order, based on one or more sort keys. A list of names could be sorted alphabetically, bank accounts could be sorted by account number, employee payroll records could be sorted by social security number, and so on. This chapter introduces two simple sorting algorithms, the selection sort and the insertion sort, along with the more efficient but more complex merge sort. Figure 16.1 summarizes the searching and sorting algorithms discussed in the examples and exercises of this book.

Chapter	Algorithm	Location
Searching Algorithms:		
16	Linear search	Section 16.2.1
	Binary search	Section 16.2.2
	Recursive linear search	Exercise 16.8
	Recursive binary search	Exercise 16.9
17	Linear search of a List	Exercise 17.21
	Binary tree search	Exercise 17.23
19	binarySearch method of class Collections	Fig. 19.14
Sorting Algorithms:		
16	Selection sort	Section 16.3.1

Fig. 16.1 | Searching and sorting algorithms in this text. (Part 1 of 2.)

Chapter	Algorithm	Location
Sorting Algorithms (continued):		
	Insertion sort	Section 16.3.2
	Recursive merge sort	Section 16.3.3
	Bubble sort	Exercises 16.3 and 16.4
	Bucket sort	Exercise 16.7
	Recursive quicksort	Exercise 16.10
17	Binary tree sort	Section 17.9
19	sort method of class Collections	Figs. 19.8–19.11
	SortedSet collection	Fig. 19.19

Fig. 16.1 | Searching and sorting algorithms in this text. (Part 2 of 2.)

16.2 Searching Algorithms

Looking up a phone number, finding a website via a search engine and checking the definition of a word in a dictionary all involve searching large amounts of data. The next two sections discuss two common search algorithms—one that is easy to program yet relatively inefficient and one that is relatively efficient but more complex and difficult to program.

16.2.1 Linear Search

The linear search algorithm searches each element in an array sequentially. If the search key does not match an element in the array, the algorithm tests each element, and when the end of the array is reached, informs the user that the search key is not present. If the search key is in the array, the algorithm tests each element until it finds one that matches the search key and returns the index of that element.

As an example, consider an array containing the following values

34 56 2 10 77 51 93 30 5 52

and a program that is searching for 51. Using the linear search algorithm, the program first checks whether 34 matches the search key. It does not, so the algorithm checks whether 56 matches the search key. The program continues moving through the array sequentially, testing 2, then 10, then 77. When the program tests 51, which matches the search key, the program returns the index 5, which is the location of 51 in the array. If, after checking every array element, the program determines that the search key does not match any element in the array, the program returns a sentinel value (e.g., -1).

Figure 16.2 declares the LinearArray class. This class has two private instance variables—an array of ints named data, and a static Random object to fill the array with randomly generated ints. When an object of class LinearArray is instantiated, the constructor (lines 12–19) creates and initializes the array data with random ints in the

```java
1    // Fig 16.2: LinearArray.java
2    // Class that contains an array of random integers and a method
3    // that will search that array sequentially
4    import java.util.Random;
5
6    public class LinearArray
7    {
8       private int[] data; // array of values
9       private static Random generator = new Random();
10
11      // create array of given size and fill with random numbers
12      public LinearArray( int size )
13      {
14         data = new int[ size ]; // create space for array
15
16         // fill array with random ints in range 10-99
17         for ( int i = 0; i < size; i++ )
18            data[ i ] = 10 + generator.nextInt( 90 );
19      } // end LinearArray constructor
20
21      // perform a linear search on the data
22      public int linearSearch( int searchKey )
23      {
24         // loop through array sequentially
25         for ( int index = 0; index < data.length; index++ )
26            if ( data[ index ] == searchKey )
27               return index; // return index of integer
28
29         return -1; // integer was not found
30      } // end method linearSearch
31
32      // method to output values in array
33      public String toString()
34      {
35         StringBuilder temporary = new StringBuilder();
36
37         // iterate through array
38         for ( int element : data )
39            temporary.append( element + " " );
40
41         temporary.append( "\n" ); // add endline character
42         return temporary.toString();
43      } // end method toString
44   } // end class LinearArray
```

Fig. 16.2 | LinearArray class.

range 10–99. If there are duplicate values in the array, linear search returns the index of the first element in the array that matches the search key.

Lines 22–30 perform the linear search. The search key is passed to parameter searchKey. Lines 25–27 loop through the elements in the array. Line 26 compares each element in the array with searchKey. If the values are equal, line 27 returns the index of the element. If the loop ends without finding the value, line 29 returns -1. Lines 33–43 declare method toString, which returns a String representation of the array for printing.

Figure 16.3 creates a LinearArray object containing an array of 10 ints (line 16) and allows the user to search the array for specific elements. Lines 20–22 prompt the user for the search key and store it in searchInt. Lines 25–41 then loop until the searchInt is equal to -1. The array holds ints from 10–99 (line 18 of Fig. 16.2). Line 28 calls method linearSearch to determine whether searchInt is in the array. If it is not, linearSearch

```
1   // Fig 16.3: LinearSearchTest.java
2   // Sequentially search an array for an item.
3   import java.util.Scanner;
4
5   public class LinearSearchTest
6   {
7      public static void main( String args[] )
8      {
9         // create Scanner object to input data
10        Scanner input = new Scanner( System.in );
11
12        int searchInt; // search key
13        int position; // location of search key in array
14
15        // create array and output it
16        LinearArray searchArray = new LinearArray( 10 );
17        System.out.println( searchArray ); // print array
18
19        // get input from user
20        System.out.print(
21           "Please enter an integer value (-1 to quit): " );
22        searchInt = input.nextInt(); // read first int from user
23
24        // repeatedly input an integer; -1 terminates the program
25        while ( searchInt != -1 )
26        {
27           // perform linear search
28           position = searchArray.linearSearch( searchInt );
29
30           if ( position == -1 ) // integer was not found
31              System.out.println( "The integer " + searchInt +
32                 " was not found.\n" );
33           else // integer was found
34              System.out.println( "The integer " + searchInt +
35                 " was found in position " + position + ".\n" );
36
37           // get input from user
38           System.out.print(
39              "Please enter an integer value (-1 to quit): " );
40           searchInt = input.nextInt(); // read next int from user
41        } // end while
42     } // end main
43  } // end class LinearSearchTest
```

Fig. 16.3 | LinearSearchTest class. (Part 1 of 2.)

```
16 35 68 10 48 36 81 60 84 21

Please enter an integer value (-1 to quit): 48
The integer 48 was found in position 4.

Please enter an integer value (-1 to quit): 60
The integer 60 was found in position 7.

Please enter an integer value (-1 to quit): 33
The integer 33 was not found.

Please enter an integer value (-1 to quit): -1
```

Fig. 16.3 | LinearSearchTest class. (Part 2 of 2.)

returns –1 and the program notifies the user (lines 31–32). If searchInt is in the array, linearSearch returns the position of the element, which the program outputs in lines 34–35. Lines 38–40 retrieve the next integer from the user.

Efficiency of Linear Search

Searching algorithms all accomplish the same goal—finding an element that matches a given search key, if such an element does, in fact, exist. There are, however, a number of things that differentiate search algorithms from one another. The major difference is the amount of effort they require to complete the search. One way to describe this effort is with **Big O notation**, which indicates the worst-case run time for an algorithm—that is, how hard an algorithm may have to work to solve a problem. For searching and sorting algorithms, this depends particularly on how many data elements there are.

Suppose an algorithm is designed to test whether the first element of an array is equal to the second element. If the array has 10 elements, this algorithm requires one comparison. If the array has 1000 elements, it still requires one comparison. In fact, the algorithm is completely independent of the number of elements in the array. This algorithm is said to have a **constant run time**, which is represented in Big O notation as $O(1)$. An algorithm that is $O(1)$ does not necessarily require only one comparison. $O(1)$ just means that the number of comparisons is *constant*—it does not grow as the size of the array increases. An algorithm that tests whether the first element of an array is equal to any of the next three elements is still $O(1)$ even though it requires three comparisons.

An algorithm that tests whether the first element of an array is equal to *any* of the other elements of the array will require at most $n – 1$ comparisons, where n is the number of elements in the array. If the array has 10 elements, this algorithm requires up to nine comparisons. If the array has 1000 elements, it requires up to 999 comparisons. As n grows larger, the n part of the expression "dominates," and subtracting one becomes inconsequential. Big O is designed to highlight these dominant terms and ignore terms that become unimportant as n grows. For this reason, an algorithm that requires a total of $n – 1$ comparisons (such as the one we described earlier) is said to be $O(n)$. An $O(n)$ algorithm is referred to as having a **linear run time**. $O(n)$ is often pronounced "on the order of n" or more simply "order n."

Now suppose you have an algorithm that tests whether *any* element of an array is duplicated elsewhere in the array. The first element must be compared with every other element in the array. The second element must be compared with every other element except the first (it was already compared to the first). The third element must be compared with every other element except the first two. In the end, this algorithm will end up making $(n-1) + (n-2) + \ldots + 2 + 1$ or $n^2/2 - n/2$ comparisons. As n increases, the n^2 term dominates and the n term becomes inconsequential. Again, Big O notation highlights the n^2 term, leaving $n^2/2$. But as we will soon see, constant factors are omitted in Big O notation.

Big O is concerned with how an algorithm's run time grows in relation to the number of items processed. Suppose an algorithm requires n^2 comparisons. With four elements, the algorithm requires 16 comparisons; with eight elements, 64 comparisons. With this algorithm, doubling the number of elements quadruples the number of comparisons. Consider a similar algorithm requiring $n^2/2$ comparisons. With four elements, the algorithm requires eight comparisons; with eight elements, 32 comparisons. Again, doubling the number of elements quadruples the number of comparisons. Both of these algorithms grow as the square of n, so Big O ignores the constant and both algorithms are considered to be $O(n^2)$, which is referred to as **quadratic run time** and pronounced "on the order of n-squared" or more simply "order n-squared."

When n is small, $O(n^2)$ algorithms (running on today's billion-operation-per-second personal computers) will not noticeably affect performance. But as n grows, you will start to notice the performance degradation. An $O(n^2)$ algorithm running on a million-element array would require a trillion "operations" (where each could actually require several machine instructions to execute). This could require several hours to execute. A billion-element array would require a quintillion operations, a number so large that the algorithm could take decades! $O(n^2)$ algorithms, unfortunately, are easy to write, as you'll see in this chapter. You'll also see algorithms with more favorable Big O measures. These efficient algorithms often take a bit more cleverness and work to create, but their superior performance can be well worth the extra effort, especially as n gets large and as algorithms are combined into larger programs.

The linear search algorithm runs in $O(n)$ time. The worst case in this algorithm is that every element must be checked to determine whether the search item exists in the array. If the size of the array is doubled, the number of comparisons that the algorithm must perform is also doubled. Note that linear search can provide outstanding performance if the element matching the search key happens to be at or near the front of the array. But we seek algorithms that perform well, on average, across all searches, including those where the element matching the search key is near the end of the array.

Linear search is the easiest search algorithm to program, but it can be slow compared to other search algorithms. If a program needs to perform many searches on large arrays, it may be better to implement a more efficient algorithm, such as the binary search, which we present in the next section.

 Performance Tip 16.1

Sometimes the simplest algorithms perform poorly. Their virtue is that they are easy to program, test and debug. Sometimes more complex algorithms are required to realize maximum performance.

16.2.2 Binary Search

The **binary search algorithm** is more efficient than the linear search algorithm, but it requires that the array be sorted. The first iteration of this algorithm tests the middle element in the array. If this matches the search key, the algorithm ends. Assuming the array is sorted in ascending order, then if the search key is less than the middle element, it cannot match any element in the second half of the array and the algorithm continues with only the first half of the array (i.e., the first element up to, but not including, the middle element). If the search key is greater than the middle element, it cannot match any element in the first half of the array and the algorithm continues with only the second half of the array (i.e., the element after the middle element through the last element). Each iteration tests the middle value of the remaining portion of the array. If the search key does not match the element, the algorithm eliminates half of the remaining elements. The algorithm ends by either finding an element that matches the search key or reducing the subarray to zero size.

As an example consider the sorted 15-element array

2 3 5 10 27 30 34 51 56 65 77 81 82 93 99

and a search key of 65. A program implementing the binary search algorithm would first check whether 51 is the search key (because 51 is the middle element of the array). The search key (65) is larger than 51, so 51 is discarded along with the first half of the array (all elements smaller than 51.) Next, the algorithm checks whether 81 (the middle element of the remainder of the array) matches the search key. The search key (65) is smaller than 81, so 81 is discarded along with the elements larger than 81. After just two tests, the algorithm has narrowed the number of values to check to three (56, 65 and 77). The algorithm then checks 65 (which indeed matches the search key), and returns the index of the array element containing 65. This algorithm required just three comparisons to determine whether the search key matched an element of the array. Using a linear search algorithm would have required 10 comparisons. [*Note:* In this example, we have chosen to use an array with 15 elements so that there will always be an obvious middle element in the array. With an even number of elements, the middle of the array lies between two elements. We implement the algorithm to chose the lower of those two elements.]

Figure 16.4 declares class `BinaryArray`. This class is similar to `LinearArray`—it has two `private` instance variables, a constructor, a search method (`binarySearch`), a remainingElements method and a `toString` method. Lines 13–22 declare the constructor. After the array has been initialized with random `int`s from 10–99 (lines 18–19), line 21 calls the `Arrays.sort` method on the array data. Method **sort** is a `static` method of class `Arrays` that sorts the elements in an array in ascending order by default; an overloaded version of this method allows you to change the sorting order. Recall that the binary search algorithm will work only on a sorted array.

```
1   // Fig 16.4: BinaryArray.java
2   // Class that contains an array of random integers and a method
3   // that uses binary search to find an integer.
4   import java.util.Random;
5   import java.util.Arrays;
6
7   public class BinaryArray
8   {
```

Fig. 16.4 | `BinaryArray` class. (Part 1 of 3.)

```
 9      private int[] data; // array of values
10      private static Random generator = new Random();
11
12      // create array of given size and fill with random integers
13      public BinaryArray( int size )
14      {
15         data = new int[ size ]; // create space for array
16
17         // fill array with random ints in range 10-99
18         for ( int i = 0; i < size; i++ )
19            data[ i ] = 10 + generator.nextInt( 90 );
20
21         Arrays.sort( data );
22      } // end BinaryArray constructor
23
24      // perform a binary search on the data
25      public int binarySearch( int searchElement )
26      {
27         int low = 0; // low end of the search area
28         int high = data.length - 1; // high end of the search area
29         int middle = ( low + high + 1 ) / 2; // middle element
30         int location = -1; // return value; -1 if not found
31
32         do // loop to search for element
33         {
34            // print remaining elements of array
35            System.out.print( remainingElements( low, high ) );
36
37            // output spaces for alignment
38            for ( int i = 0; i < middle; i++ )
39               System.out.print( "   " );
40            System.out.println( " * " ); // indicate current middle
41
42            // if the element is found at the middle
43            if ( searchElement == data[ middle ] )
44               location = middle; // location is the current middle
45
46            // middle element is too high
47            else if ( searchElement < data[ middle ] )
48               high = middle - 1; // eliminate the higher half
49            else  // middle element is too low
50               low = middle + 1; // eliminate the lower half
51
52            middle = ( low + high + 1 ) / 2; // recalculate the middle
53         } while ( ( low <= high ) && ( location == -1 ) );
54
55         return location; // return location of search key
56      } // end method binarySearch
57
58      // method to output certain values in array
59      public String remainingElements( int low, int high )
60      {
61         StringBuilder temporary = new StringBuilder();
```

Fig. 16.4 | BinaryArray class. (Part 2 of 3.)

```
62
63            // output spaces for alignment
64            for ( int i = 0; i < low; i++ )
65               temporary.append( "     " );
66
67            // output elements left in array
68            for ( int i = low; i <= high; i++ )
69               temporary.append( data[ i ] + " " );
70
71            temporary.append( "\n" );
72            return temporary.toString();
73         } // end method remainingElements
74
75         // method to output values in array
76         public String toString()
77         {
78            return remainingElements( 0, data.length - 1 );
79         } // end method toString
80   } // end class BinaryArray
```

Fig. 16.4 | `BinaryArray` class. (Part 3 of 3.)

Lines 25–56 declare method `binarySearch`. The search key is passed into parameter
`searchElement` (line 25). Lines 27–29 calculate the `low` end index, `high` end index and
`middle` index of the portion of the array that the program is currently searching. At the
beginning of the method, the `low` end is 0, the `high` end is the length of the array minus
1 and the `middle` is the average of these two values. Line 30 initializes the `location` of the
element to -1—the value that will be returned if the element is not found. Lines 32–53
loop until `low` is greater than `high` (this occurs when the element is not found) or `loca-
tion` does not equal -1 (indicating that the search key was found). Line 43 tests whether
the value in the `middle` element is equal to `searchElement`. If this is `true`, line 44 assigns
`middle` to `location`. Then the loop terminates and `location` is returned to the caller.
Each iteration of the loop tests a single value (line 43) and eliminates half of the remaining
values in the array (line 48 or 50).

Lines 26–44 of Fig. 16.5 loop until the user enters -1. For each other number the user
enters, the program performs a binary search on the data to determine whether it matches
an element in the array. The first line of output from this program is the array of `int`s, in
increasing order. When the user instructs the program to search for 23, the program first
tests the middle element, which is 42 (as indicated by *). The search key is less than 42, so
the program eliminates the second half of the array and tests the middle element from the
first half. The search key is smaller than 34, so the program eliminates the second half of
the array, leaving only three elements. Finally, the program checks 23 (which matches the
search key) and returns the index 1.

Efficiency of Binary Search

In the worst-case scenario, searching a sorted array of 1023 elements will take only 10 comparisons when using a binary search. Repeatedly dividing 1023 by 2 (because after each
comparison we are able to eliminate half of the array) and rounding down (because we also
remove the middle element) yields the values 511, 255, 127, 63, 31, 15, 7, 3, 1 and 0. The

number 1023 ($2^{10} - 1$) is divided by 2 only 10 times to get the value 0, which indicates that there are no more elements to test. Dividing by 2 is equivalent to one comparison in the binary search algorithm. Thus, an array of 1,048,575 ($2^{20} - 1$) elements takes a maximum of 20 comparisons to find the key, and an array of over one billion elements takes a

```
1   // Fig 16.5: BinarySearchTest.java
2   // Use binary search to locate an item in an array.
3   import java.util.Scanner;
4
5   public class BinarySearchTest
6   {
7      public static void main( String args[] )
8      {
9         // create Scanner object to input data
10        Scanner input = new Scanner( System.in );
11
12        int searchInt; // search key
13        int position; // location of search key in array
14
15        // create array and output it
16        BinaryArray searchArray = new BinaryArray( 15 );
17        System.out.println( searchArray );
18
19        // get input from user
20        System.out.print(
21           "Please enter an integer value (-1 to quit): " );
22        searchInt = input.nextInt(); // read an int from user
23        System.out.println();
24
25        // repeatedly input an integer; -1 terminates the program
26        while ( searchInt != -1 )
27        {
28           // use binary search to try to find integer
29           position = searchArray.binarySearch( searchInt );
30
31           // return value of -1 indicates integer was not found
32           if ( position == -1 )
33              System.out.println( "The integer " + searchInt +
34                 " was not found.\n" );
35           else
36              System.out.println( "The integer " + searchInt +
37                 " was found in position " + position + ".\n" );
38
39           // get input from user
40           System.out.print(
41              "Please enter an integer value (-1 to quit): " );
42           searchInt = input.nextInt(); // read an int from user
43           System.out.println();
44        } // end while
45     } // end main
46  } // end class BinarySearchTest
```

Fig. 16.5 | BinarySearchTest class. (Part 1 of 2.)

```
13 23 24 34 35 36 38 42 47 51 68 74 75 85 97

Please enter an integer value (-1 to quit): 23

13 23 24 34 35 36 38 42 47 51 68 74 75 85 97
                        *
13 23 24 34 35 36 38
                  *
13 23 24
      *
The integer 23 was found in position 1.

Please enter an integer value (-1 to quit): 75

13 23 24 34 35 36 38 42 47 51 68 74 75 85 97
                     *
                     47 51 68 74 75 85 97
                                 *
                                 75 85 97
                                    *
                                 75
                                  *
The integer 75 was found in position 12.

Please enter an integer value (-1 to quit): 52

13 23 24 34 35 36 38 42 47 51 68 74 75 85 97
                  *
                     47 51 68 74 75 85 97
                              *
                     47 51 68
                        *
                              68
                               *
The integer 52 was not found.

Please enter an integer value (-1 to quit): -1
```

Fig. 16.5 | BinarySearchTest class. (Part 2 of 2.)

maximum of 30 comparisons to find the key. This is a tremendous improvement in performance over the linear search. For a one-billion-element array, this is a difference between an average of 500 million comparisons for the linear search and a maximum of only 30 comparisons for the binary search! The maximum number of comparisons needed for the binary search of any sorted array is the exponent of the first power of 2 greater than the number of elements in the array, which is represented as $\log_2 n$. All logarithms grow at roughly the same rate, so in big O notation the base can be omitted. This results in a big O of $O(\log n)$ for a binary search which is also known as logarithmic run time.

16.3 Sorting Algorithms

Sorting data (i.e., placing the data into some particular order, such as ascending or descending) is one of the most important computing applications. A bank sorts all checks by account number so that it can prepare individual bank statements at the end of each month. Telephone companies sort their lists of accounts by last name and, further, by first name to make it easy to find phone numbers. Virtually every organization must sort some data, and often massive amounts of it. Sorting data is an intriguing, computer-intensive problem that has attracted intense research efforts.

An important item to understand about sorting is that the end result—the sorted array—will be the same no matter which algorithm you use to sort the array. The choice of algorithm affects only the run time and memory use of the program. The rest of the chapter introduces three common sorting algorithms. The first two—selection sort and insertion sort—are simple to program but inefficient. The last algorithm—merge sort—is much faster than selection sort and insertion sort but harder to program. We focus on sorting arrays of primitive-type data, namely ints. It is possible to sort arrays of objects of classes as well. We discuss this in Section 19.6.1.

16.3.1 Selection Sort

Selection sort is a simple, but inefficient, sorting algorithm. The first iteration of the algorithm selects the smallest element in the array and swaps it with the first element. The second iteration selects the second-smallest item (which is the smallest item of the remaining elements) and swaps it with the second element. The algorithm continues until the last iteration selects the second-largest element and swaps it with the second-to-last index, leaving the largest element in the last index. After the ith iteration, the smallest i items of the array will be sorted into increasing order in the first i elements of the array.

As an example, consider the array

| 34 | 56 | 4 | 10 | 77 | 51 | 93 | 30 | 5 | 52 |

A program that implements selection sort first determines the smallest element (4) of this array which is contained in index 2. The program swaps 4 with 34, resulting in

| 4 | 56 | 34 | 10 | 77 | 51 | 93 | 30 | 5 | 52 |

The program then determines the smallest value of the remaining elements (all elements except 4), which is 5, contained in index 8. The program swaps 5 with 56, resulting in

| 4 | 5 | 34 | 10 | 77 | 51 | 93 | 30 | 56 | 52 |

On the third iteration, the program determines the next smallest value (10) and swaps it with 34.

| 4 | 5 | 10 | 34 | 77 | 51 | 93 | 30 | 56 | 52 |

The process continues until the array is fully sorted.

| 4 | 5 | 10 | 30 | 34 | 51 | 52 | 56 | 77 | 93 |

Note that after the first iteration, the smallest element is in the first position. After the second iteration, the two smallest elements are in order in the first two positions. After the third iteration, the three smallest elements are in order in the first three positions.

Figure 16.6 declares the SelectionSort class. This class has two private instance variables—an array of ints named data, and a static Random object to generate random integers to fill the array. When an object of class SelectionSort is instantiated, the constructor (lines 12–19) creates and initializes the array data with random ints in the range 10–99.

```java
1   // Fig 16.6: SelectionSort.java
2   // Class that creates an array filled with random integers.
3   // Provides a method to sort the array with selection sort.
4   import java.util.Random;
5
6   public class SelectionSort
7   {
8      private int[] data; // array of values
9      private static Random generator = new Random();
10
11     // create array of given size and fill with random integers
12     public SelectionSort( int size )
13     {
14        data = new int[ size ]; // create space for array
15
16        // fill array with random ints in range 10-99
17        for ( int i = 0; i < size; i++ )
18           data[ i ] = 10 + generator.nextInt( 90 );
19     } // end SelectionSort constructor
20
21     // sort array using selection sort
22     public void sort()
23     {
24        int smallest; // index of smallest element
25
26        // loop over data.length - 1 elements
27        for ( int i = 0; i < data.length - 1; i++ )
28        {
29           smallest = i; // first index of remaining array
30
31           // loop to find index of smallest element
32           for ( int index = i + 1; index < data.length; index++ )
33              if ( data[ index ] < data[ smallest ] )
34                 smallest = index;
35
36           swap( i, smallest ); // swap smallest element into position
37           printPass( i + 1, smallest ); // output pass of algorithm
38        } // end outer for
39     } // end method sort
40
41     // helper method to swap values in two elements
42     public void swap( int first, int second )
43     {
44        int temporary = data[ first ]; // store first in temporary
45        data[ first ] = data[ second ]; // replace first with second
46        data[ second ] = temporary; // put temporary in second
47     } // end method swap
48
49     // print a pass of the algorithm
50     public void printPass( int pass, int index )
51     {
52        System.out.print( String.format( "after pass %2d: ", pass ) );
53
```

Fig. 16.6 | SelectionSort class. (Part 1 of 2.)

```
54          // output elements till selected item
55          for ( int i = 0; i < index; i++ )
56              System.out.print( data[ i ] + "  " );
57
58          System.out.print( data[ index ] + "* " ); // indicate swap
59
60          // finish outputting array
61          for ( int i = index + 1; i < data.length; i++ )
62              System.out.print( data[ i ] + "  " );
63
64          System.out.print( "\n                    " ); // for alignment
65
66          // indicate amount of array that is sorted
67          for ( int j = 0; j < pass; j++ )
68              System.out.print( "--  " );
69          System.out.println( "\n" ); // add endline
70      } // end method indicateSelection
71
72      // method to output values in array
73      public String toString()
74      {
75          StringBuilder temporary = new StringBuilder();
76
77          // iterate through array
78          for ( int element : data )
79              temporary.append( element + "  " );
80
81          temporary.append( "\n" ); // add endline character
82          return temporary.toString();
83      } // end method toString
84  } // end class SelectionSort
```

Fig. 16.6 | SelectionSort class. (Part 2 of 2.)

Lines 22–39 declare the sort method. Line 24 declares the variable smallest, which will store the index of the smallest element in the remaining array. Lines 27–38 loop data.length - 1 times. Line 29 initializes the index of the smallest element to the current item. Lines 32–34 loop over the remaining elements in the array. For each of these elements, line 33 compares its value to the value of the smallest element. If the current element is smaller than the smallest element, line 34 assigns the current element's index to smallest. When this loop finishes, smallest will contain the index of the smallest element in the remaining array. Line 36 calls method swap (lines 42–47) to place the smallest remaining element in the next spot in the array.

Line 9 of Fig. 16.7 creates a SelectionSort object with 10 elements. Line 12 implicitly calls method toString to output the unsorted object. Line 14 calls method sort (lines 22–39 of Fig. 16.6), which sorts the elements using selection sort. Then lines 16–17 output the sorted object. The output of this program uses dashes to indicate the portion of the array that is sorted after each pass. An asterisk is placed next to the position of the element that was swapped with the smallest element on that pass. On each pass, the element next to the asterisk and the element above the rightmost set of dashes were the two values that were swapped.

```
 1    // Fig 16.7: SelectionSortTest.java
 2    // Test the selection sort class.
 3
 4    public class SelectionSortTest
 5    {
 6       public static void main( String[] args )
 7       {
 8          // create object to perform selection sort
 9          SelectionSort sortArray = new SelectionSort( 10 );
10
11          System.out.println( "Unsorted array:" );
12          System.out.println( sortArray ); // print unsorted array
13
14          sortArray.sort(); // sort array
15
16          System.out.println( "Sorted array:" );
17          System.out.println( sortArray ); // print sorted array
18       } // end main
19    } // end class SelectionSortTest
```

```
Unsorted array:
61  87  80  58  40  50  20  13  71  45

after pass  1: 13  87  80  58  40  50  20  61* 71  45
               --

after pass  2: 13  20  80  58  40  50  87* 61  71  45
               --  --

after pass  3: 13  20  40  58  80* 50  87  61  71  45
               --  --  --

after pass  4: 13  20  40  45  80  50  87  61  71  58*
               --  --  --  --

after pass  5: 13  20  40  45  50  80* 87  61  71  58
               --  --  --  --  --

after pass  6: 13  20  40  45  50  58  87  61  71  80*
               --  --  --  --  --  --

after pass  7: 13  20  40  45  50  58  61  87* 71  80
               --  --  --  --  --  --  --

after pass  8: 13  20  40  45  50  58  61  71  87* 80
               --  --  --  --  --  --  --  --

after pass  9: 13  20  40  45  50  58  61  71  80  87*
               --  --  --  --  --  --  --  --  --

Sorted array:
13  20  40  45  50  58  61  71  80  87
```

Fig. 16.7 | SelectionSortTest class.

Efficiency of Selection Sort

The selection sort algorithm runs in $O(n^2)$ time. The sort method in lines 22–39 of Fig. 16.6, which implements the selection sort algorithm, contains two for loops. The outer for loop (lines 27–38) iterates over the first $n-1$ elements in the array, swapping the smallest remaining item into its sorted position. The inner for loop (lines 32–34) iterates over each item in the remaining array, searching for the smallest element. This loop executes $n-1$ times during the first iteration of the outer loop, $n-2$ times during the second iteration, then $n-3, \ldots , 3, 2, 1$. This inner loop will iterate a total of $n(n-1)/2$ or $(n^2-n)/2$. In Big O notation, smaller terms drop out and constants are ignored, leaving a final Big O of $O(n^2)$.

16.3.2 Insertion Sort

Insertion sort is another simple, but inefficient, sorting algorithm. The first iteration of this algorithm takes the second element in the array and, if it is less than the first element, swaps it with the first element. The second iteration looks at the third element and inserts it into the correct position with respect to the first two elements, so all three elements are in order. At the *i*th iteration of this algorithm, the first *i* elements in the original array will be sorted.

Consider as an example the following array. [*Note:* This array is identical to the one used in the discussions of selection sort and merge sort.]

| 34 | 56 | 4 | 10 | 77 | 51 | 93 | 30 | 5 | 52 |

A program that implements the insertion sort algorithm will first look at the first two elements of the array, 34 and 56. These two elements are already in order, so the program continues (if they were out of order, the program would swap them).

In the next iteration, the program looks at the third value, 4. This value is less than 56, so the program stores 4 in a temporary variable and moves 56 one element to the right. The program then checks and determines that 4 is less than 34, so it moves 34 one element to the right. The program has now reached the beginning of the array, so it places 4 in the zeroth element. The array now is

| 4 | 34 | 56 | 10 | 77 | 51 | 93 | 30 | 5 | 52 |

In the next iteration, the program stores the value 10 in a temporary variable. Then the program compares 10 to 56 and moves 56 one element to the right because it is larger than 10. The program then compares 10 to 34, moving 34 right one element. When the program compares 10 to 4, it observes that 10 is larger than 4 and places 10 in element 1. The array now is

| 4 | 10 | 34 | 56 | 77 | 51 | 93 | 30 | 5 | 52 |

Using this algorithm, at the *i*th iteration, the first *i* elements of the original array are sorted. They may not be in their final locations, however, because smaller values may be located later in the array.

Figure 16.8 declares the InsertionSort class. Lines 22–46 declare the sort method. Line 24 declares the variable insert, which holds the element you are going to insert while you move the other elements. Lines 27–45 loop over data.length - 1 items in the array.

```java
1   // Fig 16.8: InsertionSort.java
2   // Class that creates an array filled with random integers.
3   // Provides a method to sort the array with insertion sort.
4   import java.util.Random;
5
6   public class InsertionSort
7   {
8      private int[] data; // array of values
9      private static Random generator = new Random();
10
11     // create array of given size and fill with random integers
12     public InsertionSort( int size )
13     {
14        data = new int[ size ]; // create space for array
15
16        // fill array with random ints in range 10-99
17        for ( int i = 0; i < size; i++ )
18           data[ i ] = 10 + generator.nextInt( 90 );
19     } // end InsertionSort constructor
20
21     // sort array using insertion sort
22     public void sort()
23     {
24        int insert; // temporary variable to hold element to insert
25
26        // loop over data.length - 1 elements
27        for ( int next = 1; next < data.length; next++ )
28        {
29           // store value in current element
30           insert = data[ next ];
31
32           // initialize location to place element
33           int moveItem = next;
34
35           // search for place to put current element
36           while ( moveItem > 0 && data[ moveItem - 1 ] > insert )
37           {
38              // shift element right one slot
39              data[ moveItem ] = data[ moveItem - 1 ];
40              moveItem--;
41           } // end while
42
43           data[ moveItem ] = insert; // place inserted element
44           printPass( next, moveItem ); // output pass of algorithm
45        } // end for
46     } // end method sort
47
48     // print a pass of the algorithm
49     public void printPass( int pass, int index )
50     {
51        System.out.print( String.format( "after pass %2d: ", pass ) );
52
```

Fig. 16.8 | InsertionSort class. (Part 1 of 2.)

```
53            // output elements till swapped item
54            for ( int i = 0; i < index; i++ )
55                System.out.print( data[ i ] + "   " );
56
57            System.out.print( data[ index ] + "* " ); // indicate swap
58
59            // finish outputting array
60            for ( int i = index + 1; i < data.length; i++ )
61                System.out.print( data[ i ] + "   " );
62
63            System.out.print( "\n                    " ); // for alignment
64
65            // indicate amount of array that is sorted
66            for( int i = 0; i <= pass; i++ )
67                System.out.print( "--   " );
68            System.out.println( "\n" ); // add endline
69        } // end method printPass
70
71        // method to output values in array
72        public String toString()
73        {
74            StringBuilder temporary = new StringBuilder();
75
76            // iterate through array
77            for ( int element : data )
78                temporary.append( element + "   " );
79
80            temporary.append( "\n" ); // add endline character
81            return temporary.toString();
82        } // end method toString
83    } // end class InsertionSort
```

Fig. 16.8 | InsertionSort class. (Part 2 of 2.)

In each iteration, line 30 stores in insert the value of the element that will be inserted into the sorted portion of the array. Line 33 declares and initializes the variable moveItem, which keeps track of where to insert the element. Lines 36–41 loop to locate the correct position where the element should be inserted. The loop will terminate either when the program reaches the front of the array or when it reaches an element that is less than the value to be inserted. Line 39 moves an element to the right, and line 40 decrements the position at which to insert the next element. After the loop ends, line 43 inserts the element into place. Figure 16.9 is the same as Fig. 16.7 except that it creates and uses an InsertionSort object. The output of this program uses dashes to indicate the portion of the array that is sorted after each pass. An asterisk is placed next to the element that was inserted into place on that pass.

```
1    // Fig 16.9: InsertionSortTest.java
2    // Test the insertion sort class.
3
```

Fig. 16.9 | InsertionSortTest class. (Part 1 of 2.)

```
4  public class InsertionSortTest
5  {
6     public static void main( String[] args )
7     {
8        // create object to perform selection sort
9        InsertionSort sortArray = new InsertionSort( 10 );
10
11       System.out.println( "Unsorted array:" );
12       System.out.println( sortArray ); // print unsorted array
13
14       sortArray.sort(); // sort array
15
16       System.out.println( "Sorted array:" );
17       System.out.println( sortArray ); // print sorted array
18    } // end main
19 } // end class InsertionSortTest
```

```
Unsorted array:
40  17  45  82  62  32  30  44  93  10

after pass  1: 17* 40  45  82  62  32  30  44  93  10
               --          --

after pass  2: 17  40  45* 82  62  32  30  44  93  10
               --  --  --

after pass  3: 17  40  45  82* 62  32  30  44  93  10
               --  --  --  --

after pass  4: 17  40  45  62* 82  32  30  44  93  10
               --  --  --  --  --

after pass  5: 17  32* 40  45  62  82  30  44  93  10
               --  --  --  --  --  --

after pass  6: 17  30* 32  40  45  62  82  44  93  10
               --  --  --  --  --  --  --

after pass  7: 17  30  32  40  44* 45  62  82  93  10
               --  --  --  --  --  --  --  --

after pass  8: 17  30  32  40  44  45  62  82  93* 10
               --  --  --  --  --  --  --  --  --

after pass  9: 10* 17  30  32  40  44  45  62  82  93
               --  --  --  --  --  --  --  --  --  --

Sorted array:
10  17  30  32  40  44  45  62  82  93
```

Fig. 16.9 | InsertionSortTest class. (Part 2 of 2.)

Efficiency of Insertion Sort

The insertion sort algorithm also runs in $O(n^2)$ time. Like selection sort, the implementation of insertion sort (lines 22–46 of Fig. 16.8) contains two loops. The for loop (lines 27–45) iterates data.length - 1 times, inserting an element into the appropriate position in the elements sorted so far. For the purposes of this application, data.length - 1 is equivalent to $n - 1$ (as data.length is the size of the array). The while loop (lines 36–41) iterates over the preceding elements in the array. In the worst case, this while loop will require $n - 1$ comparisons. Each individual loop runs in $O(n)$ time. In Big O notation, nested loops mean that you must multiply the number of comparisons. For each iteration of an outer loop, there will be a certain number of iterations of the inner loop. In this algorithm, for each $O(n)$ iterations of the outer loop, there will be $O(n)$ iterations of the inner loop. Multiplying these values results in a Big O of $O(n^2)$.

16.3.3 Merge Sort

Merge sort is an efficient sorting algorithm, but is conceptually more complex than selection sort and insertion sort. The merge sort algorithm sorts an array by splitting it into two equal-sized subarrays, sorting each subarray and then merging them into one larger array. With an odd number of elements, the algorithm creates the two subarrays such that one has one more element than the other.

The implementation of merge sort in this example is recursive. The base case is an array with one element, which is, of course, sorted, so the merge sort immediately returns in this case. The recursion step splits the array into two approximately equal pieces, recursively sorts them, then merges the two sorted arrays into one larger, sorted array.

Suppose the algorithm has already merged smaller arrays to create sorted arrays A:

    4   10   34   56   77

and B:

    5   30   51   52   93

Merge sort combines these two arrays into one larger, sorted array. The smallest element in A is 4 (located in the zeroth index of A). The smallest element in B is 5 (located in the zeroth index of B). In order to determine the smallest element in the larger array, the algorithm compares 4 and 5. The value from A is smaller, so 4 becomes the first element in the merged array. The algorithm continues by comparing 10 (the second element in A) to 5 (the first element in B). The value from B is smaller, so 5 becomes the second element in the larger array. The algorithm continues by comparing 10 to 30, with 10 becoming the third element in the array, and so on.

Lines 22–25 of Fig. 16.10 declare the sort method. Line 24 calls method sortArray with 0 and data.length - 1 as the arguments—corresponding to the beginning and ending indices, respectively, of the array to be sorted. These values tell method sortArray to operate on the entire array.

```
1   // Figure 16.10: MergeSort.java
2   // Class that creates an array filled with random integers.
3   // Provides a method to sort the array with merge sort.
4   import java.util.Random;
5
6   public class MergeSort
7   {
8       private int[] data; // array of values
```

Fig. 16.10 | MergeSort class. (Part 1 of 3.)

```
9     private static Random generator = new Random();
10
11     // create array of given size and fill with random integers
12     public MergeSort( int size )
13     {
14        data = new int[ size ]; // create space for array
15
16        // fill array with random ints in range 10-99
17        for ( int i = 0; i < size; i++ )
18           data[ i ] = 10 + generator.nextInt( 90 );
19     } // end MergeSort constructor
20
21     // calls recursive split method to begin merge sorting
22     public void sort()
23     {
24        sortArray( 0, data.length - 1 ); // split entire array
25     } // end method sort
26
27     // splits array, sorts subarrays and merges subarrays into sorted array
28     private void sortArray( int low, int high )
29     {
30        // test base case; size of array equals 1
31        if ( ( high - low ) >= 1 ) // if not base case
32        {
33           int middle1 = ( low + high ) / 2; // calculate middle of array
34           int middle2 = middle1 + 1; // calculate next element over
35
36           // output split step
37           System.out.println( "split:   " + subarray( low, high ) );
38           System.out.println( "         " + subarray( low, middle1 ) );
39           System.out.println( "         " + subarray( middle2, high ) );
40           System.out.println();
41
42           // split array in half; sort each half (recursive calls)
43           sortArray( low, middle1 ); // first half of array
44           sortArray( middle2, high ); // second half of array
45
46           // merge two sorted arrays after split calls return
47           merge ( low, middle1, middle2, high );
48        } // end if
49     } // end method sortArray
50
51     // merge two sorted subarrays into one sorted subarray
52     private void merge( int left, int middle1, int middle2, int right )
53     {
54        int leftIndex = left; // index into left subarray
55        int rightIndex = middle2; // index into right subarray
56        int combinedIndex = left; // index into temporary working array
57        int[] combined = new int[ data.length ]; // working array
58
59        // output two subarrays before merging
60        System.out.println( "merge:   " + subarray( left, middle1 ) );
61        System.out.println( "         " + subarray( middle2, right ) );
```

Fig. 16.10 | MergeSort class. (Part 2 of 3.)

```
62
63          // merge arrays until reaching end of either
64          while ( leftIndex <= middle1 && rightIndex <= right )
65          {
66             // place smaller of two current elements into result
67             // and move to next space in arrays
68             if ( data[ leftIndex ] <= data[ rightIndex ] )
69                combined[ combinedIndex++ ] = data[ leftIndex++ ];
70             else
71                combined[ combinedIndex++ ] = data[ rightIndex++ ];
72          } // end while
73
74          // if left array is empty
75          if ( leftIndex == middle2 )
76             // copy in rest of right array
77             while ( rightIndex <= right )
78                combined[ combinedIndex++ ] = data[ rightIndex++ ];
79          else // right array is empty
80             // copy in rest of left array
81             while ( leftIndex <= middle1 )
82                combined[ combinedIndex++ ] = data[ leftIndex++ ];
83
84          // copy values back into original array
85          for ( int i = left; i <= right; i++ )
86             data[ i ] = combined[ i ];
87
88          // output merged array
89          System.out.println( "                " + subarray( left, right ) );
90          System.out.println();
91       } // end method merge
92
93       // method to output certain values in array
94       public String subarray( int low, int high )
95       {
96          StringBuilder temporary = new StringBuilder();
97
98          // output spaces for alignment
99          for ( int i = 0; i < low; i++ )
100            temporary.append( "   " );
101
102         // output elements left in array
103         for ( int i = low; i <= high; i++ )
104            temporary.append( " " + data[ i ] );
105
106         return temporary.toString();
107      } // end method subarray
108
109      // method to output values in array
110      public String toString()
111      {
112         return subarray( 0, data.length - 1 );
113      } // end method toString
114   } // end class MergeSort
```

Fig. 16.10 | MergeSort class. (Part 3 of 3.)

Method `sortArray` is declared in lines 28–49. Line 31 tests the base case. If the size of the array is 1, the array is already sorted, so the method returns immediately. If the size of the array is greater than 1, the method splits the array in two, recursively calls method `sortArray` to sort the two subarrays, then merges them. Line 43 recursively calls method `sortArray` on the first half of the array, and line 44 recursively calls method `sortArray` on the second half of the array. When these two method calls return, each half of the array has been sorted. Line 47 calls method `merge` (lines 52–91) on the two halves of the array to combine the two sorted arrays into one larger sorted array.

Lines 64–72 in method `merge` loop until the program reaches the end of either subarray. Line 68 tests which element at the beginning of the arrays is smaller. If the element in the left array is smaller, line 69 places it in position in the combined array. If the element in the right array is smaller, line 71 places it in position in the combined array. When the `while` loop has completed (line 72), one entire subarray is placed in the combined array, but the other subarray still contains data. Line 75 tests whether the left array has reached the end. If so, lines 77–78 fill the combined array with the elements of the right array. If the left array has not reached the end, then the right array must have reached the end, and lines 81–82 fill the combined array with the elements of the left array. Finally, lines 85–86 copy the combined array into the original array. Figure 16.11 creates and uses a `MergeSort` object. The fascinating output from this program displays the splits and merges performed by merge sort, showing the progress of the sort at each step of the algorithm. It is well worth your time to step through these outputs to fully understand this elegant sorting algorithm.

```java
1   // Figure 16.11: MergeSortTest.java
2   // Test the merge sort class.
3
4   public class MergeSortTest
5   {
6      public static void main( String[] args )
7      {
8         // create object to perform merge sort
9         MergeSort sortArray = new MergeSort( 10 );
10
11        // print unsorted array
12        System.out.println( "Unsorted:" + sortArray + "\n" );
13
14        sortArray.sort(); // sort array
15
16        // print sorted array
17        System.out.println( "Sorted:   " + sortArray );
18     } // end main
19  } // end class MergeSortTest
```

```
Unsorted: 75 56 85 90 49 26 12 48 40 47

split:    75 56 85 90 49 26 12 48 40 47
          75 56 85 90 49
                         26 12 48 40 47
```

Fig. 16.11 | `MergeSortTest` class. (Part 1 of 3.)

```
split:     75 56 85 90 49
           75 56 85
                    90 49

split:     75 56 85
           75 56
                 85

split:     75 56
           75
              56

merge:     75
              56
           56 75

merge:     56 75
                 85
           56 75 85

split:                 90 49
                       90
                          49

merge:                 90
                          49
                       49 90

merge:     56 75 85
                       49 90
           49 56 75 85 90

split:                     26 12 48 40 47
                           26 12 48
                                    40 47

split:                     26 12 48
                           26 12
                                 48

split:                     26 12
                           26
                              12

merge:                     26
                              12
                           12 26

merge:                     12 26
                                 48
                           12 26 48

split:                             40 47
                                   40
                                      47
```

Fig. 16.11 | MergeSortTest class. (Part 2 of 3.)

```
merge:                              40
                                       47
                                    40  47

merge:                  12  26  48
                                    40  47
                        12  26  40  47  48

merge:      49  56  75  85  90

            12  26  40  47  48  49  56  75  85  90

Sorted:     12  26  40  47  48  49  56  75  85  90
```

Fig. 16.11 | MergeSortTest class. (Part 3 of 3.)

Efficiency of Merge Sort

Merge sort is a far more efficient algorithm than either insertion or selection sort. Consider the first (nonrecursive) call to method sortArray. This results in two recursive calls to method sortArray with subarrays each approximately half the size of the original array, and a single call to method merge. This call to merge requires, at worst, $n - 1$ comparisons to fill the original array, which is $O(n)$. (Recall that each element in the array can be chosen by comparing one element from each of the subarrays.) The two calls to method sortArray result in four more recursive calls to method sortArray, each with a subarray approximately a quarter the size of the original array along with two calls to method merge. These two calls to method merge each require, at worst, $n/2 - 1$ comparisons for a total number of comparisons of $O(n)$. This process continues, each call to sortArray generating two additional calls to sortArray and a call to merge, until the algorithm has split the array into one-element subarrays. At each level, $O(n)$ comparisons are required to merge the subarrays. Each level splits the size of the arrays in half, so doubling the size of the array requires one more level. Quadrupling the size of the array requires two more levels. This pattern is logarithmic and results in $\log_2 n$ levels. This results in a total efficiency of $O(n \log n)$. Figure 16.12 summarizes many of the searching and sorting algorithms covered in this book and lists the Big O for each of them. Figure 16.13 lists the Big O values we have covered in this chapter along with a number of values for n to highlight the differences in the growth rates.

Algorithm	Location	Big O
Searching Algorithms:		
Linear search	Section 16.2.1	$O(n)$
Binary search	Section 16.2.2	$O(\log n)$
Recursive linear search	Exercise 16.8	$O(n)$
Recursive binary search	Exercise 16.9	$O(\log n)$

Fig. 16.12 | Searching and sorting algorithms with Big O values. (Part 1 of 2.)

Algorithm	Location	Big O
Sorting Algorithms:		
Selection sort	Section 16.3.1	$O(n^2)$
Insertion Sort	Section 16.3.2	$O(n^2)$
Merge sort	Section 16.3.3	$O(n \log n)$
Bubble sort	Exercises 16.3 and 16.4	$O(n^2)$

Fig. 16.12 | Searching and sorting algorithms with Big O values. (Part 2 of 2.)

$n =$	$O(\log n)$	$O(n)$	$O(n \log n)$	$O(n^2)$
1	0	1	0	1
2	1	2	2	4
3	1	3	3	9
4	1	4	4	16
5	1	5	5	25
10	1	10	10	100
100	2	100	200	10,000
1000	3	1000	3000	10^6
1,000,000	6	1,000,000	6,000,000	10^{12}
1,000,000,000	9	1,000,000,000	9,000,000,000	10^{18}

Fig. 16.13 | Number of comparisons for common Big O notations.

16.4 Invariants

After writing an application, a programmer typically tests it thoroughly. Creating an exhaustive set of tests often is quite difficult, and it is always possible that a particular case remains untested. One technique that can help you test your programs thoroughly is to use invariants. An invariant is an assertion (see Section 13.13) that is true before and after a portion of your code executes. Invariants are mathematical in nature and their concepts are more applicable to the theoretical side of computer science.

The most common type of invariant is a loop invariant, which is an assertion that remains true

- before the execution of the loop,

- after every iteration of the loop body, and

- when the loop terminates.

A properly written loop invariant can help you code a loop correctly. There are four steps to developing a loop from a loop invariant.

1. Set initial values for any loop control variables.

2. Determine the condition that causes the loop to terminate.

3. Modify the control variable(s) so the loop progresses toward termination.

4. Check that the invariant remains true at the end of each iteration.

As an example, we will examine method `linearSearch` from class `LinearArray` in Fig. 16.2. The invariant for the linear search algorithm is:

> *for all* k *such that* 0 <= k *and* k < index
>   data[k] != searchKey

For example, suppose `index` equals 3. If we pick any non-negative number less than 3, such as 1 for the value of `k`, the element in `data` at location `k` in the array does not equal the `searchKey`. This invariant basically states that the portion of the array, called a **subarray**, from the start of the array up to but not including the element at `index` does not contain the `searchKey`. A subarray can any number of elements.

According to *Step 1*, we must first initialize control variable `index`. From the invariant, we see that if we set `index` to 0, then the subarray contains zero elements. Therefore, the invariant is true because a subarray with no elements cannot contain a value that matches the `searchKey`.

The second step is to determine the condition that causes the loop to terminate. The loop should end after searching the entire array—when `index` equals the length of the array. In this case, no element of array `data` matches the `searchKey`. Once the `index` reaches the end of the array, the invariant remains true—no elements in the subarray (which in this case is the entire array) equal the `searchKey`.

For the loop to proceed to the next element, we increment control variable `index`. The last step is to ensure that the invariant remains true after each iteration. The `if` statement (lines 26–27 of Fig. 16.2) determines whether `data[ index ]` equals the `searchKey`. If so, the method finishes and returns `index`. Because `index` is the first occurrence of `searchKey` in `data`, the invariant is still true—the subarray up to `index` does not contain the `searchKey`.

16.5 Wrap-Up

This chapter introduced searching and sorting. We discussed two searching algorithms—linear search and binary search—and three sorting algorithms—selection sort, insertion sort and merge sort. We introduced Big O notation, which helps you analyze the efficiency of an algorithm. You also learned about loop invariants, which must remain true before the loop begins executing, while the loop executes and when the loop terminates. In the next chapter, you'll learn about dynamic data structures that can grow or shrink at execution time.

Summary

Section 16.1 Introduction
- Searching data involves determining whether a search key is present in the data and, if so, finding its location.
- Sorting involves arranging data into order.

Section 16.2 Searching Algorithms
- The linear search algorithm searches each element in the array sequentially until it finds the correct element. If the element is not in the array, the algorithm tests each element in the array, and when the end of the array is reached, informs the user that the element is not present. If the element is in the array, linear search tests each item until it finds the correct item.
- A major difference among searching algorithms is the amount of effort they require in order to return a result.
- One way to describe the efficiency of an algorithm is with Big O notation, which indicates how hard an algorithm may have to work to solve a problem.
- For searching and sorting algorithms, Big O is often dependent on how many elements are in the data.
- An algorithm that is $O(1)$ does not necessarily require only one comparison. It just means that the number of comparisons does not grow as the size of the array increases.
- An $O(n)$ algorithm is referred to as having a linear run time.
- Big O is designed to highlight dominant factors and ignore terms that become unimportant with high n values.
- Big O notation is concerned with the growth rate of algorithm run times, so constants are ignored.
- The linear search algorithm runs in $O(n)$ time.
- The worst case in linear search is that every element must be checked to determine whether the search item exists. This occurs if the search key is the last element in the array or is not present.
- The binary search algorithm is more efficient than the linear search algorithm, but it requires that the array be sorted.
- The first iteration of binary search tests the middle element in the array. If this is the search key, the algorithm returns its location. If the search key is less than the middle element, binary search continues with the first half of the array. If the search key is greater than the middle element, binary search continues with the second half of the array. Each iteration of binary search tests the middle value of the remaining array and, if the element is not found, eliminates half of the remaining elements.
- Binary search is a more efficient searching algorithm than linear search because each comparison eliminates from consideration half of the elements in the array.
- Binary search runs in $O(\log n)$ time because each step removes half of the remaining elements.
- If the size of the array is doubled, binary search requires only one extra comparison to complete successfully.

Section 16.3 Sorting Algorithms
- Selection sort is a simple, but inefficient, sorting algorithm.
- The first iteration of selection sort selects the smallest item in the array and swaps it with the first element. The second iteration of selection sort selects the second-smallest item (which is the

smallest remaining item) and swaps it with the second element. Selection sort continues until the last iteration selects the second-largest element and swaps it with the second-to-last element, leaving the largest element in the last index. At the ith iteration of selection sort, the smallest i items of the whole array are sorted into the first i indices.

- The selection sort algorithm runs in $O(n^2)$ time.

- The first iteration of insertion sort takes the second element in the array and, if it is less than the first element, swaps it with the first element. The second iteration of insertion sort looks at the third element and inserts it in the correct position with respect to the first two elements. After the ith iteration of insertion sort, the first i elements in the original array are sorted.

- The insertion sort algorithm runs in $O(n^2)$ time.

- Merge sort is a sorting algorithm that is faster, but more complex to implement, than selection sort and insertion sort.

- The merge sort algorithm sorts an array by splitting the array into two equal-sized subarrays, sorting each subarray recursively and merging the subarrays into one larger array.

- Merge sort's base case is an array with one element. A one-element array is already sorted, so merge sort immediately returns when it is called with a one-element array. The merge part of merge sort takes two sorted arrays (these could be one-element arrays) and combines them into one larger sorted array.

- Merge sort performs the merge by looking at the first element in each array, which is also the smallest element in the array. Merge sort takes the smallest of these and places it in the first element of the larger array. If there are still elements in the subarray, merge sort looks at the second element in that subarray (which is now the smallest element remaining) and compares it to the first element in the other subarray. Merge sort continues this process until the larger array is filled.

- In the worst case, the first call to merge sort has to make $O(n)$ comparisons to fill the n slots in the final array.

- The merging portion of the merge sort algorithm is performed on two subarrays, each of approximately size $n/2$. Creating each of these subarrays requires $n/2 - 1$ comparisons for each subarray, or $O(n)$ comparisons total. This pattern continues as each level works on twice as many arrays, but each is half the size of the previous array.

- Similar to binary search, this halving results in $\log n$ levels for a total efficiency of $O(n \log n)$.

Section 16.4 Invariants
- An invariant is an assertion that is true before and after the execution of a portion of your code.
- A loop invariant is an assertion that is true before you begin executing the loop, during each iteration of the loop and after the loop terminates.

Terminology

Big O notation	$O(1)$
binary search	$O(\log n)$
constant run time	$O(n \log n)$
insertion sort	$O(n)$
invariant	$O(n^2)$
linear run time	search key
linear search	quadratic run time
logarithmic run time	searching
loop invariant	selection sort
merge sort	sorting

Self-Review Exercises

16.1   Fill in the blanks in each of the following statements:
a) A selection sort application would take approximately _____ times as long to run on a 128-element array as on a 32-element array.
b) The efficiency of merge sort is _____.

16.2   What key aspect of both the binary search and the merge sort accounts for the logarithmic portion of their respective Big Os?

16.3   In what sense is the insertion sort superior to the merge sort? In what sense is the merge sort superior to the insertion sort?

16.4   In the text, we say that after the merge sort splits the array into two subarrays, it then sorts these two subarrays and merges them. Why might someone be puzzled by our statement that "it then sorts these two subarrays"?

Answers to Self-Review Exercises

16.1   a) 16, because an $O(n^2)$ algorithm takes 16 times as long to sort four times as much information. b) $O(n \log n)$.

16.2   Both of these algorithms incorporate "halving"—somehow reducing something by half. The binary search eliminates from consideration one half of the array after each comparison. The merge sort splits the array in half each time it is called.

16.3   The insertion sort is easier to understand and to program than the merge sort. The merge sort is far more efficient [$O(n \log n)$] than the insertion sort [$O(n^2)$].

16.4   In a sense, it does not really sort these two subarrays. It simply keeps splitting the original array in half until it provides a one-element subarray, which is, of course, sorted. It then builds up the original two subarrays by merging these one-element arrays to form larger subarrays, which are then merged, and so on.

Exercises

16.5   *(Bubble Sort)* Implement bubble sort—another simple yet inefficient sorting technique. It is called bubble sort or sinking sort because smaller values gradually "bubble" their way to the top of the array (i.e., toward the first element) like air bubbles rising in water, while the larger values sink to the bottom (end) of the array. The technique uses nested loops to make several passes through the array. Each pass compares successive pairs of elements. If a pair is in increasing order (or the values are equal), the bubble sort leaves the values as they are. If a pair is in decreasing order, the bubble sort swaps their values in the array.

The first pass compares the first two elements of the array and swaps their values if necessary. It then compares the second and third elements in the array. The end of this pass compares the last two elements in the array and swaps them if necessary. After one pass, the largest element will be in the last index. After two passes, the largest two elements will be in the last two indices. Explain why bubble sort is an $O(n^2)$ algorithm.

16.6   *(Enhanced Bubble Sort)* Make the following simple modifications to improve the performance of the bubble sort you developed in Exercise 16.5:
a) After the first pass, the largest number is guaranteed to be in the highest-numbered element of the array; after the second pass, the two highest numbers are "in place"; and so on. Instead of making nine comparisons on every pass, modify the bubble sort to make eight comparisons on the second pass, seven on the third pass, and so on.

b) The data in the array may already be in proper or near-proper order, so why make nine passes if fewer will suffice? Modify the sort to check at the end of each pass whether any swaps have been made. If none have been made, the data must already be in the proper order, so the program should terminate. If swaps have been made, at least one more pass is needed.

16.7 (*Bucket Sort*) A bucket sort begins with a one-dimensional array of positive integers to be sorted and a two-dimensional array of integers with rows indexed from 0 to 9 and columns indexed from 0 to $n-1$, where n is the number of values to be sorted. Each row of the two-dimensional array is referred to as a *bucket*. Write a class named `BucketSort` containing a method called `sort` that operates as follows:

a) Place each value of the one-dimensional array into a row of the bucket array, based on the value's "ones" (rightmost) digit. For example, 97 is placed in row 7, 3 is placed in row 3 and 100 is placed in row 0. This procedure is called a *distribution pass*.

b) Loop through the bucket array row by row, and copy the values back to the original array. This procedure is called a *gathering pass*. The new order of the preceding values in the one-dimensional array is 100, 3 and 97.

c) Repeat this process for each subsequent digit position (tens, hundreds, thousands, etc.). On the second (tens digit) pass, 100 is placed in row 0, 3 is placed in row 0 (because 3 has no tens digit) and 97 is placed in row 9. After the gathering pass, the order of the values in the one-dimensional array is 100, 3 and 97. On the third (hundreds digit) pass, 100 is placed in row 1, 3 is placed in row 0 and 97 is placed in row 0 (after the 3). After this last gathering pass, the original array is in sorted order.

   Note that the two-dimensional array of buckets is 10 times the length of the integer array being sorted. This sorting technique provides better performance than a bubble sort, but requires much more memory—the bubble sort requires space for only one additional element of data. This comparison is an example of the space–time trade-off: The bucket sort uses more memory than the bubble sort, but performs better. This version of the bucket sort requires copying all the data back to the original array on each pass. Another possibility is to create a second two-dimensional bucket array and repeatedly swap the data between the two bucket arrays.

16.8 (*Recursive Linear Search*) Modify Fig. 16.2 to use recursive method `recursiveLinearSearch` to perform a linear search of the array. The method should receive the search key and starting index as arguments. If the search key is found, return its index in the array; otherwise, return –1. Each call to the recursive method should check one index in the array.

16.9 (*Recursive Binary Search*) Modify Fig. 16.4 to use recursive method `recursiveBinarySearch` to perform a binary search of the array. The method should receive the search key, starting index and ending index as arguments. If the search key is found, return its index in the array. If the search key is not found, return –1.

16.10 (*Quicksort*) The recursive sorting technique called quicksort uses the following basic algorithm for a one-dimensional array of values:

a) *Partitioning Step*: Take the first element of the unsorted array and determine its final location in the sorted array (i.e., all values to the left of the element in the array are less than the element, and all values to the right of the element in the array are greater than the element—we show how to do this below). We now have one element in its proper location and two unsorted subarrays.

b) *Recursive Step*: Perform *Step 1* on each unsorted subarray. Each time *Step 1* is performed on a subarray, another element is placed in its final location of the sorted array, and two unsorted subarrays are created. When a subarray consists of one element, that element is in its final location (because a one-element array is already sorted).

The basic algorithm seems simple enough, but how do we determine the final position of the first element of each subarray? As an example, consider the following set of values (the element in bold is the partitioning element—it will be placed in its final location in the sorted array):

37 2 6 4 89 8 10 12 68 45

Starting from the rightmost element of the array, compare each element with 37 until an element less than 37 is found; then swap 37 and that element. The first element less than 37 is 12, so 37 and 12 are swapped. The new array is

12 2 6 4 89 8 10 37 68 45

Element 12 is in italics to indicate that it was just swapped with 37.

Starting from the left of the array, but beginning with the element after 12, compare each element with 37 until an element greater than 37 is found—then swap 37 and that element. The first element greater than 37 is 89, so 37 and 89 are swapped. The new array is

12 2 6 4 37 8 10 *89* 68 45

Starting from the right, but beginning with the element before 89, compare each element with 37 until an element less than 37 is found—then swap 37 and that element. The first element less than 37 is 10, so 37 and 10 are swapped. The new array is

12 2 6 4 *10* 8 37 89 68 45

Starting from the left, but beginning with the element after 10, compare each element with 37 until an element greater than 37 is found—then swap 37 and that element. There are no more elements greater than 37, so when we compare 37 with itself, we know that 37 has been placed in its final location in the sorted array. Every value to the left of 37 is smaller than it, and every value to the right of 37 is larger than it.

Once the partition has been applied on the previous array, there are two unsorted subarrays. The subarray with values less than 37 contains 12, 2, 6, 4, 10 and 8. The subarray with values greater than 37 contains 89, 68 and 45. The sort continues recursively with both subarrays being partitioned in the same manner as the original array.

Based on the preceding discussion, write recursive method `quickSortHelper` to sort a one-dimensional integer array. The method should receive as arguments a starting index and an ending index on the original array being sorted.

Data Structures

Much that I bound, I could not free;
Much that I freed returned to me.
—Lee Wilson Dodd

'Will you walk a little faster?' said a whiting to a snail,
'There's a porpoise close behind us, and he's treading on my tail.'
—Lewis Carroll

There is always room at the top.
—Daniel Webster

Push on—keep moving.
—Thomas Morton

I'll turn over a new leaf.
—Miguel de Cervantes

OBJECTIVES

In this chapter you will learn:

- To form linked data structures using references, self-referential classes and recursion.

- The type-wrapper classes that enable programs to process primitive data values as objects.

- To use autoboxing to convert a primitive value to an object of the corresponding type-wrapper class.

- To use auto-unboxing to convert an object of a type-wrapper class to a primitive value.

- To create and manipulate dynamic data structures, such as linked lists, queues, stacks and binary trees.

- Various important applications of linked data structures.

- How to create reusable data structures with classes, inheritance and composition.

17.1 Introduction

In previous chapters, we studied fixed-size **data structures** such as one-dimensional and multidimensional arrays. This chapter introduces **dynamic data structures** that grow and shrink at execution time. **Linked lists** are collections of data items "linked up in a chain"—insertions and deletions can be made anywhere in a linked list. **Stacks** are important in compilers and operating systems; insertions and deletions are made only at one end of a stack—its **top**. **Queues** represent waiting lines; insertions are made at the back (also referred to as the **tail**) of a queue and deletions are made from the front (also referred to as the **head**). **Binary trees** facilitate high-speed searching and sorting of data, eliminating duplicate data items efficiently, representing file-system directories, compiling expressions into machine language and many other interesting applications.

We discuss each of these major data structure types and implement programs that create and manipulate them. We use classes, inheritance and composition to create and package these data structures for reusability and maintainability. In Chapter 19, Collections, we discuss Java's predefined classes that implement the data structures discussed in this chapter.

The examples presented here are practical programs that can be used in advanced courses and in industrial applications. The exercises include a rich collection of useful applications.

This chapter's examples manipulate primitive values for simplicity. However, most of the data-structure implementations in this chapter store only `Objects`. Java has a feature called boxing that allows primitive values to be converted to and from objects for use in cases like this. The objects that represent primitive values are instances of Java's so-called type-wrapper classes in package `java.lang`. We discuss these classes and boxing in the next two sections, so that we can use them in this chapter's examples.

We encourage you to attempt the major project described in the special section entitled Building Your Own Compiler. You have been using a Java compiler to translate your Java programs to bytecodes so that you could execute these programs on your computer. In this project, you will actually build your own compiler. It will read a file of statements written in a simple, yet powerful high-level language similar to early versions of the popular language BASIC. Your compiler will translate these statements into a file of Simpletron Machine Language (SML) instructions—SML is the language you learned in the Chapter 7 special section, Building Your Own Computer. Your Simpletron Simulator program will then execute the SML program produced by your compiler! Implementing this project by using an object-oriented approach will give you a wonderful opportunity to exercise most of what you have learned in this book. The special section carefully walks you through the specifications of the high-level language and describes the algorithms you will need to convert each high-level language statement into machine-language instructions. If you enjoy being challenged, you might attempt the many enhancements to both the compiler and the Simpletron Simulator suggested in the exercises.

17.2 Type-Wrapper Classes for Primitive Types

Each primitive type (listed in Appendix D, Primitive Types) has a corresponding type-wrapper class (in package `java.lang`). These classes are called `Boolean`, `Byte`, `Character`, `Double`, `Float`, `Integer`, `Long` and `Short`. Each type-wrapper class enables you to manipulate primitive-type values as objects. Many of the data structures that we develop or reuse in Chapters 17–19 manipulate and share `Object`s. These classes cannot manipulate variables of primitive types, but they can manipulate objects of the type-wrapper classes, because every class ultimately derives from `Object`.

Each of the numeric type-wrapper classes—`Byte`, `Short`, `Integer`, `Long`, `Float` and `Double`—extends class `Number`. Also, the type-wrapper classes are `final` classes, so you cannot extend them.

Primitive types do not have methods, so the methods related to a primitive type are located in the corresponding type-wrapper class (e.g., method `parseInt`, which converts a `String` to an `int` value, is located in class `Integer`). If you need to manipulate a primitive value in your program, first refer to the documentation for the type-wrapper classes—the method you need might already be declared.

17.3 Autoboxing and Auto-Unboxing

Prior to Java SE 5, if you wanted to insert a primitive value into a data structure that could store only `Object`s, you had to create a new object of the corresponding type-wrapper class, then insert this object in the collection. Similarly, if you wanted to retrieve an object of a type-wrapper class from a collection and manipulate its primitive value, you had to invoke a method on the object to obtain its corresponding primitive-type value. For example, suppose you want to add an `int` to an array that stores only references to `Integer` objects. Prior to Java SE 5, you would be required to "wrap" an `int` value in an `Integer` object before adding the integer to the array and to "unwrap" the `int` value from the `Integer` object to retrieve the value from the array, as in

```
Integer[] integerArray = new Integer[ 5 ]; // create integerArray

// assign Integer 10 to integerArray[ 0 ]
integerArray[ 0 ] = new Integer( 10 );

// get int value of Integer
int value = integerArray[ 0 ].intValue();
```

Notice that the int primitive value 10 is used to initialize an Integer object. This achieves the desired result but requires extra code and is cumbersome. We then need to invoke method intValue of class Integer to obtain the int value in the Integer object.

Java SE 5 simplified converting between primitive-type values and type-wrapper objects, requiring no additional code on the part of the programmer. Java SE 5 introduced two new conversions—the boxing conversion and the unboxing conversion. A boxing conversion converts a value of a primitive type to an object of the corresponding type-wrapper class. An unboxing conversion converts an object of a type-wrapper class to a value of the corresponding primitive type. These conversions can be performed automatically (called autoboxing and auto-unboxing). For example, the previous statements can be rewritten as

```
Integer[] integerArray = new Integer[ 5 ]; // create integerArray
integerArray[ 0 ] = 10; // assign Integer 10 to integerArray[ 0 ]
int value = integerArray[ 0 ]; // get int value of Integer
```

In this case, autoboxing occurs when assigning an int value (10) to integerArray[0], because integerArray stores references to Integer objects, not int primitive values. Auto-unboxing occurs when assigning integerArray[0] to int variable value, because variable value stores an int value, not a reference to an Integer object. Autoboxing and auto-unboxing also occur in control statements—the condition of a control statement can evaluate to a primitive boolean type or a Boolean reference type. Many of this chapter's examples use these conversions to store primitive values in and to retrieve them from data structures that store only references to Objects.

17.4 Self-Referential Classes

A self-referential class contains an instance variable that refers to another object of the same class type. For example, the declaration

```
class Node
{
    private int data;
    private Node nextNode; // reference to next linked node

    public Node( int data ) { /* constructor body */ }
    public void setData( int data ) { /* method body */ }
    public int getData() { /* method body */ }
    public void setNext( Node next ) { /* method body */ }
    public Node getNext() { /* method body */ }
} // end class Node
```

declares class Node, which has two private instance variables—integer data and Node reference nextNode. Field nextNode references a Node object, an object of the same class being declared here—hence, the term "self-referential class." Field nextNode is a link—it "links" an object of type Node to another object of the same type. Type Node also has five methods: a constructor that receives an integer to initialize data, a setData method to set the value of data, a getData method to return the value of data, a setNext method to set the value of nextNode and a getNext method to return a reference to the next node.

Programs can link self-referential objects together to form such useful data structures as lists, queues, stacks and trees. Figure 17.1 illustrates two self-referential objects linked together to form a list. A backslash—representing a null reference—is placed in the link

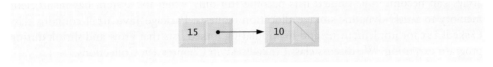

Fig. 17.1 | Self-referential-class objects linked together.

member of the second self-referential object to indicate that the link does not refer to another object. Note that the backslash is illustrative; it does not correspond to the backslash character in Java. We use the null to reference indicate the end of a data structure.

17.5 Dynamic Memory Allocation

Creating and maintaining dynamic data structures requires dynamic memory allocation—the ability for a program to obtain more memory space at execution time to hold new nodes and to release space no longer needed. Remember that Java programs do not explicitly release dynamically allocated memory. Rather, Java performs automatic garbage collection of objects that are no longer referenced in a program.

The limit for dynamic memory allocation can be as large as the amount of available physical memory in the computer or the amount of available disk space in a virtual-memory system. Often, the limits are much smaller, because the computer's available memory must be shared among many applications.

The declaration and class-instance creation expression

```
Node nodeToAdd = new Node( 10 ); // 10 is nodeToAdd's data
```

allocates the memory to store a Node object and returns a reference to the object, which is assigned to nodeToAdd. If insufficient memory is available, the expression throws an Out-OfMemoryError.

The following sections discuss lists, stacks, queues and trees that all use dynamic memory allocation and self-referential classes to create dynamic data structures.

17.6 Linked Lists

A linked list is a linear collection (i.e., a sequence) of self-referential-class objects, called nodes, connected by reference links—hence, the term "linked" list. Typically, a program accesses a linked list via a reference to the first node in the list. The program accesses each subsequent node via the link reference stored in the previous node. By convention, the link reference in the last node of the list is set to null. Data is stored in a linked list dynamically—the program creates each node as necessary. A node can contain data of any type, including references to objects of other classes. Stacks and queues are also linear data structures and, as we will see, are constrained versions of linked lists. Trees are nonlinear data structures.

Lists of data can be stored in arrays, but linked lists provide several advantages. A linked list is appropriate when the number of data elements to be represented in the data structure is unpredictable. Linked lists are dynamic, so the length of a list can increase or decrease as necessary. The size of a "conventional" Java array, however, cannot be altered—the array size is fixed at the time the program creates the array. "Conventional" arrays can become full. Linked lists become full only when the system has insufficient memory to satisfy dynamic storage allocation requests. Package java.util contains class LinkedList for implementing and manipulating linked lists that grow and shrink during program execution. We discuss class LinkedList in Chapter 19, Collections.

Performance Tip 17.1

An array can be declared to contain more elements than the number of items expected, but this wastes memory. Linked lists provide better memory utilization in these situations. Linked lists allow the program to adapt to storage needs at runtime.

Performance Tip 17.2

Insertion into a linked list is fast—only two references have to be modified (after locating the insertion point). All existing node objects remain at their current locations in memory.

Linked lists can be maintained in sorted order simply by inserting each new element at the proper point in the list. (It does, of course, take time to locate the proper insertion point.) Existing list elements do not need to be moved.

Performance Tip 17.3

Insertion and deletion in a sorted array can be time consuming—all the elements following the inserted or deleted element must be shifted appropriately.

Linked list nodes normally are not stored contiguously in memory. Rather, they are logically contiguous. Figure 17.2 illustrates a linked list with several nodes. This diagram presents a singly linked list—each node contains one reference to the next node in the list. Often, linked lists are implemented as doubly linked lists—each node contains a reference to the next node in the list and a reference to the previous node in the list. Java's LinkedList class is a doubly linked list implementation.

Performance Tip 17.4

Normally, the elements of an array are contiguous in memory. This allows immediate access to any array element, because its address can be calculated directly as its offset from the beginning of the array. Linked lists do not afford such immediate access to their elements—an element can be accessed only by traversing the list from the front (or from the back in a doubly linked list).

The program of Figs. 17.3–17.5 uses an object of our List class to manipulate a list of miscellaneous objects. The program consists of four classes—ListNode (Fig. 17.3, lines

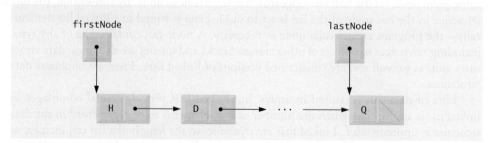

Fig. 17.2 | Linked list graphical representation.

6–37), List (Fig. 17.3, lines 40–147), EmptyListException (Fig. 17.4) and ListTest (Fig. 17.5). The List, ListNode and EmptyListException classes are placed in package com.deitel.jhtp7.ch17, so they can be reused throughout this chapter. Encapsulated in each List object is a linked list of ListNode objects. [*Note:* Many of the classes in this chapter are declared in the package com.deitel.jhtp7.ch17. Each such class should be compiled with the -d command-line option to javac. When compiling the classes that are not in this package and when running the programs, be sure to use the option -classpath to javac and java, respectively.]

Class ListNode (Fig. 17.3, lines 6–37) declares package-access fields data and next-Node. The data field is an Object reference, so it can refer to any object. ListNode member nextNode stores a reference to the next ListNode object in the linked list (or null if the node is the last one in the list).

```
1   // Fig. 17.3: List.java
2   // ListNode and List class definitions.
3   package com.deitel.jhtp7.ch17;
4
5   // class to represent one node in a list
6   class ListNode
7   {
8      // package access members; List can access these directly
9      Object data; // data for this node
10     ListNode nextNode; // reference to the next node in the list
11
12     // constructor creates a ListNode that refers to object
13     ListNode( Object object )
14     {
15        this( object, null );
16     } // end ListNode one-argument constructor
17
18     // constructor creates ListNode that refers to
19     // Object and to next ListNode
20     ListNode( Object object, ListNode node )
21     {
22        data = object;
23        nextNode = node;
24     } // end ListNode two-argument constructor
25
26     // return reference to data in node
27     Object getObject()
28     {
29        return data; // return Object in this node
30     } // end method getObject
31
32     // return reference to next node in list
33     ListNode getNext()
34     {
35        return nextNode; // get next node
36     } // end method getNext
37  } // end class ListNode
```

Fig. 17.3 | ListNode and List class declarations. (Part 1 of 4.)

```
38
39   // class List definition
40   public class List
41   {
42       private ListNode firstNode;
43       private ListNode lastNode;
44       private String name; // string like "list" used in printing
45
46       // constructor creates empty List with "list" as the name
47       public List()
48       {
49           this( "list" );
50       } // end List no-argument constructor
51
52       // constructor creates an empty List with a name
53       public List( String listName )
54       {
55           name = listName;
56           firstNode = lastNode = null;
57       } // end List one-argument constructor
58
59       // insert Object at front of List
60       public void insertAtFront( Object insertItem )
61       {
62           if ( isEmpty() ) // firstNode and lastNode refer to same object
63               firstNode = lastNode = new ListNode( insertItem );
64           else // firstNode refers to new node
65               firstNode = new ListNode( insertItem, firstNode );
66       } // end method insertAtFront
67
68       // insert Object at end of List
69       public void insertAtBack( Object insertItem )
70       {
71           if ( isEmpty() ) // firstNode and lastNode refer to same Object
72               firstNode = lastNode = new ListNode( insertItem );
73           else // lastNode's nextNode refers to new node
74               lastNode = lastNode.nextNode = new ListNode( insertItem );
75       } // end method insertAtBack
76
77       // remove first node from List
78       public Object removeFromFront() throws EmptyListException
79       {
80           if ( isEmpty() ) // throw exception if List is empty
81               throw new EmptyListException( name );
82
83           Object removedItem = firstNode.data; // retrieve data being removed
84
85           // update references firstNode and lastNode
86           if ( firstNode == lastNode )
87               firstNode = lastNode = null;
88           else
89               firstNode = firstNode.nextNode;
90
```

Fig. 17.3 | ListNode and List class declarations. (Part 2 of 4.)

```
91              return removedItem; // return removed node data
92         } // end method removeFromFront
93
94         // remove last node from List
95         public Object removeFromBack() throws EmptyListException
96         {
97              if ( isEmpty() ) // throw exception if List is empty
98                  throw new EmptyListException( name );
99
100             Object removedItem = lastNode.data; // retrieve data being removed
101
102             // update references firstNode and lastNode
103             if ( firstNode == lastNode )
104                 firstNode = lastNode = null;
105             else // locate new last node
106             {
107                 ListNode current = firstNode;
108
109                 // loop while current node does not refer to lastNode
110                 while ( current.nextNode != lastNode )
111                     current = current.nextNode;
112
113                 lastNode = current; // current is new lastNode
114                 current.nextNode = null;
115             } // end else
116
117             return removedItem; // return removed node data
118        } // end method removeFromBack
119
120        // determine whether list is empty
121        public boolean isEmpty()
122        {
123             return firstNode == null; // return true if list is empty
124        } // end method isEmpty
125
126        // output list contents
127        public void print()
128        {
129             if ( isEmpty() )
130             {
131                 System.out.printf( "Empty %s\n", name );
132                 return;
133             } // end if
134
135             System.out.printf( "The %s is: ", name );
136             ListNode current = firstNode;
137
138             // while not at end of list, output current node's data
139             while ( current != null )
140             {
141                 System.out.printf( "%s ", current.data );
142                 current = current.nextNode;
143             } // end while
```

Fig. 17.3 | ListNode and List class declarations. (Part 3 of 4.)

```
144
145          System.out.println( "\n" );
146       } // end method print
147  } // end class List
```

Fig. 17.3 | ListNode and List class declarations. (Part 4 of 4.)

Lines 42–43 of class List (Fig. 17.3, lines 40–147) declare references to the first and last ListNodes in a List (firstNode and lastNode, respectively). The constructors (lines 47–50 and 53–57) initialize both references to null. The most important methods of class List are insertAtFront (lines 60–66), insertAtBack (lines 69–75), removeFromFront (lines 78–92) and removeFromBack (lines 95–118). Method isEmpty (lines 121–124) is a *predicate method* that determines whether the list is empty (i.e., the reference to the first node of the list is null). Predicate methods typically test a condition and do not modify the object on which they are called. If the list is empty, method isEmpty returns true; otherwise, it returns false. Method print (lines 127–146) displays the list's contents. A detailed discussion of List's methods follows Fig. 17.5.

Method main of class ListTest (Fig. 17.5) inserts objects at the beginning of the list using method insertAtFront, inserts objects at the end of the list using method insertAtBack, deletes objects from the front of the list using method removeFromFront and deletes objects from the end of the list using method removeFromBack. After each insert and remove operation, ListTest calls List method print to display the current list contents. If an attempt is made to remove an item from an empty list, an EmptyListException (Fig. 17.4) is thrown, so the method calls to removeFromFront and removeFromBack are placed in a try block that is followed by an appropriate exception handler. Notice in lines 13, 15, 17 and 19 that the application passes literal primitive int

```
1   // Fig. 17.4: EmptyListException.java
2   // Class EmptyListException definition.
3   package com.deitel.jhtp7.ch17;
4
5   public class EmptyListException extends RuntimeException
6   {
7      // no-argument constructor
8      public EmptyListException()
9      {
10        this( "List" ); // call other EmptyListException constructor
11     } // end EmptyListException no-argument constructor
12
13     // one-argument constructor
14     public EmptyListException( String name )
15     {
16        super( name + " is empty" ); // call superclass constructor
17     } // end EmptyListException one-argument constructor
18  } // end class EmptyListException
```

Fig. 17.4 | EmptyListException class declaration.

values to methods insertAtFront and insertAtBack, even though each of these methods was declared with a parameter of type Object (Fig. 17.3, lines 60 and 69). In this case, the JVM autoboxes each literal value in an Integer object, and that object is actually inserted into the list. This, of course, is allowed because Object is an indirect superclass of Integer.

```java
1   // Fig. 17.5: ListTest.java
2   // ListTest class to demonstrate List capabilities.
3   import com.deitel.jhtp7.ch17.List;
4   import com.deitel.jhtp7.ch17.EmptyListException;
5
6   public class ListTest
7   {
8      public static void main( String args[] )
9      {
10        List list = new List(); // create the List container
11
12        // insert integers in list
13        list.insertAtFront( -1 );
14        list.print();
15        list.insertAtFront( 0 );
16        list.print();
17        list.insertAtBack( 1 );
18        list.print();
19        list.insertAtBack( 5 );
20        list.print();
21
22        // remove objects from list; print after each removal
23        try
24        {
25           Object removedObject = list.removeFromFront();
26           System.out.printf( "%s removed\n", removedObject );
27           list.print();
28
29           removedObject = list.removeFromFront();
30           System.out.printf( "%s removed\n", removedObject );
31           list.print();
32
33           removedObject = list.removeFromBack();
34           System.out.printf( "%s removed\n", removedObject );
35           list.print();
36
37           removedObject = list.removeFromBack();
38           System.out.printf( "%s removed\n", removedObject );
39           list.print();
40        } // end try
41        catch ( EmptyListException emptyListException )
42        {
43           emptyListException.printStackTrace();
44        } // end catch
45     } // end main
46  } // end class ListTest
```

Fig. 17.5 | Linked list manipulations. (Part 1 of 2.)

```
The list is: -1

The list is: 0 -1

The list is: 0 -1 1

The list is: 0 -1 1 5

0 removed
The list is: -1 1 5

-1 removed
The list is: 1 5

5 removed
The list is: 1

1 removed
Empty list
```

Fig. 17.5 | Linked list manipulations. (Part 2 of 2.)

Now we discuss each method of class List (Fig. 17.3) in detail and provide diagrams showing the reference manipulations performed by methods insertAtFront, insertAt-Back, removeFromFront and removeFromBack. Method insertAtFront (lines 60–66 of Fig. 17.3) places a new node at the front of the list. The steps are:

1. Call isEmpty to determine whether the list is empty (line 62).

2. If the list is empty, assign firstNode and lastNode to the new ListNode that was initialized with insertItem (line 63). The ListNode constructor at lines 13–16 calls the ListNode constructor at lines 20–24 to set instance variable data to refer to the insertItem passed as an argument and to set reference nextNode to null, because this is the first and last node in the list.

3. If the list is not empty, the new node is "linked" into the list by setting firstNode to a new ListNode object and initializing that object with insertItem and firstNode (line 65). When the ListNode constructor (lines 20–24) executes, it sets instance variable data to refer to the insertItem passed as an argument and performs the insertion by setting the nextNode reference of the new node to the ListNode passed as an argument, which previously was the first node.

In Fig. 17.6, part (a) shows a list and a new node during the insertAtFront operation and before the program links the new node into the list. The dotted arrows in part (b) illustrate *Step 3* of the insertAtFront operation that enables the node containing 12 to become the new first node in the list.

Method insertAtBack (lines 69–75 of Fig. 17.3) places a new node at the back of the list. The steps are:

1. Call isEmpty to determine whether the list is empty (line 71).

2. If the list is empty, assign firstNode and lastNode to the new ListNode that was initialized with insertItem (line 72). The ListNode constructor at lines 13–16 calls the constructor at lines 20–24 to set instance variable data to refer to the insertItem passed as an argument and to set reference nextNode to null.

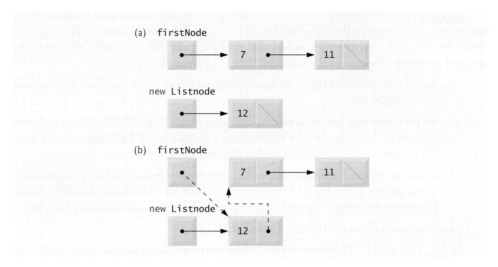

Fig. 17.6 | Graphical representation of operation `insertAtFront`.

3. If the list is not empty, line 74 links the new node into the list by assigning to `lastNode` and `lastNode.nextNode` the reference to the new `ListNode` that was initialized with `insertItem`. `ListNode`'s constructor (lines 13–16), sets instance variable `data` to refer to the `insertItem` passed as an argument and sets reference `nextNode` to `null`, because this is the last node in the list.

In Fig. 17.7, part (a) shows a list and a new node during the `insertAtBack` operation and before the program links the new node into the list. The dotted arrows in part (b) illustrate *Step 3* of method `insertAtBack`, which adds the new node to the end of a list that is not empty.

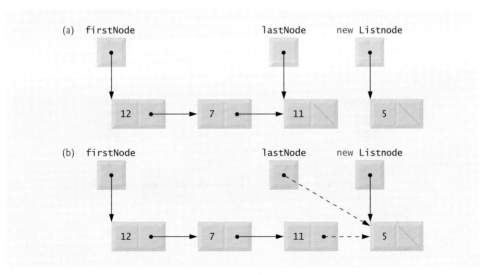

Fig. 17.7 | Graphical representation of operation `insertAtBack`.

Method removeFromFront (lines 78–92 of Fig. 17.3) removes the first node of the list and returns a reference to the removed data. The method throws an EmptyListException (lines 80–81) if the list is empty when the program calls this method. Otherwise, the method returns a reference to the removed data. The steps are:

1. Assign firstNode.data (the data being removed from the list) to reference removedItem (line 83).

2. If firstNode and lastNode refer to the same object (line 86), the list has only one element at this time. So, the method sets firstNode and lastNode to null (line 87) to remove the node from the list (leaving the list empty).

3. If the list has more than one node, then the method leaves reference lastNode as is and assigns the value of firstNode.nextNode to firstNode (line 89). Thus, firstNode references the node that was previously the second node in the list.

4. Return the removedItem reference (line 91).

In Fig. 17.8, part (a) illustrates the list before the removal operation. The dashed lines and arrows in part (b) show the reference manipulations.

Method removeFromBack (lines 95–118 of Fig. 17.3) removes the last node of a list and returns a reference to the removed data. The method throws an EmptyListException (lines 97–98) if the list is empty when the program calls this method. The steps are:

1. Assign lastNode.data (the data being removed from the list) to removedItem (line 100).

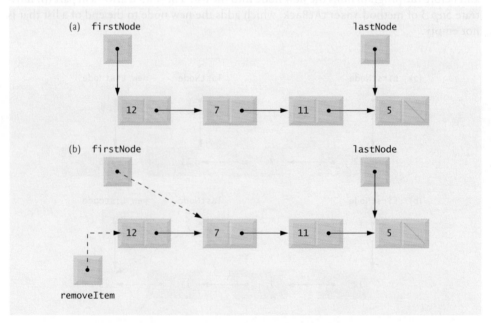

Fig. 17.8 | Graphical representation of operation removeFromFront.

2. If the `firstNode` and `lastNode` refer to the same object (line 103), the list has only one element at this time. So, line 104 sets `firstNode` and `lastNode` to `null` to remove that node from the list (leaving the list empty).

3. If the list has more than one node, create the `ListNode` reference current and assign it `firstNode` (line 107).

4. Now "walk the list" with current until it references the node before the last node. The `while` loop (lines 110–111) assigns `current.nextNode` to current as long as `current.nextNode` (the next node in the list) is not `lastNode`.

5. After locating the second-to-last node, assign current to `lastNode` (line 113) to update which node is last in the list.

6. Set the `current.nextNode` to `null` (line 114) to remove the last node from the list and terminate the list at the current node.

7. Return the `removedItem` reference (line 117).

In Fig. 17.9, part (a) illustrates the list before the removal operation. The dashed lines and arrows in part (b) show the reference manipulations.

Method `print` (lines 127–146) first determines whether the list is empty (lines 129–133). If so, `print` displays a message indicating that the list is empty and returns control to the calling method. Otherwise, `print` outputs the list's data. Line 136 creates `ListNode` current and initializes it with `firstNode`. While current is not `null`, there are more items in the list. Therefore, line 141 outputs a string representation of `current.data`. Line 142 moves to the next node in the list by assigning the value of reference `current.next-Node` to current. This printing algorithm is identical for linked lists, stacks and queues.

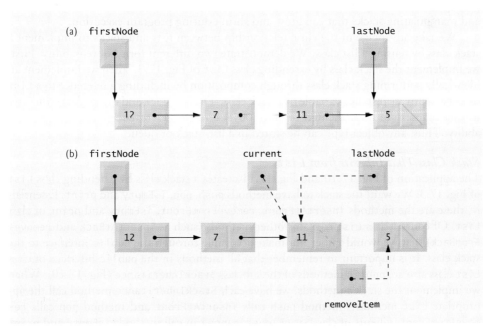

Fig. 17.9 | Graphical representation of operation `removeFromBack`.

17.7 Stacks

A stack is a constrained version of a linked list—new nodes can be added to and removed from a stack only at the top. [*Note:* A stack does not have to be implemented using a linked list.] For this reason, a stack is referred to as a last-in, first-out (LIFO) data structure. The link member in the bottom (i.e., last) node of the stack is set to null to indicate the bottom of the stack.

The primary methods for manipulating a stack are **push** and **pop**. Method push adds a new node to the top of the stack. Method pop removes a node from the top of the stack and returns the data from the popped node.

Stacks have many interesting applications. For example, when a program calls a method, the called method must know how to return to its caller, so the return address of the calling method is pushed onto the program execution stack. If a series of method calls occurs, the successive return addresses are pushed onto the stack in last-in, first-out order so that each method can return to its caller. Stacks support recursive method calls in the same manner as they do conventional nonrecursive method calls.

The program execution stack also contains the memory for local variables on each invocation of a method during a program's execution. When the method returns to its caller, the memory for that method's local variables is popped off the stack, and those variables are no longer known to the program. If the local variable is a reference, the reference count for the object to which it referred is decremented by 1. If the reference count becomes zero, the object can be garbage collected.

Compilers use stacks to evaluate arithmetic expressions and generate machine-language code to process the expressions. The exercises in this chapter explore several applications of stacks, including using them to develop a complete working compiler. Also, package java.util contains class Stack (see Chapter 19, Collections) for implementing and manipulating stacks that can grow and shrink during program execution.

We take advantage of the close relationship between lists and stacks to implement a stack class by reusing a list class. We demonstrate two different forms of reusability. First, we implement the stack class by extending class List of Fig. 17.3. Then we implement an identically performing stack class through composition by including a reference to a List object as a private instance variable of a stack class. The list, stack and queue data structures in this chapter are implemented to store Object references to encourage further reusability. Thus, any object type can be stored in a list, stack or queue.

Stack Class That Inherits from List

The application of Fig. 17.10 and Fig. 17.11 creates a stack class by extending class List of Fig. 17.3. We want the stack to have methods push, pop, isEmpty and print. Essentially, these are the methods insertAtFront, removeFromFront, isEmpty and print of class List. Of course, class List contains other methods (such as insertAtBack and remove-FromBack) that we would rather not make accessible through the public interface to the stack class. It is important to remember that all methods in the public interface of class List class also are public methods of the subclass StackInheritance (Fig. 17.10). When we implement the stack's methods, we have each StackInheritance method call the appropriate List method—method push calls insertAtFront and method pop calls removeFromFront. Clients of class StackInheritance can call methods isEmpty and print because they are inherited from List. Class StackInheritance is declared as part of pack-

```
 1   // Fig. 17.10: StackInheritance.java
 2   // Derived from class List.
 3   package com.deitel.jhtp7.ch17;
 4
 5   public class StackInheritance extends List
 6   {
 7      // no-argument constructor
 8      public StackInheritance()
 9      {
10         super( "stack" );
11      } // end StackInheritance no-argument constructor
12
13      // add object to stack
14      public void push( Object object )
15      {
16         insertAtFront( object );
17      } // end method push
18
19      // remove object from stack
20      public Object pop() throws EmptyListException
21      {
22         return removeFromFront();
23      } // end method pop
24   } // end class StackInheritance
```

Fig. 17.10 | StackInheritance extends class List.

age com.deitel.jhtp7.ch17 for reuse purposes. Note that StackInheritance does not import List, because both classes are in the same package.

Class StackInheritanceTest's method main (Fig. 17.11) creates an object of class StackInheritance called stack (line 10). The program pushes integers onto the stack (lines 13, 15, 17 and 19). Once again, note that autoboxing is used here to insert Integer objects into the data structure. Lines 27–32 pop the objects from the stack in an infinite while loop. If method pop is invoked on an empty stack, the method throws an Empty-ListException. In this case, the program displays the exception's stack trace, which shows the methods on the program execution stack at the time the exception occurred. Note that the program uses method print (inherited from List) to output the contents of the stack.

```
 1   // Fig. 17.11: StackInheritanceTest.java
 2   // Class StackInheritanceTest.
 3   import com.deitel.jhtp7.ch17.StackInheritance;
 4   import com.deitel.jhtp7.ch17.EmptyListException;
 5
 6   public class StackInheritanceTest
 7   {
 8      public static void main( String args[] )
 9      {
10         StackInheritance stack = new StackInheritance();
11
```

Fig. 17.11 | Stack manipulation program. (Part 1 of 2.)

```
12        // use push method
13        stack.push( -1 );
14        stack.print();
15        stack.push( 0 );
16        stack.print();
17        stack.push( 1 );
18        stack.print();
19        stack.push( 5 );
20        stack.print();
21
22        // remove items from stack
23        try
24        {
25           Object removedObject = null;
26
27           while ( true )
28           {
29              removedObject = stack.pop(); // use pop method
30              System.out.printf( "%s popped\n", removedObject );
31              stack.print();
32           } // end while
33        } // end try
34        catch ( EmptyListException emptyListException )
35        {
36           emptyListException.printStackTrace();
37        } // end catch
38     } // end main
39  } // end class StackInheritanceTest
```

```
The stack is: -1

The stack is: 0 -1

The stack is: 1 0 -1

The stack is: 5 1 0 -1

5 popped
The stack is: 1 0 -1

1 popped
The stack is: 0 -1

0 popped
The stack is: -1

-1 popped
Empty stack
com.deitel.jhtp7.ch17.EmptyListException: stack is empty
        at com.deitel.jhtp7.ch17.List.removeFromFront(List.java:81)
        at com.deitel.jhtp7.ch17.StackInheritance.pop(
           StackInheritance.java:22)
        at StackInheritanceTest.main(StackInheritanceTest.java:29)
```

Fig. 17.11 | Stack manipulation program. (Part 2 of 2.)

Stack Class That Contains a Reference to a List

You can also implement a class by reusing a list class through composition. Figure 17.12 uses a private List (line 7) in class StackComposition's declaration. Composition enables us to hide the List methods that should not be in our stack's public interface. We provide public interface methods that use only the required List methods. Implementing each stack method as a call to a List method is called delegation—the stack method invoked delegates the call to the appropriate List method. In particular, StackComposition delegates calls to List methods insertAtFront, removeFromFront, isEmpty and print. In this example, we do not show class StackCompositionTest, because the only difference is that we change the type of the stack from StackInheritance to StackComposition (lines 3 and 10 of Fig. 17.11). The output is identical using either version of the stack.

```java
1   // Fig. 17.12: StackComposition.java
2   // Class StackComposition definition with composed List object.
3   package com.deitel.jhtp7.ch17;
4
5   public class StackComposition
6   {
7      private List stackList;
8
9      // no-argument constructor
10     public StackComposition()
11     {
12        stackList = new List( "stack" );
13     } // end StackComposition no-argument constructor
14
15     // add object to stack
16     public void push( Object object )
17     {
18        stackList.insertAtFront( object );
19     } // end method push
20
21     // remove object from stack
22     public Object pop() throws EmptyListException
23     {
24        return stackList.removeFromFront();
25     } // end method pop
26
27     // determine if stack is empty
28     public boolean isEmpty()
29     {
30        return stackList.isEmpty();
31     } // end method isEmpty
32
33     // output stack contents
34     public void print()
35     {
36        stackList.print();
37     } // end method print
38   } // end class StackComposition
```

Fig. 17.12 | StackComposition uses a composed List object.

17.8 Queues

Another commonly used data structure is the queue. A queue is similar to a checkout line in a supermarket—the cashier services the person at the beginning of the line first. Other customers enter the line only at the end and wait for service. Queue nodes are removed only from the head (or front) of the queue and are inserted only at the tail (or end). For this reason, a queue is a **first-in, first-out (FIFO)** data structure. The insert and remove operations are known as **enqueue** and **dequeue**.

Queues have many uses in computer systems. Most computers have only a single processor, so only one application at a time can be serviced. Each application requiring processor time is placed in a queue. The application at the front of the queue is the next to receive service. Each application gradually advances to the front as the applications before it receive service.

Queues are also used to support **print spooling**. For example, a single printer might be shared by all users of a network. Many users can send print jobs to the printer, even when the printer is already busy. These print jobs are placed in a queue until the printer becomes available. A program called a **spooler** manages the queue to ensure that, as each print job completes, the next print job is sent to the printer.

Information packets also wait in queues in computer networks. Each time a packet arrives at a network node, it must be routed to the next node along the path to the packet's final destination. The routing node routes one packet at a time, so additional packets are enqueued until the router can route them.

A file server in a computer network handles file-access requests from many clients throughout the network. Servers have a limited capacity to service requests from clients. When that capacity is exceeded, client requests wait in queues.

Figure 17.13 creates a queue class that contains an object of class List (Fig. 17.3). Class Queue (Fig. 17.13) provides methods enqueue, dequeue, isEmpty and print. Class List contains other methods (e.g., insertAtFront and removeFromBack) that we would rather not make accessible through the public interface of class Queue. By using composition, these methods in the public interface of class List are not accessible to clients of class Queue. Each method of class Queue calls an appropriate List method—method enqueue calls List method insertAtBack, method dequeue calls List method removeFromFront,

```
1   // Fig. 17.13: Queue.java
2   // Class Queue.
3   package com.deitel.jhtp7.ch17;
4
5   public class Queue
6   {
7      private List queueList;
8
9      // no-argument constructor
10     public Queue()
11     {
12        queueList = new List( "queue" );
13     } // end Queue no-argument constructor
14
```

Fig. 17.13 | Queue uses class List. (Part 1 of 2.)

```
15        // add object to queue
16        public void enqueue( Object object )
17        {
18           queueList.insertAtBack( object );
19        } // end method enqueue
20
21        // remove object from queue
22        public Object dequeue() throws EmptyListException
23        {
24           return queueList.removeFromFront();
25        } // end method dequeue
26
27        // determine if queue is empty
28        public boolean isEmpty()
29        {
30           return queueList.isEmpty();
31        } // end method isEmpty
32
33        // output queue contents
34        public void print()
35        {
36           queueList.print();
37        } // end method print
38     } // end class Queue
```

Fig. 17.13 | Queue uses class List. (Part 2 of 2.)

method isEmpty calls List method isEmpty and method print calls List method print. For reuse purposes, class Queue is declared in package com.deitel.jhtp7.ch17.

Class QueueTest (Fig. 17.14) method main creates an object of class Queue called queue. Lines 13, 15, 17 and 19 enqueue four integers, taking advantage of autoboxing to insert Integer objects into the queue. Lines 27–32 use an infinite while loop to dequeue the objects in first-in, first-out order. When the queue is empty, method dequeue throws an EmptyListException, and the program displays the exception's stack trace.

```
1     // Fig. 17.14: QueueTest.java
2     // Class QueueTest.
3     import com.deitel.jhtp7.ch17.Queue;
4     import com.deitel.jhtp7.ch17.EmptyListException;
5
6     public class QueueTest
7     {
8        public static void main( String args[] )
9        {
10          Queue queue = new Queue();
11
12          // use enqueue method
13          queue.enqueue( -1 );
14          queue.print();
15          queue.enqueue( 0 );
```

Fig. 17.14 | Queue processing program. (Part 1 of 2.)

```
16          queue.print();
17          queue.enqueue( 1 );
18          queue.print();
19          queue.enqueue( 5 );
20          queue.print();
21
22          // remove objects from queue
23          try
24          {
25             Object removedObject = null;
26
27             while ( true )
28             {
29                removedObject = queue.dequeue(); // use dequeue method
30                System.out.printf( "%s dequeued\n", removedObject );
31                queue.print();
32             } // end while
33          } // end try
34          catch ( EmptyListException emptyListException )
35          {
36             emptyListException.printStackTrace();
37          } // end catch
38       } // end main
39    } // end class QueueTest
```

```
The queue is: -1

The queue is: -1 0

The queue is: -1 0 1

The queue is: -1 0 1 5

-1 dequeued
The queue is: 0 1 5

0 dequeued
The queue is: 1 5

1 dequeued
The queue is: 5

5 dequeued
Empty queue
com.deitel.jhtp7.ch17.EmptyListException: queue is empty
        at com.deitel.jhtp7.ch17.List.removeFromFront(List.java:81)
        at com.deitel.jhtp7.ch17.Queue.dequeue(Queue.java:24)
        at QueueTest.main(QueueTest.java:29)
```

Fig. 17.14 | Queue processing program. (Part 2 of 2.)

17.9 Trees

Linked lists, stacks and queues are linear data structures (i.e., sequences). A tree is a non-linear, two-dimensional data structure with special properties. Tree nodes contain two or more links. This section discusses binary trees (Fig. 17.15)—trees whose nodes each contain two links (one or both of which may be null). The root node is the first node in a tree. Each link in the root node refers to a child. The left child is the first node in the left subtree (also known as the root node of the left subtree), and the right child is the first node in the right subtree (also known as the root node of the right subtree). The children of a specific node are called siblings. A node with no children is called a leaf node. Computer scientists normally draw trees from the root node down—the opposite of the way most trees grow in nature.

In our example, we create a special binary tree called a binary search tree. A binary search tree (with no duplicate node values) has the characteristic that the values in any left subtree are less than the value in that subtree's parent node, and the values in any right subtree are greater than the value in that subtree's parent node. Figure 17.16 illustrates a binary search tree with 12 integer values. Note that the shape of the binary search tree that corresponds to a set of data can vary, depending on the order in which the values are inserted into the tree.

The application of Fig. 17.17 and Fig. 17.18 creates a binary search tree of integers and traverses it (i.e., walks through all its nodes) three ways—using recursive inorder, preorder and postorder traversals. The program generates 10 random numbers and inserts each into the tree. Class Tree is declared in package com.deitel.jhtp7.ch17 for reuse purposes.

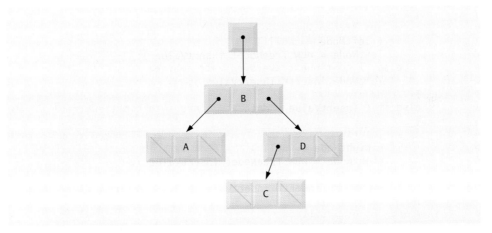

Fig. 17.15 | Binary tree graphical representation.

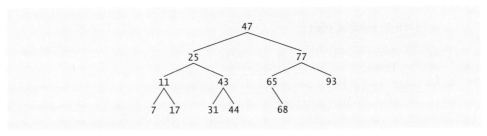

Fig. 17.16 | Binary search tree containing 12 values.

```java
1   // Fig. 17.17: Tree.java
2   // Definition of class TreeNode and class Tree.
3   package com.deitel.jhtp7.ch17;
4
5   // class TreeNode definition
6   class TreeNode
7   {
8       // package access members
9       TreeNode leftNode; // left node
10      int data; // node value
11      TreeNode rightNode; // right node
12
13      // constructor initializes data and makes this a leaf node
14      public TreeNode( int nodeData )
15      {
16          data = nodeData;
17          leftNode = rightNode = null; // node has no children
18      } // end TreeNode constructor
19
20      // locate insertion point and insert new node; ignore duplicate values
21      public void insert( int insertValue )
22      {
23          // insert in left subtree
24          if ( insertValue < data )
25          {
26              // insert new TreeNode
27              if ( leftNode == null )
28                  leftNode = new TreeNode( insertValue );
29              else // continue traversing left subtree
30                  leftNode.insert( insertValue );
31          } // end if
32          else if ( insertValue > data ) // insert in right subtree
33          {
34              // insert new TreeNode
35              if ( rightNode == null )
36                  rightNode = new TreeNode( insertValue );
37              else // continue traversing right subtree
38                  rightNode.insert( insertValue );
39          } // end else if
40      } // end method insert
41  } // end class TreeNode
42
43  // class Tree definition
44  public class Tree
45  {
46      private TreeNode root;
47
48      // constructor initializes an empty Tree of integers
49      public Tree()
50      {
51          root = null;
52      } // end Tree no-argument constructor
```

Fig. 17.17 | TreeNode and Tree class declarations for a binary search tree. (Part 1 of 3.)

```
53
54      // insert a new node in the binary search tree
55      public void insertNode( int insertValue )
56      {
57         if ( root == null )
58            root = new TreeNode( insertValue ); // create the root node here
59         else
60            root.insert( insertValue ); // call the insert method
61      } // end method insertNode
62
63      // begin preorder traversal
64      public void preorderTraversal()
65      {
66         preorderHelper( root );
67      } // end method preorderTraversal
68
69      // recursive method to perform preorder traversal
70      private void preorderHelper( TreeNode node )
71      {
72         if ( node == null )
73            return;
74
75         System.out.printf( "%d ", node.data ); // output node data
76         preorderHelper( node.leftNode );           // traverse left subtree
77         preorderHelper( node.rightNode );          // traverse right subtree
78      } // end method preorderHelper
79
80      // begin inorder traversal
81      public void inorderTraversal()
82      {
83         inorderHelper( root );
84      } // end method inorderTraversal
85
86      // recursive method to perform inorder traversal
87      private void inorderHelper( TreeNode node )
88      {
89         if ( node == null )
90            return;
91
92         inorderHelper( node.leftNode );            // traverse left subtree
93         System.out.printf( "%d ", node.data ); // output node data
94         inorderHelper( node.rightNode );           // traverse right subtree
95      } // end method inorderHelper
96
97      // begin postorder traversal
98      public void postorderTraversal()
99      {
100        postorderHelper( root );
101     } // end method postorderTraversal
102
```

Fig. 17.17 | TreeNode and Tree class declarations for a binary search tree. (Part 2 of 3.)

```
103      // recursive method to perform postorder traversal
104      private void postorderHelper( TreeNode node )
105      {
106         if ( node == null )
107            return;
108
109         postorderHelper( node.leftNode );      // traverse left subtree
110         postorderHelper( node.rightNode );     // traverse right subtree
111         System.out.printf( "%d ", node.data ); // output node data
112      } // end method postorderHelper
113   } // end class Tree
```

Fig. 17.17 | TreeNode and Tree class declarations for a binary search tree. (Part 3 of 3.)

Let us walk through the binary tree program. Method main of class TreeTest (Fig. 17.18) begins by instantiating an empty Tree object and assigning its reference to variable tree (line 10). Lines 17–22 randomly generate 10 integers, each of which is inserted into the binary tree through a call to method insertNode (line 21). The program then performs preorder, inorder and postorder traversals (these will be explained shortly) of tree (lines 25, 28 and 31, respectively).

Class Tree (Fig. 17.17, lines 44–113) has private field root (line 46)—a TreeNode reference to the root node of the tree. Tree's constructor (lines 49–52) initializes root to null to indicate that the tree is empty. The class contains method insertNode (lines 55–61) to insert a new node in the tree and methods preorderTraversal (lines 64–67), inorderTraversal (lines 81–84) and postorderTraversal (lines 98–101) to begin traversals of the tree. Each of these methods calls a recursive utility method to perform the traversal operations on the internal representation of the tree. (We discussed recursion in Chapter 15.)

Class Tree's method insertNode (lines 55–61) first determines whether the tree is empty. If so, line 58 allocates a new TreeNode, initializes the node with the integer being inserted in the tree and assigns the new node to reference root. If the tree is not empty, line 60 calls TreeNode method insert (lines 21–41). This method uses recursion to determine the location for the new node in the tree and inserts the node at that location. A node can be inserted only as a leaf node in a binary search tree.

TreeNode method insert compares the value to insert with the data value in the root node. If the insert value is less than the root node data (line 24), the program determines if the left subtree is empty (line 27). If so, line 28 allocates a new TreeNode, initializes it with the integer being inserted and assigns the new node to reference leftNode. Otherwise, line 30 recursively calls insert for the left subtree to insert the value into the left subtree. If the insert value is greater than the root node data (line 32), the program determines if the right subtree is empty (line 35). If so, line 36 allocates a new TreeNode, initializes it with the integer being inserted and assigns the new node to reference rightNode. Otherwise, line 38 recursively calls insert for the right subtree to insert the value in the right subtree. If the insertValue is already in the tree, it is simply ignored.

Methods inorderTraversal, preorderTraversal and postorderTraversal call Tree helper methods inorderHelper (lines 87–95), preorderHelper (lines 70–78) and postorderHelper (lines 104–112), respectively, to traverse the tree and print the node values. The helper methods in class Tree enable the programmer to start a traversal without having

```
1   // Fig. 17.18: TreeTest.java
2   // This program tests class Tree.
3   import java.util.Random;
4   import com.deitel.jhtp7.ch17.Tree;
5
6   public class TreeTest
7   {
8      public static void main( String args[] )
9      {
10        Tree tree = new Tree();
11        int value;
12        Random randomNumber = new Random();
13
14        System.out.println( "Inserting the following values: " );
15
16        // insert 10 random integers from 0-99 in tree
17        for ( int i = 1; i <= 10; i++ )
18        {
19           value = randomNumber.nextInt( 100 );
20           System.out.print( value + " " );
21           tree.insertNode( value );
22        } // end for
23
24        System.out.println ( "\n\nPreorder traversal" );
25        tree.preorderTraversal(); // perform preorder traversal of tree
26
27        System.out.println ( "\n\nInorder traversal" );
28        tree.inorderTraversal(); // perform inorder traversal of tree
29
30        System.out.println ( "\n\nPostorder traversal" );
31        tree.postorderTraversal(); // perform postorder traversal of tree
32        System.out.println();
33     } // end main
34  } // end class TreeTest
```

```
Inserting the following values:
92 73 77 16 30 30 94 89 26 80

Preorder traversal
92 73 16 30 26 77 89 80 94

Inorder traversal
16 26 30 73 77 80 89 92 94

Postorder traversal
26 30 16 80 89 77 73 94 92
```

Fig. 17.18 | Binary tree test program.

to pass the root node to the method. Reference root is an implementation detail that a programmer should not be able to access. Methods inorderTraversal, preorderTraversal and postorderTraversal simply take the private root reference and pass it to the appropriate helper method to initiate a traversal of the tree. The base case for each helper method determines whether the reference it receives is null and, if so, returns immediately.

Method `inorderHelper` (lines 87–95) defines the steps for an inorder traversal:

1. Traverse the left subtree with a call to `inorderHelper` (line 92).

2. Process the value in the node (line 93).

3. Traverse the right subtree with a call to `inorderHelper` (line 94).

The inorder traversal does not process the value in a node until the values in that node's left subtree are processed. The inorder traversal of the tree in Fig. 17.19 is

```
6 13 17 27 33 42 48
```

Note that the inorder traversal of a binary search tree prints the node values in ascending order. The process of creating a binary search tree actually sorts the data; thus, it is called the binary tree sort.

Method `preorderHelper` (lines 70–78) defines the steps for a preorder traversal:

1. Process the value in the node (line 75).

2. Traverse the left subtree with a call to `preorderHelper` (line 76).

3. Traverse the right subtree with a call to `preorderHelper` (line 77).

The preorder traversal processes the value in each node as the node is visited. After processing the value in a given node, the preorder traversal processes the values in the left subtree, then the values in the right subtree. The preorder traversal of the tree in Fig. 17.19 is

```
27 13 6 17 42 33 48
```

Method `postorderHelper` (lines 104–112) defines the steps for a postorder traversal:

1. Traverse the left subtree with a call to `postorderHelper` (line 109).

2. Traverse the right subtree with a call to `postorderHelper` (line 110).

3. Process the value in the node (line 111).

The postorder traversal processes the value in each node after the values of all that node's children are processed. The `postorderTraversal` of the tree in Fig. 17.19 is

```
6 17 13 33 48 42 27
```

The binary search tree facilitates duplicate elimination. While building a tree, the insertion operation recognizes attempts to insert a duplicate value, because a duplicate follows the same "go left" or "go right" decisions on each comparison as the original value did. Thus, the insertion operation eventually compares the duplicate with a node containing the same value. At this point, the insertion operation can decide to discard the duplicate value (as we do in this example).

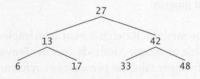

Fig. 17.19 | Binary search tree with seven values.

Searching a binary tree for a value that matches a key value is fast, especially for tightly packed (or balanced) trees. In a tightly packed tree, each level contains about twice as many elements as the previous level. Figure 17.19 is a tightly packed binary tree. A tightly packed binary search tree with n elements has $\log_2 n$ levels. Thus, at most $\log_2 n$ comparisons are required either to find a match or to determine that no match exists. Searching a (tightly packed) 1000-element binary search tree requires at most 10 comparisons, because $2^{10} > 1000$. Searching a (tightly packed) 1,000,000-element binary search tree requires at most 20 comparisons, because $2^{20} > 1,000,000$.

The chapter exercises present algorithms for several other binary tree operations, such as deleting an item from a binary tree, printing a binary tree in a two-dimensional tree format and performing a level-order traversal of a binary tree. The level-order traversal visits the nodes of the tree row by row, starting at the root node level. On each level of the tree, a level-order traversal visits the nodes from left to right. Other binary tree exercises include allowing a binary search tree to contain duplicate values, inserting string values in a binary tree and determining how many levels are contained in a binary tree. Chapter 19 continues our discussion of data structures by presenting the data structures in the Java API.

17.10 Wrap-Up

In this chapter, you learned about type-wrapper classes, boxing and dynamic data structures that grow and shrink at execution time. You learned that each primitive type has a corresponding type-wrapper class in package java.lang. You also saw that Java can convert between primitive values and objects of the type-wrapper classes using boxing.

You learned that linked lists are collections of data items that are "linked up in a chain." You also saw that an application can perform insertions and deletions anywhere in a linked list. You learned that the stack and queue data structures are constrained versions of lists. For stacks, you saw that insertions and deletions are made only at the top. For queues that represent waiting lines, you saw that insertions are made at the tail and deletions are made from the head. You also learned the binary tree data structure. You saw a binary search tree that facilitated high-speed searching and sorting of data and eliminating duplicate data items efficiently. Throughout the chapter, you learned how to create and package these data structures for reusability and maintainability.

Chapter 18, Generics, presents a mechanism for declaring classes and methods without specific type information so that the classes and methods can be used with many different types. Generics are used extensively in Java's built-in set of data structures, known as the Collections API, which we discuss in Chapter 19.

Summary

Section 17.1 Introduction
- Dynamic data structures can grow and shrink at execution time.
- Linked lists are collections of data items "linked up in a chain"—insertions and deletions can be made anywhere in a linked list.
- Stacks are important in compilers and operating systems—insertions and deletions are made only at one end of a stack, its top.

- Insertions are made at the tail of a queue and deletions are made from the head.
- Binary trees facilitate high-speed searching and sorting of data, eliminating duplicate data items efficiently, representing file-system directories and compiling expressions into machine language.

Section 17.2 Type-Wrapper Classes for Primitive Types
- Type-wrapper classes (e.g., Integer, Double, Boolean) enable programmers to manipulate primitive-type values as objects. Objects of these classes can be used in collections and data structures that can store only references to objects—not primitive-type values.

Section 17.3 Autoboxing and Auto-Unboxing
- A boxing conversion converts a value of a primitive type to an object of the corresponding type-wrapper class. An unboxing conversion converts an object of a type-wrapper class to a value of the corresponding primitive type.
- Java performs boxing conversions and unboxing conversions automatically (called autoboxing and auto-unboxing).

Section 17.4 Self-Referential Classes
- A self-referential class contains a reference that refers to another object of the same class type. Self-referential objects can be linked together to form dynamic data structures.

Section 17.5 Dynamic Memory Allocation
- The limit for dynamic memory allocation can be as large as the available physical memory in the computer or the amount of available disk space in a virtual-memory system. Often, the limits are much smaller because the computer's available memory must be shared among many users.
- If no memory is available, an OutOfMemoryError is thrown.

Section 17.6 Linked Lists
- A linked list is accessed via a reference to the first node of the list. Each subsequent node is accessed via the link-reference member stored in the previous node.
- By convention, the link reference in the last node of a list is set to null to mark the end of the list.
- A node can contain data of any type, including objects of other classes.
- A linked list is appropriate when the number of data elements to be stored is unpredictable. Linked lists are dynamic, so the length of a list can increase or decrease as necessary.
- The size of a "conventional" Java array cannot be altered—it is fixed at creation time.
- Linked lists can be maintained in sorted order simply by inserting each new element at the proper point in the list.
- List nodes normally are not stored contiguously in memory. Rather, they are logically contiguous.

Section 17.7 Stacks
- A stack is a last-in, first-out (LIFO) data structure. The primary methods used to manipulate a stack are push and pop. Method push adds a new node to the top of the stack. Method pop removes a node from the top of the stack and returns the data object from the popped node.
- Stacks have many interesting applications. When a method call is made, the called method must know how to return to its caller, so the return address is pushed onto the program execution stack. If a series of method calls occurs, the successive return values are pushed onto the stack in last-in, first-out order so that each method can return to its caller. The program execution stack contains the space created for local variables on each invocation of a method. When the method returns to its caller, the space for that method's local variables is popped off the stack, and those variables are no longer available to the program.

- Stacks are used by compilers to evaluate arithmetic expressions and generate machine-language code to process the expressions.
- The technique of implementing each stack method as a call to a `List` method is called delegation—the stack method invoked delegates the call to the appropriate `List` method.

Section 17.8 Queues
- A queue is similar to a checkout line in a supermarket—the first person in line is serviced first, and other customers enter the line only at the end and wait to be serviced.
- Queue nodes are removed only from the head of the queue and are inserted only at the tail. For this reason, a queue is referred to as a first-in, first-out (FIFO) data structure.
- The insert and remove operations for a queue are known as enqueue and dequeue.
- Queues have many uses in computer systems. Most computers have only a single processor, so only one application at a time can be serviced. Entries for the other applications are placed in a queue. The entry at the front of the queue is the next to receive service. Each entry gradually advances to the front of the queue as applications receive service.

Section 17.9 Trees
- A tree is a nonlinear, two-dimensional data structure. Tree nodes contain two or more links.
- A binary tree is a tree whose nodes all contain two links. The root node is the first node in a tree.
- Each link in the root node refers to a child. The left child is the first node in the left subtree, and the right child is the first node in the right subtree.
- The children of a node are called siblings. A node with no children is called a leaf node.
- In a binary search tree with no duplicate values, the values in any left subtree are less than the value in the subtree's parent node, and the values in any right subtree are greater than the value in the subtree's parent node. A node can be inserted only as a leaf node in a binary search tree.
- An inorder traversal of a binary search tree processes the node values in ascending order.
- In a preorder traversal, the value in each node is processed as the node is visited. Then the values in the left subtree are processed, and then the values in the right subtree.
- In a postorder traversal, the value in each node is processed after the values of its children.
- The binary search tree facilitates duplicate elimination. As the tree is created, attempts to insert a duplicate value are recognized, because a duplicate follows the same "go left" or "go right" decisions on each comparison as the original value did. Thus, the duplicate eventually is compared with a node containing the same value. The duplicate value can be discarded at this point.
- Searching a binary tree for a value that matches a key value is also fast, especially for tightly packed trees. In a tightly packed tree, each level contains about twice as many elements as the previous one. So a tightly packed binary search tree with n elements has $\log_2 n$ levels, and thus at most $\log_2 n$ comparisons would have to be made either to find a match or to determine that no match exists. Searching a (tightly packed) 1000-element binary search tree requires at most 10 comparisons, because $2^{10} > 1000$. Searching a (tightly packed) 1,000,000-element binary search tree requires at most 20 comparisons, because $2^{20} > 1,000,000$.

Terminology

autoboxing	binary tree sort
auto-unboxing	`Boolean` class
balanced tree	boxing conversion
binary search tree	`Byte` class
binary tree	`Character` class

child node
children of a node
delegate a method call
delete a node
dequeue
duplicate elimination
dynamic data structure
enqueue
FIFO (first-in, first-out)
Float class
head of a queue
inorder traversal of a binary tree
insert a node
Integer class
leaf node
left child
left subtree
level-order traversal of a binary tree
LIFO (last-in, first-out)
linear data structure
linked list
Long class
node
nonlinear data structure
null reference

OutOfMemoryError
packed tree
parent node
pop
postorder traversal of a binary tree
predicate method
preorder traversal of a binary tree
program execution stack
push
queue
recursive tree traversal algorithms
right child
right subtree
root node
self-referential class
Short class
stack
subtree
tail of a queue
top of a stack
traversal
tree
type-wrapper classes
unboxing conversion
visiting a node

Self-Review Exercises

17.1 Fill in the blanks in each of the following statements:
   a) A self-_____ class is used to form dynamic data structures that can grow and shrink at execution time.
   b) A(n) _____ is a constrained version of a linked list in which nodes can be inserted and deleted only from the start of the list.
   c) A method that does not alter a linked list, but simply looks at it to determine whether it is empty, is referred to as a(n) _____ method.
   d) A queue is referred to as a(n) _____ data structure because the first nodes inserted are the first ones removed.
   e) The reference to the next node in a linked list is referred to as a(n) _____.
   f) Automatically reclaiming dynamically allocated memory in Java is called _____.
   g) A(n) _____ is a constrained version of a linked list in which nodes can be inserted only at the end of the list and deleted only from the start of the list.
   h) A(n) _____ is a nonlinear, two-dimensional data structure that contains nodes with two or more links.
   i) A stack is referred to as a(n) _____ data structure because the last node inserted is the first node removed.
   j) The nodes of a(n) _____ tree contain two link members.
   k) The first node of a tree is the _____ node.
   l) Each link in a tree node refers to a(n) _____ or _____ of that node.
   m) A tree node that has no children is called a(n) _____ node.
   n) The three traversal algorithms we mentioned in the text for binary search trees are _____, _____ and _____.

o) Assuming that myArray contains references to Double objects, _____ occurs when the statement "double number = myArray[0];" executes.

p) Assuming that myArray contains references to Double objects, _____ occurs when the statement "myArray[0] = 1.25;" executes.

17.2   What are the differences between a linked list and a stack?

17.3   What are the differences between a stack and a queue?

17.4   Perhaps a more appropriate title for this chapter would have been Reusable Data Structures. Comment on how each of the following entities or concepts contributes to the reusability of data structures:

a) classes
b) inheritance
c) composition

17.5   Manually provide the inorder, preorder and postorder traversals of the binary search tree of Fig. 17.20.

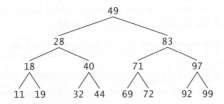

Fig. 17.20 | Binary search tree with 15 nodes.

Answers to Self-Review Exercises

17.1   a) referential. b) stack. c) predicate. d) first-in, first-out (FIFO). e) link. f) garbage collection. g) queue. h) tree   i) last-in, first-out (LIFO). j) binary. k) root. l) child or subtree. m) leaf. n) inorder, preorder, postorder. o) auto-unboxing. p) autoboxing.

17.2   It is possible to insert a node anywhere in a linked list and remove a node from anywhere in a linked list. Nodes in a stack may be inserted only at the top of the stack and removed only from the top.

17.3   A queue is a FIFO data structure that has references to both its head and its tail, so that nodes may be inserted at the tail and deleted from the head. A stack is a LIFO data structure that has a single reference to the stack's top, where both insertion and deletion of nodes are performed.

17.4   a) Classes allow us to instantiate as many data structure objects of a certain type (i.e., class) as we wish.

b) Inheritance enables a subclass to reuse the functionality from a superclass. Public and protected methods of a superclass can be accessed through a subclass to eliminate duplicate logic.

c) Composition enables a class to reuse code by storing a reference to an instance of another class in a field. Public methods of the instance can be called by methods in the class that contains the reference.

17.5   The inorder traversal is

11 18 19 28 32 40 44 49 69 71 72 83 92 97 99

The preorder traversal is

> 49 28 18 11 19 40 32 44 83 71 69 72 97 92 99

The postorder traversal is

> 11 19 18 32 44 40 28 69 72 71 92 99 97 83 49

Exercises

17.6 Write a program that concatenates two linked list objects of characters. Class `ListConcatenate` should include a method `concatenate` that takes references to both list objects as arguments and concatenates the second list to the first list.

17.7 Write a program that merges two ordered list objects of integers into a single ordered-list object of integers. Method `merge` of class `ListMerge` should receive references to each of the list objects to be merged and return a reference to the merged list object.

17.8 Write a program that inserts 25 random integers from 0 to 100 in order into a linked-list object. The program should calculate the sum of the elements and the floating-point average of the elements.

17.9 Write a program that creates a linked list object of 10 characters, then creates a second list object containing a copy of the first list, but in reverse order.

17.10 Write a program that inputs a line of text and uses a stack object to print the words of the line in reverse order.

17.11 Write a program that uses a stack to determine whether a string is a palindrome (i.e., the string is spelled identically backward and forward). The program should ignore spaces and punctuation.

17.12 Stacks are used by compilers to help in the process of evaluating expressions and generating machine-language code. In this and the next exercise, we investigate how compilers evaluate arithmetic expressions consisting only of constants, operators and parentheses.

Humans generally write expressions like 3 + 4 and 7 / 9 in which the operator (+ or / here) is written between its operands—this is called *infix notation*. Computers "prefer" *postfix notation*, in which the operator is written to the right of its two operands. The preceding infix expressions would appear in postfix notation as 3 4 + and 7 9 /, respectively.

To evaluate a complex infix expression, a compiler would first convert the expression to postfix notation and evaluate the postfix version. Each of these algorithms requires only a single left-to-right pass of the expression. Each algorithm uses a stack object in support of its operation, but each uses the stack for a different purpose.

In this exercise, you will write a Java version of the infix-to-postfix conversion algorithm. In the next exercise, you will write a Java version of the postfix expression evaluation algorithm. In a later exercise, you will discover that code you write in this exercise can help you implement a complete working compiler.

Write class `InfixToPostfixConverter` to convert an ordinary infix arithmetic expression (assume a valid expression is entered) with single-digit integers such as

> (6 + 2) * 5 - 8 / 4

to a postfix expression. The postfix version of the preceding infix expression is (note that no parentheses are needed)

> 6 2 + 5 * 8 4 / -

The program should read the expression into `StringBuffer infix` and use one of the stack classes implemented in this chapter to help create the postfix expression in `StringBuffer postfix`. The algorithm for creating a postfix expression is as follows:

a) Push a left parenthesis '(' on the stack.
b) Append a right parenthesis ')' to the end of infix.
c) While the stack is not empty, read infix from left to right and do the following:

If the current character in infix is a digit, append it to postfix.

If the current character in infix is a left parenthesis, push it onto the stack.

If the current character in infix is an operator:

Pop operators (if there are any) at the top of the stack while they have equal or higher precedence than the current operator, and append the popped operators to postfix.

Push the current character in infix onto the stack.

If the current character in infix is a right parenthesis:

Pop operators from the top of the stack and append them to postfix until a left parenthesis is at the top of the stack.

Pop (and discard) the left parenthesis from the stack.

The following arithmetic operations are allowed in an expression:

+   addition
-   subtraction
*   multiplication
/   division
^   exponentiation
%   remainder

The stack should be maintained with stack nodes that each contain an instance variable and a reference to the next stack node. Some of the methods you may want to provide are as follows:

a) Method convertToPostfix, which converts the infix expression to postfix notation.
b) Method isOperator, which determines whether c is an operator.
c) Method precedence, which determines whether the precedence of operator1 (from the infix expression) is less than, equal to or greater than the precedence of operator2 (from the stack). The method returns true if operator1 has lower precedence than operator2. Otherwise, false is returned.
d) Method stackTop (this should be added to the stack class), which returns the top value of the stack without popping the stack.

17.13 Write class PostfixEvaluator, which evaluates a postfix expression such as

    6 2 + 5 * 8 4 / -

The program should read a postfix expression consisting of digits and operators into a String-Buffer. Using modified versions of the stack methods implemented earlier in this chapter, the program should scan the expression and evaluate it (assume it is valid). The algorithm is as follows:

a) Append a right parenthesis ')' to the end of the postfix expression. When the right-parenthesis character is encountered, no further processing is necessary.
b) When the right-parenthesis character has not been encountered, read the expression from left to right.

If the current character is a digit, do the following:

Push its integer value on the stack (the integer value of a digit character is its value in the computer's character set minus the value of '0' in Unicode).

Otherwise, if the current character is an *operator*:

Pop the two top elements of the stack into variables x and y.

Calculate y *operator* x.

Push the result of the calculation onto the stack.

c) When the right parenthesis is encountered in the expression, pop the top value of the stack. This is the result of the postfix expression.

[*Note:* In b) above (based on the sample expression at the beginning of this exercise), if the operator is '/', the top of the stack is 2 and the next element in the stack is 8, then pop 2 into x, pop 8 into y, evaluate 8 / 2 and push the result, 4, back on the stack. This note also applies to operator '-'.] The arithmetic operations allowed in an expression are:

+	addition
-	subtraction
*	multiplication
/	division
^	exponentiation
%	remainder

The stack should be maintained with one of the stack classes introduced in this chapter. You may want to provide the following methods:

a) Method `evaluatePostfixExpression`, which evaluates the postfix expression.
b) Method `calculate`, which evaluates the expression op1 operator op2.
c) Method `push`, which pushes a value onto the stack.
d) Method `pop`, which pops a value off the stack.
e) Method `isEmpty`, which determines whether the stack is empty.
f) Method `printStack`, which prints the stack.

17.14   Modify the postfix evaluator program of Exercise 17.13 so that it can process integer operands larger than 9.

17.15   Modify Figs. 17.17 and 17.18 to allow the binary tree to contain duplicates.

17.16   Write a program based on the program of Figs. 17.17 and 17.18 that inputs a line of text, tokenizes the sentence into separate words (you might want to use the `StreamTokenizer` class from the `java.io` package), inserts the words in a binary search tree and prints the inorder, preorder and postorder traversals of the tree.

17.17   In this chapter, we saw that duplicate elimination is straightforward when creating a binary search tree. Describe how you would perform duplicate elimination when using only a one-dimensional array. Compare the performance of array-based duplicate elimination with the performance of binary-search-tree-based duplicate elimination.

17.18   Write a method `depth` that receives a binary tree and determines how many levels it has.

17.19   (*Recursively Print a List Backward*) Write a method `printListBackward` that recursively outputs the items in a linked list object in reverse order. Write a test program that creates a sorted list of integers and prints the list in reverse order.

17.20   (*Recursively Search a List*) Write a method `searchList` that recursively searches a linked list object for a specified value. Method `searchList` should return a reference to the value if it is found; otherwise, `null` should be returned. Use your method in a test program that creates a list of integers. The program should prompt the user for a value to locate in the list.

17.21   (*Binary Tree Search*) Write method `binaryTreeSearch`, which attempts to locate a specified value in a binary-search-tree object. The method should take as an argument a search key to be located. If the node containing the search key is found, the method should return a reference to that node; otherwise, it should return a null reference.

17.22   (*Level-Order Binary Tree Traversal*) The program of Figs. 17.17 and 17.18 illustrated three recursive methods of traversing a binary tree—inorder, preorder and postorder traversals. This exercise presents the *level-order traversal* of a binary tree, in which the node values are printed level by level, starting at the root node level. The nodes on each level are printed from left to right. The level-order traversal is not a recursive algorithm. It uses a queue object to control the output of the nodes. The algorithm is as follows:

a) Insert the root node in the queue.

b) While there are nodes left in the queue, do the following:

Get the next node in the queue.

Print the node's value.

If the reference to the left child of the node is not null:

Insert the left child node in the queue.

If the reference to the right child of the node is not null:

Insert the right child node in the queue.

Write method `levelOrder` to perform a level-order traversal of a binary tree object. Modify the program of Figs. 17.17 and 17.18 to use this method. [*Note:* You will also need to use queue-processing methods of Fig. 17.13 in this program.]

17.23   (*Printing Trees*) Write a recursive method `outputTree` to display a binary tree object on the screen. The method should output the tree row by row, with the top of the tree at the left of the screen and the bottom of the tree toward the right of the screen. Each row is output vertically. For example, the binary tree illustrated in Fig. 17.20 is output as shown in Fig. 17.21.

The rightmost leaf node appears at the top of the output in the rightmost column and the root node appears at the left of the output. Each column starts five spaces to the right of the preceding column. Method `outputTree` should receive an argument `totalSpaces` representing the number of spaces preceding the value to be output. (This variable should start at zero so that the root node is output at the left of the screen.) The method uses a modified inorder traversal to output the tree—it starts at the rightmost node in the tree and works back to the left. The algorithm is as follows:

Fig. 17.21 | Sample output of recursive method `outputTree`.

While the reference to the current node is not null, perform the following:

Recursively call `outputTree` with the right subtree of the current node and `totalSpaces + 5`.

Use a `for` statement to count from 1 to `totalSpaces` and output spaces.

Output the value in the current node.

Set the reference to the current node to refer to the left subtree of the current node.

Increment `totalSpaces` by 5.

Special Section: Building Your Own Compiler

In Exercises 7.34–7.35, we introduced Simpletron Machine Language (SML), and you implemented a Simpletron computer simulator to execute programs written in SML. In this section, we build a compiler that converts programs written in a high-level programming language to SML. This section "ties" together the entire programming process. You will write programs in this new high-level language, compile them on the compiler you build and run them on the simulator you built in Exercise 7.35. You should make every effort to implement your compiler in an object-oriented manner.

17.24 (*The Simple Language*) Before we begin building the compiler, we discuss a simple, yet powerful high-level language similar to early versions of the popular language BASIC. We call the language *Simple*. Every Simple *statement* consists of a *line number* and a Simple *instruction*. Line numbers must appear in ascending order. Each instruction begins with one of the following Simple *commands*: rem, input, let, print, goto, if/goto or end (see Fig. 17.22). All commands except end can be used repeatedly. Simple evaluates only integer expressions using the +, -, * and / operators. These operators have the same precedence as in Java. Parentheses can be used to change the order of evaluation of an expression.

Our Simple compiler recognizes only lowercase letters. All characters in a Simple file should be lowercase. (Uppercase letters result in a syntax error unless they appear in a rem statement, in which case they are ignored.) A *variable name* is a single letter. Simple does not allow descriptive variable names, so variables should be explained in remarks to indicate their use in a program. Simple uses only integer variables. Simple does not have variable declarations—merely mentioning a variable name in a program causes the variable to be declared and initialized to zero. The syntax of Simple does not allow string manipulation (reading a string, writing a string, comparing strings, and so on). If a string is encountered in a Simple program (after a command other than rem), the compiler generates a syntax error. The first version of our compiler assumes that Simple programs are entered correctly. Exercise 17.27 asks the reader to modify the compiler to perform syntax error checking.

Command	Example statement	Description
rem	50 rem this is a remark	Any text following the command rem is for documentation purposes only and is ignored by the compiler.
input	30 input x	Display a question mark to prompt the user to enter an integer. Read that integer from the keyboard and store the integer in x.
let	80 let u = 4 * (j - 56)	Assign u the value of 4 * (j - 56). Note that an arbitrarily complex expression can appear to the right of the equal sign.
print	10 print w	Display the value of w.
goto	70 goto 45	Transfer program control to line 45.
if/goto	35 if i == z goto 80	Compare i and z for equality and transfer program control to line 80 if the condition is true; otherwise, continue execution with the next statement.
end	99 end	Terminate program execution.

Fig. 17.22 | Simple commands.

Simple uses the conditional if/goto and unconditional goto statements to alter the flow of control during program execution. If the condition in the if/goto statement is true, control is transferred to a specific line of the program. The following relational and equality operators are valid in an if/goto statement: <, >, <=, >=, == or !=. The precedence of these operators is the same as in Java.

Let us now consider several programs that demonstrate Simple's features. The first program (Fig. 17.23) reads two integers from the keyboard, stores the values in variables a and b and computes and prints their sum (stored in variable c).

```
 1   10 rem    determine and print the sum of two integers
 2   15 rem
 3   20 rem    input the two integers
 4   30 input a
 5   40 input b
 6   45 rem
 7   50 rem    add integers and store result in c
 8   60 let c = a + b
 9   65 rem
10   70 rem    print the result
11   80 print c
12   90 rem    terminate program execution
13   99 end
```

Fig. 17.23 | Simple program that determines the sum of two integers.

The program of Fig. 17.24 determines and prints the larger of two integers. The integers are input from the keyboard and stored in s and t. The if/goto statement tests the condition s >= t. If the condition is true, control is transferred to line 90 and s is output; otherwise, t is output and control is transferred to the end statement in line 99, where the program terminates.

Simple does not provide a repetition statement (such as Java's for, while or do...while). However, Simple can simulate each of Java's repetition statements by using the if/goto and goto statements. Figure 17.25 uses a sentinel-controlled loop to calculate the squares of several integers. Each integer is input from the keyboard and stored in variable j. If the value entered is the sentinel value -9999, control is transferred to line 99, where the program terminates. Otherwise, k is assigned the square of j, k is output to the screen and control is passed to line 20, where the next integer is input.

Using the sample programs of Figs. 17.23–17.25 as your guide, write a Simple program to accomplish each of the following:

a) Input three integers, determine their average and print the result.
b) Use a sentinel-controlled loop to input 10 integers and compute and print their sum.
c) Use a counter-controlled loop to input 7 integers, some positive and some negative, and compute and print their average.
d) Input a series of integers and determine and print the largest. The first integer input indicates how many numbers should be processed.
e) Input 10 integers and print the smallest.
f) Calculate and print the sum of the even integers from 2 to 30.
g) Calculate and print the product of the odd integers from 1 to 9.

```
 1    10 rem    determine and print the larger of two integers
 2    20 input s
 3    30 input t
 4    32 rem
 5    35 rem    test if s >= t
 6    40 if s >= t goto 90
 7    45 rem
 8    50 rem    t is greater than s, so print t
 9    60 print t
10    70 goto 99
11    75 rem
12    80 rem    s is greater than or equal to t, so print s
13    90 print s
14    99 end
```

Fig. 17.24 | Simple program that finds the larger of two integers.

```
 1    10 rem    calculate the squares of several integers
 2    20 input j
 3    23 rem
 4    25 rem    test for sentinel value
 5    30 if j == -9999 goto 99
 6    33 rem
 7    35 rem    calculate square of j and assign result to k
 8    40 let k = j * j
 9    50 print k
10    53 rem
11    55 rem    loop to get next j
12    60 goto 20
13    99 end
```

Fig. 17.25 | Calculate the squares of several integers.

17.25 (*Building a Compiler. Prerequisites: Complete Exercise 7.34, Exercise 7.35, Exercise 17.12, Exercise 17.13 and Exercise 17.24*) Now that the Simple language has been presented (Exercise 17.24), we discuss how to build a Simple compiler. First, we consider the process by which a Simple program is converted to SML and executed by the Simpletron simulator (see Fig. 17.26). A file containing a Simple program is read by the compiler and converted to SML code. The SML code is output to a file on disk, in which SML instructions appear one per line. The SML file is then loaded into the Simpletron simulator, and the results are sent to a file on disk and to the screen. Note that the Simpletron program developed in Exercise 7.35 took its input from the keyboard. It must be modified to read from a file so it can run the programs produced by our compiler.

The Simple compiler performs two *passes* of the Simple program to convert it to SML. The first pass constructs a *symbol table* (object) in which every *line number* (object), *variable name* (object) and *constant* (object) of the Simple program is stored with its type and corresponding location in the final SML code (the symbol table is discussed in detail below). The first pass also produces the corresponding SML instruction object(s) for each of the Simple statements (object, and so on). If the Simple program contains statements that transfer control to a line later in the program, the first pass results in an SML program containing some "unfinished" instructions. The second pass of the compiler locates and completes the unfinished instructions and outputs the SML program to a file.

First Pass

The compiler begins by reading one statement of the Simple program into memory. The line must be separated into its individual *tokens* (i.e., "pieces" of a statement) for processing and compilation. (The `StreamTokenizer` class from the `java.io` package can be used.) Recall that every statement begins with a line number followed by a command. As the compiler breaks a statement into tokens, if the token is a line number, a variable or a constant, it is placed in the symbol table. A line number is placed in the symbol table only if it is the first token in a statement. The `symbolTable` object is an array of `tableEntry` objects representing each symbol in the program. There is no restriction on the number of symbols that can appear in the program. Therefore, the `symbolTable` for a particular program could be large. Make it a 100-element array for now. You can increase or decrease its size once the program is working.

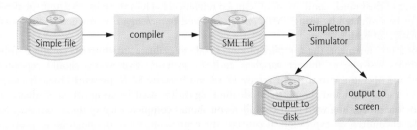

Fig. 17.26 | Writing, compiling and executing a Simple language program.

Each `tableEntry` object contains three fields. Field `symbol` is an integer containing the Unicode representation of a variable (remember that variable names are single characters), a line number or a constant. Field `type` is one of the following characters indicating the symbol's type: `'C'` for constant, `'L'` for line number or `'V'` for variable. Field `location` contains the Simpletron memory location (00 to 99) to which the symbol refers. Simpletron memory is an array of 100 integers in which SML instructions and data are stored. For a line number, the location is the element in the Simpletron memory array at which the SML instructions for the Simple statement begin. For a variable or constant, the location is the element in the Simpletron memory array in which the variable or constant is stored. Variables and constants are allocated from the end of Simpletron's memory backward. The first variable or constant is stored at location 99, the next at location 98, an so on.

The symbol table plays an integral part in converting Simple programs to SML. We learned in Chapter 7 that an SML instruction is a four-digit integer comprised of two parts—the *operation code* and the *operand*. The operation code is determined by commands in Simple. For example, the simple command `input` corresponds to SML operation code 10 (read), and the Simple command `print` corresponds to SML operation code 11 (write). The operand is a memory location containing the data on which the operation code performs its task (e.g., operation code 10 reads a value from the keyboard and stores it in the memory location specified by the operand). The compiler searches `symbolTable` to determine the Simpletron memory location for each symbol, so the corresponding location can be used to complete the SML instructions.

The compilation of each Simple statement is based on its command. For example, after the line number in a `rem` statement is inserted in the symbol table, the remainder of the statement is ignored by the compiler, because a remark is for documentation purposes only. The `input`, `print`, `goto` and `end` statements correspond to the SML *read, write, branch (*to a specific location) and *halt* instructions. Statements containing these Simple commands are converted directly to SML. [*Note:*

A goto statement may contain an unresolved reference if the specified line number refers to a statement further into the Simple program file; this is sometimes called a forward reference.]

When a goto statement is compiled with an unresolved reference, the SML instruction must be *flagged* to indicate that the second pass of the compiler must complete the instruction. The flags are stored in a 100-element array flags of type int in which each element is initialized to -1. If the memory location to which a line number in the Simple program refers is not yet known (i.e., it is not in the symbol table), the line number is stored in array flags in the element with the same index as the incomplete instruction. The operand of the incomplete instruction is set to 00 temporarily. For example, an unconditional branch instruction (making a forward reference) is left as +4000 until the second pass of the compiler. The second pass will be described shortly.

Compilation of if/goto and let statements is more complicated than for other statements—they are the only statements that produce more than one SML instruction. For an if/goto statement, the compiler produces code to test the condition and to branch to another line if necessary. The result of the branch could be an unresolved reference. Each of the relational and equality operators can be simulated by using SML's *branch zero* and *branch negative* instructions (or possibly a combination of both).

For a let statement, the compiler produces code to evaluate an arbitrarily complex arithmetic expression consisting of integer variables and/or constants. Expressions should separate each operand and operator with spaces. Exercise 17.12 and Exercise 17.13 presented the infix-to-postfix conversion algorithm and the postfix evaluation algorithm used by compilers to evaluate expressions. Before proceeding with your compiler, you should complete each of these exercises. When a compiler encounters an expression, it converts the expression from infix notation to postfix notation, then evaluates the postfix expression.

How is it that the compiler produces the machine language to evaluate an expression containing variables? The postfix evaluation algorithm contains a "hook" where the compiler can generate SML instructions rather than actually evaluating the expression. To enable this "hook" in the compiler, the postfix evaluation algorithm must be modified to search the symbol table for each symbol it encounters (and possibly insert it), determine the symbol's corresponding memory location and *push the memory location (instead of the symbol) onto the stack*. When an operator is encountered in the postfix expression, the two memory locations at the top of the stack are popped, and machine language for effecting the operation is produced by using the memory locations as operands. The result of each subexpression is stored in a temporary location in memory and pushed back onto the stack so the evaluation of the postfix expression can continue. When postfix evaluation is complete, the memory location containing the result is the only location left on the stack. This is popped, and SML instructions are generated to assign the result to the variable at the left of the let statement.

Second Pass

The second pass of the compiler performs two tasks: Resolve any unresolved references and output the SML code to a file. Resolution of references occurs as follows:
   a) Search the flags array for an unresolved reference (i.e., an element with a value other than -1).
   b) Locate the object in array symbolTable containing the symbol stored in the flags array (be sure that the type of the symbol is 'L' for line number).
   c) Insert the memory location from field location into the instruction with the unresolved reference (remember that an instruction containing an unresolved reference has operand 00).
   d) Repeat *Steps (a)*, *(b)* and *(c)* until the end of the flags array is reached.

After the resolution process is complete, the entire array containing the SML code is output to a disk file with one SML instruction per line. This file can be read by the Simpletron for execution (after the simulator is modified to read its input from a file). Compiling your first Simple program into an SML file and executing that file should give you a real sense of personal accomplishment.

A Complete Example

The following example illustrates the complete conversion of a Simple program to SML as it will be performed by the Simple compiler. Consider a Simple program that inputs an integer and sums the values from 1 to that integer. The program and the SML instructions produced by the first pass of the Simple compiler are illustrated in Fig. 17.27. The symbol table constructed by the first pass is shown in Fig. 17.28.

Simple program	SML location and instruction	Description
5 rem sum 1 to x	*none*	rem ignored
10 input x	00 +1099	read x into location 99
15 rem check y == x	*none*	rem ignored
20 if y == x goto 60	01 +2098	load y (98) into accumulator
	02 +3199	sub x (99) from accumulator
	03 +4200	branch zero to unresolved location
25 rem increment y	*none*	rem ignored
30 let y = y + 1	04 +2098	load y into accumulator
	05 +3097	add 1 (97) to accumulator
	06 +2196	store in temporary location 96
	07 +2096	load from temporary location 96
	08 +2198	store accumulator in y
35 rem add y to total	*none*	rem ignored
40 let t = t + y	09 +2095	load t (95) into accumulator
	10 +3098	add y to accumulator
	11 +2194	store in temporary location 94
	12 +2094	load from temporary location 94
	13 +2195	store accumulator in t
45 rem loop y	*none*	rem ignored
50 goto 20	14 +4001	branch to location 01
55 rem output result	*none*	rem ignored

Fig. 17.27 | SML instructions produced after the compiler's first pass. (Part 1 of 2.)

Simple program	SML location and instruction		Description
60 print t	15	+1195	output t to screen
99 end	16	+4300	terminate execution

Fig. 17.27 | SML instructions produced after the compiler's first pass. (Part 2 of 2.)

Symbol	Type	Location
5	L	00
10	L	00
'x'	V	99
15	L	01
20	L	01
'y'	V	98
25	L	04
30	L	04
1	C	97
35	L	09
40	L	09
't'	V	95
45	L	14
50	L	14
55	L	15
60	L	15
99	L	16

Fig. 17.28 | Symbol table for program of Fig. 17.27.

Most Simple statements convert directly to single SML instructions. The exceptions in this program are remarks, the if/goto statement in line 20 and the let statements. Remarks do not translate into machine language. However, the line number for a remark is placed in the symbol table in case the line number is referenced in a goto statement or an if/goto statement. Line 20 of the program specifies that, if the condition y == x is true, program control is transferred to line 60. Since line 60 appears later in the program, the first pass of the compiler has not as yet placed 60 in the symbol table. (Statement line numbers are placed in the symbol table only when they appear as the first token in a statement.) Therefore, it is not possible at this time to determine the operand of the SML *branch zero* instruction at location 03 in the array of SML instructions. The compiler places 60 in location 03 of the flags array to indicate that the second pass completes this instruction.

We must keep track of the next instruction location in the SML array because there is not a one-to-one correspondence between Simple statements and SML instructions. For example, the if/goto statement of line 20 compiles into three SML instructions. Each time an instruction is produced, we must increment the *instruction counter* to the next location in the SML array. Note that the size of Simpletron's memory could present a problem for Simple programs with many statements, variables and constants. It is conceivable that the compiler will run out of memory. To test for this case, your program should contain a *data counter* to keep track of the location at which the next variable or constant will be stored in the SML array. If the value of the instruction counter is larger than the value of the data counter, the SML array is full. In this case, the compilation process should terminate, and the compiler should print an error message indicating that it ran out of memory during compilation. This serves to emphasize that, although the programmer is freed from the burdens of managing memory by the compiler, the compiler itself must carefully determine the placement of instructions and data in memory and must check for such errors as memory being exhausted during the compilation process.

A Step-by-Step View of the Compilation Process

Let us now walk through the compilation process for the Simple program in Fig. 17.27. The compiler reads the first line of the program

```
5 rem sum 1 to x
```

into memory. The first token in the statement (the line number) is determined using the String-Tokenizer class. (See Chapter 30 for a discussion of this class.) The token returned by the String-Tokenizer is converted to an integer by using static method Integer.parseInt(), so the symbol 5 can be located in the symbol table. If the symbol is not found, it is inserted in the symbol table.

We are at the beginning of the program and this is the first line, and no symbols are in the table yet. Therefore, 5 is inserted into the symbol table as type L (line number) and assigned the first location in the SML array (00). Although this line is a remark, a space in the symbol table is still allocated for the line number (in case it is referenced by a goto or an if/goto). No SML instruction is generated for a rem statement, so the instruction counter is not incremented.

```
10 input x
```

is tokenized next. The line number 10 is placed in the symbol table as type L and assigned the first location in the SML array (00 because a remark began the program, so the instruction counter is currently 00). The command input indicates that the next token is a variable (only a variable can appear in an input statement). input corresponds directly to an SML operation code; therefore, the compiler simply has to determine the location of x in the SML array. Symbol x is not found in the symbol table, so it is inserted into the symbol table as the Unicode representation of x, given type V and assigned location 99 in the SML array (data storage begins at 99 and is allocated backward). SML code can now be generated for this statement. Operation code 10 (the SML read operation code) is multiplied by 100, and the location of x (as determined in the symbol table) is added to complete the instruction. The instruction is then stored in the SML array at location 00. The instruction counter is incremented by one, because a single SML instruction was produced.

The statement

```
15 rem   check y == x
```

is tokenized next. The symbol table is searched for line number 15 (which is not found). The line number is inserted as type L and assigned the next location in the array, 01. (Remember that rem statements do not produce code, so the instruction counter is not incremented.)

The statement

```
20 if y == x goto 60
```

is tokenized next. Line number 20 is inserted in the symbol table and given type L at the next location in the SML array 01. The command if indicates that a condition is to be evaluated. The variable y is not found in the symbol table, so it is inserted and given the type V and the SML location 98. Next, SML instructions are generated to evaluate the condition. There is no direct equivalent in SML for the if/goto; it must be simulated by performing a calculation using x and y and branching according to the result. If y is equal to x, the result of subtracting x from y is zero, so the *branch zero* instruction can be used with the result of the calculation to simulate the if/goto statement. The first step requires that y be loaded (from SML location 98) into the accumulator. This produces the instruction 01 +2098. Next, x is subtracted from the accumulator. This produces the instruction 02 +3199. The value in the accumulator may be zero, positive or negative. The operator is ==, so we want to *branch zero*. First, the symbol table is searched for the branch location (60 in this case), which is not found. So, 60 is placed in the flags array at location 03, and the instruction 03 +4200 is generated. (We cannot add the branch location because we have not yet assigned a location to line 60 in the SML array.) The instruction counter is incremented to 04.

The compiler proceeds to the statement

```
25 rem    increment y
```

The line number 25 is inserted in the symbol table as type L and assigned SML location 04. The instruction counter is not incremented.

When the statement

```
30 let y = y + 1
```

is tokenized, the line number 30 is inserted in the symbol table as type L and assigned SML location 04. Command let indicates that the line is an assignment statement. First, all the symbols on the line are inserted in the symbol table (if they are not already there). The integer 1 is added to the symbol table as type C and assigned SML location 97. Next, the right side of the assignment is converted from infix to postfix notation. Then the postfix expression (y 1 +) is evaluated. Symbol y is located in the symbol table, and its corresponding memory location is pushed onto the stack. Symbol 1 is also located in the symbol table, and its corresponding memory location is pushed onto the stack. When the operator + is encountered, the postfix evaluator pops the stack into the right operand of the operator and pops the stack again into the left operand of the operator, then produces the SML instructions

```
04 +2098    (load y)
05 +3097    (add 1)
```

The result of the expression is stored in a temporary location in memory (96) with the instruction

```
06 +2196    (store temporary)
```

and the temporary location is pushed onto the stack. Now that the expression has been evaluated, the result must be stored in y (i.e., the variable on the left side of =). So, the temporary location is loaded into the accumulator and the accumulator is stored in y with the instructions

```
07 +2096    (load temporary)
08 +2198    (store y)
```

The reader should immediately notice that SML instructions appear to be redundant. We will discuss this issue shortly.

When the statement

```
35 rem   add y to total
```

is tokenized, line number 35 is inserted in the symbol table as type L and assigned location 09.

The statement

```
40 let t = t + y
```

is similar to line 30. The variable t is inserted in the symbol table as type V and assigned SML location 95. The instructions follow the same logic and format as line 30, and the instructions 09 +2095, 10 +3098, 11 +2194, 12 +2094 and 13 +2195 are generated. Note that the result of t + y is assigned to temporary location 94 before being assigned to t (95). Once again, the reader should note that the instructions in memory locations 11 and 12 appear to be redundant. Again, we will discuss this shortly.

The statement

```
45 rem   loop y
```

is a remark, so line 45 is added to the symbol table as type L and assigned SML location 14.

The statement

```
50 goto 20
```

transfers control to line 20. Line number 50 is inserted in the symbol table as type L and assigned SML location 14. The equivalent of goto in SML is the *unconditional branch* (40) instruction that transfers control to a specific SML location. The compiler searches the symbol table for line 20 and finds that it corresponds to SML location 01. The operation code (40) is multiplied by 100, and location 01 is added to it to produce the instruction 14 +4001.

The statement

```
55 rem   output result
```

is a remark, so line 55 is inserted in the symbol table as type L and assigned SML location 15.

The statement

```
60 print t
```

is an output statement. Line number 60 is inserted in the symbol table as type L and assigned SML location 15. The equivalent of print in SML is operation code 11 (*write*). The location of t is determined from the symbol table and added to the result of the operation code multiplied by 100.

The statement

```
99 end
```

is the final line of the program. Line number 99 is stored in the symbol table as type L and assigned SML location 16. The end command produces the SML instruction +4300 (43 is *halt* in SML), which is written as the final instruction in the SML memory array.

This completes the first pass of the compiler. We now consider the second pass. The flags array is searched for values other than -1. Location 03 contains 60, so the compiler knows that instruction 03 is incomplete. The compiler completes the instruction by searching the symbol table for 60, determining its location and adding the location to the incomplete instruction. In this case, the search determines that line 60 corresponds to SML location 15, so the completed instruction 03 +4215 is produced, replacing 03 +4200. The Simple program has now been compiled successfully.

To build the compiler, you will have to perform each of the following tasks:

a) Modify the Simpletron simulator program you wrote in Exercise 7.35 to take its input from a file specified by the user (see Chapter 14). The simulator should output its results to a disk file in the same format as the screen output. Convert the simulator to an object-oriented program. In particular, make each part of the hardware an object.

Arrange the instruction types into a class hierarchy using inheritance. Then execute the program polymorphically simply by telling each instruction to execute itself with an executeInstruction message.

b) Modify the infix-to-postfix evaluation algorithm of Exercise 17.12 to process multidigit integer operands and single-letter variable-name operands. [*Hint:* Class StringTokenizer can be used to locate each constant and variable in an expression, and constants can be converted from strings to integers by using Integer class method parseInt.] [*Note:* The data representation of the postfix expression must be altered to support variable names and integer constants.]

c) Modify the postfix evaluation algorithm to process multidigit integer operands and variable-name operands. Also, the algorithm should now implement the "hook" discussed earlier so that SML instructions are produced rather than directly evaluating the expression. [*Hint:* Class StringTokenizer can be used to locate each constant and variable in an expression, and constants can be converted from strings to integers by using Integer class method parseInt.] [*Note:* The data representation of the postfix expression must be altered to support variable names and integer constants.]

d) Build the compiler. Incorporate parts b) and c) for evaluating expressions in let statements. Your program should contain a method that performs the first pass of the compiler and a method that performs the second pass of the compiler. Both methods can call other methods to accomplish their tasks. Make your compiler as object oriented as possible.

17.26 (*Optimizing the Simple Compiler*) When a program is compiled and converted into SML, a set of instructions is generated. Certain combinations of instructions often repeat themselves, usually in triplets called *productions*. A production normally consists of three instructions, such as *load*, *add* and *store*. For example, Fig. 17.29 illustrates five of the SML instructions that were produced in the compilation of the program in Fig. 17.27. The first three instructions are the production that adds 1 to y. Note that instructions 06 and 07 store the accumulator value in temporary location 96, then load the value back into the accumulator so instruction 08 can store the value in location 98. Often a production is followed by a load instruction for the same location that was just stored. This code can be *optimized* by eliminating the store instruction and the subsequent load instruction that operate on the same memory location, thus enabling the Simpletron to execute the program faster. Figure 17.30 illustrates the optimized SML for the program of Fig. 17.27. Note that there are four fewer instructions in the optimized code—a memory-space savings of 25%.

1	04	+2098	*(load)*
2	05	+3097	*(add)*
3	06	+2196	*(store)*
4	07	+2096	*(load)*
5	08	+2198	*(store)*

Fig. 17.29 | Unoptimized code from the program of Fig. 19.25.

Simple program	SML location and instruction	Description
5 rem sum 1 to x	*none*	rem ignored

Fig. 17.30 | Optimized code for the program of Fig. 17.27. (Part 1 of 2.)

Simple program	SML location and instruction	Description
10 input x	00 +1099	read x into location 99
15 rem check y == x	*none*	rem ignored
20 if y == x goto 60	01 +2098	load y (98) into accumulator
	02 +3199	sub x (99) from accumulator
	03 +4211	branch to location 11 if zero
25 rem increment y	*none*	rem ignored
30 let y = y + 1	04 +2098	load y into accumulator
	05 +3097	add 1 (97) to accumulator
	06 +2198	store accumulator in y (98)
35 rem add y to total	*none*	rem ignored
40 let t = t + y	07 +2096	load t from location (96)
	08 +3098	add y (98) accumulator
	09 +2196	store accumulator in t (96)
45 rem loop y	*none*	rem ignored
50 goto 20	10 +4001	branch to location 01
55 rem output result	*none*	rem ignored
60 print t	11 +1196	output t (96) to screen
99 end	12 +4300	terminate execution

Fig. 17.30 | Optimized code for the program of Fig. 17.27. (Part 2 of 2.)

17.27 (*Modifications to the Simple Compiler*) Perform the following modifications to the Simple compiler. Some of these modifications might also require modifications to the Simpletron simulator program written in Exercise 7.35.

a) Allow the remainder operator (%) to be used in let statements. Simpletron Machine Language must be modified to include a remainder instruction.

b) Allow exponentiation in a let statement using ^ as the exponentiation operator. Simpletron Machine Language must be modified to include an exponentiation instruction.

c) Allow the compiler to recognize uppercase and lowercase letters in Simple statements (e.g., 'A' is equivalent to 'a'). No modifications to the Simpletron simulator are required.

d) Allow input statements to read values for multiple variables such as input x, y. No modifications to the Simpletron simulator are required to perform this enhancement to the Simple compiler.

e) Allow the compiler to output multiple values from a single print statement, such as print a, b, c. No modifications to the Simpletron simulator are required to perform this enhancement.

f) Add syntax-checking capabilities to the compiler so error messages are output when syntax errors are encountered in a Simple program. No modifications to the Simpletron simulator are required.

g) Allow arrays of integers. No modifications to the Simpletron simulator are required to perform this enhancement.

h) Allow subroutines specified by the Simple commands gosub and return. Command gosub passes program control to a subroutine and command return passes control back to the statement after the gosub. This is similar to a method call in Java. The same subroutine can be called from many gosub commands distributed throughout a program. No modifications to the Simpletron simulator are required.

i) Allow repetition statements of the form

```
for x = 2 to 10 step 2
    Simple statements
next
```

This for statement loops from 2 to 10 with an increment of 2. The next line marks the end of the body of the for line. No modifications to the Simpletron simulator are required.

j) Allow repetition statements of the form

```
for x = 2 to 10
    Simple statements
next
```

This for statement loops from 2 to 10 with a default increment of 1. No modifications to the Simpletron simulator are required.

k) Allow the compiler to process string input and output. This requires the Simpletron simulator to be modified to process and store string values. [*Hint:* Each Simpletron word (i.e., memory location) can be divided into two groups, each holding a two-digit integer. Each two-digit integer represents the Unicode decimal equivalent of a character. Add a machine-language instruction that will print a string beginning at a certain Simpletron memory location. The first half of the Simpletron word at that location is a count of the number of characters in the string (i.e., the length of the string). Each succeeding half-word contains one Unicode character expressed as two decimal digits. The machine-language instruction checks the length and prints the string by translating each two-digit number into its equivalent character.]

l) Allow the compiler to process floating-point values in addition to integers. The Simpletron Simulator must also be modified to process floating-point values.

17.28 (*A Simple Interpreter*) An interpreter is a program that reads a high-level language program statement, determines the operation to be performed by the statement and executes the operation immediately. The high-level language program is not converted into machine language first. Interpreters execute more slowly than compilers do, because each statement encountered in the program being interpreted must first be deciphered at execution time. If statements are contained in a loop, the statements are deciphered each time they are encountered in the loop. Early versions of the BASIC programming language were implemented as interpreters. Most Java programs are run interpretively.

Write an interpreter for the Simple language discussed in Exercise 17.24. The program should use the infix-to-postfix converter developed in Exercise 17.12 and the postfix evaluator developed in Exercise 17.13 to evaluate expressions in a let statement. The same restrictions placed on the

Simple language in Exercise 17.24 should be adhered to in this program. Test the interpreter with the Simple programs written in Exercise 17.24. Compare the results of running these programs in the interpreter with the results of compiling the Simple programs and running them in the Simpletron simulator built in Exercise 7.35.

17.29 *(Insert/Delete Anywhere in a Linked List)* Our linked list class allowed insertions and deletions at only the front and the back of the linked list. These capabilities were convenient for us when we used inheritance or composition to produce a stack class and a queue class with a minimal amount of code simply by reusing the list class. Linked lists are normally more general than those we provided. Modify the linked list class we developed in this chapter to handle insertions and deletions anywhere in the list.

17.30 *(Lists and Queues without Tail References)* Our implementation of a linked list (Fig. 17.3) used both a firstNode and a lastNode. The lastNode was useful for the insertAtBack and removeFromBack methods of the List class. The insertAtBack method corresponds to the enqueue method of the Queue class.

   Rewrite the List class so that it does not use a lastNode. Thus, any operations on the tail of a list must begin searching the list from the front. Does this affect our implementation of the Queue class (Fig. 17.13)?

17.31 *(Performance of Binary Tree Sorting and Searching)* One problem with the binary tree sort is that the order in which the data is inserted affects the shape of the tree—for the same collection of data, different orderings can yield binary trees of dramatically different shapes. The performance of the binary tree sorting and searching algorithms is sensitive to the shape of the binary tree. What shape would a binary tree have if its data were inserted in increasing order? in decreasing order? What shape should the tree have to achieve maximal searching performance?

17.32 In Section 17.7, we created a stack class from class List with inheritance (Fig. 17.10) and with composition (Fig. 17.12). In Section 17.8 we created a queue class from class List with composition (Fig. 17.13). Create a queue class by inheriting from class List. What are the differences between this class and the one we created with composition?

18

Generics

OBJECTIVES

In this chapter you will learn:

- To create generic methods that perform identical tasks on arguments of different types.

- To create a generic `Stack` class that can be used to store objects of any class or interface type.

- To understand how to overload generic methods with non-generic methods or with other generic methods.

- To understand raw types and how they help achieve backward compatibility.

- To use wildcards when precise type information about a parameter is not required in the method body.

- The relationship between generics and inheritance.

18.1 Introduction

It would be nice if we could write a single sort method that could sort the elements in an Integer array, a String array or an array of any type that supports ordering (i.e., its elements can be compared). It would also be nice if we could write a single Stack class that could be used as a Stack of integers, a Stack of floating-point numbers, a Stack of Strings or a Stack of any other type. It would be even nicer if we could detect type mismatches at compile time—known as compile-time type safety. For example, if a Stack stores only integers, attempting to push a String on to that Stack should issue a compile-time error.

This chapter discusses generics, which provide the means to create the general models mentioned above. Generic methods and generic classes enable programmers to specify, with a single method declaration, a set of related methods or, with a single class declaration, a set of related types, respectively. Generics also provide compile-time type safety that allows programmers to catch invalid types at compile time.

We might write a generic method for sorting an array of objects, then invoke the generic method with Integer arrays, Double arrays, String arrays and so on, to sort the array elements. The compiler could perform type checking to ensure that the array passed to the sorting method contains the same type elements. We might write a single generic Stack class that manipulates a stack of objects, then instantiate Stack objects for a stack of Integers, a stack of Doubles, a stack of Strings and so on. The compiler could perform type checking to ensure that the Stack stores elements of the same type.

Software Engineering Observation 18.1

Generic methods and classes are among Java's most powerful capabilities for software reuse with compile-time type safety.

This chapter presents generic method and generic class examples. It also considers the relationships between generics and other Java features, such as overloading and inheritance. Chapter 19, Collections, presents an in-depth treatment of the Java Collections Framework's generic methods and classes. A collection is a data structure that maintains references to many objects. The Java Collections Framework uses generics to allow programmers to specify the exact types of objects that a particular collection will store in a program.

18.2 Motivation for Generic Methods

Overloaded methods are often used to perform similar operations on different types of data. To motivate generic methods, let's begin with an example (Fig. 18.1) that contains three overloaded printArray methods (lines 7–14, lines 17–24 and lines 27–34). These methods print the string representations of the elements of an Integer array, a Double array and a Character array, respectively. Note that we could have used arrays of primitive types int, double and char in this example. We chose to use arrays of type Integer, Double and Character to set up our generic method example, because only reference types can be used with generic methods and classes.

```java
 1   // Fig. 18.1: OverloadedMethods.java
 2   // Using overloaded methods to print arrays of different types.
 3
 4   public class OverloadedMethods
 5   {
 6      // method printArray to print Integer array
 7      public static void printArray( Integer[] inputArray )
 8      {
 9         // display array elements
10         for ( Integer element : inputArray )
11            System.out.printf( "%s ", element );
12
13         System.out.println();
14      } // end method printArray
15
16      // method printArray to print Double array
17      public static void printArray( Double[] inputArray )
18      {
19         // display array elements
20         for ( Double element : inputArray )
21            System.out.printf( "%s ", element );
22
23         System.out.println();
24      } // end method printArray
25
26      // method printArray to print Character array
27      public static void printArray( Character[] inputArray )
28      {
29         // display array elements
30         for ( Character element : inputArray )
31            System.out.printf( "%s ", element );
32
33         System.out.println();
34      } // end method printArray
35
36      public static void main( String args[] )
37      {
38         // create arrays of Integer, Double and Character
39         Integer[] integerArray = { 1, 2, 3, 4, 5, 6 };
40         Double[] doubleArray = { 1.1, 2.2, 3.3, 4.4, 5.5, 6.6, 7.7 };
```

Fig. 18.1 | Printing array elements using overloaded methods. (Part 1 of 2.)

```
41          Character[] characterArray = { 'H', 'E', 'L', 'L', 'O' };
42
43          System.out.println( "Array integerArray contains:" );
44          printArray( integerArray ); // pass an Integer array
45          System.out.println( "\nArray doubleArray contains:" );
46          printArray( doubleArray ); // pass a Double array
47          System.out.println( "\nArray characterArray contains:" );
48          printArray( characterArray ); // pass a Character array
49       } // end main
50   } // end class OverloadedMethods
```

```
Array integerArray contains:
1 2 3 4 5 6

Array doubleArray contains:
1.1 2.2 3.3 4.4 5.5 6.6 7.7

Array characterArray contains:
H E L L O
```

Fig. 18.1 | Printing array elements using overloaded methods. (Part 2 of 2.)

The program begins by declaring and initializing three arrays—six-element Integer array integerArray (line 39), seven-element Double array doubleArray (line 40) and five-element Character array characterArray (line 41). Then, lines 43–48 output the arrays.

When the compiler encounters a method call, it always attempts to locate a method declaration that has the same method name and parameters that match the argument types in the method call. In this example, each printArray call exactly matches one of the printArray method declarations. For example, line 44 calls printArray with integer-Array as its argument. At compile time, the compiler determines argument integer-Array's type (i.e., Integer[]) and attempts to locate a method named printArray that specifies a single Integer[] parameter (lines 7–14) and sets up a call to that method. Similarly, when the compiler encounters the printArray call at line 46, it determines argument doubleArray's type (i.e., Double[]), then attempts to locate a method named printArray that specifies a single Double[] parameter (lines 17–24) and sets up a call to that method. Finally, when the compiler encounters the printArray call at line 48, it determines argument characterArray's type (i.e., Character[]), then attempts to locate a method named printArray that specifies a single Character[] parameter (lines 27–34) and sets up a call to that method.

Study each printArray method. Note that the array element type appears in two locations in each method—the method header (lines 7, 17 and 27) and the for statement header (lines 10, 20 and 30). If we were to replace the element types in each method with a generic name—by convention we'll use E to represent the "element" type—then all three methods would look like the one in Fig. 18.2. It appears that if we can replace the array element type in each of the three methods with a single generic type, then we should be able to declare one printArray method that can display the string representations of the elements of any array that contains objects. Note that the format specifier %s can be used to output any object's string representation—the object's toString method will be called implicitly. The method in Fig. 18.2 is similar to the generic printArray method declaration we discuss in Section 18.3.

```
1   public static void printArray( E[] inputArray )
2   {
3      // display array elements
4      for ( E element : inputArray )
5         System.out.printf( "%s ", element );
6
7      System.out.println();
8   } // end method printArray
```

Fig. 18.2 | `printArray` method in which actual type names are replaced by convention with the generic name E.

18.3 Generic Methods: Implementation and Compile-Time Translation

If the operations performed by several overloaded methods are identical for each argument type, the overloaded methods can be more compactly and conveniently coded using a generic method. You can write a single generic method declaration that can be called with arguments of different types. Based on the types of the arguments passed to the generic method, the compiler handles each method call appropriately.

Figure 18.3 reimplements the application of Fig. 18.1 using a generic `printArray` method (lines 7–14). Note that the `printArray` method calls in lines 24, 26 and 28 are identical to those of Fig. 18.1 (lines 44, 46 and 48) and that the outputs of the two applications are identical. This dramatically demonstrates the expressive power of generics.

```
1    // Fig. 18.3: GenericMethodTest.java
2    // Using generic methods to print arrays of different types.
3
4    public class GenericMethodTest
5    {
6       // generic method printArray
7       public static < E > void printArray( E[] inputArray )
8       {
9          // display array elements
10         for ( E element : inputArray )
11            System.out.printf( "%s ", element );
12
13         System.out.println();
14      } // end method printArray
15
16      public static void main( String args[] )
17      {
18         // create arrays of Integer, Double and Character
19         Integer[] intArray = { 1, 2, 3, 4, 5 };
20         Double[] doubleArray = { 1.1, 2.2, 3.3, 4.4, 5.5, 6.6, 7.7 };
21         Character[] charArray = { 'H', 'E', 'L', 'L', 'O' };
22
23         System.out.println( "Array integerArray contains:" );
24         printArray( integerArray ); // pass an Integer array
```

Fig. 18.3 | Printing array elements using generic method `printArray`. (Part 1 of 2.)

```
25              System.out.println( "\nArray doubleArray contains:" );
26              printArray( doubleArray ); // pass a Double array
27              System.out.println( "\nArray characterArray contains:" );
28              printArray( characterArray ); // pass a Character array
29       } // end main
30    } // end class GenericMethodTest
```

```
Array integerArray contains:
1 2 3 4 5 6

Array doubleArray contains:
1.1 2.2 3.3 4.4 5.5 6.6 7.7

Array characterArray contains:
H E L L O
```

Fig. 18.3 | Printing array elements using generic method `printArray`. (Part 2 of 2.)

Line 7 begins method `printArray`'s declaration. All generic method declarations have a **type parameter section** delimited by **angle brackets** (< and >) that precedes the method's return type (< E > in this example). Each type parameter section contains one or more **type parameters** (also called **formal type parameters**), separated by commas. A type parameter, also known as a **type variable**, is an identifier that specifies a generic type name. The type parameters can be used to declare the return type, parameter types and local variable types in a generic method declaration, and act as placeholders for the types of the arguments passed to the generic method, which are known as **actual type arguments**. A generic method's body is declared like that of any other method. Note that type parameters can represent only reference types—not primitive types (like `int`, `double` and `char`). Note, too, that the type parameter names throughout the method declaration must match those declared in the type parameter section. For example, line 10 declares `element` as type `E`, which matches the type parameter (`E`) declared in line 7. Also, a type parameter can be declared only once in the type parameter section but can appear more than once in the method's parameter list. For example, the type parameter name `E` appears twice in the following method's parameter list:

```
public static < E > void printTwoArrays( E[] array1, E[] array2 )
```

Type-parameter names need not be unique among different generic methods.

Common Programming Error 18.1

When declaring a generic method, failing to place a type parameter section before the return type of a method is a syntax error—the compiler will not understand the type parameter name when it is encountered in the method.

Method `printArray`'s type parameter section declares type parameter, `E`, as the placeholder for the array element type that `printArray` will output. Note that `E` appears in the parameter list as the array element type (line 7). The `for` statement header (line 10) also uses `E` as the element type. These are the same two locations where the overloaded `print-Array` methods of Fig. 18.1 specified `Integer`, `Double` or `Character` as the array element type. The remainder of `printArray` is identical to the versions presented in Fig. 18.1.

Good Programming Practice 18.1

It is recommended that type parameters be specified as individual capital letters. Typically, a type parameter that represents an array element's type (or other collection) is named E for "element."

As in Fig. 18.1, the program begins by declaring and initializing six-element Integer array integerArray (line 19), seven-element Double array doubleArray (line 20) and five-element Character array characterArray (line 21). Then the program outputs each array by calling printArray (lines 24, 26 and 28)—once with argument integerArray, once with argument doubleArray and once with argument characterArray.

When the compiler encounters line 24, it first determines argument integerArray's type (i.e., Integer[]) and attempts to locate a method named printArray that specifies a single Integer[] parameter. There is no such method in this example. Next, the compiler determines whether there is a generic method named printArray that specifies a single array parameter and uses a type parameter to represent the array element type. The compiler determines that printArray (lines 7–14) is a match and sets up a call to the method. The same process is repeated for the calls to method printArray at lines 26 and 28.

Common Programming Error 18.2

If the compiler cannot match a method call to a non-generic or a generic method declaration, a compilation error occurs.

Common Programming Error 18.3

If the compiler does not find a method declaration that matches a method call exactly, but does find two or more generic methods that can satisfy the method call, a compilation error occurs.

In addition to setting up the method calls, the compiler also determines whether the operations in the method body can be applied to elements of the type stored in the array argument. The only operation performed on the array elements in this example is to output the string representation of the elements. Line 11 performs an implicit toString call on every element. To work with generics, every element of the array must be an object of a class or interface type. Since all objects have a toString method, the compiler is satisfied that line 11 performs a valid operation for any object in printArray's array argument. The toString methods of classes Integer, Double and Character return the string representation of the underlying int, double or char value, respectively.

When the compiler translates generic method printArray into Java bytecodes, it removes the type parameter section and replaces the type parameters with actual types. This process is known as erasure. By default all generic types are replaced with type Object. So the compiled version of method printArray appears as shown in Fig. 18.4—there is only one copy of this code which is used for all printArray calls in the example. This is quite different from other, similar mechanisms, such as C++'s templates, in which a separate copy of the source code is generated and compiled for every type passed as an argument to the method. As we will discuss in Section 18.4, the translation and compilation of generics is a bit more involved than what we have discussed in this section.

By declaring printArray as a generic method in Fig. 18.3, we eliminated the need for the overloaded methods of Fig. 18.1, saving 20 lines of code and creating a reusable method that can output the string representations of the elements in any array that contains objects. However, this particular example could have simply declared the printArray method as shown in Fig. 18.4 using an Object array as the parameter. This would have

```
1   public static void printArray( Object[] inputArray )
2   {
3      // display array elements
4      for ( Object element : inputArray )
5         System.out.printf( "%s ", element );
6
7      System.out.println();
8   } // end method printArray
```

Fig. 18.4 | Generic method `printArray` after erasure is performed by the compiler.

yielded the same results, because any `Object` can be output as a `String`. In a generic method, the benefits become apparent when the method also uses a type parameter as the method's return type, as we demonstrate in the next section.

18.4 Additional Compile-Time Translation Issues: Methods That Use a Type Parameter as the Return Type

Let's consider a generic method example in which type parameters are used in the return type and in the parameter list (Fig. 18.5). The application uses a generic method `maximum` to determine and return the largest of its three arguments of the same type. Unfortunately, the relational operator > cannot be used with reference types. However, it is possible to compare two objects of the same class if that class implements the generic interface `Comparable< T >` (package `java.lang`). All the type-wrapper classes for primitive types implement this interface. Like generic classes, **generic interfaces** enable programmers to specify, with a single interface declaration, a set of related types. `Comparable< T >` objects have a `compareTo` method. For example, if we have two `Integer` objects, `integer1` and `integer2`, they can be compared with the expression:

```
integer1.compareTo( integer2 )
```

It is the responsibility of the programmer who declares a class that implements `Comparable< T >` to declare method `compareTo` such that it compares the contents of two objects of that class and returns the results of the comparison. The method must return 0 if the objects are equal, -1 if `object1` is less than `object2` or 1 if `object1` is greater than `object2`. For example, class `Integer`'s `compareTo` method compares the `int` values stored in two `Integer` objects. A benefit of implementing interface `Comparable< T >` is that `Comparable< T >` objects can be used with the sorting and searching methods of class `Collections` (package `java.util`). We discuss those methods in Chapter 19, Collections. In this example, we'll use method `compareTo` in method `maximum` to help determine the largest value.

Generic method `maximum` (lines 7–18) uses type parameter `T` as the return type of the method (line 7), as the type of method parameters x, y and z (line 7), and as the type of local variable max (line 9). The type parameter section specifies that `T` extends `Comparable< T >`—only objects of classes that implement interface `Comparable< T >` can be used with this method. In this case, `Comparable` is known as the **upper bound** of the type parameter. By default, `Object` is the upper bound. Note that type parameter declarations that **bound** the parameter always use keyword `extends` regardless of whether the type

```
1    // Fig. 18.5: MaximumTest.java
2    // Generic method maximum returns the largest of three objects.
3
4    public class MaximumTest
5    {
6       // determines the largest of three Comparable objects
7       public static < T extends Comparable< T > > T maximum( T x, T y, T z )
8       {
9          T max = x; // assume x is initially the largest
10
11         if ( y.compareTo( max ) > 0 )
12            max = y; // y is the largest so far
13
14         if ( z.compareTo( max ) > 0 )
15            max = z; // z is the largest
16
17         return max; // returns the largest object
18      } // end method maximum
19
20      public static void main( String args[] )
21      {
22         System.out.printf( "Maximum of %d, %d and %d is %d\n\n", 3, 4, 5,
23            maximum( 3, 4, 5 ) );
24         System.out.printf( "Maximum of %.1f, %.1f and %.1f is %.1f\n\n",
25            6.6, 8.8, 7.7, maximum( 6.6, 8.8, 7.7 ) );
26         System.out.printf( "Maximum of %s, %s and %s is %s\n", "pear",
27            "apple", "orange", maximum( "pear", "apple", "orange" ) );
28      } // end main
29   } // end class MaximumTest
```

```
Maximum of 3, 4 and 5 is 5

Maximum of 6.6, 8.8 and 7.7 is 8.8

Maximum of pear, apple and orange is pear
```

Fig. 18.5 | Generic method maximum with an upper bound on its type parameter.

parameter extends a class or implements an interface. This type parameter is more restrictive than the one specified for printArray in Fig. 18.3, which was able to output arrays containing any type of object. The restriction of using Comparable< T > objects is important, because not all objects can be compared. However, Comparable< T > objects are guaranteed to have a compareTo method.

Method maximum uses the same algorithm that we used in Section 6.4 to determine the largest of its three arguments. The method assumes that its first argument (x) is the largest and assigns it to local variable max (line 9). Next, the if statement at lines 11–12 determines whether y is greater than max. The condition invokes y's compareTo method with the expression y.compareTo(max), which returns -1, 0 or 1, to determine y's relationship to max. If the return value of the compareTo is greater than 0, then y is greater and is assigned to variable max. Similarly, the if statement at lines 14–15 determines whether z is greater than max. If so, line 15 assigns z to max. Then, line 17 returns max to the caller.

In main (lines 20–28), line 23 calls maximum with the integers 3, 4 and 5. When the compiler encounters this call, it first looks for a maximum method that takes three arguments of type int. There is no such method, so the compiler looks for a generic method that can be used and finds generic method maximum. However, recall that the arguments to a generic method must be of a reference type. So the compiler autoboxes the three int values as Integer objects and specifies that the three Integer objects will be passed to maximum. Note that class Integer (package java.lang) implements interface Comparable< Integer > such that method compareTo compares the int values in two Integer objects. Therefore, Integers are valid arguments to method maximum. When the Integer representing the maximum is returned, we attempt to output it with the %d format specifier, which outputs an int primitive type value. So maximum's return value is output as an int value.

A similar process occurs for the three double arguments passed to maximum in line 25. Each double is autoboxed as a Double object and passed to maximum. Again, this is allowed because class Double (package java.lang) implements the Comparable< Double > interface. The Double returned by maximum is output with the format specifier %.1f, which outputs a double primitive-type value. So maximum's return value is auto-unboxed and output as a double. The call to maximum in line 27 receives three Strings, which are also Comparable< String > objects. Note that we intentionally placed the largest value in a different position in each method call (lines 23, 25 and 27) to show that the generic method always finds the maximum value, regardless of its position in the argument list.

When the compiler translates generic method maximum into Java bytecodes, it uses erasure (introduced in Section 18.3) to replace the type parameters with actual types. In Fig. 18.3, all generic types were replaced with type Object. Actually, all type parameters are replaced with the upper bound of the type parameter—unless specified otherwise, Object is the default upper bound. The upper bound of a type parameter is specified in the type parameter section. To indicate the upper bound, follow the type parameter's name with the keyword extends and the class or interface name that represents the upper bound. In method maximum's type parameter section (Fig. 18.5), we specified the upper bound as type Comparable< T >. Thus, only Comparable< T > objects can be passed as arguments to maximum—anything that is not Comparable< T > will result in compilation errors. Figure 18.6 simulates the erasure of method maximum's types by showing the method's source code after the type parameter section is removed and type parameter T is

```
1   public static Comparable maximum(Comparable x, Comparable y, Comparable z)
2   {
3      Comparable max = x; // assume x is initially the largest
4
5      if ( y.compareTo( max ) > 0 )
6         max = y; // y is the largest so far
7
8      if ( z.compareTo( max ) > 0 )
9         max = z; // z is the largest
10
11     return max; // returns the largest object
12  } // end method maximum
```

Fig. 18.6 | Generic method maximum after erasure is performed by the compiler.

replaced with the upper bound, Comparable, throughout the method declaration. Note that the erasure of Comparable< T > is simply Comparable.

After erasure, the compiled version of method maximum specifies that it returns type Comparable. However, the calling method does not expect to receive a Comparable. Rather, the caller expects to receive an object of the same type that was passed to maximum as an argument—Integer, Double or String in this example. When the compiler replaces the type parameter information with the upper bound type in the method declaration, it also inserts explicit cast operations in front of each method call to ensure that the returned value is of the type expected by the caller. Thus, the call to maximum in line 23 (Fig. 18.5) is preceded by an Integer cast, as in

```
(Integer) maximum( 3, 4, 5 )
```

the call to maximum in line 25 is preceded by a Double cast, as in

```
(Double) maximum( 6.6, 8.8, 7.7 )
```

and the call to maximum in line 27 is preceded by a String cast, as in

```
(String) maximum( "pear", "apple", "orange" )
```

In each case, the type of the cast for the return value is inferred from the types of the method arguments in the particular method call, because, according to the method declaration, the return type and the argument types match.

In this example, you cannot use a method that accepts Objects, because class Object provides only an equality comparison. Also, without generics, you would be responsible for implementing the cast operation. Using generics ensures that the inserted cast will never throw a ClassCastException, assuming that generics are used throughout your code (i.e., you do not mix old code with new generics code).

18.5 Overloading Generic Methods

A generic method may be overloaded. A class can provide two or more generic methods that specify the same method name but different method parameters. For example, generic method printArray of Fig. 18.3 could be overloaded with another printArray generic method with the additional parameters lowSubscript and highSubscript to specify the portion of the array to output (see Exercise 18.4).

A generic method can also be overloaded by non-generic methods that have the same method name and number of parameters. When the compiler encounters a method call, it searches for the method declaration that most precisely matches the method name and the argument types specified in the call. For example, generic method printArray of Fig. 18.3 could be overloaded with a version that is specific to Strings, which outputs the Strings in neat, tabular format (see Exercise 18.6).

When the compiler encounters a method call, it performs a matching process to determine which method to invoke. The compiler tries to find and use a precise match in which the method names and argument types of the method call match those of a specific method declaration. If there is no such method, the compiler determines whether there is an inexact but applicable matching method.

18.6 Generic Classes

The concept of a data structure, such as a stack, can be understood independently of the element type it manipulates. Generic classes provide a means for describing the concept of a stack (or any other class) in a type-independent manner. We can then instantiate type-specific objects of the generic class. This capability provides a wonderful opportunity for software reusability.

Once you have a generic class, you can use a simple, concise notation to indicate the actual type(s) that should be used in place of the class's type parameter(s). At compilation time, the Java compiler ensures the type safety of your code and uses the erasure techniques described in Sections 18.3–18.4 to enable your client code to interact with the generic class.

One generic Stack class, for example, could be the basis for creating many Stack classes (e.g., "Stack of Double," "Stack of Integer," "Stack of Character," "Stack of Employee"). These classes are known as parameterized classes or parameterized types because they accept one or more parameters. Recall that type parameters represent only reference types, which means the Stack generic class cannot be instantiated with primitive types. However, we can instantiate a Stack that stores objects of Java's type-wrapper classes and allow Java to use autoboxing to convert the primitive values into objects. Autoboxing occurs when a value of a primitive type (e.g., int) is pushed onto a Stack that contains wrapper-class objects (e.g., Integer). Auto-unboxing occurs when an object of the wrapper class is popped off the Stack and assigned to a primitive-type variable.

Figure 18.7 presents a generic Stack class declaration. A generic class declaration looks like a non-generic class declaration, except that the class name is followed by a type parameter section (line 4). In this case, type parameter E represents the element type the Stack will manipulate. As with generic methods, the type parameter section of a generic class can have one or more type parameters separated by commas. (You will create a generic class with two type parameters in Exercise 18.6.) Type parameter E is used throughout the Stack class declaration to represent the element type. [*Note:* This example implements a Stack as an array.]

```
1   // Fig. 18.7: Stack.java
2   // Generic class Stack.
3
4   public class Stack< E >
5   {
6      private final int size; // number of elements in the stack
7      private int top; // location of the top element
8      private E[] elements; // array that stores stack elements
9
10     // no-argument constructor creates a stack of the default size
11     public Stack()
12     {
13        this( 10 ); // default stack size
14     } // end no-argument Stack constructor
15
```

Fig. 18.7 | Generic class Stack declaration. (Part 1 of 2.)

```
16      // constructor creates a stack of the specified number of elements
17      public Stack( int s )
18      {
19          size = s > 0 ? s : 10; // set size of Stack
20          top = -1; // Stack initially empty
21
22          elements = ( E[] ) new Object[ size ]; // create array
23      } // end Stack constructor
24
25      // push element onto stack; if successful, return true;
26      // otherwise, throw FullStackException
27      public void push( E pushValue )
28      {
29          if ( top == size - 1 ) // if stack is full
30              throw new FullStackException( String.format(
31                  "Stack is full, cannot push %s", pushValue ) );
32
33          elements[ ++top ] = pushValue; // place pushValue on Stack
34      } // end method push
35
36      // return the top element if not empty; else throw EmptyStackException
37      public E pop()
38      {
39          if ( top == -1 ) // if stack is empty
40              throw new EmptyStackException( "Stack is empty, cannot pop" );
41
42          return elements[ top-- ]; // remove and return top element of Stack
43      } // end method pop
44  } // end class Stack< E >
```

Fig. 18.7 | Generic class Stack declaration. (Part 2 of 2.)

Class Stack declares variable elements as an array of type E (line 8). This array will store the Stack's elements. We would like to create an array of type E to store the elements. However, the generics mechanism does not allow type parameters in array-creation expressions because the type parameter (in this case, E) is not available at runtime. To create an array with the appropriate type, line 22 in the one-argument constructor creates the array as an array of type Object and casts the reference returned by new to type E[]. Any object could be stored in an Object array, but the compiler's type-checking mechanism ensures that only objects of the array variable's declared type can be assigned to the array via any array-access expression that uses variable elements. Yet when this class is compiled using the -Xlint:unchecked option, e.g.,

    javac -Xlint:unchecked Stack.java

the compiler issues the following warning message about line 22:

```
Stack.java:22: warning: [unchecked] unchecked cast
found    : java.lang.Object[]
required: E[]
        elements = ( E[] ) new Object[ size ]; // create array
```

The reason for this message is that the compiler cannot ensure with 100% certainty that an array of type Object will never contain objects of types other than E. Assume that E represents type Integer, so that array elements should store Integer objects. It is possible to assign variable elements to a variable of type Object[], as in

```
Object[] objectArray = elements;
```

Then any object can be placed into the array with an assignment statement like

```
objectArray[ 0 ] = "hello";
```

This places a String in an array that should contain only Integers, which would lead to runtime problems when manipulating the Stack. As long as you do not perform statements like those shown here, your Stack will contain objects of only the correct element type.

Method push (lines 27–34) first determines whether an attempt is being made to push an element onto a full Stack. If so, lines 30–31 throw a FullStackException. Class FullStackException is declared in Fig. 18.8. If the Stack is not full, line 33 increments the top counter and places the argument in that location of array elements.

Method pop (lines 37–43) first determines whether an attempt is being made to pop an element from an empty Stack. If so, line 40 throws an EmptyStackException. Class EmptyStackException is declared in Fig. 18.9. Otherwise, line 42 returns the top element of the Stack, then postdecrements the top counter to indicate the position of the next top element.

Classes FullStackException (Fig. 18.8) and EmptyStackException (Fig. 18.9) each provide the conventional no-argument constructor and one-argument constructor of exception classes (as discussed in Section 13.11). The no-argument constructor sets the default error message, and the one-argument constructor sets a custom exception message.

As with generic methods, when a generic class is compiled, the compiler performs erasure on the class's type parameters and replaces them with their upper bounds. For class Stack (Fig. 18.7), no upper bound is specified, so the default upper bound, Object, is used. The scope of a generic class's type parameter is the entire class. However, type parameters cannot be used in a class's static declarations.

```
1   // Fig. 18.8: FullStackException.java
2   // Indicates a stack is full.
3   public class FullStackException extends RuntimeException
4   {
5      // no-argument constructor
6      public FullStackException()
7      {
8         this( "Stack is full" );
9      } // end no-argument FullStackException constructor
10
11     // one-argument constructor
12     public FullStackException( String exception )
13     {
14        super( exception );
15     } // end one-argument FullStackException constructor
16  } // end class FullStackException
```

Fig. 18.8 | FullStackException class declaration.

```
1   // Fig. 18.9: EmptyStackException.java
2   // Indicates a stack is full.
3   public class EmptyStackException extends RuntimeException
4   {
5      // no-argument constructor
6      public EmptyStackException()
7      {
8         this( "Stack is empty" );
9      } // end no-argument EmptyStackException constructor
10
11     // one-argument constructor
12     public EmptyStackException( String exception )
13     {
14        super( exception );
15     } // end one-argument EmptyStackException constructor
16  } // end class EmptyStackException
```

Fig. 18.9 | EmptyStackException class declaration.

Now, let's consider the test application (Fig. 18.10) that uses the Stack generic class. Lines 9–10 declare variables of type Stack< Double > (pronounced "Stack of Double") and Stack< Integer > (pronounced "Stack of Integer"). The types Double and Integer are known as the Stack's **type arguments**. They are used by the compiler to replace the type parameters so that the compiler can perform type checking and insert cast operations as necessary. We'll discuss the cast operations in more detail shortly. Method testStack (called from main) instantiates objects doubleStack of size 5 (line 15) and integerStack of size 10 (line 16), then calls methods testPushDouble (lines 25–44), testPopDouble (lines 47–67), testPushInteger (lines 70–89) and testPopInteger (lines 92–112) to demonstrate the two Stacks in this example.

Method testPushDouble (lines 25–44) invokes method push to place the double values 1.1, 2.2, 3.3, 4.4 and 5.5 stored in array doubleElements onto doubleStack. The for loop terminates when the test program attempts to push a sixth value onto doubleStack (which is full, because doubleStack can store only five elements). In this case,

```
1   // Fig. 18.10: StackTest.java
2   // Stack generic class test program.
3
4   public class StackTest
5   {
6      private double[] doubleElements = { 1.1, 2.2, 3.3, 4.4, 5.5, 6.6 };
7      private int[] integerElements = { 1, 2, 3, 4, 5, 6, 7, 8, 9, 10, 11 };
8
9      private Stack< Double > doubleStack; // stack stores Double objects
10     private Stack< Integer > integerStack; // stack stores Integer objects
11
12     // test Stack objects
13     public void testStacks()
14     {
15        doubleStack = new Stack< Double >( 5 ); // Stack of Doubles
```

Fig. 18.10 | Generic class Stack test program. (Part 1 of 4.)

```java
16        integerStack = new Stack< Integer >( 10 ); // Stack of Integers
17
18        testPushDouble(); // push double onto doubleStack
19        testPopDouble(); // pop from doubleStack
20        testPushInteger(); // push int onto intStack
21        testPopInteger(); // pop from intStack
22     } // end method testStacks
23
24     // test push method with double stack
25     public void testPushDouble()
26     {
27        // push elements onto stack
28        try
29        {
30           System.out.println( "\nPushing elements onto doubleStack" );
31
32           // push elements to Stack
33           for ( double element : doubleElements )
34           {
35              System.out.printf( "%.1f ", element );
36              doubleStack.push( element ); // push onto doubleStack
37           } // end for
38        } // end try
39        catch ( FullStackException fullStackException )
40        {
41           System.err.println();
42           fullStackException.printStackTrace();
43        } // end catch FullStackException
44     } // end method testPushDouble
45
46     // test pop method with double stack
47     public void testPopDouble()
48     {
49        // pop elements from stack
50        try
51        {
52           System.out.println( "\nPopping elements from doubleStack" );
53           double popValue; // store element removed from stack
54
55           // remove all elements from Stack
56           while ( true )
57           {
58              popValue = doubleStack.pop(); // pop from doubleStack
59              System.out.printf( "%.1f ", popValue );
60           } // end while
61        } // end try
62        catch( EmptyStackException emptyStackException )
63        {
64           System.err.println();
65           emptyStackException.printStackTrace();
66        } // end catch EmptyStackException
67     } // end method testPopDouble
```

Fig. 18.10 | Generic class Stack test program. (Part 2 of 4.)

```
68
69      // test push method with integer stack
70      public void testPushInteger()
71      {
72         // push elements to stack
73         try
74         {
75            System.out.println( "\nPushing elements onto intStack" );
76
77            // push elements to Stack
78            for ( int element : integerElements )
79            {
80               System.out.printf( "%d ", element );
81               integerStack.push( element ); // push onto integerStack
82            } // end for
83         } // end try
84         catch ( FullStackException fullStackException )
85         {
86            System.err.println();
87            fullStackException.printStackTrace();
88         } // end catch FullStackException
89      } // end method testPushInteger
90
91      // test pop method with integer stack
92      public void testPopInteger()
93      {
94         // pop elements from stack
95         try
96         {
97            System.out.println( "\nPopping elements from intStack" );
98            int popValue; // store element removed from stack
99
100           // remove all elements from Stack
101           while ( true )
102           {
103              popValue = integerStack.pop(); // pop from intStack
104              System.out.printf( "%d ", popValue );
105           } // end while
106        } // end try
107        catch( EmptyStackException emptyStackException )
108        {
109           System.err.println();
110           emptyStackException.printStackTrace();
111        } // end catch EmptyStackException
112     } // end method testPopInteger
113
114     public static void main( String args[] )
115     {
116        StackTest application = new StackTest();
117        application.testStacks();
118     } // end main
119  } // end class StackTest
```

Fig. 18.10 | Generic class **Stack** test program. (Part 3 of 4.)

```
Pushing elements onto doubleStack
1.1 2.2 3.3 4.4 5.5 6.6
FullStackException: Stack is full, cannot push 6.6
        at Stack.push(Stack.java:30)
        at StackTest.testPushDouble(StackTest.java:36)
        at StackTest.testStacks(StackTest.java:18)
        at StackTest.main(StackTest.java:117)

Popping elements from doubleStack
5.5 4.4 3.3 2.2 1.1
EmptyStackException: Stack is empty, cannot pop
        at Stack.pop(Stack.java:40)
        at StackTest.testPopDouble(StackTest.java:58)
        at StackTest.testStacks(StackTest.java:19)
        at StackTest.main(StackTest.java:117)

Pushing elements onto integerStack
1 2 3 4 5 6 7 8 9 10 11
FullStackException: Stack is full, cannot push 11
        at Stack.push(Stack.java:30)
        at StackTest.testPushInteger(StackTest.java:81)
        at StackTest.testStacks(StackTest.java:20)
        at StackTest.main(StackTest.java:117)

Popping elements from integerStack
10 9 8 7 6 5 4 3 2 1
EmptyStackException: Stack is empty, cannot pop
        at Stack.pop(Stack.java:40)
        at StackTest.testPopInteger(StackTest.java:103)
        at StackTest.testStacks(StackTest.java:21)
        at StackTest.main(StackTest.java:117)
```

Fig. 18.10 | Generic class Stack test program. (Part 4 of 4.)

the method throws a FullStackException (Fig. 18.8) to indicate that the Stack is full. Lines 39–43 catch this exception and print the stack trace information. The stack trace indicates the exception that occurred and shows that Stack method push generated the exception at lines 30–31 of the file Stack.java (Fig. 18.7). The trace also shows that method push was called by StackTest method testPushDouble at line 36 of Stack-Test.java, that method testPushDouble was called from method testStacks at line 18 of StackTest.java and that method testStacks was called from method main at line 117 of StackTest.java. This information enables you to determine the methods that were on the method-call stack at the time that the exception occurred. Because the program catches the exception, the Java runtime environment considers the exception to have been handled and the program can continue executing. Note that autoboxing occurs in line 36 when the program tries to push a primitive double value onto the doubleStack, which stores only Double objects.

Method testPopDouble (lines 47–67) invokes Stack method pop in an infinite while loop to remove all the values from the stack. Note in the output that the values indeed pop off in last-in, first-out order (this, of course, is the defining characteristic of stacks). The while loop (lines 57–61) continues until the stack is empty (i.e., until an Empty-StackException occurs), which causes the program to proceed to the catch block (lines

62–66) and handle the exception, so the program can continue executing. When the test program attempts to pop a sixth value, the doubleStack is empty, so the pop throws an EmptyStackException. Auto-unboxing occurs in line 58 when the program assigns the Double object popped from the stack to a double primitive variable. Recall from Section 18.4 that the compiler inserts cast operations to ensure that the proper types are returned from generic methods. After erasure, Stack method pop returns type Object. However, the client code in method testPopDouble expects to receive a double when method pop returns. So the compiler inserts a Double cast, as in

```
popValue = ( Double ) doubleStack.pop();
```

to ensure that a reference of the appropriate type is returned, auto-unboxed and assigned to popValue.

Method testPushInteger (lines 70–89) invokes Stack method push to place values onto integerStack until it is full. Method testPopInteger (lines 92–112) invokes Stack method pop to remove values from integerStack until it is empty. Once again, note that the values pop off in last-in, first-out order. During the erasure process, the compiler recognizes that the client code in method testPopInteger expects to receive an int when method pop returns. So the compiler inserts an Integer cast, as in

```
popValue = ( Integer ) integerStack.pop();
```

to ensure that a reference of the appropriate type is returned, auto-unboxed and assigned to popValue.

Creating Generic Methods to Test Class Stack< E >

Note that the code in methods testPushDouble and testPushInteger is almost identical for pushing values onto a Stack< Double > or a Stack< Integer >, respectively, and the code in methods testPopDouble and testPopInteger is almost identical for popping values from a Stack< Double > or a Stack< Integer >, respectively. This presents another opportunity to use generic methods. Figure 18.11 declares generic method testPush (lines 26–46) to perform the same tasks as testPushDouble and testPushInteger in Fig. 18.10—that is, push values onto a Stack< T >. Similarly, generic method testPop (lines 49–69) performs the same tasks as testPopDouble and testPopInteger in Fig. 18.10—that is, pop values off a Stack< T >. Note that the output of Fig. 18.11 precisely matches the output of Fig. 18.10.

```
1   // Fig. 18.11: StackTest2.java
2   // Stack generic class test program.
3
4   public class StackTest2
5   {
6      private Double[] doubleElements = { 1.1, 2.2, 3.3, 4.4, 5.5, 6.6 };
7      private Integer[] integerElements =
8         { 1, 2, 3, 4, 5, 6, 7, 8, 9, 10, 11 };
9
10     private Stack< Double > doubleStack; // stack stores Double objects
11     private Stack< Integer > integerStack; // stack stores Integer objects
```

Fig. 18.11 | Passing a generic type Stack to a generic method. (Part 1 of 3.)

```
12
13      // test Stack objects
14      public void testStacks()
15      {
16         doubleStack = new Stack< Double >( 5 ); // Stack of Doubles
17         integerStack = new Stack< Integer >( 10 ); // Stack of Integers
18
19         testPush( "doubleStack", doubleStack, doubleElements );
20         testPop( "doubleStack", doubleStack );
21         testPush( "integerStack", integerStack, integerElements );
22         testPop( "integerStack", integerStack );
23      } // end method testStacks
24
25      // generic method testPush pushes elements onto a Stack
26      public < T > void testPush( String name, Stack< T > stack,
27         T[] elements )
28      {
29         // push elements onto stack
30         try
31         {
32            System.out.printf( "\nPushing elements onto %s\n", name );
33
34            // push elements onto Stack
35            for ( T element : elements )
36            {
37               System.out.printf( "%s ", element );
38               stack.push( element ); // push element onto stack
39            }
40         } // end try
41         catch ( FullStackException fullStackException )
42         {
43            System.out.println();
44            fullStackException.printStackTrace();
45         } // end catch FullStackException
46      } // end method testPush
47
48      // generic method testPop pops elements from a Stack
49      public < T > void testPop( String name, Stack< T > stack )
50      {
51         // pop elements from stack
52         try
53         {
54            System.out.printf( "\nPopping elements from %s\n", name );
55            T popValue; // store element removed from stack
56
57            // remove elements from Stack
58            while ( true )
59            {
60               popValue = stack.pop(); // pop from stack
61               System.out.printf( "%s ", popValue );
62            } // end while
63         } // end try
```

Fig. 18.11 | Passing a generic type **Stack** to a generic method. (Part 2 of 3.)

```
64              catch( EmptyStackException emptyStackException )
65              {
66                  System.out.println();
67                  emptyStackException.printStackTrace();
68              } // end catch EmptyStackException
69          } // end method testPop
70
71      public static void main( String args[] )
72      {
73          StackTest2 application = new StackTest2();
74          application.testStacks();
75      } // end main
76  } // end class StackTest2
```

```
Pushing elements onto doubleStack
1.1 2.2 3.3 4.4 5.5 6.6
FullStackException: Stack is full, cannot push 6.6
        at Stack.push(Stack.java:30)
        at StackTest2.testPush(StackTest2.java:38)
        at StackTest2.testStacks(StackTest2.java:19)
        at StackTest2.main(StackTest2.java:74)

Popping elements from doubleStack
5.5 4.4 3.3 2.2 1.1
EmptyStackException: Stack is empty, cannot pop
        at Stack.pop(Stack.java:40)
        at StackTest2.testPop(StackTest2.java:60)
        at StackTest2.testStacks(StackTest2.java:20)
        at StackTest2.main(StackTest2.java:74)

Pushing elements onto integerStack
1 2 3 4 5 6 7 8 9 10 11
FullStackException: Stack is full, cannot push 11
        at Stack.push(Stack.java:30)
        at StackTest2.testPush(StackTest2.java:38)
        at StackTest2.testStacks(StackTest2.java:21)
        at StackTest2.main(StackTest2.java:74)

Popping elements from integerStack
10 9 8 7 6 5 4 3 2 1
EmptyStackException: Stack is empty, cannot pop
        at Stack.pop(Stack.java:40)
        at StackTest2.testPop(StackTest2.java:60)
        at StackTest2.testStacks(StackTest2.java:22)
        at StackTest2.main(StackTest2.java:74)
```

Fig. 18.11 | Passing a generic type Stack to a generic method. (Part 3 of 3.)

The testStacks method (lines 14–23) creates the Stack< Double > (line 16) and Stack< Integer > (line 17) objects. Lines 19–22 invoke generic methods testPush and testPop to test the Stack objects. Recall that type parameters can represent only reference types. Therefore, to be able to pass arrays doubleElements and integerElements to generic method testPush, the arrays declared in lines 6–8 must be declared with the wrapper types Double and Integer. When these arrays are initialized with primitive values, the compiler autoboxes each primitive value.

Generic method `testPush` (lines 26–46) uses type parameter T (specified at line 26) to represent the data type stored in the Stack< T >. The generic method takes three arguments—a `String` that represents the name of the Stack< T > object for output purposes, a reference to an object of type Stack< T > and an array of type T—the type of elements that will be pushed onto Stack< T >. Note that the compiler enforces consistency between the type of the Stack and the elements that will be pushed onto the Stack when push is invoked, which is the real value of the generic method call. Generic method `testPop` (lines 49–69) takes two arguments—a `String` that represents the name of the Stack< T > object for output purposes and a reference to an object of type Stack< T >.

18.7 Raw Types

The test programs for generic class `Stack` in Section 18.6 instantiate Stacks with type arguments `Double` and `Integer`. It is also possible to instantiate generic class `Stack` without specifying a type argument, as follows:

```
Stack objectStack = new Stack( 5 ); // no type argument specified
```

In this case, the `objectStack` is said to have a **raw type**, which means that the compiler implicitly uses type `Object` throughout the generic class for each type argument. Thus the preceding statement creates a `Stack` that can store objects of any type. This is important for backward compatibility with prior versions of Java. For example, the data structures of the Java Collections Framework (see Chapter 19, Collections) all stored references to `Objects`, but are now implemented as generic types.

A raw type `Stack` variable can be assigned a `Stack` that specifies a type argument, such as a Stack< Double > object, as follows:

```
Stack rawTypeStack2 = new Stack< Double >( 5 );
```

because type `Double` is a subclass of `Object`. This assignment is allowed because the elements in a Stack< Double > (i.e., `Double` objects) are certainly objects—class `Double` is an indirect subclass of `Object`.

Similarly, a `Stack` variable that specifies a type argument in its declaration can be assigned a raw type `Stack` object, as in:

```
Stack< Integer > integerStack = new Stack( 10 );
```

Although this assignment is permitted, it is unsafe because a `Stack` of raw type might store types other than `Integer`. In this case, the compiler issues a warning message which indicates the unsafe assignment.

The test program of Fig. 18.12 uses the notion of raw type. Line 14 instantiates generic class `Stack` with raw type, which indicates that `rawTypeStack1` can hold objects of any type. Line 17 assigns a Stack< Double > to variable `rawTypeStack2`, which is declared as a `Stack` of raw type. Line 20 assigns a `Stack` of raw type to Stack< Integer > variable, which is legal but causes the compiler to issue a warning message (Fig. 18.13) indicating a potentially unsafe assignment—again, this occurs because a `Stack` of raw type might store types other than `Integer`. Also, each of the calls to generic method `testPush` and `testPop` in lines 22–25 results in a compiler warning message (Fig. 18.13). These warnings occur because variables `rawTypeStack1` and `rawTypeStack2` are declared as Stacks of

raw type, but methods `testPush` and `testPop` each expect a second argument that is a
`Stack` with a specific type argument. The warnings indicate that the compiler cannot guarantee that the types manipulated by the stacks are the correct types, because we did not
supply a variable declared with a type argument. Methods `testPush` (lines 31–51) and
`testPop` (lines 54–74) are the same as in Fig. 18.11.

```
 1   // Fig. 18.12: RawTypeTest.java
 2   // Raw type test program.
 3
 4   public class RawTypeTest
 5   {
 6      private Double[] doubleElements = { 1.1, 2.2, 3.3, 4.4, 5.5, 6.6 };
 7      private Integer[] integerElements =
 8         { 1, 2, 3, 4, 5, 6, 7, 8, 9, 10, 11 };
 9
10      // method to test Stacks with raw types
11      public void testStacks()
12      {
13         // Stack of raw types assigned to Stack of raw types variable
14         Stack rawTypeStack1 = new Stack( 5 );
15
16         // Stack< Double > assigned to Stack of raw types variable
17         Stack rawTypeStack2 = new Stack< Double >( 5 );
18
19         // Stack of raw types assigned to Stack< Integer > variable
20         Stack< Integer > integerStack = new Stack( 10 );
21
22         testPush( "rawTypeStack1", rawTypeStack1, doubleElements );
23         testPop( "rawTypeStack1", rawTypeStack1 );
24         testPush( "rawTypeStack2", rawTypeStack2, doubleElements );
25         testPop( "rawTypeStack2", rawTypeStack2 );
26         testPush( "integerStack", integerStack, integerElements );
27         testPop( "integerStack", integerStack );
28      } // end method testStacks
29
30      // generic method pushes elements onto stack
31      public < T > void testPush( String name, Stack< T > stack,
32         T[] elements )
33      {
34         // push elements onto stack
35         try
36         {
37            System.out.printf( "\nPushing elements onto %s\n", name );
38
39            // push elements onto Stack
40            for ( T element : elements )
41            {
42               System.out.printf( "%s ", element );
43               stack.push( element ); // push element onto stack
44            } // end for
45         } // end try
```

Fig. 18.12 | Raw type test program. (Part 1 of 3.)

```
46              catch ( FullStackException fullStackException )
47              {
48                  System.out.println();
49                  fullStackException.printStackTrace();
50              } // end catch FullStackException
51          } // end method testPush
52
53          // generic method testPop pops elements from stack
54          public < T > void testPop( String name, Stack< T > stack )
55          {
56              // pop elements from stack
57              try
58              {
59                  System.out.printf( "\nPopping elements from %s\n", name );
60                  T popValue; // store element removed from stack
61
62                  // remove elements from Stack
63                  while ( true )
64                  {
65                      popValue = stack.pop(); // pop from stack
66                      System.out.printf( "%s ", popValue );
67                  } // end while
68              } // end try
69              catch( EmptyStackException emptyStackException )
70              {
71                  System.out.println();
72                  emptyStackException.printStackTrace();
73              } // end catch EmptyStackException
74          } // end method testPop
75
76          public static void main( String args[] )
77          {
78              RawTypeTest application = new RawTypeTest();
79              application.testStacks();
80          } // end main
81      } // end class RawTypeTest
```

```
Pushing elements onto rawTypeStack1
1.1 2.2 3.3 4.4 5.5 6.6
FullStackException: Stack is full, cannot push 6.6
        at Stack.push(Stack.java:30)
        at RawTypeTest.testPush(RawTypeTest.java:43)
        at RawTypeTest.testStacks(RawTypeTest.java:22)
        at RawTypeTest.main(RawTypeTest.java:79)

Popping elements from rawTypeStack1
5.5 4.4 3.3 2.2 1.1
EmptyStackException: Stack is empty, cannot pop
        at Stack.pop(Stack.java:40)
        at RawTypeTest.testPop(RawTypeTest.java:65)
        at RawTypeTest.testStacks(RawTypeTest.java:23)
        at RawTypeTest.main(RawTypeTest.java:79)
```

Fig. 18.12 | Raw type test program. (Part 2 of 3.)

```
Pushing elements onto rawTypeStack2
1.1 2.2 3.3 4.4 5.5 6.6
FullStackException: Stack is full, cannot push 6.6
        at Stack.push(Stack.java:30)
        at RawTypeTest.testPush(RawTypeTest.java:43)
        at RawTypeTest.testStacks(RawTypeTest.java:24)
        at RawTypeTest.main(RawTypeTest.java:79)

Popping elements from rawTypeStack2
5.5 4.4 3.3 2.2 1.1
EmptyStackException: Stack is empty, cannot pop
        at Stack.pop(Stack.java:40)
        at RawTypeTest.testPop(RawTypeTest.java:65)
        at RawTypeTest.testStacks(RawTypeTest.java:25)
        at RawTypeTest.main(RawTypeTest.java:79)

Pushing elements onto integerStack
1 2 3 4 5 6 7 8 9 10 11
FullStackException: Stack is full, cannot push 11
        at Stack.push(Stack.java:30)
        at RawTypeTest.testPush(RawTypeTest.java:43)
        at RawTypeTest.testStacks(RawTypeTest.java:26)
        at RawTypeTest.main(RawTypeTest.java:79)

Popping elements from integerStack
10 9 8 7 6 5 4 3 2 1
EmptyStackException: Stack is empty, cannot pop
        at Stack.pop(Stack.java:40)
        at RawTypeTest.testPop(RawTypeTest.java:65)
        at RawTypeTest.testStacks(RawTypeTest.java:27)
        at RawTypeTest.main(RawTypeTest.java:79)
```

Fig. 18.12 | Raw type test program. (Part 3 of 3.)

Figure 18.13 shows the warning messages generated by the compiler (compiled with the -Xlint:unchecked option) when the file RawTypeTest.java (Fig. 18.12) is compiled. The first warning is generated for line 20, which assigned a raw type Stack to a Stack< Integer > variable—the compiler cannot ensure that all objects in the Stack will be Integer objects. The second warning is generated for line 22. Because the second method argument is a raw type Stack variable, the compiler determines the type argument for method testPush from the Double array passed as the third argument. In this case, Double is the type argument, so the compiler expects a Stack< Double > to be passed as the second argument. The warning occurs because the compiler cannot ensure that a raw type Stack contains only Double objects. The warning at line 24 occurs for the same reason, even though the actual Stack that rawTypeStack2 references is a Stack< Double >. The compiler cannot guarantee that the variable will always refer to the same Stack object, so it must use the variable's declared type to perform all type checking. Lines 23 and 25 each generate warnings because method testPop expects as an argument a Stack for which a type argument has been specified. However, in each call to testPop, we pass a raw type Stack variable. Thus, the compiler indicates a warning because it cannot check the types used in the body of the method.

```
RawTypeTest.java:20: warning: unchecked assignment
found    : Stack
required: Stack<java.lang.Integer>
     Stack< Integer > integerStack = new Stack( 10 );
                                     ^
RawTypeTest.java:22: warning: [unchecked] unchecked method invocation:
<T>testPush(java.lang.String,Stack<T>,T[]) in RawTypeTest is applied to
(java.lang.String,Stack,java.lang.Double[])
     testPush( "rawTypeStack1", rawTypeStack1, doubleElements );
     ^
RawTypeTest.java:23: warning: [unchecked] unchecked method invocation:
<T>testPop(java.lang.String,Stack<T>) in RawTypeTest is applied to
(java.lang.String,Stack)
     testPop( "rawTypeStack1", rawTypeStack1 );
     ^
RawTypeTest.java:24: warning: [unchecked] unchecked method invocation:
<T>testPush(java.lang.String,Stack<T>,T[]) in RawTypeTest is applied to
(java.lang.String,Stack,java.lang.Double[])
     testPush( "rawTypeStack2", rawTypeStack2, doubleElements );
     ^
RawTypeTest.java:25: warning: [unchecked] unchecked method invocation:
<T>testPop(java.lang.String,Stack<T>) in RawTypeTest is applied to
(java.lang.String,Stack)
     testPop( "rawTypeStack2", rawTypeStack2 );
     ^
5 warnings
```

Fig. 18.13 | Warning messages from the compiler.

18.8 Wildcards in Methods That Accept Type Parameters

In this section, we introduce a powerful generics concept known as wildcards. For this purpose, we will also introduce a new data structure from package java.util. Chapter 19, Collections, discusses the Java Collections Framework, which provides many generic data structures and algorithms that manipulate the elements of those data structures. Perhaps the simplest of these data structures is class ArrayList—a dynamically resizable, array-like data structure. As part of this discussion, you will learn how to create an ArrayList, add elements to it and traverse those elements using an enhanced for statement.

Before we introduce wildcards, let's consider an example that helps us motivate their use. Suppose that you would like to implement a generic method sum that totals the numbers in a collection, such as an ArrayList. You would begin by inserting the numbers in the collection. As you know, generic classes can be used only with class or interface types. So the numbers would be autoboxed as objects of the type-wrapper classes. For example, any int value would be autoboxed as an Integer object, and any double value would be autoboxed as a Double object. We'd like to be able to total all the numbers in the Array-List regardless of their type. For this reason, we'll declare the ArrayList with the type argument Number, which is the superclass of both Integer and Double. In addition, method sum will receive a parameter of type ArrayList< Number > and total its elements. Figure 18.14 demonstrates totaling the elements of an ArrayList of Numbers.

```
 1   // Fig. 18.14: TotalNumbers.java
 2   // Summing the elements of an ArrayList.
 3   import java.util.ArrayList;
 4
 5   public class TotalNumbers
 6   {
 7      public static void main( String args[] )
 8      {
 9         // create, initialize and output ArrayList of Numbers containing
10         // both Integers and Doubles, then display total of the elements
11         Number[] numbers = { 1, 2.4, 3, 4.1 }; // Integers and Doubles
12         ArrayList< Number > numberList = new ArrayList< Number >();
13
14         for ( Number element : numbers )
15            numberList.add( element ); // place each number in numberList
16
17         System.out.printf( "numberList contains: %s\n", numberList );
18         System.out.printf( "Total of the elements in numberList: %.1f\n",
19            sum( numberList ) );
20      } // end main
21
22      // calculate total of ArrayList elements
23      public static double sum( ArrayList< Number > list )
24      {
25         double total = 0; // initialize total
26
27         // calculate sum
28         for ( Number element : list )
29            total += element.doubleValue();
30
31         return total;
32      } // end method sum
33   } // end class TotalNumbers
```

```
numberList contains: [1, 2.4, 3, 4.1]
Total of the elements in numberList: 10.5
```

Fig. 18.14 | Totaling the numbers in an ArrayList< Number >.

Line 11 declares and initializes an array of Numbers. Because the initializers are primitive values, Java autoboxes each primitive value as an object of its corresponding wrapper type. The int values 1 and 3 are autoboxed as Integer objects, and the double values 2.4 and 4.1 are autoboxed as Double objects. Line 12 declares and creates an ArrayList object that stores Numbers and assigns it to variable numberList. Note that we do not have to specify the size of the ArrayList because it will grow automatically as we insert objects.

Lines 14–15 traverse array numbers and place each element in numberList. Method add of class ArrayList appends an element to the end of the collection. Line 17 outputs the contents of the ArrayList as a String. This statement implicitly invokes the Array-List's toString method, which returns a string of the form "[*elements*]" in which *elements* is a comma-separated list of the elements' string representations. Lines 18–19 display the sum of the elements that is returned by the call to method sum at line 19.

Method sum (lines 23–32) receives an ArrayList of Numbers and calculates the total of the Numbers in the collection. The method uses double values to perform the calculations and returns the result as a double. Line 25 declares local variable total and initializes it to 0. Lines 28–29 use the enhanced for statement, which is designed to work with both arrays and the collections of the Collections Framework, to total the elements of the ArrayList. The for statement assigns each Number in the ArrayList to variable element, then uses method doubleValue of class Number to obtain the Number's underlying primitive value as a double value. The result is added to total. When the loop terminates, the method returns the total.

Implementing Method **sum** *With a Wildcard Type Argument in Its Parameter*

Recall that the purpose of method sum in Fig. 18.14 was to total any type of Numbers stored in an ArrayList. We created an ArrayList of Numbers that contained both Integer and Double objects. The output of Fig. 18.14 demonstrates that method sum worked properly. Given that method sum can total the elements of an ArrayList of Numbers, you might expect that the method would also work for ArrayLists that contain elements of only one numeric type, such as ArrayList< Integer >. So we modified class TotalNumbers to create an ArrayList of Integers and pass it to method sum. When we compile the program, the compiler issues the following error message:

```
sum(java.util.ArrayList<java.lang.Number>) in TotalNumbersErrors
cannot be applied to (java.util.ArrayList<java.lang.Integer>)
```

Although Number is the superclass of Integer, the compiler does not consider the parameterized type ArrayList< Number > to be a supertype of ArrayList< Integer >. If it were, then every operation we could perform on ArrayList< Number > would also work on an ArrayList< Integer >. Consider the fact that you can add a Double object to an ArrayList< Number > because a Double *is a* Number, but you cannot add a Double object to an ArrayList< Integer > because a Double *is not* an Integer. Thus, the subtype relationship does not hold.

How do we create a more flexible version of method sum that can total the elements of any ArrayList that contains elements of any subclass of Number? This is where wildcard type arguments are important. Wildcards enable you to specify method parameters, return values, variables or fields, etc. that act as supertypes of parameterized types. In Fig. 18.15, method sum's parameter is declared in line 50 with the type:

```
ArrayList< ? extends Number >
```

A wildcard type argument is denoted by a question mark (?), which by itself represents an "unknown type." In this case, the wildcard extends class Number, which means that the wildcard has an upper bound of Number. Thus, the unknown type argument must be either Number or a subclass of Number. With the parameter type shown here, method sum can receive an ArrayList argument that contains any type of Number, such as ArrayList< Integer > (line 20), ArrayList< Double > (line 33) or ArrayList< Number > (line 46).

Lines 11–20 create and initialize an ArrayList< Integer > called integerList, output its elements and total its elements by calling method sum (line 20). Lines 24–33 perform the same operations for an ArrayList< Double > called doubleList. Lines 37–46 perform the same operations for an ArrayList< Number > called numberList that contains both Integers and Doubles.

```
1    // Fig. 18.15: WildcardTest.java
2    // Wildcard test program.
3    import java.util.ArrayList;
4
5    public class WildcardTest
6    {
7       public static void main( String args[] )
8       {
9          // create, initialize and output ArrayList of Integers, then
10         // display total of the elements
11         Integer[] integers = { 1, 2, 3, 4, 5 };
12         ArrayList< Integer > integerList = new ArrayList< Integer >();
13
14         // insert elements in integerList
15         for ( Integer element : integers )
16            integerList.add( element );
17
18         System.out.printf( "integerList contains: %s\n", integerList );
19         System.out.printf( "Total of the elements in integerList: %.0f\n\n",
20            sum( integerList ) );
21
22         // create, initialize and output ArrayList of Doubles, then
23         // display total of the elements
24         Double[] doubles = { 1.1, 3.3, 5.5 };
25         ArrayList< Double > doubleList = new ArrayList< Double >();
26
27         // insert elements in doubleList
28         for ( Double element : doubles )
29            doubleList.add( element );
30
31         System.out.printf( "doubleList contains: %s\n", doubleList );
32         System.out.printf( "Total of the elements in doubleList: %.1f\n\n",
33            sum( doubleList ) );
34
35         // create, initialize and output ArrayList of Numbers containing
36         // both Integers and Doubles, then display total of the elements
37         Number[] numbers = { 1, 2.4, 3, 4.1 }; // Integers and Doubles
38         ArrayList< Number > numberList = new ArrayList< Number >();
39
40         // insert elements in numberList
41         for ( Number element : numbers )
42            numberList.add( element );
43
44         System.out.printf( "numberList contains: %s\n", numberList );
45         System.out.printf( "Total of the elements in numberList: %.1f\n",
46            sum( numberList ) );
47      } // end main
48
49      // calculate total of stack elements
50      public static double sum( ArrayList< ? extends Number > list )
51      {
52         double total = 0; // initialize total
53
```

Fig. 18.15 | Wildcard test program. (Part 1 of 2.)

```
54        // calculate sum
55        for ( Number element : list )
56           total += element.doubleValue();
57
58        return total;
59    } // end method sum
60 } // end class WildcardTest
```

```
integerList contains: [1, 2, 3, 4, 5]
Total of the elements in integerList: 15

doubleList contains: [1.1, 3.3, 5.5]
Total of the elements in doubleList: 9.9

numberList contains: [1, 2.4, 3, 4.1]
Total of the elements in numberList: 10.5
```

Fig. 18.15 | Wildcard test program. (Part 2 of 2.)

In method sum (lines 50–59), although the ArrayList argument's element types are not directly known by the method, they are known to be at least of type Number, because the wildcard was specified with the upper bound Number. For this reason line 56 is allowed, because all Number objects have a doubleValue method.

Although wildcards provide flexibility when passing parameterized types to a method, they also have some disadvantages. Because the wildcard (?) in the method's header (line 50) does not specify a type-parameter name, you cannot use it as a type name throughout the method's body (i.e., you cannot replace Number with ? in line 55). You could, however, declare method sum as follows:

```
public static <T extends Number> double sum( ArrayList< T > list )
```

which allows the method to receive an ArrayList that contains elements of any Number subclass. You could then use the type parameter T throughout the method body.

If the wildcard is specified without an upper bound, then only the methods of type Object can be invoked on values of the wildcard type. Also, methods that use wildcards in their parameter's type arguments cannot be used to add elements to a collection referenced by the parameter.

Common Programming Error 18.4

Using a wildcard in a method's type parameter section or using a wildcard as an explicit type of a variable in the method body is a syntax error.

18.9 Generics and Inheritance: Notes

Generics can be used with inheritance in several ways:

- A generic class can be derived from a non-generic class. For example, the Object class is a direct or indirect superclass of every generic class.

- A generic class can be derived from another generic class. For example, generic class Stack (in package java.util) is a subclass of generic class Vector (in package java.util). We discuss these classes in Chapter 19, Collections.

- A non-generic class can be derived from a generic class. For example, non-generic class `Properties` (in package `java.util`) is a subclass of generic class `Hashtable` (in package `java.util`). We also discuss these classes in Chapter 19.

- Finally, a generic method in a subclass can override a generic method in a super-class if both methods have the same signatures.

18.10 Wrap-Up

This chapter introduced generics. You learned how to declare generic methods and classes. You learned how backward compatibility is achieved via raw types. You also learned how to use wildcards in a generic method or a generic class. In the next chapter, we demonstrate the interfaces, classes and algorithms of the Java collections framework. As you will see, the collections presented all use the generics capabilties you learned here.

18.11 Internet and Web Resources

www.jcp.org/aboutJava/communityprocess/review/jsr014/
Java Community Process download page for the generics specification document *Adding Generics to the Java Programming Language: Public Draft Specification, Version 2.0.*

www.angelikalanger.com/GenericsFAQ/JavaGenericsFAQ.html
A collection of frequently asked questions about Java generics.

java.sun.com/j2se/1.5/pdf/generics-tutorial.pdf
The tutorial *Generics in the Java Programming Language* by Gilad Bracha (the specification lead for JSR-14 and a reviewer of this book) introduces generics concepts with sample code snippets.

today.java.net/pub/a/today/2003/12/02/explorations.html
today.java.net/pub/a/today/2004/01/15/wildcards.html
The articles *Explorations: Generics, Erasure, and Bridging* and *Explorations: Wildcards in the Generics Specification*, each by William Grosso, overview generics features and how to use wildcards.

Summary

Section 18.1 Introduction

- Generic methods enable programmers to specify, with a single method declaration, a set of related methods.

- Generic classes enable programmers to specify, with a single class declaration, a set of related types.

- Generic methods and classes are among Java's most powerful capabilities for software reuse with compile-time type safety.

Section 18.2 Motivation for Generic Methods

- Overloaded methods are often used to perform similar operations on different types of data.

- When the compiler encounters a method call, it attempts to locate a method declaration that has the same method name and parameters that match the argument types in the method call.

Section 18.3 Generic Methods: Implementation and Compile-Time Translation

- If the operations performed by several overloaded methods are identical for each argument type, the overloaded methods can be more compactly and conveniently coded using a generic method. You can write a single generic method declaration, which can be called with arguments of different data types. Based on the types of the arguments passed to the generic method, the compiler handles each method call appropriately.

- All generic method declarations have a type parameter section delimited by angle brackets (< and >) that precedes the method's return type.

- Each type parameter section contains one or more type parameters (also called formal type parameters) separated by commas.

- A type parameter is an identifier that specifies a generic type name. The type parameters can be used as the return type, parameter types and local variable types in a generic method declaration, and they act as placeholders for the types of the arguments passed to the generic method, which are known as actual type arguments. Type parameters can represent only reference types.

- The names used for type parameters throughout the method declaration must match those declared in the type parameter section. The name of a type parameter can be declared only once in the type parameter section but can appear more than once in the method's parameter list. Type-parameter names need not be unique among different generic methods.

- When the compiler encounters a method call, it determines the argument types and attempts to locate a method with the same name and parameters that match the argument types. If there is no such method, the compiler determines whether there is an inexact but applicable match.

- The relational operator > cannot be used with reference types. However, it is possible to compare two objects of the same class if that class implements the generic interface Comparable (package java.lang).

- Comparable objects have a compareTo method that must return 0 if the objects are equal, -1 if the first object is less than the second or 1 if the first object is greater than the second.

- All the type-wrapper classes for primitive types implement Comparable.

- A benefit of implementing interface Comparable is that Comparable objects can be used with the sorting and searching methods of class Collections (package java.util).

- When the compiler translates a generic method into Java bytecodes, it removes the type parameter section and replaces the type parameters with actual types. This process is known as erasure. By default each type parameter is replaced with its upper bound. By default, the upper bound is type Object unless specified otherwise in the type parameter section.

Section 18.4 Additional Compile-Time Translation Issues: Methods That Use a Type Parameter as the Return Type

- When the compiler performs erasure on a method that returns a type variable, it also inserts explicit cast operations in front of each method call to ensure that the returned value is of the type expected by the caller.

Section 18.5 Overloading Generic Methods

- A generic method may be overloaded. A class can provide two or more generic methods that specify the same method name but different method parameters. A generic method can also be overloaded by non-generic methods that have the same method name and number of parameters. When the compiler encounters a method call, it searches for the method declaration that most precisely matches the method name and the argument types specified in the call.

- When the compiler encounters a method call, it performs a matching process to determine which method to call. The compiler tries to find and use a precise match in which the method names and argument types of the method call match those of a specific method declaration. If this fails, the compiler determines whether a generic method is available that provides a precise match of the method name and argument types, and if so, uses that generic method.

Section 18.6 Generic Classes

- Generic classes provide a means for describing a class in a type-independent manner. We can then instantiate type-specific objects of the generic class.

- A generic class declaration looks like a non-generic class declaration, except that the class name is followed by a type parameter section. As with generic methods, the type parameter section of a generic class can have one or more type parameters separated by commas.

- When a generic class is compiled, the compiler performs erasure on the class's type parameters and replaces them with their upper bounds.

- Type parameters cannot be used in a class's static declarations.

- When instantiating an object of a generic class, the types specified in angle brackets after the class name are known as type arguments. The compiler uses them to replace the type parameters so that it can perform type checking and insert cast operations as necessary.

Section 18.7 Raw Types

- It is possible to instantiate a generic class without specifying a type argument. In this case, the new object of the class is said to have a raw type, which means that the compiler implicitly uses type Object (or the type parameter's upper bound) throughout the generic class for each type argument.

Section 18.8 Wildcards in Methods That Accept Type Parameters

- The Java Collections Framework provides many generic data structures and algorithms that manipulate the elements of those data structures. Perhaps the simplest of the data structures is class ArrayList—a dynamically resizable, array-like data structure.

- Class Number is the superclass of both Integer and Double.

- Method add of class ArrayList appends an element to the end of the collection.

- Method toString of class ArrayList returns a string of the form "[elements]" in which elements is a comma-separated list of the elements' string representations.

- Method doubleValue of class Number obtains the Number's underlying primitive value as a double value.

- Wildcard type arguments enable you to specify method parameters, return values, variables, etc. that act as supertypes of parameterized types. A wildcard type argument is denoted by the question mark (?), which represents an "unknown type." A wildcard can also have an upper bound.

- Because a wildcard (?) is not a type parameter name, you cannot use it as a type name throughout a method's body.

- If a wildcard is specified without an upper bound, then only the methods of type Object can be invoked on values of the wildcard type.

- Methods that use wildcards as type arguments cannot be used to add elements to a collection referenced by the parameter.

Section 18.9 Generics and Inheritance: Notes

- A generic class can be derived from a non-generic class. For example, Object is a direct or indirect superclass of every generic class.

- A generic class can be derived from another generic class.

- A non-generic class can be derived from a generic class.

- A generic method in a subclass can override a generic method in a superclass if both methods have the same signatures.

Terminology

? (wildcard type argument)	Number class
actual type arguments	overloaded a generic method
add method of `ArrayList`	parameterized class
angle brackets (< and >)	parameterized type
`ArrayList` class	raw type
`Comparable<T>` interface	scope of a type parameter
`compareTo` method of `Comparable<T>`	`toString` method of `ArrayList`
default upper bound of a type parameter	type argument
`Double` class	type parameter
`doubleValue` method of `Number`	type parameter scope
erasure	type parameter section
formal type parameter	type variable
generics	upper bound of a type parameter
generic class	upper bound of a wildcard
generic interface	wildcard (?)
generic method	wildcard as a type argument
`Integer` class	wildcard without an upper bound

Self-Review Exercises

18.1 State whether each of the following is *true* or *false*. If *false*, explain why.

a) A generic method cannot have the same method name as a non-generic method.

b) All generic method declarations have a type parameter section that immediately precedes the method name.

c) A generic method can be overloaded by another generic method with the same method name but different method parameters.

d) A type parameter can be declared only once in the type parameter section but can appear more than once in the method's parameter list.

e) Type parameter names among different generic methods must be unique.

f) The scope of a generic class's type parameter is the entire class except its `static` members.

18.2 Fill in the blanks in each of the following:

a) _____ and _____ enable you to specify, with a single method declaration, a set of related methods, or with a single class declaration, a set of related types, respectively.

b) A type parameter section is delimited by _____.

c) A generic method's _____ can be used to specify the method's argument types, to specify the method's return type and to declare variables within the method.

d) The statement "`Stack objectStack = new Stack();`" indicates that `objectStack` stores _____.

e) In a generic class declaration, the class name is followed by a(n) _____.

f) The syntax _____ specifies that the upper bound of a wildcard is type `E`.

Answers to Self-Review Exercises

18.1 a) False. Generic and non-generic methods can have the same method name. A generic method can overload another generic method with the same method name but different method parameters. A generic method also can be overloaded by providing non-generic methods with the same method name and number of arguments. b) False. All generic method declarations have a type parameter section that immediately precedes the method's return type. c) True. d) True. e) False. Type parameter names among different generic methods need not be unique. f) True.

18.2 a) Generic methods, generic classes. b) angle brackets (< and >). c) type parameters. d) a raw type. e) type parameter section. f) ? extends E.

Exercises

18.3 Write a generic method selectionSort based on the sort program of Figs. 16.6–16.7. Write a test program that inputs, sorts and outputs an Integer array and a Float array. [*Hint:* Use < T extends Comparable< T > > in the type parameter section for method selectionSort, so that you can use method compareTo to compare the objects of two generic types T.]

18.4 Overload generic method printArray of Fig. 18.3 so that it takes two additional integer arguments, lowSubscript and highSubscript. A call to this method prints only the designated portion of the array. Validate lowSubscript and highSubscript. If either is out of range, or if highSubscript is less than or equal to lowSubscript, the overloaded printArray method should throw an InvalidSubscriptException; otherwise, printArray should return the number of elements printed. Then modify main to exercise both versions of printArray on arrays integerArray, doubleArray and characterArray. Test all capabilities of both versions of printArray.

18.5 Write a simple generic version of method isEqualTo that compares its two arguments with the equals method and returns true if they are equal and false otherwise. Use this generic method in a program that calls isEqualTo with a variety of built-in types, such as Object or Integer. What result do you get when you attempt to run this program?

18.6 Write a generic class Pair which has two type parameters—F and S, each representing the type of the first and second element of the pair, respectively. Add *get* and *set* methods for the first and second elements of the pair. [*Hint:* The class header should be public class Pair< F, S >.]

18.7 Convert classes TreeNode and Tree from Fig. 17.17 into generic classes. To insert an object in a Tree, the object must be compared to the objects in existing TreeNodes. For this reason, classes TreeNode and Tree should specify Comparable< E > as the upper bound of each class's type parameter. After modifying classes TreeNode and Tree, write a test application that creates three Tree objects—one that stores Integers, one that stores Doubles and one that stores Strings. Insert 10 values into each tree. Then output the preorder, inorder and postorder traversals for each Tree.

18.8 How can generic methods be overloaded?

18.9 Explain why a Java program might use the statement

```
ArrayList< Employee > workerList = new ArrayList< Employee >();
```

19

Collections

OBJECTIVES

In this chapter you will learn:

- What collections are.

- To use class **Arrays** for array manipulations.

- To use the collections framework (prepackaged data structure) implementations.

- To use collections framework algorithms to manipulate (such as **search**, **sort** and **fill**) collections.

- To use the collections framework interfaces to program with collections polymorphically.

- To use iterators to "walk through" a collection.

- To use persistent hash tables manipulated with objects of class **Properties**.

- To use synchronization and modifiability wrappers.

19.1 Introduction

In Chapter 17, we discussed how to create and manipulate data structures. The discussion was "low level" in the sense that we painstakingly created each element of each data structure dynamically and modified the data structures by directly manipulating their elements and the references to their elements. In this chapter, we consider the Java **collections framework**, which contains prepackaged data structures, interfaces and algorithms for manipulating those data structures. Some examples of collections are the cards you hold in a card game, your favorite songs stored in your computer, the members of a sports team and the real-estate records in your local registry of deeds (which map book numbers and page numbers to property owners). In this chapter, we also discuss how generics (see Chapter 18) are used in the Java collections framework.

With collections, programmers use existing data structures, without concern for how they are implemented. This is a marvelous example of code reuse. Programmers can code faster and can expect excellent performance, maximizing execution speed and minimizing memory consumption. In this chapter, we discuss the collections framework interfaces that list the capabilities of each collection type, the implementation classes, the algorithms that process the collections, and the so-called iterators and enhanced for statement syntax that "walk through" collections. This chapter provides an introduction to the collections framework. For complete details, visit java.sun.com/javase/6/docs/guide/collections.

The Java collections framework provides ready-to-go, reusable componentry—you do not need to write your own collection classes, but you can if you wish to. The collections are standardized so that applications can share them easily without concern with for details of their implementation. The collections framework encourages further reusability. As new data structures and algorithms are developed that fit this framework, a large base of programmers will already be familiar with the interfaces and algorithms implemented by those data structures.

19.2 Collections Overview

A collection is a data structure—actually, an object—that can hold references to other objects. Usually, collections contain references to objects that are all of the same type. The collections framework interfaces declare the operations to be performed generically on various types of collections. Figure 19.1 lists some of the interfaces of the collections framework. Several implementations of these interfaces are provided within the framework. Programmers may also provide implementations specific to their own requirements.

The collections framework provides high-performance, high-quality implementations of common data structures and enables software reuse. These features minimize the amount of coding programmers need to do to create and manipulate collections. The classes and interfaces of the collections framework are members of package java.util. In the next section, we begin our discussion by examining the collections framework capabilities for array manipulation.

In earlier versions of Java, the classes in the collections framework stored and manipulated Object references. Thus, you could store any object in a collection. One inconvenient aspect of storing Object references occurs when retrieving them from a collection. A program normally has the need to process specific types of objects. As a result, the Object references obtained from a collection typically need to be cast to an appropriate type to allow the program to process the objects correctly.

Interface	Description
Collection	The root interface in the collections hierarchy from which interfaces Set, Queue and List are derived.
Set	A collection that does not contain duplicates.
List	An ordered collection that can contain duplicate elements.
Map	Associates keys to values and cannot contain duplicate keys.
Queue	Typically a first-in, first-out collection that models a waiting line; other orders can be specified.

Fig. 19.1 | Some collection framework interfaces.

In Java SE 5, the collections framework was enhanced with the generics capabilities we introduced in Chapter 18. This means that you can specify the exact type that will be stored in a collection. You also receive the benefits of compile-time type checking—the compiler ensures that you are using appropriate types with your collection and, if not, issues compile-time error messages. Also, once you specify the type stored in a collection, any reference you retrieve from the collection will have the specified type. This eliminates the need for explicit type casts that can throw `ClassCastException`s if the referenced object is not of the appropriate type. Programs that were implemented with prior Java versions and that use collections can compile properly because the compiler automatically uses raw types when it encounters collections for which type arguments were not specified.

19.3 Class Arrays

Class `Arrays` provides `static` methods for manipulating arrays. In Chapter 7, our discussion of array manipulation was low level in the sense that we wrote the actual code to sort and search arrays. Class `Arrays` provides high-level methods, such as **sort** for sorting an array, `binarySearch` for searching a sorted array, **equals** for comparing arrays and `fill` for placing values into an array. These methods are overloaded for primitive-type arrays and `Object` arrays. In addition, methods `sort` and `binarySearch` are overloaded with generic versions that allow programmers to sort and search arrays containing objects of any type. Figure 19.2 demonstrates methods `fill`, `sort`, `binarySearch` and `equals`. Method `main` (lines 65–85) creates a `UsingArrays` object and invokes its methods.

Line 17 calls `static` method `fill` of class `Arrays` to populate all 10 elements of `filledIntArray` with 7s. Overloaded versions of `fill` allow the programmer to populate a specific range of elements with the same value.

Line 18 sorts the elements of array `doubleArray`. The `static` method `sort` of class `Arrays` orders the array's elements in ascending order by default. We discuss how to sort in descending order later in the chapter. Overloaded versions of `sort` allow the programmer to sort a specific range of elements.

Lines 21–22 copy array `intArray` into array `intArrayCopy`. The first argument (`intArray`) passed to `System` method `arraycopy` is the array from which elements are to be copied. The second argument (0) is the index that specifies the starting point in the range of elements to copy from the array. This value can be any valid array index. The third argument (`intArrayCopy`) specifies the destination array that will store the copy. The fourth argument (0) specifies the index in the destination array where the first copied element should be stored. The last argument specifies the number of elements to copy from the array in the first argument. In this case, we copy all the elements in the array.

Line 50 calls `static` method `binarySearch` of class `Arrays` to perform a binary search on `intArray`, using `value` as the key. If `value` is found, `binarySearch` returns the index of the element; otherwise, `binarySearch` returns a negative value. The negative value returned is based on the search key's **insertion point**—the index where the key would be inserted in the array if we were performing an insert operation. After `binarySearch` determines the insertion point, it changes its sign to negative and subtracts 1 to obtain the return value. For example, in Fig. 19.2, the insertion point for the value 8763 is the element with index 6 in the array. Method `binarySearch` changes the insertion point to –6, subtracts 1 from it and returns the value –7. Subtracting 1 from the insertion point guarantees that method `binarySearch` returns positive values (>= 0) if and only if the key is found. This return value is useful for inserting elements in a sorted array. Chapter 16, Searching and Sorting, discusses binary searching in detail.

```java
1   // Fig. 19.2: UsingArrays.java
2   // Using Java arrays.
3   import java.util.Arrays;
4
5   public class UsingArrays
6   {
7      private int intArray[] = { 1, 2, 3, 4, 5, 6 };
8      private double doubleArray[] = { 8.4, 9.3, 0.2, 7.9, 3.4 };
9      private int filledIntArray[], intArrayCopy[];
10
11     // constructor initializes arrays
12     public UsingArrays()
13     {
14        filledIntArray = new int[ 10 ]; // create int array with 10 elements
15        intArrayCopy = new int[ intArray.length ];
16
17        Arrays.fill( filledIntArray, 7 ); // fill with 7s
18        Arrays.sort( doubleArray ); // sort doubleArray ascending
19
20        // copy array intArray into array intArrayCopy
21        System.arraycopy( intArray, 0, intArrayCopy,
22           0, intArray.length );
23     } // end UsingArrays constructor
24
25     // output values in each array
26     public void printArrays()
27     {
28        System.out.print( "doubleArray: " );
29        for ( double doubleValue : doubleArray )
30           System.out.printf( "%.1f ", doubleValue );
31
32        System.out.print( "\nintArray: " );
33        for ( int intValue : intArray )
34           System.out.printf( "%d ", intValue );
35
36        System.out.print( "\nfilledIntArray: " );
37        for ( int intValue : filledIntArray )
38           System.out.printf( "%d ", intValue );
39
40        System.out.print( "\nintArrayCopy: " );
41        for ( int intValue : intArrayCopy )
42           System.out.printf( "%d ", intValue );
43
44        System.out.println( "\n" );
45     } // end method printArrays
46
47     // find value in array intArray
48     public int searchForInt( int value )
49     {
```

Fig. 19.2 | Arrays class methods. (Part 1 of 2.)

```
50          return Arrays.binarySearch( intArray, value );
51       } // end method searchForInt
52
53       // compare array contents
54       public void printEquality()
55       {
56          boolean b = Arrays.equals( intArray, intArrayCopy );
57          System.out.printf( "intArray %s intArrayCopy\n",
58             ( b ? "==" : "!=" ) );
59
60          b = Arrays.equals( intArray, filledIntArray );
61          System.out.printf( "intArray %s filledIntArray\n",
62             ( b ? "==" : "!=" ) );
63       } // end method printEquality
64
65       public static void main( String args[] )
66       {
67          UsingArrays usingArrays = new UsingArrays();
68
69          usingArrays.printArrays();
70          usingArrays.printEquality();
71
72          int location = usingArrays.searchForInt( 5 );
73          if ( location >= 0 )
74             System.out.printf(
75                "Found 5 at element %d in intArray\n", location );
76          else
77             System.out.println( "5 not found in intArray" );
78
79          location = usingArrays.searchForInt( 8763 );
80          if ( location >= 0 )
81             System.out.printf(
82                "Found 8763 at element %d in intArray\n", location );
83          else
84             System.out.println( "8763 not found in intArray" );
85       } // end main
86    } // end class UsingArrays
```

```
doubleArray: 0.2 3.4 7.9 8.4 9.3
intArray: 1 2 3 4 5 6
filledIntArray: 7 7 7 7 7 7 7 7 7 7
intArrayCopy: 1 2 3 4 5 6

intArray == intArrayCopy
intArray != filledIntArray
Found 5 at element 4 in intArray
8763 not found in intArray
```

Fig. 19.2 | Arrays class methods. (Part 2 of 2.)

 Common Programming Error 19.1

Passing an unsorted array to binarySearch is a logic error—the value returned is undefined.

Lines 56 and 60 call static method equals of class Arrays to determine whether the elements of two arrays are equivalent. If the arrays contain the same elements in the same order, the method returns true; otherwise, it returns false. The equality of each element is compared using Object method equals. Many classes override method equals to perform the comparisons in a manner specific to those classes. For example, class String declares equals to compare the individual characters in the two Strings being compared. If method equals is not overridden, the original version of method equals inherited from class Object is used.

19.4 Interface Collection and Class Collections

Interface Collection is the root interface in the collection hierarchy from which interfaces Set, Queue and List are derived. Interface **Set** defines a collection that does not contain duplicates. Interface **Queue** defines a collection that represents a waiting line—typically, insertions are made at the back of a queue and deletions are made from the front, though other orders can be specified. We discuss Queue and Set in Section 19.8 and Section 19.9, respectively. Interface Collection contains **bulk operations** (i.e., operations performed on an entire collection) for adding, clearing, comparing and retaining objects (or elements) in a collection. A Collection can also be converted to an array. In addition, interface Collection provides a method that returns an **Iterator** object, which allows a program to walk through the collection and remove elements from the collection during the iteration. We discuss class Iterator in Section 19.5.1. Other methods of interface Collection enable a program to determine a collection's size and whether a collection is empty.

Software Engineering Observation 19.1

Collection is used commonly as a method parameter type to allow polymorphic processing of all objects that implement interface Collection.

Software Engineering Observation 19.2

Most collection implementations provide a constructor that takes a Collection argument, thereby allowing a new collection to be constructed containing the elements of the specified collection.

Class Collections provides static methods that manipulate collections polymorphically. These methods implement algorithms for searching, sorting and so on. Chapter 16, Searching and Sorting, discussed and implemented various searching and sorting algorithms. Section 19.6 discusses more about the algorithms that are available in class Collections. We also cover the **wrapper methods** of class Collections that enable you to treat a collection as a **synchronized collection** (Section 19.12) or an **unmodifiable collection** (Section 19.13). Unmodifiable collections are useful when a client of a class needs to view the elements of a collection, but should not be allowed to modify the collection by adding and removing elements. Synchronized collections are for use with a powerful capability called multithreading (discussed in Chapter 23). Multithreading enables programs to perform operations in parallel. When two or more threads of a program share a collection, there is the potential for problems to occur. As a brief analogy, consider a traffic intersection. We cannot allow all cars access to one intersection at the same time— if we did, accidents would occur. For this reason, traffic lights are provided at intersections to control access to the intersection. Similarly, we can synchronize access to a collection to ensure that only one thread manipulates the collection at a time. The synchronization wrapper methods of class `Collections` return synchronized versions of collections that can be shared among threads in a program.

19.5 Lists

A `List` (sometimes called a sequence) is an ordered `Collection` that can contain duplicate elements. Like array indices, `List` indices are zero based (i.e., the first element's index is zero). In addition to the methods inherited from `Collection`, `List` provides methods for manipulating elements via their indices, manipulating a specified range of elements, searching for elements and getting a `ListIterator` to access the elements.

Interface `List` is implemented by several classes, including classes `ArrayList`, `LinkedList` and `Vector`. Autoboxing occurs when you add primitive-type values to objects of these classes, because they store only references to objects. Class `ArrayList` and `Vector` are resizable-array implementations of `List`. Class `LinkedList` is a linked list implementation of interface `List`.

Class `ArrayList`'s behavior and capabilities are similar to those of class `Vector`. The primary difference between `Vector` and `ArrayList` is that objects of class `Vector` are synchronized by default, whereas objects of class `ArrayList` are not. Also, class `Vector` is from Java 1.0, before the collections framework was added to Java. As such, `Vector` has several methods that are not part of interface `List` and are not implemented in class `ArrayList`, but perform identical tasks. For example, `Vector` methods `addElement` and `add` both append an element to a `Vector`, but only method `add` is specified in interface `List` and implemented by `ArrayList`. Unsynchronized collections provide better performance than synchronized ones. For this reason, `ArrayList` is typically preferred over `Vector` in programs that do not share a collection among threads.

Performance Tip 19.1

ArrayLists behave like Vectors without synchronization and therefore execute faster than Vectors because ArrayLists do not have the overhead of thread synchronization.

Software Engineering Observation 19.3

LinkedLists can be used to create stacks, queues, trees and deques (double-ended queues, pronounced "decks"). The collections framework provides implementations of some of these data structures.

The following three subsections demonstrate the `List` and `Collection` capabilities with several examples. Section 19.5.1 focuses on removing elements from an `ArrayList` with an `Iterator`. Section 19.5.2 focuses on `ListIterator` and several `List`- and `LinkedList`-specific methods. Section 19.5.3 introduces more `List` methods and several `Vector`-specific methods.

19.5.1 ArrayList and Iterator

Figure 19.3 uses an `ArrayList` to demonstrate several `Collection` interface capabilities. The program places two `Color` arrays in `ArrayLists` and uses an `Iterator` to remove elements in the second `ArrayList` collection from the first `ArrayList` collection.

Lines 10–13 declare and initialize two `String` array variables, which are declared `final`, so they always refer to these arrays. Recall that it is good programing practice to declare constants with keywords static and final. Lines 18–19 create ArrayList objects and assign their references to variables list and removeList, respectively. These two lists store String objects. Note that ArrayList is a generic class as of Java SE 5, so we are able to specify a type argument (String in this case) to indicate the type of the elements in each list. Both list and removeList are collections of Strings. Lines 22–23 populate list with Strings stored in array colors, and lines 26–27 populate removeList with Strings stored in array removeColors using List method **add**. Lines 32–33 output each element of list. Line 32 calls List method **size** to get the number of ArrayList elements. Line 33 uses List method **get** to retrieve individual element values. Lines 32–33 could have used the enhanced for statement. Line 36 calls method removeColors (lines 46–57), passing list and removeList as arguments. Method removeColors deletes Strings specified in removeList from the list collection. Lines 41–42 print list's elements after removeColors removes the String objects specified in removeList from the list.

```java
1   // Fig. 19.3: CollectionTest.java
2   // Using the Collection interface.
3   import java.util.List;
4   import java.util.ArrayList;
5   import java.util.Collection;
6   import java.util.Iterator;
7
8   public class CollectionTest
9   {
10     private static final String[] colors =
11        { "MAGENTA", "RED", "WHITE", "BLUE", "CYAN" };
12     private static final String[] removeColors =
13        { "RED", "WHITE", "BLUE" };
14
15     // create ArrayList, add colors to it and manipulate it
16     public CollectionTest()
17     {
18        List< String > list = new ArrayList< String >();
19        List< String > removeList = new ArrayList< String >();
20
21        // add elements in colors array to list
22        for ( String color : colors )
23           list.add( color );
24
25        // add elements in removeColors to removeList
26        for ( String color : removeColors )
27           removeList.add( color );
28
29        System.out.println( "ArrayList: " );
30
31        // output list contents
32        for ( int count = 0; count < list.size(); count++ )
33           System.out.printf( "%s ", list.get( count ) );
34
35        // remove colors contained in removeList
36        removeColors( list, removeList );
```

Fig. 19.3 | Collection interface demonstrated via an ArrayList object. (Part 1 of 2.)

```
37
38            System.out.println( "\n\nArrayList after calling removeColors: " );
39
40            // output list contents
41            for ( String color : list )
42                System.out.printf( "%s ", color );
43        } // end CollectionTest constructor
44
45        // remove colors specified in collection2 from collection1
46        private void removeColors(
47            Collection< String > collection1, Collection< String > collection2 )
48        {
49            // get iterator
50            Iterator< String > iterator = collection1.iterator();
51
52            // loop while collection has items
53            while ( iterator.hasNext() )
54
55                if ( collection2.contains( iterator.next() ) )
56                    iterator.remove(); // remove current Color
57        } // end method removeColors
58
59        public static void main( String args[] )
60        {
61            new CollectionTest();
62        } // end main
63    } // end class CollectionTest
```

```
ArrayList:
MAGENTA RED WHITE BLUE CYAN

ArrayList after calling removeColors:
MAGENTA CYAN
```

Fig. 19.3 | Collection interface demonstrated via an ArrayList object. (Part 2 of 2.)

Method removeColors declares two Collection parameters (line 47) that allow any Collections containing strings to be passed as arguments to this method. The method accesses the elements of the first Collection (collection1) via an Iterator. Line 50 calls Collection method **iterator** to get an Iterator for the Collection. Note that interfaces Collection and Iterator are generic types. The loop-continuation condition (line 53) calls Iterator method **hasNext** to determine whether the Collection contains more elements. Method hasNext returns true if another element exists and false otherwise.

The if condition in line 55 calls Iterator method **next** to obtain a reference to the next element, then uses method **contains** of the second Collection (collection2) to determine whether collection2 contains the element returned by next. If so, line 56 calls Iterator method **remove** to remove the element from the Collection collection1.

Common Programming Error 19.2

If a collection is modified by one of its methods after an iterator is created for that collection, the iterator immediately becomes invalid—any operations performed with the iterator after this point throw ConcurrentModificationExceptions. For this reason, iterators are said to be "fail fast."

19.5.2 LinkedList

Figure 19.4 demonstrates operations on LinkedLists. The program creates two LinkedLists that contain Strings. The elements of one List are added to the other. Then all the Strings are converted to uppercase, and a range of elements is deleted.

```java
1   // Fig. 19.4: ListTest.java
2   // Using LinkLists.
3   import java.util.List;
4   import java.util.LinkedList;
5   import java.util.ListIterator;
6
7   public class ListTest
8   {
9      private static final String colors[] = { "black", "yellow",
10        "green", "blue", "violet", "silver" };
11     private static final String colors2[] = { "gold", "white",
12        "brown", "blue", "gray", "silver" };
13
14     // set up and manipulate LinkedList objects
15     public ListTest()
16     {
17        List< String > list1 = new LinkedList< String >();
18        List< String > list2 = new LinkedList< String >();
19
20        // add elements to list link
21        for ( String color : colors )
22           list1.add( color );
23
24        // add elements to list link2
25        for ( String color : colors2 )
26           list2.add( color );
27
28        list1.addAll( list2 ); // concatenate lists
29        list2 = null; // release resources
30        printList( list1 ); // print list1 elements
31
32        convertToUppercaseStrings( list1 ); // convert to uppercase string
33        printList( list1 ); // print list1 elements
34
35        System.out.print( "\nDeleting elements 4 to 6..." );
36        removeItems( list1, 4, 7 ); // remove items 4-7 from list
37        printList( list1 ); // print list1 elements
38        printReversedList( list1 ); // print list in reverse order
39     } // end ListTest constructor
40
41     // output List contents
42     public void printList( List< String > list )
43     {
44        System.out.println( "\nlist: " );
45
46        for ( String color : list )
47           System.out.printf( "%s ", color );
```

Fig. 19.4 | Lists and ListIterators. (Part I of 2.)

```
48
49          System.out.println();
50       } // end method printList
51
52       // locate String objects and convert to uppercase
53       private void convertToUppercaseStrings( List< String > list )
54       {
55          ListIterator< String > iterator = list.listIterator();
56
57          while ( iterator.hasNext() )
58          {
59             String color = iterator.next();  // get item
60             iterator.set( color.toUpperCase() ); // convert to uppercase
61          } // end while
62       } // end method convertToUppercaseStrings
63
64       // obtain sublist and use clear method to delete sublist items
65       private void removeItems( List< String > list, int start, int end )
66       {
67          list.subList( start, end ).clear();  // remove items
68       } // end method removeItems
69
70       // print reversed list
71       private void printReversedList( List< String > list )
72       {
73          ListIterator< String > iterator = list.listIterator( list.size() );
74
75          System.out.println( "\nReversed List:" );
76
77          // print list in reverse order
78          while ( iterator.hasPrevious() )
79             System.out.printf( "%s ", iterator.previous() );
80       } // end method printReversedList
81
82       public static void main( String args[] )
83       {
84          new ListTest();
85       } // end main
86    } // end class ListTest
```

```
list:
black yellow green blue violet silver gold white brown blue gray silver

list:
BLACK YELLOW GREEN BLUE VIOLET SILVER GOLD WHITE BROWN BLUE GRAY SILVER

Deleting elements 4 to 6...
list:
BLACK YELLOW GREEN BLUE WHITE BROWN BLUE GRAY SILVER

Reversed List:
SILVER GRAY BLUE BROWN WHITE BLUE GREEN YELLOW BLACK
```

Fig. 19.4 | Lists and ListIterators. (Part 2 of 2.)

Lines 17–18 create LinkedLists list1 and list2 of type String. Note that LinkedList is a generic class that has one type parameter for which we specify the type argument String in this example. Lines 21–26 call List method add to append elements from arrays colors and colors2 to the end of list1 and list2, respectively.

Line 28 calls List method **addAll** to append all elements of list2 to the end of list1. Line 29 sets list2 to null, so the LinkedList to which list2 referred can be garbage collected. Line 30 calls method printList (lines 42–50) to output list list1's contents. Line 32 calls method convertToUppercaseStrings (lines 53–62) to convert each String element to uppercase, then line 33 calls printList again to display the modified Strings. Line 36 calls method removeItems (lines 65–68) to remove the elements starting at index 4 up to, but not including, index 7 of the list. Line 38 calls method printReversedList (lines 71–80) to print the list in reverse order.

Method convertToUppercaseStrings (lines 53–62) changes lowercase String elements in its List argument to uppercase Strings. Line 55 calls List method **listIterator** to get a bidirectional iterator (i.e., an iterator that can traverse a List backward or forward) for the List. Note that ListIterator is a generic class. In this example, the ListIterator contains String objects, because method listIterator is called on a List of Strings. The while condition (line 57) calls method hasNext to determine whether the List contains another element. Line 59 gets the next String in the List. Line 60 calls String method **toUpperCase** to get an uppercase version of the String and calls ListIterator method **set** to replace the current String to which iterator refers with the String returned by method toUpperCase. Like method toUpperCase, String method **toLowerCase** returns a lowercase version of the String.

Method removeItems (lines 65–68) removes a range of items from the list. Line 67 calls List method **subList** to obtain a portion of the List (called a sublist). The sublist is simply another view into the List on which subList is called. Method subList takes two arguments—the beginning and the ending index for the sublist. The ending index is not part of the range of the sublist. In this example, we pass (in line 36) 4 for the beginning index and 7 for the ending index to subList. The sublist returned is the set of elements with indices 4 through 6. Next, the program calls List method **clear** on the sublist to remove the elements of the sublist from the List. Any changes made to a sublist are also made to the original List.

Method printReversedList (lines 71–80) prints the list backward. Line 73 calls List method listIterator with the starting position as an argument (in our case, the last element in the list) to get a bidirectional iterator for the list. List method **size** returns the number of items in the List. The while condition (line 78) calls method **hasPrevious** to determine whether there are more elements while traversing the list backward. Line 79 gets the previous element from the list and outputs it to the standard output stream.

An important feature of the collections framework is the ability to manipulate the elements of one collection type (such as a set) through a different collection type (such as a list), regardless of the collection's internal implementation. The set of public methods through which collections are manipulated is called a view.

Class Arrays provides static method **asList** to view an array as a List collection (which encapsulates behavior similar to that of the linked lists created in Chapter 17). A List view allows the programmer to manipulate the array as if it were a list. This is useful for adding the elements in an array to a collection (e.g., a LinkedList) and for sorting array elements. The next example demonstrates how to create a LinkedList with a List view of an array, because we cannot pass the array to a LinkedList constructor. Sorting array elements with a List view is demonstrated in Fig. 19.9. Any modifications made through the List view change the array, and any modifications made to the array change the List view. The only operation permitted on the view returned by asList is *set*, which changes the value of the view and the backing array. Any other attempts to change the view (such as adding or removing elements) result in an UnsupportedOperationException.

Figure 19.5 uses method asList to view an array as a List collection and uses method **toArray** of a List to get an array from a LinkedList collection. The program calls method asList to create a List view of an array, which is then used for creating a LinkedList object, adds a series of strings to a LinkedList and calls method toArray to obtain an array containing references to the strings. Notice that the instantiation of LinkedList (line 13) indicates that LinkedList is a generic class that accepts one type argument—String, in this example.

```
1   // Fig. 19.5: UsingToArray.java
2   // Using method toArray.
3   import java.util.LinkedList;
4   import java.util.Arrays;
5
6   public class UsingToArray
7   {
8      // constructor creates LinkedList, adds elements and converts to array
9      public UsingToArray()
10     {
11        String colors[] = { "black", "blue", "yellow" };
12
13        LinkedList< String > links =
14           new LinkedList< String >( Arrays.asList( colors ) );
15
16        links.addLast( "red" );      // add as last item
17        links.add( "pink" );         // add to the end
18        links.add( 3, "green" );     // add at 3rd index
19        links.addFirst( "cyan" );    // add as first item
20
21        // get LinkedList elements as an array
22        colors = links.toArray( new String[ links.size() ] );
23
24        System.out.println( "colors: " );
25
26        for ( String color : colors )
27           System.out.println( color );
28     } // end UsingToArray constructor
29
30     public static void main( String args[] )
31     {
32        new UsingToArray();
33     } // end main
34  } // end class UsingToArray
```

Fig. 19.5 | List method toArray. (Part 1 of 2.)

```
colors:
cyan
black
blue
yellow
green
red
pink
```

Fig. 19.5 | List method `toArray`. (Part 2 of 2.)

Lines 13–14 construct a `LinkedList` of `Strings` containing the elements of array `colors` and assigns the `LinkedList` reference to `links`. Note the use of `Arrays` method `asList` to return a view of the array as a `List`, then initialize the `LinkedList` with the `List`. Line 16 calls `LinkedList` method **`addLast`** to add "red" to the end of `links`. Lines 17–18 call `LinkedList` method **`add`** to add "pink" as the last element and "green" as the element at index 3 (i.e., the fourth element). Note that method `addLast` (line 16) is identical in function to method `add` (line 17). Line 19 calls `LinkedList` method **`addFirst`** to add "cyan" as the new first item in the `LinkedList`. The `add` operations are permitted because they operate on the `LinkedList` object, not the view returned by `asList`. [*Note:* When "cyan" is added as the first element, "green" becomes the fifth element in the `LinkedList`.]

Line 22 calls `List` method `toArray` to get a `String` array from `links`. The array is a copy of the list's elements—modifying the array's contents does not modify the list. The array passed to method `toArray` is of the same type that you would like method `toArray` to return. If the number of elements in the array is greater than or equal to the number of elements in the `LinkedList`, `toArray` copies the list's elements into its array argument and returns that array. If the `LinkedList` has more elements than the number of elements in the array passed to `toArray`, `toArray` allocates a new array of the same type it receives as an argument, copies the list's elements into the new array and returns the new array.

 Common Programming Error 19.3

Passing an array that contains data to `toArray` can cause logic errors. If the number of elements in the array is smaller than the number of elements in the list on which `toArray` is called, a new array is allocated to store the list's elements—without preserving the array argument's elements. If the number of elements in the array is greater than the number of elements in the list, the elements of the array (starting at index zero) are overwritten with the list's elements. Array elements that are not overwritten retain their values.

19.5.3 Vector

Like `ArrayList`, class `Vector` provides the capabilities of array-like data structures that can resize themselves dynamically. Recall that class `ArrayList`'s behavior and capabilities are similar to those of class `Vector`, except that `ArrayLists` do not provide synchronization by default. We cover class `Vector` here primarily because it is the superclass of class `Stack`, which is presented in Section 19.7.

At any time, a `Vector` contains a number of elements that is less than or equal to its capacity. The capacity is the space that has been reserved for the `Vector`'s elements. If a

Vector requires additional capacity, it grows by a capacity increment that you specify or by a default capacity increment. If you do not specify a capacity increment or specify one that is less than or equal to zero, the system will double the size of a Vector each time additional capacity is needed.

Performance Tip 19.2

Inserting an element into a Vector whose current size is less than its capacity is a relatively fast operation.

Performance Tip 19.3

Inserting an element into a Vector that needs to grow larger to accommodate the new element is a relatively slow operation.

Performance Tip 19.4

The default capacity increment doubles the size of the Vector. This may seem a waste of storage, but it is actually an efficient way for many Vectors to grow quickly to be "about the right size." This operation is much more efficient than growing the Vector each time by only as much space as it takes to hold a single element. The disadvantage is that the Vector might occupy more space than it requires. This is a classic example of the space–time trade-off.

Performance Tip 19.5

If storage is at a premium, use Vector method trimToSize to trim a Vector's capacity to the Vector's exact size. This operation optimizes a Vector's use of storage. However, adding another element to the Vector will force the Vector to grow dynamically (again, a relatively slow operation)—trimming leaves no room for growth.

Figure 19.6 demonstrates class Vector and several of its methods. For complete information on class Vector, please visit java.sun.com/javase/6/docs/api/java/util/Vector.html.

```java
1   // Fig. 19.6: VectorTest.java
2   // Using the Vector class.
3   import java.util.Vector;
4   import java.util.NoSuchElementException;
5
6   public class VectorTest
7   {
8      private static final String colors[] = { "red", "white", "blue" };
9
10     public VectorTest()
11     {
12        Vector< String > vector = new Vector< String >();
13        printVector( vector ); // print vector
14
15        // add elements to the vector
16        for ( String color : colors )
17           vector.add( color );
18
```

Fig. 19.6 | Vector class of package java.util. (Part 1 of 3.)

```
19          printVector( vector ); // print vector
20
21          // output the first and last elements
22          try
23          {
24             System.out.printf( "First element: %s\n", vector.firstElement());
25             System.out.printf( "Last element: %s\n", vector.lastElement() );
26          } // end try
27          // catch exception if vector is empty
28          catch ( NoSuchElementException exception )
29          {
30             exception.printStackTrace();
31          } // end catch
32
33          // does vector contain "red"?
34          if ( vector.contains( "red" ) )
35             System.out.printf( "\n\"red\" found at index %d\n\n",
36                vector.indexOf( "red" ) );
37          else
38             System.out.println( "\n\"red\" not found\n" );
39
40          vector.remove( "red" ); // remove the string "red"
41          System.out.println( "\"red\" has been removed" );
42          printVector( vector ); // print vector
43
44          // does vector contain "red" after remove operation?
45          if ( vector.contains( "red" ) )
46             System.out.printf(
47                "\"red\" found at index %d\n", vector.indexOf( "red" ) );
48          else
49             System.out.println( "\"red\" not found" );
50
51          // print the size and capacity of vector
52          System.out.printf( "\nSize: %d\nCapacity: %d\n", vector.size(),
53             vector.capacity() );
54       } // end Vector constructor
55
56       private void printVector( Vector< String > vectorToOutput )
57       {
58          if ( vectorToOutput.isEmpty() )
59             System.out.print( "vector is empty" ); // vectorToOutput is empty
60          else  // iterate through the elements
61          {
62             System.out.print( "vector contains: " );
63
64             // output elements
65             for ( String element : vectorToOutput )
66                System.out.printf( "%s ", element );
67          } // end else
68
69          System.out.println( "\n" );
70       } // end method printVector
```

Fig. 19.6 | Vector class of package java.util. (Part 2 of 3.)

```
71
72      public static void main( String args[] )
73      {
74         new VectorTest(); // create object and call its constructor
75      } // end main
76   } // end class VectorTest
```

```
vector is empty

vector contains: red white blue

First element: red
Last element: blue

"red" found at index 0

"red" has been removed
vector contains: white blue

"red" not found

Size: 2
Capacity: 10
```

Fig. 19.6 | Vector class of package `java.util`. (Part 3 of 3.)

The application's constructor creates a Vector (line 13) of type String with an initial capacity of 10 elements and capacity increment of zero (the defaults for a Vector). Note that Vector is a generic class, which takes one argument that specifies the type of the elements stored in the Vector. A capacity increment of zero indicates that this Vector will double in size each time it needs to grow to accommodate more elements. Class Vector provides three other constructors. The constructor that takes one integer argument creates an empty Vector with the initial capacity specified by that argument. The constructor that takes two arguments creates a Vector with the initial capacity specified by the first argument and the capacity increment specified by the second argument. Each time the Vector needs to grow, it will add space for the specified number of elements in the capacity increment. The constructor that takes a Collection creates a copy of a collection's elements and stores them in the Vector.

Line 18 calls Vector method **add** to add objects (Strings in this program) to the end of the Vector. If necessary, the Vector increases its capacity to accommodate the new element. Class Vector also provides a method add that takes two arguments. This method takes an object and an integer and inserts the object at the specified index in the Vector. Method **set** will replace the element at a specified position in the Vector with a specified element. Method **insertElementAt** provides the same functionality as the method add that takes two arguments, except that the order of the parameters is reversed.

Line 25 calls Vector method **firstElement** to return a reference to the first element in the Vector. Line 26 calls Vector method **lastElement** to return a reference to the last element in the Vector. Each of these methods throws a NoSuchElementException if there are no elements in the Vector when the method is called.

Line 35 calls Vector method **contains** to determine whether the Vector contains "red". The method returns true if its argument is in the Vector—otherwise, the method returns `false`. Method `contains` uses `Object` method `equals` to determine whether the search key is equal to one of the `Vector`'s elements. Many classes override method `equals` to perform the comparisons in a manner specific to those classes. For example, class `String` declares `equals` to compare the individual characters in the two `Strings` being compared. If method `equals` is not overridden, the original version of method `equals` inherited from class `Object` is used.

Common Programming Error 19.4

Without overriding method `equals`, the program performs comparisons using operator `==` to determine whether two references refer to the same object in memory.

Line 37 calls `Vector` method `indexOf` to determine the index of the first location in the `Vector` that contains the argument. The method returns –1 if the argument is not found in the `Vector`. An overloaded version of this method takes a second argument specifying the index in the `Vector` at which the search should begin.

Performance Tip 19.6

`Vector` methods `contains` and `indexOf` perform linear searches of a `Vector`'s contents. These searches are inefficient for large `Vectors`. If a program frequently searches for elements in a collection, consider using one of the Java Collection API's `Map` implementations (Section 19.10), which provide high-speed searching capabilities.

Line 41 calls `Vector` method `remove` to remove the first occurrence of its argument from the `Vector`. The method returns `true` if it finds the element in the `Vector`; otherwise, the method returns `false`. If the element is removed, all elements after that element in the `Vector` shift one position toward the beginning of the `Vector` to fill in the position of the removed element. Class `Vector` also provides method `removeAllElements` to remove every element from a `Vector` and method `removeElementAt` to remove the element at a specified index.

Lines 53–54 use `Vector` methods `size` and `capacity` to determine the number of elements currently in the `Vector` and the number of elements that can be stored in the `Vector` without allocating more memory, respectively.

Line 59 calls `Vector` method `isEmpty` to determine whether the `Vector` is empty. The method returns `true` if there are no elements in the `Vector`; otherwise, the method returns `false`. Lines 66–67 use the enhanced `for` statement to print out all elements in the vector.

Among the methods introduced in Fig. 19.6, `firstElement`, `lastElement` and `capacity` can be used only with `Vector`. Other methods (e.g., `add`, `contains`, `indexOf`, `remove`, `size` and `isEmpty`) are declared by `List`, which means that they can be used by any class that implements `List`, such as `Vector`.

19.6 Collections Algorithms

The collections framework provides several high-performance algorithms for manipulating collection elements. These algorithms are implemented as `static` methods of class `Collections` (Fig. 19.7). Algorithms `sort`, `binarySearch`, `reverse`, `shuffle`, `fill` and `copy` operate on `Lists`. Algorithms `min`, `max`, `addAll`, `frequency` and `disjoint` operate on `Collections`.

Algorithm	Description
sort	Sorts the elements of a List.
binarySearch	Locates an object in a List.
reverse	Reverses the elements of a List.
shuffle	Randomly orders a List's elements.
fill	Sets every List element to refer to a specified object.
copy	Copies references from one List into another.
min	Returns the smallest element in a Collection.
max	Returns the largest element in a Collection.
addAll	Appends all elements in an array to a collection.
frequency	Calculates how many elements in the collection are equal to the specified element.
disjoint	Determines whether two collections have no elements in common.

Fig. 19.7 | Collections algorithms.

Software Engineering Observation 19.4

The collections framework algorithms are polymorphic. That is, each algorithm can operate on objects that implement specific interfaces, regardless of the underlying implementations.

19.6.1 Algorithm sort

Algorithm **sort** sorts the elements of a List, which must implement the Comparable interface. The order is determined by the natural order of the elements' type as implemented by a compareTo method. Method compareTo is declared in interface Comparable and is sometimes called the **natural comparison method**. The sort call may specify as a second argument a Comparator object that determines an alternative ordering of the elements.

Sorting in Ascending Order

Figure 19.8 uses algorithm sort to order the elements of a List in ascending order (line 20). Recall that List is a generic type and accepts one type argument that specifies the list element type—line 15 declares list as a List of String. Note that lines 18 and 23 each use an implicit call to the list's toString method to output the list contents in the format shown on the second and fourth lines of the output.

Sorting in Descending Order

Figure 19.9 sorts the same list of strings used in Fig. 19.8 in descending order. The example introduces the Comparator interface, which is used for sorting a Collection's elements in a different order. Line 21 calls Collections's method sort to order the List in descending order. The static Collections method **reverseOrder** returns a Comparator object that orders the collection's elements in reverse order.

```java
 1  // Fig. 19.8: Sort1.java
 2  // Using algorithm sort.
 3  import java.util.List;
 4  import java.util.Arrays;
 5  import java.util.Collections;
 6
 7  public class Sort1
 8  {
 9     private static final String suits[] =
10        { "Hearts", "Diamonds", "Clubs", "Spades" };
11
12     // display array elements
13     public void printElements()
14     {
15        List< String > list = Arrays.asList( suits ); // create List
16
17        // output list
18        System.out.printf( "Unsorted array elements:\n%s\n", list );
19
20        Collections.sort( list ); // sort ArrayList
21
22        // output list
23        System.out.printf( "Sorted array elements:\n%s\n", list );
24     } // end method printElements
25
26     public static void main( String args[] )
27     {
28        Sort1 sort1 = new Sort1();
29        sort1.printElements();
30     } // end main
31  } // end class Sort1
```

```
Unsorted array elements:
[Hearts, Diamonds, Clubs, Spades]
Sorted array elements:
[Clubs, Diamonds, Hearts, Spades]
```

Fig. 19.8 | Collections method sort.

```java
 1  // Fig. 19.9: Sort2.java
 2  // Using a Comparator object with algorithm sort.
 3  import java.util.List;
 4  import java.util.Arrays;
 5  import java.util.Collections;
 6
 7  public class Sort2
 8  {
```

Fig. 19.9 | Collections method sort with a Comparator object. (Part 1 of 2.)

```
 9      private static final String suits[] =
10         { "Hearts", "Diamonds", "Clubs", "Spades" };
11
12      // output List elements
13      public void printElements()
14      {
15         List< String > list = Arrays.asList( suits ); // create List
16
17         // output List elements
18         System.out.printf( "Unsorted array elements:\n%s\n", list );
19
20         // sort in descending order using a comparator
21         Collections.sort( list, Collections.reverseOrder() );
22
23         // output List elements
24         System.out.printf( "Sorted list elements:\n%s\n", list );
25      } // end method printElements
26
27      public static void main( String args[] )
28      {
29         Sort2 sort2 = new Sort2();
30         sort2.printElements();
31      } // end main
32   } // end class Sort2
```

```
Unsorted array elements:
[Hearts, Diamonds, Clubs, Spades]
Sorted list elements:
[Spades, Hearts, Diamonds, Clubs]
```

Fig. 19.9 | `Collections` method `sort` with a `Comparator` object. (Part 2 of 2.)

Sorting with a *Comparator*

Figure 19.10 creates a custom Comparator class, named TimeComparator, that implements interface Comparator to compare two Time2 objects. Class Time2, declared in Fig. 8.5, represents times with hours, minutes and seconds.

Class TimeComparator implements interface Comparator, a generic type that takes one argument (in this case Time2). Method compare (lines 7–26) performs comparisons between Time2 objects. Line 9 compares the two hours of the Time2 objects. If the hours are different (line 12), then we return this value. If this value is positive, then the first hour is greater than the second and the first time is greater than the second. If this value is negative, then the first hour is less than the second and the first time is less than the second. If this value is zero, the hours are the same and we must test the minutes (and maybe the seconds) to determine which time is greater.

Figure 19.11 sorts a list using the custom Comparator class TimeComparator. Line 11 creates an ArrayList of Time2 objects. Recall that both ArrayList and List are generic types and accept a type argument that specifies the element type of the collection. Lines 13–17 create five Time2 objects and add them to this list. Line 23 calls method sort, passing it an object of our TimeComparator class (Fig. 19.10).

```
 1   // Fig. 19.10: TimeComparator.java
 2   // Custom Comparator class that compares two Time2 objects.
 3   import java.util.Comparator;
 4
 5   public class TimeComparator implements Comparator< Time2 >
 6   {
 7      public int compare( Time2 time1, Time2 time2 )
 8      {
 9         int hourCompare = time1.getHour() - time2.getHour(); // compare hour
10
11         // test the hour first
12         if ( hourCompare != 0 )
13            return hourCompare;
14
15         int minuteCompare =
16            time1.getMinute() - time2.getMinute(); // compare minute
17
18         // then test the minute
19         if ( minuteCompare != 0 )
20            return minuteCompare;
21
22         int secondCompare =
23            time1.getSecond() - time2.getSecond(); // compare second
24
25         return secondCompare; // return result of comparing seconds
26      } // end method compare
27   } // end class TimeComparator
```

Fig. 19.10 | Custom `Comparator` class that compares two `Time2` objects.

```
 1   // Fig. 19.11: Sort3.java
 2   // Sort a list using the custom Comparator class TimeComparator.
 3   import java.util.List;
 4   import java.util.ArrayList;
 5   import java.util.Collections;
 6
 7   public class Sort3
 8   {
 9      public void printElements()
10      {
11         List< Time2 > list = new ArrayList< Time2 >(); // create List
12
13         list.add( new Time2(  6, 24, 34 ) );
14         list.add( new Time2( 18, 14, 58 ) );
15         list.add( new Time2(  6, 05, 34 ) );
16         list.add( new Time2( 12, 14, 58 ) );
17         list.add( new Time2(  6, 24, 22 ) );
18
19         // output List elements
20         System.out.printf( "Unsorted array elements:\n%s\n", list );
21
```

Fig. 19.11 | `Collections` method `sort` with a custom `Comparator` object. (Part 1 of 2.)

```
22          // sort in order using a comparator
23          Collections.sort( list, new TimeComparator() );
24
25          // output List elements
26          System.out.printf( "Sorted list elements:\n%s\n", list );
27       } // end method printElements
28
29       public static void main( String args[] )
30       {
31          Sort3 sort3 = new Sort3();
32          sort3.printElements();
33       } // end main
34    } // end class Sort3
```

```
Unsorted array elements:
[6:24:34 AM, 6:14:58 PM, 6:05:34 AM, 12:14:58 PM, 6:24:22 AM]
Sorted list elements:
[6:05:34 AM, 6:24:22 AM, 6:24:34 AM, 12:14:58 PM, 6:14:58 PM]
```

Fig. 19.11 | `Collections` method `sort` with a custom `Comparator` object. (Part 2 of 2.)

19.6.2 Algorithm shuffle

Algorithm `shuffle` randomly orders a `List`'s elements. In Chapter 7, we presented a card shuffling and dealing simulation that used a loop to shuffle a deck of cards. In Fig. 19.12, we use algorithm `shuffle` to shuffle a deck of `Card` objects that might be used in a card game simulator.

Class Card (lines 8–41) represents a card in a deck of cards. Each Card has a face and a suit. Lines 10–12 declare two enum types—Face and Suit—which represent the face and the suit of the card, respectively. Method toString (lines 37–40) returns a String containing the face and suit of the Card separated by the string " of ". When an enum constant is converted to a string, the constant's identifier is used as the string representation. Normally we would use all uppercase letters for enum constants. In this example, we chose to use capital letters for only the first letter of each enum constant because we want the card to be displayed with initial capital letters for the face and the suit (e.g., "Ace of Spades").

```
 1    // Fig. 19.12: DeckOfCards.java
 2    // Using algorithm shuffle.
 3    import java.util.List;
 4    import java.util.Arrays;
 5    import java.util.Collections;
 6
 7    // class to represent a Card in a deck of cards
 8    class Card
 9    {
10       public static enum Face { Ace, Deuce, Three, Four, Five, Six,
11          Seven, Eight, Nine, Ten, Jack, Queen, King };
12       public static enum Suit { Clubs, Diamonds, Hearts, Spades };
13
```

Fig. 19.12 | Card shuffling and dealing with `Collections` method `shuffle`. (Part 1 of 3.)

```
14      private final Face face; // face of card
15      private final Suit suit; // suit of card
16
17      // two-argument constructor
18      public Card( Face cardFace, Suit cardSuit )
19      {
20         face = cardFace; // initialize face of card
21         suit = cardSuit; // initialize suit of card
22      } // end two-argument Card constructor
23
24      // return face of the card
25      public Face getFace()
26      {
27         return face;
28      } // end method getFace
29
30      // return suit of Card
31      public Suit getSuit()
32      {
33         return suit;
34      } // end method getSuit
35
36      // return String representation of Card
37      public String toString()
38      {
39         return String.format( "%s of %s", face, suit );
40      } // end method toString
41   } // end class Card
42
43   // class DeckOfCards declaration
44   public class DeckOfCards
45   {
46      private List< Card > list; // declare List that will store Cards
47
48      // set up deck of Cards and shuffle
49      public DeckOfCards()
50      {
51         Card[] deck = new Card[ 52 ];
52         int count = 0; // number of cards
53
54         // populate deck with Card objects
55         for ( Card.Suit suit : Card.Suit.values() )
56         {
57            for ( Card.Face face : Card.Face.values() )
58            {
59               deck[ count ] = new Card( face, suit );
60               count++;
61            } // end for
62         } // end for
63
64         list = Arrays.asList( deck ); // get List
65         Collections.shuffle( list ); // shuffle deck
66      } // end DeckOfCards constructor
```

Fig. 19.12 | Card shuffling and dealing with `Collections` method `shuffle`. (Part 2 of 3.)

```
67
68     // output deck
69     public void printCards()
70     {
71        // display 52 cards in two columns
72        for ( int i = 0; i < list.size(); i++ )
73           System.out.printf( "%-20s%s", list.get( i ),
74              ( ( i + 1 ) % 2 == 0 ) ? "\n" : "\t" );
75     } // end method printCards
76
77     public static void main( String args[] )
78     {
79        DeckOfCards cards = new DeckOfCards();
80        cards.printCards();
81     } // end main
82  } // end class DeckOfCards
```

```
King of Diamonds     Jack of Spades
Four of Diamonds     Six of Clubs
King of Hearts       Nine of Diamonds
Three of Spades      Four of Spades
Four of Hearts       Seven of Spades
Five of Diamonds     Eight of Hearts
Queen of Diamonds    Five of Hearts
Seven of Diamonds    Seven of Hearts
Nine of Hearts       Three of Clubs
Ten of Spades        Deuce of Hearts
Three of Hearts      Ace of Spades
Six of Hearts        Eight of Diamonds
Six of Diamonds      Deuce of Clubs
Ace of Clubs         Ten of Diamonds
Eight of Clubs       Queen of Hearts
Jack of Clubs        Ten of Clubs
Seven of Clubs       Queen of Spades
Five of Clubs        Six of Spades
Nine of Spades       Nine of Clubs
King of Spades       Ace of Diamonds
Ten of Hearts        Ace of Hearts
Queen of Clubs       Deuce of Spades
Three of Diamonds    King of Clubs
Four of Clubs        Jack of Diamonds
Eight of Spades      Five of Spades
Jack of Hearts       Deuce of Diamonds
```

Fig. 19.12 | Card shuffling and dealing with `Collections` method `shuffle`. (Part 3 of 3.)

Lines 55–62 populate the deck array with cards that have unique face and suit combinations. Both Face and Suit are public static enum types of class Card. To use these enum types outside of class Card, you must qualify each enum's type name with the name of the class in which it resides (i.e., Card) and a dot (.) separator. Hence, lines 55 and 57 use Card.Suit and Card.Face to declare the control variables of the for statements. Recall that method values of an enum type returns an array that contains all the constants of the enum type. Lines 55–62 use enhanced for statements to construct 52 new Cards.

The shuffling occurs in line 65, which calls static method shuffle of class Collections to shuffle the elements of the array. Method shuffle requires a List argument, so we must obtain a List view of the array before we can shuffle it. Line 64 invokes static method asList of class Arrays to get a List view of the deck array.

Method printCards (lines 69–75) displays the deck of cards in two columns. In each iteration of the loop, lines 73–74 output a card left justified in a 20-character field followed by either a newline or an empty string based on the number of cards output so far. If the number of cards is even, a newline is output; otherwise, a tab is output.

19.6.3 Algorithms reverse, fill, copy, max and min

Class Collections provides algorithms for reversing, filling and copying Lists. Algorithm **reverse** reverses the order of the elements in a List, and algorithm **fill** overwrites elements in a List with a specified value. The fill operation is useful for reinitializing a List. Algorithm **copy** takes two arguments—a destination List and a source List. Each source List element is copied to the destination List. The destination List must be at least as long as the source List; otherwise, an IndexOutOfBoundsException occurs. If the destination List is longer, the elements not overwritten are unchanged.

Each algorithm we have seen so far operates on Lists. Algorithms **min** and **max** each operate on any Collection. Algorithm min returns the smallest element in a Collection, and algorithm max returns the largest element in a Collection. Both of these algorithms can be called with a Comparator object as a second argument to perform custom comparisons of objects, such as the TimeComparator in Fig. 19.11. Figure 19.13 demonstrates the use of algorithms reverse, fill, copy, min and max. Note that the generic type List is declared to store Characters.

```java
1   // Fig. 19.13: Algorithms1.java
2   // Using algorithms reverse, fill, copy, min and max.
3   import java.util.List;
4   import java.util.Arrays;
5   import java.util.Collections;
6
7   public class Algorithms1
8   {
9      private Character[] letters = { 'P', 'C', 'M' };
10     private Character[] lettersCopy;
11     private List< Character > list;
12     private List< Character > copyList;
13
14     // create a List and manipulate it with methods from Collections
15     public Algorithms1()
16     {
17        list = Arrays.asList( letters ); // get List
18        lettersCopy = new Character[ 3 ];
19        copyList = Arrays.asList( lettersCopy ); // list view of lettersCopy
20
21        System.out.println( "Initial list: " );
22        output( list );
```

Fig. 19.13 | Collections methods reverse, fill, copy, max and min. (Part I of 2.)

```
23
24        Collections.reverse( list ); // reverse order
25        System.out.println( "\nAfter calling reverse: " );
26        output( list );
27
28        Collections.copy( copyList, list ); // copy List
29        System.out.println( "\nAfter copying: " );
30        output( copyList );
31
32        Collections.fill( list, 'R' ); // fill list with Rs
33        System.out.println( "\nAfter calling fill: " );
34        output( list );
35     } // end Algorithms1 constructor
36
37     // output List information
38     private void output( List< Character > listRef )
39     {
40        System.out.print( "The list is: " );
41
42        for ( Character element : listRef )
43           System.out.printf( "%s ", element );
44
45        System.out.printf( "\nMax: %s", Collections.max( listRef ) );
46        System.out.printf( "  Min: %s\n", Collections.min( listRef ) );
47     } // end method output
48
49     public static void main( String args[] )
50     {
51        new Algorithms1();
52     } // end main
53  } // end class Algorithms1
```

```
Initial list:
The list is: P C M
Max: P  Min: C

After calling reverse:
The list is: M C P
Max: P  Min: C

After copying:
The list is: M C P
Max: P  Min: C

After calling fill:
The list is: R R R
Max: R  Min: R
```

Fig. 19.13 | Collections methods reverse, fill, copy, max and min. (Part 2 of 2.)

Line 24 calls Collections method reverse to reverse the order of list. Method reverse takes one List argument. In this case, list is a List view of array letters. Array letters now has its elements in reverse order. Line 28 copies the elements of list into copyList, using Collections method copy. Changes to copyList do not change letters, because copyList is a separate List that is not a List view for letters. Method copy requires two List arguments. Line 32 calls Collections method fill to place the string "R" in each element of list. Because list is a List view of letters, this operation changes each element in letters to "R". Method fill requires a List for the first argument and an Object for the second argument. Lines 45–46 call Collections methods max and min to find the largest and the smallest element of the collection, respectively. Recall that a List is a Collection, so lines 45–46 can pass a List to methods max and min.

19.6.4 Algorithm binarySearch

In Section 16.2.2, we studied the high-speed binary search algorithm. This algorithm is built into the Java collections framework as a static method of class Collections. The binarySearch algorithm locates an object in a List (i.e., a LinkedList, a Vector or an ArrayList). If the object is found, its index is returned. If the object is not found, binarySearch returns a negative value. Algorithm binarySearch determines this negative value by first calculating the insertion point and making its sign negative. Then, binarySearch subtracts 1 from the insertion point to obtain the return value, which guarantees that method binarySearch returns positive numbers (>= 0) if and only if the object is found. If multiple elements in the list match the search key, there is no guarantee which one will be located first. Figure 19.14 uses the binarySearch algorithm to search for a series of strings in an ArrayList.

```
1   // Fig. 19.14: BinarySearchTest.java
2   // Using algorithm binarySearch.
3   import java.util.List;
4   import java.util.Arrays;
5   import java.util.Collections;
6   import java.util.ArrayList;
7
8   public class BinarySearchTest
9   {
10      private static final String colors[] = { "red", "white",
11         "blue", "black", "yellow", "purple", "tan", "pink" };
12      private List< String > list; // ArrayList reference
13
14      // create, sort and output list
15      public BinarySearchTest()
16      {
17         list = new ArrayList< String >( Arrays.asList( colors ) );
18         Collections.sort( list ); // sort the ArrayList
19         System.out.printf( "Sorted ArrayList: %s\n", list );
20      } // end BinarySearchTest constructor
21
22      // search list for various values
23      private void search()
24      {
25         printSearchResults( colors[ 3 ] ); // first item
26         printSearchResults( colors[ 0 ] ); // middle item
27         printSearchResults( colors[ 7 ] ); // last item
```

Fig. 19.14 | Collections method binarySearch. (Part 1 of 2.)

```
28          printSearchResults( "aqua" ); // below lowest
29          printSearchResults( "gray" ); // does not exist
30          printSearchResults( "teal" ); // does not exist
31       } // end method search
32
33       // perform searches and display search result
34       private void printSearchResults( String key )
35       {
36          int result = 0;
37
38          System.out.printf( "\nSearching for: %s\n", key );
39          result = Collections.binarySearch( list, key );
40
41          if ( result >= 0 )
42             System.out.printf( "Found at index %d\n", result );
43          else
44             System.out.printf( "Not Found (%d)\n",result );
45       } // end method printSearchResults
46
47       public static void main( String args[] )
48       {
49          BinarySearchTest binarySearchTest = new BinarySearchTest();
50          binarySearchTest.search();
51       } // end main
52    } // end class BinarySearchTest
```

```
Sorted ArrayList: [black, blue, pink, purple, red, tan, white, yellow]

Searching for: black
Found at index 0

Searching for: red
Found at index 4

Searching for: pink
Found at index 2

Searching for: aqua
Not Found (-1)

Searching for: gray
Not Found (-3)

Searching for: teal
Not Found (-7)
```

Fig. 19.14 | Collections method binarySearch. (Part 2 of 2.)

Recall that both List and ArrayList are generic types (lines 12 and 17). Collections method binarySearch expects the list's elements to be sorted in ascending order, so line 18 in the constructor sorts the list with Collections method sort. If the list's elements are not sorted, the result is undefined. Line 19 outputs the sorted list. Method search (lines 23–31) is called from main to perform the searches. Each search calls method print-SearchResults (lines 34–45) to perform the search and output the results. Line 39 calls

Collections method binarySearch to search list for the specified key. Method binarySearch takes a List as the first argument and an Object as the second argument. Lines 41–44 output the results of the search. An overloaded version of binarySearch takes a Comparator object as its third argument, which specifies how binarySearch should compare elements.

19.6.5 Algorithms addAll, frequency and disjoint

Class Collections also provides the algorithms **addAll**, **frequency** and **disjoint**. Algorithm addAll takes two arguments—a Collection into which to insert the new element(s) and an array that provides elements to be inserted. Algorithm frequency takes two arguments—a Collection to be searched and an Object to be searched for in the collection. Method frequency returns the number of times that the second argument appears in the collection. Algorithm disjoint takes two Collections and returns true if they have no elements in common. Figure 19.15 demonstrates the use of algorithms addAll, frequency and disjoint.

```
1    // Fig. 19.15: Algorithms2.java
2    // Using algorithms addAll, frequency and disjoint.
3    import java.util.List;
4    import java.util.Vector;
5    import java.util.Arrays;
6    import java.util.Collections;
7
8    public class Algorithms2
9    {
10       private String[] colors = { "red", "white", "yellow", "blue" };
11       private List< String > list;
12       private Vector< String > vector = new Vector< String >();
13
14       // create List and Vector
15       // and manipulate them with methods from Collections
16       public Algorithms2()
17       {
18          // initialize list and vector
19          list = Arrays.asList( colors );
20          vector.add( "black" );
21          vector.add( "red" );
22          vector.add( "green" );
23
24          System.out.println( "Before addAll, vector contains: " );
25
26          // display elements in vector
27          for ( String s : vector )
28             System.out.printf( "%s ", s );
29
30          // add elements in colors to list
31          Collections.addAll( vector, colors );
32
33          System.out.println( "\n\nAfter addAll, vector contains: " );
```

Fig. 19.15 | Collections method addAll, frequency and disjoint. (Part 1 of 2.)

```
34
35        // display elements in vector
36        for ( String s : vector )
37           System.out.printf( "%s ", s );
38
39        // get frequency of "red"
40        int frequency = Collections.frequency( vector, "red" );
41        System.out.printf(
42           "\n\nFrequency of red in vector: %d\n", frequency );
43
44        // check whether list and vector have elements in common
45        boolean disjoint = Collections.disjoint( list, vector );
46
47        System.out.printf( "\nlist and vector %s elements in common\n",
48           ( disjoint ? "do not have" : "have"  ) );
49     } // end Algorithms2 constructor
50
51     public static void main( String args[] )
52     {
53        new Algorithms2();
54     } // end main
55  } // end class Algorithms2
```

```
Before addAll, vector contains:
black red green

After addAll, vector contains:
black red green red white yellow blue

Frequency of red in vector: 2

list and vector have elements in common
```

Fig. 19.15 | Collections method addAll, frequency and disjoint. (Part 2 of 2.)

Line 19 initializes list with elements in array colors, and lines 20–22 add Strings "black", "red" and "green" to vector. Line 31 invokes method addAll to add elements in array colors to vector. Line 40 gets the frequency of String "red" in Collection vector using method frequency. Note that lines 41–42 use the new printf method to print the frequency. Line 45 invokes method disjoint to test whether Collections list and vector have elements in common.

19.7 Stack Class of Package java.util

In Chapter 17, Data Structures, we learned how to build fundamental data structures, including linked lists, stacks, queues and trees. In a world of software reuse, rather than building data structures as we need them, we can often take advantage of existing data structures. In this section, we investigate class Stack in the Java utilities package (java.util).

Section 19.5.3 discussed class Vector, which implements a dynamically resizable array. Class Stack extends class Vector to implement a stack data structure. Autoboxing occurs when you add a primitive type to a Stack, because class Stack stores only references to objects. Figure 19.16 demonstrates several Stack methods. For the details of class Stack, visit java.sun.com/javase/6/docs/api/java/util/Stack.html.

```java
1  // Fig. 19.16: StackTest.java
2  // Program to test java.util.Stack.
3  import java.util.Stack;
4  import java.util.EmptyStackException;
5
6  public class StackTest
7  {
8     public StackTest()
9     {
10        Stack< Number > stack = new Stack< Number >();
11
12        // create numbers to store in the stack
13        Long longNumber = 12L;
14        Integer intNumber = 34567;
15        Float floatNumber = 1.0F;
16        Double doubleNumber = 1234.5678;
17
18        // use push method
19        stack.push( longNumber ); // push a long
20        printStack( stack );
21        stack.push( intNumber ); // push an int
22        printStack( stack );
23        stack.push( floatNumber ); // push a float
24        printStack( stack );
25        stack.push( doubleNumber ); // push a double
26        printStack( stack );
27
28        // remove items from stack
29        try
30        {
31           Number removedObject = null;
32
33           // pop elements from stack
34           while ( true )
35           {
36              removedObject = stack.pop(); // use pop method
37              System.out.printf( "%s popped\n", removedObject );
38              printStack( stack );
39           } // end while
40        } // end try
41        catch ( EmptyStackException emptyStackException )
42        {
43           emptyStackException.printStackTrace();
44        } // end catch
45     } // end StackTest constructor
46
47     private void printStack( Stack< Number > stack )
48     {
```

Fig. 19.16 | Stack class of package java.util. (Part 1 of 2.)

```
49        if ( stack.isEmpty() )
50            System.out.print( "stack is empty\n\n" ); // the stack is empty
51        else  // stack is not empty
52        {
53            System.out.print( "stack contains: " );
54
55            // iterate through the elements
56            for ( Number number : stack )
57                System.out.printf( "%s ", number );
58
59            System.out.print( "(top) \n\n" ); // indicates top of the stack
60        } // end else
61    } // end method printStack
62
63    public static void main( String args[] )
64    {
65        new StackTest();
66    } // end main
67 } // end class StackTest
```

```
stack contains: 12 (top)

stack contains: 12 34567 (top)

stack contains: 12 34567 1.0 (top)

stack contains: 12 34567 1.0 1234.5678 (top)

1234.5678 popped
stack contains: 12 34567 1.0 (top)

1.0 popped
stack contains: 12 34567 (top)

34567 popped
stack contains: 12 (top)

12 popped
stack is empty

java.util.EmptyStackException
        at java.util.Stack.peek(Unknown Source)
        at java.util.Stack.pop(Unknown Source)
        at StackTest.<init>(StackTest.java:36)
        at StackTest.main(StackTest.java:65)
```

Fig. 19.16 | Stack class of package java.util. (Part 2 of 2.)

Line 10 of the constructor creates an empty Stack of type Number. Class Number (in package java.lang) is the superclass of most wrapper classes (e.g., Integer, Double) for the primitive types. By creating a Stack of Number, objects of any class that extends the Number class can be pushed onto the stack. Lines 19, 21, 23 and 25 each call Stack method **push** to add objects to the top of the stack. Note the literals 12L (line 13) and 1.0F (line 15). Any integer literal that has the **suffix L** is a long value. An integer literal without a suffix is an `int` value. Similarly, any floating-point literal that has the suffix `F` is a `float` value. A floating-point literal without a suffix is a `double` value. You can learn more about numeric literals in the *Java Language Specification* at `java.sun.com/docs/books/jls/second_edition/html/expressions.doc.html#224125`.

An infinite loop (lines 34–39) calls `Stack` method **pop** to remove the top element of the stack. The method returns a `Number` reference to the removed element. If there are no elements in the `Stack`, method pop throws an `EmptyStackException`, which terminates the loop. Class `Stack` also declares method **peek**. This method returns the top element of the stack without popping the element off the stack.

Line 49 calls `Stack` method `isEmpty` (inherited by `Stack` from class `Vector`) to determine whether the stack is empty. If it is empty, the method returns `true`; otherwise, the method returns `false`.

Method `printStack` (lines 47–61) uses the enhanced `for` statement to iterate through the elements in the stack. The current top of the stack (the last value pushed onto the stack) is the first value printed. Because class `Stack` extends class `Vector`, the entire `public` interface of class `Vector` is available to clients of class `Stack`.

Error-Prevention Tip 19.1

Because `Stack` extends `Vector`, all `public` `Vector` methods can be called on `Stack` objects, even if the methods do not represent conventional stack operations. For example, `Vector` method `add` can be used to insert an element anywhere in a stack—an operation that could "corrupt" the stack. When manipulating a `Stack`, only methods `push` and `pop` should be used to add elements to and remove elements from the `Stack`, respectively.

19.8 Class `PriorityQueue` and Interface `Queue`

In Section 17.8, we introduced the queue data structure and created our own implementation of it. In this section we investigate interface `Queue` and class `PriorityQueue` in the Java utilities package (`java.util`). Queue, a new collection interface introduced in Java SE 5, extends interface `Collection` and provides additional operations for inserting, removing and inspecting elements in a queue. `PriorityQueue`, one of the classes that implements the `Queue` interface, orders elements by their natural ordering as specified by `Comparable` elements' `compareTo` method or by a `Comparator` object that is supplied through the constructor.

Class `PriorityQueue` provides functionality that enables insertions in sorted order into the underlying data structure and deletions from the front of the underlying data structure. When adding elements to a `PriorityQueue`, the elements are inserted in priority order such that the highest-priority element (i.e., the largest value) will be the first element removed from the `PriorityQueue`.

The common `PriorityQueue` operations are **offer** to insert an element at the appropriate location based on priority order, **poll** to remove the highest-priority element of the priority queue (i.e., the head of the queue), **peek** to get a reference to the highest-priority element of the priority queue (without removing that element), **clear** to remove all elements in the priority queue and **size** to get the number of elements in the priority queue. Figure 19.17 demonstrates the `PriorityQueue` class.

Line 10 creates a `PriorityQueue` that stores `Double`s with an initial capacity of 11 elements and orders the elements according to the object's natural ordering (the defaults for

```
 1   // Fig. 19.17: PriorityQueueTest.java
 2   // Standard library class PriorityQueue test program.
 3   import java.util.PriorityQueue;
 4
 5   public class PriorityQueueTest
 6   {
 7      public static void main( String args[] )
 8      {
 9         // queue of capacity 11
10         PriorityQueue< Double > queue = new PriorityQueue< Double >();
11
12         // insert elements to queue
13         queue.offer( 3.2 );
14         queue.offer( 9.8 );
15         queue.offer( 5.4 );
16
17         System.out.print( "Polling from queue: " );
18
19         // display elements in queue
20         while ( queue.size() > 0 )
21         {
22            System.out.printf( "%.1f ", queue.peek() ); // view top element
23            queue.poll(); // remove top element
24         } // end while
25      } // end main
26   } // end class PriorityQueueTest
```

```
Polling from queue: 3.2 5.4 9.8
```

Fig. 19.17 | PriorityQueue test program.

a PriorityQueue). Note that PriorityQueue is a generic class and that line 10 instantiates a PriorityQueue with a type argument Double. Class PriorityQueue provides five additional constructors. One of these takes an int and a Comparator object to create a PriorityQueue with the initial capacity specified by the int and the ordering by the Comparator. Lines 13–15 use method offer to add elements to the priority queue. Method offer throws a NullPointException if the program attempts to add a null object to the queue. The loop in lines 20–24 uses method size to determine whether the priority queue is empty (line 20). While there are more elements, line 22 uses Priority-Queue method peek to retrieve the highest-priority element in the queue for output (without actually removing the element from the queue). Line 23 removes the highest-priority element in the queue with method poll.

19.9 Sets

A Set is a Collection that contains unique elements (i.e., no duplicate elements). The collections framework contains several Set implementations, including HashSet and TreeSet. HashSet stores its elements in a hash table, and TreeSet stores its elements in a tree. The concept of hash tables is presented in Section 19.10. Figure 19.18 uses a HashSet to remove duplicate strings from a List. Recall that both List and Collection are generic

```
1    // Fig. 19.18: SetTest.java
2    // Using a HashSet to remove duplicates.
3    import java.util.List;
4    import java.util.Arrays;
5    import java.util.HashSet;
6    import java.util.Set;
7    import java.util.Collection;
8
9    public class SetTest
10   {
11      private static final String colors[] = { "red", "white", "blue",
12         "green", "gray", "orange", "tan", "white", "cyan",
13         "peach", "gray", "orange" };
14
15      // create and output ArrayList
16      public SetTest()
17      {
18         List< String > list = Arrays.asList( colors );
19         System.out.printf( "ArrayList: %s\n", list );
20         printNonDuplicates( list );
21      } // end SetTest constructor
22
23      // create set from array to eliminate duplicates
24      private void printNonDuplicates( Collection< String > collection )
25      {
26         // create a HashSet
27         Set< String > set = new HashSet< String >( collection );
28
29         System.out.println( "\nNonduplicates are: " );
30
31         for ( String s : set )
32            System.out.printf( "%s ", s );
33
34         System.out.println();
35      } // end method printNonDuplicates
36
37      public static void main( String args[] )
38      {
39         new SetTest();
40      } // end main
41   } // end class SetTest
```

```
ArrayList: [red, white, blue, green, gray, orange, tan, white, cyan, peach,
gray, orange]

Nonduplicates are:
red cyan white tan gray green orange blue peach
```

Fig. 19.18 | HashSet used to remove duplicate values from array of strings.

types, so line 18 creates a List that contains String objects, and line 24 passes a Collection of Strings to method printNonDuplicates.

Method `printNonDuplicates` (lines 24–35), which is called from the constructor, takes a `Collection` argument. Line 27 constructs a `HashSet` from the `Collection` argument. Note that both `Set` and `HashSet` are generic types. By definition, `Set`s do not contain any duplicates, so when the `HashSet` is constructed, it removes any duplicates in the `Collection`. Lines 31–32 output elements in the `Set`.

Sorted Sets

The collections framework also includes interface **SortedSet** (which extends `Set`) for sets that maintain their elements in sorted order—either the elements' natural order (e.g., numbers are in ascending order) or an order specified by a `Comparator`. Class `TreeSet` implements `SortedSet`. The program in Fig. 19.19 places strings into a `TreeSet`. The strings are sorted as they are added to the `TreeSet`. This example also demonstrates range-view methods, which enable a program to view a portion of a collection.

Lines 16–17 of the constructor create a `TreeSet` of `String`s that contains the elements of array `names` and assigns the `SortedSet` to variable `tree`. Both `SortedSet` and `TreeSet`

```
1   // Fig. 19.19: SortedSetTest.java
2   // Using TreeSet and SortedSet.
3   import java.util.Arrays;
4   import java.util.SortedSet;
5   import java.util.TreeSet;
6
7   public class SortedSetTest
8   {
9      private static final String names[] = { "yellow", "green",
10         "black", "tan", "grey", "white", "orange", "red", "green" };
11
12      // create a sorted set with TreeSet, then manipulate it
13      public SortedSetTest()
14      {
15         // create TreeSet
16         SortedSet< String > tree =
17            new TreeSet< String >( Arrays.asList( names ) );
18
19         System.out.println( "sorted set: " );
20         printSet( tree ); // output contents of tree
21
22         // get headSet based on "orange"
23         System.out.print( "\nheadSet (\"orange\"):  " );
24         printSet( tree.headSet( "orange" ) );
25
26         // get tailSet based upon "orange"
27         System.out.print( "tailSet (\"orange\"):  " );
28         printSet( tree.tailSet( "orange" ) );
29
30         // get first and last elements
31         System.out.printf( "first: %s\n", tree.first() );
32         System.out.printf( "last : %s\n", tree.last() );
33      } // end SortedSetTest constructor
34
```

Fig. 19.19 | Using `SortedSet`s and `TreeSet`s. (Part 1 of 2.)

```
35      // output set
36      private void printSet( SortedSet< String > set )
37      {
38         for ( String s : set )
39            System.out.printf( "%s ",  s );
40
41         System.out.println();
42      } // end method printSet
43
44      public static void main( String args[] )
45      {
46         new SortedSetTest();
47      } // end main
48   } // end class SortedSetTest
```

```
sorted set:
black green grey orange red tan white yellow

headSet ("orange"):  black green grey
tailSet ("orange"):  orange red tan white yellow
first: black
last : yellow
```

Fig. 19.19 | Using SortedSets and TreeSets. (Part 2 of 2.)

are generic types. Line 20 outputs the initial set of strings using method printSet (lines 36–42), which we discuss momentarily. Line 24 calls TreeSet method **headSet** to get a subset of the TreeSet in which every element is less than "orange". The view returned from headSet is then output with printSet. If any changes are made to the subset, they will also be made to the original TreeSet, because the subset returned by headSet is a view of the TreeSet.

Line 28 calls TreeSet method **tailSet** to get a subset in which each element is greater than or equal to "orange", then outputs the result. Any changes made through the tailSet view are made to the original TreeSet. Lines 31–32 call SortedSet methods first and last to get the smallest and largest elements of the set, respectively.

Method printSet (lines 36–42) accepts a SortedSet as an argument and prints it. Lines 38–39 print each element of the SortedSet using the enhanced for statement.

19.10 Maps

Maps associate keys to values and cannot contain duplicate keys (i.e., each key can map to only one value; this is called **one-to-one mapping**). Maps differ from Sets in that Maps contain keys and values, whereas Sets contain only values. Three of the several classes that implement interface Map are **Hashtable**, **HashMap** and **TreeMap**. Hashtables and HashMaps store elements in hash tables, and TreeMaps store elements in trees. This section discusses hash tables and provides an example that uses a HashMap to store keyPvalue pairs. Interface SortedMap extends Map and maintains its keys in sorted order—either the elements' natural order or an order specified by a Comparator. Class TreeMap implements SortedMap.

Map *Implementation with Hash Tables*

Object-oriented programming languages facilitate creating new types. When a program creates objects of new or existing types, it may need to store and retrieve them efficiently. Storing and retrieving information with arrays is efficient if some aspect of your data directly matches a numerical key value and if the keys are unique and tightly packed. If you have 100 employees with nine-digit social security numbers and you want to store and retrieve employee data by using the social security number as a key, the task would require an array with one billion elements, because there are one billion unique nine-digit numbers (000,000,000–999,999,999). This is impractical for virtually all applications that use social security numbers as keys. A program that had an array that large could achieve high performance for both storing and retrieving employee records by simply using the social security number as the array index.

Numerous applications have this problem—namely, that either the keys are of the wrong type (e.g., not positive integers that correspond to array subscripts) or they are of the right type, but sparsely spread over a huge range. What is needed is a high-speed scheme for converting keys such as social security numbers, inventory part numbers and the like into unique array indices. Then, when an application needs to store something, the scheme could convert the application's key rapidly into an index, and the record could be stored at that slot in the array. Retrieval is accomplished the same way: Once the application has a key for which it wants to retrieve a data record, the application simply applies the conversion to the key—this produces the array index where the data is stored and retrieved.

The scheme we describe here is the basis of a technique called hashing. Why the name? When we convert a key into an array index, we literally scramble the bits, forming a kind of "mishmashed," or hashed, number. The number actually has no real significance beyond its usefulness in storing and retrieving a particular data record.

A glitch in the scheme is called a collision—this occurs when two different keys "hash into" the same cell (or element) in the array. We cannot store two values in the same space, so we need to find an alternative home for all values beyond the first that hash to a particular array index. There are many schemes for doing this. One is to "hash again" (i.e., to apply another hashing transformation to the key to provide a next candidate cell in the array). The hashing process is designed to distribute the values throughout the table, so the assumption is that an available cell will be found with just a few hashes.

Another scheme uses one hash to locate the first candidate cell. If that cell is occupied, successive cells are searched in order until an available cell is found. Retrieval works the same way: The key is hashed once to determine the initial location and check whether it contains the desired data. If it does, the search is finished. If it does not, successive cells are searched linearly until the desired data is found.

The most popular solution to hash-table collisions is to have each cell of the table be a hash "bucket," typically a linked list of all the key/value pairs that hash to that cell. This is the solution that Java's `Hashtable` and `HashMap` classes (from package `java.util`) implement. Both `Hashtable` and `HashMap` implement the `Map` interface. The primary differences between them are that `HashMap` is unsynchronized (multiple threads should not modify a `HashMap` concurrently), and allows `null` keys and `null` values.

A hash table's load factor affects the performance of hashing schemes. The load factor is the ratio of the number of occupied cells in the hash table to the total number of cells in the hash table. The closer this ratio gets to 1.0, the greater the chance of collisions.

Performance Tip 19.7

The load factor in a hash table is a classic example of a memory-space/execution-time trade-off: By increasing the load factor, we get better memory utilization, but the program runs slower, due to increased hashing collisions. By decreasing the load factor, we get better program speed, because of reduced hashing collisions, but we get poorer memory utilization, because a larger portion of the hash table remains empty.

Hash tables are complex to program. Computer science students study hashing schemes in courses called "Data Structures" and "Algorithms." Java provides classes Hashtable and HashMap to enable programmers to use hashing without having to implement hash table mechanisms. This concept is profoundly important in our study of object-oriented programming. As discussed in earlier chapters, classes encapsulate and hide complexity (i.e., implementation details) and offer user-friendly interfaces. Properly crafting classes to exhibit such behavior is one of the most valued skills in the field of object-oriented programming. Figure 19.20 uses a HashMap to count the number of occurrences of each word in a string.

Line 17 creates an empty HashMap with a default initial capacity (16 elements) and a default load factor (0.75)—these defaults are built into the implementation of HashMap. When the number of occupied slots in the HashMap becomes greater than the capacity times the load factor, the capacity is doubled automatically. Note that HashMap is a generic class that takes two type arguments. The first specifies the type of key (i.e., String), and the second the type of value (i.e., Integer). Recall that the type arguments passed to a generic class must be reference types, hence the second type argument is Integer, not int. Line 18 creates a Scanner that reads user input from the standard input stream. Line 19 calls method createMap (lines 24–46), which uses a map to store the number of occurrences of each word in the sentence. Line 27 invokes method nextLine of scanner to obtain the user input, and line 30 creates a StringTokenizer to break the input string into

```java
 1   // Fig. 19.20: WordTypeCount.java
 2   // Program counts the number of occurrences of each word in a string
 3   import java.util.StringTokenizer;
 4   import java.util.Map;
 5   import java.util.HashMap;
 6   import java.util.Set;
 7   import java.util.TreeSet;
 8   import java.util.Scanner;
 9
10   public class WordTypeCount
11   {
12      private Map< String, Integer > map;
13      private Scanner scanner;
14
15      public WordTypeCount()
16      {
17         map = new HashMap< String, Integer >(); // create HashMap
18         scanner = new Scanner( System.in ); // create scanner
```

Fig. 19.20 | HashMaps and Maps. (Part 1 of 3.)

```
19              createMap(); // create map based on user input
20              displayMap(); // display map content
21          } // end WordTypeCount constructor
22
23          // create map from user input
24          private void createMap()
25          {
26              System.out.println( "Enter a string:" ); // prompt for user input
27              String input = scanner.nextLine();
28
29              // create StringTokenizer for input
30              StringTokenizer tokenizer = new StringTokenizer( input );
31
32              // processing input text
33              while ( tokenizer.hasMoreTokens() ) // while more input
34              {
35                  String word = tokenizer.nextToken().toLowerCase(); // get word
36
37                  // if the map contains the word
38                  if ( map.containsKey( word ) ) // is word in map
39                  {
40                      int count = map.get( word ); // get current count
41                      map.put( word, count + 1 );  // increment count
42                  } // end if
43                  else
44                      map.put( word, 1 ); // add new word with a count of 1 to map
45              } // end while
46          } // end method createMap
47
48          // display map content
49          private void displayMap()
50          {
51              Set< String > keys = map.keySet(); // get keys
52
53              // sort keys
54              TreeSet< String > sortedKeys = new TreeSet< String >( keys );
55
56              System.out.println( "Map contains:\nKey\t\tValue" );
57
58              // generate output for each key in map
59              for ( String key : sortedKeys )
60                  System.out.printf( "%-10s%10s\n", key, map.get( key ) );
61
62              System.out.printf(
63                  "\nsize:%d\nisEmpty:%b\n", map.size(), map.isEmpty() );
64          } // end method displayMap
65
66          public static void main( String args[] )
67          {
68              new WordTypeCount();
69          } // end main
70      } // end class WordTypeCount
```

Fig. 19.20 | HashMaps and Maps. (Part 2 of 3.)

```
Enter a string:
To be or not to be: that is the question Whether 'tis nobler to suffer
Map contains:
Key                    Value
'tis                       1
be                         1
be:                        1
is                         1
nobler                     1
not                        1
or                         1
question                   1
suffer                     1
that                       1
the                        1
to                         3
whether                    1

size:13
isEmpty:false
```

Fig. 19.20 | HashMaps and Maps. (Part 3 of 3.)

its component individual words. This StringTokenizer constructor takes a string argument and creates a StringTokenizer for that string and will use the white space to separate the string. The condition in the while statement in lines 33–45 uses StringTokenizer method hasMoreTokens to determine whether there are more tokens in the string being tokenized. If so, line 35 converts the next token to lowercase letters. The next token is obtained with a call to StringTokenizer method nextToken that returns a String. [*Note:* Section 30.6 discusses class StringTokenizer in detail.] Then line 38 calls Map method containsKey to determine whether the word is in the map (and thus has occurred previously in the string). If the Map does not contain a mapping for the word, line 44 uses Map method put to create a new entry in the map, with the word as the key and an Integer object containing 1 as the value. Note that autoboxing occurs when the program passes integer 1 to method put, because the map stores the number of occurrences of the word as Integer. If the word does exist in the map, line 40 uses Map method get to obtain the key's associated value (the count) in the map. Line 41 increments that value and uses put to replace the key's associated value in the map. Method put returns the prior value associated with the key, or null if the key was not in the map.

Method displayMap (lines 49–64) displays all the entries in the map. It uses HashMap method keySet (line 51) to get a set of the keys. The keys have type String in the map, so method keySet returns a generic type Set with type parameter specified to be String. Line 54 creates a TreeSet of the keys, in which the keys are sorted. The loop in lines 59–60 accesses each key and its value in the map. Line 60 displays each key and its value using format specifier %-10s to left justify each key and format specifier %10s to right justify each value. Note that the keys are displayed in ascending order. Line 63 calls Map method size to get the number of key–value pairs in the Map. Line 64 calls isEmpty, which returns a boolean indicating whether the Map is empty.

19.11 Properties Class

A `Properties` object is a persistent `Hashtable` that normally stores key–value pairs of strings—assuming that you use methods `setProperty` and `getProperty` to manipulate the table rather than inherited `Hashtable` methods put and get. By "persistent," we mean that the `Properties` object can be written to an output stream (possibly a file) and read back in through an input stream. A common use of `Properties` objects in prior versions of Java was to maintain application-configuration data or user preferences for applications. [*Note:* The Preferences API (package `java.util.prefs`) is meant to replace this particular use of class `Properties` but is beyond the scope of this book. To learn more, visit `java.sun.com/javase/6/docs/technotes/guides/preferences/index.html`.]

Class `Properties` extends class `Hashtable`. Figure 19.21 demonstrates several methods of class `Properties`.

Line 16 uses the no-argument constructor to create an empty `Properties` table with no default properties. Class `Properties` also provides an overloaded constructor that receives a reference to a `Properties` object containing default property values. Lines 19 and 20 each call `Properties` method `setProperty` to store a value for the specified key. If the key does not exist in the `table`, `setProperty` returns `null`; otherwise, it returns the previous value for that key.

Line 41 calls `Properties` method `getProperty` to locate the value associated with the specified key. If the key is not found in this `Properties` object, `getProperty` returns `null`. An overloaded version of this method receives a second argument that specifies the default value to return if `getProperty` cannot locate the key.

Line 57 calls `Properties` method **store** to save the contents of the `Properties` object to the `OutputStream` object specified as the first argument (in this case, `FileOutputStream`

```
1   // Fig. 19.21: PropertiesTest.java
2   // Demonstrates class Properties of the java.util package.
3   import java.io.FileOutputStream;
4   import java.io.FileInputStream;
5   import java.io.IOException;
6   import java.util.Properties;
7   import java.util.Set;
8
9   public class PropertiesTest
10  {
11     private Properties table;
12
13     // set up GUI to test Properties table
14     public PropertiesTest()
15     {
16        table = new Properties(); // create Properties table
17
18        // set properties
19        table.setProperty( "color", "blue" );
20        table.setProperty( "width", "200" );
21
```

Fig. 19.21 | Properties class of package `java.util`. (Part 1 of 3.)

```
22        System.out.println( "After setting properties" );
23        listProperties(); // display property values
24
25        // replace property value
26        table.setProperty( "color", "red" );
27
28        System.out.println( "After replacing properties" );
29        listProperties(); // display property values
30
31        saveProperties(); // save properties
32
33        table.clear(); // empty table
34
35        System.out.println( "After clearing properties" );
36        listProperties(); // display property values
37
38        loadProperties(); // load properties
39
40        // get value of property color
41        Object value = table.getProperty( "color" );
42
43        // check if value is in table
44        if ( value != null )
45           System.out.printf( "Property color's value is %s\n", value );
46        else
47           System.out.println( "Property color is not in table" );
48     } // end PropertiesTest constructor
49
50     // save properties to a file
51     public void saveProperties()
52     {
53        // save contents of table
54        try
55        {
56           FileOutputStream output = new FileOutputStream( "props.dat" );
57           table.store( output, "Sample Properties" ); // save properties
58           output.close();
59           System.out.println( "After saving properties" );
60           listProperties();
61        } // end try
62        catch ( IOException ioException )
63        {
64           ioException.printStackTrace();
65        } // end catch
66     } // end method saveProperties
67
68     // load properties from a file
69     public void loadProperties()
70     {
71        // load contents of table
72        try
73        {
```

Fig. 19.21 | Properties class of package java.util. (Part 2 of 3.)

```
74          FileInputStream input = new FileInputStream( "props.dat" );
75          table.load( input ); // load properties
76          input.close();
77          System.out.println( "After loading properties" );
78          listProperties(); // display property values
79       } // end try
80       catch ( IOException ioException )
81       {
82          ioException.printStackTrace();
83       } // end catch
84    } // end method loadProperties
85
86    // output property values
87    public void listProperties()
88    {
89       Set< Object > keys = table.keySet(); // get property names
90
91       // output name/value pairs
92       for ( Object key : keys )
93       {
94          System.out.printf(
95             "%s\t%s\n", key, table.getProperty( ( String ) key ) );
96       } // end for
97
98       System.out.println();
99    } // end method listProperties
100
101   public static void main( String args[] )
102   {
103      new PropertiesTest();
104   } // end main
105 } // end class PropertiesTest
```

```
After setting properties
color    blue
width    200

After replacing properties
color    red
width    200

After saving properties
color    red
width    200

After clearing properties

After loading properties
color    red
width    200

Property color's value is red
```

Fig. 19.21 | Properties class of package java.util. (Part 3 of 3.)

output). The second argument, a `String`, is a description of the `Properties` object. Class `Properties` also provides method `list`, which takes a `PrintStream` argument. This method is useful for displaying the list of properties.

Line 75 calls `Properties` method `load` to restore the contents of the `Properties` object from the `InputStream` specified as the first argument (in this case, a `FileInput-Stream`). Line 89 calls `Properties` method `keySet` to obtain a `Set` of the property names. Line 94 obtains the value of a property by passing a key to method `getProperty`.

19.12 **Synchronized Collections**

In Chapter 23, we discuss multithreading. Except for `Vector` and `Hashtable`, the collections in the collections framework are unsynchronized by default, so they can operate efficiently when multithreading is not required. Because they are unsynchronized, however, concurrent access to a `Collection` by multiple threads could cause indeterminate results or fatal errors. To prevent potential threading problems, synchronization wrappers are used for collections that might be accessed by multiple threads. A **wrapper** object receives method calls, adds thread synchronization (to prevent concurrent access to the collection) and delegates the calls to the wrapped collection object. The `Collections` API provides a set of `static` methods for wrapping collections as synchronized versions. Method headers for the synchronization wrappers are listed in Fig. 19.22. Details about these methods are available at `java.sun.com/javase/6/docs/api/java/util/Collections.html`. All these methods take a generic type and return a synchronized view of the generic type. For example, the following code creates a synchronized `List` (`list2`) that stores `String` objects:

```
List< String > list1 = new ArrayList< String >();
List< String > list2 = Collections.synchronizedList( list1 );
```

public static method headers
< T > Collection< T > synchronizedCollection(Collection< T > c)
< T > List< T > synchronizedList(List< T > aList)
< T > Set< T > synchronizedSet(Set< T > s)
< T > SortedSet< T > synchronizedSortedSet(SortedSet< T > s)
< K, V > Map< K, V > synchronizedMap(Map< K, V > m)
< K, V > SortedMap< K, V > synchronizedSortedMap(SortedMap< K, V > m)

Fig. 19.22 | Synchronization wrapper methods.

19.13 **Unmodifiable Collections**

The `Collections` API provides a set of `static` methods that create **unmodifiable wrappers** for collections. Unmodifiable wrappers throw `UnsupportedOperationExceptions` if attempts are made to modify the collection. Headers for these methods are listed in Fig. 19.23. Details about these methods are available at `java.sun.com/javase/6/docs/`

```
public static method headers

< T > Collection< T > unmodifiableCollection( Collection< T > c )

< T > List< T > unmodifiableList( List< T > aList )

< T > Set< T > unmodifiableSet( Set< T > s )

< T > SortedSet< T > unmodifiableSortedSet( SortedSet< T > s )

< K, V > Map< K, V > unmodifiableMap( Map< K, V > m )

< K, V > SortedMap< K, V > unmodifiableSortedMap( SortedMap< K, V > m )
```

Fig. 19.23 | Unmodifiable wrapper methods.

api/java/util/Collections.html. All these methods take a generic type and return an unmodifiable view of the generic type. For example, the following code creates an unmodifiable List (list2) that stores String objects:

```
List< String > list1 = new ArrayList< String >();
List< String > list2 = Collections.unmodifiableList( list1 );
```

> **Software Engineering Observation 19.5**
>
> *You can use an unmodifiable wrapper to create a collection that offers read-only access to others, while allowing read–write access to yourself. You do this simply by giving others a reference to the unmodifiable wrapper while retaining for yourself a reference to the original collection.*

19.14 Abstract Implementations

The collections framework provides various abstract implementations of Collection interfaces from which the programmer can quickly "flesh out" complete customized implementations. These abstract implementations include a thin Collection implementation called an AbstractCollection, a thin List implementation that allows random access to its elements called an AbstractList, a thin Map implementation called an AbstractMap, a thin List implementation that allows sequential access to its elements called an Abstract-SequentialList, a thin Set implementation called an AbstractSet and a thin Queue implementation called AbstractQueue. You can learn more about these classes at java.sun.com/javase/6/docs/api/java/util/package-summary.html.

To write a custom implementation, you can extend the abstract implementation that best meets your needs, and implement each of the class's abstract methods. Then, if your collection is to be modifiable, override any concrete methods that prevent modification.

19.15 Wrap-Up

This chapter introduced the Java collections framework. You learned how to use class Arrays to perform array manipulations. You learned the collection hierarchy and how to use the collections framework interfaces to program with collections polymorphically. You also learned several predefined algorithms for manipulating collections. In the next chapter, we introduce Java applets, which are Java programs that typically execute in a web browser. We start with sample applets that come with the JDK, then show you how to write and execute your own applets.

Summary

Section 19.1 Introduction
- The Java collections framework gives the programmer access to prepackaged data structures as well as to algorithms for manipulating them.

Section 19.2 Collections Overview
- A collection is an object that can hold references to other objects. The collection interfaces declare the operations that can be performed on each type of collection.
- The classes and interfaces of the collections framework are in package java.util.

Section 19.3 Class Arrays
- Class Arrays provides static methods for manipulating arrays, including sort for sorting an array, binarySearch for searching a sorted array, equals for comparing arrays and fill for placing items in an array.
- Arrays method asList returns a List view of an array, which enables a program to manipulate the array as if it were a List. Any modifications made through the List view change the array, and any modifications to the array change the List view.
- Method size gets the number of items in a List, and method get returns a List element.

Section 19.4 Interface Collection and Class Collections
- Interface Collection is the root interface in the collection hierarchy from which interfaces Set and List are derived. Interface Collection contains bulk operations for adding, clearing, comparing and retaining objects in a collection. Interface Collection provides a method iterator for getting an Iterator.
- Class Collections provides static methods for manipulating collections. Many of the methods are implementations of polymorphic algorithms for searching, sorting and so on.

Section 19.5 Lists
- A List is an ordered Collection that can contain duplicate elements.
- Interface List is implemented by classes ArrayList, LinkedList and Vector. Class ArrayList is a resizable-array implementation of a List. A LinkedList is a linked list implementation of a List.
- Iterator method hasNext determines whether a Collection contains another element. Method next returns a reference to the next object in the Collection and advances the Iterator.
- Method subList returns a view of a portion of a List. Any changes made to this view are also made to the List.
- Method clear removes elements from a List.
- Method toArray returns the contents of a collection as an array.
- Class Vector manages dynamically resizable arrays. At any time, a Vector contains a number of elements that is less than or equal to its capacity. If a Vector needs to grow, it grows by its capacity increment. If no capacity increment is specified, Java doubles the size of the Vector each time additional capacity is required. The default capacity is 10 elements.

- Vector method add adds its argument to the end of the Vector. Method insertElementAt inserts an element at the specified position. Method set sets the element at a specific position.

- Vector method remove removes the first occurrence of its argument from the Vector. Method removeAllElements removes every element from the Vector. Method removeElementAt removes the element at the specified index.

- Vector method firstElement returns a reference to the first element. Method lastElement returns a reference to the last element.

- Vector method contains determines whether the Vector contains the searchKey specified as an argument. Vector method indexOf gets the index of the first location of its argument. The method returns –1 if the argument is not found in the Vector.

- Vector method isEmpty determines whether the Vector is empty. Methods size and capacity determine the number of elements currently in the Vector and the number of elements that can be stored in the Vector without allocating more memory, respectively.

Section 19.6 Collections Algorithms

- Algorithms sort, binarySearch, reverse, shuffle, fill and copy operate on Lists. Algorithms min and max operate on Collections. Algorithm reverse reverses the elements of a List, fill sets every List element to a specified Object, and copy copies elements from one List into another List. Algorithm sort sorts the elements of a List.

- Algorithms addAll appends all the elements in an array to a collection, frequency calculates how many elements in the collection are equal to the specified element, and disjoint determines whether two collections have elements in common.

- Algorithms min and max find the smallest and largest items in a collection.

- The Comparator interface provides a means of sorting a Collection's elements in an order other than their natural order.

- Collections method reverseOrder returns a Comparator object that can be used with sort to sort elements of a collection in reverse order.

- Algorithm shuffle randomly orders the elements of a List.

- Algorithm binarySearch locates an Object in a sorted List.

Section 19.7 Stack Class of Package java.util

- Class Stack extends Vector. Stack method push adds its argument to the top of the stack. Method pop removes the top element of the stack. Method peek returns a reference to the top element without removing it. Stack method empty determines whether the stack is empty.

Section 19.8 Class PriorityQueue and Interface Queue

- Queue, a new collection interface introduced in Java SE 5, extends interface Collection and provides additional operations for inserting, removing and inspecting elements in a queue.

- PriorityQueue, one of the Queue implementations, orders elements by their natural ordering (i.e., the implementation of the compareTo method) or by a Comparator object that is supplied through the constructor.

- The common PriorityQueue operations are offer to insert an element at the appropriate location based on priority order, poll to remove the highest-priority element of the priority queue (i.e., the head of the queue), peek to get a reference to the highest-priority element of the priority queue, clear to remove all elements in the priority queue and size to get the number of elements in the priority queue.

Section 19.9 Sets

- A Set is a Collection that contains no duplicate elements. HashSet stores its elements in a hash table. TreeSet stores its elements in a tree.

- Interface SortedSet extends Set and represents a set that maintains its elements in sorted order. Class TreeSet implements SortedSet.

- TreeSet method headSet gets a view of a TreeSet that is less than a specified element. Method tailSet gets a view that is greater than or equal to a specified element. Any changes made to the view are made to the TreeSet.

Section 19.10 Maps

- Maps map keys to values and cannot contain duplicate keys. Maps differ from Sets in that Maps contain both keys and values, whereas Sets contain only values. HashMaps store elements in a hash table, and TreeMaps store elements in a tree.

- Hashtables and HashMaps store elements in hash tables, and TreeMaps store elements in trees.

- HashMap is a generic class that takes two type arguments. The first type argument specifies the type of key, and the second the type of value.

- HashMap method put adds a key and a value into a HashMap. Method get locates the value associated with the specified key. Method isEmpty determines whether the map is empty.

- HashMap method keySet returns a set of the keys. Map methods size and isEmpty return the number of key–value pairs in the Map and a boolean indicating whether the Map is empty, respectively.

- Interface SortedMap extends Map and represents a map that maintains its keys in sorted order. Class TreeMap implements SortedMap.

Section 19.11 *Properties Class*

- A Properties object is a persistent Hashtable object. Class Properties extends Hashtable.

- The Properties no-argument constructor creates an empty Properties table with no default properties. There is also an overloaded constructor that is passed a reference to a default Properties object containing default property values.

- Properties method setProperty specifies the value associated with the key argument. Properties method getProperty locates the value of the key specified as an argument. Method store saves the contents of the Properties object to the OutputStream object specified as the first argument. Method load restores the contents of the Properties object from the InputStream object specified as the argument.

Section 19.12 *Synchronized Collections*

- Collections from the collections framework are unsynchronized. Synchronization wrappers are provided for collections that can be accessed by multiple threads simultaneously.

Section 19.13 *Unmodifiable Collections*

- The Collections API provides a set of public static methods for converting collections to unmodifiable versions. Unmodifiable wrappers throw UnsupportedOperationExceptions if attempts are made to modify the collection.

Section 19.14 *Abstract Implementations*

- The collections framework provides various abstract implementations of collection interfaces from which the programmer can quickly flesh out complete customized implementations.

Terminology

AbstractCollection class	hasNext method of Iterator
AbstractList class	hasPrevious method of ListIterator
AbstractMap class	insert an element into a collection
AbstractQueue class	indexOf method of Vector
AbstractSequentialList class	isEmpty method of Map
AbstractSet class	isEmpty method of Vector
add method of List	iterate through container elements
add method of Vector	iterator
addAll method of Collections	Iterator interface
addFirst method of List	key in HashMap
addLast method of List	keySet method of HashMap
algorithms in Collections	key/value pair
ArrayList	lastElement method of Vector
array	lexicographical comparison
arrays as collections	LinkedList class
asList method of Arrays	List interface
bidirectional iterator	ListIterator interface
binarySearch method of Arrays	load factor in hashing
binarySearch method of Collections	map
capacity increment of a Vector	Map collection interface
capacity method of Vector	mapping keys to values
clear method of List	mappings
clear method of PriorityQueue	max method of Collections
collection	min method of Collections
Collection interface	modifiable collections
Collections class	natural comparison method
collections framework	natural ordering
collections placed in arrays	next method of Iterator
collision in hashing	nextToken method of StringTokenizer
contains method of Vector	NoSuchElementException class
containsKey method of HashMap	offer method of PriorityQueue
Comparable interface	one-to-one mapping
Comparator interface	ordered collection
compareTo method of Comparable	ordering
copy method of Collections	peek method of PriorityQueue
delete an element from a collection	peek method of Stack
disjoint method of Collections	poll method of PriorityQueue
duplicate elements	pop method of Stack
fill method of Arrays	PriorityQueue class
fill method of Collections	Properties class
firstElement method of Vector	put method of HashMap
frequency method of Collections	Queue interface
get method of HashMap	range-view methods
getProperty method of class Properties	removeAllElements method of Vector
hashing	removeElement method of Vector
HashMap class	removeElementAt method of Vector
HashSet class	reverse method of Collections
Hashtable class	reverseOrder method of Collections
hasMoreTokens method of StringTokenizer	sequence

Set interface

shuffle method of Collections

size method of List

size method of PriorityQueue

sort a List

sort method of Arrays

sort method of Collections

SortedMap collection interface

SortedSet collection interface

stable sort

Stack class

StringTokenizer class

synchronization wrappers

TreeMap class

TreeSet class

unmodifiable collections

view

view an array as a List

wrapper class

Self-Review Exercises

19.1 Fill in the blanks in each of the following statements:

a) A(n) _____ is used to walk through a collection and can remove elements from the collection during the iteration.

b) An element in a List can be accessed by using the element's _____.

c) Lists are sometimes called _____.

d) Java classes _____ and _____ provide the capabilities of array-like data structures that can resize themselves dynamically.

e) If you do not specify a capacity increment, the system will _____ the size of the Vector each time additional capacity is needed.

f) You can use a(n) _____ to create a collection that offers only read-only access to others while allowing read–write access to yourself.

g) _____ can be used to create stacks, queues, trees and deques (double-ended queues).

h) Algorithm _____ of Collections determines whether two collections have elements in common.

19.2 Determine whether each statement is *true* or *false*. If *false*, explain why.

a) Values of primitive types may be stored directly in a Vector.

b) A Set can contain duplicate values.

c) A Map can contain duplicate keys.

d) A LinkedList can contain duplicate values.

e) Collections is an interface.

f) Iterators can remove elements.

g) With hashing, as the load factor increases, the chance of collisions decreases.

h) A PriorityQueue permits null elements.

Answers to Self-Review Exercises

19.1 a) Iterator. b) index. c) sequences. d) ArrayList, Vector. e) double. f) unmodifiable wrapper. g) LinkedLists. h) disjoint.

19.2 a) False; a Vector stores only objects. Autoboxing occurs when adding a primitive type to the Vector, which means the primitive type is converted to its corresponding type-wrapper class.

b) False. A Set cannot contain duplicate values.

c) False. A Map cannot contain duplicate keys.

d) True.

e) False. Collections is a class; Collection is an interface.

f) True.

g) False. With hashing, as the load factor increases, fewer slots are available relative to the total number of slots, so the chance of selecting an occupied slot (a collision) with a hashing operation increases.

h) False. A `NullPointerException` is thrown if the program attempts to add `null` to a `PriorityQueue`.

Exercises

19.3 Explain briefly the operation of each of the following methods of class `Vector`:
a) `add`
b) `insertElementAt`
c) `set`
d) `remove`
e) `removeAllElements`
f) `removeElementAt`
g) `firstElement`
h) `lastElement`
i) `isEmpty`
j) `contains`
k) `indexOf`
l) `size`
m) `capacity`

19.4 Explain why inserting additional elements into a `Vector` object whose current size is less than its capacity is a relatively fast operation and why inserting additional elements into a `Vector` object whose current size is at capacity is a relatively slow operation.

19.5 Briefly answer the following questions:
a) What is the primary difference between a `Set` and a `Map`?
b) Can a two-dimensional array be passed to `Arrays` method `asList`? If yes, how would an individual element be accessed?
c) What happens when you add a primitive type (e.g., `double`) value to a collection?
d) Can you print all the elements in a collection without using an `Iterator`? If yes, how?

19.6 Explain briefly the operation of each of the following `Iterator`-related methods:
a) `iterator`
b) `hasNext`
c) `next`

19.7 Explain briefly the operation of each of the following methods of class `HashMap`:
a) `put`
b) `get`
c) `isEmpty`
d) `containsKey`
e) `keySet`

19.8 Explain the operation of each of the following methods of the `Properties` class:
a) `load`
b) `store`
c) `getProperty`
d) `list`

19.9 Rewrite lines 17–26 in Fig. 19.4 to be more concise by using the `asList` method and the `LinkedList` constructor that takes a `Collection` argument.

19.10 Modify the program of Fig. 19.20 to count the number of occurrences of each letter rather than of each word. For example, the string `"HELLO THERE"` contains two Hs, three Es, two Ls, one O, one T and one R. Display the results.

19.11 Write a program that determines and prints the number of duplicate words in a sentence. Treat uppercase and lowercase letters the same. Ignore punctuation.

19.12 Rewrite your solution to Exercise 17.8 to use a LinkedList collection.

19.13 Rewrite your solution to Exercise 17.9 to use a LinkedList collection.

19.14 Write a program that takes a whole number input from a user and determines whether it is prime. If the number is not prime, display its unique prime factors. Remember that a prime number's factors are only 1 and the prime number itself. Every number that is not prime has a unique prime factorization. For example, consider the number 54. The prime factors of 54 are 2, 3, 3 and 3. When the values are multiplied together, the result is 54. For the number 54, the prime factors output should be 2 and 3. Use Sets as part of your solution.

19.15 Write a program that uses a StringTokenizer to tokenize a line of text input by the user and places each token in a TreeSet. Print the elements of the TreeSet. [*Note:* This should cause the elements to be printed in ascending sorted order.]

19.16 The output of Fig. 19.17 (PriorityQueueTest) shows that PriorityQueue orders Double elements in ascending order. Rewrite Fig. 19.17 so that it orders Double elements in descending order (i.e., 9.8 should be the highest-priority element rather than 3.2).

20

Introduction to Java Applets

OBJECTIVES

In this chapter you will learn:

- To differentiate between applets and applications.
- To observe some of Java's exciting capabilities through the JDK's demonstration applets.
- To write simple applets.
- To write a simple HyperText Markup Language (HTML) document to load an applet into an applet container and execute the applet.
- Five methods that are called automatically by an applet container during an applet's life cycle.

20.1 Introduction

[*Note:* This chapter and its exercises are intentionally small and simple for readers who wish to learn about applets after reading only the first few chapters of the book—possibly just Chapters 2 and 3. We present more complex applets in Chapter 21, Multimedia: Applets and Applications, Chapter 23, Multithreading and Chapter 24, Networking.]

This chapter introduces applets—Java programs that can be embedded in HyperText Markup Language (HTML) documents (i.e., web pages). When a browser loads a web page containing an applet, the applet downloads into the web browser and executes.

The browser that executes an applet is known as the applet container. The JDK includes the `appletviewer` applet container for testing applets as you develop them and before you embed them in web pages. We typically demonstrate applets using the `appletviewer`. If you would like to execute your applets in a web browser, be aware that some web browsers do not support Java by default. You can visit `java.com` and click the **Download Now** button to install Java for your browser. Several popular browsers are supported.

20.2 Sample Applets Provided with the JDK

Let's consider several demonstration applets provided with the JDK. Each sample applet comes with its source code. Some programmers find it interesting to read this source code to learn new and exciting Java features.

The demonstration programs provided with the JDK are located in a directory called demo. For Windows, the default location of the JDK 6.0's demo directory is

```
C:\Program Files\Java\jdk1.6.0\demo
```

On UNIX/Linux/Mac OS X, the default location is the directory in which you install the JDK followed by jdk1.6.0/demo—for example,

```
/usr/local/jdk1.6.0/demo
```

For other platforms, there will be a similar directory (or folder) structure. This chapter assumes that the JDK is installed in C:\Program Files\Java\jdk1.6.0\demo on Windows or in your home directory in ~/jdk1.6.0 on UNIX/Linux/Max OS X. You may need to update the locations specified here to reflect your chosen installation directory and disk drive, or a different version of the JDK.

If you are using a Java development tool that does not come with the Sun Java demos, you can download the JDK (with the demos) from the Sun Microsystems Java website

```
java.sun.com/javase/6/
```

TicTacToe *Applet*

The TicTacToe demonstration applet allows you to play Tic-Tac-Toe against the computer. To execute this applet, open a command window and change directories to the JDK's demo directory.

The demo directory contains several subdirectories. You can list them by issuing the dir command on Windows or the ls command on UNIX/Linux/Max OS X. We discuss sample programs in the applets and jfc directories. The applets directory contains several demonstration applets. The jfc (Java Foundation Classes) directory contains applets and applications that demonstrate Java's graphics and GUI features.

Change directories to the applets directory and list its contents to see the directory names for the demonstration applets. Figure 20.1 provides a brief description of each sample applet. If your browser supports Java, you can test these applets by opening the site java.sun.com/javase/6/docs/technotes/samples/demos.html in your browser and clicking the **Applets Page** link. We will demonstrate three of these applets by using the appletviewer command in a command window.

Example	Description
Animator	Performs one of four separate animations.
ArcTest	Demonstrates drawing arcs. You can interact with the applet to change attributes of the arc that is displayed.
BarChart	Draws a simple bar chart.
Blink	Displays blinking text in different colors.
CardTest	Demonstrates several GUI components and layouts.
Clock	Draws a clock with rotating hands, the current date and the current time. The clock updates once per second.
DitherTest	Demonstrates drawing with a graphics technique known as dithering that allows gradual transformation from one color to another.
DrawTest	Allows the user mouse to draw lines and points in different colors by dragging the mouse.
Fractal	Draws a fractal. Fractals typically require complex calculations to determine how they are displayed.
GraphicsTest	Draws shapes to illustrate graphics capabilities.

Fig. 20.1 | The examples from the applets directory. (Part 1 of 2.)

Example	Description
GraphLayout	Draws a graph consisting of many nodes (represented as rectangles) connected by lines. Drag a node to see the other nodes in the graph adjust on the screen and demonstrate complex graphical interactions.
ImageMap	Demonstrates an image with hot spots. Positioning the mouse pointer over certain areas of the image highlights the area and displays a message in the lower-left corner of the applet container window. Position over the mouth in the image to hear the applet say "hi."
JumpingBox	Moves a rectangle randomly around the screen. Try to catch it by clicking it with the mouse!
MoleculeViewer	Presents a three-dimensional view of several chemical molecules. Drag the mouse to view the molecule from different angles.
NervousText	Draws text that jumps around the applet.
SimpleGraph	Draws a complex curve.
SortDemo	Compares three sorting techniques. Sorting (described in Chapter 16) arranges information in order—like alphabetizing words. When you execute this example from a command window, three appletviewer windows appear. When you execute this example in a browser, the three demos appear side by side. Click in each demo to start the sort. Note that the sorts all operate at different speeds.
SpreadSheet	Demonstrates a simple spreadsheet of rows and columns.
TicTacToe	Allows the user to play Tic-Tac-Toe against the computer.
WireFrame	Draws a three-dimensional shape as a wire frame. Drag the mouse to view the shape from different angles.

Fig. 20.1 | The examples from the applets directory. (Part 2 of 2.)

Change directories to subdirectory TicTacToe, where you will find the HTML document example1.html that is used to execute the applet. In the command window, type the command

```
appletviewer example1.html
```

and press *Enter*. This executes the appletviewer applet container, which loads the HTML document example1.html specified as its command-line argument. The appletviewer determines from the document which applet to load and executes the applet. Figure 20.2 shows several screen captures of playing Tic-Tac-Toe with this applet.

You are player **X**. To interact with the applet, point the mouse at the square where you want to place an **X** and click the mouse button. The applet plays a sound and places an **X** in the square if the square is open. If the square is occupied, this is an invalid move, and the applet plays a different sound indicating that you cannot make the specified move. After you make a valid move, the applet responds by making its own move.

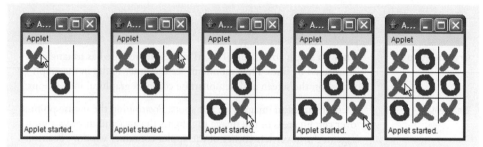

Fig. 20.2 | TicTacToe applet sample execution.

To play again, click the appletviewer's **Applet** menu and select the **Reload** menu item (Fig. 20.3). To terminate the appletviewer, click the appletviewer's **Applet** menu and select the **Quit** menu item.

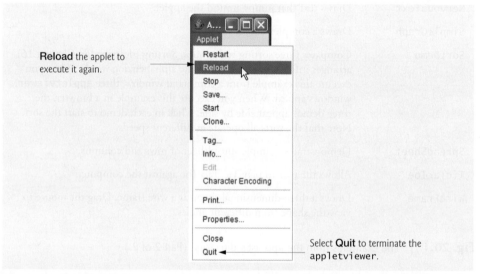

Reload the applet to execute it again.

Select **Quit** to terminate the appletviewer.

Fig. 20.3 | **Applet** menu in the appletviewer.

DrawTest *Applet*

The DrawTest applet allows you to draw lines and points in different colors. In the command window, change directories to directory applets, then to subdirectory DrawTest. You can move up the directory tree incrementally toward demo by issuing the command "cd .." in the command window. The DrawTest directory contains the example1.html document that is used to execute the applet. In the command window, type the command

```
appletviewer example1.html
```

and press *Enter*. The appletviewer loads example1.html, determines from the document which applet to load and executes the applet. Figure 20.4 shows a screen capture after some lines and points have been drawn.

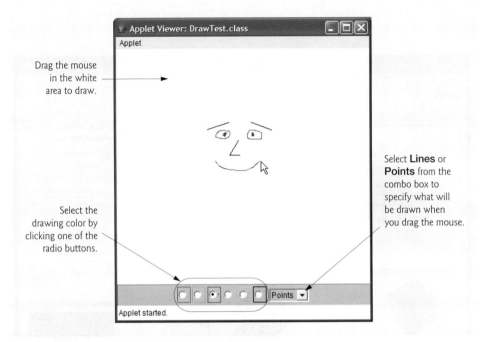

Drag the mouse in the white area to draw.

Select **Lines** or **Points** from the combo box to specify what will be drawn when you drag the mouse.

Select the drawing color by clicking one of the radio buttons.

Fig. 20.4 | `DrawTest` applet sample execution.

By default the applet allows you to draw black lines by dragging the mouse across the applet. When you drag the mouse, note that the start point of the line always remains in the same place and the endpoint of the line follows the mouse pointer around the applet. The line is not permanent until you release the mouse button.

Select a color by clicking one of the radio buttons at the bottom of the applet. You can select from red, green, blue, pink, orange and black. Change the shape to draw from **Lines** to **Points** by selecting **Points** from the combo box. To start a new drawing, select **Reload** from the `appletviewer`'s **Applet** menu.

Java2D Applet

The `Java2D` applet demonstrates many features of the Java 2D API (which we introduced in Chapter 12). Change directories to the `jfc` directory in the JDK's `demo` directory, then change to the `Java2D` directory. In the command window, type the command

```
appletviewer Java2Demo.html
```

and press *Enter*. The `appletviewer` loads `Java2Demo.html`, determines from the document which applet to load and executes the applet. Figure 20.5 shows a screen capture of one of this applet's many demonstrations of Java's two-dimensional graphics capabilities.

At the top of the applet are tabs that look like file folders in a filing cabinet. This demo provides 12 tabs with Java 2D API features demonstrated on each tab. To change to a different part of the demo, simply click a different tab. Also, try changing the options in the upper-right corner of the applet. Some of these affect the speed with which the applet draws the graphics. For example, click the checkbox to the left of the word **Anti-Aliasing** to

Click a tab to select a
two-dimensional graphics demo.

Try changing the options to see
their effect on the demonstration.

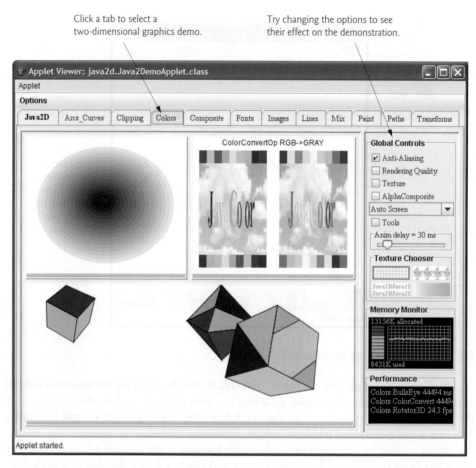

Fig. 20.5 | Java2D applet sample execution.

turn off anti-aliasing (a graphics technique for producing smoother on-screen graphics in which the edges of the graphic are blurred). When this feature is turned off, the animation speed increases for the animated shapes at the bottom of the demo (Fig. 20.5). This performance increase occurs because shapes that are not anti-aliased are less complex to draw.

20.3 Simple Java Applet: Drawing a String

Every Java applet is a graphical user interface on which you can place GUI components using the techniques introduced in Chapter 11 or draw using the techniques demonstrated in Chapter 12. In this chapter, we will demonstrate drawing on an applet. Examples in Chapters 21, 23 and 24 demonstrate building an applet's graphical user interface.

Now let's build an applet of our own. We begin with a simple applet (Fig. 20.6) that draws "Welcome to Java Programming!" on the applet. Figure 20.7 shows this applet executing in two applet containers—the appletviewer and the Microsoft Internet Explorer web browser. At the end of this section, you will learn how to execute the applet in a web browser.

```
 1    // Fig. 20.6: WelcomeApplet.java
 2    // A first applet in Java.
 3    import java.awt.Graphics;   // program uses class Graphics
 4    import javax.swing.JApplet; // program uses class JApplet
 5
 6    public class WelcomeApplet extends JApplet
 7    {
 8       // draw text on applet's background
 9       public void paint( Graphics g )
10       {
11          // call superclass version of method paint
12          super.paint( g );
13
14          // draw a String at x-coordinate 25 and y-coordinate 25
15          g.drawString( "Welcome to Java Programming!", 25, 25 );
16       } // end method paint
17    } // end class WelcomeApplet
```

Fig. 20.6 | Applet that draws a string.

WelcomeApplet executing in the appletviewer

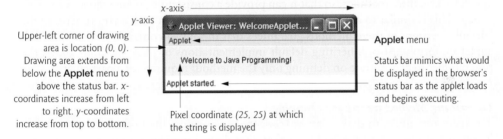

Upper-left corner of drawing area is location *(0, 0)*. Drawing area extends from below the **Applet** menu to above the status bar. *x*-coordinates increase from left to right. *y*-coordinates increase from top to bottom.

Pixel coordinate *(25, 25)* at which the string is displayed

Applet menu

Status bar mimics what would be displayed in the browser's status bar as the applet loads and begins executing.

WelcomeApplet executing in Microsoft Internet Explorer

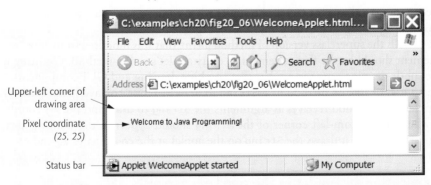

Upper-left corner of drawing area

Pixel coordinate *(25, 25)*

Status bar

Fig. 20.7 | Sample outputs of the WelcomeApplet in Fig. 20.6.

Creating the Applet Class

Line 3 imports class Graphics to enable the applet to draw graphics, such as lines, rectangles, ovals and strings of characters. Class **JApplet** (imported at line 4) from package javax.swing is used to create applets. As with applications, every Java applet contains at least one public class declaration. An applet container can create only objects of classes that are public and extend JApplet (or the Applet class from early versions of Java). For this reason, class WelcomeApplet (lines 6–17) extends JApplet.

An applet container expects every Java applet to have methods named **init**, **start**, **paint**, **stop** and **destroy**, each of which is declared in class JApplet. Each new applet class you create inherits default implementations of these methods from class JApplet. These methods can be overridden (redefined) to perform tasks that are specific to your applet. Section 20.4 discusses each of these methods in more detail.

When an applet container loads class WelcomeApplet, the container creates an object of type WelcomeApplet, then calls three of the applet's methods. In sequence, these three methods are init, start and paint. If you do not declare these methods in your applet, the applet container calls the inherited versions. The superclass methods init and start have empty bodies, so they do not perform any tasks. The superclass method paint does not draw anything on the applet.

You might wonder why it is necessary to inherit methods init, start and paint if their default implementations do not perform tasks. Some applets do not use all three of these methods. However, the applet container does not know that. Thus, it expects every applet to have these methods, so that it can provide a consistent start-up sequence for each applet. This is similar to applications' always starting execution with main. Inheriting the "default" versions of these methods guarantees that the applet container can execute each applet uniformly. Also, inheriting default implementations of these methods allows the programmer to concentrate on defining only the methods required for a particular applet.

*Overriding Method **paint** for Drawing*

To enable our applet to draw, class WelcomeApplet overrides method paint (lines 9–16) by placing statements in the body of paint that draw a message on the screen. Method paint receives a parameter of type Graphics (called g by convention), which is used to draw graphics on the applet. You do not call method paint explicitly in an applet. Rather, the applet container calls paint to tell the applet when to draw, and the applet container is responsible for passing a Graphics object as an argument.

Line 12 calls the superclass version of method paint that was inherited from JApplet. This statement should be the first statement in every applet's paint method. Omitting it can cause subtle drawing errors in applets that combine drawing and GUI components.

Line 15 uses Graphics method drawString to draw Welcome to Java Programming! on the applet. The method receives as arguments the String to draw and the x-y coordinates at which the bottom-left corner of the String should appear in the drawing area. When line 15 executes, it draws the String on the applet at the coordinates 25 and 25.

20.3.1 Executing an Applet in the appletviewer

As with application classes, you must compile an applet class before it can execute. After creating class WelcomeApplet and saving it in the file WelcomeApplet.java, open a command window, change to the directory in which you saved the applet class declaration and compile class WelcomeApplet.

Recall that applets are embedded in web pages for execution in an applet container (appletviewer or a browser). Before you can execute the applet, you must create an HTML (HyperText Markup Language) document that specifies which applet to execute in the applet container. Typically, an HTML document ends with an ".html" or ".htm" file-name extension. Figure 20.8 shows a simple HTML document—WelcomeApplet.html—that loads the applet defined in Fig. 20.6 into an applet container. [*Note:* If you are interested in learning more about HTML, the CD that accompanies this book contains three chapters from our book *Internet and World Wide Web How to Program, Third Edition*, that introduce the current version of HTML (known as XHTML) and the web page formatting capability known as Cascading Style Sheets (CSS).]

Most HTML elements are delimited by pairs of tags. For example, lines 1 and 4 of Fig. 20.8 indicate the beginning and the end, respectively, of the HTML document. All HTML tags begin with a left angle bracket, <, and end with a right angle bracket, >. Lines 2–3 specify an applet element that tells the applet container to load a specific applet and defines the size of the applet's display area (its width and height in pixels) in the applet container. Normally, the applet and its corresponding HTML document are stored in the same directory on disk. Typically, a browser loads an HTML document from a computer (other than your own) connected to the Internet. However, HTML documents also can reside on your computer (as you saw in Section 20.2). When an applet container encounters an HTML document that contains an applet, the applet container automatically loads the applet's .class file (or files) from the same directory on the computer in which the HTML document resides.

The applet element has several attributes. The first attribute in line 2, code = "WelcomeApplet.class", indicates that the file WelcomeApplet.class contains the compiled applet class. The second and third attributes in line 2 indicate the width (300) and the height (45) of the applet in pixels. The </applet> tag (line 3) terminates the applet element that began at line 2. The </html> tag (line 4) terminates the HTML document.

Look-and-Feel Observation 20.1

To ensure that it can be viewed properly on most computer screens, an applet should generally be less than 1024 pixels wide and 768 pixels tall—dimensions supported by most computer screens.

Common Programming Error 20.1

Forgetting the ending </applet> tag prevents the applet from executing in some applet containers. The appletviewer terminates without indicating an error. Some web browsers simply ignore the incomplete applet element.

```
1   <html>
2   <applet code = "WelcomeApplet.class" width = "300" height = "45">
3   </applet>
4   </html>
```

Fig. 20.8 | WelcomeApplet.html loads WelcomeApplet (Fig. 20.6) into an applet container.

Error-Prevention Tip 20.1

If you receive a MissingResourceException *error message when loading an applet into the* appletviewer *or a browser, check the* <applet> *tag in the HTML document carefully for syntax errors, such as commas (,) between the attributes.*

The appletviewer understands only the <applet> and </applet> HTML tags and ignores all other tags in the document. The appletviewer is an ideal place to test an applet and ensure that it executes properly. Once the applet's execution is verified, you can add its HTML tags to a web page that others can view in their web browsers.

To execute WelcomeApplet in the appletviewer, open a command window, change to the directory containing your applet and HTML document, then type

```
appletviewer WelcomeApplet.html
```

Error-Prevention Tip 20.2

Test your applets in the appletviewer *applet container before executing them in a web browser. Browsers often save a copy of an applet in memory until all the browser's windows are closed. If you change an applet, recompile it, then reload it in your browser, the browser may still execute the original version of the applet. Close all your browser windows to remove the old applet from memory. Open a new browser window and load the applet to see your changes.*

Error-Prevention Tip 20.3

Test your applets in every web browser in which they will execute to ensure that they operate correctly.

20.3.2 Executing an Applet in a Web Browser

The sample program executions in Fig. 20.6 demonstrate WelcomeApplet executing in the appletviewer and in Microsoft Internet Explorer web browser. To execute an applet in Internet Explorer, perform the following steps:

1. Select **Open...** from the **File** menu.

2. In the dialog box that appears, click the **Browse...** button.

3. In the dialog box that appears, locate the directory containing the HTML document for the applet you wish to execute.

4. Select the HTML document.

5. Click the **Open** button.

6. Click the **OK** button.

[*Note:* The steps for executing applets in other web browsers are similar.]

If your applet executes in the appletviewer, but does not execute in your web browser, Java may not be installed and configured for your browser. In this case, visit the website java.com and click the **Download Now** button to install Java for your browser. In Internet Explorer, if this does not fix the problem, you might need to manually configure Internet Explorer to use Java. To do so, click the **Tools** menu and select **Internet Options...**, then click the **Advanced** tab in the window that appears. Locate the option "**Use JRE v1.6.0 for <applet> (requires restart)**" and ensure that it is checked, then click **OK**. Close all your browser windows before attempting to execute another applet in the browser.

20.4 Applet Life-Cycle Methods

Now that you have created an applet, let's consider the five applet methods that are called by the applet container from the time the applet is loaded into the browser to the time that it is terminated by the browser. These methods correspond to various aspects of an applet's life cycle. Figure 20.9 lists these methods, which are inherited into your applet classes from class JApplet. The table specifies when each method gets called and explains its purpose. Other than method paint, these methods have empty bodies by default. If you would like to declare any of these methods in your applets and have the applet container call them, you must use the method headers shown in Fig. 20.9. If you modify the method headers (e.g., by changing the method names or by providing additional parameters), the applet container will not call your methods. Instead, it will call the superclass methods inherited from JApplet.

Common Programming Error 20.2

Declaring methods init, start, paint, stop or destroy with method headers that differ from those shown in Figure 20.9 results in methods that will not be called by the applet container. The code specified in your versions of the methods will not execute.

Method	When the method is called and its purpose
public void init()	Called once by the applet container when an applet is loaded for execution. This method initializes an applet. Typical actions performed here are initializing fields, creating GUI components, loading sounds to play, loading images to display (see Chapter 20, Multimedia: Applets and Applications) and creating threads (see Chapter 23, Multithreading).
public void start()	Called by the applet container after method init completes execution. In addition, if the user browses to another website and later returns to the applet's HTML page, method start is called again. The method performs any tasks that must be completed when the applet is loaded for the first time and that must be performed every time the applet's HTML page is revisited. Actions performed here might include starting an animation (see Chapter 21) or starting other threads of execution (see Chapter 23).
public void paint(Graphics g)	Called by the applet container after methods init and start. Method paint is also called when the applet needs to be repainted. For example, if the user covers the applet with another open window on the screen and later uncovers the applet, the paint method is called. Typical actions performed here involve drawing with the Graphics object g that is passed to the paint method by the applet container.

Fig. 20.9 | JApplet life-cycle methods that are called by an applet container during an applet's execution. (Part 1 of 2.)

Method	When the method is called and its purpose

`public void stop()`

> This method is called by the applet container when the user leaves the applet's web page by browsing to another web page. Since it is possible that the user might return to the web page containing the applet, method `stop` performs tasks that might be required to suspend the applet's execution, so that the applet does not use computer processing time when it is not displayed on the screen. Typical actions performed here would stop the execution of animations and threads.

`public void destroy()`

> This method is called by the applet container when the applet is being removed from memory. This occurs when the user exits the browsing session by closing all the browser windows and may also occur at the browser's discretion when the user has browsed to other web pages. The method performs any tasks that are required to clean up resources allocated to the applet.

Fig. 20.9 | `JApplet` life-cycle methods that are called by an applet container during an applet's execution. (Part 2 of 2.)

20.5 Initializing an Instance Variable with Method `init`

Our next applet (Fig. 20.10) computes the sum of two values input by the user and displays the result by drawing a `String` inside a rectangle on the applet. The sum is stored in an instance variable of class `AdditionApplet`, so it can be used in both method `init` and method `paint`. The HTML document to load this applet into the `appletviewer` is shown in Fig. 20.11.

```
 1   // Fig. 20.10: AdditionApplet.java
 2   // Adding two floating-point numbers.
 3   import java.awt.Graphics;      // program uses class Graphics
 4   import javax.swing.JApplet;    // program uses class JApplet
 5   import javax.swing.JOptionPane; // program uses class JOptionPane
 6
 7   public class AdditionApplet extends JApplet
 8   {
 9      private double sum; // sum of values entered by user
10
11      // initialize applet by obtaining values from user
12      public void init()
13      {
14         String firstNumber;  // first string entered by user
15         String secondNumber; // second string entered by user
16
17         double number1; // first number to add
18         double number2; // second number to add
```

Fig. 20.10 | Adding `double` values. (Part 1 of 2.)

```
19
20          // obtain first number from user
21          firstNumber = JOptionPane.showInputDialog(
22             "Enter first floating-point value" );
23
24          // obtain second number from user
25          secondNumber = JOptionPane.showInputDialog(
26             "Enter second floating-point value" );
27
28          // convert numbers from type String to type double
29          number1 = Double.parseDouble( firstNumber );
30          number2 = Double.parseDouble( secondNumber );
31
32          sum = number1 + number2; // add numbers
33       } // end method init
34
35       // draw results in a rectangle on applet's background
36       public void paint( Graphics g )
37       {
38          super.paint( g ); // call superclass version of method paint
39
40          // draw rectangle starting from (15, 10) that is 270
41          // pixels wide and 20 pixels tall
42          g.drawRect( 15, 10, 270, 20 );
43
44          // draw results as a String at (25, 25)
45          g.drawString( "The sum is " + sum, 25, 25 );
46       } // end method paint
47    } // end class AdditionApplet
```

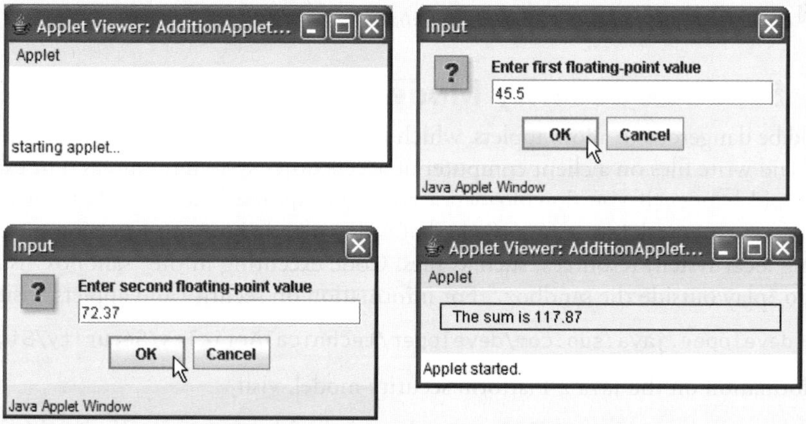

Fig. 20.10 | Adding `double` values. (Part 2 of 2.)

The applet requests that the user enter two floating-point numbers. Line 9 (Fig. 20.10) declares instance variable sum of type double. The applet contains two methods—init (lines 12–33) and paint (lines 36–46). When an applet container loads this applet, the container creates an instance of class AdditionApplet and calls its init method—this occurs only once during an applet's execution. Method init normally initializes the applet's fields

```
1   <html>
2   <applet code = "AdditionApplet.class" width = "300" height = "65">
3   </applet>
4   </html>
```

Fig. 20.11 | `AdditionApplet.html` loads class `AdditionApplet` of Fig. 20.10 into an applet container.

(if they need to be initialized to values other than their defaults) and performs other tasks that should occur only once when the applet begins execution. The first line of `init` always appears as shown in line 12, which indicates that `init` is a `public` method that receives no arguments and returns no information when it completes.

Lines 14–30 declare variables to store the values entered by the user, obtain the user input and convert the `String`s entered by the user to `double` values.

The assignment statement at line 32 sums the values stored in variables `number1` and `number2`, and assigns the result to instance variable `sum`. At this point, the applet's `init` method returns program control to the applet container, which then calls the applet's `start` method. We did not declare `start` in this applet, so the one inherited from class `JApplet` is called here. You will see typical uses of method `start` in Chapters 21 and 23.

Next, the applet container calls the applet's `paint` method, which draws a rectangle (line 42) where the addition result will appear. Line 45 calls the `Graphics` object's `drawString` method to display the results. The statement concatenates the value of instance variable `sum` to the `String` "The sum is " and displays the concatenated `String`.

Software Engineering Observation 20.1

The only statements that should be placed in an applet's `init` method are those that should execute only once when the applet is initialized.

20.6 Sandbox Security Model

It would be dangerous to allow applets, which are typically downloaded from the Internet, to read and write files on a client computer or access other system resources. For example, what would happen if you downloaded a malicious applet? The Java platform uses the sandbox security model to prevent code that is downloaded to your local computer from accessing local system resources, such as files. Code executing in the "sandbox" is not allowed to "play outside the sandbox." For information on security and applets, visit

developer.java.sun.com/developer/technicalArticles/Security/Signed

For information on the Java 2 Platform security model, visit

java.sun.com/javase/6/docs/technotes/guides/security/index.html

20.7 Internet and Web Resources

If you have access to the Internet, a large number of Java applet resources are available to you. The best place to start is at the source—the Sun Microsystems Java website, java.sun.com. The web page

java.sun.com/applets

contains several Java applet resources, including the demonstration applets from the JDK and other applets (many of which you can download).

If you do not have Java installed and configured for your browser, you can visit

    java.com

and click the **Download Now** button to download and install Java in your browser. Instructions are provided for various versions of Windows, Linux, Solaris and Mac OS.

The Sun Microsystems Java website

    java.sun.com

includes technical support, discussion forums, technical articles, resources, announcements of new Java features and early access to new Java technologies.

For various free online tutorials, visit the site

    java.sun.com/learning

Another useful website is JARS—originally called the Java Applet Rating Service. The JARS site

    www.jars.com

was a Java applet repository that rated every applet registered at the site, so you could view the best applets on the web. Early in the development of the Java language, having your applet rated here was a great way to demonstrate your Java programming abilities. JARS is now an all-around ratings site for Java programmers.

The resources listed in this section provide hyperlinks to many other Java-related websites. Spend some time browsing these sites, executing applets and reading the applets' source code when it is available. This will help you to rapidly expand your Java knowledge.

20.8 Wrap-Up

In this chapter, you learned the fundamentals of Java applets. You leaned basic HTML concepts that allowed you to embed an applet in a web page and execute the applet in an applet container such as the `appletviewer` or a web browser. In addition, you learned the five methods that are called automatically by the applet container during an applet's life cycle. In the next chapter, you will see several additional applets as we present basic multimedia capabilities. In Chapter 23, Multithreading, you will see an applet with `start` and `stop` methods that are used to control multiple threads of execution. In Chapter 24, Networking, we demonstrate how to customize an applet via parameters that are specified in an `applet` HTML element.

Summary

Section 20.1 Introduction
- Applets are Java programs that can be embedded in HTML documents.
- When a browser loads a web page containing an applet, the applet downloads into the web browser and executes.
- The browser that executes an applet is known as the applet container. The JDK includes the `appletviewer` applet container for testing applets before you embed them in a web page.

Section 20.2 Sample Applets Provided with the JDK

- To reexecute an applet in the `appletviewer`, click the `appletviewer`'s **Applet** menu and select the **Reload** menu item.
- To terminate the `appletviewer`, select **Quit** from the `appletviewer`'s **Applet** menu.

Section 20.3 Simple Java Applet: Drawing a String

- Every Java applet is a graphical user interface on which you can place GUI components or draw.
- Class `JApplet` from package `javax.swing` is used to create applets.
- An applet container can create only objects of classes that are `public` and extend `JApplet` (or the `Applet` class from early versions of Java).
- An applet container expects every Java applet to have methods named `init`, `start`, `paint`, `stop` and `destroy`, each of which is declared in class `JApplet`. Each new applet class you create inherits default implementations of these methods from class `JApplet`.
- When an applet container loads an applet, the container creates an object of the applet's type, then calls the applet's `init`, `start` and `paint` methods. If you do not declare these methods in your applet, the applet container calls the inherited versions.
- The superclass methods `init` and `start` have empty bodies, so they do not perform any tasks. The superclass method `paint` does not draw anything on the applet.
- To enable an applet to draw, override its method `paint`. You do not call method `paint` explicitly in an applet. Rather, the applet container calls `paint` to tell the applet when to draw, and the applet container is responsible for passing a `Graphics` object as an argument.
- The first statement in method `paint` should be a call to the superclass method `paint`. Omitting this can cause subtle drawing errors in applets that combine drawing and GUI components.
- Before you can execute an applet, you must create an HTML (HyperText Markup Language) document that specifies which applet to execute in the applet container. Typically, an HTML document ends with an ".html" or ".htm" file-name extension.
- Most HTML elements are delimited by pairs of tags. All HTML tags begin with a left angle bracket, <, and end with a right angle bracket, >.
- An `applet` element tells the applet container to load a specific applet and defines the size of the applet's display area (its width and height in pixels) in the applet container.
- Normally, an applet and its corresponding HTML document are stored in the same directory.
- Typically, a browser loads an HTML document from a computer (other than your own) connected to the Internet.
- When an applet container encounters an HTML document that contains an applet, the applet container automatically loads the applet's `.class` file(s) from the same directory on the computer in which the HTML document resides.
- The `appletviewer` understands only the `<applet>` and `</applet>` HTML tags and ignores all other tags in the document.
- The `appletviewer` is an ideal place to test an applet and ensure that it executes properly. Once the applet's execution is verified, you can add its HTML tags to a web page that others can view in their web browsers.

Section 20.4 Applet Life-Cycle Methods

- There are five applet methods that are called by the applet container from the time the applet is loaded into the browser to the time that the applet is terminated by the browser. These methods correspond to various aspects of an applet's life cycle.

- Method `init` is called once by the applet container when an applet is loaded for execution. This method initializes the applet.
- Method `start` is called by the applet container after method `init` completes execution. In addition, if the user browses to another website and later returns to the applet's HTML page, method `start` is called again.
- Method `paint` is called by the applet container after methods `init` and `start`. Method `paint` is also called when the applet needs to be repainted.
- Method `stop` is called by the applet container when the user leaves the applet's web page by browsing to another web page.
- Method `destroy` is called by the applet container when the applet is being removed from memory. This occurs when the user exits the browsing session by closing all the browser windows and may also occur at the browser's discretion when the user has browsed to other web pages.

Terminology

applet	`init` method of `JApplet`
applet container	`JApplet` class
`applet` HTML element	left angle bracket (<)
Applet menu in `appletviewer`	`paint` method of `JApplet`
`<applet>` tag	`parseDouble` method of `Double`
`appletviewer`	**Quit** menu item in `appletviewer`
attribute	**Reload** menu item in `appletviewer`
demo directory of the JDK	right angle bracket (>)
height of an applet	`start` method of `JApplet`
`.htm` file-name extension	`stop` method of `JApplet`
HTML element	tag
`.html` file-name extension	width of an applet
HyperText Markup Language (HTML)	

Self-Review Exercise

20.1 Fill in the blanks in each of the following:
  a) Java applets begin execution with a series of three method calls: _____, _____ and _____.
  b) The _____ method is invoked for an applet each time the user of a browser leaves an HTML page on which the applet resides.
  c) Every applet should extend class _____.
  d) The _____ or a browser can be used to execute a Java applet.
  e) The _____ method is called each time the user of a browser revisits the HTML page on which an applet resides.
  f) To load an applet into a browser, you must first define a(n) _____ file.
  g) Method _____ is called once when an applet begins execution.
  h) Method _____ is invoked to draw on an applet.
  i) Method _____ is invoked for an applet when the browser removes it from memory.
  j) The _____ and _____ HTML tags specify that an applet should be loaded into an applet container and executed.

Answers to Self-Review Exercise

20.1   a) init, start, paint. b) stop. c) JApplet (or Applet). d) appletviewer. e) start. f) HTML. g) init. h) paint. i) destroy. j) `<applet>`, `</applet>`.

Exercises

20.2   Write an applet that asks the user to enter two floating-point numbers, obtains the numbers from the user and displays the two numbers first and then the larger number followed by the words "is larger" as a string on the applet. If the numbers are equal, the applet should print the message "These numbers are equal." Use the techniques shown in Fig. 20.10.

20.3   Write an applet that asks the user to input the radius of a circle as a floating-point number and draws the circle's diameter, circumference and area. Use the value 3.14159 for π. Use the techniques shown in Fig. 20.10. [*Note:* You may also use the predefined constant Math.PI for the value of π. This constant is more precise than the value 3.14159. Class Math is defined in the java.lang package, so you do not need to import it.] Use the following formulas (*r* is the radius):

$$diameter = 2r$$
$$circumference = 2\pi r$$
$$area = \pi r^2$$

20.4   Write an applet that draws a checkerboard pattern as follows:

```
*  *  *  *  *  *  *  *
 *  *  *  *  *  *  *  *
*  *  *  *  *  *  *  *
 *  *  *  *  *  *  *  *
*  *  *  *  *  *  *  *
 *  *  *  *  *  *  *  *
*  *  *  *  *  *  *  *
 *  *  *  *  *  *  *  *
```

20.5   Write an applet that allows the user to input values for the arguments required by method drawRect, then draws a rectangle using the four input values.

20.6   Modify the solution to Exercise 20.10 to output ovals of different shapes and sizes.

20.7   Write an applet that allows the user to input the four arguments required by method drawOval, then draws an oval using the four input values.

21

Multimedia: Applets and Applications

OBJECTIVES

In this chapter you will learn:

- How to get, display and scale images.
- How to create animations from sequences of images.
- How to create image maps.
- How to get, play, loop and stop sounds, using an **AudioClip**.
- How to play video using interface **Player**.

21.1 Introduction

Welcome to what may be the largest revolution in the history of the computer industry. Those who entered the field decades ago were interested in using computers primarily to perform arithmetic calculations at high speed. As the computer field evolved, we began to realize that the data-manipulation capabilities of computers are equally important. The "sizzle" of Java is multimedia—the use of sound, images, graphics and video to make applications "come alive." Although most multimedia in Java applications is two-dimensional, Java programmers already can use the Java 3D API to create substantial 3D graphics applications (Sun provides an online tutorial for the Java 3D API at java.sun.com/ developer/onlineTraining/java3d).

Multimedia programming offers many new challenges. The field is already enormous and is growing rapidly. Most new computers sold today are "multimedia ready," with CD-RW and DVD drives, audio boards and special video capabilities. Economical desktop and laptop computers are so powerful that they can store and play DVD-quality sound and video, and we expect to see further advances in the kinds of programmable multimedia capabilities available through programming languages. One thing that we have learned is to plan for the "impossible"—in the computer and communications fields, the "impossible" has repeatedly become reality.

Among users who want graphics, many now want three-dimensional, high-resolution, color graphics. True three-dimensional imaging may become available within the next decade. Imagine having high-resolution, "theater-in-the-round," three-dimensional television. Sporting and entertainment events will seem to take place on your living room floor! Medical students worldwide will see operations being performed thousands of miles away, as if they were occurring in the same room. People will be able to learn how to drive with extremely realistic driving simulators in their homes before they get behind the wheel. The possibilities are exciting and endless.

Multimedia demands extraordinary computing power. Until recently, affordable computers with that kind of power were not available. Today's ultrapowerful processors make effective multimedia possible. The computer and communications industries will be primary beneficiaries of the multimedia revolution. Users will be willing to pay for the faster processors, larger memories and wider communications bandwidths that support demanding multimedia applications. Ironically, users may not have to pay more, because the fierce competition in these industries has historically driven prices down.

We need programming languages that make creating multimedia applications easy. Most programming languages do not incorporate such capabilities. However, Java, through its class libraries, provides extensive multimedia facilities that enable you to start developing powerful multimedia applications immediately.

This chapter presents several examples of interesting multimedia features that you will need to build useful applications, including:

1. the basics of manipulating images.

2. creating smooth animations.

3. playing audio files with the `AudioClip` interface.

4. creating image maps that can sense when the cursor is over them, even without a mouse click.

5. playing video files using the `Player` interface.

This chapter's exercises suggest dozens of challenging and interesting projects. When we were creating these exercises, the ideas just kept flowing. Multimedia leverages creativity in ways that we did not experience with "conventional" computer capabilities. [*Note:* Java's multimedia capabilities go far beyond those presented in this chapter. They include the Java Media Framework (JMF) API (for adding audio and video media to an application), Java Sound API (for playing, recording and modifying audio), Java 3D API (for creating and modifying 3D graphics), Java Advanced Imaging API (for image-processing capabilities, such as cropping and scaling), Java Speech API (for inputting voice commands from the user or outputting voice commands to the user), Java 2D API (for creating and modifying 2D graphics, covered in Chapter 12) and Java Image I/O API (for reading from and outputting images to files). Section 21.8 provides web links for each of these APIs.]

21.2 **Loading, Displaying and Scaling Images**

Java's multimedia capabilities include graphics, images, animations, sounds and video. We begin our discussion with images. We will use several different images in this chapter. Developers can create such images with any image software, such as Adobe® Photoshop™, Jasc® Paint Shop Pro™ or Microsoft® Paint.

The applet of Fig. 21.1 demonstrates loading an `Image` (package java.awt) and loading an `ImageIcon` (package javax.swing). Both classes are used to load and display images. The applet displays the `Image` in its original size and scaled to a larger size, using

```
1   // Fig. 21.1: LoadImageAndScale.java
2   // Load an image and display it in its original size and twice its
3   // original size. Load and display the same image as an ImageIcon.
4   import java.awt.Graphics;
5   import java.awt.Image;
6   import javax.swing.ImageIcon;
7   import javax.swing.JApplet;
8
9   public class LoadImageAndScale extends JApplet
10  {
```

Fig. 21.1 | Loading and displaying an image in an applet. (Part 1 of 2.)

```
11      private Image image1; // create Image object
12      private ImageIcon image2; // create ImageIcon object
13
14      // load image when applet is loaded
15      public void init()
16      {
17         image1 = getImage( getDocumentBase(), "redflowers.png" );
18         image2 = new ImageIcon( "yellowflowers.png" );
19      } // end method init
20
21      // display image
22      public void paint( Graphics g )
23      {
24         super.paint( g );
25
26         g.drawImage( image1, 0, 0, this ); // draw original image
27
28         // draw image to fit the width and the height less 120 pixels
29         g.drawImage( image1, 0, 120, getWidth(), getHeight() - 120, this );
30
31         // draw icon using its paintIcon method
32         image2.paintIcon( this, g, 180, 0 );
33      } // end method paint
34   } // end class LoadImageAndScale
```

Fig. 21.1 | Loading and displaying an image in an applet. (Part 2 of 2.)

two versions of Graphics method **drawImage**. The applet also draws the ImageIcon, using the icon's method **paintIcon**. Class ImageIcon implements interface Serializable, which allows ImageIcon objects to be easily written to a file or sent across the Internet. Class ImageIcon is also easier to use than Image, because its constructor can receive arguments of several different formats, including a byte array containing the bytes of an image, an Image already loaded in memory, and a String or a URL object, which both can be used to represent the location of the image. A URL object represents a Uniform Resource Locator that serves as a pointer to a resource on the World Wide Web, on your computer or on any networked machine. A URL object is more often used when accessing data over the Internet, while a simple string is more often used when accessing data on the current machine. Using a URL object also enables the programmer to access information from the web, such as searching for information from a database or through a search engine.

Lines 11 and 12 declare Image and ImageIcon variables, respectively. Class Image is an abstract class—the applet cannot create an object of class Image directly. Rather, we must call a method that causes the applet container to load and return the Image for use in the program. Class Applet (the direct superclass of JApplet) provides method getImage (line 17, in method init) that loads an Image into an applet. This version of getImage takes two arguments—the location of the image file and the file name of the image. In the first argument, Applet method getDocumentBase returns a URL representing the location of the image on the Internet (or on your computer if the applet was loaded from your computer). Method getDocumentBase returns the location of the HTML file as an object of class URL. The second argument specifies an image file name. The two arguments together specify the unique name and path of the file being loaded (in this case, the file red-flowers.png stored in the same directory as the HTML file that invoked the applet). Java supports several image formats, including Graphics Interchange Format (GIF), Joint Photographic Experts Group (JPEG) and Portable Network Graphics (PNG). File names for these types end with .gif, .jpg (or .jpeg) and .png, respectively.

Portability Tip 21.1

Class Image is an abstract class—as a result, programs cannot instantiate class Image to create objects. To achieve platform independence, the Java implementation on each platform provides its own subclass of Image to store image information. Methods that return references to Images actually return references to objects of the Java implementation's Image subclass.

Line 17 begins loading the image from the local computer (or downloading it from the Internet). When the image is required by the program, it is loaded in a separate thread. Remember that a thread is a parallel activity, and that threads will be discussed in detail in Chapter 23, Multithreading. By using a separate thread to load an image, the program can continue execution while the image loads. [*Note:* If the requested file is not available, method getImage does not throw an exception. An Image object is returned, but when this Image is displayed using method drawImage, nothing will be displayed.]

Class ImageIcon is not an abstract class—a program can create an ImageIcon object. At line 18, in method init creates an ImageIcon object that loads yellowflowers.png. Class ImageIcon provides several constructors that enable programs to initialize Image-Icon objects with images from the local computer or stored on the Internet.

The applet's paint method (lines 22–33) displays the images. Line 26 uses Graphics method drawImage to display an Image. Method drawImage accepts four arguments. The first is a reference to the Image object to display (image1). The second and third are the *x*- and *y*-coordinates at which to display the image on the applet—the coordinates specify the location of the upper-left corner of the image. The last argument is a reference to an ImageObserver—an interface implemented by class Component. Since class JApplet indirectly extends Component, all JApplets are ImageObservers. This argument is important when displaying large images that require a long time to download from the Internet. It is possible that a program will attempt to display the image before it has downloaded completely. The ImageObserver receives notifications as the Image is loaded and updates the image on the screen if the image was not complete when it was displayed. When executing this applet, watch carefully as pieces of the image display while the image loads. [*Note:* On faster computers, you might not notice this effect.]

Line 29 uses an overloaded version method drawImage to output a scaled version of the image. The fourth and fifth arguments specify the *width* and *height* of the image for display purposes. Method drawImage scales the image to fit the specified width and height. In this example, the fourth argument indicates that the width of the scaled image should be the width of the applet, and the fifth argument indicates that the height should be 120 pixels less than the height of the applet. The width and height of the applet are determined by calling methods getWidth and getHeight (inherited from class Component).

Line 32 uses ImageIcon method paintIcon to display the image. The method requires four arguments—a reference to the Component on which to display the image, a reference to the Graphics object that will render the image, the *x*-coordinate of the upper-left corner of the image and the *y*-coordinate of the upper-left corner of the image.

21.3 Animating a Series of Images

The next example demonstrates animating a series of images that are stored in an array of ImageIcons. The animation presented in Figs. 21.2–21.3 is implemented using a subclass of JPanel called LogoAnimatorJPanel (Fig. 21.2) that can be attached to an application window or a JApplet. Class LogoAnimator (Fig. 21.3) declares a main method (lines 8–20 of Fig. 21.3) to execute the animation as an application. Method main declares an instance of class JFrame and attaches a LogoAnimatorJPanel object to the JFrame to display the animation.

```
 1   // Fig. 21.2: LogoAnimatorJPanel.java
 2   // Animation of a series of images.
 3   import java.awt.Dimension;
 4   import java.awt.event.ActionEvent;
 5   import java.awt.event.ActionListener;
 6   import java.awt.Graphics;
 7   import javax.swing.ImageIcon;
 8   import javax.swing.JPanel;
 9   import javax.swing.Timer;
10
11   public class LogoAnimatorJPanel extends JPanel
12   {
13      private final static String IMAGE_NAME = "deitel"; // base image name
14      protected ImageIcon images[]; // array of images
15      private final int TOTAL_IMAGES = 30; // number of images
16      private int currentImage = 0; // current image index
17      private final int ANIMATION_DELAY = 50; // millisecond delay
18      private int width; // image width
19      private int height; // image height
```

Fig. 21.2 | Animating a series of images. (Part 1 of 3.)

```
20
21      private Timer animationTimer; // Timer drives animation
22
23      // constructor initializes LogoAnimatorJPanel by loading images
24      public LogoAnimatorJPanel()
25      {
26         images = new ImageIcon[ TOTAL_IMAGES ];
27
28         // load 30 images
29         for ( int count = 0; count < images.length; count++ )
30            images[ count ] = new ImageIcon( getClass().getResource(
31               "images/" + IMAGE_NAME + count + ".gif" ) );
32
33         // this example assumes all images have the same width and height
34         width = images[ 0 ].getIconWidth();   // get icon width
35         height = images[ 0 ].getIconHeight(); // get icon height
36      } // end LogoAnimatorJPanel constructor
37
38      // display current image
39      public void paintComponent( Graphics g )
40      {
41         super.paintComponent( g ); // call superclass paintComponent
42
43         images[ currentImage ].paintIcon( this, g, 0, 0 );
44
45         // set next image to be drawn only if Timer is running
46         if ( animationTimer.isRunning() )
47            currentImage = ( currentImage + 1 ) % TOTAL_IMAGES;
48      } // end method paintComponent
49
50      // start animation, or restart if window is redisplayed
51      public void startAnimation()
52      {
53         if ( animationTimer == null )
54         {
55            currentImage = 0; // display first image
56
57            // create timer
58            animationTimer =
59               new Timer( ANIMATION_DELAY, new TimerHandler() );
60
61            animationTimer.start(); // start Timer
62         } // end if
63         else // animationTimer already exists, restart animation
64         {
65            if ( ! animationTimer.isRunning() )
66               animationTimer.restart();
67         } // end else
68      } // end method startAnimation
69
70      // stop animation Timer
71      public void stopAnimation()
72      {
```

Fig. 21.2 | Animating a series of images. (Part 2 of 3.)

```
73          animationTimer.stop();
74       } // end method stopAnimation
75
76       // return minimum size of animation
77       public Dimension getMinimumSize()
78       {
79          return getPreferredSize();
80       } // end method getMinimumSize
81
82       // return preferred size of animation
83       public Dimension getPreferredSize()
84       {
85          return new Dimension( width, height );
86       } // end method getPreferredSize
87
88       // inner class to handle action events from Timer
89       private class TimerHandler implements ActionListener
90       {
91          // respond to Timer's event
92          public void actionPerformed( ActionEvent actionEvent )
93          {
94             repaint(); // repaint animator
95          } // end method actionPerformed
96       } // end class TimerHandler
97    } // end class LogoAnimatorJPanel
```

Fig. 21.2 | Animating a series of images. (Part 3 of 3.)

```
1    // Fig. 21.3: LogoAnimator.java
2    // Animation of a series of images.
3    import javax.swing.JFrame;
4
5    public class LogoAnimator
6    {
7       // execute animation in a JFrame
8       public static void main( String args[] )
9       {
10          LogoAnimatorJPanel animation = new LogoAnimatorJPanel();
11
12          JFrame window = new JFrame( "Animator test" ); // set up window
13          window.setDefaultCloseOperation( JFrame.EXIT_ON_CLOSE );
14          window.add( animation ); // add panel to frame
15
16          window.pack();  // make window just large enough for its GUI
17          window.setVisible( true );   // display window
18
19          animation.startAnimation();  // begin animation
20       } // end main
21    } // end class LogoAnimator
```

Fig. 21.3 | Displaying animated images on a JFrame. (Part 1 of 2.)

Fig. 21.3 | Displaying animated images on a JFrame. (Part 2 of 2.)

Class LogoAnimatorJPanel (Fig. 21.2) maintains an array of ImageIcons that are loaded in the constructor (lines 24–36). Lines 29–31 create each ImageIcon object and store the animation's 30 images in array images. The constructor argument uses string concatenation to assemble the file name from the pieces "images/", IMAGE_NAME, count and ".gif". Each image in the animation is in a file called deitel#.gif, where # is a value in the range 0–29 specified by the loop's control variable count. Lines 34–35 determine the width and height of the animation from the size of the first image in array images— we assume that all the images have the same width and height.

After the LogoAnimatorJPanel constructor loads the images, method main of Fig. 21.3 sets up the window in which the animation will appear (lines 12–17), and line 19 calls the LogoAnimatorJPanel's startAnimation method (declared at lines 51–68 of Fig. 21.2). This method starts the program's animation for the first time or restarts the animation that the program stopped previously. [*Note:* This method is called when the program is first run, to begin the animation. Although we provide the functionality for this method to restart the animation if it has been stopped, the example does not call the method for this purpose. We have added the functionality, however, should the reader choose to add GUI components that enable the user to start and stop the animation.] For example, to make an animation "browser friendly" in an applet, the animation should stop when the user switches web pages. If the user returns to the web page with the animation, method startAnimation can be called to restart the animation. The animation is driven by an instance of class Timer (from package javax.swing).

A Timer generates ActionEvents at a fixed interval in milliseconds (normally specified as an argument to the Timer's constructor) and notifies all its ActionListeners each time an ActionEvent occurs. Line 53 determines whether the Timer reference animationTimer is null. If it is, method startAnimation is being called for the first time, and a Timer needs to be created so that the animation can begin. Line 55 sets currentImage to 0, which indicates that the animation should begin with the image in the first element of array images. Lines 58–59 assign a new Timer object to animationTimer. The Timer constructor receives two arguments—the delay in milliseconds (ANIMATION_DELAY is 50, as specified in line 17) and the ActionListener that will respond to the Timer's Action-Events. For the second argument, an object of class TimerHandler is created. This class, which implements ActionListener, is declared in lines 89–96. Line 61 starts the Timer object. Once started, animationTimer will generate an ActionEvent every 50 milliseconds. Each time an ActionEvent is generated, the Timer's event handler actionPerformed (lines 92–95) is called. Line 94 calls LogoAnimatorJPanel's repaint method to schedule a call to LogoAnimatorJPanel's paintComponent method (lines 39–48). Remember that any subclass of JComponent that draws should do so in its paintComponent method. Recall from Chapter 11 that the first statement in any paintComponent method should be a call to the superclass's paintComponent method, to ensure that Swing components are displayed correctly.

If the animation started earlier, then our Timer was created and the condition in line 53 evaluates to false. The program continues with lines 65–66, which restarts the animation that the program stopped previously. The if condition at line 65 uses Timer method isRunning to determine whether the Timer is running (i.e., generating events). If it is not running, line 66 calls Timer method restart to indicate that the Timer should start generating events again. Once this occurs, method actionPerformed (the Timer's event handler) is again called at regular intervals. Each time, a call is made to method repaint (line 94), causing method paintComponent to be called and the next image to be displayed.

Line 43 paints the ImageIcon stored at element currentImage in the array. Lines 46–47 determine whether the animationTimer is running and, if so, prepare for the next image to be displayed by incrementing currentImage by 1. The remainder calculation ensures that the value of currentImage is set to 0 (to repeat the animation sequence) when it is incremented past 29 (the last element index in the array). The if statement ensures that the same image will be displayed if paintComponent is called while the Timer is stopped. This could be useful if a GUI is provided that enables the user to start and stop the animation. For example, if the animation is stopped and the user covers it with another window, then uncovers it, method paintComponent will be called. In this case, we do not want the animation to show the next image (because the animation has been stopped). We simply want the window to display the same image until the animation is restarted.

Method stopAnimation (lines 71–74) stops the animation by calling Timer method stop to indicate that the Timer should stop generating events. This prevents actionPerformed from calling repaint to initiate the painting of the next image in the array. [*Note: Just as with restarting the animation, this example defines but does not use method stopAnimation. We have provided this method for demonstration purposes, or if the user wishes to modify this example so that the user can stop and restart the animation.*]

Software Engineering Observation 21.1

When creating an animation for use in an applet, provide a mechanism for disabling the animation when the user browses a new web page different from the one on which the animation applet resides.

Remember that by extending class JPanel, we are creating a new GUI component. Thus, we must ensure that our new component works like other components for layout purposes. Layout managers often use a GUI component's getPreferredSize method (inherited from class java.awt.Component) to determine the preferred width and height of the component when laying it out as part of a GUI. If a new component has a preferred width and height, it should override method getPreferredSize (lines 83–86) to return that width and height as an object of class Dimension (package java.awt). The Dimension class represents the width and height of a GUI component. In this example, the images are 160 pixels wide and 80 pixels tall, so method getPreferredSize returns a Dimension object containing the numbers 160 and 80 (determined at lines 34–35).

Look-and-Feel Observation 21.1

The default size of a JPanel object is 10 pixels wide and 10 pixels tall.

Look-and-Feel Observation 21.2

When subclassing JPanel (or any other JComponent), override method getPreferredSize if the new component is to have a specific preferred width and height.

Lines 77–80 override method **getMinimumSize**. This method determines the minimum width and height of the component. As with method getPreferredSize, new components should override method getMinimumSize (also inherited from class Component). Method getMinimumSize simply calls getPreferredSize (a common programming practice) to indicate that the minimum size and preferred size are the same. Some layout managers ignore the dimensions specified by these methods. For example, a BorderLayout's NORTH and SOUTH regions use only the component's preferred height.

Look-and-Feel Observation 21.3

If a new GUI component has a minimum width and height (i.e., smaller dimensions would render the component ineffective on the display), override method getMinimumSize to return the minimum width and height as an instance of class Dimension.

Look-and-Feel Observation 21.4

For many GUI components, method getMinimumSize is implemented to return the result of a call to the component's getPreferredSize method.

21.4 Image Maps

Image maps are commonly used to create interactive web pages. An image map is an image with hot areas that the user can click to accomplish a task, such as loading a different web page into a browser. When the user positions the mouse pointer over a hot area, normally a descriptive message appears in the status area of the browser or in a tool tip.

Figure 21.4 loads an image containing several of the programming-tip icons used in this book. The program allows the user to position the mouse pointer over an icon to display a descriptive message associated with it. Event handler mouseMoved (lines 39–43) takes the mouse coordinates and passes them to method translateLocation (lines 58–69). Method translateLocation tests the coordinates to determine the icon over which the mouse was positioned when the mouseMoved event occurred—the method then returns a message indicating what the icon represents. This message is displayed in the applet container's status bar using method **showStatus** of class Applet.

```
 1   // Fig. 21.4: ImageMap.java
 2   // Demonstrating an image map.
 3   import java.awt.event.MouseAdapter;
 4   import java.awt.event.MouseEvent;
 5   import java.awt.event.MouseMotionAdapter;
 6   import java.awt.Graphics;
 7   import javax.swing.ImageIcon;
 8   import javax.swing.JApplet;
 9
10   public class ImageMap extends JApplet
11   {
```

Fig. 21.4 | Image map. (Part 1 of 4.)

```
12      private ImageIcon mapImage;
13
14      private static final String captions[] = { "Common Programming Error",
15         "Good Programming Practice", "Look and Feel Observation",
16         "Performance Tip", "Portability Tip",
17         "Software Engineering Observation", "Error-Prevention Tip" };
18
19      // sets up mouse listeners
20      public void init()
21      {
22         addMouseListener(
23
24            new MouseAdapter() // anonymous inner class
25            {
26               // indicate when mouse pointer exits applet area
27               public void mouseExited( MouseEvent event )
28               {
29                  showStatus( "Pointer outside applet" );
30               } // end method mouseExited
31            } // end anonymous inner class
32         ); // end call to addMouseListener
33
34         addMouseMotionListener(
35
36            new MouseMotionAdapter() // anonymous inner class
37            {
38               // determine icon over which mouse appears
39               public void mouseMoved( MouseEvent event )
40               {
41                  showStatus( translateLocation(
42                     event.getX(), event.getY() ) );
43               } // end method mouseMoved
44            } // end anonymous inner class
45         ); // end call to addMouseMotionListener
46
47         mapImage = new ImageIcon( "icons.png" ); // get image
48      } // end method init
49
50      // display mapImage
51      public void paint( Graphics g )
52      {
53         super.paint( g );
54         mapImage.paintIcon( this, g, 0, 0 );
55      } // end method paint
56
57      // return tip caption based on mouse coordinates
58      public String translateLocation( int x, int y )
59      {
60         // if coordinates outside image, return immediately
61         if ( x >= mapImage.getIconWidth() || y >= mapImage.getIconHeight() )
62            return "";
63
```

Fig. 21.4 | Image map. (Part 2 of 4.)

```
64          // determine icon number (0 - 6)
65          double iconWidth = ( double ) mapImage.getIconWidth() / 7.0;
66          int iconNumber = ( int )( ( double ) x / iconWidth );
67
68          return captions[ iconNumber ]; // return appropriate icon caption
69       } // end method translateLocation
70    } // end class ImageMap
```

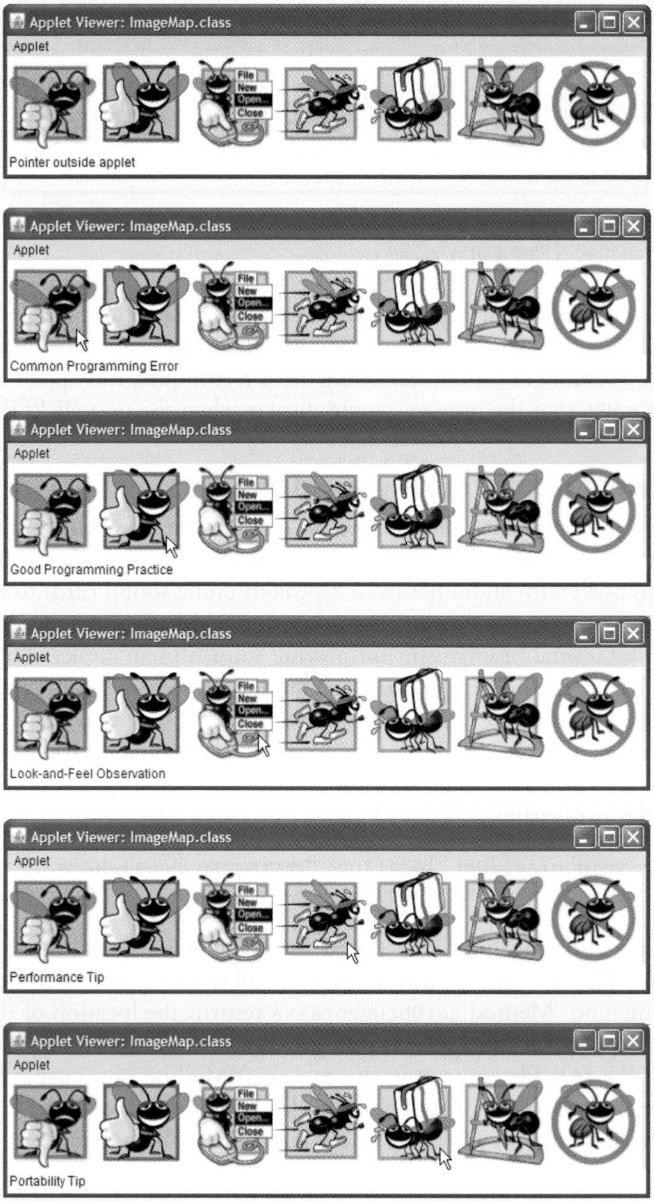

Fig. 21.4 | Image map. (Part 3 of 4.)

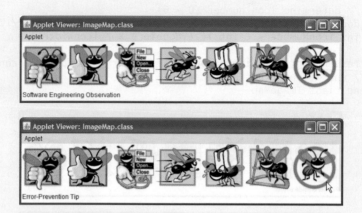

Fig. 21.4 | Image map. (Part 4 of 4.)

Clicking in the applet of Fig. 21.4 will not cause any action. In Chapter 24, Networking, we discuss the techniques required to load another web page into a browser via URLs and the AppletContext interface. Using those techniques, this applet could associate each icon with a URL that the browser would display when the user clicks the icon.

21.5 Loading and Playing Audio Clips

Java programs can manipulate and play audio clips. Users can capture their own audio clips, and many clips are available in software products and over the Internet. Your system needs to be equipped with audio hardware (speakers and a sound card) to be able to play the audio clips.

Java provides several mechanisms for playing sounds in an applet. The two simplest are the Applet's **play** method and the **play** method of the **AudioClip** interface. Additional audio capabilities are available in the Java Media Framework and Java Sound APIs. If you would like to play a sound once in a program, the Applet method play loads the sound and plays it once—the sound is marked for garbage collection after it plays. The Applet method play has two versions:

```
public void play( URL location, String soundFileName );
public void play( URL soundURL );
```

The first version loads the audio clip stored in file soundFileName from location and plays the sound. The first argument is normally a call to the applet's getDocumentBase or getCodeBase method. Method getDocumentBase returns the location of the HTML file that loaded the applet. (If the applet is in a package, the method returns the location of the package or the JAR file containing the package.) Method getCodeBase indicates the location of the applet's .class file. The second version of method play takes a URL that contains the location and the file name of the audio clip. The statement

```
play( getDocumentBase(), "hi.au" );
```

loads the audio clip in file hi.au and plays the clip once.

The sound engine that plays the audio clips supports several audio file formats, including Sun Audio file format (.au extension), Windows Wave file format (.wav extension), Macintosh AIFF file format (.aif or .aiff extensions) and Musical Instrument Digital Interface (MIDI) file format (.mid or .rmi extensions). The Java Media Framework (JMF) and Java Sound APIs support additional formats.

The program of Fig. 21.5 demonstrates loading and playing an AudioClip (package java.applet). This technique is more flexible than Applet method play. An applet can use an AudioClip to store audio for repeated use throughout a program's execution. Applet method getAudioClip has two forms that take the same arguments as method play described previously. Method getAudioClip returns a reference to an AudioClip. An AudioClip has three methods—play, loop and stop. As mentioned earlier, method play plays the audio clip once. Method loop continuously loops through the audio clip in the background. Method stop terminates an audio clip that is currently playing. In the program, each of these methods is associated with a button on the applet.

```
1   // Fig. 21.5: LoadAudioAndPlay.java
2   // Load an audio clip and play it.
3   import java.applet.AudioClip;
4   import java.awt.event.ItemListener;
5   import java.awt.event.ItemEvent;
6   import java.awt.event.ActionListener;
7   import java.awt.event.ActionEvent;
8   import java.awt.FlowLayout;
9   import javax.swing.JApplet;
10  import javax.swing.JButton;
11  import javax.swing.JComboBox;
12
13  public class LoadAudioAndPlay extends JApplet
14  {
15     private AudioClip sound1, sound2, currentSound;
16     private JButton playJButton, loopJButton, stopJButton;
17     private JComboBox soundJComboBox;
18
19     // load the image when the applet begins executing
20     public void init()
21     {
22        setLayout( new FlowLayout() );
23
24        String choices[] = { "Welcome", "Hi" };
25        soundJComboBox = new JComboBox( choices ); // create JComboBox
26
27        soundJComboBox.addItemListener(
28
29           new ItemListener() // anonymous inner class
30           {
31              // stop sound and change sound to user's selection
32              public void itemStateChanged( ItemEvent e )
33              {
34                 currentSound.stop();
```

Fig. 21.5 | Loading and playing an AudioClip. (Part 1 of 3.)

```
35              currentSound = soundJComboBox.getSelectedIndex() == 0 ?
36                 sound1 : sound2;
37           } // end method itemStateChanged
38        } // end anonymous inner class
39     ); // end addItemListener method call
40
41     add( soundJComboBox ); // add JComboBox to applet
42
43     // set up button event handler and buttons
44     ButtonHandler handler = new ButtonHandler();
45
46     // create Play JButton
47     playJButton = new JButton( "Play" );
48     playJButton.addActionListener( handler );
49     add( playJButton );
50
51     // create Loop JButton
52     loopJButton = new JButton( "Loop" );
53     loopJButton.addActionListener( handler );
54     add( loopJButton );
55
56     // create Stop JButton
57     stopJButton = new JButton( "Stop" );
58     stopJButton.addActionListener( handler );
59     add( stopJButton );
60
61     // load sounds and set currentSound
62     sound1 = getAudioClip( getDocumentBase(), "welcome.wav" );
63     sound2 = getAudioClip( getDocumentBase(), "hi.au" );
64     currentSound = sound1;
65   } // end method init
66
67   // stop the sound when the user switches web pages
68   public void stop()
69   {
70     currentSound.stop(); // stop AudioClip
71   } // end method stop
72
73   // private inner class to handle button events
74   private class ButtonHandler implements ActionListener
75   {
76     // process play, loop and stop button events
77     public void actionPerformed( ActionEvent actionEvent )
78     {
79       if ( actionEvent.getSource() == playJButton )
80         currentSound.play(); // play AudioClip once
81       else if ( actionEvent.getSource() == loopJButton )
82         currentSound.loop(); // play AudioClip continuously
83       else if ( actionEvent.getSource() == stopJButton )
84         currentSound.stop(); // stop AudioClip
85     } // end method actionPerformed
86   } // end class ButtonHandler
87 } // end class LoadAudioAndPlay
```

Fig. 21.5 | Loading and playing an AudioClip. (Part 2 of 3.)

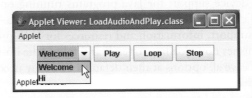

Fig. 21.5 | Loading and playing an `AudioClip`. (Part 3 of 3.)

Lines 62–63 in the applet's `init` method use `getAudioClip` to load two audio files—a Windows Wave file (`welcome.wav`) and a Sun Audio file (`hi.au`). The user can select which audio clip to play from the `JComboBox soundJComboBox`. Note that the applet's `stop` method is overridden at lines 68–71. When the user switches web pages, the applet container calls the applet's `stop` method. This enables the applet to stop playing the audio clip. Otherwise, it continues to play in the background—even if the applet is not displayed in the browser. This is not necessarily a problem, but it can be annoying to the user if the audio clip is looping. The `stop` method is provided here as a convenience to the user.

Look-and-Feel Observation 21.5

When playing audio clips in an applet or application, provide a mechanism for the user to disable the audio.

21.6 Playing Video and Other Media with Java Media Framework

A simple video can concisely and effectively convey a great deal of information. Recognizing the value of bringing extensible multimedia capabilities to Java, Sun Microsystems, Intel and Silicon Graphics worked together to produce the multimedia API Java Media Framework (JMF), discussed briefly in Section 21.1. Using the JMF API, programmers can create Java applications that play, edit, stream and capture many popular media types. While the features of JMF are quite extensive, this section briefly introduces some popular media formats and demonstrates playing video using the JMF API.

IBM and Sun developed the latest JMF specification—version 2.0. Sun also provides a reference implementation of the JMF specification—JMF 2.1.1e—that supports media file types such as Microsoft Audio/Video Interleave (`.avi`), Macromedia Flash 2 movies (`.swf`), Future Splash (`.spl`), MPEG Layer 3 Audio (`.mp3`), Musical Instrument Digital Interface (MIDI; `.mid` or `.rmi` extensions), MPEG-1 videos (`.mpeg`, `.mpg`), QuickTime (`.mov`), Sun Audio file format (`.au` extension), and Macintosh AIFF file format (`.aif` or `.aiff` extensions). You have already seen some of these file types.

Currently, JMF is available as an extension separate from the Java 2 Software Development Kit. The most recent JMF implementation (2.1.1e) can be downloaded from:

```
java.sun.com/products/java-media/jmf/2.1.1/download.html
```

You need to accept the license agreement prior to downloading.

The JMF website provides versions of the JMF that take advantage of the performance features of certain platforms. For example, the JMF Windows Performance Pack provides extensive media and device support for Java programs running on Microsoft Windows platforms. JMF's official website (java.sun.com/products/java-media/jmf) provides continually updated support, information and resources for JMF programmers.

Once the file finishes downloading, open it and follow the on-screen instructions to install the program. Leave all options at their defaults. You may need to restart your computer to finish the installation.

Creating a Simple Media Player

The JMF offers several mechanisms for playing media. The simplest mechanism is using objects that implement interface **Player** declared in package **javax.media**. Package javax.media and its subpackages contain the classes that compose the Java Media Framework. To play a media clip you must first create a URL object that refers to it. Then pass the URL as an argument to static method **createRealizedPlayer** of class Manager to obtain a Player for the media clip. Class **Manager** declares utility methods for accessing system resources to play and to manipulate media. Figure 21.6 declares a JPanel that demonstrates some of these methods.

```
 1   // Fig. 21.6: MediaPanel.java
 2   // A JPanel the plays media from a URL
 3   import java.awt.BorderLayout;
 4   import java.awt.Component;
 5   import java.io.IOException;
 6   import java.net.URL;
 7   import javax.media.CannotRealizeException;
 8   import javax.media.Manager;
 9   import javax.media.NoPlayerException;
10   import javax.media.Player;
11   import javax.swing.JPanel;
12
13   public class MediaPanel extends JPanel
14   {
15      public MediaPanel( URL mediaURL )
16      {
17         setLayout( new BorderLayout() ); // use a BorderLayout
18
19         // Use lightweight components for Swing compatibility
20         Manager.setHint( Manager.LIGHTWEIGHT_RENDERER, true );
21
22         try
23         {
24            // create a player to play the media specified in the URL
25            Player mediaPlayer = Manager.createRealizedPlayer( mediaURL );
26
27            // get the components for the video and the playback controls
28            Component video = mediaPlayer.getVisualComponent();
29            Component controls = mediaPlayer.getControlPanelComponent();
30
31            if ( video != null )
32               add( video, BorderLayout.CENTER ); // add video component
33
```

Fig. 21.6 | JPanel that plays a media file from a URL. (Part 1 of 2.)

```
34          if ( controls != null )
35             add( controls, BorderLayout.SOUTH ); // add controls
36
37          mediaPlayer.start(); // start playing the media clip
38       } // end try
39       catch ( NoPlayerException noPlayerException )
40       {
41          System.err.println( "No media player found" );
42       } // end catch
43       catch ( CannotRealizeException cannotRealizeException )
44       {
45          System.err.println( "Could not realize media player" );
46       } // end catch
47       catch ( IOException ioException )
48       {
49          System.err.println( "Error reading from the source" );
50       } // end catch
51    } // end MediaPanel constructor
52 } // end class MediaPanel
```

Fig. 21.6 | JPanel that plays a media file from a URL. (Part 2 of 2.)

The constructor (lines 15–51) sets up the JPanel to play the media file specified by the constructor's URL parameter. MediaPanel uses a BorderLayout (line 17). Line 20 invokes static method **setHint** to set the flag **Manager.LIGHTWEIGHT_RENDERER** to true. This instructs the Manager to use a lightweight renderer that is compatible with lightweight Swing components, as opposed to the default heavyweight renderer. Inside the try block (lines 22–38), line 25 invokes static method createRealizedPlayer of class Manager to create and realize a Player that plays the media file. When a Player realizes, it identifies the system resources it needs to play the media. Depending on the file, realizing can be a resource-consuming and time-consuming process. Method createRealized-Player throws three checked exceptions, **NoPlayerException**, **CannotRealizeException** and IOException. A NoPlayerException indicates that the system could not find a player that can play the file format. A CannotRealizeException indicates that the system could not properly identify the resources a media file needs. An IOException indicates that there was an error while reading the file. These exceptions are handled in the catch block in lines 39–50.

Line 28 invokes method **getVisualComponent** of Player to get a Component that displays the visual (generally video) aspect of the media file. Line 29 invokes method **getControlPanelComponent** of Player to get a Component that provides playback and media controls. These components are assigned to local variables video and control, respectively. The if statements in lines 31–32 and lines 34–35 add the video and the controls if they exist. The video Component is added to the CENTER region (line 32), so it fills any available space on the JPanel. The controls Component, which is added to the SOUTH region, typically provides the following controls:

1. A positioning slider to jump to certain points in the media clip.

2. A pause button.

3. A volume button that provides volume control by right clicking and a mute function by left clicking.

4. A media properties button that provides detailed media information by left clicking and frame rate control by right clicking.

Line 37 calls Player method **start** to begin playing the media file. Lines 39–50 handle the various exceptions that createRealizedPlayer throws.

The application in Fig. 21.7 displays a JFileChooser dialog for the user to choose a media file. It then creates a MediaPanel that plays the selected file and creates a JFrame to display the MediaPanel.

```java
1   // Fig. 21.7: MediaTest.java
2   // A simple media player
3   import java.io.File;
4   import java.net.MalformedURLException;
5   import java.net.URL;
6   import javax.swing.JFileChooser;
7   import javax.swing.JFrame;
8
9   public class MediaTest
10  {
11     // launch the application
12     public static void main( String args[] )
13     {
14        // create a file chooser
15        JFileChooser fileChooser = new JFileChooser();
16
17        // show open file dialog
18        int result = fileChooser.showOpenDialog( null );
19
20        if ( result == JFileChooser.APPROVE_OPTION ) // user chose a file
21        {
22           URL mediaURL = null;
23
24           try
25           {
26              // get the file as URL
27              mediaURL = fileChooser.getSelectedFile().toURL();
28           } // end try
29           catch ( MalformedURLException malformedURLException )
30           {
31              System.err.println( "Could not create URL for the file" );
32           } // end catch
33
34           if ( mediaURL != null ) // only display if there is a valid URL
35           {
36              JFrame mediaTest = new JFrame( "Media Tester" );
37              mediaTest.setDefaultCloseOperation( JFrame.EXIT_ON_CLOSE );
38
39              MediaPanel mediaPanel = new MediaPanel( mediaURL );
40              mediaTest.add( mediaPanel );
```

Fig. 21.7 | Test application that creates a MediaPanel from a user-selected file. (Part 1 of 2.)

```
41
42              mediaTest.setSize( 300, 300 );
43              mediaTest.setVisible( true );
44           } // end inner if
45        } // end outer if
46     } // end main
47  } // end class MediaTest
```

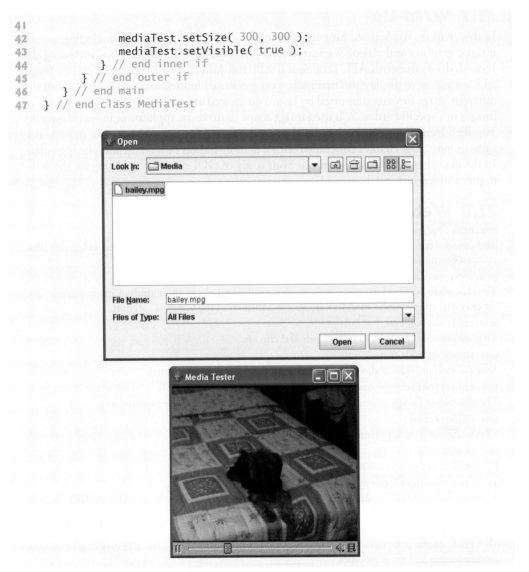

Fig. 21.7 | Test application that creates a MediaPanel from a user-selected file. (Part 2 of 2.)

Method main (lines 12–46) assigns a new JFileChooser to local variable fileChooser (line 15), shows an open file dialog (line 18) and assigns the return value to result. Line 20 checks result to determine whether the user chose a file. To create a Player to play the selected media file, you must convert the File object returned by JFileChooser to a URL object. Method **toURL** of class File returns a URL that points to the File on the system, possibly throwing a MalformedURLException if it cannot create a URL object for the File. The try statement (lines 24–32) creates a URL for the selected file and assigns it to mediaURL. The if statement in lines 34–44 checks that mediaURL is not null and creates the GUI components to play the media.

21.7 **Wrap-Up**

In this chapter, you learned how to make applications more exciting by including sound, images, graphics and video. We introduced Java's multimedia capabilities, including the Java Media Framework API, Java Sound API and Java 3D API. You used classes `Image` and `ImageIcon` to display and manipulate images stored in files, and you learned about the different image formats supported by Java. You created animation by displaying a series of images in a specific order. You used image maps to make an application more interactive. You then learned how to load audio clips, and how to play them either once or in a continuous loop. The chapter concluded with a demonstration of loading and playing video. In the next chapter, you will continue your study of GUI concepts, building on the techniques you learned in Chapter 11.

21.8 **Web Resources**

`www.nasa.gov/multimedia/highlights/index.html`
The *NASA Multimedia Gallery* contains a wide variety of images, audio clips and video clips that you can download and use to test your Java multimedia programs.

`www.anbg.gov.au/anbg/index.html`
The *Australian National Botanic Gardens* website provides links to the sounds of many animals. Try, for example, the *Common Birds* link under the "Animals in the Gardens" section.

`www.thefreesite.com`
TheFreeSite.com has links to free sounds and clip art.

`www.soundcentral.com`
SoundCentral provides audio clips in WAV, AU, AIFF and MIDI formats.

`www.animationfactory.com`
The *Animation Factory* provides thousands of free GIF animations for personal use.

`www.clipart.com`
ClipArt.com is a subscription-based service for images and sounds.

`www.pngart.com`
PNGART.com provides over 50,000 free images in PNG format.

`java.sun.com/developer/techDocs/hi/repository/`
The *Java look and feel Graphics Repository* provides images designed for use in a Swing GUI, including toolbar button images.

`www.freebyte.com/graphicprograms/`
This guide contains links to several free graphics software programs. The software can be used to modify images and draw graphics.

`graphicssoft.about.com/od/pixelbasedfreewin/`
This site provides links for free graphics programs designed for use on Windows machines.

Java Multimedia API References

`java.sun.com/products/java-media/jmf/`
This is the *Java Media Framework (JMF) API* home page. Here you can download the latest Sun implementation of the JMF. The site also contains the documentation for the JMF.

`java.sun.com/products/java-media/sound/`
The *Java Sound API* home page. Java Sound provides capabilities for playing and recording audio.

`java3d.dev.java.net/`
The *Java 3D API* home page. This API can be used to produce three-dimensional images typical of today's video games.

`java.sun.com/developer/onlineTraining/java3d/`
This site provides a *Java 3D API* tutorial.

`java.sun.com/products/java-media/jai/`
The *Java Advanced Imaging API* home page. This API provides image-processing capabilities, such as contrast enhancement, cropping, scaling and geometric warping.

`java.sun.com/products/java-media/speech/`
The *Java Speech API* enables programs to perform speech synthesis and speech recognition.

`freetts.sourceforge.net/docs/index.php`
FreeTTS is an implementation of the Java Speech API.

`java.sun.com/products/java-media/2D/`
This is the *Java 2D API* home page. This API (introduced in Chapter 12) provides complex two-dimensional graphics capabilities.

`java.sun.com/javase/6/docs/technotes/guides/imageio/index.html`
This site contains a guide to the *Java Image I/O API*, which enables programs to load and save images using formats that are not currently supported by the Java APIs.

Summary

Section 21.2 Loading, Displaying and Scaling Images

- `Applet` method `getImage` loads an `Image`.

- `Applet` method `getDocumentBase` returns the location of the applet's HTML file on the Internet as an object of class `URL`.

- Java supports several image formats, including Graphics Interchange Format (GIF), Joint Photographic Experts Group (JPEG) and Portable Network Graphics (PNG). The file names for these types end with `.gif`, `.jpg` (or `.jpeg`) and `.png`, respectively.

- Class `ImageIcon` provides constructors that allow an `ImageIcon` object to be initialized with an image from the local computer or stored on a web server on the Internet.

- `Graphics` method `drawImage` accepts four arguments—a reference to the `Image` object in which the image is stored, the *x*- and *y*-coordinates where the image should be displayed and a reference to an `ImageObserver` object.

- Another version of `Graphics` method `drawImage` outputs a scaled image. The fourth and fifth arguments specify the width and height of the image for display purposes.

- Interface `ImageObserver` is implemented by class `Component`. `ImageObserver`s receive notifications as an `Image` is loaded and update it on the screen if it was not complete when it was displayed.

- `ImageIcon` method `paintIcon` displays the `ImageIcon`'s image. The method requires four arguments—a reference to the `Component` on which the image will be displayed, a reference to the `Graphics` object used to render the image, the *x*-coordinate of the upper-left corner of the image and the *y*-coordinate of the upper-left corner of the image.

- A `URL` object represents a Uniform Resource Locator, which is as a pointer to a resource on the World Wide Web, on your computer or on any networked machine.

Section 21.3 Animating a Series of Images

- `Timer` objects generate `ActionEvent`s at fixed millisecond intervals. The `Timer` constructor receives a delay in milliseconds and an `ActionListener`. `Timer` method `start` starts the `Timer`. Method `stop` indicates that the `Timer` should stop generating events. Method `restart` indicates that the `Timer` should start generating events again.

Section 21.4 Image Maps
- An image map is an image that has hot areas that the user can click to accomplish a task, such as loading a different web page into a browser.

Section 21.5 Loading and Playing Audio Clips
- Applet method play has two forms:

```
public void play( URL location, String soundFileName );
public void play( URL soundURL );
```

One version loads the audio clip stored in file soundFileName from location and plays the sound. The other version takes a URL that contains the location and the file name of the audio clip.

- Applet method getDocumentBase indicates the location of the HTML file that loaded the applet. Method getCodeBase indicates where the .class file for an applet is located.

- The sound engine that plays audio clips supports several audio file formats, including Sun Audio file format (.au extension), Windows Wave file format (.wav extension), Macintosh AIFF file format (.aif or .aiff extensions) and Musical Instrument Digital Interface (MIDI) file format (.mid or .rmi extensions). The Java Media Framework (JMF) supports additional formats.

- Applet method getAudioClip has two forms that take the same arguments as the play method. Method getAudioClip returns a reference to an AudioClip. AudioClips have three methods—play, loop and stop. Method play plays the audio clip once. Method loop continuously loops the audio clip. Method stop terminates an audio clip that is currently playing.

Section 21.6 Playing Video and Other Media with Java Media Framework
- Sun Microsystems, Intel and Silicon Graphics worked together to produce the Java Media Framework (JMF).

- Package javax.media and its subpackages contain the classes that compose the Java Media Framework.

- Class Manager declares utility methods for accessing system resources to play and to manipulate media.

- Method toURL of class File returns a URL that points to the File on the system.

Terminology

.aif file extension	getMinimumSize method of class Component
.aiff file extension	getPreferredSize method of class Component
.au file extension	getVisualComponent method of interface
audio clip	Player
AudioClip interface	.gif file extension
.avi file extension	Graphics class
CannotRealizePlayerException exception	Graphics Interchange Format (GIF)
createRealizedPlayer method of class Manager	hot area
Dimension class	Image class
drawImage method of class Graphics	image map
Future Splash (.spl) files	ImageIcon class
getAudioClip method of class Applet	ImageObserver interface
getCodeBase method of class Applet	Java 3D API
getControlPanelComponent method of inter- face Player	Java Advanced Imaging API
	Java Image I/O API
getDocumentBase method of class Applet	Java Media Framework (JMF) API
getImage method of class Applet	Java Sound API

Java Speech API
javax.media package
Joint Photographic Experts Group (JPEG)
.jpeg file extension
.jpg file extension
LIGHTWEIGHT_RENDERER constant of class
  Manager
loop method of interface AudioClip
Macintosh AIFF file format (.aif or .aiff
  extensions)
Macromedia Flash 2 movies (.swf)
Manager class
Microsoft Audio/Video Interleave (.avi) file
.mid file extension
.mov file extension
.mp3 file extension
.mpeg file extension
MPEG Layer 3 Audio (.mp3) files
MPEG-1 videos (.mpeg, .mpg)
.mpg file extension
multimedia
Musical Instrument Digital Interface (MIDI)
  file format (.mid or .rmi extensions)
NoPlayerException exception

paintIcon method of class ImageIcon
play method of class Applet
play method of interface AudioClip
Player interface
.png file extension
Portable Network Graphics (PNG)
QuickTime (.mov) files
.rmi file extension
setHint method of class Manager
showStatus method of class Applet
sound
sound engine
.spl file extension
start method of interface Player
stop method of class Timer
stop method of interface AudioClip
Sun Audio file format (.au extension)
.swf file extension
toURL method of class File
URL class
video
.wav file extension
Windows Wave file format (.wav extension)

Self-Review Exercises

21.1 Fill in the blanks in each of the following statements:
  a) Applet method _____ loads an image into an applet.
  b) Graphics method _____ displays an image on an applet.
  c) Java provides two mechanisms for playing sounds in an applet—the Applet's play
    method and the play method of the _____ interface.
  d) A(n) _____ is an image that has hot areas that the user can click to accomplish a task
    such as loading a web page.
  e) Method _____ of class ImageIcon displays the ImageIcon's image.
  f) Java supports several image formats, including _____, _____ and _____.

21.2 Determine whether each of the following statements is *true* or *false*. If *false*, explain why.
  a) A sound is marked for garbage collection after it plays.
  b) Class ImageIcon provides constructors that allow an ImageIcon object to be initialized
    only with an image from the local computer.
  c) Method play of class AudioClip continuously loops an audio clip.
  d) The Java Image I/O API is used for adding 3D graphics to a Java application.
  e) Applet method getDocumentBase returns, as an object of class URL, the location on the
    Internet of the HTML file that invoked the applet.

Answers to Self-Review Exercises

21.1 a) getImage. b) drawImage. c) AudioClip. d) image map. e) paintIcon. f) Graphics Interchange Format (GIF), Joint Photographic Experts Group (JPEG), Portable Network Graphics
(PNG).

21.2 a) True. b) False. ImageIcon can load images from the Internet as well. c) False. Method play of class AudioClip plays an audio clip once. Method loop of class AudioClip continuously loops an audio clip. d) False. The Java 3D API is used for creating and modifying 3D graphics. The Java Image I/O API is used for reading from and outputting images to files. e) True.

Exercises

21.3 Describe the Java methods for playing and manipulating audio clips.

21.4 *(Randomly Erasing an Image)* Suppose an image is displayed in a rectangular screen area. One way to erase the image is simply to set every pixel to the same color immediately, but this is a dull visual effect. Write a Java program that displays an image and then erases it by using random-number generation to select individual pixels to erase. After most of the image is erased, erase all the remaining pixels at once. You can draw individual pixels as a line that starts and ends at the same coordinates. You might try several variants of this problem. For example, you might display lines randomly or display shapes randomly to erase regions of the screen.

21.5 *(Image Flasher)* Create a Java program that repeatedly flashes an image on the screen. Do this by alternating the image with a plain background-color image.

21.6 *(Digital Clock)* Implement a program that displays a digital clock on the screen.

21.7 *(Image Zooming)* Create a program that enables you to zoom in on or out from an image.

Special Section: Challenging Multimedia Projects

The preceding exercises are keyed to the text and designed to test the reader's understanding of fundamental multimedia concepts. This section includes a collection of advanced multimedia projects. The reader should find these problems challenging, yet entertaining. The problems vary considerably in difficulty. Some require an hour or two of program writing and implementation. Others are useful for lab assignments that might require two or three weeks of study and implementation. Some are challenging term projects. [*Note to Instructors:* Solutions are not provided for these exercises.]

21.8 *(Animation)* Create a general-purpose Java animation program. It should allow the user to specify the sequence of frames to be displayed, the speed at which the images are displayed, audios to be played while the animation is running and so on.

21.9 *(Random Interimage Transition)* This provides a nice visual effect. If you are displaying one image in a given area on the screen and you would like to transition to another image in the same area, store the new screen image in an off-screen buffer and randomly copy pixels from it to the display area, overlaying the pixels already at those locations. When the vast majority of the pixels have been copied, copy the entire new image to the display area to be sure you are displaying the complete new image. To implement this program, you may need to use the PixelGrabber and MemoryImage-Source classes (see the Java API documentation for descriptions of these classes). You might try several variants of this problem. For example, try selecting all the pixels in a randomly selected straight line or shape in the new image, and overlay them above the corresponding positions of the old image.

21.10 *(Scrolling Marquee Sign)* Create a Java program that scrolls dotted characters from right to left (or from left to right if that is appropriate for your language) across a marquee-like display sign. As an option, display the text in a continuous loop, so that after the text disappears at one end, it reappears at the other.

21.11 *(Analog Clock)* Create a Java program that displays an analog clock with hour, minute and second hands that move appropriately as the time changes.

21.12 *(Automatic Jigsaw Puzzle Generator)* Create a Java jigsaw puzzle generator and manipulator. The user specifies an image. Your program loads and displays the image, then breaks it into randomly selected shapes and shuffles them. The user then uses the mouse to move the pieces around to solve the puzzle. Add appropriate audio sounds as the pieces are moved around and snapped back into place. You might keep tabs on each piece and where it really belongs—then use audio effects to help the user get the pieces into the correct positions.

21.13 *(One-Armed Bandit)* Develop a multimedia simulation of a "one-armed bandit." Have three spinning wheels. Place images of various fruits and symbols on each wheel. Use true random-number generation to simulate the spinning of each wheel and the stopping of each wheel on a symbol.

21.14 *(Shuffleboard)* Develop a multimedia-based simulation of the game of shuffleboard. Use appropriate audio and visual effects.

21.15 *(Artist)* Design a Java art program that will give an artist a great variety of capabilities to draw, use images and use animations to create a dynamic multimedia art display.

21.16 *(Floor Planner)* Develop a Java program that will help someone arrange furniture in a home. Add features that enable the person to achieve the best possible arrangement.

21.17 *(15 Puzzle)* Write a multimedia-based Java program that enables the user to play the game of 15. The game is played on a 4-by-4 board for a total of 16 slots. One slot is empty, the others are occupied by 15 tiles numbered 1 through 15. Any tile next to the currently empty slot can be moved into that slot by clicking on the tile. Your program should create the board with the tiles out of order. The goal is to arrange the tiles into sequential order, row by row.

21.18 *(Calendar/Tickler File)* Using both audio and images, create a general-purpose calendar and "tickler" file. For example, the program should sing "Happy Birthday" when you use it on your birthday. Have the program display images and play audios associated with important events. Also, have the program remind you in advance of these important events. It would be nice, for example, to have the program give you a week's notice so you can pick up an appropriate greeting card for that special person.

21.19 *(Coloring Black-and-White Photographs and Images)* Create a Java program that lets you paint a black-and-white photograph with color. Provide a color palette for selecting colors. Your program should let you apply different colors to different regions of the image.

21.20 *(Multimedia-Based Simpletron Simulator)* Modify the Simpletron simulator that you developed in the exercises in the previous chapters (Exercises 7.34—7.36 and Exercises 17.26—17.30) to include multimedia features. Add computer-like sounds to indicate that the Simpletron is executing instructions. Add a breaking-glass sound when a fatal error occurs. Use flashing lights to indicate which cells of memory or which registers are currently being manipulated. Use other multimedia techniques, as appropriate, to make your Simpletron simulator more valuable to its users as an educational tool.

22

GUI Components: Part 2

OBJECTIVES

In this chapter you will learn:

- To create and manipulate sliders, menus, pop-up menus and windows.
- To change the look-and-feel of a GUI, using Swing's pluggable look-and-feel.
- To create a multiple-document interface with **JDesktopPane** and **JInternalFrame**.
- To use additional layout managers.

An actor entering through the door, you've got nothing. But if he enters through the window, you've got a situation.

—Billy Wilder

...the force of events wakes slumberous talents.

—Edward Hoagland

You and I would see more interesting photography if they would stop worrying, and instead, apply horse-sense to the problem of recording the look and feel of their own era.

—Jessie Tarbox Beals

22.1 Introduction

In this chapter, we continue our study of GUIs. We discuss additional components and layout managers and lay the groundwork for building more complex GUIs.

We begin our discussion with menus that enable the user to effectively perform tasks in the program. The look-and-feel of a Swing GUI can be uniform across all platforms on which a Java program executes, or the GUI can be customized by using Swing's pluggable look-and-feel (PLAF). We provide an example that illustrates how to change between Swing's default metal look-and-feel (which looks and behaves the same across platforms), a look-and-feel that simulates Motif (a popular UNIX look-and-feel) and one that simulates Microsoft's Windows look-and-feel.

Many of today's applications use a multiple-document interface (MDI)—a main window (often called the parent window) containing other windows (often called child windows) to manage several open documents in parallel. For example, many e-mail programs allow you to have several e-mail windows open at the same time so that you can compose or read multiple e-mail messages. We demonstrate Swing's classes for creating multiple-document interfaces. The chapter finishes with a series of examples discussing additional layout managers for organizing graphical user interfaces.

Swing is a large and complex topic. There are many more GUI components and capabilities than can be presented here. Several more Swing GUI components are introduced in the remaining chapters of this book as they are needed. Our book *Advanced Java 2 Platform How to Program* discusses other, more advanced Swing components and capabilities.

22.2 JSlider

JSliders enable a user to select from a range of integer values. Class JSlider inherits from JComponent. Figure 22.1 shows a horizontal JSlider with tick marks and the thumb that allows a user to select a value. JSliders can be customized to display major tick marks,

Fig. 22.1 | JSlider component with horizontal orientation.

minor tick marks and labels for the tick marks. They also support snap-to ticks, which cause the thumb, when positioned between two tick marks, to snap to the closest one.

Most Swing GUI components support user interactions through the mouse and the keyboard. For example, if a JSlider has the focus (i.e., it is the currently selected GUI component in the user interface), the left arrow key and right arrow key cause the thumb of the JSlider to decrease or increase by 1, respectively. The down arrow key and up arrow key also cause the thumb of the JSlider to decrease or increase by 1 tick, respectively. The *PgDn* (page down) *key* and *PgUp* (page up) *key* cause the thumb of the JSlider to decrease or increase by block increments of one-tenth of the range of values, respectively. The *Home key* moves the thumb to the minimum value of the JSlider, and the *End key* moves the thumb to the maximum value of the JSlider.

JSliders have either a horizontal orientation or a vertical orientation. For a horizontal JSlider, the minimum value is at the left end of the JSlider and the maximum is at the right end. For a vertical JSlider, the minimum value is at the bottom and the maximum is at the top. The minimum and maximum value positions on a JSlider can be reversed by invoking JSlider method **setInverted** with boolean argument true. The relative position of the thumb indicates the current value of the JSlider.

The program in Figs. 22.2–22.4 allows the user to size a circle drawn on a subclass of JPanel called OvalPanel (Fig. 22.2). The user specifies the circle's diameter with a horizontal JSlider. Class OvalPanel knows how to draw a circle on itself, using its own instance variable diameter to determine the diameter of the circle—the diameter is used as the width and height of the bounding box in which the circle is displayed. The diameter value is set when the user interacts with the JSlider. The event handler calls method setDiameter in class OvalPanel to set the diameter and calls repaint to draw the new circle. The repaint call results in a call to OvalPanel's paintComponent method.

```
1   // Fig. 22.2: OvalPanel.java
2   // A customized JPanel class.
3   import java.awt.Graphics;
4   import java.awt.Dimension;
5   import javax.swing.JPanel;
6
7   public class OvalPanel extends JPanel
8   {
9      private int diameter = 10; // default diameter of 10
10
11     // draw an oval of the specified diameter
12     public void paintComponent( Graphics g )
13     {
14        super.paintComponent( g );
15
16        g.fillOval( 10, 10, diameter, diameter ); // draw circle
17     } // end method paintComponent
18
19     // validate and set diameter, then repaint
20     public void setDiameter( int newDiameter )
21     {
```

Fig. 22.2 | JPanel subclass for drawing circles of a specified diameter. (Part 1 of 2.)

```
22          // if diameter invalid, default to 10
23          diameter = ( newDiameter >= 0 ? newDiameter : 10 );
24          repaint(); // repaint panel
25       } // end method setDiameter
26
27       // used by layout manager to determine preferred size
28       public Dimension getPreferredSize()
29       {
30          return new Dimension( 200, 200 );
31       } // end method getPreferredSize
32
33       // used by layout manager to determine minimum size
34       public Dimension getMinimumSize()
35       {
36          return getPreferredSize();
37       } // end method getMinimumSize
38    } // end class OvalPanel
```

Fig. 22.2 | `JPanel` subclass for drawing circles of a specified diameter. (Part 2 of 2.)

Class `OvalPanel` (Fig. 22.2) contains a `paintComponent` method (lines 12–17) that draws a filled oval (a circle in this example), a `setDiameter` method (lines 20–25) that changes the circle's `diameter` and repaints the `OvalPanel`, a `getPreferredSize` method (lines 28–31) that returns the preferred width and height of an `OvalPanel` and a `getMinimumSize` method (lines 34–37) that returns an `OvalPanel`'s minimum width and height.

 **Look-and-Feel Observation 22.1**

If a new GUI component has a minimum width and height (i.e., smaller dimensions would render the component ineffective on the display), override method `getMinimumSize` to return the minimum width and height as an instance of class `Dimension`.

Software Engineering Observation 22.1

For many GUI components, method `getMinimumSize` is implemented to return the result of a call to the component's `getPreferredSize` method.

Class `SliderFrame` (Fig. 22.3) creates the `JSlider` that controls the diameter of the circle. Class `SliderFrame`'s constructor (lines 17–45) creates `OvalPanel` object `myPanel` (line 21) and sets its background color (line 22). Lines 25–26 create `JSlider` object `diameterSlider` to control the diameter of the circle drawn on the `OvalPanel`. The `JSlider` constructor takes four arguments. The first argument specifies the orientation of `diameterSlider`, which is `HORIZONTAL` (a constant in interface `SwingConstants`). The second and third arguments indicate the minimum and maximum integer values in the range of values for this `JSlider`. The last argument indicates that the initial value of the `JSlider` (i.e., where the thumb is displayed) should be 10.

Lines 27–28 customize the appearance of the `JSlider`. Method `setMajorTickSpacing` indicates that each major tick mark represents 10 values in the range of values supported by the `JSlider`. Method `setPaintTicks` with a `true` argument indicates that the tick marks should be displayed (they are not displayed by default). For other methods that are used to customize a `JSlider`'s appearance, see the `JSlider` on-line documentation (`java.sun.com/javase/6/docs/api/javax/swing/JSlider.html`).

```
1   // Fig. 22.3: SliderFrame.java
2   // Using JSliders to size an oval.
3   import java.awt.BorderLayout;
4   import java.awt.Color;
5   import javax.swing.JFrame;
6   import javax.swing.JSlider;
7   import javax.swing.SwingConstants;
8   import javax.swing.event.ChangeListener;
9   import javax.swing.event.ChangeEvent;
10
11  public class SliderFrame extends JFrame
12  {
13     private JSlider diameterJSlider; // slider to select diameter
14     private OvalPanel myPanel; // panel to draw circle
15
16     // no-argument constructor
17     public SliderFrame()
18     {
19        super( "Slider Demo" );
20
21        myPanel = new OvalPanel(); // create panel to draw circle
22        myPanel.setBackground( Color.YELLOW ); // set background to yellow
23
24        // set up JSlider to control diameter value
25        diameterJSlider =
26           new JSlider( SwingConstants.HORIZONTAL, 0, 200, 10 );
27        diameterJSlider.setMajorTickSpacing( 10 ); // create tick every 10
28        diameterJSlider.setPaintTicks( true ); // paint ticks on slider
29
30        // register JSlider event listener
31        diameterJSlider.addChangeListener(
32
33           new ChangeListener() // anonymous inner class
34           {
35              // handle change in slider value
36              public void stateChanged( ChangeEvent e )
37              {
38                 myPanel.setDiameter( diameterJSlider.getValue() );
39              } // end method stateChanged
40           } // end anonymous inner class
41        ); // end call to addChangeListener
42
43        add( diameterJSlider, BorderLayout.SOUTH ); // add slider to frame
44        add( myPanel, BorderLayout.CENTER ); // add panel to frame
45     } // end SliderFrame constructor
46  } // end class SliderFrame
```

Fig. 22.3 | JSlider value used to determine the diameter of a circle.

JSliders generate ChangeEvents (package javax.swing.event) in response to user interactions. An object of a class that implements interface ChangeListener (package javax.swing.event) and declares method stateChanged can respond to ChangeEvents. Lines 31–41 register a ChangeListener to handle diameterSlider's events. When

```
 1   // Fig. 22.4: SliderDemo.java
 2   // Testing SliderFrame.
 3   import javax.swing.JFrame;
 4
 5   public class SliderDemo
 6   {
 7      public static void main( String args[] )
 8      {
 9         SliderFrame sliderFrame = new SliderFrame();
10         sliderFrame.setDefaultCloseOperation( JFrame.EXIT_ON_CLOSE );
11         sliderFrame.setSize( 220, 270 ); // set frame size
12         sliderFrame.setVisible( true ); // display frame
13      } // end main
14   } // end class SliderDemo
```

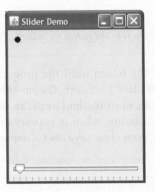

Fig. 22.4 | Test class for `SliderFrame`.

method `stateChanged` (lines 36–39) is called in response to a user interaction, line 38 calls myPanel's `setDiameter` method and passes the current value of the `JSlider` as an argument. `JSlider` method `getValue` returns the current thumb position.

22.3 Windows: Additional Notes

In this section, we discuss several important `JFrame` issues. A `JFrame` is a *window* with a *title bar* and a *border*. Class `JFrame` is a subclass of `java.awt.Frame` (which is a subclass of `java.awt.Window`). As such, `JFrame` is one of the few Swing GUI components that is not a lightweight GUI component. When you display a window from a Java program, the window is provided by the local platform's windowing toolkit, and therefore the window will look like every other window displayed on that platform. When a Java application executes on a Macintosh and displays a window, the window's title bar and borders will look like those of other Macintosh applications. When a Java application executes on a Microsoft Windows system and displays a window, the window's title bar and borders will look like those of other Microsoft Windows applications. And when a Java application executes on a UNIX platform and displays a window, the window's title bar and borders will look like other UNIX applications on that platform.

Class `JFrame` supports three operations when the user closes the window. By default, a window is hidden (i.e., removed from the screen). This can be controlled with `JFrame` method `setDefaultCloseOperation`. Interface `WindowConstants` (package `javax.swing`), which class `JFrame` implements, declares three constants—`DISPOSE_ON_CLOSE`, `DO_NOTHING_ON_CLOSE` and `HIDE_ON_CLOSE` (the default)—for use with this method. Some platforms allow only a limited number of windows to be displayed on the screen. Thus, a window is a valuable resource that should be given back to the system when it is no longer needed. Class `Window` (an indirect superclass of `JFrame`) declares method `dispose` for this purpose. When a `Window` is no longer needed in an application, you should explicitly dispose of it. This can be done by calling the `Window`'s `dispose` method or by calling method `setDefaultCloseOperation` with the argument `WindowConstants.DISPOSE_ON_CLOSE`. Terminating an application will return window resources to the system. Setting the default close operation to `DO_NOTHING_ON_CLOSE` indicates that the program will determine what to do when the user indicates that the window should be closed.

Performance Tip 22.1

A window is an expensive system resource. Return it to the system by calling its `dispose` method when the window is no longer needed.

By default, a window is not displayed on the screen until the program invokes the window's `setVisible` method (inherited from class `java.awt.Component`) with a `true` argument. A window's size should be set with a call to method `setSize` (inherited from class `java.awt.Component`). The position of a window when it appears on the screen is specified with method `setLocation` (inherited from class `java.awt.Component`).

Common Programming Error 22.1

Forgetting to call method `setVisible` on a window is a runtime logic error—the window is not displayed.

Common Programming Error 22.2

Forgetting to call the `setSize` method on a window is a runtime logic error—only the title bar appears.

When the user manipulates the window, this action generates window events. Event listeners are registered for window events with `Window` method `addWindowListener`. Interface `WindowListener` provides seven window-event-handling methods—`windowActivated` (called when the user makes a window the active window), `windowClosed` (called after the window is closed), `windowClosing` (called when the user initiates closing of the window), `windowDeactivated` (called when the user makes another window the active window), `windowDeiconified` (called when the user restores a window from being minimized), `windowIconified` (called when the user minimizes a window) and `windowOpened` (called when a program first displays a window on the screen).

22.4 Using Menus with Frames

Menus are an integral part of GUIs. Menus allow the user to perform actions without unnecessarily cluttering a GUI with extra components. In Swing GUIs, menus can be attached only to objects of the classes that provide method `setJMenuBar`. Two such classes are `JFrame` and `JApplet`. The classes used to declare menus are `JMenuBar`, `JMenu`, `JMenuItem`, `JCheckBoxMenuItem` and class `JRadioButtonMenuItem`.

Look-and-Feel Observation 22.2

Menus simplify GUIs because components can be hidden within them. These components will be visible only when the user looks for them by selecting the menu.

Class `JMenuBar` (a subclass of `JComponent`) contains the methods necessary to manage a menu bar, which is a container for menus. Class `JMenu` (a subclass of `javax.swing.JMenuItem`) contains the methods necessary for managing menus. Menus contain menu items and are added to menu bars or to other menus as submenus. When a menu is clicked, it expands to show its list of menu items.

Class `JMenuItem` (a subclass of `javax.swing.AbstractButton`) contains the methods necessary to manage menu items. A menu item is a GUI component inside a menu that, when selected, causes an action event. A menu item can be used to initiate an action, or it can be a submenu that provides more menu items from which the user can select. Submenus are useful for grouping related menu items in a menu.

Class `JCheckBoxMenuItem` (a subclass of `javax.swing.JMenuItem`) contains the methods necessary to manage menu items that can be toggled on or off. When a `JCheck-BoxMenuItem` is selected, a check appears to the left of the menu item. When the `JCheck-BoxMenuItem` is selected again, the check is removed.

Class `JRadioButtonMenuItem` (a subclass of `javax.swing.JMenuItem`) contains the methods necessary to manage menu items that can be toggled on or off like `JCheckBox-MenuItems`. When multiple `JRadioButtonMenuItems` are maintained as part of a `Button-Group`, only one item in the group can be selected at a given time. When a `JRadioButtonMenuItem` is selected, a filled circle appears to the left of the menu item. When another `JRadioButtonMenuItem` is selected, the filled circle of the previously selected menu item is removed.

The application in Figs. 22.5–22.6 demonstrates various menu items and how to specify special characters called **mnemonics** that can provide quick access to a menu or menu item from the keyboard. Mnemonics can be used with all subclasses of `javax.swing.AbstractButton`.

Class `MenuFrame` (Fig. 22.5) declares the GUI components and event handling for the menu items. Most of the code in this application appears in the class's constructor (lines 34–151).

```java
1   // Fig. 22.5: MenuFrame.java
2   // Demonstrating menus.
3   import java.awt.Color;
4   import java.awt.Font;
5   import java.awt.BorderLayout;
6   import java.awt.event.ActionListener;
7   import java.awt.event.ActionEvent;
8   import java.awt.event.ItemListener;
9   import java.awt.event.ItemEvent;
10  import javax.swing.JFrame;
11  import javax.swing.JRadioButtonMenuItem;
12  import javax.swing.JCheckBoxMenuItem;
13  import javax.swing.JOptionPane;
```

Fig. 22.5 | `JMenus` and mnemonics. (Part I of 5.)

```
14   import javax.swing.JLabel;
15   import javax.swing.SwingConstants;
16   import javax.swing.ButtonGroup;
17   import javax.swing.JMenu;
18   import javax.swing.JMenuItem;
19   import javax.swing.JMenuBar;
20
21   public class MenuFrame extends JFrame
22   {
23      private final Color colorValues[] =
24         { Color.BLACK, Color.BLUE, Color.RED, Color.GREEN };
25      private JRadioButtonMenuItem colorItems[]; // color menu items
26      private JRadioButtonMenuItem fonts[]; // font menu items
27      private JCheckBoxMenuItem styleItems[]; // font style menu items
28      private JLabel displayJLabel; // displays sample text
29      private ButtonGroup fontButtonGroup; // manages font menu items
30      private ButtonGroup colorButtonGroup; // manages color menu items
31      private int style; // used to create style for font
32
33      // no-argument constructor set up GUI
34      public MenuFrame()
35      {
36         super( "Using JMenus" );
37
38         JMenu fileMenu = new JMenu( "File" ); // create file menu
39         fileMenu.setMnemonic( 'F' ); // set mnemonic to F
40
41         // create About... menu item
42         JMenuItem aboutItem = new JMenuItem( "About..." );
43         aboutItem.setMnemonic( 'A' ); // set mnemonic to A
44         fileMenu.add( aboutItem ); // add about item to file menu
45         aboutItem.addActionListener(
46
47            new ActionListener() // anonymous inner class
48            {
49               // display message dialog when user selects About...
50               public void actionPerformed( ActionEvent event )
51               {
52                  JOptionPane.showMessageDialog( MenuFrame.this,
53                     "This is an example\nof using menus",
54                     "About", JOptionPane.PLAIN_MESSAGE );
55               } // end method actionPerformed
56            } // end anonymous inner class
57         ); // end call to addActionListener
58
59         JMenuItem exitItem = new JMenuItem( "Exit" ); // create exit item
60         exitItem.setMnemonic( 'x' ); // set mnemonic to x
61         fileMenu.add( exitItem ); // add exit item to file menu
62         exitItem.addActionListener(
63
64            new ActionListener() // anonymous inner class
65            {
```

Fig. 22.5 | JMenus and mnemonics. (Part 2 of 5.)

```
66        // terminate application when user clicks exitItem
67        public void actionPerformed( ActionEvent event )
68        {
69           System.exit( 0 ); // exit application
70        } // end method actionPerformed
71     } // end anonymous inner class
72   ); // end call to addActionListener
73
74   JMenuBar bar = new JMenuBar(); // create menu bar
75   setJMenuBar( bar ); // add menu bar to application
76   bar.add( fileMenu ); // add file menu to menu bar
77
78   JMenu formatMenu = new JMenu( "Format" ); // create format menu
79   formatMenu.setMnemonic( 'r' ); // set mnemonic to r
80
81   // array listing string colors
82   String colors[] = { "Black", "Blue", "Red", "Green" };
83
84   JMenu colorMenu = new JMenu( "Color" ); // create color menu
85   colorMenu.setMnemonic( 'C' ); // set mnemonic to C
86
87   // create radio button menu items for colors
88   colorItems = new JRadioButtonMenuItem[ colors.length ];
89   colorButtonGroup = new ButtonGroup(); // manages colors
90   ItemHandler itemHandler = new ItemHandler(); // handler for colors
91
92   // create color radio button menu items
93   for ( int count = 0; count < colors.length; count++ )
94   {
95      colorItems[ count ] =
96         new JRadioButtonMenuItem( colors[ count ] ); // create item
97      colorMenu.add( colorItems[ count ] ); // add item to color menu
98      colorButtonGroup.add( colorItems[ count ] ); // add to group
99      colorItems[ count ].addActionListener( itemHandler );
100  } // end for
101
102  colorItems[ 0 ].setSelected( true ); // select first Color item
103
104  formatMenu.add( colorMenu ); // add color menu to format menu
105  formatMenu.addSeparator(); // add separator in menu
106
107  // array listing font names
108  String fontNames[] = { "Serif", "Monospaced", "SansSerif" };
109  JMenu fontMenu = new JMenu( "Font" ); // create font menu
110  fontMenu.setMnemonic( 'n' ); // set mnemonic to n
111
112  // create radio button menu items for font names
113  fonts = new JRadioButtonMenuItem[ fontNames.length ];
114  fontButtonGroup = new ButtonGroup(); // manages font names
115
116  // create Font radio button menu items
117  for ( int count = 0; count < fonts.length; count++ )
118  {
```

Fig. 22.5 | JMenus and mnemonics. (Part 3 of 5.)

```
119         fonts[ count ] = new JRadioButtonMenuItem( fontNames[ count ] );
120         fontMenu.add( fonts[ count ] ); // add font to font menu
121         fontButtonGroup.add( fonts[ count ] ); // add to button group
122         fonts[ count ].addActionListener( itemHandler ); // add handler
123      } // end for
124
125      fonts[ 0 ].setSelected( true ); // select first Font menu item
126      fontMenu.addSeparator(); // add separator bar to font menu
127
128      String styleNames[] = { "Bold", "Italic" }; // names of styles
129      styleItems = new JCheckBoxMenuItem[ styleNames.length ];
130      StyleHandler styleHandler = new StyleHandler(); // style handler
131
132      // create style checkbox menu items
133      for ( int count = 0; count < styleNames.length; count++ )
134      {
135         styleItems[ count ] =
136            new JCheckBoxMenuItem( styleNames[ count ] ); // for style
137         fontMenu.add( styleItems[ count ] ); // add to font menu
138         styleItems[ count ].addItemListener( styleHandler ); // handler
139      } // end for
140
141      formatMenu.add( fontMenu ); // add Font menu to Format menu
142      bar.add( formatMenu ); // add Format menu to menu bar
143
144      // set up label to display text
145      displayJLabel = new JLabel( "Sample Text", SwingConstants.CENTER );
146      displayJLabel.setForeground( colorValues[ 0 ] );
147      displayJLabel.setFont( new Font( "Serif", Font.PLAIN, 72 ) );
148
149      getContentPane().setBackground( Color.CYAN ); // set background
150      add( displayJLabel, BorderLayout.CENTER ); // add displayJLabel
151   } // end MenuFrame constructor
152
153   // inner class to handle action events from menu items
154   private class ItemHandler implements ActionListener
155   {
156      // process color and font selections
157      public void actionPerformed( ActionEvent event )
158      {
159         // process color selection
160         for ( int count = 0; count < colorItems.length; count++ )
161         {
162            if ( colorItems[ count ].isSelected() )
163            {
164               displayJLabel.setForeground( colorValues[ count ] );
165               break;
166            } // end if
167         } // end for
168
169         // process font selection
170         for ( int count = 0; count < fonts.length; count++ )
171         {
```

Fig. 22.5 | JMenus and mnemonics. (Part 4 of 5.)

```
172                     if ( event.getSource() == fonts[ count ] )
173                     {
174                         displayJLabel.setFont(
175                             new Font( fonts[ count ].getText(), style, 72 ) );
176                     } // end if
177                 } // end for
178
179                 repaint(); // redraw application
180             } // end method actionPerformed
181         } // end class ItemHandler
182
183         // inner class to handle item events from check box menu items
184         private class StyleHandler implements ItemListener
185         {
186             // process font style selections
187             public void itemStateChanged( ItemEvent e )
188             {
189                 style = 0; // initialize style
190
191                 // check for bold selection
192                 if ( styleItems[ 0 ].isSelected() )
193                     style += Font.BOLD; // add bold to style
194
195                 // check for italic selection
196                 if ( styleItems[ 1 ].isSelected() )
197                     style += Font.ITALIC; // add italic to style
198
199                 displayJLabel.setFont(
200                     new Font( displayJLabel.getFont().getName(), style, 72 ) );
201                 repaint(); // redraw application
202             } // end method itemStateChanged
203         } // end class StyleHandler
204     } // end class MenuFrame
```

Fig. 22.5 | JMenus and mnemonics. (Part 5 of 5.)

```
1   // Fig. 22.6: MenuTest.java
2   // Testing MenuFrame.
3   import javax.swing.JFrame;
4
5   public class MenuTest
6   {
7       public static void main( String args[] )
8       {
9           MenuFrame menuFrame = new MenuFrame(); // create MenuFrame
10          menuFrame.setDefaultCloseOperation( JFrame.EXIT_ON_CLOSE );
11          menuFrame.setSize( 500, 200 ); // set frame size
12          menuFrame.setVisible( true ); // display frame
13      } // end main
14  } // end class MenuTest
```

Fig. 22.6 | Test class for MenuFrame. (Part 1 of 2.)

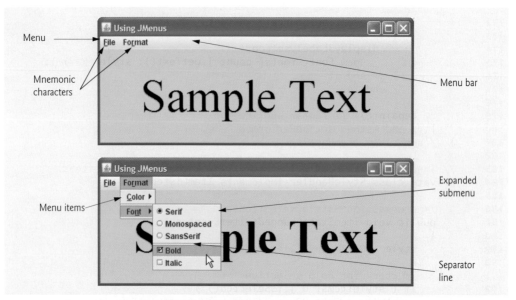

Fig. 22.6 | Test class for `MenuFrame`. (Part 2 of 2.)

Lines 38–76 set up the **File** menu and attach it to the menu bar. The **File** menu contains an **About...** menu item that displays a message dialog when the menu item is selected and an **Exit** menu item that can be selected to terminate the application.

Line 38 creates a `JMenu` and passes to the constructor the string `"File"` as the name of the menu. Line 39 uses `JMenu` method `setMnemonic` (inherited from class `Abstract-Button`) to indicate that `F` is the mnemonic for this menu. Pressing the *Alt* key and the letter *F* opens the menu, just as clicking the menu name with the mouse would. In the GUI, the mnemonic character in the menu's name is displayed with an underline. (See the screen captures in Fig. 22.6.)

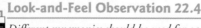

Look-and-Feel Observation 22.3

Mnemonics provide quick access to menu commands and button commands through the keyboard.

Look-and-Feel Observation 22.4

*Different mnemonics should be used for each button or menu item. Normally, the first letter in the label on the menu item or button is used as the mnemonic. If several buttons or menu items start with the same letter, choose the next most prominent letter in the name (e.g., x is commonly chosen for a button or menu item called **Exit**).*

Lines 42–43 create `JMenuItem aboutItem` with the text "`About...`" and set its mnemonic to the letter `A`. This menu item is added to `fileMenu` at line 44 with `JMenu` method `add`. To access the **About...** menu item through the keyboard, press the *Alt* key and letter *F* to open the **File** menu, then press *A* to select the **About...** menu item. Lines 47–56 create an `ActionListener` to process `aboutItem`'s action event. Lines 52–54 display a message dialog box. In most prior uses of `showMessageDialog`, the first argument was `null`. The purpose of the first argument is to specify the parent window that helps determine where the dialog box will be displayed. If the parent window is specified as null, the dialog box appears in the center of the screen. Otherwise, it appears centered over the specified parent window. In this example, the program specifies the parent window with MenuTest.this— the this reference of the MenuTest object. When using the this reference in an inner class, specifying this by itself refers to the inner-class object. To reference the outer-class object's this reference, qualify this with the outer-class name and a dot (.).

Dialog boxes are typically modal. A modal dialog box does not allow any other window in the application to be accessed until the dialog box is dismissed. The dialogs displayed with class JOptionPane are modal dialogs. Class JDialog can be used to create your own modal or nonmodal dialogs.

Lines 59–72 create menu item exitItem, set its mnemonic to x, add it to fileMenu and register an ActionListener that terminates the application when the user selects exitItem.

Lines 74–76 create the JMenuBar, attach it to the application window with JFrame method setJMenuBar and use JMenuBar method add to attach the fileMenu to the JMenuBar.

Common Programming Error 22.3

Forgetting to set the menu bar with JFrame method setJMenuBar prevents the menu bar from displaying in the JFrame.

Look-and-Feel Observation 22.5

Menus appear left to right in the order that they are added to a JMenuBar.

Lines 78–79 create menu formatMenu and set its mnemonic to r. (F is not used because that is the **File** menu's mnemonic.)

Lines 84–85 create menu colorMenu (this will be a submenu in the **Format** menu) and set its mnemonic to C. Line 88 creates JRadioButtonMenuItem array colorItems, which refers to the menu items in colorMenu. Line 89 creates ButtonGroup colorGroup, which will ensure that only one of the menu items in the **Color** submenu is selected at a time. Line 90 creates an instance of inner class ItemHandler (declared at lines 154–181) that responds to selections from the **Color** and **Font** submenus (discussed shortly). The for statement at lines 93–100 creates each JRadioButtonMenuItem in array colorItems, adds each menu item to colorMenu and to colorGroup and registers the ActionListener for each menu item.

Line 102 invokes AbstractButton method setSelected to select the first element in array colorItems. Line 104 adds colorMenu as a submenu of formatMenu. Line 105 invokes JMenu method addSeparator to add a horizontal separator line to the menu.

Look-and-Feel Observation 22.6

A submenu is created by adding a menu as a menu item in another menu. When the mouse is positioned over a submenu (or the submenu's mnemonic is pressed), the submenu expands to show its menu items.

Look-and-Feel Observation 22.7

Separators can be added to a menu to group menu items logically.

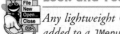

Look-and-Feel Observation 22.8

Any lightweight GUI component (i.e., a component that is a subclass of JComponent) can be added to a JMenu or to a JMenuBar.

Lines 108–126 create the **Font** submenu and several JRadioButtonMenuItems and select the first element of JRadioButtonMenuItem array fonts. Line 129 creates a JCheck-BoxMenuItem array to represent the menu items for specifying bold and italic styles for the fonts. Line 130 creates an instance of inner class StyleHandler (declared at lines 184–203) to respond to the JCheckBoxMenuItem events. The for statement at lines 133–139 creates each JCheckBoxMenuItem, adds each menu item to fontMenu and registers the ItemListener for each menu item. Line 141 adds fontMenu as a submenu of formatMenu. Line 142 adds the formatMenu to bar (the menu bar).

Lines 145–147 create a JLabel for which the **Format** menu items control the font, font color and font style. The initial foreground color is set to the first element of array colorValues (Color.BLACK) by invoking JComponent method **setForeground**, and the initial font is set to Serif with PLAIN style and 72-point size. Line 149 sets the background color of the window's content pane to cyan, and line 150 attaches the JLabel to the CENTER of the content pane's BorderLayout.

ItemHandler method actionPerformed (lines 157–180) uses two for statements to determine which font or color menu item generated the event and sets the font or color of the JLabel displayLabel, respectively. The if condition at line 162 uses Abstract-Button method **isSelected** to determine the selected JRadioButtonMenuItem. The if condition at line 172 invokes the event object's getSource method to get a reference to the JRadioButtonMenuItem that generated the event. Line 175 invokes AbstractButton method getText to obtain the name of the font from the menu item.

The program calls StyleHandler method itemStateChanged (lines 187–202) if the user selects a JCheckBoxMenuItem in the fontMenu. Lines 192 and 196 determine whether either or both of the JCheckBoxMenuItems are selected and use their combined state to determine the new style of the font.

22.5 JPopupMenu

Many of today's computer applications provide so-called **context-sensitive pop-up menus**. In Swing, such menus are created with class **JPopupMenu** (a subclass of JCompo-nent). These menus provide options that are specific to the component for which the **pop-up trigger event** was generated. On most systems, the pop-up trigger event occurs when the user presses and releases the right mouse button.

Look-and-Feel Observation 22.9

The pop-up trigger event is platform specific. On most platforms that use a mouse with multiple buttons, the pop-up trigger event occurs when the user clicks the right mouse button on a component that supports a pop-up menu.

The application in Figs. 22.7–22.8 creates a JPopupMenu that allows the user to select one of three colors and change the background color of the window. When the user clicks the right mouse button on the PopupTest window's background, a JPopupMenu containing colors appears. If the user clicks a JRadioButtonMenuItem for a color, ItemHandler method actionPerformed changes the background color of the window's content pane.

```
1   // Fig. 22.7: PopupFrame.java
2   // Demonstrating JPopupMenus.
3   import java.awt.Color;
4   import java.awt.event.MouseAdapter;
5   import java.awt.event.MouseEvent;
6   import java.awt.event.ActionListener;
7   import java.awt.event.ActionEvent;
8   import javax.swing.JFrame;
9   import javax.swing.JRadioButtonMenuItem;
10  import javax.swing.JPopupMenu;
11  import javax.swing.ButtonGroup;
12
13  public class PopupFrame extends JFrame
14  {
15     private JRadioButtonMenuItem items[]; // holds items for colors
16     private final Color colorValues[] =
17        { Color.BLUE, Color.YELLOW, Color.RED }; // colors to be used
18     private JPopupMenu popupMenu; // allows user to select color
19
20     // no-argument constructor sets up GUI
21     public PopupFrame()
22     {
23        super( "Using JPopupMenus" );
24
25        ItemHandler handler = new ItemHandler(); // handler for menu items
26        String colors[] = { "Blue", "Yellow", "Red" }; // array of colors
27
28        ButtonGroup colorGroup = new ButtonGroup(); // manages color items
29        popupMenu = new JPopupMenu(); // create pop-up menu
30        items = new JRadioButtonMenuItem[ 3 ]; // items for selecting color
31
32        // construct menu item, add to popup menu, enable event handling
33        for ( int count = 0; count < items.length; count++ )
34        {
35           items[ count ] = new JRadioButtonMenuItem( colors[ count ] );
36           popupMenu.add( items[ count ] ); // add item to pop-up menu
37           colorGroup.add( items[ count ] ); // add item to button group
38           items[ count ].addActionListener( handler ); // add handler
39        } // end for
40
41        setBackground( Color.WHITE ); // set background to white
42
43        // declare a MouseListener for the window to display pop-up menu
44        addMouseListener(
45
46           new MouseAdapter() // anonymous inner class
47           {
48              // handle mouse press event
49              public void mousePressed( MouseEvent event )
50              {
51                 checkForTriggerEvent( event ); // check for trigger
52              } // end method mousePressed
```

Fig. 22.7 | JPopupMenu for selecting colors. (Part 1 of 2.)

```
53
54            // handle mouse release event
55            public void mouseReleased( MouseEvent event )
56            {
57               checkForTriggerEvent( event ); // check for trigger
58            } // end method mouseReleased
59
60            // determine whether event should trigger popup menu
61            private void checkForTriggerEvent( MouseEvent event )
62            {
63               if ( event.isPopupTrigger() )
64                  popupMenu.show(
65                     event.getComponent(), event.getX(), event.getY() );
66            } // end method checkForTriggerEvent
67         } // end anonymous inner class
68      ); // end call to addMouseListener
69   } // end PopupFrame constructor
70
71   // private inner class to handle menu item events
72   private class ItemHandler implements ActionListener
73   {
74      // process menu item selections
75      public void actionPerformed( ActionEvent event )
76      {
77         // determine which menu item was selected
78         for ( int i = 0; i < items.length; i++ )
79         {
80            if ( event.getSource() == items[ i ] )
81            {
82               getContentPane().setBackground( colorValues[ i ] );
83               return;
84            } // end if
85         } // end for
86      } // end method actionPerformed
87   } // end private inner class ItemHandler
88 } // end class PopupFrame
```

Fig. 22.7 | JPopupMenu for selecting colors. (Part 2 of 2.)

Line 25 of the PopupFrame constructor (lines 21–69) creates an instance of class Item-Handler (declared in lines 72–87) that will process the item events from the menu items in the pop-up menu. Line 29 creates the JPopupMenu. The for statement (lines 33–39) creates a JRadioButtonMenuItem object (line 35), adds it to popupMenu (line 36), adds it to ButtonGroup colorGroup (line 37) to maintain one selected JRadioButtonMenuItem at a time and registers its ActionListener (line 38). Line 41 sets the initial background to white by invoking method setBackground.

Lines 44–68 register a MouseListener to handle the mouse events of the application window. Methods mousePressed (lines 49–52) and mouseReleased (lines 55–58) check for the pop-up trigger event. Each method calls private utility method checkForTrigger-Event (lines 61–66) to determine whether the pop-up trigger event occurred. If it did, MouseEvent method **isPopupTrigger** returns true, and JPopupMenu method **show** displays the JPopupMenu. The first argument to method show specifies the **origin component**,

```
 1   // Fig. 22.8: PopupTest.java
 2   // Testing PopupFrame.
 3   import javax.swing.JFrame;
 4
 5   public class PopupTest
 6   {
 7      public static void main( String args[] )
 8      {
 9         PopupFrame popupFrame = new PopupFrame(); // create PopupFrame
10         popupFrame.setDefaultCloseOperation( JFrame.EXIT_ON_CLOSE );
11         popupFrame.setSize( 300, 200 ); // set frame size
12         popupFrame.setVisible( true ); // display frame
13      } // end main
14   } // end class PopupTest
```

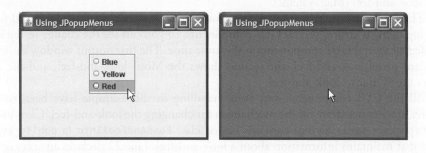

Fig. 22.8 | Test class for `PopupFrame`.

whose position helps determine where the `JPopupMenu` will appear on the screen. The last two arguments are the *x-y* coordinates (measured from the origin component's upper-left corner) at which the `JPopupMenu` is to appear.

Look-and-Feel Observation 22.10

Displaying a `JPopupMenu` for the pop-up trigger event of multiple GUI components requires registering mouse-event handlers for each of those GUI components.

When the user selects a menu item from the pop-up menu, class `ItemHandler`'s method `actionPerformed` (lines 75–86) determines which `JRadioButtonMenuItem` the user selected and sets the background color of the window's content pane.

22.6 Pluggable Look-and-Feel

A program that uses Java's Abstract Window Toolkit GUI components (package `java.awt`) takes on the look-and-feel of the platform on which the program executes. A Java application running on a Macintosh looks like other applications running on a Macintosh. A Java application running on Microsoft Windows looks like other applications running on Microsoft Windows. A Java application running on a UNIX platform looks like other applications running on that UNIX platform. This is sometimes desirable, because it allows users of the application on each platform to use GUI components with which they are already familiar. However, it also introduces interesting portability issues.

Portability Tip 22.1

GUI components look different on different platforms and may require different amounts of space to display. This could change their layout and alignments.

Portability Tip 22.2

GUI components on different platforms have different default functionality (e.g., some platforms allow a button with the focus to be "pressed" with the space bar, and some do not).

Swing's lightweight GUI components eliminate many of these issues by providing uniform functionality across platforms and by defining a uniform cross-platform look-and-feel (known as the metal look-and-feel). Swing also provides the flexibility to customize the look-and-feel to appear as a Microsoft Windows-style look-and-feel (on Window systems), a Motif-style (UNIX) look-and-feel (across all platforms) or a Macintosh look-and-feel (Mac systems).

The application in Figs. 22.9–22.10 demonstrates how to change the look-and-feel of a Swing GUI. It creates several GUI components, so you can see the change in the look-and-feel of several GUI components at the same time. The first output window shows the standard metal look-and-feel, the second shows the Motif look-and-feel, and the third shows the Windows look-and-feel.

All the GUI components and event handling in this example have been covered before, so we concentrate on the mechanism for changing the look-and-feel. Class **UIManager** (package `javax.swing`) contains nested class **LookAndFeelInfo** (a public static class) that maintains information about a look-and-feel. Line 22 declares an array of type `UIManager.LookAndFeelInfo` (note the syntax used to identify the inner class `LookAndFeelInfo`). Line 68 uses `UIManager` static method **getInstalledLookAndFeels** to get the array of `UIManager.LookAndFeelInfo` objects that describe each look-and-feel available on your system.

Performance Tip 22.2

Each look-and-feel is represented by a Java class. `UIManager` method `getInstalledLookAndFeels` does not load each class. Rather, it provides the names of the available look-and-feel classes so that a choice can be made (presumably once at program start-up). This reduces the overhead of having to load all the look-and-feel classes even if the program will not use some of them.

```
1   // Fig. 22.9: LookAndFeelFrame.java
2   // Changing the look and feel.
3   import java.awt.GridLayout;
4   import java.awt.BorderLayout;
5   import java.awt.event.ItemListener;
6   import java.awt.event.ItemEvent;
7   import javax.swing.JFrame;
8   import javax.swing.UIManager;
9   import javax.swing.JRadioButton;
10  import javax.swing.ButtonGroup;
11  import javax.swing.JButton;
12  import javax.swing.JLabel;
13  import javax.swing.JComboBox;
```

Fig. 22.9 | Look-and-feel of a Swing-based GUI. (Part 1 of 3.)

```
14    import javax.swing.JPanel;
15    import javax.swing.SwingConstants;
16    import javax.swing.SwingUtilities;
17
18    public class LookAndFeelFrame extends JFrame
19    {
20       // string names of look and feels
21       private final String strings[] = { "Metal", "Motif", "Windows" };
22       private UIManager.LookAndFeelInfo looks[]; // look and feels
23       private JRadioButton radio[]; // radio buttons to select look-and-feel
24       private ButtonGroup group; // group for radio buttons
25       private JButton button; // displays look of button
26       private JLabel label; // displays look of label
27       private JComboBox comboBox; // displays look of combo box
28
29       // set up GUI
30       public LookAndFeelFrame()
31       {
32          super( "Look and Feel Demo" );
33
34          JPanel northPanel = new JPanel(); // create north panel
35          northPanel.setLayout( new GridLayout( 3, 1, 0, 5 ) );
36
37          label = new JLabel( "This is a Metal look-and-feel",
38             SwingConstants.CENTER ); // create label
39          northPanel.add( label ); // add label to panel
40
41          button = new JButton( "JButton" ); // create button
42          northPanel.add( button ); // add button to panel
43
44          comboBox = new JComboBox( strings ); // create combobox
45          northPanel.add( comboBox ); // add combobox to panel
46
47          // create array for radio buttons
48          radio = new JRadioButton[ strings.length ];
49
50          JPanel southPanel = new JPanel(); // create south panel
51          southPanel.setLayout( new GridLayout( 1, radio.length ) );
52
53          group = new ButtonGroup(); // button group for looks-and-feels
54          ItemHandler handler = new ItemHandler(); // look-and-feel handler
55
56          for ( int count = 0; count < radio.length; count++ )
57          {
58             radio[ count ] = new JRadioButton( strings[ count ] );
59             radio[ count ].addItemListener( handler ); // add handler
60             group.add( radio[ count ] ); // add radio button to group
61             southPanel.add( radio[ count ] ); // add radio button to panel
62          } // end for
63
64          add( northPanel, BorderLayout.NORTH ); // add north panel
65          add( southPanel, BorderLayout.SOUTH ); // add south panel
66
```

Fig. 22.9 | Look-and-feel of a Swing-based GUI. (Part 2 of 3.)

```
67          // get installed look-and-feel information
68          looks = UIManager.getInstalledLookAndFeels();
69          radio[ 0 ].setSelected( true ); // set default selection
70       } // end LookAndFeelFrame constructor
71
72       // use UIManager to change look-and-feel of GUI
73       private void changeTheLookAndFeel( int value )
74       {
75          try // change look-and-feel
76          {
77             // set look-and-feel for this application
78             UIManager.setLookAndFeel( looks[ value ].getClassName() );
79
80             // update components in this application
81             SwingUtilities.updateComponentTreeUI( this );
82          } // end try
83          catch ( Exception exception )
84          {
85             exception.printStackTrace();
86          } // end catch
87       } // end method changeTheLookAndFeel
88
89       // private inner class to handle radio button events
90       private class ItemHandler implements ItemListener
91       {
92          // process user's look-and-feel selection
93          public void itemStateChanged( ItemEvent event )
94          {
95             for ( int count = 0; count < radio.length; count++ )
96             {
97                if ( radio[ count ].isSelected() )
98                {
99                   label.setText( String.format( "This is a %s look-and-feel",
100                     strings[ count ] ) );
101                  comboBox.setSelectedIndex( count ); // set combobox index
102                  changeTheLookAndFeel( count ); // change look-and-feel
103               } // end if
104            } // end for
105         } // end method itemStateChanged
106      } // end private inner class ItemHandler
107 } // end class LookAndFeelFrame
```

Fig. 22.9 | Look-and-feel of a Swing-based GUI. (Part 3 of 3.)

Our utility method changeTheLookAndFeel (lines 73–87) is called by the event handler for the JRadioButtons at the bottom of the user interface. The event handler (declared in private inner class ItemHandler at lines 90–106) passes an integer representing the element in array looks that should be used to change the look-and-feel. Line 78 invokes static method setLookAndFeel of UIManager to change the look-and-feel. Method getClassName of class UIManager.LookAndFeelInfo determines the name of the look-and-feel class that corresponds to the UIManager.LookAndFeelInfo object. If the look-and-feel class is not already loaded, it will be loaded as part of the call to setLookAndFeel. Line 81 invokes static method updateComponentTreeUI of class SwingUtilities (package

```
 1    // Fig. 22.10: LookAndFeelDemo.java
 2    // Changing the look and feel.
 3    import javax.swing.JFrame;
 4
 5    public class LookAndFeelDemo
 6    {
 7       public static void main( String args[] )
 8       {
 9          LookAndFeelFrame lookAndFeelFrame = new LookAndFeelFrame();
10          lookAndFeelFrame.setDefaultCloseOperation( JFrame.EXIT_ON_CLOSE );
11          lookAndFeelFrame.setSize( 300, 200 ); // set frame size
12          lookAndFeelFrame.setVisible( true ); // display frame
13       } // end main
14    } // end class LookAndFeelDemo
```

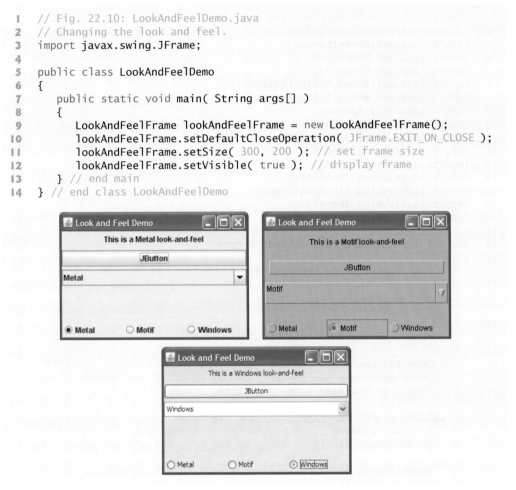

Fig. 22.10 | Test class for LookAndFeelFrame.

javax.swing) to change the look-and-feel of every GUI component attached to its argument (this instance of our application class LookAndFeelDemo) to the new look-and-feel.

22.7 JDesktopPane and JInternalFrame

Many of today's applications use a multiple-document interface (MDI)—a main window (called the parent window) containing other windows (called child windows), to manage several open documents that are being processed in parallel. For example, many e-mail programs allow you to have several windows open at the same time, so you can compose or read multiple e-mail messages simultaneously. Similarly, many word processors allow the user to open multiple documents in separate windows, making it possible to switch between them without having to close one to open another. The application in Figs. 22.11–22.12 demonstrates Swing's JDesktopPane and JInternalFrame classes for implementing multiple-document interfaces.

```
1   // Fig. 22.11: DesktopFrame.java
2   // Demonstrating JDesktopPane.
3   import java.awt.BorderLayout;
4   import java.awt.Dimension;
5   import java.awt.Graphics;
6   import java.awt.event.ActionListener;
7   import java.awt.event.ActionEvent;
8   import java.util.Random;
9   import javax.swing.JFrame;
10  import javax.swing.JDesktopPane;
11  import javax.swing.JMenuBar;
12  import javax.swing.JMenu;
13  import javax.swing.JMenuItem;
14  import javax.swing.JInternalFrame;
15  import javax.swing.JPanel;
16  import javax.swing.ImageIcon;
17
18  public class DesktopFrame extends JFrame
19  {
20     private JDesktopPane theDesktop;
21
22     // set up GUI
23     public DesktopFrame()
24     {
25        super( "Using a JDesktopPane" );
26
27        JMenuBar bar = new JMenuBar(); // create menu bar
28        JMenu addMenu = new JMenu( "Add" ); // create Add menu
29        JMenuItem newFrame = new JMenuItem( "Internal Frame" );
30
31        addMenu.add( newFrame ); // add new frame item to Add menu
32        bar.add( addMenu ); // add Add menu to menu bar
33        setJMenuBar( bar ); // set menu bar for this application
34
35        theDesktop = new JDesktopPane(); // create desktop pane
36        add( theDesktop ); // add desktop pane to frame
37
38        // set up listener for newFrame menu item
39        newFrame.addActionListener(
40
41           new ActionListener() // anonymous inner class
42           {
43              // display new internal window
44              public void actionPerformed( ActionEvent event )
45              {
46                 // create internal frame
47                 JInternalFrame frame = new JInternalFrame(
48                    "Internal Frame", true, true, true, true );
49
50                 MyJPanel panel = new MyJPanel(); // create new panel
51                 frame.add( panel, BorderLayout.CENTER ); // add panel
52                 frame.pack(); // set internal frame to size of contents
```

Fig. 22.11 | Multiple-document interface. (Part 1 of 2.)

```
53
54                      theDesktop.add( frame ); // attach internal frame
55                      frame.setVisible( true ); // show internal frame
56                 } // end method actionPerformed
57            } // end anonymous inner class
58         ); // end call to addActionListener
59      } // end DesktopFrame constructor
60   } // end class DesktopFrame
61
62   // class to display an ImageIcon on a panel
63   class MyJPanel extends JPanel
64   {
65      private static Random generator = new Random();
66      private ImageIcon picture; // image to be displayed
67      private String[] images = { "yellowflowers.png", "purpleflowers.png",
68         "redflowers.png", "redflowers2.png", "lavenderflowers.png" };
69
70      // load image
71      public MyJPanel()
72      {
73         int randomNumber = generator.nextInt( 5 );
74         picture = new ImageIcon( images[ randomNumber ] ); // set icon
75      } // end MyJPanel constructor
76
77      // display imageIcon on panel
78      public void paintComponent( Graphics g )
79      {
80         super.paintComponent( g );
81         picture.paintIcon( this, g, 0, 0 ); // display icon
82      } // end method paintComponent
83
84      // return image dimensions
85      public Dimension getPreferredSize()
86      {
87         return new Dimension( picture.getIconWidth(),
88            picture.getIconHeight() );
89      } // end method getPreferredSize
90   } // end class MyJPanel
```

Fig. 22.11 | Multiple-document interface. (Part 2 of 2.)

```
1   // Fig. 22.12: DesktopTest.java
2   // Demonstrating JDesktopPane.
3   import javax.swing.JFrame;
4
5   public class DesktopTest
6   {
7      public static void main( String args[] )
8      {
9         DesktopFrame desktopFrame = new DesktopFrame();
10        desktopFrame.setDefaultCloseOperation( JFrame.EXIT_ON_CLOSE );
```

Fig. 22.12 | Test class for DeskTopFrame. (Part 1 of 2.)

```
11          desktopFrame.setSize( 600, 480 ); // set frame size
12          desktopFrame.setVisible( true ); // display frame
13      } // end main
14  } // end class DesktopTest
```

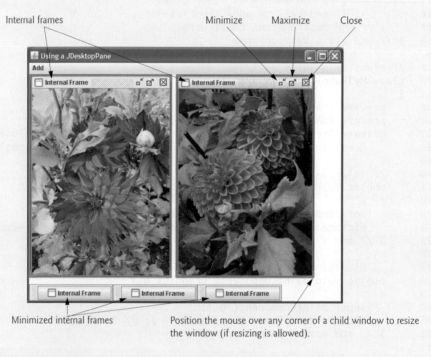

Internal frames   Minimize   Maximize   Close

Minimized internal frames   Position the mouse over any corner of a child window to resize the window (if resizing is allowed).

Maximized internal frame

Fig. 22.12 | Test class for DeskTopFrame. (Part 2 of 2.)

Lines 27–33 create a JMenuBar, a JMenu and a JMenuItem, add the JMenuItem to the JMenu, add the JMenu to the JMenuBar and set the JMenuBar for the application window. When the user selects the JMenuItem newFrame, the application creates and displays a new JInternalFrame object containing an image.

Line 35 assigns JDesktopPane (package javax.swing) variable theDesktop a new JDesktopPane object that will be used to manage the JInternalFrame child windows. Line 36 adds the JDesktopPane to the JFrame. By default, the JDesktopPane is added to the center of the content pane's BorderLayout, so the JDesktopPane expands to fill the entire application window.

Lines 39–58 register an ActionListener to handle the event when the user selects the newFrame menu item. When the event occurs, method actionPerformed (lines 44–56) creates a JInternalFrame object in lines 47–48. The JInternalFrame constructor used here takes five arguments—a string for the title bar of the internal window, a boolean indicating whether the internal frame can be resized by the user, a boolean indicating whether the internal frame can be closed by the user, a boolean indicating whether the internal frame can be maximized by the user and a boolean indicating whether the internal frame can be minimized by the user. For each of the boolean arguments, a true value indicates that the operation should be allowed (as is the case here).

As with JFrames and JApplets, a JInternalFrame has a content pane to which GUI components can be attached. Line 50 creates an instance of our class MyJPanel (declared at lines 63–90) that is added to the JInternalFrame at line 51.

Line 52 uses JInternalFrame method **pack** to set the size of the child window. Method pack uses the preferred sizes of the components to determine the window's size. Class MyJPanel declares method **getPreferredSize** (lines 85–89) to specify the panel's preferred size for use by the pack method. Line 54 adds the JInternalFrame to the JDesktopPane, and line 55 displays the JInternalFrame.

Classes JInternalFrame and JDesktopPane provide many methods for managing child windows. See the JInternalFrame and JDesktopPane online API documentation for complete lists of these methods:

```
java.sun.com/javase/6/docs/api/javax/swing/JInternalFrame.html
java.sun.com/javase/6/docs/api/javax/swing/JDesktopPane.html
```

22.8 JTabbedPane

A JTabbedPane arranges GUI components into layers, of which only one is visible at a time. Users access each layer via a tab—similar to folders in a file cabinet. When the user clicks a tab, the appropriate layer is displayed. The tabs appear at the top by default but also can be positioned at the left, right or bottom of the JTabbedPane. Any component can be placed on a tab. If the component is a container, such as a panel, it can use any layout manager to lay out several components on the tab. Class JTabbedPane is a subclass of JComponent. The application in Figs. 22.13–22.14 creates one tabbed pane with three tabs. Each tab displays one of the JPanels—panel1, panel2 or panel3.

The constructor (lines 15–46) builds the GUI. Line 19 creates an empty JTabbedPane with default settings—that is, tabs across the top. If the tabs do not fit on one line, they will wrap to form additional lines of tabs. Next the constructor creates the JPanels panel1, panel2 and panel3 and their GUI components. As we set up each panel, we add it to tabbedPane, using JTabbedPane method **addTab** with four arguments. The first argument

```java
1    // Fig. 22.13: JTabbedPaneFrame.java
2    // Demonstrating JTabbedPane.
3    import java.awt.BorderLayout;
4    import java.awt.Color;
5    import javax.swing.JFrame;
6    import javax.swing.JTabbedPane;
7    import javax.swing.JLabel;
8    import javax.swing.JPanel;
9    import javax.swing.JButton;
10   import javax.swing.SwingConstants;
11
12   public class JTabbedPaneFrame extends JFrame
13   {
14      // set up GUI
15      public JTabbedPaneFrame()
16      {
17         super( "JTabbedPane Demo " );
18
19         JTabbedPane tabbedPane = new JTabbedPane(); // create JTabbedPane
20
21         // set up panel1 and add it to JTabbedPane
22         JLabel label1 = new JLabel( "panel one", SwingConstants.CENTER );
23         JPanel panel1 = new JPanel(); // create first panel
24         panel1.add( label1 ); // add label to panel
25         tabbedPane.addTab( "Tab One", null, panel1, "First Panel" );
26
27         // set up panel2 and add it to JTabbedPane
28         JLabel label2 = new JLabel( "panel two", SwingConstants.CENTER );
29         JPanel panel2 = new JPanel(); // create second panel
30         panel2.setBackground( Color.YELLOW ); // set background to yellow
31         panel2.add( label2 ); // add label to panel
32         tabbedPane.addTab( "Tab Two", null, panel2, "Second Panel" );
33
34         // set up panel3 and add it to JTabbedPane
35         JLabel label3 = new JLabel( "panel three" );
36         JPanel panel3 = new JPanel(); // create third panel
37         panel3.setLayout( new BorderLayout() ); // use borderlayout
38         panel3.add( new JButton( "North" ), BorderLayout.NORTH );
39         panel3.add( new JButton( "West" ), BorderLayout.WEST );
40         panel3.add( new JButton( "East" ), BorderLayout.EAST );
41         panel3.add( new JButton( "South" ), BorderLayout.SOUTH );
42         panel3.add( label3, BorderLayout.CENTER );
43         tabbedPane.addTab( "Tab Three", null, panel3, "Third Panel" );
44
45         add( tabbedPane ); // add JTabbedPane to frame
46      } // end JTabbedPaneFrame constructor
47   } // end class JTabbedPaneFrame
```

Fig. 22.13 | JTabbedPane used to organize GUI components.

is a string that specifies the title of the tab. The second argument is an Icon reference that specifies an icon to display on the tab. If the Icon is a null reference, no image is displayed. The third argument is a Component reference that represents the GUI component to display when the user clicks the tab. The last argument is a string that specifies the tool tip

```
 1   // Fig. 22.14: JTabbedPaneDemo.java
 2   // Demonstrating JTabbedPane.
 3   import javax.swing.JFrame;
 4
 5   public class JTabbedPaneDemo
 6   {
 7      public static void main( String args[] )
 8      {
 9         JTabbedPaneFrame tabbedPaneFrame = new JTabbedPaneFrame();
10         tabbedPaneFrame.setDefaultCloseOperation( JFrame.EXIT_ON_CLOSE );
11         tabbedPaneFrame.setSize( 250, 200 ); // set frame size
12         tabbedPaneFrame.setVisible( true ); // display frame
13      } // end main
14   } // end class JTabbedPaneDemo
```

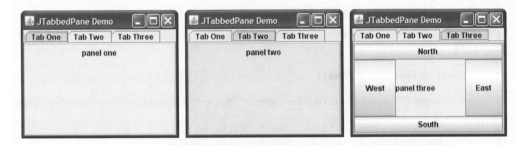

Fig. 22.14 | Test class for JTabbedPaneFrame.

for the tab. For example, line 25 adds JPanel panel1 to tabbedPane with title "Tab One" and the tool tip "First Panel". JPanels panel2 and panel3 are added to tabbedPane at lines 32 and 43. To view a tab, click it with the mouse or use the arrow keys to cycle through the tabs.

22.9 Layout Managers: BoxLayout and GridBagLayout

In Chapter 11, we introduced three layout managers—FlowLayout, BorderLayout and GridLayout. This section presents two additional layout managers (summarized in Fig. 22.15). We discuss these layout managers in the examples that follow.

Layout manager	Description
BoxLayout	A layout manager that allows GUI components to be arranged left-to-right or top-to-bottom in a container. Class Box declares a container with BoxLayout as its default layout manager and provides **static** methods to create a Box with a horizontal or vertical BoxLayout.
GridBagLayout	A layout manager similar to GridLayout, but unlike it in that components can vary in size and can be added in any order.

Fig. 22.15 | Additional layout managers.

BoxLayout *Layout Manager*

The BoxLayout layout manager (in package javax.swing) arranges GUI components horizontally along a container's *x*-axis or vertically along its *y*-axis. The application in Figs. 22.16–22.17 demonstrates BoxLayout and the container class Box that uses BoxLayout as its default layout manager.

```
1   // Fig. 22.16: BoxLayoutFrame.java
2   // Demonstrating BoxLayout.
3   import java.awt.Dimension;
4   import javax.swing.JFrame;
5   import javax.swing.Box;
6   import javax.swing.JButton;
7   import javax.swing.BoxLayout;
8   import javax.swing.JPanel;
9   import javax.swing.JTabbedPane;
10
11  public class BoxLayoutFrame extends JFrame
12  {
13     // set up GUI
14     public BoxLayoutFrame()
15     {
16        super( "Demonstrating BoxLayout" );
17
18        // create Box containers with BoxLayout
19        Box horizontal1 = Box.createHorizontalBox();
20        Box vertical1 = Box.createVerticalBox();
21        Box horizontal2 = Box.createHorizontalBox();
22        Box vertical2 = Box.createVerticalBox();
23
24        final int SIZE = 3; // number of buttons on each Box
25
26        // add buttons to Box horizontal1
27        for ( int count = 0; count < SIZE; count++ )
28           horizontal1.add( new JButton( "Button " + count ) );
29
30        // create strut and add buttons to Box vertical1
31        for ( int count = 0; count < SIZE; count++ )
32        {
33           vertical1.add( Box.createVerticalStrut( 25 ) );
34           vertical1.add( new JButton( "Button " + count ) );
35        } // end for
36
37        // create horizontal glue and add buttons to Box horizontal2
38        for ( int count = 0; count < SIZE; count++ )
39        {
40           horizontal2.add( Box.createHorizontalGlue() );
41           horizontal2.add( new JButton( "Button " + count ) );
42        } // end for
43
44        // create rigid area and add buttons to Box vertical2
45        for ( int count = 0; count < SIZE; count++ )
46        {
```

Fig. 22.16 | BoxLayout layout manager. (Part 1 of 2.)

```
47          vertical2.add( Box.createRigidArea( new Dimension( 12, 8 ) ) );
48          vertical2.add( new JButton( "Button " + count ) );
49       } // end for
50
51       // create vertical glue and add buttons to panel
52       JPanel panel = new JPanel();
53       panel.setLayout( new BoxLayout( panel, BoxLayout.Y_AXIS ) );
54
55       for ( int count = 0; count < SIZE; count++ )
56       {
57          panel.add( Box.createGlue() );
58          panel.add( new JButton( "Button " + count ) );
59       } // end for
60
61       // create a JTabbedPane
62       JTabbedPane tabs = new JTabbedPane(
63          JTabbedPane.TOP, JTabbedPane.SCROLL_TAB_LAYOUT );
64
65       // place each container on tabbed pane
66       tabs.addTab( "Horizontal Box", horizontal1 );
67       tabs.addTab( "Vertical Box with Struts", vertical1 );
68       tabs.addTab( "Horizontal Box with Glue", horizontal2 );
69       tabs.addTab( "Vertical Box with Rigid Areas", vertical2 );
70       tabs.addTab( "Vertical Box with Glue", panel );
71
72       add( tabs ); // place tabbed pane on frame
73    } // end BoxLayoutFrame constructor
74 } // end class BoxLayoutFrame
```

Fig. 22.16 | BoxLayout layout manager. (Part 2 of 2.)

Lines 19–22 create Box containers. References horizontal1 and horizontal2 are initialized with static Box method createHorizontalBox, which returns a Box container with a horizontal BoxLayout in which GUI components are arranged left-to-right. Variables vertical1 and vertical2 are initialized with static Box method createVerticalBox, which returns references to Box containers with a vertical BoxLayout in which GUI components are arranged top-to-bottom.

The for statement at lines 27–28 adds three JButtons to horizontal1. The for statement at lines 31–35 adds three JButtons to vertical1. Before adding each button, line 33 adds a vertical strut to the container with static Box method createVerticalStrut. A vertical strut is an invisible GUI component that has a fixed pixel height and is used to guarantee a fixed amount of space between GUI components. The int argument to method createVerticalStrut determines the height of the strut in pixels. When the container is resized, the distance between GUI components separated by struts does not change. Class Box also declares method createHorizontalStrut for horizontal BoxLayouts.

The for statement at lines 38–42 adds three JButtons to horizontal2. Before adding each button, line 40 adds horizontal glue to the container with static Box method createHorizontalGlue. Horizontal glue is an invisible GUI component that can be used between fixed-size GUI components to occupy additional space. Normally, extra space appears to the right of the last horizontal GUI component or below the last vertical one in

```
 1   // Fig. 22.17: BoxLayoutDemo.java
 2   // Demonstrating BoxLayout.
 3   import javax.swing.JFrame;
 4
 5   public class BoxLayoutDemo
 6   {
 7      public static void main( String args[] )
 8      {
 9         BoxLayoutFrame boxLayoutFrame = new BoxLayoutFrame();
10         boxLayoutFrame.setDefaultCloseOperation( JFrame.EXIT_ON_CLOSE );
11         boxLayoutFrame.setSize( 400, 220 ); // set frame size
12         boxLayoutFrame.setVisible( true ); // display frame
13      } // end main
14   } // end class BoxLayoutDemo
```

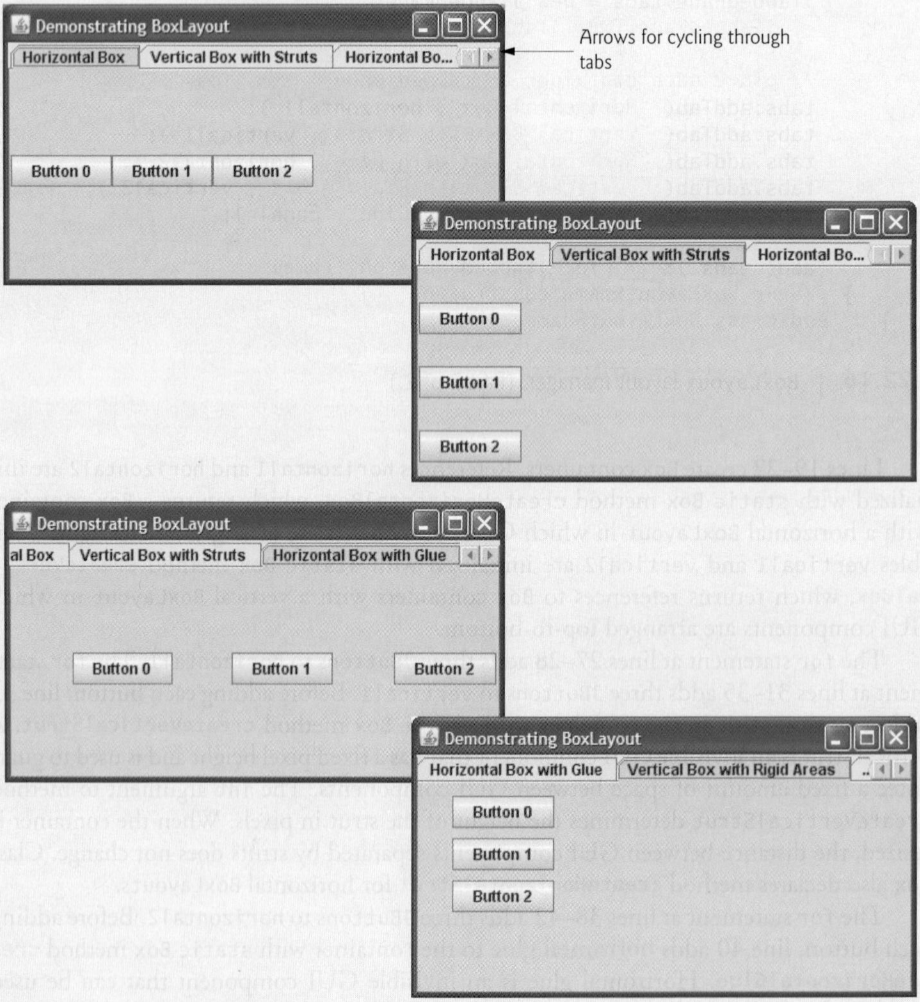

Fig. 22.17 | Test class for **BoxLayoutFrame**. (Part 1 of 2.)

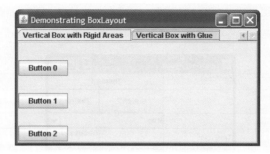

Fig. 22.17 | Test class for BoxLayoutFrame. (Part 2 of 2.)

a BoxLayout. Glue allows the extra space to be placed between GUI components. When the container is resized, components separated by glue components remain the same size, but the glue stretches or contracts to occupy the space between them. Class Box also declares method createVerticalGlue for vertical BoxLayouts.

The for statement at lines 45–49 adds three JButtons to vertical2. Before each button is added, line 47 adds a rigid area to the container with static Box method createRigidArea. A rigid area is an invisible GUI component that always has a fixed pixel width and height. The argument to method createRigidArea is a Dimension object that specifies the area's width and height.

Lines 52–53 create a JPanel object and set its layout to a BoxLayout in the conventional manner, using Container method setLayout. The BoxLayout constructor receives a reference to the container for which it controls the layout and a constant indicating whether the layout is horizontal (BoxLayout.X_AXIS) or vertical (BoxLayout.Y_AXIS).

The for statement at lines 55–59 adds three JButtons to panel. Before adding each button, line 57 adds a glue component to the container with static Box method create-Glue. This component expands or contracts based on the size of the Box.

Lines 62–63 create a JTabbedPane to display the five containers in this program. The argument JTabbedPane.TOP sent to the constructor indicates that the tabs should appear The argument JTabbedPane.SCROLL_TAB_LAYOUT specifies that the tabs should scroll if there are too many to fit on one line.

The Box containers and the JPanel are attached to the JTabbedPane at lines 66–70. Try executing the application. When the window appears, resize the window to see how the glue components, strut components and rigid area affect the layout on each tab.

GridBagLayout Layout Manager

One of the most powerful predefined layout managers is GridBagLayout (in package java.awt). This layout is similar to GridLayout in that it arranges components in a grid. However, GridBagLayout is more flexible. The components can vary in size (i.e., they can occupy multiple rows and columns) and can be added in any order.

The first step in using GridBagLayout is determining the appearance of the GUI. For this step you need only a piece of paper. Draw the GUI and then draw a grid over it, dividing the components into rows and columns. The initial row and column numbers should be 0, so that the GridBagLayout layout manager can use the row and column numbers to properly place the components in the grid. Figure 22.18 demonstrates drawing the lines for the rows and columns over a GUI.

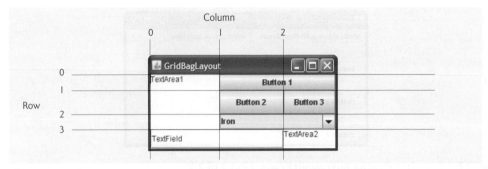

Fig. 22.18 | Designing a GUI that will use `GridBagLayout`.

A `GridBagConstraints` object describes how a component is placed in a `GridBag-Layout`. Several `GridBagConstraints` fields are summarized in Fig. 22.19.

`GridBagConstraints` field **anchor** specifies the relative position of the component in an area that it does not fill. The variable anchor is assigned one of the following `GridBag-Constraints` constants: NORTH, NORTHEAST, EAST, SOUTHEAST, SOUTH, SOUTHWEST, WEST, NORTHWEST or CENTER. The default value is CENTER.

`GridBagConstraints` field **fill** defines how the component grows if the area in which it can be displayed is larger than the component. The variable fill is assigned one of the following `GridBagConstraints` constants: NONE, VERTICAL, HORIZONTAL or BOTH. The default value is NONE, which indicates that the component will not grow in either direction. VERTICAL indicates that it will grow vertically. HORIZONTAL indicates that it will grow horizontally. BOTH indicates that it will grow in both directions.

GridBagCon-straints field	Description
anchor	Specifies the relative position (NORTH, NORTHEAST, EAST, SOUTH-EAST, SOUTH, SOUTHWEST, WEST, NORTHWEST, CENTER) of the component in an area that it does not fill.
fill	Resizes the component in specified direction (NONE, HORIZONTAL, VERTICAL, BOTH) when the display area is larger than the component.
gridx	The column in which the component will be placed.
gridy	The row in which the component will be placed.
gridwidth	The number of columns the component occupies.
gridheight	The number of rows the component occupies.
weightx	The amount of extra space to allocate horizontally. The grid slot can become wider when extra space is available.
weighty	The amount of extra space to allocate vertically. The grid slot can become taller when extra space is available.

Fig. 22.19 | `GridBagConstraints` fields.

Variables `gridx` and `gridy` specify where the upper-left corner of the component is placed in the grid. Variable `gridx` corresponds to the column, and variable `gridy` corresponds to the row. In Fig. 22.18, the JComboBox (displaying "Iron") has a `gridx` value of 1 and a `gridy` value of 2.

Variable `gridwidth` specifies the number of columns a component occupies. The JComboBox occupies two columns. Variable `gridheight` specifies the number of rows a component occupies. The JTextArea on the left side of Fig. 22.18 occupies three rows.

Variable `weightx` specifies how to distribute extra horizontal space to grid slots in a GridBagLayout when the container is resized. A zero value indicates that the grid slot does not grow horizontally on its own. However, if the component spans a column containing a component with nonzero `weightx` value, the component with zero `weightx` value will grow horizontally in the same proportion as the other component(s) in the same column. This is because each component must be maintained in the same row and column in which it was originally placed.

Variable `weighty` specifies how to distribute extra vertical space to grid slots in a GridBagLayout when the container is resized. A zero value indicates that the grid slot does not grow vertically on its own. However, if the component spans a row containing a component with nonzero `weighty` value, the component with zero `weighty` value grows vertically in the same proportion as the other component(s) in the same row.

In Fig. 22.18, the effects of `weighty` and `weightx` cannot easily be seen until the container is resized and additional space becomes available. Components with larger weight values occupy more of the additional space than those with smaller weight values.

Components should be given nonzero positive weight values—otherwise they will "huddle" together in the middle of the container. Figure 22.20 shows the GUI of Fig. 22.18 with all weights set to zero.

The application in Figs. 22.21–22.22 uses the GridBagLayout layout manager to arrange the components of the GUI in Fig. 22.18. The application does nothing except demonstrate how to use GridBagLayout.

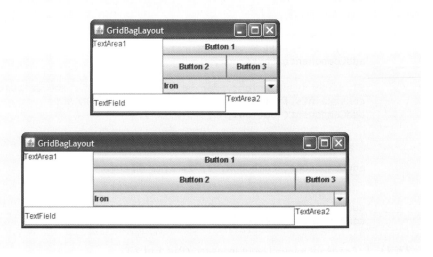

Fig. 22.20 | `GridBagLayout` with the weights set to zero.

```
1   // Fig. 22.21: GridBagFrame.java
2   // Demonstrating GridBagLayout.
3   import java.awt.GridBagLayout;
4   import java.awt.GridBagConstraints;
5   import java.awt.Component;
6   import javax.swing.JFrame;
7   import javax.swing.JTextArea;
8   import javax.swing.JTextField;
9   import javax.swing.JButton;
10  import javax.swing.JComboBox;
11
12  public class GridBagFrame extends JFrame
13  {
14     private GridBagLayout layout; // layout of this frame
15     private GridBagConstraints constraints; // constraints of this layout
16
17     // set up GUI
18     public GridBagFrame()
19     {
20        super( "GridBagLayout" );
21        layout = new GridBagLayout();
22        setLayout( layout ); // set frame layout
23        constraints = new GridBagConstraints(); // instantiate constraints
24
25        // create GUI components
26        JTextArea textArea1 = new JTextArea( "TextArea1", 5, 10 );
27        JTextArea textArea2 = new JTextArea( "TextArea2", 2, 2 );
28
29        String names[] = { "Iron", "Steel", "Brass" };
30        JComboBox comboBox = new JComboBox( names );
31
32        JTextField textField = new JTextField( "TextField" );
33        JButton button1 = new JButton( "Button 1" );
34        JButton button2 = new JButton( "Button 2" );
35        JButton button3 = new JButton( "Button 3" );
36
37        // weightx and weighty for textArea1 are both 0: the default
38        // anchor for all components is CENTER: the default
39        constraints.fill = GridBagConstraints.BOTH;
40        addComponent( textArea1, 0, 0, 1, 3 );
41
42        // weightx and weighty for button1 are both 0: the default
43        constraints.fill = GridBagConstraints.HORIZONTAL;
44        addComponent( button1, 0, 1, 2, 1 );
45
46        // weightx and weighty for comboBox are both 0: the default
47        // fill is HORIZONTAL
48        addComponent( comboBox, 2, 1, 2, 1 );
49
50        // button2
51        constraints.weightx = 1000;  // can grow wider
52        constraints.weighty = 1;     // can grow taller
```

Fig. 22.21 | GridBagLayout layout manager. (Part 1 of 2.)

```
53          constraints.fill = GridBagConstraints.BOTH;
54          addComponent( button2, 1, 1, 1, 1 );
55
56          // fill is BOTH for button3
57          constraints.weightx = 0;
58          constraints.weighty = 0;
59          addComponent( button3, 1, 2, 1, 1 );
60
61          // weightx and weighty for textField are both 0, fill is BOTH
62          addComponent( textField, 3, 0, 2, 1 );
63
64          // weightx and weighty for textArea2 are both 0, fill is BOTH
65          addComponent( textArea2, 3, 2, 1, 1 );
66       } // end GridBagFrame constructor
67
68       // method to set constraints on
69       private void addComponent( Component component,
70          int row, int column, int width, int height )
71       {
72          constraints.gridx = column; // set gridx
73          constraints.gridy = row; // set gridy
74          constraints.gridwidth = width; // set gridwidth
75          constraints.gridheight = height; // set gridheight
76          layout.setConstraints( component, constraints ); // set constraints
77          add( component ); // add component
78       } // end method addComponent
79    } // end class GridBagFrame
```

Fig. 22.21 | GridBagLayout layout manager. (Part 2 of 2.)

The GUI consists of three JButtons, two JTextAreas, a JComboBox and a JTextField. The layout manager for the content pane is GridBagLayout. Lines 21–22 create the Grid-BagLayout object and set the layout manager for the JFrame to layout. Line 23 creates the GridBagConstraints object used to determine the location and size of each component in the grid. Lines 26–35 create each GUI component that will be added to the content pane.

Lines 39–40 configure JTextArea textArea1 and add it to the content pane. The values for weightx and weighty values are not specified in constraints, so each has the value zero by default. Thus, the JTextArea will not resize itself even if space is available. However, it spans multiple rows, so the vertical size is subject to the weighty values of JButtons button2 and button3. When either button is resized vertically based on its weighty value, the JTextArea is also resized.

Line 39 sets variable fill in constraints to GridBagConstraints.BOTH, causing the JTextArea to always fill its entire allocated area in the grid. An anchor value is not specified in constraints, so the default CENTER is used. We do not use variable anchor in this application, so all the components will use the default. Line 40 calls our utility method addComponent (declared at lines 69–78). The JTextArea object, the row, the column, the number of columns to span and the number of rows to span are passed as arguments.

JButton button1 is the next component added (lines 43–44). By default, the weightx and weighty values are still zero. The fill variable is set to HORIZONTAL—the component will always fill its area in the horizontal direction. The vertical direction is not filled. The

```
1   // Fig. 22.22: GridBagDemo.java
2   // Demonstrating GridBagLayout.
3   import javax.swing.JFrame;
4
5   public class GridBagDemo
6   {
7      public static void main( String args[] )
8      {
9         GridBagFrame gridBagFrame = new GridBagFrame();
10        gridBagFrame.setDefaultCloseOperation( JFrame.EXIT_ON_CLOSE );
11        gridBagFrame.setSize( 300, 150 ); // set frame size
12        gridBagFrame.setVisible( true ); // display frame
13     } // end main
14  } // end class GridBagDemo
```

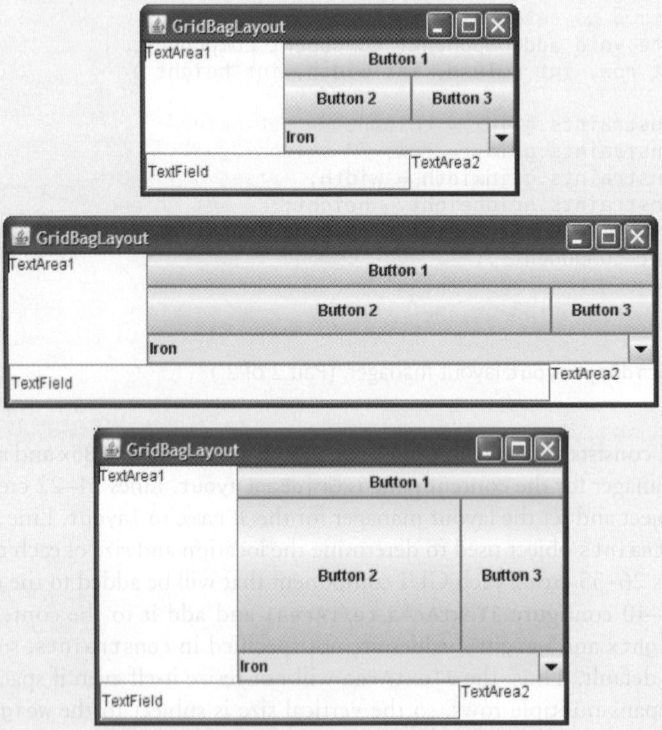

Fig. 22.22 | Test class for GridBagFrame.

weighty value is zero, so the button will become taller only if another component in the same row has a nonzero weighty value. JButton button1 is located at row 0, column 1. One row and two columns are occupied.

JComboBox comboBox is the next component added (line 48). By default, the weightx and weighty values are zero, and the fill variable is set to HORIZONTAL. The JComboBox button will grow only in the horizontal direction. Note that the weightx, weighty and fill variables retain the values set in constraints until they are changed. The JComboBox button is placed at row 2, column 1. One row and two columns are occupied.

`JButton button2` is the next component added (lines 51–54). It is given a `weightx` value of 1000 and a `weighty` value of 1. The area occupied by the button is capable of growing in the vertical and horizontal directions. The `fill` variable is set to `BOTH`, which specifies that the button will always fill the entire area. When the window is resized, `button2` will grow. The button is placed at row 1, column 1. One row and one column are occupied.

`JButton button3` is added next (lines 57–59). Both the `weightx` value and `weighty` value are set to zero, and the value of `fill` is `BOTH`. `JButton button3` will grow if the window is resized—it is affected by the weight values of `button2`. Note that the `weightx` value for `button2` is much larger than that for `button3`. When resizing occurs, `button2` will occupy a larger percentage of the new space. The button is placed at row 1, column 2. One row and one column are occupied.

Both the `JTextField textField` (line 62) and `JTextArea textArea2` (line 65) have a `weightx` value of 0 and a `weighty` value of 0. The value of `fill` is `BOTH`. The `JTextField` is placed at row 3, column 0, and the `JTextArea` at row 3, column 2. The `JTextField` occupies one row and two columns, the `JTextArea` one row and one column.

Method addComponent's parameters are a `Component` reference component and integers `row`, `column`, `width` and `height`. Lines 72–73 set the `GridBagConstraints` variables `gridx` and `gridy`. The `gridx` variable is assigned the column in which the `Component` will be placed, and the `gridy` value is assigned the row in which the `Component` will be placed. Lines 74–75 set the `GridBagConstraints` variables `gridwidth` and `gridheight`. The `gridwidth` variable specifies the number of columns the `Component` will span in the grid, and the `gridheight` variable specifies the number of rows the `Component` will span in the grid. Line 76 sets the `GridBagConstraints` for a component in the `GridBagLayout`. Method `setConstraints` of class `GridBagLayout` takes a `Component` argument and a `GridBagConstraints` argument. Line 77 adds the component to the `JFrame`.

When you execute this application, try resizing the window to see how the constraints for each GUI component affect its position and size in the window.

GridBagConstraints *Constants* RELATIVE *and* REMAINDER

Instead of `gridx` and `gridy`, a variation of `GridBagLayout` uses `GridBagConstraints` constants **RELATIVE** and **REMAINDER**. RELATIVE specifies that the next-to-last component in a particular row should be placed to the right of the previous component in the row. REMAINDER specifies that a component is the last component in a row. Any component that is not the second-to-last or last component on a row must specify values for `GridbagConstraints` variables `gridwidth` and `gridheight`. The application in Figs. 22.23–22.24 arranges components in `GridBagLayout`, using these constants.

Lines 21–22 create a `GridBagLayout` and use it to set the `JFrame`'s layout manager. The components that are placed in `GridBagLayout` are created in lines 27–38—they are a `JComboBox`, a `JTextField`, a `JList` and five `JButtons`.

The `JTextField` is added first (lines 41–45). The `weightx` and `weighty` values are set to 1. The `fill` variable is set to `BOTH`. Line 44 specifies that the `JTextField` is the last component on the line. The `JTextField` is added to the content pane with a call to our utility method addComponent (declared at lines 79–83). Method addComponent takes a `Component` argument and uses `GridBagLayout` method `setConstraints` to set the constraints for the `Component`. Method add attaches the component to the content pane.

```
1    // Fig. 22.23: GridBagFrame2.java
2    // Demonstrating GridBagLayout constants.
3    import java.awt.GridBagLayout;
4    import java.awt.GridBagConstraints;
5    import java.awt.Component;
6    import javax.swing.JFrame;
7    import javax.swing.JComboBox;
8    import javax.swing.JTextField;
9    import javax.swing.JList;
10   import javax.swing.JButton;
11
12   public class GridBagFrame2 extends JFrame
13   {
14      private GridBagLayout layout; // layout of this frame
15      private GridBagConstraints constraints; // constraints of this layout
16
17      // set up GUI
18      public GridBagFrame2()
19      {
20         super( "GridBagLayout" );
21         layout = new GridBagLayout();
22         setLayout( layout ); // set frame layout
23         constraints = new GridBagConstraints(); // instantiate constraints
24
25         // create GUI components
26         String metals[] = { "Copper", "Aluminum", "Silver" };
27         JComboBox comboBox = new JComboBox( metals );
28
29         JTextField textField = new JTextField( "TextField" );
30
31         String fonts[] = { "Serif", "Monospaced" };T
32         JList list = new JList( fonts );
33
34         String names[] = { "zero", "one", "two", "three", "four" };
35         JButton buttons[] = new JButton[ names.length ];
36
37         for ( int count = 0; count < buttons.length; count++ )
38            buttons[ count ] = new JButton( names[ count ] );
39
40         // define GUI component constraints for textField
41         constraints.weightx = 1;
42         constraints.weighty = 1;
43         constraints.fill = GridBagConstraints.BOTH;
44         constraints.gridwidth = GridBagConstraints.REMAINDER;
45         addComponent( textField );
46
47         // buttons[0] -- weightx and weighty are 1: fill is BOTH
48         constraints.gridwidth = 1;
49         addComponent( buttons[ 0 ] );
50
51         // buttons[1] -- weightx and weighty are 1: fill is BOTH
52         constraints.gridwidth = GridBagConstraints.RELATIVE;
53         addComponent( buttons[ 1 ] );
```

Fig. 22.23 | GridBagConstraints constants RELATIVE and REMAINDER. (Part 1 of 2.)

```
54
55          // buttons[2] -- weightx and weighty are 1: fill is BOTH
56          constraints.gridwidth = GridBagConstraints.REMAINDER;
57          addComponent( buttons[ 2 ] );
58
59          // comboBox -- weightx is 1: fill is BOTH
60          constraints.weighty = 0;
61          constraints.gridwidth = GridBagConstraints.REMAINDER;
62          addComponent( comboBox );
63
64          // buttons[3] -- weightx is 1: fill is BOTH
65          constraints.weighty = 1;
66          constraints.gridwidth = GridBagConstraints.REMAINDER;
67          addComponent( buttons[ 3 ] );
68
69          // buttons[4] -- weightx and weighty are 1: fill is BOTH
70          constraints.gridwidth = GridBagConstraints.RELATIVE;
71          addComponent( buttons[ 4 ] );
72
73          // list -- weightx and weighty are 1: fill is BOTH
74          constraints.gridwidth = GridBagConstraints.REMAINDER;
75          addComponent( list );
76      } // end GridBagFrame2 constructor
77
78      // add a component to the container
79      private void addComponent( Component component )
80      {
81          layout.setConstraints( component, constraints );
82          add( component ); // add component
83      } // end method addComponent
84  } // end class GridBagFrame2
```

Fig. 22.23 | GridBagConstraints constants RELATIVE and REMAINDER. (Part 2 of 2.)

JButton buttons[0] (lines 48–49) has weightx and weighty values of 1. The fill variable is BOTH. Because buttons[0] is not one of the last two components on the row, it is given a gridwidth of 1 and so will occupy one column. The JButton is added to the content pane with a call to utility method addComponent.

JButton buttons[1] (lines 52–53) has weightx and weighty values of 1. The fill variable is BOTH. Line 52 specifies that the JButton is to be placed relative to the previous component. The Button is added to the JFrame with a call to addComponent.

JButton buttons[2] (lines 56–57) has weightx and weighty values of 1. The fill variable is BOTH. This JButton is the last component on the line, so REMAINDER is used. The JButton is added to the content pane with a call to addComponent.

The JComboBox (lines 60–62) has a weightx of 1 and a weighty of 0. The JComboBox will not grow in the vertical direction. The JComboBox is the only component on the line, so REMAINDER is used. The JComboBox is added to the content pane with a call to addComponent.

JButton buttons[3] (lines 65–67) has weightx and weighty values of 1. The fill variable is BOTH. This JButton is the only component on the line, so REMAINDER is used. The JButton is added to the content pane with a call to addComponent.

```
 1   // Fig. 22.24: GridBagDemo2.java
 2   // Demonstrating GridBagLayout constants.
 3   import javax.swing.JFrame;
 4
 5   public class GridBagDemo2
 6   {
 7      public static void main( String args[] )
 8      {
 9         GridBagFrame2 gridBagFrame = new GridBagFrame2();
10         gridBagFrame.setDefaultCloseOperation( JFrame.EXIT_ON_CLOSE );
11         gridBagFrame.setSize( 300, 200 ); // set frame size
12         gridBagFrame.setVisible( true ); // display frame
13      } // end main
14   } // end class GridBagDemo2
```

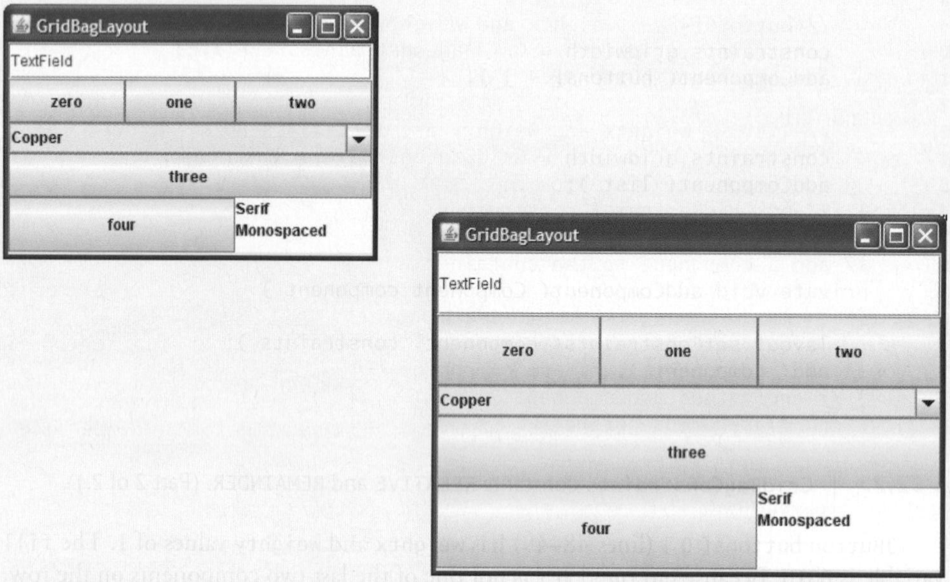

Fig. 22.24 | Test class for `GridBagDemo2`.

JButton buttons[4] (lines 70–71) has weightx and weighty values of 1. The fill variable is BOTH. This JButton is the next-to-last component on the line, so RELATIVE is used. The JButton is added to the content pane with a call to addComponent.

The JList (lines 74–75) has weightx and weighty values of 1. The fill variable is BOTH. The JList is added to the content pane with a call to addComponent.

22.10 Wrap-Up

This chapter completes our introduction to GUI. In this chapter, you learned about more advanced GUI topics, such as menus, sliders, pop-up menus and the multiple-document interface. All these components can be added to existing applications to make them easier to use and understand. In the next chapter, you will learn about multithreading, a powerful capability that allows applications to use threads to perform multiple tasks at once.

Summary

Section 22.2 *JSlider*

- JSliders enable the user to select from a range of integer values. JSliders can display major tick marks, minor tick marks and labels for the tick marks. They also support snap-to ticks, where positioning the thumb between two tick marks causes the thumb to snap to the closest tick mark.

- If a JSlider has the focus, the left and right arrow keys cause the thumb of the JSlider to decrease or increase by 1. The down and up arrow keys also cause the thumb of the JSlider to decrease or increase by 1, respectively. The *PgDn* (page down) *key* and *PgUp* (page up) *key* cause the thumb of the JSlider to decrease or increase by block increments of one-tenth of the range of values, respectively. The *Home key* moves the thumb to the minimum value of the JSlider, and the *End key* moves it to the maximum value.

- JSliders have either horizontal or vertical orientation. For a horizontal JSlider, the minimum value is at the extreme left and the maximum value at the extreme right. For a vertical JSlider, the minimum value is at the extreme bottom and the maximum value at the extreme top. The position of the thumb indicates the current value of the JSlider. Method getValue of class JSlider returns the current thumb position.

- Method setMajorTickSpacing of class JSlider sets the spacing for tick marks on a JSlider. Method setPaintTicks with a true argument indicates that the tick marks should be displayed.

- JSliders generate ChangeEvents when the user interacts with a JSlider. A ChangeListener declares method stateChanged that can respond to ChangeEvents.

Section 22.3 *Windows: Additional Notes*

- Every window generates window events when the user manipulates it. Interface WindowListener provides seven window-event-handling methods—windowActivated, windowClosed, windowClosing, windowDeactivated, windowDeiconified, windowIconified and windowOpened.

- Menus are an integral part of GUIs. Menus allow the user to perform actions without unnecessarily cluttering a graphical user interface with extra GUI components. In Swing GUIs, menus can be attached only to objects of classes with method setJMenuBar (e.g., JFrame and JApplet).

Section 22.4 *Using Menus with Frames*

- The classes used to declare menus are JMenuBar, JMenuItem, JMenu, JCheckBoxMenuItem and JRadioButtonMenuItem.

- A JMenuBar is a container for menus. A JMenuItem is a GUI component inside a menu that, when selected, causes an action to be performed. A JMenu contains menu items and can be added to a JMenuBar or to other JMenus as submenus.

- When a menu is clicked, it expands to show its list of menu items. JMenu method addSeparator adds a separator line to a menu.

- When a JCheckBoxMenuItem is selected, a check appears to the left of the menu item. When the JCheckBoxMenuItem is selected again, the check is removed.

- When multiple JRadioButtonMenuItems are maintained as part of a ButtonGroup, only one item in the group can be selected at a given time. When an item is selected, a filled circle appears to its left. When another JRadioButtonMenuItem is selected, the filled circle to the left of the previously selected item is removed.

- AbstractButton method setMnemonic specifies the mnemonic for an AbstractButton. Mnemonic characters are normally displayed with an underline.

- A modal dialog box does not allow access to any other window in the application until the dialog is dismissed. The dialogs displayed with class JOptionPane are modal dialogs. Class JDialog can be used to create your own modal or nonmodal dialogs.

Section 22.5 *JPopupMenu*

- Context-sensitive pop-up menus are created with class JPopupMenu. On most systems, the pop-up trigger event occurs when the user presses and releases the right mouse button. MouseEvent method isPopupTrigger returns true if the pop-up trigger event occurred.

- JPopupMenu method show displays a JPopupMenu. The first argument specifies the origin component, which helps determine where the JPopupMenu will appear. The last two arguments are the coordinates from the origin component's upper-left corner, at which the JPopupMenu appears.

Section 22.6 *Pluggable Look-and-Feel*

- Class UIManager contains nested class LookAndFeelInfo that maintains information about a look-and-feel.

- UIManager static method getInstalledLookAndFeels gets an array of UIManager.LookAndFeelInfo objects that describe the available look-and-feels.

- UIManager static method setLookAndFeel changes the look-and-feel. SwingUtilities static method updateComponentTreeUI changes the look-and-feel of every component attached to its Component argument to the new look-and-feel.

Section 22.7 *JDesktopPane and JInternalFrame*

- Many of today's applications use a multiple-document interface (MDI) to manage several open documents that are being processed in parallel. Swing's JDesktopPane and JInternalFrame classes provide support for creating multiple-document interfaces.

Section 22.8 *JTabbedPane*

- A JTabbedPane arranges GUI components into layers, of which only one is visible at a time. Users access each layer via a tab similar to those on folders in a file cabinet. When the user clicks a tab, the appropriate layer is displayed.

Section 22.9 *Layout Managers: BoxLayout and GridBagLayout*

- BoxLayout is a layout manager that allows GUI components to be arranged left-to-right or top-to-bottom in a container.

- Class Box declares a container with BoxLayout as its default layout manager and provides static methods to create a Box with a horizontal or vertical BoxLayout.

- GridBagLayout is a layout manager similar to GridLayout. It differs in that each component size can vary, and components can be added in any order.

- A GridBagConstraints object specifies how a component is placed in a GridBagLayout. Method setConstraints of class GridBagLayout takes a Component argument and a GridBagConstraints argument and sets the constraints of the Component.

Terminology

add method of class JMenuBar
addWindowListener method of class Window
anchor field of class GridBagConstraints
border
BOTH constant of class GridBagConstraints

Box class
BoxLayout class
CENTER constant of class GridBagConstraints
ChangeEvent class
ChangeListener interface

child window

context-sensitive pop-up menu

createGlue method of class Box

createHorizontalBox method of class Box

createHorizontalGlue method of class Box

createHorizontalStrut method of class Box

createRigidArea method of class Box

createVerticalBox method of class Box

createVerticalGlue method of class Box

createVerticalStrut method of class Box

Dimension class

dispose method of class Window

document

EAST constant of class GridBagConstraints

getClassName method of class
    UIManager.LookAndFeelInfo

getInstalledLookAndFeels method of class
    UIManager

getPreferredSize method of class Component

getSelectedText method of class
    JTextComponent

getValue method of class JSlider

GridBagConstraints class

GridBagLayout class

gridheight field of class GridBagConstraints

gridwidth field of class GridBagConstraints

gridx field of class GridBagConstraints

gridy field of class GridBagConstraints

HORIZONTAL constant of GridBagConstraints

horizontal glue

isPopupTrigger method of class MouseEvent

isSelected method of class AbstractButton

JCheckBoxMenuItem class

JDesktopPane class

JDialog class

JFrame class

JInternalFrame class

JMenu class

JMenuBar class

JMenuItem class

JRadioButtonMenuItem class

JSlider class

JTabbedPane class

line wrapping

LookAndFeelInfo nested class of class UIManager

major tick marks

menu

menu bar

menu item

metal look-and-feel

minor tick marks of JSlider

mnemonic

modal dialog box

multiple document interface (MDI)

NONE constant of class GridBagConstraints

NORTH constant of class GridBagConstraints

NORTHEAST constant of class
    GridBagConstraints

NORTHWEST constant of class
    GridBagConstraints

opaque

origin component

pack method of class Window

paintComponent method of class JComponent

parent window

parent window for a dialog box

pluggable look and feel (PLAF)

pop-up trigger event

RELATIVE constant of class GridBagConstraints

REMAINDER constant of class
    GridBagConstraints

rigid area

scrollbar policies

separator line in a menu

setConstraints method of class GridBagLayout

setDefaultCloseOperation method of class
    JFrame

setInverted method of class JSlider

setJMenuBar method of class JFrame

setLocation method of class Component

setLookAndFeel method of class UIManager

setMajorTickSpacing method of class JSlider

setMnemonic method of class AbstractButton

setOpaque method of class JComponent

setPaintTicks method of class JSlider

setSelected method of class AbstractButton

setVerticalScrollBarPolicy method of
    JSlider

shortcut key

show method of class JPopupMenu

snap-to ticks for JSlider

SOUTH constant of class GridBagConstraints

SOUTHEAST constant of class
    GridBagConstraints

SOUTHWEST constant of class
    GridBagConstraints

stateChanged method of interface
    ChangeListener

submenu

SwingUtilities class

thumb of JSlider

tick marks on JSlider

title bar

transparency of a JComponent

UIManager class

updateComponentTreeUI method of class
    SwingUtilities

VERTICAL constant of class GridBagConstraints

vertical strut

weightx field of class GridBagConstraints

weighty field of class GridBagConstraints

WEST constant of class GridBagConstraints

window events

windowActivated method of interface
    WindowListener

windowClosing method of interface
    WindowListener

WindowConstants interface

windowDeactivated method of interface
    WindowListener

windowDeiconified method of interface
    WindowListener

windowIconified method of interface
    WindowListener

WindowListener interface

windowOpened method of interface
    WindowListener

X_AXIS constant of class Box

Y_AXIS constant of class Box

Self-Review Exercises

22.1 Fill in the blanks in each of the following statements:

  a) The _____ class is used to create a menu object.

  b) The _____ method of class JMenu places a separator bar in a menu.

  c) JSlider events are handled by the _____ method of interface _____.

  d) The GridBagConstraints instance variable _____ is set to CENTER by default.

22.2 State whether each of the following is *true* or *false*. If *false*, explain why.

  a) When the programmer creates a JFrame, a minimum of one menu must be created and added to the JFrame.

  b) The variable fill belongs to the GridBagLayout class.

  c) Drawing on a GUI component is performed with respect to the (0, 0) upper-left corner coordinate of the component.

  d) The default layout for a Box is BoxLayout.

22.3 Find the error(s) in each of the following and explain how to correct the error(s).

  a) `JMenubar b;`

  b) `mySlider = JSlider( 1000, 222, 100, 450 );`

  c) `gbc.fill = GridBagConstraints.NORTHWEST;  // set fill`

  d)
```
// override to paint on a customized Swing component
public void paintcomponent( Graphics g )
{
    g.drawString( "HELLO", 50, 50 );
} // end method paintComponent
```

  e)
```
// create a JFrame and display it
JFrame f = new JFrame( "A Window" );
f.setVisible( true );
```

Answers to Self-Review Exercises

22.1 a) JMenu. b) addSeparator. c) stateChanged, ChangeListener. d) anchor.

22.2 a) False. A JFrame does not require any menus.

  b) False. The variable fill belongs to the GridBagConstraints class.

  c) True.

  d) True.

22.3 a) JMenubar should be JMenuBar.

b) The first argument to the constructor should be either SwingConstants.HORIZONTAL or SwingConstants.VERTICAL, and the keyword new must be used after the = operator.

c) The constant should be either BOTH, HORIZONTAL, VERTICAL or NONE.

d) paintcomponent should be paintComponent, and the method should call super.paintComponent(g) as its first statement.

e) The JFrame's setSize method must also be called to establish the size of the window.

Exercises

22.4 State whether each of the following is *true* or *false*. If *false*, explain why.

a) Menus require a JMenuBar object so they can be attached to a JFrame.

b) BoxLayout is the default layout manager for a JFrame.

c) Method setEditable is a JTextComponent method.

d) Class JFrame directly extends class Container.

e) JApplets can contain menus.

22.5 Write a program that displays a circle of random size and calculates and displays the area, radius, diameter and circumference. Use the following equations: *diameter = 2 ∞ radius, area = π ∞ radius²*, *circumference = 2 ∞ π ∞ radius*. Use the constant Math.PI for pi (π). All drawing should be done on a subclass of JPanel, and the results of the calculations should be displayed in a read-only JTextArea.

22.6 Explore the effects of varying the weightx and weighty values of the program in Fig. 22.21. What happens when a slot has a nonzero weight but is not allowed to fill the whole area (i.e., the fill value is not BOTH)?

22.7 Modify the program in Fig. 22.13 by adding a minimum of two new tabs.

22.8 Declare a subclass of JPanel called MyColorChooser that provides three JSlider objects and three JTextField objects. Each JSlider represents the values from 0 to 255 for the red, green and blue parts of a color. Use these values as the arguments to the Color constructor to create a new Color object. Display the current value of each JSlider in the corresponding JTextField. When the user changes the value of the JSlider, the JTextField should be changed accordingly. Use your new GUI component as part of an application that displays the current Color value by drawing a filled rectangle.

22.9 Modify the MyColorChooser class of Exercise 22.8 to allow the user to enter an integer value into a JTextField to set the red, green or blue value. When the user presses *Enter* in the JTextField, the corresponding JSlider should be set to the appropriate value.

22.10 Modify the application in Exercise 22.9 to draw the current color as a rectangle on an instance of a subclass of JPanel which provides its own paintComponent method to draw the rectangle and provides *set* methods to set the red, green and blue values for the current color. When any *set* method is invoked, the drawing panel should automatically repaint itself.

22.11 Modify the application in Exercise 22.10 to allow the user to drag the mouse across the drawing panel (a subclass of JPanel) to draw a shape in the current color. Enable the user to choose what shape to draw.

22.12 Modify the application in Exercise 22.11 to provide the user with the ability to terminate the application by clicking the close box on the window that is displayed and by selecting Exit from a File menu. Use the techniques shown in Fig. 22.5.

22.13 *(Complete Drawing Application)* Using the techniques developed in this chapter and Chapter 11, create a complete drawing application. The program should use the GUI components from Chapter 11 and Chapter 22 to enable the user to select the shape, color and fill characteristics. Each shape should be stored in an array of MyShape objects, where MyShape is the superclass in your hierarchy of shape classes. Use a JDesktopPane and JInternalFrames to allow the user to create multiple separate drawings in separate child windows. Create the user interface as a separate child window containing all the GUI components that allow the user to determine the characteristics of the shape to be drawn. The user can then click in any JInternalFrame to draw the shape.

23

Multithreading

OBJECTIVES

In this chapter you will learn:

- What threads are and why they are useful.

- How threads enable you to manage concurrent activities.

- The life cycle of a thread.

- Thread priorities and scheduling.

- To create and execute **Runnable**s.

- Thread synchronization.

- What producer/consumer relationships are and how they are implemented with multithreading.

- To enable multiple threads to update Swing GUI components in a thread-safe manner.

- About interfaces **Callable** and **Future**, which you can use with threading to execute tasks that return results.

23.1 Introduction

It would be nice if we could focus our attention on performing only one action at a time and performing it well, but that is usually difficult to do. The human body performs a great variety of operations in parallel—or, as we will say throughout this chapter, concurrently. Respiration, blood circulation, digestion, thinking and walking, for example, can occur concurrently. All the senses—sight, touch, smell, taste and hearing—can be employed at once. Computers, too, can perform operations concurrently. It is common for personal computers to compile a program, send a file to a printer and receive electronic mail messages over a network concurrently. Only computers that have multiple processors can truly execute multiple instructions concurrently. Operating systems on single-processor computers create the illusion of concurrent execution by rapidly switching between activities, but on such computers only a single instruction can execute at once.

Most programming languages do not enable you to specify concurrent activities. Rather, the languages provide sequential control statements which enable you to specify that only one action at a time should be performed, with execution proceeding to the next action after the previous one has finished. Historically, concurrency has been implemented with operating system primitives available only to experienced systems programmers.

The Ada programming language, developed by the United States Department of Defense, made concurrency primitives widely available to defense contractors building military command-and-control systems. However, Ada has not been widely used in academia and industry.

Java makes concurrency available to you through the language and APIs. You specify that an application contains separate threads of execution, where each thread has its own method-call stack and program counter, allowing it to execute concurrently with other threads while sharing application-wide resources such as memory with these other threads. This capability, called multithreading, is not available in the core C and C++ languages, which influenced the design of Java.

Performance Tip 23.1

A problem with single-threaded applications that can lead to poor responsiveness is that lengthy activities must complete before others can begin. In a multithreaded application, threads can be distributed across multiple processors (if available) so that multiple tasks execute concurrently and the application can operate more efficiently. Multithreading can also increase performance on single-processor systems that simulate concurrency—when one thread cannot proceed (because, for example, it is waiting for the result of an I/O operation), another can use the processor.

Unlike languages that do not have built-in multithreading capabilities (such as C and C++) and must therefore make nonportable calls to operating system multithreading primitives, Java includes multithreading primitives as part of the language itself and as part of its libraries. This facilitates manipulating threads in a portable manner across platforms.

We'll discuss many applications of concurrent programming. For example, when downloading a large file (e.g., an image, an audio clip or a video clip) over the Internet, the user may not want to wait until the entire clip downloads before starting the playback. To solve this problem, we can put multiple threads to work—one to download the clip, and another to play it. These activities proceed concurrently. To avoid choppy playback, we synchronize (coordinate the actions of) the threads so that the player thread doesn't begin until there is a sufficient amount of the clip in memory to keep the player thread busy.

The Java Virtual Machine (JVM) uses threads as well. In addition to creating threads to run a program, the JVM also may create threads for performing housekeeping tasks such as garbage collection.

Writing multithreaded programs can be tricky. Although the human mind can perform functions concurrently, people find it difficult to jump between parallel trains of thought. To see why multithreaded programs can be difficult to write and understand, try the following experiment: Open three books to page 1, and try reading the books concurrently. Read a few words from the first book, then a few from the second, then a few from the third, then loop back and read the next few words from the first book, and so on. After this experiment, you will appreciate many of the challenges of multithreading—switching between the books, reading briefly, remembering your place in each book, moving the book you're reading closer so that you can see it and pushing the books you are not reading aside—and, amid all this chaos, trying to comprehend the content of the books!

Programming concurrent applications is a difficult and error-prone undertaking. If you find that you must use synchronization in a program, you should follow some simple guidelines. First, *use existing classes from the Java API* (such as the ArrayBlockingQueue class we discuss in Section 23.7, Producer/Consumer Relationship: ArrayBlockingQueue) *that manage synchronization for you*. The classes in the Java API are written by experts, have been fully tested and debugged, operate efficiently and help you avoid common traps and pitfalls. Second, if you find that you need more custom functionality than that provided in the Java APIs, you should use the synchronized keyword and Object methods wait, notify and `notifyAll` (discussed in Section 23.5 and Section 23.8). Finally, if you need even more complex capabilities, then you should use the `Lock` and `Condition` interfaces that are introduced in Section 23.10.

The `Lock` and `Condition` interfaces should be used only by advanced programmers who are familiar with the common traps and pitfalls of concurrent programming. We explain these topics in this chapter for several reasons—they provide a solid basis for understanding how concurrent applications synchronize access to shared memory; the concepts are important to understand, even if an application does not use these tools explicitly; and by showing you the complexity involved in using these low-level features, we hope to impress upon you the importance of using prepackaged concurrency capabilities whenever possible.

23.2 Thread States: Life Cycle of a Thread

At any time, a thread is said to be in one of several thread states—illustrated in the UML state diagram in Fig. 23.1. Several of the terms in the diagram are defined in later sections.

A new thread begins its life cycle in the *new* state. It remains in this state until the program starts the thread, which places it in the *runnable* state. A thread in the *runnable* state is considered to be executing its task.

Sometimes a *runnable* thread transitions to the *waiting* state while it waits for another thread to perform a task. A *waiting* thread transitions back to the *runnable* state only when another thread notifies the waiting thread to continue executing.

A *runnable* thread can enter the *timed waiting* state for a specified interval of time. It transitions back to the *runnable* state when that time interval expires or when the event it is waiting for occurs. *Timed waiting* and *waiting* threads cannot use a processor, even if one is available. A *runnable* thread can transition to the *timed waiting* state if it provides an optional wait interval when it is waiting for another thread to perform a task. Such a thread returns to the *runnable* state when it is notified by another thread or when the timed

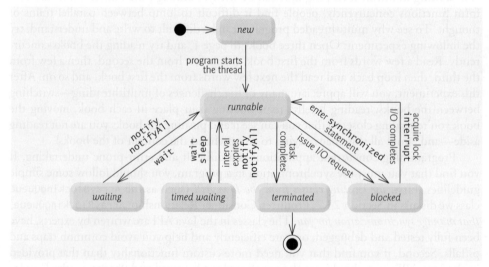

Fig. 23.1 | Thread life-cycle UML state diagram.

interval expires—whichever comes first. Another way to place a thread in the *timed waiting* state is to put a *runnable* thread to sleep. A sleeping thread remains in the *timed waiting* state for a designated period of time (called a sleep interval), after which it returns to the *runnable* state. Threads sleep when they momentarily do not have work to perform. For example, a word processor may contain a thread that periodically backs up (i.e., writes a copy of) the current document to disk for recovery purposes. If the thread did not sleep between successive backups, it would require a loop in which it continually tested whether it should write a copy of the document to disk. This loop would consume processor time without performing productive work, thus reducing system performance. In this case, it is more efficient for the thread to specify a sleep interval (equal to the period between successive backups) and enter the *timed waiting* state. This thread is returned to the *runnable* state when its sleep interval expires, at which point it writes a copy of the document to disk and reenters the *timed waiting* state.

A *runnable* thread transitions to the *blocked* state when it attempts to perform a task that cannot be completed immediately and it must temporarily wait until that task completes. For example, when a thread issues an input/output request, the operating system blocks the thread from executing until that I/O request completes—at that point, the *blocked* thread transitions to the *runnable* state, so it can resume execution. A *blocked* thread cannot use a processor, even if one is available.

A *runnable* thread enters the *terminated* state (sometimes called the *dead* state) when it successfully completes its task or otherwise terminates (perhaps due to an error). In the UML state diagram of Fig. 23.1, the *terminated* state is followed by the UML final state (the bull's-eye symbol) to indicate the end of the state transitions.

At the operating system level, Java's *runnable* state typically encompasses two separate states (Fig. 23.2). The operating system hides these states from the Java Virtual Machine (JVM), which sees only the *runnable* state. When a thread first transitions to the *runnable* state from the *new* state, the thread is in the *ready* state. A *ready* thread enters the *running* state (i.e., begins executing) when the operating system assigns the thread to a processor— also known as dispatching the thread. In most operating systems, each thread is given a small amount of processor time—called a quantum or timeslice—with which to perform its task. (Deciding how large the quantum should be is a key topic in operating systems courses.) When its quantum expires, the thread returns to the *ready* state and the operating system assigns another thread to the processor (see Section 23.3). Transitions between the *ready* and *running* states are handled solely by the operating system. The JVM does not "see" the transitions—it simply views the thread as being *runnable* and leaves it up to the operating system to transition the thread between *ready* and *running*. The process that an operating system uses to determine which thread to dispatch is called thread scheduling and is dependent on thread priorities (discussed in the next section).

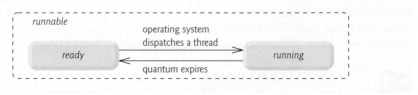

Fig. 23.2 | Operating system's internal view of Java's *runnable* state.

23.3 **Thread Priorities and Thread Scheduling**

Every Java thread has a thread priority that helps the operating system determine the order in which threads are scheduled. Java priorities range between MIN_PRIORITY (a constant of 1) and MAX_PRIORITY (a constant of 10). By default, every thread is given priority NORM_PRIORITY (a constant of 5). Each new thread inherits the priority of the thread that created it. Informally, higher-priority threads are more important to a program and should be allocated processor time before lower-priority threads. However, thread priorities cannot guarantee the order in which threads execute.

[*Note:* The constants (MAX_PRIORITY, MIN_PRIORITY and NORM_PRIORITY) are declared in the Thread class. It is recommended that you do not explicitly create and use Thread objects to implement concurrency, but rather use the Executor interface (which is described in Section 23.4.2). The Thread class contains some useful static methods, which we discuss later in the chapter.]

Most operating systems support timeslicing, which enables threads of equal priority to share a processor. Without timeslicing, each thread in a set of equal-priority threads runs to completion (unless it leaves the *runnable* state and enters the *waiting* or *timed waiting* state, or gets interrupted by a higher-priority thread) before other threads of equal priority get a chance to execute. With timeslicing, even if a thread has not finished executing when its quantum expires, the processor is taken away from the thread and given to the next thread of equal priority, if one is available.

An operating system's thread scheduler determines which thread runs next. One simple thread scheduler implementation keeps the highest-priority thread *running* at all times and, if there is more than one highest-priority thread, ensures that all such threads execute for a quantum each in round-robin fashion. Figure 23.3 illustrates a multilevel priority queue for threads. In the figure, assuming a single-processor computer, threads A and B each execute for a quantum in round-robin fashion until both threads complete execution. This means that A gets a quantum of time to run. Then B gets a quantum. Then A gets another quantum. Then B gets another quantum. This continues until one thread completes. The processor then devotes all its power to the thread that remains (unless another priority 10 thread becomes ready). Next, thread C runs to completion (assuming that no higher-priority threads arrive). Threads D, E and F each execute for a quantum in round-robin fashion until they all complete execution (again assuming that no higher-priority threads arrive). This process continues until all threads run to completion.

When a higher-priority thread enters the *ready* state, the operating system generally preempts the currently *running* thread (an operation known as preemptive scheduling). Depending on the operating system, higher-priority threads could postpone—possibly indefinitely—the execution of lower-priority threads. Such indefinite postponement is sometimes referred to more colorfully as starvation.

Java provides higher-level concurrency utilities to hide some of this complexity and make multithreaded programs less error prone. Thread priorities are used behind the scenes to interact with the operating system, but most programmers who use Java multithreading will not be concerned with setting and adjusting thread priorities.

Portability Tip 23.1

Thread scheduling is platform dependent—the behavior of a multithreaded program could vary across different Java implementations.

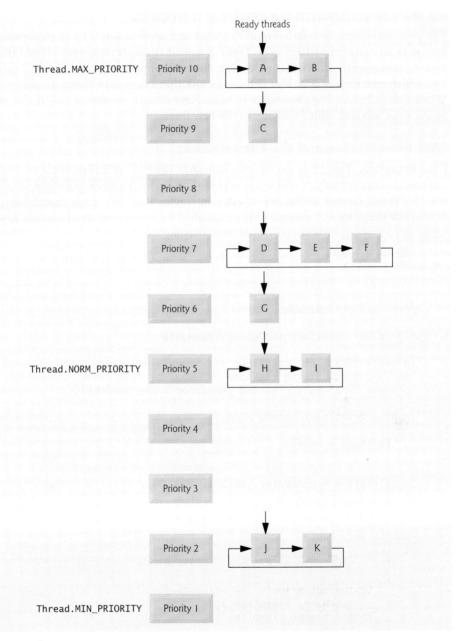

Fig. 23.3 | Thread-priority scheduling.

 Portability Tip 23.2

When designing multithreaded programs consider the threading capabilities of all the platforms on which the programs will execute. Using priorities other than the default will make your programs' behavior platform specific. If portability is your goal, don't adjust thread priorities.

23.4 Creating and Executing Threads

The preferred means of creating multithreaded Java applications is by implementing the Runnable interface (of package java.lang). A Runnable object represents a "task" that can execute concurrently with other tasks. The Runnable interface declares a single method, run, which contains the code that defines the task that a Runnable object should perform. When a thread executing a Runnable is created and started, the thread calls the Runnable object's run method, which executes in the new thread.

23.4.1 Runnables and the Thread Class

Class PrintTask (Fig. 23.4) implements Runnable (line 5), so that multiple PrintTasks can execute concurrently. Variable sleepTime (line 7) stores a random integer value from 0 to 5 seconds created in the PrintTask constructor (line 16). Each thread running a PrintTask sleeps for the amount of time specified by sleepTime, then outputs its task's name and a message indicating that it's done sleeping.

```java
1   // Fig. 23.4: PrintTask.java
2   // PrintTask class sleeps for a random time from 0 to 5 seconds
3   import java.util.Random;
4
5   public class PrintTask implements Runnable
6   {
7      private final int sleepTime; // random sleep time for thread
8      private final String taskName; // name of task
9      private final static Random generator = new Random();
10
11     public PrintTask( String name )
12     {
13        taskName = name; // set task name
14
15        // pick random sleep time between 0 and 5 seconds
16        sleepTime = generator.nextInt( 5000 ); // milliseconds
17     } // end PrintTask constructor
18
19     // method run contains the code that a thread will execute
20     public void run()
21     {
22        try // put thread to sleep for sleepTime amount of time
23        {
24           System.out.printf( "%s going to sleep for %d milliseconds.\n",
25              taskName, sleepTime );
26           Thread.sleep( sleepTime ); // put thread to sleep
27        } // end try
28        catch ( InterruptedException exception )
29        {
30           System.out.printf( "%s %s\n", taskName,
31              "terminated prematurely due to interruption" );
32        } // end catch
33
```

Fig. 23.4 | PrintTask class sleeps for a random time from 0 to 5 seconds. (Part 1 of 2.)

```
34              // print task name
35              System.out.printf( "%s done sleeping\n", taskName );
36          } // end method run
37      } // end class PrintTask
```

Fig. 23.4 | PrintTask class sleeps for a random time from 0 to 5 seconds. (Part 2 of 2.)

A PrintTask executes when a thread calls the PrintTask's run method. Lines 24–25 display a message indicating the name of the currently executing task and that the task is going to sleep for sleepTime milliseconds. Line 26 invokes static method sleep of class Thread to place the thread in the *timed waiting* state for the specified amount of time. At this point, the thread loses the processor, and the system allows another thread to execute. When the thread awakens, it reenters the *runnable* state. When the PrintTask is assigned to a processor again, line 35 outputs a message indicating that the task is done sleeping, then method run terminates. Note that the catch at lines 28–32 is required because method sleep might throw a (checked) InterruptedException if the sleeping thread's interrupt method is called.

Figure 23.5 creates Thread objects to execute PrintTasks. Lines 12–14 create three threads, each of which specifies a new PrintTask to execute. Lines 19–21 call Thread method start on each of the threads—each call invokes the corresponding Runnable's run method to execute the task. Line 23 outputs a message indicating that all of the threads' tasks have been started and that the main method is finished executing.

```
 1  // Fig. 23.5: ThreadCreator.java
 2  // Creating and starting three threads to execute Runnables.
 3  import java.lang.Thread;
 4
 5  public class ThreadCreator
 6  {
 7     public static void main( String[] args )
 8     {
 9        System.out.println( "Creating threads" );
10
11        // create each thread with a new targeted runnable
12        Thread thread1 = new Thread( new PrintTask( "task1" ) );
13        Thread thread2 = new Thread( new PrintTask( "task2" ) );
14        Thread thread3 = new Thread( new PrintTask( "task3" ) );
15
16        System.out.println( "Threads created, starting tasks." );
17
18        // start threads and place in runnable state
19        thread1.start(); // invokes task1's run method
20        thread2.start(); // invokes task2's run method
21        thread3.start(); // invokes task3's run method
22
23        System.out.println( "Tasks started, main ends.\n" );
24     } // end main
25  } // end class RunnableTester
```

Fig. 23.5 | Creating and starting three threads to execute Runnables. (Part 1 of 2.)

```
Creating threads
Threads created, starting tasks
Tasks started, main ends

task3 going to sleep for 491 milliseconds
task2 going to sleep for 71 milliseconds
task1 going to sleep for 3549 milliseconds
task2 done sleeping
task3 done sleeping
task1 done sleeping
```

```
Creating threads
Threads created, starting tasks
task1 going to sleep for 4666 milliseconds
task2 going to sleep for 48 milliseconds
task3 going to sleep for 3924 milliseconds
Tasks started, main ends

thread2 done sleeping
thread3 done sleeping
thread1 done sleeping
```

Fig. 23.5 | Creating and starting three threads to execute `Runnable`s. (Part 2 of 2.)

The code in method `main` executes in the **main thread**, a thread created by the JVM. The code in the `run` method of `PrintTask` (lines 20–36 of Fig. 23.4) executes in the threads created in lines 12–14 of Fig. 23.5. When method `main` terminates, the program itself continues running because there are still threads that are alive (i.e., any of the three threads we created that have not yet reached the *terminated* state). The program will not terminate until its last thread completes execution, at which point the JVM will also terminate.

The sample outputs for this program show each task's name and sleep time as the thread goes to sleep. The thread with the shortest sleep time normally awakens first, indicates that it's done sleeping and terminates. In Section 23.9, we discuss multithreading issues that could prevent the thread with the shortest sleep time from awakening first. In the first output, the main thread terminates before any of the other threads output their names and sleep times. This shows that the main thread runs to completion before any of the other threads get a chance to run. In the second output, all of the threads output their names and sleep times before the main thread terminates. This shows that the operating system allowed other threads to execute before the main thread terminated. This is an example of the round-robin scheduling we discussed in Section 23.3. Also notice that in the first example output, `task3` goes to sleep first and `task1` goes to sleep last, even though we started `task1`'s thread first. This illustrates the fact that we cannot predict the order in which threads will be scheduled, even if we know the order in which they were created and started. Finally, in each of the outputs, notice that the order in which the threads indicate that they are done sleeping matches the smallest to largest sleep times of the three threads. Although this is the reasonable and intuitive order for these threads to finish their tasks, the threads are not guaranteed to finish in this order.

23.4.2 Thread Management with the Executor Framework

Though it is possible to create threads explicitly as in Figure 23.5, it is recommended that you use the Executor interface to manage the execution of Runnable objects for you. An Executor object typically creates and manages a group of threads called a **thread pool** to execute Runnables. Using an Executor has many advantages over creating threads yourself. Executors can reuse existing threads to eliminate the overhead of creating a new thread for each task and can improve performance by optimizing the number of threads to ensure that the processor stays busy, without creating so many threads that the application runs out of resources.

The Executor interface declares a single method named **execute** which accepts a Runnable as an argument. The Executor assigns every Runnable passed to its execute method to one of the available threads in the thread pool. If there are no available threads, the Executor creates a new thread or waits for a thread to become available and assigns that thread the Runnable that was passed to method execute.

Interface **ExecutorService** (of package java.util.concurrent) is an interface that extends Executor and declares a number of other methods for managing the life cycle of an Executor. An object that implements the ExecutorService interface can be created using static methods declared in class Executors (of package java.util.concurrent). We use interface ExecutorService and a method of class **Executors** in the next application, which executes three tasks.

Figure 23.6 uses an ExecutorService object to manage threads that execute Print-Tasks. Method main (lines 8–29) creates and names three PrintTask objects (lines 11–13). Line 18 uses Executors method **newCachedThreadPool** to obtain an ExecutorService that creates new threads as they are needed by the application. These threads are used by threadExecutor to execute the Runnables.

```
1   // Fig. 23.6: TaskExecutor.java
2   // Using an ExecutorService to execute Runnables.
3   import java.util.concurrent.Executors;
4   import java.util.concurrent.ExecutorService;
5
6   public class TaskExecutor
7   {
8      public static void main( String[] args )
9      {
10        // create and name each runnable
11        PrintTask task1 = new PrintTask( "task1" );
12        PrintTask task2 = new PrintTask( "task2" );
13        PrintTask task3 = new PrintTask( "task3" );
14
15        System.out.println( "Starting Executor" );
16
17        // create ExecutorService to manage threads
18        ExecutorService threadExecutor = Executors.newCachedThreadPool();
19
20        // start threads and place in runnable state
21        threadExecutor.execute( task1 ); // start task1
```

Fig. 23.6 | Using an ExecutorService to execute Runnables. (Part 1 of 2.)

```
22        threadExecutor.execute( task2 ); // start task2
23        threadExecutor.execute( task3 ); // start task3
24
25        // shut down worker threads when their tasks complete
26        threadExecutor.shutdown();
27
28        System.out.println( "Tasks started, main ends.\n" );
29    } // end main
30 } // end class TaskExecutor
```

```
Starting Executor
Tasks started, main ends

task1 going to sleep for 4806 milliseconds
task2 going to sleep for 2513 milliseconds
task3 going to sleep for 1132 milliseconds
thread3 done sleeping
thread2 done sleeping
thread1 done sleeping
```

```
Starting Executor
task1 going to sleep for 1342 milliseconds
task2 going to sleep for 277 milliseconds
task3 going to sleep for 2737 milliseconds
Tasks started, main ends

task2 done sleeping
task1 done sleeping
task3 done sleeping
```

Fig. 23.6 | Using an ExecutorService to execute Runnables. (Part 2 of 2.)

Lines 21–23 each invoke the ExecutorService's execute method. This method executes the Runnable passed to it as an argument (in this case a PrintTask) some time in the future. The specified task may execute in one of the threads in the ExecutorService's thread pool, in a new thread created to execute it, or in the thread that called the execute method; the ExecutorService manages these details. Method execute returns immediately from each invocation—the program does not wait for each PrintTask to finish. Line 26 calls ExecutorService method **shutdown**, which notifies the ExecutorService to stop accepting new tasks, but continues executing tasks that have already been submitted. Once all of the previously submitted Runnables have completed, the threadExecutor terminates. Line 28 outputs a message indicating that the tasks were started and the main thread is finishing its execution. The sample outputs for this program are similar to those of the previous program and again demonstrate the nondeterminism of thread scheduling.

23.5 Thread Synchronization

When multiple threads share an object and that object is modified by one or more of the threads, indeterminate results may occur (as we will see in the examples) unless access to the shared object is managed properly. If one thread is in the process of updating a shared object and another thread also tries to update it, it is unclear which thread's update takes effect. When this happens, the program's behavior cannot be trusted—sometimes the program will produce the correct results, and sometimes it won't. In either case, there will be no indication that the shared object was manipulated incorrectly.

The problem can be solved by giving only one thread at a time *exclusive access* to code that manipulates the shared object. During that time, other threads desiring to manipulate the object are kept waiting. When the thread with exclusive access to the object finishes manipulating it, one of the threads that was waiting is allowed to proceed. This process, called thread synchronization, coordinates access to shared data by multiple concurrent threads. By synchronizing threads in this manner, you can ensure that each thread accessing a shared object excludes all other threads from doing so simultaneously—this is called mutual exclusion.

A common way to perform synchronization is to use Java's built-in monitors. Every object has a monitor and a monitor lock (or intrinsic lock). The monitor ensures that its object's monitor lock is held by a maximum of only one thread at any time. Monitors and monitor locks can thus be used to enforce mutual exclusion. If an operation requires the executing thread to hold a lock while the operation is performed, a thread must acquire the lock before proceeding with the operation. Other threads attempting to perform an operation that requires the same lock will be *blocked* until the first thread releases the lock, at which point the *blocked* threads may attempt to acquire the lock and proceed with the operation.

To specify that a thread must hold a monitor lock to execute a block of code, the code should be placed in a synchronized statement. Such code is said to be guarded by the monitor lock; a thread must acquire the lock to execute the synchronized statements. The monitor allows only one thread at a time to execute statements within synchronized blocks that lock on the same object, as only one thread at a time can hold the monitor lock. The synchronized statements are declared using the synchronized keyword:

```
synchronized ( object )
{
    statements
} // end synchronized statement
```

where *object* is the object whose monitor lock will be acquired; *object* is normally this if it is the object in which the synchronized statement appears. If several synchronized statements are trying to execute on an object at the same time, only one of them may be active on the object—all the other threads attempting to enter a synchronized statement on the same object are placed in the *blocked* state.

When a synchronized statement finishes executing, the object's monitor lock is released and the operating system can allow one of the *blocked* threads attempting to enter a synchronized statement to acquire the lock to proceed. Java also allows synchronized methods. Such a method is equivalent to a synchronized statement enclosing the entire body of a method and using this as the object whose monitor lock will be acquired. You can specify a method as synchronized by placing the synchronized keyword before the method's return type in the method declaration.

23.5.1 Unsynchronized Data Sharing

We now present an example to illustrate the dangers of sharing an object across threads without proper synchronization. In this example, two Runnables maintain references to a single integer array. Each `Runnable` writes five values to the array, then terminates. This may seem harmless, but it can result in errors if the array is manipulated without synchronization.

Class SimpleArray

An object of class `SimpleArray` (Fig. 23.7) will be shared across multiple threads. `SimpleArray` will enable those threads to place `int` values into `array` (declared at line 7). Line 8 initializes variable `writeIndex`, which will be used to determine the array element that should be written to next. The constructor (lines 12–15) creates an integer array of the desired size.

```java
1   // Fig. 23.7: SimpleArray.java
2   // Class that manages an integer array to be shared by multiple threads.
3   import java.util.Random;
4
5   public class SimpleArray // CAUTION: NOT THREAD SAFE!
6   {
7      private final int array[]; // the shared integer array
8      private int writeIndex = 0; // index of next element to be written
9      private final static Random generator = new Random();
10
11     // construct a SimpleArray of a given size
12     public SimpleArray( int size )
13     {
14        array = new int[ size ];
15     } // end constructor
16
17     // add a value to the shared array
18     public void add( int value )
19     {
20        int position = writeIndex; // store the write index
21
22        try
23        {
24           // put thread to sleep for 0-499 milliseconds
25           Thread.sleep( generator.nextInt( 500 ) );
26        } // end try
27        catch ( InterruptedException ex )
28        {
29           ex.printStackTrace();
30        } // end catch
31
32        // put value in the appropriate element
33        array[ position ] = value;
34        System.out.printf( "%s wrote %2d to element %d.\n",
35           Thread.currentThread().getName(), value, position );
36
37        ++writeIndex; // increment index of element to be written next
38        System.out.printf( "Next write index: %d\n", writeIndex );
39     } // end method add
40
```

Fig. 23.7 | Class that manages an integer array to be shared by multiple threads. (Part 1 of 2.)

```
41        // used for outputting the contents of the shared integer array
42        public String toString()
43        {
44            String arrayString = "\nContents of SimpleArray:\n";
45
46            for ( int i = 0; i < array.length; i++ )
47                arrayString += array[ i ] + " ";
48
49            return arrayString;
50        } // end method toString
51    } // end class SimpleArray
```

Fig. 23.7 | Class that manages an integer array to be shared by multiple threads. (Part 2 of 2.)

Method add (lines 18–39) allows new values to be inserted at the end of the array. Line 20 stores the current writeIndex value. Line 25 puts the thread that invokes add to sleep for a random interval from 0 to 499 milliseconds. This is done to make the problems associated with unsynchronized access to shared data more obvious. After the thread is done sleeping, line 33 inserts the value passed to add into the array at the element specified by position. Lines 34–35 output a message indicating the executing thread's name, the value that was inserted in the array and where it was inserted. Line 37 increments writeIndex so that the next call to add will insert a value in the array's next element. Lines 42–50 override method toString to create a String representation of the array's contents.

Class *ArrayWriter*

Class ArrayWriter (Fig. 23.8) implements the interface Runnable to define a task for inserting values in a SimpleArray object. The constructor (lines 10–14) takes two arguments—an integer value, which is the first value this task will insert in the SimpleArray object, and a reference to the SimpleArray object. Line 20 invokes method add on the SimpleArray object. The task completes after three consecutive integers beginning with startValue are added to the SimpleArray object.

```
1    // Fig. 23.8: ArrayWriter.java
2    // Adds integers to an array shared with other Runnables
3    import java.lang.Runnable;
4
5    public class ArrayWriter implements Runnable
6    {
7        private final SimpleArray sharedSimpleArray;
8        private final int startValue;
9
10       public ArrayWriter( int value, SimpleArray array )
11       {
12           startValue = value;
13           sharedSimpleArray = array;
14       } // end constructor
15
```

Fig. 23.8 | Adds integers to an array shared with other Runnables. (Part 1 of 2.)

```
16      public void run()
17      {
18         for ( int i = startValue; i < startValue + 3; i++ )
19         {
20            sharedSimpleArray.add( i ); // add an element to the shared array
21         } // end for
22      } // end method run
23   } // end class ArrayWriter
```

Fig. 23.8 | Adds integers to an array shared with other Runnables. (Part 2 of 2.)

Class *SharedArrayTest*

Class SharedArrayTest executes two ArrayWriter tasks that add values to a single SimpleArray object. Line 12 constructs a six-element SimpleArray object. Lines 15–16 create two new ArrayWriter tasks, one that places the values 1–3 in the SimpleArray object, and one that places the values 11–13. Lines 19–21 create an ExecutorService and execute the two ArrayWriters. Line 23 invokes the ExecutorService's shutDown method to prevent additional tasks from starting and to enable the application to terminate when the currently executing tasks complete execution.

```
1    // Fig 23.9: SharedArrayTest.java
2    // Executes two Runnables to add elements to a shared SimpleArray.
3    import java.util.concurrent.Executors;
4    import java.util.concurrent.ExecutorService;
5    import java.util.concurrent.TimeUnit;
6
7    public class SharedArrayTest
8    {
9       public static void main( String[] arg )
10      {
11         // construct the shared object
12         SimpleArray sharedSimpleArray = new SimpleArray( 6 );
13
14         // create two tasks to write to the shared SimpleArray
15         ArrayWriter writer1 = new ArrayWriter( 1, sharedSimpleArray );
16         ArrayWriter writer2 = new ArrayWriter( 11, sharedSimpleArray );
17
18         // execute the tasks with an ExecutorService
19         ExecutorService executor = Executors.newCachedThreadPool();
20         executor.execute( writer1 );
21         executor.execute( writer2 );
22
23         executor.shutdown();
24
25         try
26         {
27            // wait 1 minute for both writers to finish executing
28            boolean tasksEnded = executor.awaitTermination(
29               1, TimeUnit.MINUTES );
30
```

Fig. 23.9 | Executes two Runnables to insert values in a shared array. (Part 1 of 2.)

```
31          if ( tasksEnded )
32              System.out.println( sharedSimpleArray ); // print contents
33          else
34              System.out.println(
35                  "Timed out while waiting for tasks to finish." );
36      } // end try
37      catch ( InterruptedException ex )
38      {
39          System.out.println(
40              "Interrupted while wait for tasks to finish." );
41      } // end catch
42   } // end main
43 } // end class SharedArrayTest
```

```
pool-1-thread-1 wrote  1 to element 0.
Next write index: 1
pool-1-thread-1 wrote  2 to element 1.
Next write index: 2
pool-1-thread-1 wrote  3 to element 2.
Next write index: 3
pool-1-thread-2 wrote 11 to element 0.
Next write index: 4
pool-1-thread-2 wrote 12 to element 4.
Next write index: 5
pool-1-thread-2 wrote 13 to element 5.
Next write index: 6

Contents of SimpleArray:
11 2 3 0 12 13
```

First `pool-1-thread-1` wrote the value 1 to element 0. Later `pool-1-thread-2` wrote the value 11 to element 0, thus overwriting the previously stored value.

Fig. 23.9 | Executes two `Runnable`s to insert values in a shared array. (Part 2 of 2.)

Recall that `ExecutorService` method `shutdown` returns immediately. Thus any code that appears after the call to `ExecutorService` method `shutdown` in line 23 will continue executing as long as the `main` thread is still assigned to a processor. We'd like to output the `SimpleArray` object to show you the results *after* the threads complete their tasks. So, we need the program to wait for the threads to complete before `main` outputs the `SimpleArray` object's contents. Interface `ExecutorService` provides the `awaitTermination` method for this purpose. This method returns control to its caller either when all tasks executing in the `ExecutorService` complete or when the specified timeout elapses. If all tasks are completed before `awaitTermination` times out, this method returns `true`; otherwise it returns `false`. The two arguments to `awaitTermination` represent a timeout value and a unit of measure specified with a constant from class `TimeUnit` (in this case, `TimeUnit.MINUTES`). In this example, if both tasks complete before `awaitTermination` times out, line 32 displays the `SimpleArray` object's contents. Otherwise, lines 34–35 print a message indicating that the tasks did not finish executing before `awaitTermination` timed out.

The output in Fig. 23.9 demonstrates the problems (highlighted in the output) that can be caused by failure to synchronize access to shared data. The value 1 was written to element 0, then overwritten later by the value 11. Also, when `writeIndex` was incremented to 3, nothing was written to that element, as indicated by the 0 in that element of the printed array.

Recall that we have added calls to Thread method sleep between operations on the shared data to emphasize the unpredictability of thread scheduling and increase the likelihood of producing erroneous output. It is important to note that even if these operations were allowed to proceed at their normal pace, you could still see errors in the program's output. However, modern processors can handle the simple operations of the Simple-Array method add so quickly that you might not see the errors caused by the two threads executing this method concurrently, even if you tested the program dozens of times. One of the challenges of multithreaded programming is spotting the errors—they may occur so infrequently that a broken program does not produce incorrect results during testing, creating the illusion that the program is correct.

23.5.2 Synchronized Data Sharing—Making Operations Atomic

The output errors of Fig. 23.9 can be attributed to the fact that the shared object, Simple-Array, is not thread safe—SimpleArray is susceptible to errors if it is accessed concurrently by multiple threads. The problem lies in method add, which stores the value of writeIndex, places a new value in that element, then increments writeIndex. Such a method would present no problem in a single-threaded program. However, if one thread obtains the value of writeIndex, there is no guarantee that another thread cannot come along and increment writeIndex before the first thread has had a chance to place a value in the array. If this happens, the first thread will be writing to the array based on a stale value of writeIndex—a value that is no longer valid. Another possibility is that one thread might obtain the value of writeIndex after another thread adds an element to the array but before writeIndex is incremented. In this case, too, the first thread would write to the array based on an invalid value for writeIndex.

SimpleArray is not thread safe because it allows any number of threads to read and modify shared data concurrently, which can cause errors. To make SimpleArray thread safe, we must ensure that no two threads can access it at the same time. We also must ensure that while one thread is in the process of storing writeIndex, adding a value to the array, and incrementing writeIndex, no other thread may read or change the value of writeIndex or modify the contents of the array at any point during these three operations. In other words, we want these three operations—storing writeIndex, writing to the array, incrementing writeIndex—to be an atomic operation, which cannot be divided into smaller suboperations. While no processor can carry out all three stages of the add method in a single clock cycle to make the operation truly atomic, we can simulate atomicity by ensuring that only one thread carries out the three operations at a time. Any other threads that need to perform the operation must wait until the first thread has finished the add operation in its entirety.

Atomicity can be achieved using the synchronized keyword. By placing our three suboperations in a synchronized statement or synchronized method, only one thread at a time will be allowed to acquire the lock and perform the operations. When that thread has completed all of the operations in the synchronized block and releases the lock, another thread may acquire the lock and begin executing the operations. This ensures that a thread executing the operations will see the actual values of the shared data and that these values will not change unexpectedly in the middle of the operations as a result of another thread's modifying them.

Software Engineering Observation 23.1

Place all accesses to mutable data that may be shared by multiple threads inside synchronized statements or synchronized methods that synchronize on the same lock. When performing multiple operations on shared data, hold the lock for the entirety of the operation to ensure that the operation is effectively atomic.

Figure 23.10 displays class `SimpleArray` with the proper synchronization. Notice that it's identical to the `SimpleArray` class of Fig. 23.7, except that add is now a `synchronized` method (line 19). So, only one thread at a time can execute this method. We reuse classes `ArrayWriter` (Fig. 23.8) and `SharedArrayTest` (Fig. 23.9) from the previous example.

```java
 1   // Fig. 23.10: SimpleArray.java
 2   // Class that manages an integer array to be shared by multiple threads.
 3   import java.util.Random;
 4
 5   public class SimpleArray
 6   {
 7      private final int array[]; // the shared integer array
 8      private int writeIndex = 0; // index of next element to be written
 9      private final static Random generator = new Random();
10
11      // construct a SimpleArray of a given size
12      public SimpleArray( int size )
13      {
14         array = new int[ size ];
15      } // end constructor
16
17      // add a value to the shared array
18      public synchronized void add( int value )
19      {
20         int position = writeIndex; // store the write index
21
22         try
23         {
24            // put thread to sleep for 0-499 milliseconds
25            Thread.sleep( generator.nextInt( 500 ) );
26         } // end try
27         catch ( InterruptedException ex )
28         {
29            ex.printStackTrace();
30         } // end catch
31
32         // put value in the appropriate element
33         array[ position ] = value;
34         System.out.printf( "%s wrote %2d to element %d.\n",
35            Thread.currentThread().getName(), value, position );
36
37         ++writeIndex; // increment index of element to be written next
38         System.out.printf( "Next write index: %d\n", writeIndex );
39      } // end method add
```

Fig. 23.10 | Class that manages an integer array to be shared by multiple threads with synchronization. (Part 1 of 2.)

```
40
41      // used for outputting the contents of the shared integer array
42      public String toString()
43      {
44         String arrayString = "\nContents of SimpleArray:\n";
45
46         for ( int i = 0; i < array.length; i++ )
47            arrayString += array[ i ] + " ";
48
49         return arrayString;
50      } // end method toString
51   } // end class SimpleArray
```

```
pool-1-thread-1 wrote  1 to element 0.
Next write index: 1
pool-1-thread-2 wrote 11 to element 1.
Next write index: 2
pool-1-thread-2 wrote 12 to element 2.
Next write index: 3
pool-1-thread-2 wrote 13 to element 3.
Next write index: 4
pool-1-thread-1 wrote  2 to element 4.
Next write index: 5
pool-1-thread-1 wrote  3 to element 5.
Next write index: 6

Contents of SimpleArray:
1 11 12 13 2 3
```

Fig. 23.10 | Class that manages an integer array to be shared by multiple threads with synchronization. (Part 2 of 2.)

Line 18 declares method as synchronized, making all of the operations in this method behave as a single, atomic operation. Line 20 performs the first suboperation—storing the value of writeIndex. Line 33 defines the second suboperation, writing an element to the element at the index position. Line 37 increments writeIndex. When the method finishes executing at line 39, the executing thread releases the SimpleArray lock, making it possible for another thread to begin executing the add method.

In the synchronized add method, we print messages to the console indicating the progress of threads as they execute this method, in addition to performing the actual operations required to insert a value in the array. We do this so that the messages will be printed in the correct order, allowing you to see whether the method is properly synchronized by comparing these outputs with those of the previous, unsynchronized example. We continue to output messages from synchronized blocks in later examples for demonstration purposes; typically, however, I/O *should not* be performed in synchronized blocks, because it's important to minimize the amount of time that an object is "locked."

Performance Tip 23.2

Keep the duration of synchronized statements as short as possible while maintaining the needed synchronization. This minimizes the wait time for blocked threads. Avoid performing I/O, lengthy calculations and operations that do not require synchronization with a lock held.

Another note on thread safety: We have said that it is necessary to synchronize access to all data that may be shared across multiple threads. Actually, this synchronization is necessary only for mutable data, or data that may change in its lifetime. If the shared data will not change in a multithreaded program, then it is not possible for a thread to see old or incorrect values as a result of another thread's manipulating that data.

When you share immutable data across threads, declare the corresponding data fields final to indicate that variables' values will not change after they are initialized. This prevents accidental modification of the shared data later in a program, which could compromise thread safety. Labeling object references as final indicates that the reference will not change, but it does not guarantee that the object itself is immutable—this depends entirely on the properties of the object. However, it is still good practice to mark references that will not change as final, as doing so forces the object's constructor to be atomic—the object will be fully constructed with all its fields initialized before it is accessed by the program.

Good Programming Practice 23.1

Always declare data fields that you do not expect to change as final. Primitive variables that are declared as final can safely be shared across threads. An object reference that is declared as final ensures that the object it refers to will be fully constructed and initialized before it is used by the program and prevents the reference from pointing to another object.

23.6 Producer/Consumer Relationship without Synchronization

In a producer/consumer relationship, the producer portion of an application generates data and stores it in a shared object, and the consumer portion of an application reads data from the shared object. The producer/consumer relationship separates the task of identifying work to be done from the tasks involved in actually carrying out the work. One example of a common producer/consumer relationship is print spooling. Although a printer might not be available when you want to print from an application (i.e., the producer), you can still "complete" the print task, as the data is temporarily placed on disk until the printer becomes available. Similarly, when the printer (i.e., a consumer) is available, it doesn't have to wait until a current user wants to print. The spooled print jobs can be printed as soon as the printer becomes available. Another example of the producer/consumer relationship is an application that copies data onto CDs by placing data in a fixed-size buffer, which is emptied as the CD-RW drive "burns" the data onto the CD.

In a multithreaded producer/consumer relationship, a producer thread generates data and places it in a shared object called a buffer. A consumer thread reads data from the buffer. This relationship requires synchronization to ensure that values are produced and consumed properly. All operations on mutable data that is shared by multiple threads (e.g., the data in the buffer) must be guarded with a lock to prevent corruption, as discussed in Section 23.5. Operations on the buffer data shared by a producer and consumer thread are also state dependent—the operations should proceed only if the buffer is in the correct state. If the buffer is in a not-full state, the producer may produce; if the buffer is in a not-empty state, the consumer may consume. All operations that access the buffer must use synchronization to ensure that data is written to the buffer or read from the buffer only if the buffer is in the proper state. If the producer attempting to put the next data into the buffer determines that it is full, the producer thread should wait until there is space to write a new value. If a consumer thread finds the buffer empty or finds that the previous data has already been read, the consumer must also wait for new data to become available.

Consider how logic errors can arise if we do not synchronize access among multiple threads manipulating shared data. Our next example (Fig. 23.11–Fig. 23.15) implements a producer/consumer relationship without the proper synchronization. A producer thread writes the numbers 1 through 10 into a shared buffer—a single memory location shared between two threads (a single int variable called buffer in line 6 of Fig. 23.14 in this example). The consumer thread reads this data from the shared buffer and displays the data. The program's output shows the values that the producer writes (produces) into the shared buffer and the values that the consumer reads (consumes) from the shared buffer.

Each value the producer thread writes to the shared buffer must be consumed exactly once by the consumer thread. However, the threads in this example erroneously are not synchronized. Therefore, data can be lost or garbled if the producer places new data into the shared buffer before the consumer reads the previous data. Also, data can be incorrectly duplicated if the consumer consumes data again before the producer produces the next value. To show these possibilities, the consumer thread in the following example keeps a total of all the values it reads. The producer thread produces values from 1 through 10. If the consumer reads each value produced once and only once, the total will be 55. However, if you execute this program several times, you will see that the total is not always 55 (as shown in the outputs in Fig. 23.10). To emphasize the point, the producer and consumer threads in the example each sleep for random intervals of up to three seconds between performing their tasks. Thus, we do not know when the producer thread will attempt to write a new value, or when the consumer thread will attempt to read a value.

The program consists of interface Buffer (Fig. 23.11) and four classes—Producer (Fig. 23.12), Consumer (Fig. 23.13), UnsynchronizedBuffer (Fig. 23.14) and Shared-BufferTest (Fig. 23.15). Interface Buffer declares methods set (line 6) and get (line 9) that a Buffer must implement to enable the Producer thread to place a value in the Buffer and the Consumer thread to retrieve a value from the Buffer, respectively. Some programmers prefer to call these methods put and take, respectively. In subsequent examples, methods set and get will call methods that throw InterruptedExceptions. We declare each method with a throws clause here so that we don't have to modify this interface for the later examples Figure 23.14 shows the implementation of this interface.

Class Producer (Fig. 23.12) implements the Runnable interface, allowing it to be executed as a task in a separate thread. The constructor (lines 11–14) initializes the Buffer reference sharedLocation with an object created in main (line 14 of Fig. 23.15) and

```
1    // Fig. 23.11: Buffer.java
2    // Buffer interface specifies methods called by Producer and Consumer.
3    public interface Buffer
4    {
5        // place int value into Buffer
6        public void set( int value ) throws InterruptedException;
7
8        // return int value from Buffer
9        public int get() throws InterruptedException;
10   } // end interface Buffer
```

Fig. 23.11 | Buffer interface specifies methods called by Producer and Consumer.

passed to the constructor in the parameter shared. As we will see, this is an Unsynchro-nizedBuffer object that implements the interface Buffer without synchronizing access to the shared object. The Producer thread in this program executes the tasks specified in the method run (lines 17–39). Each iteration of the loop (lines 21–35) invokes Thread method sleep (line 25) to place the Producer thread into the *timed waiting* state for a random time interval between 0 and 3 seconds. When the thread awakens, line 26 passes the value of control variable count to the Buffer object's set method to set the shared buffer's value. Line 27 keeps a total of all the values produced so far and line 28 outputs that value. When the loop completes, lines 37–38 display a message indicating that the Producer has finished producing data and is terminating. Next, method run terminates, which indicates that the Producer completed its task. It is important to note that any method called from a Runnable's run method (e.g., Buffer method set) executes as part of that task's thread of execution. This fact becomes important in Section 23.7 when we add synchronization to the producer/consumer relationship.

```java
1   // Fig. 23.12: Producer.java
2   // Producer with a run method that inserts the values 1 to 10 in buffer.
3   import java.util.Random;
4
5   public class Producer implements Runnable
6   {
7      private final static Random generator = new Random();
8      private final Buffer sharedLocation; // reference to shared object
9
10     // constructor
11     public Producer( Buffer shared )
12     {
13        sharedLocation = shared;
14     } // end Producer constructor
15
16     // store values from 1 to 10 in sharedLocation
17     public void run()
18     {
19        int sum = 0;
20
21        for ( int count = 1; count <= 10; count++ )
22        {
23           try // sleep 0 to 3 seconds, then place value in Buffer
24           {
25              Thread.sleep( generator.nextInt( 3000 ) ); // random sleep
26              sharedLocation.set( count ); // set value in buffer
27              sum += count; // increment sum of values
28              System.out.printf( "\t%2d\n", sum );
29           } // end try
30           // if lines 25 or 26 get interrupted, print stack trace
31           catch ( InterruptedException exception )
32           {
33              exception.printStackTrace();
34           } // end catch
35        } // end for
```

Fig. 23.12 | Producer with a run method that inserts the values 1 to 10 in buffer. (Part 1 of 2.)

```
36
37          System.out.println(
38             "Producer done producing\nTerminating Producer" );
39       } // end method run
40    } // end class Producer
```

Fig. 23.12 | Producer with a run method that inserts the values I to 10 in buffer. (Part 2 of 2.)

Class Consumer (Fig. 23.13) also implements interface Runnable, allowing the Consumer to execute concurrently with the Producer. The constructor (lines 11–14) initializes Buffer reference sharedLocation with an object that implements the Buffer interface created in main (Fig. 23.15) and passed to the constructor as the parameter shared. As we will see, this is the same UnsynchronizedBuffer object that is used to initialize the Producer object—thus, the two threads share the same object. The Consumer thread in this program performs the tasks specified in method run (lines 17–39). The loop at lines 21–35 iterates 10 times. Each iteration invokes Thread method sleep (line 26) to put the Consumer thread into the *timed waiting* state for up to 3 seconds. Next, line 27 uses the Buffer's get method to retrieve the value in the shared buffer, then adds the value to variable sum. Line 28 displays the total of all the values consumed so far. When the loop completes, lines 37–38 display a line indicating the sum of the consumed values. Then method run terminates, which indicates that the Consumer completed its task. Once both threads enter the *terminated* state, the program ends.

```
 1    // Fig. 23.13: Consumer.java
 2    // Consumer with a run method that loops, reading 10 values from buffer.
 3    import java.util.Random;
 4
 5    public class Consumer implements Runnable
 6    {
 7       private final static Random generator = new Random();
 8       private final Buffer sharedLocation; // reference to shared object
 9
10       // constructor
11       public Consumer( Buffer shared )
12       {
13          sharedLocation = shared;
14       } // end Consumer constructor
15
16       // read sharedLocation's value 10 times and sum the values
17       public void run()
18       {
19          int sum = 0;
20
21          for ( int count = 1; count <= 10; count++ )
22          {
23             // sleep 0 to 3 seconds, read value from buffer and add to sum
24             try
25             {
26                Thread.sleep( generator.nextInt( 3000 ) );
```

Fig. 23.13 | Consumer with a run method that loops, reading 10 values from buffer. (Part 1 of 2.)

```
27                    sum += sharedLocation.get();
28                    System.out.printf( "\t\t\t%2d\n", sum );
29                } // end try
30                // if lines 26 or 27 get interrupted, print stack trace
31                catch ( InterruptedException exception )
32                {
33                    exception.printStackTrace();
34                } // end catch
35            } // end for
36
37            System.out.printf( "\n%s %d\n%s\n",
38                "Consumer read values totaling", sum, "Terminating Consumer" );
39        } // end method run
40    } // end class Consumer
```

Fig. 23.13 | Consumer with a `run` method that loops, reading 10 values from buffer. (Part 2 of 2.)

[*Note:* We call method `sleep` in method `run` of the Producer and Consumer classes to emphasize the fact that in multithreaded applications, it is unpredictable when each thread will perform its task and for how long it will perform the task when it has a processor. Normally, these thread scheduling issues are the job of the computer's operating system, beyond the control of the Java developer. In this program, our thread's tasks are quite simple—the Producer writes the values 1 to 10 to the buffer, and the Consumer reads 10 values from the buffer and adds each value to variable `sum`. Without the `sleep` method call, and if the Producer executes first, given today's phenomenally fast processors, the Producer would likely complete its task before the Consumer got a chance to execute. If the Consumer executed first, it would likely consume garbage data ten times, then terminate before the Producer could produce the first real value.]

Class `UnsynchronizedBuffer` (Fig. 23.14) implements interface `Buffer` (line 4). An object of this class is shared between the Producer and the Consumer. Line 6 declares instance variable `buffer` and initializes it with the value –1. This value is used to demonstrate the case in which the Consumer attempts to consume a value before the Producer ever places a value in `buffer`. Methods `set` (lines 9–13) and `get` (lines 16–20) do not synchronize access to the field `buffer`. Method `set` simply assigns its argument to `buffer` (line 12), and method `get` simply returns the value of `buffer` (line 19).

```
1   // Fig. Fig. 23.14: UnsynchronizedBuffer.java
2   // UnsynchronizedBuffer maintains the shared integer that is accessed by
3   // a producer thread and a consumer thread via methods set and get.
4   public class UnsynchronizedBuffer implements Buffer
5   {
6       private int buffer = -1; // shared by producer and consumer threads
7
8       // place value into buffer
9       public void set( int value ) throws InterruptedException
10      {
11          System.out.printf( "Producer writes\t%2d", value );
```

Fig. 23.14 | `UnsynchronizedBuffer` maintains the shared integer that is accessed by a producer thread and a consumer thread via methods `set` and `get`. (Part 1 of 2.)

```
12          buffer = value;
13      } // end method set
14
15      // return value from buffer
16      public int get() throws InterruptedException
17      {
18          System.out.printf( "Consumer reads\t%2d", buffer );
19          return buffer;
20      } // end method get
21  } // end class UnsynchronizedBuffer
```

Fig. 23.14 | `UnsynchronizedBuffer` maintains the shared integer that is accessed by a producer thread and a consumer thread via methods `set` and `get`. (Part 2 of 2.)

Class `SharedBufferTest` contains method `main` (lines 9–25). Line 11 creates an `ExecutorService` to execute the Producer and Consumer `Runnable`s. Line 14 creates an `UnsynchronizedBuffer` object and assigns it to `Buffer` variable `sharedLocation`. This object stores the data that the Producer and Consumer threads will share. Lines 23–24 create and execute the Producer and Consumer. Note that the Producer and Consumer constructors are each passed the same `Buffer` object (`sharedLocation`), so each object is initialized with a reference to the same `Buffer`. These lines also implicitly launch the threads and call each `Runnable`'s run method. Finally, line 26 calls method `shutdown` so that the application can terminate when the threads executing the Producer and Consumer complete their tasks. When `main` terminates (line 27), the main thread of execution enters the *terminated* state. Recall from the overview of this example that we would like the Producer to execute first and every value produced by the Producer to be consumed exactly once by the Consumer. However, when we study the first output of Fig. 23.15, we see that the Producer writes the values 1, 2 and 3 before the Consumer reads its first value (3). Therefore, the values 1 and 2 are lost. Later, the values 5, 6 and 9 are lost, while 7 and 8 are read twice and 10 is read four times. So the first output produces an incorrect total of 77, instead of the correct total of 55. In the second output, the Consumer reads the value -1 before the Producer ever writes a value. The Consumer reads the value 1 five times before the Producer writes the value 2. Meanwhile, the values 5, 7, 8, 9 and 10 are all lost—the last four because the Consumer terminates before the Producer. An incorrect consumer total of 19 is displayed. (Lines in the output where the Producer or Consumer has acted out of order are highlighted.) This example clearly demonstrates that access to a shared object by concurrent threads must be controlled carefully or a program may produce incorrect results.

To solve the problems of lost and duplicated data, Section 23.7 presents an example in which we use an `ArrayBlockingQueue` (from package `java.util.concurrent`) to synchronize access to the shared object, guaranteeing that each and every value will be processed once and only once.

```
1   // Fig. 23.15: SharedBufferTest.java
2   // Application with two threads manipulating an unsynchronized buffer.
3   import java.util.concurrent.ExecutorService;
4   import java.util.concurrent.Executors;
```

Fig. 23.15 | Application with two threads manipulating an unsynchronized buffer. (Part 1 of 3.)

```
5
6    public class SharedBufferTest
7    {
8       public static void main( String[] args )
9       {
10          // create new thread pool with two threads
11          ExecutorService application = Executors.newCachedThreadPool();
12
13          // create UnsynchronizedBuffer to store ints
14          Buffer sharedLocation = new UnsynchronizedBuffer();
15
16          System.out.println(
17             "Action\t\tValue\tSum of Produced\tSum of Consumed" );
18          System.out.println(
19             "------\t\t-----\t---------------\t---------------\n" );
20
21          // execute the Producer and Consumer, giving each of them access
22          // to sharedLocation
23          application.execute( new Producer( sharedLocation ) );
24          application.execute( new Consumer( sharedLocation ) );
25
26          application.shutdown(); // terminate application when tasks complete
27       } // end main
28    } // end class SharedBufferTest
```

Action	Value	Sum of Produced	Sum of Consumed	
Producer writes	1	1		
Producer writes	2	3		—— 1 is lost
Producer writes	3	6		—— 2 is lost
Consumer reads	3		3	
Producer writes	4	10		
Consumer reads	4		7	
Producer writes	5	15		
Producer writes	6	21		—— 5 is lost
Producer writes	7	28		—— 6 is lost
Consumer reads	7		14	
Consumer reads	7		21	—— 7 read again
Producer writes	8	36		
Consumer reads	8		29	
Consumer reads	8		37	—— 8 read again
Producer writes	9	45		
Producer writes	10	55		—— 9 is lost
Producer done producing				
Terminating Producer				
Consumer reads	10		47	
Consumer reads	10		57	—— 10 read again
Consumer reads	10		67	—— 10 read again
Consumer reads	10		77	—— 10 read again
Consumer read values totaling 77				
Terminating Consumer				

Fig. 23.15 | Application with two threads manipulating an unsynchronized buffer. (Part 2 of 3.)

```
Action           Value   Sum of Produced Sum of Consumed
------           -----   --------------- ---------------

Consumer reads   -1                      -1 ---- reads -1 bad data
Producer writes   1        1
Consumer reads    1                       0
Consumer reads    1                       1 ---- I read again
Consumer reads    1                       2 ---- I read again
Consumer reads    1                       3 ---- I read again
Consumer reads    1                       4 ---- I read again
Producer writes   2        3
Consumer reads    2                       6
Producer writes   3        6
Consumer reads    3                       9
Producer writes   4       10
Consumer reads    4                      13
Producer writes   5       15
Producer writes   6       21              ---- 5 is lost
Consumer reads    6                      19

Consumer read values totaling 19
Terminating Consumer
Producer writes   7       28              ---- 7 never read
Producer writes   8       36              ---- 8 never read
Producer writes   9       45              ---- 9 never read
Producer writes  10       55              ---- 10 never read

Producer done producing
Terminating Producer
```

Fig. 23.15 | Application with two threads manipulating an unsynchronized buffer. (Part 3 of 3.)

23.7 Producer/Consumer Relationship: ArrayBlockingQueue

One way to synchronize producer and consumer threads is to use classes from Java's concurrency package that encapsulate the synchronization for you. Java includes the class ArrayBlockingQueue (from package java.util.concurrent)—a fully implemented, thread-safe buffer class that implements interface BlockingQueue. This interface extends the Queue interface discussed in Chapter 19 and declares methods put and take, the blocking equivalents of Queue methods offer and poll, respectively. Method put places an element at the end of the BlockingQueue, waiting if the queue is full. Method take removes an element from the head of the BlockingQueue, waiting if the queue is empty. These methods make class ArrayBlockingQueue a good choice for implementing a shared buffer. Because method put blocks until there is room in the buffer to write data, and method take blocks until there is new data to read, the producer must produce a value first, the consumer correctly consumes only after the producer writes a value and the producer correctly produces the next value (after the first) only after the consumer reads the previous (or first) value. ArrayBlockingQueue stores the shared data in an array. The array's size is specified as an argument to the ArrayBlockingQueue constructor. Once created, an ArrayBlocking-Queue is fixed in size and will not expand to accommodate extra elements.

The program in Fig. 23.16 and Fig. 23.17 demonstrates a Producer and a Consumer accessing an ArrayBlockingQueue. Class BlockingBuffer (Fig. 23.16) uses an Array-

`BlockingQueue` object that stores an `Integer` (line 7). Line 11 creates the `ArrayBlocking-Queue` and passes 1 to the constructor so that the object holds a single value, as we did with the `UnsynchronizedBuffer` of Fig. 23.14. Note that lines 7 and 11 use generics, which we discussed in Chapters 18–19. We discuss multiple-element buffers in Section 23.9. Because our `BlockingBuffer` class uses the thread-safe `ArrayBlockingQueue` class to manage access to the shared buffer, `BlockingBuffer` is itself thread safe, even though we have not implemented the synchronization ourselves.

   `BlockingBuffer` implements interface `Buffer` (Fig. 23.11) and use classes `Producer` (Fig. 23.12 modified to remove line 28) and `Consumer` (Fig. 23.13 modified to remove line 28) from the example in Section 23.6. This approach demonstrates that the threads accessing the shared object are unaware that their buffer accesses are now synchronized. The synchronization is handled entirely in the `set` and `get` methods of `BlockingBuffer` by calling the synchronized `ArrayBlockingQueue` methods `put` and `take`, respectively. Thus, the `Producer` and `Consumer` `Runnable`s are properly synchronized simply by calling the shared object's `set` and `get` methods.

```java
1   // Fig. 23.16: BlockingBuffer.java
2   // Creates a synchronized buffer using an ArrayBlockingQueue.
3   import java.util.concurrent.ArrayBlockingQueue;
4
5   public class BlockingBuffer implements Buffer
6   {
7      private final ArrayBlockingQueue<Integer> buffer; // shared buffer
8
9      public BlockingBuffer()
10     {
11        buffer = new ArrayBlockingQueue<Integer>( 1 );
12     } // end BlockingBuffer constructor
13
14     // place value into buffer
15     public void set( int value ) throws InterruptedException
16     {
17        buffer.put( value ); // place value in buffer
18        System.out.printf( "%s%2d\t%s%d\n", "Producer writes ", value,
19           "Buffer cells occupied: ", buffer.size() );
20     } // end method set
21
22     // return value from buffer
23     public int get() throws InterruptedException
24     {
25        int readValue = 0; // initialize value read from buffer
26
27        readValue = buffer.take(); // remove value from buffer
28        System.out.printf( "%s %2d\t%s%d\n", "Consumer reads ",
29           readValue, "Buffer cells occupied: ", buffer.size() );
30
31        return readValue;
32     } // end method get
33  } // end class BlockingBuffer
```

Fig. 23.16 | Creates a synchronized buffer using an `ArrayBlockingQueue`.

Line 17 in method set (lines 15–20) calls the ArrayBlockingQueue object's put method. This method call blocks if necessary until there is room in the buffer to place the value. Method get (lines 23–32) calls the ArrayBlockingQueue object's take method (line 27). This method call blocks if necessary until there is an element in the buffer to remove. Lines 18–19 and 28–29 use the ArrayBlockingQueue object's size method to display the total number of elements currently in the ArrayBlockingQueue.

Class BlockingBufferTest (Fig. 23.17) contains the main method that launches the application. Line 11 creates an ExecutorService, and line 14 creates a BlockingBuffer object and assigns its reference to the Buffer variable sharedLocation. Lines 16–17 execute the Producer and Consumer Runnables. Line 19 calls method shutdown to end the application when the threads finish executing the Producer and Consumer tasks.

Note that while methods put and take of ArrayBlockingQueue are properly synchronized, BlockingBuffer methods set and get (Fig. 23.16) are not declared to be synchronized. Thus, the statements performed in method set—the put operation (line 19) and the output (lines 20–21)—are not atomic; nor are the statements in method get—the take operation (line 36) and the output (lines 37–38). So there is no guarantee that each output will occur immediately after the corresponding put or take operation, and the outputs may appear out of order. Even they do, the ArrayBlockingQueue object is properly synchronizing access to the data, as evidenced by the fact that the sum of values read by the consumer is always correct.

```java
1   // Fig. 23.17: BlockingBufferTest.java
2   // Two threads manipulating a blocking buffer.
3   import java.util.concurrent.ExecutorService;
4   import java.util.concurrent.Executors;
5
6   public class BlockingBufferTest
7   {
8      public static void main( String[] args )
9      {
10        // create new thread pool with two threads
11        ExecutorService application = Executors.newCachedThreadPool();
12
13        // create BlockingBuffer to store ints
14        Buffer sharedLocation = new BlockingBuffer();
15
16        application.execute( new Producer( sharedLocation ) );
17        application.execute( new Consumer( sharedLocation ) );
18
19        application.shutdown();
20     } // end main
21   } // end class BlockingBufferTest
```

```
Producer writes   1    Buffer cells occupied: 1
Consumer reads    1    Buffer cells occupied: 0
Producer writes   2    Buffer cells occupied: 1
Consumer reads    2    Buffer cells occupied: 0
```

Fig. 23.17 | Two threads manipulating a blocking buffer. (Part 1 of 2.)

```
Producer writes   3       Buffer cells occupied: 1
Consumer reads    3       Buffer cells occupied: 0
Producer writes   4       Buffer cells occupied: 1
Consumer reads    4       Buffer cells occupied: 0
Producer writes   5       Buffer cells occupied: 1
Consumer reads    5       Buffer cells occupied: 0
Producer writes   6       Buffer cells occupied: 1
Consumer reads    6       Buffer cells occupied: 0
Producer writes   7       Buffer cells occupied: 1
Consumer reads    7       Buffer cells occupied: 0
Producer writes   8       Buffer cells occupied: 1
Consumer reads    8       Buffer cells occupied: 0
Producer writes   9       Buffer cells occupied: 1
Consumer reads    9       Buffer cells occupied: 0
Producer writes  10       Buffer cells occupied: 1

Producer done producing
Terminating Producer
Consumer reads   10       Buffer cells occupied: 0

Consumer read values totaling 55
Terminating Consumer
```

Fig. 23.17 | Two threads manipulating a blocking buffer. (Part 2 of 2.)

23.8 Producer/Consumer Relationship with Synchronization

The previous example showed how multiple threads can share a single-element buffer in a thread-safe manner by using the ArrayBlockingQueue class that encapsulates the synchronization necessary to protect the shared data. For educational purposes, we now explain how you can implement a shared buffer yourself using the synchronized keyword. Using an ArrayBlockingQueue will result in more maintainable and better performing code.

The first step in synchronizing access to the buffer is to implement methods get and set as synchronized methods. This requires that a thread obtain the monitor lock on the Buffer object before attempting to access the buffer data, but it does not solve the state-dependence problem associated with producer/consumer relationships. We must ensure that threads proceed with an operation only if the buffer is in the proper state. We need a way to allow our threads to wait, depending on whether certain conditions are true. In the case of placing a new item in the buffer, the condition that allows the operation to proceed is that the buffer is not full. In the case of fetching an item from the buffer, the condition that allows the operation to proceed is that the buffer is not empty. If the condition in question is true, the operation may proceed; if it is false, the thread must wait until it becomes true. When a thread is waiting on a condition, it is removed from contention for the processor, placed in the object's wait queue and the lock it holds is released.

Methods *wait, notify* and *notifyAll*

Methods wait, notify and notifyAll, which are declared in class Object and inherited by all other classes, can be used with conditions to make threads wait when they cannot perform their tasks. If a thread obtains the monitor lock on an object, then determines that it cannot continue with its task on that object until some condition is satisfied, the thread can call Object method `wait`; this releases the monitor lock on the object, and the thread waits in the *waiting* state while the other threads try to enter the object's synchronized statement(s) or method(s). When a thread executing a synchronized statement (or method) completes or satisfies the condition on which another thread may be waiting, it can call Object method `notify` to allow a waiting thread to transition to the *runnable* state again. At this point, the thread that was transitioned from the *wait* state to the *runnable* state can attempt to reacquire the monitor lock on the object. Even if the thread is able to reacquire the monitor lock, it still might not be able to perform its task at this time—in which case the thread will reenter the *waiting* state and implicitly release the monitor lock. If a thread calls `notifyAll`, then all the threads waiting for the monitor lock become eligible to reacquire the lock (that is, they all transition to the *runnable* state). Remember that only one thread at a time can obtain the monitor lock on the object—other threads that attempt to acquire the same monitor lock will be *blocked* until the monitor lock becomes available again (i.e., until no other thread is executing in a synchronized statement on that object).

Common Programming Error 23.1

It is an error if a thread issues a wait, a notify or a notifyAll on an object without having acquired a lock for it. This causes an `IllegalMonitorStateException`.

Error-Prevention Tip 23.1

It is a good practice to use `notifyAll` to notify waiting threads to become runnable. Doing so avoids the possibility that your program would forget about waiting threads, which would otherwise starve.

The application in Fig. 23.18 and Fig. 23.19 demonstrates a Producer and a Consumer accessing a shared buffer with synchronization. In this case, the Producer always produces a value first, the Consumer correctly consumes only after the Producer produces a value and the Producer correctly produces the next value only after the Consumer consumes the previous (or first) value. We reuse interface Buffer and classes Producer and Consumer from the example in Section 23.6. The synchronization is handled in the set and get methods of class SynchronizedBuffer (Fig. 23.18), which implements interface Buffer (line 4). Thus, the Producer's and Consumer's run methods simply call the shared object's synchronized set and get methods.

```
1   // Fig. 23.18: SynchronizedBuffer.java
2   // Synchronizing access to shared data using Object
3   // methods wait and notify.
4   public class SynchronizedBuffer implements Buffer
5   {
6      private int buffer = -1; // shared by producer and consumer threads
7      private boolean occupied = false; // whether the buffer is occupied
8
9      // place value into buffer
10     public synchronized void set( int value )
11     {
```

Fig. 23.18 | Synchronizing access to shared data using Object methods wait and notify. (Part 1 of 2.)

```
12          // while there are no empty locations, place thread in waiting state
13          while ( occupied )
14          {
15              // output thread information and buffer information, then wait
16              System.out.println( "Producer tries to write." );
17              displayState( "Buffer full. Producer waits." );
18              wait();
19          } // end while
20
21          buffer = value; // set new buffer value
22
23          // indicate producer cannot store another value
24          // until consumer retrieves current buffer value
25          occupied = true;
26
27          displayState( "Producer writes " + buffer );
28
29          notifyAll(); // tell waiting thread(s) to enter runnable state
30      } // end method set; releases lock on SynchronizedBuffer
31
32      // return value from buffer
33      public synchronized int get()
34      {
35          // while no data to read, place thread in waiting state
36          while ( !occupied )
37          {
38              // output thread information and buffer information, then wait
39              System.out.println( "Consumer tries to read." );
40              displayState( "Buffer empty. Consumer waits." );
41              wait();
42          } // end while
43
44          // indicate that producer can store another value
45          // because consumer just retrieved buffer value
46          occupied = false;
47
48          displayState( "Consumer reads " + buffer );
49
50          notifyAll(); // tell waiting thread(s) to enter runnable state
51
52          return buffer;
53      } // end method get; releases lock on SynchronizedBuffer
54
55      // display current operation and buffer state
56      public void displayState( String operation )
57      {
58          System.out.printf( "%-40s%d\t\t%b\n\n", operation, buffer,
59              occupied );
60      } // end method displayState
61  } // end class SynchronizedBuffer
```

Fig. 23.18 | Synchronizing access to shared data using `Object` methods `wait` and `notify`.
(Part 2 of 2.)

*Fields and Methods of Class **SynchronizedBuffer***

Class SynchronizedBuffer contains two fields—buffer (line 6) and occupied (line 7). Method set (lines 10–30) and method get (lines 33–53) are declared as synchronized—only one thread can call either of these methods at a time on a particular Synchronized-Buffer object. Field occupied is used to determine whether it is the Producer's or the Consumer's turn to perform a task. This field is used in conditional expressions in both the set and get methods. If occupied is false, then buffer is empty, so the Consumer cannot read the value of buffer, but the Producer can place a value into buffer. If occupied is true, the Consumer can read a value from buffer, but the Producer cannot place a value into buffer.

*Method **set** and the **Producer** Thread*

When the Producer thread's run method invokes synchronized method set, the thread implicitly attempts to acquire the SynchronizedBuffer object's monitor lock. If the monitor lock is available, the Producer thread implicitly acquires the lock. Then the loop at lines 13–19 first determines whether occupied is true. If so, buffer is full, so line 16 outputs a message indicating that the Producer thread is trying to write a value, and line 17 invokes method displayState (lines 56–60) to output another message indicating that buffer is full and that the Producer thread is waiting until there is space. Line 18 invokes method wait (inherited from Object by SynchronizedBuffer) to place the thread that called method set (i.e., the Producer thread) in the *waiting* state for the SynchronizedBuffer object. The call to wait causes the calling thread to implicitly release the lock on the SynchronizedBuffer object. This is important because the thread cannot currently perform its task and because other threads (in this case, the Consumer) should be allowed to access the object to allow the condition (occupied) to change. Now another thread can attempt to acquire the SynchronizedBuffer object's lock and invoke the object's set or get method.

The Producer thread remains in the *waiting* state until another thread notifies the Producer that it may proceed—at which point the Producer returns to the *runnable* state and attempts to implicitly reacquire the lock on the SynchronizedBuffer object. If the lock is available, the Producer thread reacquires the lock, and method set continues executing with the next statement after the wait call. Because wait is called in a loop, the loop-continuation condition is tested again to determine whether the thread can proceed. If not, then wait is invoked again—otherwise, method set continues with the next statement after the loop.

Line 21 in method set assigns the value to the buffer. Line 25 sets occupied to true to indicate that the buffer now contains a value (i.e., a consumer can read the value, but a Producer cannot yet put another value there). Line 27 invokes method displayState to output a message indicating that the Producer is writing a new value into the buffer. Line 29 invokes method notifyAll (inherited from Object). If any threads are waiting on the SynchronizedBuffer object's monitor lock, those threads enter the *runnable* state and can now attempt to reacquire the lock. Method notifyAll returns immediately, and method set then returns to the calling method (i.e., the Producer's run method). When method set returns, it implicitly releases the monitor lock on the SynchronizedBuffer object.

*Method **get** and the **Consumer** Thread*

Methods get and set are implemented similarly. When the Consumer thread's run method invokes synchronized method get, the thread attempts to acquire the monitor lock on the SynchronizedBuffer object. If the lock is available, the Consumer thread acquires it. Then the while loop at lines 36–42 determines whether occupied is false. If so, the buffer is empty, so line 39 outputs a message indicating that the Consumer thread is trying to read a value, and line 40 invokes method displayState to output a message indicating that the buffer is empty and that the Consumer thread is waiting. Line 41 invokes method wait to place the thread that called method get (i.e., the Consumer) in the *waiting* state for the SynchronizedBuffer object. Again, the call to wait causes the calling thread to implicitly release the lock on the SynchronizedBuffer object, so another thread can attempt to acquire the SynchronizedBuffer object's lock and invoke the object's set or get method. If the lock on the SynchronizedBuffer is not available (e.g., if the Producer has not yet returned from method set), the Consumer is blocked until the lock becomes available.

The Consumer thread remains in the *waiting* state until it is notified by another thread that it may proceed—at which point the Consumer thread returns to the *runnable* state and attempts to implicitly reacquire the lock on the SynchronizedBuffer object. If the lock is available, the Consumer reacquires the lock, and method get continues executing with the next statement after wait. Because wait is called in a loop, the loop-continuation condition is tested again to determine whether the thread can proceed with its execution. If not, wait is invoked again—otherwise, method get continues with the next statement after the loop. Line 46 sets occupied to false to indicate that buffer is now empty (i.e., a Consumer cannot read the value, but a Producer can place another value in buffer), line 48 calls method displayState to indicate that the consumer is reading and line 50 invokes method notifyAll. If any threads are in the *waiting* state for the lock on this SynchronizedBuffer object, they enter the *runnable* state and can now attempt to reacquire the lock. Method notifyAll returns immediately, then method get returns the value of buffer to its caller. When method get returns, the lock on the SynchronizedBuffer object is implicitly released.

Error-Prevention Tip 23.2

Always invoke method wait in a loop that tests the condition the task is waiting on. It is possible that a thread will reenter the runnable *state (via a timed wait or another thread calling notify-All) before the condition is satisfied. Testing the condition again ensures that the thread will not erroneously execute if it was notified early.*

Testing Class SynchronizedBuffer

Class SharedBufferTest2 (Fig. 23.19) is similar to class SharedBufferTest (Fig. 23.15). SharedBufferTest2 contains method main (lines 8–24), which launches the application. Line 11 creates an ExecutorService to run the Producer and Consumer tasks. Line 14 creates a SynchronizedBuffer object and assigns its reference to Buffer variable shared-Location. This object stores the data that will be shared between the Producer and

```
1   // Fig. 23.19: SharedBufferTest2.java
2   // Two threads manipulating a synchronized buffer.
3   import java.util.concurrent.ExecutorService;
4   import java.util.concurrent.Executors;
5
```

Fig. 23.19 | Two threads manipulating a synchronized buffer. (Part 1 of 3.)

```
 6   public class SharedBufferTest2
 7   {
 8      public static void main( String[] args )
 9      {
10         // create a newCachedThreadPool
11         ExecutorService application = Executors.newCachedThreadPool();
12
13         // create SynchronizedBuffer to store ints
14         Buffer sharedLocation = new SynchronizedBuffer();
15
16         System.out.printf( "%-40s%s\t\t%s\n%-40s%s\n\n", "Operation",
17            "Buffer", "Occupied", "---------", "------\t\t--------" );
18
19         // execute the Producer and Consumer tasks
20         application.execute( new Producer( sharedLocation ) );
21         application.execute( new Consumer( sharedLocation ) );
22
23         application.shutdown();
24      } // end main
25   } // end class SharedBufferTest2
```

Operation	Buffer	Occupied
---------	------	--------
Consumer tries to read.		
Buffer empty. Consumer waits.	-1	false
Producer writes 1	1	true
Consumer reads 1	1	false
Consumer tries to read.		
Buffer empty. Consumer waits.	1	false
Producer writes 2	2	true
Consumer reads 2	2	false
Producer writes 3	3	true
Consumer reads 3	3	false
Producer writes 4	4	true
Producer tries to write.		
Buffer full. Producer waits.	4	true
Consumer reads 4	4	false
Producer writes 5	5	true
Consumer reads 5	5	false
Producer writes 6	6	true
Producer tries to write.		
Buffer full. Producer waits.	6	true

Fig. 23.19 | Two threads manipulating a synchronized buffer. (Part 2 of 3.)

```
Consumer reads 6                        6              false

Producer writes 7                       7              true

Producer tries to write.
Buffer full. Producer waits.            7              true

Consumer reads 7                        7              false

Producer writes 8                       8              true

Consumer reads 8                        8              false

Consumer tries to read.
Buffer empty. Consumer waits.           8              false

Producer writes 9                       9              true

Consumer reads 9                        9              false

Consumer tries to read.
Buffer empty. Consumer waits.           9              false

Producer writes 10                      10             true

Consumer reads 10                       10             false


Producer done producing
Terminating Producer

Consumer read values totaling 55
Terminating Consumer
```

Fig. 23.19 | Two threads manipulating a synchronized buffer. (Part 3 of 3.)

Consumer. Lines 16–17 display the column heads for the output. Lines 20–21 execute a Producer and a Consumer. Finally, line 23 calls method shutdown to end the application when the Producer and Consumer complete their tasks. When method main ends (line 24), the main thread of execution terminates.

Study the outputs in Fig. 23.19. Observe that every integer produced is consumed exactly once—no values are lost, and no values are consumed more than once. The synchronization ensures that the Producer produces a value only when the buffer is empty and the Consumer consumes only when the buffer is full. The Producer always goes first, the Consumer waits if the Producer has not produced since the Consumer last consumed, and the Producer waits if the Consumer has not yet consumed the value that the Producer most recently produced. Execute this program several times to confirm that every integer produced is consumed exactly once. In the sample output, note the highlighted lines indicating when the Producer and Consumer must wait to perform their respective tasks.

23.9 Producer/Consumer Relationship: Bounded Buffers

The program in Section 23.8 uses thread synchronization to guarantee that two threads manipulate data in a shared buffer correctly. However, the application may not perform optimally. If the two threads operate at different speeds, one of the threads will spend more (or most) of its time waiting. For example, in the program in Section 23.8 we shared a single integer variable between the two threads. If the Producer thread produces values faster than the Consumer can consume them, then the Producer thread waits for the Consumer, because there are no other locations in the buffer in which to place the next value. Similarly, if the Consumer consumes values faster than the Producer produces them, the Consumer waits until the Producer places the next value in the shared buffer. Even when we have threads that operate at the same relative speeds, those threads may occasionally become "out of sync" over a period of time, causing one of them to wait for the other. We cannot make assumptions about the relative speeds of concurrent threads—interactions that occur with the operating system, the network, the user and other components can cause the threads to operate at different speeds. When this happens, threads wait. When threads wait excessively, programs become less efficient, interactive programs become less responsive and applications suffer longer delays.

Bounded Buffers

To minimize the amount of waiting time for threads that share resources and operate at the same average speeds, we can implement a bounded buffer that provides a fixed number of buffer cells into which the Producer can place values, and from which the Consumer can retrieve those values. (In fact, we have already done this with the ArrayBlockingQueue class in Section 23.7.) If the Producer temporarily produces values faster than the Consumer can consume them, the Producer can write additional values into the extra buffer space (if any are available). This capability enables the Producer to perform its task even though the Consumer is not ready to retrieve the current value being produced. Similarly, if the Consumer consumes faster than the Producer produces new values, the Consumer can read additional values (if there are any) from the buffer. This enables the Consumer to keep busy even though the Producer is not ready to produce additional values.

Note that even a bounded buffer is inappropriate if the Producer and the Consumer operate consistently at different speeds. If the Consumer always executes faster than the Producer, then a buffer containing one location is enough. Additional locations would simply waste memory. If the Producer always executes faster, only a buffer with an "infinite" number of locations would be able to absorb the extra production. However, if the Producer and Consumer execute at about the same average speed, a bounded buffer helps to smooth the effects of any occasional speeding up or slowing down in either thread's execution.

The key to using a bounded buffer with a Producer and Consumer that operate at about the same speed is to provide the buffer with enough locations to handle the anticipated "extra" production. If, over a period of time, we determine that the Producer often produces as many as three more values than the Consumer can consume, we can provide a buffer of at least three cells to handle the extra production. Making the buffer too small would cause threads to wait longer; making the buffer too large would waste memory.

Performance Tip 23.3

Even when using a bounded buffer, it is possible that a producer thread could fill the buffer, which would force the producer to wait until a consumer consumed a value to free an element in the buffer. Similarly, if the buffer is empty at any given time, a consumer thread must wait until the producer produces another value. The key to using a bounded buffer is to optimize the buffer size to minimize the amount of thread wait time, while not wasting space..

Bounded Buffers Using `ArrayBlockingQueue`

The simplest way to implement a bounded buffer is to use an `ArrayBlockingQueue` for the buffer so that all of the synchronization details are handled for you. This can be done by reusing the example from Section 23.7 and simply passing the desired size for the bounded buffer into the `ArrayBlockingQueue` constructor. Rather than repeat our previous Array-BlockingQueue example with a different size, we instead present an example that illustrates how you can build a bounded buffer yourself. Again, note that using an `ArrayBlockingQueue` will result in more maintainable and better performing code.

Implementing Your Own Bounded Buffer as a Circular Buffer

The program in Fig. 23.20 and Fig. 23.21 demonstrates a `Producer` and a `Consumer` accessing a bounded buffer with synchronization. We implement the bounded buffer in class `CircularBuffer` (Fig. 23.20) as a circular buffer that uses a shared array of three elements. A circular buffer writes into and reads from the array elements in order, beginning at the

```java
1   // Fig. 23.20: CircularBuffer.java
2   // Synchronizing access to a shared three-element bounded buffer.
3   public class CircularBuffer implements Buffer
4   {
5      private final int[] buffer = { -1, -1, -1 }; // shared buffer
6
7      private int occupiedCells = 0; // count number of buffers used
8      private int writeIndex = 0; // index of next element to write to
9      private int readIndex = 0; // index of next element to read
10
11     // place value into buffer
12     public synchronized void set( int value ) throws InterruptedException
13     {
14        // output thread information and buffer information, then wait;
15        // while no empty locations, place thread in blocked state
16        while ( occupiedCells == buffer.length )
17        {
18           System.out.printf( "Buffer is full. Producer waits.\n" );
19           wait(); // wait until a buffer cell is free
20        } // end while
21
22        buffer[ writeIndex ] = value; // set new buffer value
23
24        // update circular write index
25        writeIndex = ( writeIndex + 1 ) % buffer.length;
26
27        ++occupiedCells; // one more buffer cell is full
28        displayState( "Producer writes " + value );
29        notifyAll(); // notify threads waiting to read from buffer
30     } // end method set
31
32     // return value from buffer
33     public synchronized int get() throws InterruptedException
34     {
```

Fig. 23.20 | Synchronizing access to a shared three-element bounded buffer. (Part 1 of 2.)

```
35          // wait until buffer has data, then read value;
36          // while no data to read, place thread in waiting state
37          while ( occupiedCells == 0 )
38          {
39             System.out.printf( "Buffer is empty. Consumer waits.\n" );
40             wait(); // wait until a buffer cell is filled
41          } // end while
42
43          int readValue = buffer[ readIndex ]; // read value from buffer
44
45          // update circular read index
46          readIndex = ( readIndex + 1 ) % buffer.length;
47
48          --occupiedCells; // one fewer buffer cells are occupied
49          displayState( "Consumer reads " + readValue );
50          notifyAll(); // notify threads waiting to write to buffer
51
52          return readValue;
53       } // end method get
54
55       // display current operation and buffer state
56       public void displayState( String operation )
57       {
58          // output operation and number of occupied buffer cells
59          System.out.printf( "%s%s%d)\n%s", operation,
60             " (buffer cells occupied: ", occupiedCells, "buffer cells:  " );
61
62          for ( int value : buffer )
63             System.out.printf( " %2d  ", value ); // output values in buffer
64
65          System.out.print( "\n                    " );
66
67          for ( int i = 0; i < buffer.length; i++ )
68             System.out.print( "---- " );
69
70          System.out.print( "\n                    " );
71
72          for ( int i = 0; i < buffer.length; i++ )
73          {
74             if ( i == writeIndex && i == readIndex )
75                System.out.print( " WR" ); // both write and read index
76             else if ( i == writeIndex )
77                System.out.print( " W  " ); // just write index
78             else if ( i == readIndex )
79                System.out.print( "  R " ); // just read index
80             else
81                System.out.print( "    " ); // neither index
82          } // end for
83
84          System.out.println( "\n" );
85       } // end method displayState
86    } // end class CircularBuffer
```

Fig. 23.20 | Synchronizing access to a shared three-element bounded buffer. (Part 2 of 2.)

first cell and moving toward the last. When a Producer or Consumer reaches the last element, it returns to the first and begins writing or reading, respectively, from there. In this version of the producer/consumer relationship, the Consumer consumes a value only when the array is not empty and the Producer produces a value only when the array is not full. The statements that created and started the thread objects in the main method of class SharedBufferTest2 (Fig. 23.19) now appear in class CircularBufferTest (Fig. 23.21).

Line 5 initializes array buffer as a three-element integer array that represents the circular buffer. Variable occupiedCells (line 7) counts the number of elements in buffer that contain data to be read. When occupiedBuffers is 0, there is no data in the circular buffer and the Consumer must wait—when occupiedCells is 3 (the size of the circular buffer), the circular buffer is full and the Producer must wait. Variable writeIndex (line 8) indicates the next location in which a value can be placed by a Producer. Variable read-Index (line 9) indicates the position from which the next value can be read by a Consumer.

CircularBuffer method set (lines 12–30) performs the same tasks as in Fig. 23.18, with a few modifications. The loop at lines 16–20 determines whether the Producer must wait (i.e., all buffers are full). If so, line 18 indicates that the Producer is waiting to perform its task. Then line 19 invokes method wait, causing the Producer thread to release the CircularBuffer's lock and wait until there is space for a new value to be written into the buffer. When execution continues at line 22 after the while loop, the value written by the Producer is placed in the circular buffer at location writeIndex. Then line 25 updates writeIndex for the next call to CircularBuffer method set. This line is the key to the "circularity" of the buffer. When writeIndex is incremented past the end of the buffer, the line sets it to 0. Line 27 increments occupiedCells, because there is now one more value in the buffer that the Consumer can read. Next, line 28 invokes method displayState (lines 56–85) to update the output with the value produced, the number of occupied buffers, the contents of the buffers and the current writeIndex and readIndex. Line 29 invokes method notifyAll to transition *waiting* threads to the runnable state, so that a waiting Consumer thread (if there is one) can try again to read a value from the buffer.

CircularBuffer method get (lines 33–53) also performs the same tasks as it did in Fig. 23.18, with a few minor modifications. The loop at lines 37–41 determines whether the Consumer must wait (i.e., all buffer cells are empty). If the Consumer must wait, line 39 updates the output to indicate that the Consumer is waiting to perform its task. Then line 40 invokes method wait, causing the current thread to release the lock on the Circular-Buffer and wait until data is available to read. When execution eventually continues at line 43 after a notifyAll call from the Producer, readValue is assigned the value at location readIndex in the circular buffer. Then line 46 updates readIndex for the next call to CircularBuffer method get. This line and line 25 implement the "circularity" of the buffer. Line 48 decrements occupiedCells, because there is now one more position in the buffer in which the Producer thread can place a value. Line 49 invokes method display-State to update the output with the consumed value, the number of occupied buffers, the contents of the buffers and the current writeIndex and readIndex. Line 50 invokes method notifyAll to allow any Producer threads waiting to write into the Circular-Buffer object to attempt to write again. Then line 52 returns the consumed value to the caller.

Method displayState (lines 56–85) outputs the state of the application. Lines 62–63 output the current values of the buffer cells. Line 63 uses method printf with a "%2d" format specifier to print the contents of each buffer with a leading space if it is a single digit. Lines 70–82 output the current writeIndex and readIndex with the letters W and R, respectively.

Testing Class CircularBuffer

Class CircularBufferTest (Fig. 23.21) contains the main method that launches the application. Line 11 creates the ExecutorService, and line 14 creates a CircularBuffer object and assigns its reference to CircularBuffer variable sharedLocation. Line 17 invokes the CircularBuffer's displayState method to show the initial state of the buffer. Lines 20–21 execute the Producer and Consumer tasks. Line 23 calls method shutdown to end the application when the threads complete the Producer and Consumer tasks.

Each time the Producer writes a value or the Consumer reads a value, the program outputs a message indicating the action performed (a read or a write), the contents of buffer, and the location of writeIndex and readIndex. In the output of Fig. 23.21, the Producer first writes the value 1. The buffer then contains the value 1 in the first cell and the value –1 (the default value that we use for output purposes) in the other two cells. The write index is updated to the second cell, while the read index stays at the first cell. Next, the Consumer reads 1. The buffer contains the same values, but the read index has been updated to the second cell. The Consumer then tries to read again, but the buffer is empty and the Consumer is forced to wait. Note that only once in this execution of the program was it necessary for either thread to wait.

```
1   // Fig. 23.21: CircularBufferTest.java
2   // Producer and Consumer threads manipulating a circular buffer.
3   import java.util.concurrent.ExecutorService;
4   import java.util.concurrent.Executors;
5
6   public class CircularBufferTest
7   {
8      public static void main( String[] args )
9      {
10        // create new thread pool with two threads
11        ExecutorService application = Executors.newCachedThreadPool();
12
13        // create CircularBuffer to store ints
14        CircularBuffer sharedLocation = new CircularBuffer();
15
16        // display the initial state of the CircularBuffer
17        sharedLocation.displayState( "Initial State" );
18
19        // execute the Producer and Consumer tasks
20        application.execute( new Producer( sharedLocation ) );
21        application.execute( new Consumer( sharedLocation ) );
22
23        application.shutdown();
24     } // end main
25  } // end class CircularBufferTest
```

Fig. 23.21 | Producer and Consumer threads manipulating a circular buffer. (Part 1 of 3.)

```
Initial State (buffer cells occupied: 0)
buffer cells:   -1   -1   -1
                ---- ---- ----
                 WR

Producer writes 1 (buffer cells occupied: 1)
buffer cells:    1   -1   -1
                ---- ---- ----
                 R    W

Consumer reads 1 (buffer cells occupied: 0)
buffer cells:    1   -1   -1
                ---- ---- ----
                      WR

Buffer is empty. Consumer waits.
Producer writes 2 (buffer cells occupied: 1)
buffer cells:    1    2   -1
                ---- ---- ----
                      R    W

Consumer reads 2 (buffer cells occupied: 0)
buffer cells:    1    2   -1
                ---- ---- ----
                           WR

Producer writes 3 (buffer cells occupied: 1)
buffer cells:    1    2    3
                ---- ---- ----
                 W         R

Consumer reads 3 (buffer cells occupied: 0)
buffer cells:    1    2    3
                ---- ---- ----
                 WR

Producer writes 4 (buffer cells occupied: 1)
buffer cells:    4    2    3
                ---- ---- ----
                 R    W

Producer writes 5 (buffer cells occupied: 2)
buffer cells:    4    5    3
                ---- ---- ----
                 R         W

Consumer reads 4 (buffer cells occupied: 1)
buffer cells:    4    5    3
                ---- ---- ----
                      R    W

Producer writes 6 (buffer cells occupied: 2)
buffer cells:    4    5    6
                ---- ---- ----
                 W         R
```

Fig. 23.21 | Producer and Consumer threads manipulating a circular buffer. (Part 2 of 3.)

```
Producer writes 7 (buffer cells occupied: 3)
buffer cells:    7    5    6
                ---- ---- ----
                      WR

Consumer reads 5 (buffer cells occupied: 2)
buffer cells:    7    5    6
                ---- ---- ----
                 W         R

Producer writes 8 (buffer cells occupied: 3)
buffer cells:    7    8    6
                ---- ---- ----
                           WR

Consumer reads 6 (buffer cells occupied: 2)
buffer cells:    7    8    6
                ---- ---- ----
                 R         W

Consumer reads 7 (buffer cells occupied: 1)
buffer cells:    7    8    6
                ---- ---- ----
                      R    W

Producer writes 9 (buffer cells occupied: 2)
buffer cells:    7    8    9
                ---- ---- ----
                 W    R

Consumer reads 8 (buffer cells occupied: 1)
buffer cells:    7    8    9
                ---- ---- ----
                 W         R

Consumer reads 9 (buffer cells occupied: 0)
buffer cells:    7    8    9
                ---- ---- ----
                 WR

Producer writes 10 (buffer cells occupied: 1)
buffer cells:   10    8    9
                ---- ---- ----
                 R    W


Producer done producing
Terminating Producer
Consumer reads 10 (buffer cells occupied: 0)
buffer cells:   10    8    9
                ---- ---- ----
                      WR


Consumer read values totaling: 55
Terminating Consumer
```

Fig. 23.21 | Producer and Consumer threads manipulating a circular buffer. (Part 3 of 3.)

23.10 Producer/Consumer Relationship: The Lock and Condition Interfaces

Though the synchronized keyword provides for most basic thread synchronization needs, Java provides other tools to assist in developing concurrent programs. In this section, we discuss the Lock and Condition interfaces, which were introduced in Java SE 5. These interfaces give programmers more precise control over thread synchronization, but are more complicated to use.

Interface *Lock* and Class *ReentrantLock*

Any object can contain a reference to an object that implements the Lock interface (of package java.util.concurrent.locks). A thread calls the Lock's lock method to acquire the lock. Once a Lock has been obtained by one thread, the Lock object will not allow another thread to obtain the Lock until the first thread releases the Lock (by calling the Lock's unlock method). If several threads are trying to call method lock on the same Lock object at the same time, only one of these threads can obtain the lock—all the others are placed in the *waiting* state for that lock. When a thread calls method unlock, the lock on the object is released and a waiting thread attempting to lock the object proceeds.

Class ReentrantLock (of package java.util.concurrent.locks) is a basic implementation of the Lock interface. The constructor for a ReentrantLock takes a boolean argument that specifies whether the lock has a fairness policy. If the argument is true, the ReentrantLock's fairness policy is "the longest-waiting thread will acquire the lock when it is available." Such a fairness policy guarantees that indefinite postponement (also called starvation) cannot occur. If the fairness policy argument is set to false, there is no guarantee as to which waiting thread will acquire the lock when it is available.

Software Engineering Observation 23.2

Using a ReentrantLock with a fairness policy avoids indefinite postponement.

Performance Tip 23.4

Using a ReentrantLock with a fairness policy can decrease program performance significantly.

Condition Objects and Interface *Condition*

If a thread that owns a Lock determines that it cannot continue with its task until some condition is satisfied, the thread can wait on a condition object. Using Lock objects allows you to explicitly declare the condition objects on which a thread may need to wait. For example, in the producer/consumer relationship, producers can wait on one object and consumers can wait on another. This is not possible when using the synchronized keywords and an object's built-in monitor lock. Condition objects are associated with a specific Lock and are created by calling a Lock's newCondition method, which returns an object that implements the Condition interface (of package java.util.concurrent.locks). To wait on a condition object, the thread can call the Condition's await method. This immediately releases the associated Lock and places the thread in the *waiting* state for that Condition. Other threads can then try to obtain the Lock. When a *runnable* thread completes a task and determines that the *waiting* thread can now continue, the *runnable* thread can call Condition method signal to allow a thread in that Condition's *waiting* state to return to the *runnable* state. At this point, the thread that transitioned from the *waiting* state to the *runnable* state can attempt to reacquire the Lock. Even if it is able to reacquire the Lock, the thread still might not be able to perform its task at this time—in which case the thread can call the Condition's await method to release the Lock and reenter the *waiting* state. If multiple threads are in a Condition's *waiting* state when signal is called, the default implementation of Condition signals the longest-waiting thread to transition to the *runnable* state. If a thread calls Condition method signalAll, then all the threads waiting for that condition transition to the *runnable* state and become eligible to reacquire the Lock. Only one of those threads can obtain the Lock on the object—the others will wait until the Lock becomes available again. If the Lock has a fairness policy, the longest-waiting thread acquires the Lock. When a thread is finished with a shared object, it must call method unlock to release the Lock.

Common Programming Error 23.2

Deadlock occurs when a waiting thread (let us call this thread1) cannot proceed because it is waiting (either directly or indirectly) for another thread (let us call this thread2) to proceed, while simultaneously thread2 cannot proceed because it is waiting (either directly or indirectly) for thread1 to proceed. The two threads are waiting for each other, so the actions that would enable each thread to continue execution can never occur.

Error-Prevention Tip 23.3

When multiple threads manipulate a shared object using locks, ensure that if one thread calls method await to enter the waiting *state for a condition object, a separate thread eventually will call Condition method signal to transition the thread waiting on the condition object back to the* runnable *state. If multiple threads may be waiting on the condition object, a separate thread can call Condition method signalAll as a safeguard to ensure that all the waiting threads have another opportunity to perform their tasks. If this is not done, starvation might occur.*

Common Programming Error 23.3

An IllegalMonitorStateException occurs if a thread issues an await, a signal, or a signalAll on a condition object without having acquired the lock for that condition object.

Lock and Condition vs. the synchronized Keyword

In some applications, using Lock and Condition objects may be preferable to using the synchronized keyword. Locks allow you to interrupt waiting threads or to specify a timeout for waiting to acquire a lock, which is not possible using the synchronized keyword. Also, a Lock is not constrained to be acquired and released in the same block of code, which is the case with the synchronized keyword. Condition objects allow you to specify multiple condition objects on which threads may wait. Thus, it is possible indicate to waiting threads that a specific condition object is now true by calling signal or signallAll on that Condition object. With the synchronized keyword, there is no way to explicitly state the condition on which threads are waiting, and thus there is no way to notify threads waiting on one condition that they may proceed without also signaling threads waiting on any other conditions. There are other possible advantages to using Lock and Condition objects, but note that generally it is best to use the synchronized keyword unless your application requires advanced synchronization capabilities. Using interfaces Lock and Condition is error prone—unlock is not guaranteed to be called, whereas the monitor in a synchronized statement will always be released when the statement completes execution.

*Using **Locks** and **Conditions** to Implement Synchronization*

To illustrate how to use the Lock and Condition interfaces, we now implement the producer/consumer relationship using Lock and Condition objects to coordinate access to a shared single-element buffer (Fig. 23.22 and Fig. 23.23). In this case, each produced value is correctly consumed exactly once.

Class SynchronizedBuffer (Fig. 23.22) contains five fields. Line 11 creates a new object of type ReentrantLock and assigns its reference to Lock variable accessLock. The ReentrantLock is created without the fairness policy because at any time only a single Producer or Consumer will be waiting to acquire the Lock in this example. Lines 14–15 create two Conditions using Lock method newCondition. Condition canWrite contains a queue for a Producer thread waiting while the buffer is full (i.e., there is data in the buffer that the Consumer has not read yet). If the buffer is full, the Producer calls method await on this Condition. When the Consumer reads data from a full buffer, it calls method signal on this Condition. Condition canRead contains a queue for a Consumer thread waiting while the buffer is empty (i.e., there is no data in the buffer for the Consumer to read). If the buffer is empty, the Consumer calls method await on this Condition. When the Producer writes to the empty buffer, it calls method signal on this Condition. The int variable buffer (line 17) holds the shared data. The boolean variable occupied (line 18) keeps track of whether the buffer currently holds data (that the Consumer should read).

```java
1   // Fig. 23.22: SynchronizedBuffer.java
2   // Synchronizing access to a shared integer using the Lock and Condition
3   // interfaces
4   import java.util.concurrent.locks.Lock;
5   import java.util.concurrent.locks.ReentrantLock;
6   import java.util.concurrent.locks.Condition;
7
8   public class SynchronizedBuffer implements Buffer
9   {
10      // Lock to control synchronization with this buffer
11      private final Lock accessLock = new ReentrantLock();
12
13      // conditions to control reading and writing
14      private final Condition canWrite = accessLock.newCondition();
15      private final Condition canRead = accessLock.newCondition();
16
17      private int buffer = -1; // shared by producer and consumer threads
18      private boolean occupied = false; // whether buffer is occupied
19
20      // place int value into buffer
21      public void set( int value ) throws InterruptedException
22      {
23         accessLock.lock(); // lock this object
24
25         // output thread information and buffer information, then wait
26         try
27         {
```

Fig. 23.22 | Synchronizing access to a shared integer using the Lock and Condition interfaces. (Part 1 of 3.)

```
28              // while buffer is not empty, place thread in waiting state
29              while ( occupied )
30              {
31                 System.out.println( "Producer tries to write." );
32                 displayState( "Buffer full. Producer waits." );
33                 canWrite.await(); // wait until buffer is empty
34              } // end while
35
36              buffer = value; // set new buffer value
37
38              // indicate producer cannot store another value
39              // until consumer retrieves current buffer value
40              occupied = true;
41
42              displayState( "Producer writes " + buffer );
43
44              // signal thread waiting to read from buffer
45              canRead.signal();
46           } // end try
47           finally
48           {
49              accessLock.unlock(); // unlock this object
50           } // end finally
51        } // end method set
52
53        // return value from buffer
54        public int get() throws InterruptedException
55        {
56           int readValue = 0; // initialize value read from buffer
57           accessLock.lock(); // lock this object
58
59           // output thread information and buffer information, then wait
60           try
61           {
62              // while no data to read, place thread in waiting state
63              while ( !occupied )
64              {
65                 System.out.println( "Consumer tries to read." );
66                 displayState( "Buffer empty. Consumer waits." );
67                 canRead.await(); // wait until buffer is full
68              } // end while
69
70              // indicate that producer can store another value
71              // because consumer just retrieved buffer value
72              occupied = false;
73
74              readValue = buffer; // retrieve value from buffer
75              displayState( "Consumer reads " + readValue );
76
77              // signal thread waiting for buffer to be empty
78              canWrite.signal();
79           } // end try
```

Fig. 23.22 | Synchronizing access to a shared integer using the Lock and Condition interfaces. (Part 2 of 3.)

```
80            finally
81            {
82                accessLock.unlock(); // unlock this object
83            } // end finally
84
85            return readValue;
86        } // end method get
87
88        // display current operation and buffer state
89        public void displayState( String operation )
90        {
91            System.out.printf( "%-40s%d\t\t%b\n\n", operation, buffer,
92                occupied );
93        } // end method displayState
94    } // end class SynchronizedBuffer
```

Fig. 23.22 | Synchronizing access to a shared integer using the Lock and Condition interfaces. (Part 3 of 3.)

Line 23 in method set calls method lock on the SynchronizedBuffer's accessLock. If the lock is available (i.e., no other thread has acquired this lock), method lock returns immediately (this thread now owns the lock) and the thread continues. If the lock is unavailable (i.e., it is held by another thread), this method waits until the lock is released by the other thread. After the lock is acquired, the try block in lines 26–46 executes. Line 29 tests occupied to determine whether buffer is full. If it is, lines 31–32 display a message indicating that the thread will wait. Line 33 calls Condition method await on the canWrite condition object, which temporarily releases the SynchronizedBuffer's Lock and waits for a signal from the Consumer that buffer is available for writing. When buffer is available, the method proceeds, writing to buffer (line 36), setting occupied to true (line 40) and displaying a message indicating that the producer wrote a value (line 42). Line 45 calls Condition method signal on condition object canRead to notify the waiting Consumer (if there is one) that the buffer has new data to be read. Line 49 calls method unlock from a finally block to release the lock and allow the Consumer to proceed.

Error-Prevention Tip 23.4

Place calls to Lock method unlock in a finally block. If an exception is thrown, unlock must still be called or deadlock could occur.

Line 57 of method get (lines 54–86) calls method lock to acquire the Lock. This method waits until the Lock is available. Once the Lock is acquired, line 63 tests whether occupied is false, indicating that the buffer is empty. If the buffer is empty, line 67 calls method await on condition object canRead. Recall that method signal is called on variable canRead in the set method (line 45). When the Condition object is signaled, the get method continues. Line 72 sets occupied to false, line 74 stores the value of buffer in readValue and line 75 outputs the readValue. Then line 78 signals the condition object canWrite. This will awaken the Producer if it is indeed waiting for the buffer to be emptied. Line 82 calls method unlock from a finally block to release the lock, and line 85 returns readValue to the calling method.

Common Programming Error 23.4

Forgetting to signal a waiting thread is a logic error. The thread will remain in the waiting state, which will prevent the thread from proceeding. Such waiting can lead to indefinite postponement or deadlock.

Class SharedBufferTest2 (Fig. 23.23) is identical to that of Fig. 23.19. Study the outputs in Fig. 23.23. Observe that every integer produced is consumed exactly once—no values are lost, and no values are consumed more than once. The Lock and Condition objects ensure that the Producer and Consumer cannot perform their tasks unless it is their turn. The Producer must go first, the Consumer must wait if the Producer has not produced since the Consumer last consumed and the Producer must wait if the Consumer has not yet consumed the value that the Producer most recently produced. Execute this program several times to confirm that every integer produced is consumed exactly once. In the sample output, note the highlighted lines indicating when the Producer and Consumer must wait to perform their respective tasks.

```
1   // Fig. 23.23: SharedBufferTest2.java
2   // Two threads manipulating a synchronized buffer.
3   import java.util.concurrent.ExecutorService;
4   import java.util.concurrent.Executors;
5
6   public class SharedBufferTest2
7   {
8      public static void main( String[] args )
9      {
10        // create new thread pool with two threads
11        ExecutorService application = Executors.newCachedThreadPool();
12
13        // create SynchronizedBuffer to store ints
14        Buffer sharedLocation = new SynchronizedBuffer();
15
16        System.out.printf( "%-40s%s\t\t%s\n%-40s%s\n\n", "Operation",
17           "Buffer", "Occupied", "---------", "------\t\t--------" );
18
19        // execute the Producer and Consumer tasks
20        application.execute( new Producer( sharedLocation ) );
21        application.execute( new Consumer( sharedLocation ) );
22
23        application.shutdown();
24     } // end main
25  } // end class SharedBufferTest2
```

Operation	Buffer	Occupied
---------	------	--------
Producer writes 1	1	true
Producer tries to write. Buffer full. Producer waits.	1	true

Fig. 23.23 | Two threads manipulating a synchronized buffer. (Part 1 of 2.)

Consumer reads 1	1	false
Producer writes 2	2	true
Producer tries to write. Buffer full. Producer waits.	2	true
Consumer reads 2	2	false
Producer writes 3	3	true
Consumer reads 3	3	false
Producer writes 4	4	true
Consumer reads 4	4	false
Consumer tries to read. Buffer empty. Consumer waits.	4	false
Producer writes 5	5	true
Consumer reads 5	5	false
Consumer tries to read. Buffer empty. Consumer waits.	5	false
Producer writes 6	6	true
Consumer reads 6	6	false
Producer writes 7	7	true
Consumer reads 7	7	false
Producer writes 8	8	true
Consumer reads 8	8	false
Producer writes 9	9	true
Consumer reads 9	9	false
Producer writes 10	10	true
Producer done producing Terminating Producer Consumer reads 10	10	false
Consumer read values totaling 55 Terminating Consumer		

Fig. 23.23 | Two threads manipulating a synchronized buffer. (Part 2 of 2.)

23.11 Multithreading with GUI

Swing applications present a unique set of challenges for multithreaded programming. All Swing applications have a single thread, called the **event dispatch thread**, to handle interactions with the application's GUI components. Typical interactions include updating GUI components or processing user actions such as mouse clicks. All tasks that require interaction with an application's GUI are placed in an event queue and are executed sequentially by the event dispatch thread.

Swing GUI components are not thread safe—they cannot be manipulated by multiple threads without the risk of incorrect results. Unlike the other examples presented in this chapter, thread safety in GUI applications is achieved not by synchronizing thread actions, but by ensuring that Swing components are accessed from only a single thread—the event dispatch thread. This technique is called thread confinement. Allowing just one thread to access non-thread-safe objects eliminates the possibility of corruption due to multiple threads accessing these objects concurrently.

Usually it is sufficient to perform simple calculations on the event dispatch thread in sequence with GUI component manipulations. If an application must perform a lengthy computation in response to a user interface interaction, the event dispatch thread cannot attend to other tasks in the event queue while the thread is tied up in that computation. This causes the GUI components to become unresponsive. It is preferable to handle a long-running computation in a separate thread, freeing the event dispatch thread to continue managing other GUI interactions. Of course, to update the GUI based on the computation's results, you must update the GUI from the event dispatch thread, rather than from the worker thread that performed the computation.

Class *SwingWorker*

Java SE 6 provides class SwingWorker (in package javax.swing) to perform long-running computations in a worker thread and to update Swing components from the event dispatch thread based on the computations' results. SwingWorker implements the Runnable interface, meaning that a SwingWorker object can be scheduled to execute in a separate thread. The SwingWorker class provides several methods to simplify performing computations in a worker thread and making the results available for display in a GUI. Some common SwingWorker methods are described in Fig. 23.24.

Method	Description
doInBackground	Defines a long computation and is called in a worker thread.
done	Executes on the event dispatch thread when doInBackground returns.
execute	Schedules the SwingWorker object to be executed in a worker thread.
get	Waits for the computation to complete, then returns the result of the computation (i.e., the return value of doInBackground).
publish	Sends intermediate results from the doInBackground method to the process method for processing on the event dispatch thread.
process	Receives intermediate results from the publish method and processes these results on the event dispatch thread.
setProgress	Sets the progress property to notify any property change listeners on the event dispatch thread of progress bar updates.

Fig. 23.24 | Commonly used SwingWorker methods.

23.11.1 Performing Computations in a Worker Thread

In the next example, a GUI provides components for a user to enter a number n and get the nth Fibonacci number, which we calculate using the recursive algorithm discussed in Section 15.4. Since the recursive algorithm is time consuming for large values, we use a SwingWorker object to perform the calculation in a worker thread. The GUI also provides a separate set of components that get the next Fibonacci number in the sequence with each click of a button, beginning with fibonacci(1). This set of components performs its short computation directly in the event dispatch thread.

Class BackgroundCalculator (Fig. 23.25) performs the recursive Fibonacci calculation in a worker thread. This class extends SwingWorker (line 8), overriding the methods doInBackground and done. Method doInBackground (lines 21–25) computes the nth Fibonacci number in a worker thread and returns the result. Method done (lines 28–44) displays the result in a JLabel.

```
 1   // Fig. 23.25: BackgroundCalculator.java
 2   // SwingWorker subclass for calculating Fibonacci numbers
 3   // in a background thread.
 4   import javax.swing.SwingWorker;
 5   import javax.swing.JLabel;
 6   import java.util.concurrent.ExecutionException;
 7
 8   public class BackgroundCalculator extends SwingWorker< String, Object >
 9   {
10      private final int n; // Fibonacci number to calculate
11      private final JLabel resultJLabel; // JLabel to display the result
12
13      // constructor
14      public BackgroundCalculator( int number, JLabel label )
15      {
16         n = number;
17         resultJLabel = label;
18      } // end BackgroundCalculator constructor
19
20      // long-running code to be run in a worker thread
21      public String doInBackground()
22      {
23         long nthFib = fibonacci( n );
24         return String.valueOf( nthFib );
25      } // end method doInBackground
26
27      // code to run on the event dispatch thread when doInBackground returns
28      protected void done()
29      {
30         try
31         {
32            // get the result of doInBackground and display it
33            resultJLabel.setText( get() );
34         } // end try
```

Fig. 23.25 | SwingWorker subclass for calculating Fibonacci numbers in a background thread. (Part 1 of 2.)

```
35          catch ( InterruptedException ex )
36          {
37              resultJLabel.setText( "Interrupted while waiting for results." );
38          } // end catch
39          catch ( ExecutionException ex )
40          {
41              resultJLabel.setText(
42                  "Error encountered while performing calculation." );
43          } // end catch
44      } // end method done
45
46      // recursive method fibonacci; calculates nth Fibonacci number
47      public long fibonacci( long number )
48      {
49          if ( number == 0 || number == 1 )
50              return number;
51          else
52              return fibonacci( number - 1 ) + fibonacci( number - 2 );
53      } // end method fibonacci
54  } // end class BackgroundCalculator
```

Fig. 23.25 | `SwingWorker` subclass for calculating Fibonacci numbers in a background thread. (Part 2 of 2.)

Note that SwingWorker is a generic class. In line 8, the first type parameter is String and the second is Object. The first type parameter indicates the type returned by the doIn-Background method; the second indicates the type that is passed between the publish and process methods to handle intermediate results. Since we do not use publish and process in this example, we simply use Object as the second type parameter. We discuss publish and process in Section 23.11.2.

A BackgroundCalculator object can be instantiated from a class that controls a GUI. A BackgroundCalculator maintains instance variables for an integer that represents the Fibonacci number to be calculated and a JLabel that displays the results of the calculation (lines 10–11). The BackgroundCalculator constructor (lines 14–18) initializes these instance variables with the arguments that are passed to the constructor.

Software Engineering Observation 23.3

Any GUI components that will be manipulated by SwingWorker methods, such as components that will be updated from methods process or done, should be passed to the SwingWorker subclass's constructor and stored in the subclass object. This gives these methods access to the GUI components they will manipulate.

When method execute is called on a BackgroundCalculator object, the object is scheduled for execution in a worker thread. Method doInBackground is called from the worker thread and invokes the fibonacci method (lines 47–53), passing instance variable n as an argument (line 23). Method fibonacci uses recursion to compute the Fibonacci of n. When fibonacci returns, method doInBackground returns the result.

After doInBackground returns, method done is called from the event dispatch thread. This method attempts to set the result JLabel to the return value of doInBackground by calling method get to retrieve this return value (line 33). Method get waits for the result to be ready if necessary, but since we call it from method done, the computation will be complete before get is called. Lines 35–38 catch InterruptedException if the current thread is interrupted while waiting for get to return. Lines 39–43 catch ExecutionException, which is thrown if an exception occurs during the computation.

Class FibonacciNumbers (Fig. 23.26) displays a window containing two sets of GUI components—one set to compute a Fibonacci number in a worker thread and another to get the next Fibonacci number in response to the user's clicking a JButton. The constructor (lines 38–109) places these components in separate titled JPanels. Lines 46–47 and 78–79 add two JLabels, a JTextField and a JButton to the workerJPanel to allow the user to enter an integer whose Fibonacci number will be calculated by the BackgroundWorker. Lines 84–85 and 103 add two JLabels and a JButton to the event dispatch thread panel to allow the user to get the next Fibonacci number in the sequence. Instance variables n1 and n2 contain the previous two Fibonacci numbers in the sequence and are initialized to 0 and 1, respectively (lines 29–30). Instance variable count stores the most recently computed sequence number and is initialized to 1 (line 31). The two JLabels display count and n2 initially, so that the user will see the text Fibonacci of 1: 1 in the eventThreadJPanel when the GUI starts.

```
1    // Fig. 23.26: FibonacciNumbers.java
2    // Using SwingWorker to perform a long calculation with
3    // intermediate results displayed in a GUI.
4    import java.awt.GridLayout;
5    import java.awt.event.ActionEvent;
6    import java.awt.event.ActionListener;
7    import javax.swing.JButton;
8    import javax.swing.JFrame;
9    import javax.swing.JPanel;
10   import javax.swing.JLabel;
11   import javax.swing.JTextField;
12   import javax.swing.border.TitledBorder;
13   import javax.swing.border.LineBorder;
14   import java.awt.Color;
15   import java.util.concurrent.ExecutionException;
16
17   public class FibonacciNumbers extends JFrame
18   {
19      // components for calculating the Fibonacci of a user-entered number
20      private final JPanel workerJPanel =
21         new JPanel( new GridLayout( 2, 2, 5, 5 ) );
22      private final JTextField numberJTextField = new JTextField();
23      private final JButton goJButton = new JButton( "Go" );
24      private final JLabel fibonacciJLabel = new JLabel();
25
26      // components and variables for getting the next Fibonacci number
27      private final JPanel eventThreadJPanel =
28         new JPanel( new GridLayout( 2, 2, 5, 5 ) );
29      private int n1 = 0; // initialize with first Fibonacci number
```

Fig. 23.26 | Using SwingWorker to perform a long calculation with intermediate results displayed in a GUI. (Part 1 of 4.)

```
30     private int n2 = 1; // initialize with second Fibonacci number
31     private int count = 1;
32     private final JLabel nJLabel = new JLabel( "Fibonacci of 1: " );
33     private final JLabel nFibonacciJLabel =
34        new JLabel( String.valueOf( n2 ) );
35     private final JButton nextNumberJButton = new JButton( "Next Number" );
36
37     // constructor
38     public FibonacciNumbers()
39     {
40        super( "Fibonacci Numbers" );
41        setLayout( new GridLayout( 2, 1, 10, 10 ) );
42
43        // add GUI components to the SwingWorker panel
44        workerJPanel.setBorder( new TitledBorder(
45           new LineBorder( Color.BLACK ), "With SwingWorker" ) );
46        workerJPanel.add( new JLabel( "Get Fibonacci of:" ) );
47        workerJPanel.add( numberJTextField );
48        goJButton.addActionListener(
49           new ActionListener()
50           {
51              public void actionPerformed( ActionEvent event )
52              {
53                 int n;
54
55                 try
56                 {
57                    // retrieve user's input as an integer
58                    n = Integer.parseInt( numberJTextField.getText() );
59                 } // end try
60                 catch( NumberFormatException ex )
61                 {
62                    // display an error message if the user did not
63                    // enter an integer
64                    fibonacciJLabel.setText( "Enter an integer." );
65                    return;
66                 } // end catch
67
68                 // indicate that the calculation has begun
69                 fibonacciJLabel.setText( "Calculating..." );
70
71                 // create a task to perform calculation in background
72                 BackgroundCalculator task =
73                    new BackgroundCalculator( n, fibonacciJLabel );
74                 task.execute(); // execute the task
75              } // end method actionPerformed
76           } // end anonymous inner class
77        ); // end call to addActionListener
78        workerJPanel.add( goJButton );
79        workerJPanel.add( fibonacciJLabel );
80
```

Fig. 23.26 | Using SwingWorker to perform a long calculation with intermediate results displayed in a GUI. (Part 2 of 4.)

```
81          // add GUI components to the event-dispatching thread panel
82          eventThreadJPanel.setBorder( new TitledBorder(
83             new LineBorder( Color.BLACK ), "Without SwingWorker" ) );
84          eventThreadJPanel.add( nJLabel );
85          eventThreadJPanel.add( nFibonacciJLabel );
86          nextNumberJButton.addActionListener(
87             new ActionListener()
88             {
89                public void actionPerformed( ActionEvent event )
90                {
91                   // calculate the Fibonacci number after n2
92                   int temp = n1 + n2;
93                   n1 = n2;
94                   n2 = temp;
95                   ++count;
96
97                   // display the next Fibonacci number
98                   nJLabel.setText( "Fibonacci of " + count + ": " );
99                   nFibonacciJLabel.setText( String.valueOf( n2 ) );
100               } // end method actionPerformed
101            } // end anonymous inner class
102         ); // end call to addActionListener
103         eventThreadJPanel.add( nextNumberJButton );
104
105         add( workerJPanel );
106         add( eventThreadJPanel );
107         setSize( 275, 200 );
108         setVisible( true );
109      } // end constructor
110
111      // main method begins program execution
112      public static void main( String[] args )
113      {
114         FibonacciNumbers application = new FibonacciNumbers();
115         application.setDefaultCloseOperation( EXIT_ON_CLOSE );
116      } // end main
117   } // end class FibonacciNumbers
```

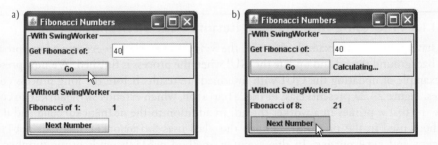

Fig. 23.26 | Using `SwingWorker` to perform a long calculation with intermediate results displayed in a GUI. (Part 3 of 4.)

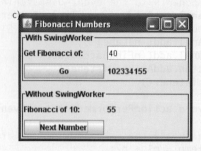

Fig. 23.26 | Using SwingWorker to perform a long calculation with intermediate results displayed in a GUI. (Part 4 of 4.)

Lines 48–77 register the event handler for the goJButton. If the user clicks this JButton, line 58 gets the value entered in the numberJTextField and attempts to parse it as an integer. Lines 72–73 create a new BackgroundCalculator object, passing in the user-entered value and the fibonacciJLabel that is used to display the calculation's results. Line 74 calls method execute on the BackgroundCalculator, scheduling it for execution in a separate worker thread. Method execute does not wait for the BackgroundCalculator to finish executing. It returns immediately, allowing the GUI to continue processing other events while the computation is performed.

If the user clicks the nextNumberJButton in the eventThreadJPanel, the event handler registered in lines 86–102 executes. The previous two Fibonacci numbers stored in n1 and n2 are added together and count is incremented to determine the next number in the sequence (lines 92–95). Then lines 98–99 update the GUI to display the next number. The code to perform these calculations is written directly in method actionPerformed, so these calculations are performed on the event dispatch thread. Handling such short computations in the event dispatch thread does not cause the GUI to become unresponsive, like the recursive algorithm for calculating the Fibonacci of a large number. Because the longer Fibonacci computation is performed in a separate worker thread using the Swing-Worker, it is possible to get the next Fibonacci number while the recursive computation is still in progress.

23.11.2 Processing Intermediate Results with SwingWorker

We have presented an example that uses the SwingWorker class to execute a long process in a background thread and update the GUI when the process is finished. We now present an example of updating the GUI with intermediate results before the long process completes. Figure 23.27 presents class PrimeCalculator, which extends SwingWorker to compute the first *n* primes in a worker thread. In addition to the doInBackground and done methods used in the previous example, this class uses SwingWorker methods publish, process and setProgress. In this example, method publish sends prime numbers to method process as they are found, method process displays these primes in a GUI component and method setProgress updates the progress property. We later show how to use this property to update a JProgressBar.

```
1    // Fig. 23.27: PrimeCalculator.java
2    // Calculates the first n primes, displaying them as they are found.
3    import javax.swing.JTextArea;
4    import javax.swing.JLabel;
5    import javax.swing.JButton;
6    import javax.swing.SwingWorker;
7    import java.util.Random;
8    import java.util.List;
9    import java.util.concurrent.ExecutionException;
10
11   public class PrimeCalculator extends SwingWorker< Integer, Integer >
12   {
13      private final Random generator = new Random();
14      private final JTextArea intermediateJTextArea; // displays found primes
15      private final JButton getPrimesJButton;
16      private final JButton cancelJButton;
17      private final JLabel statusJLabel; // displays status of calculation
18      private final boolean primes[]; // boolean array for finding primes
19      private boolean stopped = false; // flag indicating cancelation
20
21      // constructor
22      public PrimeCalculator( int max, JTextArea intermediate, JLabel status,
23         JButton getPrimes, JButton cancel )
24      {
25         intermediateJTextArea = intermediate;
26         statusJLabel = status;
27         getPrimesJButton = getPrimes;
28         cancelJButton = cancel;
29         primes = new boolean[ max ];
30
31         // initialize all primes array values to true
32         for ( int i = 0; i < max; i ++ )
33            primes[ i ] = true;
34      } // end constructor
35
36      // finds all primes up to max using the Sieve of Eratosthenes
37      public Integer doInBackground()
38      {
39         int count = 0; // the number of primes found
40
41         // starting at the third value, cycle through the array and put
42         // false as the value of any greater number that is a multiple
43         for ( int i = 2; i < primes.length; i++ )
44         {
45            if ( stopped ) // if calculation has been canceled
46               return count;
47            else
48            {
49               setProgress( 100 * ( i + 1 ) / primes.length );
50
51               try
52               {
```

Fig. 23.27 | Calculates the first *n* primes, displaying them as they are found. (Part 1 of 3.)

```
53              Thread.currentThread().sleep( generator.nextInt( 5 ) );
54           } // end try
55           catch ( InterruptedException ex )
56           {
57              statusJLabel.setText( "Worker thread interrupted" );
58              return count;
59           } // end catch
60
61           if ( primes[ i ] ) // i is prime
62           {
63              publish( i ); // make i available for display in prime list
64              ++count;
65
66              for ( int j = i + i; j < primes.length; j += i )
67                 primes[ j ] = false; // i is not prime
68           } // end if
69        } // end else
70     } // end for
71
72     return count;
73  } // end method doInBackground
74
75  // displays published values in primes list
76  protected void process( List< Integer > publishedVals )
77  {
78     for ( int i = 0; i < publishedVals.size(); i++ )
79        intermediateJTextArea.append( publishedVals.get( i ) + "\n" );
80  } // end method process
81
82  // code to execute when doInBackground completes
83  protected void done()
84  {
85     getPrimesJButton.setEnabled( true ); // enable Get Primes button
86     cancelJButton.setEnabled( false ); // disable Cancel button
87
88     int numPrimes;
89
90     try
91     {
92        numPrimes = get(); // retrieve doInBackground return value
93     } // end try
94     catch ( InterruptedException ex )
95     {
96        statusJLabel.setText( "Interrupted while waiting for results." );
97        return;
98     } // end catch
99     catch ( ExecutionException ex )
100    {
101       statusJLabel.setText( "Error performing computation." );
102       return;
103    } // end catch
104
```

Fig. 23.27 | Calculates the first *n* primes, displaying them as they are found. (Part 2 of 3.)

```
105          statusJLabel.setText( "Found " + numPrimes + " primes." );
106       } // end method done
107
108       // sets flag to stop looking for primes
109       public void stopCalculation()
110       {
111          stopped = true;
112       } // end method stopCalculation
113    } // end class PrimeCalculator
```

Fig. 23.27 | Calculates the first *n* primes, displaying them as they are found. (Part 3 of 3.)

Class `PrimeCalculator` extends `SwingWorker` (line 11), with the first type parameter indicating the return type of method `doInBackground` and the second indicating the type of intermediate results passed between methods `publish` and `process`. In this case, both type parameters are `Integer`s. The constructor (lines 22–34) takes as arguments an integer that indicates the upper limit of the prime numbers to locate, a `JTextArea` used to display primes in the GUI, one `JButton` for initiating a calculation and one for canceling it, and a `JLabel` used to display the status of the calculation.

Lines 32–33 initialize the elements of the `boolean` array primes to `true`. `PrimeCalculator` uses this array and the Sieve of Eratosthenes algorithm (described in Exercise 7.27) to find all primes less than `max`. The Sieve of Eratosthenes takes a list of natural numbers of any length and, beginning with the first prime number, filters out all multiples of that prime. It then moves to the next prime, which will be the next number that is not yet filtered out, and eliminates all of its multiples. It continues until the end of the list is reached and all non-primes have been filtered out. Algorithmically, we begin with element 2 of the `boolean` array and set the cells corresponding to all values that are multiples of 2 to `false` to indicate that they are divisible by 2 and thus not prime. We then move to the next array element, check whether it is `true`, and if so set all of its multiples to `false` to indicate that they are divisible by the current index. When the whole array has been traversed in this way, all indices that contain `true` are prime, as they have no divisors.

In method `doInBackground` (lines 37–73), the control variable i for the loop (lines 43–70) controls the current index for implementing the Sieve of Eratosthenes. Line 45 tests the `stopped` `boolean` flag, which indicates whether the user has clicked the **Cancel** button. If `stopped` is `true`, the method returns the number of primes found so far (line 46) without finishing the computation.

If the calculation is not canceled, line 49 calls method `setProgress` to update the progress property with the percentage of the array that has been traversed so far. Line 53 puts the currently executing thread to sleep for up to 4 milliseconds. We discuss the reason for this shortly. Line 61 tests whether the element of array primes at the current index is `true` (and thus prime). If so, line 63 passes the index to method `publish` so that it can be displayed as an intermediate result in the GUI and line 64 increments the number of primes found. Lines 66–67 set all multiples of the current index to `false` to indicate that they are not prime. When the entire `boolean` array has been traversed, the number of primes found is returned at line 72.

Lines 76–80 declare method `process`, which executes in the event dispatch thread and receives its argument `publishedVals` from method `publish`. The passing of values between publish in the worker thread and process in the event dispatch thread is asynchronous; process is not necessarily invoked for every call to publish. All Integers published since the last call to process are received as a List by method process. Lines 78–79 iterate through this list and display the published values in a JTextArea. Because the computation in method doInBackground progresses quickly, publishing values often, updates to the JTextArea can pile up on the event dispatch thread, causing the GUI to become sluggish. In fact, when searching for a large enough number of primes, the event dispatch thread may receive so many requests in quick succession to update the JTextArea that the thread will run out of memory in its event queue. This is why we put the worker thread to sleep for a few milliseconds between each potential call to publish. The calculation is slowed just enough to allow the event dispatch thread to keep up with requests to update the JTextArea with new primes, enabling the GUI to update smoothly and remain responsive.

Lines 83–106 define method done. When the calculation is finished or canceled, method done enables the **Get Primes** button and disables the **Cancel** button (lines 85–86). Line 92 gets the return value—the number of primes found—from method doInBackground. Lines 94–103 catch the exceptions thrown by method get and display an appropriate error message in the statusJLabel. If no exceptions occur, line 105 sets the statusJLabel to indicate the number of primes found.

Lines 109–112 define public method stopCalculation, which is invoked when the **Cancel** button is clicked. This method sets the flag stopped at line 111 so that doInBackground will return without finishing its calculation the next time it tests this flag. Though SwingWorker provides a method cancel, this method simply calls Thread method interrupt on the worker thread. Using the boolean flag instead of cancel allows us to stop the calculation cleanly, return a value from doInBackground and ensure that method done is called even though the calculation did not run to completion, without the risk of throwing an InterruptedException associated with interrupting the worker thread.

Class FindPrimes (Fig. 23.28) displays a JTextField that allows the user to enter a number, a JButton to begin finding all primes less than that number and a JTextArea to display the primes. A JButton allows the user to cancel the calculation, and a JProgressBar indicates the calculation's progress. The FindPrimes constructor (lines 32–125) initializes these components and displays them in a JFrame using BorderLayout.

Lines 42–94 register the event handler for the getPrimesJButton. When the user clicks this JButton, lines 47–49 reset the JProgressBar and clear the displayPrimesJTextArea and the statusJLabel. Lines 53–63 parse the value in the JTextField and display an error message if the value is not an integer. Lines 66–68 construct a new PrimeCalculator object, passing as arguments the integer the user entered, the displayPrimesJTextArea for displaying the primes, the statusJLabel and the two JButtons.

Lines 71–85 register a PropertyChangeListener for the new PrimeCalculator object using an anonymous inner class. **PropertyChangeListener** is an interface from package java.beans that defines a single method, propertyChange. Every time method setProgress is invoked on a PrimeCalculator, the PrimeCalculator generates a PropertyChangeEvent to indicate that the progress property has changed. Method propertyChange listens for these events. Line 78 tests whether a given PropertyChangeEvent indicates a change to the progress property. If so, line 80 gets the new value of the property and line 81 updates the JProgressBar with the new progress property value. The **Get Primes**

JButton is disabled (line 88) so that only one calculation that updates the GUI can execute at a time, and the **Cancel** JButton is enabled (line 89) to allow the user to stop the computation before it completes. Line 91 executes the PrimesCalculator to begin finding primes. If the user clicks the cancelJButton, the event handler registered at lines 107–115 calls PrimeCalculator method stopCalculation (line 112) and the calculation returns early.

```
1   // Fig 23.28: FindPrimes.java
2   // Using a SwingWorker to display prime numbers and update a JProgressBar
3   // while the prime numbers are being calculated.
4   import javax.swing.JFrame;
5   import javax.swing.JTextField;
6   import javax.swing.JTextArea;
7   import javax.swing.JButton;
8   import javax.swing.JProgressBar;
9   import javax.swing.JLabel;
10  import javax.swing.JPanel;
11  import javax.swing.JScrollPane;
12  import javax.swing.ScrollPaneConstants;
13  import java.awt.BorderLayout;
14  import java.awt.GridLayout;
15  import java.awt.event.ActionListener;
16  import java.awt.event.ActionEvent;
17  import java.util.concurrent.ExecutionException;
18  import java.beans.PropertyChangeListener;
19  import java.beans.PropertyChangeEvent;
20
21  public class FindPrimes extends JFrame
22  {
23     private final JTextField highestPrimeJTextField = new JTextField();
24     private final JButton getPrimesJButton = new JButton( "Get Primes" );
25     private final JTextArea displayPrimesJTextArea = new JTextArea();
26     private final JButton cancelJButton = new JButton( "Cancel" );
27     private final JProgressBar progressJProgressBar = new JProgressBar();
28     private final JLabel statusJLabel = new JLabel();
29     private PrimeCalculator calculator;
30
31     // constructor
32     public FindPrimes()
33     {
34        super( "Finding Primes with SwingWorker" );
35        setLayout( new BorderLayout() );
36
37        // initialize panel to get a number from the user
38        JPanel northJPanel = new JPanel();
39        northJPanel.add( new JLabel( "Find primes less than: " ) );
40        highestPrimeJTextField.setColumns( 5 );
41        northJPanel.add( highestPrimeJTextField );
42        getPrimesJButton.addActionListener(
43           new ActionListener()
44           {
```

Fig. 23.28 | Using a SwingWorker to display prime numbers and update a JProgressBar while the prime numbers are being calculated. (Part 1 of 4.)

```
45          public void actionPerformed( ActionEvent e )
46          {
47              progressJProgressBar.setValue( 0 ); // reset JProgressBar
48              displayPrimesJTextArea.setText( "" ); // clear JTextArea
49              statusJLabel.setText( "" ); // clear JLabel
50
51              int number;
52
53              try
54              {
55                  // get user input
56                  number = Integer.parseInt(
57                      highestPrimeJTextField.getText() );
58              } // end try
59              catch ( NumberFormatException ex )
60              {
61                  statusJLabel.setText( "Enter an integer." );
62                  return;
63              } // end catch
64
65              // construct a new PrimeCalculator object
66              calculator = new PrimeCalculator( number,
67                  displayPrimesJTextArea, statusJLabel, getPrimesJButton,
68                  cancelJButton );
69
70              // listen for progress bar property changes
71              calculator.addPropertyChangeListener(
72                  new PropertyChangeListener()
73                  {
74                      public void propertyChange( PropertyChangeEvent e )
75                      {
76                          // if the changed property is progress,
77                          // update the progress bar
78                          if ( e.getPropertyName().equals( "progress" ) )
79                          {
80                              int newValue = ( Integer ) e.getNewValue();
81                              progressJProgressBar.setValue( newValue );
82                          } // end if
83                      } // end method propertyChange
84                  } // end anonymous inner class
85              ); // end call to addPropertyChangeListener
86
87              // disable Get Primes button and enable Cancel button
88              getPrimesJButton.setEnabled( false );
89              cancelJButton.setEnabled( true );
90
91              calculator.execute(); // execute the PrimeCalculator object
92          } // end method ActionPerformed
93      } // end anonymous inner class
94  ); // end call to addActionListener
95  northJPanel.add( getPrimesJButton );
```

Fig. 23.28 | Using a SwingWorker to display prime numbers and update a JProgressBar while the prime numbers are being calculated. (Part 2 of 4.)

```
96
97        // add a scrollable JList to display results of calculation
98        displayPrimesJTextArea.setEditable( false );
99        add( new JScrollPane( displayPrimesJTextArea,
100          ScrollPaneConstants.VERTICAL_SCROLLBAR_ALWAYS,
101          ScrollPaneConstants.HORIZONTAL_SCROLLBAR_NEVER ) );
102
103       // initialize a panel to display cancelJButton,
104       // progressJProgressBar, and statusJLabel
105       JPanel southJPanel = new JPanel( new GridLayout( 1, 3, 10, 10 ) );
106       cancelJButton.setEnabled( false );
107       cancelJButton.addActionListener(
108         new ActionListener()
109         {
110           public void actionPerformed( ActionEvent e )
111           {
112             calculator.stopCalculation(); // cancel the calculation
113           } // end method ActionPerformed
114         } // end anonymous inner class
115       ); // end call to addActionListener
116       southJPanel.add( cancelJButton );
117       progressJProgressBar.setStringPainted( true );
118       southJPanel.add( progressJProgressBar );
119       southJPanel.add( statusJLabel );
120
121       add( northJPanel, BorderLayout.NORTH );
122       add( southJPanel, BorderLayout.SOUTH );
123       setSize( 350, 300 );
124       setVisible( true );
125     } // end constructor
126
127     // main method begins program execution
128     public static void main( String[] args )
129     {
130       FindPrimes application = new FindPrimes();
131       application.setDefaultCloseOperation( EXIT_ON_CLOSE );
132     } // end main
133   } // end class FindPrimes
```

Fig. 23.28 | Using a SwingWorker to display prime numbers and update a JProgressBar while the prime numbers are being calculated. (Part 3 of 4.)

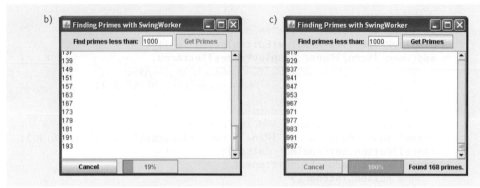

Fig. 23.28 | Using a `SwingWorker` to display prime numbers and update a `JProgressBar` while the prime numbers are being calculated. (Part 4 of 4.)

23.12 Other Classes and Interfaces in java.util.concurrent

Interface `Runnable` provides only the most basic functionality for multithreaded programming. In fact, this interface has several limitations. Suppose a `Runnable` encounters a problem and tries to throw a checked exception. The run method is not declared to throw any exceptions, so the problem must be handled within the `Runnable`—the exception cannot be passed to the calling thread. Now suppose a `Runnable` is performing a long calculation and the application wants to retrieve the result of that calculation. The run method cannot return a value, so the application must use shared data to pass the value back to the calling thread. This also involves the overhead of synchronizing access to the data. The developers of the concurrency APIs introduced in Java SE 5 recognized these limitations and created a new interface to fix them. The `Callable` interface (of package java.util.concurrent) declares a single method named `call`. This interface is designed to be similar to the Runnable interface—allowing an action to be performed concurrently in a separate thread—but the `call` method allows the thread to return a value or to throw a checked exception.

An application that creates a `Callable` likely wants to run the `Callable` concurrently with other `Runnables` and `Callables`. The `ExecutorService` interface provides method **submit**, which will execute a `Callable` passed in as its argument. The submit method returns an object of type **Future** (of package java.util.concurrent), which is an interface that represents the executing `Callable`. The `Future` interface declares method **get** to return the result of the `Callable` and provides other methods to manage a `Callable`'s execution.

23.13 Wrap-Up

In this chapter, you learned that concurrency has historically been implemented with operating system primitives available only to experienced systems programmers, but that Java makes concurrency available to you through the language and APIs. You also learned that the JVM itself creates threads to run a program, and that it also may create threads to perform housekeeping tasks such as garbage collection.

We discussed the life cycle of a thread and the states that a thread may occupy during its lifetime. We also discussed Java's thread priorities, which help the system schedule threads for execution. You learned that you should avoid manipulating Java thread priorities directly and you learned about problems associated with thread priorities, such as indefinite postponement (sometimes called starvation).

Next, we presented the interface `Runnable`, which is used to specify a task that can execute concurrently with other tasks. This interface's `run` method is invoked by the thread executing the task. We showed how to execute a `Runnable` object by associating it with an object of class `Thread`. Then we showed how to use the `Executor` interface to manage the execution of `Runnable` objects via thread pools, which can reuse existing threads to eliminate the overhead of creating a new thread for each task and can improve performance by optimizing the number of threads to ensure that the processor stays busy.

You learned that when multiple threads share an object and one or more of them modify that object, indeterminate results may occur unless access to the shared object is managed properly. We showed you how to solve this problem via thread synchronization, which coordinates access to shared data by multiple concurrent threads. You learned several techniques for performing synchronization—first with the built-in class `ArrayBlockingQueue` (which handles all the synchronization details for you), then with Java's built-in monitors and the `synchronized` keyword, and finally with interfaces `Lock` and `Condition`.

We discussed the fact that Swing GUIs are not thread safe, so all interactions with and modifications to the GUI must be performed in the event dispatch thread. We also discussed the problems associated with performing long-running calculations in the event dispatch thread. Then we showed how you can use Java SE 6's `SwingWorker` class to perform long-running calculations in worker threads. You learned how to display the results of a `SwingWorker` in a GUI when the calculation completed and how to display intermediate results while the calculation was still in process.

Finally, we discussed the `Callable` and `Future` interfaces, which enable you to execute tasks that return results and to obtain those results, respectively. We use the multithreading techniques introduced here again in Chapter 24, Networking, to help build multithreaded servers that can interact with multiple clients concurrently.

Summary

Section 23.1 Introduction
- Historically, concurrency has been implemented with operating system primitives available only to experienced systems programmers.
- The Ada programming language, developed by the United States Department of Defense, made concurrency primitives widely available to defense contractors building military command-and-control systems.
- Java makes concurrency available to you through the language and APIs. You specify that an application contains separate threads of execution, where each thread has its own method-call stack and program counter, allowing it to execute concurrently with other threads while sharing application-wide resources such as memory with these other threads.
- In addition to creating threads to run a program, the JVM also may create threads for performing housekeeping tasks such as garbage collection.

Section 23.2 Thread States: Life Cycle of a Thread
- At any time, a thread is said to be in one of several thread states.

- A new thread begins its life cycle in the *new* state. It remains in this state until the program starts the thread, which places the thread in the *runnable* state. A thread in the *runnable* state is considered to be executing its task.

- Sometimes a *runnable* thread transitions to the *waiting* state while it waits for another thread to perform a task. A *waiting* thread transitions back to the *runnable* state only when another thread notifies it to continue executing.

- A *runnable* thread can enter the *timed waiting* state for a specified interval of time. A *timed waiting* thread transitions back to the *runnable* state when that time interval expires or when the event it is waiting for occurs.

- A *runnable* thread can transition to the *timed waiting* state if it provides an optional wait interval when it is waiting for another thread to perform a task. Such a thread will return to the *runnable* state when it is notified by another thread or when the timed interval expires.

- A sleeping thread remains in the *timed waiting* state for a designated period of time, after which it returns to the *runnable* state.

- A *runnable* thread transitions to the *blocked* state when it attempts to perform a task that cannot be completed immediately and the thread must temporarily wait until that task completes. At that point, the *blocked* thread transitions to the *runnable* state, so it can resume execution. A *blocked* thread cannot use a processor, even if one is available.

- A *runnable* thread enters the *terminated* state when it successfully completes its task or otherwise terminates (perhaps due to an error).

- At the operating system level, Java's *runnable* state typically encompasses two separate states. When a thread first transitions to the *runnable* state from the *new* state, the thread is in the *ready* state. A *ready* thread enters the *running* state when the operating system assigns the thread to a processor—also known as dispatching the thread.

- In most operating systems, each thread is given a small amount of processor time—called a quantum or timeslice—with which to perform its task. When the thread's quantum expires, the thread returns to the *ready* state and the operating system assigns another thread to the processor.

- The process that an operating system uses to determine which thread to dispatch is called thread scheduling and is dependent on thread priorities (discussed in the next section).

Section 23.3 Thread Priorities and Thread Scheduling

- Every Java thread has a thread priority (from MIN_PRIORITY to MAX_PRIORITY) that helps the operating system determine the order in which threads are scheduled.

- By default, every thread is given priority NORM_PRIORITY (a constant of 5). Each new thread inherits the priority of the thread that created it.

- Most operating systems enable threads of equal priority to share a processor with timeslicing.

- The job of an operating system's thread scheduler is to determine which thread runs next.

- When a higher-priority thread enters the *ready* state, the operating system generally preempts the currently *running* thread (an operation known as preemptive scheduling).

- Depending on the operating system, higher-priority threads could postpone—possibly indefinitely—the execution of lower-priority threads. Such indefinite postponement is sometimes referred to more colorfully as starvation.

Section 23.4 Creating and Executing Threads

- The preferred means of creating multithreaded Java applications is by implementing interface Runnable (of package java.lang). A Runnable object represents a "task" that can execute concurrently with other tasks.

- Interface `Runnable` declares method `run` in which you place the code that defines the task to perform. The thread executing a `Runnable` calls method `run` to perform the task.

- A program will not terminate until its last thread completes execution, at which point the JVM will also terminate.

- You cannot predict the order in which threads will be scheduled, even if you know the order in which they were created and started.

- Though it is possible to create threads explicitly, it is recommended that you use the `Executor` interface to manage the execution of `Runnable` objects for you. An `Executor` object typically creates and manages a group of threads called a thread pool to execute `Runnable`s.

- Executors can reuse existing threads to eliminate the overhead of creating a new thread for each task and can improve performance by optimizing the number of threads to ensure that the processor stays busy.

- Interface `Executor` declares method `execute`, which accepts a `Runnable` as an argument and assigns it to one of the available threads in the thread pool. If there are no available threads, the `Executor` creates a new thread or waits for a thread to become available.

- Interface `ExecutorService` (of package `java.util.concurrent`) extends interface `Executor` and declares other methods for managing the life cycle of an `Executor`.

- An object that implements the `ExecutorService` interface can be created using `static` methods declared in class `Executors` (of package `java.util.concurrent`).

- Executors method `newCachedThreadPool` returns an `ExecutorService` that creates new threads as they are needed by the application.

- `ExecutorService` method `execute` executes its `Runnable` sometime in the future. The method returns immediately from each invocation—the program does not wait for each task to finish.

- `ExecutorService` method `shutdown` notifies the `ExecutorService` to stop accepting new tasks, but continues executing tasks that have already been submitted. Once all of the previously submitted `Runnable`s have completed, the `ExecutorService` terminates.

Section 23.5 Thread Synchronization

- When multiple threads share an object and one or more of them modify that object, indeterminate results may occur unless access to the shared object is managed properly. The problem can be solved by giving only one thread at a time *exclusive access* to code that manipulates the shared object. During that time, other threads desiring to manipulate the object are kept waiting. When the thread with exclusive access to the object finishes manipulating it, one of the threads that was waiting is allowed to proceed. This process, called thread synchronization, coordinates access to shared data by multiple concurrent threads.

- By synchronizing threads, you can ensure that each thread accessing a shared object excludes all other threads from doing so simultaneously—this is called mutual exclusion.

- A common way to perform synchronization is to use Java's built-in monitors. Every object has a monitor and a monitor lock. The monitor ensures that its object's monitor lock is held by a maximum of only one thread at any time, and thus can be used to enforce mutual exclusion.

- If an operation requires the executing thread to hold a lock while the operation is performed, a thread must acquire the lock before it can proceed with the operation. Any other threads attempting to perform an operation that requires the same lock will be *blocked* until the first thread releases the lock, at which point the *blocked* threads may attempt to acquire the lock.

- To specify that a thread must hold a monitor lock in order to execute a block of code, the code should be placed in a `synchronized` statement. Such code is said to be guarded by the monitor lock; a thread must acquire the lock to execute the `synchronized` statements.

- The synchronized statements are declared using the synchronized keyword:

```
synchronized ( object )
{
    statements
} // end synchronized statement
```

  where *object* is the object whose monitor lock will be acquired; *object* is normally this if it's the object in which the synchronized statement appears.

- A synchronized methods is equivalent to a synchronized statement that encloses the entire body of a method and with this as the object whose monitor lock will be acquired.

- Interface ExecutorService provides the awaitTermination method to force a program to wait for threads to complete execution. This method returns control to its caller either when all tasks executing in the ExecutorService complete or when the specified timeout elapses. If all tasks are completed before awaitTermination times out, this method returns true; otherwise it returns false. The two arguments to awaitTermination represent a timeout value and a unit of measure specified with a constant from class TimeUnit.

- You can simulate atomicity by ensuring that only one thread carries out a set of operations at a time. Atomicity can be achieved using the synchronized keyword to create a synchronized statement or synchronized method.

- When you share immutable data across threads, you should declare the corresponding data fields final to indicate that variables' values will not change after they are initialized.

Section 23.6 Producer/Consumer Relationship Without Synchronization
- In a multithreaded producer/consumer relationship, a producer thread generates data and places it in a shared object called a buffer. A consumer thread reads data from the buffer.

- Operations on the buffer data shared by a producer and a consumer are state dependent—they should proceed only if the buffer is in the correct state. If the buffer is in a not-full state, the producer may produce; if the buffer is in a not-empty state, the consumer may consume.

- Threads with access to a buffer must be synchronized to ensure that data is written to the buffer or read from the buffer only if the buffer is in the proper state. If the producer attempting to put the next data into the buffer determines that the buffer is full, the producer thread should wait until there is space. If a consumer thread finds the buffer empty or finds that the previous data has already been read, the consumer must also wait for new data to become available.

Section 23.7 Producer/Consumer Relationship: *ArrayBlockingQueue*
- Java includes a fully implemented buffer class named ArrayBlockingQueue in package java.util.concurrent, which implements the BlockingQueue interface. The BlockingQueue interface extends the Queue interface and declares methods put and take, the blocking equivalents of Queue methods offer and poll, respectively.

- Method put places an element at the end of the BlockingQueue, waiting if the queue is full. Method take removes an element from the head of the BlockingQueue, waiting if the queue is empty. These methods make class ArrayBlockingQueue a good choice for implementing a shared buffer. Because method put blocks until there is room in the buffer to write data and method take blocks until there is new data to read, the producer must produce a value first, the consumer correctly consumes only after the producer writes a value and the producer correctly produces the next value (after the first) only after the consumer reads the previous (or first) value.

- ArrayBlockingQueue stores shared data in an array. The array's size is specified as an argument to the ArrayBlockingQueue constructor. Once created, an ArrayBlockingQueue is fixed in size and will not expand to accommodate extra elements.

Section 23.8 Producer/Consumer Relationship with Synchronization

- You can implement a shared buffer yourself using the synchronized keyword and Object methods wait, notify and notifyAll, which can be used with conditions to make threads wait when they cannot perform their tasks.

- If a thread obtains the monitor lock on an object, then determines that it cannot continue with its task on that object until some condition is satisfied, the thread can call Object method wait; this releases the monitor lock on the object, and the thread waits in the *waiting* state while the other threads try to enter the object's synchronized statement(s) or method(s).

- When a thread executing a synchronized statement (or method) completes or satisfies the condition on which another thread may be waiting, it can call Object method notify to allow a waiting thread to transition to the *runnable* state again. At this point, the thread that was transitioned from the *wait* state to the *runnable* state can attempt to reacquire the monitor lock on the object.

- If a thread calls notifyAll, then all the threads waiting for the monitor lock become eligible to reacquire the lock (that is, they all transition to the *runnable* state).

Section 23.9 Producer/Consumer Relationship: Bounded Buffers

- You cannot make assumptions about the relative speeds of concurrent threads—interactions that occur with the operating system, the network, the user and other components can cause the threads to operate at different speeds. When this happens, threads wait.

- A bounded buffer can be used to minimize the amount of waiting time for threads that share resources and operate at the same average speeds. If the producer temporarily produces values faster than the consumer can consume them, the producer can write additional values into the extra buffer space (if any are available). If the consumer consumes faster than the producer produces new values, the consumer can read additional values (if there are any) from the buffer.

- The key to using a bounded buffer with a producer and consumer that operate at about the same speed is to provide the buffer with enough locations to handle the anticipated "extra" production.

- The simplest way to implement a bounded buffer is to use an ArrayBlockingQueue for the buffer so that all of the synchronization details are handled for you.

Section 23.10 Producer/Consumer Relationship: The **Lock** and **Condition** Interfaces

- The Lock and Condition interfaces, which were introduced in Java SE 5, give programmers more precise control over thread synchronization, but are more complicated to use.

- Any object can contain a reference to an object that implements the Lock interface (of package java.util.concurrent.locks). A thread calls the Lock's lock method to acquire the lock. Once a Lock has been obtained by one thread, the Lock object will not allow another thread to obtain the Lock until the first thread releases the Lock (by calling the Lock's unlock method).

- If several threads are trying to call method lock on the same Lock object at the same time, only one thread can obtain the lock—all other threads attempting to obtain that Lock are placed in the *waiting* state. When a thread calls method unlock, the lock on the object is released and a waiting thread attempting to lock the object proceeds.

- Class ReentrantLock (of package java.util.concurrent.locks) is a basic implementation of the Lock interface.

- The constructor for a ReentrantLock takes a boolean argument that specifies whether the lock has a fairness policy. If the argument is true, the ReentrantLock's fairness policy is "the longest-waiting thread will acquire the lock when it is available." This guarantees that indefinite postponement (also called starvation) cannot occur. If the fairness policy argument is set to false, there is no guarantee as to which waiting thread will acquire the lock when it is available.

- If a thread that owns a Lock determines that it cannot continue with its task until some condition is satisfied, the thread can wait on a condition object. Using Lock objects allows you to explicitly declare the condition objects on which a thread may need to wait.

- Condition objects are associated with a specific Lock and are created by calling a Lock's newCondition method, which returns an object that implements the Condition interface (of package java.util.concurrent.locks). To wait on a condition object, the thread can call the Condition's await method. This immediately releases the associated Lock and places the thread in the *waiting* state for that Condition. Other threads can then try to obtain the Lock.

- When a *runnable* thread completes a task and determines that the *waiting* thread can now continue, the *runnable* thread can call Condition method signal to allow a thread in that Condition's *waiting* state to return to the *runnable* state. At this point, the thread that transitioned from the *waiting* state to the *runnable* state can attempt to reacquire the Lock.

- If multiple threads are in a Condition's *waiting* state when signal is called, the default implementation of Condition signals the longest-waiting thread to transition to the *runnable* state.

- If a thread calls Condition method signalAll, then all the threads waiting for that condition transition to the *runnable* state and become eligible to reacquire the Lock.

- When a thread is finished with a shared object, it must call method unlock to release the Lock.

- In some applications, using Lock and Condition objects may be preferable to using the synchronized keyword. Lock objects allow you to interrupt waiting threads or to specify a timeout for waiting to acquire a lock, which is not possible using the synchronized keyword. Also, a Lock object is not constrained to be acquired and released in the same block of code, which is the case with the synchronized keyword.

- Condition objects allow you to specify multiple conditions on which threads may wait. Thus, it is possible to indicate to waiting threads that a specific condition object is now true by calling signal or signallAll on that Condition object. With synchronized, there is no way to explicitly state the condition on which threads are waiting, so there is no way to notify threads waiting on one condition that they may proceed without also notifying threads waiting on any other conditions.

Section 23.11 Multithreading with GUI

- Swing applications have a thread, called the event dispatch thread, to handle interactions with the application's GUI components. All tasks that require interaction with an application's GUI are placed in an event queue and are executed sequentially by the event dispatch thread.

- Swing GUI components are not thread safe. Thread safety in GUI applications is achieved by ensuring that Swing components are accessed from only the event dispatch thread. This technique is called thread confinement.

- If an application must perform a lengthy computation in response to a user interface interaction, the event dispatch thread cannot attend to other tasks in the event queue while the thread is tied up in that computation. This causes the GUI components to become unresponsive. It is preferable to handle a long-running computation in a separate thread, freeing the event dispatch thread to continue managing other GUI interactions.

- Java SE 6 provides class SwingWorker (in package javax.swing), which implements the Runnable interface, to perform long-running computations in a worker thread and to update Swing components from the event dispatch thread based on the computations' results.

- To use SwingWorker's capabilities, create a class that extends SwingWorker and overrides the methods doInBackground and done. Method doInBackground performs the computation and returns the result. Method done displays the results in the GUI.

- `SwingWorker` is a generic class. Its first type parameter indicates the type returned by the `doIn-Background` method; the second indicates the type that is passed between the `publish` and `process` methods to handle intermediate results.

- Method `doInBackground` is called from a worker thread. After `doInBackground` returns, method `done` is called from the event dispatch thread to display the results.

- An `ExecutionException` is thrown if an exception occurs during the computation.

- `SwingWorker` also provides methods `publish`, `process` and `setProgress`. Method `publish` repeatedly sends intermediate results to method `process`, which displays the results in a GUI component. Method `setProgress` updates the progress property.

- Method `process` executes in the event dispatch thread and receives data from method `publish`. The passing of values between `publish` in the worker thread and `process` in the event dispatch thread is asynchronous; `process` is not necessarily invoked for every call to `publish`.

- `PropertyChangeListener` is an interface from package `java.beans` that defines a single method, `propertyChange`. Every time method `setProgress` is invoked, a `PropertyChangeEvent` is generated to indicate that the progress property has changed.

Section 23.12 Other Classes and Interfaces in `java.util.concurrent`

- The `Callable` interface (of package `java.util.concurrent`) declares a single method named `call`. This interface is designed to be similar to the `Runnable` interface—allowing an action to be performed concurrently in a separate thread—but the `call` method allows the thread to return a value or to throw a checked exception.

- An application that creates a `Callable` likely wants to run it concurrently with other `Runnables` and `Callables`. The `ExecutorService` interface provides method `submit`, which will execute a `Callable` passed in as its argument.

- Method `submit` returns an object of type `Future` (of package `java.util.concurrent`) that represents the executing `Callable`. Interface `Future` declares method `get` to return the result of the `Callable` and provides other methods to manage a `Callable`'s execution.

Terminology

acquire the lock
`ArrayBlockingQueue` class
atomic operation
`await` method of interface `Condition`
`awaitTermination` method of interface `Executor-`
    `torService`
blocked state
`BlockingQueue` interface
bounded buffer
buffer
`call` method of interface `Callable`
`Callable` interface
circular buffer
concurrency
concurrent programming
`Condition` interface
condition object
consumer
consumer thread

deadlock
dispatching a thread
event dispatch thread
execute method of interface `Executor`
`Executor` interface
`Executors` class
`ExecutorService` interface
fairness policy of a lock
`Future` interface
garbage collection
`get` method of interface `Future`
guarded by a lock
`IllegalMonitorStateException` class
indefinite postponement
`interrupt` method of class `Thread`
`InterruptedException` class
intrinsic lock
`java.util.concurrent` package
`java.util.concurrent.locks` package

Lock interface

lock method of interface Lock

main thread

monitor

monitor lock

multilevel priority queue

multithreading

mutable data

mutual exclusion

new state

newCachedThreadPool method of class Executors

newCondition method of interface Lock

notify method of class Object

notifyAll method of class Object

parallel operations

preemptive scheduling

producer

producer thread

producer/consumer relationship

propertyChange method of interface PropertyChangeListener

PropertyChangeListener interface

put method of interface BlockingQueue

quantum

ready state

ReentrantLock class

round-robin scheduling

run method of interface Runnable

Runnable interface

runnable state

running state

shutdown method of class ExecutorService

signal method of class Condition

signalAll method of class Condition

size method of class ArrayBlockingQueue

sleep interval

sleep method of class Thread

sleeping thread

stale value

starvation

state dependence

submit method of class ExecutorService

SwingWorker class

synchronization

synchronized keyword

synchronized method

synchronized statement

take method of interface BlockingQueue

terminated state

thread

Thread class

thread confinement

thread pool

thread priority

thread safe

thread scheduler

thread scheduling

thread state

thread synchronization

timed waiting state

timeslice

unlock method of interface Lock

wait method of class Object

waiting state

Self-Review Exercises

23.1   Fill in the blanks in each of the following statements:

a)   C and C++ are _____-threaded languages, whereas Java is a(n) _____-threaded language.

b)   A thread enters the *terminated* state when _____.

c)   To pause for a designated number of milliseconds and resume execution, a thread should call method _____ of class _____.

d)   Method _____ of class Condition moves a single thread in an object's *waiting* state to the *runnable* state.

e)   Method _____ of class Condition moves every thread in an object's *waiting* state to the *runnable* state.

f)   A(n) _____ thread enters the _____ state when it completes its task or otherwise terminates.

g)   A *runnable* thread can enter the _____ state for a specified interval of time.

h)   At the operating system level, the *runnable* state actually encompasses two separate states, _____ and _____.

    i)   Runnables are executed using a class that implements the _____ interface.

    j)   `ExecutorService` method _____ ends each thread in an `ExecutorService` as soon as it finishes executing its current `Runnable`, if any.

    k)   A thread can call method _____ on a `Condition` object to release the associated `Lock` and place that thread in the _____ state.

    l)   In a(n) _____ relationship, the _____ portion of an application generates data and stores it in a shared object, and the _____ portion of an application reads data from the shared object.

    m) Class _____ implements the `BlockingQueue` interface using an array.

    n)   The keyword _____ indicates that only one thread at a time should execute on an object.

23.2 State whether each of the following is *true* or *false*. If *false*, explain why.

    a)   A thread is not *runnable* if it has terminated.

    b)   A higher-priority *runnable* thread preempts threads of lower priority.

    c)   Some operating systems use timeslicing with threads. Therefore, they can enable threads to preempt threads of the same priority.

    d)   When the thread's quantum expires, the thread returns to the *running* state as the operating system assigns the thread to a processor.

    e)   On a single-processor system without timeslicing, each thread in a set of equal-priority threads (with no other threads present) runs to completion before other threads of equal priority get a chance to execute.

Answers to Self-Review Exercises

23.1   a) single, multi. b) its run method ends. c) `sleep`, `Thread`. d) `signal`. e) `signalAll`. f) *runnable, terminated.* g) *timed waiting.* h) *ready, running.* i) Executor. j) `shutdown`. k) `await`, *waiting.* l) producer/consumer, producer, consumer. m) `ArrayBlockingQueue`. n) `synchronized`.

23.2   a) True. b) True. c) False. Timeslicing allows a thread to execute until its timeslice (or quantum) expires. Then other threads of equal priority can execute. d) False. When a thread's quantum expires, the thread returns to the *ready* state and the operating system assigns to the processor another thread. e) True.

Exercises

23.3   Define each of the following terms.

    a)   thread

    b)   multithreading

    c)   *runnable* state

    d)   *timed waiting* state

    e)   preemptive scheduling

    f)   `Runnable` interface

    g)   `notifyAll` method

    h)   producer/consumer relationship

    i)   quantum

23.4   Discuss each of the following terms in the context of Java's threading mechanisms:

    a)   `synchronized`

    b)   producer

    c)   consumer

    d)   `wait`

    e)   `notify`

f) Lock

g) Condition

23.5 Write a program that bounces a blue ball inside a JPanel. The ball should begin moving with a mousePressed event. When the ball hits the edge of the JPanel, it should bounce off the edge and continue in the opposite direction. The ball should be updated using a Runnable.

23.6 Modify the program in Exercise 23.5 to add a new ball each time the user clicks the mouse. Provide for a minimum of 20 balls. Randomly choose the color for each new ball.

23.7 Modify the program in Exercise 23.6 to add shadows. As a ball moves, draw a solid black oval at the bottom of the JPanel. You may consider adding a 3-D effect by increasing or decreasing the size of each ball when it hits the edge of the JPanel.

24

Networking

If the presence of electricity can be made visible in any part of a circuit, I see no reason why intelligence may not be transmitted instantaneously by electricity.
—Samuel F. B. Morse

Protocol is everything.
—Francois Giuliani

What networks of railroads, highways and canals were in another age, the networks of telecommunications, information and computerization … are today.
—Bruno Kreisky

The port is near, the bells I hear, the people all exulting.
—Walt Whitman

OBJECTIVES

In this chapter you will learn:

- To understand Java networking with URLs, sockets and datagrams.
- To implement Java networking applications by using sockets and datagrams.
- To understand how to implement Java clients and servers that communicate with one another.
- To understand how to implement network-based collaborative applications.
- To construct a multithreaded server.

24.1 Introduction

There is much excitement about the Internet and the World Wide Web. The Internet ties the information world together. The World Wide Web makes the Internet easy to use and gives it the flair and sizzle of multimedia. Organizations see the Internet and the web as crucial to their information-systems strategies. Java provides a number of built-in networking capabilities that make it easy to develop Internet-based and web-based applications. Java can enable programs to search the world for information and to collaborate with programs running on other computers internationally, nationally or just within an organization. Java can enable applets and applications to communicate with one another (subject to security constraints).

Networking is a massive and complex topic. Computer science and computer engineering students typically take a full-semester, upper-level course in computer networking and continue with further study at the graduate level. Java is often used as an implementation vehicle in computer networking courses. In *Java How to Program, Seventh Edition*, we introduce a portion of Java's networking concepts and capabilities.

Java's fundamental networking capabilities are declared by classes and interfaces of package `java.net`, through which Java offers stream-based communications that enable applications to view networking as streams of data. The classes and interfaces of package java.net also offer packet-based communications for transmitting individual packets of information—commonly used to transmit audio and video over the Internet. In this chapter, we show how to create and manipulate sockets and how to communicate with packets and streams of data.

Our discussion of networking focuses on both sides of the client/server relationship. The client requests that some action be performed, and the server performs the action and responds to the client. A common implementation of the request-response model is between web browsers and web servers. When a user selects a website to browse through a browser (the client application), a request is sent to the appropriate web server (the server application). The server normally responds to the client by sending an appropriate HTML web page.

We introduce Java's socket-based communications, which enable applications to view networking as if it were file I/O—a program can read from a socket or write to a socket as simply as reading from a file or writing to a file. The socket is simply a software construct that represents one endpoint of a connection. We show how to create and manipulate stream sockets and datagram sockets.

With stream sockets, a process establishes a connection to another process. While the connection is in place, data flows between the processes in continuous streams. Stream sockets are said to provide a connection-oriented service. The protocol used for transmission is the popular TCP (Transmission Control Protocol).

With datagram sockets, individual packets of information are transmitted. This is not appropriate for everyday programmers, because the protocol used—UDP, the User Datagram Protocol—is a connectionless service, and thus does not guarantee that packets arrive in any particular order. With UDP, packets can even be lost or duplicated. Significant extra programming is required on your part to deal with these problems (if you choose to do so). UDP is most appropriate for network applications that do not require the error checking and reliability of TCP. Stream sockets and the TCP protocol will be more desirable for the vast majority of Java programmers.

Performance Tip 24.1

Connectionless services generally offer greater performance but less reliability than connection-oriented services.

Portability Tip 24.1

TCP, UDP and related protocols enable a great variety of heterogeneous computer systems (i.e., computer systems with different processors and different operating systems) to intercommunicate.

We also introduce a case study in which we implement a client/server chat application similar to the instant-messaging services popular on the web today. This case study is provided as a web bonus at www.deitel.com/books/jhtp7/. The application incorporates many networking techniques introduced in this chapter. It also introduces multicasting, in which a server can publish information and clients can subscribe to that information. Each time the server publishes more information, all subscribers receive it. Throughout the examples of this chapter, we will see that many of the networking details are handled by the Java APIs.

24.2 Manipulating URLs

The Internet offers many protocols. The Hypertext Transfer Protocol (HTTP), which forms the basis of the World Wide Web, uses URIs (Uniform Resource Identifiers) to identify data on the Internet. URIs that specify the locations of documents are called URLs (Uniform Resource Locators). Common URLs refer to files or directories and can reference objects that perform complex tasks, such as database lookups and Internet searches. If you know the HTTP URL of a publicly available HTML document anywhere on the web, you can access it through HTTP.

Java makes it easy to manipulate URLs. When you use a URL that refers to the exact location of a resource (e.g., a web page) as an argument to the showDocument method of interface AppletContext, the browser in which the applet is executing will display that resource. The applet in Figs. 24.1–24.2 demonstrates simple networking capabilities. It enables the user to select a web page from a JList and causes the browser to display the corresponding page. In this example, the networking is performed by the browser.

```
1   <html>
2   <title>Site Selector</title>
3   <body>
4      <applet code = "SiteSelector.class" width = "300" height = "75">
5         <param name = "title0" value = "Java Home Page">
6         <param name = "location0" value = "http://java.sun.com/">
7         <param name = "title1" value = "Deitel">
8         <param name = "location1" value = "http://www.deitel.com/">
9         <param name = "title2" value = "JGuru">
10        <param name = "location2" value = "http://www.jGuru.com/">
11        <param name = "title3" value = "JavaWorld">
12        <param name = "location3" value = "http://www.javaworld.com/">
13     </applet>
14  </body>
15  </html>
```

Fig. 24.1 | HTML document to load SiteSelector applet.

```
1   // Fig. 24.2: SiteSelector.java
2   // This program loads a document from a URL.
3   import java.net.MalformedURLException;
4   import java.net.URL;
5   import java.util.HashMap;
6   import java.util.ArrayList;
7   import java.awt.BorderLayout;
8   import java.applet.AppletContext;
9   import javax.swing.JApplet;
10  import javax.swing.JLabel;
11  import javax.swing.JList;
12  import javax.swing.JScrollPane;
13  import javax.swing.event.ListSelectionEvent;
14  import javax.swing.event.ListSelectionListener;
15
16  public class SiteSelector extends JApplet
17  {
18     private HashMap< Object, URL > sites; // site names and URLs
19     private ArrayList< String > siteNames; // site names
20     private JList siteChooser; // list of sites to choose from
21
22     // read HTML parameters and set up GUI
23     public void init()
24     {
25        sites = new HashMap< Object, URL >(); // create HashMap
26        siteNames = new ArrayList< String >(); // create ArrayList
27
```

Fig. 24.2 | Loading a document from a URL into a browser. (Part 1 of 3.)

```
28          // obtain parameters from HTML document
29          getSitesFromHTMLParameters();
30
31          // create GUI components and layout interface
32          add( new JLabel( "Choose a site to browse" ), BorderLayout.NORTH );
33
34          siteChooser = new JList( siteNames.toArray() ); // populate JList
35          siteChooser.addListSelectionListener(
36             new ListSelectionListener() // anonymous inner class
37             {
38                // go to site user selected
39                public void valueChanged( ListSelectionEvent event )
40                {
41                   // get selected site name
42                   Object object = siteChooser.getSelectedValue();
43
44                   // use site name to locate corresponding URL
45                   URL newDocument = sites.get( object );
46
47                   // get applet container
48                   AppletContext browser = getAppletContext();
49
50                   // tell applet container to change pages
51                   browser.showDocument( newDocument );
52                } // end method valueChanged
53             } // end anonymous inner class
54          ); // end call to addListSelectionListener
55
56          add( new JScrollPane( siteChooser ), BorderLayout.CENTER );
57       } // end method init
58
59       // obtain parameters from HTML document
60       private void getSitesFromHTMLParameters()
61       {
62          String title; // site title
63          String location; // location of site
64          URL url; // URL of location
65          int counter = 0; // count number of sites
66
67          title = getParameter( "title" + counter ); // get first site title
68
69          // loop until no more parameters in HTML document
70          while ( title != null )
71          {
72             // obtain site location
73             location = getParameter( "location" + counter );
74
75             try // place title/URL in HashMap and title in ArrayList
76             {
77                url = new URL( location ); // convert location to URL
78                sites.put( title, url ); // put title/URL in HashMap
79                siteNames.add( title ); // put title in ArrayList
80             } // end try
```

Fig. 24.2 | Loading a document from a URL into a browser. (Part 2 of 3.)

```
81                    catch ( MalformedURLException urlException )
82                    {
83                       urlException.printStackTrace();
84                    } // end catch
85
86                    counter++;
87                    title = getParameter( "title" + counter ); // get next site title
88              } // end while
89           } // end method getSitesFromHTMLParameters
90    } // end class SiteSelector
```

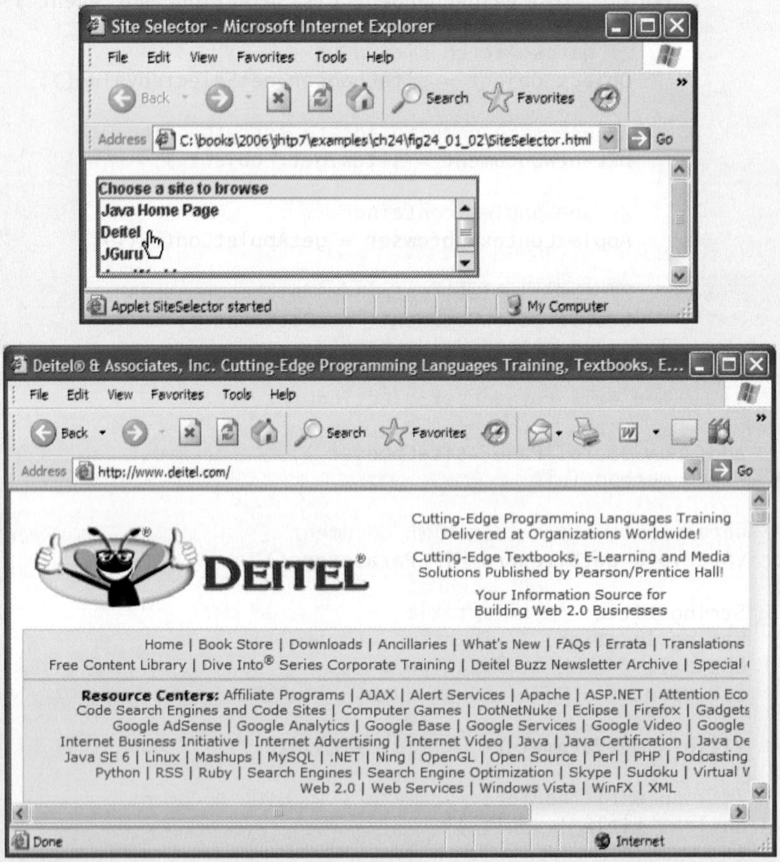

Fig. 24.2 | Loading a document from a URL into a browser. (Part 3 of 3.)

This applet takes advantage of applet parameters specified in the HTML document that invokes the applet. When browsing the World Wide Web, you will often come across applets that are in the public domain—you can use them free of charge on your own web pages (normally in exchange for crediting the applet's creator). Many applets can be customized via parameters supplied from the HTML file that invokes the applet. For example, Fig. 24.1 contains the HTML that invokes the applet SiteSelector in Fig. 24.2.

The HTML document contains eight parameters specified with the `param` tag—these lines must appear between the starting and ending `applet` tags. The applet can read these values and use them to customize itself. Any number of `param` tags can appear between the starting and ending `applet` tags. Each parameter has a `name` and a `value`. `Applet` method `getParameter` retrieves the `value` associated with a specific parameter name and returns it as a string. The argument passed to `getParameter` is a string containing the name of the parameter in the `param` element. In this example, parameters represent the title and location of each website the user can select. Parameters specified for this applet are named `title#`, where the value of # starts at 0 and increments by 1 for each new title. Each title should have a corresponding location parameter of the form `location#`, where the value of # starts at 0 and increments by 1 for each new location. The statement

```
String title = getParameter( "title0" );
```

gets the value associated with parameter "title0" and assigns it to reference `title`. If there is no `param` tag containing the specified parameter, `getParameter` returns `null`.

The applet (Fig. 24.2) obtains from the HTML document (Fig. 24.1) the choices that will be displayed in the applet's `JList`. Class `SiteSelector` uses a `HashMap` (package `java.util`) to store the website names and URLs. In this example, the *key* is the string in the `JList` that represents the website name, and the *value* is a URL object that stores the location of the website to display in the browser.

Class `SiteSelector` also contains an `ArrayList` (package `java.util`) in which the site names are placed so that they can be used to initialize the `JList` (one version of the `JList` constructor receives an array of `Objects` which is returned by `ArrayList`'s `toArray` method). An `ArrayList` is a dynamically resizable array of references. Class `ArrayList` provides method `add` to add a new element to the end of the `ArrayList`. (We provide discussions of classes `ArrayList` and `HashMap` in Chapter 19.)

Lines 25–26 in the applet's `init` method (lines 23–57) create a `HashMap` object and an `ArrayList` object. Line 29 calls our utility method `getSitesFromHTMLParameters` (declared at lines 60–89) to obtain the HTML parameters from the HTML document that invoked the applet.

Method `getSitesFromHTMLParameters` uses `Applet` method `getParameter` (line 67) to obtain a website title. If the `title` is not `null`, the loop in lines 70–88 begins executing. Line 73 uses `Applet` method `getParameter` to obtain the website location. Line 77 uses the `location` as the value of a new URL object. The URL constructor determines whether its argument represents a valid URL. If not, the URL constructor throws a `Malformed-URLException`. Note that the URL constructor must be called in a `try` block. If the URL constructor generates a `MalformedURLException`, the call to `printStackTrace` (line 83) causes the program to output a stack trace to the Java console. On Windows machines, the Java console can be viewed by right clicking the Java icon in the notification area of the taskbar. Then the program attempts to obtain the next website title. The program does not add the site for the invalid URL to the `HashMap`, so the title will not be displayed in the `JList`.

For a proper URL, line 78 places the `title` and URL into the `HashMap`, and line 79 adds the `title` to the `ArrayList`. Line 87 gets the next title from the HTML document. When the call to `getParameter` at line 87 returns `null`, the loop terminates.

When method `getSitesFromHTMLParameters` returns to `init`, lines 32–56 construct the applet's GUI. Line 32 adds the `JLabel` "Choose a site to browse" to the NORTH of the

JFrame's BorderLayout. Line 34 creates JList siteChooser to allow the user to select a
web page to view. Lines 35–54 register a ListSelectionListener to handle the
siteChooser's events. Line 56 adds siteChooser to the CENTER of the JFrame's Border-
Layout.

When the user selects one of the websites listed in siteChooser, the program calls
method valueChanged (lines 39–52). Line 42 obtains the selected site name from the
JList. Line 45 passes the selected site name (the *key*) to HashMap method get, which
locates and returns a reference to the corresponding URL object (the *value*) that is assigned
to reference newDocument.

Line 48 uses Applet method getAppletContext to get a reference to an AppletContext object that represents the applet container. Line 51 uses the AppletContext reference
browser to invoke method showDocument, which receives a URL object as an argument and
passes it to the AppletContext (i.e., the browser). The browser displays in the current
browser window the World Wide Web resource associated with that URL. In this example,
all the resources are HTML documents.

For programmers familiar with HTML frames, there is a second version of Applet-
Context method showDocument that enables an applet to specify the so-called target frame
in which to display the web resource. This second version takes two arguments—a URL
object specifying the resource to display and a string representing the target frame. There
are some special target frames that can be used as the second argument. The target frame
_blank results in a new web browser window to display the content from the specified
URL. The target frame _self specifies that the content from the specified URL should be
displayed in the same frame as the applet (the applet's HTML page is replaced in this case).
The target frame _top specifies that the browser should remove the current frames in the
browser window, then display the content from the specified URL in the current window.
[*Note:* If you are interested in learning more about HTML, the CD that accompanies this
book contains three chapters from our book *Internet and World Wide Web How to Program,
Third Edition* that introduce the current version of HTML (known as XHTML) and the
web page formatting capability known as Cascading Style Sheets (CSS).]

Error-Prevention Tip 24.1

*The applet in Fig. 24.2 must be run from a web browser, such as Mozilla or Microsoft Internet
Explorer, to see the results of displaying another web page. The appletviewer is capable only of
executing applets—it ignores all other HTML tags. If the websites in the program contained
Java applets, only those applets would appear in the appletviewer when the user selected a website. Each applet would execute in a separate appletviewer window.*

24.3 Reading a File on a Web Server

Our next example once again hides the networking details from us. The application in
Fig. 24.3 uses Swing GUI component JEditorPane (from package javax.swing) to display the contents of a file on a web server. The user enters a URL in the JTextField at the
top of the window, and the application displays the corresponding document (if it exists)
in the JEditorPane. Class JEditorPane is able to render both plain text and HTML-for-
matted text, as illustrated in the two screen captures (Fig. 24.4), so this application acts as
a simple web browser. The application also demonstrates how to process HyperlinkEvents
when the user clicks a hyperlink in the HTML document. The techniques shown in this

```
 1    // Fig. 24.3: ReadServerFile.java
 2    // Use a JEditorPane to display the contents of a file on a web server.
 3    import java.awt.BorderLayout;
 4    import java.awt.event.ActionEvent;
 5    import java.awt.event.ActionListener;
 6    import java.io.IOException;
 7    import javax.swing.JEditorPane;
 8    import javax.swing.JFrame;
 9    import javax.swing.JOptionPane;
10    import javax.swing.JScrollPane;
11    import javax.swing.JTextField;
12    import javax.swing.event.HyperlinkEvent;
13    import javax.swing.event.HyperlinkListener;
14
15    public class ReadServerFile extends JFrame
16    {
17       private JTextField enterField; // JTextField to enter site name
18       private JEditorPane contentsArea; // to display website
19
20       // set up GUI
21       public ReadServerFile()
22       {
23          super( "Simple Web Browser" );
24
25          // create enterField and register its listener
26          enterField = new JTextField( "Enter file URL here" );
27          enterField.addActionListener(
28             new ActionListener()
29             {
30                // get document specified by user
31                public void actionPerformed( ActionEvent event )
32                {
33                   getThePage( event.getActionCommand() );
34                } // end method actionPerformed
35             } // end inner class
36          ); // end call to addActionListener
37
38          add( enterField, BorderLayout.NORTH );
39
40          contentsArea = new JEditorPane(); // create contentsArea
41          contentsArea.setEditable( false );
42          contentsArea.addHyperlinkListener(
43             new HyperlinkListener()
44             {
45                // if user clicked hyperlink, go to specified page
46                public void hyperlinkUpdate( HyperlinkEvent event )
47                {
48                   if ( event.getEventType() ==
49                      HyperlinkEvent.EventType.ACTIVATED )
50                      getThePage( event.getURL().toString() );
51                } // end method hyperlinkUpdate
52             } // end inner class
53          ); // end call to addHyperlinkListener
```

Fig. 24.3 | Reading a file by opening a connection through a URL. (Part 1 of 2.)

```
54
55          add( new JScrollPane( contentsArea ), BorderLayout.CENTER );
56          setSize( 400, 300 ); // set size of window
57          setVisible( true ); // show window
58       } // end ReadServerFile constructor
59
60       // load document
61       private void getThePage( String location )
62       {
63          try // load document and display location
64          {
65             contentsArea.setPage( location ); // set the page
66             enterField.setText( location ); // set the text
67          } // end try
68          catch ( IOException ioException )
69          {
70             JOptionPane.showMessageDialog( this,
71                "Error retrieving specified URL", "Bad URL",
72                JOptionPane.ERROR_MESSAGE );
73          } // end catch
74       } // end method getThePage
75    } // end class ReadServerFile
```

Fig. 24.3 | Reading a file by opening a connection through a URL. (Part 2 of 2.)

```
 1    // Fig. 24.4: ReadServerFileTest.java
 2    // Create and start a ReadServerFile.
 3    import javax.swing.JFrame;
 4
 5    public class ReadServerFileTest
 6    {
 7       public static void main( String args[] )
 8       {
 9          ReadServerFile application = new ReadServerFile();
10          application.setDefaultCloseOperation( JFrame.EXIT_ON_CLOSE );
11       } // end main
12    } // end class ReadServerFileTest
```

Fig. 24.4 | Test class for ReadServerFile. (Part 1 of 2.)

Fig. 24.4 | Test class for `ReadServerFile`. (Part 2 of 2.)

example can also be used in applets. However, an applet is allowed to read files only on the server from which it was downloaded.

The application class `ReadServerFile` contains `JTextField enterField`, in which the user enters the URL of the file to read and `JEditorPane contentsArea` to display the contents of the file. When the user presses the *Enter* key in `enterField`, the application calls method `actionPerformed` (lines 31–34). Line 33 uses `ActionEvent` method `getAc-tionCommand` to get the string the user input in the `JTextField` and passes the string to utility method `getThePage` (lines 61–74).

Line 65 invokes `JEditorPane` method **`setPage`** to download the document specified by `location` and display it in the `JEditorPane`. If there is an error downloading the document, method `setPage` throws an `IOException`. Also, if an invalid URL is specified, a `MalformedURLException` (a subclass of `IOException`) occurs. If the document loads successfully, line 66 displays the current location in `enterField`.

Typically, an HTML document contains hyperlinks—text, images or GUI components which, when clicked, provide quick access to another document on the web. If a `JEditorPane` contains an HTML document and the user clicks a hyperlink, the `JEditor-Pane` generates a **`HyperlinkEvent`** (package `javax.swing.event`) and notifies all registered **`HyperlinkListeners`** (package `javax.swing.event`) of that event. Lines 42–53 register a `HyperlinkListener` to handle `HyperlinkEvents`. When a `HyperlinkEvent` occurs, the program calls method **`hyperlinkUpdate`** (lines 46–51). Lines 48–49 use `HyperlinkEvent` method **`getEventType`** to determine the type of the `HyperlinkEvent`. Class `Hyper-linkEvent` contains a `public` nested class called **`EventType`** that declares three `static` `EventType` objects, which represent the hyperlink event types. **`ACTIVATED`** indicates that the user clicked a hyperlink to change web pages, **`ENTERED`** indicates that the user moved the mouse over a hyperlink and **`EXITED`** indicates that the user moved the mouse away from a hyperlink. If a hyperlink was `ACTIVATED`, line 50 uses `HyperlinkEvent` method **`getURL`** to obtain the URL represented by the hyperlink. Method `toString` converts the returned URL to a string that can be passed to utility method `getThePage`.

Look-and-Feel Observation 24.1

A JEditorPane generates HyperlinkEvents only if it is uneditable.

24.4 Establishing a Simple Server Using Stream Sockets

The two examples discussed so far use high-level Java networking capabilities to communicate between applications. In the examples, it was not your responsibility to establish the connection between a client and a server. The first program relied on the web browser to communicate with a web server. The second program relied on a JEditorPane to perform the connection. This section begins our discussion of creating your own applications that can communicate with one another.

Establishing a simple server in Java requires five steps. *Step 1* is to create a **Server-Socket** object. A call to the ServerSocket constructor, such as

```
ServerSocket server = new ServerSocket( portNumber, queueLength );
```

registers an available TCP **port number** and specifies the maximum number of clients that can wait to connect to the server (i.e., the **queue length**). The port number is used by clients to locate the server application on the server computer. This is often called the **handshake point**. If the queue is full, the server refuses client connections. The constructor establishes the port where the server waits for connections from clients—a process known as **binding the server to the port**. Each client will ask to connect to the server on this **port**. Only one application at a time can be bound to a specific port on the server.

Software Engineering Observation 24.1

Port numbers can be between 0 and 65,535. Most operating systems reserve port numbers below 1024 for system services (e.g., e-mail and World Wide Web servers). Generally, these ports should not be specified as connection ports in user programs. In fact, some operating systems require special access privileges to bind to port numbers below 1024.

Programs manage each client connection with a **Socket** object. In *Step 2*, the server listens indefinitely (or **blocks**) for an attempt by a client to connect. To listen for a client connection, the program calls ServerSocket method **accept**, as in

```
Socket connection = server.accept();
```

which returns a Socket when a connection with a client is established. The Socket allows the server to interact with the client. The interactions with the client actually occur at a different server port from the handshake point. This allows the port specified in *Step 1* to be used again in a multithreaded server to accept another client connection. We demonstrate this concept in Section 24.8.

Step 3 is to get the OutputStream and InputStream objects that enable the server to communicate with the client by sending and receiving bytes. The server sends information to the client via an OutputStream and receives information from the client via an Input-Stream. The server invokes method **getOutputStream** on the Socket to get a reference to the Socket's OutputStream and invokes method **getInputStream** on the Socket to get a reference to the Socket's InputStream.

The stream objects can be used to send or receive individual bytes or sequences of bytes with the OutputStream's method **write** and the InputStream's method **read**, respectively. Often it is useful to send or receive values of primitive types (e.g., int and double) or Serializable objects (e.g., Strings or other serializable types) rather than sending bytes. In this case, we can use the techniques discussed in Chapter 14 to wrap other stream types (e.g., ObjectOutputStream and ObjectInputStream) around the OutputStream and InputStream associated with the Socket. For example,

```
ObjectInputStream input =
    new ObjectInputStream( connection.getInputStream() );

ObjectOutputStream output =
    new ObjectOutputStream( connection.getOutputStream() );
```

The beauty of establishing these relationships is that whatever the server writes to the ObjectOutputStream is sent via the OutputStream and is available at the client's InputStream, and whatever the client writes to its OutputStream (with a corresponding ObjectOutputStream) is available via the server's InputStream. The transmission of the data over the network is seamless and is handled completely by Java.

Step 4 is the *processing* phase, in which the server and the client communicate via the OutputStream and InputStream objects. In *Step 5*, when the transmission is complete, the server closes the connection by invoking the `close` method on the streams and on the Socket.

Software Engineering Observation 24.2

With sockets, network I/O appears to Java programs to be similar to sequential file I/O. Sockets hide much of the complexity of network programming from the programmer.

Software Engineering Observation 24.3

With Java's multithreading, we can create multithreaded servers that can manage many simultaneous connections with many clients. This multithreaded-server architecture is precisely what popular network servers use.

Software Engineering Observation 24.4

A multithreaded server can take the Socket returned by each call to accept and create a new thread that manages network I/O across that Socket. Alternatively, a multithreaded server can maintain a pool of threads (a set of already existing threads) ready to manage network I/O across the new Sockets as they are created. See Chapter 23 for more information on multithreading.

Performance Tip 24.2

In high-performance systems in which memory is abundant, a multithreaded server can be implemented to create a pool of threads that can be assigned quickly to handle network I/O across each new Socket as it is created. Thus, when the server receives a connection, it need not incur the overhead of thread creation. When the connection is closed, the thread is returned to the pool for reuse.

24.5 Establishing a Simple Client Using Stream Sockets

Establishing a simple client in Java requires four steps. In *Step 1*, we create a Socket to connect to the server. The Socket constructor establishes the connection to the server. For example, the statement

```
Socket connection = new Socket( serverAddress, port );
```

uses the Socket constructor with two arguments—the server's address (*serverAddress*) and the *port* number. If the connection attempt is successful, this statement returns a Socket. A connection attempt that fails throws an instance of a subclass of IOException, so many programs simply catch IOException. An UnknownHostException occurs specifically when the system is unable to resolve the server address specified in the call to the Socket constructor to a corresponding IP address.

In *Step 2*, the client uses Socket methods getInputStream and getOutputStream to obtain references to the Socket's InputStream and OutputStream. As we mentioned in the preceding section, we can use the techniques of Chapter 14 to wrap other stream types around the InputStream and OutputStream associated with the Socket. If the server is sending information in the form of actual types, the client should receive the information in the same format. Thus, if the server sends values with an ObjectOutputStream, the client should read those values with an ObjectInputStream.

Step 3 is the processing phase in which the client and the server communicate via the InputStream and OutputStream objects. In *Step 4*, the client closes the connection when the transmission is complete by invoking the close method on the streams and on the Socket. The client must determine when the server is finished sending information so that it can call close to close the Socket connection. For example, the InputStream method read returns the value –1 when it detects end-of-stream (also called EOF—end-of-file). If an ObjectInputStream is used to read information from the server, an EOFException occurs when the client attempts to read a value from a stream on which end-of-stream is detected.

24.6 Client/Server Interaction with Stream Socket Connections

Figures 24.5 and 24.7 use stream sockets to demonstrate a simple client/server chat application. The server waits for a client connection attempt. When a client connects to the server, the server application sends the client a String object (recall that Strings are Serializable objects) indicating that the connection was successful. Then the client displays the message. The client and server applications each provide textfields that allow the user to type a message and send it to the other application. When the client or the server sends the string "TERMINATE", the connection terminates. Then the server waits for the next client to connect. The declaration of class Server appears in Fig. 24.5. The declaration of class Client appears in Fig. 24.7. The screen captures showing the execution between the client and the server are shown as part of Fig. 24.7.

Server Class
Server's constructor (lines 30–55) creates the server's GUI, which contains a JTextField and a JTextArea. Server displays its output in the JTextArea. When the main method (lines 7–12 of Fig. 24.6) executes, it creates a Server object, specifies the window's default close operation and calls method runServer (declared at lines 58–87).

Method runServer sets up the server to receive a connection and processes one connection at a time. Line 62 creates a ServerSocket called server to wait for connections. The ServerSocket listens for a connection from a client at port 12345. The second argument to the constructor is the number of connections that can wait in a queue to connect to the server (100 in this example). If the queue is full when a client attempts to connect, the server refuses the connection.

```
1   // Fig. 24.5: Server.java
2   // Set up a server that will receive a connection from a client, send
3   // a string to the client, and close the connection.
4   import java.io.EOFException;
5   import java.io.IOException;
6   import java.io.ObjectInputStream;
7   import java.io.ObjectOutputStream;
8   import java.net.ServerSocket;
9   import java.net.Socket;
10  import java.awt.BorderLayout;
11  import java.awt.event.ActionEvent;
12  import java.awt.event.ActionListener;
13  import javax.swing.JFrame;
14  import javax.swing.JScrollPane;
15  import javax.swing.JTextArea;
16  import javax.swing.JTextField;
17  import javax.swing.SwingUtilities;
18
19  public class Server extends JFrame
20  {
21     private JTextField enterField; // inputs message from user
22     private JTextArea displayArea; // display information to user
23     private ObjectOutputStream output; // output stream to client
24     private ObjectInputStream input; // input stream from client
25     private ServerSocket server; // server socket
26     private Socket connection; // connection to client
27     private int counter = 1; // counter of number of connections
28
29     // set up GUI
30     public Server()
31     {
32        super( "Server" );
33
34        enterField = new JTextField(); // create enterField
35        enterField.setEditable( false );
36        enterField.addActionListener(
37           new ActionListener()
38           {
39              // send message to client
40              public void actionPerformed( ActionEvent event )
41              {
42                 sendData( event.getActionCommand() );
43                 enterField.setText( "" );
44              } // end method actionPerformed
45           } // end anonymous inner class
46        ); // end call to addActionListener
47
48        add( enterField, BorderLayout.NORTH );
```

Fig. 24.5 | Server portion of a client/server stream-socket connection. (Part 1 of 4.)

```
49
50       displayArea = new JTextArea(); // create displayArea
51       add( new JScrollPane( displayArea ), BorderLayout.CENTER );
52
53       setSize( 300, 150 ); // set size of window
54       setVisible( true ); // show window
55    } // end Server constructor
56
57    // set up and run server
58    public void runServer()
59    {
60       try // set up server to receive connections; process connections
61       {
62          server = new ServerSocket( 12345, 100 ); // create ServerSocket
63
64          while ( true )
65          {
66             try
67             {
68                waitForConnection(); // wait for a connection
69                getStreams(); // get input & output streams
70                processConnection(); // process connection
71             } // end try
72             catch ( EOFException eofException )
73             {
74                displayMessage( "\nServer terminated connection" );
75             } // end catch
76             finally
77             {
78                closeConnection(); // close connection
79                counter++;
80             } // end finally
81          } // end while
82       } // end try
83       catch ( IOException ioException )
84       {
85          ioException.printStackTrace();
86       } // end catch
87    } // end method runServer
88
89    // wait for connection to arrive, then display connection info
90    private void waitForConnection() throws IOException
91    {
92       displayMessage( "Waiting for connection\n" );
93       connection = server.accept(); // allow server to accept connection
94       displayMessage( "Connection " + counter + " received from: " +
95          connection.getInetAddress().getHostName() );
96    } // end method waitForConnection
97
98    // get streams to send and receive data
99    private void getStreams() throws IOException
100   {
```

Fig. 24.5 | Server portion of a client/server stream-socket connection. (Part 2 of 4.)

```
101          // set up output stream for objects
102          output = new ObjectOutputStream( connection.getOutputStream() );
103          output.flush(); // flush output buffer to send header information
104
105          // set up input stream for objects
106          input = new ObjectInputStream( connection.getInputStream() );
107
108          displayMessage( "\nGot I/O streams\n" );
109       } // end method getStreams
110
111       // process connection with client
112       private void processConnection() throws IOException
113       {
114          String message = "Connection successful";
115          sendData( message ); // send connection successful message
116
117          // enable enterField so server user can send messages
118          setTextFieldEditable( true );
119
120          do // process messages sent from client
121          {
122             try // read message and display it
123             {
124                message = ( String ) input.readObject(); // read new message
125                displayMessage( "\n" + message ); // display message
126             } // end try
127             catch ( ClassNotFoundException classNotFoundException )
128             {
129                displayMessage( "\nUnknown object type received" );
130             } // end catch
131
132          } while ( !message.equals( "CLIENT>>> TERMINATE" ) );
133       } // end method processConnection
134
135       // close streams and socket
136       private void closeConnection()
137       {
138          displayMessage( "\nTerminating connection\n" );
139          setTextFieldEditable( false ); // disable enterField
140
141          try
142          {
143             output.close(); // close output stream
144             input.close(); // close input stream
145             connection.close(); // close socket
146          } // end try
147          catch ( IOException ioException )
148          {
149             ioException.printStackTrace();
150          } // end catch
151       } // end method closeConnection
152
```

Fig. 24.5 | Server portion of a client/server stream-socket connection. (Part 3 of 4.)

```
153     // send message to client
154     private void sendData( String message )
155     {
156        try // send object to client
157        {
158           output.writeObject( "SERVER>>> " + message );
159           output.flush(); // flush output to client
160           displayMessage( "\nSERVER>>> " + message );
161        } // end try
162        catch ( IOException ioException )
163        {
164           displayArea.append( "\nError writing object" );
165        } // end catch
166     } // end method sendData
167
168     // manipulates displayArea in the event-dispatch thread
169     private void displayMessage( final String messageToDisplay )
170     {
171        SwingUtilities.invokeLater(
172           new Runnable()
173           {
174              public void run() // updates displayArea
175              {
176                 displayArea.append( messageToDisplay ); // append message
177              } // end method run
178           } // end anonymous inner class
179        ); // end call to SwingUtilities.invokeLater
180     } // end method displayMessage
181
182     // manipulates enterField in the event-dispatch thread
183     private void setTextFieldEditable( final boolean editable )
184     {
185        SwingUtilities.invokeLater(
186           new Runnable()
187           {
188              public void run() // sets enterField's editability
189              {
190                 enterField.setEditable( editable );
191              } // end method run
192           } // end inner class
193        ); // end call to SwingUtilities.invokeLater
194     } // end method setTextFieldEditable
195  } // end class Server
```

Fig. 24.5 | Server portion of a client/server stream-socket connection. (Part 4 of 4.)

```
1   // Fig. 24.6: ServerTest.java
2   // Test the Server application.
3   import javax.swing.JFrame;
4
5   public class ServerTest
6   {
```

Fig. 24.6 | Test class for Server. (Part 1 of 2.)

```
7        public static void main( String args[] )
8        {
9           Server application = new Server(); // create server
10          application.setDefaultCloseOperation( JFrame.EXIT_ON_CLOSE );
11          application.runServer(); // run server application
12       } // end main
13   } // end class ServerTest
```

Fig. 24.6 | Test class for `Server`. (Part 2 of 2.)

Common Programming Error 24.1

Specifying a port that is already in use or specifying an invalid port number when creating a `ServerSocket` results in a `BindException`.

Line 68 calls method `waitForConnection` (declared at lines 90–96) to wait for a client connection. After the connection is established, line 69 calls method `getStreams` (declared at lines 99–109) to obtain references to the streams for the connection. Line 70 calls method `processConnection` (declared at lines 112–133) to send the initial connection message to the client and to process all messages received from the client. The `finally` block (lines 76–80) terminates the client connection by calling method `closeConnection` (lines 136–151) even if an exception occurs. Method `displayMessage` (lines 169–180) is called from these methods to use the event dispatch thread to display messages in the application's `JTextArea`.

Method `waitForConnection` (lines 90–96) uses `ServerSocket` method `accept` (line 93) to wait for a connection from a client. When a connection occurs, the resulting `Socket` is assigned to `connection`. Method `accept` blocks until a connection is received (i.e., the thread in which `accept` is called stops executing until a client connects). Lines 94–95 output the host name of the computer that made the connection. `Socket` method `getInet-Address` returns an `InetAddress` (package `java.net`) containing information about the client computer. `InetAddress` method `getHostName` returns the host name of the client computer. For example, there is a special IP address (127.0.0.1) and host name (local-host) that is useful for testing networking applications on your local computer (this is also known as the loopback address). If `getHostName` is called on an `InetAddress` containing 127.0.0.1, the corresponding host name returned by the method would be `localhost`.

Method `getStreams` (lines 99–109) obtains the `Socket`'s streams and uses them to initialize an `ObjectOutputStream` (line 102) and an `ObjectInputStream` (line 106), respectively. Note the call to `ObjectOutputStream` method `flush` at line 103. This statement causes the `ObjectOutputStream` on the server to send a stream header to the corresponding client's `ObjectInputStream`. The stream header contains such information as the version of object serialization being used to send objects. This information is required by the `ObjectInputStream` so that it can prepare to receive those objects correctly.

Software Engineering Observation 24.5

When using an `ObjectOutputStream` and `ObjectInputStream` to send and receive data over a network connection, always create the `ObjectOutputStream` first and `flush` the stream so that the client's `ObjectInputStream` can prepare to receive the data. This is required only for networking applications that communicate using `ObjectOutputStream` and `ObjectInputStream`.

Performance Tip 24.3

A computer's input and output components are typically much slower than its memory. Output buffers typically are used to increase the efficiency of an application by sending larger amounts of data fewer times, thus reducing the number of times an application accesses the computer's input and output components.

Line 114 of method `processConnection` (lines 112–133) calls method `sendData` to send `"SERVER>>> Connection successful"` as a string to the client. The loop at lines 120–132 executes until the server receives the message `"CLIENT>>> TERMINATE"`. Line 124 uses `ObjectInputStream` method `readObject` to read a `String` from the client. Line 125 invokes method `displayMessage` to append the message to the `JTextArea`.

When the transmission is complete, method `processConnection` returns, and the program calls method `closeConnection` (lines 136–151) to close the streams associated with the `Socket` and close the `Socket`. Then the server waits for the next connection attempt from a client by continuing with line 68 at the beginning of the `while` loop.

When the user of the server application enters a string in the text field and presses the *Enter* key, the program calls method `actionPerformed` (lines 40–44), which reads the string from the text field and calls utility method `sendData` (lines 154–166) to send the string to the client. Method `sendData` writes the object, flushes the output buffer and appends the same string to the textarea in the server window. It is not necessary to invoke `displayMessage` to modify the textarea here, because method `sendData` is called from an event handler—thus, `sendData` executes as part of the event-dispatch thread.

Note that `Server` receives a connection, processes it, closes it and waits for the next connection. A more likely scenario would be a `Server` that receives a connection, sets it up to be processed as a separate thread of execution, then immediately waits for new connections. The separate threads that process existing connections can continue to execute while the `Server` concentrates on new connection requests. This makes the server more efficient, because multiple client requests can be processed concurrently. We demonstrate a multithreaded server in Section 24.8.

Client Class

Like class `Server`, class `Client`'s (Fig. 24.7) constructor (lines 29–56) creates the GUI of the application (a `JTextField` and a `JTextArea`). `Client` displays its output in the textarea. When method `main` (lines 7–19 of Fig. 24.8) executes, it creates an instance of class `Client`, specifies the window's default close operation and calls method `runClient` (declared at lines 59–79). In this example, you can execute the client from any computer on the Internet and specify the IP address or host name of the server computer as a command-line argument to the program. For example, the command

    java Client 192.168.1.15

attempts to connect to the `Server` on the computer with IP address `192.168.1.15`.

`Client` method `runClient` (lines 59–79) sets up the connection to the server, processes messages received from the server and closes the connection when communication is complete. Line 63 calls method `connectToServer` (declared at lines 82–92) to perform the connection. After connecting, line 64 calls method `getStreams` (declared at lines 95–105) to obtain references to the `Socket`'s stream objects. Then line 65 calls method `processConnection` (declared at lines 108–126) to receive and display messages sent from the server. The `finally` block (lines 75–78) calls `closeConnection` (lines 129–144) to close the streams and the `Socket` even if an exception has occurred. Method `displayMessage` (lines 162–173) is called from these methods to use the event-dispatch thread to display messages in the application's textarea.

```java
1   // Fig. 24.7: Client.java
2   // Client that reads and displays information sent from a Server.
3   import java.io.EOFException;
4   import java.io.IOException;
5   import java.io.ObjectInputStream;
6   import java.io.ObjectOutputStream;
7   import java.net.InetAddress;
8   import java.net.Socket;
9   import java.awt.BorderLayout;
10  import java.awt.event.ActionEvent;
11  import java.awt.event.ActionListener;
12  import javax.swing.JFrame;
13  import javax.swing.JScrollPane;
14  import javax.swing.JTextArea;
15  import javax.swing.JTextField;
16  import javax.swing.SwingUtilities;
17
18  public class Client extends JFrame
19  {
20     private JTextField enterField; // enters information from user
21     private JTextArea displayArea; // display information to user
22     private ObjectOutputStream output; // output stream to server
23     private ObjectInputStream input; // input stream from server
24     private String message = ""; // message from server
25     private String chatServer; // host server for this application
26     private Socket client; // socket to communicate with server
27
28     // initialize chatServer and set up GUI
29     public Client( String host )
30     {
31        super( "Client" );
32
33        chatServer = host; // set server to which this client connects
34
35        enterField = new JTextField(); // create enterField
36        enterField.setEditable( false );
37        enterField.addActionListener(
38           new ActionListener()
39           {
40              // send message to server
41              public void actionPerformed( ActionEvent event )
42              {
43                 sendData( event.getActionCommand() );
44                 enterField.setText( "" );
45              } // end method actionPerformed
46           } // end anonymous inner class
47        ); // end call to addActionListener
```

Fig. 24.7 | Client portion of a stream-socket connection between client and server. (Part 1 of 4.)

```
48
49        add( enterField, BorderLayout.NORTH );
50
51        displayArea = new JTextArea(); // create displayArea
52        add( new JScrollPane( displayArea ), BorderLayout.CENTER );
53
54        setSize( 300, 150 ); // set size of window
55        setVisible( true ); // show window
56    } // end Client constructor
57
58    // connect to server and process messages from server
59    public void runClient()
60    {
61        try // connect to server, get streams, process connection
62        {
63            connectToServer(); // create a Socket to make connection
64            getStreams(); // get the input and output streams
65            processConnection(); // process connection
66        } // end try
67        catch ( EOFException eofException )
68        {
69            displayMessage( "\nClient terminated connection" );
70        } // end catch
71        catch ( IOException ioException )
72        {
73            ioException.printStackTrace();
74        } // end catch
75        finally
76        {
77            closeConnection(); // close connection
78        } // end finally
79    } // end method runClient
80
81    // connect to server
82    private void connectToServer() throws IOException
83    {
84        displayMessage( "Attempting connection\n" );
85
86        // create Socket to make connection to server
87        client = new Socket( InetAddress.getByName( chatServer ), 12345 );
88
89        // display connection information
90        displayMessage( "Connected to: " +
91            client.getInetAddress().getHostName() );
92    } // end method connectToServer
93
94    // get streams to send and receive data
95    private void getStreams() throws IOException
96    {
97        // set up output stream for objects
98        output = new ObjectOutputStream( client.getOutputStream() );
99        output.flush(); // flush output buffer to send header information
```

Fig. 24.7 | Client portion of a stream-socket connection between client and server. (Part 2 of 4.)

```
100
101        // set up input stream for objects
102        input = new ObjectInputStream( client.getInputStream() );
103
104        displayMessage( "\nGot I/O streams\n" );
105     } // end method getStreams
106
107     // process connection with server
108     private void processConnection() throws IOException
109     {
110        // enable enterField so client user can send messages
111        setTextFieldEditable( true );
112
113        do // process messages sent from server
114        {
115           try // read message and display it
116           {
117              message = ( String ) input.readObject(); // read new message
118              displayMessage( "\n" + message ); // display message
119           } // end try
120           catch ( ClassNotFoundException classNotFoundException )
121           {
122              displayMessage( "\nUnknown object type received" );
123           } // end catch
124
125        } while ( !message.equals( "SERVER>>> TERMINATE" ) );
126     } // end method processConnection
127
128     // close streams and socket
129     private void closeConnection()
130     {
131        displayMessage( "\nClosing connection" );
132        setTextFieldEditable( false ); // disable enterField
133
134        try
135        {
136           output.close(); // close output stream
137           input.close(); // close input stream    1
138           client.close(); // close socket
139        } // end try
140        catch ( IOException ioException )
141        {
142           ioException.printStackTrace();
143        } // end catch
144     } // end method closeConnection
145
146     // send message to server
147     private void sendData( String message )
148     {
149        try // send object to server
150        {
151           output.writeObject( "CLIENT>>> " + message );
```

Fig. 24.7 | Client portion of a stream-socket connection between client and server. (Part 3 of 4.)

```
152            output.flush(); // flush data to output
153            displayMessage( "\nCLIENT>>> " + message );
154         } // end try
155         catch ( IOException ioException )
156         {
157            displayArea.append( "\nError writing object" );
158         } // end catch
159      } // end method sendData
160
161      // manipulates displayArea in the event-dispatch thread
162      private void displayMessage( final String messageToDisplay )
163      {
164         SwingUtilities.invokeLater(
165            new Runnable()
166            {
167               public void run() // updates displayArea
168               {
169                  displayArea.append( messageToDisplay );
170               } // end method run
171            }  // end anonymous inner class
172         ); // end call to SwingUtilities.invokeLater
173      } // end method displayMessage
174
175      // manipulates enterField in the event-dispatch thread
176      private void setTextFieldEditable( final boolean editable )
177      {
178         SwingUtilities.invokeLater(
179            new Runnable()
180            {
181               public void run() // sets enterField's editability
182               {
183                  enterField.setEditable( editable );
184               } // end method run
185            } // end anonymous inner class
186         ); // end call to SwingUtilities.invokeLater
187      } // end method setTextFieldEditable
188 } // end class Client
```

Fig. 24.7 | Client portion of a stream-socket connection between client and server. (Part 4 of 4.)

Method connectToServer (lines 82–92) creates a Socket called client (line 87) to establish a connection. The method passes two arguments to the Socket constructor—the IP address of the server computer and the port number (12345) where the server application is awaiting client connections. In the first argument, InetAddress static method getByName returns an InetAddress object containing the IP address specified as a command-line argument to the application (or 127.0.0.1 if no command-line arguments are specified). Method getByName can receive a string containing either the actual IP address or the host name of the server. The first argument also could have been written other ways. For the localhost address 127.0.0.1, the first argument could be specified with either of the following expressions:

```
InetAddress.getByName( "localhost" )
InetAddress.getLocalHost()
```

```
 1   // Fig. 24.8: ClientTest.java
 2   // Test the Client class.
 3   import javax.swing.JFrame;
 4
 5   public class ClientTest
 6   {
 7      public static void main( String args[] )
 8      {
 9         Client application; // declare client application
10
11         // if no command line args
12         if ( args.length == 0 )
13            application = new Client( "127.0.0.1" ); // connect to localhost
14         else
15            application = new Client( args[ 0 ] ); // use args to connect
16
17         application.setDefaultCloseOperation( JFrame.EXIT_ON_CLOSE );
18         application.runClient(); // run client application
19      } // end main
20   } // end class ClientTest
```

Fig. 24.8 | Class that tests the `Client`.

Also, there are versions of the `Socket` constructor that receive a string for the IP address or host name. The first argument could have been specified as `"127.0.0.1"` or `"localhost"`. We chose to demonstrate the client/server relationship by connecting between applications executing on the same computer (`localhost`). Normally, this first argument would be the IP address of another computer. The `InetAddress` object for another computer can be obtained by specifying the computer's IP address or host name as the argument to `InetAddress` method `getByName`. The `Socket` constructor's second argument is the server port number. This must match the port number at which the server is waiting for connections (called the handshake point). Once the connection is made, lines 90–91 display a message in the text area indicating the name of the server computer to which the client has connected.

The `Client` uses an `ObjectOutputStream` to send data to the server and an `Object-InputStream` to receive data from the server. Method `getStreams` (lines 95–105) creates the `ObjectOutputStream` and `ObjectInputStream` objects that use the streams associated with the client socket.

Method `processConnection` (lines 108–126) contains a loop that executes until the client receives the message `"SERVER>>> TERMINATE"`. Line 117 reads a `String` object from the server. Line 118 invokes `displayMessage` to append the message to the textarea.

When the transmission is complete, method `closeConnection` (lines 129–144) closes the streams and the `Socket`.

When the user of the client application enters a string in the text field and presses the *Enter* key, the program calls method `actionPerformed` (lines 41–45) to read the string and invoke utility method `sendData` (147–159) to send the string to the server. Method `sendData` writes the object, flushes the output buffer and appends the same string to the `JTextArea` in the client window. Once again, it is not necessary to invoke utility method `displayMessage` to modify the textarea here, because method `sendData` is called from an event handler.

24.7 Connectionless Client/Server Interaction with Datagrams

We have been discussing connection-oriented, streams-based transmission. Now we consider connectionless transmission with datagrams.

Connection-oriented transmission is like the telephone system in which you dial and are given a connection to the telephone of the person with whom you wish to communicate. The connection is maintained for the duration of your phone call, even when you are not talking.

Connectionless transmission with datagrams is more like the way mail is carried via the postal service. If a large message will not fit in one envelope, you break it into separate message pieces that you place in separate, sequentially numbered envelopes. Each of the letters is then mailed at the same time. The letters could arrive in order, out of order or not at all (the last case is rare, but it does happen). The person at the receiving end reassembles the message pieces into sequential order before attempting to make sense of the message. If your message is small enough to fit in one envelope, you need not worry about the "out-of-sequence" problem, but it is still possible that your message might not arrive. One difference between datagrams and postal mail is that duplicates of datagrams can arrive at the receiving computer.

Figures 24.9–24.12 use datagrams to send packets of information via the User Datagram Protocol (UDP) between a client application and a server application. In the `Client` application (Fig. 24.11), the user types a message into a text field and presses *Enter*. The program converts the message into a `byte` array and places it in a datagram packet that is sent to the server. The `Server` (Fig. 24.9) receives the packet and displays the information in it, then echoes the packet back to the client. Upon receiving the packet, the client displays the information it contains.

Server Class

Class `Server` (Fig. 24.9) declares two `DatagramPackets` that the server uses to send and receive information and one `DatagramSocket` that sends and receives the packets. The `Server` constructor (lines 19–37) creates the graphical user interface in which the packets of information will be displayed. Line 30 creates the `DatagramSocket` in a `try` block. Line 30 uses the `DatagramSocket` constructor that takes an integer port number argument (5000 in this example) to bind the server to a port where it can receive packets from clients. `Clients` sending packets to this `Server` specify the same port number in the packets they send. A `SocketException` is thrown if the `DatagramSocket` constructor fails to bind the `DatagramSocket` to the specified port.

```java
 1   // Fig. 24.9: Server.java
 2   // Server that receives and sends packets from/to a client.
 3   import java.io.IOException;
 4   import java.net.DatagramPacket;
 5   import java.net.DatagramSocket;
 6   import java.net.SocketException;
 7   import java.awt.BorderLayout;
 8   import javax.swing.JFrame;
 9   import javax.swing.JScrollPane;
10   import javax.swing.JTextArea;
11   import javax.swing.SwingUtilities;
12
13   public class Server extends JFrame
14   {
15      private JTextArea displayArea; // displays packets received
16      private DatagramSocket socket; // socket to connect to client
17
18      // set up GUI and DatagramSocket
19      public Server()
20      {
21         super( "Server" );
22
23         displayArea = new JTextArea(); // create displayArea
24         add( new JScrollPane( displayArea ), BorderLayout.CENTER );
25         setSize( 400, 300 ); // set size of window
26         setVisible( true ); // show window
27
28         try // create DatagramSocket for sending and receiving packets
29         {
30            socket = new DatagramSocket( 5000 );
31         } // end try
32         catch ( SocketException socketException )
33         {
34            socketException.printStackTrace();
35            System.exit( 1 );
36         } // end catch
37      } // end Server constructor
38
39      // wait for packets to arrive, display data and echo packet to client
40      public void waitForPackets()
41      {
42         while ( true )
43         {
44            try // receive packet, display contents, return copy to client
45            {
46               byte data[] = new byte[ 100 ]; // set up packet
47               DatagramPacket receivePacket =
48                  new DatagramPacket( data, data.length );
49
50               socket.receive( receivePacket ); // wait to receive packet
51
```

Fig. 24.9 | Server side of connectionless client/server computing with datagrams. (Part 1 of 2.)

```
52                    // display information from received packet
53                    displayMessage( "\nPacket received:" +
54                       "\nFrom host: " + receivePacket.getAddress() +
55                       "\nHost port: " + receivePacket.getPort() +
56                       "\nLength: " + receivePacket.getLength() +
57                       "\nContaining:\n\t" + new String( receivePacket.getData(),
58                          0, receivePacket.getLength() ) );
59
60                    sendPacketToClient( receivePacket ); // send packet to client
61                 } // end try
62                 catch ( IOException ioException )
63                 {
64                    displayMessage( ioException.toString() + "\n" );
65                    ioException.printStackTrace();
66                 } // end catch
67              } // end while
68        } // end method waitForPackets
69
70        // echo packet to client
71        private void sendPacketToClient( DatagramPacket receivePacket )
72           throws IOException
73        {
74           displayMessage( "\n\nEcho data to client..." );
75
76           // create packet to send
77           DatagramPacket sendPacket = new DatagramPacket(
78              receivePacket.getData(), receivePacket.getLength(),
79              receivePacket.getAddress(), receivePacket.getPort() );
80
81           socket.send( sendPacket ); // send packet to client
82           displayMessage( "Packet sent\n" );
83        } // end method sendPacketToClient
84
85        // manipulates displayArea in the event-dispatch thread
86        private void displayMessage( final String messageToDisplay )
87        {
88           SwingUtilities.invokeLater(
89              new Runnable()
90              {
91                 public void run() // updates displayArea
92                 {
93                    displayArea.append( messageToDisplay ); // display message
94                 } // end method run
95              } // end anonymous inner class
96           ); // end call to SwingUtilities.invokeLater
97        } // end method displayMessage
98  } // end class Server
```

Fig. 24.9 | Server side of connectionless client/server computing with datagrams. (Part 2 of 2.)

Common Programming Error 24.2

Specifying a port that is already in use or specifying an invalid port number when creating a DatagramSocket results in a SocketException.

```
1    // Fig. 24.10: ServerTest.java
2    // Tests the Server class.
3    import javax.swing.JFrame;
4
5    public class ServerTest
6    {
7       public static void main( String args[] )
8       {
9          Server application = new Server(); // create server
10         application.setDefaultCloseOperation( JFrame.EXIT_ON_CLOSE );
11         application.waitForPackets(); // run server application
12      } // end main
13   } // end class ServerTest
```

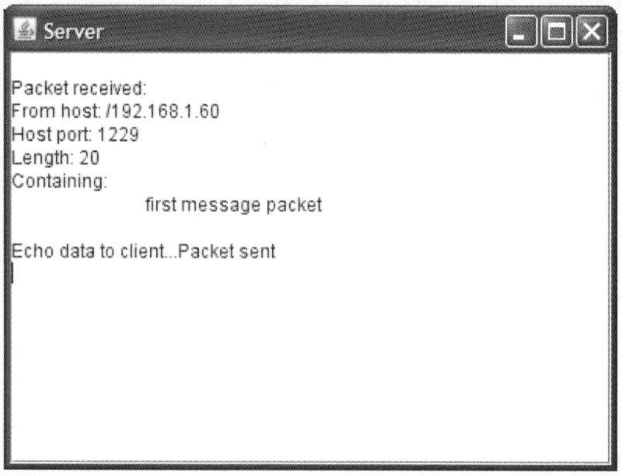

Server window after packet of data is received from Client

Server

Packet received:
From host: /192.168.1.60
Host port: 1229
Length: 20
Containing:
                first message packet

Echo data to client...Packet sent

Fig. 24.10 | Class that tests the Server.

Server method waitForPackets (lines 40–68) uses an infinite loop to wait for packets to arrive at the Server. Lines 47–48 create a DatagramPacket in which a received packet of information can be stored. The DatagramPacket constructor for this purpose receives two arguments—a byte array in which the data will be stored and the length of the array. Line 50 uses DatagramSocket method receive to wait for a packet to arrive at the Server. Method receive blocks until a packet arrives, then stores the packet in its DatagramPacket argument. The method throws an IOException if an error occurs while receiving a packet.

When a packet arrives, lines 53–58 call method displayMessage (declared at lines 86–97) to append the packet's contents to the textarea. DatagramPacket method getAddress (line 54) returns an InetAddress object containing the host name of the computer from which the packet was sent. Method getPort (line 55) returns an integer specifying the port number through which the host computer sent the packet. Method getLength (line 56) returns an integer representing the number of bytes of data sent. Method getData (line 57) returns a byte array containing the data. Lines 57–58 initialize a String object using a three-argument constructor that takes a byte array, the offset and the length. This String is then appended to the text to display.

After displaying a packet, line 60 calls method sendPacketToClient (declared at lines 71–83) to create a new packet and send it to the client. Lines 77–79 create a Datagram-

Packet and pass four arguments to its constructor. The first argument specifies the byte array to send. The second argument specifies the number of bytes to send. The third argument specifies the client computer's Internet address, to which the packet will be sent. The fourth argument specifies the port where the client is waiting to receive packets. Line 81 sends the packet over the network. Method **send** of DatagramSocket throws an IOException if an error occurs while sending a packet.

Client Class

Class Client (Fig. 24.11) works similarly to class Server, except that the Client sends packets only when the user types a message in a text field and presses the *Enter* key. When this occurs, the program calls method actionPerformed (lines 32–57), which converts the string the user entered into a byte array (line 41). Lines 44–45 create a DatagramPacket and initialize it with the byte array, the length of the string that was entered by the user, the IP address to which the packet is to be sent (InetAddress.getLocalHost() in this example) and the port number at which the Server is waiting for packets (5000 in this example). Line 47 sends the packet. Note that the client in this example must know that the server is receiving packets at port 5000—otherwise, the server will not receive the packets.

```java
 1   // Fig. 24.11: Client.java
 2   // Client that sends and receives packets to/from a server.
 3   import java.io.IOException;
 4   import java.net.DatagramPacket;
 5   import java.net.DatagramSocket;
 6   import java.net.InetAddress;
 7   import java.net.SocketException;
 8   import java.awt.BorderLayout;
 9   import java.awt.event.ActionEvent;
10   import java.awt.event.ActionListener;
11   import javax.swing.JFrame;
12   import javax.swing.JScrollPane;
13   import javax.swing.JTextArea;
14   import javax.swing.JTextField;
15   import javax.swing.SwingUtilities;
16
17   public class Client extends JFrame
18   {
19      private JTextField enterField; // for entering messages
20      private JTextArea displayArea; // for displaying messages
21      private DatagramSocket socket; // socket to connect to server
22
23      // set up GUI and DatagramSocket
24      public Client()
25      {
26         super( "Client" );
27
28         enterField = new JTextField( "Type message here" );
29         enterField.addActionListener(
30            new ActionListener()
31            {
```

Fig. 24.11 | Client side of connectionless client/server computing with datagrams. (Part 1 of 3.)

```
32          public void actionPerformed( ActionEvent event )
33          {
34              try // create and send packet
35              {
36                  // get message from textfield
37                  String message = event.getActionCommand();
38                  displayArea.append( "\nSending packet containing: " +
39                      message + "\n" );
40
41                  byte data[] = message.getBytes(); // convert to bytes
42
43                  // create sendPacket
44                  DatagramPacket sendPacket = new DatagramPacket( data,
45                      data.length, InetAddress.getLocalHost(), 5000 );
46
47                  socket.send( sendPacket ); // send packet
48                  displayArea.append( "Packet sent\n" );
49                  displayArea.setCaretPosition(
50                      displayArea.getText().length() );
51              } // end try
52              catch ( IOException ioException )
53              {
54                  displayMessage( ioException.toString() + "\n" );
55                  ioException.printStackTrace();
56              } // end catch
57          } // end actionPerformed
58      } // end inner class
59    ); // end call to addActionListener
60
61    add( enterField, BorderLayout.NORTH );
62
63    displayArea = new JTextArea();
64    add( new JScrollPane( displayArea ), BorderLayout.CENTER );
65
66    setSize( 400, 300 ); // set window size
67    setVisible( true ); // show window
68
69    try // create DatagramSocket for sending and receiving packets
70    {
71        socket = new DatagramSocket();
72    } // end try
73    catch ( SocketException socketException )
74    {
75        socketException.printStackTrace();
76        System.exit( 1 );
77    } // end catch
78  } // end Client constructor
79
80  // wait for packets to arrive from Server, display packet contents
81  public void waitForPackets()
82  {
83      while ( true )
84      {
```

Fig. 24.11 | Client side of connectionless client/server computing with datagrams. (Part 2 of 3.)

```
85          try // receive packet and display contents
86          {
87              byte data[] = new byte[ 100 ]; // set up packet
88              DatagramPacket receivePacket = new DatagramPacket(
89                  data, data.length );
90
91              socket.receive( receivePacket ); // wait for packet
92
93              // display packet contents
94              displayMessage( "\nPacket received:" +
95                  "\nFrom host: " + receivePacket.getAddress() +
96                  "\nHost port: " + receivePacket.getPort() +
97                  "\nLength: " + receivePacket.getLength() +
98                  "\nContaining:\n\t" + new String( receivePacket.getData(),
99                      0, receivePacket.getLength() ) );
100         } // end try
101         catch ( IOException exception )
102         {
103             displayMessage( exception.toString() + "\n" );
104             exception.printStackTrace();
105         } // end catch
106     } // end while
107 } // end method waitForPackets
108
109 // manipulates displayArea in the event-dispatch thread
110 private void displayMessage( final String messageToDisplay )
111 {
112     SwingUtilities.invokeLater(
113         new Runnable()
114         {
115             public void run() // updates displayArea
116             {
117                 displayArea.append( messageToDisplay );
118             } // end method run
119         } // end inner class
120     ); // end call to SwingUtilities.invokeLater
121 } // end method displayMessage
122 } // end class Client
```

Fig. 24.11 | Client side of connectionless client/server computing with datagrams. (Part 3 of 3.)

Note that the DatagramSocket constructor call (line 71) in this application does not specify any arguments. This no-argument constructor allows the computer to select the next available port number for the DatagramSocket. The client does not need a specific port number, because the server receives the client's port number as part of each DatagramPacket sent by the client. Thus, the server can send packets back to the same computer and port number from which it receives a packet of information.

Client method waitForPackets (lines 81–107) uses an infinite loop to wait for packets from the server. Line 91 blocks until a packet arrives. This does not prevent the user from sending a packet, because the GUI events are handled in the event-dispatch thread. It only prevents the while loop from continuing until a packet arrives at the Client. When a packet arrives, line 91 stores it in receivePacket, and lines 94–99 call

```
1   // Fig. 24.12: ClientTest.java
2   // Tests the Client class.
3   import javax.swing.JFrame;
4
5   public class ClientTest
6   {
7      public static void main( String args[] )
8      {
9         Client application = new Client(); // create client
10        application.setDefaultCloseOperation( JFrame.EXIT_ON_CLOSE );
11        application.waitForPackets(); // run client application
12     } // end main
13  } // end class ClientTest
```

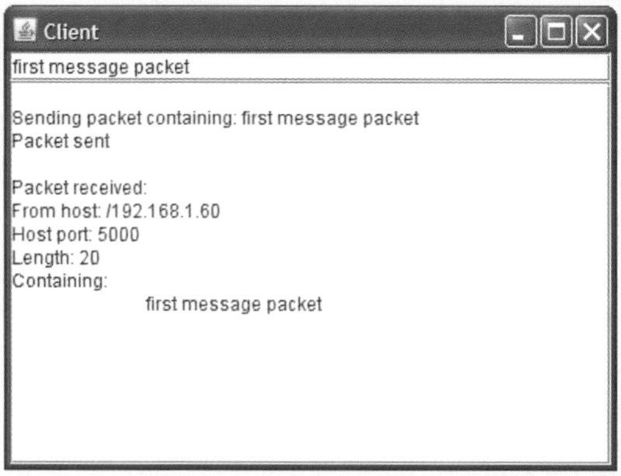

Client window after sending
packet to Server and receiving packet back
from Server

```
Client
first message packet

Sending packet containing: first message packet
Packet sent

Packet received:
From host: /192.168.1.60
Host port: 5000
Length: 20
Containing:
         first message packet
```

Fig. 24.12 | Class that tests the Client.

method displayMessage (declared at lines 110–121) to display the packet's contents in the textarea.

24.8 Client/Server Tic-Tac-Toe Using a Multithreaded Server

In this section, we present the popular game Tic-Tac-Toe implemented by using client/server techniques with stream sockets. The program consists of a TicTacToeServer application (Figs. 24.13–24.14) that allows two TicTacToeClient applications (Figs. 24.15–24.16) to connect to the server and play Tic-Tac-Toe. Sample outputs are shown in Fig. 24.17.

TicTacToeServer Class

As the TicTacToeServer receives each client connection, it creates an instance of inner-class Player (lines 182–301 of Fig. 24.13) to process the client in a separate thread. These threads enable the clients to play the game independently. The first client to connect to the server is player X and the second is player O. Player X makes the first move. The server maintains the information about the board so it can determine whether a player's move is valid or invalid.

```
1    // Fig. 24.13: TicTacToeServer.java
2    // This class maintains a game of Tic-Tac-Toe for two clients.
3    import java.awt.BorderLayout;
4    import java.net.ServerSocket;
5    import java.net.Socket;
6    import java.io.IOException;
7    import java.util.Formatter;
8    import java.util.Scanner;
9    import java.util.concurrent.ExecutorService;
10   import java.util.concurrent.Executors;
11   import java.util.concurrent.locks.Lock;
12   import java.util.concurrent.locks.ReentrantLock;
13   import java.util.concurrent.locks.Condition;
14   import javax.swing.JFrame;
15   import javax.swing.JTextArea;
16   import javax.swing.SwingUtilities;
17
18   public class TicTacToeServer extends JFrame
19   {
20      private String[] board = new String[ 9 ]; // tic-tac-toe board
21      private JTextArea outputArea; // for outputting moves
22      private Player[] players; // array of Players
23      private ServerSocket server; // server socket to connect with clients
24      private int currentPlayer; // keeps track of player with current move
25      private final static int PLAYER_X = 0; // constant for first player
26      private final static int PLAYER_O = 1; // constant for second player
27      private final static String[] MARKS = { "X", "O" }; // array of marks
28      private ExecutorService runGame; // will run players
29      private Lock gameLock; // to lock game for synchronization
30      private Condition otherPlayerConnected; // to wait for other player
31      private Condition otherPlayerTurn; // to wait for other player's turn
32
33      // set up tic-tac-toe server and GUI that displays messages
34      public TicTacToeServer()
35      {
36         super( "Tic-Tac-Toe Server" ); // set title of window
37
38         // create ExecutorService with a thread for each player
39         runGame = Executors.newFixedThreadPool( 2 );
40         gameLock = new ReentrantLock(); // create lock for game
41
42         // condition variable for both players being connected
43         otherPlayerConnected = gameLock.newCondition();
44
45         // condition variable for the other player's turn
46         otherPlayerTurn = gameLock.newCondition();
47
48         for ( int i = 0; i < 9; i++ )
49            board[ i ] = new String( "" ); // create tic-tac-toe board
50         players = new Player[ 2 ]; // create array of players
51         currentPlayer = PLAYER_X; // set current player to first player
52
```

Fig. 24.13 | Server side of client/server Tic-Tac-Toe program. (Part 1 of 6.)

```
53        try
54        {
55            server = new ServerSocket( 12345, 2 ); // set up ServerSocket
56        } // end try
57        catch ( IOException ioException )
58        {
59            ioException.printStackTrace();
60            System.exit( 1 );
61        } // end catch
62
63        outputArea = new JTextArea(); // create JTextArea for output
64        add( outputArea, BorderLayout.CENTER );
65        outputArea.setText( "Server awaiting connections\n" );
66
67        setSize( 300, 300 ); // set size of window
68        setVisible( true ); // show window
69     } // end TicTacToeServer constructor
70
71     // wait for two connections so game can be played
72     public void execute()
73     {
74        // wait for each client to connect
75        for ( int i = 0; i < players.length; i++ )
76        {
77           try // wait for connection, create Player, start runnable
78           {
79              players[ i ] = new Player( server.accept(), i );
80              runGame.execute( players[ i ] ); // execute player runnable
81           } // end try
82           catch ( IOException ioException )
83           {
84              ioException.printStackTrace();
85              System.exit( 1 );
86           } // end catch
87        } // end for
88
89        gameLock.lock(); // lock game to signal player X's thread
90
91        try
92        {
93           players[ PLAYER_X ].setSuspended( false ); // resume player X
94           otherPlayerConnected.signal(); // wake up player X's thread
95        } // end try
96        finally
97        {
98           gameLock.unlock(); // unlock game after signalling player X
99        } // end finally
100    } // end method execute
101
102    // display message in outputArea
103    private void displayMessage( final String messageToDisplay )
104    {
```

Fig. 24.13 | Server side of client/server Tic-Tac-Toe program. (Part 2 of 6.)

```
105         // display message from event-dispatch thread of execution
106         SwingUtilities.invokeLater(
107            new Runnable()
108            {
109               public void run() // updates outputArea
110               {
111                  outputArea.append( messageToDisplay ); // add message
112               } // end  method run
113            } // end inner class
114         ); // end call to SwingUtilities.invokeLater
115      } // end method displayMessage
116
117      // determine if move is valid
118      public boolean validateAndMove( int location, int player )
119      {
120         // while not current player, must wait for turn
121         while ( player != currentPlayer )
122         {
123            gameLock.lock(); // lock game to wait for other player to go
124
125            try
126            {
127               otherPlayerTurn.await(); // wait for player's turn
128            } // end try
129            catch ( InterruptedException exception )
130            {
131               exception.printStackTrace();
132            } // end catch
133            finally
134            {
135               gameLock.unlock(); // unlock game after waiting
136            } // end finally
137         } // end while
138
139         // if location not occupied, make move
140         if ( !isOccupied( location ) )
141         {
142            board[ location ] = MARKS[ currentPlayer ]; // set move on board
143            currentPlayer = ( currentPlayer + 1 ) % 2; // change player
144
145            // let new current player know that move occurred
146            players[ currentPlayer ].otherPlayerMoved( location );
147
148            gameLock.lock(); // lock game to signal other player to go
149
150            try
151            {
152               otherPlayerTurn.signal(); // signal other player to continue
153            } // end try
154            finally
155            {
156               gameLock.unlock(); // unlock game after signaling
157            } // end finally
```

Fig. 24.13 | Server side of client/server Tic-Tac-Toe program. (Part 3 of 6.)

```
158
159            return true; // notify player that move was valid
160        } // end if
161        else // move was not valid
162            return false; // notify player that move was invalid
163    } // end method validateAndMove
164
165    // determine whether location is occupied
166    public boolean isOccupied( int location )
167    {
168        if ( board[ location ].equals( MARKS[ PLAYER_X ] ) ||
169            board [ location ].equals( MARKS[ PLAYER_O ] ) )
170            return true; // location is occupied
171        else
172            return false; // location is not occupied
173    } // end method isOccupied
174
175    // place code in this method to determine whether game over
176    public boolean isGameOver()
177    {
178        return false; // this is left as an exercise
179    } // end method isGameOver
180
181    // private inner class Player manages each Player as a runnable
182    private class Player implements Runnable
183    {
184        private Socket connection; // connection to client
185        private Scanner input; // input from client
186        private Formatter output; // output to client
187        private int playerNumber; // tracks which player this is
188        private String mark; // mark for this player
189        private boolean suspended = true; // whether thread is suspended
190
191        // set up Player thread
192        public Player( Socket socket, int number )
193        {
194            playerNumber = number; // store this player's number
195            mark = MARKS[ playerNumber ]; // specify player's mark
196            connection = socket; // store socket for client
197
198            try // obtain streams from Socket
199            {
200                input = new Scanner( connection.getInputStream() );
201                output = new Formatter( connection.getOutputStream() );
202            } // end try
203            catch ( IOException ioException )
204            {
205                ioException.printStackTrace();
206                System.exit( 1 );
207            } // end catch
208        } // end Player constructor
209
```

Fig. 24.13 | Server side of client/server Tic-Tac-Toe program. (Part 4 of 6.)

```
210        // send message that other player moved
211        public void otherPlayerMoved( int location )
212        {
213           output.format( "Opponent moved\n" );
214           output.format( "%d\n", location ); // send location of move
215           output.flush(); // flush output
216        } // end method otherPlayerMoved
217
218        // control thread's execution
219        public void run()
220        {
221           // send client its mark (X or O), process messages from client
222           try
223           {
224              displayMessage( "Player " + mark + " connected\n" );
225              output.format( "%s\n", mark ); // send player's mark
226              output.flush(); // flush output
227
228              // if player X, wait for another player to arrive
229              if ( playerNumber == PLAYER_X )
230              {
231                 output.format( "%s\n%s", "Player X connected",
232                    "Waiting for another player\n" );
233                 output.flush(); // flush output
234
235                 gameLock.lock(); // lock game to  wait for second player
236
237                 try
238                 {
239                    while( suspended )
240                    {
241                       otherPlayerConnected.await(); // wait for player O
242                    } // end while
243                 } // end try
244                 catch ( InterruptedException exception )
245                 {
246                    exception.printStackTrace();
247                 } // end catch
248                 finally
249                 {
250                    gameLock.unlock(); // unlock game after second player
251                 } // end finally
252
253                 // send message that other player connected
254                 output.format( "Other player connected. Your move.\n" );
255                 output.flush(); // flush output
256              } // end if
257              else
258              {
259                 output.format( "Player O connected, please wait\n" );
260                 output.flush(); // flush output
261              } // end else
262
```

Fig. 24.13 | Server side of client/server Tic-Tac-Toe program. (Part 5 of 6.)

```
263                // while game not over
264                while ( !isGameOver() )
265                {
266                    int location = 0; // initialize move location
267
268                    if ( input.hasNext() )
269                        location = input.nextInt(); // get move location
270
271                    // check for valid move
272                    if ( validateAndMove( location, playerNumber ) )
273                    {
274                        displayMessage( "\nlocation: " + location );
275                        output.format( "Valid move.\n" ); // notify client
276                        output.flush(); // flush output
277                    } // end if
278                    else // move was invalid
279                    {
280                        output.format( "Invalid move, try again\n" );
281                        output.flush(); // flush output
282                    } // end else
283                } // end while
284            } // end try
285            finally
286            {
287                try
288                {
289                    connection.close(); // close connection to client
290                } // end try
291                catch ( IOException ioException )
292                {
293                    ioException.printStackTrace();
294                    System.exit( 1 );
295                } // end catch
296            } // end finally
297        } // end method run
298
299        // set whether or not thread is suspended
300        public void setSuspended( boolean status )
301        {
302            suspended = status; // set value of suspended
303        } // end method setSuspended
304    } // end class Player
305 } // end class TicTacToeServer
```

Fig. 24.13 | Server side of client/server Tic-Tac-Toe program. (Part 6 of 6.)

We begin with a discussion of the server side of the Tic-Tac-Toe game. When the
TicTacToeServer application executes, the main method (lines 7–12 of Fig. 24.14) creates
a TicTacToeServer object called application. The constructor (lines 34–69 of
Fig. 24.13) attempts to set up a ServerSocket. If successful, the program displays the
server window, then main invokes the TicTacToeServer method execute (lines 72–100).
Method execute loops twice, blocking at line 79 each time while waiting for a client con-

nection. When a client connects, line 79 creates a new Player object to manage the connection as a separate thread, and line 80 executes the Player in the runGame thread pool.

When the TicTacToeServer creates a Player, the Player constructor (lines 192–208) receives the Socket object representing the connection to the client and gets the associated input and output streams. Line 201 creates a Formatter (see Chapter 28) by wrapping it around the output stream of the socket. The Player's run method (lines 219–297) controls the information that is sent to and received from the client. First, it passes to the client the character that the client will place on the board when a move is made (line 225). Line 226 calls Formatter method **flush** to force this output to the client. Line 241 suspends player X's thread as it starts executing, because player X can move only after player O connects.

After player O connects, the game can be played, and the run method begins executing its while statement (lines 264–283). Each iteration of this loop reads an integer (line 269) representing the location where the client wants to place a mark, and line 272 invokes the TicTacToeServer method validateAndMove (declared at lines 118–163) to check the move. If the move is valid, line 275 sends a message to the client to this effect. If not, line 280 sends a message indicating that the move was invalid. The program maintains board locations as numbers from 0 to 8 (0 through 2 for the first row, 3 through 5 for the second row and 6 through 8 for the third row).

```
1   // Fig. 24.14: TicTacToeServerTest.java
2   // Tests the TicTacToeServer.
3   import javax.swing.JFrame;
4
5   public class TicTacToeServerTest
6   {
7      public static void main( String args[] )
8      {
9         TicTacToeServer application = new TicTacToeServer();
10        application.setDefaultCloseOperation( JFrame.EXIT_ON_CLOSE );
11        application.execute();
12     } // end main
13  } // end class TicTacToeServerTest
```

Tic-Tac-Toe Server
```
Server awaiting connections
Player X connected
Player O connected

location: 0
location: 4
location: 2
location: 1
location: 7
location: 5
location: 6
location: 8
location: 3
```

Fig. 24.14 | Class that tests Tic-Tac-Toe server.

Method validateAndMove (lines 118–163 in class TicTacToeServer) allows only one player at a time to move, thereby preventing them from modifying the state information of the game simultaneously. If the Player attempting to validate a move is not the current player (i.e., the one allowed to make a move), it is placed in a *wait* state until its turn to move. If the position for the move being validated is already occupied on the board, validMove returns false. Otherwise, the server places a mark for the player in its local representation of the board (line 142), notifies the other Player object (line 146) that a move has been made (so that the client can be sent a message), invokes method signal (line 152) so that the waiting Player (if there is one) can validate a move and returns true (line 159) to indicate that the move is valid.

TicTacToeClient *Class*
Each TicTacToeClient application (Fig. 24.15) maintains its own GUI version of the Tic-Tac-Toe board on which it displays the state of the game. The clients can place a mark only in an empty square on the board. Inner class Square (lines 205–262 of Fig. 24.15) implements each of the nine squares on the board. When a TicTacToeClient begins execution, it creates a JTextArea in which messages from the server and a representation of the board using nine Square objects are displayed. The startClient method (lines 80–100) opens a connection to the server and gets the associated input and output streams from the Socket object. Lines 85–86 make a connection to the server. Class TicTacToeClient implements interface Runnable so that a separate thread can read messages from the server. This approach enables the user to interact with the board (in the event dispatch thread) while waiting for messages from the server. After establishing the connection to the server, line 99 executes the client with the worker ExecutorService. The run method (lines 103–124) controls the separate thread of execution. The method first reads the mark character (X or O) from the server (line 105), then loops continuously (lines 121–125) and reads messages from the server (line 124). Each message is passed to the processMessage method (lines 129–156) for processing.

```
1   // Fig. 24.15: TicTacToeClient.java
2   // Client that let a user play Tic-Tac-Toe with another across a network.
3   import java.awt.BorderLayout;
4   import java.awt.Dimension;
5   import java.awt.Graphics;
6   import java.awt.GridLayout;
7   import java.awt.event.MouseAdapter;
8   import java.awt.event.MouseEvent;
9   import java.net.Socket;
10  import java.net.InetAddress;
11  import java.io.IOException;
12  import javax.swing.JFrame;
13  import javax.swing.JPanel;
14  import javax.swing.JScrollPane;
15  import javax.swing.JTextArea;
16  import javax.swing.JTextField;
17  import javax.swing.SwingUtilities;
18  import java.util.Formatter;
```

Fig. 24.15 | Client side of client/server Tic-Tac-Toe program. (Part 1 of 6.)

```
19    import java.util.Scanner;
20    import java.util.concurrent.Executors;
21    import java.util.concurrent.ExecutorService;
22
23    public class TicTacToeClient extends JFrame implements Runnable
24    {
25       private JTextField idField; // textfield to display player's mark
26       private JTextArea displayArea; // JTextArea to display output
27       private JPanel boardPanel; // panel for tic-tac-toe board
28       private JPanel panel2; // panel to hold board
29       private Square board[][]; // tic-tac-toe board
30       private Square currentSquare; // current square
31       private Socket connection; // connection to server
32       private Scanner input; // input from server
33       private Formatter output; // output to server
34       private String ticTacToeHost; // host name for server
35       private String myMark; // this client's mark
36       private boolean myTurn; // determines which client's turn it is
37       private final String X_MARK = "X"; // mark for first client
38       private final String O_MARK = "O"; // mark for second client
39
40       // set up user-interface and board
41       public TicTacToeClient( String host )
42       {
43          ticTacToeHost = host; // set name of server
44          displayArea = new JTextArea( 4, 30 ); // set up JTextArea
45          displayArea.setEditable( false );
46          add( new JScrollPane( displayArea ), BorderLayout.SOUTH );
47
48          boardPanel = new JPanel(); // set up panel for squares in board
49          boardPanel.setLayout( new GridLayout( 3, 3, 0, 0 ) );
50
51          board = new Square[ 3 ][ 3 ]; // create board
52
53          // loop over the rows in the board
54          for ( int row = 0; row < board.length; row++ )
55          {
56             // loop over the columns in the board
57             for ( int column = 0; column < board[ row ].length; column++ )
58             {
59                // create square
60                board[ row ][ column ] = new Square( ' ', row * 3 + column );
61                boardPanel.add( board[ row ][ column ] ); // add square
62             } // end inner for
63          } // end outer for
64
65          idField = new JTextField(); // set up textfield
66          idField.setEditable( false );
67          add( idField, BorderLayout.NORTH );
68
69          panel2 = new JPanel(); // set up panel to contain boardPanel
70          panel2.add( boardPanel, BorderLayout.CENTER ); // add board panel
```

Fig. 24.15 | Client side of client/server Tic-Tac-Toe program. (Part 2 of 6.)

```
71          add( panel2, BorderLayout.CENTER ); // add container panel
72
73          setSize( 300, 225 ); // set size of window
74          setVisible( true ); // show window
75
76          startClient();
77       } // end TicTacToeClient constructor
78
79       // start the client thread
80       public void startClient()
81       {
82          try // connect to server, get streams and start outputThread
83          {
84             // make connection to server
85             connection = new Socket(
86                InetAddress.getByName( ticTacToeHost ), 12345 );
87
88             // get streams for input and output
89             input = new Scanner( connection.getInputStream() );
90             output = new Formatter( connection.getOutputStream() );
91          } // end try
92          catch ( IOException ioException )
93          {
94             ioException.printStackTrace();
95          } // end catch
96
97          // create and start worker thread for this client
98          ExecutorService worker = Executors.newFixedThreadPool( 1 );
99          worker.execute( this ); // execute client
100      } // end method startClient
101
102      // control thread that allows continuous update of displayArea
103      public void run()
104      {
105         myMark = input.nextLine(); // get player's mark (X or O)
106
107         SwingUtilities.invokeLater(
108            new Runnable()
109            {
110               public void run()
111               {
112                  // display player's mark
113                  idField.setText( "You are player \"" + myMark + "\"" );
114               } // end method run
115            } // end anonymous inner class
116         ); // end call to SwingUtilities.invokeLater
117
118         myTurn = ( myMark.equals( X_MARK ) ); // determine if client's turn
119
120         // receive messages sent to client and output them
121         while ( true )
122         {
```

Fig. 24.15 | Client side of client/server Tic-Tac-Toe program. (Part 3 of 6.)

```
123                 if ( input.hasNextLine() )
124                     processMessage( input.nextLine() );
125             } // end while
126         } // end method run
127
128         // process messages received by client
129         private void processMessage( String message )
130         {
131             // valid move occurred
132             if ( message.equals( "Valid move." ) )
133             {
134                 displayMessage( "Valid move, please wait.\n" );
135                 setMark( currentSquare, myMark ); // set mark in square
136             } // end if
137             else if ( message.equals( "Invalid move, try again" ) )
138             {
139                 displayMessage( message + "\n" ); // display invalid move
140                 myTurn = true; // still this client's turn
141             } // end else if
142             else if ( message.equals( "Opponent moved" ) )
143             {
144                 int location = input.nextInt(); // get move location
145                 input.nextLine(); // skip newline after int location
146                 int row = location / 3; // calculate row
147                 int column = location % 3; // calculate column
148
149                 setMark( board[ row ][ column ],
150                     ( myMark.equals( X_MARK ) ? O_MARK : X_MARK ) ); // mark move
151                 displayMessage( "Opponent moved. Your turn.\n" );
152                 myTurn = true; // now this client's turn
153             } // end else if
154             else
155                 displayMessage( message + "\n" ); // display the message
156         } // end method processMessage
157
158         // manipulate outputArea in event-dispatch thread
159         private void displayMessage( final String messageToDisplay )
160         {
161             SwingUtilities.invokeLater(
162                 new Runnable()
163                 {
164                     public void run()
165                     {
166                         displayArea.append( messageToDisplay ); // updates output
167                     } // end method run
168                 } // end inner class
169             ); // end call to SwingUtilities.invokeLater
170         } // end method displayMessage
171
172         // utility method to set mark on board in event-dispatch thread
173         private void setMark( final Square squareToMark, final String mark )
174         {
```

Fig. 24.15 | Client side of client/server Tic-Tac-Toe program. (Part 4 of 6.)

```
175            SwingUtilities.invokeLater(
176               new Runnable()
177               {
178                  public void run()
179                  {
180                     squareToMark.setMark( mark ); // set mark in square
181                  } // end method run
182               } // end anonymous inner class
183            ); // end call to SwingUtilities.invokeLater
184      } // end method setMark
185
186      // send message to server indicating clicked square
187      public void sendClickedSquare( int location )
188      {
189         // if it is my turn
190         if ( myTurn )
191         {
192            output.format( "%d\n", location ); // send location to server
193            output.flush();
194            myTurn = false; // not my turn anymore
195         } // end if
196      } // end method sendClickedSquare
197
198      // set current Square
199      public void setCurrentSquare( Square square )
200      {
201         currentSquare = square; // set current square to argument
202      } // end method setCurrentSquare
203
204      // private inner class for the squares on the board
205      private class Square extends JPanel
206      {
207         private String mark; // mark to be drawn in this square
208         private int location; // location of square
209
210         public Square( String squareMark, int squareLocation )
211         {
212            mark = squareMark; // set mark for this square
213            location = squareLocation; // set location of this square
214
215            addMouseListener(
216               new MouseAdapter()
217               {
218                  public void mouseReleased( MouseEvent e )
219                  {
220                     setCurrentSquare( Square.this ); // set current square
221
222                     // send location of this square
223                     sendClickedSquare( getSquareLocation() );
224                  } // end method mouseReleased
225               } // end anonymous inner class
226            ); // end call to addMouseListener
227         } // end Square constructor
```

Fig. 24.15 | Client side of client/server Tic-Tac-Toe program. (Part 5 of 6.)

```
228
229        // return preferred size of Square
230        public Dimension getPreferredSize()
231        {
232            return new Dimension( 30, 30 ); // return preferred size
233        } // end method getPreferredSize
234
235        // return minimum size of Square
236        public Dimension getMinimumSize()
237        {
238            return getPreferredSize(); // return preferred size
239        } // end method getMinimumSize
240
241        // set mark for Square
242        public void setMark( String newMark )
243        {
244            mark = newMark; // set mark of square
245            repaint(); // repaint square
246        } // end method setMark
247
248        // return Square location
249        public int getSquareLocation()
250        {
251            return location; // return location of square
252        } // end method getSquareLocation
253
254        // draw Square
255        public void paintComponent( Graphics g )
256        {
257            super.paintComponent( g );
258
259            g.drawRect( 0, 0, 29, 29 ); // draw square
260            g.drawString( mark, 11, 20 ); // draw mark
261        } // end method paintComponent
262    } // end inner-class Square
263 } // end class TicTacToeClient
```

Fig. 24.15 | Client side of client/server Tic-Tac-Toe program. (Part 6 of 6.)

If the message received is "Valid move.", lines 134–135 display the message "Valid move, please wait." and call method setMark (lines 173–184) to set the client's mark in the current square (the one in which the user clicked), using SwingUtilities method invokeLater to ensure that the GUI updates occur in the event dispatch thread. If the message received is "Invalid move, try again.", line 139 displays the message so that the user can click a different square. If the message received is "Opponent moved.", line 145 reads an integer from the server indicating where the opponent moved, and lines 149–150 place a mark in that square of the board (again using SwingUtilities method invoke-Later to ensure that the GUI updates occur in the event dispatch thread). If any other message is received, line 155 simply displays the message. Figure 24.17 shows sample screen captures of two applications interacting via the TicTacToeServer.

```
1   // Fig. 24.16: TicTacToeClientTest.java
2   // Tests the TicTacToeClient class.
3   import javax.swing.JFrame;
4
5   public class TicTacToeClientTest
6   {
7      public static void main( String args[] )
8      {
9         TicTacToeClient application; // declare client application
10
11         // if no command line args
12         if ( args.length == 0 )
13            application = new TicTacToeClient( "127.0.0.1" ); // localhost
14         else
15            application = new TicTacToeClient( args[ 0 ] ); // use args
16
17         application.setDefaultCloseOperation( JFrame.EXIT_ON_CLOSE );
18      } // end main
19   } // end class TicTacToeClientTest
```

Fig. 24.16 | Test class for Tic-Tac-Toe client.

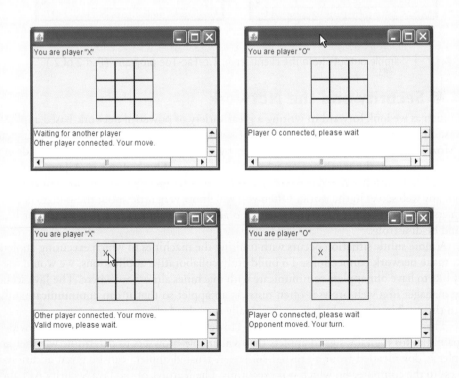

Fig. 24.17 | Sample outputs from the client/server Tic-Tac-Toe program. (Part 1 of 2.)

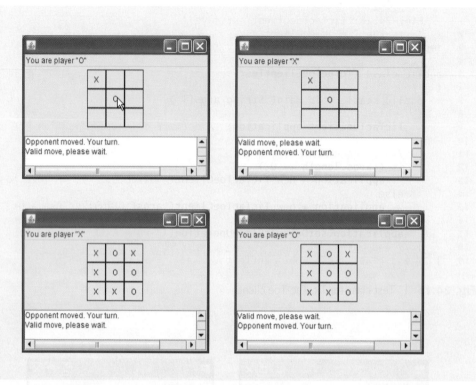

Fig. 24.17 | Sample outputs from the client/server Tic-Tac-Toe program. (Part 2 of 2.)

24.9 Security and the Network

As much as we look forward to writing a great variety of powerful network-based applications, our efforts may be limited because of security concerns. Many web browsers, such as Mozilla and Microsoft Internet Explorer, by default prohibit Java applets from doing file processing on the machines on which they execute. Think about it. A Java applet is designed to be sent to your browser via an HTML document that could be downloaded from any web server in the world. Often you will know very little about the sources of Java applets that will execute on your system. To allow these applets free rein with your files could be disastrous.

A more subtle situation occurs with limiting the machines to which executing applets can make network connections. To build truly collaborative applications, we would ideally like to have our applets communicate with machines almost anywhere. The Java security manager in a web browser often restricts an applet so that it can communicate only with the machine from which it was originally downloaded.

These restrictions may seem too strict. However, the Java Security API now provides capabilities for digitally signed applets that will enable browsers to determine whether an applet is downloaded from a trusted source. A trusted applet can be given additional access to the computer on which it is executing. The features of the Java Security API and additional networking capabilities are discussed in our text *Advanced Java 2 Platform How to Program*.

24.10 [Web Bonus] Case Study: DeitelMessenger Server and Client

[*Note:* This case study is available at www.deitel.com/books/jhtp7/.] Chat rooms have become common on the Internet. They provide a central location where users can chat with each other via short text messages. Each participant can see all messages that the other users post, and each user can post messages. This case study integrates many of the Java networking, multithreading and Swing GUI features you have learned thus far to build an online chat system. We also introduce multicasting, which enables an application to send DatagramPackets to groups of clients.

The DeitelMessenger case study is a significant application that uses many intermediate Java features, such as networking with Sockets, DatagramPackets and Multicast-Sockets, multithreading and Swing GUI. The case study also demonstrates good software engineering practices by separating interface from implementation, enabling developers to support different network protocols and provide different user interfaces. After reading this case study, you will be able to build more significant networking applications.

24.11 Wrap-Up

In this chapter, you have learned the basics of network programming in Java. You learned two different methods of sending data over a network: streams-based networking using TCP/IP and datagrams-based networking using UDP. In the next chapter, you will learn basic database concepts, how to interact with data in a database using SQL and how to use JDBC to allow Java applications to manipulate database data.

Summary

Section 24.1 Introduction

- Java provides stream sockets and datagram sockets. With stream sockets, a process establishes a connection to another process. While the connection is in place, data flows between the processes in streams. Stream sockets are said to provide a connection-oriented service. The protocol used for transmission is the popular TCP (Transmission Control Protocol).

- With datagram sockets, individual packets of information are transmitted. UDP (User Datagram Protocol) is a connectionless service that does not guarantee that packets will not be lost, duplicated or arrive out of sequence. Extra programming is required on your part to deal with these problems.

Section 24.2 Manipulating URLs

- The HTTP protocol (Hypertext Transfer Protocol) that forms the basis of the web uses URIs (Uniform Resource Identifiers) to locate data on the Internet. Common URIs represent files or directories and can represent complex tasks such as database lookups and Internet searches. A URI that represents a document is called a URL (Uniform Resource Locator).

- Applet method getAppletContext returns a reference to an AppletContext object that represents the applet's environment (i.e., the browser in which the applet is executing). AppletContext method showDocument receives a URL as an argument and passes it to the AppletContext (i.e., the browser), which displays the web resource associated with that URL. A second version of showDocument enables an applet to specify the target frame in which to display a web resource. Special target frames include _blank (display in a new web browser window), _self (display in the same frame as the applet) and _top (remove the current frames, then display in the current window).

Section 24.3 Reading a File on a Web Server

- JEditorPane method setPage downloads the document specified by its argument and displays it in the JEditorPane.

- Typically, an HTML document contains hyperlinks—text, images or GUI components that, when clicked, link to another document on the web. If an HTML document is displayed in a JEditorPane and the user clicks a hyperlink, the JEditorPane generates a HyperlinkEvent and notifies all registered HyperlinkListeners of the event.

- HyperlinkEvent method getEventType determines the event type. HyperlinkEvent contains nested class EventType, which declares three hyperlink event types: ACTIVATED (hyperlink clicked), ENTERED (mouse over a hyperlink) and EXITED (mouse moved away from a hyperlink). HyperlinkEvent method getURL obtains the URL represented by the hyperlink.

Section 24.4 Establishing a Simple Server Using Stream Sockets

- Stream-based connections are managed with Socket objects.

- A ServerSocket object establishes the port where a server waits for connections from clients. The second argument to the ServerSocket constructor is the number of connections that can wait in a queue to connect to the server. If the queue of clients is full, client connections are refused. The ServerSocket method accept waits indefinitely (i.e., blocks) for a connection from a client and returns a Socket object when a connection is established.

- Socket methods getOutputStream and getInputStream get references to a Socket's Output-Stream and InputStream, respectively. Socket method close terminates a connection.

Section 24.5 Establishing a Simple Client Using Stream Sockets

- A server name and port number are specified when creating a Socket object to enable it to connect a client to the server. A failed connection attempt throws an IOException.

- InetAddress method getByName returns an InetAddress object containing the host name of the computer for which the host name or IP address is specified as an argument. InetAddress method getLocalHost returns an InetAddress object containing the host name of the local computer executing the program.

Section 24.7 Connectionless Client/Server Interaction with Datagrams

- Connection-oriented transmission is like the telephone system—you dial and are given a connection to the telephone of the person with whom you wish to communicate. The connection is maintained for the duration of your phone call, even when you are not talking.

- Connectionless transmission with datagrams is similar to mail carried via the postal service. A large message that will not fit in one envelope can be broken into separate message pieces that are placed in separate, sequentially numbered envelopes. All the letters are then mailed at once. They could arrive in order, out of order or not at all.

- DatagramPacket objects store packets of data that are to be sent or that are received by an application. DatagramSockets send and receive DatagramPackets.

- The DatagramSocket constructor that takes no arguments binds the application to a port chosen by the computer on which the program executes. The DatagramSocket constructor that takes an integer port number argument binds the application to the specified port. If a DatagramSocket constructor fails to bind the application to a port, a SocketException occurs. DatagramSocket method receive blocks (waits) until a packet arrives, then stores the packet in its argument.

- `DatagramPacket` method `getAddress` returns an `InetAddress` object containing information about the host computer from which the packet was sent. Method `getPort` returns an integer specifying the port number through which the host computer sent the `DatagramPacket`. Method `getLength` returns an integer representing the number of bytes of data in a `DatagramPacket`. Method `getData` returns a byte array containing the data in a `DatagramPacket`.

- The `DatagramPacket` constructor for a packet to be sent takes four arguments—the byte array to be sent, the number of bytes to be sent, the client address to which the packet will be sent and the port number where the client is waiting to receive packets.

- `DatagramSocket` method `send` sends a `DatagramPacket` out over the network.

- If an error occurs when receiving or sending a `DatagramPacket`, an `IOException` occurs.

Section 24.9 Security and the Network
- Web browsers often restrict an applet so that it can communicate only with the machine from which it was originally downloaded.

Terminology

accept method of class `ServerSocket`
`ACTIVATED` constant of nested class `EventType`
applet parameter
`AppletContext` interface
binding the server to the port
`_blank` target frame
block to listen for a connection
class loader
client
client/server relationship
`close` method of class `Socket`
connection
connection-oriented service
connection-oriented, streams-based
    transmission
connectionless service
connectionless transmission
datagram packet
datagram socket
`DatagramPacket` class
`DatagramSocket` class
echoes a packet back to the client
`ENTERED` constant of nested class `EventType`
`EventType` nested class of `HyperlinkEvent`
`EXITED` constant of nested class `EventType`
getAddress method of class `DatagramPacket`
getAppletContext method of class `Applet`
getByName method of class `InetAddress`
getData method of class `DatagramPacket`
getEventType method of class `HyperlinkEvent`
getHostName method of class `InetAddress`
getInetAddress method of class `Socket`
getInputStream method of class `Socket`

getLength method of class `DatagramPacket`
getLocalHost method of class `InetAddress`
getOutputStream method of class `Socket`
getParameter method of class `Applet`
getPort method of class `DatagramPacket`
getResource method of class `Class`
getURL method of class `HyperlinkEvent`
handshake point
HTML frame
hyperlink
`HyperlinkEvent` class
`HyperlinkListener` interface
hyperlinkUpdate method of interface
     `HyperlinkListener`
HyperText Transfer Protocol (HTTP)
`InetAddress` class
`java.net` package
`JEditorPane` class
loopback address
`MalformedURLException` class
packet
packet-based communications
param tag
port
port number
queue length
receive method of class `DatagramSocket`
register a port
`_self` target frame
send method of class `DatagramSocket`
server
`ServerSocket` class
setPage method of class `JEditorPane`

showDocument method of class `AppletContext`	target frame
socket	TCP (Transmission Control Protocol)
socket-based communication	_top target frame
`Socket` class	trusted source
`SocketException` class	UDP (User Datagram Protocol)
stream header	Uniform Resource Identifier (URI)
stream socket	`UnknownHostException` class
stream-based communication	User Datagram Protocol (UDP)
stream-based transmission	World Wide Web Consortium (W3C)

Self-Review Exercises

24.1 Fill in the blanks in each of the following statements:

a) Exception _____ occurs when an input/output error occurs when closing a socket.

b) Exception _____ occurs when a host name indicated by a client cannot be resolved to an address.

c) If a `DatagramSocket` constructor fails to set up a `DatagramSocket` properly, an exception of type _____ occurs.

d) Many of Java's networking classes are contained in package _____.

e) Class _____ binds the application to a port for datagram transmission.

f) An object of class _____ contains an IP address.

g) The two types of sockets we discussed in this chapter are _____ and _____.

h) The acronym URL stands for _____.

i) The acronym URI stands for _____.

j) The key protocol that forms the basis of the World Wide Web is _____.

k) `AppletContext` method _____ receives a `URL` object as an argument and displays in a browser the World Wide Web resource associated with that `URL`.

l) Method `getLocalHost` returns a(n) _____ object containing the local host name of the computer on which the program is executing.

m) The `URL` constructor determines whether its string argument is a valid URL. If so, the `URL` object is initialized with that location. If not, a(n) _____ exception occurs.

24.2 State whether each of the following is *true or false*. If *false*, explain why.

a) UDP is a connection-oriented protocol.

b) With stream sockets a process establishes a connection to another process.

c) A server waits at a port for connections from a client.

d) Datagram packet transmission over a network is reliable—packets are guaranteed to arrive in sequence.

e) For security reasons, many web browsers, such as Mozilla, allow Java applets to do file processing only on the machines on which they execute.

f) Web browsers often restrict an applet so that it can communicate only with the machine from which it was originally downloaded.

Answers to Self-Review Exercises

24.1 a) `IOException`. b) `UnknownHostException`. c) `SocketException`. d) `java.net`. e) `DatagramSocket`. f) `InetAddress`. g) stream sockets, datagram sockets. h) Uniform Resource Locator. i) Uniform Resource Identifier. j) HTTP. k) `showDocument`. l) `InetAddress`. m) `MalformedURLException`.

24.2 a) False; UDP is a connectionless protocol and TCP is a connection-oriented protocol. b) True. c) True. d) False; packets can be lost, arrive out of order or be duplicated. e) False; most browsers prevent applets from doing file processing on the client machine. f) True.

Exercises

24.3 How does a client determine the host name of the client computer?

24.4 How can a client get a line of text from a server?

24.5 Describe how a server sends data to a client.

24.6 How does a server listen for streams-based socket connections at a port?

24.7 As described in the text, what reasons might cause a server to refuse a connection request from a client?

24.8 Multithreaded servers are quite popular today, especially because of the increasing use of multiprocessing servers. Modify the simple server application presented in Section 24.6 to be a multithreaded server. Then use several client applications and have each of them connect to the server simultaneously. Use an `ArrayList` to store the client threads. `ArrayList` provides several methods of use in this exercise. Method `size` determines the number of elements in an `ArrayList`. Method `get` returns the element in the location specified by its argument. Method `add` places its argument at the end of the `ArrayList`. Method `remove` deletes its argument from the `ArrayList`.

24.9 (*Blackjack Game*) Develop a blackjack card game program in which the server application deals cards to each of the client applets. The server should deal additional cards (as per the rules of the game) to each player as requested.

24.10 (*Poker Game*) Develop a poker card game in which the server application deals cards to each of the client applets. The server should deal additional cards (as per the rules of the game) to each player as requested.

24.11 (*Modifications to the Multithreaded Tic-Tac-Toe Program*) The programs in Figs. 24.13 and 24.15 implemented a multithreaded, client/server version of the game of Tic-Tac-Toe. Our goal in developing this game was to demonstrate a multithreaded server that could process multiple connections from clients at the same time. The server in the example is really a mediator between the two client applets—it makes sure that each move is valid and that each client moves in the proper order. The server does not determine who won or lost or whether there was a draw. Also, there is no capability to allow a new game to be played or to terminate an existing game.

The following is a list of suggested modifications to Figs. 24.13 and 24.15:

    a) Modify the `TicTacToeServer` class to test for a win, loss or draw on each move in the game. Send a message to each client applet that indicates the result of the game when the game is over.

    b) Modify the `TicTacToeClient` class to display a button that when clicked allows the client to play another game. The button should be enabled only when a game completes. Note that both class `TicTacToeClient` and class `TicTacToeServer` must be modified to reset the board and all state information. Also, the other `TicTacToeClient` should be notified that a new game is about to begin so that its board and state can be reset.

    c) Modify the `TicTacToeClient` class to provide a button that allows a client to terminate the program at any time. When the user clicks the button, the server and the other client should be notified. The server should then wait for a connection from another client so that a new game can begin.

    d) Modify the `TicTacToeClient` class and the `TicTacToeServer` class so that the winner of a game can choose game piece X or O for the next game. Remember: X always goes first.

    e) If you would like to be ambitious, allow a client to play against the server while the server waits for a connection from another client.

24.12 *(Networked Morse Code)* Perhaps the most famous of all coding schemes is the Morse code, developed by Samuel Morse in 1832 for use with the telegraph system. The Morse code assigns a series of dots and dashes to each letter of the alphabet, each digit, and a few special characters (e.g., period, comma, colon and semicolon). In sound-oriented systems, the dot represents a short sound and the dash represents a long sound. Other representations of dots and dashes are used with light-oriented systems and signal-flag systems. Separation between words is indicated by a space or, simply, the absence of a dot or dash. In a sound-oriented system, a space is indicated by a short time during which no sound is transmitted. The international version of the Morse code appears in Fig. 24.18.

Write a client/server application in which two clients can send Morse-code messages to each other through a multithreaded server application. The client application should allow the user to type English-language phrases in a JTextArea. When the user sends the message, the client application encodes the text into Morse code and sends the coded message through the server to the other client. Use one blank between each Morse-coded letter and three blanks between each Morse-coded word. When messages are received, they should be decoded and displayed as normal characters and as Morse code. The client should have one JTextField for typing and one JTextArea for displaying the other client's messages.

Character	Code	Character	Code
A	.-	T	-
B	-...	U	..-
C	-.-.	V	...-
D	-..	W	.--
E	.	X	-..-
F	..-.	Y	-.--
G	--.	Z	--..
H	....		
I	..	*Digits*	
J	.---	1	.----
K	-.-	2	..---
L	.-..	3	...--
M	--	4	....-
N	-.	5	.....
O	---	6	-....
P	.--.	7	--...
Q	--.-	8	---..

Fig. 24.18 | The letters of the alphabet as expressed in international Morse code. (Part 1 of 2.)

Character	Code	Character	Code
R	.-.	9	----.
S	...	0	-----

Fig. 24.18 | The letters of the alphabet as expressed in international Morse code. (Part 2 of 2.)

25

Accessing Databases with JDBC

OBJECTIVES

In this chapter you will learn:

- Relational database concepts.

- To use Structured Query Language (SQL) to retrieve data from and manipulate data in a database.

- To use the JDBC™ API of package `java.sql` to access databases.

- To use the `RowSet` interface from package `javax.sql` to manipulate databases.

- To use JDBC 4.0's automatic JDBC driver discovery.

- To use `PreparedStatement`s to create precompiled SQL statements with parameters.

- How transaction processing makes database applications more robust.

25.1 Introduction

A database is an organized collection of data. There are many different strategies for organizing data to facilitate easy access and manipulation. A database management system (DBMS) provides mechanisms for storing, organizing, retrieving and modifying data for many users. Database management systems allow for the access and storage of data without concern for the internal representation of data.

Today's most popular database systems are relational databases, where the data is stored without consideration of its physical structure (Section 25.2). A language called SQL—pronounced "sequel," or as its individual letters—is the international standard language used almost universally with relational databases to perform queries (i.e., to request information that satisfies given criteria) and to manipulate data. [*Note:* As you learn about SQL, you will see some authors writing "a SQL statement" (which assumes the pronunciation "sequel") and others writing "an SQL statement" (which assumes that the individual letters are pronounced). In this book we pronounce SQL as "sequel."]

Some popular relational database management systems (RDBMSs) are Microsoft SQL Server, Oracle, Sybase, IBM DB2, Informix, PostgreSQL and MySQL. The JDK now comes with a pure-Java RDBMS called Java DB—Sun's version of Apache Derby. In this chapter, we present examples using MySQL and Java DB.[1]

Java programs communicate with databases and manipulate their data using the JDBC™ API. A JDBC driver enables Java applications to connect to a database in a particular DBMS and allows you to manipulate that database using the JDBC API.

Software Engineering Observation 25.1

Using the JDBC API enables developers to change the underlying DBMS without modifying the Java code that accesses the database.

Most popular database management systems now provide JDBC drivers. There are also many third-party JDBC drivers available. In this chapter, we introduce JDBC and use it to manipulate MySQL and Java DB databases. The techniques demonstrated here can also be used to manipulate other databases that have JDBC drivers. Check your DBMS's documentation to determine whether your DBMS comes with a JDBC driver. If not, third-party vendors provide JDBC drivers for many DBMSs.

For more information on JDBC, visit

```
java.sun.com/javase/technologies/database/index.jsp
```

This site contains JDBC information including the JDBC specification, FAQs, a learning resource center and software downloads to search for JDBC drivers for your DBMS,

```
developers.sun.com/product/jdbc/drivers/
```

This site provides a search engine to help you locate drivers appropriate for your DBMS.

25.2 Relational Databases

A relational database is a logical representation of data that allows the data to be accessed without consideration of its physical structure. A relational database stores data in tables. Figure 25.1 illustrates a sample table that might be used in a personnel system. The table name is Employee, and its primary purpose is to store the attributes of an employee. Tables are composed of rows, and rows are composed of columns in which values are stored. This table consists of six rows. The Number column of each row in this table is the table's primary key—a column (or group of columns) in a table with a unique value that cannot be duplicated in other rows. This guarantees that each row can be identified by its primary key. Good examples of primary key columns are a social security number, an employee ID number and a part number in an inventory system, as values in each of these columns are guaranteed to be unique. The rows in Fig. 25.1 are displayed in order by primary key. In this case, the rows are listed in increasing order, but we could also use decreasing order.

---

1. MySQL is one of the most popular open-source database management systems in use today. As of this writing, it does not yet support JDBC 4, which is part of Java SE 6 (Mustang). However, Sun's Java DB, which is based on the open-source Apache Derby database management system and bundled with Sun's JDK 1.6.0, does support JDBC 4. We use MySQL and JDBC 3 in Sections 25.8–25.10, and we use Java DB and JDBC 4 in Section 25.11.

Number	Name	Department	Salary	Location
23603	Jones	413	1100	New Jersey
24568	Kerwin	413	2000	New Jersey
34589	Larson	642	1800	Los Angeles
35761	Myers	611	1400	Orlando
47132	Neumann	413	9000	New Jersey
78321	Stephens	611	8500	Orlando

Row { (rows 34589 Larson 642 1800 Los Angeles highlighted)

Primary key — Column

Fig. 25.1 | Employee table sample data.

Rows in tables are not guaranteed to be stored in any particular order. As we will demonstrate in an upcoming example, programs can specify ordering criteria when requesting data from a database.

Each column represents a different data attribute. Rows are normally unique (by primary key) within a table, but particular column values may be duplicated between rows. For example, three different rows in the Employee table's Department column contain number 413.

Different users of a database are often interested in different data and different relationships among the data. Most users require only subsets of the rows and columns. To obtain these subsets, we use queries to specify which data to select from a table. You use SQL to define complex queries that select data from a table. For example, you might select data from the Employee table to create a result that shows where each department is located, and present the data sorted in increasing order by department number. This result is shown in Fig. 25.2. SQL queries are discussed in Section 25.4.

Department	Location
413	New Jersey
611	Orlando
642	Los Angeles

Fig. 25.2 | Result of selecting distinct Department and Location data from table Employee.

25.3 Relational Database Overview: The books Database

We now overview relational databases in the context of a sample books database we created for this chapter. Before we discuss SQL, we overview the tables of the books database. We use this database to introduce various database concepts, including how to use SQL to obtain information from the database and to manipulate the data. We provide a script to create the database. You can find the script in the examples directory for this chapter on the CD that accompanies this book. Section 25.5 explains how to use this script.

The database consists of three tables: authors, authorISBN and titles. The authors table (described in Fig. 25.3) consists of three columns that maintain each author's unique ID number, first name and last name. Figure 25.4 contains sample data from the authors table of the books database.

Column	Description
authorID	Author's ID number in the database. In the books database, this integer column is defined as autoincremented—for each row inserted in this table, the authorID value is increased by 1 automatically to ensure that each row has a unique authorID. This column represents the table's primary key.
firstName	Author's first name (a string).
lastName	Author's last name (a string).

Fig. 25.3 | authors table from the books database.

authorID	firstName	lastName
1	Harvey	Deitel
2	Paul	Deitel
3	Andrew	Goldberg
4	David	Choffnes

Fig. 25.4 | Sample data from the authors table.

The authorISBN table (described in Fig. 25.5) consists of two columns that maintain each ISBN and the corresponding author's ID number. This table associates authors with their books. Both columns are foreign keys that represent the relationship between the tables authors and titles—one row in table authors may be associated with many rows in table titles, and vice versa. Figure 25.6 contains sample data from the authorISBN

Column	Description
authorID	The author's ID number, a foreign key to the authors table.
isbn	The ISBN for a book, a foreign key to the titles table.

Fig. 25.5 | authorISBN table from the books database.

authorID	isbn	authorID	isbn
1	0131869000	2	0131450913
2	0131869000	1	0131828274
1	0131483986	2	0131828274
2	0131483986	3	0131450913
1	0131450913	4	0131828274

Fig. 25.6 | Sample data from the authorISBN table of books.

table of the books database. [*Note:* To save space, we have split the contents of this table into two columns, each containing the authorID and isbn columns.] The authorID column is a foreign key—a column in this table that matches the primary key column in another table (i.e., authorID in the authors table). Foreign keys are specified when creating a table. The foreign key helps maintain the Rule of Referential Integrity: Every foreign-key value must appear as another table's primary-key value. This enables the DBMS to determine whether the authorID value for a particular book is valid. Foreign keys also allow related data in multiple tables to be selected from those tables for analytic purposes—this is known as joining the data.

The titles table described in Fig. 25.7 consists of four columns that stand for the ISBN, the title, the edition number and the copyright year. The table is in Fig. 25.8.

There is a one-to-many relationship between a primary key and a corresponding foreign key (e.g., one publisher can publish many books). A foreign key can appear many times in its own table, but can appear only once (as the primary key) in another table. Figure 25.9 is an entity-relationship (ER) diagram for the books database. This diagram shows the database tables and the relationships among them. The first compartment in each box contains the table's name. The names in italic are primary keys. A table's primary key uniquely identifies each row in the table. Every row must have a primary-key value, and that value must be unique in the table. This is known as the Rule of Entity Integrity.

Column	Description
isbn	ISBN of the book (a string). The table's primary key. ISBN is an abbreviation for "International Standard Book Number"—a numbering scheme that publishers use to give every book a unique identification number.
title	Title of the book (a string).
editionNumber	Edition number of the book (an integer).
copyright	Copyright year of the book (a string).

Fig. 25.7 | titles table from the books database.

isbn	title	editionNumber	copyright
0131869000	Visual Basic How to Program	3	2006
0131525239	Visual C# How to Program	2	2006
0132222205	Java How to Program	7	2007
0131857576	C++ How to Program	5	2005
0132404168	C How to Program	5	2007
0131450913	Internet & World Wide Web How to Program	3	2004

Fig. 25.8 | Sample data from the titles table of the books database .

Fig. 25.9 | Table relationships in the books database.

Common Programming Error 25.1

Not providing a value for every column in a primary key breaks the Rule of Entity Integrity and causes the DBMS to report an error.

Common Programming Error 25.2

Providing the same value for the primary key in multiple rows causes the DBMS to report an error.

The lines connecting the tables in Fig. 25.9 represent the relationships between the tables. Consider the line between the authorISBN and authors tables. On the authors end of the line, there is a 1, and on the authorISBN end, there is an infinity symbol (∞), indicating a one-to-many relationship in which every author in the authors table can have an arbitrary number of books in the authorISBN table. Note that the relationship line links the authorID column in the table authors (i.e., its primary key) to the authorID column in table authorISBN (i.e., its foreign key). The authorID column in the authorISBN table is a foreign key.

Common Programming Error 25.3

Providing a foreign-key value that does not appear as a primary-key value in another table breaks the Rule of Referential Integrity and causes the DBMS to report an error.

The line between the titles and authorISBN tables illustrates another one-to-many relationship; a title can be written by any number of authors. In fact, the sole purpose of the authorISBN table is to provide a many-to-many relationship between the authors and titles tables—an author can write any number of books and a book can have any number of authors.

25.4 SQL

We now provide an overview of SQL in the context of our books database. You will be able to use the SQL discussed here in the examples later in the chapter and in examples in Chapters 26–28.

The next several subsections discuss the SQL keywords listed in Fig. 25.10 in the context of SQL queries and statements. Other SQL keywords are beyond this text's scope. To learn other keywords, refer to the SQL reference guide supplied by the vendor of the RDBMS you are using. [*Note:* For more information on SQL, refer to the web resources in Section 25.15 and the recommended readings listed at the end of this chapter.]

SQL keyword	Description
SELECT	Retrieves data from one or more tables.
FROM	Tables involved in the query. Required in every SELECT.
WHERE	Criteria for selection that determine the rows to be retrieved, deleted or updated. Optional in a SQL query or a SQL statement.
GROUP BY	Criteria for grouping rows. Optional in a SELECT query.
ORDER BY	Criteria for ordering rows. Optional in a SELECT query.
INNER JOIN	Merge rows from multiple tables.
INSERT	Insert rows into a specified table.
UPDATE	Update rows in a specified table.
DELETE	Delete rows from a specified table.

Fig. 25.10 | SQL query keywords.

25.4.1 Basic SELECT Query

Let us consider several SQL queries that extract information from database books. A SQL query "selects" rows and columns from one or more tables in a database. Such selections are performed by queries with the SELECT keyword. The basic form of a SELECT query is

SELECT * FROM *tableName*

in which the asterisk (*) indicates that all columns from the *tableName* table should be retrieved. For example, to retrieve all the data in the authors table, use

SELECT * FROM authors

Most programs do not require all the data in a table. To retrieve only specific columns from a table, replace the asterisk (*) with a comma-separated list of the column names. For example, to retrieve only the columns authorID and lastName for all rows in the authors table, use the query

SELECT authorID, lastName FROM authors

This query returns the data listed in Fig. 25.11.

authorID	lastName
1	Deitel
2	Deitel
3	Goldberg
4	Choffnes

Fig. 25.11 | Sample authorID and lastName data from the authors table.

Software Engineering Observation 25.2

For most queries, the asterisk (*) should not be used to specify column names. In general, you process results by knowing in advance the order of the columns in the result—for example, selecting authorID and lastName from table authors ensures that the columns will appear in the result with authorID as the first column and lastName as the second column. Programs typically process result columns by specifying the column number in the result (starting from number 1 for the first column). Selecting columns by name also avoids returning unneeded columns and protects against changes in the actual order of the columns in the table(s).

Common Programming Error 25.4

If you assume that the columns are always returned in the same order from a query that uses the asterisk (*), the program may process the results incorrectly. If the column order in the table(s) changes or if additional columns are added at a later time, the order of the columns in the result would change accordingly.

25.4.2 WHERE Clause

In most cases, it is necessary to locate rows in a database that satisfy certain selection criteria. Only rows that satisfy the selection criteria (formally called predicates) are selected. SQL uses the optional WHERE clause in a query to specify the selection criteria for the query. The basic form of a query with selection criteria is

SELECT *columnName1*, *columnName2*, ... FROM *tableName* WHERE *criteria*

For example, to select the title, editionNumber and copyright columns from table titles for which the copyright date is greater than 2005, use the query

```
SELECT title, editionNumber, copyright
   FROM titles
   WHERE copyright > '2005'
```

Figure 25.12 shows the result of the preceding query. The WHERE clause criteria can contain the operators <, >, <=, >=, =, <> and LIKE. Operator LIKE is used for pattern matching with wildcard characters percent (%) and underscore (_). Pattern matching allows SQL to search for strings that match a given pattern.

A pattern that contains a percent character (%) searches for strings that have zero or more characters at the percent character's position in the pattern. For example, the next query locates the rows of all the authors whose last name starts with the letter D:

```
SELECT authorID, firstName, lastName
   FROM authors
   WHERE lastName LIKE 'D%'
```

This query selects the two rows shown in Fig. 25.13—two of the four authors have a last name starting with the letter D (followed by zero or more characters). The % in the WHERE clause's LIKE pattern indicates that any number of characters can appear after the letter D in the lastName. Note that the pattern string is surrounded by single-quote characters.

Portability Tip 25.1

See the documentation for your database system to determine whether SQL is case sensitive on your system and to determine the syntax for SQL keywords (i.e., should they be all uppercase letters, all lowercase letters or some combination of the two?).

title	editionNumber	copyright
Visual C# How to Program	2	2006
Visual Basic 2005 How to Program	3	2006
Java How to Program	7	2007
C How to Program	5	2007

Fig. 25.12 | Sampling of titles with copyrights after 2005 from table `titles`.

authorID	firstName	lastName
1	Harvey	Deitel
2	Paul	Deitel

Fig. 25.13 | Authors whose last name starts with D from the `authors` table.

Portability Tip 25.2

Read your database system's documentation carefully to determine whether your system supports the LIKE *operator. The SQL we discuss is supported by most RDBMSs, but it is always a good idea to check the features of SQL that are supported by your RDBMS.*

An underscore (_) in the pattern string indicates a single wildcard character at that position in the pattern. For example, the following query locates the rows of all the authors whose last names start with any character (specified by _), followed by the letter o, followed by any number of additional characters (specified by %):

```
SELECT authorID, firstName, lastName
    FROM authors
    WHERE lastName LIKE '_o%'
```

The preceding query produces the row shown in Fig. 25.14, because only one author in our database has a last name that contains the letter o as its second letter.

authorID	firstName	lastName
3	Andrew	Goldberg

Fig. 25.14 | The only author from the `authors` table whose last name contains o as the second letter.

25.4.3 ORDER BY Clause

The rows in the result of a query can be sorted into ascending or descending order by using the optional ORDER BY clause. The basic form of a query with an ORDER BY clause is

SELECT *columnName1*, *columnName2*, ... FROM *tableName* ORDER BY *column* ASC
SELECT *columnName1*, *columnName2*, ... FROM *tableName* ORDER BY *column* DESC

where ASC specifies ascending order (lowest to highest), DESC specifies descending order (highest to lowest) and *column* specifies the column on which the sort is based. For example, to obtain the list of authors in ascending order by last name (Fig. 25.15), use the query

```
SELECT authorID, firstName, lastName
   FROM authors
   ORDER BY lastName ASC
```

Note that the default sorting order is ascending, so ASC is optional. To obtain the same list of authors in descending order by last name (Fig. 25.16), use the query

```
SELECT authorID, firstName, lastName
   FROM authors
   ORDER BY lastName DESC
```

Multiple columns can be used for sorting with an ORDER BY clause of the form

```
ORDER BY column1 sortingOrder, column2 sortingOrder, ...
```

where *sortingOrder* is either ASC or DESC. Note that the *sortingOrder* does not have to be identical for each column. The query

```
SELECT authorID, firstName, lastName
   FROM authors
   ORDER BY lastName, firstName
```

authorID	firstName	lastName
4	David	Choffnes
1	Harvey	Deitel
2	Paul	Deitel
3	Andrew	Goldberg

Fig. 25.15 | Sample data from table authors in ascending order by lastName.

authorID	firstName	lastName
3	Andrew	Goldberg
1	Harvey	Deitel
2	Paul	Deitel
4	David	Choffnes

Fig. 25.16 | Sample data from table authors in descending order by lastName.

sorts all the rows in ascending order by last name, then by first name. If any rows have the same last name value, they are returned sorted by first name (Fig. 25.17).

The WHERE and ORDER BY clauses can be combined in one query, as in

```
SELECT isbn, title, editionNumber, copyright
    FROM titles
    WHERE title LIKE '%How to Program'
    ORDER BY title ASC
```

which returns the isbn, title, editionNumber and copyright of each book in the titles table that has a title ending with "How to Program" and sorts them in ascending order by title. A portion of the query results are shown in Fig. 25.18.

authorID	firstName	lastName
4	David	Choffnes
1	Harvey	Deitel
2	Paul	Deitel
4	Andrew	Goldberg

Fig. 25.17 | Sample data from authors in ascending order by lastName and firstName.

isbn	title	edition -Number	copy- right
0132404168	C How to Program	5	2007
0131857576	C++ How to Program	5	2005
0131450913	Internet and World Wide Web How to Program	3	2004
0132222205	Java How to Program	7	2007
0131869000	Visual Basic 2005 How to Program	3	2006
013152539	Visual C# How to Program	2	2006

Fig. 25.18 | Sampling of books from table titles whose titles end with How to Program in ascending order by title.

25.4.4 Merging Data from Multiple Tables: INNER JOIN

Database designers often split related data into separate tables to ensure that a database does not store data redundantly. For example, the books database has tables authors and titles. We use an authorISBN table to store the relationship data between authors and their corresponding titles. If we did not separate this information into individual tables, we would need to include author information with each entry in the titles table. This would result in the database storing duplicate author information for authors who wrote multiple books. Often, it is necessary to merge data from multiple tables into a single result. Referred to as joining the tables, this is specified by an INNER JOIN operator in the query. An INNER JOIN merges rows from two tables by matching values in columns that are common to the tables. The basic form of an INNER JOIN is:

```
SELECT columnName1, columnName2, …
FROM table1
INNER JOIN table2
    ON table1.columnName = table2.columnName
```

The ON clause of the INNER JOIN specifies the columns from each table that are compared to determine which rows are merged. For example, the following query produces a list of authors accompanied by the ISBNs for books written by each author:

```
SELECT firstName, lastName, isbn
FROM authors
INNER JOIN authorISBN
    ON authors.authorID = authorISBN.authorID
ORDER BY lastName, firstName
```

The query merges the firstName and lastName columns from table authors with the isbn column from table authorISBN, sorting the result in ascending order by lastName and firstName. Note the use of the syntax *tableName.columnName* in the ON clause. This syntax, called a **qualified name**, specifies the columns from each table that should be compared to join the tables. The "*tableName.*" syntax is required if the columns have the same name in both tables. The same syntax can be used in any query to distinguish columns in different tables that have the same name. In some systems, table names qualified with the database name can be used to perform cross-database queries. As always, the query can contain an ORDER BY clause. Figure 25.19 depicts a portion of the results of the preceding query, ordered by lastName and firstName. [*Note:* To save space, we split the result of the query into two columns, each containing the firstName, lastName and isbn columns.]

firstName	lastName	isbn	firstName	lastName	isbn
David	Choffnes	0131828274	Paul	Deitel	0131525239
Harvey	Deitel	0131525239	Paul	Deitel	0132404168
Harvey	Deitel	0132404168	Paul	Deitel	0131869000
Harvey	Deitel	0131869000	Paul	Deitel	0132222205
Harvey	Deitel	0132222205	Paul	Deitel	0131450913
Harvey	Deitel	0131450913	Paul	Deitel	0131525239
Harvey	Deitel	0131525239	Paul	Deitel	0131857576
Harvey	Deitel	0131857576	Paul	Deitel	0131828274
Harvey	Deitel	0131828274	Andrew	Goldberg	0131450913

Fig. 25.19 | Sampling of authors and ISBNs for the books they have written in ascending order by lastName and firstName.

Software Engineering Observation 25.3

If a SQL statement includes columns with the same name from multiple tables, the statement must precede those column names with their table names and a dot (e.g., `authors.authorID`).

Common Programming Error 25.5

Failure to qualify names for columns that have the same name in two or more tables is an error.

25.4.5 INSERT Statement

The `INSERT` statement inserts a row into a table. The basic form of this statement is

```
INSERT INTO tableName ( columnName1, columnName2, ..., columnNameN )
    VALUES ( value1, value2, ..., valueN )
```

where *tableName* is the table in which to insert the row. The *tableName* is followed by a comma-separated list of column names in parentheses (this list is not required if the INSERT operation specifies a value for every column of the table in the correct order). The list of column names is followed by the SQL keyword `VALUES` and a comma-separated list of values in parentheses. The values specified here must match the columns specified after the table name in both order and type (e.g., if *columnName1* is supposed to be the firstName column, then *value1* should be a string in single quotes representing the first name). Always explicitly list the columns when inserting rows. If the table's column order changes or a new column is added, using only `VALUES` may cause an error. The INSERT statement

```
INSERT INTO authors ( firstName, lastName )
    VALUES ( 'Sue', 'Smith' )
```

inserts a row into the `authors` table. The statement indicates that values are provided for the firstName and lastName columns. The corresponding values are `'Sue'` and `'Smith'`. We do not specify an authorID in this example because authorID is an autoincremented column in the authors table. For every row added to this table, MySQL assigns a unique authorID value that is the next value in the autoincremented sequence (i.e., 1, 2, 3 and so on). In this case, Sue Smith would be assigned authorID number 5. Figure 25.20 shows the authors table after the INSERT operation. [*Note:* Not every database management system supports autoincremented columns. Check the documentation for your DBMS for alternatives to autoincremented columns.]

authorID	firstName	lastName
1	Harvey	Deitel
2	Paul	Deitel
3	Andrew	Goldberg
4	David	Choffnes
5	Sue	Smith

Fig. 25.20 | Sample data from table `Authors` after an `INSERT` operation.

Common Programming Error 25.6

It is normally an error to specify a value for an autoincrement column.

Common Programming Error 25.7

SQL uses the single-quote (') character as a delimiter for strings. To specify a string containing a single quote (e.g., O'Malley) in a SQL statement, the string must have two single quotes in the position where the single-quote character appears in the string (e.g., 'O''Malley'). The first of the two single-quote characters acts as an escape character for the second. Not escaping single-quote characters in a string that is part of a SQL statement is a SQL syntax error.

25.4.6 UPDATE Statement

An UPDATE statement modifies data in a table. The basic form of the UPDATE statement is

```
UPDATE tableName
    SET columnName1 = value1, columnName2 = value2, ..., columnNameN = valueN
    WHERE criteria
```

where *tableName* is the table to update. The *tableName* is followed by keyword SET and a comma-separated list of column name/value pairs in the format *columnName = value*. The optional WHERE clause provides criteria that determine which rows to update. Though not required, the WHERE clause is typically used, unless a change is to be made to every row. The UPDATE statement

```
UPDATE authors
    SET lastName = 'Jones'
    WHERE lastName = 'Smith' AND firstName = 'Sue'
```

updates a row in the authors table. The statement indicates that lastName will be assigned the value Jones for the row in which lastName is equal to Smith and firstName is equal to Sue. [*Note:* If there are multiple rows with the first name "Sue" and the last name "Smith," this statement will modify all such rows to have the last name "Jones."] If we know the authorID in advance of the UPDATE operation (possibly because we searched for it previously), the WHERE clause can be simplified as follows:

```
WHERE AuthorID = 5
```

Figure 25.21 shows the authors table after the UPDATE operation has taken place.

authorID	firstName	lastName
1	Harvey	Deitel
2	Paul	Deitel
3	Andrew	Goldberg
4	David	Choffnes
5	Sue	Jones

Fig. 25.21 | Sample data from table authors after an UPDATE operation.

25.4.7 DELETE Statement

A SQL DELETE statement removes rows from a table. The basic form of a DELETE is

```
DELETE FROM tableName WHERE criteria
```

where *tableName* is the table from which to delete. The optional WHERE clause specifies the criteria used to determine which rows to delete. If this clause is omitted, all the table's rows are deleted. The DELETE statement

```
DELETE FROM authors
    WHERE lastName = 'Jones' AND firstName = 'Sue'
```

deletes the row for Sue Jones in the authors table. If we know the authorID in advance of the DELETE operation, the WHERE clause can be simplified as follows:

```
WHERE authorID = 5
```

Figure 25.22 shows the authors table after the DELETE operation has taken place.

authorID	firstName	lastName
1	Harvey	Deitel
2	Paul	Deitel
3	Andrew	Goldberg
4	David	Choffnes

Fig. 25.22 | Sample data from table authors after a DELETE operation.

25.5 Instructions for installing MySQL and MySQL Connector/J

MySQL 5.0 Community Edition is an open-source database management system that executes on many platforms, including Windows, Solaris, Linux, and Macintosh. Complete information about MySQL is available from www.mysql.com. The examples in Section 25.8 and Section 25.9 manipulate MySQL databases.

Installing MySQL
To install MySQL Community Edition:

1. To learn about the installation requirements for your platform, visit the site dev.mysql.com/doc/refman/5.0/en/general-installation-issues.html.

2. Visit dev.mysql.com/downloads/mysql/5.0.html and download the installer for your platform. For the MySQL examples in this chapter, you need only the Windows Essentials package on Microsoft Windows, or the Standard package on most other platforms. [*Note:* For these instructions, we assume you are running Microsoft Windows. Complete installation instructions for other platforms are available at dev.mysql.com/doc/refman/5.0/en/installing.html.]

3. Double click mysql-essential-5.0.27-win32.msi to start the installer. [*Note:* This file name may differ based on the current version of MySQL 5.0.]

4. Choose **Typical** for the **Setup Type** and click **Next >**. Then click **Install**.

When the installation completes, you will be asked to set up an account on MySQL.com. If you do not wish to do this, select **Skip Sign-up** and click **Next >**. After completing the sign-up process or skipping it, you can configure the MySQL Server. Click **Finish** to start the **MySQL Server Instance Configuration Wizard**. To configure the server:

1. Click **Next >** then select **Standard Configuration** and click **Next >** again.

2. You have the option of installing MySQL as a Windows service, which enables the MySQL server to begin executing automatically each time your system starts. For our examples, this is unnecessary, so uncheck **Install as a Windows Service**, then check **Include Bin Directory in Windows PATH**. This will enable you to use the MySQL commands in the Windows Command Prompt.

3. Click **Next >** then click **Execute** to perform the server configuration.

4. Click **Finish** to close the wizard.

Installing MySQL Connector/J

To use MySQL with JDBC, you also need to install **MySQL Connector/J** (the J stands for Java)—a JDBC driver that allows programs to use JDBC to interact with MySQL. MySQL Connector/J can be downloaded from

```
dev.mysql.com/downloads/connector/j/5.0.html
```

The documentation for Connector/J is located at dev.mysql.com/doc/connector/j/en/ connector-j.html. At the time of this writing, the current generally available release of MySQL Connector/J is 5.0.4. To install MySQL Connector/J:

1. Download mysql-connector-java-5.0.4.zip.

2. Open mysql-connector-java-5.0.4.zip with a file extractor, such as WinZip (www.winzip.com). Extract its contents to the C:\ drive. This will create a directory named mysql-connector-java-5.0.4. The documentation for MySQL Connector/J is in connector-j.pdf in the docs subdirectory of mysql-connec-tor-java-5.0.4 or you can view it online at dev.mysql.com/doc/connector/j/ en/connector-j.html.

25.6 Instructions for Setting Up a MySQL User Account

For the MySQL examples to execute correctly, you need to set up a user account that allows users to create, delete and modify a database. After MySQL is installed, follow the steps below to set up a user account (these steps assume MySQL is installed in its default installation directory):

1. Open a Command Prompt and start the database server by executing the command mysqld-nt.exe. Note that this command has no output—it simply starts the MySQL server. Do not close this window—doing so terminates the server.

2. Next, you'll start the MySQL monitor so you can set up a user account, open another Command Prompt and execute the command

```
mysql -h localhost -u root
```

The -h option indicates the host (i.e., computer) on which the MySQL server is running—in this case your local computer (localhost). The -u option indicates the user account that will be used to log in to the server—root is the default user account that is created during installation to allow you to configure the server. Once you've logged in, you'll see a mysql> prompt at which you can type commands to interact with the MySQL server.

3. At the mysql> prompt, type

```
USE mysql;
```

to select the built-in database named mysql, which stores server information, such as user accounts and their privileges for interacting with the server. Note that each command must end with a semicolon. To confirm the command, MySQL issues the message "Database changed."

4. Next, you'll add the jhtp7 user account to the mysql built-in database. The mysql database contains a table called user with columns that represent the user's name, password and various privileges. To create the jhtp7 user account with the password jhtp7, execute the following commands from the mysql> prompt:

```
create user 'jhtp7'@'localhost' identified by 'jhtp7';

grant select, insert, update, delete, create, drop, references,
    execute on *.* to 'jhtp7'@'localhost';
```

This creates the jhtp7 user with the privileges needed to create the databases used in this chapter and manipulate those databases. Next, type

5. Type the command

```
exit;
```

to terminate the MySQL monitor.

25.7 Creating Database books in MySQL

For each MySQL database we discuss in this book, we provide a SQL script in a file with the .sql extension that sets up the database and its tables. You can execute these scripts in the MySQL monitor. In the examples directory for this chapter, you'll find the SQL script books.sql to create the books database. For the following steps, we assume that the MySQL server (mysqld-nt.exe) is still running. To execute the books.sql script:

1. Open a Command Prompt and use the cd command to change directories to the location that contains the books.sql script.

2. Start the MySQL monitor by typing

```
mysql -h localhost -u jhtp7 -p
```

The -p option prompts you for the password for the jhtp7 user account. When prompted, enter the password jhtp7.

3. Execute the script by typing

```
source books.sql;
```

This creates a new directory named books in the server's data directory—located on Windows at `C:\Program Files\MySQL\MySQL Server 5.0\data` by default. This new directory contains the books database.

4. Type the command

```
exit;
```

to terminate the MySQL monitor. You are now ready to proceed to the first JDBC example.

25.8 Manipulating Databases with JDBC

In this section, we present two examples. The first example introduces how to connect to a database and query the database. The second example demonstrates how to display the result of the query in a JTable.

25.8.1 Connecting to and Querying a Database

The example of Fig. 25.23 performs a simple query on the books database that retrieves the entire authors table and displays the data. The program illustrates connecting to the database, querying the database and processing the result. The following discussion presents the key JDBC aspects of the program. [*Note:* Sections 25.5—25.7 demonstrate how to start the MySQL server, configure a user account and create the books database. These steps *must* be performed before executing the program of Fig. 25.23.]

```
 1   // Fig. 25.23: DisplayAuthors.java
 2   // Displaying the contents of the authors table.
 3   import java.sql.Connection;
 4   import java.sql.Statement;
 5   import java.sql.DriverManager;
 6   import java.sql.ResultSet;
 7   import java.sql.ResultSetMetaData;
 8   import java.sql.SQLException;
 9
10   public class DisplayAuthors
11   {
12      // JDBC driver name and database URL
13      static final String DRIVER = "com.mysql.jdbc.Driver";
14      static final String DATABASE_URL = "jdbc:mysql://localhost/books";
15
16      // launch the application
17      public static void main( String args[] )
18      {
19         Connection connection = null; // manages connection
20         Statement statement = null; // query statement
21         ResultSet resultSet = null; // manages results
22
23         // connect to database books and query database
24         try
25         {
```

Fig. 25.23 | Displaying the contents of the authors table. (Part 1 of 3.)

```
26        // load the driver class
27        Class.forName( DRIVER );
28
29        // establish connection to database
30        connection =
31           DriverManager.getConnection( DATABASE_URL, "jhtp7", "jhtp7" );
32
33        // create Statement for querying database
34        statement = connection.createStatement();
35
36        // query database
37        resultSet = statement.executeQuery(
38           "SELECT authorID, firstName, lastName FROM authors" );
39
40        // process query results
41        ResultSetMetaData metaData = resultSet.getMetaData();
42        int numberOfColumns = metaData.getColumnCount();
43        System.out.println( "Authors Table of Books Database:\n" );
44
45        for ( int i = 1; i <= numberOfColumns; i++ )
46           System.out.printf( "%-8s\t", metaData.getColumnName( i ) );
47        System.out.println();
48
49        while ( resultSet.next() )
50        {
51           for ( int i = 1; i <= numberOfColumns; i++ )
52              System.out.printf( "%-8s\t", resultSet.getObject( i ) );
53           System.out.println();
54        } // end while
55     }  // end try
56     catch ( SQLException sqlException )
57     {
58        sqlException.printStackTrace();
59     } // end catch
60     catch ( ClassNotFoundException classNotFound )
61     {
62        classNotFound.printStackTrace();
63     } // end catch
64     finally // ensure resultSet, statement and connection are closed
65     {
66        try
67        {
68           resultSet.close();
69           statement.close();
70           connection.close();
71        } // end try
72        catch ( Exception exception )
73        {
74           exception.printStackTrace();
75        } // end catch
76     } // end finally
77  } // end main
78 } // end class DisplayAuthors
```

Fig. 25.23 | Displaying the contents of the **authors** table. (Part 2 of 3.)

```
Authors Table of Books Database:

authorID        firstName       lastName
1               Harvey          Deitel
2               Paul            Deitel
3               Andrew          Goldberg
4               David           Choffnes
```

Fig. 25.23 | Displaying the contents of the authors table. (Part 3 of 3.)

Lines 3–8 import the JDBC interfaces and classes from package java.sql used in this program. Line 13 declares a string constant for the database driver, and line 14 declares a string constant for the database URL. This identifies the name of the database to connect to, as well as information about the protocol used by the JDBC driver (discussed shortly). Method main (lines 17–77) connects to the books database, queries the database, displays the result of the query and closes the database connection.

The program must load the database driver before connecting to the database. Line 27 uses the static method **forName** of class Class to load the class for the database driver. This line throws a checked exception of type **java.lang.ClassNotFoundException** if the class loader cannot locate the driver class. To avoid this exception, you need to include the mysql-connector-java-5.0.4-bin.jar (in the C:\mysql-connector-java-5.0.4 directory) in your program's classpath when you execute the program, as in:

```
java -classpath
    .;c:\mysql-connector-java-5.0.4\mysql-connector-java-5.0.4-bin.jar
    DisplayAuthors
```

In the classpath of the preceding command, notice the period (.) at the beginning of the classpath information. If this period is missing, the JVM will not look for classes in the current directory and thus will not find the DisplayAuthors class file. You may also copy the mysql-connector-java-5.0.4-bin.jar file to the directory C:\Program Files\Java \jdk1.6.0\jre\lib\ext. After doing so, you can run the application simply using the command java DisplayAuthors.

Software Engineering Observation 25.4

Most major database vendors provide their own JDBC database drivers, and many third-party vendors provide JDBC drivers as well. For more information on JDBC drivers, visit the Sun Microsystems JDBC Web site, servlet.java.sun.com/products/jdbc/drivers.

Lines 30–31 of Fig. 25.23 create a Connection object (package java.sql) referenced by connection. An object that implements interface Connection manages the connection between the Java program and the database. Connection objects enable programs to create SQL statements that manipulate databases. The program initializes connection with the result of a call to static method getConnection of class DriverManager (package java.sql), which attempts to connect to the database specified by its URL. Method get-Connection takes three arguments—a String that specifies the database URL, a String that specifies the username and a String that specifies the password. The username and password are set in Section 25.6. If you used a different username and password, you need to replace the username (second argument) and password (third argument) passed to method getConnection in line 31. The URL locates the database (possibly on a network or in the local file system of the computer). The URL jdbc:mysql://localhost/books specifies the protocol for communication (jdbc), the **subprotocol** for communication (mysql) and the location of the database (//localhost/books, where localhost is the host running the MySQL server and books is the database name). The subprotocol mysql indicates that the program uses a MySQL-specific subprotocol to connect to the MySQL database. If the DriverManager cannot connect to the database, method getConnection throws a SQLException (package java.sql). Figure 25.24 lists the JDBC driver names and database URL formats of several popular RDBMSs.

Software Engineering Observation 25.5

Most database management systems require the user to log in before accessing the database contents. DriverManager method getConnection is overloaded with versions that enable the program to supply the user name and password to gain access.

Line 34 invokes Connection method createStatement to obtain an object that implements interface Statement (package java.sql). The program uses the Statement object to submit SQL to the database.

Lines 37–38 use the Statement object's executeQuery method to submit a query that selects all the author information from table authors. This method returns an object that implements interface ResultSet and contains the query results. The ResultSet methods enable the program to manipulate the query result.

Lines 41–54 process the ResultSet. Line 41 obtains the metadata for the ResultSet as a ResultSetMetaData (package java.sql) object. The **metadata** describes the ResultSet's contents. Programs can use metadata programmatically to obtain information about the ResultSet's column names and types. Line 42 uses ResultSetMetaData method getColumnCount to retrieve the number of columns in the ResultSet. Lines 45–46 display the column names.

RDBMS	Database URL format
MySQL	jdbc:mysql://*hostname*:*portNumber*/*databaseName*
ORACLE	jdbc:oracle:thin:@*hostname*:*portNumber*:*databaseName*
DB2	jdbc:db2:*hostname*:*portNumber*/*databaseName*
Java DB/Apache Derby	jdbc:derby:*dataBaseName* (embedded) jdbc:derby://*hostname*:*portNumber*/*databaseName* (network)
Microsoft SQL Server	jdbc:sqlserver://*hostname*:*portNumber*;databaseName=*dataBaseName*
Sybase	jdbc:sybase:Tds:*hostname*:*portNumber*/*databaseName*

Fig. 25.24 | Popular JDBC database URL formats.

Software Engineering Observation 25.6

Metadata enables programs to process ResultSet contents dynamically when detailed information about the ResultSet is not known in advance.

Lines 49–54 display the data in each ResultSet row. First, the program positions the ResultSet cursor (which points to the row being processed) to the first row in the ResultSet with method next (line 49). Method next returns boolean value true if it is able to position to the next row; otherwise, the method returns false.

Common Programming Error 25.8

Initially, a ResultSet cursor is positioned before the first row. Attempting to access a Result-Set's contents before positioning the ResultSet cursor to the first row with method next causes a SQLException.

If there are rows in the ResultSet, line 52 extracts the contents of one column in the current row. When processing a ResultSet, it is possible to extract each column of the ResultSet as a specific Java type. In fact, ResultSetMetaData method getColumnType returns a constant integer from class Types (package java.sql) indicating the type of a specified column. Programs can use these values in a switch statement to invoke ResultSet methods that return the column values as appropriate Java types. If the type of a column is Types.INTEGER, ResultSet method getInt returns the column value as an int. ResultSet *get* methods typically receive as an argument either a column number (as an int) or a column name (as a String) indicating which column's value to obtain. Visit

```
java.sun.com/javase/6/docs/technotes/guides/jdbc/getstart/
   GettingStartedTOC.fm.html
```

for detailed mappings of SQL data types to Java types and to determine the appropriate ResultSet method to call for each SQL data type.

Performance Tip 25.1

If a query specifies the exact columns to select from the database, the ResultSet contains the columns in the specified order. In this case, using the column number to obtain the column's value is more efficient than using the column name. The column number provides direct access to the specified column. Using the column name requires a search of the column names to locate the appropriate column.

For simplicity, this example treats each value as an Object. The program retrieves each column value with ResultSet method getObject (line 52) and prints the String representation of the Object. Note that, unlike array indices, which start at 0, ResultSet column numbers start at 1. The finally block (lines 64–76) closes the ResultSet (line 68), the Statement (line 69) and the database Connection (line 70). [*Note:* Lines 68–70 will throw NullPointerExceptions if the ResultSet, Statement or Connection objects were not created properly. In production code, you should check the variables that refer to these objects to see if they are null before you call close.]

Common Programming Error 25.9

Specifying column number 0 when obtaining values from a ResultSet causes a SQLException.

Common Programming Error 25.10

Attempting to manipulate a ResultSet after closing the Statement that created the ResultSet causes a SQLException. The program discards the ResultSet when the corresponding Statement is closed.

Software Engineering Observation 25.7

Each Statement object can open only one ResultSet object at a time. When a Statement returns a new ResultSet, the Statement closes the prior ResultSet. To use multiple ResultSets in parallel, separate Statement objects must return the ResultSets.

25.8.2 Querying the books Database

The next example (Fig. 25.25 and Fig. 25.28) allows the user to enter any query into the program. The example displays the result of a query in a JTable, using a TableModel object to provide the ResultSet data to the JTable. A JTable is a swing GUI component that can be bound to a database to display the results of a query. Class ResultSetTableModel (Fig. 25.25) performs the connection to the database via a TableModel and maintains the ResultSet. Class DisplayQueryResults (Fig. 25.28) creates the GUI and specifies an instance of class ResultSetTableModel to provide data for the JTable.

ResultSetTableModel Class

Class ResultSetTableModel (Fig. 25.25) extends class AbstractTableModel (package javax.swing.table), which implements interface TableModel. Class ResultSetTableModel overrides TableModel methods getColumnClass, getColumnCount, getColumnName, getRowCount and getValueAt. The default implementations of TableModel methods isCellEditable and setValueAt (provided by AbstractTableModel) are not overridden, because this example does not support editing the JTable cells. The default implementations of TableModel methods addTableModelListener and removeTableModelListener (provided by AbstractTableModel) are not overridden, because the implementations of these methods in AbstractTableModel properly add and remove event listeners.

```
1   // Fig. 25.25: ResultSetTableModel.java
2   // A TableModel that supplies ResultSet data to a JTable.
3   import java.sql.Connection;
4   import java.sql.Statement;
5   import java.sql.DriverManager;
6   import java.sql.ResultSet;
7   import java.sql.ResultSetMetaData;
8   import java.sql.SQLException;
9   import javax.swing.table.AbstractTableModel;
10
11  // ResultSet rows and columns are counted from 1 and JTable
12  // rows and columns are counted from 0. When processing
13  // ResultSet rows or columns for use in a JTable, it is
14  // necessary to add 1 to the row or column number to manipulate
15  // the appropriate ResultSet column (i.e., JTable column 0 is
16  // ResultSet column 1 and JTable row 0 is ResultSet row 1).
```

Fig. 25.25 | A TableModel that supplies ResultSet data to a JTable. (Part 1 of 5.)

```
17   public class ResultSetTableModel extends AbstractTableModel
18   {
19      private Connection connection;
20      private Statement statement;
21      private ResultSet resultSet;
22      private ResultSetMetaData metaData;
23      private int numberOfRows;
24
25      // keep track of database connection status
26      private boolean connectedToDatabase = false;
27
28      // constructor initializes resultSet and obtains its meta data object;
29      // determines number of rows
30      public ResultSetTableModel( String driver, String url, String username,
31         String password, String query )
32         throws SQLException, ClassNotFoundException
33      {
34         Class.forName( driver );
35         // connect to database
36         connection = DriverManager.getConnection( url, username, password );
37
38         // create Statement to query database
39         statement = connection.createStatement(
40            ResultSet.TYPE_SCROLL_INSENSITIVE,
41            ResultSet.CONCUR_READ_ONLY );
42
43         // update database connection status
44         connectedToDatabase = true;
45
46         // set query and execute it
47         setQuery( query );
48      } // end constructor ResultSetTableModel
49
50      // get class that represents column type
51      public Class getColumnClass( int column ) throws IllegalStateException
52      {
53         // ensure database connection is available
54         if ( !connectedToDatabase )
55            throw new IllegalStateException( "Not Connected to Database" );
56
57         // determine Java class of column
58         try
59         {
60            String className = metaData.getColumnClassName( column + 1 );
61
62            // return Class object that represents className
63            return Class.forName( className );
64         } // end try
65         catch ( Exception exception )
66         {
67            exception.printStackTrace();
68         } // end catch
```

Fig. 25.25 | A TableModel that supplies ResultSet data to a JTable. (Part 2 of 5.)

```
69
70          return Object.class; // if problems occur above, assume type Object
71       } // end method getColumnClass
72
73       // get number of columns in ResultSet
74       public int getColumnCount() throws IllegalStateException
75       {
76          // ensure database connection is available
77          if ( !connectedToDatabase )
78             throw new IllegalStateException( "Not Connected to Database" );
79
80          // determine number of columns
81          try
82          {
83             return metaData.getColumnCount();
84          } // end try
85          catch ( SQLException sqlException )
86          {
87             sqlException.printStackTrace();
88          } // end catch
89
90          return 0; // if problems occur above, return 0 for number of columns
91       } // end method getColumnCount
92
93       // get name of a particular column in ResultSet
94       public String getColumnName( int column ) throws IllegalStateException
95       {
96          // ensure database connection is available
97          if ( !connectedToDatabase )
98             throw new IllegalStateException( "Not Connected to Database" );
99
100         // determine column name
101         try
102         {
103            return metaData.getColumnName( column + 1 );
104         } // end try
105         catch ( SQLException sqlException )
106         {
107            sqlException.printStackTrace();
108         } // end catch
109
110         return ""; // if problems, return empty string for column name
111      } // end method getColumnName
112
113      // return number of rows in ResultSet
114      public int getRowCount() throws IllegalStateException
115      {
116         // ensure database connection is available
117         if ( !connectedToDatabase )
118            throw new IllegalStateException( "Not Connected to Database" );
119
120         return numberOfRows;
121      } // end method getRowCount
```

Fig. 25.25 | A `TableModel` that supplies `ResultSet` data to a `JTable`. (Part 3 of 5.)

```
122
123        // obtain value in particular row and column
124        public Object getValueAt( int row, int column )
125           throws IllegalStateException
126        {
127           // ensure database connection is available
128           if ( !connectedToDatabase )
129              throw new IllegalStateException( "Not Connected to Database" );
130
131           // obtain a value at specified ResultSet row and column
132           try
133           {
134              resultSet.absolute( row + 1 );
135              return resultSet.getObject( column + 1 );
136           } // end try
137           catch ( SQLException sqlException )
138           {
139              sqlException.printStackTrace();
140           } // end catch
141
142           return ""; // if problems, return empty string object
143        } // end method getValueAt
144
145        // set new database query string
146        public void setQuery( String query )
147           throws SQLException, IllegalStateException
148        {
149           // ensure database connection is available
150           if ( !connectedToDatabase )
151              throw new IllegalStateException( "Not Connected to Database" );
152
153           // specify query and execute it
154           resultSet = statement.executeQuery( query );
155
156           // obtain meta data for ResultSet
157           metaData = resultSet.getMetaData();
158
159           // determine number of rows in ResultSet
160           resultSet.last(); // move to last row
161           numberOfRows = resultSet.getRow(); // get row number
162
163           // notify JTable that model has changed
164           fireTableStructureChanged();
165        } // end method setQuery
166
167        // close Statement and Connection
168        public void disconnectFromDatabase()
169        {
170           if ( connectedToDatabase )
171           {
172              // close Statement and Connection
173              try
174              {
```

Fig. 25.25 | A `TableModel` that supplies `ResultSet` data to a `JTable`. (Part 4 of 5.)

```
175                resultSet.close();
176                statement.close();
177                connection.close();
178           } // end try
179           catch ( SQLException sqlException )
180           {
181                sqlException.printStackTrace();
182           } // end catch
183           finally  // update database connection status
184           {
185                connectedToDatabase = false;
186           } // end finally
187        } // end if
188     } // end method disconnectFromDatabase
189  } // end class ResultSetTableModel
```

Fig. 25.25 | A `TableModel` that supplies `ResultSet` data to a `JTable`. (Part 5 of 5.)

The `ResultSetTableModel` constructor (lines 30–48) accepts five `String` arguments—the name of the MySQL driver, the URL of the database, the username, the password and the default query to perform. The constructor throws any exceptions that occur in its body back to the application that created the `ResultSetTableModel` object, so that the application can determine how to handle the exception (e.g., report an error and terminate the application). Line 34 loads the driver. Line 36 establishes a connection to the database. Lines 39–41 invoke `Connection` method `createStatement` to create a `Statement` object. This example uses a version of method `createStatement` that takes two arguments—the result set type and the result set concurrency. The result set type (Fig. 25.26) specifies whether the `ResultSet`'s cursor is able to scroll in both directions or forward only and whether the `ResultSet` is sensitive to changes. `ResultSet`s that are sensitive to changes reflect those changes immediately after they are made with methods of interface `ResultSet`. If a `ResultSet` is insensitive to changes, the query that produced the `ResultSet` must be

ResultSet static type constant	Description
TYPE_FORWARD_ONLY	Specifies that a `ResultSet`'s cursor can move only in the forward direction (i.e., from the first row to the last row in the Result-Set).
TYPE_SCROLL_INSENSITIVE	Specifies that a `ResultSet`'s cursor can scroll in either direction and that the changes made to the `ResultSet` during `ResultSet` processing are not reflected in the `ResultSet` unless the program queries the database again.
TYPE_SCROLL_SENSITIVE	Specifies that a `ResultSet`'s cursor can scroll in either direction and that the changes made to the `ResultSet` during `ResultSet` processing are reflected immediately in the `ResultSet`.

Fig. 25.26 | ResultSet constants for specifying ResultSet type.

executed again to reflect any changes made. The **result set concurrency** (Fig. 25.27) specifies whether the `ResultSet` can be updated with `ResultSet`'s update methods. This example uses a `ResultSet` that is scrollable, insensitive to changes and read only. Line 47 invokes our method `setQuery` (lines 146–165) to perform the default query.

Portability Tip 25.3

Some JDBC drivers do not support scrollable ResultSets. In such cases, the driver typically returns a ResultSet in which the cursor can move only forward. For more information, see your database driver documentation.

Portability Tip 25.4

Some JDBC drivers do not support updatable ResultSets. In such cases, the driver typically returns a read-only ResultSet. For more information, see your database driver documentation.

Common Programming Error 25.11

Attempting to update a ResultSet when the database driver does not support updatable ResultSets causes SQLFeatureNotSupportedExceptions.

Common Programming Error 25.12

Attempting to move the cursor backward through a ResultSet when the database driver does not support backward scrolling causes a SQLException.

Method `getColumnClass` (lines 51–71) returns a `Class` object that represents the superclass of all objects in a particular column. The `JTable` uses this information to configure the default cell renderer and cell editor for that column in the `JTable`. Line 60 uses `ResultSetMetaData` method `getColumnClassName` to obtain the fully qualified class name for the specified column. Line 63 loads the class and returns the corresponding `Class` object. If an exception occurs, the `catch` in lines 65–68 prints a stack trace and line 70 returns `Object.class`—the `Class` instance that represents class `Object`—as the default type. [*Note:* Line 60 uses the argument `column + 1`. Like arrays, `JTable` row and column numbers are counted from 0. However, `ResultSet` row and column numbers are counted from 1. Thus, when processing `ResultSet` rows or columns for use in a `JTable`, it is necessary to add 1 to the row or column number to manipulate the appropriate `ResultSet` row or column.]

ResultSet static concurrency constant	Description
CONCUR_READ_ONLY	Specifies that a `ResultSet` cannot be updated (i.e., changes to the `ResultSet` contents cannot be reflected in the database with `ResultSet`'s update methods).
CONCUR_UPDATABLE	Specifies that a `ResultSet` can be updated (i.e., changes to the `ResultSet` contents can be reflected in the database with `ResultSet`'s update methods).

Fig. 25.27 | `ResultSet` constants for specifying result properties.

Method getColumnCount (lines 74–91) returns the number of columns in the model's underlying ResultSet. Line 83 uses ResultSetMetaData method getColumnCount to obtain the number of columns in the ResultSet. If an exception occurs, the catch in lines 85–88 prints a stack trace and line 93 returns 0 as the default number of columns.

Method getColumnName (lines 94–111) returns the name of the column in the model's underlying ResultSet. Line 103 uses ResultSetMetaData method getColumn-Name to obtain the column name from the ResultSet. If an exception occurs, the catch in lines 105–108 prints a stack trace and line 110 returns the empty string as the default column name.

Method getRowCount (lines 114–121) returns the number of rows in the model's underlying ResultSet. When method setQuery (lines 146–165) performs a query, it stores the number of rows in variable numberOfRows.

Method getValueAt (lines 124–143) returns the Object in a particular row and column of the model's underlying ResultSet. Line 134 uses ResultSet method absolute to position the ResultSet cursor at a specific row. Line 135 uses ResultSet method get-Object to obtain the Object in a specific column of the current row. If an exception occurs, the catch in lines 137–140 prints a stack trace and line 142 returns an empty string as the default value.

Method setQuery (lines 146–165) executes the query it receives as an argument to obtain a new ResultSet (line 154). Line 157 gets the ResultSetMetaData for the new ResultSet. Line 160 uses ResultSet method last to position the ResultSet cursor at the last row in the ResultSet. [*Note:* This can be slow if the table contains many rows.] Line 161 uses ResultSet method getRow to obtain the row number for the current row in the ResultSet. Line 164 invokes method fireTableStructureChanged (inherited from class AbstractTableModel) to notify any JTable using this ResultSetTableModel object as its model that the structure of the model has changed. This causes the JTable to repopulate its rows and columns with the new ResultSet data. Method setQuery throws any exceptions that occur in its body back to the application that invoked setQuery.

Method disconnectFromDatabase (lines 168–188) implements an appropriate termination method for class ResultSetTableModel. A class designer should provide a public method that clients of the class must invoke explicitly to free resources that an object has used. In this case, method disconnectFromDatabase closes the ResultSet, Statement and Connection (lines 175–177), which are considered limited resources. Clients of the ResultSetTableModel class should always invoke this method when the instance of this class is no longer needed. Before releasing resources, line 170 verifies whether the connection is already terminated. If not, the method proceeds. Note that the other methods in class ResultSetTableModel each throw an IllegalStateException if connectedToDatabase is false. Method disconnectFromDatabase sets connectedTo-Database to false (line 185) to ensure that clients do not use an instance of ResultSet-TableModel after that instance has already been terminated. IllegalStateException is an exception from the Java libraries that is appropriate for indicating this error condition.

DisplayQueryResults Class
Class DisplayQueryResults (Fig. 25.28) implements the application's GUI and interacts with the ResultSetTableModel via a JTable object. This application also demonstrates the new JTable sorting and filtering capabilities introduced in Java SE 6.

Lines 27–30 and 33 declare the database driver, URL, username, password and default query that are passed to the `ResultSetTableModel` constructor to make the initial connection to the database and perform the default query. The `DisplayQueryResults` constructor (lines 39–198) creates a `ResultSetTableModel` object and the GUI for the application. Line 69 creates the `JTable` object and passes a `ResultSetTableModel` object to the `JTable` constructor, which then registers the `JTable` as a listener for `TableModelEvents` generated by the `ResultSetTableModel`.

```
 1   // Fig. 25.28: DisplayQueryResults.java
 2   // Display the contents of the Authors table in the books database.
 3   import java.awt.BorderLayout;
 4   import java.awt.event.ActionListener;
 5   import java.awt.event.ActionEvent;
 6   import java.awt.event.WindowAdapter;
 7   import java.awt.event.WindowEvent;
 8   import java.sql.SQLException;
 9   import java.util.regex.PatternSyntaxException;
10   import javax.swing.JFrame;
11   import javax.swing.JTextArea;
12   import javax.swing.JScrollPane;
13   import javax.swing.ScrollPaneConstants;
14   import javax.swing.JTable;
15   import javax.swing.JOptionPane;
16   import javax.swing.JButton;
17   import javax.swing.Box;
18   import javax.swing.JLabel;
19   import javax.swing.JTextField;
20   import javax.swing.RowFilter;
21   import javax.swing.table.TableRowSorter;
22   import javax.swing.table.TableModel;
23
24   public class DisplayQueryResults extends JFrame
25   {
26      // JDBC database URL, username and password
27      static final String DRIVER = "com.mysql.jdbc.Driver";
28      static final String DATABASE_URL = "jdbc:mysql://localhost/books";
29      static final String USERNAME = "jhtp7";
30      static final String PASSWORD = "jhtp7";
31
32      // default query retrieves all data from authors table
33      static final String DEFAULT_QUERY = "SELECT * FROM authors";
34
35      private ResultSetTableModel tableModel;
36      private JTextArea queryArea;
37
38      // create ResultSetTableModel and GUI
39      public DisplayQueryResults()
40      {
41         super( "Displaying Query Results" );
42
```

Fig. 25.28 | Displays contents of the database **books**. (Part 1 of 5.)

```
43          // create ResultSetTableModel and display database table
44          try
45          {
46             // create TableModel for results of query SELECT * FROM authors
47             tableModel = new ResultSetTableModel( DRIVER, DATABASE_URL,
48                USERNAME, PASSWORD, DEFAULT_QUERY );
49
50             // set up JTextArea in which user types queries
51             queryArea = new JTextArea( DEFAULT_QUERY, 3, 100 );
52             queryArea.setWrapStyleWord( true );
53             queryArea.setLineWrap( true );
54
55             JScrollPane scrollPane = new JScrollPane( queryArea,
56                ScrollPaneConstants.VERTICAL_SCROLLBAR_AS_NEEDED,
57                ScrollPaneConstants.HORIZONTAL_SCROLLBAR_NEVER );
58
59             // set up JButton for submitting queries
60             JButton submitButton = new JButton( "Submit Query" );
61
62             // create Box to manage placement of queryArea and
63             // submitButton in GUI
64             Box boxNorth = Box.createHorizontalBox();
65             boxNorth.add( scrollPane );
66             boxNorth.add( submitButton );
67
68             // create JTable delegate for tableModel
69             JTable resultTable = new JTable( tableModel );
70
71             JLabel filterLabel = new JLabel( "Filter:" );
72             final JTextField filterText = new JTextField();
73             JButton filterButton = new JButton( "Apply Filter" );
74             Box boxSouth = boxNorth.createHorizontalBox();
75
76             boxSouth.add( filterLabel );
77             boxSouth.add( filterText );
78             boxSouth.add( filterButton );
79
80             // place GUI components on content pane
81             add( boxNorth, BorderLayout.NORTH );
82             add( new JScrollPane( resultTable ), BorderLayout.CENTER );
83             add( boxSouth, BorderLayout.SOUTH );
84
85             // create event listener for submitButton
86             submitButton.addActionListener(
87
88                new ActionListener()
89                {
90                   // pass query to table model
91                   public void actionPerformed( ActionEvent event )
92                   {
93                      // perform a new query
94                      try
95                      {
```

Fig. 25.28 | Displays contents of the database books. (Part 2 of 5.)

```
 96                      tableModel.setQuery( queryArea.getText() );
 97                   } // end try
 98                   catch ( SQLException sqlException )
 99                   {
100                      JOptionPane.showMessageDialog( null,
101                         sqlException.getMessage(), "Database error",
102                         JOptionPane.ERROR_MESSAGE );
103
104                      // try to recover from invalid user query
105                      // by executing default query
106                      try
107                      {
108                         tableModel.setQuery( DEFAULT_QUERY );
109                         queryArea.setText( DEFAULT_QUERY );
110                      } // end try
111                      catch ( SQLException sqlException2 )
112                      {
113                         JOptionPane.showMessageDialog( null,
114                            sqlException2.getMessage(), "Database error",
115                            JOptionPane.ERROR_MESSAGE );
116
117                         // ensure database connection is closed
118                         tableModel.disconnectFromDatabase();
119
120                         System.exit( 1 ); // terminate application
121                      } // end inner catch
122                   } // end outer catch
123                } // end actionPerformed
124             } // end ActionListener inner class
125          ); // end call to addActionListener
126
127          final TableRowSorter< TableModel > sorter =
128             new TableRowSorter< TableModel >( tableModel );
129          resultTable.setRowSorter( sorter );
130          setSize( 500, 250 ); // set window size
131          setVisible( true ); // display window
132
133          // create listener for filterButton
134          filterButton.addActionListener(
135             new ActionListener()
136             {
137                // pass filter text to listener
138                public void actionPerformed( ActionEvent e )
139                {
140                   String text = filterText.getText();
141
142                   if ( text.length() == 0 )
143                      sorter.setRowFilter( null );
144                   else
145                   {
146                      try
147                      {
```

Fig. 25.28 | Displays contents of the database books. (Part 3 of 5.)

```
148                        sorter.setRowFilter(
149                           RowFilter.regexFilter( text ) );
150                     } // end try
151                     catch ( PatternSyntaxException pse )
152                     {
153                        JOptionPane.showMessageDialog( null,
154                           "Bad regex pattern", "Bad regex pattern",
155                           JOptionPane.ERROR_MESSAGE );
156                     } // end catch
157                  } // end else
158               } // end method actionPerfomed
159            } // end annonymous inner class
160         ); // end call to addActionLister
161      } // end try
162      catch ( ClassNotFoundException classNotFound )
163      {
164         JOptionPane.showMessageDialog( null,
165            "Database Driver not found", "Driver not found",
166            JOptionPane.ERROR_MESSAGE );
167
168         System.exit( 1 ); // terminate application
169      } // end catch
170      catch ( SQLException sqlException )
171      {
172         JOptionPane.showMessageDialog( null, sqlException.getMessage(),
173            "Database error", JOptionPane.ERROR_MESSAGE );
174
175         // ensure database connection is closed
176         tableModel.disconnectFromDatabase();
177
178         System.exit( 1 ); // terminate application
179      } // end catch
180
181      // dispose of window when user quits application (this overrides
182      // the default of HIDE_ON_CLOSE)
183      setDefaultCloseOperation( DISPOSE_ON_CLOSE );
184
185      // ensure database connection is closed when user quits application
186      addWindowListener(
187
188         new WindowAdapter()
189         {
190            // disconnect from database and exit when window has closed
191            public void windowClosed( WindowEvent event )
192            {
193               tableModel.disconnectFromDatabase();
194               System.exit( 0 );
195            } // end method windowClosed
196         } // end WindowAdapter inner class
197      ); // end call to addWindowListener
198   } // end DisplayQueryResults constructor
199
```

Fig. 25.28 | Displays contents of the database books. (Part 4 of 5.)

```
200      // execute application
201      public static void main( String args[] )
202      {
203         new DisplayQueryResults();
204      } // end main
205   } // end class DisplayQueryResults
```

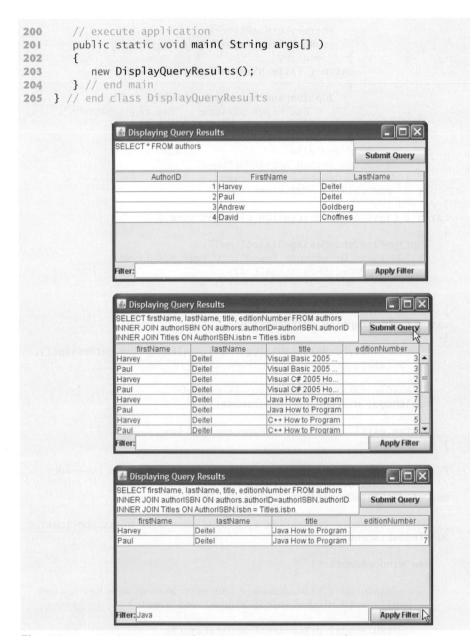

Fig. 25.28 | Displays contents of the database **books**. (Part 5 of 5.)

Lines 86–125 register an event handler for the submitButton that the user clicks to submit a query to the database. When the user clicks the button, method actionPerformed (lines 91–123) invokes method setQuery from the class ResultSetTableModel to execute the new query. If the user's query fails (e.g., because of a syntax error in the user's input), lines 108–109 execute the default query. If the default query also fails, there could be a more serious error, so line 118 ensures that the database connection is closed and line

120 exits the program. The screen captures in Fig. 25.28 show the results of two queries. The first screen capture shows the default query that retrieves all the data from table authors of database books. The second screen capture shows a query that selects each author's first name and last name from the authors table and combines that information with the title and edition number from the titles table. Try entering your own queries in the text area and clicking the **Submit Query** button to execute the query.

As of Java SE 6, JTables now allow users to sort rows by the data in a specific column. Lines 127–128 use the TableRowSorter class (from package javax.swing.table) to create an object that uses our ResultSetTableModel to sort rows in the JTable that displays query results. When the user clicks the title of a particular JTable column, the TableRowSorter interacts with the underlying TableModel to reorder the rows based on the data in that column. Line 129 uses JTable method setRowSorter to specify the TableRowSorter for resultTable.

Another new feature of JTables is the ability to view subsets of the data from the underlying TableModel. This is known as filtering the data. Lines 134–160 register an event handler for the filterButton that the user clicks to filter the data. In method actionPerformed (lines 138–158), line 140 obtains the filter text. If the user did not specify filter text, line 143 uses JTable method setRowFilter to remove any prior filter by setting the filter to null. Otherwise, lines 148–149, use setRowFilter to specify a RowFilter (from package javax.swing) based on the user's input. Class RowFilter provides several methods for creating filters. The static method regexFilter receives a String containing a regular expression pattern as its argument and an optional set of indices that specify which columns to filter. If no indices are specified, then all the columns are searched. In this example, the regular expression pattern is the text the user typed. Once the filter is set, the data displayed in the JTable is updated based on the filtered TableModel.

25.9 RowSet Interface

In the previous examples, you learned how to query a database by explicitly establishing a Connection to the database, preparing a Statement for querying the database and executing the query. In this section, we demonstrate the RowSet interface, which configures the database connection and prepares query statements automatically. The interface RowSet provides several *set* methods that allow you to specify the properties needed to establish a connection (such as the database URL, user name and password of the database) and create a Statement (such as a query). RowSet also provides several *get* methods that return these properties.

There are two types of RowSet objects—connected and disconnected. A connected RowSet object connects to the database once and remains connected until the application terminates. A disconnected RowSet object connects to the database, executes a query to retrieve the data from the database and then closes the connection. A program may change the data in a disconnected RowSet while it is disconnected. Modified data can be updated in the database after a disconnected RowSet reestablishes the connection with the database.

Package javax.sql.rowset contains two subinterfaces of RowSet—JdbcRowSet and CachedRowSet. JdbcRowSet, a connected RowSet, acts as a wrapper around a ResultSet object, and allows you to scroll through and update the rows in the ResultSet. Recall that by default, a ResultSet object is non-scrollable and read only—you must explicitly set the result set type constant to TYPE_SCROLL_INSENSITIVE and set the result set concurrency constant to CONCUR_UPDATABLE to make a ResultSet object scrollable and updatable. A JdbcRowSet object is scrollable and updatable by default. **CachedRowSet**, a disconnected RowSet, caches the data of a ResultSet in memory and disconnects from the database. Like JdbcRowSet, a CachedRowSet object is scrollable and updatable by default. A Cached-RowSet object is also serializable, so it can be passed between Java applications through a network, such as the Internet. However, CachedRowSet has a limitation—the amount of data that can be stored in memory is limited. Package javax.sql.rowset contains three other subinterfaces of RowSet. For details of these interfaces, visit java.sun.com/javase/6/docs/technotes/guides/jdbc/getstart/rowsetImpl.html.

Portability Tip 25.5

A RowSet can provide scrolling capability for drivers that do not support scrollable ResultSets.

Figure 25.29 reimplements the example of Fig. 25.23 using a RowSet. Rather than establish the connection and create a Statement explicitly, Fig. 25.29 uses a JdbcRowSet object to create a Connection and a Statement automatically.

```
1   // Fig. 25.29: JdbcRowSetTest.java
2   // Displaying the contents of the authors table using JdbcRowSet.
3   import java.sql.ResultSetMetaData;
4   import java.sql.SQLException;
5   import javax.sql.rowset.JdbcRowSet;
6   import com.sun.rowset.JdbcRowSetImpl; // Sun's JdbcRowSet implementation
7
8   public class JdbcRowSetTest
9   {
10     // JDBC driver name and database URL
11     static final String DRIVER = "com.mysql.jdbc.Driver";
12     static final String DATABASE_URL = "jdbc:mysql://localhost/books";
13     static final String USERNAME = "jhtp7";
14     static final String PASSWORD = "jhtp7";
15
16     // constructor connects to database, queries database, processes
17     // results and displays results in window
18     public JdbcRowSetTest()
19     {
20       // connect to database books and query database
21       try
22       {
23         Class.forName( DRIVER );
24
25         // specify properties of JdbcRowSet
26         JdbcRowSet rowSet = new JdbcRowSetImpl();
27         rowSet.setUrl( DATABASE_URL ); // set database URL
28         rowSet.setUsername( USERNAME ); // set username
29         rowSet.setPassword( PASSWORD ); // set password
30         rowSet.setCommand( "SELECT * FROM authors" ); // set query
31         rowSet.execute(); // execute query
32
```

Fig. 25.29 | Displaying the authors table using JdbcRowSet. (Part 1 of 2.)

```
33              // process query results
34              ResultSetMetaData metaData = rowSet.getMetaData();
35              int numberOfColumns = metaData.getColumnCount();
36              System.out.println( "Authors Table of Books Database:\n" );
37
38              // display rowset header
39              for ( int i = 1; i <= numberOfColumns; i++ )
40                 System.out.printf( "%-8s\t", metaData.getColumnName( i ) );
41              System.out.println();
42
43              // display each row
44              while ( rowSet.next() )
45              {
46                 for ( int i = 1; i <= numberOfColumns; i++ )
47                    System.out.printf( "%-8s\t", rowSet.getObject( i ) );
48                 System.out.println();
49              } // end while
50
51              // close the underlying ResultSet, Statement and Connection
52              rowSet.close();
53           } // end try
54           catch ( SQLException sqlException )
55           {
56              sqlException.printStackTrace();
57              System.exit( 1 );
58           } // end catch
59           catch ( ClassNotFoundException classNotFound )
60           {
61              classNotFound.printStackTrace();
62              System.exit( 1 );
63           } // end catch
64        } // end DisplayAuthors constructor
65
66        // launch the application
67        public static void main( String args[] )
68        {
69           JdbcRowSetTest application = new JdbcRowSetTest();
70        } // end main
71     } // end class JdbcRowSetTest
```

```
Authors Table of Books Database:

authorID        firstName       lastName
1               Harvey          Deitel
2               Paul            Deitel
3               Andrew          Goldberg
4               David           Choffnes
```

Fig. 25.29 | Displaying the authors table using JdbcRowSet. (Part 2 of 2.)

The package **com.sun.rowset** provides Sun's reference implementations of the interfaces in package javax.sql.rowset. Line 26 uses Sun's reference implementation of the
JdbcRowSet interface—**JdbcRowSetImpl**—to create a JdbcRowSet object. We used class

JdbcRowSetImpl here to demonstrate the capability of the JdbcRowSet interface. Other databases may provide their own RowSet implementations.

Lines 27–29 set the RowSet properties that are used by the DriverManager to establish a connection to the database. Line 27 invokes JdbcRowSet method setUrl to specify the database URL. Line 28 invokes JdbcRowSet method setUsername to specify the username. Line 29 invokes JdbcRowSet method setPassword to specify the password. Line 30 invokes JdbcRowSet method setCommand to specify the SQL query that will be used to populate the RowSet. Line 31 invokes JdbcRowSet method execute to execute the SQL query. Method execute performs four actions—it establishes a Connection, prepares the query Statement, executes the query and stores the ResultSet returned by query. The Connection, Statement and ResultSet are encapsulated in the JdbcRowSet object.

The remaining code is almost identical to Fig. 25.23, except that line 34 obtains a ResultSetMetaData object from the JdbcRowSet, line 44 uses the JdbcRowSet's next method to get the next row of the result and line 47 uses the JdbcRowSet's getObject method to obtain a column's value. Line 52 invokes JdbcRowSet method close, which closes the RowSet's encapsulated ResultSet, Statement and Connection. In a Cached-RowSet, invoking close also releases the memory held by that RowSet. Note that the output of this application is the same as that of Fig. 25.23.

25.10 Java DB/Apache Derby

As of JDK 6, Sun Microsystems now bundles the open-source, pure Java database Java DB (the Sun branded version of Apache Derby) with the JDK. In Section 25.11, we use Java DB to demonstrate a new JDBC 4.0 feature and to demonstrate so called PreparedStatements. Before you can execute the application in the next section, you must set up the AddressBook database in Java DB. In Section 25.11, we use the embedded version of Java DB. There is also a network version that executes similarly to the MySQL DBMS introduced earlier in the chapter. For the purpose of the following steps, we assume you are running Microsoft Windows with Java installed in its default location.

1. Java DB comes with several batch files to configure and run it. Before executing these batch files from a command prompt, you must set the environment variable JAVA_HOME to refer to the JDK's C:\Program Files\Java\jdk1.6.0 installation directory. For information on setting an environment variable's value, see the *Before You Begin* section of this book.

2. Open the batch file setEmbeddedCP.bat (located in C:\Program Files\Java\jdk1.6.0\db\frameworks\embedded\bin) in a text editor such as Notepad. Locate the line

   ```
   rem set DERBY_INSTALL=
   ```

   and change it to

   ```
   set DERBY_INSTALL=C:\Program Files\Java\jdk1.6.0\db
   ```

   Also, comment out the line

   ```
   @FOR %%X in ("%DERBY_HOME%") DO SET DERBY_HOME=%%~sX
   ```

   by preceding it with REM as in

```
REM @FOR %%X in ("%DERBY_HOME%") DO SET DERBY_HOME=%%~sX
```

Save your changes and close this file.

3. Open a Command Prompt and change directories to `C:\Program Files\Java\ jdk1.6.0\db\frameworks\embedded\bin\`. Then, type `setEmbeddedCP.bat` and press *Enter* to set the environment variables required by Java DB.

4. An embedded Java DB database must reside in the same location as the application that manipulates the database. For this reason, change to the directory that contains the code for Figs. 25.30–25.32. This directory contains a SQL script `address.sql` that builds the `AddressBook` database.

5. Execute the command

```
"C:\Program Files\Java\jdk1.6.0\db\frameworks\embedded\bin\ij"
```

to start the command-line tool for interacting with Java DB. The double quotes are necessary because the path contains a space. This will display the `ij>` prompt

6. At the `ij>` prompt type

```
connect 'jdbc:derby:AddressBook;create=true;user=jhtp7;
    password=jhtp7';
```

to create the `AddressBook` database in the current directory. This command also creates the user `jhtp7` with the password `jhtp7` for accessing the database.

7. To create the database table and insert sample data in the database type

```
run 'address.sql';
```

8. To terminate the Java DB command-line tool, type

```
exit;
```

You are now ready to execute the `AddressBook` application in Section 25.12.

25.11 PreparedStatements

Interface `PreparedStatement` enables you to create compiled SQL statements that execute more efficiently than `Statement` objects. `PreparedStatements` also can specify parameters, making them more flexible than `Statements`. Programs can execute the same query repeatedly with different parameter values. For example, in the `books` database, you might want to locate all book titles for an author with a specific last name and first name, and you might want to execute that query for several authors. With a `PreparedStatement`, that query is defined as follows:

```
PreparedStatement authorBooks = connection.prepareStatement(
    "SELECT lastName, firstName, title " +
    "FROM authors INNER JOIN authorISBN " +
       "ON authors.authorID=authorISBN.authorID " +
    "INNER JOIN titles " +
       "ON authorISBN.isbn=titles.isbn " +
    "WHERE lastName = ? AND firstName = ?" );
```

The two question marks (?) in the the preceding SQL statement's last line are placeholders for values that will be passed as part of the query to the database. Before executing a PreparedStatement, the program must specify the parameter values by using the Prepared-Statement interface's *set* methods.

For the preceding query, both parameters are strings that can be set with Prepared-Statement method **setString** as follows:

```
authorBooks.setString( 1, "Deitel" );
authorBooks.setString( 2, "Paul" );
```

Method setString's first argument represents the number of the parameter being set and the second argument is that parameter's value. Parameter numbers are counted from 1, starting with the first question mark (?). When the program executes the preceding Pre-paredStatement with the parameter values shown here, the SQL statement passed to the database is

```
SELECT lastName, firstName, title
FROM authors INNER JOIN authorISBN
    ON authors.authorID=authorISBN.authorID
INNER JOIN titles
    ON authorISBN.isbn=titles.isbn
WHERE lastName = 'Deitel' AND firstName = 'Paul'
```

Method setString automatically escapes String parameter values as necessary. For example, if the last name is O'Brien, the statement

```
authorBooks.setString( 1, "O'Brien" );
```

escapes the ' character in O'Brien by replacing it with two single-quote characters.

Performance Tip 25.2

PreparedStatements are more efficient than Statements when executing SQL statements multiple times and with different parameter values.

Error-Prevention Tip 25.1

Use PreparedStatements with parameters for queries that receive String values as arguments to ensure that the Strings are quoted properly in the SQL statement.

Interface PreparedStatement provides *set* methods for each supported SQL type. It is important to use the *set* method that is appropriate for the parameter's SQL type in the database—SQLExceptions occur when a program attempts to convert a parameter value to an incorrect type. For a complete list of interface PreparedStatement's *set* methods, see java.sun.com/javase/6/docs/api/java/sql/PreparedStatement.html.

Address Book Application that Uses *PreparedStatements*

We now present an address book application that enables you to browse existing entries, add new entries and search for entries with a specific last name. Our AddressBook Java DB database contains an Addresses table with the columns addressID, firstName, lastName, email and phoneNumber. The column addressID is a so-called identity column. This is the SQL standard way to represent an autoincremented column. The SQL script we provide for this database uses the SQL **IDENTITY** keyword to mark the addressID column as an identity column. For more information on using the IDENTITY keyword and creating databases, see the Java DB Developer's Guide at developers.sun.com/prodtech/java-adb/reference/docs/10.2.1.6/devguide/index.html.

Our address book application consists of three classes—Person (Fig. 25.30), Person-Queries (Fig. 25.31) and AddressBookDisplay (Fig. 25.32). Class Person is a simple class that represents one person in the address book. The class contains fields for the address ID, first name, last name, email address and phone number, as well as *set* and *get* methods for manipulating these fields.

```java
1   // Fig. 25.30: Person.java
2   // Person class that represents an entry in an address book.
3   public class Person
4   {
5      private int addressID;
6      private String firstName;
7      private String lastName;
8      private String email;
9      private String phoneNumber;
10
11     // no-argument constructor
12     public Person()
13     {
14     } // end no-argument Person constructor
15
16     // constructor
17     public Person( int id, String first, String last,
18        String emailAddress, String phone )
19     {
20        setAddressID( id );
21        setFirstName( first );
22        setLastName( last );
23        setEmail( emailAddress );
24        setPhoneNumber( phone );
25     } // end five-argument Person constructor
26
27     // sets the addressID
28     public void setAddressID( int id )
29     {
30        addressID = id;
31     } // end method setAddressID
32
33     // returns the addressID
34     public int getAddressID()
35     {
36        return addressID;
37     } // end method getAddressID
38
39     // sets the firstName
40     public void setFirstName( String first )
41     {
42        firstName = first;
43     } // end method setFirstName
44
```

Fig. 25.30 | Person class that represents an entry in an AddressBook. (Part I of 2.)

```
45     // returns the first name
46     public String getFirstName()
47     {
48        return firstName;
49     } // end method getFirstName
50
51     // sets the lastName
52     public void setLastName( String last )
53     {
54        lastName = last;
55     } // end method setLastName
56
57     // returns the first name
58     public String getLastName()
59     {
60        return lastName;
61     } // end method getLastName
62
63     // sets the email address
64     public void setEmail( String emailAddress )
65     {
66        email = emailAddress;
67     } // end method setEmail
68
69     // returns the email address
70     public String getEmail()
71     {
72        return email;
73     } // end method getEmail
74
75     // sets the phone number
76     public void setPhoneNumber( String phone )
77     {
78        phoneNumber = phone;
79     } // end method setPhoneNumber
80
81     // returns the email address
82     public String getPhoneNumber()
83     {
84        return phoneNumber;
85     } // end method getPhoneNumber
86  } // end class Person
```

Fig. 25.30 | Person class that represents an entry in an AddressBook. (Part 2 of 2.)

Class *PersonQueries*

Class PersonQueries (Fig. 25.31) manages the address book application's database connection and creates the PreparedStatements that the application uses to interact with the database. Lines 18–20 declare three PreparedStatement variables. The constructor (lines 23–49) connects to the database at lines 27–28. Notice that we do not use Class.forName to load the database driver for Java DB as we did in the examples that use MySQL earlier in the chapter. JDBC 4.0, part of Java SE 6, supports automatic driver discovery—you are no longer required to load the database driver in advance. At the time of this writing, this feature in the process of being implemented in MySQL.

```java
1   // Fig. 25.31: PersonQueries.java
2   // PreparedStatements used by the Address Book application
3   import java.sql.Connection;
4   import java.sql.DriverManager;
5   import java.sql.PreparedStatement;
6   import java.sql.ResultSet;
7   import java.sql.SQLException;
8   import java.util.List;
9   import java.util.ArrayList;
10
11  public class PersonQueries
12  {
13     private static final String URL = "jdbc:derby:AddressBook";
14     private static final String USERNAME = "jhtp7";
15     private static final String PASSWORD = "jhtp7";
16
17     private Connection connection = null; // manages connection
18     private PreparedStatement selectAllPeople = null;
19     private PreparedStatement selectPeopleByLastName = null;
20     private PreparedStatement insertNewPerson = null;
21
22     // constructor
23     public PersonQueries()
24     {
25        try
26        {
27           connection =
28              DriverManager.getConnection( URL, USERNAME, PASSWORD );
29
30           // create query that selects all entries in the AddressBook
31           selectAllPeople =
32              connection.prepareStatement( "SELECT * FROM Addresses" );
33
34           // create query that selects entries with a specific last name
35           selectPeopleByLastName = connection.prepareStatement(
36              "SELECT * FROM Addresses WHERE LastName = ?" );
37
38           // create insert that adds a new entry into the database
39           insertNewPerson = connection.prepareStatement(
40              "INSERT INTO Addresses " +
41              "( FirstName, LastName, Email, PhoneNumber ) " +
42              "VALUES ( ?, ?, ?, ? )" );
43        } // end try
44        catch ( SQLException sqlException )
45        {
46           sqlException.printStackTrace();
47           System.exit( 1 );
48        } // end catch
49     } // end PersonQueries constructor
```

Fig. 25.31 | An interface that stores all the queries to be used by AddressBook. (Part 1 of 4.)

```
50
51     // select all of the addresses in the database
52     public List< Person > getAllPeople()
53     {
54         List< Person > results = null;
55         ResultSet resultSet = null;
56
57         try
58         {
59             // executeQuery returns ResultSet containing matching entries
60             resultSet = selectAllPeople.executeQuery();
61             results = new ArrayList< Person >();
62
63             while ( resultSet.next() )
64             {
65                 results.add( new Person(
66                     resultSet.getInt( "addressID" ),
67                     resultSet.getString( "firstName" ),
68                     resultSet.getString( "lastName" ),
69                     resultSet.getString( "email" ),
70                     resultSet.getString( "phoneNumber" ) ) );
71             } // end while
72         } // end try
73         catch ( SQLException sqlException )
74         {
75             sqlException.printStackTrace();
76         } // end catch
77         finally
78         {
79             try
80             {
81                 resultSet.close();
82             } // end try
83             catch ( SQLException sqlException )
84             {
85                 sqlException.printStackTrace();
86                 close();
87             } // end catch
88         } // end finally
89
90         return results;
91     } // end method getAllPeople
92
93     // select person by last name
94
95     public List< Person > getPeopleByLastName( String name )
96     {
97         List< Person > results = null;
98         ResultSet resultSet = null;
99
100        try
101        {
102            selectPeopleByLastName.setString( 1, name ); // specify last name
```

Fig. 25.31 | An interface that stores all the queries to be used by AddressBook. (Part 2 of 4.)

```
103
104              // executeQuery returns ResultSet containing matching entries
105              resultSet = selectPeopleByLastName.executeQuery();
106
107              results = new ArrayList< Person >();
108
109              while ( resultSet.next() )
110              {
111                 results.add( new Person(
112                    resultSet.getInt( "addressID" ),
113                    resultSet.getString( "firstName" ),
114                    resultSet.getString( "lastName" ),
115                    resultSet.getString( "email" ),
116                    resultSet.getString( "phoneNumber" ) ) );
117              } // end while
118           } // end try
119           catch ( SQLException sqlException )
120           {
121              sqlException.printStackTrace();
122           } // end catch
123           finally
124           {
125              try
126              {
127                 resultSet.close();
128              } // end try
129              catch ( SQLException sqlException )
130              {
131                 sqlException.printStackTrace();
132                 close();
133              } // end catch
134           } // end finally
135
136           return results;
137        } // end method getPeopleByName
138
139        // add an entry
140        public int addPerson(
141           String fname, String lname, String email, String num )
142        {
143           int result = 0;
144
145           // set parameters, then execute insertNewPerson
146           try
147           {
148              insertNewPerson.setString( 1, fname );
149              insertNewPerson.setString( 2, lname );
150              insertNewPerson.setString( 3, email );
151              insertNewPerson.setString( 4, num );
152
153              // insert the new entry; returns # of rows updated
154              result = insertNewPerson.executeUpdate();
155           } // end try
```

Fig. 25.31 | An interface that stores all the queries to be used by AddressBook. (Part 3 of 4.)

```
156            catch ( SQLException sqlException )
157            {
158               sqlException.printStackTrace();
159               close();
160            } // end catch
161
162            return result;
163         } // end method addPerson
164
165         // close the database connection
166         public void close()
167         {
168            try
169            {
170               connection.close();
171            } // end try
172            catch ( SQLException sqlException )
173            {
174               sqlException.printStackTrace();
175            } // end catch
176         } // end method close
177      } // end interface PersonQueries
```

Fig. 25.31 | An interface that stores all the queries to be used by `AddressBook`. (Part 4 of 4.)

Lines 31–32 invoke `Connection` method **prepareStatement** to create the Prepared-Statement named `selectAllPeople` that selects all the rows in the `Addresses` table. Lines 35–36 create the `PreparedStatement` named `selectPeopleByLastName` with a parameter. This statement selects all the rows in the `Addresses` table that match a particular last name. Notice the ? character that is used to specify the last name parameter. Lines 39–42 create the `PreparedStatement` named `insertNewPerson` with four parameters that represent the first name, last name, email address and phone number for a new entry. Again, notice the ? characters used to represent these parameters.

Method `getAllPeople` (lines 52–91) executes `PreparedStatement` `selectAllPeople` (line 60) by calling method **executeQuery**, which returns a `ResultSet` containing the rows that match the query (in this case, all the rows in the `Addresses` table). Lines 61–71 place the query results in an `ArrayList` of `Person` objects, which is returned to the caller at line 90. Method `getPeopleByLastName` (lines 95–137) uses `PreparedStatement` method **setString** to set the parameter to `selectPeopleByLastName`. Then, line 105 executes the query and lines 107–117 place the query results in an `ArrayList` of `Person` objects. Line 136 returns the `ArrayList` to the caller.

Method `addPerson` (lines 140–163) uses `PreparedStatement` method `setString` (lines 148–151) to set the parameters for the `insertNewPerson` `PreparedStatement`. Line 154 uses `PreparedStatement` method **executeUpdate** to insert the new record. This method returns an integer indicating the number of rows that were updated (or inserted) in the database. Method `close` (lines 166–176) simply closes the database connection.

Class *AddressBookDisplay*
The `AddressBookDisplay` (Fig. 25.32) application uses an object of class `PersonQueries` to interact with the database. Line 59 creates the `PersonQueries` object used throughout

class AddressBookDisplay. When the user presses the **Browse All Entries** JButton, the browseButtonActionPerformed handler (lines 309–335) is called. Line 313 calls the method getAllPeople on the PersonQueries object to obtain all the entries in the database. The user can then scroll through the entries using the **Previous** and **Next** JButtons. When the user presses the **Find** JButton, the queryButtonActionPerformed handler (lines 265–287) is called. Lines 267–268 call method getPeopleByLastName on the PersonQueries object to obtain the entries in the database that match the specified last name. If there are several such entries, the user can then scroll through them using the **Previous** and **Next** JButtons.

To add a new entry into the AddressBook database, the user can enter the first name, last name, email and phone number (the AddressID will autoincrement) in the JTextFields and press the **Insert New Entry** JButton. When the user presses **Insert New Entry**, the insertButtonActionPerformed handler (lines 338–352) is called. Lines 340–342 call the method addPerson on the PersonQueries object to add a new entry to the database.

The user can then view different entries by pressing the **Previous** JButton or **Next** JButton, which results in calls to methods previousButtonActionPerformed (lines 241–250) or nextButtonActionPerformed (lines 253–262), respectively. Alternatively, the user can enter a number in the indexTextField and press *Enter* to view a particular entry.

```
1   // Fig. 25.32: AddressBookDisplay.java
2   // A simple address book
3   import java.awt.event.ActionEvent;
4   import java.awt.event.ActionListener;
5   import java.awt.event.WindowAdapter;
6   import java.awt.event.WindowEvent;
7   import java.awt.FlowLayout;
8   import java.awt.GridLayout;
9   import java.util.List;
10  import javax.swing.JButton;
11  import javax.swing.Box;
12  import javax.swing.JFrame;
13  import javax.swing.JLabel;
14  import javax.swing.JPanel;
15  import javax.swing.JTextField;
16  import javax.swing.WindowConstants;
17  import javax.swing.BoxLayout;
18  import javax.swing.BorderFactory;
19  import javax.swing.JOptionPane;
20
21  public class AddressBookDisplay extends JFrame
22  {
23     private Person currentEntry;
24     private PersonQueries personQueries;
25     private List< Person > results;
26     private int numberOfEntries = 0;
27     private int currentEntryIndex;
28
29     private JButton browseButton;
30     private JLabel emailLabel;
31     private JTextField emailTextField;
```

Fig. 25.32 | A simple address book. (Part 1 of 8.)

```
32        private JLabel firstNameLabel;
33        private JTextField firstNameTextField;
34        private JLabel idLabel;
35        private JTextField idTextField;
36        private JTextField indexTextField;
37        private JLabel lastNameLabel;
38        private JTextField lastNameTextField;
39        private JTextField maxTextField;
40        private JButton nextButton;
41        private JLabel ofLabel;
42        private JLabel phoneLabel;
43        private JTextField phoneTextField;
44        private JButton previousButton;
45        private JButton queryButton;
46        private JLabel queryLabel;
47        private JPanel queryPanel;
48        private JPanel navigatePanel;
49        private JPanel displayPanel;
50        private JTextField queryTextField;
51        private JButton insertButton;
52
53        // no-argument constructor
54        public AddressBookDisplay()
55        {
56           super( "Address Book" );
57
58           // establish database connection and set up PreparedStatements
59           personQueries = new PersonQueries();
60
61           // create GUI
62           navigatePanel = new JPanel();
63           previousButton = new JButton();
64           indexTextField = new JTextField( 2 );
65           ofLabel = new JLabel();
66           maxTextField = new JTextField( 2 );
67           nextButton = new JButton();
68           displayPanel = new JPanel();
69           idLabel = new JLabel();
70           idTextField = new JTextField( 10 );
71           firstNameLabel = new JLabel();
72           firstNameTextField = new JTextField( 10 );
73           lastNameLabel = new JLabel();
74           lastNameTextField = new JTextField( 10 );
75           emailLabel = new JLabel();
76           emailTextField = new JTextField( 10 );
77           phoneLabel = new JLabel();
78           phoneTextField = new JTextField( 10 );
79           queryPanel = new JPanel();
80           queryLabel = new JLabel();
81           queryTextField = new JTextField( 10 );
82           queryButton = new JButton();
83           browseButton = new JButton();
84           insertButton = new JButton();
```

Fig. 25.32 | A simple address book. (Part 2 of 8.)

```
85
86          setLayout( new FlowLayout( FlowLayout.CENTER, 10, 10 ) );
87          setSize( 400, 300 );
88          setResizable( false );
89
90          navigatePanel.setLayout(
91             new BoxLayout( navigatePanel, BoxLayout.X_AXIS ) );
92
93          previousButton.setText( "Previous" );
94          previousButton.setEnabled( false );
95          previousButton.addActionListener(
96             new ActionListener()
97             {
98                public void actionPerformed( ActionEvent evt )
99                {
100                   previousButtonActionPerformed( evt );
101                } // end method actionPerformed
102             } // end anonymous inner class
103          ); // end call to addActionListener
104
105          navigatePanel.add( previousButton );
106          navigatePanel.add( Box.createHorizontalStrut( 10 ) );
107
108          indexTextField.setHorizontalAlignment(
109             JTextField.CENTER );
110          indexTextField.addActionListener(
111             new ActionListener()
112             {
113                public void actionPerformed( ActionEvent evt )
114                {
115                   indexTextFieldActionPerformed( evt );
116                } // end method actionPerformed
117             } // end anonymous inner class
118          ); // end call to addActionListener
119
120          navigatePanel.add( indexTextField );
121          navigatePanel.add( Box.createHorizontalStrut( 10 ) );
122
123          ofLabel.setText( "of" );
124          navigatePanel.add( ofLabel );
125          navigatePanel.add( Box.createHorizontalStrut( 10 ) );
126
127          maxTextField.setHorizontalAlignment(
128             JTextField.CENTER );
129          maxTextField.setEditable( false );
130          navigatePanel.add( maxTextField );
131          navigatePanel.add( Box.createHorizontalStrut( 10 ) );
132
133          nextButton.setText( "Next" );
134          nextButton.setEnabled( false );
135          nextButton.addActionListener(
136             new ActionListener()
137             {
```

Fig. 25.32 | A simple address book. (Part 3 of 8.)

```
138              public void actionPerformed( ActionEvent evt )
139              {
140                 nextButtonActionPerformed( evt );
141              } // end method actionPerformed
142           } // end anonymous inner class
143        ); // end call to addActionListener
144
145     navigatePanel.add( nextButton );
146     add( navigatePanel );
147
148     displayPanel.setLayout( new GridLayout( 5, 2, 4, 4 ) );
149
150     idLabel.setText( "Address ID:" );
151     displayPanel.add( idLabel );
152
153     idTextField.setEditable( false );
154     displayPanel.add( idTextField );
155
156     firstNameLabel.setText( "First Name:" );
157     displayPanel.add( firstNameLabel );
158     displayPanel.add( firstNameTextField );
159
160     lastNameLabel.setText( "Last Name:" );
161     displayPanel.add( lastNameLabel );
162     displayPanel.add( lastNameTextField );
163
164     emailLabel.setText( "Email:" );
165     displayPanel.add( emailLabel );
166     displayPanel.add( emailTextField );
167
168     phoneLabel.setText( "Phone Number:" );
169     displayPanel.add( phoneLabel );
170     displayPanel.add( phoneTextField );
171     add( displayPanel );
172
173     queryPanel.setLayout(
174        new BoxLayout( queryPanel, BoxLayout.X_AXIS) );
175
176     queryPanel.setBorder( BorderFactory.createTitledBorder(
177        "Find an entry by last name" ) );
178     queryLabel.setText( "Last Name:" );
179     queryPanel.add( Box.createHorizontalStrut( 5 ) );
180     queryPanel.add( queryLabel );
181     queryPanel.add( Box.createHorizontalStrut( 10 ) );
182     queryPanel.add( queryTextField );
183     queryPanel.add( Box.createHorizontalStrut( 10 ) );
184
185     queryButton.setText( "Find" );
186     queryButton.addActionListener(
187        new ActionListener()
188        {
189           public void actionPerformed( ActionEvent evt )
190           {
```

Fig. 25.32 | A simple address book. (Part 4 of 8.)

```
191                    queryButtonActionPerformed( evt );
192                 } // end method actionPerformed
193              } // end anonymous inner class
194          ); // end call to addActionListener
195
196          queryPanel.add( queryButton );
197          queryPanel.add( Box.createHorizontalStrut( 5 ) );
198          add( queryPanel );
199
200          browseButton.setText( "Browse All Entries" );
201          browseButton.addActionListener(
202             new ActionListener()
203             {
204                public void actionPerformed( ActionEvent evt )
205                {
206                   browseButtonActionPerformed( evt );
207                } // end method actionPerformed
208             } // end anonymous inner class
209          ); // end call to addActionListener
210
211          add( browseButton );
212
213          insertButton.setText( "Insert New Entry" );
214          insertButton.addActionListener(
215             new ActionListener()
216             {
217                public void actionPerformed( ActionEvent evt )
218                {
219                   insertButtonActionPerformed( evt );
220                } // end method actionPerformed
221             } // end anonymous inner class
222          ); // end call to addActionListener
223
224          add( insertButton );
225
226          addWindowListener(
227             new WindowAdapter()
228             {
229                public void windowClosing( WindowEvent evt )
230                {
231                   personQueries.close(); // close database connection
232                   System.exit( 0 );
233                } // end method windowClosing
234             } // end anonymous inner class
235          ); // end call to addWindowListener
236
237          setVisible( true );
238       } // end no-argument constructor
239
240       // handles call when previousButton is clicked
241       private void previousButtonActionPerformed( ActionEvent evt )
242       {
243          currentEntryIndex--;
```

Fig. 25.32 | A simple address book. (Part 5 of 8.)

```
244
245       if ( currentEntryIndex < 0 )
246          currentEntryIndex = numberOfEntries - 1;
247
248       indexTextField.setText( "" + ( currentEntryIndex + 1 ) );
249       indexTextFieldActionPerformed( evt );
250    } // end method previousButtonActionPerformed
251
252    // handles call when nextButton is clicked
253    private void nextButtonActionPerformed( ActionEvent evt )
254    {
255       currentEntryIndex++;
256
257       if ( currentEntryIndex >= numberOfEntries )
258          currentEntryIndex = 0;
259
260       indexTextField.setText( "" + ( currentEntryIndex + 1 ) );
261       indexTextFieldActionPerformed( evt );
262    } // end method nextButtonActionPerformed
263
264    // handles call when queryButton is clicked
265    private void queryButtonActionPerformed( ActionEvent evt )
266    {
267       results =
268          personQueries.getPeopleByLastName( queryTextField.getText() );
269       numberOfEntries = results.size();
270
271       if ( numberOfEntries != 0 )
272       {
273          currentEntryIndex = 0;
274          currentEntry = results.get( currentEntryIndex );
275          idTextField.setText( "" + currentEntry.getAddressID() );
276          firstNameTextField.setText( currentEntry.getFirstName() );
277          lastNameTextField.setText( currentEntry.getLastName() );
278          emailTextField.setText( currentEntry.getEmail() );
279          phoneTextField.setText( currentEntry.getPhoneNumber() );
280          maxTextField.setText( "" + numberOfEntries );
281          indexTextField.setText( "" + ( currentEntryIndex + 1 ) );
282          nextButton.setEnabled( true );
283          previousButton.setEnabled( true );
284       } // end if
285       else
286          browseButtonActionPerformed( evt );
287    } // end method queryButtonActionPerformed
288
289    // handles call when a new value is entered in indextTextField
290    private void indexTextFieldActionPerformed( ActionEvent evt )
291    {
292       currentEntryIndex =
293          ( Integer.parseInt( indexTextField.getText() ) - 1 );
294
295       if ( numberOfEntries != 0 && currentEntryIndex < numberOfEntries )
296       {
```

Fig. 25.32 | A simple address book. (Part 6 of 8.)

```
297             currentEntry = results.get( currentEntryIndex );
298             idTextField.setText("" + currentEntry.getAddressID() );
299             firstNameTextField.setText( currentEntry.getFirstName() );
300             lastNameTextField.setText( currentEntry.getLastName() );
301             emailTextField.setText( currentEntry.getEmail() );
302             phoneTextField.setText( currentEntry.getPhoneNumber() );
303             maxTextField.setText( "" + numberOfEntries );
304             indexTextField.setText( "" + ( currentEntryIndex + 1 ) );
305          } // end if
306       } // end method indexTextFieldActionPerformed
307
308       // handles call when browseButton is clicked
309       private void browseButtonActionPerformed( ActionEvent evt )
310       {
311          try
312          {
313             results = personQueries.getAllPeople();
314             numberOfEntries = results.size();
315
316             if ( numberOfEntries != 0 )
317             {
318                currentEntryIndex = 0;
319                currentEntry = results.get( currentEntryIndex );
320                idTextField.setText( "" + currentEntry.getAddressID() );
321                firstNameTextField.setText( currentEntry.getFirstName() );
322                lastNameTextField.setText( currentEntry.getLastName() );
323                emailTextField.setText( currentEntry.getEmail() );
324                phoneTextField.setText( currentEntry.getPhoneNumber() );
325                maxTextField.setText( "" + numberOfEntries );
326                indexTextField.setText( "" + ( currentEntryIndex + 1 ) );
327                nextButton.setEnabled( true );
328                previousButton.setEnabled( true );
329             } // end if
330          } // end try
331          catch ( Exception e )
332          {
333             e.printStackTrace();
334          } // end catch
335       } // end method browseButtonActionPerformed
336
337       // handles call when insertButton is clicked
338       private void insertButtonActionPerformed( ActionEvent evt )
339       {
340          int result = personQueries.addPerson( firstNameTextField.getText(),
341             lastNameTextField.getText(), emailTextField.getText(),
342             phoneTextField.getText() );
343
344          if ( result == 1 )
345             JOptionPane.showMessageDialog( this, "Person added!",
346                "Person added", JOptionPane.PLAIN_MESSAGE );
347          else
348             JOptionPane.showMessageDialog( this, "Person not added!",
349                "Error", JOptionPane.PLAIN_MESSAGE );
```

Fig. 25.32 | A simple address book. (Part 7 of 8.)

```
350            browseButtonActionPerformed( evt );
351        } // end method insertButtonActionPerformed
352
353
354        // main method
355        public static void main( String args[] )
356        {
357            new AddressBookDisplay();
358        } // end method main
359    } // end class AddressBookDisplay
```

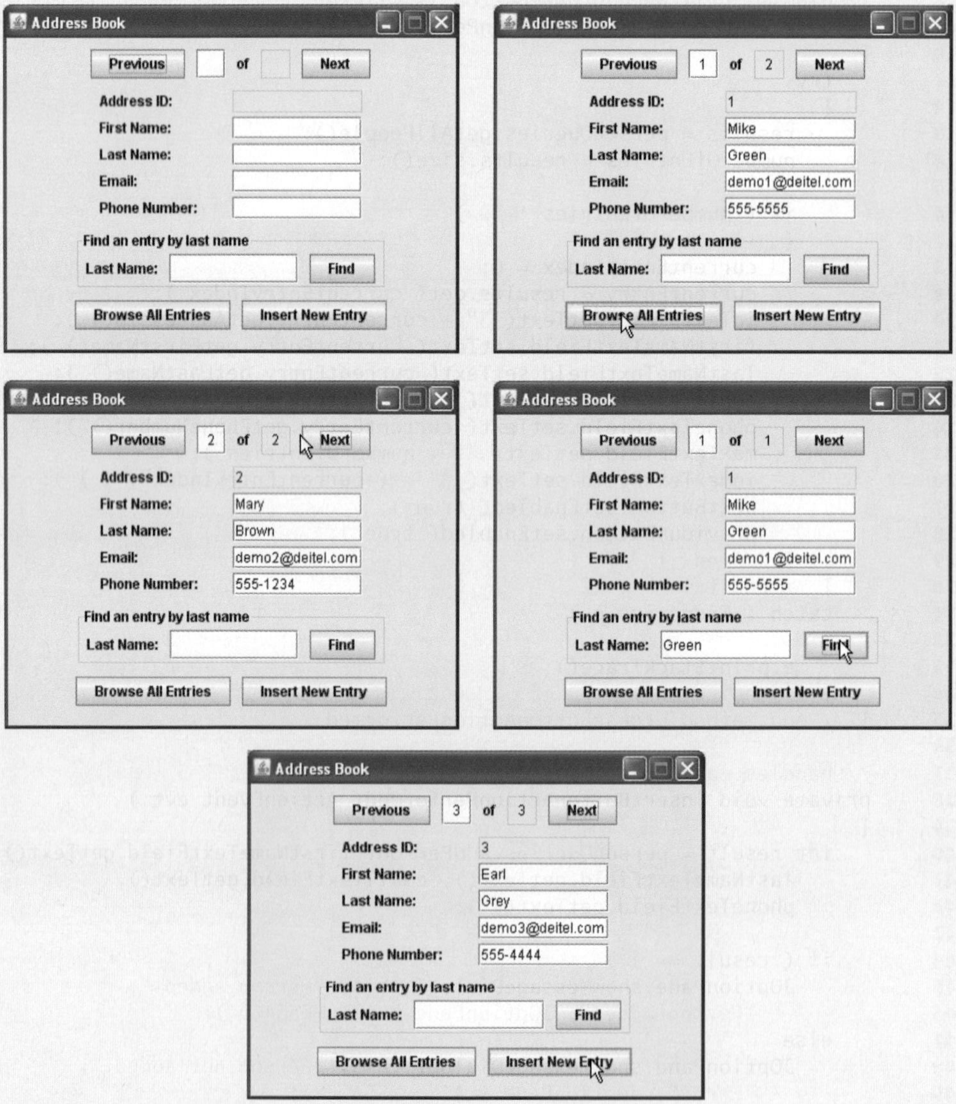

Fig. 25.32 | A simple address book. (Part 8 of 8.)

25.12 **Stored Procedures**

Many database management systems can store individual SQL statements or sets of SQL statements in a database, so that programs accessing that database can invoke them. Such named collections of SQL statements are called stored procedures. JDBC enables programs to invoke stored procedures using objects that implement the interface `CallableStatement`. `CallableStatements` can receive arguments specified with the methods inherited from interface `PreparedStatement`. In addition, `CallableStatements` can specify output parameters in which a stored procedure can place return values. Interface `CallableStatement` includes methods to specify which parameters in a stored procedure are output parameters. The interface also includes methods to obtain the values of output parameters returned from a stored procedure.

Portability Tip 25.6

Although the syntax for creating stored procedures differs across database management systems, the interface `CallableStatement` provides a uniform interface for specifying input and output parameters for stored procedures and for invoking stored procedures.

Portability Tip 25.7

According to the Java API documentation for interface `CallableStatement`, for maximum portability between database systems, programs should process the update counts or `ResultSets` returned from a `CallableStatement` before obtaining the values of any output parameters.

25.13 **Transaction Processing**

Many database applications require guarantees that a series of database insertions, updates and deletions executes properly before the applications continue processing the next database operation. For example, when you transfer money electronically between bank accounts, several factors determine if the transaction is successful. You begin by specifying the source account and the amount you wish to transfer from that account to a destination account. Next, you specify the destination account. The bank checks the source account to determine if there are sufficient funds in the account to complete the transfer. If so, the bank withdraws the specified amount from the source account and, if all goes well, deposits the money into the destination account to complete the transfer. What happens if the transfer fails after the bank withdraws the money from the source account? In a proper banking system, the bank redeposits the money in the source account. How would you feel if the money was subtracted from your source account and the bank *did not* deposit the money in the destination account?

Transaction processing enables a program that interacts with a database to treat a database operation (or set of operations) as a single operation. Such an operation also is known as an atomic operation or a transaction. At the end of a transaction, a decision can be made either to commit the transaction or roll back the transaction. Committing the transaction finalizes the database operation(s); all insertions, updates and deletions performed as part of the transaction cannot be reversed without performing a new database operation. Rolling back the transaction leaves the database in its state prior to the database operation. This is useful when a portion of a transaction fails to complete properly. In our bank-account-transfer discussion, the transaction would be rolled back if the deposit could not be made into the destination account.

Java provides transaction processing via methods of interface `Connection`. Method `setAutoCommit` specifies whether each SQL statement commits after it completes (a `true` argument) or if several SQL statements should be grouped as a transaction (a `false` argument). If the argument to `setAutoCommit` is `false`, the program must follow the last SQL statement in the transaction with a call to `Connection` method `commit` (to commit the changes to the database) or `Connection` method `rollback` (to return the database to its state prior to the transaction). Interface `Connection` also provides method `getAutoCommit` to determine the autocommit state for the `Connection`.

25.14 Wrap-Up

In this chapter, you learned basic database concepts, how to interact with data in a database using SQL and how to use JDBC to allow Java applications to manipulate MySQL and Java DB databases. You learned about the SQL commands `SELECT`, `INSERT`, `UPDATE` and `DELETE`, as well as clauses such as `WHERE`, `ORDER BY` and `INNER JOIN`. You learned the explicit steps for obtaining a `Connection` to the database, creating a `Statement` to interact with the database's data, executing the statement and processing the results. Then you saw how to use a `RowSet` to simplify the process of connecting to a database and creating statements. You used `PreparedStatements` to create precompiled SQL statements. You also learned how to create and configure databases in both MySQL and Java DB. We also provided overviews of `CallableStatements` and transaction processing. In the next chapter, you will learn about web application development with JavaServer Faces. Web-based applications create content that is typically displayed in web browser clients. As you'll see in Chapter 27, web applications can also use the JDBC API to access databases to create more dynamic web content.

25.15 Web Resources and Recommended Readings

java.sun.com/products/jdbc
Sun Microsystems, Inc.'s JDBC home page.

java.sun.com/docs/books/tutorial/jdbc/index.html
The Java Tutorial's JDBC track.

industry.java.sun.com/products/jdbc/drivers
Sun Microsystems search engine for locating JDBC drivers.

www.sql.org
This SQL portal provides links to many resources, including SQL syntax, tips, tutorials, books, magazines, discussion groups, companies with SQL services, SQL consultants and free software.

www.datadirect.com/developer/jdbc/topics/perfoptjdbc/index.ssp
White paper that discusses designing a good JDBC application.

java.sun.com/javase/6/docs/technotes/guides/jdbc/index.html
Sun Microsystems JDBC API documentation.

java.sun.com/products/jdbc/faq.html
Sun Microsystems FAQs on JDBC.

www.jguru.com/faq/JDBC
The JGuru JDBC FAQs.

www.mysql.com
This site is the MySQL database home page. You can download the latest versions of MySQL and MySQL Connector/J and access their online documentation.

`www.mysql.com/products/enterprise/server.html`
Introduction to the MySQL database server and links to its documentation and download sites.
`dev.mysql.com/doc/mysql/en/index.html`
MySQL reference manual.
`dev.mysql.com/doc/connector/j/en/index.html`
MySQL Connector/J documentation, including the installation instructions and examples.
`developers.sun.com/prodtech/javadb/reference/docs/10.2.1.6/devguide/index.html`
The *Java DB Developer's Guide.*
`java.sun.com/javase/6/docs/technotes/guides/jdbc/getstart/rowsetImpl.html`
Overviews the RowSet interface and its subinterfaces. This site also discusses the reference implementations of these interfaces from Sun and their usage.
`developer.java.sun.com/developer/Books/JDBCTutorial/chapter5.html`
Chapter 5 (RowSet Tutorial) of the book *The JDBC 2.0 API Tutorial and Reference, Second Edition.*

Recommended Readings

Ashmore, D. C. "Best Practices for JDBC Programming." *Java Developers Journal*, 5: no. 4 (2000), 42–54.

Blaha, M. R., W. J. Premerlani and J. E. Rumbaugh. "Relational Database Design Using an Object-Oriented Methodology." *Communications of the ACM*, 31: no. 4 (1988): 414–427.

Brunner, R. J. "The Evolution of Connecting." *Java Developers Journal*, 5: no. 10 (2000): 24–26.

Brunner, R. J. "After the Connection." *Java Developers Journal*, 5: no. 11 (2000): 42–46.

Callahan, T. "So You Want a Stand-Alone Database for Java." *Java Developers Journal*, 3: no. 12 (1998): 28–36.

Codd, E. F. "A Relational Model of Data for Large Shared Data Banks." *Communications of the ACM*, June 1970.

Codd, E. F. "Further Normalization of the Data Base Relational Model." *Courant Computer Science Symposia*, Vol. 6, *Data Base Systems*. Upper Saddle River, NJ: Prentice Hall, 1972.

Codd, E. F. "Fatal Flaws in SQL." *Datamation*, 34: no. 16 (1988): 45–48.

Cooper, J. W. "Making Databases Easier for Your Users." *Java Pro*, 4: no. 10 (2000): 47–54.

Date, C. J. *An Introduction to Database Systems, 8/e.* Reading, MA: Pearson Education, 2003.

Deitel, H. M., P. J. Deitel and D. R. Choffnes. *Operating Systems, Third Edition.* Upper Saddle River, NJ: Prentice Hall, 2004.

Duguay, C. "Electronic Mail Merge." *Java Pro*, Winter 1999/2000, 22–32.

Ergul, S. "Transaction Processing with Java." *Java Report*, January 2001, 30–36.

Fisher, M. "JDBC Database Access," (a trail in *The Java Tutorial*), <`java.sun.com/docs/books/tutorial/jdbc/index.html`>.

Harrison, G., "Browsing the JDBC API." *Java Developers Journal*, 3: no. 2 (1998): 44–52.

Jasnowski, M. "Persistence Frameworks." *Java Developers Journal*, 5: no. 11 (2000): 82–86.

"JDBC API Documentation." <`java.sun.com/javase/6/docs/technotes/guides/jdbc/`>.

Jordan, D. "An Overview of Sun's Java Data Objects Specification." *Java Pro*, 4: no. 6 (2000): 102–108.

Khanna, P. "Managing Object Persistence with JDBC." *Java Pro*, 4: no. 5 (2000): 28–33.

Reese, G. *Database Programming with JDBC and Java, Second Edition.* Cambridge, MA: O'Reilly, 2001.

Spell, B. "Create Enterprise Applications with JDBC 2.0." *Java Pro*, 4: no. 4 (2000): 40–44.

Stonebraker, M. "Operating System Support for Database Management." *Communications of the ACM*, 24: no. 7 (1981): 412–418.

Taylor, A. *JDBC Developer's Resource: Database Programming on the Internet.* Upper Saddle River, NJ: Prentice Hall, 1999.

Thilmany, C. "Applying Patterns to JDBC Development." *Java Developers Journal*, 5: no. 6 (2000): 80–90.

Venugopal, S. 2000. "Cross-Database Portability with JDBC." *Java Developers Journal*, 5: no. 1 (2000): 58–62.

White, S., M. Fisher, R. Cattell, G. Hamilton and M. Hapner. *JDBC API Tutorial and Reference, Second Edition.* Boston, MA: Addison Wesley, 1999.

Winston, A. "A Distributed Database Primer." *UNIX World*, April 1988, 54–63.

Summary

Section 25.1 Introduction

- A database is an integrated collection of data. A database management system (DBMS) provides mechanisms for storing, organizing, retrieving and modifying data for many users.

- Today's most popular database management systems are relational database systems.

- SQL is the international standard language used almost universally with relational database systems to perform queries and manipulate data.

- Programs connect to, and interact with, relational databases via an interface—software that facilitates communications between a database management system and a program.

- Java programs communicate with databases and manipulate their data using the JDBC API. A JDBC driver enables Java applications to connect to a database in a particular DBMS and allows you to retrieve and manipulate database data.

Section 25.2 Relational Databases

- A relational database stores data in tables. Tables are composed of rows, and rows are composed of columns in which values are stored.

- A primary key provides a unique value that cannot be duplicated in other rows of the same table.

- Each column of a table represents a different attribute.

- The primary key can be composed of more than one column.

- SQL provides a rich set of language constructs that enable you to define complex queries to retrieve data from a database.

- Every column in a primary key must have a value, and the value of the primary key must be unique. This is known as the Rule of Entity Integrity.

- A one-to-many relationship between tables indicates that a row in one table can have many related rows in a separate table.

- A foreign key is a column in a table that matches the primary-key column in another table.

- The foreign key helps maintain the Rule of Referential Integrity: Every foreign-key value must appear as another table's primary-key value. Foreign keys enable information from multiple tables to be joined together. There is a one-to-many relationship between a primary key and its corresponding foreign key.

Section 25.4.1 Basic **SELECT** Query

- The basic form of a query is

      SELECT * FROM *tableName*

  where the asterisk (*) indicates that all columns from *tableName* should be selected, and *tableName* specifies the table in the database from which rows will be retrieved.
- To retrieve specific columns from a table, replace the asterisk (*) with a comma-separated list of column names.
- You process query results by knowing in advance the order of the columns in the result. Specifying columns explicitly guarantees that they are always returned in the specified order, even if the actual order in the table(s) is different.

Section 25.4.2 **WHERE** Clause

- The optional WHERE clause in a query specifies the selection criteria for the query. The basic form of a query with selection criteria is

      SELECT *columnName1*, *columnName2*, ... FROM *tableName* WHERE *criteria*

- The WHERE clause can contain operators <, >, <=, >=, =, <> and LIKE. Operator LIKE is used for string pattern matching with wildcard characters percent (%) and underscore (_).
- A percent character (%) in a pattern indicates that a string matching the pattern can have zero or more characters at the percent character's location in the pattern.
- An underscore (_) in the pattern string indicates a single character at that position in the pattern.

Section 25.4.3 **ORDER BY** Clause

- The result of a query can be sorted in ascending or descending order using the optional ORDER BY clause. The simplest form of an ORDER BY clause is

      SELECT *columnName1*, *columnName2*, ... FROM *tableName* ORDER BY *column* ASC
      SELECT *columnName1*, *columnName2*, ... FROM *tableName* ORDER BY *column* DESC

  where ASC specifies ascending order, DESC specifies descending order and *column* specifies the column on which the sort is based. The default sorting order is ascending, so ASC is optional.
- Multiple columns can be used for ordering purposes with an ORDER BY clause of the form

      ORDER BY *column1* *sortingOrder*, *column2* *sortingOrder*, ...

- The WHERE and ORDER BY clauses can be combined in one query. If used, ORDER BY must be the last clause in the query.

Section 25.4.4 Merging Data from Multiple Tables: **INNER JOIN**

- An INNER JOIN merges rows from two tables by matching values in columns that are common to the tables. The basic form for the INNER JOIN operator is:

      SELECT *columnName1*, *columnName2*, ...
      FROM *table1*
      INNER JOIN *table2*
         ON *table1.columnName* = *table2.columnName*

  The ON clause specifies the columns from each table that are compared to determine which rows are joined. If a SQL statement uses columns with the same name from multiple tables, the column names must be fully qualified by prefixing them with their table names and a dot (.).

Section 25.4.5 *INSERT Statement*

- An INSERT statement inserts a new row into a table. The basic form of this statement is

    > INSERT INTO *tableName* (*columnName1*, *columnName2*, ..., *columnNameN*)
    >   VALUES (*value1*, *value2*, ..., *valueN*)

    where *tableName* is the table in which to insert the row. The *tableName* is followed by a comma-separated list of column names in parentheses. The list of column names is followed by the SQL keyword VALUES and a comma-separated list of values in parentheses.

- SQL uses single quotes (') as the delimiter for strings. To specify a string containing a single quote in SQL, the single quote must be escaped with another single quote.

Section 25.4.6 *UPDATE Statement*

- An UPDATE statement modifies data in a table. The basic form of an UPDATE statement is

    > UPDATE *tableName*
    >   SET *columnName1* = *value1*, *columnName2* = *value2*, ..., *columnNameN* = *valueN*
    >   WHERE *criteria*

    where *tableName* is the table in which to update data. The *tableName* is followed by keyword SET and a comma-separated list of column name/value pairs in the format *columnName* = *value*. The optional WHERE clause *criteria* determines which rows to update.

Section 25.4.7 *DELETE Statement*

- A DELETE statement removes rows from a table. The simplest form for a DELETE statement is

    > DELETE FROM *tableName* WHERE *criteria*

    where *tableName* is the table from which to delete a row (or rows). The optional WHERE *criteria* determines which rows to delete. If this clause is omitted, all the table's rows are deleted.

Section 25.8.1 *Connecting to and Querying a Database*

- Package java.sql contains classes and interfaces for accessing relational databases in Java.

- An object that implements interface Connection manages the connection between a Java program and a database. Connection objects enable programs to create SQL statements that access data.

- Method getConnection of class DriverManager attempts to connect to a database specified by its URL argument. The URL helps the program locate the database. The URL includes the protocol for communication, the subprotocol for communication and the name of the database.

- Connection method createStatement creates an object of type Statement. The program uses the Statement object to submit SQL statements to the database.

- Statement method executeQuery executes a query and returns an object that implements interface ResultSet containing the query result. ResultSet methods enable a program to manipulate query results.

- A ResultSetMetaData object describes a ResultSet's contents. Programs can use metadata programmatically to obtain information about the ResultSet column names and types.

- ResultSetMetaData method getColumnCount retrieves the number of ResultSet columns.

- ResultSet method next positions the ResultSet cursor to the next row in the ResultSet. The cursor points to the current row. Method next returns boolean value true if it is able to position to the next row; otherwise, the method returns false. This method must be called to begin processing a ResultSet.

- When processing ResultSets, it is possible to extract each column of the ResultSet as a specific Java type. ResultSetMetaData method getColumnType returns a constant integer from class Types (package java.sql) indicating the type of the data for a specific column.

- ResultSet *get* methods typically receive as an argument either a column number (as an int) or a column name (as a String) indicating which column's value to obtain.

- ResultSet row and column numbers start at 1.

- Each Statement object can open only one ResultSet object at a time. When a Statement returns a new ResultSet, the Statement closes the prior ResultSet.

- Connection method createStatement has an overloaded version that takes two arguments: the result type and the result concurrency. The result type specifies whether the ResultSet's cursor is able to scroll in both directions or forward only and whether the ResultSet is sensitive to changes. The result concurrency specifies whether the ResultSet can be updated with Result-Set's update methods.

- Some JDBC drivers do not support scrollable or updatable ResultSets.

Section 25.8.2 Querying the **books** Database

- TableModel method getColumnClass returns a Class object that represents the superclass of all objects in a particular column. JTable uses this information to set up the default cell renderer and cell editor for that column in a JTable.

- ResultSetMetaData method getColumnClassName obtains the fully qualified class name of the specified column.

- TableModel method getColumnCount returns the number of columns in the model's underlying ResultSet.

- TableModel method getColumnName returns the name of the column in the model's underlying ResultSet.

- ResultSetMetaData method getColumnName obtains the column name from the ResultSet.

- TableModel method getRowCount returns the number of rows in the model's ResultSet.

- TableModel method getValueAt returns the Object at a particular row and column of the model's underlying ResultSet.

- ResultSet method absolute positions the ResultSet cursor at a specific row.

- AbstractTableModel method fireTableStructureChanged notifies any JTable using a particular TableModel object as its model that the data in the model has changed.

Section 25.9 RowSet Interface

- Interface RowSet configures the database connection and executes the query automatically.

- There are two types of RowSets—connected and disconnected.

- A connected RowSet connects to the database once and remains connected until the application terminates.

- A disconnected RowSet connects to the database, executes a query to retrieve the data from the database and then closes the connection.

- JdbcRowSet, a connected RowSet, acts as a wrapper for a ResultSet object and allows you to scroll and update the rows in the ResultSet. Unlike a ResultSet object, a JdbcRowSet object is scrollable and updatable by default.

- CachedRowSet, a disconnected RowSet, caches the data of a ResultSet in memory. Like Jdbc-RowSet, a CachedRowSet object is scrollable and updatable. A CachedRowSet object is also serializable, so it can be passed between Java applications through a network, such as the Internet.

Section 25.10 Java DB/Apache Derby
- As of JDK 6, Sun Microsystems now bundles the open-source, pure Java database Java DB (the Sun branded version of Apache Derby) with the JDK.
- Java DB has both an embedded version and a network version.

Section 25.11 PreparedStatements
- Interface PreparedStatement enables you to create compiled SQL statements that execute more efficiently than Statement objects.
- PreparedStatements also can specify parameters, making them more flexible than Statements. Programs can execute the same query repeatedly with different parameter values.
- A parameter is specified with a question mark (?) in the SQL statement. Before executing a PreparedStatement, the program must specify the parameter values by using the PreparedStatement interface's *set* methods.
- PreparedStatement method setString's first argument represents the number of the parameter being set and the second argument is that parameter's value.
- Parameter numbers are counted from 1, starting with the first question mark (?).
- Method setString automatically escapes String parameter values as necessary.
- Interface PreparedStatement provides set methods for each supported SQL type.
- An identity column is the SQL standard way to represent an autoincremented column. The SQL IDENTITY keyword to mark a column as an identity column.

Section 25.12 Stored Procedures
- JDBC enables programs to invoke stored procedures using objects that implement interface CallableStatement.
- CallableStatement can specify input parameters, like PreparedStatement. In addition, CallableStatement can specify output parameters in which a stored procedure can place return values.

Section 25.13 Transaction Processing
- Transaction processing enables a program that interacts with a database to treat a database operation (or set of operations) as a single operation. Such an operation is also known as an atomic operation or a transaction.
- At the end of a transaction, a decision can be made either to commit the transaction or roll back the transaction.
- Committing the transaction finalizes the database operation(s); all insertions, updates and deletions performed as part of the transaction cannot be reversed without performing a new database operation.
- Rolling back a transaction leaves the database in its state prior to the database operation. This is useful when a portion of a transaction fails to complete properly.
- Java provides transaction processing via methods of interface Connection.
- Method setAutoCommit specifies whether each SQL statement commits after it completes (a true argument) or if several SQL statements should be grouped as a transaction (a false argument).
- If the argument to setAutoCommit is false, the program must follow the last SQL statement in the transaction with a call to Connection method commit (to commit the changes to the database) or Connection method rollback (to return the database to its state prior to the transaction).
- Method getAutoCommit determines the autocommit state for the Connection.

Terminology

% SQL wildcard character

_ SQL wildcard character

* SQL wildcard character

absolute method of ResultSet

AbstractTableModel class

addTableModelListener method of interface
    TableModel

automatic driver discovery

CachedRowSet interface

CallableStatement interface

close method of Connection

close method of Statement

com.mysql.jdbc.Driver

column

connect to a database

connected RowSet

Connection interface

createStatement method of interface
    Connection

database

DELETE SQL statement

deleteRow method of interface ResultSet

disconnected RowSet

DriverManager class

execute method of interface JdbcRowSet

execute method of interface Statement

executeQuery method of interface Statement

executeUpdate method of interface Statement

filter the data in a TableModel

fireTableStructureChanged method of class
    AbstractTableModel

foreign key

getColumnClass method of interface
    TableModel

getColumnClassName method of interface
    ResultSetMetaData

getColumnCount method of interface
    ResultSetMetaData

getColumnCount method of interface
    TableModel

getColumnName method of interface
    ResultSetMetaData

getColumnName method of interface TableModel

getColumnType method of interface
    ResultSetMetaData

getConnection method of class DriverManager

getMetaData method of interface ResultSet

getMoreResults method of interface Statement

getObject method of interface ResultSet

getResultSet method of interface Statement

getRow method of interface ResultSet

getRowCount method of interface TableModel

getUpdateCount method of interface Statement

getValueAt method of interface TableModel

INNER JOIN SQL operator

INSERT SQL statement

insertRow method of interface ResultSet

java.sql package

javax.sql package

javax.sql.rowset package

javax.swing.table package

JDBC

JDBC driver

JdbcRowSet interface

JdbcRowSetImpl class

join

last method of interface ResultSet

metadata

moveToCurrentRow method of ResultSet

moveToInsertRow method of ResultSet

MySQL Connector/J

MySQL database

next method of interface ResultSet

ON clause

one-to-many relationship

ORDER BY clause

ordering rows

output parameter

pattern matching

PreparedStatement interface

primary key

query a database

regexFilter method of class RowFilter

relational database

removeTableModelListener method of inter-
    face TableModel

result

ResultSet interface

ResultSetMetaData interface

row

RowFilter class

Rule of Entity Integrity

Rule of Referential Integrity

SELECT SQL keyword

selection criteria

setCommand method of interface JdbcRowSet

setPassword method of interface JdbcRowSet

setRowFilter method of class JTable

setRowSorter method of class JTable
setString method of interface
    PreparedStatement
setUsername method of interface JdbcRowSet
setUrl method of interface JdbcRowSet
SQL (Structured Query Language)
SQL script
SQLException class
Statement interface
stored procedure

sun.jdbc.odbc.JdbcOdbcDriver
table
TableModel interface
TableModelEvent class
TableRowSorter class
Types class
updatable ResultSet
UPDATE SQL statement
updateRow method of interface ResultSet
WHERE clause of a SQL statement

Self-Review Exercise

25.1 Fill in the blanks in each of the following statements:
    a) The international standard database language is _____.
    b) A table in a database consists of _____ and _____.
    c) Statement objects return SQL query results as _____ objects.
    d) The _____ uniquely identifies each row in a table.
    e) SQL keyword _____ is followed by the selection criteria that specify the rows to select in a query.
    f) SQL keywords _____ specify the order in which rows are sorted in a query.
    g) Merging rows from multiple database tables is called _____ the tables.
    h) A(n) _____ is an organized collection of data.
    i) A(n) _____ is a set of columns whose values match the primary key values of another table.
    j) A(n) _____ object is used to obtain a Connection to a database.
    k) Interface _____ helps manage the connection between a Java program and a database.
    l) A(n) _____ object is used to submit a query to a database.
    m) Unlike a ResultSet object, _____ and _____ objects are scrollable and updatable by default.
    n) _____, a disconnected RowSet, caches the data of a ResultSet in memory.

Answers to Self-Review Exercise

25.1 a) SQL. b) rows, columns. c) ResultSet. d) primary key. e) WHERE. f) ORDER BY. g) joining. h) database. i) foreign key. j) DriverManager. k) Connection. l) Statement. m) Jdbc-RowSet, CachedRowSet n) CachedRowSet.

Exercises

25.2 Using the techniques shown in this chapter, define a complete query application for the books database. Provide the following predefined queries:
    a) Select all authors from the authors table.
    b) Select a specific author and list all books for that author. Include each book's title, year and ISBN. Order the information alphabetically by the author's last then first name.
    c) Select a specific publisher and list all books published by that publisher. Include the title, year and ISBN. Order the information alphabetically by title.
    d) Provide any other queries you feel are appropriate.

Display a JComboBox with appropriate names for each predefined query. Also allow users to supply their own queries.

25.3 In Section 10.7, we introduced an employee-payroll hierarchy to calculate each employee's payroll. In this exercise, we provide a database of employees that corresponds to the employee payroll hierarchy. (A SQL script to create the `employees` database is provided with the examples for this chapter on the CD that accompanies this text and on our website, www.deitel.com.) Write an application that allows the user to:

    a) Add employees to the `employee` table.

    b) Add payroll information to the appropriate table for each new employee. For example, for a salaried employee add the payroll information to the `salariedEmployees` table.

Figure 25.33 is the entity-relationship diagram for the `employees` database.

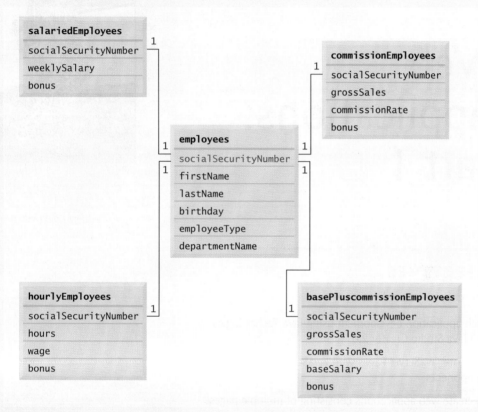

Fig. 25.33 | Table relationships in `employees`.

25.4 Modify Exercise 25.3 to provide a `JComboBox` and a `JTextArea` to allow the user to perform a query that is either selected from the `JComboBox` or defined in the `JTextArea`. Sample predefined queries are:

    a) Select all employees working in Department SALES.

    b) Select hourly employees working over 30 hours.

    c) Select all commission employees in descending order of the commission rate.

25.5 Modify Exercise 25.4 to perform the following tasks:

    a) Increase base salary by 10% for all base-plus-commission employees.

    b) If the employee's birthday is in the current month, add a $100 bonus.

    c) For all commission employees with gross sales over $10,000, add a $100 bonus.

26

Web Applications: Part 1

Outline

26.1 Introduction

In this chapter, we introduce web application development with Java-based technology. Web-based applications create web content for web browser clients. This web content includes Extensible HyperText Markup Language (XHTML), client-side scripting, images and binary data. For those who are not familiar with XHTML, we've provided on the CD that accompanies this book three chapters from our book *Internet & World Wide Web How to Program, 3/e*—Introduction to XHTML: Part 1, Introduction to XHTML: Part 2 and Cascading Style Sheets (CSS). In Chapters 26–28, we assume you already know XHTML.

This chapter begins with an overview of multitier application architecture and Java's web technologies for implementing multitier applications. We then present several examples that demonstrate web application development. The first example introduces you to Java web development. In the second example, we build a web application that simply shows the look-and-feel of several web-application GUI components. Next, we demonstrate how to use validation components and custom validation methods to ensure that user input is valid before it is submitted for processing on the server. The chapter finishes with two examples of customizing a user's experience with session tracking.

In Chapter 27, we continue our discussion of web application development with more advanced concepts, including the AJAX-enabled components from Sun's Java Blue-Prints. AJAX helps web-based applications provide the interactivity and responsiveness that users typically expect of desktop applications.

Throughout this chapter and Chapter 27, we use Sun Java Studio Creator 2.0—an IDE that helps you build web applications using Java technologies such as JavaServer Pages and JavaServer Faces. To implement the examples presented in this chapter, you must install Java Studio Creator 2.0, which is available for download at developers.sun.com/prodtech/javatools/jscreator/downloads/index.jsp. The features of Java Studio Creator 2.0 are being incorporated into Netbeans 5.5 via an add-on called the Netbeans Visual Web Pack 5.5 (www.netbeans.org/products/visualweb/).

26.2 Simple HTTP Transactions

Web application development requires a basic understanding of networking and the World Wide Web. In this section, we discuss the Hypertext Transfer Protocol (HTTP) and what occurs behind the scenes when a user requests a web page in a browser. HTTP specifies a set of methods and headers that allow clients and servers to interact and exchange information in a uniform and reliable manner.

In its simplest form, a web page is nothing more than an XHTML document—a plain text file containing markup (i.e., tags) that describe to a web browser how to display and format the document's information. For example, the XHTML markup

```
<title>My Web Page</title>
```

indicates that the browser should display the text between the `<title>` start tag and the `</title>` end tag in the browser's title bar. XHTML documents also can contain hypertext data (usually called hyperlinks) that link to different pages or to other parts of the same page. When the user activates a hyperlink (usually by clicking it with the mouse), the requested web page loads into the user's web browser.

HTTP uses URIs (Uniform Resource Identifiers) to identify data on the Internet. URIs that specify document locations are called URLs (Uniform Resource Locators). Common URLs refer to files, directories or objects that perform complex tasks, such as database lookups and Internet searches. If you know the HTTP URL of a publicly available XHTML document anywhere on the web, you can access it through HTTP.

A URL contains information that directs a browser to the resource that the user wishes to access. Computers that run web server software make such resources available. Let's examine the components of the URL

```
http://www.deitel.com/books/downloads.html
```

The `http://` indicates that the resource is to be obtained using the HTTP protocol. The middle portion, www.deitel.com, is the server's fully qualified hostname—the name of the server on which the resource resides. This computer usually is referred to as the host, because it houses and maintains resources. The hostname www.deitel.com is translated into an IP address (68.236.123.125), which identifies the server in a manner similar to how a telephone number uniquely defines a particular phone line. This translation is performed by a domain name system (DNS) server—a computer that maintains a database of host-names and their corresponding IP addresses—and the process is called a DNS lookup.

The remainder of the URL (i.e., /books/downloads.html) specifies both the name of the requested resource (the XHTML document downloads.html) and its path, or location (/books), on the web server. The path could specify the location of an actual directory on the web server's file system. However, for security reasons, the path normally specifies the location of a **virtual directory**. The server translates the virtual directory into a real location on the server (or on another computer on the server's network), thus hiding the true location of the resource. Some resources are created dynamically and do not reside anywhere on the server. The hostname in the URL for such a resource specifies the correct server; the path and resource information identify the location of the resource with which to respond to the client's request.

When given a URL, a web browser performs a simple HTTP transaction to retrieve and display the web page found at that address. Figure 26.1 illustrates the transaction in detail, showing the interaction between the web browser (the client side) and the web server application (the server side).

In Fig. 26.1, the web browser sends an HTTP request to the server. The request (in its simplest form) is

```
GET /books/downloads.html HTTP/1.1
```

The word GET is an **HTTP method** indicating that the client wishes to obtain a resource from the server. The remainder of the request provides the path name of the resource (an XHTML document) and the protocol's name and version number (HTTP/1.1).

Any server that understands HTTP (version 1.1) can translate this request and respond appropriately. Figure 26.2 depicts the results of a successful request. The server first responds by sending a line of text that indicates the HTTP version, followed by a numeric code and a phrase describing the status of the transaction. For example,

```
HTTP/1.1 200 OK
```

indicates success, whereas

```
HTTP/1.1 404 Not found
```

informs the client that the web server could not locate the requested resource. A complete list of numeric codes indicating the status of an HTTP transaction can be found at www.w3.org/Protocols/HTTP/HTRESP.html.

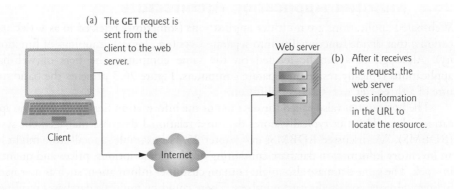

(a) The GET request is sent from the client to the web server.

Web server

(b) After it receives the request, the web server uses information in the URL to locate the resource.

Client

Internet

Fig. 26.1 | Client interacting with web server. *Step 1:* The GET request.

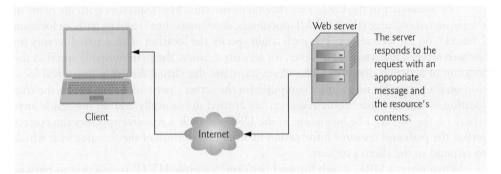

Fig. 26.2 | Client interacting with web server. *Step 2:* The HTTP response.

The server then sends one or more HTTP headers, which provide additional information about the data that will be sent. In this case, the server is sending an XHTML text document, so the HTTP header for this example reads:

```
Content-type: text/html
```

The information provided in this header specifies the Multipurpose Internet Mail Extensions (MIME) type of the content that the server is transmitting to the browser. MIME is an Internet standard that specifies data formats so that programs can interpret data correctly. For example, the MIME type text/plain indicates that the sent information is text that can be displayed directly, without any interpretation of the content as XHTML markup. Similarly, the MIME type image/jpeg indicates that the content is a JPEG image. When the browser receives this MIME type, it attempts to display the image.

The header or set of headers is followed by a blank line, which indicates to the client that the server is finished sending HTTP headers. The server then sends the contents of the requested XHTML document (downloads.html). The server terminates the connection when the resource transfer is complete. The client-side browser parses the XHTML markup it receives and renders (or displays) the results.

26.3 Multitier Application Architecture

Web-based applications are multitier applications (sometimes referred to as *n*-tier applications) that divide functionality into separate tiers (i.e., logical groupings of functionality). Although tiers can be located on the same computer, the tiers of web-based applications typically reside on separate computers. Figure 26.3 presents the basic structure of a three-tier web-based application.

The bottom tier (also called the data tier or the information tier) maintains the application's data. This tier typically stores data in a relational database management system (RDBMS). We discussed RDBMSs in Chapter 25. For example, a retail store might have an inventory information database containing product descriptions, prices and quantities in stock. The same database also might contain customer information, such as user names, billing addresses and credit card numbers. There could be multiple databases residing on one or more computers, which together comprise the application's data.

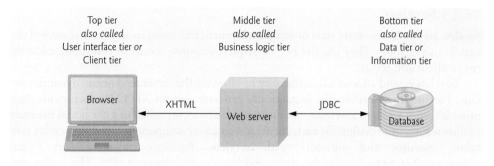

Fig. 26.3 | Three-tier architecture.

The middle tier implements business logic, controller logic and presentation logic to control interactions between the application's clients and its data. The middle tier acts as an intermediary between data in the information tier and the application's clients. The middle-tier controller logic processes client requests (such as requests to view a product catalog) and retrieves data from the database. The middle-tier presentation logic then processes data from the information tier and presents the content to the client. Web applications typically present data to clients as XHTML documents.

Business logic in the middle tier enforces business rules and ensures that data is reliable before the server application updates the database or presents the data to users. Business rules dictate how clients can and cannot access application data, and how applications process data. For example, a business rule in the middle tier of a retail store's web-based application might ensure that all product quantities remain positive. A client request to set a negative quantity in the bottom tier's product information database would be rejected by the middle tier's business logic.

The top tier, or client tier, is the application's user interface, which gathers input and displays output. Users interact directly with the application through the user interface, which is typically a web browser, keyboard and mouse. In response to user actions (e.g., clicking a hyperlink), the client tier interacts with the middle tier to make requests and to retrieve data from the information tier. The client tier then displays the data retrieved for the user. The client tier never directly interacts with the information tier.

Java multitier applications are typically implemented using the features of Java Enterprise Edition (Java EE). The technologies we use to develop web applications in Chapters 26–28 are part of Java EE 5 (java.sun.com/javaee).

26.4 Java Web Technologies

Java web technologies continually evolve to provide developers with higher levels of abstraction and greater separation of the application's tiers. This separation makes web applications more maintainable and extensible. It also allows for an effective division of labor. A graphic designer can build the application's user interface without concern for the underlying page logic, which will be handled by a programmer. Meanwhile, the programmer is free to focus on the application's business logic, leaving the details of building an attractive and easy-to-use application to the designer. Java Studio Creator 2 is the latest step in this evolution, allowing you to develop a web application's GUI in a drag-and-drop design tool, while handling the business logic in separate Java classes.

26.4.1 Servlets

Servlets are the lowest-level view of web development technologies in Java that we will discuss in this chapter. They use the HTTP request-response model of communication between client and server.

Servlets extend a server's functionality by allowing the server to generate dynamic content. For instance, servlets can dynamically generate custom XHTML documents, help provide secure access to a website, interact with databases on behalf of a client and maintain unique session information for each client. A web server component called the servlet container executes and interacts with servlets. Packages `javax.servlet` and `javax.servlet.http` provide the classes and interfaces to define servlets. The servlet container receives HTTP requests from a client and directs each request to the appropriate servlet. The servlet processes the request and returns an appropriate response to the client—usually in the form of an XHTML or XML (Extensible Markup Language) document to display in the browser. XML is a language used to exchange structured data on the web.

Architecturally, all servlets must implement the `Servlet` interface of package `javax.servlet`, which ensures that each servlet can execute in the framework provided by the servlet container. Interface `Servlet` declares methods used by the servlet container to manage the servlet's life cycle. A servlet's life cycle begins when the servlet container loads it into memory—usually in response to the first request for the servlet. Before the servlet can handle that request, the container invokes the servlet's `init` method, which is called only once during a servlet's life-cycle to initialize the servlet. After `init` completes execution, the servlet is ready to respond to its first request. All requests are handled by a servlet's **service method**, which is the key method in defining a servlet's functionality. The service method receives the request, processes it and sends a response to the client. During a servlet's life cycle, `service` is called once per request. Each new request is typically handled in a separate thread of execution (managed by the servlet container), so each servlet must be thread safe. When the servlet container terminates the servlet (e.g. when the servlet container needs more memory or when it is shut down), the servlet's `destroy` method is called to release any resources held by the servlet.

26.4.2 JavaServer Pages

JavaServer Pages (JSP) technology is an extension of servlet technology. Each JSP is translated by the JSP container into a servlet. Unlike servlets, JSPs help you separate presentation from content. JavaServer Pages enable web application programmers to create dynamic content by reusing predefined components and by interacting with components using server-side scripting. JSP programmers can use special software components called JavaBeans and custom tag libraries that encapsulate complex, dynamic functionality. A JavaBean is a reusable component that follows certain conventions for class design. For example, JavaBeans classes that allow reading and writing of instance variables must provide appropriate *get* and *set* methods. The complete set of class design conventions is discussed in the JavaBeans specification (`java.sun.com/products/javabeans/glasgow/index.html`).

Custom Tag Libraries

Custom tag libraries are a powerful feature of JSP that allows Java developers to hide code for database access and other complex operations in **custom tags**. To use such capabilities, you simply add the custom tags to the page. This simplicity enables web-page designers who are not familiar with Java to enhance web pages with powerful dynamic content and processing capabilities. The JSP classes and interfaces are located in packages `javax.servlet.jsp` and `javax.servlet.jsp.tagext`.

JSP Components

There are four key components to JSPs—directives, actions, scripting elements and tag libraries. Directives are messages to the JSP container—the web server component that executes JSPs. Directives enable you to specify page settings, to include content from other resources and to specify custom tag libraries for use in JSPs. Actions encapsulate functionality in predefined tags that programmers can embed in JSPs. Actions often are performed based on the information sent to the server as part of a particular client request. They also can create Java objects for use in JSPs. Scripting elements enable you to insert Java code that interacts with components in a JSP (and possibly other web application components) to perform request processing. Tag libraries are part of the tag extension mechanism that enables programmers to create custom tags. Such tags enable web-page designers to manipulate JSP content without prior Java knowledge. The JavaServer Pages Standard Tag Library (JSTL) provides the functionality for many common web application tasks, such as iterating over a collection of objects and executing SQL statements.

Static Content

JSPs can contain other static content. For example JSPs normally include XHTML or XML markup. Such markup is known as fixed-template data or fixed-template text. Any literal text in a JSP is translated to a `String` literal in the servlet representation of the JSP.

Processing a JSP Request

When a JSP-enabled server receives the first request for a JSP, the JSP container translates the JSP into a servlet that handles the current request and future requests to the JSP. JSPs thus rely on the same request-response mechanism as servlets to process requests from and send responses to clients.

Performance Tip 26.1

Some JSP containers translate JSPs into servlets at the JSP's deployment time (i.e., when the application is placed on a web server). This eliminates the translation overhead for the first client that requests each JSP, as the JSP will be translated before it is ever requested by a client.

26.4.3 JavaServer Faces

JavaServer Faces (JSF) is a web application framework that simplifies the design of an application's user interface and further separates a web application's presentation from its business logic. A framework simplifies application development by providing libraries and sometimes software tools to help you organize and build your applications. Though the JSF framework can use many technologies to define the pages in web applications, this chapter focuses on JSF applications that use JavaServer Pages. JSF provides a set of user interface components, or JSF components that simplify web-page design. These components are similar to the Swing components used to build GUI applications. JSF provides two JSP custom tag libraries for adding these components to a JSP page. JSF also includes APIs for handling component events (such as processing component state changes and validating user input), navigating between web application pages and more. You design the look-and-feel of a page with JSF by adding tags to a JSP file and manipulating their attributes. You define the page's behavior separately in a related Java source-code file.

Though the standard JSF components are sufficient for most basic web applications, you can also write custom component libraries. Additional component libraries are available through the Java BluePrints project—which shows best practices for developing Java applications. Many other vendors provide JSF component libraries. For example, Oracle provides almost 100 components in its ADF Faces library. We discuss one such component library, the BluePrints AJAX components library (blueprints.dev.java.net/ajax-components.html). We discuss the Java BluePrints components for building AJAX-enabled JSF applications in the next chapter.

26.4.4 Web Technologies in Java Studio Creator 2

Java Studio Creator 2 web applications consist of one or more JSP web pages built in the JavaServer Faces framework. These JSP files have the file-name extension .jsp and contain the web page's GUI elements. The JSPs can also contain JavaScript to add functionality to the page. JSPs can be customized in Java Studio Creator 2 by adding JSF components, including labels, text fields, images, buttons and other GUI components. The IDE allows you to design pages visually by dragging and dropping these components onto a page; you can also customize a web page by editing the .jsp file manually.

Every JSP file created in Java Studio Creator 2 represents a web page and has a corresponding JavaBean class called the page bean. A JavaBean class must have a default (or no-argument) constructor, and *get* and *set* methods for all of the bean's properties (i.e., instance variables). The page bean defines properties for each of the page's elements. The page bean also contains event handlers and page life-cycle methods for managing tasks such as page initialization and rendering, and other supporting code for the web application.

Every web application built with Java Studio Creator 2 has three other JavaBeans. The RequestBean object is maintained in request scope—this object exists only for the duration of an HTTP request. A SessionBean object has session scope—the object exists throughout a user's browsing session or until the session times out. There is a unique SessionBean object for each user. Finally, the ApplicationBean object has application scope—this object is shared by all instances of an application and exists as long as the application remains deployed on a web server. This object is used for application-wide data storage or processing; only one instance exists for the application, regardless of the number of open sessions.

26.5 Creating and Running a Simple Application in Java Studio Creator 2

Our first example displays the web server's time of day in a browser window. When run, this program displays the text "Current Time on the Web Server", followed by the web server's time. The application contains a single web page and, as mentioned previously, consists of two related files—a JSP file (Fig. 26.4) and a supporting page bean file (Fig. 26.6). The application also has the three scoped data beans for request, session, and application scopes. Since this application does not store data, these beans are not used in this example. We first discuss the markup in the JSP file, the code in the page bean file and the application output, then we provide step-by-step instructions for creating the program. [*Note:* The markup in Fig. 26.4 and other JSP file listings in this chapter is the same as the markup that appears in Java Studio Creator 2, but we have reformatted these listings for presentation purposes to make the code more readable.]

Java Studio Creator 2 generates all the markup shown in Fig. 26.4 when you set the web page's title, drag two **Static Text** components onto the page and set the properties of the **Static Text** components. **Static Text** components display text that cannot be edited by the user. We show these steps shortly.

```
1   <?xml version = "1.0" encoding = "UTF-8"?>
2
3   <!-- Fig. 26.4: Time.jsp -->
4   <!-- JSP file generated by Java Studio Creator 2 that displays -->
5   <!-- the current time on the web server -->
6   <jsp:root version = "1.2"
7      xmlns:f = "http://java.sun.com/jsf/core"
8      xmlns:h = "http://java.sun.com/jsf/html"
9      xmlns:jsp = "http://java.sun.com/JSP/Page"
10     xmlns:ui = "http://www.sun.com/web/ui">
11     <jsp:directive.page contentType = "text/html; charset = UTF-8"
12        pageEncoding = "UTF-8"/>
13     <f:view>
14        <ui:page binding = "#{Time.page}" id = "page">
15           <ui:html binding = "#{Time.html}" id = "html">
16              <ui:head binding = "#{Time.head}" id = "head"
17                 title = "Web Time: A Simple Example">
18                 <ui:link binding = "#{Time.link}" id = "link"
19                    url = "/resources/stylesheet.css"/>
20              </ui:head>
21              <ui:meta content = "60" httpEquiv = "refresh"/>
22              <ui:body binding = "#{Time.body}" id = "body"
23                 style = "-rave-layout: grid">
24                 <ui:form binding = "#{Time.form}" id = "form">
25                    <ui:staticText binding = "#{Time.timeHeader}" id =
26                       "timeHeader" style = "font-size: 18px; left: 24px;
27                       top: 24px; position: absolute" text = "Current time
28                       on the Web Server:"/>
29                    <ui:staticText binding = "#{Time.clockText}" id =
30                       "clockText" style = "background-color: black;
31                       color: yellow; font-size: 18px; left: 24px; top:
32                       48px; position: absolute"/>
33                 </ui:form>
34              </ui:body>
35           </ui:html>
36        </ui:page>
37     </f:view>
38  </jsp:root>
```

Fig. 26.4 | JSP file generated by Java Studio Creator 2 that displays the current time on the web server.

26.5.1 Examining a JSP File

The JSP files used in this and the following examples are generated almost entirely by Java Studio Creator 2, which provides a Visual Editor that allows you to build a page's GUI by dragging and dropping components onto a design area. The IDE generates a JSP file in response to your interactions. Line 1 of Fig. 26.4 is the XML declaration, indicating that the JSP is expressed in XML syntax and the version of XML that is used. Lines 3–5 are comments that we added to the JSP to indicate its figure number, file name and purpose.

Line 6 begins the root element for the JSP. All JSPs must have this `jsp:root` element, which has a `version` attribute to indicate the version of JSP being used (line 6) and one or more `xmlns` attributes (lines 7–10). Each `xmlns` attribute specifies a prefix and a URL for a tag library, allowing the page to use tags specified in that library. For example, line 9 allows the page to use the standard JSP elements. To use these elements, each element's tag must be preceded by the `jsp` prefix. All JSPs generated by Java Studio Creator 2 include the tag libraries specified in lines 7–10 (the JSF core components library, the JSF HTML components library, the JSP standard components library and the JSF user interface components library).

Lines 11–12 are the `jsp:directive.page` element. Its `contentType` attribute specifies the MIME type (`text/html`) and the character set (`UTF-8`) the page uses. The `page-Encoding` attribute specifies the character encoding used by the page source. These attributes help the client (typically a web browser) determine how to render the content.

All pages containing JSF components are represented in a component tree (Fig. 26.5) with the root JSF element `f:view`, which is of type `UIViewRoot`. This component tree

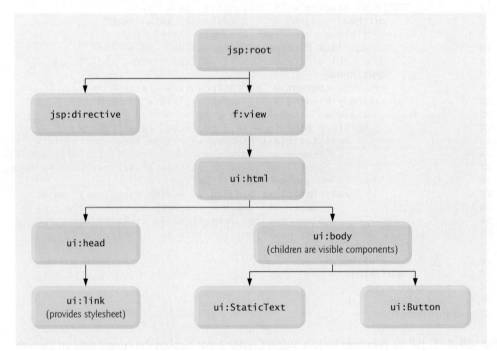

Fig. 26.5 | Sample JSF component tree.

structure is represented in a JSP by enclosing all JSF component tags inside the f:view element (lines 13–37).

Lines 14–20 begin the definition of the JSP with the **ui:page**, **ui:html**, and **ui:head** tags, all from the ui (JSF user interface components) tag library. These, and many other ui page elements, have a binding attribute. For example, the ui:head element (line 16) has the attribute binding = "#{Time.head}." This attribute uses JSF Expression Language notation (i.e., #{Time.head}) to reference the head property in the Time class that represents the page bean (you'll see this class in Fig. 26.6). It is possible to bind a single attribute of a JSP element to a property in any of the web application's JavaBeans. For instance, the text attribute of a ui:label component can be bound to a String property in the application's SessionBean. We will see an example of this in Section 26.7.2.

The ui:head element (lines 16–20) has a title attribute that specifies the page's title. This element also contains a ui:link element (lines 18–19) that specifies the CSS stylesheet used by the page. The ui:body element (lines 22–34) contains a ui:form element (lines 24–33), which contains two ui:staticText components (lines 25–28 and 29–32). These components display the page's text. The timeHeader component (lines 25–28) has a text attribute (lines 27–28) that specifies the text to display (i.e., "Current Time on the Web Server"). The clockText component (lines 29–32) does not specify a text attribute because this component's text will be set programmatically.

For the markup in this file to be displayed in a web browser, all of the JSP's elements are automatically mapped to XHTML elements that the browser recognizes. The same web component can map to different XHTML elements, depending on the client browser and the component's property settings. In this example, the ui:staticText components (lines 25–28, 29–32) map to XHTML **span** elements. A span element contains text that is displayed on a web page and is typically used to control the formatting of the text. The style attributes of a JSP's ui:staticText element will be represented as part of the corresponding span element's style attribute when the browser renders the page. We show momentarily the XHTML document that results when Time.jsp is requested by a browser.

26.5.2 Examining a Page Bean File

Figure 26.6 presents the page bean file. Line 3 indicates that this class belongs to package webtime. This line is autogenerated and specifies the project's name as the package name. Line 17 begins class Time's declaration and indicates that it inherits from class **Abstract-PageBean** (from package com.sun.rave.web.ui.appbase). All page bean classes that support JSP files with JSF components must inherit from the abstract class AbstractPageBean, which provides page life-cycle methods. Note that the IDE makes the class name match the page name. Package **com.sun.rave.web.ui.component** includes classes for many of the basic JSF components (see the import statements at lines 6–11 and 13).

```
1   // Fig. 26.6: Time.java
2   // Page bean file that sets clockText to the time on the web server.
3   package webtime;
4
5   import com.sun.rave.web.ui.appbase.AbstractPageBean;
6   import com.sun.rave.web.ui.component.Body;
```

Fig. 26.6 | Page bean file that sets clockText to the time on the web server. (Part 1 of 5.)

```
7    import com.sun.rave.web.ui.component.Form;
8    import com.sun.rave.web.ui.component.Head;
9    import com.sun.rave.web.ui.component.Html;
10   import com.sun.rave.web.ui.component.Link;
11   import com.sun.rave.web.ui.component.Page;
12   import javax.faces.FacesException;
13   import com.sun.rave.web.ui.component.StaticText;
14   import java.text.DateFormat;
15   import java.util.Date;
16
17   public class Time extends AbstractPageBean
18   {
19       private int __placeholder;
20
21       // auto-generated component initialization method.
22       private void _init() throws Exception
23       {
24           // empty body
25       } // end method _init
26
27       private Page page = new Page();
28
29       public Page getPage()
30       {
31           return page;
32       } // end method getPage
33
34       public void setPage( Page page )
35       {
36           this.page = page;
37       } // end method setPage
38
39       private Html html = new Html();
40
41       public Html getHtml )
42       {
43           return html;
44       } // end method getHtml
45
46       public void setHtml( Html html )
47       {
48           this.html = html;
49       } // end method setHtml
50
51       private Head head = new Head();
52
53       public Head getHead()
54       {
55           return head;
56       } // end method getHead
57
58       public void setHead( Head head )
59       {
```

Fig. 26.6 | Page bean file that sets `clockText` to the time on the web server. (Part 2 of 5.)

```
60            this.head = head;
61         } // end method setHead
62
63         private Link link = new Link();
64
65         public Link getLink()
66         {
67            return link;
68         } // end method getLink
69
70         public void setLink( Link link )
71         {
72            this.link = link;
73         } // end method setLink
74
75         private Body body = new Body();
76
77         public Body getBody()
78         {
79            return body;
80         } // end method getBody
81
82         public void setBody( Body body )
83         {
84            this.body = body;
85         } // end method setBody
86
87         private Form form = new Form();
88
89         public Form getForm()
90         {
91            return form;
92         } // end method getForm
93
94         public void setForm( Form form )
95         {
96            this.form = form;
97         } // end method setForm
98
99         private StaticText timeHeader = new StaticText();
100
101         public StaticText getTimeHeader()
102         {
103            return timeHeader;
104         } // end method getStaticText1
105
106         public void setTimeHeader( StaticText st )
107         {
108            this.timeHeader = st;
109         } // end method setTimeHeader
110
111         private StaticText clockText = new StaticText();
112
```

Fig. 26.6 | Page bean file that sets clockText to the time on the web server. (Part 3 of 5.)

```
113        public StaticText getClockText()
114        {
115           return clockText;
116        } // end method getClockText
117
118        public void setClockText( StaticText st )
119        {
120           this.clockText = st;
121        } // end method setClockText
122
123        // Construct a new page bean instance.
124        public Time()
125        {
126           // empty constructor
127        } // end constructor
128
129        // Return a reference to the scoped data bean.
130        protected RequestBean getRequestBean()
131        {
132           return (RequestBean) getBean( "RequestBean" );
133        } // end method getRequestBean
134
135        // Return a reference to the scoped data bean.
136        protected ApplicationBean getApplicationBean()
137        {
138           return (ApplicationBean) getBean( "ApplicationBean" );
139        } // end method getApplicationBean
140
141        // Return a reference to the scoped data bean.
142        protected SessionBean getSessionBean()
143        {
144           return (SessionBean) getBean( "SessionBean" );
145        } // end method getSessionBean
146
147        // initializes page content
148        public void init()
149        {
150           super.init();
151           try
152           {
153              _init();
154           } // end try
155           catch ( Exception e )
156           {
157              log( "Time Initialization Failure", e );
158              throw e instanceof FacesException ? ( FacesException ) e:
159                 new FacesException( e );
160           } // end catch
161        } // end method init
162
163        // method called when a postback occurs.
164        public void preprocess()
165        {
```

Fig. 26.6 | Page bean file that sets clockText to the time on the web server. (Part 4 of 5.)

```
166        // empty body
167     } // end method preprocess
168
169     // method called before the page is rendered.
170     public void prerender()
171     {
172        clockText.setValue( DateFormat.getTimeInstance(
173           DateFormat.LONG ).format( new Date() ) );
174     } // end method prerender
175
176     // method called after rendering completes, if init was called.
177     public void destroy()
178     {
179        // empty body
180     } // end method destroy
181  } // end class Time
```

Fig. 26.6 | Page bean file that sets clockText to the time on the web server. (Part 5 of 5.)

This page bean file provides *get* and *set* methods for every element of the JSP file of Fig. 26.4. These methods are generated automatically by the IDE. We included the complete page bean file in this first example, but in future examples these properties and their *get* and *set* methods will be omitted to save space. Lines 99–109 and 111–121 of the page bean file define the two **Static Text** components that we dropped onto the page and their *get* and *set* methods. These components are objects of class StaticText in package com.sun.rave.web.ui.component.

The only logic required in this page is to set the clockText component's text to read the current time on the server. We do this in the prerender method (lines 170–174). The meaning of this and other page bean methods will be discussed shortly. Lines 172–173 fetch and format the time on the server and set the value of clockText to that time.

26.5.3 Event-Processing Life Cycle

Java Studio Creator 2's application model places several methods in the page bean that tie into the JSF event-processing life cycle. These methods represent four major stages—initialization, preprocessing, prerendering and destruction. Each corresponds to a method in the page bean class—init, preprocess, prerender and destroy, respectively. Java Studio Creator 2 automatically creates these methods, but you can customize them to handle life-cycle processing tasks, such as rendering an element on a page only if a user clicks a button.

The init method (Fig. 26.6, lines 148–161) is called by the JSP container the first time the page is requested and on postbacks. A postback occurs when form data is submitted, and the page and its contents are sent to the server to be processed. Method init invokes its superclass version (line 150) then tries to call the method _init (declared in lines 22–25). The _init method is also automatically generated and handles component initialization tasks (if there are any), such as setting the options for a group of radio buttons.

The preprocess method (lines 164–167) is called after init, but only if the page is processing a postback. The prerender method (lines 170–174) is called just before a page is rendered (i.e., displayed) by the browser. This method should be used to set component properties; properties that are set sooner (such as in method init) may be overwritten before the page is actually rendered by the browser. For this reason, we set the value of clockText in the prerender method.

Finally, the destroy method (lines 177–180) is called after the page has been rendered, but only if the init method was called. This method handles tasks such as freeing resources used to render the page.

26.5.4 Relationship Between the JSP and Page Bean Files

The page bean has a property for every element that appears in the JSP file of Fig. 26.4, from the html element to the two Static Text components. Recall that the elements in the JSP file were explicitly bound to these properties by each element's binding attribute using a JSF Expression Language statement. Because this is a JavaBean class, *get* and *set* methods for each of these properties are also included (lines 27–121). This code is automatically generated by the IDE for every web application project.

26.5.5 Examining the XHTML Generated by a Java Web Application

Figure 26.7 shows the XHTML generated when Time.jsp (Fig. 26.4) is requested by a client web browser. To view this XHTML, select **View > Source** in Internet Explorer. [*Note:* We added the XHTML comments in lines 3–4 and reformatted the XHTML to conform to our coding conventions.]

The XHTML document in Fig. 26.7 is similar in structure to the JSP file of Fig. 26.4. Lines 5–6 are the document type declaration, which declares this document to be an XHTML 1.0 Transitional document. The ui:meta tags in lines 9–13 are equivalent to HTTP headers and are used to control browser behavior.

```
1    <?xml version = "1.0"?>
2
3    <!-- Fig. 26.7: Time.html -->
4    <!-- The XHTML response generated when the browser requests Time.jsp. -->
5    <!DOCTYPE html PUBLIC "-//W3C//DTD XHTML 1.0 Transitional//EN"
6       "http://www.w3.org/TR/xhtml1/DTD/xhtml1-transitional.dtd">
7    <html xmlns = "http://www.w3.org/1999/xhtml">
8       <head>
9          <meta content = "no-cache" http-equiv = "Pragma" />
10         <meta content = "no-cache" http-equiv = "Cache-Control" />
11         <meta content = "no-store" http-equiv = "Cache-Control" />
```

Fig. 26.7 | XHTML response generated when the browser requests Time.jsp. (Part I of 2.)

```
12        <meta content = "max-age=0" http-equiv = "Cache-Control" />
13        <meta content = "1" http-equiv = "Expires" />
14        <title>Web Time: A Simple Example</title>
15        <script type = "text/javascript"
16           src = "/WebTime/theme/com/sun/rave/web/ui/defaulttheme/
17           javascript/formElements.js"></script>
18        <link rel = "stylesheet" type = "text/css" href = "/WebTime/theme/
19           com/sun/rave/web/ui/defaulttheme/css/css_master.css" />
20        <link rel = "stylesheet" type = "text/css" href = "/WebTime/theme/
21           com/sun/rave/web/ui/defaulttheme/css/css_ie55up.css" />
22        <script type = "text/javascript">
23           var sjwuic_ScrollCookie = new sjwuic_ScrollCookie(
24           '/Time.jsp', '/WebTime/faces/Time.jsp' );
25        </script>
26        <link id = "link" rel = "stylesheet" type = "text/css"
27           href = "/WebTime/resources/stylesheet.css" />
28     </head>
29     <meta id = "_id0" http-equiv = "refresh" content = "5" />
30     <body id = "body" style = "-rave-layout: grid">
31     <form id = "form" class = "form" method = "post"
32        action = "/WebTime/faces/Time.jsp"
33        enctype = "application/x-www-form-urlencoded">
34        <span id = "form:timeHeader" style = "font-size: 18px; left: 24px;
35           top: 24px; position: absolute">Current time on the Web Server:
36        </span>
37        <span id = "form:clockText" style = "background-color: black;
38           color: yellow; font-size: 18px; left: 24px; top: 48px; position:
39           absolute">1:18:58 AM EDT</span>
40        <input id = "form_hidden" name = "form_hidden"
41           value = "form_hidden" type = "hidden" />
42     </form>
43     </body>
44  </html>
```

Fig. 26.7 | XHTML response generated when the browser requests `Time.jsp`. (Part 2 of 2.)

Lines 30–43 define the body of the document. Line 31 begins the form, a mechanism for collecting user information and sending it to the web server. In this particular program, the user does not submit data to the web server for processing; however, processing user data is a crucial part of many web applications that is facilitated by forms. We demonstrate how to submit data to the server in later examples.

XHTML forms can contain visual and nonvisual components. Visual components include clickable buttons and other GUI components with which users interact. Nonvisual components, called **hidden form elements**, store data, such as e-mail addresses, that the document author specifies. One of these hidden inputs is defined in lines 40–41. We discuss the precise meaning of this hidden input later in the chapter. Attribute method of the form element (line 31) specifies the method by which the web browser submits the form to the server. By default, JSPs use the post method. The two most common HTTP request types (also known as request methods) are get and post. A get request gets (or retrieves) information from a server. Such requests often retrieve an HTML document or an image. A post request posts (or sends) data to a server, such as authentication information or data from a form that gathers user input. Usually, post requests are used to post a message to a news group or a discussion forum, pass user input to a data-handling process on the server and store or update the data on a server. The form's `action` attribute (line 32) identifies the resource that will be requested when this form is submitted—in this case, `/WebTime/faces/Time.jsp`.

Note that the two **Static Text** components (i.e., timeHeader and clockText) are represented by two span elements in the XHTML document (lines 34–36, 37–39) as previously discussed. The formatting options that were specified as properties of timeHeader and clockText, such as the font size and text color in the components, are now specified in each span element's `style` attribute.

26.5.6 Building a Web Application in Java Studio Creator 2

Now that we have presented the JSP file, the page bean file and the resulting XHTML web page sent to the web browser, we discuss the steps to create this application. To build the WebTime application, perform the following steps in Java Studio Creator 2:

Step 1: Creating the Web Application Project
Select **File > New Project...** to display the **New Project** dialog. In this dialog, select **Web** in the **Categories** pane, **JSF Web Application** in the **Projects** pane and click **Next**. Change the project name to WebTime and use the default project location and Java package. These settings will create a WebTime directory in your My Documents\Creator\Projects directory to store the project's files. Click **Finish** to create the web application project.

Step 2: Examining the Visual Editor Window of the New Project
The next several figures describe important features of the IDE, beginning with the Visual Editor window (Fig. 26.8). Java Studio Creator 2 creates a single web page named Page1 when a new project is created. This page is open by default in the Visual Editor in **Design** mode when the project first loads. As you drag and drop new components onto the page,

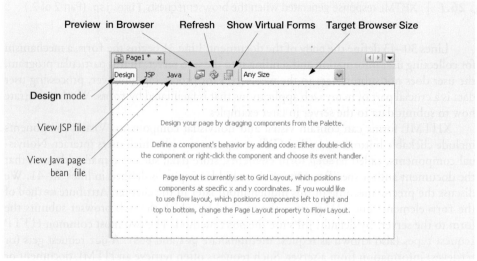

Fig. 26.8 | Visual Editor window in **Design** mode.

Design mode allows you to see how your page will be rendered in the browser. The JSP file for this page, named `Page1.jsp`, can be viewed by clicking the **JSP** button at the top of the Visual Editor or by right clicking anywhere in the Visual Editor and selecting **Edit JSP Source**. As mentioned previously, each web page is supported by a page bean file. Java Studio Creator 2 creates a file named `Page1.java` when a new project is created. To open this file, click the **Java** button at the top of the Visual Editor or right click anywhere in the Visual Editor and select **Edit Page1 Java Source**.

The **Preview in Browser** button at the top of the Visual Editor window allows you to view your pages in a browser without having to build and run the application. The **Refresh** button redraws the page in the Visual Editor. The **Show Virtual Forms** button allows you to see which form elements are participating in virtual forms (we discuss this concept in Chapter 27). The **Target Browser Size** drop-down list lets you specify the optimal browser resolution for viewing the page and lets you see what the page will look like in different screen resolutions.

Step 3: Examining the **Palette** in Java Studio Creator 2

Figure 26.9 shows the **Palette** displayed in the IDE when the project loads. Part (a) displays the beginning of the **Basic** list of web components, and part (b) displays the remaining **Basic** components, as well as the list of **Layout** components. We discuss specific components in Fig. 26.9 as they are used throughout the chapter.

Step 4: Examining the **Projects** Window

Figure 26.10 displays the **Projects** window, which appears in the lower-right corner of the IDE. This window displays the hierarchy of all files included in the project. The JSP files for each page are listed under the **Web Pages** node. This node also includes the **resources**

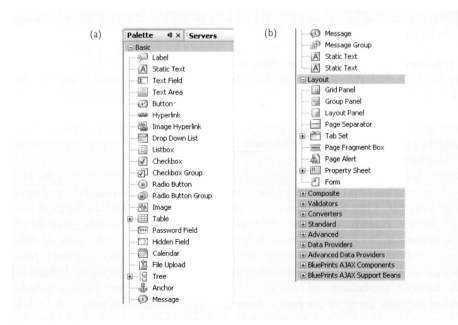

Fig. 26.9 | **Palette** in Java Studio Creator 2.

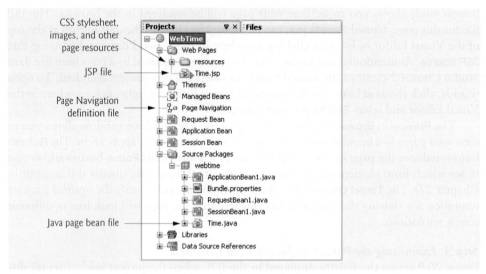

CSS stylesheet, images, and other page resources

JSP file

Page Navigation definition file

Java page bean file

Fig. 26.10 | **Projects** window for the `WebTime` project.

folder, which contains the CSS stylesheet for the project and any other files the pages may need to display properly, such as image files. All of the Java source code, including the page bean file for each web page and the application, session and request scope beans, can be found under the **Source Packages** node. Another useful file displayed in the project window is the **Page Navigation** file, which defines rules for navigating the project's pages based on the outcome of some user-initiated event, such as clicking a button or a link. The **Page Navigation** file can also be accessed by right clicking in the Visual Editor while in **Design** mode and selecting **Page Navigation…**.

Step 5: Examining the JSP and Java Files in the IDE
Figure 26.11 displays `Page1.jsp`—the JSP file generated by Java Studio Creator 2 for `Page1`. [*Note:* We reformatted the code to match our coding conventions.] Click the **JSP** button at the top of the Visual Editor to open the JSP file. When it is first created, this file contains some tags for setting up the page, including linking to the page's stylesheet and defining the necessary JSF libraries. Otherwise, the JSP file's tags are empty, as no components have been added to the page yet.

Figure 26.12 displays part of `Page1.java`—the page bean file generated by Java Studio Creator 2 for `Page1`. Click the **Java** button at the top of the Visual Editor to open the page bean file. This file contains a Java class with the same name as the page (i.e., `Page1`), which extends the class `AbstractPageBean`. As previously mentioned, `AbstractPageBean` has several methods that manage the page's life cycle. Four of these methods—`init`, `preprocess`, `prerender` and `destroy`—are overridden by `Page1.java`. Other than method `init`, these methods are initially empty. They serve as placeholders for you to customize the behavior of your web application. The page bean file also includes *get* and *set* methods for all of the page's elements—page, `html`, `head`, `body` and `link` to start. You can view these *get* and *set* methods by clicking the plus (+) sign on the line that says **Creator-managed Component Definition**.

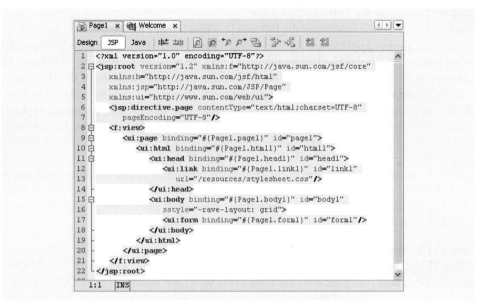

Fig. 26.11 | JSP file generated for Page1 by Java Studio Creator 2.

Click this plus (+) sign to display the hidden generated code

Fig. 26.12 | Page bean file for `Page1.jsp` generated by Java Studio Creator 2.

Step 6: Renaming the JSP and JSF Files

Typically, you'll want to rename the JSP and Java files in your project, so that their names are relevant to your application. Right click the `Page1.jsp` file in the **Projects Window** and select **Rename** to display the **Rename** dialog. Enter the new file name `Time`. If **Preview All Changes** is checked, the **Refactoring Window** will appear at the bottom of the IDE when you click **Next >**. Refactoring is the process of modifying source code to improve its readability and reusability without changing its behavior—for example, by renaming methods or variables, or breaking long methods into shorter ones. Java Studio Creator 2 has built-in refactoring tools that automate some refactoring tasks. Using these tools to rename the project files updates the name of both the JSP file and the page bean file. The refactoring tool also changes the class name in the page bean file and all of the attribute bindings in the JSP file to reflect the new class name. Note that none of these changes will be made until you click **Do Refactoring** in the **Refactoring Window**. If you do not preview the changes, refactoring occurs when you click **Next >** in the **Rename** dialog.

Step 7: Changing the Title of the Page

Before designing the content of the web page, we give it the title `"Web Time: A Simple Example"`. By default, the page does not have a title when it is generated by the IDE. To add a title, open the JSP file in **Design** mode. In the **Properties** window, enter the new title next to the **Title** property and press *Enter*. View the JSP to see that the attribute `title = "Web Time: A Simple Example"` was automatically added to the `ui:head` tag.

Step 8: Designing the Page

Designing a web page is simple in Java Studio Creator 2. To add components to the page, you can drag and drop them from the **Palette** onto the page in **Design** mode. Like the web page itself, each component is an object that has properties, methods and events. You can set these properties and events visually using the **Properties** window or programmatically in the page bean file. *Get* and *set* methods are automatically added to the page bean file for each component you add to the page.

The IDE generates the JSP tags for the components you drag and drop using a grid layout, as specified in the `ui:body` tag. This means that components will be rendered to the browser using absolute positioning, so that they appear exactly where they are dropped on the page. As you add components to the page, the `style` attribute in each component's JSP element will include the number of pixels from the top and left margins of the page at which the component is positioned.

In this example, we use two **Static Text** components. To add the first one to the web page, drag and drop it from the **Palette's Basic** components list to the page in **Design** mode. Edit the component's text by typing `"Current time on the Web Server:"` directly into the component. The text can also be edited by changing the component's `text` property in the **Properties** window. Java Studio Creator 2 is a WYSIWYG (What You See Is What You Get) editor—whenever you make a change to a web page in **Design** mode, the IDE creates the markup (visible in **JSP** mode) necessary to achieve the desired visual effects seen in **Design** mode. After adding the text to the web page, switch to **JSP** mode. You should see that the IDE added a `ui:staticText` element to the page body, which is bound to the object `staticText1`, in the page bean file and whose `text` attribute matches the text you just entered. Back in **Design** mode, click the **Static Text** component to select it. In the **Properties** window, click the ellipsis button next to the style property to open a dialog box to edit the text's style. Select 18 px for the font size and click **OK**. Again in the **Properties** window, change the id property to timeHeader. Setting the id property also changes the name of the component's corresponding property in the page bean and updates its binding attribute in the JSP accordingly. Notice that font-size: 18 px has been added to style attribute and the id attribute has been changed to timeHeader in the component's tag in the JSP file. The IDE should now appear as in Fig. 26.13.

Drop a second **Static Text** component onto the page and set its id to clockText. Edit its style property so that the font size is 18 px, the text color is yellow, and the background color is black. Do not edit the component's text, as this will be set programmatically in the page bean file. The component will display with the text *Static Text* in the IDE, but will not display any text at runtime unless the text is set programmatically. Figure 26.14 shows the IDE after the second component is added.

Step 9: Adding Page Logic

After designing the user interface, you can modify the page bean file to set the text of the clockText element. In this example, we add a statement to method prerender (lines 170–174 of Fig. 26.6). Recall that we use method prerender to ensure that clockText will be updated each time the page is refreshed. Lines 172–173 of Fig. 26.6 programmatically set the text of clockText to the current time on the server.

We would like this page to refresh automatically to display an up-to-date time. To accomplish this, add the empty tag <ui:meta content = "60" httpEquiv = "refresh" /> to the JSP file, between the end of the ui:head tag and the beginning of the ui:body tag. This tag tells browser to reload the page automatically every 60 seconds. You can also add this tag by dragging a **Meta** component from the **Advanced** section of the **Palette** to your page, then setting the component's content attribute to 60 and its httpEquiv attribute to refresh.

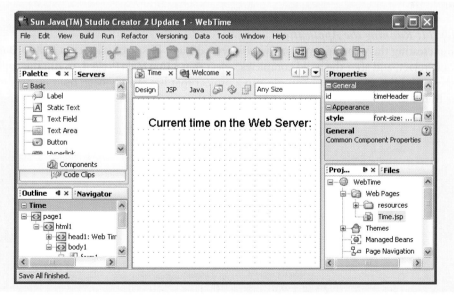

Fig. 26.13 | Time.jsp after inserting the first **Static Text** component.

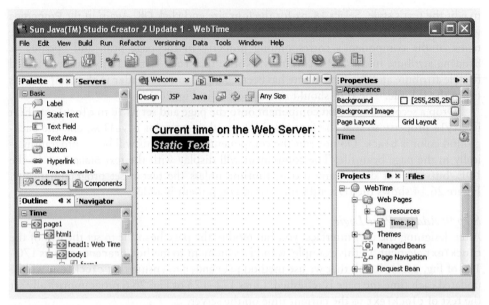

Fig. 26.14 | `Time.jsp` after adding the second `Static Text` component.

Step 10: Examining the Outline Window

Figure 26.15 displays the **Outline window** in Java Studio Creator 2. The project's four Java files are displayed as gray nodes. The **Time** node representing the page bean file is expanded and shows the contents of the component tree. The request, session and application scope beans are collapsed by default, as we have not added any properties to these beans in this example. Clicking an item in the page's component tree selects the item in the Visual Editor.

Step 11: Running the Application

After creating the web page, you can view it several ways. First, you can select **Build > Build Main Project**, and after the build completes, select **Run > Run Main Project**, to run the application in a browser window. You can run a project that has already been built by pressing the **Run Main Project** icon (⬦) in the toolbar at the top of the IDE. Note that if changes

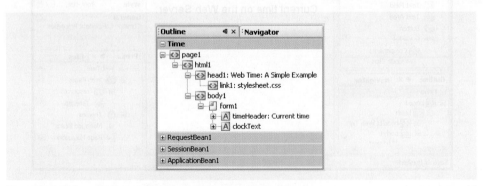

Fig. 26.15 | **Outline** window in Java Studio Creator 2.

are made to a project, the project must be rebuilt before they will be reflected when the application is viewed in a browser. Because this application was built on the local file system, the URL displayed in the address bar of the browser when the application is run will be `http://localhost:29080/WebTime/` (Fig. 26.6), where 29080 is the port number on which Java Studio Creator 2's built-in test server—Sun Application Server 8—runs by default. When you run a program on the test server, a tray icon appears near the bottom-right of your screen to show that the Sun Application Server is running. To shut down the server after you exit Java Studio Creator 2, right click the tray icon and select **Stop Domain creator**.

Alternatively, you can press *F5* to build the application, then run it in debug mode—the Java Studio Creator 2 built-in debugger can help you troubleshoot applications. If you type *<Ctrl> F5*, the program executes without debugging enabled.

Error-Prevention Tip 26.1

*If you have trouble building your project due to errors in the Java Studio Creator-generated XML files used for building, try cleaning the project and building again. You can do this by selecting **Build > Clean and Build Main Project** or by pressing <Alt> B.*

Finally, you can run your built application by opening a browser window and typing the web page's URL in the **Address** field. Since your application resides on the local file system, you must first start the Sun Application Server. If you have previously run the application using one of the methods above, the server will already be started. Otherwise, you can start the server from the IDE by opening the **Servers** tab (located in the same panel as the **Palette**), right clicking the **Deployment Server**, selecting **Start/Stop Server**, and clicking **Start** in the dialog that appears. Then you can type the URL (including the port number for the application server, 29080) in the browser to execute the application. For this example it is not necessary to type the entire URL, `http://localhost:29080/WebTime/faces/Time.jsp`. The path to the file `Time.jsp` (i.e., `faces/Time.jsp`) can be omitted, because this file was set by default as the project's start page. For projects with multiple pages, you can change the start page by right clicking the desired page in the **Projects** window and selecting **Set As Start Page**. The start page is indicated by a green arrow next to the page's name in the **Projects** window. [*Note:* If you use the Netbeans Visual Web Pack 5.5, the port number will depend on the server to which you deploy your web application. Also, the **Servers** tab is called **Runtime** in Netbeans.]

26.6 **JSF Components**

This section introduces some of the JSF components featured in the **Palette** (Fig. 26.9). Figure 26.16 summarizes some of the JSF components used in the chapter examples.

JSF Components	Description
Label	Displays text that can be associated with an input element.
Static Text	Displays text that the user cannot edit.
Text Field	Gathers user input and displays text.

Fig. 26.16 | Commonly used JSF components. (Part 1 of 2.)

JSF Components	Description
Button	Triggers an event when clicked.
Hyperlink	Displays a hyperlink.
Drop Down List	Displays a drop-down list of choices.
Radio Button Group	Groups radio buttons.
Image	Displays images (e.g., GIF and JPG).

Fig. 26.16 | Commonly used JSF components. (Part 2 of 2.)

26.6.1 Text and Graphics Components

Figure 26.17 displays a simple form for gathering user input. This example uses all the components listed in Fig. 26.16, except Label, which you will see in later examples. All the code in Fig. 26.17 was generated by Java Studio Creator 2 in response to actions performed in **Design** mode. This example does not perform any tasks when the user clicks **Register**. We ask you to add functionality to this example as an exercise. In successive examples, we demonstrate how to add functionality to many of these JSF components.

```
1   <?xml version = "1.0" encoding = "UTF-8"?>
2
3   <!-- Fig. 26.17: WebComponents.jsp -->
4   <!-- Registration form that demonstrates JSF components. -->
5   <jsp:root version = "1.2" xmlns:f = "http://java.sun.com/jsf/core"
6      xmlns:h = "http://java.sun.com/jsf/html" xmlns:jsp =
7      "http://java.sun.com/JSP/Page" xmlns:ui = "http://www.sun.com/web/ui">
8      <jsp:directive.page contentType = "text/html; charset = UTF-8"
9         pageEncoding = "UTF-8"/>
10     <f:view>
11        <ui:page binding = "#{WebComponents.page}" id = "page">
12           <ui:html binding = "#{WebComponents.html}" id = "html">
13              <ui:head binding = "#{WebComponents.head}" id = "head">
14                 <ui:link binding = "#{WebComponents.link}" id = "link"
15                    url = "/resources/stylesheet.css"/>
16              </ui:head>
17              <ui:body binding = "#{WebComponents.body}" id = "body"
18                 style = "-rave-layout: grid">
19                 <ui:form binding = "#{WebComponents.form}" id = "form">
20                    <ui:staticText binding = "#{WebComponents.header}"
21                       id = "header" style = "font-size: 18px; left: 24px;
22                       top: 24px; position: absolute" text = "This is a
23                       sample registration form."/>
24                    <ui:staticText binding = "#{WebComponents.instructions}"
25                       id = "instructions" style = "font-style: italic;
26                       left: 24px; top: 72px; position: absolute" text =
27                       "Please fill in all fields and click Register."/>
```

Fig. 26.17 | Registration form that demonstrates JSF components. (Part 1 of 3.)

```
28      <ui:image binding = "#{WebComponents.userImage}" id =
29         "userImage" style = "left: 24px; top: 120px;
30         position: absolute" url = "/resources/user.JPG"/>
31      <h:panelGrid binding = "#{WebComponents.gridPanel}"
32         columns = "4" id = "gridPanel" style = "height: 96px;
33         left: 24px; top: 168px; position: absolute"
34         width = "576">
35         <ui:image binding = "#{WebComponents.fnameImage}"
36            id = "fnameImage" url = "/resources/fname.png"/>
37         <ui:textField binding = "#{WebComponents.fnameTf}"
38            id = "fnameTf"/>
39         <ui:image binding = "#{WebComponents.lnameImage}"
40            id = "lnameImage" url = "/resources/lname.JPG"/>
41         <ui:textField binding = "#{WebComponents.lnameTF}"
42            id = "lnameTF"/>
43         <ui:image binding = "#{WebComponents.emailImage}"
44            id = "emailImage" url = "/resources/email.JPG"/>
45         <ui:textField binding = "#{WebComponents.emailTF}"
46            id = "emailTF"/>
47         <ui:image binding = "#{WebComponents.phoneImage}"
48            id = "phoneImage" url = "/resources/phone.JPG"/>
49         <ui:textField binding = "#{WebComponents.phoneTF}"
50            id = "phoneTF" label = "Must be in the form (555)
51            555-5555"/>
52      </h:panelGrid>
53      <ui:image binding = "#{WebComponents.publicationsImage}"
54         id = "publicationsImage" style = "position: absolute;
55         left: 24px; top: 288px" url =
56         "/resources/publications.JPG"/>
57      <ui:staticText binding =
58         "#{WebComponents.publicationLabel}" id =
59         "publicationLabel" style = "left: 240px; top: 288px;
60         position: absolute" text = "Which book would you like
61         information about?"/>
62      <ui:dropDown binding = "#{WebComponents.booksDropDown}"
63         id = "bookcDropDown" items = "#{WebComponents.
64         booksDropDownDefaultOptions.options}" style = "left:
65         24px; top: 336px; position: absolute; width: 240px"/>
66      <ui:hyperlink binding = "#{WebComponents.deitelLink}"
67         id = "deitelLink" style = "left: 24px; top: 384px;
68         position: absolute" target = "_blank" text = "Click
69         here for more information about our books."
70         url = "http://www.deitel.com"/>
71      <ui:image binding = "#{WebComponents.osImage}" id =
72         "osImage" style = "position: absolute; left: 24px;
73         top: 432px" url = "/resources/os.JPG"/>
74      <ui:staticText binding = "#{WebComponents.osLabel}" id =
75         "osLabel" style = "left: 240px; top: 432px; position:
76         absolute" text = "Which operating system are you
77         using?"/>
78      <ui:radioButtonGroup binding =
79         "#{WebComponents.osRadioButtonGroup}" id =
80         "osRadioButtonGroup" items = "#{WebComponents.
```

Fig. 26.17 | Registration form that demonstrates JSF components. (Part 2 of 3.)

```
81                          osRadioButtonGroupDefaultOptions.options}"  style =
82                          "left: 24px; top: 504px; position: absolute"/>
83                       <ui:button binding = "#{WebComponents.registerButton}"
84                          id = "registerButton" style = "left: 23px; top:
85                          648px; position: absolute" text = "Register"/>
86                    </ui:form>
87                 </ui:body>
88              </ui:html>
89           </ui:page>
90        </f:view>
91     </jsp:root>
```

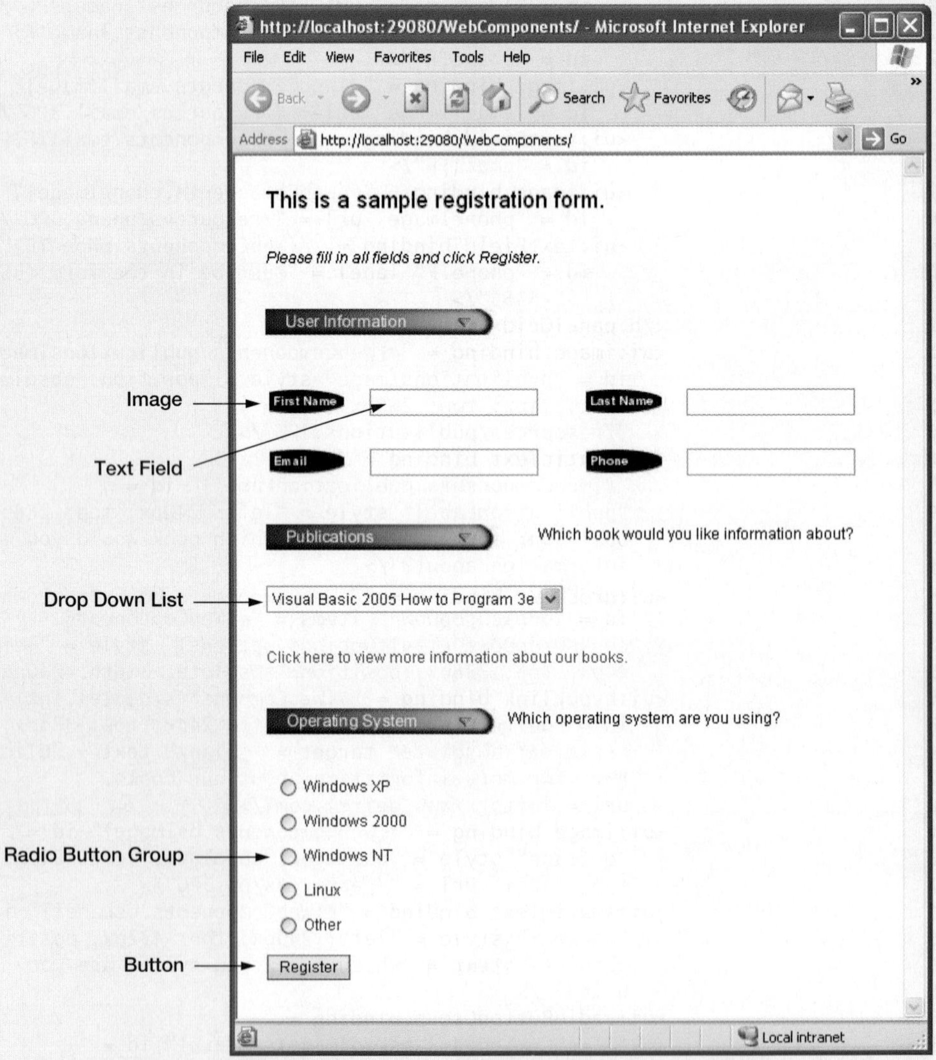

Fig. 26.17 | Registration form that demonstrates JSF components. (Part 3 of 3.)

Before discussing the JSF components used in this JSP file, we explain the XHTML that creates the layout in Fig. 26.17. As discussed previously, Java Studio Creator 2 uses absolute positioning, so components are rendered wherever they were dropped in the Visual Editor. In this example, in addition to absolute positioning, we use a Grid Panel component (lines 31–52) from the **Palette**'s **Layout** component group. The h: prefix indicates that it can be found in the JSF HTML tag library. This component, an object of class HtmlPanelGrid in package javax.faces.component.html, controls the positioning of the components it contains. The **Grid Panel** component allows the designer to specify the number of columns the grid should contain. Components may then be dropped anywhere inside the panel, and they will automatically be repositioned into evenly spaced columns in the order in which they are dropped. When the number of components exceeds the number of columns, the panel moves the additional components to a new row. In this way, the **Grid Panel** behaves like an XHTML table, and is in fact rendered to the browser as an XHTML table. In this example, we use the **Grid Panel** to control the positions of the **Image** and **Text Field** components in the user information section of the page.

Adding a Formatting Component to a Web Page

To create the layout for the **User Information** section of the form shown in Fig. 26.17, drag a **Grid Panel** component onto the page. In the **Properties** window, set the component's columns property to 4. The component also has properties to control the cell padding, cell spacing and other elements of the component's appearance. In this case, accept the defaults for these properties. Now you can simply drag the **Images** and **Text Fields** for user information into the **Grid Panel**. The **Grid Panel** will manage their spacing and their organization into rows and columns.

Examining Web Components on a Sample Registration Form

Lines 28–30 of Fig. 26.17 define an Image component, an object of class Image which inserts an image into a web page. The images used in this example are located in this chapter's examples directory. Images to be displayed on a web page must be placed in the project's resources folder. To add images to the project, drop an **Image** component onto the page and click the ellipsis button next to the url property in the **Properties** window. This opens a dialog in which you can select the image to display. Since no images have been added to the resources folder yet, click the **Add File** button, locate the image on your computer's file system and click **Add File**. This copies the file you selected into the project's resources directory. Now you can select the image from the list of files in the resources folder and click **OK** to insert the image into the page.

Lines 31–52 contain an h:panelGrid element representing the **Grid Panel** component. Within this element, there are eight **Image** and Text Field components. **Text Field**s allow you to obtain text input from the user. For example, lines 37–38 define a **Text Field** control used to collect the user's first name. Lines 49–51 define a **Text Field** with the label property set to "Must be in the form (555) 555-5555". Setting the label property of a **Text Field** places text directly above the **Text Field**. Alternatively, you can label a **Text Field** by dragging and dropping a **Label** component onto the page, which allows you to customize the **Label**'s position and style.

The order in which **Text Fields** are dragged to the page is important, because their JSP tags are added to the JSP file in that order. When a user presses the *Tab* key to navigate between input fields, they will navigate the fields in the order in which the JSP tags occur in the JSP file. To specify the navigation order, you should drag components onto the page in that order. Alternatively, you can set each input field's **Tab Index** property in the **Properties** window to control the order in which the user will tab through the fields. A component with a tab index of 1 will be the first in the tab sequence.

Lines 62–65 define a **Drop Down List**. When a user clicks the drop-down list, it expands and displays a list from which the user can make a selection. This component is an object of class DropDownList and is bound to the object booksDropDown, a SingleSelectOptionsList object that controls the list of options. This object can be configured automatically by right clicking the drop-down list in **Design** mode and selecting **Configure Default Options**, which opens the **Options Customizer** dialog box to add options to the list. Each option consists of a display String that will represent the option in the browser and a value String that will be returned when programmatically retrieving the user's selection from the drop-down list. Java Studio Creator 2 constructs the SingleSelectOptionsList object in the page bean file based on the display-value pairs entered in the **Options Customizer** dialog box. To view the code that constructs the object, close the dialog box by clicking **OK**, open the page bean file, and expand the **Creator-managed Component Definition** node near the top of the file. The object is constructed in the _init method, which is called from method init the first time the page loads.

The **Hyperlink** component (lines 66–70) of class Hyperlink adds a link to a web page. The url property of this component specifies the resource (http://www.deitel.com in this case) that is requested when a user clicks the hyperlink. Setting the target property to _blank specifies that the requested web page should open in a new browser window. By default, **Hyperlink** components cause pages to open in the same browser window.

Lines 78–82 define a **Radio Button Group** component of class RadioButtonGroup, which provides a series of radio buttons from which the user can select only one. Like **Drop Down List**, a **Radio Button Group** is bound to a SingleSelectOptionList object. The options can be edited by right clicking the component and selecting **Configure Default Options**. Also like the drop-down list, the SingleSelectOptionsList constructor is automatically generated by the IDE and placed in the _init method of the page bean class.

The final web control in Fig. 26.17 is a **Button** (lines 83–85), a JSF component of class Button that triggers an action when clicked. A **Button** component typically maps to an input XHTML element with attribute type set to submit. As stated earlier, clicking the **Register** button in this example does not do anything.

26.6.2 Validation Using Validator Components and Custom Validators

This section introduces form validation. Validating user input is an important step in collecting information from users. Validation helps prevent processing errors due to incomplete or improperly formatted user input. For example, you may perform validation to ensure that all required fields have been filled out or that a ZIP-code field contains exactly five digits. Java Studio Creator 2 provides three validator components. A **Length Validator** determines whether a field contains an acceptable number of characters. **Double Range Validators** and **Long Range Validators** determine whether numeric input falls within acceptable ranges. Package javax.faces.validators contains the classes for these validators. Studio Creator 2 also allows custom validation with validator methods in the page bean file. The following example demonstrates validation using both a validator component and custom validation.

Validating Form Data in a Web Application

The example in this section prompts the user to enter a name, e-mail address and phone number. After the user enters any data, but before the data is sent to the web server, validation ensures that the user entered a value in each field, that the entered name does not exceed 30 characters, and that the e-mail address and phone number values are in an acceptable format. In this example, (555) 123-4567, 555-123-4567 and 123-4567 are all considered valid phone numbers. Once the data is submitted, the web server responds by displaying an appropriate message and a **Grid Panel** component repeating the submitted information. Note that a real business application would typically store the submitted data in a database or in a file on the server. We simply send the data back to the page to demonstrate that the server received the data.

Building the Web Page

This web application introduces two additional JSF components—**Label** and **Message** from the **Basic** section of the **Palette**. Each of the page's three text fields should have its own label and message. **Label** components describe other components and can be associated with user input fields by setting their for property. **Message** components display error messages when validation fails. This page requires three **Text Fields**, three **Labels** and three **Messages**, as well as a submit **Button**. To associate the **Label** components and **Message** components with their corresponding **Text Field** components, hold the *Ctrl* and *Shift* keys, then drag the label or message to the appropriate **Text Field**. In the **Properties** window, notice that each **Label** and **Message** component's for property is set to the appropriate **Text Field**.

You should also add a **Static Text** component to display a validation success message at the bottom of the page. Set the text to "Thank you for your submission.
We received the following information:" and change the component's id to resultText. In the **Properties** window, unset the component's rendered and escaped properties. The rendered property controls whether the component will be displayed the first time the page loads. Setting escaped to false enables the browser to recognize the <br/> tag so it can start a new line of text rather than display the characters "<br/>" in the web page.

Finally, add a **Grid Panel** component below the resultText component. The panel should have two columns, one for displaying **Static Text** components that label the user's validated data, and one for displaying **Static Text** components that echo back that data.

The JSP file for this page is displayed in Fig. 26.18. Lines 30–34, 35–39 and 40–44 define ui:textFields for retrieving the user's name, e-mail address and phone number, respectively. Lines 45–48, 49–53, and 54–58 define ui:labels for each of these text fields. Lines 63–74 define the text fields' ui:message elements. Lines 59–62 define a **Submit** ui:button. Lines 75–80 create a ui:staticText named resultText that displays the response from the server when the user successfully submits the form, and lines 81–101 define a ui:panelGrid that contains components for echoing validated user input to the browser.

*Setting the **Required** Property of an Input Component*

Ensuring that the user has made a selection or entered some text in a required input element is a basic type of validation. This is accomplished by checking the required box in the element's **Properties** window. If you add a validator component or custom validator method to an input field, the field's required property must be set to true for validation to occur. Notice that the three input ui:textFields in this example (Fig. 26.18, lines 30–44) all have their required property set to true. Also note in the Visual Editor that the label for a required field is automatically marked by a red asterisk. If a user submits this form with empty text fields, the default error message for a required field will be displayed in the empty field's associated ui:message component.

```
1    <?xml version = "1.0" encoding = "UTF-8"?>
2
3    <!-- Fig. 26.18: Validation.jsp -->
4    <!-- JSP that demonstrates validation of user input. -->
5    <jsp:root version = "1.2" xmlns:f = "http://java.sun.com/jsf/core"
6       xmlns:h = "http://java.sun.com/jsf/html" xmlns:jsp =
7       "http://java.sun.com/JSP/Page" xmlns:ui = "http://www.sun.com/web/ui">
8       <jsp:directive.page contentType = "text/html; charset = UTF-8"
9          pageEncoding = "UTF-8"/>
10      <f:view>
11         <ui:page binding = "#{Validation.page}" id = "page">
12            <ui:html binding = "#{Validation.html}" id = "html">
13               <ui:head binding = "#{Validation.head}" id = "head"
14                  title = "Validation">
15                  <ui:link binding = "#{Validation.link}" id = "link"
16                     url = "/resources/stylesheet.css"/>
17               </ui:head>
18               <ui:body binding = "#{Validation.body}" focus = "form1:nameTF"
19                  id = "body" style = "-rave-layout: grid">
20                  <ui:form binding = "#{Validation.form}" id = "form">
21                     <ui:staticText binding = "#{Validation.header}" id =
22                        "header" style = "font-size: 16px; height: 22px;
23                        left: 24px; top: 24px; position: absolute; width:
24                        456px" text = "Please fill out the following form."/>
25                     <ui:staticText binding = "#{Validation.instructions}"
26                        id = "instructions" style = "font-size: 14px;
27                        font-style: italic; left: 24px; top: 48px; position:
28                        absolute; width: 406px" text = "All fields are
29                        required and must contain valid information."/>
30                     <ui:textField binding = "#{Validation.nameTF}" columns =
31                        "30" id = "nameTF" required = "true" style = "left:
32                        168px; top: 96px; position: absolute; width: 216px"
33                        validator =
34                        "#{Validation.nameLengthValidator.validate}"/>
35                     <ui:textField binding = "#{Validation.emailTF}"
36                        columns = "28" id = "emailTF" required = "true"
37                        style = "left: 168px; top: 144px; position: absolute;
38                        width: 216px" validator =
39                        "#{Validation.emailTF_validate}"/>
40                     <ui:textField binding = "#{Validation.phoneTF}"
41                        columns = "30" id = "phoneTF" required = "true"
42                        style = "left: 168px; top: 192px; position: absolute;
43                        width: 216px" validator =
44                        "#{Validation.phoneTF_validate}"/>
45                     <ui:label binding = "#{Validation.nameLabel}" for =
46                        "nameTF" id = "nameLabel" style = "font-weight:
```

Fig. 26.18 | JSP that demonstrates validation of user input. (Part 1 of 4.)

```
47          normal; height: 24px; left: 24px; top: 96px;
48          position: absolute; width: 94px" text = "Name:"/>
49      <ui:label binding = "#{Validation.emailLabel}" for =
50          "emailTF" id = "emailLabel" style = "font-weight:
51          normal; height: 24px; left: 24px; top: 144px;
52          position: absolute; width: 142px" text =
53          "Email Address:"/>
54      <ui:label binding = "#{Validation.phoneLabel}" for =
55          "phoneTF" id = "phoneLabel" style = "font-weight:
56          normal; height: 24px; left: 24px; top: 192px;
57          position: absolute; width: 142px" text =
58          "Phone number:"/>
59      <ui:button action = "#{Validation.submitButton_action}"
60          binding = "#{Validation.submitButton}" id =
61          "submitButton" style = "left: 23px; top: 240px;
62          position: absolute; width: 72px" text = "Submit"/>
63      <ui:message binding = "#{Validation.emailMessage}" for =
64          "emailTF" id = "emailMessage" showDetail = "false"
65          showSummary = "true" style = "left: 408px; top:
66          144px; position: absolute"/>
67      <ui:message binding = "#{Validation.phoneMessage}" for =
68          "phoneTF" id = "phoneMessage" showDetail = "false"
69          showSummary = "true" style = "left: 408px; top:
70          192px; position: absolute"/>
71      <ui:message binding = "#{Validation.nameMessage}" for =
72          "nameTF" id = "nameMessage" showDetail = "false"
73          showSummary = "true" style = "left: 408px; top: 96px;
74          position: absolute"/>
75      <ui:staticText binding = "#{Validation.resultText}"
76          escape = "false" id = "resultText" rendered = "false"
77          style = "height: 46px; left: 24px; top: 288px;
78          position: absolute; width: 312px" text = "Thank you
79          for your submission.&#xa;&lt;br/&gt;We received the
80          following information:"/>
81      <h:panelGrid bgcolor = "seashell" binding =
82          "#{Validation.gridPanel}" columns = "2" id =
83          "gridPanel" rendered = "false" style = "height: 96px;
84          left: 24px; top: 336px; position: absolute"
85          width = "312">
86          <ui:staticText binding =
87              "#{Validation.nameResultLabel}" id =
88              "nameResultLabel" text = "Name:"/>
89          <ui:staticText binding = "#{Validation.nameResult}"
90              id = "nameResult"/>
91          <ui:staticText binding =
92              "#{Validation.emailResultLabel}" id =
93              "emailResultLabel" text = "E-mail address:"/>
94          <ui:staticText binding = "#{Validation.emailResult}"
95              id = "emailResult"/>
96          <ui:staticText binding =
97              "#{Validation.phoneResultLabel}" id =
98              "phoneResultLabel" text ="Phone number:"/>
```

Fig. 26.18 | JSP that demonstrates validation of user input. (Part 2 of 4.)

```
99                        <ui:staticText binding = "#{Validation.phoneResult}"
100                            id = "phoneResult"/>
101                  </h:panelGrid>
102               </ui:form>
103            </ui:body>
104         </ui:html>
105      </ui:page>
106   </f:view>
107 </jsp:root>
```

(a)

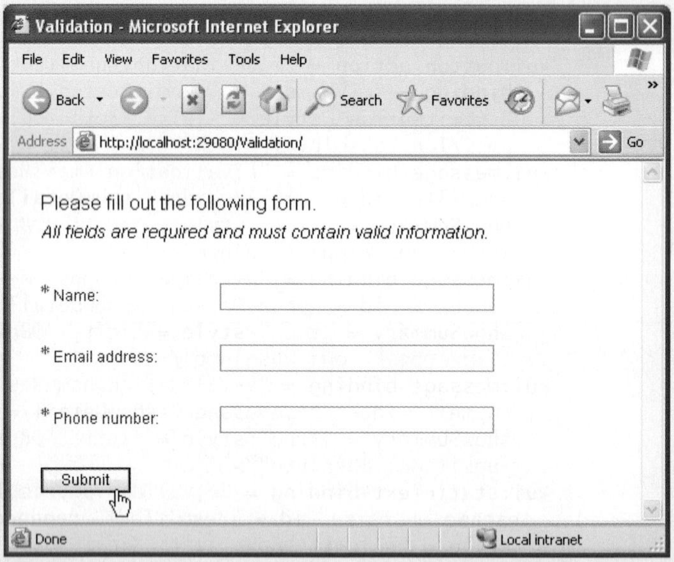

(b)

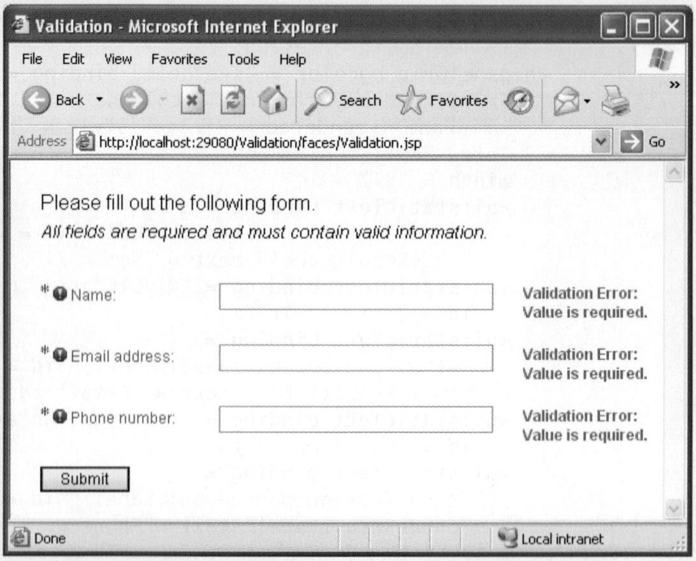

Fig. 26.18 | JSP that demonstrates validation of user input. (Part 3 of 4.)

(c)

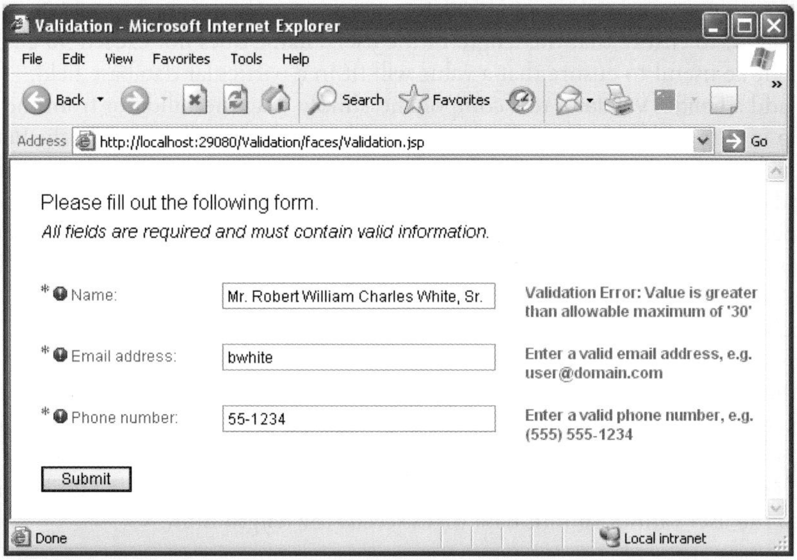

(d)

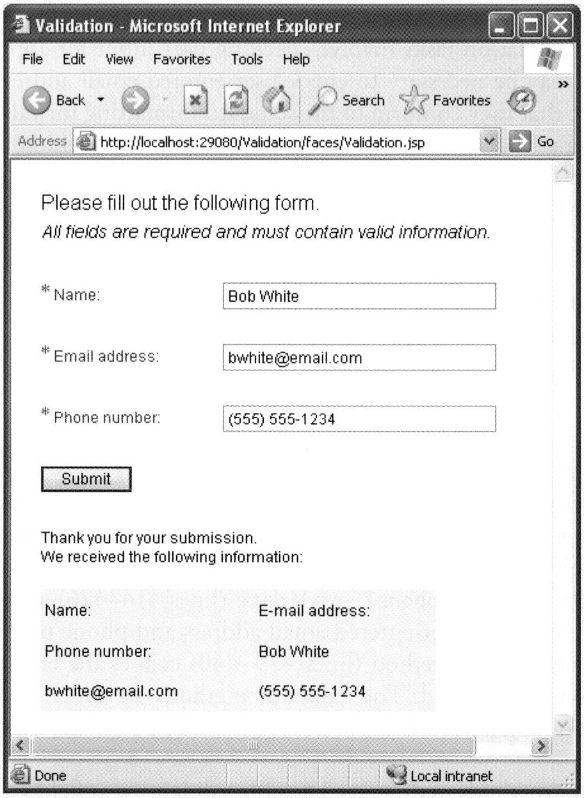

Fig. 26.18 | JSP that demonstrates validation of user input. (Part 4 of 4.)

Using the **LengthValidator** *Component*

In this example, we use the **Length Validator** component (found in the **Validators** section of the **Palette**) to ensure that the length of the user's name does not exceed 30 characters. This might be useful to ensure that a value will fit in a particular database field.

To add a **Length Validator** to a component, simply drag the validator from the **Palette** and drop it onto the field to validate. A **lengthValidator** node will appear in the **Validation** section of the **Outline** window. To edit the validation component's properties, click this node and set the maximum and minimum properties to the desired number of characters in the **Properties** window. Here, we set only the maximum property to 30. We also changed the component's id to nameLengthValidator. Notice that the nameTF input field in the JSP file has been bound to the validate method of the property nameLengthValidator in the page bean file (lines 33–34).

This validator allows users to type as much text in the field as they wish, and if they exceed the limit, the default length validation error message will be displayed in the field's ui:message component after the user clicks the **Submit** button. It is possible to limit the length of user input without using validation. By setting a **Text Field**'s maxLength property, the **Text Field**'s cursor will not advance beyond the maximum allowable number of characters, so the user cannot submit data that exceeds the length limit.

Using Regular Expressions to Perform Custom Validation

Some of the most common validation tasks involve checking user input for appropriate formatting. For instance, it may be necessary to check user-entered email addresses and telephone numbers to ensure that they conform to the standard formatting for valid email addresses and phone numbers. Matching user input against a regular expression is an effective way to ensure that the input is properly formatted. (We discuss regular expressions in Section 30.7.) Java Studio Creator 2 does not provide components for validation using regular expressions, so we will add our own custom validator methods to the page bean file. To add a custom validator to an input component, right-click the component and select **Edit Event Handler > validate**. This creates a validation method for the component with an empty body in the page bean file. We'll add code to this method shortly. Note that both emailTF and phoneTF's validate attributes are bound to their respective custom validation methods in the page bean file (lines 38–39 and 43–44).

Examining the Page Bean File for a Form That Receives User Input

Figure 26.19 contains the page bean file for the JSP file in Fig. 26.18. Line 33 sets the maximum length for the nameLengthValidator, which is a property of this page bean. Recall that the name text field was bound to this property in the JSP file. Method emailTF_validate (lines 398–410) and phoneTF_validate (lines 414–426) are the custom validator methods that verify the user-entered email address and phone number, respectively. The submitButton_action method (lines 429–440) echoes the entered data back to the user if validation is successful. The validator methods are called before the event handler, so if validation fails, submitButton_action will not be called and the user input will not be echoed.

The two custom validator methods in this page bean file validate a text field's contents against a regular expression using the String method match, which takes a regular expression as an argument and returns true if the String conforms to the specified format.

```java
 1   // Fig. 26.19: Validation.java
 2   // Page bean for validating user input and redisplaying that input if
 3   // valid.
 4   package validation;
 5
 6   import com.sun.rave.web.ui.appbase.AbstractPageBean;
 7   import com.sun.rave.web.ui.component.Body;
 8   import com.sun.rave.web.ui.component.Form;
 9   import com.sun.rave.web.ui.component.Head;
10   import com.sun.rave.web.ui.component.Html;
11   import com.sun.rave.web.ui.component.Link;
12   import com.sun.rave.web.ui.component.Page;
13   import javax.faces.FacesException;
14   import com.sun.rave.web.ui.component.StaticText;
15   import com.sun.rave.web.ui.component.TextField;
16   import com.sun.rave.web.ui.component.TextArea;
17   import com.sun.rave.web.ui.component.Label;
18   import com.sun.rave.web.ui.component.Button;
19   import com.sun.rave.web.ui.component.Message;
20   import javax.faces.component.UIComponent;
21   import javax.faces.context.FacesContext;
22   import javax.faces.validator.ValidatorException;
23   import javax.faces.application.FacesMessage;
24   import javax.faces.component.html.HtmlPanelGrid;
25   import javax.faces.validator.LengthValidator;
26
27   public class Validation extends AbstractPageBean
28   {
29       private int __placeholder;
30
31       private void _init() throws Exception
32       {
33           nameLengthValidator.setMaximum( 30 );
34       } // end method _init
35
36       // To save space, we omitted the code in lines 36-345. The complete
37       // source code is provided with this chapter's examples.
38
346      public Validation()
347      {
348          // empty constructor
349      } // end constructor
350
351      protected RequestBean getRequestBean()
352      {
353          return (RequestBean) getBean( "RequestBean" );
354      } // end method getRequestBean
355
356      protected ApplicationBean getApplicationBean()
357      {
358          return (ApplicationBean) getBean( "ApplicationBean" );
359      } // end method getApplicationBean
360
```

Fig. 26.19 | Page bean for validating user input and redisplaying that input if valid. (Part 1 of 3.)

```
361     protected SessionBean getSessionBean()
362     {
363        return (SessionBean) getBean( "SessionBean" );
364     } // end method getSessionBean
365
366     public void init()
367     {
368        super.init();
369        try
370        {
371           _init();
372        } // end try
373        catch ( Exception e )
374        {
375           log( "Validation Initialization Failure", e );
376           throw e instanceof FacesException ? (FacesException) e:
377              new FacesException( e );
378        } // end catch
379     } // end method init
380
381     public void preprocess()
382     {
383        // empty body
384     } // end method preprocess
385
386     public void prerender()
387     {
388        // empty body
389     } // end method prerender
390
391     public void destroy()
392     {
393        // empty body
394     } // end method destroy
395
396     // validates entered email address against the regular expression
397     // that represents the form of a valid email address.
398     public void emailTF_validate( FacesContext context,
399        UIComponent component, Object value )
400     {
401        String email = String.valueOf( value );
402
403        // if entered email address is not in a valid format
404        if ( !email.matches(
405           "\\w+([-+.']\\w+)*@\\w+([-.]\\w+)*\\.\\w+([-.]\\w+)*" ) )
406        {
407           throw new ValidatorException( new FacesMessage(
408              "Enter a valid email address, e.g. user@domain.com" ) );
409        } // end if
410     } // end method emailTF_validate
411
412     // validates entered email address against the regular expression
413     // that represents the form of a valid email address.
```

Fig. 26.19 | Page bean for validating user input and redisplaying that input if valid. (Part 2 of 3.)

```
414    public void phoneTF_validate( FacesContext context,
415       UIComponent component, Object value )
416    {
417       String phone = String.valueOf( value );
418
419       // if entered phone number is not in a valid format
420       if ( !phone.matches(
421          "((\\(\\d{3}\\) ?)|(\\d{3}-))?\\d{3}-\\d{4}" ) )
422       {
423          throw new ValidatorException( new FacesMessage(
424             "Enter a valid phone number, e.g. (555) 555-1234" ) );
425       } // end if
426    } // end method phoneTF_validate
427
428    // displays validated form entries in a Grid Panel.
429    public String submitButton_action()
430    {
431       String name = String.valueOf( nameTF.getValue() );
432       String email = String.valueOf( emailTF.getValue() );
433       String phone = String.valueOf( phoneTF.getValue() );
434       nameResult.setValue( name );
435       emailResult.setValue( email );
436       phoneResult.setValue( phone );
437       gridPanel.setRendered( true );
438       resultText.setRendered( true );
439       return null;
440    } // end method submitButton_action
441 } // end class Validation
```

Fig. 26.19 | Page bean for validating user input and redisplaying that input if valid. (Part 3 of 3.)

For the emailTF_validate method, we use the validation expression

```
\w+([-+.']\w+)*@\w+([-.]\w+)*\.\w+([-.]\w+)*
```

Note that each backslash in the regular expression String (line 405) must be escaped with another backslash (as in \\), because the backslash character normally represents the beginning of an escape sequence. This regular expression indicates that an e-mail address is valid if the part before the @ symbol contains one or more word characters (i.e., alphanumeric characters or underscores), followed by zero or more Strings comprised of a hyphen, plus sign, period or apostrophe and additional word characters. After the @ symbol, a valid e-mail address must contain one or more groups of word characters potentially separated by hyphens or periods, followed by a required period and another group of one or more word characters potentially separated by hyphens or periods. For example, the e-mail addresses bob's-personal.email@white.email.com, bob-white@my-email.com and bob.white@email.com are all valid. If the user enters text in emailTF that does not have the correct format and attempts to submit the form, lines 408–408 throw a ValidatorException. The emailMessage component will catch this exception and display the message in red.

The regular expression in phoneTF_validate ensures that the phoneTextBox contains a valid phone number before the form is submitted. The user input is matched against the regular expression

```
((\(\d{3}\) ?)|(\d{3}-))?\d{3}-\d{4}
```

(Again, each backslash is escaped in the regular expression `String` in line 421.) This expression indicates that a phone number can contain a three-digit area code either in parentheses and followed by an optional space or without parentheses and followed by required hyphen. After an optional area code, a phone number must contain three digits, a hyphen and another four digits. For example, (555) 123-4567, 555-123-4567 and 123-4567 are all valid phone numbers. If a user enters an invalid phone number, lines 423–424 throw a `ValidatorException` The `emailMessage` component catches this exception and displays the error message in red.

If all six validators are successful (i.e., each `TextField` contains data, the name is less than 30 characters and the e-mail address and phone number are valid), clicking the **Submit** button sends the form's data to the server. As shown in Fig. 26.18(d), the `submitButton_action` method displays the submitted data in a `gridPanel` (lines 434–437) and a success message in `resultsText` (line 128).

26.7 Session Tracking

In the early days of the internet, e-businesses could not provide the kind of customized service typically experienced in "brick-and-mortar" stores. To address this problem, e-businesses began to establish mechanisms by which they could personalize users' browsing experiences, tailoring content to individual users while enabling them to bypass irrelevant information. Businesses achieve this level of service by tracking each customer's movement through their websites and combining the collected data with information provided by the consumer, including billing information, personal preferences, interests and hobbies.

Personalization
Personalization makes it possible for e-businesses to communicate effectively with their customers and also improves the user's ability to locate desired products and services. Companies that provide content of particular interest to users can establish relationships with customers and build on those relationships over time. Furthermore, by targeting consumers with personal offers, recommendations, advertisements, promotions and services, e-businesses create customer loyalty. Websites can use sophisticated technology to allow visitors to customize home pages to suit their individual needs and preferences. Similarly, online shopping sites often store personal information for customers, tailoring notifications and special offers to their interests. Such services encourage customers to visit sites and make purchases more frequently.

Privacy
A trade-off exists, however, between personalized e-business service and protection of privacy. Some consumers embrace the idea of tailored content, but others fear the possible adverse consequences if the info they provide to e-businesses is released or collected by tracking technologies. Consumers and privacy advocates ask: What if the e-business to which we give personal data sells or gives that information to another organization without our knowledge? What if we do not want our actions on the Internet—a supposedly anonymous medium—to be tracked and recorded by unknown parties? What if unauthorized parties gain access to sensitive private data, such as credit-card numbers or medical history?

All of these are questions that must be debated and addressed by programmers, consumers, e-businesses and lawmakers alike.

Recognizing Clients

To provide personalized services to consumers, e-businesses must be able to recognize clients when they request information from a site. As we have discussed, the request/response system on which the web operates is facilitated by HTTP. Unfortunately, HTTP is a stateless protocol—it does not support persistent connections that would enable web servers to maintain state information regarding particular clients. So, web servers cannot determine whether a request comes from a particular client or whether a series of requests comes from one or several clients. To circumvent this problem, sites can provide mechanisms to identify individual clients. A session represents a unique client on a website. If the client leaves a site and then returns later, the client will still be recognized as the same user. To help the server distinguish among clients, each client must identify itself to the server. Tracking individual clients, known as **session tracking**, can be achieved in a number of ways. One popular technique uses cookies (Section 26.7.1); another uses the SessionBean object (Section 26.7.2). Additional session-tracking techniques include using input form elements of type "hidden" and URL rewriting. With "hidden" form elements, a web form can write session-tracking data into a form in the web page that it returns to the client in response to a prior request. When the user submits the form in the new web page, all the form data, including the "hidden" fields, is sent to the form handler on the web server. With URL rewriting, the web server embeds session-tracking information directly in the URLs of hyperlinks that the user clicks to send subsequent requests to the web server.

26.7.1 Cookies

Cookies provide web developers with a tool for personalizing web pages. A cookie is a piece of data typically stored in a text file on the user's computer. A cookie maintains information about the client during and between browser sessions. The first time a user visits the website, the user's computer might receive a cookie; this cookie is then reactivated each time the user revisits that site. The collected information is intended to be an anonymous record containing data that is used to personalize the user's future visits to the site. For example, cookies in a shopping application might store unique identifiers for users. When a user adds items to an online shopping cart or performs another task resulting in a request to the web server, the server receives a cookie from the client containing the user's unique identifier. The server then uses the unique identifier to locate the shopping cart and perform any necessary processing.

In addition to identifying users, cookies also can indicate clients' shopping preferences. When a web server receives a request from a client, the server can examine the cookie(s) it sent to the client during previous communications, identify the client's preferences and immediately display products of interest to the client.

Every HTTP-based interaction between a client and a server includes a header containing information either about the request (when the communication is from the client to the server) or about the response (when the communication is from the server to the client). When a page receives a request, the header includes information such as the request type (e.g., GET or POST) and any cookies that have been sent previously from the server to be stored on the client machine. When the server formulates its response, the header information contains any cookies the server wants to store on the client computer and other information, such as the MIME type of the response.

The **expiration date** of a cookie determines how long the cookie remains on the client's computer. If you do not set an expiration date for a cookie, the web browser maintains the cookie for the duration of the browsing session. Otherwise, the web browser maintains the cookie until the expiration date occurs. When the browser requests a resource from a web server, cookies previously sent to the client by that web server are returned to the web server as part of the request formulated by the browser. Cookies are deleted when they **expire**.

> **Portability Tip 26.1**
>
> *Clients may disable cookies in their web browsers for more privacy. When such clients use web applications that depend on cookies to maintain state information, the applications will not execute correctly.*

Using Cookies to Provide Book Recommendations

The next web application shows how to use cookies. The example contains two pages. In the first page (Figs. 26.20 and 26.22), users select a favorite programming language from a group of radio buttons and submit the form to the web server for processing. The web server responds by creating a cookie that stores the selected language and the ISBN number for a recommended book on that topic. The server then renders new components in the browser that allow the user either to select another favorite programming language or to view the second page in our application (Figs. 26.23–26.24), which lists recommended books pertaining to the programming language(s) that the user selected. When the user clicks the hyperlink, the cookies previously stored on the client are read and used to form the list of book recommendations.

The JSP file in Fig. 26.20 contains a **Radio Button Group** (lines 26–39) with the options **Java, C, C++, Visual Basic 2005**, and **Visual C# 2005**. Recall that you can set the display and value Strings of radio buttons by right clicking the **Radio Button Group** and selecting **Configure Default Options**. The user selects a programming language by clicking one of the radio buttons. When the user presses the **Submit** button, the web application creates a cookie containing the selected language. This cookie is added to the HTTP response header and sent to the client as part of the response.

When **Submit** is clicked, the ui:label, ui:radioButtonGroup and ui:button elements used to select a language are hidden, and a ui:staticText and two ui:hyperlink elements are displayed. Each ui:staticText and ui:hyperlink initially has its rendered property set to false (lines 31, 37, and 43). This indicates that these components are not visible the first time the page loads, as we want the user's first view of the page to include only the components for selecting a programming language and submitting the selection.

```
1   <?xml version = "1.0" encoding = "UTF-8"?>
2
3   <!-- Fig. 26.20: Options.jsp -->
4   <!-- JSP file that allows the user to select a programming language. -->
```

Fig. 26.20 | JSP file that allows the user to select a programming language. (Part 1 of 4.)

```jsp
5    <jsp:root version = "1.2" xmlns:f = "http://java.sun.com/jsf/core"
6       xmlns:h = "http://java.sun.com/jsf/html" xmlns:jsp =
7       "http://java.sun.com/JSP/Page" xmlns:ui = "http://www.sun.com/web/ui">
8       <jsp:directive.page contentType = "text/html; charset = UTF-8"
9          pageEncoding = "UTF-8"/>
10      <f:view>
11         <ui:page binding = "#{Options.page}" id = "page">
12            <ui:html binding = "#{Options.html}" id = "html">
13               <ui:head binding = "#{Options.head}" id = "head" title =
14                  "Options">
15                  <ui:link binding = "#{Options.link}" id = "link"
16                     url = "/resources/stylesheet.css"/>
17               </ui:head>
18               <ui:body binding = "#{Options.body}" id = "body"
19                  style = "-rave-layout: grid">
20                  <ui:form binding = "#{Options.form}" id = "form">
21                     <ui:label binding = "#{Options.languageLabel}" for =
22                        "languageList" id = "languageLabel" style =
23                        "font-size: 16px; font-weight: bold; left: 24px; top:
24                        24px; position: absolute" text = "Select a
25                        programming language:"/>
26                     <ui:radioButtonGroup binding = "#{Options.languageList}"
27                        id = "languageList" items =
28                        "#{Options.languageListOptions.options}" style =
29                        "left: 24px; top: 48px; position: absolute"/>
30                     <ui:staticText binding = "#{Options.responseLabel}" id =
31                        "responseLabel" rendered = "false" style =
32                        "font-size: 16px; font-weight: bold; height: 24px;
33                        left: 24px; top: 24px; position: absolute;
34                        width: 216px"/>
35                     <ui:hyperlink action = "#{Options.languagesLink_action}"
36                        binding = "#{Options.languagesLink}" id =
37                        "languagesLink" rendered = "false" style = "left:
38                        24px; top: 96px; position: absolute" text = "Click
39                        here to choose another language."/>
40                     <ui:hyperlink action =
41                        "#{Options.recommendationsLink_action}" binding =
42                        "#{Options.recommendationsLink}" id =
43                        "recommendationsLink" rendered = "false" style =
44                        "left: 24px; top: 120px; position: absolute" text =
45                        "Click here to get book recommendations." url =
46                        "/faces/Recommendations.jsp"/>
47                     <ui:button action = "#{Options.submit_action}" binding =
48                        "#{Options.submit}" id = "submit" style = "left:
49                        23px; top: 192px; position: absolute" text =
50                        "Submit"/>
51                  </ui:form>
52               </ui:body>
53            </ui:html>
54         </ui:page>
55      </f:view>
56   </jsp:root>
```

Fig. 26.20 | JSP file that allows the user to select a programming language. (Part 2 of 4.)

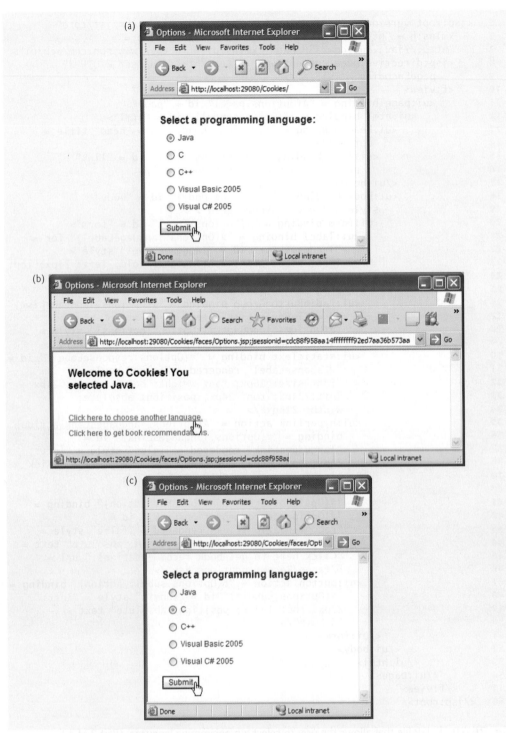

Fig. 26.20 | JSP file that allows the user to select a programming language. (Part 3 of 4.)

(d)

Fig. 26.20 | JSP file that allows the user to select a programming language. (Part 4 of 4.)

The first hyperlink (lines 35–39) requests this page, and the second (lines 40–47) requests Recommendations.jsp. The url property is not set for the first link; we discuss this momentarily. The second link's url property is set to /faces/Recommendations.jsp. Recall that earlier in the chapter, we set a url property to a remote website (http://www.deitel.com). To set this property to a page within the current application, click the ellipsis button next to the url property in the **Properties** window to open a dialog. Use this dialog to select a page within your project as the destination for the link.

Adding and Linking to a New Web Page
Setting the url property to a page in the current application requires that the destination page already exists. To set the url property of a link to Recommendations.jsp, you must first create this page. Right click the **Web Pages** node in the **Projects** window and select **New > Page** from the menu that appears. In the **New Page** dialog, change the name of the page to Recommendations and click **Finish** to create the files Recommendations.jsp and Recommendations.java. (We discuss the contents of these files shortly.) Once the Recommendations.jsp file exists, you can select it as the url value for recommendationsLink.

For Options.jsp, rather than setting the languagesLink's url property, we will add an action handler for this component to the page bean. The action handler will enable us to show and hide components of the page without redirecting the user to another page. Specifying a destination url would override the component's action handler and redirect the user to the specified page, so it is important that we do not set the url property in this case. Since we use this link to reload the current page, we simply return null from the action handler, causing Options.jsp to reload.

To add an action handler to a hyperlink that should also direct the user to another page, you must add a rule to the **Page Navigation** file (Fig. 26.21). To edit this file, right click anywhere in the Visual Designer and select **Page Navigation...** Locate the link whose navigation rule you would like to set and drag it to the destination page. Now the link can direct the user to a new page without overriding its action handler. Editing the **Page Navigation** file is also useful when you would like action elements that cannot specify a url property, such as buttons, to direct users to another page.

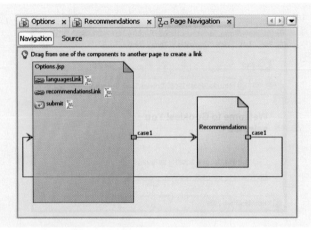

Fig. 26.21 | Editing the **Page Navigation** file.

Figure 26.22 contains the code that writes a cookie to the client machine when the user selects a programming language. The file also determines which components appear on the page, displaying either the components for choosing a language or the links for navigating the application, depending on the user's actions.

```java
 1   // Fig. 26.22: Options.java
 2   // Page bean that stores the user's language selection as a cookie on the
 3   // client.
 4   package cookies;
 5
 6   import com.sun.rave.web.ui.appbase.AbstractPageBean;
 7   import com.sun.rave.web.ui.component.Body;
 8   import com.sun.rave.web.ui.component.Form;
 9   import com.sun.rave.web.ui.component.Head;
10   import com.sun.rave.web.ui.component.Html;
11   import com.sun.rave.web.ui.component.Link;
12   import com.sun.rave.web.ui.component.Page;
13   import javax.faces.FacesException;
14   import com.sun.rave.web.ui.component.StaticText;
15   import com.sun.rave.web.ui.component.Label;
16   import com.sun.rave.web.ui.component.RadioButtonGroup;
17   import com.sun.rave.web.ui.model.SingleSelectOptionsList;
18   import com.sun.rave.web.ui.component.Hyperlink;
19   import com.sun.rave.web.ui.component.Button;
20   import javax.servlet.http.HttpServletResponse;
21   import javax.servlet.http.Cookie;
22   import java.util.Properties;
23
24   public class Options extends AbstractPageBean
25   {
26      private int __placeholder;
```

Fig. 26.22 | Page bean that stores the user's language selection in a cookie on the client. (Part 1 of 4.)

```
27
28      // method _init initializes components and sets the
29      // options for the radio button group.
30      private void _init() throws Exception
31      {
32          languageListOptions.setOptions(
33              new com.sun.rave.web.ui.model.Option[]
34              {
35                  new com.sun.rave.web.ui.model.Option( "Java", "Java" ),
36                  new com.sun.rave.web.ui.model.Option( "C", "C" ),
37                  new com.sun.rave.web.ui.model.Option( "C++", "C++" ),
38                  new com.sun.rave.web.ui.model.Option( "Visual/Basic/2005",
39                      "Visual Basic 2005" ),
40                  new com.sun.rave.web.ui.model.Option( "Visual/C#/2005",
41                      "Visual C# 2005" )
42              }
43          );
44      } // end method _init
45
46      // To save space, we omitted the code in lines 46-203. The complete
47      // source code is provided with this chapter's examples.
48
204     private Properties books = new Properties();
205
206     // Construct a new page bean instance and initialize the properties
207     // that map languages to ISBN numbers of recommended books.
208     public Options()
209     {
210         // initialze the Properties object of values to be stored as
211         // cookies.
212         books.setProperty( "Java", "0-13-222220-5" );
213         books.setProperty( "C", "0-13-142644-3" );
214         books.setProperty( "C++", "0-13-185757-6" );
215         books.setProperty( "Visual/Basic/2005", "0-13-186900-0" );
216         books.setProperty( "Visual/C#/2005", "0-13-152523-9" );
217     } // end Options constructor
218
219     protected ApplicationBean getApplicationBean()
220     {
221         return (ApplicationBean) getBean( "ApplicationBean" );
222     } // end method getApplicationBean
223
224     protected RequestBean getRequestBean()
225     {
226         return (RequestBean) getBean( "RequestBean" );
227     } // end method getRequestBean
228
229     protected SessionBean getSessionBean()
230     {
231         return (SessionBean) getBean( "SessionBean" );
232     } // end method getSessionBean
```

Fig. 26.22 | Page bean that stores the user's language selection in a cookie on the client. (Part 2 of 4.)

```
233
234    public void init()
235    {
236       super.init();
237       try
238       {
239          _init();
240       } // end try
241       catch ( Exception e )
242       {
243          log( "Options Initialization Failure", e );
244          throw e instanceof FacesException ? ( FacesException ) e:
245             new FacesException( e );
246       } // end catch
247    } // end method init
248
249    public void preprocess()
250    {
251       // empty body
252    } // end method preprocess
253
254    public void prerender()
255    {
256       // empty body
257    } // end method prerender
258
259    public void destroy()
260    {
261       // empty body
262    } // end method destroy
263
264    // Action handler for the Submit button.  Checks to see if a language
265    // was selected and if so, registers a cookie for that language and
266    // sets the responseLabel to indicate the chosen language.
267    public String submit_action()
268    {
269       String msg = "Welcome to Cookies!  You ";
270
271       // if the user made a selection
272       if ( languageList.getSelected() != null )
273       {
274          String language = languageList.getSelected().toString();
275          String displayLanguage = language.replace( '/', ' ' );
276          msg += "selected " + displayLanguage + ".";
277
278          // get ISBN number of book for the given language.
279          String ISBN = books.getProperty( language );
280
281          // create cookie using language-ISBN name-value pair
282          Cookie cookie = new Cookie( language, ISBN );
283
```

Fig. 26.22 | Page bean that stores the user's language selection in a cookie on the client. (Part 3 of 4.)

```
284          // add cookie to the response header to place it on the user's
285          // machine
286          HttpServletResponse response =
287             (HttpServletResponse) getExternalContext().getResponse();
288          response.addCookie( cookie );
289       } // end if
290       else
291          msg += "did not select a language.";
292
293       responseLabel.setValue( msg );
294       languageList.setRendered( false );
295       languageLabel.setRendered( false );
296       submit.setRendered( false );
297       responseLabel.setRendered( true );
298       languagesLink.setRendered( true );
299       recommendationsLink.setRendered( true );
300       return null; // reloads the page
301    } // end method submit_action
302
303    // redisplay the components used to allow the user to select a
304    // language.
305    public String languagesLink_action()
306    {
307       responseLabel.setRendered( false );
308       languagesLink.setRendered( false );
309       recommendationsLink.setRendered( false );
310       languageList.setRendered( true );
311       languageLabel.setRendered( true );
312       submit.setRendered( true );
313       return null;
314    } // end method languagesLink_action
315 } // end class Options
```

Fig. 26.22 | Page bean that stores the user's language selection in a cookie on the client. (Part 4 of 4.)

As mentioned previously, the _init method handles component initialization. Since this page contains a RadioButtonGroup object that requires initialization, method _init (lines 30–44) constructs an array of Option objects to be displayed by the buttons. The option's names contain slashes rather than spaces in lines 38 and 40, because we later use these names as cookie names and Java does not allow cookie names to contain spaces.

Lines 212–216 in the constructor initialize a Properties object—a data structure that stores String key-value pairs. The application uses the key to store and retrieve the associated value in the Properties object. In this example, the keys are Strings containing the programming language names, and the values are Strings containing the ISBN numbers for the recommended books. Class Properties provides method set-Property, which takes as arguments a key and a value. A value that is added via method setProperty is placed in the Properties at a location determined by the key. The value for a specific Properties entry can be determined by invoking the method getProperty on the Properties object with that value's key as an argument.

Software Engineering Observation 26.1

Java Studio Creator 2 can automatically import any missing packages your Java file needs. For example, after adding the Properties *object to* Options.java, *you can right click in the Java editor window and select* **Fix Imports** *to automatically import* java.util.Properties.

Clicking **Submit** invokes the event handler submit_action (lines 267–301), which display a message indicating the selected language in the responseLabel element and adds a new cookie to the response. If a language was selected (line 272), the selected value is retrieved (line 274). Line 275 converts the selection to a String that can be displayed in the responseLabel, replacing the slashes with spaces. Line 276 adds the selected language to the results message.

Line 279 retrieves the ISBN for the selected language from the books Properties. Then line 282 creates a new cookie object (of class Cookie in package javax.servlet.http), using the selected language as the cookie's name and a corresponding ISBN number as the cookie's value. This cookie is added to the HTTP response header in lines 286–288. An object of class HttpServletResponse (from package javax.servlet.http) represents the response. This object can be accessed by invoking the method getExternalContext on the page bean then invoking getResponse on the resulting object. If a language was not selected, line 291 sets the results message to indicate that no selection was made.

Lines 293–299 control the appearance of the page after the user clicks **Submit**. Line 293 sets the responseLabel to display the String msg. Since the user has just submitted a language selection, the components used to collect the selection are hidden (lines 294–296) and responseLabel and the links used to navigate the application are displayed (lines 297–299). The action handler returns null at line 300, which reloads Options.jsp.

Lines 305–311 contain the languagesLink's event handler. When the user clicks this link, responseLabel and the two links are hidden (lines 307–309), and the components that allow the user to select a language are redisplayed (lines 310–312). The method returns null at line 313, causing Options.jsp to reload.

Displaying Book Recommendations Based on Cookie Values

After clicking **Submit**, the user may request a book recommendation. The book recommendations hyperlink forwards the user to Recommendations.jsp (Fig. 26.23) to display recommendations based on the user's language selections.

```
1    <?xml version = "1.0" encoding = "UTF-8"?>
2
3    <!-- Fig. 26.23: Recommendations.jsp -->
4    <!-- JSP file that displays book recommendations based on cookies. -->
5    <jsp:root version = "1.2" xmlns:f = "http://java.sun.com/jsf/core"
6       xmlns:h = "http://java.sun.com/jsf/html" xmlns:jsp =
7       "http://java.sun.com/JSP/Page" xmlns:ui = "http://www.sun.com/web/ui">
8       <jsp:directive.page contentType = "text/html; charset = UTF-8"
9          pageEncoding = "UTF-8"/>
10      <f:view>
11         <ui:page binding = "#{Recommendations.page}" id = "page">
```

Fig. 26.23 | JSP file that displays book recommendations based on cookies. (Part 1 of 2.)

```
12          <ui:html binding = "#{Recommendations.html}" id = "html">
13            <ui:head binding = "#{Recommendations.head}" id = "head"
14              title = "Recommendations">
15              <ui:link binding = "#{Recommendations.link}" id = "link"
16              url = "/resources/stylesheet.css"/>
17            </ui:head>
18            <ui:body binding = "#{Recommendations.body}" id = "body"
19              style = "-rave-layout: grid">
20              <ui:form binding = "#{Recommendations.form}" id = "form">
21                <ui:label binding = "#{Recommendations.languageLabel}"
22                  for = "booksListBox" id = "languageLabel" style =
23                  "font-size: 20px; font-weight: bold; left: 24px; top:
24                  24px; position: absolute" text = "Recommendations"/>
25                <ui:listbox binding = "#{Recommendations.booksListBox}"
26                  id = "booksListBox" items = "#{Recommendations.
27                  booksListBoxOptions.options}" rows = "6" style =
28                  "left: 24px; top: 72px; position: absolute;
29                  width: 360px"/>
30                <ui:hyperlink action = "case1" binding =
31                  "#{Recommendations.optionsLink}" id = "optionsLink"
32                  style = "left: 24px; top: 192px; position: absolute"
33                  text = "Click here to choose another language."/>
34              </ui:form>
35            </ui:body>
36          </ui:html>
37        </ui:page>
38      </f:view>
39    </jsp:root>
```

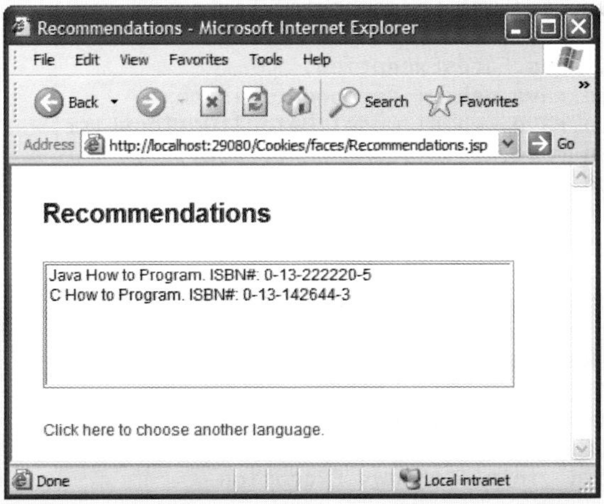

Fig. 26.23 | JSP file that displays book recommendations based on cookies. (Part 2 of 2.)

Recommendations.jsp contains a **Label** (lines 21–24), a **List Box** (lines 25–29) and a **Hyperlink** (lines 30–33). The **Label** displays the text Recommendations at the top of the page. A **List Box** component displays a list of options from which a user can make multiple selections. The **List Box** in this example displays the recommendations created by the Recommendation.java page bean (Fig. 26.24), or the text "No Recommendations. Please select a language." The **Hyperlink** allows the user to return to Options.jsp to select additional languages.

Page Bean That Creates Book Recommendations from Cookies

In Recommendations.java (Fig. 26.24), method prerender (lines 192–223) retrieves the cookies from the client, using the request object's getCookies method (lines 195–197). An object of class HttpServletRequest (from package javax.servlet.http) represents the request. This object can be obtained by invoking method getExternalContext on the page bean, then invoking getRequest on the resulting object. The call to getCookies returns an array of the cookies previously written to the client. Cookies can be read by an application only if they were created by a server in the domain in which the application is running—a web server cannot access cookies created by servers in other domains. For example, a cookie created by a web server in the deitel.com domain cannot be read by a web server in any other domain.

```
 1   // Fig. 26.24: Recommendations.java
 2   // Page bean that displays book recommendations based on cookies storing
 3   // user's selected programming languages.
 4   package cookies;
 5
 6   import com.sun.rave.web.ui.appbase.AbstractPageBean;
 7   import com.sun.rave.web.ui.component.Body;
 8   import com.sun.rave.web.ui.component.Form;
 9   import com.sun.rave.web.ui.component.Head;
10   import com.sun.rave.web.ui.component.Html;
11   import com.sun.rave.web.ui.component.Link;
12   import com.sun.rave.web.ui.component.Page;
13   import javax.faces.FacesException;
14   import com.sun.rave.web.ui.component.Listbox;
15   import com.sun.rave.web.ui.model.DefaultOptionsList;
16   import com.sun.rave.web.ui.component.Label;
17   import com.sun.rave.web.ui.component.Hyperlink;
18   import com.sun.rave.web.ui.model.Option;
19   import javax.servlet.http.HttpServletRequest;
20   import javax.servlet.http.Cookie;
21   import com.sun.rave.web.ui.component.HiddenField;
22
23   public class Recommendations extends AbstractPageBean
24   {
25      private int __placeholder;
26
27      private void _init() throws Exception
28      {
29         // empty body
30      } // end method _init()
31
32      // To save space, we omitted the code in lines 32-151. The complete
33      // source code is provided with this chapter's examples.
```

Fig. 26.24 | Page bean that displays book recommendations based on cookies storing user's selected languages. (Part 1 of 3.)

```
34
152      public Recommendations()
153      {
154         // empty body
155      } // end constructor
156
157      protected RequestBean getRequestBean()
158      {
159         return (RequestBean) getBean( "RequestBean" );
160      } // end method getRequestBean
161
162      protected ApplicationBean getApplicationBean()
163      {
164         return (ApplicationBean) getBean( "ApplicationBean" );
165      } // end method getApplicationBean
166
167      protected SessionBean getSessionBean()
168      {
169         return (SessionBean) getBean( "SessionBean" );
170      } // end method getSessionBean
171
172      public void init()
173      {
174         super.init();
175         try
176         {
177            _init();
178         } // end try
179         catch ( Exception e )
180         {
181            log( "Recommendations Initialization Failure", e );
182            throw e instanceof FacesException ? (FacesException) e:
183               new FacesException( e );
184         } // end catch
185      } // end method init
186
187      public void preprocess()
188      {
189         // empty body
190      } // end method preprocess
191
192      public void prerender()
193      {
194         //retrieve client's cookies
195         HttpServletRequest request =
196            (HttpServletRequest)getExternalContext().getRequest();
197         Cookie [] cookies = request.getCookies();
198
199         // if there are cookies, store the corresponding books and ISBN
200         // numbers in an array of Options
201         Option [] recommendations;
```

Fig. 26.24 | Page bean that displays book recommendations based on cookies storing user's selected languages. (Part 2 of 3.)

```
202
203              if ( cookies.length > 1 )
204              {
205                 recommendations = new Option[ cookies.length - 1 ];
206                 for ( int i = 0; i < cookies.length - 1; i++ )
207                 {
208                    String language =
209                       cookies[ i ].getName().replace( '/', ' ' );
210                    recommendations[ i ] = new Option( language + " How to "
211                       "Program.   ISBN#: " + cookies[ i ].getValue() );
212                 } // end for
213              } // end if
214
215              // otherwise store a message indicating no language was selected
216              else
217              {
218                 recommendations = new Option[ 1 ];
219                 recommendations[ 0 ] = new Option( "No recommendations.  " +
220                    "Please select a language." ) ;
221              } // end else
222
223              booksListBox.setItems( recommendations );
224           } // end method prerender
225
226           public void destroy()
227           {
228              // empty body
229           } // end method destroy
230        } // end class Recommendations
```

Fig. 26.24 | Page bean that displays book recommendations based on cookies storing user's selected languages. (Part 3 of 3.)

Line 203 determines whether at least one cookie exists. (We ignore the first cookie in the array which contains information that is not specific to our application.) Lines 205–213 add the information in the cookie(s) to an Option array. Arrays of Option objects can be displayed as a list of items in a **List Box** component. The loop retrieves the name and value of each cookie using the control variable to determine the current value in the cookie array. If no language was selected, lines 215–220 add to an Options array a message instructing the user to select a language. Line 222 sets booksListBox to display the resulting Options array. We summarize commonly used Cookie methods in Fig. 26.25.

Methods	Description
getDomain	Returns a String containing the cookie's domain (i.e., the domain from which the cookie was written). This determines which web servers can receive the cookie. By default, cookies are sent to the web server that originally sent the cookie to the client. Changing the Domain property causes the cookie to be returned to a web server other than the one that originally wrote it.

Fig. 26.25 | javax.servlet.http.Cookie methods. (Part 1 of 2.)

Methods	Description
getMaxAge	Returns an `int` indicating how many seconds the cookie will persist on the browser. This is –1 by default, meaning the cookie will persist until the browser is shut down.
getName	Returns a `String` containing the cookie's name.
getPath	Returns a `String` containing the path to a directory on the server to which the cookie applies. Cookies can be "targeted" to specific directories on the web server. By default, a cookie is returned only to applications operating in the same directory as the application that sent the cookie or a subdirectory of that directory. Changing the `Path` property causes the cookie to be returned to a directory other than the one from which it was originally written.
getSecure	Returns a `bool` value indicating whether the cookie should be transmitted through a secure protocol. The value `true` causes a secure protocol to be used.
getValue	Returns a `String` containing the cookie's value.

Fig. 26.25 | `javax.servlet.http.Cookie` methods. (Part 2 of 2.)

26.7.2 Session Tracking with the SessionBean Object

You can also perform session tracking with the `SessionBean` class that is provided in each web application created with Java Studio Creator 2. When a web page in the project is requested, a `SessionBean` object is created. Properties of this object can be accessed throughout a browser session by invoking the method `getSessionBean` on the page bean. To demonstrate session-tracking techniques using the `SessionBean`, we modified the page bean files in Figs. 26.22 and 26.24 so that they use the `SessionBean` to store the user's selected languages. We begin with the updated `Options.jsp` file (Fig. 26.27). Figure 26.29 presents the `SessionBean.java` file, and Fig. 26.30 presents the modified page bean file for `Options.jsp`.

The `Options.jsp` file in Fig. 26.26 is similar to that presented in Fig. 26.20 for the cookies example. Lines 38–45 define two `ui:staticText` elements that were not present in the cookies example. The first element displays the text `"Number of selections so far:"`. The second element's `text` attribute is bound to property `numSelections` in the `SessionBean` (lines 44–45). We discuss how to bind the `text` attribute to a `SessionBean` property momentarily.

```
1   <?xml version = "1.0" encoding = "UTF-8"?>
2
3   <!-- Fig. 26.26: Options.jsp -->
4   <!-- JSP file that allows the user to select a programming language. -->
5   <jsp:root version = "1.2" xmlns:f = "http://java.sun.com/jsf/core"
6      xmlns:h = "http://java.sun.com/jsf/html" xmlns:jsp =
7      "http://java.sun.com/JSP/Page" xmlns:ui = "http://www.sun.com/web/ui">
8      <jsp:directive.page contentType = "text/html; charset = UTF-8"
9         pageEncoding = "UTF-8"/>
```

Fig. 26.26 | JSP file that allows the user to select a programming language. (Part 1 of 4.)

```
10      <f:view>
11        <ui:page binding = "#{Options.page}" id = "page">
12          <ui:html binding = "#{Options.html}" id = "html">
13            <ui:head binding = "#{Options.head}" id = "head">
14              <ui:link binding = "#{Options.link}" id = "link"
15                url = "/resources/stylesheet.css"/>
16            </ui:head>
17            <ui:body binding = "#{Options.body}" id = "body"
18              style = "-rave-layout: grid">
19              <ui:form binding = "#{Options.form}" id = "form">
20                <ui:label binding = "#{Options.languageLabel}" for =
21                  "languageList" id = "languageLabel" style =
22                  "font-size: 16px; font-weight: bold; left: 24px; top:
23                  24px; position: absolute" text = "Select a
24                  programming language:"/>
25                <ui:radioButtonGroup binding = "#{Options.languageList}"
26                  id = "languageList" items =
27                  "#{Options.languageListOptions.options}" style =
28                  "left: 24px; top: 48px; position: absolute"/>
29                <ui:button action = "#{Options.submit_action}" binding =
30                  "#{Options.submit}" id = "submit" style = "left:
31                  23px; top: 192px; position: absolute" text =
32                  "Submit"/>
33                <ui:staticText binding = "#{Options.responseLabel}" id =
34                  "responseLabel" rendered = "false" style =
35                  "font-size: 16px; font-weight: bold; height: 24px;
36                  left: 24px; top: 24px; position: absolute;
37                  width: 216px"/>
38                <ui:staticText binding = "#{Options.numSelectedLabel}"
39                  id = "numSelectedLabel" rendered = "false" style =
40                  "left: 24px; top: 96px; position: absolute" text =
41                  "Number of selections so far:"/>
42                <ui:staticText binding = "#{Options.numSelected}" id =
43                  "numSelected" rendered = "false" style = "left:
44                  192px; top: 96px; position: absolute" text =
45                  "#{SessionBean.numSelections}"/>
46                <ui:hyperlink action = "#{Options.languagesLink_action}"
47                  binding = "#{Options.languagesLink}" id =
48                  "languagesLink" rendered = "false" style = "left:
49                  24px; top: 144px; position: absolute" text = "Click
50                  here to choose another language."/>
51                <ui:hyperlink binding = "#{Options.recommendationsLink}"
52                  id = "recommendationsLink" rendered = "false" style =
53                  "left: 24px; top: 168px; position: absolute" text =
54                  "Click here to get book recommendations." url =
55                  "/faces/Recommendations.jsp"/>
56              </ui:form>
57            </ui:body>
58          </ui:html>
59        </ui:page>
60      </f:view>
61    </jsp:root>
```

Fig. 26.26 | JSP file that allows the user to select a programming language. (Part 2 of 4.)

(a)

(b)

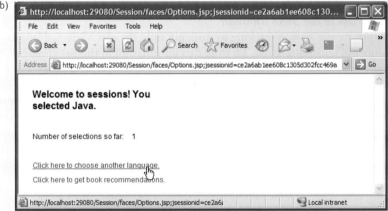

(c)

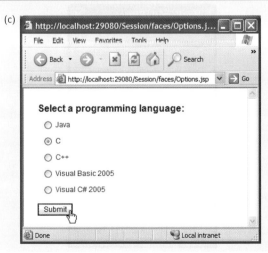

Fig. 26.26 | JSP file that allows the user to select a programming language. (Part 3 of 4.)

(d)

Fig. 26.26 | JSP file that allows the user to select a programming language. (Part 4 of 4.)

Adding Properties to the SessionBean

In this example, we use session tracking to store not only the user's selected languages, but also the number of selections made. To store this information in the SessionBean, we add properties to the SessionBean class.

To add a property that will store the number of selections so far, right click the SessionBean node in the **Outline** window and select **Add > Property** to display the **New Property Pattern** dialog (Fig. 26.27). This dialog allows you to add primitive, String or primitive type-wrapper properties to the SessionBean. Add an int property named numSelections and click **OK** to accept the default settings for this property. Open the SessionBean file and you will see a new property definition, a *get* and *set* method for numSelections.

Fig. 26.27 | **New Property** dialog for adding a property to the SessionBean.

Property `numSelections` will be manipulated in the page bean file to store the number of languages the user selected. To display the value of this property in the `numSelected` **Static Text** element in the JSP file, right click the **Static Text** component in the **Outline** window in **Design** mode and select **Bind to Data…**. In the **Bind to Data** dialog (Fig. 26.28), select the **Bind to an Object** tab, locate property `numSelections` under the `SessionBean` node and click **OK**. The **Static Text** element will now always display the value of `SessionBean`'s `numSelections` property. If the property's value changes, the text changes as well, so that you need not programmatically set the text in the page bean file.

Now that we have added a property to store the number of selections in the `SessionBean`, we must add a second property to store the selections themselves. We would like to store selections as key-value pairs of the selected language and the ISBN number of a related book, similar to the way selections were stored using cookies. To do this, we add a `Properties` object named `selectedLanguages` to the `SessionBean`. We manually added this property to the `SessionBean` file, but you can add it using the **New Property** dialog in Fig. 26.27. Simply type `java.util.Properties` in the **Type** drop down list's field, configure the property and click **OK**. The final `SessionBean` file after the two properties have been added is displayed in Fig. 26.29.

Fig. 26.28 | **Bind to Data** dialog

```
1   // Fig. 26.29: SessionBean.java
2   // SessionBean file for storing language selections.
3   package session;
4
5   import com.sun.rave.web.ui.appbase.AbstractSessionBean;
6   import java.util.Properties;
7   import javax.faces.FacesException;
8
```

Fig. 26.29 | `SessionBean` file for storing language selections. (Part 1 of 3.)

```
 9   public class SessionBean extends AbstractSessionBean
10   {
11      private int __placeholder;
12
13      private void _init() throws Exception
14      {
15         // empty body
16      } // end method _init
17
18      public SessionBean()
19      {
20         // empty constructor
21      } // end constructor
22
23      protected ApplicationBean getApplicationBean()
24      {
25         return (ApplicationBean1) getBean( "ApplicationBean" );
26      } // end method getApplicationBean
27
28      public void init()
29      {
30         super.init();
31         try
32         {
33            _init();
34         } // end try
35         catch ( Exception e )
36         {
37            log( "SessionBean Initialization Failure", e);
38            throw e instanceof FacesException ? (FacesException) e:
39               new FacesException( e ) ;
40         } // end catch
41      } // end method init
42
43      public void passivate()
44      {
45         // empty body
46      } // end method passivate
47
48      public void activate()
49      {
50         // empty body
51      } // end method activate
52
53      public void destroy()
54      {
55         // empty body
56      } // end method destroy
57
58      private int numSelections = 0; // stores number of unique selections
59
60      public int getNumSelections()
61      {
```

Fig. 26.29 | SessionBean file for storing language selections. (Part 2 of 3.)

```
62            return this.numSelections;
63        } // end method getNumSelections
64
65        public void setNumSelections( int numSelections )
66        {
67            this.numSelections = numSelections;
68        } // end method setNumSelections
69
70        // Stores key-value pairs of selected languages
71        private Properties selectedLanguages = new Properties();
72
73        public Properties getSelectedLanguages()
74        {
75            return this.selectedLanguages;
76        } // end method getSelectedLanguages
77
78        public void setSelectedLanguages( Properties selectedLanguages )
79        {
80            this.selectedLanguages = selectedLanguages;
81        } // end method setSelectedLanguages
82    } // end class SessionBean
```

Fig. 26.29 | `SessionBean` file for storing language selections. (Part 3 of 3.)

Line 58 declares the `numSelections` property, and lines 60–63 and 65–68 declare its *get* and *set* methods, respectively. This portion of the code was generated automatically when we used the **New Property** dialog. Line 71 defines the `Properties` object `selected-Languages` that will store user selections. Lines 73–76 and 78–81 are the *get* and *set* methods for this property.

Manipulating **SessionBean** *Properties in a Page Bean File*

The page bean file for the `Options.jsp` page is displayed in Fig. 26.30. Because much of this example is identical to the preceding one, we concentrate on the new features.

```
1    // Fig. 26.30: Options.java
2    // Page bean that stores language selections in a SessionBean property.
3    package session;
4
5    import com.sun.rave.web.ui.appbase.AbstractPageBean;
6    import com.sun.rave.web.ui.component.Body;
7    import com.sun.rave.web.ui.component.Form;
8    import com.sun.rave.web.ui.component.Head;
9    import com.sun.rave.web.ui.component.Html;
10   import com.sun.rave.web.ui.component.Link;
11   import com.sun.rave.web.ui.component.Page;
12   import javax.faces.FacesException;
13   import com.sun.rave.web.ui.component.RadioButtonGroup;
14   import com.sun.rave.web.ui.component.Hyperlink;
15   import com.sun.rave.web.ui.component.Button;
16   import com.sun.rave.web.ui.component.Label;
```

Fig. 26.30 | Page bean that stores language selections in a `SessionBean` property. (Part 1 of 4.)

```
17   import com.sun.rave.web.ui.component.StaticText;
18   import com.sun.rave.web.ui.model.SingleSelectOptionsList;
19   import java.util.Properties;
20   import javax.servlet.http.Cookie;
21   import javax.servlet.http.HttpServletRequest;
22   import javax.servlet.http.HttpSession;
23
24   public class Options extends AbstractPageBean
25   {
26      private int __placeholder;
27
28      private void _init() throws Exception
29      {
30         languageListOptions.setOptions(
31            new com.sun.rave.web.ui.model.Option[]
32            {
33               new com.sun.rave.web.ui.model.Option( "Java", "Java" ),
34               new com.sun.rave.web.ui.model.Option( "C", "C" ),
35               new com.sun.rave.web.ui.model.Option( "C++", "C++" ),
36               new com.sun.rave.web.ui.model.Option( "Visual Basic 2005",
37                  "Visual Basic 2005" ),
38               new com.sun.rave.web.ui.model.Option( "Visual C# 2005",
39                  "Visual C# 2005" )
40            }
41         );
42      } // end method init
43
44      // To save space, we omitted the code in lines 44-219. The complete
45      // source code is provided with this chapter's examples.
46
220     private Properties books = new Properties();
221
222     public Options()
223     {
224        // initialze the Properties object of values to be stored in
225        // the session bean.
226        books.setProperty( "Java", "0-13-148398-6" );
227        books.setProperty( "C", "0-13-142644-3" );
228        books.setProperty( "C++", "0-13-185757-6" );
229        books.setProperty( "Visual Basic 2005", "0-13-186900-0" );
230        books.setProperty( "Visual C# 2005", "0-13-152523-9" );
231     } // end constructor
232
233     protected ApplicationBean getApplicationBean()
234     {
235        return (ApplicationBean) getBean( "ApplicationBean" );
236     } // end method getApplicationBean
237
238     protected RequestBean getRequestBean()
239     {
240        return (RequestBean) getBean( "RequestBean" );
241     } // end method getRequestBean
242
```

Fig. 26.30 | Page bean that stores language selections in a SessionBean property. (Part 2 of 4.)

```
243      protected SessionBean getSessionBean()
244      {
245         return (SessionBean) getBean( "SessionBean" );
246      } // end method getSessionBean
247
248      public void init()
249      {
250         super.init();
251         try
252         {
253            _init();
254         } // end try
255         catch ( Exception e )
256         {
257            log( "Options Initialization Failure", e );
258            throw e instanceof FacesException ? (FacesException) e:
259               new FacesException( e );
260         } // end catch
261      } // end method init
262
263      public void preprocess()
264      {
265         // empty body
266      } // end method preprocess
267
268      public void prerender()
269      {
270         // empty body
271      } // end method prerender
272
273      public void destroy()
274      {
275         // empty body
276      } // end method destroy
277
278      // action handler for the submit button, stores selected languages
279      // in session scope for retrieval when making book recommendations.
280      public String submit_action()
281      {
282         String msg = "Welcome to sessions!  You ";
283
284         // if the user made a selection
285         if ( getLanguageList().getSelected() != null )
286         {
287            String language = languageList.getSelected().toString();
288            msg += "selected " + language + ".";
289
290            // get ISBN number of book for the given language.
291            String ISBN = books.getProperty( language );
292
293            // add the selection to the SessionBean's Properties object
294            Properties selections = getSessionBean().getSelectedLanguages();
295            Object result = selections.setProperty( language, ISBN );
```

Fig. 26.30 | Page bean that stores language selections in a SessionBean property. (Part 3 of 4.)

```
296
297          // increment numSelections in the SessionBean and update
298          // selectedLanguages if the user has not made this selection
299          // before
300          if ( result == null )
301          {
302             int numSelected = getSessionBean().getNumSelections();
303             getSessionBean().setNumSelections( ++numSelected );
304          } // end if
305       } // end if
306       else
307          msg += "did not select a language.";
308
309       responseLabel.setValue( msg );
310       languageList.setRendered( false );
311       languageLabel.setRendered( false );
312       submit.setRendered( false );
313       responseLabel.setRendered( true );
314       numSelectedLabel.setRendered( true );
315       numSelected.setRendered( true );
316       languagesLink.setRendered( true );
317       recommendationsLink.setRendered( true );
318       return null;
319    } // end method submit_action
320
321    // redisplay the components used to allow the user to select a
322    // language.
323    public String languagesLink_action() {
324       responseLabel.setRendered( false );
325       numSelectedLabel.setRendered( false );
326       numSelected.setRendered( false );
327       languagesLink.setRendered( false );
328       recommendationsLink.setRendered( false );
329       languageList.setRendered( true );
330       languageLabel.setRendered( true );
331       submit.setRendered( true );
332       return null;
333    } // end method languagesLink_action
334 } // end class Options
```

Fig. 26.30 | Page bean that stores language selections in a `SessionBean` property. (Part 4 of 4.)

The submit `Button`'s action handler (lines 280–319) stores the user's selections in the `SessionBean` and increments the number of selections made, if necessary. Line 294 retrieves from the `SessionBean` the `Properties` object that contains the user's selections. Line 295 adds the current selection to the `Properties` object. Method `setProperty` returns the value previously associated with the new key, or `null` if this key was not already stored in the `Properties` object. If adding the new property returns `null`, then the user has made a new selection. In this case, lines 302–303 increment the `numSelections` property in the `SessionBean`. Lines 309–317 and the `languaguesLink` action handler (lines 323–334) control the components that will be displayed on the page, just as in the cookies examples.

Software Engineering Observation 26.2

A benefit of using SessionBean properties (rather than cookies) is that they can store any type of object (not just Strings) as attribute values. This provides you with increased flexibility in maintaining client state information.

Displaying Recommendations Based on Session Values

As in the cookies example, this application provides a link to Recommendations.jsp (Fig. 26.31), which displays a list of book recommendations based on the user's language selections. It is identical to recommendation.jsp from the cookies example (Fig. 26.23).

```
1   <?xml version = "1.0" encoding = "UTF-8"?>
2
3   <!-- Fig. 26.31: Recommendations.jsp -->
4   <!-- JSP file that displays book recommendations based on language
5   <!-- selections stored in session scope. -->
6   <jsp:root version = "1.2" xmlns:f = "http://java.sun.com/jsf/core"
7       xmlns:h = "http://java.sun.com/jsf/html" xmlns:jsp =
8       "http://java.sun.com/JSP/Page" xmlns:ui = "http://www.sun.com/web/ui">
9       <jsp:directive.page contentType = "text/html; charset = UTF-8"
10          pageEncoding = "UTF-8"/>
11      <f:view>
12          <ui:page binding = "#{Recommendations.page}" id = "page">
13              <ui:html binding = "#{Recommendations.html}" id = "html">
14                  <ui:head binding = "#{Recommendations.head}" id = "head">
15                      <ui:link binding = "#{Recommendations.link}" id = "link"
16                          url = "/resources/stylesheet.css"/>
17                  </ui:head>
18                  <ui:body binding = "#{Recommendations.body}" id = "body"
19                      style = "-rave-layout: grid">
20                      <ui:form binding = "#{Recommendations.form}" id = "form">
21                          <ui:label binding = "#{Recommendations.languageLabel}"
22                              for = "booksListBox" id = "languageLabel" style =
23                              "font-size: 20px; font-weight: bold; left: 24px; top:
24                              24px; position: absolute" text = "Recommendations"/>
25                          <ui:listbox binding = "#{Recommendations.booksListBox}"
26                              id = "booksListBox" items = "#{Recommendations.
27                              booksListBoxDefaultOptions.options}" rows = "6"
28                              style = "left: 24px; top: 72px; position: absolute;
29                              width: 360px"/>
30                          <ui:hyperlink action = "case1" binding =
31                              "#{Recommendations.optionsLink}" id = "optionsLink"
32                              style = "left: 24px; top: 192px; position: absolute"
33                              text = "Click here to choose another language."/>
34                      </ui:form>
35                  </ui:body>
36              </ui:html>
37          </ui:page>
38      </f:view>
39  </jsp:root>
```

Fig. 26.31 | JSP file that displays book recommendations based on language selections stored in session scope. (Part 1 of 2.)

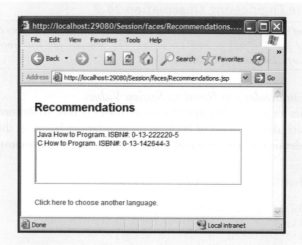

Fig. 26.31 | JSP file that displays book recommendations based on language selections stored in session scope. (Part 2 of 2.)

Page Bean That Creates Book Recommendations from a* SessionBean *Property
Figure 26.32 presents the page bean for Recommendations.jsp. Again, much of it is similar to the page bean used in the cookies example. We discuss only the new features.

```
1   // Fig. 26.32: Recommendations.java
2   // Page bean that displays book recommendations based on a SessionBean
3   // property.
4   package session;
5
6   import com.sun.rave.web.ui.appbase.AbstractPageBean;
7   import com.sun.rave.web.ui.component.Body;
8   import com.sun.rave.web.ui.component.Form;
9   import com.sun.rave.web.ui.component.Head;
10  import com.sun.rave.web.ui.component.Html;
11  import com.sun.rave.web.ui.component.Link;
12  import com.sun.rave.web.ui.component.Page;
13  import javax.faces.FacesException;
14  import com.sun.rave.web.ui.component.Listbox;
15  import com.sun.rave.web.ui.component.Label;
16  import com.sun.rave.web.ui.component.Hyperlink;
17  import com.sun.rave.web.ui.model.DefaultOptionsList;
18  import java.util.Enumeration;
19  import com.sun.rave.web.ui.model.Option;
20  import java.util.Properties;
21
22  public class Recommendations extends AbstractPageBean
23  {
24      private int __placeholder;
```

Fig. 26.32 | Page bean that displays book recommendations based on a SessionBean property. (Part 1 of 3.)

```
25
26     private void _init() throws Exception
27     {
28        // empty body
29     } // end method _init
30
31     // To save space, we omitted the code in lines 31-150. The complete
32     // source code is provided with this chapter's examples.
33
151    public Recommendations()
152    {
153       // empty constructor
154    } // end constructor
155
156    protected RequestBean getRequestBean()
157    {
158       return (RequestBean) getBean( "RequestBean" );
159    } // end method getRequestBean
160
161    protected ApplicationBean getApplicationBean()
162    {
163       return (ApplicationBean) getBean( "ApplicationBean" );
164    } // end method getApplicationBean
165
166    protected SessionBean getSessionBean()
167    {
168       return (SessionBean) getBean( "SessionBean" );
169    } // end method getSessionBean
170
171    public void init()
172    {
173       super.init();
174       try
175       {
176          _init();
177       } // end try
178       catch ( Exception e )
179       {
180          log( "Recommendations Initialization Failure", e );
181          throw e instanceof FacesException ? (FacesException) e:
182             new FacesException( e );
183       } // end catch
184    } // end method init
185
186    public void preprocess()
187    {
188       // empty body
189    } // end method preprocess
190
191    public void prerender()
192    {
```

Fig. 26.32 | Page bean that displays book recommendations based on a SessionBean property. (Part 2 of 3.)

```
193          //retrieve user's selections and number of selections made
194          Properties languages = getSessionBean().getSelectedLanguages();
195          Enumeration selectionsEnum = languages.propertyNames();
196          int numSelected = getSessionBean().getNumSelections();
197
198          Option [] recommendations;
199
200          // if at least one selection was made
201          if ( numSelected > 0 )
202          {
203             recommendations = new Option[ numSelected ];
204
205             for ( int i = 0; i < numSelected; i++ )
206             {
207                String language = (String) selectionsEnum.nextElement() ;
208                recommendations[ i ] = new Option( language +
209                   "How to Program.   ISBN#:" +
210                   languages.getProperty( language ) );
211             } // end for
212          } // end if
213          else
214          {
215             recommendations = new Option[ 1 ];
216             recommendations[ 0 ] = new Option( "No recommendations.   " +
217                "Please select a language." );
218          } // end else
219
220          booksListBox.setItems( recommendations );
221       } // end method prerender
222
223       public void destroy()
224       {
225          // empty body
226       } // end method destroy
227    } // end class Recommendations
```

Fig. 26.32 | Page bean that displays book recommendations based on a `SessionBean` property. (Part 3 of 3.)

Line 194 retrieves the `Properties` object containing the user's selections from the `SessionBean`, and line 195 gets an enumeration of all of the keys in that `Properties` object. Line 196 retrieves the number of selections made from the `SessionBean`. If any selections were made, line 208 constructs an appropriately sized `Option` array to display the selections in the `ui:listBox` element of `Recommendations.jsp`. Lines 205–211 add each of the user's selections to this `Option` array. Line 207 gets the next key from the enumeration of keys, and lines 208–210 add a recommendation to the `Option` array.

26.8 Wrap-Up

In this chapter, we introduced web application development using JavaServer Pages and JavaServer Faces in Java Studio Creator 2. We began by discussing the simple HTTP transactions that take place when you request and receive a web page through a web browser. We then discussed the three tiers (i.e., the client or top tier, the business logic or middle tier and the information or bottom tier) that comprise most web applications.

You learned the role of JSP files and page bean files, and the relationship between them. You learned how to use Java Studio Creator 2 to compile and execute web applications. You also learned how to build web applications visually using Java Studio Creator 2's drag-and-drop capabilities.

We demonstrated several common JSF components used for displaying text and images on web pages. We also discussed validation components and custom validator methods, which allow you to ensure that user input satisfies certain requirements.

We discussed the benefits of maintaining user information across multiple pages of a website. We then demonstrated how you can include such functionality in a web application using either cookies or properties in the SessionBean class. In the next chapter, we continue our discussion of web application development. You'll learn how to access a database from a web application, how to use several of the AJAX-enabled JSF components from Sun's Java Blueprints and how to use virtual forms.

26.9 Web Resources

developers.sun.com/prodtech/javatools/jscreator
Overviews Java Studio Creator 2 and includes articles, forums, product demonstrations and links to useful resources relevant to building web applications in Java Studio Creator 2.

developers.sun.com/prodtech/javatools/jscreator/index.jsp
Sun's Java Studio Creator center, has everything you need to get started. Download the IDE for free and check out the Learning tab for Java Studio Creator tutorials.

developers.sun.com/prodtech/javatools/jscreator/learning/tutorials/index.jsp
Provides dozens of tutorials, ranging from tips on getting started with Java Studio Creator 2 to feature-specific instructions on how to use many facets of the IDE.

developers.sun.com/prodtech/javatools/jscreator/reference/docs/apis/
The documentation for Java Studio Creator 2.

java.sun.com/javaee/javaserverfaces/
This official Sun site provides the documentation for JavaServer Faces and links to relevant articles and tutorials.

www.netbeans.org/products/visualweb/
Get the Netbeans Visual Web Pack 5.5 for Netbeans 5.5 here.

java.sun.com/javaee/5/docs/tutorial/doc/JSFPage.html#wp114889
The Java EE 5 JavaServer Faces tutorial.

jsftutorials.net/
Links to tutorials and general articles on JavaServer Faces.

javaserverfaces.dev.java.net
Download the latest version of Sun's JavaServer Faces implementation.

java.sun.com/javaee/javaserverfaces/reference/api/
Tag Library, API, and Standard RenderKit documentation for all versions of JSF.

java.sun.com/javaee/5/docs/tutorial/doc/JSFCustom.html
A tutorial on building custom JSF components.

bpcatalog.dev.java.net/nonav/webtier/index.html
The Java BluePrints solution catalog contains reusable code examples for designing web applications using JavaServer Faces and AJAX.

Summary

Section 26.1 Introduction
- Web-based applications create web content for web browser clients.
- AJAX helps web-based applications provide the interactivity and responsiveness that users typically expect of desktop applications.

Section 26.2 Simple HTTP Transactions
- Hypertext Transfer Protocol (HTTP) specifies a set of methods and headers that allow clients and servers to interact and exchange information in a uniform and reliable manner.
- In its simplest form, a web page is nothing more than an XHTML document containing markup that describes to a web browser how to display and format the document's information.
- XHTML documents can contain hypertext data (hyperlinks) that link to different pages or to other parts of the same page when the user clicks the link.
- HTTP uses URIs (Uniform Resource Identifiers) to identify data on the Internet.
- URIs that specify the locations of documents are called URLs (Uniform Resource Locators). Common URLs refer to files or directories and can reference objects that perform complex tasks.
- A URL contains information that directs a browser to the resource that the user wishes to access. Computers that run web server software make such resources available.
- When given a URL, a web browser performs a simple HTTP transaction to retrieve and display the web page found at that address.
- The HTTP GET method indicates that the client wishes to obtain a resource from the server.
- HTTP headers provide information about the data sent to a client, such as the MIME type.
- Multipurpose Internet Mail Extensions (MIME) is an Internet standard that specifies data formats so that programs can interpret data correctly.

Section 26.3 Multitier Application Architecture
- Web-based applications are multitier (or *n*-tier) applications that divide functionality into separate tiers that typically reside on separate computers.
- The bottom tier (also called the data tier or the information tier) maintains the application's data. This tier typically stores data in a relational database management system (RDBMS).
- The middle tier implements business logic, controller logic and presentation logic to control interactions between the application's clients and the its data. The middle tier acts as an intermediary between data in the information tier and the application's clients.
- The middle-tier controller logic processes client requests and retrieves data from the database.
- The middle-tier presentation logic processes data from the information tier and presents the content to the client.
- Web applications typically present data to clients as XHTML documents.
- Business logic in the middle tier enforces business rules and ensures that data is reliable before the server application updates the database or presents the data to users.
- Business rules dictate how clients can and cannot access application data, and how applications process data.
- The top tier, or client tier, is the application's user interface, which gathers input and displays output. Users interact with the application through the user interface, typically in a web browser.

- In response to user actions, the client tier interacts with the middle tier to make requests and to retrieve data from the information tier. The client tier then displays the data retrieved for the user. The client tier never directly interacts with the information tier.

Section 26.4 Java Web Technologies

- Java web technologies continually evolve to provide developers with higher levels of abstraction and greater separation of the application's tiers. This separation makes web applications more maintainable and extensible.

- Java Studio Creator 2 allows you to develop a web application's GUI in a drag-and-drop design tool, while handling the business logic in separate Java classes.

Section 26.4.1 Servlets

- Servlets use the HTTP request-response model of communication between client and server.

- Servlets extend a server's functionality by allowing the server to generate dynamic content. A servlet container executes and interacts with servlets.

- Packages `javax.servlet` and `javax.servlet.http` contain the servlet classes and interfaces.

- The servlet container receives HTTP requests from a client and directs each request to the appropriate servlet. The servlet processes the request and returns an appropriate response to the client—usually in the form of an XHTML or XML document.

- All servlets implement the `Servlet` interface of package `javax.servlet`, which ensures that each servlet can execute in the framework provided by the servlet container. Interface `Servlet` declares methods used by the servlet container to manage the servlet's life cycle.

- A servlet's life cycle begins when the servlet container loads it into memory—usually in response to the first request for the servlet. The container invokes the servlet's `init` method, which is called only once during a servlet's life-cycle to initialize the servlet. After `init` completes execution, the servlet is ready to respond to its first request. All requests are handled by a servlet's `service` method, which receives the request, processes it and sends a response to the client. Method `service` is called once per request. When the servlet container terminates the servlet, the servlet's `destroy` method is called to release any resources held by the servlet.

Section 26.4.2 JavaServer Pages

- JavaServer Pages (JSP) are an extension of servlet technology. Each JSP is translated by the JSP container into a servlet.

- Unlike servlets, JSPs help you separate presentation from content.

- JavaServer Pages enable web application programmers to create dynamic content by reusing predefined components and by interacting with components using server-side scripting.

- JSP programmers can use special software components called JavaBeans and custom tag libraries that encapsulate complex, dynamic functionality.

- Custom tag libraries allow Java developers to hide code for database access and other complex operations in custom tags. To use such capabilities, you simply add the custom tags to the page. This simplicity enables web-page designers who are not familiar with Java to enhance web pages with powerful dynamic content and processing capabilities.

- The JSP classes and interfaces are located in packages `javax.servlet.jsp` and `javax.servlet.jsp.tagext`.

- There are four key components to JSPs—directives, actions, scripting elements and tag libraries.

- Directives are messages to the JSP container that enable you to specify page settings, to include content from other resources and to specify custom tag libraries for use in JSPs.

- Actions encapsulate functionality in predefined tags that programmers can embed in JSPs. Actions often are performed based on the information sent to the server as part of a particular client request. They also can create Java objects for use in JSPs.

- Scripting elements enable you to insert Java code that interacts with components in a JSP to perform request processing.

- Tag libraries enable programmers to create custom tags and web-page designers to manipulate JSP content without prior Java knowledge.

- The JavaServer Pages Standard Tag Library (JSTL) provides the functionality for many common web application tasks.

- JSPs can contain static content such as XHTML or XML markup, which is known as fixed-template data or fixed-template text. Any literal text in a JSP is translated to a String literal in the servlet representation of the JSP.

- When a JSP-enabled server receives the first request for a JSP, the JSP container translates the JSP into a servlet that handles the current request and future requests to the JSP.

- JSPs rely on the same request/response mechanism as servlets to process requests from and send responses to clients.

Section 26.4.3 JavaServer Faces
- JavaServer Faces (JSF) is a web application framework that simplifies the design of an application's user interface and further separates a web application's presentation from its business logic.

- A framework simplifies application development by providing libraries and sometimes software tools to help you organize and build your applications.

- JSF provides custom tag libraries containing user interface components that simplify web-page design. JSF also includes a set of APIs for handling component events.

- You design the look-and-feel of a page with JSF by adding custom tags to a JSP file and manipulating their attributes. You define the page's behavior in a separate Java source-code file.

Section 26.4.4 Web Technologies in Java Studio Creator 2
- Java Studio Creator 2 web applications consist of one or more JSPs built in the JavaServer Faces framework. Each has the file-name extension .jsp and contains the web page's GUI elements.

- Java Studio Creator 2 allows you to design pages visually by dragging and dropping JSF components onto a page; you can also customize a web page by editing its .jsp file manually.

- Every JSP file created in Java Studio Creator 2 represents a web page and has a corresponding JavaBean class called the page bean.

- A JavaBean class must have a default (or no-argument) constructor, and *get* and *set* methods for all of its properties.

- The page bean defines properties for each of the page's elements, and contains event handlers, page life-cycle methods and other supporting code for the web application.

- Every web application built with Java Studio Creator 2 has a page bean, a RequestBean, a SessionBean and an ApplicationBean.

- The RequestBean object is maintained in request scope—this object exists only for the duration of an HTTP request.

- A SessionBean object has session scope—the object exists throughout a user's browsing session or until the session times out. There is a unique SessionBean object for each user.

- The ApplicationBean object has application scope—this object is shared by all instances of an application and exists as long as the application remains deployed on a web server. This object is used for application-wide data storage or processing; only one instance exists for the application, regardless of the number of open sessions.

Section 26.5.1 Examining a JSP File
- Java Studio Creator 2 generates a JSP file in response to your interactions with the Visual Editor.
- All JSPs have a `jsp:root` element with a `version` attribute to indicate the version of JSP being used and one or more `xmlns` attributes. Each `xmlns` attribute specifies a prefix and a URL for a tag library, allowing the page to use tags specified in that library.
- All JSPs generated by Java Studio Creator 2 include the tag libraries for the JSF core components library, the JSF HTML components library, the JSP standard components library and the JSP user interface components library.
- The `jsp:directive.page` element's `contentType` attribute specifies the MIME type and the character set the page uses. The `pageEncoding` attribute specifies the character encoding used by the page source. These attributes help the client determine how to render the content.
- All pages containing JSF components are represented in a component tree with the root JSF element `f:view` (of type `UIViewRoot`). All JSF component elements are placed in this element.
- Many `ui` page elements have a `binding` attribute to bind their values to properties in the web application's JavaBeans. JSF Expression Language is used to perform these bindings.
- The `ui:head` element has a `title` attribute that specifies the page's title.
- A `ui:link` element can be used to specify the CSS stylesheet used by a page.
- A `ui:body` element defines the body of the page.
- A `ui:form` element defines a form in a page.
- A `ui:staticText` component displays text that does not change.
- JSP elements are mapped to XHTML elements for rendering in a browser. The same JSP element can map to different XHTML elements, depending on the client browser and the component's property settings.
- A `ui:staticText` component typically maps to an XHTML `span` element. A `span` element contains text that is displayed on a web page and is used to control the formatting of the text. The `style` attribute of a `ui:staticText` element will be represented as part of the corresponding `span` element's `style` attribute when the browser renders the page.

Section 26.5.2 Examining a Page Bean File
- Page bean classes inherit from class `AbstractPageBean` (package `com.sun.rave.web.ui.appbase`), which provides page life-cycle methods.
- Package `com.sun.rave.web.ui.component` includes classes for many basic JSF components.
- A `ui:staticText` component is a `StaticText` object (package `com.sun.rave.web.ui.component`).

Section 26.5.3 Event-Processing Life Cycle
- Java Studio Creator 2's application model places several methods (`init`, `preprocess`, `prerender` and `destroy`) in the page bean that tie into the JSF event-processing life cycle. These methods represent four major stages—initialization, preprocessing, prerendering and destruction.
- The `init` method is called by the JSP container the first time the page is requested and on postbacks. A postback occurs when form data is submitted, and the page and its contents are sent to the server to be processed.
- Method `init` invokes its superclass version, then tries to call the method `_init`, which handles component initialization tasks.

- The preprocess method is called after init, but only if the page is processing a postback. The prerender method is called just before a page is rendered by the browser. This method should be used to set component properties; properties that are set sooner (such is in method init) may be overwritten before the page is actually rendered by the browser.

- The destroy method is called after the page has been rendered, but only if the init method was called. This method handles tasks such as freeing resources used to render the page.

Section 26.5.4 Relationship Between the JSP and Page Bean Files

- The page bean has a property for every element that appears in the JSP file.

Section 26.5.5 Examining the XHTML Generated by a Java Web Application

- To create a new web application, select **File > New Project...** to display the **New Project** dialog. In this dialog, select **Web** in the **Categories** pane, **JSF Web Application** in the **Projects** pane and click **Next**. Specify the project name and location. Click **Finish** to create the web application project.

- Java Studio Creator 2 creates a single web page named Page1 when you create a new project. This page is open by default in the Visual Editor in **Design** mode when the project first loads. As you drag and drop new components onto the page, **Design** mode allows you to see how your page will be rendered in the browser. The JSP file for this page, named Page1.jsp, can be viewed by clicking the **JSP** button at the top of the Visual Editor or by right clicking anywhere in the Visual Editor and selecting **Edit JSP Source**.

- To open the corresponding page bean file, click the **Java** button at the top of the Visual Editor or right click anywhere in the Visual Editor and select **Edit Page1 Java Source**.

- The **Preview in Browser** button at the top of the Visual Editor window allows you to view your pages in a browser without having to build and run the application.

- The **Refresh** button redraws the page in the Visual Editor.

- The **Target Browser Size** drop-down list allows you to specify the optimal browser resolution for viewing the page and allows you to see what the page will look like in different screen resolutions.

- The **Projects** window in the lower-right corner of the IDE displays the hierarchy of all the project's files. The **Web Pages** node contains the JSP files and includes the **resources** folder, which contains the project's CSS stylesheet and any other files the pages may need to display properly (e.g., images). The Java source code, including the page bean file for each web page and the application, session and request scope beans, can be found under the **Source Packages** node.

- The **Page Navigation** file defines rules for navigating the project's pages based on the outcome of user-initiated events, such as clicking a button or a link. This file can also be accessed by right clicking in the Visual Editor while in **Design** mode and selecting **Page Navigation...**.

- Methods init, preprocess, prerender and destroy are overridden in each page bean. Other than method init, these methods are initially empty. They serve as placeholders for you to customize the behavior of your web application.

- Typically, you'll want to rename the JSP and Java files in your project, so that their names are relevant to your application. To do so, right click the JSP file in the **Projects Window** and select **Rename** to display the **Rename** dialog. Enter the new file name. If **Preview All Changes** is checked, the **Refactoring Window** will appear at the bottom of the IDE when you click **Next >**. No changes will be made until you click **Do Refactoring** in the **Refactoring Window**. If you do not preview the changes, refactoring occurs when you click **Next >** in the **Rename** dialog.

- Refactoring is the process of modifying source code to improve its readability and reusability without changing its behavior—for example, by renaming methods or variables, or breaking long methods into shorter ones. Java Studio Creator 2 has built-in refactoring tools that automate some refactoring tasks.

- To add a title, open the JSP file in **Design** mode. In the **Properties** window, enter the new title next to the **Title** property and press *Enter*.

- To add components to a page, drag and drop them from the **Palette** onto the page in **Design** mode. Each component is an object that has properties, methods and events. You can set these properties and events in the **Properties** window or programmatically in the page bean file. *Get* and *set* methods are added to the page bean file for each component you add to the page.

- Components are rendered using absolute positioning, so that they appear exactly where they are dropped on the page.

- Java Studio Creator 2 is a WYSIWYG (What You See Is What You Get) editor—whenever you make a change to a web page in **Design** mode, the IDE creates the markup (visible in **JSP** mode) necessary to achieve the desired visual effects seen in **Design** mode.

- After designing the user interface, you can modify the page bean to add your business logic.

- The **Outline** window displays the page bean and the request, session and application scope beans. Clicking an item in the page bean's component tree selects the item in the Visual Editor.

- Select **Build > Build Main Project** then **Run > Run Main Project** to run the application.

- You can run a project that has already been built by pressing the **Run Main Project** icon (◈) in the toolbar at the top of the IDE.

- If changes are made to a project, the project must be rebuilt before the changes will be reflected when the application is viewed in a browser.

- Press *F5* to build the application, then run it in debug mode. If you type *<Ctrl> F5*, the program executes without debugging enabled.

Section 26.5.6 Building a Web Application in Java Studio Creator 2
- The **Grid Panel** component allows the designer to specify the number of columns the grid should contain. Components may then be dropped anywhere inside the panel, and they will automatically be repositioned into evenly spaced columns in the order in which they are dropped. When the number of components exceeds the number of columns, the panel moves the additional components to a new row.

- An **Image** component (of class Image) inserts an image into a web page. Images to be displayed on a web page must be placed in the project's resources folder. To add images to the project, drop an **Image** component onto the page and click the ellipsis button next to the url property in the **Properties** window. This opens a dialog in which you can select the image to display.

- **Text Fields** allow you to obtain text input from the user.

- Note that the order in which components are dragged to the page is important, because their JSP tags will be added to the JSP file in that order. Tabbing between components navigates the components in the order in which the JSP tags occur in the JSP file. If you would like the user to navigate the components in a certain order, you should drag them onto the page in that order. Alternatively, you can set each input field's **Tab Index** property in the **Properties** window. A component with a tab index of 1 will be the first in the tab sequence.

- A **Drop Down List** displays a list from which the user can make a selection. This object can be configured by right clicking the drop-down list in **Design** mode and selecting **Configure Default Options**, which opens the **Options Customizer** dialog box to add options to the list.

- A **Hyperlink** component of class Hyperlink adds a link to a web page. The url property of this component specifies the resource that is requested when a user clicks the hyperlink.

- A **Radio Button Group** component of class RadioButtonGroup provides a series of radio buttons from which the user can select only one. The options can be edited by right clicking the component and selecting **Configure Default Options**.

- A **Button** is a JSF component of class Button that triggers an action when clicked. A **Button** component typically maps to an input XHTML element with attribute type set to submit.

Section 26.6.2 Validation Using Validator Components and Custom Validators

- Validation helps prevent processing errors due to incomplete or improperly formatted user input.
- A **Length Validator** determines whether a field contains an acceptable number of characters.
- **Double Range Validator**s and **Long Range Validator**s determine whether numeric input falls within acceptable ranges.
- Package javax.faces.validators contains the classes for these validators.
- **Label** components describe other components and can be associated with user input fields by setting their for property.
- **Message** components display error messages when validation fails.
- To associate a **Label** or **Message** component with another component, hold the *Ctrl* and *Shift* keys, then drag the label or message to the appropriate component.
- Set the required property of a component to ensure that the user enters data for it.
- If you add a validator component or custom validator method to an input field, the field's required property must be set to true for validation to occur.
- In the Visual Editor the label for a required field is automatically marked by a red asterisk.
- If a user submits a form with an empty text field for which a value is required, the default error message for that field will be displayed in its associated ui:message component.
- To edit a **Double Range Validator**'s or a **Long Range Validator**'s properties, click its node in the **Outline** window in **Design** mode and set the maximum and minimum properties in the **Properties** window.
- It is possible to limit the length of user input without using validation by setting a **Text Field**'s maxLength property.
- Matching user input against a regular expression is an effective way to ensure that the input is properly formatted.
- Java Studio Creator 2 does not provide components for validation using regular expressions, but you can add your own custom validator methods to the page bean file.
- To add a custom validator method to an input component, right click the component and select **Edit Event Handler > validate** to create a validation method for the component in the page bean file.

Section 26.7 Session Tracking

- Personalization makes it possible for e-businesses to communicate effectively with their customers and also improves the user's ability to locate desired products and services.
- A trade-off exists between personalized e-business service and protection of privacy. Some consumers embrace the idea of tailored content, but others fear the possible adverse consequences if the information they provide to e-businesses is released or collected by tracking technologies.
- To provide personalized services to consumers, e-businesses must be able to recognize clients when they request information from a site. Unfortunately, HTTP is a stateless protocol—it does not support persistent connections that would enable web servers to maintain state information regarding particular clients. So, web servers cannot determine whether a request comes from a particular client or whether a series of requests comes from one or several clients.
- To help the server distinguish among clients, each client must identify itself to the server. Tracking individual clients, known as session tracking, can be achieved in a number of ways. One popular technique uses cookies; another uses the SessionBean object.

- With "hidden" form elements, a web form can write session-tracking data into a form in the web page that it returns to the client in response to a prior request. When the user submits the form in the new web page, all the form data, including the "hidden" fields, is sent to the form handler on the web server. With URL rewriting, the web server embeds session-tracking information directly in the URLs of hyperlinks that the user clicks to send subsequent requests.

Section 26.7.1 Cookies

- A cookie is a piece of data typically stored in a text file on the user's computer. A cookie maintains information about the client during and between browser sessions.

- The first time a user visits the website, the user's computer might receive a cookie; this cookie is then reactivated each time the user revisits that site. The collected information is intended to be an anonymous record containing data that is used to personalize the user's future visits to the site.

- Every HTTP-based interaction between a client and a server includes a header containing information either about the request (when the communication is from the client to the server) or about the response (when the communication is from the server to the client).

- When a page receives a request, the header includes information such as the request type and any cookies that have been sent previously from the server to be stored on the client machine. When the server formulates its response, the header information contains any cookies the server wants to store on the client computer and other information, such as the MIME type of the response.

- A cookie's expiration date determines how long the cookie remains on the client's computer. If you do not set a cookie's expiration date, the web browser maintains the cookie for the browsing session's duration. Otherwise, it maintains the cookie until the expiration date.

- Setting the action handler for a **Hyperlink** enables you to respond to a click without redirecting the user to another page.

- To add an action handler to a **Hyperlink** that should also direct the user to another page, you must add a rule to the **Page Navigation** file. To edit this file, right click in the Visual Designer and select **Page Navigation...**, then drag the appropriate **Hyperlink** to the destination page.

- A cookie object is an instance of class `Cookie` in package `javax.servlet.http`.

- An object of class `HttpServletResponse` (from package `javax.servlet.http`) represents the response. This object can be accessed by invoking the method `getExternalContext` on the page bean, then invoking `getResponse` on the resulting object.

- An object of class `HttpServletRequest` (from package `javax.servlet.http`) represents the request. This object can be obtained by invoking method `getExternalContext` on the page bean, then invoking `getRequest` on the resulting object.

- `HttpServletRequest` method `getCookies` returns an array of the cookies previously written to the client.

- A web server cannot access cookies created by servers in other domains.

Section 26.7.2 Session Tracking with the **SessionBean** Object

- You can perform session tracking with the `SessionBean` class that is provided in each web application created with Java Studio Creator 2. When a new client requests a web page in the project, a `SessionBean` object is created.

- The `SessionBean` can be accessed throughout a session by invoking the method `getSessionBean` on the page bean. You can then use the `SessionBean` object to access stored session properties.

- To store information in the `SessionBean`, add properties to the `SessionBean` class. To add a property, right click the `SessionBean` node in the **Outline** window and select **Add > Property** to display the **New Property Pattern** dialog. Configure the property and click **OK** to create it.

Terminology

absolute positioning
AbstractPageBean
action attribute of XHTML element form
action in a JSP
ApplicationBean
bottom tier
business logic
business rule
Button JSF component
client tier
com.sun.rave.web.ui.component
component tree
controller logic
cookie
custom tag library
custom tag
data tier
Design mode
destroy event-processing life-cycle method
directive in a JSP
DNS (domain name system) server
DNS lookup
Double Range Validator JSF component
Drop Down List JSF component
end tag
escaped property
event-processing life cycle
expiration date of a cookie
fixed-template data
fixed-template text
framework
GET HTTP request
Grid Panel JSF component
hidden input in an XHTML form
host
hostname
HTTP header
HTTP method
Hyperlink JSF component
hyperlink
hypertext
Image JSF component
information tier
init event-processing life-cycle method
IP address
JavaBeans
Java BluePrints
Java Studio Creator 2
javax.servlet package

javax.servlet.http package
JSF (JavaServer Faces)
JSF components
JSF Expression Language
JSP (JavaServer Pages)
.jsp filename extension
JSP container
JSTL (JSP Standard Tag Library)
Label JSF component
Length Validator JSF component
List Box JSF component
localhost
Long Range Validator JSF component
Message JSF component
method attribute of XHTML element form
middle tier
MIME (Multipurpose Internet Mail Extensions)
multitier application
n-tier application
Outline window
page bean
Palette
personalization
postback
preprocess event-processing life-cycle method
prerender event-processing life-cycle method
presentation logic
Radio Button Group JSF component
refactoring
rendered property
rendering XHTML in a web browser
RequestBean
required property
scripting element in a JSP
service method of Interface Servlet
servlet
Servlet interface
servlet container
SessionBean
session tracking
span element
start tag
Static Text JSF component
Sun Application Server 8
tag extension mechanism
tag library
Text Field JSF component
three-tier web-based application

tier in a multitier application
title XHTML element
top tier
validation
virtual directory
Visual Editor
web application development

web server
WYSIWYG (What You See Is What You Get)
   editor
XHTML markup
XHTML tag
XML
xmlns attributes

Self-Review Exercises

26.1 State whether each of the following is *true* or *false*. If *false*, explain why.
  a) Every JSP web page created in Java Studio Creator 2 has its own `ApplicationBean`, `SessionBean`, and `RequestBean` files.
  b) Event-processing life-cycle method `init` is invoked every time a page loads.
  c) Every component on a JSP web page is bound to a property in the Java page bean file.
  d) A single JSF component may have multiple validation components placed on it.
  e) If no expiration date is set for a cookie, that cookie will be destroyed at the end of the browser session.
  f) Each JSF component maps to exactly one corresponding XHTML element.
  g) Expressions in the JSF Expression Language syntax are delimited by `<!--` and `-->`.
  h) The `SessionBean` can store only primitive properties and properties of type `String`.

26.2 Fill in the blanks in each of the following statements:
  a) Web applications contain three basic tiers: _____, _____, and _____.
  b) The _____ JSF component is used to display error messages if validation fails.
  c) A component that checks the input in another component before submitting that input to the server is called a(n) _____.
  d) Every page bean class inherits from class _____.
  e) When a page loads the first time, the _____ event occurs first, followed by the _____ event.
  f) The _____ file contains the functionality for a JSP.
  g) A(n) _____ can be used in a custom validator method to validate the format of user input.
  h) The array of `Cookie` objects stored on the client can be obtained by calling `getCookies` on the _____ object.
  i) In a multitier application, the _____ tier controls interactions between the application's clients and the application's data.

Answers to Self-Review Exercises

26.1 a) False. If an application contains multiple JSPs, those JSPs will share the scoped data beans. b) False. `init` is invoked the first time the page is requested, but not on page refreshes. c) True. d) True. e) True. f) False. A web component can map to a group of XHTML elements—JSPs can generate complex XHTML markup from simple components. g) False. `#{` and `}` delimit JSF Expression Language statements. h) False. The scoped data beans may store any type of property.

26.2 a) bottom (information), middle (business logic), top (client). b) **Message**. c) validator. d) `AbstractPageBean`. e) `init`, `prerender`. f) page bean. g) regular expression. h) Request (`HttpServletRequest`). i) middle.

Exercises

26.3 *(Registration Form Modification)* Modify the WebComponents application to add functionality to the **Register** button. When the user clicks **Submit**, validate all input fields to make sure the user has filled out the form completely and entered a valid email address and phone number. Then, direct the user to another page that displays a message indicating successful registration and echoes back the user's registration information.

26.4 *(Page Hit Counter with **ApplicationBean**)* Create a JSP that uses the ApplicationBean to keep track of how many times a page has been visited. [*Note:* if you were to deploy this page on the web, it would count the number of times that any computer requested the page, unlike in the previous exercise.] Display the number of page hits (i.e., the value of an int property in the ApplicationBean) every time the page loads.

27

Web Applications: Part 2

OBJECTIVES

In this chapter you will learn:

- To use data providers to access databases from web applications built in Java Studio Creator 2.

- The basic principles and advantages of Ajax technology.

- To include Ajax-enabled JSF components in a Java Studio Creator 2 web application project.

- To configure virtual forms that enable subsets of a form's input components to be submitted to the server.

27.1   Introduction

This chapter continues our discussion of web application development with several advanced concepts. We discuss accessing, updating and searching databases in a web application, adding virtual forms to web pages to enable subsets of a form's input components to be submitted to the server, and using Ajax-enabled component libraries to improve application performance and component responsiveness.

We present a single address book application developed in three stages to illustrate these concepts. The application is backed by a Java DB database for storing the contact names and their addresses.

The address book application presents a form that allows the user to enter a new name and address to store in the address book and displays the contents of the address book in table format. It also provides a search form that allows the user to search for a contact and, if found, display the contact's address on a map. The first version of this application demonstrates how to add contacts to the database and how to display the list of contacts in a JSF **Table** component. In the second version, we add an Ajax-enabled **Auto Complete Text Field** component and enable it to suggest a list of contact names as the user types. The last version allows you to search the address book for a contact and display the corresponding address on a map using the Ajax-enabled `MapViewer` component that is powered by Google Maps (`maps.google.com`).

As in Chapter 26, the examples in this chapter were developed in Java Studio Creator 2.0. We installed a supplementary component library—the Java BluePrints Ajax component library—which provides the Ajax-enabled components used in the address book application. Instructions for installing this library are included in Section 27.3.1.

27.2 Accessing Databases in Web Applications

Many web applications access databases to store and retrieve persistent data. In this section, we build a web application that uses a Java DB database to store contacts in the address book and display contacts from the address book on a web page.

The web page enables the user to enter new contacts in a form. This form consists of **Text Field** components for the contact's first name, last name, street address, city, state and zip code. The form also has a **Submit** button to send the data to the server and a **Clear** button to reset the form's fields. The application stores the address book information in a database named AddressBook, which has a single table named Addresses. (We provide this database in the examples directory for this chapter. You can download the examples from www.deitel.com/books/jhtp7). This example also introduces the Table JSF component, which displays the addresses from the database in tabular format. We show how to configure the **Table** component shortly.

27.2.1 Building a Web Application That Displays Data from a Database

We now explain how to build the AddressBook application's GUI and set up a data binding that allows the **Table** component to display information from the database. We present the generated JSP file later in the section, and we discuss the related page bean file in Section 27.2.2. To build the AddressBook application, perform the following steps:

Step 1: Creating the Project
In Java Studio Creator 2, create a **JSF Web Application** project named AddressBook. Rename the JSP and page bean files to AddressBook using the refactoring tools.

Step 2: Creating the Form for User Input
In **Design** mode, add a **Static Text** component to the top of the page that reads "Add a contact to the address book:" and use the component's style property to set the font size to 18px. Add six **Text Field** components to the page and rename them fnameTextField, lnameTextField, streetTextField, cityTextField, stateTextField and zipTextField. Set each **Text Field**'s required property to true by selecting the **Text Field**, then clicking the required property's checkbox. Label each **Text Field** with a **Label** component and associate the **Label** with its corresponding **Text Field**. Finally, add a **Submit** and a **Clear** button. Set the **Submit** button's primary property to true to make it stand out more on the page than the **Clear** button and to allow the user to submit a new contact by pressing *Enter* rather than by clicking the **Submit** button. Set the **Clear** button's reset property to true to prevent validation when the user clicks the **Clear** button. Since we are clearing the fields, we don't want to ensure that they contain information. We discuss the action handler for the **Submit** button after we present the page bean file. The **Clear** button does not need an action handler method, because setting the reset property to true automatically configures the button to reset all of the page's input fields. When you have finished these steps, your form should look like Fig. 27.1.

Step 3: Adding a Table Component to the Page
Drag a **Table** component from the **Basic** section of the **Palette** to the page and place it just below the two **Button** components. Name it addressesTable. The **Table** component formats and displays data from database tables. In the **Properties** window, change the **Table**'s

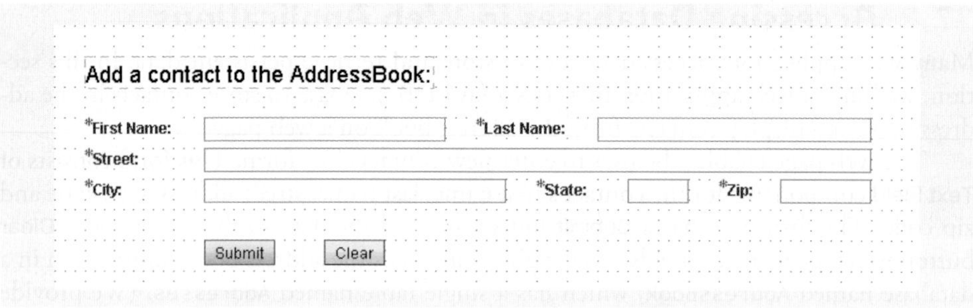

Add a contact to the AddressBook:

*First Name:		*Last Name:
*Street:		
*City:		*State: *Zip:

Submit   Clear

Fig. 27.1 | AddressBook application form for adding a contact.

title property to Contacts. We show how to configure the **Table** to interact with the AddressBook database shortly.

Step 4: Adding a Database to a Java Studio Creator 2 Web Application
For this example, we use a Java DB database named AddressBook with a single database table named Addresses. To make this database available in your projects, copy the AddressBook folder from the chapter's examples folder into your Java Studio Creator 2 installation folder's SunAppServer8\derby\databases folder.

To use a database in a Java Studio Creator 2 web application, you must first start the IDE's bundled database server, which allows database connections to be used in Java Studio Creator 2 projects. The server includes drivers for many databases, including Java DB. Click the **Servers** tab below the **File** menu, right click **Bundled Database Server** at the bottom of the **Servers** window and select **Start Bundled Database Server**. You can now use databases that run on this server in your applications.

To add the AddressBook database to this project, right click the **Data Sources** node at the top of the **Servers** window and select **Add Data Source....** In the **Add Data Source** dialog (Fig. 27.2), enter AddressBook for the data source name and select **Derby** for the server type. (Recall from Chapter 25 that Java DB is the Sun-branded version of Apache Derby.) The user ID and password for this database are both jhtp7. For the database

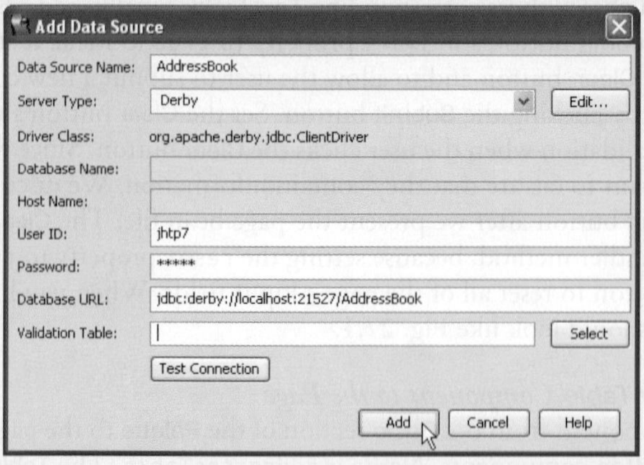

Add Data Source	
Data Source Name:	AddressBook
Server Type:	Derby Edit...
Driver Class:	org.apache.derby.jdbc.ClientDriver
Database Name:	
Host Name:	
User ID:	jhtp7
Password:	*****
Database URL:	jdbc:derby://localhost:21527/AddressBook
Validation Table:	Select
	Test Connection
	Add Cancel Help

Fig. 27.2 | Dialog to add a data source.

URL, enter `jdbc:derby://localhost:21527/AddressBook`. This URL indicates that the database resides on the local machine and accepts connections on port 21527. Click the **Select** button to choose a table that will be used to validate the database. In the dialog that appears, choose the **JHTP7.ADDRESSES** table, as this is the only table in the database. Click **Select** to close this dialog, then click **Add** to add the database as a data source for the project and close the dialog. [*Note:* Java Studio Creator 2 displays database and table names in capital letters.]

Step 5: Binding the Table Component to the Addresses Table of the AddressBook Database

Now that we've configured a data source for the `Addresses` database table, we can configure the **Table** component to display the `AddressBook` data. Simply drag the database table from the Servers tab and drop it on the **Table** component to create the binding.

If you need more precise control over the columns to display, you can bind to a database table as follows: Right click the **Table** component and select **Bind to Data** to display the **Table Layout** dialog. Click the **Add Data Provider...** button to display the **Add Data Provider** dialog, which contains a list of the available data sources. Expand the **AddressBook** node, expand the **Tables** node, select **ADDRESSES** and click **Add**. The **Table Layout** dialog now displays a list of the columns in the `Addresses` database table (Fig. 27.3). All of the items under the **Selected** heading will be displayed in the **Table**. To remove a column from the **Table**, you can select it and click the < button. Since we want to display all of these columns in our **Table**, simply click **OK** to exit the dialog.

By default, the **Table** uses the database table's column names in all uppercase letters as headings. To change these headings, select a column and edit its `headerText` property in the **Properties** window. To select a column, expand the `addressesTable` node in the **Outline** window (while in **Design** mode), then select the appropriate column object. We also changed the `id` property of each column to make the variable names in the code more readable. In **Design** mode, your **Table**'s column heads should appear as in Fig. 27.4.

An address book might contain many contacts, so we'd like to display only a few at a time. Clicking the checkbox next to the table's `paginationControls` property in the **Properties** window configures this **Table** for automatic pagination. Five rows will be displayed at a time, and buttons for moving forward and backward between groups of five contacts

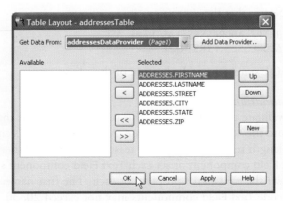

Fig. 27.3 | Dialog for binding to the `Addresses` table.

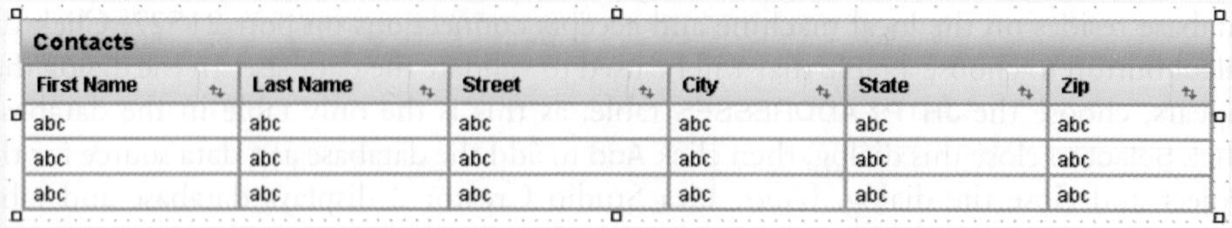

Fig. 27.4 | `Table` component after binding it to a database table and editing its column names for display purposes.

will be added to the bottom of the **Table**. (You may also use the **Table Layout** dialog's **Options** tab to select the pagination and number of rows. To view this tab, right click the **Table**, select **Table Layout...**, then click the **Options** tab.) Next, set the addressesTable's internalVirtualForm property. Virtual forms allow subsets of a form's input components to be submitted to the server. Setting this property prevents the pagination control buttons on the **Table** from submitting the **Text Field**s on the form every time the user wishes to view the next group of contacts. Virtual forms are discussed in Section 27.4.1.

Notice that binding the **Table** to a data provider added a new addressesDataProvider object (an instance of class **CachedRowSetDataProvider**) to the **AddressBook** node in the **Outline** window. A CachedRowSetDataProvider provides a scrollable RowSet that can be bound to a **Table** component to display the RowSet's data. This data provider is a wrapper for a CachedRowSet object. If you click the **addressesDataProvider** element in the **Outline** window, you will see in the **Properties** window that its CachedRowSet property is set to addressesRowSet, an object that implements interface CachedRowSet.

Step 6: Modifying *addressesRowSet's* SQL Statement
The CachedRowSet object wrapped by our addressesDataProvider is configured by default to execute a SQL query that selects all the data in the Addresses table of the AddressBook database. You can edit this SQL query by expanding the SessionBean node in the **Outline** window and double clicking the addressesRowSet element to open the query editor window (Fig. 27.5). We'd like to edit the SQL statement so that records with duplicate last names are sorted by last name, then by first name. To do this, click in the **Sort Type** column next to the **LASTNAME** row and select **Ascending**. Then, repeat this for the **FIRSTNAME** row. Notice that the expression

```
ORDER BY JHTP7.ADDRESSES.LASTNAME ASC,
    JHTP7.ADDRESSES.FIRSTNAME ASC
```

was added to the SQL statement at the bottom of the editor.

Step 7: Adding Validation
It is important to validate the form data on this page to ensure that the data can be successfully inserted into the AddressBook database. All of the database's columns are of type varchar and have length restrictions. For this reason, you should either add a **Length Validator** to each **Text Field** component or set each **Text Field** component's maxLength property. We chose to set the maxLength property of each. The first name, last name, street, city, state and zip code **Text Field** components may not exceed 20, 30, 100, 30, 2 and 5 characters, respectively.

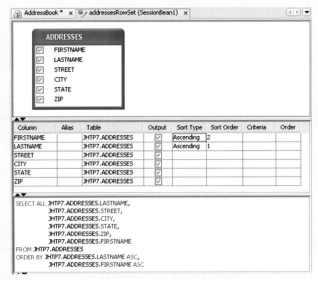

Fig. 27.5 | Editing addressesRowSet's SQL statement.

Finally, drag a **Message Group** component onto your page to the right of the **Table**. A **Message Group** component displays system messages. We use this component to display an error message when an attempt to add a contact to the database fails. Set the **Message Group**'s showGlobalOnly property to true to prevent component-level validation error messages from being displayed here.

JSP File for a Web Page that Interacts with a Database
The JSP file for the application is shown in Fig. 27.6. This file contains a large amount of generated markup for components you learned in Chapter 26. We discuss the markup for only the components that are new in this example.

```
 1   <?xml version="1.0" encoding="UTF-8"?>
 2
 3   <!-- Fig. 27.6: AddressBook.jsp -->
 4   <!-- AddressBook JSP with an add form and a Table JSF component. -->
 5
 6   <jsp:root version="1.2" xmlns:f="http://java.sun.com/jsf/core"
 7      xmlns:h="http://java.sun.com/jsf/html" xmlns:jsp=
 8      "http://java.sun.com/JSP/Page" xmlns:ui="http://www.sun.com/web/ui">
 9      <jsp:directive.page contentType="text/html;charset = UTF-8"
10         pageEncoding="UTF-8"/>
11      <f:view>
12         <ui:page binding="#{AddressBook.page1}" id="page1">
13            <ui:html binding="#{AddressBook.html1}" id="html1">
14               <ui:head binding="#{AddressBook.head1}" id="head1">
15                  <ui:link binding="#{AddressBook.link1}" id="link1"
16                     url="/resources/stylesheet.css"/>
```

Fig. 27.6 | AddressBook JSP with an add form and a **Table** JSF component (Part 1 of 5.)

```
17              </ui:head>
18              <ui:body binding="#{AddressBook.body1}" id="body1"
19                 style="-rave-layout: grid">
20                 <ui:form binding="#{AddressBook.form1}" id="form1">
21                    <ui:staticText binding="#{AddressBook.staticText1}" id=
22                       "staticText1" style="font-size: 18px; left: 24px;
23                       top: 24px; position: absolute"
24                       text="Add a contact to the address book:"/>
25                    <ui:textField binding="#{AddressBook.fnameTextField}"
26                       id="fnameTextField" maxLength="20" required="true"
27                       style="left: 120px; top: 72px; position: absolute;
28                       width: 192px"/>
29                    <ui:textField binding="#{AddressBook.lnameTextField}"
30                       id="lnameTextField" maxLength="30" required="true"
31                       style="left: 432px; top: 72px; position: absolute;
32                       width: 240px"/>
33                    <ui:textField binding="#{AddressBook.streetTextField}"
34                       id="streetTextField" maxLength="100" required="true"
35                       style="left: 120px; top: 96px; position: absolute;
36                       width: 552px"/>
37                    <ui:textField binding="#{AddressBook.cityTextField}"
38                       id="cityTextField" maxLength="30" required="true"
39                       style="left: 120px; top: 120px; position: absolute"/>
40                    <ui:textField binding="#{AddressBook.stateTextField}"
41                       id="stateTextField" maxLength="2" required="true"
42                       style="left: 456px; top: 120px; position: absolute;
43                       width: 48px"/>
44                    <ui:textField binding="#{AddressBook.zipTextField}"
45                       id="zipTextField" maxLength="5" required="true"
46                       style="left: 576px; top: 120px; position: absolute;
47                       width: 96px"/>
48                    <ui:label binding="#{AddressBook.fnameLabel}" for=
49                       "fnameTextField" id="fnameLabel" style="position:
50                       absolute; left: 24px; top: 72px" text="First Name:"/>
51                    <ui:label binding="#{AddressBook.lnameLabel}" for=
52                       "lnameTextField" id="lnameLabel" style="left: 336px;
53                       top: 72px; position: absolute" text="Last Name:"/>
54                    <ui:label binding="#{AddressBook.streetLabel}" for=
55                       "streetTextField" id="streetLabel" style="position:
56                       absolute; left: 24px; top: 96px" text="Street:"/>
57                    <ui:label binding="#{AddressBook.cityLabel}" for=
58                       "cityTextField" id="cityLabel" style="position:
59                       absolute; left: 24px; top: 120px" text="City:"/>
60                    <ui:label binding="#{AddressBook.stateLabel}" for=
61                       "stateTextField" id="stateLabel" style="position:
62                       absolute; left: 384px; top: 120px" text="State:"/>
63                    <ui:label binding="#{AddressBook.zipLabel}" for=
64                       "zipTextField" id="zipLabel" style="left: 528px; top:
65                       120px; position: absolute" text="Zip:"/>
66                    <ui:button action="#{AddressBook.submitButton_action}"
67                       binding="#{AddressBook.submitButton}" id=
68                       "submitButton" primary="true" style="position:
69                       absolute; left: 120px; top: 168px" text="Submit"/>
```

Fig. 27.6 | AddressBook JSP with an add form and a **Table** JSF component (Part 2 of 5.)

```
70                        <ui:button binding="#{AddressBook.clearButton}" id=
71                           "clearButton" reset="true" style="left: 215px; top:
72                           168px; position: absolute" text="Clear"/>
73                        <ui:table augmentTitle="false" binding=
74                           "#{AddressBook.addressesTable}" id="addressesTable"
75                           paginationControls="true" style="left: 24px; top:
76                           216px; position: absolute; width: 360px"
77                           title="Contacts" width="720">
78                           <script><![CDATA[
79   <!-- Lines 79-140 contain JavaScript code that was removed to save space.
80        The complete source code is provided in this example's folder. -->
141                          ]]></script>
142                          <ui:tableRowGroup binding=
143                             "#{AddressBook.tableRowGroup1}" id=
144                             "tableRowGroup1" rows="5" sourceData=
145                             "#{AddressBook.addressesDataProvider}"
146                             sourceVar="currentRow">
147                             <ui:tableColumn binding=
148                                "#{AddressBook.fnameColumn}" headerText=
149                                "First Name" id="fnameColumn" sort=
150                                "ADDRESSES.FIRSTNAME">
151                                <ui:staticText binding=
152                                   "#{AddressBook.fnameHeader}" id=
153                                   "fnameHeader" text="#{currentRow.value[
154                                   'ADDRESSES.FIRSTNAME']}"/>
155                             </ui:tableColumn>
156                             <ui:tableColumn binding=
157                                "#{AddressBook.lnameColumn}" headerText=
158                                "Last Name" id="lnameColumn"
159                                sort="ADDRESSES.LASTNAME">
160                                <ui:staticText binding=
161                                   "#{AddressBook.lnameHeader}" id=
162                                   "lnameHeader" text="#{currentRow.value[
163                                   'ADDRESSES.LASTNAME']}"/>
164                             </ui:tableColumn>
165                             <ui:tableColumn binding=
166                                "#{AddressBook.streetColumn}" headerText=
167                                "Street" id="streetColumn"
168                                sort="ADDRESSES.STREET">
169                                <ui:staticText binding=
170                                   "#{AddressBook.streetHeader}" id=
171                                   "streetHeader" text="#{currentRow.value[
172                                   'ADDRESSES.STREET']}"/>
173                             </ui:tableColumn>
174                             <ui:tableColumn binding=
175                                "#{AddressBook.cityColumn}" headerText="City"
176                                id="cityColumn" sort="ADDRESSES.CITY">
177                                <ui:staticText binding=
178                                   "#{AddressBook.cityHeader}" id="cityHeader"
179                                   text="#{currentRow.value[
180                                   'ADDRESSES.CITY']}"/>
181                             </ui:tableColumn>
```

Fig. 27.6 | AddressBook JSP with an add form and a **Table** JSF component (Part 3 of 5.)

```
182                          <ui:tableColumn binding=
183                             "#{AddressBook.stateColumn}" headerText="State"
184                             id="stateColumn" sort="ADDRESSES.STATE">
185                             <ui:staticText binding=
186                                "#{AddressBook.stateHeader}" id=
187                                "stateHeader" text="#{currentRow.value[
188                                'ADDRESSES.STATE']}"/>
189                          </ui:tableColumn>
190                          <ui:tableColumn binding=
191                             "#{AddressBook.zipColumn}" headerText="Zip"
192                             id="zipColumn" sort="ADDRESSES.ZIP">
193                             <ui:staticText binding=
194                                "#{AddressBook.zipHeader}" id="zipHeader"
195                                text="#{currentRow.value[
196                                'ADDRESSES.ZIP']}"/>
197                          </ui:tableColumn>
198                       </ui:tableRowGroup>
199                    </ui:table>
200                    <ui:messageGroup binding="#{AddressBook.messageGroup1}"
201                       id="messageGroup1" showGlobalOnly="true" style=
202                       "position: absolute; left: 24px; top: 624px"/>
203                 </ui:form>
204              </ui:body>
205           </ui:html>
206        </ui:page>
207     </f:view>
208  </jsp:root>
```

a)

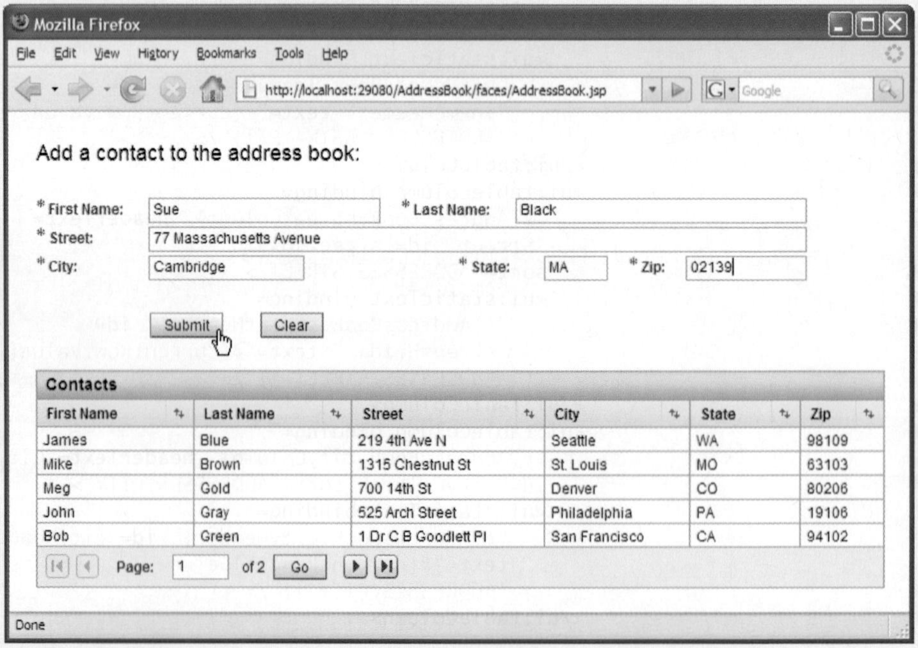

Fig. 27.6 | AddressBook JSP with an add form and a **Table** JSF component (Part 4 of 5.)

b)

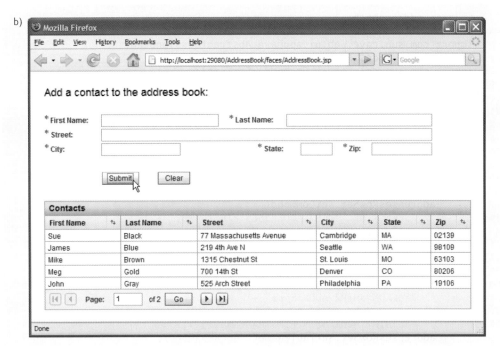

Fig. 27.6 | `AddressBook` JSP with an add form and a **Table** JSF component (Part 5 of 5.)

Lines 21–72 contain the JSF components that comprise the form that gathers user input. Lines 73–199 define the **Table** element (`ui:table`) that displays address information from the database. Lines 79–140 (not shown here) contain JavaScript functions generated by the IDE to handle **Table** actions, such as a change in the current row's state. JSF **Table**s may have multiple groups of rows displaying different data. This **Table** has a single `ui:tableRowGroup` with a start tag in lines 142–146. The row group's `sourceData` attribute is bound to our `addressesDataProvider` and given the variable name `currentRow`. The row group also defines the **Table**'s columns. Each `ui:tableColumn` element contains a `ui:staticText` element with its `text` attribute bound to a column in the data provider `currentRow`. These `ui:staticText` elements enable the **Table** to display each row's data.

Session Bean for the *AddressBook* Application
Figure 27.7 displays the `SessionBean1.java` file generated by Java Studio Creator 2 for the `AddressBook` application. The `CachedRowSet` that the **Table** component's data provider uses to access the `AddressBook` database is a property of this class (lines 31–41).

```
 1   // Fig. 27.7: SessionBean1.java
 2   // Session bean that initializes the data source for the
 3   // AddressBook database.
```

Fig. 27.7 | Session Bean that initializes the data source for the `AddressBook` database. (Part 1 of 2.)

```
 4   package addressbook;
 5
 6   import com.sun.rave.web.ui.appbase.AbstractSessionBean;
 7   import javax.faces.FacesException;
 8   import com.sun.sql.rowset.CachedRowSetXImpl;
 9
10   public class SessionBean1 extends AbstractSessionBean
11   {
12      private int __placeholder;
13
14      private void _init() throws Exception
15      {
16         addressesRowSet.setDataSourceName(
17            "java:comp/env/jdbc/AddressBook" );
18         addressesRowSet.setCommand(
19            "SELECT ALL JHTP7.ADDRESSES.FIRSTNAME," +
20            "\nJHTP7.ADDRESSES.LASTNAME," +
21            "\nJHTP7.ADDRESSES.STREET," +
22            "\nJHTP7.ADDRESSES.CITY," +
23            "\nJHTP7.ADDRESSES.STATE," +
24            "\nJHTP7.ADDRESSES.ZIP" +
25            "\nFROM JHTP7.ADDRESSES" +
26            "\nORDER BY JHTP7.ADDRESSES.LASTNAME ASC," +
27            "\nJHTP7.ADDRESSES.FIRSTNAME ASC " );
28         addressesRowSet.setTableName( "ADDRESSES" );
29      } // end method _init
30
31      private CachedRowSetXImpl addressesRowSet = new CachedRowSetXImpl();
32
33      public CachedRowSetXImpl getAddressesRowSet()
34      {
35         return addressesRowSet;
36      }
37
38      public void setAddressesRowSet( CachedRowSetXImpl crsxi )
39      {
40         this.addressesRowSet = crsxi;
41      }
42
43      // Lines 43-76 of the autogenerated code were removed to save space.
44      // The complete source code is provided in this example's folder.
45   } // end class SessionBean1
```

Fig. 27.7 | Session Bean that initializes the data source for the AddressBook database. (Part 2 of 2.)

The _init method (lines 14–29) configures addressesRowSet to interact with the AddressBook database (lines 16–27). Lines 16–17 connect the row set to the database. Lines 18–27 set addressesRowSet's SQL command to the query configured in Fig. 27.5.

27.2.2 Modifying the Page Bean File for the AddressBook Application

After building the web page and configuring the components used in this example, double click the **Submit** button to create an action event handler for this button in the page bean file. The code to insert a contact into the database will be placed in this method. The page bean with the completed event handler is shown in Fig. 27.8 below.

```java
1   // Fig. 27.8: AddressBook.java
2   // Page bean for adding a contact to the address book.
3   package addressbook;
4
5   import com.sun.data.provider.RowKey;
6   import com.sun.rave.web.ui.appbase.AbstractPageBean;
7   import com.sun.rave.web.ui.component.Body;
8   import com.sun.rave.web.ui.component.Form;
9   import com.sun.rave.web.ui.component.Head;
10  import com.sun.rave.web.ui.component.Html;
11  import com.sun.rave.web.ui.component.Link;
12  import com.sun.rave.web.ui.component.Page;
13  import javax.faces.FacesException;
14  import com.sun.rave.web.ui.component.StaticText;
15  import com.sun.rave.web.ui.component.TextField;
16  import com.sun.rave.web.ui.component.Label;
17  import com.sun.rave.web.ui.component.Button;
18  import com.sun.rave.web.ui.component.Table;
19  import com.sun.rave.web.ui.component.TableRowGroup;
20  import com.sun.rave.web.ui.component.TableColumn;
21  import com.sun.data.provider.impl.CachedRowSetDataProvider;
22  import com.sun.rave.web.ui.component.MessageGroup;
23
24  public class AddressBook extends AbstractPageBean
25  {
26     private int __placeholder;
27
28     private void _init() throws Exception
29     {
30        addressesDataProvider.setCachedRowSet(
31           (javax.sql.rowset.CachedRowSet)
32              getValue( "#{SessionBean1.addressesRowSet}" ) );
33        addressesTable.setInternalVirtualForm( true );
34     }
35
36     // Lines 36-521 of the autogenerated code were removed to save space.
37     // The complete source code is provided in this example's folder.
38
522     public void prerender()
523     {
524        addressesDataProvider.refresh();
525     } // end method prerender
526
527     public void destroy()
528     {
529        addressesDataProvider.close();
530     } // end method destroy
531
```

Fig. 27.8 | Page bean for adding a contact to the address book. (Part 1 of 2.)

```
532    // action handler that adds a contact to the AddressBook database
533    // when the user clicks submit
534    public String submitButton_action()
535    {
536       if ( addressesDataProvider.canAppendRow() )
537       {
538          try
539          {
540             RowKey rk = addressesDataProvider.appendRow();
541             addressesDataProvider.setCursorRow( rk );
542
543             addressesDataProvider.setValue( "ADDRESSES.FIRSTNAME",
544                fnameTextField.getValue() );
545             addressesDataProvider.setValue( "ADDRESSES.LASTNAME",
546                lnameTextField.getValue() );
547             addressesDataProvider.setValue( "ADDRESSES.STREET",
548                streetTextField.getValue() );
549             addressesDataProvider.setValue( "ADDRESSES.CITY",
550                cityTextField.getValue() );
551             addressesDataProvider.setValue( "ADDRESSES.STATE",
552                stateTextField.getValue() );
553             addressesDataProvider.setValue( "ADDRESSES.ZIP",
554                zipTextField.getValue());
555             addressesDataProvider.commitChanges();
556
557             // reset text fields
558             lnameTextField.setValue( "" );
559             fnameTextField.setValue( "" );
560             streetTextField.setValue( "" );
561             cityTextField.setValue( "" );
562             stateTextField.setValue( "" );
563             zipTextField.setValue( "" );
564          } // end try
565          catch ( Exception ex )
566          {
567             error( "The address book was not updated.  " +
568                ex.getMessage() );
569          } // end catch
570       } // end if
571
572       return null;
573    } // end method submitButton_action
574 } // end class AddressBook
```

Fig. 27.8 | Page bean for adding a contact to the address book. (Part 2 of 2.)

Lines 534–573 contain the event-handling code for the **Submit** button. Line 536 determines whether a new row can be appended to the data provider. If so, a new row is appended at line 540. Every row in a CachedRowSetDataProvider has its own key; method **appendRow** returns the key for the new row. Line 541 sets the data provider's cursor to the new row, so that any changes we make to the data provider affect that row. Lines 543–554 set each of the row's columns to the values entered by the user in the corresponding **Text Field**s. Line 555 stores the new contact by calling method `commitChanges` of class `CachedRowSetDataProvider` to insert the new row into the `AddressBook` database.

Lines 558–563 clear all of the form's **Text Field**s. If these lines are omitted, the fields will retain their current values after the database is updated and the page reloads. Also, the **Clear** button will not work properly if the **Text Field**s are not cleared. Rather than emptying the **Text Field**s, it will reset them to the values they held the last time form was submitted.

Lines 565–569 catch any exceptions that might occur while updating the `Address-Book` database. Lines 567–568 display a message indicating that the database was not updated as well as the exception's error message in the page's `MessageGroup` component.

In method `prerender`, line 524 calls `CachedRowSetDataProvider` method `refresh`. This re-executes the wrapped `CachedRowSet`'s SQL statement and re-sorts the **Table**'s rows so that the new row is displayed in the proper order. If you do not call `refresh`, the new address is displayed at the end of the **Table** (since we appended the new row to the end of the data provider). The IDE automatically generated code to free resources used by the data provider (line 529) in the `destroy` method.

27.3 Ajax-Enabled JSF Components

The term Ajax—short for Asynchronous JavaScript and XML—was coined by Jesse James Garrett of Adaptive Path, Inc. in February 2005 to describe a range of technologies for developing highly responsive, dynamic web applications. Ajax applications include Google Maps, Yahoo's FlickR and many more. Ajax separates the user interaction portion of an application from its server interaction, enabling both to proceed asynchronously in parallel. This enables Ajax web-based applications to perform at speeds approaching those of desktop applications, reducing or even eliminating the performance advantage that desktop applications have traditionally had over web-based applications. This has huge ramifications for the desktop applications industry—the applications platform of choice is starting to shift from the desktop to the web. Many people believe that the web—especially in the context of abundant open-source software, inexpensive computers and exploding Internet bandwidth—will create the next major growth phase for Internet companies.

Ajax makes asynchronous calls to the server to exchange small amounts of data with each call. Where normally the entire page would be submitted and reloaded with every user interaction on a web page, Ajax allows only the necessary portions of the page to reload, saving time and resources.

Ajax applications are marked up in XHTML and CSS as any other web page and make use of client-side scripting technologies such as JavaScript to interact with page elements. The `XMLHttpRequestObject` enables the asynchronous exchanges with the web server that make Ajax applications so responsive. This object can be used by most scripting languages to pass XML data from the client to the server and to process XML data sent from the server back to the client.

While using Ajax technologies in web applications can dramatically improve performance, programming in Ajax is complex and error prone. It requires page designers to know both scripting and markup languages. Ajax libraries make it possible to reap Ajax's benefits in web applications without the labor of writing "raw" Ajax. These libraries provide Ajax-enabled page elements that can be included in web pages simply by adding library-defined tags to the page's markup. We limit our discussion of building Ajax applications to the use of one such library in Java Studio Creator 2.

27.3.1 Java BluePrints Component Library

The Java BluePrints Ajax component library provides Ajax-enabled JSF components. These components rely on Ajax technology to deliver the feel and responsiveness of a desktop application over the web. Figure 27.9 summarizes the current set of components that you can download and use with Java Studio Creator 2. We demonstrate the **AutoComplete Text Field** and **Map Viewer** components in the next two sections.

To use the Java BluePrints Ajax-enabled components in Java Studio Creator 2, you must download and import them. The IDE provides a wizard for installing this group of components. To access it, choose **Tools > Update Center** to display the **Update Center Wizard** dialog. Click **Next >** to search for available updates. In the **Available Updates and New Modules** area of the dialog, select **BluePrints AJAX Components** and click the right arrow (>) button to add it to the list of items you'd like to install. Click **Next >** and follow the prompts to accept the terms of use and download the components. When the download completes, click **Next >** then click **Finish**. Click **OK** to restart the IDE.

Next, you must import the components into the **Palette**. Select **Tools > Component Library Manager**, then click **Import....** Click **Browse...** in the **Import Component Library** dialog that appears. Select the `ui.complib` file and click **Open**. Click **OK** to import both the **BluePrints AJAX Components** and the **BluePrints AJAX SupportBeans**. Close the Component Library Manager to return to the IDE.

You should now see two new nodes at the bottom of the **Palette**. The first, **BluePrints AJAX Components**, provides the eight components listed in Fig. 27.9. The second, **Blue-**

Component	Description
AutoComplete Text Field	Makes Ajax requests to display a list of suggestions as the user types in the text field.
Buy Now Button	Initiates a transaction through the PayPal web site.
Map Viewer	Uses the Google Maps API to display a map that pans, zooms, and can display markers for locations of interest.
Popup Calendar	Provides a calendar that enables a user to scroll between months and years. Fills a **Text Field** with a formatted date when the user selects a day.
Progress Bar	Visually displays the progress of a long-running operation. Uses a programmer-supplied calculation to determine the progress percentage.
Rating	Provides a customizable five-star rating bar that can display messages as the user moves the mouse over the ratings.
Rich Textarea Editor	Provides an editable text area that allows the user to format text with fonts, colors, hyperlinks and backgrounds.
Select Value Text Field	Displays a list of suggestions in a drop-down list as the user types, similar to the **AutoComplete Text Field**.

Fig. 27.9 | Ajax-enabled components provided by the Java BluePrints Ajax component library.

Prints AJAX Support Beans, includes components that support the Ajax components. You can now build high-performance Ajax web applications by dragging, dropping and configuring the component's properties, just as you do with other components in the **Palette**.

27.4 AutoComplete Text Field and Virtual Forms

We demonstrate the **AutoComplete Text Field** component from the BluePrints catalog by adding a new form to our AddressBook application. The **AutoComplete Text Field** provides a list of suggestions as the user types. It obtains the suggestions from a data source, such as a database or web service. Eventually, the new form will allow users to search the address book by last name, then first name. If the user selects a contact, the application will display the contact's name and address on a map of the neighborhood. We build this form in two stages. First, we'll add the **AutoComplete Text Field** that will display suggestions as the user types a contact's last name. Then we'll add the search functionality and map display in the next step.

Adding Search Components to the AddressBook.jsp Page

Using the AddressBook application from Section 27.2, drop a **Static Text** component named searchHeader below addressesTable. Change its text to "Search the address book by last name:" and change its font size to 18 px. Now drag an **AutoComplete Text Field** component to the page and name it nameAutoComplete. Set this field's required property to true. Add a **Label** named nameSearchLabel containing the text "Last Name:" to the left of the **AutoComplete Text Field**. Finally, add a button called lookUpButton with the text Look Up to the right of the **AutoComplete Text Field**.

27.4.1 Configuring Virtual Forms

Virtual forms are used when you would like a button to submit a subset of the page's input fields to the server. Recall that the **Table**'s internal virtual forms were enabled so that clicking the pagination buttons would not submit any of the data in the **Text Field**s used to add a contact to the AddressBook database. Virtual forms are particularly useful for displaying multiple forms on the same page. They allow you to specify a submitter and one or more participants for a form. When the virtual form's submitter component is clicked, only the values of its participant components will be submitted to the server. We use virtual forms in our AddressBook application to separate the form for adding a contact to the AddressBook database from the form for searching the database.

To add virtual forms to the page, right click the **Submit** button on the upper form and choose **Configure Virtual Forms...** from the popup menu to display the **Configure Virtual Forms** dialog. Click **New** to add a virtual form, then click in the **Name** column and change the new form's name to addForm. Double click the **Submit** column and change the option to **Yes** to indicate that this button should be used to submit the addForm virtual form. Click **OK** to exit the dialog. Next, select all the **Text Field**s used to enter a contact's information in the upper form. You can do this by holding the *Ctrl* key while you click each **Text Field**. Right click one of the selected **Text Field**s and choose **Configure Virtual Forms....** In the **Participate** column of the addForm, change the option to **Yes** to indicate that the values in these **Text Field**s should be submitted to the server when the form is submitted. Figure 27.10 shows the **Configure Virtual Forms** dialog after both virtual forms have been added. Click **OK** to exit.

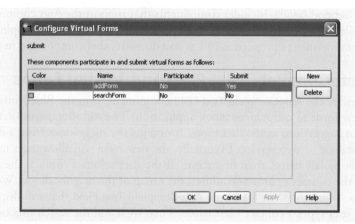

Fig. 27.10 | **Configure Virtual Forms** dialog.

Repeat the process described above to create a second virtual form named searchForm for the lower form. The **Look Up** Button should submit the searchForm, and nameAuto-Complete should participate in the searchForm. Next, return to **Design** mode and click the **Show Virtual Forms** button (▦) at the top of the Visual Designer panel to display a legend of the virtual forms on the page. Your virtual forms should be configured as in Fig. 27.11. The **Text Field**s outlined in blue participate in the virtual form addForm. Those outlined in green participate in the virtual form searchForm. The components outlined with a

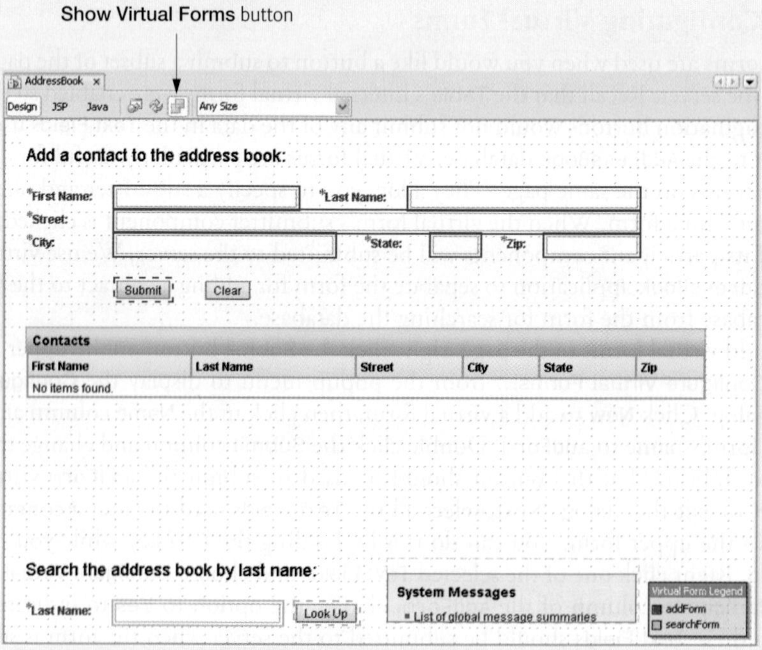

Fig. 27.11 | Virtual forms legend.

dashed line submit their respective forms. A color key is provided at the bottom right of the **Design** area so that you know which components belong to each virtual form.

27.4.2 JSP File with Virtual Forms and an AutoComplete Text Field

Figure 27.12 presents the JSP file generated by Java Studio Creator 2 for this stage of the AddressBook application. Notice that a new tag library is specified in the root element (xmlns:bp="http://java.sun.com/blueprints/ui/14"; line 6). This is the BluePrints catalog library that provides Ajax-enabled components such as the **AutoComplete Text Field** component. We focus only on the new features of this JSP.

```
1    <?xml version="1.0" encoding="UTF-8"?>
2
3    <!-- Fig. 27.12: AddressBook.jsp -->
4    <!-- AddressBook JSP with an AutoComplete Text Field component -->
5
6    <jsp:root version="1.2" xmlns:bp="http://java.sun.com/blueprints/ui/14"
7       xmlns:f="http://java.sun.com/jsf/core" xmlns:h=
8       "http://java.sun.com/jsf/html" xmlns:jsp="http://java.sun.com/JSP/Page"
9       xmlns:ui="http://www.sun.com/web/ui">
10      <jsp:directive.page contentType="text/html;charset = UTF-8"
11         pageEncoding="UTF-8"/>
12      <f:view>
13        <ui:page binding="#{AddressBook.page1}" id="page1">
14          <ui:html binding="#{AddressBook.html1}" id="html1">
15            <ui:head binding="#{AddressBook.head1}" id="head1">
16              <ui:link binding="#{AddressBook.link1}" id="link1"
17                 url="/resources/stylesheet.css"/>
18            </ui:head>
19            <ui:body binding="#{AddressBook.body1}" id="body1"
20               style="-rave-layout: grid">
21              <ui:form binding="#{AddressBook.form1}" id="form1"
22                 virtualFormsConfig="addForm | lnameTextField
23                 streetTextField fnameTextField cityTextField
24                 stateTextField zipTextField | submitButton , searchForm
25                 | nameAutoComplete | lookUpButton">
26                <ui:staticText binding="#{AddressBook.staticText1}" id=
27                   "staticText1" style="font-size: 18px; left: 24px;
28                   top: 24px; position: absolute" text=
29                   "Add a contact to the address book:"/>
30                <ui:textField binding="#{AddressBook.fnameTextField}"
31                   id="fnameTextField" maxLength="20" required="true"
32                   style="left: 120px; top: 72px; position: absolute;
33                   width: 192px"/>
34                <ui:textField binding="#{AddressBook.lnameTextField}"
35                   id="lnameTextField" maxLength="30" required="true"
36                   style="left: 432px; top: 72px; position: absolute;
37                   width: 240px"/>
38                <ui:textField binding="#{AddressBook.streetTextField}"
39                   id="streetTextField" maxLength="100" required="true"
40                   style="left: 120px; top: 96px; position: absolute;
41                   width: 552px"/>
```

Fig. 27.12 | AddressBook JSP with an **AutoComplete Text Field** component. (Part 1 of 4.)

```
42          <ui:textField binding="#{AddressBook.cityTextField}"
43              id="cityTextField" maxLength="30" required="true"
44              style="left: 120px; top: 120px; position: absolute"/>
45          <ui:textField binding="#{AddressBook.stateTextField}"
46              id="stateTextField" maxLength="2" required="true"
47              style="left: 456px; top: 120px; position: absolute;
48              width: 48px"/>
49          <ui:textField binding="#{AddressBook.zipTextField}"
50              id="zipTextField" maxLength="5" required="true"
51              style="left: 576px; top: 120px; position: absolute;
52              width: 96px"/>
53          <ui:label binding="#{AddressBook.fnameLabel}" for=
54              "fnameTextField" id="fnameLabel" style="position:
55              absolute; left: 24px; top: 72px" text="First Name:"/>
56          <ui:label binding="#{AddressBook.lnameLabel}" for=
57              "lnameTextField" id="lnameLabel" style="left: 336px;
58              top: 72px; position: absolute" text="Last Name:"/>
59          <ui:label binding="#{AddressBook.streetLabel}" for=
60              "streetTextField" id="streetLabel" style="position:
61              absolute; left: 24px; top: 96px" text="Street:"/>
62          <ui:label binding="#{AddressBook.cityLabel}" for=
63              "cityTextField" id="cityLabel" style="position:
64              absolute; left: 24px; top: 120px" text="City:"/>
65          <ui:label binding="#{AddressBook.stateLabel}" for=
66              "stateTextField" id="stateLabel" style="position:
67              absolute; left: 384px; top: 120px" text="State:"/>
68          <ui:label binding="#{AddressBook.zipLabel}" for=
69              "zipTextField" id="zipLabel" style="left: 528px;
70              top: 120px; position: absolute" text="Zip:"/>
71          <ui:button action="#{AddressBook.submitButton_action}"
72              binding="#{AddressBook.submitButton}" id=
73              "submitButton" primary="true" style="position:
74              absolute; left: 120px; top: 168px" text="Submit"/>
75          <ui:button binding="#{AddressBook.clearButton}" id=
76              "clearButton" reset="true" style="left: 215px;
77              top: 168px; position: absolute" text="Clear"/>
78          <ui:table augmentTitle="false" binding=
79              "#{AddressBook.addressesTable}" id="addressesTable"
80              paginationControls="true" style="left: 24px;
81              top: 216px; position: absolute; width: 360px"
82              title="Contacts" width="720">
83          <script><![CDATA[
84  <!-- Lines 84-145 contain JavaScript code that was removed to save space.
85      The complete source code is provided in this example's folder. -->
146         ]]></script>
147         <ui:tableRowGroup binding=
148             "#{AddressBook.tableRowGroup1}"
149             id="tableRowGroup1" rows="5" sourceData=
150             "#{AddressBook.addressesDataProvider}"
151             sourceVar="currentRow">
152         <ui:tableColumn binding=
153             "#{AddressBook.fnameColumn}" headerText=
154             "First Name" id="fnameColumn"
```

Fig. 27.12 | AddressBook JSP with an **AutoComplete Text Field** component. (Part 2 of 4.)

```
155          sort="ADDRESSES.FIRSTNAME">
156          <ui:staticText binding=
157             "#{AddressBook.fnameHeader}" id=
158             "fnameHeader" text="#{currentRow.value[
159             'ADDRESSES.FIRSTNAME']}"/>
160       </ui:tableColumn>
161       <ui:tableColumn binding=
162          "#{AddressBook.lnameColumn}" headerText=
163          "Last Name" id="lnameColumn"
164          sort="ADDRESSES.LASTNAME">
165          <ui:staticText binding=
166             "#{AddressBook.lnameHeader}" id=
167             "lnameHeader" text="#{currentRow.value[
168             'ADDRESSES.LASTNAME']}"/>
169       </ui:tableColumn>
170       <ui:tableColumn binding=
171          "#{AddressBook.streetColumn}" headerText=
172          "Street" id="streetColumn"
173          sort="ADDRESSES.STREET">
174          <ui:staticText binding=
175             "#{AddressBook.streetHeader}" id=
176             "streetHeader" text="#{currentRow.value[
177             'ADDRESSES.STREET']}"/>
178       </ui:tableColumn>
179       <ui:tableColumn binding=
180          "#{AddressBook.cityColumn}" headerText="City"
181          id="cityColumn" sort="ADDRESSES.CITY">
182          <ui:staticText binding=
183             "#{AddressBook.cityHeader}" id="cityHeader"
184             text="#{currentRow.value[
185             'ADDRESSES.CITY']}"/>
186       </ui:tableColumn>
187       <ui:tableColumn binding=
188          "#{AddressBook.stateColumn}" headerText="State"
189          id="stateColumn" sort="ADDRESSES.STATE">
190          <ui:staticText binding=
191             "#{AddressBook.stateHeader}" id=
192             "stateHeader" text="#{currentRow.value[
193             'ADDRESSES.STATE']}"/>
194       </ui:tableColumn>
195       <ui:tableColumn binding="#{AddressBook.zipColumn}"
196          headerText="Zip" id="zipColumn"
197          sort="ADDRESSES.ZIP">
198          <ui:staticText binding=
199             "#{AddressBook.zipHeader}" id="zipHeader"
200             text="#{currentRow.value[
201             'ADDRESSES.ZIP']}"/>
202       </ui:tableColumn>
203    </ui:tableRowGroup>
204 </ui:table>
205 <ui:messageGroup binding="#{AddressBook.messageGroup1}"
206    id="messageGroup1" showGlobalOnly="true" style="left:
207    408px; top: 456px; position: absolute"/>
```

Fig. 27.12 | AddressBook JSP with an **AutoComplete Text Field** component. (Part 3 of 4.)

```
208                              <ui:staticText binding="#{AddressBook.searchHeader}"
209                                  id="searchHeader" style="font-size: 18px; left: 24px;
210                                   top: 456px; position: absolute"
211                                  text="Search the address book by last name:"/>
212                              <ui:label binding="#{AddressBook.nameSearchLabel}"
213                                  for="nameAutoComplete" id="nameSearchLabel"
214                                  requiredIndicator="true"
215                                  style="position: absolute; left: 24px; top: 504px"
216                                  text="Last Name:"/>
217                              <bp:autoComplete binding=
218                                  "#{AddressBook.nameAutoComplete}" completionMethod=
219                                  "#{AddressBook.nameAutoComplete_complete}" id=
220                                  "nameAutoComplete" required="true" style="left:
221                                  120px; top: 504px; position: absolute"/>
222                              <ui:button binding="#{AddressBook.lookUpButton}"
223                                  id="lookUpButton" style="position: absolute; left:
224                                  312px; top: 504px" text="Look Up"/>
225                          </ui:form>
226                      </ui:body>
227                  </ui:html>
228              </ui:page>
229          </f:view>
230  </jsp:root>
```

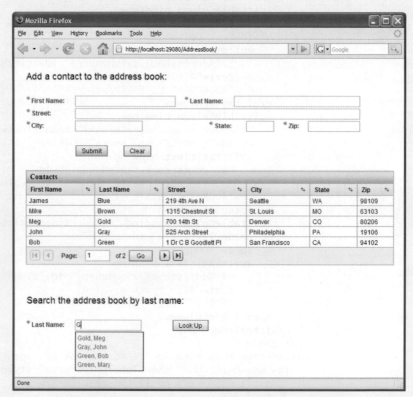

Fig. 27.12 | AddressBook JSP with an **AutoComplete Text Field** component. (Part 4 of 4.)

Lines 21–25 configure the virtual forms for this page. Lines 217–221 define the **Auto-Complete Text Field** component. This component's completionMethod attribute is bound to the page bean's nameAutoComplete_complete method (discussed in Section 27.4.3), which provides the list of options the **AutoComplete Text Field** component should suggest. To create this method, right click the nameAutoComplete component in **Design** view and select **Edit Event Handler > complete**. Notice that the **Look Up** button (lines 222–224) does not specify an action handler method binding; we'll add this in Section 27.5.

27.4.3 Providing Suggestions for an AutoComplete Text Field

Figure 27.13 displays the page bean file for the JSP in Fig. 27.12. It includes the method nameAutoComplete_complete, which provides the functionality for the **AutoComplete Text Field**. Otherwise, this page bean is identical to the one in Fig. 27.8.

```
 1   // Fig. 27.8: AddressBook.java
 2   // Page bean that suggests names in the AutoComplete Text Field.
 3   package addressbook;
 4
 5   import com.sun.data.provider.RowKey;
 6   import com.sun.rave.web.ui.appbase.AbstractPageBean;
 7   import com.sun.rave.web.ui.component.Body;
 8   import com.sun.rave.web.ui.component.Form;
 9   import com.sun.rave.web.ui.component.Head;
10   import com.sun.rave.web.ui.component.Html;
11   import com.sun.rave.web.ui.component.Link;
12   import com.sun.rave.web.ui.component.Page;
13   import javax.faces.FacesException;
14   import com.sun.rave.web.ui.component.StaticText;
15   import com.sun.rave.web.ui.component.TextField;
16   import com.sun.rave.web.ui.component.Label;
17   import com.sun.rave.web.ui.component.Button;
18   import com.sun.rave.web.ui.component.Table;
19   import com.sun.rave.web.ui.component.TableRowGroup;
20   import com.sun.rave.web.ui.component.TableColumn;
21   import com.sun.data.provider.impl.CachedRowSetDataProvider;
22   import com.sun.rave.web.ui.component.MessageGroup;
23   import com.sun.j2ee.blueprints.ui.autocomplete.AutoCompleteComponent;
24   import com.sun.j2ee.blueprints.ui.autocomplete.CompletionResult;
25   import javax.faces.context.FacesContext;
26
27   public class AddressBook extends AbstractPageBean
28   {
29      private int __placeholder;
30
31      private void _init() throws Exception
32      {
33         addressesDataProvider.setCachedRowSet(
34            (javax.sql.rowset.CachedRowSet)
35               getValue( "#{SessionBean1.addressesRowSet}" ) );
36         addressesTable.setInternalVirtualForm( true );
37      }
```

Fig. 27.13 | Page bean that suggests names in the **AutoComplete Text Field**. (Part 1 of 3.)

```
38
39      // Lines 39-572 of the autogenerated code were removed to save space.
40      // The complete source code is provided in this example's folder.
41
573     public void prerender()
574     {
575        addressesDataProvider.refresh();
576     } // end method prerender
577
578     public void destroy()
579     {
580        addressesDataProvider.close();
581     } // end method destroy
582
583     // action handler that adds a contact to the AddressBook database
584     // when the user clicks submit
585     public String submitButton_action()
586     {
587        if ( addressesDataProvider.canAppendRow() )
588        {
589           try
590           {
591              RowKey rk = addressesDataProvider.appendRow();
592              addressesDataProvider.setCursorRow( rk );
593
594              addressesDataProvider.setValue( "ADDRESSES.FIRSTNAME",
595                 fnameTextField.getValue() );
596              addressesDataProvider.setValue( "ADDRESSES.LASTNAME",
597                 lnameTextField.getValue() );
598              addressesDataProvider.setValue( "ADDRESSES.STREET",
599                 streetTextField.getValue() );
600              addressesDataProvider.setValue( "ADDRESSES.CITY",
601                 cityTextField.getValue() );
602              addressesDataProvider.setValue( "ADDRESSES.STATE",
603                 stateTextField.getValue() );
604              addressesDataProvider.setValue( "ADDRESSES.ZIP",
605                 zipTextField.getValue() );
606              addressesDataProvider.commitChanges();
607
608              // reset text fields
609              lnameTextField.setValue( "" );
610              fnameTextField.setValue( "" );
611              streetTextField.setValue( "" );
612              cityTextField.setValue( "" );
613              stateTextField.setValue( "" );
614              zipTextField.setValue( "" );
615           } // end try
616           catch ( Exception ex )
617           {
618              error( "The address book was not updated.  " +
619                 ex.getMessage() );
620           } // end catch
621        } // end if
```

Fig. 27.13 | Page bean that suggests names in the **AutoComplete Text Field**. (Part 2 of 3.)

```
622
623        return null;
624     } // end method submitButton_action
625
626
627     // action handler for the autocomplete box that fetches names
628     // from the address book whose prefixes match the letters typed so far
629     // and displays them in a suggestion list.
630     public void nameAutoComplete_complete( FacesContext context, String
631        prefix, CompletionResult result )
632     {
633        try
634        {
635           boolean hasNext = addressesDataProvider.cursorFirst();
636
637           while ( hasNext )
638           {
639              // get a name from the database
640              String name =
641                 (String) addressesDataProvider.getValue(
642                 "ADDRESSES.LASTNAME" ) + ", " +
643                 (String) addressesDataProvider.getValue(
644                 "ADDRESSES.FIRSTNAME" ) ;
645
646              // if the name in the database starts with the prefix, add it
647              // to the list of suggestions
648              if ( name.toLowerCase().startsWith( prefix.toLowerCase() ) )
649              {
650                 result.addItem( name );
651              } // end if
652              else
653              {
654                 // terminate the loop if the rest of the names are
655                 // alphabetically less than the prefix
656                 if ( prefix.compareTo( name ) < 0 )
657                 {
658                    break;
659                 } // end if
660              } // end else
661
662              // move cursor to next row of database
663              hasNext = addressesDataProvider.cursorNext();
664           } // end while
665        } // end try
666        catch ( Exception ex )
667        {
668           result.addItem( "Exception getting matching names." );
669        } // end catch
670     } // end method nameAutoComplete_complete
671 } // end class AddressBook
```

Fig. 27.13 | Page bean that suggests names in the **AutoComplete Text Field**. (Part 3 of 3.)

Method `nameAutoComplete_complete` (lines 630–670) is invoked after every keystroke in the **AutoComplete Text Field** to update the list of suggestions based on the text the user has typed so far. The method receives a string (`prefix`) containing the text the user has entered and a `CompletionResult` object (`result`) that is used to display suggestions to the user. The method loops through the rows of the `addressesDataProvider`, retrieves the name from each row, checks whether the name begins with the letters typed so far and, if so, adds the name to `result`. Line 635 sets the cursor to the first row in the data provider. Line 637 determines whether there are more rows in the data provider. If so, lines 640–644 retrieve the last name and first name from the current row and create a `String` in the format *last name, first name*. Line 648 compares the lowercase versions of `name` and `prefix` to determine whether the `name` starts with the characters typed so far. If so, the name is a match and line 650 adds it to `result`.

Recall that the data provider wraps a `CachedRowSet` object that contains a SQL query which returns the rows in the database sorted by last name, then first name. This allows us to stop iterating through the data provider once we reach a row whose name comes alphabetically after the text entered by the user—names in the rows beyond this will all be alphabetically greater and thus are not potential matches. If the `name` does not match the text entered so far, line 656 tests whether the current name is alphabetically greater than the `prefix`. If so, line 658 terminates the loop.

> ![bee icon] **Performance Tip 27.1**
>
> *When using database columns to provide suggestions in an **AutoComplete Text Field**, sorting the columns eliminates the need to check every row in the database for potential matches. This significantly improves performance when dealing with a large database.*

If the name is neither a match nor alphabetically greater than `prefix`, then line 663 moves the cursor to the next row in the data provider. If there is another row, the loop iterates again, checking whether the name in the next row matches the `prefix` and should be added to `results`.

Lines 666–669 catch any exceptions generated while searching the database. Line 668 adds text to the suggestion box indicating the error to the user.

27.5 Google Maps Map Viewer Component

We now complete the `AddressBook` application by adding functionality to the **Look Up Button**. When the user clicks this **Button**, the name in the **AutoComplete Text Field** is used to search the `AddressBook` database. We also add a **Map Viewer** Ajax-enabled JSF component to the page to display a map of the area for the address. A **Map Viewer** uses the Google Maps API web service to find and display maps. (The details of web services are covered in Chapter 28.) In this example, using the Google Maps API is analogous to making ordinary method calls on a **Map Viewer** object and its supporting bean in the page bean file. When a contact is found, we display a map of the neighborhood with a **Map Marker** that points to the location and indicates the contact's name and address.

27.5.1 Obtaining a Google Maps API Key

To use the **Map Viewer** component, you must have an account with Google. Visit the site `https://www.google.com/accounts/ManageAccount` to register for a free account if you do not have one. Once you have logged in to your account, you must obtain a key to use the Google Maps API from www.google.com/apis/maps. The key you receive will be specific to this web application and will limit the number of maps the application can display per day. When you sign up for the key, you will be asked to enter the URL for the application that will be using the Google Maps API. If you are deploying the application only on Java Studio Creator 2's built-in Sun Application Server 8 test server, enter http://localhost:29080/ as the URL.

After you accept Google's terms and conditions, you'll be redirected to a page containing your new Google Maps API key. Save this key in a text file in a convenient location for future reference.

27.5.2 Adding a **Map Viewer** Component to a Page

Now that you have a key to use the Google Maps API, you are ready to complete the AddressBook application. With AddressBook.jsp open in **Design** mode, add a **Map Viewer** component named mapViewer below the nameAutoComplete. In the **Properties** window, set the **Map Viewer**'s key property to the key you obtained for accessing the Google Maps API. Set the rendered property to false so that the map will not be displayed when the user has not yet searched for an address. Set the zoomLevel property to 1 (In) so the user can see the street names on the map.

Drop a **Map Marker** (named mapMarker) from the **AJAX Support Beans** section of the **Palette** anywhere on the page. This component (which is not visible in **Design** view) marks the contact's location on the map. You must bind the marker to the map so that the marker will display on the map. To do so, right click the **Map Viewer** in **Design** mode component and choose **Property Bindings...** to display the **Property Bindings** dialog. Select info from the **Select bindable property** column of the dialog, then select mapMarker from the **Select binding target** column. Click **Apply**, then **Close**.

Finally, drop a **Geocoding Service Object** (named geoCoder) from the **AJAX Support Beans** section of the **Palette** anywhere on the page. This object (which is not visible in **Design** view) converts street addresses into latitudes and longitudes that the **Map Viewer** component uses to display an appropriate map.

Adding a Data Provider to the Page

To complete this application, you need a second data provider to search the AddressBook database based on the first and last name entered in the **AutoComplete Text Field**. Open the **Servers** window and expand the **AddressBook** node and its **Tables** node to reveal the **Addresses** table. Right click the table's node and select **Add To Page** to display the **Add New Data Provider with RowSet** dialog (Fig. 27.14). We want to create a new data source rather than reuse the existing one, because the query to search for contacts is different from the query to display all the contacts. Select the **Create** option for the SessionBean and enter the name addressesSearch for the data provider. Click **OK** to create the new data provider. In the **Outline** window, a new node named addressesSearchDataProvider has been added to the AddressBook node, and a node named addressesSearch has been added to the SessionBean node.

Double click the addressesSearch node to edit the SQL statement for this RowSet. Since we will use this row set to search the database for a given last and first name, we need to add search parameters to the SELECT statement the RowSet will execute. To do this,

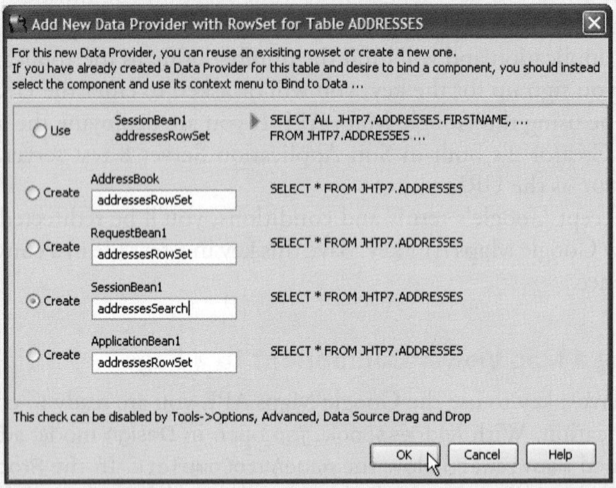

Fig. 27.14 | Dialog to create a new data provider.

enter the text "= ?" in the **Criteria** column of both the first-name and last-name rows in the SQL statement editor table. The number 1 should appear in the **Order** column for first name and 2 should appear for last name. Notice that the lines

```
WHERE JHTP7.ADDRESSES.FIRSTNAME = ?
   AND JHTP7.ADDRESSES.LASTNAME = ?
```

have been added to the SQL statement. This indicates that the RowSet now executes a parameterized SQL statement. The parameters can be set programmatically, with the first name as the first parameter and the last name as the second.

27.5.3 JSP File with a Map Viewer Component

Figure 27.15 presents the JSP file for the completed address book application. It is nearly identical to the JSP for the previous two versions of this application. The new feature is the **Map Viewer** component (and its supporting components) used to display a map with the contact's location. We discuss only the new elements of this file. [*Note:* This code will not run until you have specified your own Google Maps key in lines 227–229. You can paste your key into the **Map Viewer** component's key property in the **Properties** window.]

```
1   <?xml version="1.0" encoding="UTF-8"?>
2
3   <!-- Fig. 27.15: AddressBook.jsp -->
4   <!-- AddressBook JSP page with a Map Viewer component. -->
5
6   <jsp:root version="1.2" xmlns:bp="http://java.sun.com/blueprints/ui/14"
7      xmlns:f="http://java.sun.com/jsf/core" xmlns:h=
8      "http://java.sun.com/jsf/html" xmlns:jsp="http://java.sun.com/JSP/Page"
9      xmlns:ui="http://www.sun.com/web/ui">
```

Fig. 27.15 | AddressBook JSP with a **Map Viewer** component. (Part 1 of 5.)

```
10        <jsp:directive.page contentType="text/html;charset = UTF-8"
11          pageEncoding="UTF-8"/>
12        <f:view>
13          <ui:page binding="#{AddressBook.page1}" id="page1">
14            <ui:html binding="#{AddressBook.html1}" id="html1">
15              <ui:head binding="#{AddressBook.head1}" id="head1">
16                <ui:link binding="#{AddressBook.link1}" id="link1"
17                  url="/resources/stylesheet.css"/>
18              </ui:head>
19              <ui:body binding="#{AddressBook.body1}" id="body1"
20                style="-rave-layout: grid">
21                <ui:form binding="#{AddressBook.form1}" id="form1"
22                  virtualFormsConfig="addForm | streetTextField
23                  fnameTextField cityTextField zipTextField stateTextField
24                  lnameTextField | submitButton , searchForm |
25                  nameAutoComplete | lookUpButton">
26                  <ui:staticText binding="#{AddressBook.staticText1}" id=
27                    "staticText1" style="font-size: 18px; left: 24px;
28                    top: 24px; position: absolute"
29                    text="Add a contact to the address book:"/>
30                  <ui:textField binding="#{AddressBook.fnameTextField}"
31                    id="fnameTextField" maxLength="20" required="true"
32                    style="left: 120px; top: 72px; position: absolute;
33                    width: 192px"/>
34                  <ui:textField binding="#{AddressBook.lnameTextField}"
35                    id="lnameTextField" maxLength="30" required="true"
36                    style="left: 432px; top: 72px; position: absolute;
37                    width: 240px"/>
38                  <ui:textField binding="#{AddressBook.streetTextField}"
39                    id="streetTextField" maxLength="100" required="true"
40                    style="left: 120px; top: 96px; position: absolute;
41                    width: 552px"/>
42                  <ui:textField binding="#{AddressBook.cityTextField}"
43                    id="cityTextField" maxLength="30" required="true"
44                    style="left: 120px; top: 120px; position: absolute"/>
45                  <ui:textField binding="#{AddressBook.stateTextField}"
46                    id="stateTextField" maxLength="2" required="true"
47                    style="left: 456px; top: 120px; position: absolute;
48                    width: 48px"/>
49                  <ui:textField binding="#{AddressBook.zipTextField}"
50                    id="zipTextField" maxLength="5" required="true"
51                    style="left: 576px; top: 120px; position: absolute;
52                    width: 96px"/>
53                  <ui:label binding="#{AddressBook.fnameLabel}" for=
54                    "fnameTextField" id="fnameLabel" style="position:
55                    absolute; left: 24px; top: 72px" text="First Name:"/>
56                  <ui:label binding="#{AddressBook.lnameLabel}" for=
57                    "lnameTextField" id="lnameLabel" style="left: 336px;
58                    top: 72px; position: absolute" text="Last Name:"/>
59                  <ui:label binding="#{AddressBook.streetLabel}" for=
60                    "streetTextField" id="streetLabel" style="position:
61                    absolute; left: 24px; top: 96px" text="Street:"/>
```

Fig. 27.15 | AddressBook JSP with a **Map Viewer** component. (Part 2 of 5.)

```
62              <ui:label binding="#{AddressBook.cityLabel}" for=
63                  "cityTextField" id="cityLabel" style="position:
64                  absolute; left: 24px; top: 120px" text="City:"/>
65              <ui:label binding="#{AddressBook.stateLabel}" for=
66                  "stateTextField" id="stateLabel" style="position:
67                  absolute; left: 384px; top: 120px" text="State:"/>
68              <ui:label binding="#{AddressBook.zipLabel}" for=
69                  "zipTextField" id="zipLabel" style="left: 528px;
70                  top: 120px; position: absolute" text="Zip:"/>
71              <ui:button action="#{AddressBook.submitButton_action}"
72                  binding="#{AddressBook.submitButton}" id=
73                  "submitButton" primary="true" style="position:
74                  absolute; left: 120px; top: 168px" text="Submit"/>
75              <ui:button binding="#{AddressBook.clearButton}" id=
76                  "clearButton" reset="true" style="left: 215px;
77                  top: 168px; position: absolute" text="Clear"/>
78              <ui:table augmentTitle="false" binding=
79                  "#{AddressBook.addressesTable}" id="addressesTable"
80                  paginationControls="true" style="left: 24px; top:
81                  216px; position: absolute; width: 360px"
82                  title="Contacts" width="720">
83              <script><![CDATA[
84 <!-- Lines 84-145 contain JavaScript code that was removed to save space.
85     The complete source code is provided in this example's folder. -->
146             ]]></script>
147             <ui:tableRowGroup binding=
148                 "#{AddressBook.tableRowGroup1}" id=
149                 "tableRowGroup1" rows="5" sourceData=
150                 "#{AddressBook.addressesDataProvider}"
151                 sourceVar="currentRow">
152                 <ui:tableColumn binding=
153                     "#{AddressBook.fnameColumn}" headerText=
154                     "First Name" id="fnameColumn"
155                     sort="ADDRESSES.FIRSTNAME">
156                     <ui:staticText binding=
157                         "#{AddressBook.fnameHeader}"
158                         id="fnameHeader" text="#{currentRow.value[
159                         'ADDRESSES.FIRSTNAME']}"/>
160                 </ui:tableColumn>
161                 <ui:tableColumn binding=
162                     "#{AddressBook.lnameColumn}" headerText=
163                     "Last Name" id="lnameColumn"
164                     sort="ADDRESSES.LASTNAME">
165                     <ui:staticText binding=
166                         "#{AddressBook.lnameHeader}" id=
167                         "lnameHeader" text="#{currentRow.value[
168                         'ADDRESSES.LASTNAME']}"/>
169                 </ui:tableColumn>
170                 <ui:tableColumn binding=
171                     "#{AddressBook.streetColumn}" headerText=
172                     "Street" id="streetColumn"
173                     sort="ADDRESSES.STREET">
```

Fig. 27.15 | AddressBook JSP with a **Map Viewer** component. (Part 3 of 5.)

```
174            <ui:staticText binding=
175              "#{AddressBook.streetHeader}" id=
176              "streetHeader" text="#{currentRow.value[
177              'ADDRESSES.STREET']}"/>
178            </ui:tableColumn>
179            <ui:tableColumn binding=
180              "#{AddressBook.cityColumn}" headerText=
181              "City" id="cityColumn" sort="ADDRESSES.CITY">
182            <ui:staticText binding=
183              "#{AddressBook.cityHeader}" id="cityHeader"
184              text="#{currentRow.value[
185              'ADDRESSES.CITY']}"/>
186            </ui:tableColumn>
187            <ui:tableColumn binding=
188              "#{AddressBook.stateColumn}" headerText="State"
189              id="stateColumn" sort="ADDRESSES.STATE">
190            <ui:staticText binding=
191              "#{AddressBook.stateHeader}" id=
192              "stateHeader" text="#{currentRow.value[
193              'ADDRESSES.STATE']}"/>
194            </ui:tableColumn>
195            <ui:tableColumn binding="#{AddressBook.zipColumn}"
196              headerText="Zip" id="zipColumn"
197              sort="ADDRESSES.ZIP">
198            <ui:staticText binding=
199              "#{AddressBook.zipHeader}" id="zipHeader"
200              text="#{currentRow.value[
201              'ADDRESSES.ZIP']}"/>
202            </ui:tableColumn>
203          </ui:tableRowGroup>
204        </ui:table>
205        <ui:messageGroup binding="#{AddressBook.messageGroup1}"
206          id="messageGroup1" showGlobalOnly="true" style="left:
207          408px; top: 456px; position: absolute"/>
208        <ui:staticText binding="#{AddressBook.searchHeader}" id=
209          "searchHeader" style="font-size: 18px; left: 24px;
210          top: 456px; position: absolute"
211          text="Search the address book by last name:"/>
212        <ui:label binding="#{AddressBook.nameSearchLabel}" for=
213          "nameAutoComplete" id="nameSearchLabel"
214          requiredIndicator="true" style="position: absolute;
215          left: 24px; top: 504px" text="Last Name:"/>
216        <bp:autoComplete binding=
217          "#{AddressBook.nameAutoComplete}" completionMethod=
218          "#{AddressBook.nameAutoComplete_complete}"
219          id="nameAutoComplete" required="true" style="left:
220          120px; top: 504px; position: absolute"/>
221        <ui:button action="#{AddressBook.lookUpButton_action}"
222          binding="#{AddressBook.lookUpButton}" id=
223          "lookUpButton" style="position: absolute; left:
224          312px; top: 504px" text="Look Up"/>
225        <bp:mapViewer binding="#{AddressBook.mapViewer}" center=
226          "#{AddressBook.mapViewer_center}" id="mapViewer"
```

Fig. 27.15 | AddressBook JSP with a **Map Viewer** component. (Part 4 of 5.)

```
227                          info="#{AddressBook.mapMarker}" key=
228                          "ABQIAAAABbS__0A19lFlFZyI1XlCjBRv3hXvfLy8rd_zkEeAYi6q
229                          FBadthTMv2w53yW0G-vPtzO1VdEEPgYwqA" mapControls=
230                          "false" style="height: 600px; left: 24px; top: 552px;
231                          position: absolute; width: 718px" zoomLevel="1"/>
232                      </ui:form>
233                  </ui:body>
234              </ui:html>
235          </ui:page>
236      </f:view>
237 </jsp:root>
```

Fig. 27.15 | AddressBook JSP with a **Map Viewer** component. (Part 5 of 5.)

Lines 242–247 define the mapViewer component that displays a map of the area surrounding the address. The component's center attribute is bound to the page bean property mapViewer_center. This property is manipulated in the page bean file to center the map on the desired address.

The **Look Up** Button's action attribute is now bound to method `lookUp_action` in the page bean (line 226). This action handler searches the `AddressBook` database for the name entered in the **AutoComplete Text Field** and displays the contact's name and address on a map of the contact's location. We discuss this method in Section 27.5.3.

27.5.4 Page Bean that Displays a Map in the Map Viewer Component

Figure 27.16 presents the page bean for the completed `AddressBook` application. Most of this file is identical to the page beans for the first two versions of this application. We discuss only the new action-handler method, `lookUpButton_action`.

Method `lookUpButton_action` (lines 646–704) is invoked when the user clicks the **Look Up** button in the lower form on the page. Lines 649–652 retrieve the name from the **AutoComplete Text Field** and split it into `String`s for the first and last name. Lines 662–669 each obtain the `addressesSearchDataProvider`'s `CachedRowSet`, then use its method `setObject` to set the parameters for the query to the first and last name. The `setObject` method replaces a parameter in the SQL query with a specified string. Line 661 refreshes the data provider, which executes the wrapped `RowSet`'s query with the new parameters. The result set now contains only rows that match the first and last name from the **Auto-Complete Text Field**. Lines 662–669 fetch the street address, city, state and zip code for this contact from the database. Note that in this example, we assume there are not multiple entries in the address book for the same first and last name, as we fetch only the address information for the first row in the data provider. Any additional rows that match the first and last name are ignored.

```
1   // Fig. 27.16: AddressBook.java
2   // Page bean for adding a contact to the address books.
3   package addressbook;
4
5   import com.sun.data.provider.RowKey;
6   import com.sun.rave.web.ui.appbase.AbstractPageBean;
7   import com.sun.rave.web.ui.component.Body;
8   import com.sun.rave.web.ui.component.Form;
9   import com.sun.rave.web.ui.component.Head;
10  import com.sun.rave.web.ui.component.Html;
11  import com.sun.rave.web.ui.component.Link;
12  import com.sun.rave.web.ui.component.Page;
13  import javax.faces.FacesException;
14  import com.sun.rave.web.ui.component.StaticText;
15  import com.sun.rave.web.ui.component.TextField;
16  import com.sun.rave.web.ui.component.Label;
17  import com.sun.rave.web.ui.component.Button;
18  import com.sun.rave.web.ui.component.Table;
19  import com.sun.rave.web.ui.component.TableRowGroup;
20  import com.sun.rave.web.ui.component.TableColumn;
21  import com.sun.data.provider.impl.CachedRowSetDataProvider;
22  import com.sun.rave.web.ui.component.MessageGroup;
23  import com.sun.j2ee.blueprints.ui.autocomplete.AutoCompleteComponent;
24  import com.sun.j2ee.blueprints.ui.autocomplete.CompletionResult;
25  import javax.faces.context.FacesContext;
```

Fig. 27.16 | Page bean that gets a map to display in the `MapViewer` component. (Part 1 of 5.)

```
26   import com.sun.j2ee.blueprints.ui.mapviewer.MapComponent;
27   import com.sun.j2ee.blueprints.ui.mapviewer.MapPoint;
28   import com.sun.j2ee.blueprints.ui.geocoder.GeoCoder;
29   import com.sun.j2ee.blueprints.ui.geocoder.GeoPoint;
30   import com.sun.j2ee.blueprints.ui.mapviewer.MapMarker;
31
32   public class AddressBook extends AbstractPageBean
33   {
34      private int __placeholder;
35
36      private void _init() throws Exception
37      {
38         addressesDataProvider.setCachedRowSet(
39            (javax.sql.rowset.CachedRowSet)
40               getValue( "#{SessionBean1.addressesRowSet}" ) );
41         addressesTable.setInternalVirtualForm( true );
42         addressesSearchDataProvider.setCachedRowSet(
43            (javax.sql.rowset.CachedRowSet)
44               getValue( "#{SessionBean1.addressesSearch}" ) );
45         mapViewer.setRendered( false );
46      } // end method _init
47
48      // Lines 48-544 of the autogenerated code were removed to save space.
49      // The complete source code is provided in this example's folder.
50
545      public void prerender()
546      {
547         addressesDataProvider.refresh();
548      } // end method prerender
549
550      public void destroy()
551      {
552         addressesSearchDataProvider.close();
553         addressesDataProvider.close();
554      } // end method destroy
555
556      // action handler that adds a contact to the AddressBook database
557      // when the user clicks submit
558      public String submitButton_action()
559      {
560         if ( addressesDataProvider.canAppendRow() )
561         {
562            try
563            {
564               RowKey rk = addressesDataProvider.appendRow();
565               addressesDataProvider.setCursorRow( rk );
566
567               addressesDataProvider.setValue( "ADDRESSES.FIRSTNAME",
568                  fnameTextField.getValue() );
569               addressesDataProvider.setValue( "ADDRESSES.LASTNAME",
570                  lnameTextField.getValue() );
571               addressesDataProvider.setValue( "ADDRESSES.STREET",
572                  streetTextField.getValue() );
```

Fig. 27.16 | Page bean that gets a map to display in the `MapViewer` component. (Part 2 of 5.)

```
573          addressesDataProvider.setValue( "ADDRESSES.CITY",
574             cityTextField.getValue() );
575          addressesDataProvider.setValue( "ADDRESSES.STATE",
576             stateTextField.getValue() );
577          addressesDataProvider.setValue( "ADDRESSES.ZIP",
578             zipTextField.getValue());
579          addressesDataProvider.commitChanges();
580
581          // reset text fields
582          lnameTextField.setValue( "" );
583          fnameTextField.setValue( "" );
584          streetTextField.setValue( "" );
585          cityTextField.setValue( "" );
586          stateTextField.setValue( "" );
587          zipTextField.setValue( "" );
588       } // end try
589       catch ( Exception ex )
590       {
591          error( "The address book was not updated.  " +
592             ex.getMessage() );
593       } // end catch
594    } // end if
595
596    return null;
597 } // end method submitButton_action
598
599 // action handler for the autocomplete box that fetches names
600 // from the address book whose prefixes match the letters typed so far
601 // and displays them in a suggestion list.
602 public void nameAutoComplete_complete( FacesContext context, String
603    prefix, CompletionResult result )
604 {
605    try
606    {
607       boolean hasNext = addressesDataProvider.cursorFirst();
608
609       while ( hasNext )
610       {
611          // get a name from the database
612          String name =
613             (String) addressesDataProvider.getValue(
614             "ADDRESSES.LASTNAME" ) + ", " +
615             (String) addressesDataProvider.getValue(
616             "ADDRESSES.FIRSTNAME" ) ;
617
618          // if the name in the database starts with the prefix, add it
619          // to the list of suggestions
620          if ( name.toLowerCase().startsWith( prefix.toLowerCase() ) )
621          {
622             result.addItem( name );
623          } // end if
624          else
625          {
```

Fig. 27.16 | Page bean that gets a map to display in the `MapViewer` component. (Part 3 of 5.)

```
626              // terminate the loop if the rest of the names are
627              // alphabetically less than the prefix
628              if ( prefix.compareTo( name ) < 0 )
629              {
630                 break;
631              } // end if
632           } // end else
633
634           // move cursor to next row of database
635           hasNext = addressesDataProvider.cursorNext();
636        } // end while
637     } // end try
638     catch ( Exception ex )
639     {
640        result.addItem( "Exception getting matching names." );
641     } // end catch
642  } // end method nameAutoComplete_complete
643
644  // action handler for the lookUpButton that searches the address book
645  // database and displays the requested address on a corresponding map.
646  public String lookUpButton_action()
647  {
648     // split text in autcomplete field into first and last name
649     String name = String.valueOf( nameAutoComplete.getValue() );
650     int splitIndex = name.indexOf( "," );
651     String lname = name.substring( 0, splitIndex );
652     String fname = name.substring( splitIndex + 2 );
653
654     try
655     {
656        // set the parameters for the addressesSelected query
657        addressesSearchDataProvider.getCachedRowSet().setObject(
658           1, fname );
659        addressesSearchDataProvider.getCachedRowSet().setObject(
660           2, lname );
661        addressesSearchDataProvider.refresh();
662        String street = (String) addressesSearchDataProvider.getValue(
663           "ADDRESSES.STREET" );
664        String city = (String) addressesSearchDataProvider.getValue(
665           "ADDRESSES.CITY" );
666        String state = (String) addressesSearchDataProvider.getValue(
667           "ADDRESSES.STATE" );
668        String zip =  (String) addressesSearchDataProvider.getValue(
669           "ADDRESSES.ZIP" );
670
671        // format the address for Google Maps
672        String googleAddress = street + ", " + city + ", " + state +
673           " " + zip;
674
675        // get the geopoints for the address
676        GeoPoint points[] = geoCoder.geoCode( googleAddress );
677
```

Fig. 27.16 | Page bean that gets a map to display in the MapViewer component. (Part 4 of 5.)

```
678                // if Google Maps cannot find the address
679             if ( points == null )
680             {
681                error( "Map for " + googleAddress + " could not be found" );
682                mapViewer.setRendered( false ); // hide map
683                return null;
684             } // end if
685
686                // center the map for the given address
687             mapViewer_center.setLatitude( points[ 0 ].getLatitude() );
688             mapViewer_center.setLongitude( points[ 0 ].getLongitude() );
689
690                // create a marker for the address and set its display text
691             mapMarker.setLatitude( points[ 0 ].getLatitude() );
692             mapMarker.setLongitude( points[ 0 ].getLongitude() );
693             mapMarker.setMarkup(  fname + " " + lname + "<br/>" + street +
694                "<br/>" + city + ", " + state + " " + zip );
695
696             mapViewer.setRendered( true ); // show map
697          } // end try
698          catch ( Exception e )
699          {
700             error( "Error processing search. " + e.getMessage() );
701          } // end catch
702
703          return null;
704       } // end method lookUpButton_action
705    } // end class AddressBook
```

Fig. 27.16 | Page bean that gets a map to display in the `MapViewer` component. (Part 5 of 5.)

Lines 672–673 format the address as a String for use with the Google Maps API. Line 219 calls the **Geocoding Service Object**'s geoCode method with the address as an argument. This method returns an array of GeoPoint objects representing locations that match the address parameter. GeoPoint objects provide the latitude and longitude of a given location. We supply a complete address with a street, city, state and zip code as an argument to geoCode, so the returned array will contain just one GeoPoint object. Line 679 determines whether the array of GeoPoint objects is null. If so, the address could not be found, and lines 681–683 display a message in the **Message Group** informing the user of the search error, hide the **Map Viewer** and return null to terminate the processing.

Lines 687–688 set the latitude and longitude of the **Map Viewer**'s center to the latitude and longitude of the GeoPoint that represents the selected address. Lines 691–694 set the **Map Marker**'s latitude and longitude, and set the text to display on the marker. Line 696 displays the recentered map containing the **Map Marker** that indicates the contact's location.

Lines 698–701 catch any exceptions generated throughout the method body and display an error message in the **Message Group**. If the user has simply selected a name from the list of selections in the **AutoComplete Text Field**, there will be no errors in searching the database, as the name is guaranteed to be in the proper *last name, first name* format and included in the AddressBook database. We did not include any special error-handling code for cases in which the user types a name that cannot be found in the AddressBook or for improperly formatted names.

27.6 Wrap-Up

In this chapter, we presented a three-part case study on building a web application that interacts with a database and provides rich user interaction using Ajax-enabled JSF components. We first showed how to build an AddressBook application that allows a user to add addresses to the AddressBook and browse its contents. Through this example, you learned how to insert user input into a Java DB database and how to display the contents of a database on a web page using a **Table** JSF component.

You learned how to download and import the Java BluePrints Ajax-enabled component library. We then extended the AddressBook application to include an **AutoComplete Text Field** component. We showed how to use a database to display suggestions in the **AutoComplete Text Field**. You also learned how to use virtual forms to submit subsets of a form's input components to the server for processing.

Finally, we completed the third part of the AddressBook application by adding functionality to the search form. You learned how to use a Map Viewer, a Map Marker and a Geocoding Service Object from the Java BluePrints Ajax-enabled component library to display a Google map that shows a contact's location.

In the next chapter, you'll learn how to create and consume web services with Java. You'll use the Netbeans 5.5 IDE to create web services and consume them from desktop applications, and you'll use the Java Studio Creator IDE to consume a web service from a web application. If you would prefer to perform all these tasks in one IDE, you can download the Netbeans Visual Web Pack 5.5 (www.netbeans.org/products/visualweb/) for Netbeans 5.5.

27.7 Web Resources

www.deitel.com/ajax/Ajax_resourcecenter.html
Explore our Ajax Resource Center for links to Ajax articles, tutorials, applications, community websites, and more.

developers.sun.com/prodtech/javatools/jscreator/learning/tutorials/index.jsp
Provides dozens of tutorials on Java Studio Creator 2. Particularly useful for this chapter are the Access Databases and Work with Ajax Components sections.

developers.sun.com/prodtech/javadb/
Sun's official site on Java DB—overviews the technology and provides links to technical articles and a manual on using Apache Derby databases.

java.sun.com/reference/blueprints/
The Sun Developer Network reference site for the Java BluePrints.

blueprints.dev.java.net/
The java.net site for the Java BluePrints project.

blueprints.dev.java.net/ajaxcomponents.html
Information about the Ajax-enabled components provided by the Java BluePrints library

developers.sun.com/prodtech/javatools/jscreator/reference/code/samplecomps/index.html
Demonstrates the eight Ajax-enabled components provided by the Java BluePrints library.

google.com/apis/maps
Google account holders can sign up here for a key to use the Google Maps API.

ajax.dev.java.net/
The Project jMaki Ajax framework for building your own Ajax-enabled components.

Summary

Section 27.2 Accessing Databases in Web Applications

- Many web applications access databases to store and retrieve persistent data. In this section, we build a web application that uses a Java DB database to store contacts in the address book and display contacts from the address book on a web page.

- The web page enables the user to enter new contacts in a form. This form consists of **Text Field** components for the contact's first name, last name, street address, city, state and zip code. The form also has a **Submit** button to send the data to the server and a **Clear** button to reset the form's fields. The application stores the address book information in a database named AddressBook, which has a single table named Addresses. (We provide this database in the examples directory for this chapter. You can download the examples from www.deitel.com/books/jhtp7.) This example also introduces the **Table** JSF component, which displays the addresses from the database in tabular format. We show how to configure the **Table** component shortly.

- The **Table** component formats and displays data from database tables.

- Change the **Table**'s title property to specify the text displayed at the top of the **Table**.

- To use a database in a Java Studio Creator 2 web application, you must first start the IDE's bundled database server, which includes drivers for many types of databases, including Java DB.

- To start the server, click the **Servers** tab below the **File** menu, right click **Bundled Database Server** at the bottom of the **Servers** window and select **Start Bundled Database Server**.

- To add a Java DB database to a project, right click the **Data Sources** node at the top of the **Servers** window and select **Add Data Source....** In the **Add Data Source** dialog, enter the data source name and select **Derby** for the server type. Specify the user ID and password for the database. For the database URL, enter jdbc:derby://localhost:21527/*YourDatabaseNameHere*. This URL indicates that the database resides on the local machine and accepts connections on port 21527. Click the **Select** button to choose a table that will be used to validate the database. Click **Select** to close this dialog, then click **Add** to add the database as a data source for the project and close the dialog.

- To configure a **Table** component to display database data, right click the **Table** and select **Bind to Data** to display the **Table Layout** dialog. Click the **Add Data Provider...** button to display the **Add Data Provider** dialog, which contains a list of the available data sources. Expand the database's node, expand the **Tables** node, select a table and click **Add**. The **Table Layout** dialog displays a list of the columns in the database table. All of the items under the **Selected** heading will be displayed in the **Table**. To remove a column from the **Table**, you can select it and click the < button.

- By default, the **Table**'s column headings are the column names in the database table displayed in all capital letters. You can change these headings by selecting a column and editing its headerText property in the **Properties** window. To select a column, expand the table's node in the **Outline** window (while in **Design** mode), then select the appropriate column object.

- Clicking the checkbox next to a **Table**'s paginationControls property in the **Properties** window configures a **Table** for automatic pagination. Five rows will be displayed at a time, and buttons for moving forward and backward between groups of five contacts will be added to the bottom of the **Table**.

- Binding a **Table** to a data provider adds a new CachedRowSetDataProvider to the application's node in the **Outline** window. A CachedRowSetDataProvider provides a scrollable RowSet that can be bound to a **Table** component to display the RowSet's data.

- The CachedRowSet object wrapped by our addressesDataProvider is configured by default to execute a SQL query that selects all the data in the database table. You can edit this SQL query by expanding the SessionBean node in the **Outline** window and double clicking the RowSet element to open the query editor window.

- Every row in a `CachedRowSetDataProvider` has its own key; method `appendRow`, which adds a new row to the `CachedRowSet`, returns the key for the new row.

- Method `commitChanges` of class `CachedRowSetDataProvider` applies any changes to the `CachedRowSet` to the database.

- `CachedRowSetDataProvider` method `refresh` re-executes the wrapped `CachedRowSet`'s SQL statement.

Section 27.3 Ajax-Enabled JSF Components

- The term Ajax—short for Asynchronous JavaScript and XML—was coined by Jesse James Garrett of Adaptive Path, Inc. in February 2005 to describe a range of technologies for developing highly responsive, dynamic web applications.

- Ajax separates the user interaction portion of an application from its server interaction, enabling both to proceed asynchronously in parallel. This enables Ajax web-based applications to perform at speeds approaching those of desktop applications.

- Ajax makes asynchronous calls to the server to exchange small amounts of data with each call.

- Ajax allows only the necessary portions of the page to reload, saving time and resources.

- Ajax applications are marked up in XHTML and CSS as any other web page and make use of client-side scripting technologies such as JavaScript to interact with page elements.

- The `XMLHttpRequestObject` enables the asynchronous exchanges with the web server that make Ajax applications so responsive. This object can be used by most scripting languages to pass XML data from the client to the server and to process XML data sent from the server to the client.

- Ajax libraries make it possible to reap Ajax's benefits in web applications without the labor of writing "raw" Ajax.

- The Java BluePrints Ajax component library provides Ajax-enabled JSF components.

- To use the Java BluePrints Ajax-enabled components in Java Studio Creator 2, you must download and import them. Choose **Tools > Update Center** to display the **Update Center Wizard** dialog. Click **Next >** to search for available updates. In the **Available Updates and New Modules** area of the dialog, select **BluePrints AJAX Components** and click the right arrow (>) button to add it to the list of items you'd like to install. Click **Next >** and follow the prompts to accept the terms of use and download the components. When the download completes, click **Next >** then click **Finish**. Click **OK** to restart the IDE.

- Next, you must import the components into the **Palette**. Select **Tools > Component Library Manager**, then click **Import....** Click **Browse...** in the **Import Component Library** dialog that appears. Select the `ui.complib` file and click **Open**. Click **OK** to import both the **BluePrints AJAX Components** and the **BluePrints AJAX SupportBeans**.

Section 27.4 AutoComplete Text Field and Virtual Forms

- The **AutoComplete Text Field** provides a list of suggestions from a data source (such as a database or web service) as the user types.

- Virtual forms are used when you would like a button to submit a subset of the page's input fields to the server.

- Virtual forms enable you to display multiple forms on the same page. They allow you to specify a submitter and one or more participants for each form. When the virtual form's submitter component is clicked, only the values of its participant components will be submitted to the server.

- To add virtual forms to a page, right click the submitter component on the form and choose **Configure Virtual Forms...** from the pop-up menu to display the **Configure Virtual Forms** dialog. Click **New** to add a virtual form, then click in the **Name** column and specify the new form's name. Double click the **Submit** column and change the option to **Yes** to indicate that this button should be used to submit the virtual form. Click **OK** to exit the dialog. Next, select all the input components that will participate in the virtual form. Right click one of the selected components and choose **Configure Virtual Forms…**. In the **Participate** column of the appropriate virtual form, change the option to **Yes** to indicate that the values in these components should be submitted to the server when the form is submitted.

- To see the virtual forms in the **Design** mode, click the **Show Virtual Forms** button ( ) at the top of the Visual Designer panel to display a legend of the virtual forms on the page.

- An **AutoComplete Text Field** component's `completionMethod` attribute is bound to a page bean's `complete` event handler. To create this method, right click the **AutoComplete Text Field** component in **Design** view and select **Edit Event Handler > complete**.

- The `complete` event handler is invoked after every keystroke in an **AutoComplete Text Field** to update the list of suggestions based on the text the user has typed so far. The method receives a string containing the text the user has entered and a `CompletionResult` object that is used to display suggestions to the user.

Section 27.5 Google Maps *Map Viewer Component*
- A **Map Viewer** Ajax-enabled JSF component uses the Google Maps API web service to find and display maps. A **Map Marker** points to a location on a map.

- To use the **Map Viewer** component, you must have an account with Google. Register for a free account at `https://www.google.com/accounts/ManageAccount`. You must obtain a key to use the Google Maps API from `www.google.com/apis/maps`. The key you receive will be specific to your web application and will limit the number of maps the application can display per day. When you sign up for the key, you will be asked to enter the URL for the application that will be using the Google Maps API. If you are deploying the application only on Java Studio Creator 2's built-in test server, enter the URL `http://localhost:29080/`.

- To use a **Map Viewer**, set its key property to the Google Maps API key you obtained.

- A **Map Marker** (from the **AJAX Support Beans** section of the **Palette**) marks a location on a map. You must bind the marker to the map so that the marker will display on the map. To do so, right click the **Map Viewer** in **Design** mode component and choose **Property Bindings…** to display the **Property Bindings** dialog. Select `info` from the **Select bindable property** column of the dialog, then select the **Map Marker** from the **Select binding target** column. Click **Apply**, then **Close**.

- A **Geocoding Service Object** (from the **AJAX Support Beans** section of the **Palette**) converts street addresses into latitudes and longitudes that the **Map Viewer** component uses to display an appropriate map.

- The **Map Viewer**'s center attribute is bound to the page bean property `mapViewer_center`. This property is manipulated in the page bean file to center the map on the desired address.

- The **Geocoding Service Object**'s geoCode method receives an address as an argument and returns an array of `GeoPoint` objects representing locations that match the address parameter. `GeoPoint` objects provide the latitude and longitude of a given location.

Terminology

Ajax (Asynchronous JavaScript and XML)
Ajax-enabled component libraries
Ajax-enabled JSF components
Apache Derby
AutoComplete Text Field JSF component

binding a JSF **Table** to a database table
bundled database server
Button JSF component
Buy Now Button JSF component
CachedRowSet interface

CachedRowSetDataProvider class

commitChanges method of classCachedRowSet-
    DataProvider

data provider

event-processing life cycle

Geocoding Service Object

geoCode method of a **Geocoding Service Object**

Google Maps

Google Maps API

Java BluePrints

Java BluePrints Ajax component library

Java DB

JavaServer Faces (JSF)

Jesse James Garrett

JSF element

Map Marker JSF component

Map Viewer JSF component

Message Group JSF component

participant in a virtual form

Popup Calendar JSF component

primary property of a JSF **Button**

Progress Bar JSF component

Rating JSF component

refresh method of
    classCachedRowSetDataProvider

reset property of a JSF **Button**

Rich Textarea Editor JSF component

Select Value Text Field JSF component

Servers tab in Java Studio Creator 2

submitter in a virtual form

Table JSF component

ui:staticText JSF element

ui:table JSF element

ui:tableRowGroup JSF element

virtual form

XMLHttpRequestObject

Self-Review Exercises

27.1 State whether each of the following is *true* or *false*. If *false*, explain why.
  a) The **Table** JSF component allows you to lay out other components and text in tabular format.
  b) Virtual forms allow multiple forms, each with its own **Submit** button, to be displayed on the same web page.
  c) A CachedRowSetDataProvider is stored in the SessionBean and executes SQL queries to provide Table components with data to display.
  d) The XMLHttpRequestObject provides access to a page's request object.
  e) The complete event handler for an **AutoComplete Text Field** is called after every keystroke in the text field to provide a list of suggestions based on what has already been typed.
  f) A data provider automatically re-executes its SQL command to provide updated database information at every page refresh.
  g) To recenter a **Map Viewer** component, you must set the longitude and latitude of the map's center.

27.2 Fill in the blanks in each of the following statements.
  a) Ajax is an acronym for _____.
  b) Method _____ of class _____ updates a database to reflect any changes made in the database's data provider.
  c) A(n) _____ is a supporting component used to translate addresses into latitudes and longitudes for display in a **Map Viewer** component.
  d) A virtual form specifies that certain JSF components are _____ whose data will be submitted when the submitter component is clicked.
  e) Ajax components for Java Studio Creator 2 such as the **AutoComplete Text Field** and **Map Viewer** are provided by the _____.

Answers to Self-Review Exercises

27.1 a) False. Table components are used to display data from databases. b) True. c) False. The CachedRowSetDataProvider is a property of the page bean. It wraps a CachedRowSet, which is stored in the SessionBean and executes SQL queries. d) False. The XMLHttpRequestObject is an object that allows asynchronous exchanges with a web server. e) True. f) False. You must call method refresh on the data provider to re-execute the SQL command. g) True.

27.2 a) Asynchronous JavaScript and XML. b) commitChanges, CachedRowSetDataProvider. c) **Geocoding Service Object**. d) participants. e) Java BluePrints Ajax component library.

Exercises

27.3 *(Guestbook Application)* Create a JSF web page that allows users to sign and view a guestbook. Use the Guestbook database (provided in the examples directory for this chapter) to store guestbook entries. The Guestbook database has a single table, Messages, which has four columns: date, name, email and message. The database already contains a few sample entries. On the web page, provide **Text Field**s for the user's name and email address and a **Text Area** for the message. Add a **Submit Button** and a **Table** component and configure the **Table** to display guestbook entries. Use the **Submit Button**'s action-handler method to insert a new row containing the user's input and to-day's date into the Guestbook database.

27.4 *(Map Search Application)* Create a JSF web page that allows users to obtain a map of any address. Recall that a search for a location using the Google Maps API returns an array of GeoPoint objects. Search for locations a user enters in a **Text Field** and display a map of the first location in the resulting GeoPoint array. To handle multiple search results, display all results in a **Listbox** component. You can obtain a string representation of each result by invoking method toString on a GeoPoint object. Add a **Button** that allows users to select a result from the **Listbox** and displays a map for that result with a **Map Marker** showing the location on the map. Finally, use a **Message Group** to display messages regarding search errors. In case of an error, and when the page loads for the first time, recenter the map on a default location of your choosing.

28

JAX-WS Web Services, Web 2.0 and Mash-Ups

A client is to me a mere unit, a factor in a problem.
—Sir Arthur Conan Doyle

They also serve who only stand and wait.
—John Milton

...if the simplest things of nature have a message that you understand, rejoice, for your soul is alive.
—Eleonora Duse

Protocol is everything.
—Francoise Giuliani

OBJECTIVES

In this chapter you will learn:

- What a web service is.

- How to publish and consume web services in Netbeans.

- The elements that comprise web services, such as service descriptions and classes that implement web services.

- How to create client desktop and web applications that invoke web service methods.

- The important part that XML and the Simple Object Access Protocol (SOAP) play in enabling web services.

- How to use session tracking in web services to maintain client state information.

- How to use JDBC with web services to connect to databases.

- How to pass objects of user-defined types to and return them from a web service.

28.1 Introduction

This chapter introduces web services, which promote software portability and reusability in applications that operate over the Internet. A web service is a software component stored on one computer that can be accessed via method calls by an application (or other software component) on another computer over a network. Web services communicate using such technologies as XML and HTTP. Several Java APIs facilitate web services. In this chapter, we'll be dealing with APIs that are based on the Simple Object Access Protocol (SOAP)—an XML-based protocol that allows web services and clients to communicate, even if the client and the web service are written in different languages. There are other web services technologies, such as Representational State Transfer (REST), which we do not cover in this chapter. For information on REST, see the web resources in Section 28.10 and visit our Web Services Resource Center at

> www.deitel.com/WebServices

The Deitel Free Content Library includes the following tutorials that introduce XML:

> www.deitel.com/articles/xml_tutorials/20060401/XMLBasics/
> www.deitel.com/articles/xml_tutorials/20060401/XMLStructuringData/

Web services have important implications for **business-to-business (B2B)** **transactions**. They enable businesses to conduct transactions via standardized, widely available web services rather than relying on proprietary applications. Web services and SOAP are platform and language independent, so companies can collaborate via web services without worrying about the compatibility of their hardware, software and communications technologies. Companies such as Amazon, Google, eBay, PayPal and many others are using web services to their advantage by making their server-side applications available to partners via web services.

By purchasing web services and using extensive free web services that are relevant to their businesses, companies can spend less time developing new applications and can create innovative new applications. E-businesses can use web services to provide their customers with enhanced shopping experiences. Consider an online music store. The store's website links to information about various CDs, enabling users to purchase the CDs, to learn about the artists, to find more titles by those artists, to find other artists' music the users may enjoy, and more. Another company that sells concert tickets provides a web service that displays upcoming concert dates for various artists, and allows users to buy tickets. By consuming the concert-ticket web service on its site, the online music store can provide an additional service to its customers and increase its site traffic and perhaps earn a commission on concert-ticket sales. The company that sells concert tickets also benefits from the business relationship by selling more tickets and possibly by receiving revenue from the online music store for the use of the web service.

Any Java programmer with a knowledge of web services can write applications that can "consume" web services. The resulting applications would call web service methods of objects running on servers which could be thousands of miles away. To learn more about Java web services read the Java Technology and Web Services Overview at java.sun.com/webservices/overview.html.

Netbeans 5.5 and Sun Java Studio Creator 2

Netbeans 5.5 and Sun Java Studio Creator 2—both developed by Sun—are two of the many tools that enable programmers to "publish" and/or "consume" web services. We demonstrate how to use these tools to implement web services and invoke them from client applications. For each example, we provide the code for the web service, then present a client application that uses the web service. Our first examples build web services and client applications in Netbeans. Then we demonstrate web services that use more sophisticated features, such as manipulating databases with JDBC (which was introduced in Chapter 25, Accessing Databases with JDBC) and manipulating class objects.

Sun Java Studio Creator 2 facilitates web application development and consuming web services. Netbeans provides broader capabilities, including the ability to create, publish and consume web services. We use Netbeans to create and publish web services, and to build desktop applications that consume them. We use Sun Java Studio Creator 2 to build web applications that consume web services. The capabilities of Sun Java Studio Creator 2 can be added to Netbeans via the Netbeans Visual Web Pack. For more information on this Netbeans add-on, visit `www.netbeans.org/products/visualweb/`.

28.1.1 Downloading, Installing and Configuring Netbeans 5.5 and the Sun Java System Application Server

To develop the web services in this chapter, we use Netbeans 5.5 and the Sun Java System Application Server with the default installation options. The Netbeans website provides a bundled installer for both of these products. To download the installer, go to

> `www.netbeans.org/products/ide/`

then click the **Download Netbeans IDE** button. On the next page, select your operating system and language, then click the **Next** button. Download the installer with the title **NetBeans IDE 5.5 with Java EE Application Server 9.0 U1 bundle**.

Once you've downloaded and installed these tools, run the Netbeans IDE. On Windows XP, the installer will place an entry for Netbeans in **Start > All Programs**. Before proceeding with the rest of the chapter, perform the following steps to configure Netbeans to allow testing with the Sun Java System Application Server:

1. Select **Tools > Server Manager** to display the **Server Manager** dialog. If Sun Java System Application Server already appears in the list of servers, skip *Steps 2–6*.

2. Click the **Add Server...** button in the lower-left corner of the dialog to display the **Add Server Instance** dialog.

3. Choose **Sun Java System Application Server** from the **Server** drop-down list, then click **Next >**.

4. In the **Platform Location** field, specify the install location of Sun Java System Application Server—by default, `C:\Sun\AppServer` on Windows. Click **Next >**.

5. Specify the username and password for the server—by default, these are set to `admin` and `adminadmin`, respectively. Click **Finish**.

6. Click **Close** to close the **Server Manager** dialog.

28.1.2 Web Services Resource Center and Java Resource Centers at www.deitel.com

Visit our Web Services Resource Center at `www.deitel.com/WebServices/` for information on designing and implementing web services in many languages, and information about web services offered by companies such as Google, Amazon and eBay. You'll also find many additional Java tools for publishing and consuming web services.

Our Java Resource Centers at

> `www.deitel.com/java/`
> `www.deitel.com/JavaSE6/`
> `www.deitel.com/JavaEE5/`

provide additional Java-specific information, such as books, papers, articles, journals, websites and blogs that cover a broad range of Java topics (including Java web services).

28.2 Java Web Services Basics

The computer on which a web service resides is referred to as a remote machine or server. The application (i.e., the client) that accesses the web service sends a method call over a network to the remote machine, which processes the call and returns a response over the network to the application. This kind of distributed computing is beneficial in many applications. For example, a client application without direct access to a database on a remote server might be able to retrieve the data via a web service. Similarly, an application lacking the processing power to perform specific computations could use a web service to take advantage of another system's superior resources.

In Java, a web service is implemented as a class. In previous chapters, all the pieces of an application resided on one machine. The class that represents the web service resides on a server—it's not part of the client application.

Making a web service available to receive client requests is known as publishing a web service; using a web service from a client application is known as consuming a web service. An application that consumes a web service consists of two parts—an object of a proxy class for interacting with the web service and a client application that consumes the web service by invoking methods on the object of the proxy class. The client code invokes methods on the proxy object, which handles the details of communicating with the web service (such as passing method arguments to the web service and receiving return values from the web service) on the client's behalf. This communication can occur over a local network, over the Internet or even with a web service on the same computer. The web service performs the corresponding task and returns the results to the proxy object, which then returns the results to the client code. Figure 28.1 depicts the interactions among the client code, the proxy class and the web service. As you'll soon see, Netbeans and Sun Java Studio Creator 2 create these proxy classes for you in your client applications.

Requests to and responses from web services created with JAX-WS 2.0—the most recent Java web services framework—are typically transmitted via SOAP. Any client capable of generating and processing SOAP messages can interact with a web service, regardless of the language in which the web service is written. We discuss SOAP in Section 28.5.

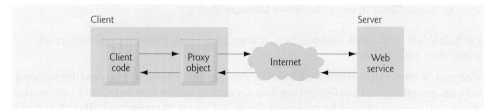

Fig. 28.1 | Interaction between a web service client and a web service.

28.3 Creating, Publishing, Testing and Describing a Web Service

The following subsections demonstrate how to create, publish and test a HugeInteger web service that performs calculations with positive integers up to 100 digits long (maintained as arrays of digits). Such integers are much larger than Java's integral primitive types can represent. The `HugeInteger` web service provides methods that take two "huge integers" (represented as `String`s) and determine their sum, their difference, which is larger, which is smaller or whether the two numbers are equal. These methods will be services available to other applications via the web—hence the term web services.

28.3.1 Creating a Web Application Project and Adding a Web Service Class in Netbeans

When you create a web service in Netbeans, you focus on the logic of the web service and let the IDE handle the web service's infrastructure. To create a web service in Netbeans, you first create a project of type **Web Application**. Netbeans uses this project type for web applications that execute in browser-based clients and for web services that are invoked by other applications.

Creating a Web Application Project in Netbeans 5.5
To create a web application, perform the following steps:

1. Select **File > New Project** to open the **New Project** dialog.

2. Select **Web** from the dialog's **Categories** list, then select **Web Application** from the **Projects** list. Click **Next >**.

3. Specify the name of your project (`HugeInteger`) in the **Project Name** field and specify where you'd like to store the project in the **Project Location** field. You can click the **Browse** button to select the location.

4. Select **Sun Java System Application Server** from the **Server** drop-down list.

5. Select **Java EE 5** from the **J2EE Version** drop-down list.

6. Click **Finish** to dismiss the **New Project** dialog.

This creates a web application that will run in a web browser. When you create a **Web Application** in Netbeans, the IDE generates additional files that support the web application. In this chapter, we discuss only the files that are specific to web services.

Adding a Web Service Class to a Web Application Project
To create a web service, perform the following steps to add a web service class to the project:

1. Under the **Projects** tab in Netbeans (just below the **File** menu), right click the **HugeInteger** project's node and select **New > Web Service...** to open the **New Web Service** dialog.

2. Specify `HugeInteger` in the **Web Service Name** field.

3. Specify `com.deitel.jhtp7.ch28.hugeinteger` in the **Package** field.

4. Click **Finish** to dismiss the **New Web Service** dialog.

The IDE generates a sample web service class with the name you specified in *Step 2*. In this class, you'll define the methods that your web service makes available to client applications. When you eventually build your application, the IDE will generate other supporting files (which we'll discuss shortly) for your web service.

28.3.2 Defining the HugeInteger Web Service in Netbeans

Figure 28.2 contains the HugeInteger web service's code. You can implement this code yourself in the HugeInteger.java file created in Section 28.3.1, or you can simply replace the code in HugeInteger.java with a copy of our code from this example's folder. You can find this file in the project's src\java\com\deitel\jhtp7\ch28\hugeinteger folder. The book's examples can be downloaded from www.deitel.com/books/jhtp7.

```java
1   // Fig. 28.2: HugeInteger.java
2   // HugeInteger web service that performs operations on large integers.
3   package com.deitel.jhtp7.ch28.hugeinteger;
4
5   import javax.jws.WebService; // program uses the annotation @WebService
6   import javax.jws.WebMethod; // program uses the annotation @WebMethod
7   import javax.jws.WebParam; // program uses the annotation @WebParam
8
9   @WebService( // annotates the class as a web service
10     name = "HugeInteger", // sets class name
11     serviceName = "HugeIntegerService" ) // sets the service name
12  public class HugeInteger
13  {
14     private final static int MAXIMUM = 100; // maximum number of digits
15     public int[] number = new int[ MAXIMUM ]; // stores the huge integer
16
17     // returns a String representation of a HugeInteger
18     public String toString()
19     {
20        String value = "";
21
22        // convert HugeInteger to a String
23        for ( int digit : number )
24           value = digit + value; // places next digit at beginning of value
25
26        // locate position of first non-zero digit
27        int length = value.length();
28        int position = -1;
29
30        for ( int i = 0; i < length; i++ )
31        {
32           if ( value.charAt( i ) != '0' )
33           {
34              position = i; // first non-zero digit
35              break;
36           }
37        } // end for
38
39        return ( position != -1 ? value.substring( position ) : "0" );
40     } // end method toString
41
42     // creates a HugeInteger from a String
43     public static HugeInteger parseHugeInteger( String s )
44     {
```

Fig. 28.2 | HugeInteger web service that performs operations on large integers. (Part I of 3.)

```
45         HugeInteger temp = new HugeInteger();
46         int size = s.length();
47
48         for ( int i = 0; i < size; i++ )
49            temp.number[ i ] = s.charAt( size - i - 1 ) - '0';
50
51         return temp;
52      } // end method parseHugeInteger
53
54      // WebMethod that adds huge integers represented by String arguments
55      @WebMethod( operationName = "add" )
56      public String add( @WebParam( name = "first" ) String first,
57         @WebParam( name = "second" ) String second )
58      {
59         int carry = 0; // the value to be carried
60         HugeInteger operand1 = HugeInteger.parseHugeInteger( first );
61         HugeInteger operand2 = HugeInteger.parseHugeInteger( second );
62         HugeInteger result = new HugeInteger(); // stores addition result
63
64         // perform addition on each digit
65         for ( int i = 0; i < MAXIMUM; i++ )
66         {
67            // add corresponding digits in each number and the carried value;
68            // store result in the corresponding column of HugeInteger result
69            result.number[ i ] =
70               ( operand1.number[ i ] + operand2.number[ i ] + carry ) % 10;
71
72            // set carry for next column
73            carry =
74               ( operand1.number[ i ] + operand2.number[ i ] + carry ) / 10;
75         } // end for
76
77         return result.toString();
78      } // end WebMethod add
79
80      // WebMethod that subtracts integers represented by String arguments
81      @WebMethod( operationName = "subtract" )
82      public String subtract( @WebParam( name = "first" ) String first,
83         @WebParam( name = "second" ) String second )
84      {
85         HugeInteger operand1 = HugeInteger.parseHugeInteger( first );
86         HugeInteger operand2 = HugeInteger.parseHugeInteger( second );
87         HugeInteger result = new HugeInteger(); // stores difference
88
89         // subtract bottom digit from top digit
90         for ( int i = 0; i < MAXIMUM; i++ )
91         {
92            // if the digit in operand1 is smaller than the corresponding
93            // digit in operand2, borrow from the next digit
94            if ( operand1.number[ i ] < operand2.number[ i ] )
95               operand1.borrow( i );
96
```

Fig. 28.2 | HugeInteger web service that performs operations on large integers. (Part 2 of 3.)

```
 97              // subtract digits
 98              result.number[ i ] = operand1.number[ i ] - operand2.number[ i ];
 99         } // end for
100
101         return result.toString();
102      } // end WebMethod subtract
103
104      // borrow 1 from next digit
105      private void borrow( int place )
106      {
107         if ( place >= MAXIMUM )
108            throw new IndexOutOfBoundsException();
109         else if ( number[ place + 1 ] == 0 ) // if next digit is zero
110            borrow( place + 1 ); // borrow from next digit
111
112         number[ place ] += 10; // add 10 to the borrowing digit
113         --number[ place + 1 ]; // subtract one from the digit to the left
114      } // end method borrow
115
116      // WebMethod that returns true if first integer is greater than second
117      @WebMethod( operationName = "bigger" )
118      public boolean bigger( @WebParam( name = "first" ) String first,
119         @WebParam( name = "second" ) String second )
120      {
121         try // try subtracting first from second
122         {
123            String difference = subtract( first, second );
124            return !difference.matches( "^[0]+$" );
125         } // end try
126         catch ( IndexOutOfBoundsException e ) // first is less than second
127         {
128            return false;
129         } // end catch
130      } // end WebMethod bigger
131
132      // WebMethod that returns true if the first integer is less than second
133      @WebMethod( operationName = "smaller" )
134      public boolean smaller( @WebParam( name = "first" ) String first,
135         @WebParam( name = "second" ) String second )
136      {
137         return bigger( second, first );
138      } // end WebMethod smaller
139
140      // WebMethod that returns true if the first integer equals the second
141      @WebMethod( operationName = "equals" )
142      public boolean equals( @WebParam( name = "first" ) String first,
143         @WebParam( name = "second" ) String second )
144      {
145         return !( bigger( first, second ) || smaller( first, second ) );
146      } // end WebMethod equals
147   } // end class HugeInteger
```

Fig. 28.2 | HugeInteger web service that performs operations on large integers. (Part 3 of 3.)

Lines 5–7 import the annotations used in this example. By default, each new web service class created with the JAX-WS APIs is a POJO (plain old Java object), meaning that—unlike prior Java web service APIs—you do not need to extend a class or implement an interface to create a Web service. When you compile a class that uses these JAX-WS 2.0 annotations, the compiler creates all the server-side artifacts that support the web service—that is, the compiled code framework that allows the web service to wait for client requests and respond to those requests once the service is deployed on an application server. Popular application servers that support Java web services include the Sun Java System Application Server (www.sun.com/software/products/appsrvr/index.xml), GlassFish (glassfish.dev.java.net), Apache Tomcat (tomcat.apache.org), BEA Weblogic Server (www.bea.com) and JBoss Application Server (www.jboss.org/products/jbossas). We use Sun Java System Application Server in this chapter.

Lines 9–11 contain a @WebService annotation (imported at line 5) with properties name and serviceName. The @WebService annotation indicates that class HugeInteger represents a web service. The annotation is followed by a set of parentheses containing optional elements. The annotation's name element (line 10) specifies the name of the proxy class that will be generated for the client. The annotation's serviceName element (line 11) specifies the name of the class that the client uses to obtain an object of the proxy class. [*Note:* If the serviceName element is not specified, the web service's name is assumed to be the class name followed by the word Service.] Netbeans places the @WebService annotation at the beginning of each new web service class you create. You can then add the name and serviceName properties in the parentheses following the annotation.

Line 14 declares the constant MAXIMUM that specifies the maximum number of digits for a HugeInteger (i.e., 100 in this example). Line 15 creates the array that stores the digits in a huge integer. Lines 18–40 declare method toString, which returns a String representation of a HugeInteger without any leading 0s. Lines 43–52 declare static method parseHugeInteger, which converts a String into a HugeInteger. The web service's methods add, subtract, bigger, smaller and equals use parseHugeInteger to convert their String arguments to HugeIntegers for processing.

HugeInteger methods add, subtract, bigger, smaller and equals are tagged with the @WebMethod annotation (lines 55, 81, 117, 133 and 141) to indicate that they can be called remotely. Any methods that are not tagged with @WebMethod are not accessible to clients that consume the web service. Such methods are typically utility methods within the web service class. Note that the @WebMethod annotations each use the operationName element to specify the method name that is exposed to the web service's client.

Common Programming Error 28.1

Failing to expose a method as a web method by declaring it with the @WebMethod annotation prevents clients of the web service from accessing the method.

Common Programming Error 28.2

Methods with the @WebMethod annotation cannot be static. An object of the web service class must exist for a client to access the service's web methods.

Each of the web methods in class HugeInteger specifies parameters that are annotated with the @WebParam annotation (e.g., lines 56–57 of method add). The optional @WebParam element name indicates the parameter name that is exposed to the web service's clients.

Lines 55–78 and 81–102 declare HugeInteger web methods add and subtract. We assume for simplicity that add does not result in overflow (i.e., the result will be 100 digits or fewer) and that the first argument to subtract will always be larger than the second. The subtract method calls method borrow (lines 105–114) when it is necessary to borrow 1 from the next digit to the left in the first argument—that is, when a particular digit in the left operand is smaller than the corresponding digit in the right operand. Method borrow adds 10 to the appropriate digit and subtracts 1 from the next digit to the left. This utility method is not intended to be called remotely, so it is not tagged with @WebMethod.

Lines 117–130 declare HugeInteger web method bigger. Line 123 invokes method subtract to calculate the difference between the numbers. If the first number is less than the second, this results in an exception. In this case, bigger returns false. If subtract does not throw an exception, then line 124 returns the result of the expression

```
    !difference.matches( "^[0]+$" )
```

This expression calls String method matches to determine whether the String difference matches the regular expression "^[0]+$", which determines if the String consists only of one or more 0s. The symbols ^ and $ indicate that matches should return true only if the entire String difference matches the regular expression. We then use the logical negation operator (!) to return the opposite boolean value. Thus, if the numbers are equal (i.e., their difference is 0), the preceding expression returns false—the first number is not greater than the second. Otherwise, the expression returns true. We discuss regular expressions in more detail in Section 30.7.

Lines 133–146 declare methods smaller and equals. Method smaller returns the result of invoking method bigger (line 137) with the arguments reversed—if first is less than second, then second is greater than first. Method equals invokes methods bigger and smaller (line 145). If either bigger or smaller returns true, line 145 returns false because the numbers are not equal. If both methods return false, the numbers are equal and line 145 returns true.

28.3.3 Publishing the HugeInteger Web Service from Netbeans

Now that we've created the HugeInteger web service class, we'll use Netbeans to build and publish (i.e., deploy) the web service so that clients can consume its services. Netbeans handles all the details of building and deploying a web service for you. This includes creating the framework required to support the web service. Right click the project name (HugeInteger) in the Netbeans **Projects** tab to display the pop-up menu shown in Fig. 28.3. To determine if there are any compilation errors in your project, select the **Build Project** option. When the project compiles successfully, you can select **Deploy Project** to deploy the project to the server you selected when you set up the web application in Section 28.3.1. If the code in the project has changed since the last build, selecting **Deploy Project** also builds the project. Selecting **Run Project** executes the web application. If the web application was not previously built or deployed, this option performs these tasks first. Note that both the **Deploy Project** and **Run Project** options also start the application server (in our case Sun Java System Application Server) if it is not already running. To ensure that all source-code files in a project are recompiled during the next build operation, you can use the **Clean Project** or **Clean and Build Project** options. If you have not already done so, select **Deploy Project** now.

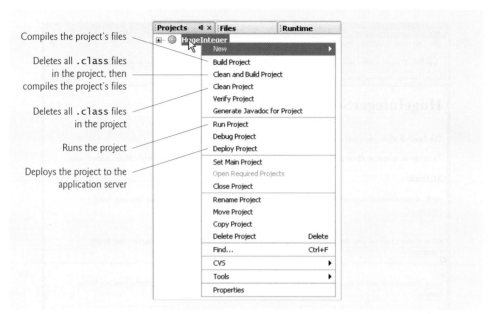

Compiles the project's files

Deletes all .class files in the project, then compiles the project's files

Deletes all .class files in the project

Runs the project

Deploys the project to the application server

Fig. 28.3 | Pop-up menu that appears when you right click a project name in the Netbeans **Projects** tab.

28.3.4 Testing the HugeInteger Web Service with Sun Java System Application Server's Tester Web page

The next step is to test the HugeInteger web service. We previously selected the Sun Java System Application Server to execute this web application. This server can dynamically create a web page for testing a web service's methods from a web browser. To enable this capability:

1. Right click the project name (HugeInteger) in the Netbeans **Projects** tab and select **Properties** from the pop-up menu to display the **Project Properties** dialog.

2. Click **Run** under **Categories** to display the options for running the project.

3. In the **Relative URL** field, type /HugeIntegerService?Tester.

4. Click **OK** to dismiss the **Project Properties** dialog.

The **Relative URL** field specifies what should happen when the web application executes. If this field is empty, then the web application's default JSP displays when you run the project. When you specify /HugeIntegerService?Tester in this field, then run the project, Sun Java System Application Server builds the Tester web page and loads it into your web browser. Figure 28.4 shows the Tester web page for the HugeInteger web service. Once you've deployed the web service, you can also type the URL

```
http://localhost:8080/HugeInteger/HugeIntegerService?Tester
```

in your web browser to view the Tester web page. Note that HugeIntegerService is the name (specified in line 11 of Fig. 28.2) that clients, including the Tester web page, use to access the web service.

Fig. 28.4 | Tester web page created by Sun Java System Application Server for the HugeInteger web service.

To test HugeInteger's web methods, type two positive integers into the textfields to the right of a particular method's button, then click the button to invoke the web method and see the result. Figure 28.5 shows the results of invoking HugeInteger's add method with the values 99999999999999999 and 1. Note that the number 99999999999999999 is larger than primitive type long can represent.

a) Invoking the HugeInteger web service's add method.

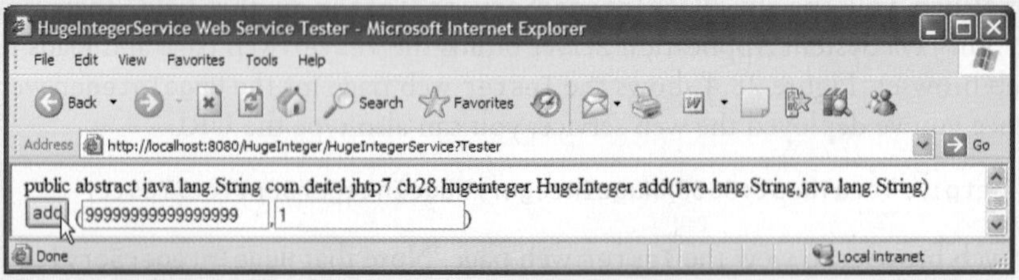

Fig. 28.5 | Testing HugeInteger's add method. (Part 1 of 2.)

b) Results of calling the `HugeInteger` web service's **add** method with `"99999999999999999"` and `"1"`

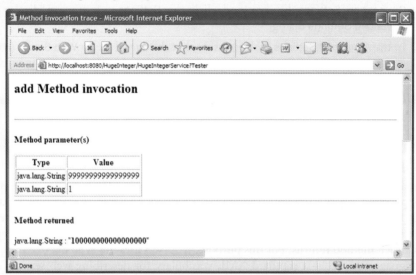

Fig. 28.5 | Testing `HugeInteger`'s add method. (Part 2 of 2.)

Note that you can access the web service only when the application server is running. If Netbeans launches the application server for you, it will automatically shut it down when you close Netbeans. To keep the application server up and running, you can launch it independently of Netbeans before you deploy or run web applications in Netbeans. For Sun Java System Application Server running on Windows, you can do this by selecting **Start > All Programs > Sun Microsystems > Application Server PE 9 > Start Default Server**. To shut down the application server, you can select the **Stop Default Server** option from the same location.

Testing the *HugeInteger* Web Service from Another Computer

If your computer is connected to a network and your computer allows HTTP requests, then you can test the web service from another computer on the network by typing the following URL into a browser on another computer:

```
http://host:8080/HugeInteger/HugeIntegerService?Tester
```

where *host* is the hostname or IP address of the computer on which the web service is deployed.

Note to *Windows XP Service Pack 2 Users*

For security reasons, computers running Windows XP Service Pack 2 do not allow HTTP requests from other computers by default. If you wish to allow other computers to connect to your computer using HTTP, perform the following steps:

1. Select **Start > Control Panel** to open your system's **Control Panel** window, then double click **Windows Firewall** to view the **Windows Firewall** settings dialog.

2. In the **Windows Firewall** settings dialog, click the **Advanced** tab, select **Local Area Connection** (or your network connection's name, if it is different) in the **Network Connection Settings** list box and click the **Settings...** button to display the **Advanced Settings** dialog.

3. In the **Advanced Settings** dialog, ensure that the checkbox for **Web Server (HTTP)** is checked to allow clients on other computers to submit requests to your computer's web server.

4. Click **OK** in the **Advanced Settings** dialog, then click **OK** in the **Windows Firewall** settings dialog.

28.3.5 Describing a Web Service with the Web Service Description Language (WSDL)

Once you implement a web service, compile it and deploy it on an application server, a client application can consume the web service. To do so, however, the client must know where to find the web service and must be provided with a description of how to interact with the web service—that is, what methods are available, what parameters they expect and what each method returns. For this purpose, JAX-WS uses the Web Service Description Language (WSDL)—a standard XML vocabulary for describing web services in a platform-independent manner.

You do not need to understand the details of WSDL to take advantage of it—the server generates a web service's WSDL dynamically for you, and client tools can parse the WSDL to help create the client-side proxy class that a client uses to access the web service. Since the WSDL is created dynamically, clients always receive a deployed web service's most up-to-date description. To view the WSDL for the HugeInteger web service (Fig. 28.6), enter the following URL in your browser:

```
http://localhost:8080/HugeInteger/HugeIntegerService?WSDL
```

or click the **WSDL File** link in the Tester web page (shown in Fig. 28.4).

Accessing the HugeInteger Web Service's WSDL from Another Computer
Eventually, you'll want clients on other computers to use your web service. Such clients need access to your web service's WSDL, which they would access with the following URL:

```
http://host:8080/HugeInteger/HugeIntegerService?WSDL
```

where *host* is the hostname or IP address of the computer on which the web service is deployed. As we discussed in Section 28.3.4, this will work only if your computer allows HTTP connections from other computers—as is the case for publicly accessible web and application servers.

28.4 Consuming a Web Service

Now that we have defined and deployed our web service, we can consume it from a client application. A web service client can be any type of application or even another web service. You enable a client application to consume a web service by adding a web service

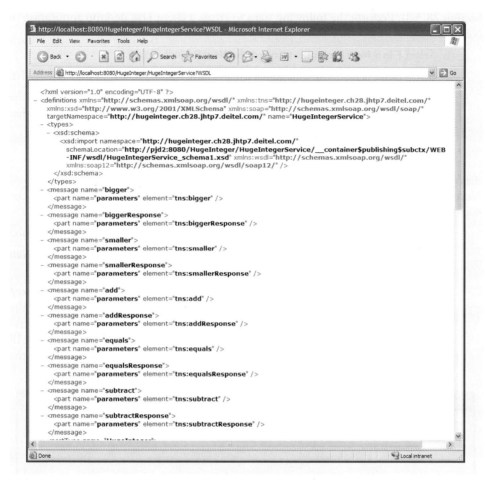

Fig. 28.6 | A portion of the `.wsdl` file for the `HugeInteger` web service.

reference to the application. This process defines the proxy class that allows the client to access the web service.

28.4.1 Creating a Client in Netbeans to Consume the HugeInteger Web Service

In this section, you'll use Netbeans to create a client Java desktop GUI application, then you'll add a web service reference to the project so the client can access the web service. When you add the web service reference, the IDE creates and compiles the client-side artifacts—the framework of Java code that supports the client-side proxy class. The client then calls methods on an object of the proxy class, which uses the rest of the artifacts to interact with the Web service.

Creating a Desktop Application Project in Netbeans 5.5
Before performing the steps in this section, ensure that the `HugeInteger` web service has been deployed and that the Sun Java System Application Server is running (see

Section 28.3.3). Perform the following steps to create a client Java desktop application in Netbeans:

1. Select **File > New Project...** to open the **New Project** dialog.

2. Select **General** from the **Categories** list and **Java Application** from the **Projects** list.

3. Specify the name UsingHugeInteger in the **Project Name** field and uncheck the **Create Main Class** checkbox. In a moment, you'll add a subclass of JFrame that contains a main method.

4. Click **Finish** to create the project.

Adding a Web Service Reference to an Application

Next, you'll add a web service reference to your application so that it can interact with the HugeInteger web service. To add a web service reference, perform the following steps.

1. Right click the project name (UsingHugeInteger) in the Netbeans **Projects** tab.

2. Select **New > Web Service Client...** from the pop-up menu to display the **New Web Service Client** dialog (Fig. 28.7).

3. In the **WSDL URL** field, specify the URL http://localhost:8080/HugeInteger/ HugeIntegerService?WSDL (Fig. 28.7). This URL tells the IDE where to find the web service's WSDL description. [*Note:* If the Sun Java System Application Server is located on a different computer, replace localhost with the hostname or IP address of that computer.] The IDE uses this WSDL description to generate the

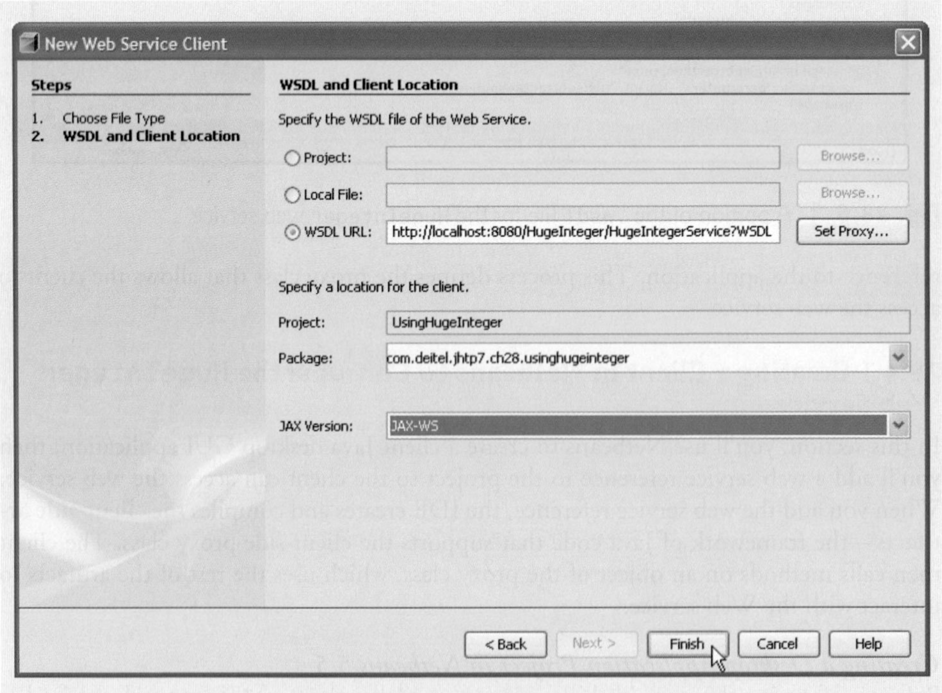

Fig. 28.7 | **New Web Service Client** dialog.

client-side artifacts that compose and support the proxy. Note that the **New Web Service Client** dialog enables you to search for web services in several locations. Many companies simply distribute the exact WSDL URLs for their web services, which you can place in the **WSDL URL** field.

4. In the **Package** field, specify `com.deitel.jhtp7.ch28.usinghugeinteger` as the package name.

5. Click **Finish** to dismiss the **New Web Service Client** dialog.

In the Netbeans **Projects** tab, the `UsingHugeInteger` project now contains a `Web Service References` folder with the proxy for the `HugeInteger` web service (Fig. 28.8). Note that the proxy's name is listed as `HugeIntegerService`, as we specified in line 11 of Fig. 28.2.

When you specify the web service you want to consume, Netbeans accesses the web service's WSDL information and copies it into a file in your project (named `HugeIntegerService.wsdl` in this example). You can view this file from the Netbeans **Files** tab by expanding the nodes in the `UsingHugeInteger` project's `xml-resources` folder as shown in Fig. 28.9. If the web service changes, the client-side artifacts and the client's copy of the WSDL file can be regenerated by right clicking the `HugeIntegerService` node shown in Fig. 28.8 and selecting **Refresh Client**.

You can view the IDE-generated client-side artifacts by selecting the Netbeans **Files** tab and expanding the `UsingHugeInteger` project's **build** folder as shown in Fig. 28.10.

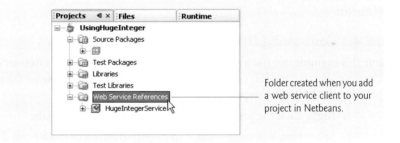

Fig. 28.8 | Netbeans **Project** tab after adding a web service reference to the project.

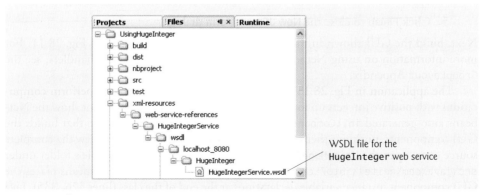

Fig. 28.9 | Locating the `HugeIntegerService.wsdl` file in the Netbeans **Files** tab.

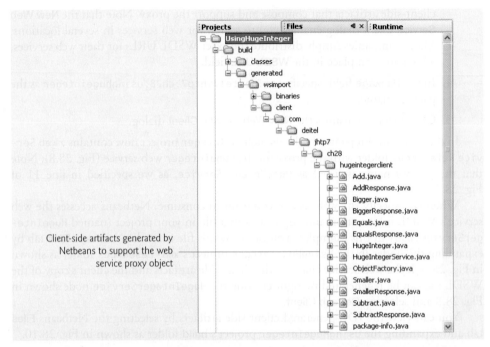

Client-side artifacts generated by Netbeans to support the web service proxy object

Fig. 28.10 | Viewing the HugeInteger web service's client-side artifacts generated by Netbeans.

28.4.2 Consuming the HugeInteger Web Service

For this example, we use a GUI application to interact with the web service. To build the client application's GUI, you must first add a subclass of JFrame to the project. To do so, perform the following steps:

1. Right click the project name in the Netbeans **Project** tab.

2. Select **New > JFrame Form...** to display the **New JFrame Form** dialog.

3. Specify UsingHugeIntegerJFrame in the **Class Name** field.

4. Specify com.deitel.jhtp7.ch28.hugeintegerclient in the **Package** field.

5. Click **Finish** to close the **New JFrame Form** dialog.

Next, build the GUI shown in the sample screen captures at the end of Fig. 28.11. For more information on using Netbeans to build a GUI and create event handlers, see the GroupLayout Appendix.

The application in Fig. 28.11 uses the HugeInteger web service to perform computations with positive integers up to 100 digits long. To save space, we do not show the Netbeans auto-generated initComponents method, which contains the code that builds the GUI components, positions them and registers their event handlers. To view the complete source code, open the UsingHugeIntegerJFrame.java file in this example's folder under src\java\com\deitel\jhtp7\ch28\hugeintegerclient. Note that Netbeans places the GUI component instance variable declarations at the end of the class (lines 326–335). Java allows instance variables to be declared anywhere in a class's body as long as they are placed outside the class's methods. We continue to declare our own instance variables at the top of the class.

```java
1   // Fig. 28.11: UsingHugeIntegerJFrame.java
2   // Client desktop application for the HugeInteger web service.
3   package com.deitel.jhtp7.ch28.hugeintegerclient;
4
5   // import classes for accessing HugeInteger web service's proxy
6   import com.deitel.jhtp7.ch28.hugeintegerclient.HugeInteger;
7   import com.deitel.jhtp7.ch28.hugeintegerclient.HugeIntegerService;
8
9   import javax.swing.JOptionPane; // used to display errors to the user
10
11  public class UsingHugeIntegerJFrame extends javax.swing.JFrame
12  {
13     private HugeIntegerService hugeIntegerService; // used to obtain proxy
14     private HugeInteger hugeIntegerProxy; // used to access the web service
15
16     // no-argument constructor
17     public UsingHugeIntegerJFrame()
18     {
19        initComponents();
20
21        try
22        {
23           // create the objects for accessing the HugeInteger web service
24           hugeIntegerService = new HugeIntegerService();
25           hugeIntegerProxy = hugeIntegerService.getHugeIntegerPort();
26        }
27        catch ( Exception exception )
28        {
29           exception.printStackTrace();
30        }
31     } // end UsingHugeIntegerJFrame constructor
32
33     // The initComponents method is autogenerated by Netbeans and is called
34     // from the constructor to initialize the GUI. This method is not shown
35     // here to save space. Open UsingHugeIntegerJFrame.java in this
36     // example's folder to view the complete generated code (lines 37-153).
37
154    // invokes HugeInteger web service's add method to add HugeIntegers
155    private void addJButtonActionPerformed(
156       java.awt.event.ActionEvent evt )
157    {
158       String firstNumber = firstJTextField.getText();
159       String secondNumber = secondJTextField.getText();
160
161       if ( isValid( firstNumber ) && isValid( secondNumber ) )
162       {
163          try
164          {
```

Fig. 28.11 | Client desktop application for the `HugeInteger` web service. (Part 1 of 6.)

```
165              resultsJTextArea.setText(
166                 hugeIntegerProxy.add( firstNumber, secondNumber ) );
167          } // end try
168          catch ( Exception e )
169          {
170             JOptionPane.showMessageDialog( this, e.toString(),
171                "Add method failed", JOptionPane.ERROR_MESSAGE );
172             e.printStackTrace();
173          } // end catch
174       } // end if
175    } // end method addJButtonActionPerformed
176
177    // invokes HugeInteger web service's subtract method to subtract the
178    // second HugeInteger from the first
179    private void subtractJButtonActionPerformed(
180       java.awt.event.ActionEvent evt )
181    {
182       String firstNumber = firstJTextField.getText();
183       String secondNumber = secondJTextField.getText();
184
185       if ( isValid( firstNumber ) && isValid( secondNumber ) )
186       {
187          try
188          {
189             resultsJTextArea.setText(
190                hugeIntegerProxy.subtract( firstNumber, secondNumber ) );
191          } // end try
192          catch ( Exception e )
193          {
194             JOptionPane.showMessageDialog( this, e.toString(),
195                "Subtract method failed", JOptionPane.ERROR_MESSAGE );
196             e.printStackTrace();
197          } // end catch
198       } // end if
199    } // end method subtractJButtonActionPerformed
200
201    // invokes HugeInteger web service's bigger method to determine whether
202    // the first HugeInteger is greater than the second
203    private void biggerJButtonActionPerformed(
204       java.awt.event.ActionEvent evt )
205    {
206       String firstNumber = firstJTextField.getText();
207       String secondNumber = secondJTextField.getText();
208
209       if ( isValid( firstNumber ) && isValid( secondNumber ) )
210       {
211          try
212          {
213             boolean result =
214                hugeIntegerProxy.bigger( firstNumber, secondNumber );
```

Fig. 28.11 | Client desktop application for the HugeInteger web service. (Part 2 of 6.)

```
215              resultsJTextArea.setText( String.format( "%s %s %s %s",
216                 firstNumber, ( result ? "is" : "is not" ), "greater than",
217                 secondNumber ) );
218           } // end try
219           catch ( Exception e )
220           {
221              JOptionPane.showMessageDialog( this, e.toString(),
222                 "Bigger method failed", JOptionPane.ERROR_MESSAGE );
223              e.printStackTrace();
224           } // end catch
225        } // end if
226     } // end method biggerJButtonActionPerformed
227
228     // invokes HugeInteger web service's smaller method to determine
229     // whether the first HugeInteger is less than the second
230     private void smallerJButtonActionPerformed(
231        java.awt.event.ActionEvent evt )
232     {
233        String firstNumber = firstJTextField.getText();
234        String secondNumber = secondJTextField.getText();
235
236        if ( isValid( firstNumber ) && isValid( secondNumber ) )
237        {
238           try
239           {
240              boolean result =
241                 hugeIntegerProxy.smaller( firstNumber, secondNumber );
242              resultsJTextArea.setText( String.format( "%s %s %s %s",
243                 firstNumber, ( result ? "is" : "is not" ), "less than",
244                 secondNumber ) );
245           } // end try
246           catch ( Exception e )
247           {
248              JOptionPane.showMessageDialog( this, e.toString(),
249                 "Smaller method failed", JOptionPane.ERROR_MESSAGE );
250              e.printStackTrace();
251           } // end catch
252        } // end if
253     } // end method smallerJButtonActionPerformed
254
255     // invokes HugeInteger web service's equals method to determine whether
256     // the first HugeInteger is equal to the second
257     private void equalsJButtonActionPerformed(
258        java.awt.event.ActionEvent evt )
259     {
260        String firstNumber = firstJTextField.getText();
261        String secondNumber = secondJTextField.getText();
262
263        if ( isValid( firstNumber ) && isValid( secondNumber ) )
264        {
265           try
266           {
```

Fig. 28.11 | Client desktop application for the `HugeInteger` web service. (Part 3 of 6.)

```
267            boolean result =
268               hugeIntegerProxy.equals( firstNumber, secondNumber );
269            resultsJTextArea.setText( String.format( "%s %s %s %s",
270               firstNumber, ( result ? "is" : "is not" ), "equal to",
271               secondNumber ) );
272         } // end try
273         catch ( Exception e )
274         {
275            JOptionPane.showMessageDialog( this, e.toString(),
276               "Equals method failed", JOptionPane.ERROR_MESSAGE );
277            e.printStackTrace();
278         } // end catch
279      } // end if
280   } // end method equalsJButtonActionPerformed
281
282   // checks the size of a String to ensure that it is not too big
283   // to be used as a HugeInteger; ensure only digits in String
284   private boolean isValid( String number )
285   {
286      // check String's length
287      if ( number.length() > 100 )
288      {
289         JOptionPane.showMessageDialog( this,
290            "HugeIntegers must be <= 100 digits.", "HugeInteger Overflow",
291            JOptionPane.ERROR_MESSAGE );
292         return false;
293      } // end if
294
295      // look for nondigit characters in String
296      for ( char c : number.toCharArray() )
297      {
298         if ( !Character.isDigit( c ) )
299         {
300            JOptionPane.showMessageDialog( this,
301               "There are nondigits in the String",
302               "HugeInteger Contains Nondigit Characters",
303               JOptionPane.ERROR_MESSAGE );
304            return false;
305         } // end if
306      } // end for
307
308      return true; // number can be used as a HugeInteger
309   } // end method validate
310
311   // main method begins execution
312   public static void main( String args[] )
313   {
314      java.awt.EventQueue.invokeLater(
315         new Runnable()
316         {
317            public void run()
318            {
```

Fig. 28.11 | Client desktop application for the `HugeInteger` web service. (Part 4 of 6.)

```
319              new UsingHugeIntegerJFrame().setVisible( true );
320           } // end method run
321        } // end anonymous inner class
322      ); // end call to java.awt.EventQueue.invokeLater
323    } // end method main
324
325    // Variables declaration - do not modify
326    private javax.swing.JButton addJButton;
327    private javax.swing.JButton biggerJButton;
328    private javax.swing.JLabel directionsJLabel;
329    private javax.swing.JButton equalsJButton;
330    private javax.swing.JTextField firstJTextField;
331    private javax.swing.JScrollPane resultsJScrollPane;
332    private javax.swing.JTextArea resultsJTextArea;
333    private javax.swing.JTextField secondJTextField;
334    private javax.swing.JButton smallerJButton;
335    private javax.swing.JButton subtractJButton;
336    // End of variables declaration
337 } // end class UsingHugeIntegerJFrame
```

Fig. 28.11 | Client desktop application for the HugeInteger web service. (Part 5 of 6.)

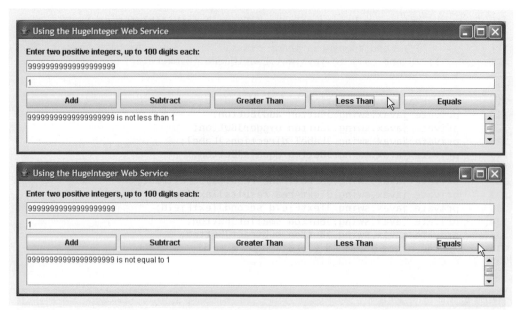

Fig. 28.11 | Client desktop application for the `HugeInteger` web service. (Part 6 of 6.)

Lines 6–7 import the classes `HugeInteger` and `HugeIntegerService` that enable the client application to interact with the web service. We include these import declarations only for documentation purposes here. These classes are in the same package as `Using-HugeIntegerJFrame`, so these import declarations are not necessary. Notice that we do not have import declarations for most of the GUI components used in this example. When you create a GUI in Netbeans, it uses fully qualified class names (such as `javax.swing.JFrame` in line 11), so import declarations are unnecessary.

Lines 13–14 declare the variables of type `HugeIntegerService` and `HugeInteger`, respectively. Line 24 in the constructor creates a `HugeIntegerService` object. Line 25 uses this object's `getHugeIntegerPort` method to obtain the `HugeInteger` proxy object that the application uses to invoke the web service's method.

Lines 165–166, 189–190, 213–214, 240–241 and 267–268 in the various `JButton` event handlers invoke the `HugeInteger` web service's web methods. Note that each call is made on the local proxy object that is referenced by `hugeIntegerProxy`. The proxy object then communicates with the web service on the client's behalf.

The user enters two integers, each up to 100 digits long. Clicking any of the five `JBut-tons` causes the application to invoke a web method to perform the corresponding task and return the result. Our client application cannot process 100-digit numbers directly. Instead the client passes `String` representations of these numbers to the web service's web methods, which perform tasks for the client. The client application then uses the return value of each operation to display an appropriate message.

28.5 SOAP

SOAP (an acronym for Simple Object Access Protocol) is a platform-independent proto-col that uses XML to facilitate remote procedure calls, typically over HTTP. SOAP is one common protocol for passing information between web service clients and web services. The protocol that transmits request-and-response messages is also known as the web service's wire format or wire protocol, because it defines how information is sent "along the wire."

Each request and response is packaged in a SOAP message (also known as a SOAP envelope)—an XML "wrapper" containing the information that a web service requires to process the message. SOAP messages are written in XML so that they are platform independent. With a few exceptions, most firewalls—security barriers that restrict communication among networks—allow HTTP traffic to pass through so that clients can browse websites on web servers behind firewalls. Thus, XML and HTTP enable computers on different platforms to send and receive SOAP messages with few limitations.

Web services also use SOAP for the extensive set of types it supports. The wire format used to transmit requests and responses must support all types passed between the applications. SOAP supports primitive types (e.g., `int`) and their wrapper types (e.g., `Integer`), as well as `Date`, `Time` and others. SOAP can also transmit arrays and objects of user-defined types (as you'll see in Section 28.8). For more information on SOAP, visit `www.w3.org/TR/soap/`.

When a program invokes a web method, the request and all relevant information are packaged in a SOAP message and sent to the server on which the web service resides. The web service processes the SOAP message's contents (contained in a SOAP envelope), which specify the method that the client wishes to invoke and the method's arguments. This process of interpreting a SOAP message's contents is known as parsing a SOAP message. After the web service receives and parses a request, the proper method is called with any specified arguments, and the response is sent back to the client in another SOAP message. The client-side proxy parses the response, which contains the result of the method call, and returns the result to the client application.

Figure 28.5 used the `HugeInteger` web service's `Tester` web page to show the result of invoking `HugeInteger`'s `add` method with the values 9999999999999999 and 1. The `Tester` web page also shows the SOAP request and response messages (which were not previously shown). Figure 28.12 shows the same result with the SOAP messages that are displayed by the `Tester` application. In the request message from Fig. 28.12, the text

```
<ns1:add>
<first>9999999999999999</first>
<second>1</second>
</ns1:add>
```

specifies the method to call (`add`), the method's arguments (`first` and `second`) and the arguments' values (9999999999999999 and 1). Similarly, the text

```
<ns1:addResponse>
<return>10000000000000000</return>
</ns1:addResponse>
```

from the response message in Fig. 28.12 specifies the return value of method add.

As with the WSDL for a web service, the SOAP messages are generated for you automatically. So you don't need to understand the details of SOAP or XML to take advantage of it when publishing and consuming web services.

Fig. 28.12 | SOAP messages for the HugeInteger web service's add method as shown by the Sun Java System Application Server's Tester web page.

28.6 Session Tracking in Web Services

Section 26.7 described the advantages of using session tracking to maintain client state information so you can personalize the users' browsing experiences. Now we'll incorporate session tracking into a web service. Suppose a client application needs to call several methods from the same web service, possibly several times each. In such a case, it can be beneficial for the web service to maintain state information for the client, thus eliminating the need for client information to be passed between the client and the web service multiple times. For example, a web service that provides local restaurant reviews could store the client user's street address during the initial request, then use it to return personalized, localized results in subsequent requests. Storing session information also enables a web service to distinguish between clients.

28.6.1 Creating a `Blackjack` Web Service

Our next example is a web service that assists you in developing a blackjack card game. The `Blackjack` web service (Fig. 28.13) provides web methods to shuffle a deck of cards, deal a card from the deck and evaluate a hand of cards. After presenting the web service, we use it to serve as the dealer for a game of blackjack (Fig. 28.14). The `Blackjack` web service uses an `HttpSession` object to maintain a unique deck of cards for each client application. Several clients can use the service at the same time, but web method calls made by a specific client use only the deck of cards stored in that client's session. Our example uses the following blackjack rules:

> *Two cards each are dealt to the dealer and the player. The player's cards are dealt face up. Only the first of the dealer's cards is dealt face up. Each card has a value. A card numbered 2 through 10 is worth its face value. Jacks, queens and kings each count as 10. Aces can count as 1 or 11—whichever value is more beneficial to the player (as we will soon see). If the sum of the player's two initial cards is 21 (i.e., the player was dealt a card valued at 10 and an ace, which counts as 11 in this situation), the player has "blackjack" and immediately wins the game—if the dealer does not also have blackjack (which would result in a "push"—i.e., a tie). Otherwise, the player can begin taking additional cards one at a time. These cards are dealt face up, and the player decides when to stop taking cards. If the player "busts" (i.e., the sum of the player's cards exceeds 21), the game is over, and the player loses. When the player is satisfied with the current set of cards, the player "stands" (i.e., stops taking cards), and the dealer's hidden card is revealed. If the dealer's total is 16 or less, the dealer must take another card; otherwise, the dealer must stand. The dealer must continue taking cards until the sum of the dealer's cards is greater than or equal to 17. If the dealer exceeds 21, the player wins. Otherwise, the hand with the higher point total wins. If the dealer and the player have the same point total, the game is a "push," and no one wins. Note that the value of an ace for a dealer depends on the dealer's other card(s) and the casino's house rules. A dealer typically must hit for totals of 16 or less and must stand for totals of 17 or more. However, for a "soft 17"—a hand with a total of 17 with one ace counted as 11—some casinos require the dealer to hit and some require the dealer to stand (we require the dealer to stand). Such a hand is known as a "soft 17" because taking another card cannot bust the hand.*

The web service (Fig. 28.13) stores each card as a `String` consisting of a number, 1–13, representing the card's face (ace through king, respectively), followed by a space and a digit, 0–3, representing the card's suit (hearts, diamonds, clubs or spades, respectively). For example, the jack of clubs is represented as `"11 2"`, and the two of hearts is represented as `"2 0"`. To create and deploy this web service, follow the steps presented in Sections 28.3.3–28.3.4 for the `HugeInteger` service.

```
1   // Fig. 28.13: Blackjack.java
2   // Blackjack web service that deals cards and evaluates hands
3   package com.deitel.jhtp7.ch28.blackjack;
```

Fig. 28.13 | `Blackjack` web service that deals cards and evaluates hands. (Part 1 of 4.)

```
4
5    import java.util.ArrayList;
6    import java.util.Random;
7    import javax.annotation.Resource;
8    import javax.jws.WebService;
9    import javax.jws.WebMethod;
10   import javax.jws.WebParam;
11   import javax.servlet.http.HttpSession;
12   import javax.servlet.http.HttpServletRequest;
13   import javax.xml.ws.WebServiceContext;
14   import javax.xml.ws.handler.MessageContext;
15
16   @WebService( name = "Blackjack", serviceName = "BlackjackService" )
17   public class Blackjack
18   {
19      // use @Resource to create a WebServiceContext for session tracking
20      private @Resource WebServiceContext webServiceContext;
21      private MessageContext messageContext; // used in session tracking
22      private HttpSession session; // stores attributes of the session
23
24      // deal one card
25      @WebMethod( operationName = "dealCard" )
26      public String dealCard()
27      {
28         String card = "";
29
30         ArrayList< String > deck =
31            ( ArrayList< String > ) session.getAttribute( "deck" );
32
33         card = deck.get( 0 ); // get top card of deck
34         deck.remove( 0 ); // remove top card of deck
35
36         return card;
37      } // end WebMethod dealCard
38
39      // shuffle the deck
40      @WebMethod( operationName = "shuffle" )
41      public void shuffle()
42      {
43         // obtain the HttpSession object to store deck for current client
44         messageContext = webServiceContext.getMessageContext();
45         session = ( ( HttpServletRequest ) messageContext.get(
46            MessageContext.SERVLET_REQUEST ) ).getSession();
47
48         // populate deck of cards
49         ArrayList< String > deck = new ArrayList< String >();
50
51         for ( int face = 1; face <= 13; face++ ) // loop through faces
52            for ( int suit = 0; suit <= 3; suit++ ) // loop through suits
53               deck.add( face + " " + suit ); // add each card to deck
54
55         String tempCard; // holds card temporarily durring swapping
```

Fig. 28.13 | Blackjack web service that deals cards and evaluates hands. (Part 2 of 4.)

```
56          Random randomObject = new Random(); // generates random numbers
57          int index; // index of randomly selected card
58
59          for ( int i = 0; i < deck.size() ; i++ ) // shuffle
60          {
61             index = randomObject.nextInt( deck.size() - 1 );
62
63             // swap card at position i with randomly selected card
64             tempCard = deck.get( i );
65             deck.set( i, deck.get( index ) );
66             deck.set( index, tempCard );
67          } // end for
68
69          // add this deck to user's session
70          session.setAttribute( "deck", deck );
71       } // end WebMethod shuffle
72
73       // determine a hand's value
74       @WebMethod( operationName = "getHandValue" )
75       public int getHandValue( @WebParam( name = "hand" ) String hand )
76       {
77          // split hand into cards
78          String[] cards = hand.split( "\t" );
79          int total = 0; // total value of cards in hand
80          int face; // face of current card
81          int aceCount = 0; // number of aces in hand
82
83          for ( int i = 0; i < cards.length; i++ )
84          {
85             // parse string and get first int in String
86             face = Integer.parseInt(
87                cards[ i ].substring( 0, cards[ i ].indexOf( " " ) ) );
88
89             switch ( face )
90             {
91                case 1: // in ace, increment aceCount
92                   ++aceCount;
93                   break;
94                case 11: // jack
95                case 12: // queen
96                case 13: // king
97                   total += 10;
98                   break;
99                default: // otherwise, add face
100                  total += face;
101                  break;
102            } // end switch
103         } // end for
104
105         // calculate optimal use of aces
106         if ( aceCount > 0 )
107         {
```

Fig. 28.13 | Blackjack web service that deals cards and evaluates hands. (Part 3 of 4.)

```
108                // if possible, count one ace as 11
109                if ( total + 11 + aceCount - 1 <= 21 )
110                    total += 11 + aceCount - 1;
111                else // otherwise, count all aces as 1
112                    total += aceCount;
113            } // end if
114
115        return total;
116    } // end WebMethod getHandValue
117 } // end class Blackjack
```

Fig. 28.13 | `Blackjack` web service that deals cards and evaluates hands. (Part 4 of 4.)

Session Tracking in Web Services

The `Blackjack` web service client first calls method `shuffle` (lines 40–71) to shuffle the deck of cards. This method also places the deck of cards into an `HttpSession` object that is specific to the client that called `shuffle`. To use session tracking in a Web service, you must include code for the resources that maintain the session state information. In the past, you had to write the sometimes tedious code to create these resources. JAX-WS, however, handles this for you via the `@Resource` annotation. This annotation enables tools like Netbeans to "inject" complex support code into your class, thus allowing you to focus on your business logic rather than the support code. The concept of using annotations to add code that supports your classes is known as dependency injection. Annotations like `@Web-Service`, `@WebMethod` and `@WebParam` also perform dependency injection.

Line 20 injects a `WebServiceContext` object into your class. A `WebServiceContext` object enables a web service to access and maintain information for a specific request, such as session state. As you look through the code in Fig. 28.13, you'll notice that we never create the `WebServiceContext` object. All of the code necessary to create it is injected into the class by the `@Resource` annotation. Line 21 declares a variable of interface type `MessaqgeContext` that the web service will use to obtain an `HttpSession` object for the current client. Line 22 declares the `HttpSession` variable that the web service will use to manipulate the session state information.

Line 44 in method `shuffle` uses the `WebServiceContext` object that was injected in line 20 to obtain a `MessageContext` object. Lines 45–46 then use the `MessageContext` object's get method to obtain the `HttpSession` object for the current client. Method get receives a constant indicating what to get from the `MessageContext`. In this case, the constant `MessageContext.SERVLET_REQUEST` indicates that we'd like to get the `HttpServlet-Request` object for the current client. We then call method `getSession` to get the `HttpSession` object from the `HttpServletRequest` object.

Lines 49–70 generate an `ArrayList` representing a deck of cards, shuffle the deck and store the deck in the client's `session` object. Lines 51–53 use nested loops to generate `Strings` in the form "*face suit*" to represent each possible card in the deck. Lines 59–67 shuffle the deck by swapping each card with another card selected at random. Line 70 inserts the `ArrayList` in the `session` object to maintain the deck between method calls from a particular client.

Lines 25–37 define method `dealCard` as a web method. Lines 30–31 use the `session` object to obtain the `"deck"` session attribute that was stored in line 70 of method shuffle. Method `getAttribute` takes as a parameter a `String` that identifies the `Object` to obtain from the session state. The HttpSession can store many Objects, provided that each has a unique identifier. Note that method shuffle must be called before method dealCard is called the first time for a client—otherwise, an exception occurs at lines 30–31 because getAttribute returns null. After obtaining the user's deck, dealCard gets the top card from the deck (line 33), removes it from the deck (line 34) and returns the card's value as a String (line 36). Without using session tracking, the deck of cards would need to be passed back and forth with each method call. Session tracking makes the dealCard method easy to call (it requires no arguments) and eliminates the overhead of sending the deck over the network multiple times.

Method getHandValue (lines 74–116) determines the total value of the cards in a hand by trying to attain the highest score possible without going over 21. Recall that an ace can be counted as either 1 or 11, and all face cards count as 10. This method does not use the session object because the deck of cards is not used in this method.

As you'll soon see, the client application maintains a hand of cards as a String in which each card is separated by a tab character. Line 78 tokenizes the hand of cards (represented by dealt) into individual cards by calling String method split and passing to it a String containing the delimiter characters (in this case, just a tab). Method split uses the delimiter characters to separate tokens in the String. Lines 83–103 count the value of each card. Lines 86–87 retrieve the first integer—the face—and use that value in the switch statement (lines 89–102). If the card is an ace, the method increments variable aceCount. We discuss how this variable is used shortly. If the card is an 11, 12 or 13 (jack, queen or king), the method adds 10 to the total value of the hand (line 97). If the card is anything else, the method increases the total by that value (line 100).

Because an ace can have either of two values, additional logic is required to process aces. Lines 106–113 of method getHandValue process the aces after all the other cards. If a hand contains several aces, only one ace can be counted as 11. The condition in line 109 determines whether counting one ace as 11 and the rest as 1 will result in a total that does not exceed 21. If this is possible, line 110 adjusts the total accordingly. Otherwise, line 112 adjusts the total, counting each ace as 1.

Method getHandValue maximizes the value of the current cards without exceeding 21. Imagine, for example, that the dealer has a 7 and receives an ace. The new total could be either 8 or 18. However, getHandValue always maximizes the value of the cards without going over 21, so the new total is 18.

28.6.2 Consuming the Blackjack Web Service

Now we use the Blackjack web service in a Java application (Fig. 28.14). The application keeps track of the player's and the dealer's cards, and the web service tracks the cards that have been dealt.

The constructor (lines 34–83) sets up the GUI (line 36), changes the background color of the window (line 40) and creates the Blackjack web service's proxy object (lines 46–47). In the GUI, each player has 11 JLabels—the maximum number of cards that can be dealt without automatically exceeding 21 (i.e., four aces, four twos and three threes). These JLabels are placed in an ArrayList of JLabels, (lines 59–82), so we can index the ArrayList during the game to determine the JLabel that will display a particular card image.

In the JAX-WS 2.0 framework, the client must indicate whether it wants to allow the web service to maintain session information. Lines 50–51 in the constructor perform this task. We first cast the proxy object to interface type BindingProvider. A **BindingProvider** enables the client to manipulate the request information that will be sent to the server. This information is stored in an object that implements interface **RequestContext**. The BindingProvider and RequestContext are part of the framework that is created by the IDE when you add a web service client to the application. Next, lines 50–51 invoke the BindingProvider's **getRequestContext** method to obtain the RequestContext object. Then the RequestContext's **put method** is called to set the property BindingProvider.SESSION_MAINTAIN_PROPERTY to true, which enables session tracking from the client side so that the web service knows which client is invoking the service's web methods.

```java
1   // Fig. 28.14: BlackjackGameJFrame.java
2   // Blackjack game that uses the Blackjack Web Service
3   package com.deitel.jhtp7.ch28.blackjackclient;
4
5   import java.awt.Color;
6   import java.util.ArrayList;
7   import javax.swing.ImageIcon;
8   import javax.swing.JLabel;
9   import javax.swing.JOptionPane;
10  import javax.xml.ws.BindingProvider;
11  import com.deitel.jhtp7.ch28.blackjackclient.Blackjack;
12  import com.deitel.jhtp7.ch28.blackjackclient.BlackjackService;
13
14  public class BlackjackGameJFrame extends javax.swing.JFrame
15  {
16     private String playerCards;
17     private String dealerCards;
18     private ArrayList< JLabel > cardboxes; // list of card image JLabels
19     private int currentPlayerCard; // player's current card number
20     private int currentDealerCard; // blackjackProxy's current card number
21     private BlackjackService blackjackService; // used to obtain proxy
22     private Blackjack blackjackProxy; // used to access the web service
23
24     // enumeration of game states
25     private enum GameStatus
26     {
27        PUSH, // game ends in a tie
28        LOSE, // player loses
29        WIN, // player wins
30        BLACKJACK // player has blackjack
31     } // end enum GameStatus
32
33     // no-argument constructor
34     public BlackjackGameJFrame()
35     {
36        initComponents();
37
```

Fig. 28.14 | Blackjack game that uses the Blackjack web service. (Part 1 of 10.)

```
38        // due to a bug in Netbeans, we must change the JFrame's background
39        // color here rather than in the designer
40        getContentPane().setBackground( new Color( 0, 180, 0 ) );
41
42        // initialize the blackjack proxy
43        try
44        {
45           // create the objects for accessing the Blackjack web service
46           blackjackService = new BlackjackService();
47           blackjackProxy = blackjackService.getBlackjackPort();
48
49           // enable session tracking
50           ( ( BindingProvider ) blackjackProxy ).getRequestContext().put(
51              BindingProvider.SESSION_MAINTAIN_PROPERTY, true );
52        } // end try
53        catch ( Exception e )
54        {
55           e.printStackTrace();
56        } // end catch
57
58        // add JLabels to cardBoxes ArrayList for programmatic manipulation
59        cardboxes = new ArrayList< JLabel >();
60
61        cardboxes.add( 0, dealerCard1JLabel );
62        cardboxes.add( dealerCard2JLabel );
63        cardboxes.add( dealerCard3JLabel );
64        cardboxes.add( dealerCard4JLabel );
65        cardboxes.add( dealerCard5JLabel );
66        cardboxes.add( dealerCard6JLabel );
67        cardboxes.add( dealerCard7JLabel );
68        cardboxes.add( dealerCard8JLabel );
69        cardboxes.add( dealerCard9JLabel );
70        cardboxes.add( dealerCard10JLabel );
71        cardboxes.add( dealerCard11JLabel );
72        cardboxes.add( playerCard1JLabel );
73        cardboxes.add( playerCard2JLabel );
74        cardboxes.add( playerCard3JLabel );
75        cardboxes.add( playerCard4JLabel );
76        cardboxes.add( playerCard5JLabel );
77        cardboxes.add( playerCard6JLabel );
78        cardboxes.add( playerCard7JLabel );
79        cardboxes.add( playerCard8JLabel );
80        cardboxes.add( playerCard9JLabel );
81        cardboxes.add( playerCard10JLabel );
82        cardboxes.add( playerCard11JLabel );
83     } // end no-argument constructor
84
85     // play the dealer's hand
86     private void dealerPlay()
87     {
88        try
89        {
```

Fig. 28.14 | Blackjack game that uses the Blackjack web service. (Part 2 of 10.)

```
90          // while the value of the dealers's hand is below 17
91          // the dealer must continue to take cards
92          String[] cards = dealerCards.split( "\t" );
93
94          // display dealers's cards
95          for ( int i = 0; i < cards.length; i++ )
96             displayCard( i, cards[ i ] );
97
98          while ( blackjackProxy.getHandValue( dealerCards ) < 17 )
99          {
100            String newCard = blackjackProxy.dealCard();
101            dealerCards += "\t" + newCard; // deal new card
102            displayCard( currentDealerCard, newCard );
103            ++currentDealerCard;
104            JOptionPane.showMessageDialog( this, "Dealer takes a card",
105               "Dealer's turn", JOptionPane.PLAIN_MESSAGE );
106         } // end while
107
108         int dealersTotal = blackjackProxy.getHandValue( dealerCards );
109         int playersTotal = blackjackProxy.getHandValue( playerCards );
110
111         // if dealer busted, player wins
112         if ( dealersTotal > 21 )
113         {
114            gameOver( GameStatus.WIN );
115            return;
116         } // end if
117
118         // if dealer and player are below 21
119         // higher score wins, equal scores is a push
120         if ( dealersTotal > playersTotal )
121            gameOver( GameStatus.LOSE );
122         else if ( dealersTotal < playersTotal )
123            gameOver( GameStatus.WIN );
124         else
125            gameOver( GameStatus.PUSH );
126      } // end try
127      catch ( Exception e )
128      {
129         e.printStackTrace();
130      } // end catch
131   } // end method dealerPlay
132
133   // displays the card represented by cardValue in specified JLabel
134   public void displayCard( int card, String cardValue )
135   {
136      try
137      {
138         // retrieve correct JLabel from cardBoxes
139         JLabel displayLabel = cardboxes.get( card );
140
```

Fig. 28.14 | Blackjack game that uses the Blackjack web service. (Part 3 of 10.)

```
141            // if string representing card is empty, display back of card
142            if ( cardValue.equals( "" ) )
143            {
144                displayLabel.setIcon( new ImageIcon( getClass().getResource(
145                    "/com/deitel/jhtp7/ch28/blackjackclient/" +
146                    "blackjack_images/cardback.png" ) ) ) ;
147                return;
148            } // end if
149
150            // retrieve the face value of the card
151            String face = cardValue.substring( 0, cardValue.indexOf( " " ) );
152
153            // retrieve the suit of the card
154            String suit =
155                cardValue.substring( cardValue. indexOf( " " ) + 1 );
156
157            char suitLetter; // suit letter used to form image file
158
159            switch ( Integer.parseInt( suit ) )
160            {
161                case 0: // hearts
162                    suitLetter = 'h';
163                    break;
164                case 1: // diamonds
165                    suitLetter = 'd';
166                    break;
167                case 2: // clubs
168                    suitLetter = 'c';
169                    break;
170                default: // spades
171                    suitLetter = 's';
172                    break;
173            } // end switch
174
175            // set image for displayLabel
176            displayLabel.setIcon( new ImageIcon( getClass().getResource(
177                "/com/deitel/jhtp7/ch28/blackjackclient/blackjack_images/" +
178                face + suitLetter + ".png" ) ) );
179        } // end try
180        catch ( Exception e )
181        {
182            e.printStackTrace();
183        } // end catch
184    } // end method displayCard
185
186    // displays all player cards and shows appropriate message
187    public void gameOver( GameStatus winner )
188    {
189        String[] cards = dealerCards.split( "\t" );
190
191        // display blackjackProxy's cards
192        for ( int i = 0; i < cards.length; i++ )
193            displayCard( i, cards[ i ]);
```

Fig. 28.14 | Blackjack game that uses the Blackjack web service. (Part 4 of 10.)

```
194
195        // display appropriate status image
196        if ( winner == GameStatus.WIN )
197           statusJLabel.setText( "You win!" );
198        else if ( winner == GameStatus.LOSE )
199           statusJLabel.setText( "You lose." );
200        else if ( winner == GameStatus.PUSH )
201           statusJLabel.setText( "It's a push." );
202        else // blackjack
203           statusJLabel.setText( "Blackjack!" );
204
205        // display final scores
206        int dealersTotal = blackjackProxy.getHandValue( dealerCards );
207        int playersTotal = blackjackProxy.getHandValue( playerCards );
208        dealerTotalJLabel.setText( "Dealer: " + dealersTotal );
209        playerTotalJLabel.setText( "Player: " + playersTotal );
210
211        // reset for new game
212        standJButton.setEnabled( false );
213        hitJButton.setEnabled( false );
214        dealJButton.setEnabled( true );
215     } // end method gameOver
216
217     // The initComponents method is autogenerated by Netbeans and is called
218     // from the constructor to initialize the GUI. This method is not shown
219     // here to save space. Open BlackjackGameJFrame.java in this
220     // example's folder to view the complete generated code (lines 221-531)
221
532     // handles standJButton click
533     private void standJButtonActionPerformed(
534        java.awt.event.ActionEvent evt )
535     {
536        standJButton.setEnabled( false );
537        hitJButton.setEnabled( false );
538        dealJButton.setEnabled( true );
539        dealerPlay();
540     } // end method standJButtonActionPerformed
541
542     // handles hitJButton click
543     private void hitJButtonActionPerformed(
544        java.awt.event.ActionEvent evt )
545     {
546        // get player another card
547        String card = blackjackProxy.dealCard(); // deal new card
548        playerCards += "\t" + card; // add card to hand
549
550        // update GUI to display new card
551        displayCard( currentPlayerCard, card );
552        ++currentPlayerCard;
553
554        // determine new value of player's hand
555        int total = blackjackProxy.getHandValue( playerCards );
```

Fig. 28.14 | Blackjack game that uses the Blackjack web service. (Part 5 of 10.)

```
556
557        if ( total > 21 ) // player busts
558            gameOver( GameStatus.LOSE );
559        if ( total == 21 ) // player cannot take any more cards
560        {
561            hitJButton.setEnabled( false );
562            dealerPlay();
563        } // end if
564    } // end method hitJButtonActionPerformed
565
566    // handles dealJButton click
567    private void dealJButtonActionPerformed(
568        java.awt.event.ActionEvent evt )
569    {
570        String card; // stores a card temporarily until it's added to a hand
571
572        // clear card images
573        for ( int i = 0; i < cardboxes.size(); i++ )
574            cardboxes.get( i ).setIcon( null );
575
576        statusJLabel.setText( "" );
577        dealerTotalJLabel.setText( "" );
578        playerTotalJLabel.setText( "" );
579
580        // create a new, shuffled deck on remote machine
581        blackjackProxy.shuffle();
582
583        // deal two cards to player
584        playerCards = blackjackProxy.dealCard(); // add first card to hand
585        displayCard( 11, playerCards ); // display first card
586        card = blackjackProxy.dealCard(); // deal second card
587        displayCard( 12, card ); // display second card
588        playerCards += "\t" + card; // add second card to hand
589
590        // deal two cards to blackjackProxy, but only show first
591        dealerCards = blackjackProxy.dealCard(); // add first card to hand
592        displayCard( 0, dealerCards ); // display first card
593        card = blackjackProxy.dealCard(); // deal second card
594        displayCard( 1, "" ); // display back of card
595        dealerCards += "\t" + card; // add second card to hand
596
597        standJButton.setEnabled( true );
598        hitJButton.setEnabled( true );
599        dealJButton.setEnabled( false );
600
601        // determine the value of the two hands
602        int dealersTotal = blackjackProxy.getHandValue( dealerCards );
603        int playersTotal = blackjackProxy.getHandValue( playerCards );
604
605        // if hands both equal 21, it is a push
606        if ( playersTotal == dealersTotal && playersTotal == 21 )
607            gameOver( GameStatus.PUSH );
```

Fig. 28.14 | Blackjack game that uses the Blackjack web service. (Part 6 of 10.)

```
608       else if ( dealersTotal == 21 ) // blackjackProxy has blackjack
609          gameOver( GameStatus.LOSE );
610       else if ( playersTotal == 21 ) // blackjack
611          gameOver( GameStatus.BLACKJACK );
612
613       // next card for blackjackProxy has index 2
614       currentDealerCard = 2;
615
616       // next card for player has index 13
617       currentPlayerCard = 13;
618    } // end method dealJButtonActionPerformed
619
620    // begins application execution
621    public static void main( String args[] )
622    {
623       java.awt.EventQueue.invokeLater(
624          new Runnable()
625          {
626             public void run()
627             {
628                new BlackjackGameJFrame().setVisible(true);
629             }
630          }
631       ); // end call to java.awt.EventQueue.invokeLater
632    } // end method main
633
634    // Variables declaration - do not modify
635    private javax.swing.JButton dealJButton;
636    private javax.swing.JLabel dealerCard10JLabel;
637    private javax.swing.JLabel dealerCard11JLabel;
638    private javax.swing.JLabel dealerCard1JLabel;
639    private javax.swing.JLabel dealerCard2JLabel;
640    private javax.swing.JLabel dealerCard3JLabel;
641    private javax.swing.JLabel dealerCard4JLabel;
642    private javax.swing.JLabel dealerCard5JLabel;
643    private javax.swing.JLabel dealerCard6JLabel;
644    private javax.swing.JLabel dealerCard7JLabel;
645    private javax.swing.JLabel dealerCard8JLabel;
646    private javax.swing.JLabel dealerCard9JLabel;
647    private javax.swing.JLabel dealerJLabel;
648    private javax.swing.JLabel dealerTotalJLabel;
649    private javax.swing.JButton hitJButton;
650    private javax.swing.JLabel playerCard10JLabel;
651    private javax.swing.JLabel playerCard11JLabel;
652    private javax.swing.JLabel playerCard1JLabel;
653    private javax.swing.JLabel playerCard2JLabel;
654    private javax.swing.JLabel playerCard3JLabel;
655    private javax.swing.JLabel playerCard4JLabel;
656    private javax.swing.JLabel playerCard5JLabel;
657    private javax.swing.JLabel playerCard6JLabel;
658    private javax.swing.JLabel playerCard7JLabel;
659    private javax.swing.JLabel playerCard8JLabel;
660    private javax.swing.JLabel playerCard9JLabel;
```

Fig. 28.14 | Blackjack game that uses the Blackjack web service. (Part 7 of 10.)

```
661     private javax.swing.JLabel playerJLabel;
662     private javax.swing.JLabel playerTotalJLabel;
663     private javax.swing.JButton standJButton;
664     private javax.swing.JLabel statusJLabel;
665     // End of variables declaration
666  } // end class BlackjackGameJFrame
```

a) Dealer and player hands after the user clicks the **Deal** JButton.

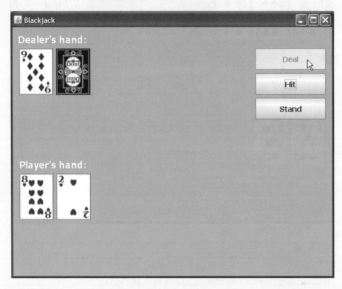

b) Dealer and player hands after the user clicks **Hit** twice, then clicks **Stand**. In this case, the player wins.

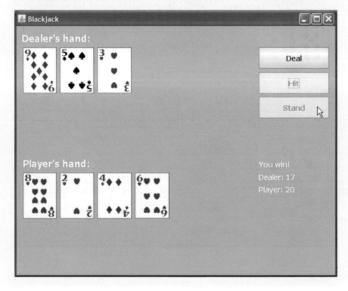

Fig. 28.14 | Blackjack game that uses the Blackjack web service. (Part 8 of 10.)

c) Dealer and player hands after the user clicks **Stand** based on the initial hand. In this case, the player loses.

d) Dealer and player hands after the user is dealt blackjack.

Fig. 28.14 | Blackjack game that uses the `Blackjack` web service. (Part 9 of 10.)

d) Dealer and player hands after the dealer is dealt blackjack.

Fig. 28.14 | Blackjack game that uses the Blackjack web service. (Part 10 of 10.)

Method gameOver (lines 178–215) displays all the dealer's cards, shows the appropriate message in statusJLabel and displays the final point totals of both the dealer and the player. Method gameOver receives as an argument a member of the GameStatus enumeration (defined in lines 25–31). The enumeration represents whether the player tied, lost or won the game; its four members are PUSH, LOSE, WIN and BLACKJACK.

When the player clicks the **Deal** JButton, method dealJButtonActionPerformed (lines 567–618) clears all of the JLabels that display cards or game status information. Next, the deck is shuffled (line 581), and the player and dealer receive two cards each (lines 584–595). Lines 602–603 then total each hand. If the player and the dealer both obtain scores of 21, the program calls method gameOver, passing GameStatus.PUSH (line 607). If only the dealer has 21, the program passes GameStatus.LOSE to method gameOver (line 609). If only the player has 21 after the first two cards are dealt, the program passes GameStatus.BLACKJACK to method gameOver (line 611).

If dealJButtonActionPerformed does not call gameOver, the player can take more cards by clicking the **Hit** JButton, which calls hitJButtonActionPerformed in lines 543–564. Each time a player clicks **Hit**, the program deals the player one more card and displays it in the GUI. If the player exceeds 21, the game is over and the player loses. If the player has exactly 21, the player is not allowed to take any more cards, and method dealerPlay (lines 86–131) is called, causing the dealer to take cards until the dealer's hand has a value of 17 or more (lines 98–106). If the dealer exceeds 21, the player wins (line 114); otherwise, the values of the hands are compared, and gameOver is called with the appropriate argument (lines 120–125).

Clicking the **Stand** JButton indicates that a player does not want to be dealt another card. Method standJButtonActionPerformed (lines 533–540) disables the **Hit** and **Stand** buttons, enables the **Deal** button then calls method dealerPlay.

Method `displayCard` (lines 134–184) updates the GUI to display a newly dealt card. The method takes as arguments an integer index for the `JLabel` in the `ArrayList` that must have its image set and a `String` representing the card. An empty `String` indicates that we wish to display the card face down. If method `displayCard` receives a `String` that's not empty, the program extracts the face and suit from the `String` and uses this information to display the correct image. The `switch` statement (lines 159–173) converts the number representing the suit to an integer and assigns the appropriate character to `suitLetter` (h for hearts, d for diamonds, c for clubs and s for spades). The character in `suitLetter` is used to complete the image's file name (lines 176–178).

In this example, you learned how to set up a web service to support session handling so that you could keep track of each client's session state. You also learned how to indicate from a desktop client application that it wishes to take part in session tracking. You'll now learn how to access a database from a web service and how to consume a web service from a client web application.

28.7 Consuming a Database-Driven Web Service from a Web Application

Our prior examples accessed web services from desktop applications created in Netbeans. However, we can just as easily use them in web applications created with Netbeans or Sun Java Studio Creator 2. In fact, because web-based businesses are becoming increasingly prevalent, it is common for web applications to consume web services. In this section, we present an airline reservation web service that receives information regarding the type of seat a customer wishes to reserve and makes a reservation if such a seat is available. Later in the section, we present a web application that allows a customer to specify a reservation request, then uses the airline reservation web service to attempt to execute the request. We use Sun Java Studio Creator 2 to create the Web application.

28.7.1 Configuring Java DB in Netbeans and Creating the Reservation Database

In this example, our web service uses a `Reservation` database containing a single table named `Seats` to locate a seat matching a client's request. You'll build the `Reservation` database using the tools provided in Netbeans to create and manipulate Java DB databases.

Adding a Java DB Database
To add a Java DB database server in Netbeans, perform the following steps:

1. Select **Tools > Options...** to display the Netbeans **Options** dialog.

2. Click the **Advanced Options** button to display the **Advanced Options** dialog.

3. Under **IDE Configuration**, expand the **Server and External Tool Settings** node and select **Java DB Database**.

4. If the Java DB properties are not already configured, set the **Java DB Location** property to the location of Java DB on your system. JDK 6 comes with a bundled version of Java DB, which is located on Windows in the directory `C:\Program Files\Java\jdk1.6.0\db`. Sun Java System Application Server also comes bun-

dled with Java DB at C:\Sun\AppServer\javadb. Also, set the **Database Location** property to the location where you'd like the Java DB databases to be stored.

Creating a Java DB Database

Now that database software is configured, create a new database as follows:

1. Select **Tools > Java DB Database > Create Java DB Database…**.

2. Enter the name of the database to create (Reservation), a username (jhtp7) and a password (jhtp7), then click **OK** to create the database.

Adding a Table and Data to the Seats Database

You can use the Netbeans **Runtime** tab (to the right of the **Projects** and **Files** tabs) to create tables and to execute SQL statements that populate the database with data:

1. Click Netbeans **Runtime** tab and expand the **Databases** node.

2. Netbeans must be connected to the database to execute SQL statements. If Netbeans is already connected, proceed to *Step 3*. If Netbeans is not connected to the database, the icon 🔌 appears next to the database's URL (jdbc:derby://localhost:1527/Reservation). In this case, right click the icon and click **Connect…**. Once connected, the icon changes to 🖳 .

3. Expand the node for the Reservation database, right click the **Tables** node and select **Create Table…** to display the **Create Table** dialog. Add a table named Seats to the database, and set up the columns Number, Location, Class and Taken, as shown in Fig. 28.15. Use the **Add column** button to add a row in the dialog for each column in the database.

4. Next, use INSERT INTO commands to populate the database with the data shown in Fig. 28.16. To do this, right click the Seats table in the **Runtime** tab and select **Execute Command…** to display a **SQL Command** tab in Netbeans editor. The file SQLStatementsForFig28_16.txt provided with this chapter's examples contains the 10 INSERT INTO commands that store the data shown in Fig. 28.16. Simply copy the text in that file and paste it into the **SQL Command** tab, then press the

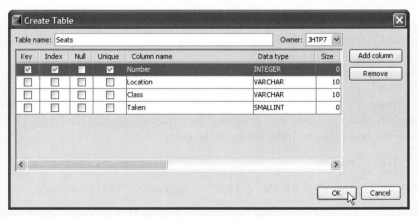

Fig. 28.15 | Seats table configuration.

Number	Location	Class	Taken
1	Aisle	Economy	0
2	Aisle	Economy	0
3	Aisle	First	0
4	Middle	Economy	0
5	Middle	Economy	0
6	Middle	First	0
7	Window	Economy	0
8	Window	Economy	0
9	Window	First	0
10	Window	First	0

Fig. 28.16 | Seats table's data.

Run **SQL** button ( ) to the right of the **Connection** drop-down list in the **SQL Command** tab to execute the commands. You can confirm that the data was inserted properly by right clicking the Seats table in the **Runtime** tab and selecting **View Data....**

Creating the Reservation Web Service

You can now create a web service that uses the Reservation database (Fig. 28.17). The airline reservation web service has a single web method—reserve (lines 25–73)—which searches a Reservation database containing a single table named Seats to locate a seat matching a user's request. The method takes two arguments—a String representing the desired seat type (i.e., "Window", "Middle" or "Aisle") and a String representing the desired class type (i.e., "Economy" or "First"). If it finds an appropriate seat, method reserve updates the database to make the reservation and returns true; otherwise, no reservation is made, and the method returns false. Note that the statements at lines 34–37 and lines 43–44 that query and update the database use objects of types ResultSet and Statement (introduced in Chapter 25).

Our database contains four columns—the seat number (i.e., 1–10), the seat type (i.e., Window, Middle or Aisle), the class type (i.e., Economy or First) and a column containing either 1 (true) or 0 (false) to indicate whether the seat is taken. Lines 34–37 retrieve the seat numbers of any available seats matching the requested seat and class type. This statement fills the resultSet with the results of the query

```
SELECT "Number"
FROM "Seats"
WHERE ("Taken" = 0) AND ("Type" = type) AND ("Class" = class)
```

The parameters *type* and *class* in the query are replaced with values of method reserve's seatType and classType parameters. When you use the Netbeans tools to create a database table and its columns, the Netbeans tools automatically place the table and column names in double quotes. For this reason, you must place the table and column names in double quotes in the SQL statements that interact with the Reservation database.

If resultSet is not empty (i.e., there at least one seat is available that matches the selected criteria), the condition in line 40 is true and the web service reserves the first matching seat number. Recall that ResultSet method next returns true if a nonempty row exists, and positions the cursor on that row. We obtain the seat number (line 42) by accessing resultSet's first column (i.e., resultSet.getInt(1)—the first column in the row). Then lines 43–44 invoke statement's executeUpdate method to execute the SQL:

```
UPDATE "Seats"
SET "Taken" = 1
WHERE ("Number" = number)
```

which marks the seat as taken in the database. The parameter *number* is replaced with the value of seatNumber. Method reserve returns true (line 45) to indicate that the reservation was successful. If there are no matching seats, or if an exception occurred, method reserve returns false (lines 48, 53, 58 and 70) to indicate that no seats matched the user's request.

```
 1   // Fig. 28.17: Reservation.java
 2   // Airline reservation web service.
 3   package com.deitel.jhtp7.ch28.reservationservice;
 4
 5   import java.sql.Connection;
 6   import java.sql.Statement;
 7   import java.sql.DriverManager;
 8   import java.sql.ResultSet;
 9   import java.sql.SQLException;
10   import javax.jws.WebService;
11   import javax.jws.WebMethod;
12   import javax.jws.WebParam;
13
14   @WebService( name = "Reservation", serviceName = "ReservationService" )
15   public class Reservation
16   {
17      private static final String DATABASE_URL =
18         "jdbc:derby://localhost:1527/Reservation";
19      private static final String USERNAME = "jhtp7";
20      private static final String PASSWORD = "jhtp7";
21      private Connection connection;
22      private Statement statement;
23
24      // a WebMethod that can reserve a seat
25      @WebMethod( operationName = "reserve" )
26      public boolean reserve( @WebParam( name = "seatType" ) String seatType,
27         @WebParam( name = "classType" ) String classType )
28      {
29         try
30         {
```

Fig. 28.17 | Airline reservation web service. (Part 1 of 2.)

```
31        connection = DriverManager.getConnection(
32           DATABASE_URL, USERNAME, PASSWORD );
33        statement = connection.createStatement();
34        ResultSet resultSet = statement.executeQuery(
35           "SELECT \"Number\" FROM \"Seats\"" +
36           "WHERE (\"Taken\" = 0) AND (\"Location\" = '" + seatType +
37           "') AND (\"Class\" = '" + classType + "')" );
38
39        // if requested seat is available, reserve it
40        if ( resultSet.next() )
41        {
42           int seat = resultSet.getInt( 1 );
43           statement.executeUpdate( "UPDATE \"Seats\" " +
44              "SET \"Taken\" = 1 WHERE \"Number\" = " + seat );
45           return true;
46        } // end if
47
48        return false;
49     } // end try
50     catch ( SQLException e )
51     {
52        e.printStackTrace();
53        return false;
54     } // end catch
55     catch ( Exception e )
56     {
57        e.printStackTrace();
58        return false;
59     } // end catch
60     finally
61     {
62        try
63        {
64           statement.close();
65           connection.close();
66        } // end try
67        catch ( Exception e )
68        {
69           e.printStackTrace();
70           return false;
71        } // end catch
72     } // end finally
73  } // end WebMethod reserve
74 } // end class Reservation
```

Fig. 28.17 | Airline reservation web service. (Part 2 of 2.)

28.7.2 Creating a Web Application to Interact with the Reservation Web Service

This section presents a ReservationClient web application that consumes the Reservation web service. The application allows users to select seats based on class ("Economy" or "First") and location ("Aisle", "Middle" or "Window"), then submit their requests to the airline reservation web service. If the database request is not successful, the application instructs the user to modify the request and try again. The application presented here was built using Sun Java Studio Creator 2, JavaServer Faces (JSF) and the techniques presented in Chapters 26–27.

Adding a Web Service Reference to a Project Sun Java Studio Creator 2

You can add a web service to a web application in Java Studio Creator 2 by performing the following steps:

1. Click the **Add Web Service...** button (🔘) to display the **Add Web Service** dialog.

2. Click the **Get Web Service Information** button.

3. Click **Add** to dismiss the dialog and add the web service's proxy to the web application. The web service now appears in Java Studio Creator 2's **Servers** tab under the **Web Services** node.

4. Right click the **ReservationService** node under the **Web Services** node and select **Add to Page** to create an instance of the web service's proxy class that you can use in the Reserve class that provides the logic of the JSP.

For the purpose of this example, we assume that you've already read Chapters 26–27, and thus know how to build a web application's GUI, create event handlers and add properties to a web application's session bean (introduced in Section 26.4.4).

Reserve.jsp

Reserve.jsp (Fig. 28.18) defines two DropDownList objects and a Button. The seat-TypeDropDownList (lines 26–31) displays all the seat types from which users can select. The classDropDownList (lines 32–37) provides choices for the class type. Users click the Button named reserveButton (lines 38–41) to submit requests after making selections from the DropDownLists. The page also defines three Labels—instructionLabel (lines 21–25) to display instructions, successLabel (lines 42–45) to indicate a successful reservation and errorLabel (lines 46–50) to display an appropriate message if no seat matching the user's selection is available. The page bean file (Fig. 28.19) attaches event handlers to seatTypeDropDownList, classDropDownList and reserveButton.

```
1   <?xml version="1.0" encoding="UTF-8"?>
2   <!-- Fig. 28.18 Reserve.jsp -->
3   <!-- JSP that allows a user to select a seat -->
4
5   <jsp:root version="1.2" xmlns:f="http://java.sun.com/jsf/core"
6      xmlns:h="http://java.sun.com/jsf/html"
7      xmlns:jsp="http://java.sun.com/JSP/Page"
8      xmlns:ui="http://www.sun.com/web/ui">
9      <jsp:directive.page contentType="text/html;charset=UTF-8"
10        pageEncoding="UTF-8"/>
11     <f:view>
12        <ui:page binding="#{Reserve.page1}" id="page1">
13           <ui:html binding="#{Reserve.html1}" id="html1">
14              <ui:head binding="#{Reserve.head1}" id="head1">
15                 <ui:link binding="#{Reserve.link1}" id="link1"
```

Fig. 28.18 | JSP that allows a user to select a seat. (Part 1 of 3.)

```
16              url="/resources/stylesheet.css"/>
17          </ui:head>
18          <ui:body binding="#{Reserve.body1}" id="body1"
19              style="-rave-layout: grid">
20              <ui:form binding="#{Reserve.form1}" id="form1">
21                  <ui:label binding="#{Reserve.instructionLabel}"
22                      id="instructionLabel"
23                      style="left: 24px; top: 24px; position: absolute"
24                      text="Please select the seat type and class to
25                      reserve:"/>
26                  <ui:dropDown binding="#{Reserve.seatTypeDropDownList}"
27                      id="seatTypeDropDownList" items=
28                      "#{Reserve.seatTypeDropDownListDefaultOptions.options}"
29                      style="left: 24px; top: 48px; position: absolute;
30                      width: 96px" valueChangeListener=
31                      "#{Reserve.seatTypeDropDownList_processValueChange}"/>
32                  <ui:dropDown binding="#{Reserve.classDropDownList}"
33                      id="classDropDownList" items=
34                      "#{Reserve.classDropDownListDefaultOptions.options}"
35                      style="left: 144px; top: 48px; position: absolute;
36                      width: 96px" valueChangeListener=
37                      "#{Reserve.classDropDownList_processValueChange}"/>
38                  <ui:button action="#{Reserve.reserveButton_action}"
39                      binding="#{Reserve.reserveButton}" id="reserveButton"
40                      primary="true" style="height: 22px; left: 263px;
41                      top: 48px; position: absolute" text="Reserve"/>
42                  <ui:label binding="#{Reserve.successLabel}"
43                      id="successLabel" style="left: 24px; top: 24px;
44                      position: absolute" text="Your reservation has been
45                      made. Thank you!" visible="false"/>
46                  <ui:label binding="#{Reserve.errorLabel}" id="errorLabel"
47                      style="color: red; left: 24px; top: 96px;
48                      position: absolute" text="This type of seat is not
49                      available. Please modify your request and try again."
50                      visible="false"/>
51              </ui:form>
52          </ui:body>
53          </ui:html>
54      </ui:page>
55  </f:view>
56  </jsp:root>
```

a) Selecting a seat:

Fig. 28.18 | JSP that allows a user to select a seat. (Part 2 of 3.)

b) Seat reserved successfully:

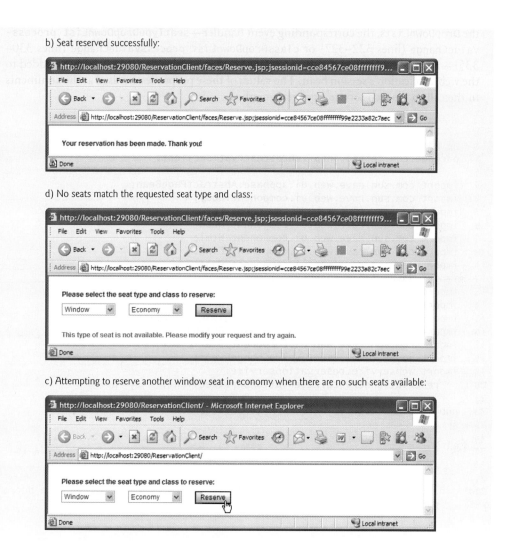

d) No seats match the requested seat type and class:

c) Attempting to reserve another window seat in economy when there are no such seats available:

Fig. 28.18 | JSP that allows a user to select a seat. (Part 3 of 3.)

Reserve.java

Figure 28.19 contains the page bean code that provides the logic for Reserve.jsp. (To save space, we do not show the autogenerated code in lines 28–283.) As discussed in Section 26.5.2, the class that represents the page's bean extends AbstractPageBean. When the user clicks **Reserve** in the JSP, the event handler reserveButton_action (lines 285–319) executes. Line 289 creates a ReservationServiceClient proxy object. Lines 290–292 use this object to invoke the web service's reserve method, passing the selected seat type and class type as arguments. If reserve returns true, lines 296–301 hide the GUI components in the JSP and display the successLabel (line 300) to thank the user for making a reservation; otherwise, lines 305–310 ensure that the GUI components remain displayed and display the errorLabel (line 310) to notify the user that the requested seat type is not available and instructs the user to try again. When the user selects a value in one of the DropDownLists, the corresponding event handler—seatTypeDropDownList_process-ValueChange (lines 322–327) or classDropDownList_processValueChange (lines 330–335)—is called to set the session properties seatType and classType, which we added to the web application's session bean. The values of these properties are used as the arguments in the call to the web service's reserve method.

```java
 1   // Fig. 28.19: Reserve.java
 2   // Page scope backing bean class for seat reservation client
 3   package com.deitel.jhtp7.ch28.reservationclient;
 4
 5   import com.sun.rave.web.ui.appbase.AbstractPageBean;
 6   import com.sun.rave.web.ui.component.Body;
 7   import com.sun.rave.web.ui.component.Form;
 8   import com.sun.rave.web.ui.component.Head;
 9   import com.sun.rave.web.ui.component.Html;
10   import com.sun.rave.web.ui.component.Link;
11   import com.sun.rave.web.ui.component.Page;
12   import javax.faces.FacesException;
13   import com.sun.rave.web.ui.component.Label;
14   import com.sun.rave.web.ui.component.DropDown;
15   import com.sun.rave.web.ui.model.SingleSelectOptionsList;
16   import com.sun.rave.web.ui.component.Button;
17   import com.sun.rave.web.ui.component.StaticText;
18   import javax.faces.event.ValueChangeEvent;
19   import webservice.reservationservice.
20      reservationservice.ReservationServiceClient;
21
22   public class Reserve extends AbstractPageBean
23   {
24      // To save space, we do not show lines 24-283 of the Java Studio
25      // Creator 2 generated code here. You can view the complete code in
26      // the file Reserve.java with this chapter's examples.
27
284      // method that invokes the web service when user clicks Reserve button
285      public String reserveButton_action()
286      {
287         try
288         {
289            ReservationServiceClient client = getReservationServiceClient1();
290            boolean reserved =
291               client.reserve( getSessionBean1().getSeatType(),
292                  getSessionBean1().getClassType() );
293
294            if ( reserved )
295            {
296               instructionLabel.setVisible( false );
297               seatTypeDropDownList.setVisible( false );
298               classDropDownList.setVisible( false );
299               reserveButton.setVisible( false );
300               successLabel.setVisible( true );
301               errorLabel.setVisible( false );
302            } // end if
```

Fig. 28.19 | Page scope backing bean class for seat reservation client. (Part 1 of 2.)

```
303          else
304          {
305              instructionLabel.setVisible( true );
306              seatTypeDropDownList.setVisible( true );
307              classDropDownList.setVisible( true );
308              reserveButton.setVisible( true );
309              successLabel.setVisible( false );
310              errorLabel.setVisible( true );
311          } // end else
312      } // end try
313      catch ( Exception e )
314      {
315          e.printStackTrace();
316      } // end catch
317
318      return null;
319   } // end method reserveButton_action
320
321   // stores selected seat type in session bean
322   public void seatTypeDropDownList_processValueChange(
323      ValueChangeEvent event )
324   {
325      getSessionBean1().setSeatType(
326          ( String ) seatTypeDropDownList.getSelected() );
327   } // end method seatTypeDropDownList_processValueChange
328
329   // stores selected class in session bean
330   public void classDropDownList_processValueChange(
331      ValueChangeEvent event )
332   {
333      getSessionBean1().setClassType(
334          ( String ) classDropDownList.getSelected() );
335   } // end method classDropDownList_processValueChange
336 } // end class Reserve
```

Fig. 28.19 | Page scope backing bean class for seat reservation client. (Part 2 of 2.)

28.8 Passing an Object of a User-Defined Type to a Web Service

The web methods we've demonstrated so far each receive and return only primitive values or Strings. Web services also can receive and return objects of user-defined types—known as **custom types**. This section presents an EquationGenerator web service that generates random arithmetic questions of type Equation. The client is a math-tutoring desktop application in which the user selects the type of mathematical question to attempt (addition, subtraction or multiplication) and the skill level of the user—level 1 uses one-digit numbers in each question, level 2 uses two-digit numbers and level 3 uses three-digit numbers. The client passes this information to the web service, which then generates an Equation consisting of random numbers with the proper number of digits. The client application receives the Equation, displays the sample question to the user in a Java application, allows the user to provide an answer and checks the answer to determine whether it is correct.

Serialization of User-Defined Types

We mentioned earlier that all types passed to and from SOAP web services must be supported by SOAP. How, then, can SOAP support a type that is not even created yet? Custom types that are sent to or from a web service are serialized into XML format. This process is referred to as XML serialization. The process of serializing objects to XML and deserializing objects from XML is handled for you automatically.

Requirements for User-Defined Types Used with Web Methods

A class that is used to specify parameter or return types in web methods must meet several requirements:

1. It must provide a `public` default or no-argument constructor. When a web service or web service consumer receives an XML serialized object, the JAX-WS 2.0 Framework must be able to call this constructor when deserializing the object (i.e., converting it from XML back to a Java object).

2. Instance variables that should be serialized in XML format must have `public` *set* and *get* methods to access the `private` instance variables (recommended), or the instance variables must be declared `public` (not recommended).

3. Non-`public` instance variables that should be serialized must provide both *set* and *get* methods (even if they have empty bodies); otherwise, they are not serialized.

Any instance variable that is not serialized simply receives its default value (or the value provided by the no-argument constructor) when an object of the class is deserialized.

Common Programming Error 28.3

A runtime error occurs if an attempt is made to deserialize an object of a class that does not have a default or no-argument constructor.

Defining Class **Equation**

We define class `Equation` in Fig. 28.20. Lines 18–31 define a constructor that takes three arguments—two `int`s representing the left and right operands and a `String` that represents the arithmetic operation to perform. The constructor sets the `leftOperand`, `rightOperand` and `operationType` instance variables, then calculates the appropriate result. The no-argument constructor (lines 13–16) calls the three-argument constructor (lines 18–31) and passes default values. We do not use the no-argument constructor explicitly, but the XML serialization mechanism uses it when objects of this class are deserialized. Because we provide a constructor with parameters, we must explicitly define the no-argument constructor in this class so that objects of the class can be passed to or returned from web methods.

```
1   // Fig. 28.20: Equation.java
2   // Class Equation that contains information about an equation
3   package com.deitel.jhtp7.generator;
4
5   public class Equation
6   {
7      private int leftOperand;
8      private int rightOperand;
```

Fig. 28.20 | Class `Equation` that stores information about an equation. (Part 1 of 3.)

```java
 9        private int resultValue;
10        private String operationType;
11
12        // required no-argument constructor
13        public Equation()
14        {
15           this( 0, 0, "+" );
16        } // end no-argument constructor
17
18        public Equation( int leftValue, int rightValue, String type )
19        {
20           leftOperand = leftValue;
21           rightOperand = rightValue;
22           operationType = type;
23
24           //determine resultValue
25           if( operationType.equals( "+" ) ) // addition
26              resultValue = leftOperand + rightOperand;
27           else if ( operationType.equals( "-" ) ) // subtraction
28              resultValue = leftOperand - rightOperand;
29           else // multiplication
30              resultValue = leftOperand * rightOperand;
31        } // end three argument constructor
32
33        // method that overrides Object.toString()
34        public String toString()
35        {
36           return leftOperand + " " + operationType + " " +
37              rightOperand + " = " + resultValue;
38        } // end method toString
39
40        // returns the left hand side of the equation as a String
41        public String getLeftHandSide()
42        {
43           return leftOperand + " " + operationType + " " + rightOperand;
44        } // end method getLeftHandSide
45
46        // returns the right hand side of the equation as a String
47        public String getRightHandSide()
48        {
49           return "" + resultValue;
50        } // end method getRightHandSide
51
52        // gets the leftOperand
53        public int getLeftOperand()
54        {
55           return leftOperand;
56        } // end method getLeftOperand
57
58        // gets the rightOperand
59        public int getRightOperand()
60        {
```

Fig. 28.20 | Class Equation that stores information about an equation. (Part 2 of 3.)

```
61          return rightOperand;
62       } // end method getRightOperand
63
64       // gets the resultValue
65       public int getReturnValue()
66       {
67          return resultValue;
68       } // end method getResultValue
69
70       // gets the operationType
71       public String getOperationType()
72       {
73          return operationType;
74       } // end method getOperationType
75
76       // required setter
77       public void setLeftHandSide( String value )
78       {
79          // empty body
80       } // end setLeftHandSide
81
82       // required setter
83       public void setRightHandSide( String value )
84       {
85          // empty body
86       } // end setRightHandSide
87
88       // required setter
89       public void setLeftOperand( int value )
90       {
91          // empty body
92       } // end method setLeftOperand
93
94       // required setter
95       public void setRightOperand( int value )
96       {
97          // empty body
98       } // end method setRightOperand
99
100      // required setter
101      public void setReturnValue( int value )
102      {
103         // empty body
104      } // end method setResultOperand
105
106      // required setter
107      public void setOperationType( String value )
108      {
109         // empty body
110      } // end method setOperationType
111   } // end class Equation
```

Fig. 28.20 | Class Equation that stores information about an equation. (Part 3 of 3.)

Class `Equation` defines methods `getLeftHandSide` and `setLeftHandSide` (lines 41–44 and 77–80); `getRightHandSide` and `setRightHandSide` (lines 47–50 and 83–86); `getLeftOperand` and `setLeftOperand` (lines 53–56 and 89–92); `getRightOperand` and `setRightOperand` (lines 59–62 and 95–98); `getReturnValue` and `setReturnValue` (lines 65–68 and 101–104); and `getOperationType` and `setOperationType` (lines 71–74 and 107–110). The client of the web service does not need to modify the values of the instance variables. However, recall that a property can be serialized only if it has both a *get* and a *set* accessor, or if it is `public`. So we provided *set* methods with empty bodies for each of the class's instance variables. Method `getLeftHandSide` (lines 41–44) returns a `String` representing everything to the left of the equals (=) sign in the equation, and `getRightHandSide` (lines 47–50) returns a `String` representing everything to the right of the equals (=) sign. Method `getLeftOperand` (lines 53–56) returns the integer to the left of the operator, and `getRightOperand` (lines 59–62) returns the integer to the right of the operator. Method `getResultValue` (lines 65–68) returns the solution to the equation, and `getOperationType` (lines 71–74) returns the operator in the equation. The client in this example does not use the `rightHandSide` property, but we included it so future clients can use it.

Creating the *EquationGenerator* Web Service
Figure 28.21 presents the `EquationGenerator` web service, which creates random, customized `Equation`s. This web service contains only method `generateEquation` (lines 18–31), which takes two parameters—the mathematical operation (one of "+", "-" or "*") and an `int` representing the difficulty level (1–3).

```
1    // Fig. 22.20: Generator.java
2    // Web service that generates random equations
3    package com.deitel.jhtp7.ch28.equationgenerator;
4
5    import java.util.Random;
6    import javax.jws.WebService;
7    import javax.jws.WebMethod;
8    import javax.jws.WebParam;
9
10   @WebService( name = "EquationGenerator",
11      serviceName = "EquationGeneratorService" )
12   public class EquationGenerator
13   {
14      private int minimum;
15      private int maximum;
16
17      // generates a math equation and returns it as an Equation object
18      @WebMethod( operationName = "generateEquation" )
19      public Equation generateEquation(
20         @WebParam( name = "operation" ) String operation,
21         @WebParam( name = "difficulty" ) int difficulty )
22      {
23         minimum = ( int ) Math.pow( 10, difficulty - 1 );
24         maximum = ( int ) Math.pow( 10, difficulty );
25
```

Fig. 28.21 | Web service that generates random equations. (Part 1 of 2.)

```
26          Random randomObject = new Random();
27
28          return new Equation(
29             randomObject.nextInt( maximum - minimum ) + minimum,
30             randomObject.nextInt( maximum - minimum ) + minimum, operation );
31       } // end method generateEquation
32   } // end class EquationGenerator
```

Fig. 28.21 | Web service that generates random equations. (Part 2 of 2.)

Testing the *EquationGenerator* Web Service

Figure 28.22 shows the result of testing the EquationGenerator web service with the Tester web page. In *part (b)* of the figure, note that the return value from our web method is XML encoded. However, this example differs from previous ones in that the XML specifies the values for all the data of the XML serialized object that is returned. The proxy class receives this return value and deserializes it into an object of class Equation, then passes it to the client.

Note that an Equation object is *not* being passed between the web service and the client. Rather, the information in the object is being sent as XML-encoded data. Clients created using Java will take the information and create a new Equation object. Clients created on other platforms, however, may use the information differently. Readers creating clients on other platforms should check the web services documentation for the specific platform they are using, to see how their clients may process custom types.

Details of the *EquationGenerator* Web Service

Let's examine web method generateEquation more closely. Lines 23–24 of Fig. 28.21 define the upper and lower bounds of the random numbers that the method uses to generate an Equation. To set these limits, the program first calls static method pow of class Math—this method raises its first argument to the power of its second argument. Variable

a) Using the EquationGenerator web service's Tester web page to generate an Equation.

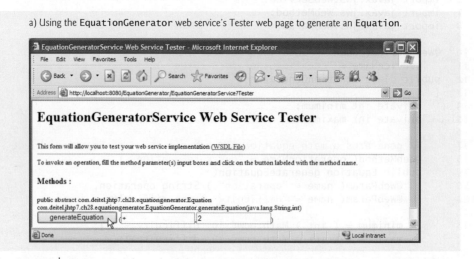

Fig. 28.22 | Testing a web method that returns an XML serialized Equation object. (Part 1 of 2.)

b) Result of generating an Equation.

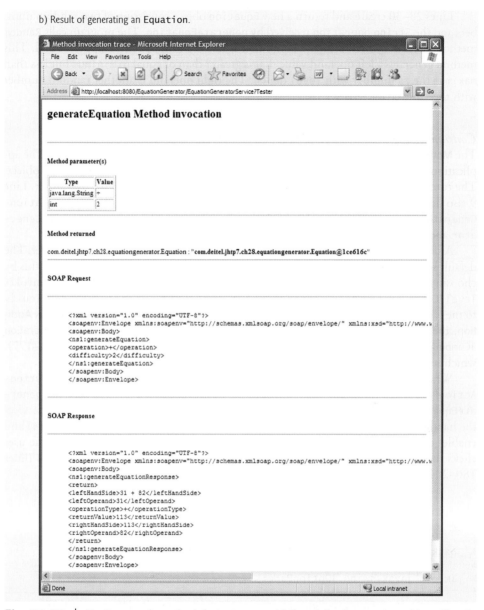

Fig. 28.22 | Testing a web method that returns an XML serialized Equation object. (Part 2 of 2.)

minimum's value is determined by raising 10 to a power one less than level (line 23). This calculates the smallest number with level digits. If level is 1, minimum is 1; if level is 2, minimum is 10; and if level is 3, minimum is 100. To calculate the value of maximum (the upper bound for any randomly generated numbers used to form an Equation), the program raises 10 to the power of the specified level argument (line 23). If level is 1, maximum is 10; if level is 2, maximum is 100; and if level is 3, maximum is 1000.

Lines 28–30 create and return a new Equation object consisting of two random numbers and the String operation received by generateEquation. The program calls Random method nextInt, which returns an int that is less than the specified upper bound. This method generates a left operand value that is greater than or equal to minimum but less than maximum (i.e., a number with level digits). The right operand is another random number with the same characteristics.

Consuming the *EquationGenerator* Web Service

The **Math Tutor** application (Fig. 28.23) uses the EquationGenerator web service. The application calls the web service's generateEquation method to create an Equation object. The tutor then displays the left-hand side of the Equation and waits for user input. Line 9 also declares a GeneratorService instance variable that we use to obtain an EquationGenerator proxy object. Lines 10–11 declare instance variables of types EquationGenerator and Equation.

After displaying an equation, the application waits for the user to enter an answer. The default setting for the difficulty level is **One-digit numbers**, but the user can change this by choosing a level from the **Choose level** JComboBox. Clicking any of the levels invokes levelJComboBoxItemStateChanged (lines 158–163), which sets the variable difficulty to the level selected by the user. Although the default setting for the question type is **Addition**, the user also can change this by selecting an operation from the **Choose operation** JComboBox. Doing so invokes operationJComboBoxItemStateChanged (lines 166–177), which sets the String operation to the appropriate mathematical symbol.

When the user clicks the **Generate Equation** JButton, method generateButtonActionPerformed (lines 207–221) invokes the EquationGenerator web service's generateEquation (line 212) method. After receiving an Equation object from the web service, the handler displays the left-hand side of the equation in equationJLabel (line 214) and enables the checkAnswerJButton so that the user can submit an answer. When the user clicks the **Check Answer** JButton, method checkAnswerJButtonActionPerformed (lines 180–204) determines whether the user provided the correct answer.

```
 1   // Fig. 28.23: EquationGeneratorClientJFrame.java
 2   // Math tutoring program using web services to generate equations
 3   package com.deitel.jhtp7.ch28.equationgeneratorclient;
 4
 5   import javax.swing.JOptionPane;
 6
 7   public class EquationGeneratorClientJFrame extends javax.swing.JFrame
 8   {
 9      private EquationGeneratorService service; // used to obtain proxy
10      private EquationGenerator proxy; // used to access the web service
11      private Equation equation; // represents an equation
12      private int answer; // the user's answer to the question
13      private String operation = "+"; // mathematical operation +, - or *
14      private int difficulty = 1; // 1, 2 or 3 digits in each number
15
```

Fig. 28.23 | Math tutoring application. (Part 1 of 4.)

```java
16      // no-argument constructor
17      public EquationGeneratorClientJFrame()
18      {
19         initComponents();
20
21         try
22         {
23            // create the objects for accessing the EquationGenerator service
24            service = new EquationGeneratorService();
25            proxy = service.getEquationGeneratorPort();
26         } // end try
27         catch ( Exception ex )
28         {
29            ex.printStackTrace();
30         } // end catch
31      } // end no-argument constructors
32
33      // The initComponents method is autogenerated by Netbeans and is called
34      // from the constructor to initialize the GUI. This method is not shown
35      // here to save space. Open EquationGeneratorClientJFrame.java in this
36      // example's folder to view the complete generated code (lines 37-156).
37
157     // obtains the difficulty level selected by the user
158     private void levelJComboBoxItemStateChanged(
159        java.awt.event.ItemEvent evt )
160     {
161        // indices start at 0, so add 1 to get the difficulty level
162        difficulty = levelJComboBox.getSelectedIndex() + 1;
163     } // end method levelJComboBoxItemStateChanged
164
165     // obtains the mathematical operation selected by the user
166     private void operationJComboBoxItemStateChanged(
167        java.awt.event.ItemEvent evt )
168     {
169        String item = ( String ) operationJComboBox.getSelectedItem();
170
171        if ( item.equals( "Addition" ) )
172           operation = "+"; // user selected addition
173        else if ( item.equals( "Subtraction" ) )
174           operation = "-"; // user selected subtraction
175        else
176           operation = "*"; // user selected multiplication
177     } // end method operationJComboBoxItemStateChanged
178
179     // checks the user's answer
180     private void checkAnswerJButtonActionPerformed(
181        java.awt.event.ActionEvent evt )
182     {
183        if ( answerJTextField.getText().equals( "" ) )
184        {
185           JOptionPane.showMessageDialog(
186              this, "Please enter your answer." );
187        } // end if
```

Fig. 28.23 | Math tutoring application. (Part 2 of 4.)

```
188
189        int userAnswer = Integer.parseInt( answerJTextField.getText() );
190
191        if ( userAnswer == answer )
192        {
193           equationJLabel.setText( "" );
194           answerJTextField.setText( "" );
195           checkAnswerJButton.setEnabled( false );
196           JOptionPane.showMessageDialog( this, "Correct! Good Job!",
197              "Correct", JOptionPane.PLAIN_MESSAGE );
198        } // end if
199        else
200        {
201           JOptionPane.showMessageDialog( this, "Incorrect. Try again.",
202              "Incorrect", JOptionPane.PLAIN_MESSAGE );
203        } // end else
204     } // end method checkAnswerJButtonActionPerformed
205
206     // generates a new Equation based on user's selections
207     private void generateJButtonActionPerformed(
208        java.awt.event.ActionEvent evt )
209     {
210        try
211        {
212           equation = proxy.generateEquation( operation, difficulty );
213           answer = equation.getReturnValue();
214           equationJLabel.setText( equation.getLeftHandSide() + " =" );
215           checkAnswerJButton.setEnabled( true );
216        } // end try
217        catch ( Exception e )
218        {
219           e.printStackTrace();
220        } // end catch
221     } // end method generateJButtonActionPerformed
222
223     // begins program execution
224     public static void main( String args[] )
225     {
226        java.awt.EventQueue.invokeLater(
227           new Runnable()
228           {
229              public void run()
230              {
231                 new EquationGeneratorClientJFrame().setVisible( true );
232              } // end method run
233           } // end anonymous inner class
234        ); // end call to java.awt.EventQueue.invokeLater
235     } // end method main
236
237     // Variables declaration - do not modify
238     private javax.swing.JLabel answerJLabel;
239     private javax.swing.JTextField answerJTextField;
240     private javax.swing.JButton checkAnswerJButton;
```

Fig. 28.23 | Math tutoring application. (Part 3 of 4.)

```
241      private javax.swing.JLabel equationJLabel;
242      private javax.swing.JButton generateJButton;
243      private javax.swing.JComboBox levelJComboBox;
244      private javax.swing.JLabel levelJLabel;
245      private javax.swing.JComboBox operationJComboBox;
246      private javax.swing.JLabel operationJLabel;
247      private javax.swing.JLabel questionJLabel;
248      // End of variables declaration
249  } // end class EquationGeneratorClientJFrame
```

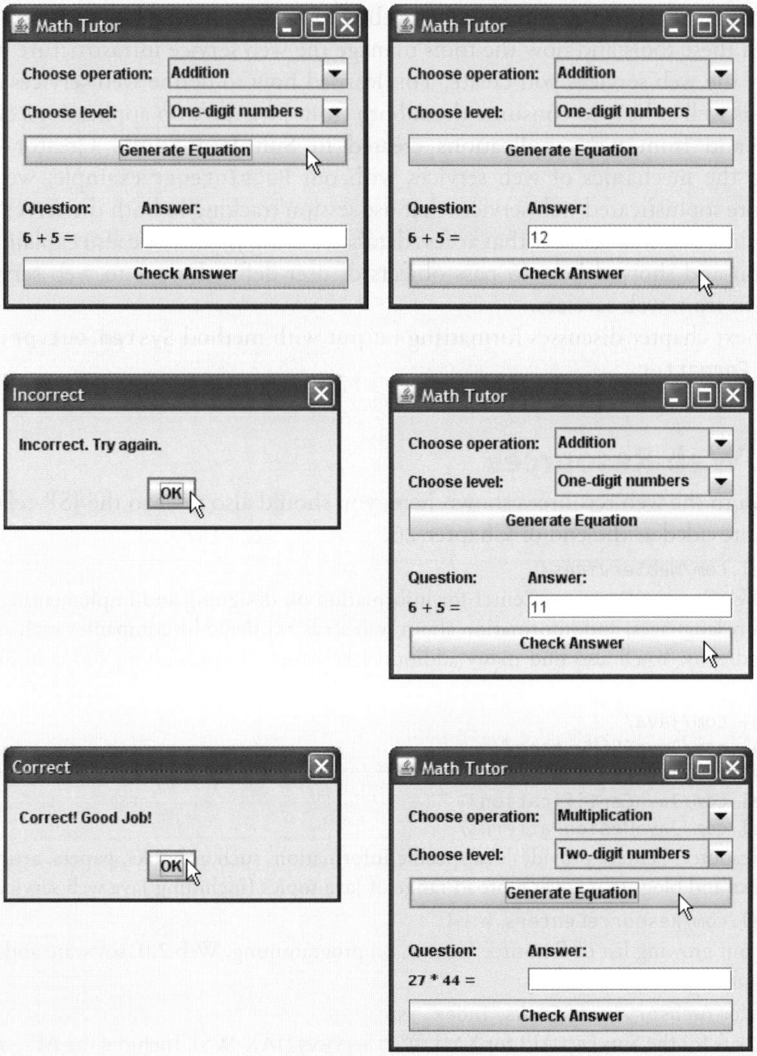

Fig. 28.23 | Math tutoring application. (Part 4 of 4.)

28.9 Wrap-Up

This chapter introduced JAX-WS 2.0 web services, which promote software portability and reusability in applications that operate over the Internet. You learned that a web service is a software component stored on one computer that can be accessed by an application (or other software component) on another computer over a network, communicating via such technologies as XML, SOAP and HTTP. We discussed several benefits of this kind of distributed computing—e.g., clients can access data on remote machines, clients lacking the processing power to perform specific computations can leverage remote machines' resources and entirely new types of innovative applications can be developed.

We explained how Netbeans, Sun Java Studio Creator 2 and the JAX-WS 2.0 APIs facilitate the creation and consumption of web services. We showed how to set up projects and files in these tools and how the tools manage the web service infrastructure necessary to support the web services you create. You learned how to define web services and web methods, as well as how to consume them both from Java desktop applications created in Netbeans and from web applications created in Sun Java Studio Creator 2. After explaining the mechanics of web services with our `HugeInteger` example, we demonstrated more sophisticated web services that use session tracking in both the server side and the client side, and web services that access databases using JDBC. We also explained XML serialization and showed how to pass objects of user-defined types to web services and return them from web services.

The next chapter discusses formatting output with method `System.out.printf` and with class `Formatter`.

28.10 Web Resources

In addition to the web resources shown here, you should also refer to the JSP-related web resources provided at the end of Chapter 26.

`www.deitel.com/WebServices/`
Visit our Web Services Resource Center for information on designing and implementing web services in many languages, and information about web services offered by companies such as Google, Amazon and eBay. You'll also find many additional Java tools for publishing and consuming web services.

`www.deitel.com/java/`
`www.deitel.com/JavaSE6Mustang/`
`www.deitel.com/JavaEE5/`
`www.deitel.com/JavaCertification/`
`www.deitel.com/JavaDesignPatterns/`
Our Java Resource Centers provide Java-specific information, such as books, papers, articles, journals, websites and blogs that cover a broad range of Java topics (including Java web services).

`www.deitel.com/ResourceCenters.html`
Check out our growing list of Resource Centers on programming, Web 2.0, software and other interesting topics.

`java.sun.com/webservices/jaxws/index.jsp`
The official site for the Sun Java API for XML Web Services (JAX-WS). Includes the API, documentation, tutorials and other useful links.

`www.webservices.org`
Provides industry-related news, articles and resources for web services.

`www-130.ibm.com/developerworks/webservices`
IBM's site for service-oriented architecture (SOA) and web services includes articles, downloads, demos and discussion forums regarding web services technology.

`www.w3.org/TR/wsdl`
Provides extensive documentation on WSDL, including a thorough discussion of web services and related technologies such as XML, SOAP, HTTP and MIME types in the context of WSDL.

`www.w3.org/TR/soap`
Provides extensive documentation on SOAP messages, using SOAP with HTTP and SOAP security issues.

`www.ws-i.org`
The Web Services Interoperability Organization's website provides detailed information regarding building web services based on standards that promote interoperability and true platform independence.

`webservices.xml.com/security`
Articles about web services security and standard security protocols.

REST-Based Web Services

`en.wikipedia.org/wiki/REST`
Wikipedia resource explaining Representational State Transfer (REST).

`www.xfront.com/REST-Web-Services.html`
Article entitled "Building Web Services the REST Way."

`www.ics.uci.edu/~fielding/pubs/dissertation/rest_arch_style.htm`
The dissertation that originally proposed the concept of REST-based services.

`rest.blueoxen.net/cgi-bin/wiki.pl?ShortSummaryOfRest`
A short introduction to REST.

`www.prescod.net/rest`
Links to many REST resources.

Summary

Section 28.1 Introduction

- A web service is a software component stored on one computer that can be accessed via method calls by an application (or other software component) on another computer over a network.
- Web services communicate using such technologies as XML and HTTP.
- The Simple Object Access Protocol (SOAP) is an XML-based protocol that allows web services and clients to communicate in a platform-independent manner.
- Web services enable businesses to conduct transactions via standardized, widely available web services rather than relying on proprietary applications.
- Companies such as Amazon, Google, eBay, PayPal and many others are using web services to their advantage by making their server-side applications available to partners via web services.
- By purchasing web services and using extensive free web services, companies can spend less time developing new applications and can create innovative new applications.
- Netbeans 5.5 and Sun Java Studio Creator 2—both developed by Sun—are two of the many tools that enable programmers to "publish" and/or "consume" web services.

Section 28.2 Java Web Services Basics

- The computer on which a web service resides is referred to as a remote machine or server. A client application that accesses a web service sends a method call over a network to the remote machine, which processes the call and returns a response over the network to the application.

- In Java, a web service is implemented as a class. The class that represents the web service resides on a server—it's not part of the client application.

- Making a web service available to receive client requests is known as publishing a web service; using a web service from a client application is known as consuming a web service.

- An application that consumes a web service consists of two parts—an object of a proxy class for interacting with the web service and a client application that consumes the web service by invoking methods on the proxy object. The proxy object handles the details of communicating with the web service on the client's behalf.

- Requests to and responses from web services created with JAX-WS 2.0 are typically transmitted via SOAP. Any client capable of generating and processing SOAP messages can interact with a web service, regardless of the language in which the web service is written.

Section 28.3.1 Creating a Web Application Project and Adding a Web Service Class in Netbeans

- When you create a web service in Netbeans, you focus on the logic of the web service and let the IDE handle the web service's infrastructure.

- To create a web service in Netbeans, you first create a project of type **Web Application**. Netbeans uses this project type for web applications that execute in browser-based clients and for web services that are invoked by other applications.

- When you create a **Web Application** in Netbeans, the IDE generates additional files that support the web application.

Section 28.3.2 Defining the **HugeInteger** Web Service in Netbeans

- By default, each new web service class created with the JAX-WS APIs is a POJO (plain old Java object)—you do not need to extend a class or implement an interface to create a Web service.

- When you compile a class that uses these JAX-WS 2.0 annotations, the compiler creates the compiled code framework that allows the web service to wait for and respond to client requests.

- The @WebService annotation indicates that a class represents a web service. Optional element name specifies the name of the proxy class that will be generated for the client. Optional element serviceName specifies the name of the class that the client uses to obtain a proxy object.

- Netbeans places the @WebService annotation at the beginning of each new web service class you create. You can add the optional name and serviceName elements in the annotation's parentheses.

- Methods that are tagged with the @WebMethod annotation can be called remotely.

- Methods that are not tagged with @WebMethod are not accessible to clients that consume the web service. Such methods are typically utility methods within the web service class.

- The @WebMethod annotation has an optional operationName element to specify the method name that is exposed to the web service's client.

- Parameters of web methods are annotated with the @WebParam annotation. The optional element name indicates the parameter name that is exposed to the web service's clients.

Section 28.3.3 Publishing the **HugeInteger** Web Service from Netbeans

- Netbeans handles all the details of building and deploying a web service for you. This includes creating the framework required to support the web service.

- To determine if there are any compilation errors in your project, right click the project name in the Netbeans **Projects** tab, then select the **Build Project** option.

- Select **Deploy Project** to deploy the project to the server you selected during application setup.

- Select **Run Project** to execute the web application.

- Both the **Deploy Project** and **Run Project** options also build the project if it has changed and start the application server if it is not already running.

- To ensure that all source-code files in a project are recompiled during the next build operation, you can use the **Clean Project** or **Clean and Build Project** options.

Section 28.3.4 Testing the **HugeInteger** Web Service with Sun Java System Application Server's **Tester** Web page

- Sun Java System Application Server can dynamically create a Tester web page for testing a web service's methods from a web browser. You can enable this feature via the project's **Run** options.

- To display the Tester web page, run the web application from Netbeans or type the URL of the web service in the browser's address field followed by ?Tester.

- A client can access a web service only when the application server is running. If Netbeans launches the application server for you, the server will shut down when you close Netbeans. To keep the application server up and running, you can launch it independently of Netbeans.

Section 28.3.5 Describing a Web Service with the Web Service Description Language (WSDL)

- To consume a web service, a client must know where to find the web service and must be provided with the web service's description.

- JAX-WS uses the Web Service Description Language (WSDL)—a standard XML vocabulary for describing web services in a platform-independent manner.

- You do not need to understand WSDL to take advantage of it—the server generates a web service's WSDL dynamically for you and client tools can parse the WSDL to help create the client-side proxy class that a client uses to access the web service.

- Since the WSDL is created dynamically, clients always receive a deployed web service's most up-to-date description.

- To view the WSDL for a web service, type its URL in the browser's address field followed by ?WSDL or click the **WSDL File** link in the Sun Java System Application Server's Tester web page.

Section 28.4 Consuming a Web Service

- A web service client can be any type of application or even another web service.

- In Netbeans, you enable a client application to consume a web service by adding a web service reference to the application, which defines the client-side proxy class.

Section 28.4.1 Creating a Client in Netbeans to Consume the **HugeInteger** Web Service

- When you add a web service reference, the IDE creates and compiles the client-side artifacts—the framework of Java code that supports the client-side proxy class.

- The client calls methods on a proxy object, which uses the client-side artifacts to interact with the web service.

- To add a web service reference, right click the client project name in the Netbeans **Projects** tab, then select **New > Web Service Client....** In the dialog's **WSDL URL** field, specify the URL of the web service's WSDL.

- Netbeans uses the WSDL description to generate the client-side proxy class and artifacts.

- When you specify the web service you want to consume, Netbeans copies the web service's WSDL into a file in your project. You can view this file from the Netbeans **Files** tab by expanding the nodes in the project's xml-resources folder.

- The client-side artifacts and the client's copy of the WSDL file can be regenerated by right clicking the web service's node in the Netbeans **Projects** tab and selecting **Refresh Client**.

- You can view the IDE-generated client-side artifacts by selecting the Netbeans **Files** tab and expanding the project's build folder.

Section 28.5 SOAP

- SOAP is a commonly used, platform-independent, XML-based protocol that facilitates remote procedure calls, typically over HTTP.

- The protocol that transmits request-and-response messages is also known as the web service's wire format or wire protocol, because it defines how information is sent "along the wire."

- Each request and response is packaged in a SOAP message (also known as a SOAP envelope) containing the information that a web service requires to process the message.

- The wire format used to transmit requests and responses must support all types passed between the applications. SOAP supports primitive types and their wrapper types, as well as Date, Time and others. SOAP can also transmit arrays and objects of user-defined types.

- When a program invokes a web method, the request and all relevant information are packaged in a SOAP message and sent to the server on which the web service resides. The web service processes the SOAP message's contents, which specify the method to invoke and its arguments. After the web service receives and parses a request, the proper method is called, and the response is sent back to the client in another SOAP message. The client-side proxy parses the response, which contains the result of the method call, and returns the result to the client application.

- The SOAP messages are generated for you automatically. So you don't need to understand the details of SOAP or XML to take advantage of it when publishing and consuming web services.

Section 28.6 Session Tracking in Web Services

- It can be beneficial for a web service to maintain client state information, thus eliminating the need to pass client information between the client and the web service multiple times. Storing session information also enables a web service to distinguish between clients.

Section 28.6.1 Creating a **Blackjack** Web Service

- To use session tracking in a Web service, you must include code for the resources that maintain the session state information. In the past, you had to write the sometimes tedious code to create these resources. JAX-WS, however, handles this for you via the @Resource annotation. This annotation enables tools like Netbeans to "inject" complex support code into your class, thus allowing you to focus on your business logic rather than the support code.

- Using annotations to add code that supports your classes is known as dependency injection. Annotations like @WebService, @WebMethod and @WebParam also perform dependency injection.

- A WebServiceContext object enables a web service to access and maintain information for a specific request, such as session state. The code that creates a WebServiceContext object is injected into the class by an @Resource annotation.

- The WebServiceContext object is used to obtain a MessageContext object. A web service uses a MessageContext to obtain an HttpSession object for the current client.

- The MessageContext object's get method is used to obtain the HttpSession object for the current client. Method get receives a constant indicating what to get from the MessageContext. The constant MessageContext.SERVLET_REQUEST indicates that we'd like to get the HttpServlet-Request object for the current client. We then call method getSession to get the HttpSession object from the HttpServletRequest object.

- HttpSession method getAttribute receives a String that identifies the Object to obtain from the session state.

Section 28.6.2 Consuming the **Blackjack** Web Service

- In the JAX-WS 2.0 framework, the client must indicate whether it wants to allow the web service to maintain session information. To do this, first cast the proxy object to interface type Binding-Provider. A BindingProvider enables the client to manipulate the request information that will be sent to the server. This information is stored in an object that implements interface Request-Context. The BindingProvider and RequestContext are part of the framework that is created by the IDE when you add a web service client to the application.

- Next, invoke the BindingProvider's getRequestContext method to obtain the RequestContext object. Then call the RequestContext's put method to set the property BindingProvid-er.SESSION_MAINTAIN_PROPERTY to true, which enables session tracking from the client side so that the web service knows which client is invoking the service's web methods.

Section 28.7.1 Configuring Java DB in Netbeans and Creating the **Reservation** Database

- To add a Java DB database server in Netbeans, perform the following steps: Select **Tools > Options...** to display the Netbeans **Options** dialog. Click the **Advanced Options** button to display the **Advanced Options** dialog. Under **IDE Configuration**, expand the **Server and External Tool Settings** node and select **Java DB Database**. If the Java DB properties are not already configured, set the **Java DB Location** property to the location of Java DB on your system. Also, set the **Database Location** property to the location where you'd like the Java DB databases to be stored.

- To create a new database: Select **Tools > Java DB Database > Create Java DB Database....** Enter the name of the database to create, a username and a password, then click **OK** to create the database.

- You can use the Netbeans **Runtime** tab to create tables and to execute SQL statements that populate the database with data. Click the Netbeans **Runtime** tab and expand the **Databases** node.

- Netbeans must be connected to the database to execute SQL statements. If Netbeans is not connected to the database, the icon 🔌 appears next to the database's URL. In this case, right click the icon and click **Connect....** Once connected, the icon changes to 🔌 .

Section 28.7.2 Creating a Web Application to Interact with the **Reservation** Web Service

- You can add a web service to a web application in Java Studio Creator 2 by clicking the **Add Web Service...** button (🔘). You can then specify the web service's WSDL in the dialog that appears.

Section 28.8 Passing an Object of a User-Defined Type to a Web Service

- Web services can receive and return objects of user-defined types—known as custom types.

- Custom types that are sent to or from a web service using SOAP are serialized into XML format. This process is referred to as XML serialization and is handled for you automatically.

- A class that is used to specify parameter or return types in web methods must provide a public default or no-argument constructor. Also, any instance variables that should be serialized must have public *set* and *get* methods or the instance variables must be declared public.

- Any instance variable that is not serialized simply receives its default value (or the value provided by the no-argument constructor) when an object of the class is deserialized.

Terminology

AbstractPageBean class
Add Server Instance dialog
adding a web service reference to a project in
    Netbeans
Apache Tomcat server
application server
B2B (business-to-business) transactions
BEA Weblogic Server
BindingProvider interface
Build Project option in Netbeans
business-to-business (B2B) transactions
Clean and Build Project option in Netbeans
Clean Project option in Netbeans
client-side artifacts
consume a web service
custom type
dependency injection
Deploy Project option in Netbeans
deploy a web service
get method of interface MessageContext
getRequestContext method of interface
    BindingProvider
GlassFish server
JAX-WS 2.0
JBoss Application Server
MessageContext interface
Netbeans 5.5 IDE
New Project dialog in Netbeans
New Web Service Client dialog in Netbeans
New Web Service dialog in Netbeans
parse a SOAP message
POJO (plain old Java object)
Project Properties dialog in Netbeans
proxy class for a web service
proxy object handles the details of
    communicating with the web service

publish a web service
put method of interface RequestContext
remote machine
Representational State Transfer (REST)
RequestContext interface
@Resource annotation
REST (Representational State Transfer)
Run Project option in Netbeans
Server Manager dialog in Netbeans
server-side artifacts
session tracking in web services
SOAP envelope
SOAP message
SOAP (Simple Object Access Protocol)
Sun Java Studio Creator 2
Sun Java System Application Server
Sun Java System Application Server Tester web
    page
test a web service
Web Application project in Netbeans
Web Service Description Language (WSDL)
web service reference
Web Services Interoperability Organization
    (WS-I)
@WebMethod annotation
@WebMethod annotation operationName element
@WebParam annotation
@WebParam annotation name element
@WebService annotation
@WebService annotation name element
@WebService annotation serviceName element
WebServiceContext interface
wire format
wire protocol
WS-I Basic Profile 1.1 (BP 1.1)
XML serialization

Self-Review Exercises

28.1 State whether each of the following is *true* or *false*. If *false*, explain why.
    a) All methods of a web service class can be invoked by clients of that web service.
    b) When consuming a web service in a client application created in Netbeans, you must create the proxy class that enables the client to communicate with the web service.
    c) A proxy class communicating with a web service normally uses SOAP to send and receive messages.
    d) Session tracking is automatically enabled in a client of a web service.
    e) Web methods cannot be declared static.
    f) A user-defined type used in a web service must define both *get* and *set* methods for any property that will be serialized.

28.2 Fill in the blanks for each of the following statements:
   a) When messages are sent between an application and a web service using SOAP, each message is placed in a(n) _____.
   b) A web service in Java is a(n) _____—it does not need to implement any interfaces or extend any classes.
   c) Web service requests are typically transported over the Internet via the _____ protocol.
   d) To set the exposed name of a web method, use the _____ element of the @WebMethod annotation.
   e) _____ transforms an object into a format that can be sent between a web service and a client.

Answers to Self-Review Exercises

28.1 a) False. Only methods declared with the @WebMethod annotation can be invoked by a web service's clients. b) False. The proxy class is created by Netbeans when you add a web service client to the application. c) True. d) False. In the JAX-WS 2.0 framework, the client must indicate whether it wants to allow the web service to maintain session information. First, you must cast the proxy object to interface type BindingProvider, then use the BindingProvider's getRequestContext method to obtain the RequestContext object. Finally, you must use the RequestContext's put method to set the property BindingProvider.SESSION_MAINTAIN_PROPERTY to true. e) True. f) True.

28.2 a) SOAP message or SOAP envelope. b) POJO (plain old Java object) c) HTTP. d) operationName. e) XML serialization.

Exercises

28.3 *(Phone Book Web Service)* Create a web service that stores phone book entries in the database PhoneBookDB and a web client application that consumes this service. Use the steps in Section 28.7.1 to create the PhoneBook database. The database should contain one table—PhoneBook—with three columns—LastName, FirstName and PhoneNumber—each of type VARCHAR. The LastName and FirstName columns should store up to 30 characters. The PhoneNumber column should support phone numbers of the form (800) 555-1212 that contain 14 characters.

Give the client user the capability to enter a new contact (web method addEntry) and to find contacts by last name (web method getEntries). Pass only Strings as arguments to the web service. The getEntries web method should return an array of Strings that contains the matching phone book entries. Each String in the array should consist of the last name, first name and phone number for one phone book entry. These values should be separated by commas.

The SELECT query that will find a PhoneBook entry by last name should be:

```
SELECT LastName, FirstName, PhoneNumber
FROM PhoneBook
WHERE (LastName = LastName)
```

The INSERT statement that inserts a new entry into the PhoneBook database should be:

```
INSERT INTO PhoneBook (LastName, FirstName, PhoneNumber)
VALUES (LastName, FirstName, PhoneNumber)
```

28.4 *(Phone Book Web Service Modification)* Modify Exercise 28.3 so that it uses a class named PhoneBookEntry to represent a row in the database. The client application should provide objects of type PhoneBookEntry to the web service when adding contacts and should receive objects of type PhoneBookEntry when searching for contacts.

29

Formatted Output

OBJECTIVES

In this chapter you will learn:

- To understand input and output streams.
- To use **printf** formatting.
- To print with field widths and precisions.
- To use formatting flags in the **printf** format string.
- To print with an argument index.
- To output literals and escape sequences.
- To format output with class **Formatter**.

29.1 Introduction

An important part of the solution to any problem is the presentation of the results. In this chapter, we discuss the formatting features of method `printf` and class `Formatter` (package `java.util`). Method `printf` formats and outputs data to the standard output stream—System.out. Class `Formatter` formats and outputs data to a specified destination, such as a string or a file output stream.

Many features of `printf` were discussed earlier in the text. This chapter summarizes those features and introduces others, such as displaying date and time data in various formats, reordering output based on the index of the argument and displaying numbers and strings with various flags.

29.2 Streams

Input and output are usually performed with streams, which are sequences of bytes. In input operations, the bytes flow from a device (e.g., a keyboard, a disk drive, a network connection) to main memory. In output operations, bytes flow from main memory to a device (e.g., a display screen, a printer, a disk drive, a network connection).

When program execution begins, three streams are connected to the program automatically. Normally, the standard input stream is connected to the keyboard, and the standard output stream is connected to the screen. A third stream, the standard error stream (System.err), is typically connected to the screen and is used to output error messages to the screen so they can be viewed immediately—even when the standard output stream is writing into a file. Operating systems typically allow these streams to be redirected to other devices. Streams are discussed in detail in Chapter 14, Files and Streams, and Chapter 24, Networking.

29.3 Formatting Output with `printf`

Precise output formatting is accomplished with `printf`. [*Note:* Java SE 5 borrowed this feature from the C programming language.] Method `printf` can perform the following formatting capabilities, each of which is discussed in this chapter:

1. Rounding floating-point values to an indicated number of decimal places.

2. Aligning a column of numbers with decimal points appearing one above the other.

3. Right justification and left justification of outputs.

4. Inserting literal characters at precise locations in a line of output.

5. Representing floating-point numbers in exponential format.

6. Representing integers in octal and hexadecimal format. (See Appendix E, Number Systems, for more information on octal and hexadecimal values.)

7. Displaying all types of data with fixed-size field widths and precisions.

8. Displaying dates and times in various formats.

Every call to `printf` supplies as the first argument a format string that describes the output format. The format string may consist of fixed text and format specifiers. Fixed text is output by `printf` just as it would be output by `System.out` methods `print` or `println`. Each format specifier is a placeholder for a value and specifies the type of data to output. Format specifiers also may include optional formatting information.

In the simplest form, each format specifier begins with a percent sign (%) and is followed by a conversion character that represents the data type of the value to output. For example, the format specifier `%s` is a placeholder for a string, and the format specifier `%d` is a placeholder for an `int` value. The optional formatting information is specified between the percent sign and the conversion character. The optional formatting information includes an argument index, flags, field width and precision. We define each of these and show examples of them throughout this chapter.

29.4 Printing Integers

An integer is a whole number, such as 776, 0 or –52, that contains no decimal point. Integer values are displayed in one of several formats. Figure 29.1 describes the integral conversion characters.

Figure 29.2 prints an integer using each of the integral conversions. In lines 9–10, note that the plus sign is not displayed by default, but the minus sign is. Later in this chapter (Fig. 29.14) we will see how to force plus signs to print.

The `printf` method has the form

```
printf( format-string, argument-list );
```

where *format-string* describes the output format, and *argument-list* contains the values that correspond to each format specifier in *format-string*. There can be many format specifiers in one format string.

Each format string in lines 8–10 specifies that `printf` should output a decimal integer (`%d`) followed by a newline character. At the format specifier's position, `printf` substitutes the value of the first argument after the format string. If the format string contained mul-

Conversion character	Description
d	Display a decimal (base 10) integer.
o	Display an octal (base 8) integer.
x or X	Display a hexadecimal (base 16) integer. X causes the digits 0–9 and the letters A–F to be displayed and x causes the digits 0–9 and a–f to be displayed.

Fig. 29.1 | Integer conversion characters.

```
1   // Fig. 29.2: IntegerConversionTest.java
2   // Using the integral conversion characters.
3
4   public class IntegerConversionTest
5   {
6      public static void main( String args[] )
7      {
8         System.out.printf( "%d\n", 26 );
9         System.out.printf( "%d\n", +26 );
10        System.out.printf( "%d\n", -26 );
11        System.out.printf( "%o\n", 26 );
12        System.out.printf( "%x\n", 26 );
13        System.out.printf( "%X\n", 26 );
14     } // end main
15  } // end class IntegerConversionTest
```

```
26
26
-26
32
1a
1A
```

Fig. 29.2 | Using integer conversion characters.

tiple format specifiers, at each subsequent format specifier's position, printf would substitute the value of the next argument in the argument list. The %o format specifier in line 11 outputs the integer in octal format. The %x format specifier in line 12 outputs the integer in hexadecimal format. The %X format specifier in line 13 outputs the integer in hexadecimal format with capital letters.

29.5 Printing Floating-Point Numbers

A floating-point value contains a decimal point, as in 33.5, 0.0 or -657.983. Floating-point values are displayed in one of several formats. Figure 29.3 describes the floating-point conversions. The conversion characters e and E display floating-point values in computerized scientific notation (also called exponential notation). Exponential notation

Conversion character	Description
e or E	Display a floating-point value in exponential notation. When conversion character E is used, the output is displayed in uppercase letters.
f	Display a floating-point value in decimal format.
g or G	Display a floating-point value in either the floating-point format f or the exponential format e based on the magnitude of the value. If the magnitude is less than 10^{-3}, or greater than or equal to 10^7, the floating-point value is printed with e (or E). Otherwise, the value is printed in format f. When conversion character G is used, the output is displayed in uppercase letters.
a or A	Display a floating-point number in hexadecimal format. When conversion character A is used, the output is displayed in uppercase letters.

Fig. 29.3 | Floating-point conversion characters.

is the computer equivalent of the scientific notation used in mathematics. For example, the value 150.4582 is represented in scientific notation in mathematics as

$$1.504582 \times 10^2$$

and is represented in exponential notation as

1.504582e+02

in Java. This notation indicates that 1.504582 is multiplied by 10 raised to the second power (e+02). The e stands for "exponent."

Values printed with the conversion characters e, E and f are output with six digits of precision to the right of the decimal point by default (e.g., 1.045921)—other precisions must be specified explicitly. For values printed with the conversion character g, the precision represents the total number of digits displayed, excluding the exponent. The default is six digits (e.g., 12345678.9 is displayed as 1.23457e+07). Conversion character f always prints at least one digit to the left of the decimal point. Conversion characters e and E print lowercase e and uppercase E preceding the exponent and always print exactly one digit to the left of the decimal point. Rounding occurs if the value being formatted has more significant digits than the precision.

Conversion character g (or G) prints in either e (E) or f format, depending on the floating-point value. For example, the values 0.0000875, 87500000.0, 8.75, 87.50 and 875.0 are printed as 8.750000e-05, 8.750000e+07, 8.750000, 87.500000 and 875.000000 with the conversion character g. The value 0.0000875 uses e notation because the magnitude is less than 10-3. The value 87500000.0 uses e notation because the magnitude is greater than 107. Figure 29.4 demonstrates each of the floating-point conversion characters.

```
 1   // Fig. 29.4: FloatingNumberTest.java
 2   // Using floating-point conversion characters.
 3
 4   public class FloatingNumberTest
 5   {
 6      public static void main( String args[] )
 7      {
 8         System.out.printf( "%e\n", 12345678.9 );
 9         System.out.printf( "%e\n", +12345678.9 );
10         System.out.printf( "%e\n", -12345678.9 );
11         System.out.printf( "%E\n", 12345678.9 );
12         System.out.printf( "%f\n", 12345678.9 );
13         System.out.printf( "%g\n", 12345678.9 );
14         System.out.printf( "%G\n", 12345678.9 );
15      } // end main
16   } // end class FloatingNumberTest
```

```
1.234568e+07
1.234568e+07
-1.234568e+07
1.234568E+07
12345678.900000
1.23457e+07
1.23457E+07
```

Fig. 29.4 | Using floating-point conversion characters.

29.6 Printing Strings and Characters

The c and s conversion characters are used to print individual characters and strings, respectively. Conversion character s can also print objects with the results of implicit calls to method toString. Conversion characters c and C require a char argument. Conversion characters s and S can take a String or any Object (this includes all subclasses of Object) as an argument. When an object is passed to the conversion character s, the program implicitly uses the object's toString method to obtain the String representation of the object. When conversion characters C and S are used, the output is displayed in uppercase letters. The program shown in Fig. 29.5 displays characters, strings and objects with conversion characters c and s. Note that autoboxing occurs at line 10 when an int constant is assigned to an Integer object. Line 15 associates an Integer object argument to the conversion character s, which implicitly invokes the toString method to get the integer value. Note that you can also output an Integer object using the %d format specifier. In this case, the int value in the Integer object will be unboxed and output.

```
 1   // Fig. 29.5: CharStringConversion.java
 2   // Using character and string conversion characters.
 3
 4   public class CharStringConversion
 5   {
```

Fig. 29.5 | Using character and string conversion characters. (Part 1 of 2.)

```
 6        public static void main( String args[] )
 7        {
 8            char character = 'A';  // initialize char
 9            String string = "This is also a string";  // String object
10            Integer integer = 1234;  // initialize integer (autoboxing)
11
12            System.out.printf( "%c\n", character );
13            System.out.printf( "%s\n", "This is a string" );
14            System.out.printf( "%s\n", string );
15            System.out.printf( "%S\n", string );
16            System.out.printf( "%s\n", integer ); // implicit call to toString
17        } // end main
18    } // end class CharStringConversion
```

```
A
This is a string
This is also a string
THIS IS ALSO A STRING
1234
```

Fig. 29.5 | Using character and string conversion characters. (Part 2 of 2.)

Common Programming Error 29.1

Using %c to print a string causes an IllegalFormatConversionException—a string cannot be converted to a character.

29.7 Printing Dates and Times

With the conversion character t or T, we can print dates and times in various formats. Conversion character t or T is always followed by a conversion suffix character that specifies the date and/or time format. When conversion character T is used, the output is displayed in uppercase letters. Figure 29.6 lists the common conversion suffix characters for formatting date and time compositions that display both the date and the time. Figure 29.7 lists the common conversion suffix characters for formatting dates. Figure 29.8 lists the common conversion suffix characters for formatting times. To view the complete list of conversion suffix characters, visit the website java.sun.com/javase/6/docs/api/java/util/Formatter.html.

Conversion suffix character	Description
c	Display date and time formatted as day month date hour:minute:second time-zone year with three characters for day and month, two digits for date, hour, minute and second and four digits for year—for example, Wed Mar 03 16:30:25 GMT-05:00 2004. The 24-hour clock is used. In this example, GMT-05:00 is the time zone.

Fig. 29.6 | Date and time composition conversion suffix characters. (Part 1 of 2.)

Conversion suffix character	Description
F	Display date formatted as year-month-date with four digits for the year and two digits each for the month and the date (e.g., 2004-05-04).
D	Display date formatted as month/day/year with two digits each for the month, day and year (e.g., 03/03/04).
r	Display time formatted as hour:minute:second AM|PM with two digits each for the hour, minute and second (e.g., 04:30:25 PM). The 12-hour clock is used.
R	Display time formatted as hour:minute with two digits each for the hour and minute (e.g., 16:30). The 24-hour clock is used.
T	Display time formatted as hour:minute:second with two digits for the hour, minute and second (e.g., 16:30:25). The 24-hour clock is used.

Fig. 29.6 | Date and time composition conversion suffix characters. (Part 2 of 2.)

Conversion suffix character	Description
A	Display full name of the day of the week (e.g., Wednesday).
a	Display the three-character short name of the day of the week (e.g., Wed).
B	Display full name of the month (e.g., March).
b	Display the three-character short name of the month (e.g., Mar).
d	Display the day of the month with two digits, padding with leading zeros as necessary (e.g., 03).
m	Display the month with two digits, padding with leading zeros as necessary (e.g., 07).
e	Display the day of month without leading zeros (e.g., 3).
Y	Display the year with four digits (e.g., 2004).
y	Display the last two digits of the year with leading zeros as necessary (e.g., 04).
j	Display the day of the year with three digits, padding with leading zeros as necessary (e.g., 016).

Fig. 29.7 | Date formatting conversion suffix characters.

Conversion suffix character	Description
H	Display hour in 24-hour clock with a leading zero as necessary (e.g., 16).
I	Display hour in 12-hour clock with a leading zero as necessary (e.g., 04).
k	Display hour in 24-hour clock without leading zeros (e.g., 16).
l	Display hour in 12-hour clock without leading zeros (e.g., 4).
M	Display minute with a leading zero as necessary (e.g., 06).
S	Display second with a leading zero as necessary (e.g., 05).
Z	Display the abbreviation for the time zone (e.g., GMT-05:00, stands for Eastern Standard Time, which is 5 hours behind Greenwich Mean Time).
p	Display morning or afternoon marker in lowercase (e.g., pm).
P	Display morning or afternoon marker in uppercase (e.g., PM).

Fig. 29.8 | Time formatting conversion suffix characters.

Figure 29.9 uses the conversion character t with the conversion suffix characters to display dates and times in various formats. Conversion character t requires the corresponding argument to be of type long, Long, Calendar or Date (both in package java.util)—objects of each of these classes can represent dates and times. Class Calendar is the preferred class for this purpose because some constructors and methods in class Date are replaced by those in class Calendar. Line 10 invokes static method getInstance of Calendar to obtain a calendar with the current date and time. Lines 13–17, 20–22 and 25–26 use this Calendar object in printf statements as the value to be formatted with conversion character t. Note that lines 20–22 and 25–26 use the optional argument index ("1$") to indicate that all format specifiers in the format string use the first argument after the format string in the argument list. You will learn more about argument indices in Section 29.11. Using the argument index eliminates the need to repeatedly list the same argument.

```
1   // Fig. 29.9: DateTimeTest.java
2   // Formatting dates and times with conversion character t and T.
3   import java.util.Calendar;
4
5   public class DateTimeTest
6   {
7      public static void main( String args[] )
8      {
9         // get current date and time
10        Calendar dateTime = Calendar.getInstance();
11
12        // printing with conversion characters for date/time compositions
13        System.out.printf( "%tc\n", dateTime );
```

Fig. 29.9 | Formatting dates and times with conversion character t. (Part 1 of 2.)

```
14        System.out.printf( "%tF\n", dateTime );
15        System.out.printf( "%tD\n", dateTime );
16        System.out.printf( "%tr\n", dateTime );
17        System.out.printf( "%tT\n", dateTime );
18
19        // printing with conversion characters for date
20        System.out.printf( "%1$tA, %1$tB %1$td, %1$tY\n", dateTime );
21        System.out.printf( "%1$TA, %1$TB %1$Td, %1$TY\n", dateTime );
22        System.out.printf( "%1$ta, %1$tb %1$te, %1$ty\n", dateTime );
23
24        // printing with conversion characters for time
25        System.out.printf( "%1$tH:%1$tM:%1$tS\n", dateTime );
26        System.out.printf( "%1$tZ %1$tI:%1$tM:%1$tS %tP", dateTime );
27     } // end main
28  } // end class DateTimeTest
```

```
Thu Nov 30 18:23:10 EST 2006
2006-11-30
11/30/06
06:23:10 PM
18:23:10
Thursday, November 30, 2006
THURSDAY, NOVEMBER 30, 2006
Thu, Nov 30, 06
18:23:10
EST 06:23:10 PM
```

Fig. 29.9 | Formatting dates and times with conversion character **t**. (Part 2 of 2.)

29.8 Other Conversion Characters

The remaining conversion characters are **b**, **B**, **h**, **H**, **%** and **n**. These are described in Fig. 29.10.

Conversion character	Description
b or B	Print "true" or "false" for the value of a boolean or Boolean. These conversion characters can also format the value of any reference. If the reference is non-null, "true" is output; otherwise, "false" is output. When conversion character B is used, the output is displayed in uppercase letters.
h or H	Print the string representation of an object's hash-code value in hexadecimal format. If the corresponding argument is null, "null" is printed. When conversion character H is used, the output is displayed in uppercase letters.
%	Print the percent character.
n	Print the platform-specific line separator (e.g., \r\n on Windows or \n on UNIX/LINUX).

Fig. 29.10 | Other conversion specifiers.

Lines 9–10 of Fig. 29.11 use %b to print the value of boolean values false and true. Line 11 associates a String to %b, which returns true because it is not null. Line 12 associates a null object to %B, which displays FALSE because test is null. Lines 13–14 use %h to print the string representations of the hash-code values for strings "hello" and "Hello". These values could be used to store or locate the strings in a Hashtable or HashMap (both discussed in Chapter 19, Collections). Note that the hash-code values for these two strings differ because one string starts with a lowercase letter and the other with an uppercase letter. Line 15 uses %H to print null in uppercase letters. The last two printf statements (lines 16–17) use %% to print the % character in a string and %n to print a platform-specific line separator.

Common Programming Error 29.2

Trying to print a literal percent character using % rather than %% in the format string might cause a difficult-to-detect logic error. When % appears in a format string, it must be followed by a conversion character in the string. The single percent could accidentally be followed by a legitimate conversion character, thus causing a logic error.

```java
1   // Fig. 29.11: OtherConversion.java
2   // Using the b, B, h, H, % and n conversion characters.
3
4   public class OtherConversion
5   {
6      public static void main( String args[] )
7      {
8         Object test = null;
9         System.out.printf( "%b\n", false );
10        System.out.printf( "%b\n", true );
11        System.out.printf( "%b\n", "Test" );
12        System.out.printf( "%B\n", test );
13        System.out.printf( "Hashcode of \"hello\" is %h\n", "hello" );
14        System.out.printf( "Hashcode of \"Hello\" is %h\n", "Hello" );
15        System.out.printf( "Hashcode of null is %H\n", test );
16        System.out.printf( "Printing a %% in a format string\n" );
17        System.out.printf( "Printing a new line %nnext line starts here" );
18     } // end main
19  } // end class OtherConversion
```

```
false
true
true
FALSE
Hashcode of "hello" is 5e918d2
Hashcode of "Hello" is 42628b2
Hashcode of null is NULL
Printing a % in a format string
Printing a new line
next line starts here
```

Fig. 29.11 | Using the b, B, h, H, % and n conversion characters.

29.9 Printing with Field Widths and Precisions

The exact size of a field in which data is printed is specified by a field width. If the field width is larger than the data being printed, the data will be right justified within that field by default. (We demonstrate left justification in Section 29.10.) The programmer inserts an integer representing the field width between the percent sign (%) and the conversion character (e.g., %4d) in the format specifier. Figure 29.12 prints two groups of five numbers each, right justifying those numbers that contain fewer digits than the field width. Note that the field width is increased to print values wider than the field and that the minus sign for a negative value uses one character position in the field. Also, if no field width is specified, the data prints in exactly as many positions as it needs. Field widths can be used with all format specifiers except the line separator (%n).

Common Programming Error 29.3

Not providing a sufficiently large field width to handle a value to be printed can offset other data being printed and produce confusing outputs. Know your data!

```
1   // Fig. 29.12: FieldWidthTest.java
2   // Right justifying integers in fields.
3
4   public class FieldWidthTest
5   {
6      public static void main( String args[] )
7      {
8         System.out.printf( "%4d\n", 1 );
9         System.out.printf( "%4d\n", 12 );
10        System.out.printf( "%4d\n", 123 );
11        System.out.printf( "%4d\n", 1234 );
12        System.out.printf( "%4d\n\n", 12345 ); // data too large
13
14        System.out.printf( "%4d\n", -1 );
15        System.out.printf( "%4d\n", -12 );
16        System.out.printf( "%4d\n", -123 );
17        System.out.printf( "%4d\n", -1234 ); // data too large
18        System.out.printf( "%4d\n", -12345 ); // data too large
19     } // end main
20  } // end class RightJustifyTest
```

```
   1
  12
 123
1234
12345

  -1
 -12
-123
-1234
-12345
```

Fig. 29.12 | Right justifying integers in fields.

Method `printf` also provides the ability to specify the precision with which data is printed. Precision has different meanings for different types. When used with floating-point conversion characters e and f, the precision is the number of digits that appear after the decimal point. When used with conversion character g, the precision is the maximum number of significant digits to be printed. When used with conversion character s, the precision is the maximum number of characters to be written from the string. To use precision, place between the percent sign and the conversion specifier a decimal point (.) followed by an integer representing the precision. Figure 29.13 demonstrates the use of precision in format strings. Note that when a floating-point value is printed with a precision smaller than the original number of decimal places in the value, the value is rounded. Also note that the format specifier %.3g indicates that the total number of digits used to display the floating-point value is 3. Because the value has three digits to the left of the decimal point, the value is rounded to the ones position.

The field width and the precision can be combined by placing the field width, followed by a decimal point, followed by a precision between the percent sign and the conversion character, as in the statement

```
printf( "%9.3f", 123.456789 );
```

which displays 123.457 with three digits to the right of the decimal point right justified in a nine-digit field—this number will be preceded in its field by two blanks.

```
 1   // Fig. 29.13: PrecisionTest.java
 2   // Using precision for floating-point numbers and strings.
 3   public class PrecisionTest
 4   {
 5      public static void main( String args[] )
 6      {
 7         double f = 123.94536;
 8         String s = "Happy Birthday";
 9
10         System.out.printf( "Using precision for floating-point numbers\n" );
11         System.out.printf( "\t%.3f\n\t%.3e\n\t%.3g\n\n", f, f, f );
12
13         System.out.printf( "Using precision for strings\n" );
14         System.out.printf( "\t%.11s\n", s );
15      } // end main
16   } // end class PrecisionTest
```

```
Using precision for floating-point numbers
        123.945
        1.239e+02
        124

Using precision for strings
        Happy Birth
```

Fig. 29.13 | Using precision for floating-point numbers and strings.

29.10 Using Flags in the `printf` Format String

Various flags may be used with method `printf` to supplement its output formatting capabilities. Seven flags are available for use in format strings (Fig. 29.14).

To use a flag in a format string, place the flag immediately to the right of the percent sign. Several flags may be used in the same format specifier. Figure 29.15 demonstrates right justification and left justification of a string, an integer, a character and a floating-point number. Note that line 9 serves as a counting mechanism for the screen output.

Figure 29.16 prints a positive number and a negative number, each with and without the + flag. Note that the minus sign is displayed in both cases, but the plus sign is displayed only when the + flag is used.

Flag	Description
– (minus sign)	Left justify the output within the specified field.
+ (plus sign)	Display a plus sign preceding positive values and a minus sign preceding negative values.
space	Print a space before a positive value not printed with the + flag.
#	Prefix 0 to the output value when used with the octal conversion character o. Prefix 0x to the output value when used with the hexadecimal conversion character x.
0 (zero)	Pad a field with leading zeros.
, (comma)	Use the locale-specific thousands separator (i.e., ',' for U.S. locale) to display decimal and floating-point numbers.
(	Enclose negative numbers in parentheses.

Fig. 29.14 | Format string flags.

```
1   // Fig. 29.15: MinusFlagTest.java
2   // Right justifying and left justifying values.
3
4   public class MinusFlagTest
5   {
6      public static void main( String args[] )
7      {
8         System.out.println( "Columns:" );
9         System.out.println( "0123456789012345678901234567890123456789\n" );
10        System.out.printf( "%10s%10d%10c%10f\n\n", "hello", 7, 'a', 1.23 );
11        System.out.printf(
12           "%-10s%-10d%-10c%-10f\n", "hello", 7, 'a', 1.23 );
13     } // end main
14  } // end class MinusFlagTest
```

Fig. 29.15 | Right justifying and left justifying values. (Part 1 of 2.)

```
Columns:
012345678901234567890123456789012345678
      hello             7             a  1.230000

hello          7            a          1.230000
```

Fig. 29.15 | Right justifying and left justifying values. (Part 2 of 2.)

```
 1   // Fig. 29.16: PlusFlagTest.java
 2   // Printing numbers with and without the + flag.
 3
 4   public class PlusFlagTest
 5   {
 6      public static void main( String args[] )
 7      {
 8         System.out.printf( "%d\t%d\n", 786, -786 );
 9         System.out.printf( "%+d\t%+d\n", 786, -786 );
10      } // end main
11   } // end class PlusFlagTest
```

```
786        -786
+786       -786
```

Fig. 29.16 | Printing numbers with and without the + flag.

Figure 29.17 prefixes a space to the positive number with the space flag. This is useful for aligning positive and negative numbers with the same number of digits. Note that the value -547 is not preceded by a space in the output because of its minus sign. Figure 29.18 uses the # flag to prefix 0 to the octal value and 0x to the hexadecimal value.

Figure 29.19 combines the + flag, the 0 flag and the space flag to print 452 in a field of width 9 with a + sign and leading zeros, next prints 452 in a field of width 9 using only the 0 flag, then prints 452 in a field of width 9 using only the space flag.

```
 1   // Fig. 29.17: SpaceFlagTest.java
 2   // Printing a space before non-negative values.
 3
 4   public class SpaceFlagTest
 5   {
 6      public static void main( String args[] )
 7      {
 8         System.out.printf( "% d\n% d\n", 547, -547 );
 9      } // end main
10   } // end class SpaceFlagTest
```

```
 547
-547
```

Fig. 29.17 | Using the space flag to print a space before nonnegative values.

```
1   // Fig. 29.18: PoundFlagTest.java
2   // Using the # flag with conversion characters o and x.
3
4   public class PoundFlagTest
5   {
6      public static void main( String args[] )
7      {
8         int c = 31;        // initialize c
9
10        System.out.printf( "%#o\n", c );
11        System.out.printf( "%#x\n", c );
12     } // end main
13  } // end class PoundFlagTest
```

```
037
0x1f
```

Fig. 29.18 | Using the # flag with conversion characters o and x.

```
1   // Fig. 29.19: ZeroFlagTest.java
2   // Printing with the 0 (zero) flag fills in leading zeros.
3
4   public class ZeroFlagTest
5   {
6      public static void main( String args[] )
7      {
8         System.out.printf( "%+09d\n", 452 );
9         System.out.printf( "%09d\n", 452 );
10        System.out.printf( "% 9d\n", 452 );
11     } // end main
12  } // end class ZeroFlagTest
```

```
+00000452
000000452
      452
```

Fig. 29.19 | Printing with the 0 (zero) flag fills in leading zeros.

Figure 29.20 uses the comma (,) flag to display a decimal and a floating-point number with the thousands separator. Figure 29.21 encloses negative numbers in parentheses using the (flag. Note that the value 50 is not enclosed in parentheses in the output because it is a positive number.

```
1   // Fig. 29.20: CommaFlagTest.java
2   // Using the comma (,) flag to display numbers with thousands separator.
3
4   public class CommaFlagTest
5   {
```

Fig. 29.20 | Using the comma (,) flag to display numbers with the thousands separator. (Part 1 of 2.)

```
 6        public static void main( String args[] )
 7        {
 8           System.out.printf( "%,d\n", 58625 );
 9           System.out.printf( "%,.2f", 58625.21 );
10           System.out.printf( "%,.2f", 12345678.9 );
11        } // end main
12     } // end class CommaFlagTest
```

```
58,625
58,625.21
12,345,678.90
```

Fig. 29.20 | Using the comma (,) flag to display numbers with the thousands separator. (Part 2 of 2.)

```
 1     // Fig. 29.21: ParenthesesFlagTest.java
 2     // Using the ( flag to place parentheses around negative numbers.
 3
 4     public class ParenthesesFlagTest
 5     {
 6        public static void main( String args[] )
 7        {
 8           System.out.printf( "%(d\n", 50 );
 9           System.out.printf( "%(d\n", -50 );
10           System.out.printf( "%(.1e\n", -50.0 );
11        } // end main
12     } // end class ParenthesesFlagTest
```

```
50
(50)
(5.0e+01)
```

Fig. 29.21 | Using the (flag to place parentheses around negative numbers.

29.11 Printing with Argument Indices

An argument index is an optional integer followed by a $ sign that indicates the argument's position in the argument list. For example, lines 20–21 and 24–25 in Fig. 29.9 use argument index "1$" to indicate that all format specifiers use the first argument in the argument list. Argument indices enable programmers to reorder the output so that the arguments in the argument list are not necessarily in the order of their corresponding format specifiers. Argument indices also help avoid duplicating arguments. Figure 29.22 demonstrates how to print arguments in the argument list in reverse order using the argument index.

```
 1     // Fig. 29.22: ArgumentIndexTest
 2     // Reordering output with argument indices.
 3
```

Fig. 29.22 | Reordering output with argument indices. (Part 1 of 2.)

```
4   public class ArgumentIndexTest
5   {
6      public static void main( String args[] )
7      {
8         System.out.printf(
9            "Parameter list without reordering: %s %s %s %s\n",
10           "first", "second", "third", "fourth" );
11        System.out.printf(
12           "Parameter list after reordering: %4$s %3$s %2$s %1$s\n",
13           "first", "second", "third", "fourth" );
14     } // end main
15  } // end class ArgumentIndexTest
```

```
Parameter list without reordering: first second third fourth
Parameter list after reordering: fourth third second first
```

Fig. 29.22 | Reordering output with argument indices. (Part 2 of 2.)

29.12 **Printing Literals and Escape Sequences**

Most literal characters to be printed in a printf statement can simply be included in the format string. However, there are several "problem" characters, such as the quotation mark (") that delimits the format string itself. Various control characters, such as newline and tab, must be represented by escape sequences. An escape sequence is represented by a backslash (\), followed by an escape character. Figure 29.23 lists the escape sequences and the actions they cause.

Common Programming Error 29.4

Attempting to print as literal data in a printf statement a double quote or backslash character without preceding that character with a backslash to form a proper escape sequence might result in a syntax error.

Escape sequence	Description
\' (single quote)	Output the single quote (') character.
\" (double quote)	Output the double quote (") character.
\\ (backslash)	Output the backslash (\) character.
\b (backspace)	Move the cursor back one position on the current line.
\f (new page or form feed)	Move the cursor to the start of the next logical page.
\n (newline)	Move the cursor to the beginning of the next line.
\r (carriage return)	Move the cursor to the beginning of the current line.
\t (horizontal tab)	Move the cursor to the next horizontal tab position.

Fig. 29.23 | Escape sequences.

29.13 Formatting Output with Class Formatter

So far, we have discussed displaying formatted output to the standard output stream. What should we do if we want to send formatted outputs to other output streams or devices, such as a JTextArea or a file? The solution relies on class Formatter (in package java.util), which provides the same formatting capabilities as printf. Formatter is a utility class that enables programmers to output formatted data to a specified destination, such as a file on disk. By default, a Formatter creates a string in memory. Figure 29.24 demonstrates how to use a Formatter to build a formatted string, which is then displayed in a message dialog.

Line 11 creates a Formatter object using the default constructor, so this object will build a string in memory. Other constructors are provided to allow you to specify the destination to which the formatted data should be output. For details, see java.sun.com/javase/6/docs/api/java/util/Formatter.html.

Line 12 invokes method **format** to format the output. Like printf, method format takes a format string and an argument list. The difference is that printf sends the formatted output directly to the standard output stream, while format sends the formatted output to the destination specified by its constructor (a string in memory in this program). Line 15 invokes the Formatter's toString method to get the formatted data as a string, which is then displayed in a message dialog.

Note that class String also provides a static convenience method named format that enables you to create a string in memory without the need to first create a Formatter object. Lines 11–12 and line 15 in Fig. 29.24 could have been replaced by

```
String s = String.format( "%d = %#o = %#^x", 10, 10, 10 );
JOptionPane.showMessageDialog( null, s );
```

```
 1   // Fig. Fig. 29.24: FormatterTest.java
 2   // Format string with class Formatter.
 3   import java.util.Formatter;
 4   import javax.swing.JOptionPane;
 5
 6   public class FormatterTest
 7   {
 8      public static void main( String args[] )
 9      {
10         // create Formatter and format output
11         Formatter formatter = new Formatter();
12         formatter.format( "%d = %#o = %#X", 10, 10, 10 );
13
14         // display output in JOptionPane
15         JOptionPane.showMessageDialog( null, formatter.toString() );
16      } // end main
17   } // end class FormatterTest
```

Fig. 29.24 | Formatting output with class Formatter.

29.14 Wrap-Up

This chapter summarized how to display formatted output with various format characters and flags. We displayed decimal numbers using format characters d, o, x and X. We displayed floating-point numbers using format characters e, E, f, g and G. We displayed date and time in various format using format characters t and T and their conversion suffix characters. You learned how to display output with field widths and precisions. We introduced the flags +, -, space, #, 0, comma and (that are used together with the format characters to produce output. We also demonstrated how to format output with class Formatter. In the next chapter, we discuss the String class's methods for manipulating strings. We also introduce regular expressions and demonstrate how to validate user input with regular expressions.

Summary

Section 29.2 Streams

- Input and output are usually performed with streams, which are sequences of bytes. In input operations, the bytes flow from a device to main memory. In output operations, bytes flow from main memory to a device.
- Normally, the standard input stream is connected to the keyboard, and the standard output stream is connected to the computer screen.

Section 29.3 Formatting Output with printf

- The printf format string describes the formats in which the output values appear. The format specifier consists of argument index, flags, field widths, precisions and conversion characters.

Section 29.4 Printing Integers

- Integers are printed with the conversion characters d for decimal integers, o for integers in octal form and x (or X) for integers in hexadecimal form. When the conversion character X is used, the output is displayed in uppercase letters.

Section 29.5 Printing Floating-Point Numbers

- Floating-point values are printed with the conversion characters e (or E) for exponential notation, f for regular floating-point notation, and g (or G) for either e (or E) notation or f notation. When the g conversion specifier is indicated, the e conversion character is used if the value is less than 10^{-3} or greater than or equal to 10^7; otherwise, the f conversion character is used. When the conversion characters E and G are used, the output is displayed in uppercase letters.

Section 29.6 Printing Strings and Characters

- The conversion character c prints a character.
- The conversion character s (or S) prints a string of characters. When the conversion character S is used, the output is displayed in uppercase letters.

Section 29.7 Printing Dates and Times

- The conversion character t (or T) followed by a conversion suffix character prints the date and time in various forms. When the conversion character T is used, the output is displayed in uppercase letters.
- Conversion character t (or T) requires the argument to be of type long, Long, Calendar or Date.

Section 29.8 Other Conversion Characters

- Conversion character b (or B) outputs the string representation of a boolean or Boolean. These conversion characters also output "true" for non-null references and "false" for null references. When conversion character B is used, the output is displayed in uppercase letters.

- Conversion character h (or H) returns null for a null reference and a String representation of the hash-code value (in base 16) of the object. Hash codes are used to store and retrieve objects in Hashtables and HashMaps. When conversion character H is used, the output is displayed in uppercase letters.

- The conversion character n prints the platform-specific line separator.

- The conversion character % is used to display a literal %.

Section 29.9 Printing with Field Widths and Precisions

- If the field width is larger than the object being printed, the object is right justified in the field.

- Field widths can be used with all conversion characters except the line-separator conversion.

- Precision used with floating-point conversion characters e and f indicates the number of digits that appear after the decimal point. Precision used with floating-point conversion character g indicates the number of significant digits to appear.

- Precision used with conversion character s indicates the number of characters to be printed.

- The field width and the precision can be combined by placing the field width, followed by a decimal point, followed by the precision between the percent sign and the conversion character.

Section 29.10 Using Flags in the `printf` Format String

- The - flag left justifies its argument in a field.

- The + flag prints a plus sign for positive values and a minus sign for negative values.

- The space flag prints a space preceding a positive value. The space flag and the + flag cannot be used together in an integral conversion character.

- The # flag prefixes 0 to octal values and 0x to hexadecimal values.

- The 0 flag prints leading zeros for a value that does not occupy its entire field.

- The comma (,) flag uses the locale-specific thousands separator (i.e., ',' for U.S. locale) to display integer and floating-point numbers.

- The (flag encloses a negative number in parentheses.

Section 29.11 Printing with Argument Indices

- An argument index is an optional decimal integer followed by a $ sign that indicates the position of the argument in the argument list.

- Argument indices enable programmers to reorder the output so that the arguments in the argument list are not necessarily in the order of their corresponding format specifiers. Argument indices also help avoid duplicating arguments.

Section 29.13 Formatting Output with Class `Formatter`

- Class Formatter (in package java.util) provides the same formatting capabilities as printf. Formatter is a utility class that enables programmers to print formatted output to various destinations, including GUI components, files and other output streams.

- Class Formatter's method format outputs formatted data to the destination specified by the Formatter constructor.

- The static method format of class String formats data and returns the formatted data as a String.

Terminology

flag
% conversion character
(flag
+ (plus) flag
- (minus) flag
, (comma) flag
0 (zero) flag
A conversion suffix character
a conversion suffix character
alignment
argument index
b conversion character
B conversion character
B conversion suffix character
b conversion suffix character
c conversion character
C conversion suffix character
conversion character
d conversion character
D conversion suffix character
e conversion character
E conversion character
e conversion suffix character
exponential floating-point format
f conversion character
F conversion suffix character
field width
flag
floating-point
floating-point number conversion
format method of Formatter
format method of String
format specifier
format string
Formatter class
g conversion character
G conversion character
h conversion character

H conversion character
H conversion suffix character
hexadecimal format
I conversion suffix character
integer conversion
j conversion suffix character
K conversion suffix character
left justification
m conversion suffix character
M conversion suffix character
n conversion character
o conversion character
octal format
P conversion suffix character
p conversion suffix character
precision
printf method
r conversion suffix character
redirect a stream
right justification
rounding
s conversion character
S conversion character
S conversion suffix character
scientific notation
space flag
standard error stream
standard input stream
standard output stream
stream
t conversion character
T conversion character
T conversion suffix character
toString method of Formatter
x conversion character
Y conversion suffix character
y conversion suffix character
Z conversion suffix character

Self-Review Exercises

29.1 Fill in the blanks in each of the following:
  a) All input and output is dealt with in the form of _____.
  b) The _____ stream is normally connected to the keyboard.
  c) The _____ stream is normally connected to the computer screen.
  d) `System.out`'s _____ method can be used to format text that is displayed on the standard output.
  e) The conversion character _____ may be used to output a decimal integer.

f) The conversion characters _____ and _____ are used to display integers in octal and hexadecimal form, respectively.

g) The conversion character _____ is used to display a floating-point value in exponential notation.

h) The conversion characters e and f are displayed with _____ digits of precision to the right of the decimal point if no precision is specified.

i) The conversion characters _____ and _____ are used to print strings and characters, respectively.

j) The conversion character _____ and conversion suffix character _____ are used to print time for the 24-hour clock as hour:minute:second.

k) The _____ flag causes output to be left justified in a field.

l) The _____ flag causes values to be displayed with either a plus sign or a minus sign.

m) The argument index _____ corresponds to the second argument in the argument list.

n) Class _____ has the same capability as printf, but allows programmers to print formatted output to various destinations besides the standard output stream.

29.2 Find the error in each of the following and explain how it can be corrected.

a) The following statement should print the character 'c'.
```
System.out.printf( "%c\n", "c" );
```

b) The following statement should print 9.375%.
```
System.out.printf( "%.3f%", 9.375 );
```

c) The following statement should print the third argument in the argument list.
```
System.out.printf( "%2$s\n", "Mon", "Tue", "Wed", "Thu", "Fri" );
```

d) `System.out.printf( ""A string in quotes"" );`

e) `System.out.printf( %d %d, 12, 20 );`

f) `System.out.printf( "%s\n", 'Richard' );`

29.3 Write a statement for each of the following:

a) Print 1234 right justified in a 10-digit field.

b) Print 123.456789 in exponential notation with a sign (+ or -) and 3 digits of precision.

c) Print 100 in octal form preceded by 0.

d) Given a Calendar object calendar, print a date formatted as month/day/year (each with two digits).

e) Given a Calendar object calendar, print a time for the 24-hour clock as hour:minute:second (each with two digits) using argument index and conversion suffix characters for formatting time.

f) Print 3.333333 with a sign (+ or -) in a field of 20 characters with a precision of 3.

Answers to Self-Review Exercises

29.1   a) Streams. b) Standard input. c) Standard output. d) printf. e) d. f) o, x or X. g) e or E. h) 6. i) s or S, c or C. j) t, T. k) - (minus). l) + (plus). m) 2$. n) Formatter.

29.2   a) Error: Conversion character c expects an argument of primitive type char.
   Correction: To print the character 'c', change "c" to 'c'.

b) Error: Trying to print the literal character % without using the format specifier %%.
   Correction: Use %% to print a literal % character.

c) Error: Argument index does not start with 0; e.g., the first argument is 1$.
   Correction: To print the third argument use 3$.

d) Error: Trying to print the literal character " without using the \" escape sequence.
   Correction: Replace each quote in the inner set of quotes with \".

e) Error: The format string is not enclosed in double quotes.
   Correction: Enclose %d %d in double quotes.

f)   Error: The string to be printed is enclosed in single quotes.
     Correction: Use double quotes instead of single quotes to represent a string.

29.3   a) `System.out.printf( "%10d\n", 1234 );`
b) `System.out.printf( "%+.3e\n", 123.456789 );`
c) `System.out.printf( "%#o\n", 100 );`
d) `System.out.printf( "%tD\n", calendar );`
e) `System.out.printf( "%1$tH:%1$tM:%1$tS\n", calendar );`
f) `System.out.printf( "%+20.3f\n", 3.333333 );`

Exercises

29.4   Show what is printed by each of the following statements. If a statement is incorrect, indicate why.

a) `System.out.printf( "%-10d\n", 10000 );`
b) `System.out.printf( "%c\n", "This is a string" );`
c) `System.out.printf( "%8.3f\n", 1024.987654 );`
d) `System.out.printf( "%#o\n%#X\n", 17, 17 );`
e) `System.out.printf( "% d\n%+d\n", 1000000, 1000000 );`
f) `System.out.printf( "%10.2e\n", 444.93738 );`
g) `System.out.printf( "%d\n", 10.987 );`

29.5   *(Printing Dates and Times)* Write a program that prints dates and times in the following forms:

```
GMT-05:00 04/30/04 09:55:09 AM
GMT-05:00 April 30 2004 09:55:09
2004-04-30 day-of-the-month:30
2004-04-30 day-of-the-year:121
Fri Apr 30 09:55:09 GMT-05:00 2004
```

[*Note:* Depending on your location, you may get a time zone other than GMT-05:00.]

29.6   *(Rounding Numbers)* Write a program that prints the value 100.453627 rounded to the nearest digit, tenth, hundredth, thousandth and ten thousandth.

29.7   *(Converting Fahrenheit Temperature to Celsius)* Write a program that converts integer Fahrenheit temperatures from 0 to 212 degrees to floating-point Celsius temperatures with three digits of precision. Use the formula

```
celsius = 5.0 / 9.0 * ( fahrenheit - 32 );
```

to perform the calculation. The output should be printed in two right-justified columns of 10 characters each, and the Celsius temperatures should be preceded by a sign for both positive and negative values.

29.8   Write a program that uses the conversion character g to output the value 9876.12345. Print the value with precisions ranging from 1 to 9.

30

Strings, Characters and Regular Expressions

*The chief defect of Henry King
Was chewing little bits of string.*
—Hilaire Belloc

*Vigorous writing is concise.
A sentence should contain no unnecessary words, a paragraph no unnecessary sentences.*
—William Strunk, Jr.

I have made this letter longer than usual, because I lack the time to make it short.
—Blaise Pascal

OBJECTIVES

In this chapter you will learn:

■ To create and manipulate immutable character string objects of class **String**.

■ To create and manipulates mutable character string objects of class **StringBuilder**.

■ To create and manipulate objects of class **Character**.

■ To use a **StringTokenizer** object to break a **String** object into tokens.

■ To use regular expressions to validate **String** data entered into an application.

30.1 Introduction

This chapter introduces Java's string- and character-processing capabilities. The techniques discussed here are appropriate for validating program input, displaying information to users and other text-based manipulations. They are also appropriate for developing text editors, word processors, page-layout software, computerized typesetting systems and other kinds of text-processing software. We have already presented several string-processing capabilities in earlier chapters. This chapter discusses in detail the capabilities of class String, class StringBuilder and class Character from the java.lang package and class StringTokenizer from the java.util package. These classes provide the foundation for string and character manipulation in Java.

The chapter also discusses regular expressions that provide applications with the capability to validate input. The functionality is located in the String class along with classes Matcher and Pattern located in the java.util.regex package.

30.2 Fundamentals of Characters and Strings

Characters are the fundamental building blocks of Java source programs. Every program is composed of a sequence of characters that—when grouped together meaningfully—are interpreted by the computer as a series of instructions used to accomplish a task. A program may contain character literals. A character literal is an integer value represented as a character in single quotes. For example, `'z'` represents the integer value of z, and `'\n'` represents the integer value of newline. The value of a character literal is the integer value of the character in the Unicode character set. Appendix B presents the integer equivalents of the characters in the ASCII character set, which is a subset of Unicode (discussed in Appendix I). For detailed information on Unicode, visit www.unicode.org.

Recall from Section 2.2 that a string is a sequence of characters treated as a single unit. A string may include letters, digits and various special characters, such as +, -, *, / and $. A string is an object of class `String`. String literals (stored in memory as `String` objects) are written as a sequence of characters in double quotation marks, as in:

```
"John Q. Doe"                (a name)
"9999 Main Street"           (a street address)
"Waltham, Massachusetts"     (a city and state)
"(201) 555-1212"             (a telephone number)
```

A string may be assigned to a `String` reference. The declaration

```
String color = "blue";
```

initializes `String` variable `color` to refer to a `String` object that contains the string `"blue"`.

Performance Tip 30.1

Java treats all string literals with the same contents as a single `String` object that has many references to it. This conserves memory.

30.3 Class String

Class `String` is used to represent strings in Java. The next several subsections cover many of class `String`'s capabilities.

30.3.1 String Constructors

Class `String` provides constructors for initializing `String` objects in a variety of ways. Four of the constructors are demonstrated in the `main` method of Fig. 30.1.

Line 12 instantiates a new `String` object using class `String`'s no-argument constructor and assigns its reference to `s1`. The new `String` object contains no characters (the empty string) and has a length of 0.

Line 13 instantiates a new `String` object using class `String`'s constructor that takes a `String` object as an argument and assigns its reference to `s2`. The new `String` object contains the same sequence of characters as the `String` object `s` that is passed as an argument to the constructor.

Software Engineering Observation 30.1

It is not necessary to copy an existing `String` object. `String` objects are immutable—their character contents cannot be changed after they are created, because class `String` does not provide any methods that allow the contents of a `String` object to be modified.

```
 1   // Fig. 30.1: StringConstructors.java
 2   // String class constructors.
 3
 4   public class StringConstructors
 5   {
 6      public static void main( String args[] )
 7      {
 8         char charArray[] = { 'b', 'i', 'r', 't', 'h', ' ', 'd', 'a', 'y' };
 9         String s = new String( "hello" );
10
11         // use String constructors
12         String s1 = new String();
13         String s2 = new String( s );
14         String s3 = new String( charArray );
15         String s4 = new String( charArray, 6, 3 );
16
17         System.out.printf(
18            "s1 = %s\ns2 = %s\ns3 = %s\ns4 = %s\n",
19            s1, s2, s3, s4 ); // display strings
20      } // end main
21   } // end class StringConstructors
```

```
s1 =
s2 = hello
s3 = birth day
s4 = day
```

Fig. 30.1 | String class constructors.

Line 14 instantiates a new String object and assigns its reference to s3 using class String's constructor that takes a char array as an argument. The new String object contains a copy of the characters in the array.

Line 15 instantiates a new String object and assigns its reference to s4 using class String's constructor that takes a char array and two integers as arguments. The second argument specifies the starting position (the offset) from which characters in the array are accessed. Remember that the first character is at position 0. The third argument specifies the number of characters (the count) to access in the array. The new String object contains a string formed from the accessed characters. If the offset or the count specified as an argument results in accessing an element outside the bounds of the character array, a StringIndexOutOfBoundsException is thrown.

Common Programming Error 30.1

Attempting to access a character that is outside the bounds of a string (i.e., an index less than 0 or an index greater than or equal to the string's length) results in a StringIndexOutOfBounds-Exception.

30.3.2 String Methods length, charAt and getChars

String methods length, charAt and getChars return the length of a string, obtain the character at a specific location in a string and retrieve a set of characters from a string as a char array, respectively. The application in Fig. 30.2 demonstrates each of these methods.

```
 1   // Fig. 30.2: StringMiscellaneous.java
 2   // This application demonstrates the length, charAt and getChars
 3   // methods of the String class.
 4
 5   public class StringMiscellaneous
 6   {
 7      public static void main( String args[] )
 8      {
 9         String s1 = "hello there";
10         char charArray[] = new char[ 5 ];
11
12         System.out.printf( "s1: %s", s1 );
13
14         // test length method
15         System.out.printf( "\nLength of s1: %d", s1.length() );
16
17         // loop through characters in s1 with charAt and display reversed
18         System.out.print( "\nThe string reversed is: " );
19
20         for ( int count = s1.length() - 1; count >= 0; count-- )
21            System.out.printf( "%s ", s1.charAt( count ) );
22
23         // copy characters from string into charArray
24         s1.getChars( 0, 5, charArray, 0 );
25         System.out.print( "\nThe character array is: " );
26
27         for ( char character : charArray )
28            System.out.print( character );
29
30         System.out.println();
31      } // end main
32   } // end class StringMiscellaneous
```

```
s1: hello there
Length of s1: 11
The string reversed is: e r e h t   o l l e h
The character array is: hello
```

Fig. 30.2 | String class character-manipulation methods.

Line 15 uses String method length to determine the number of characters in string s1. Like arrays, strings know their own length. However, unlike arrays, you cannot access a String's length via a length field—instead you must call the String's length method.

Lines 20–21 print the characters of the string s1 in reverse order (and separated by spaces). String method charAt (line 21) returns the character at a specific position in the string. Method charAt receives an integer argument that is used as the index and returns the character at that position. Like arrays, the first element of a string is at position 0.

Line 24 uses String method getChars to copy the characters of a string into a character array. The first argument is the starting index in the string from which characters are to be copied. The second argument is the index that is one past the last character to be copied from the string. The third argument is the character array into which the characters are to be copied. The last argument is the starting index where the copied characters are placed in the target character array. Next, line 28 prints the char array contents one character at a time.

30.3.3 Comparing Strings

Chapter 7 discussed sorting and searching arrays. Frequently, the information being sorted or searched consists of strings that must be compared to place them into the proper order or to determine whether a string appears in an array (or other collection). Class String provides several methods for comparing strings—these are demonstrated in the next two examples.

To understand what it means for one string to be greater than or less than another, consider the process of alphabetizing a series of last names. You would, no doubt, place "Jones" before "Smith" because the first letter of "Jones" comes before the first letter of "Smith" in the alphabet. But the alphabet is more than just a list of 26 letters—it is an ordered set of characters. Each letter occurs in a specific position within the set. Z is more than just a letter of the alphabet—it is specifically the twenty-sixth letter of the alphabet.

How does the computer know that one letter comes before another? All characters are represented in the computer as numeric codes (see Appendix B). When the computer compares strings, it actually compares the numeric codes of the characters in the strings.

Figure 30.3 demonstrates String methods equals, equalsIgnoreCase, compareTo and **regionMatches** and using the equality operator == to compare String objects.

```
 1   // Fig. 30.3: StringCompare.java
 2   // String methods equals, equalsIgnoreCase, compareTo and regionMatches.
 3
 4   public class StringCompare
 5   {
 6      public static void main( String args[] )
 7      {
 8         String s1 = new String( "hello" ); // s1 is a copy of "hello"
 9         String s2 = "goodbye";
10         String s3 = "Happy Birthday";
11         String s4 = "happy birthday";
12
13         System.out.printf(
14            "s1 = %s\ns2 = %s\ns3 = %s\ns4 = %s\n\n", s1, s2, s3, s4 );
15
16         // test for equality
17         if ( s1.equals( "hello" ) )   // true
18            System.out.println( "s1 equals \"hello\"" );
19         else
20            System.out.println( "s1 does not equal \"hello\"" );
21
22         // test for equality with ==
23         if ( s1 == "hello" )   // false; they are not the same object
24            System.out.println( "s1 is the same object as \"hello\"" );
25         else
26            System.out.println( "s1 is not the same object as \"hello\"" );
```

Fig. 30.3 | String comparisons. (Part 1 of 2.)

```
27
28        // test for equality (ignore case)
29        if ( s3.equalsIgnoreCase( s4 ) )   // true
30           System.out.printf( "%s equals %s with case ignored\n", s3, s4 );
31        else
32           System.out.println( "s3 does not equal s4" );
33
34        // test compareTo
35        System.out.printf(
36           "\ns1.compareTo( s2 ) is %d", s1.compareTo( s2 ) );
37        System.out.printf(
38           "\ns2.compareTo( s1 ) is %d", s2.compareTo( s1 ) );
39        System.out.printf(
40           "\ns1.compareTo( s1 ) is %d", s1.compareTo( s1 ) );
41        System.out.printf(
42           "\ns3.compareTo( s4 ) is %d", s3.compareTo( s4 ) );
43        System.out.printf(
44           "\ns4.compareTo( s3 ) is %d\n\n", s4.compareTo( s3 ) );
45
46        // test regionMatches (case sensitive)
47        if ( s3.regionMatches( 0, s4, 0, 5 ) )
48           System.out.println( "First 5 characters of s3 and s4 match" );
49        else
50           System.out.println(
51              "First 5 characters of s3 and s4 do not match" );
52
53        // test regionMatches (ignore case)
54        if ( s3.regionMatches( true, 0, s4, 0, 5 ) )
55           System.out.println( "First 5 characters of s3 and s4 match" );
56        else
57           System.out.println(
58              "First 5 characters of s3 and s4 do not match" );
59     } // end main
60  } // end class StringCompare
```

```
s1 = hello
s2 = goodbye
s3 = Happy Birthday
s4 = happy birthday

s1 equals "hello"
s1 is not the same object as "hello"
Happy Birthday equals happy birthday with case ignored

s1.compareTo( s2 ) is 1
s2.compareTo( s1 ) is -1
s1.compareTo( s1 ) is 0
s3.compareTo( s4 ) is -32
s4.compareTo( s3 ) is 32

First 5 characters of s3 and s4 do not match
First 5 characters of s3 and s4 match
```

Fig. 30.3 | String comparisons. (Part 2 of 2.)

The condition at line 17 uses method `equals` to compare string `s1` and the string literal `"hello"` for equality. Method `equals` (a method of class `Object` overridden in `String`) tests any two objects for equality—the strings contained in the two objects are identical. The method returns `true` if the contents of the objects are equal, and `false` otherwise. The preceding condition is `true` because string `s1` was initialized with the string literal `"hello"`. Method `equals` uses a lexicographical comparison—it compares the integer Unicode values (see Appendix I, Unicode®, for more information) that represent each character in each string. Thus, if the string `"hello"` is compared with the string `"HELLO"`, the result is `false`, because the integer representation of a lowercase letter is different from that of the corresponding uppercase letter.

The condition at line 23 uses the equality operator `==` to compare string `s1` for equality with the string literal `"hello"`. Operator `==` has different functionality when it is used to compare references than when it is used to compare values of primitive types. When primitive-type values are compared with `==`, the result is `true` if both values are identical. When references are compared with `==`, the result is `true` if both references refer to the same object in memory. To compare the actual contents (or state information) of objects for equality, a method must be invoked. In the case of `Strings`, that method is `equals`. The preceding condition evaluates to `false` at line 23 because the reference `s1` was initialized with the statement

```
s1 = new String( "hello" );
```

which creates a new `String` object with a copy of string literal `"hello"` and assigns the new object to variable `s1`. If `s1` had been initialized with the statement

```
s1 = "hello";
```

which directly assigns the string literal `"hello"` to variable `s1`, the condition would be `true`. Remember that Java treats all string literal objects with the same contents as one `String` object to which there can be many references. Thus, lines 8, 17 and 23 all refer to the same `String` object `"hello"` in memory.

Common Programming Error 30.2

Comparing references with `==` can lead to logic errors, because `==` compares the references to determine whether they refer to the same object, not whether two objects have the same contents. When two identical (but separate) objects are compared with `==`, the result will be `false`. When comparing objects to determine whether they have the same contents, use method `equals`.

If you are sorting `Strings`, you may compare them for equality with method `equals-IgnoreCase`, which ignores whether the letters in each string are uppercase or lowercase when performing the comparison. Thus, the string `"hello"` and the string `"HELLO"` compare as equal. Line 29 uses `String` method `equalsIgnoreCase` to compare string `s3`—Happy Birthday—for equality with string `s4`—happy birthday. The result of this comparison is `true` because the comparison ignores case sensitivity.

Lines 35–44 use method `compareTo` to compare strings. Method `compareTo` is declared in the `Comparable` interface and implemented in the `String` class. Line 36 compares string `s1` to string `s2`. Method `compareTo` returns 0 if the strings are equal, a negative number if the string that invokes `compareTo` is less than the string that is passed as an argument and a positive number if the string that invokes compareTo is greater than the string that is passed as an argument. Method compareTo uses a lexicographical comparison—it compares the numeric values of corresponding characters in each string. (For more information on the exact value returned by the compareTo method, see java.sun.com/javase/6/docs/api/java/lang/String.html.)

The condition at line 47 uses String method regionMatches to compare portions of two strings for equality. The first argument is the starting index in the string that invokes the method. The second argument is a comparison string. The third argument is the starting index in the comparison string. The last argument is the number of characters to compare between the two strings. The method returns true only if the specified number of characters are lexicographically equal.

Finally, the condition at line 54 uses a five-argument version of String method regionMatches to compare portions of two strings for equality. When the first argument is true, the method ignores the case of the characters being compared. The remaining arguments are identical to those described for the four-argument regionMatches method.

The next example (Fig. 30.4) demonstrates String methods startsWith and endsWith. Method main creates array strings containing the strings "started", "starting", "ended" and "ending". The remainder of method main consists of three for statements that test the elements of the array to determine whether they start with or end with a particular set of characters.

```java
 1   // Fig. 30.4: StringStartEnd.java
 2   // String methods startsWith and endsWith.
 3
 4   public class StringStartEnd
 5   {
 6      public static void main( String args[] )
 7      {
 8         String strings[] = { "started", "starting", "ended", "ending" };
 9
10         // test method startsWith
11         for ( String string : strings )
12         {
13            if ( string.startsWith( "st" ) )
14               System.out.printf( "\"%s\" starts with \"st\"\n", string );
15         } // end for
16
17         System.out.println();
18
19         // test method startsWith starting from position 2 of string
20         for ( String string : strings )
21         {
22            if ( string.startsWith( "art", 2 ) )
23               System.out.printf(
24                  "\"%s\" starts with \"art\" at position 2\n", string );
25         } // end for
26
27         System.out.println();
```

Fig. 30.4 | String class startsWith and endsWith methods. (Part 1 of 2.)

```
28
29          // test method endsWith
30          for ( String string : strings )
31          {
32             if ( string.endsWith( "ed" ) )
33                System.out.printf( "\"%s\" ends with \"ed\"\n", string );
34          } // end for
35       } // end main
36    } // end class StringStartEnd
```

```
"started" starts with "st"
"starting" starts with "st"

"started" starts with "art" at position 2
"starting" starts with "art" at position 2

"started" ends with "ed"
"ended" ends with "ed"
```

Fig. 30.4 | String class startsWith and endsWith methods. (Part 2 of 2.)

Lines 11–15 use the version of method startsWith that takes a String argument. The condition in the if statement (line 13) determines whether each String in the array starts with the characters "st". If so, the method returns true and the application prints that String. Otherwise, the method returns false and nothing happens.

Lines 20–25 use the startsWith method that takes a String and an integer as arguments. The integer specifies the index at which the comparison should begin in the string. The condition in the if statement (line 22) determines whether each String in the array has the characters "art" beginning with the third character in each string. If so, the method returns true and the application prints the String.

The third for statement (lines 30–34) uses method endsWith, which takes a String argument. The condition at line 32 determines whether each String in the array ends with the characters "ed". If so, the method returns true and the application prints the String.

30.3.4 Locating Characters and Substrings in Strings

Often it is useful to search for a character or set of characters in a string. For example, if you are creating your own word processor, you might want to provide a capability for searching through documents. Figure 30.5 demonstrates the many versions of String methods **indexOf** and **lastIndexOf** that search for a specified character or substring in a string. All the searches in this example are performed on the string letters (initialized with "abcdefghijklmabcdefghijklm") in method main. Lines 11–16 use method index-Of to locate the first occurrence of a character in a string. If method indexOf finds the character, it returns the character's index in the string—otherwise, indexOf returns –1. There are two versions of indexOf that search for characters in a string. The expression in line 12 uses the version of method indexOf that takes an integer representation of the character to find. The expression at line 14 uses another version of method indexOf, which takes two integer arguments—the character and the starting index at which the search of the string should begin.

The statements at lines 19–24 use method lastIndexOf to locate the last occurrence of a character in a string. Method lastIndexOf performs the search from the end of the string toward the beginning. If method lastIndexOf finds the character, it returns the index of the character in the string—otherwise, lastIndexOf returns –1. There are two versions of lastIndexOf that search for characters in a string. The expression at line 20 uses the version that takes the integer representation of the character. The expression at line 22 uses the version that takes two integer arguments—the integer representation of the character and the index from which to begin searching backward.

```
1    // Fig. 30.5: StringIndexMethods.java
2    // String searching methods indexOf and lastIndexOf.
3
4    public class StringIndexMethods
5    {
6       public static void main( String args[] )
7       {
8          String letters = "abcdefghijklmabcdefghijklm";
9
10         // test indexOf to locate a character in a string
11         System.out.printf(
12            "'c' is located at index %d\n", letters.indexOf( 'c' ) );
13         System.out.printf(
14            "'a' is located at index %d\n", letters.indexOf( 'a', 1 ) );
15         System.out.printf(
16            "'$' is located at index %d\n\n", letters.indexOf( '$' ) );
17
18         // test lastIndexOf to find a character in a string
19         System.out.printf( "Last 'c' is located at index %d\n",
20            letters.lastIndexOf( 'c' ) );
21         System.out.printf( "Last 'a' is located at index %d\n",
22            letters.lastIndexOf( 'a', 25 ) );
23         System.out.printf( "Last '$' is located at index %d\n\n",
24            letters.lastIndexOf( '$' ) );
25
26         // test indexOf to locate a substring in a string
27         System.out.printf( "\"def\" is located at index %d\n",
28            letters.indexOf( "def" ) );
29         System.out.printf( "\"def\" is located at index %d\n",
30            letters.indexOf( "def", 7 ) );
31         System.out.printf( "\"hello\" is located at index %d\n\n",
32            letters.indexOf( "hello" ) );
33
34         // test lastIndexOf to find a substring in a string
35         System.out.printf( "Last \"def\" is located at index %d\n",
36            letters.lastIndexOf( "def" ) );
37         System.out.printf( "Last \"def\" is located at index %d\n",
38            letters.lastIndexOf( "def", 25 ) );
39         System.out.printf( "Last \"hello\" is located at index %d\n",
40            letters.lastIndexOf( "hello" ) );
41      } // end main
42   } // end class StringIndexMethods
```

Fig. 30.5 | String class searching methods. (Part 1 of 2.)

```
'c' is located at index 2
'a' is located at index 13
'$' is located at index -1

Last 'c' is located at index 15
Last 'a' is located at index 13
Last '$' is located at index -1

"def" is located at index 3
"def" is located at index 16
"hello" is located at index -1

Last "def" is located at index 16
Last "def" is located at index 16
Last "hello" is located at index -1
```

Fig. 30.5 | String class searching methods. (Part 2 of 2.)

Lines 27–40 demonstrate versions of methods indexOf and lastIndexOf that each take a String as the first argument. These versions perform identically to those described earlier except that they search for sequences of characters (or substrings) that are specified by their String arguments. If the substring is found, these methods return the index in the string of the first character in the substring.

30.3.5 Extracting Substrings from Strings

Class String provides two substring methods to enable a new String object to be created by copying part of an existing String object. Each method returns a new String object. Both methods are demonstrated in Fig. 30.6.

```
 1  // Fig. 30.6: SubString.java
 2  // String class substring methods.
 3
 4  public class SubString
 5  {
 6     public static void main( String args[] )
 7     {
 8        String letters = "abcdefghijklmabcdefghijklm";
 9
10        // test substring methods
11        System.out.printf( "Substring from index 20 to end is \"%s\"\n",
12           letters.substring( 20 ) );
13        System.out.printf( "%s \"%s\"\n",
14           "Substring from index 3 up to, but not including 6 is",
15           letters.substring( 3, 6 ) );
16     } // end main
17  } // end class SubString
```

```
Substring from index 20 to end is "hijklm"
Substring from index 3 up to, but not including 6 is "def"
```

Fig. 30.6 | String class substring methods.

The expression `letters.substring( 20 )` at line 12 uses the `substring` method that takes one integer argument. The argument specifies the starting index in the original string `letters` from which characters are to be copied. The substring returned contains a copy of the characters from the starting index to the end of the string. Specifying an index outside the bounds of the string causes a `StringIndexOutOfBoundsException`.

The expression `letters.substring( 3, 6 )` at line 15 uses the `substring` method that takes two integer arguments. The first argument specifies the starting index from which characters are copied in the original string. The second argument specifies the index one beyond the last character to be copied (i.e., copy up to, but not including, that index in the string). The substring returned contains a copy of the specified characters from the original string. Specifying an index outside the bounds of the string causes a `StringIndexOutOfBoundsException`.

30.3.6 Concatenating Strings

String method `concat` (Fig. 30.7) concatenates two `String` objects and returns a new `String` object containing the characters from both original strings. The expression `s1.concat( s2 )` at line 13 forms a string by appending the characters in string s2 to the characters in string s1. The original `Strings` to which s1 and s2 refer are not modified.

```
1   // Fig. 30.7: StringConcatenation.java
2   // String concat method.
3
4   public class StringConcatenation
5   {
6      public static void main( String args[] )
7      {
8         String s1 = new String( "Happy " );
9         String s2 = new String( "Birthday" );
10
11        System.out.printf( "s1 = %s\ns2 = %s\n\n",s1, s2 );
12        System.out.printf(
13           "Result of s1.concat( s2 ) = %s\n", s1.concat( s2 ) );
14        System.out.printf( "s1 after concatenation = %s\n", s1 );
15     } // end main
16  } // end class StringConcatenation
```

```
s1 = Happy
s2 = Birthday

Result of s1.concat( s2 ) = Happy Birthday
s1 after concatenation = Happy
```

Fig. 30.7 | String method `concat`.

30.3.7 Miscellaneous String Methods

Class `String` provides several methods that return modified copies of strings or that return character arrays. These methods are demonstrated in the application in Fig. 30.8.

```
1   // Fig. 30.8: StringMiscellaneous2.java
2   // String methods replace, toLowerCase, toUpperCase, trim and toCharArray.
3
4   public class StringMiscellaneous2
5   {
6      public static void main( String args[] )
7      {
8         String s1 = new String( "hello" );
9         String s2 = new String( "GOODBYE" );
10        String s3 = new String( "   spaces   " );
11
12        System.out.printf( "s1 = %s\ns2 = %s\ns3 = %s\n\n", s1, s2, s3 );
13
14        // test method replace
15        System.out.printf(
16           "Replace 'l' with 'L' in s1: %s\n\n", s1.replace( 'l', 'L' ) );
17
18        // test toLowerCase and toUpperCase
19        System.out.printf( "s1.toUpperCase() = %s\n", s1.toUpperCase() );
20        System.out.printf( "s2.toLowerCase() = %s\n\n", s2.toLowerCase() );
21
22        // test trim method
23        System.out.printf( "s3 after trim = \"%s\"\n\n", s3.trim() );
24
25        // test toCharArray method
26        char charArray[] = s1.toCharArray();
27        System.out.print( "s1 as a character array = " );
28
29        for ( char character : charArray )
30           System.out.print( character );
31
32        System.out.println();
33     } // end main
34  } // end class StringMiscellaneous2
```

```
s1 = hello
s2 = GOODBYE
s3 =    spaces

Replace 'l' with 'L' in s1: heLLo

s1.toUpperCase() = HELLO
s2.toLowerCase() = goodbye

s3 after trim = "spaces"

s1 as a character array = hello
```

Fig. 30.8 | String methods `replace`, `toLowerCase`, `toUpperCase`, `trim` and `toCharArray`.

Line 16 uses `String` method `replace` to return a new `String` object in which every occurrence in string `s1` of character `'l'` (lowercase el) is replaced with character `'L'`. Method `replace` leaves the original string unchanged. If there are no occurrences of the first argument in the string, method `replace` returns the original string.

Line 19 uses String method **toUpperCase** to generate a new String with uppercase letters where corresponding lowercase letters exist in s1. The method returns a new String object containing the converted string and leaves the original string unchanged. If there are no characters to convert, method toUpperCase returns the original string.

Line 20 uses String method **toLowerCase** to return a new String object with lower-case letters where corresponding uppercase letters exist in s2. The original string remains unchanged. If there are no characters in the original string to convert, toLowerCase returns the original string.

Line 23 uses String method **trim** to generate a new String object that removes all white-space characters that appear at the beginning or end of the string on which trim operates. The method returns a new String object containing the string without leading or trailing white space. The original string remains unchanged.

Line 26 uses String method **toCharArray** to create a new character array containing a copy of the characters in string s1. Lines 29–30 output each char in the array.

30.3.8 String Method valueOf

As we have seen, every object in Java has a toString method that enables a program to obtain the object's string representation. Unfortunately, this technique cannot be used with primitive types because they do not have methods. Class String provides static methods that take an argument of any type and convert the argument to a String object. Figure 30.9 demonstrates the String class valueOf methods.

```java
 1   // Fig. 30.9: StringValueOf.java
 2   // String valueOf methods.
 3
 4   public class StringValueOf
 5   {
 6      public static void main( String args[] )
 7      {
 8         char charArray[] = { 'a', 'b', 'c', 'd', 'e', 'f' };
 9         boolean booleanValue = true;
10         char characterValue = 'Z';
11         int integerValue = 7;
12         long longValue = 10000000000L; // L suffix indicates long
13         float floatValue = 2.5f; // f indicates that 2.5 is a float
14         double doubleValue = 33.333; // no suffix, double is default
15         Object objectRef = "hello"; // assign string to an Object reference
16
17         System.out.printf(
18            "char array = %s\n", String.valueOf( charArray ) );
19         System.out.printf( "part of char array = %s\n",
20            String.valueOf( charArray, 3, 3 ) );
21         System.out.printf(
22            "boolean = %s\n", String.valueOf( booleanValue ) );
23         System.out.printf(
24            "char = %s\n", String.valueOf( characterValue ) );
25         System.out.printf( "int = %s\n", String.valueOf( integerValue ) );
26         System.out.printf( "long = %s\n", String.valueOf( longValue ) );
```

Fig. 30.9 | String class valueOf methods. (Part 1 of 2.)

```
27          System.out.printf( "float = %s\n", String.valueOf( floatValue ) );
28          System.out.printf(
29             "double = %s\n", String.valueOf( doubleValue ) );
30          System.out.printf( "Object = %s", String.valueOf( objectRef ) );
31       } // end main
32    } // end class StringValueOf
```

```
char array = abcdef
part of char array = def
boolean = true
char = Z
int = 7
long = 10000000000
float = 2.5
double = 33.333
Object = hello
```

Fig. 30.9 | String class valueOf methods. (Part 2 of 2.)

The expression String.valueOf(charArray) at line 18 uses the character array charArray to create a new String object. The expression String.valueOf(charArray, 3, 3) at line 20 uses a portion of the character array charArray to create a new String object. The second argument specifies the starting index from which the characters are used. The third argument specifies the number of characters to be used.

There are seven other versions of method valueOf, which take arguments of type boolean, char, int, long, float, double and Object, respectively. These are demonstrated in lines 21–30. Note that the version of valueOf that takes an Object as an argument can do so because all Objects can be converted to Strings with method toString.

[*Note:* Lines 12–13 use literal values 10000000000L and 2.5f as the initial values of long variable longValue and float variable floatValue, respectively. By default, Java treats integer literals as type int and floating-point literals as type double. Appending the letter L to the literal 10000000000 and appending letter f to the literal 2.5 indicates to the compiler that 10000000000 should be treated as a long and that 2.5 should be treated as a float. An uppercase L or lowercase l can be used to denote a variable of type long and an uppercase F or lowercase f can be used to denote a variable of type float.]

30.4 Class StringBuilder

Once a String object is created, its contents can never change. We now discuss the features of class StringBuilder for creating and manipulating dynamic string information— that is, modifiable strings. Every StringBuilder is capable of storing a number of characters specified by its capacity. If the capacity of a StringBuilder is exceeded, the capacity is automatically expanded to accommodate the additional characters. Class StringBuilder is also used to implement operators + and += for String concatenation.

Performance Tip 30.2

Java can perform certain optimizations involving String objects (such as sharing one String object among multiple references) because it knows these objects will not change. Strings (not StringBuilders) should be used if the data will not change.

Performance Tip 30.3

In programs that frequently perform string concatenation, or other string modifications, it is often more efficient to implement the modifications with class StringBuilder.

Software Engineering Observation 30.2

StringBuilders are not thread safe. If multiple threads require access to the same dynamic string information, use class StringBuffer in your code. Classes StringBuilder and StringBuffer are identical, but class StringBuffer is thread safe.

30.4.1 StringBuilder Constructors

Class StringBuilder provides four constructors. We demonstrate three of these in Fig. 30.10. Line 8 uses the no-argument StringBuilder constructor to create a StringBuilder with no characters in it and an initial capacity of 16 characters (the default for a StringBuilder). Line 9 uses the StringBuilder constructor that takes an integer argument to create a StringBuilder with no characters in it and the initial capacity specified by the integer argument (i.e., 10). Line 10 uses the StringBuilder constructor that takes a String argument (in this case, a string literal) to create a StringBuilder containing the characters in the String argument. The initial capacity is the number of characters in the String argument plus 16.

The statements in lines 12–14 use the method toString of class StringBuilder to output the StringBuilders with the printf method. In Section 30.4.4, we discuss how Java uses StringBuilder objects to implement the + and += operators for string concatenation.

```java
1   // Fig. 30.10: StringBuilderConstructors.java
2   // StringBuilder constructors.
3
4   public class StringBuilderConstructors
5   {
6      public static void main( String args[] )
7      {
8         StringBuilder buffer1 = new StringBuilder();
9         StringBuilder buffer2 = new StringBuilder( 10 );
10        StringBuilder buffer3 = new StringBuilder( "hello" );
11
12        System.out.printf( "buffer1 = \"%s\"\n", buffer1.toString() );
13        System.out.printf( "buffer2 = \"%s\"\n", buffer2.toString() );
14        System.out.printf( "buffer3 = \"%s\"\n", buffer3.toString() );
15     } // end main
16  } // end class StringBuilderConstructors
```

```
buffer1 = ""
buffer2 = ""
buffer3 = "hello"
```

Fig. 30.10 │ StringBuilder class constructors.

30.4.2 StringBuilder Methods length, capacity, setLength and ensureCapacity

Class StringBuilder provides methods length and capacity to return the number of characters currently in a StringBuilder and the number of characters that can be stored in a StringBuilder without allocating more memory, respectively. Method ensureCapacity guarantees that a StringBuilder has at least the specified capacity. Method setLength increases or decreases the length of a StringBuilder. Figure 30.11 demonstrates these methods.

The application contains one StringBuilder called buffer. Line 8 uses the StringBuilder constructor that takes a String argument to initialize the StringBuilder with "Hello, how are you?". Lines 10–11 print the contents, length and capacity of the StringBuilder. Note in the output window that the capacity of the StringBuilder is initially 35. Recall that the StringBuilder constructor that takes a String argument initializes the capacity to the length of the string passed as an argument plus 16.

Line 13 uses method ensureCapacity to expand the capacity of the StringBuilder to a minimum of 75 characters. Actually, if the original capacity is less than the argument, the method ensures a capacity that is the greater of the number specified as an argument and twice the original capacity plus 2. The StringBuilder's current capacity remains unchanged if it is more than the specified capacity.

```java
1   // Fig. 30.11: StringBuilderCapLen.java
2   // StringBuilder length, setLength, capacity and ensureCapacity methods.
3
4   public class StringBuilderCapLen
5   {
6      public static void main( String args[] )
7      {
8         StringBuilder buffer = new StringBuilder( "Hello, how are you?" );
9
10        System.out.printf( "buffer = %s\nlength = %d\ncapacity = %d\n\n",
11           buffer.toString(), buffer.length(), buffer.capacity() );
12
13        buffer.ensureCapacity( 75 );
14        System.out.printf( "New capacity = %d\n\n", buffer.capacity() );
15
16        buffer.setLength( 10 );
17        System.out.printf( "New length = %d\nbuffer = %s\n",
18           buffer.length(), buffer.toString() );
19     } // end main
20  } // end class StringBuilderCapLen
```

```
buffer = Hello, how are you?
length = 19
capacity = 35

New capacity = 75

New length = 10
buffer = Hello, how
```

Fig. 30.11 | StringBuilder methods length and capacity.

> **Performance Tip 30.4**
>
> *Dynamically increasing the capacity of a StringBuilder can take a relatively long time. Executing a large number of these operations can degrade the performance of an application. If a StringBuilder is going to increase greatly in size, possibly multiple times, setting its capacity high at the beginning will increase performance.*

Line 16 uses method setLength to set the length of the StringBuilder to 10. If the specified length is less than the current number of characters in the StringBuilder, the buffer is truncated to the specified length (i.e., the characters in the StringBuilder after the specified length are discarded). If the specified length is greater than the number of characters currently in the StringBuilder, null characters (characters with the numeric representation 0) are appended until the total number of characters in the StringBuilder is equal to the specified length.

30.4.3 StringBuilder Methods charAt, setCharAt, getChars and reverse

Class StringBuilder provides methods charAt, setCharAt, getChars and reverse to manipulate the characters in a StringBuilder. Each of these methods is demonstrated in Fig. 30.12.

```java
1   // Fig. 30.12: StringBuilderChars.java
2   // StringBuilder methods charAt, setCharAt, getChars and reverse.
3
4   public class StringBuilderChars
5   {
6      public static void main( String args[] )
7      {
8         StringBuilder buffer = new StringBuilder( "hello there" );
9
10        System.out.printf( "buffer = %s\n", buffer.toString() );
11        System.out.printf( "Character at 0: %s\nCharacter at 4: %s\n\n",
12           buffer.charAt( 0 ), buffer.charAt( 4 ) );
13
14        char charArray[] = new char[ buffer.length() ];
15        buffer.getChars( 0, buffer.length(), charArray, 0 );
16        System.out.print( "The characters are: " );
17
18        for ( char character : charArray )
19           System.out.print( character );
20
21        buffer.setCharAt( 0, 'H' );
22        buffer.setCharAt( 6, 'T' );
23        System.out.printf( "\n\nbuffer = %s", buffer.toString() );
24
25        buffer.reverse();
26        System.out.printf( "\n\nbuffer = %s\n", buffer.toString() );
27     } // end main
28  } // end class StringBuilderChars
```

Fig. 30.12 | StringBuilder class character-manipulation methods. (Part 1 of 2.)

```
buffer = hello there
Character at 0: h
Character at 4: o

The characters are: hello there

buffer = Hello There

buffer = erehT olleH
```

Fig. 30.12 | `StringBuilder` class character-manipulation methods. (Part 2 of 2.)

Method `charAt` (line 12) takes an integer argument and returns the character in the `StringBuilder` at that index. Method `getChars` (line 15) copies characters from a `StringBuilder` into the character array passed as an argument. This method takes four arguments—the starting index from which characters should be copied in the `String-Builder`, the index one past the last character to be copied from the `StringBuilder`, the character array into which the characters are to be copied and the starting location in the character array where the first character should be placed. Method `setCharAt` (lines 21 and 22) takes an integer and a character argument and sets the character at the specified position in the `StringBuilder` to the character argument. Method `reverse` (line 25) reverses the contents of the `StringBuilder`.

Common Programming Error 30.3

Attempting to access a character that is outside the bounds of a `StringBuilder` (i.e., with an index less than 0 or greater than or equal to the `StringBuilder`'s length) results in a `StringIndexOutOfBoundsException`.

30.4.4 `StringBuilder` append Methods

Class `StringBuilder` provides overloaded **append** methods (demonstrated in Fig. 30.13) to allow values of various types to be appended to the end of a `StringBuilder`. Versions are provided for each of the primitive types and for character arrays, `Strings`, `Objects`, `StringBuilders` and `CharSequences`. (Remember that method `toString` produces a string representation of any `Object`.) Each of the methods takes its argument, converts it to a string and appends it to the `StringBuilder`.

```
1   // Fig. 30.13: StringBuilderAppend.java
2   // StringBuilder append methods.
3
4   public class StringBuilderAppend
5   {
6      public static void main( String args[] )
7      {
8         Object objectRef = "hello";
9         String string = "goodbye";
10        char charArray[] = { 'a', 'b', 'c', 'd', 'e', 'f' };
11        boolean booleanValue = true;
12        char characterValue = 'Z';
```

Fig. 30.13 | `StringBuilder` class append methods. (Part 1 of 2.)

```
13          int integerValue = 7;
14          long longValue = 10000000000L;
15          float floatValue = 2.5f; // f suffix indicates 2.5 is a float
16          double doubleValue = 33.333;
17
18          StringBuilder lastBuffer = new StringBuilder( "last buffer" );
19          StringBuilder buffer = new StringBuilder();
20
21          buffer.append( objectRef );
22          buffer.append( "\n" ); // each of these contains new line
23          buffer.append( string );
24          buffer.append( "\n" );
25          buffer.append( charArray );
26          buffer.append( "\n" );
27          buffer.append( charArray, 0, 3 );
28          buffer.append( "\n" );
29          buffer.append( booleanValue );
30          buffer.append( "\n" );
31          buffer.append( characterValue );
32          buffer.append( "\n" );
33          buffer.append( integerValue );
34          buffer.append( "\n" );
35          buffer.append( longValue );
36          buffer.append( "\n" );
37          buffer.append( floatValue );
38          buffer.append( "\n" );
39          buffer.append( doubleValue );
40          buffer.append( "\n" );
41          buffer.append( lastBuffer );
42
43          System.out.printf( "buffer contains %s\n", buffer.toString() );
44      } // end main
45  } // end StringBuilderAppend
```

```
buffer contains hello
goodbye
abcdef
abc
true
Z
7
10000000000
2.5
33.333
last buffer
```

Fig. 30.13 | StringBuilder class append methods. (Part 2 of 2.)

Actually, the compiler uses StringBuilder and the append methods to implement the + and += operators for String concatenation. For example, assuming the declarations

```
String string1 = "hello";
String string2 = "BC";
int value = 22;
```

the statement

```
String s = string1 + string2 + value;
```

concatenates "hello", "BC" and 22. The concatenation is performed as follows:

```
new StringBuilder().append( "hello" ).append( "BC" ).append(
    22 ).toString();
```

First, Java creates an empty `StringBuilder`, then appends to it the string "hello", the string "BC" and the integer 22. Next, `StringBuilder`'s method `toString` converts the `StringBuilder` to a `String` object to be assigned to `String s`. The statement

```
s += "!";
```

is performed as follows:

```
s = new StringBuilder().append( s ).append( "!" ).toString();
```

First, Java creates an empty `StringBuilder`, then it appends to the `StringBuilder` the current contents of s followed by "!". Next, `StringBuilder`'s method `toString` converts the `StringBuilder` to a string representation, and the result is assigned to s.

30.4.5 `StringBuilder` Insertion and Deletion Methods

Class `StringBuilder` provides overloaded `insert` methods to allow values of various types to be inserted at any position in a `StringBuilder`. Versions are provided for each of the primitive types and for character arrays, `Strings`, `Objects` and `CharSequences`. Each method takes its second argument, converts it to a string and inserts it immediately preceding the index specified by the first argument. The first argument must be greater than or equal to 0 and less than the length of the `StringBuilder`—otherwise, a `StringIndexOutOf-BoundsException` occurs. Class `StringBuilder` also provides methods **`delete`** and **`deleteCharAt`** for deleting characters at any position in a `StringBuilder`. Method `delete` takes two arguments—the starting index and the index one past the end of the characters to delete. All characters beginning at the starting index up to but not including the ending index are deleted. Method `deleteCharAt` takes one argument—the index of the character to delete. Invalid indices cause both methods to throw a `StringIndexOutOfBoundsException`. Methods `insert`, `delete` and `deleteCharAt` are demonstrated in Fig. 30.14.

```
 1    // Fig. 30.14: StringBuilderInsert.java
 2    // StringBuilder methods insert, delete and deleteCharAt.
 3
 4    public class StringBuilderInsert
 5    {
 6       public static void main( String args[] )
 7       {
 8          Object objectRef = "hello";
 9          String string = "goodbye";
10          char charArray[] = { 'a', 'b', 'c', 'd', 'e', 'f' };
11          boolean booleanValue = true;
12          char characterValue = 'K';
```

Fig. 30.14 | `StringBuilder` methods `insert` and `delete`. (Part 1 of 2.)

```
13          int integerValue = 7;
14          long longValue = 10000000;
15          float floatValue = 2.5f; // f suffix indicates that 2.5 is a float
16          double doubleValue = 33.333;
17
18          StringBuilder buffer = new StringBuilder();
19
20          buffer.insert( 0, objectRef );
21          buffer.insert( 0, "  " ); // each of these contains two spaces
22          buffer.insert( 0, string );
23          buffer.insert( 0, "  " );
24          buffer.insert( 0, charArray );
25          buffer.insert( 0, "  " );
26          buffer.insert( 0, charArray, 3, 3 );
27          buffer.insert( 0, "  " );
28          buffer.insert( 0, booleanValue );
29          buffer.insert( 0, "  " );
30          buffer.insert( 0, characterValue );
31          buffer.insert( 0, "  " );
32          buffer.insert( 0, integerValue );
33          buffer.insert( 0, "  " );
34          buffer.insert( 0, longValue );
35          buffer.insert( 0, "  " );
36          buffer.insert( 0, floatValue );
37          buffer.insert( 0, "  " );
38          buffer.insert( 0, doubleValue );
39
40          System.out.printf(
41             "buffer after inserts:\n%s\n\n", buffer.toString() );
42
43          buffer.deleteCharAt( 10 ); // delete 5 in 2.5
44          buffer.delete( 2, 6 ); // delete .333 in 33.333
45
46          System.out.printf(
47             "buffer after deletes:\n%s\n", buffer.toString() );
48       } // end main
49    } // end class StringBuilderInsert
```

```
buffer after inserts:
33.333  2.5  10000000  7  K  true  def  abcdef  goodbye  hello

buffer after deletes:
33  2.  10000000  7  K  true  def  abcdef  goodbye  hello
```

Fig. 30.14 | StringBuilder methods insert and delete. (Part 2 of 2.)

30.5 Class Character

Recall from Chapter 17 that Java provides eight type-wrapper classes—Boolean, Charac-ter, Double, Float, Byte, Short, Integer and Long—that enable primitive-type values to be treated as objects. In this section, we present class Character—the type-wrapper class for primitive type char.

Most Character methods are static methods designed for convenience in processing individual char values. These methods take at least a character argument and perform either a test or a manipulation of the character. Class Character also contains a constructor that receives a char argument to initialize a Character object. Most of the methods of class Character are presented in the next three examples. For more information on class Character (and all the type-wrapper classes), see the java.lang package in the Java API documentation.

Figure 30.15 demonstrates some static methods that test characters to determine whether they are a specific character type and the static methods that perform case conversions on characters. You can enter any character and apply the methods to the character.

Line 15 uses Character method **isDefined** to determine whether character c is defined in the Unicode character set. If so, the method returns true, and otherwise, it returns false. Line 16 uses Character method **isDigit** to determine whether character c is a defined Unicode digit. If so, the method returns true, and otherwise, it returns false.

```java
1   // Fig. 30.15: StaticCharMethods.java
2   // Static Character testing methods and case conversion methods.
3   import java.util.Scanner;
4
5   public class StaticCharMethods
6   {
7      public static void main( String args[] )
8      {
9         Scanner scanner = new Scanner( System.in ); // create scanner
10        System.out.println( "Enter a character and press Enter" );
11        String input = scanner.next();
12        char c = input.charAt( 0 ); // get input character
13
14        // display character info
15        System.out.printf( "is defined: %b\n", Character.isDefined( c ) );
16        System.out.printf( "is digit: %b\n", Character.isDigit( c ) );
17        System.out.printf( "is first character in a Java identifier: %b\n",
18           Character.isJavaIdentifierStart( c ) );
19        System.out.printf( "is part of a Java identifier: %b\n",
20           Character.isJavaIdentifierPart( c ) );
21        System.out.printf( "is letter: %b\n", Character.isLetter( c ) );
22        System.out.printf(
23           "is letter or digit: %b\n", Character.isLetterOrDigit( c ) );
24        System.out.printf(
25           "is lower case: %b\n", Character.isLowerCase( c ) );
26        System.out.printf(
27           "is upper case: %b\n", Character.isUpperCase( c ) );
28        System.out.printf(
29           "to upper case: %s\n", Character.toUpperCase( c ) );
30        System.out.printf(
31           "to lower case: %s\n", Character.toLowerCase( c ) );
32     } // end main
33  } // end class StaticCharMethods
```

Fig. 30.15 | Character class static methods for testing characters and converting character case. (Part 1 of 2.)

```
Enter a character and press Enter
A
is defined: true
is digit: false
is first character in a Java identifier: true
is part of a Java identifier: true
is letter: true
is letter or digit: true
is lower case: false
is upper case: true
to upper case: A
to lower case: a
```

```
Enter a character and press Enter
8
is defined: true
is digit: true
is first character in a Java identifier: false
is part of a Java identifier: true
is letter: false
is letter or digit: true
is lower case: false
is upper case: false
to upper case: 8
to lower case: 8
```

```
Enter a character and press Enter
$
is defined: true
is digit: false
is first character in a Java identifier: true
is part of a Java identifier: true
is letter: false
is letter or digit: false
is lower case: false
is upper case: false
to upper case: $
to lower case: $
```

Fig. 30.15 | Character class static methods for testing characters and converting character case. (Part 2 of 2.)

Line 18 uses Character method isJavaIdentifierStart to determine whether c is a character that can be the first character of an identifier in Java—that is, a letter, an underscore (_) or a dollar sign ($). If so, the method returns true, and otherwise, it returns false. Line 20 uses Character method isJavaIdentifierPart to determine whether character c is a character that can be used in an identifier in Java—that is, a digit, a letter, an underscore (_) or a dollar sign ($). If so, the method returns true, and otherwise, false.

Line 21 uses Character method isLetter to determine whether character c is a letter. If so, the method returns true, and otherwise, false. Line 23 uses Character method isLetterOrDigit to determine whether character c is a letter or a digit. If so, the method returns true, and otherwise, false.

Line 25 uses Character method isLowerCase to determine whether character c is a lowercase letter. If so, the method returns true, and otherwise, false. Line 27 uses Character method isUpperCase to determine whether character c is an uppercase letter. If so, the method returns true, and otherwise, false.

Line 29 uses Character method toUpperCase to convert the character c to its uppercase equivalent. The method returns the converted character if the character has an uppercase equivalent, and otherwise, the method returns its original argument. Line 31 uses Character method toLowerCase to convert the character c to its lowercase equivalent. The method returns the converted character if the character has a lowercase equivalent, and otherwise, the method returns its original argument.

Figure 30.16 demonstrates static Character methods digit and forDigit, which convert characters to digits and digits to characters, respectively, in different number systems. Common number systems include decimal (base 10), octal (base 8), hexadecimal (base 16) and binary (base 2). The base of a number is also known as its radix. For more information on conversions between number systems, see Appendix E.

```java
 1   // Fig. 30.16: StaticCharMethods2.java
 2   // Static Character conversion methods.
 3   import java.util.Scanner;
 4
 5   public class StaticCharMethods2
 6   {
 7      // create StaticCharMethods2 object execute application
 8      public static void main( String args[] )
 9      {
10         Scanner scanner = new Scanner( System.in );
11
12         // get radix
13         System.out.println( "Please enter a radix:" );
14         int radix = scanner.nextInt();
15
16         // get user choice
17         System.out.printf( "Please choose one:\n1 -- %s\n2 -- %s\n",
18            "Convert digit to character", "Convert character to digit" );
19         int choice = scanner.nextInt();
20
21         // process request
22         switch ( choice )
23         {
24            case 1: // convert digit to character
25               System.out.println( "Enter a digit:" );
26               int digit = scanner.nextInt();
27               System.out.printf( "Convert digit to character: %s\n",
28                  Character.forDigit( digit, radix ) );
29               break;
30
```

Fig. 30.16 | Character class static conversion methods. (Part 1 of 2.)

```
31              case 2: // convert character to digit
32                  System.out.println( "Enter a character:" );
33                  char character = scanner.next().charAt( 0 );
34                  System.out.printf( "Convert character to digit: %s\n",
35                      Character.digit( character, radix ) );
36                  break;
37          } // end switch
38      } // end main
39  } // end class StaticCharMethods2
```

```
Please enter a radix:
16
Please choose one:
1 -- Convert digit to character
2 -- Convert character to digit
2
Enter a character:
A
Convert character to digit: 10
```

```
Please enter a radix:
16
Please choose one:
1 -- Convert digit to character
2 -- Convert character to digit
1
Enter a digit:
13
Convert digit to character: d
```

Fig. 30.16 | Character class static conversion methods. (Part 2 of 2.)

Line 28 uses method forDigit to convert the integer digit into a character in the number system specified by the integer radix (the base of the number). For example, the decimal integer 13 in base 16 (the radix) has the character value 'd'. Lowercase and uppercase letters represent the same value in number systems. Line 35 uses method digit to convert the character c into an integer in the number system specified by the integer radix (the base of the number). For example, the character 'A' is the base 16 (the radix) representation of the base 10 value 10. The radix must be between 2 and 36, inclusive.

Figure 30.17 demonstrates the constructor and several non-static methods of class Character—charValue, toString and equals. Lines 8–9 instantiate two Character objects by autoboxing the character constants 'A' and 'a', respectively. Line 12 uses Character method charValue to return the char value stored in Character object c1. Line 12 returns a string representation of Character object c2 using method toString. The condition in the if...else statement at lines 14–17 uses method equals to determine whether the object c1 has the same contents as the object c2 (i.e., the characters inside each object are equal).

```
 1   // Fig. 30.17: OtherCharMethods.java
 2   // Non-static Character methods.
 3
 4   public class OtherCharMethods
 5   {
 6      public static void main( String args[] )
 7      {
 8         Character c1 = 'A';
 9         Character c2 = 'a';
10
11         System.out.printf(
12            "c1 = %s\nc2 = %s\n\n", c1.charValue(), c2.toString() );
13
14         if ( c1.equals( c2 ) )
15            System.out.println( "c1 and c2 are equal\n" );
16         else
17            System.out.println( "c1 and c2 are not equal\n" );
18      } // end main
19   } // end class OtherCharMethods
```

```
c1 = A
c2 = a

c1 and c2 are not equal
```

Fig. 30.17 | `Character` class non-`static` methods.

30.6 Class `StringTokenizer`

When you read a sentence, your mind breaks the sentence into tokens—individual words and punctuation marks, each of which conveys meaning to you. Compilers also perform tokenization. They break up statements into individual pieces like keywords, identifiers, operators and other programming-language elements. We now study Java's `StringToken-izer` class (from package `java.util`), which breaks a string into its component tokens. Tokens are separated from one another by delimiters, typically white-space characters such as space, tab, newline and carriage return. Other characters can also be used as delimiters to separate tokens. The application in Fig. 30.18 demonstrates class `StringTokenizer`.

When the user presses the *Enter* key, the input sentence is stored in variable `sentence`. Line 17 creates a `StringTokenizer` for `sentence`. This `StringTokenizer` constructor takes a string argument and creates a `StringTokenizer` for it, and will use the default delimiter string " \t\n\r\f" consisting of a space, a tab, a carriage return and a newline for tokenization. There are two other constructors for class `StringTokenizer`. In the version that takes two `String` arguments, the second `String` is the delimiter string. In the version that takes three arguments, the second `String` is the delimiter string and the third argument (a `boolean`) determines whether the delimiters are also returned as tokens (only if the argument is `true`). This is useful if you need to know what the delimiters are.

Line 19 uses `StringTokenizer` method `countTokens` to determine the number of tokens in the string to be tokenized. The condition at line 21 uses `StringTokenizer` method **hasMoreTokens** to determine whether there are more tokens in the string being tokenized. If so, line 22 prints the next token in the `String`. The next token is obtained

```
 1   // Fig. 30.18: TokenTest.java
 2   // StringTokenizer class.
 3   import java.util.Scanner;
 4   import java.util.StringTokenizer;
 5
 6   public class TokenTest
 7   {
 8      // execute application
 9      public static void main( String args[] )
10      {
11         // get sentence
12         Scanner scanner = new Scanner( System.in );
13         System.out.println( "Enter a sentence and press Enter" );
14         String sentence = scanner.nextLine();
15
16         // process user sentence
17         StringTokenizer tokens = new StringTokenizer( sentence );
18         System.out.printf( "Number of elements: %d\nThe tokens are:\n",
19            tokens.countTokens() );
20
21         while ( tokens.hasMoreTokens() )
22            System.out.println( tokens.nextToken() );
23      } // end main
24   } // end class TokenTest
```

```
Enter a sentence and press Enter
This is a sentence with seven tokens
Number of elements: 7
The tokens are:
This
is
a
sentence
with
seven
tokens
```

Fig. 30.18 | StringTokenizer object used to tokenize strings.

with a call to StringTokenizer method **nextToken**, which returns a String. The token is output using println, so subsequent tokens appear on separate lines.

If you would like to change the delimiter string while tokenizing a string, you may do so by specifying a new delimiter string in a nextToken call as follows:

```
tokens.nextToken( newDelimiterString );
```

This feature is not demonstrated in Fig. 30.18.

30.7 Regular Expressions, Class Pattern and Class Matcher

Regular expressions are sequences of characters and symbols that define a set of strings. They are useful for validating input and ensuring that data is in a particular format. For example, a ZIP code must consist of five digits, and a last name must contain only letters, spaces, apostrophes and hyphens. One application of regular expressions is to facilitate the construction of a compiler. Often, a large and complex regular expression is used to validate the syntax of a program. If the program code does not match the regular expression, the compiler knows that there is a syntax error within the code.

Class String provides several methods for performing regular-expression operations, the simplest of which is the matching operation. String method matches receives a string that specifies the regular expression and matches the contents of the String object on which it is called to the regular expression. The method returns a boolean indicating whether the match succeeded.

A regular expression consists of literal characters and special symbols. Figure 30.19 specifies some predefined character classes that can be used with regular expressions. A character class is an escape sequence that represents a group of characters. A digit is any numeric character. A word character is any letter (uppercase or lowercase), any digit or the underscore character. A whitespace character is a space, a tab, a carriage return, a newline or a form feed. Each character class matches a single character in the string we are attempting to match with the regular expression.

Regular expressions are not limited to these predefined character classes. The expressions employ various operators and other forms of notation to match complex patterns. We examine several of these techniques in the application in Figs. 30.20 and 30.21 which validates user input via regular expressions. [*Note:* This application is not designed to match all possible valid user input.]

Figure 30.20 validates user input. Line 9 validates the first name. To match a set of characters that does not have a predefined character class, use square brackets, []. For example, the pattern "[aeiou]" matches a single character that is a vowel. Character ranges are represented by placing a dash (-) between two characters. In the example, "[A-Z]" matches a single uppercase letter. If the first character in the brackets is "^", the expression accepts any character other than those indicated. However, it is important to note that "[^Z]" is not the same as "[A-Y]", which matches uppercase letters A–Y—"[^Z]" matches any character other than capital Z, including lowercase letters and non-letters such as the newline character. Ranges in character classes are determined by the letters' integer values. In this example, "[A-Za-z]" matches all uppercase and lowercase letters. The range "[A-z]" matches all letters and also matches those characters (such as % and 6) with an integer value between uppercase Z and lowercase a (for more information on integer values of characters see Appendix B, ASCII Character Set). Like predefined character classes, character classes delimited by square brackets match a single character in the search object.

Character	Matches	Character	Matches
\d	any digit	\D	any nondigit
\w	any word character	\W	any nonword character
\s	any white-space character	\S	any nonwhite-space

Fig. 30.19 | Predefined character classes.

```
1    // Fig. 30.20: ValidateInput.java
2    // Validate user information using regular expressions.
3
4    public class ValidateInput
5    {
6       // validate first name
7       public static boolean validateFirstName( String firstName )
8       {
9          return firstName.matches( "[A-Z][a-zA-Z]*" );
10      } // end method validateFirstName
11
12      // validate last name
13      public static boolean validateLastName( String lastName )
14      {
15         return lastName.matches( "[a-zA-z]+([ '-][a-zA-Z]+)*" );
16      } // end method validateLastName
17
18      // validate address
19      public static boolean validateAddress( String address )
20      {
21         return address.matches(
22            "\\d+\\s+([a-zA-Z]+|[a-zA-Z]+\\s[a-zA-Z]+)" );
23      } // end method validateAddress
24
25      // validate city
26      public static boolean validateCity( String city )
27      {
28         return city.matches( "([a-zA-Z]+|[a-zA-Z]+\\s[a-zA-Z]+)" );
29      } // end method validateCity
30
31      // validate state
32      public static boolean validateState( String state )
33      {
34         return state.matches( "([a-zA-Z]+|[a-zA-Z]+\\s[a-zA-Z]+)" ) ;
35      } // end method validateState
36
37      // validate zip
38      public static boolean validateZip( String zip )
39      {
40         return zip.matches( "\\d{5}" );
41      } // end method validateZip
42
43      // validate phone
44      public static boolean validatePhone( String phone )
45      {
46         return phone.matches( "[1-9]\\d{2}-[1-9]\\d{2}-\\d{4}" );
47      } // end method validatePhone
48   } // end class ValidateInput
```

Fig. 30.20 | Validating user information using regular expressions.

In line 9, the asterisk after the second character class indicates that any number of let-ters can be matched. In general, when the regular-expression operator "*" appears in a reg-ular expression, the application attempts to match zero or more occurrences of the subexpression immediately preceding the "*". Operator "+" attempts to match one or more occurrences of the subexpression immediately preceding "+". So both "A*" and "A+" will match "AAA", but only "A*" will match an empty string.

If method validateFirstName returns true (line 29), the application attempts to validate the last name (line 31) by calling validateLastName (lines 13–16 of Fig. 30.20). The

```java
 1   // Fig. 30.21: Validate.java
 2   // Validate user information using regular expressions.
 3   import java.util.Scanner;
 4
 5   public class Validate
 6   {
 7      public static void main( String[] args )
 8      {
 9         // get user input
10         Scanner scanner = new Scanner( System.in );
11         System.out.println( "Please enter first name:" );
12         String firstName = scanner.nextLine();
13         System.out.println( "Please enter last name:" );
14         String lastName = scanner.nextLine();
15         System.out.println( "Please enter address:" );
16         String address = scanner.nextLine();
17         System.out.println( "Please enter city:" );
18         String city = scanner.nextLine();
19         System.out.println( "Please enter state:" );
20         String state = scanner.nextLine();
21         System.out.println( "Please enter zip:" );
22         String zip = scanner.nextLine();
23         System.out.println( "Please enter phone:" );
24         String phone = scanner.nextLine();
25
26         // validate user input and display error message
27         System.out.println( "\nValidate Result:" );
28
29         if ( !ValidateInput.validateFirstName( firstName ) )
30            System.out.println( "Invalid first name" );
31         else if ( !ValidateInput.validateLastName( lastName ) )
32            System.out.println( "Invalid last name" );
33         else if ( !ValidateInput.validateAddress( address ) )
34            System.out.println( "Invalid address" );
35         else if ( !ValidateInput.validateCity( city ) )
36            System.out.println( "Invalid city" );
37         else if ( !ValidateInput.validateState( state ) )
38            System.out.println( "Invalid state" );
39         else if ( !ValidateInput.validateZip( zip ) )
40            System.out.println( "Invalid zip code" );
41         else if ( !ValidateInput.validatePhone( phone ) )
42            System.out.println( "Invalid phone number" );
43         else
44            System.out.println( "Valid input.  Thank you." );
45      } // end main
46   } // end class Validate
```

Fig. 30.21 | Inputs and validates data from user using the ValidateInput class. (Part 1 of 2.)

```
Please enter first name:
Jane
Please enter last name:
Doe
Please enter address:
123 Some Street
Please enter city:
Some City
Please enter state:
SS
Please enter zip:
123
Please enter phone:
123-456-7890

Validate Result:
Invalid zip code
```

```
Please enter first name:
Jane
Please enter last name:
Doe
Please enter address:
123 Some Street
Please enter city:
Some City
Please enter state:
SS
Please enter zip:
12345
Please enter phone:
123-456-7890

Validate Result:
Valid input.  Thank you.
```

Fig. 30.21 | Inputs and validates data from user using the `ValidateInput` class. (Part 2 of 2.)

regular expression to validate the last name matches any number of letters split by spaces, apostrophes or hyphens.

Line 33 validates the address by calling method `validateAddress` (lines 19–23 of Fig. 30.20). The first character class matches any digit one or more times (\\d+). Note that two \ characters are used, because \ normally starts an escape sequences in a string. So \\d in a Java string represents the regular expression pattern \d. Then we match one or more white-space characters (\\s+). The character "|" allows a match of the expression to its left or to its right. For example, "Hi (John|Jane)" matches both "Hi John" and "Hi Jane". The parentheses are used to group parts of the regular expression. In this example, the left side of | matches a single word, and the right side matches two words separated by any amount of white space. So the address must contain a number followed by one or two words. Therefore, "10 Broadway" and "10 Main Street" are both valid addresses in this example. The city (lines 26–29 of Fig. 30.20) and state (lines 32–35 of Fig. 30.20) methods also match any word of at least one character or, alternatively, any two words of at least one character if the words are separated by a single space. This means both Waltham and West Newton would match.

Quantifiers

The asterisk (*) and plus (+) are formally called **quantifiers**. Figure 30.22 lists all the quantifiers. We have already discussed how the asterisk (*) and plus (+) quantifiers work. All quantifiers affect only the subexpression immediately preceding the quantifier. Quantifier question mark (?) matches zero or one occurrences of the expression that it quantifies. A set of braces containing one number ({n}) matches exactly n occurrences of the expression it quantifies. We demonstrate this quantifier to validate the zip code in Fig. 30.20 at line 40. Including a comma after the number enclosed in braces matches at least n occurrences of the quantified expression. The set of braces containing two numbers ({n,m}), matches between n and m occurrences of the expression that it qualifies. Quantifiers may be applied to patterns enclosed in parentheses to create more complex regular expressions.

All of the quantifiers are **greedy**. This means that they will match as many occurrences as they can as long as the match is still successful. However, if any of these quantifiers is followed by a question mark (?), the quantifier becomes **reluctant** (sometimes called **lazy**). It then will match as few occurrences as possible as long as the match is still successful.

The zip code (line 40 in Fig. 30.20) matches a digit five times. This regular expression uses the digit character class and a quantifier with the digit 5 between braces. The phone number (line 46 in Fig. 30.20) matches three digits (the first one cannot be zero) followed by a dash followed by three more digits (again the first one cannot be zero) followed by four more digits.

String Method matches checks whether an entire string conforms to a regular expression. For example, we want to accept "Smith" as a last name, but not "9@Smith#". If only a substring matches the regular expression, method matches returns false.

Replacing Substrings and Splitting Strings

Sometimes it is useful to replace parts of a string or to split a string into pieces. For this purpose, class String provides methods replaceAll, replaceFirst and split. These methods are demonstrated in Fig. 30.23.

Quantifier	Matches
*	Matches zero or more occurrences of the pattern.
+	Matches one or more occurrences of the pattern.
?	Matches zero or one occurrences of the pattern.
{n}	Matches exactly n occurrences.
{n,}	Matches at least n occurrences.
{n,m}	Matches between n and m (inclusive) occurrences.

Fig. 30.22 | Quantifiers used in regular expressions.

Method `replaceAll` replaces text in a string with new text (the second argument) wherever the original string matches a regular expression (the first argument). Line 14 replaces every instance of "*" in `firstString` with "^". Note that the regular expression ("*") precedes character * with two backslashes. Normally, * is a quantifier indicating

```
 1   // Fig. 30.23: RegexSubstitution.java
 2   // Using methods replaceFirst, replaceAll and split.
 3
 4   public class RegexSubstitution
 5   {
 6      public static void main( String args[] )
 7      {
 8         String firstString = "This sentence ends in 5 stars *****";
 9         String secondString = "1, 2, 3, 4, 5, 6, 7, 8";
10
11         System.out.printf( "Original String 1: %s\n", firstString );
12
13         // replace '*' with '^'
14         firstString = firstString.replaceAll( "\\*", "^" );
15
16         System.out.printf( "^ substituted for *: %s\n", firstString );
17
18         // replace 'stars' with 'carets'
19         firstString = firstString.replaceAll( "stars", "carets" );
20
21         System.out.printf(
22            "\"carets\" substituted for \"stars\": %s\n", firstString );
23
24         // replace words with 'word'
25         System.out.printf( "Every word replaced by \"word\": %s\n\n",
26            firstString.replaceAll( "\\w+", "word" ) );
27
28         System.out.printf( "Original String 2: %s\n", secondString );
29
30         // replace first three digits with 'digit'
31         for ( int i = 0; i < 3; i++ )
32            secondString = secondString.replaceFirst( "\\d", "digit" );
33
34         System.out.printf(
35            "First 3 digits replaced by \"digit\" : %s\n", secondString );
36         String output = "String split at commas: [";
37
38         String[] results = secondString.split( ",\\s*" ); // split on commas
39
40         for ( String string : results )
41            output += "\"" + string + "\", "; // output results
42
43         // remove the extra comma and add a bracket
44         output = output.substring( 0, output.length() - 2 ) + "]";
45         System.out.println( output );
46      } // end main
47   } // end class RegexSubstitution
```

Fig. 30.23 | Methods `replaceFirst`, `replaceAll` and `split`. (Part 1 of 2.)

```
Original String 1: This sentence ends in 5 stars *****
^ substituted for *: This sentence ends in 5 stars ^^^^^
"carets" substituted for "stars": This sentence ends in 5 carets ^^^^^
Every word replaced by "word": word word word word word word ^^^^^

Original String 2: 1, 2, 3, 4, 5, 6, 7, 8
First 3 digits replaced by "digit" : digit, digit, digit, 4, 5, 6, 7, 8
String split at commas: ["digit", "digit", "digit", "4", "5", "6", "7", "8"]
```

Fig. 30.23 | Methods replaceFirst, replaceAll and split. (Part 2 of 2.)

that a regular expression should match any number of occurrences of a preceding pattern. However, in line 14, we want to find all occurrences of the literal character *—to do this, we must escape character * with character \. Escaping a special regular-expression character with \ instructs the matching engine to find the actual character. Since the expression is stored in a Java string and \ is a special character in Java strings, we must include an additional \. So the Java string "*" represents the regular-expression pattern * which matches a single * character in the search string. In line 19, every match for the regular expression "stars" in firstString is replaced with "carets".

Method replaceFirst (line 32) replaces the first occurrence of a pattern match. Java Strings are immutable, therefore method replaceFirst returns a new string in which the appropriate characters have been replaced. This line takes the original string and replaces it with the string returned by replaceFirst. By iterating three times we replace the first three instances of a digit (\d) in secondString with the text "digit".

Method split divides a string into several substrings. The original string is broken in any location that matches a specified regular expression. Method split returns an array of strings containing the substrings between matches for the regular expression. In line 38, we use method split to tokenize a string of comma-separated integers. The argument is the regular expression that locates the delimiter. In this case, we use the regular expression ",\\s*" to separate the substrings wherever a comma occurs. By matching any white-space characters, we eliminate extra spaces from the resulting substrings. Note that the commas and white-space characters are not returned as part of the substrings. Again, note that the Java string ",\\s*" represents the regular expression ,\s*.

Classes Pattern and Matcher

In addition to the regular-expression capabilities of class String, Java provides other classes in package java.util.regex that help developers manipulate regular expressions. Class Pattern represents a regular expression. Class Matcher contains both a regular-expression pattern and a CharSequence in which to search for the pattern.

CharSequence is an interface that allows read access to a sequence of characters. The interface requires that the methods charAt, length, subSequence and toString be declared. Both String and StringBuilder implement interface CharSequence, so an instance of either of these classes can be used with class Matcher.

Common Programming Error 30.4

A regular expression can be tested against an object of any class that implements interface CharSequence, but the regular expression must be a String. Attempting to create a regular expression as a StringBuilder is an error.

If a regular expression will be used only once, static Pattern method **matches** can be used. This method takes a string that specifies the regular expression and a CharSequence on which to perform the match. This method returns a boolean indicating whether the search object (the second argument) matches the regular expression.

If a regular expression will be used more than once, it is more efficient to use static Pattern method **compile** to create a specific Pattern object for that regular expression. This method receives a string representing the pattern and returns a new Pattern object, which can then be used to call method **matcher**. This method receives a CharSequence to search and returns a Matcher object.

Matcher provides method **matches**, which performs the same task as Pattern method matches, but receives no arguments—the search pattern and search object are encapsulated in the Matcher object. Class Matcher provides other methods, including **find**, **lookingAt**, **replaceFirst** and **replaceAll**.

Figure 30.24 presents a simple example that employs regular expressions. This program matches birthdays against a regular expression. The expression matches only birthdays that do not occur in April and that belong to people whose names begin with "J".

Lines 11–12 create a Pattern by invoking static Pattern method compile. The dot character "." in the regular expression (line 12) matches any single character except a newline character.

```java
1   // Fig. 30.24: RegexMatches.java
2   // Demonstrating Classes Pattern and Matcher.
3   import java.util.regex.Matcher;
4   import java.util.regex.Pattern;
5
6   public class RegexMatches
7   {
8      public static void main( String args[] )
9      {
10        // create regular expression
11        Pattern expression =
12           Pattern.compile( "J.*\\d[0-35-9]-\\d\\d-\\d\\d" );
13
14        String string1 = "Jane's Birthday is 05-12-75\n" +
15           "Dave's Birthday is 11-04-68\n" +
16           "John's Birthday is 04-28-73\n" +
17           "Joe's Birthday is 12-17-77";
18
19        // match regular expression to string and print matches
20        Matcher matcher = expression.matcher( string1 );
21
22        while ( matcher.find() )
23           System.out.println( matcher.group() );
24     } // end main
25  } // end class RegexMatches
```

```
Jane's Birthday is 05-12-75
Joe's Birthday is 12-17-77
```

Fig. 30.24 | Regular expressions checking birthdays.

Line 20 creates the `Matcher` object for the compiled regular expression and the matching sequence (`string1`). Lines 22–23 use a `while` loop to iterate through the string. Line 22 uses `Matcher` method `find` to attempt to match a piece of the search object to the search pattern. Each call to this method starts at the point where the last call ended, so multiple matches can be found. `Matcher` method `lookingAt` performs the same way, except that it always starts from the beginning of the search object and will always find the first match if there is one.

> **Common Programming Error 30.5**
>
> *Method* `matches` *(from class* `String`, `Pattern` *or* `Matcher`*) will return* `true` *only if the entire search object matches the regular expression. Methods* `find` *and* `lookingAt` *(from class* `Matcher`*) will return* `true` *if a portion of the search object matches the regular expression.*

Line 23 uses `Matcher` method **group**, which returns the string from the search object that matches the search pattern. The string that is returned is the one that was last matched by a call to `find` or `lookingAt`. The output in Fig. 30.24 shows the two matches that were found in `string1`.

Regular Expression Web Resources

The following websites provide more information on regular expressions.

`java.sun.com/docs/books/tutorial/extra/regex/index.html`
This tutorial explains how to use Java's regular-expression API.

`java.sun.com/javase/6/docs/api/java/util/regex/package-summary.html`
This page is the javadoc overview of package `java.util.regex`.

`developer.java.sun.com/developer/technicalArticles/releases/1.4regex`
Thoroughly describes Java's regular-expression capabilities.

30.8 Wrap-Up

In this chapter, you learned about more `String` methods for selecting portions of `Strings` and manipulating `Strings`. You also learned about the `Character` class and some of the methods it declares to handle `chars`. The chapter also discussed the capabilities of the `StringBuilder` class for creating `Strings`. The end of the chapter discussed regular expressions, which provide a powerful capability to search and match portions of `Strings` that fit a particular pattern.

Summary

Section 30.2 Fundamentals of Characters and Strings

• A character literal's value is its integer value in the Unicode character set. Strings can include letters, digits and special characters such as +, -, *, / and $. A string in Java is an object of class `String`. `String` literals are often referred to as `String` objects and are written in double quotes in a program.

Section 30.3 Class `String`

• `String` objects are immutable—their character contents cannot be changed after they are created.

- String method `length` returns the number of characters in a `String`.
- String method `charAt` returns the character at a specific position.
- String method `equals` tests any two objects for equality. The method returns `true` if the contents of the `Strings` are equal, `false` otherwise. Method `equals` uses a lexicographical comparison for `Strings`.
- When primitive-type values are compared with `==`, the result is `true` if both values are identical. When references are compared with `==`, the result is `true` if both references refer to the same object in memory.
- Java treats all string literals with the same contents as a single `String` object.
- String method `equalsIgnoreCase` performs a case-insensitive string comparison.
- String method `compareTo` uses a lexicographical comparison and returns 0 if the strings it is comparing are equal, a negative number if the string that `compareTo` is invoked on is less than the `String` that is passed as an argument and a positive number if the string that `compareTo` is invoked on is greater than the string that is passed as an argument.
- String method `regionMatches` compares portions of two strings for equality.
- String method `startsWith` determines whether a string starts with the characters specified as an argument. String method `endsWith` determines whether a string ends with the characters specified as an argument.
- String method `indexOf` locates the first occurrence of a character or a substring in a string. String method `lastIndexOf` locates the last occurrence of a character or a substring in a string.
- String method `substring` copies and returns part of an existing string object.
- String method `concat` concatenates two string objects and returns a new string object containing the characters from both original strings.
- String method `replace` returns a new string object that replaces every occurrence in a `String` of its first character argument with its second character argument.
- String method `toUpperCase` returns a new string with uppercase letters in the positions where the original string had lowercase letters. String method `toLowerCase` returns a new string with lowercase letters in the positions where the original string had uppercase letters.
- String method `trim` returns a new string object in which all white-space characters (e.g., spaces, newlines and tabs) have been removed from the beginning and end of a string.
- String method `toCharArray` returns a char array containing a copy of the string's characters.
- String class static method `valueOf` returns its argument converted to a string.

Section 30.4 Class *StringBuilder*

- Class `StringBuilder` provides constructors that enable `StringBuilders` to be initialized with no characters and an initial capacity of 16 characters, with no characters and an initial capacity specified in the integer argument, or with a copy of the characters of the `String` argument and an initial capacity that is the number of characters in the `String` argument plus 16.
- `StringBuilder` method `length` returns the number of characters currently stored in a `StringBuilder`. `StringBuilder` method `capacity` returns the number of characters that can be stored in a `StringBuilder` without allocating more memory.
- `StringBuilder` method `ensureCapacity` ensures that a `StringBuilder` has at least the specified capacity. `StringBuilder` method `setLength` increases or decreases the length of a `StringBuilder`.
- `StringBuilder` method `charAt` returns the character at the specified index. `StringBuilder` method `setCharAt` sets the character at the specified position. `StringBuilder` method `getChars` copies characters in the `StringBuilder` into the character array passed as an argument.

- Class `StringBuilder` provides overloaded append methods to add primitive-type, character array, `String`, `Object` and `CharSequence` values to the end of a `StringBuilder`. `StringBuilder`s and the append methods are used by the Java compiler to implement the + and += concatenation operators.

- Class `StringBuilder` provides overloaded `insert` methods to insert primitive-type, character array, `String`, `Object` and `CharSequence` values at any position in a `StringBuilder`.

Section 30.5 Class *Character*

- Class `Character` provides a constructor that takes a `char` argument.

- `Character` method `isDefined` determines whether a character is defined in the Unicode character set. If so, the method returns `true`—otherwise, it returns `false`.

- `Character` method `isDigit` determines whether a character is a defined Unicode digit. If so, the method returns `true`—otherwise, it returns `false`.

- `Character` method `isJavaIdentifierStart` determines whether a character can be used as the first character of an identifier in Java [i.e., a letter, an underscore (_) or a dollar sign ($)]. If so, the method returns `true`—otherwise, it returns `false`.

- `Character` method `isJavaIdentifierPart` determines whether a character can be used in an identifier in Java [i.e., a digit, a letter, an underscore (_) or a dollar sign ($)]. `Character` method `isLetter` determines whether a character is a letter. `Character` method `isLetterOrDigit` determines whether a character is a letter or a digit. In each case, if so, the method returns `true`—otherwise, it returns `false`.

- `Character` method `isLowerCase` determines whether a character is a lowercase letter. `Character` method `isUpperCase` determines whether a character is an uppercase letter. In both cases, if so, the method returns `true`—otherwise, `false`.

- `Character` method `toUpperCase` converts a character to its uppercase equivalent. `Character` method `toLowerCase` converts a character to its lowercase equivalent.

- `Character` method `digit` converts its character argument into an integer in the number system specified by its integer argument `radix`. `Character` method `forDigit` converts its integer argument `digit` into a character in the number system specified by its integer argument `radix`.

- `Character` method `charValue` returns the `char` stored in a `Character` object. `Character` method `toString` returns a `String` representation of a `Character`.

Section 30.6 Class *StringTokenizer*

- `StringTokenizer`'s default constructor creates a `StringTokenizer` for its string argument that will use the default delimiter string " \t\n\r\f", consisting of a space, a tab, a newline and a carriage return for tokenization.

- `StringTokenizer` method `countTokens` returns the number of tokens in a string to be tokenized.

- `StringTokenizer` method `hasMoreTokens` determines whether there are more tokens in the string being tokenized.

- `StringTokenizer` method `nextToken` returns a `String` with the next token.

Section 30.7 Regular Expressions, Class *Pattern* and Class *Matcher*

- Regular expressions are sequences of characters and symbols that define a set of strings. They are useful for validating input and ensuring that data is in a particular format.

- `String` method `matches` receives a string that specifies the regular expression and matches the contents of the `String` object on which it is called to the regular expression. The method returns a `boolean` indicating whether the match succeeded.

- A character class is an escape sequence that represents a group of characters. Each character class matches a single character in the string we are attempting to match with the regular expression.
- A word character (\w) is any letter (uppercase or lowercase), any digit or the underscorecharacter.
- A whitespace character (\s) is a space, a tab, a carriage return, a newline or a form feed.
- A digit (\d) is any numeric character.
- To match a set of characters that does not have a predefined character class, use square brackets, []. Ranges can be represented by placing a dash (-) between two characters. If the first character in the brackets is "^", the expression accepts any character other than those indicated.
- When the regular expression operator "*" appears in a regular expression, the program attempts to match zero or more occurrences of the subexpression immediately preceding the "*".
- Operator "+" attempts to match one or more occurrences of the subexpression preceding it.
- The character "|" allows a match of the expression to its left or to its right.
- The parentheses ( ) are used to group parts of the regular expression.
- The asterisk (*) and plus (+) are formally called quantifiers.
- All quantifiers affect only the subexpression immediately preceding the quantifier.
- Quantifier question mark (?) matches zero or one occurrences of the expression that it quantifies.
- A set of braces containing one number ({n}) matches exactly n occurrences of the expression it quantifies. Including a comma after the number enclosed in braces matches at least n occurrences of the quantified expression.
- A set of braces containing two numbers ({n,m}) matches between n and m occurrences of the expression that it qualifies.
- All of the quantifiers are greedy, which means that they will match as many occurrences as they can as long as the match is successful.
- If any of these quantifiers is followed by a question mark (?), the quantifier becomes reluctant, matching as few occurrences as possible as long as the match is successful.
- String method replaceAll replaces text in a string with new text (the second argument) wherever the original string matches a regular expression (the first argument).
- Escaping a special regular-expression character with a \ instructs the regular-expression matching engine to find the actual character, as opposed to what it represents in a regular expression.
- String method replaceFirst replaces the first occurrence of a pattern match. Java Strings are immutable, therefore method replaceFirst returns a new string in which the appropriate characters have been replaced.
- String method split divides a string into several substrings. The original string is broken in any location that matches a specified regular expression. Method split returns an array of strings containing the substrings between matches for the regular expression.
- Class Pattern represents a regular expression.
- Class Matcher contains both a regular-expression pattern and a CharSequence in which to search for the pattern.
- CharSequence is an interface that allows read access to a sequence of characters. Both String and StringBuilder implement interface CharSequence, so an instance of either of these classes can be used with class Matcher.
- If a regular expression will be used only once, static Pattern method matches takes a string that specifies the regular expression and a CharSequence on which to perform the match. This method returns a boolean indicating whether the search object matches the regular expression.

- If a regular expression will be used more than once, it is more efficient to use static `Pattern` method `compile` to create a specific `Pattern` object for that regular expression. This method receives a string representing the pattern and returns a new `Pattern` object.
- `Pattern` method `matcher` receives a `CharSequence` to search and returns a `Matcher` object.
- `Matcher` method `matches` performs the same task as `Pattern` method `matches`, but receives no arguments.
- `Matcher` method `find` attempts to match a piece of the search object to the search pattern. Each call to this method starts at the point where the last call ended, so multiple matches can be found.
- `Matcher` method `lookingAt` performs the same as `find`, except that it always starts from the beginning of the search object and will always find the first match if there is one.
- `Matcher` method `group` returns the string from the search object that matches the search pattern. The string that is returned is the one that was last matched by a call to `find` or `lookingAt`.

Terminology

append method of class `StringBuilder`
capacity method of class `StringBuilder`
character literal
charAt method of class `StringBuilder`
`CharSequence` interface
charValue method of class `Character`
concat method of class `String`
delete method of class `StringBuilder`
deleteCharAt method of class `String`
delimiter for tokens
digit method of class `Character`
empty string
endsWith method of class `String`
ensureCapacity method of class `StringBuilder`
find method of class `Matcher`
forDigit method of class `Character`
getChars method of class `String`
getChars method of class `StringBuilder`
greedy quantifier
hasMoreTokens method of class
    `StringTokenizer`
immutable
indexOf method of class `String`
isDefined method of class `Character`
isDigit method of class `Character`
isJavaIdentifierPart method of class
    `Character`
isJavaIdentifierStart method of class
    `Character`
isLetter method of class `Character`
isLetterOrDigit method of class `Character`
isLowerCase method of class `Character`
isUpperCase method of class `Character`
lastIndexOf method of class `String`

lazy quantifier
length method of class `String`
length method of class `StringBuilder`
lexicographical comparison
lookingAt method of class `Matcher`
`Matcher` class
matcher method of class `Pattern`
matches method of class `Matcher`
matches method of class `Pattern`
matches method of class `String`
nextToken method of class `StringTokenizer`
`Pattern` class
predefined character class
quantifier for regular expression
radix
regionMatches method of class `String`
regular expressions
reluctant quantifier
replaceAll method of class `String`
replaceFirst method of class `String`
reverse method of class `StringBuilder`
setCharAt method of class `StringBuilder`
special character
split method of class `String`
startsWith method of class `String`
string literal
`StringIndexOutOfBoundsException` class
token of a `String`
toLowerCase method of class `Character`
toUpperCase method of class `Character`
trim method of class `StringBuilder`
Unicode character set
valueOf method of class `String`
word character

Self-Review Exercises

30.1 State whether each of the following is *true* or *false*. If *false*, explain why.

a) When String objects are compared using ==, the result is true if the Strings contain the same values.

b) A String can be modified after it is created.

30.2 For each of the following, write a single statement that performs the indicated task:

a) Compare the string in s1 to the string in s2 for equality of contents.

b) Append the string s2 to the string s1, using +=.

c) Determine the length of the string in s1.

Answers to Self-Review Exercises

30.1 a) False. String objects are compared using operator == to determine whether they are the same object in memory.

b) False. String objects are immutable and cannot be modified after they are created. StringBuilder objects can be modified after they are created.

30.2 a) `s1.equals( s2 )`

b) `s1 += s2;`

c) `s1.length()`

Exercises

30.3 Write an application that uses String method compareTo to compare two strings input by the user. Output whether the first string is less than, equal to or greater than the second.

30.4 Write an application that uses String method regionMatches to compare two strings input by the user. The application should input the number of characters to be compared and the starting index of the comparison. The application should state whether the strings are equal. Ignore the case of the characters when performing the comparison.

30.5 *(Limericks)* A limerick is a humorous five-line verse in which the first and second lines rhyme with the fifth, and the third line rhymes with the fourth. Using techniques similar to those developed in Exercise 30.5, write a Java application that produces random limericks. Polishing this application to produce good limericks is a challenging problem, but the result will be worth the effort!

30.6 *(Pig Latin)* Write an application that encodes English-language phrases into pig Latin. Pig Latin is a form of coded language. There are many different ways to form pig Latin phrases. For simplicity, use the following algorithm:

To form a pig Latin phrase from an English-language phrase, tokenize the phrase into words with an object of class StringTokenizer. To translate each English word into a pig Latin word, place the first letter of the English word at the end of the word and add the letters "ay." Thus, the word "jump" becomes "umpjay," the word "the" becomes "hetay," and the word "computer" becomes "omputercay." Blanks between words remain as blanks. Assume the following: The English phrase consists of words separated by blanks, there are no punctuation marks and all words have two or more letters. Method printLatinWord should display each word. Each token returned from nextToken is passed to method printLatinWord to print the pig Latin word. Enable the user to input the sentence. Keep a running display of all the converted sentences in a textarea.

30.7 Write an application that inputs a line of text, tokenizes the line with an object of class StringTokenizer and outputs the tokens in reverse order. Use space characters as delimiters.

30.8   Use the string-comparison methods discussed in this chapter and the techniques for sorting arrays developed in Chapter 16 to write an application that alphabetizes a list of strings. Allow the user to enter the strings in a text field. Display the results in a textarea.

30.9   Write an application that inputs a line of text and a search character and uses `String` method `indexOf` to determine the number of occurrences of the character in the text.

30.10   Write an application based on the application in Exercise 30.9 that inputs a line of text and uses `String` method `indexOf` to determine the total number of occurrences of each letter of the alphabet in the text. Uppercase and lowercase letters should be counted together. Store the totals for each letter in an array, and print the values in tabular format after the totals have been determined.

30.11   Write an application that reads a line of text, tokenizes it using space characters as delimiters and outputs only those words ending with the letters `"ED"`.

30.12   Write an application that inputs an integer code for a character and displays the corresponding character. Modify this application so that it generates all possible three-digit codes in the range from 000 to 255 and attempts to print the corresponding characters.

30.13   Write an application that reads a five-letter word from the user and produces every possible three-letter string that can be derived from the letters of that word. For example, the three-letter words produced from the word "bathe" include "ate," "bat," "bet," "tab," "hat," "the" and "tea."

Special Section: Advanced String-Manipulation Exercises

The preceding exercises are keyed to the text and designed to test your understanding of fundamental string-manipulation concepts. This section includes a collection of intermediate and advanced string-manipulation exercises. You should find these problems challenging, yet entertaining. The problems vary considerably in difficulty. Some require an hour or two of application writing and implementation. Others are useful for lab assignments that might require two or three weeks of study and implementation. Some are challenging term projects.

30.14   *(Text Analysis)* The availability of computers with string-manipulation capabilities has resulted in some rather interesting approaches to analyzing the writings of great authors. Much attention has been focused on whether William Shakespeare ever lived. Some scholars believe there is substantial evidence indicating that Christopher Marlowe actually penned the masterpieces attributed to Shakespeare. Researchers have used computers to find similarities in the writings of these two authors. This exercise examines three methods for analyzing texts with a computer.

    a)   Write an application that reads a line of text from the keyboard and prints a table indicating the number of occurrences of each letter of the alphabet in the text. For example, the phrase

```
To be, or not to be: that is the question:
```

        contains one "a," two "b's," no "c's," and so on.

    b)   Write an application that reads a line of text and prints a table indicating the number of one-letter words, two-letter words, three-letter words, and so on, appearing in the text. For example, Fig. 30.25 shows the counts for the phrase

```
Whether 'tis nobler in the mind to suffer
```

    c)   Write an application that reads a line of text and prints a table indicating the number of occurrences of each different word in the text. The first version of your application should include the words in the table in the same order in which they appear in the text. For example, the lines

```
To be, or not to be: that is the question:
Whether 'tis nobler in the mind to suffer
```

contain the word "to" three times, the word "be" two times, the word "or" once, and so on. A more interesting (and useful) printout should then be attempted in which the words are sorted alphabetically.

30.15 *(Printing Dates in Various Formats)* Dates are printed in several common formats. Two of the more common formats are

```
04/25/1955 and April 25, 1955
```

Write an application that reads a date in the first format and prints it in the second format.

Word length	Occurrences
1	0
2	2
3	1
4	2 (including 'tis)
5	0
6	2
7	1

Fig. 30.25 | Word-length counts for the string
"Whether 'tis nobler in the mind to suffer".

30.16 *(Check Protection)* Computers are frequently employed in check-writing systems, such as payroll and accounts payable applications. There are many strange stories about weekly paychecks being printed (by mistake) for amounts in excess of $1 million. Incorrect amounts are printed by computerized check-writing systems because of human error or machine failure. Systems designers build controls into their systems to prevent such erroneous checks from being issued.

Another serious problem is the intentional alteration of a check amount by someone who plans to cash a check fraudulently. To prevent a dollar amount from being altered, some computerized check-writing systems employ a technique called check protection. Checks designed for imprinting by computer contain a fixed number of spaces in which the computer may print an amount. Suppose a paycheck contains eight blank spaces in which the computer is supposed to print the amount of a weekly paycheck. If the amount is large, then all eight of the spaces will be filled. For example,

```
1,230.60 (check amount)
--------
12345678 (position numbers)
```

On the other hand, if the amount is less than $1000, then several of the spaces would ordinarily be left blank. For example,

```
   99.87
--------
12345678
```

contains three blank spaces. If a check is printed with blank spaces, it is easier for someone to alter the amount of the check. To prevent a check from being altered, many check-writing systems insert *leading asterisks* to protect the amount as follows:

```
***99.87
--------
12345678
```

Write an application that inputs a dollar amount to be printed on a check, then prints the amount in check-protected format with leading asterisks if necessary. Assume that nine spaces are available for printing the amount.

30.17 *(Writing the Word Equivalent of a Check Amount)* Continuing the discussion in Exercise 30.16, we reiterate the importance of designing check-writing systems to prevent alteration of check amounts. One common security method requires that the check amount be written in numbers and spelled out in words as well. Even if someone is able to alter the numerical amount of the check, it is extremely difficult to change the amount in words. Write an application that inputs a numeric check amount and writes the word equivalent of the amount. For example, the amount 112.43 should be written as

```
ONE hundred TWELVE and 43/100
```

30.18 *(Metric Conversion Application)* Write an application that will assist the user with metric conversions. Your application should allow the user to specify the names of the units as strings (i.e., centimeters, liters, grams, and so on, for the metric system and inches, quarts, pounds, and so on, for the English system) and should respond to simple questions, such as

```
"How many inches are in 2 meters?"
"How many liters are in 10 quarts?"
```

Your application should recognize invalid conversions. For example, the question

```
"How many feet are in 5 kilograms?"
```

is not meaningful because "feet" is a unit of length, whereas "kilograms" is a unit of mass.

Special Section: Challenging String-Manipulation Projects

30.19 *(Project: A Spelling Checker)* Many popular word-processing software packages have built-in spell checkers. In this project, you are asked to develop your own spell-checker utility. We make suggestions to help get you started. You should then consider adding more capabilities. Use a computerized dictionary (if you have access to one) as a source of words.

Why do we type so many words with incorrect spellings? In some cases, it is because we simply do not know the correct spelling, so we make a best guess. In some cases, it is because we transpose two letters (e.g., "defualt" instead of "default"). Sometimes we double-type a letter accidentally (e.g., "hanndy" instead of "handy"). Sometimes we type a nearby key instead of the one we intended (e.g., "biryhday" instead of "birthday"), and so on.

Design and implement a spell-checker application in Java. Your application should maintain an array wordList of strings. Enable the user to enter these strings. [*Note:* In Chapter 14, we have introduced file processing. With this capability, you can obtain the words for the spell checker from a computerized dictionary stored in a file.]

Your application should ask a user to enter a word. The application should then look up that word in the wordList array. If the word is in the array, your application should print "Word is spelled correctly." If the word is not in the array, your application should print "Word is not spelled correctly." Then your application should try to locate other words in wordList that might be the word the user intended to type. For example, you can try all possible single transpositions of adjacent letters to discover that the word "default" is a direct match to a word in wordList. Of course, this implies that your application will check all other single transpositions, such as "edfault," "dfeault," "deafult," "defalut" and "defautl." When you find a new word that matches one in wordList, print it in a message, such as

> Did you mean "default"?

Implement other tests, such as replacing each double letter with a single letter, and any other tests you can develop to improve the value of your spell checker.

30.20 *(Project: A Crossword Puzzle Generator)* Most people have worked a crossword puzzle, but few have ever attempted to generate one. Generating a crossword puzzle is suggested here as a string-manipulation project requiring substantial sophistication and effort.

There are many issues the programmer must resolve to get even the simplest crossword-puzzle-generator application working. For example, how do you represent the grid of a crossword puzzle inside the computer? Should you use a series of strings or two-dimensional arrays?

The programmer needs a source of words (i.e., a computerized dictionary) that can be directly referenced by the application. In what form should these words be stored to facilitate the complex manipulations required by the application?

If you are really ambitious, you will want to generate the clues portion of the puzzle, in which the brief hints for each across word and each down word are printed. Merely printing a version of the blank puzzle itself is not a simple problem.

Operator Precedence Chart

A.1 Operator Precedence

Operators are shown in decreasing order of precedence from top to bottom (Fig. A.1).

Operator	Description	Associativity
++ --	unary postfix increment unary postfix decrement	right to left
++ -- + - ! ~ (*type*)	unary prefix increment unary prefix decrement unary plus unary minus unary logical negation unary bitwise complement unary cast	right to left
* / %	multiplication division remainder	left to right
+ -	addition or string concatenation subtraction	left to right
<< >> >>>	left shift signed right shift unsigned right shift	left to right

Fig. A.1 | Operator precedence chart. (Part 1 of 2.)

Operator	Description	Associativity
 <= > >= instanceof	less than less than or equal to greater than greater than or equal to type comparison	left to right
== !=	is equal to is not equal to	left to right
&	bitwise AND boolean logical AND	left to right
^	bitwise exclusive OR boolean logical exclusive OR	left to right
|	bitwise inclusive OR boolean logical inclusive OR	left to right
&&	conditional AND	left to right
||	conditional OR	left to right
?:	conditional	right to left
= += -= *= /= %= &= ^= |= <<= >>= >>>=	assignment addition assignment subtraction assignment multiplication assignment division assignment remainder assignment bitwise AND assignment bitwise exclusive OR assignment bitwise inclusive OR assignment bitwise left shift assignment bitwise signed-right-shift assignment bitwise unsigned-right-shift assignment	right to left

Fig. A.1 | Operator precedence chart. (Part 2 of 2.)

ASCII Character Set

	0	1	2	3	4	5	6	7	8	9
0	nul	soh	stx	etx	eot	enq	ack	bel	bs	ht
1	nl	vt	ff	cr	so	si	dle	dc1	dc2	dc3
2	dc4	nak	syn	etb	can	em	sub	esc	fs	gs
3	rs	us	sp	!	"	#	$	%	&	'
4	(	)	*	+	,	-	.	/	0	1
5	2	3	4	5	6	7	8	9	:	;
6	<	=	>	?	@	A	B	C	D	E
7	F	G	H	I	J	K	L	M	N	O
8	P	Q	R	S	T	U	V	W	X	Y
9	Z	[	\	]	^	_	'	a	b	c
10	d	e	f	g	h	i	j	k	l	m
11	n	o	p	q	r	s	t	u	v	w
12	x	y	z	{			}	~	del		

Fig. B.1 | ASCII character set.

The digits at the left of the table are the left digits of the decimal equivalent (0–127) of the character code, and the digits at the top of the table are the right digits of the character code. For example, the character code for "F" is 70, and the character code for "&" is 38.

Most users of this book are interested in the ASCII character set used to represent English characters on many computers. The ASCII character set is a subset of the Unicode character set used by Java to represent characters from most of the world's languages. For more information on the Unicode character set, see the web bonus Appendix I, Unicode®.

Keywords and Reserved Words

Java Keywords				
abstract	assert	boolean	break	byte
case	catch	char	class	continue
default	do	double	else	enum
extends	final	finally	float	for
if	implements	import	instanceof	int
interface	long	native	new	package
private	protected	public	return	short
static	strictfp	super	switch	synchronized
this	throw	throws	transient	try
void	volatile	while		
Keywords that are not currently used				
const	goto			

Fig. C.1 | Java keywords.

Java also contains the reserved words true and false, which are boolean literals, and null, which is the literal that represents a reference to nothing. Like keywords, these reserved words cannot be used as identifiers.

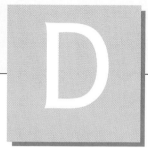

Primitive Types

Type	Size in bits	Values	Standard
boolean		true or false	
[Note: A boolean's representation is specific to the Java Virtual Machine on each platform.*]*			
char	16	'\u0000' to '\uFFFF' (0 to 65535)	(ISO Unicode character set)
byte	8	-128 to $+127$ (-2^7 to $2^7 - 1$)	
short	16	$-32,768$ to $+32,767$ (-2^{15} to $2^{15} - 1$)	
int	32	$-2,147,483,648$ to $+2,147,483,647$ (-2^{31} to $2^{31} - 1$)	
long	64	$-9,223,372,036,854,775,808$ to $+9,223,372,036,854,775,807$ (-2^{63} to $2^{63} - 1$)	
float	32	*Negative range:* $-3.4028234663852886E+38$ to $-1.40129846432481707e-45$ *Positive range:* $1.40129846432481707e-45$ to $3.4028234663852886E+38$	(IEEE 754 floating point)
double	64	*Negative range:* $-1.7976931348623157E+308$ to $-4.94065645841246544e-324$ *Positive range:* $4.94065645841246544e-324$ to $1.7976931348623157E+308$	(IEEE 754 floating point)

Fig. D.1 | Java primitive types.

For more information on IEEE 754 visit grouper.ieee.org/groups/754/. For more information on Unicode, see Appendix I, Unicode®.

E

Number Systems

OBJECTIVES

In this appendix you will learn:

- To understand basic number systems concepts, such as base, positional value and symbol value.

- To understand how to work with numbers represented in the binary, octal and hexadecimal number systems.

- To abbreviate binary numbers as octal numbers or hexadecimal numbers.

- To convert octal numbers and hexadecimal numbers to binary numbers.

- To convert back and forth between decimal numbers and their binary, octal and hexadecimal equivalents.

- To understand binary arithmetic and how negative binary numbers are represented using two's complement notation.

E.1 Introduction

In this appendix, we introduce the key number systems that Java programmers use, especially when they are working on software projects that require close interaction with machine-level hardware. Projects like this include operating systems, computer networking software, compilers, database systems and applications requiring high performance.

When we write an integer such as 227 or –63 in a Java program, the number is assumed to be in the decimal (base 10) number system. The digits in the decimal number system are 0, 1, 2, 3, 4, 5, 6, 7, 8 and 9. The lowest digit is 0 and the highest digit is 9—one less than the base of 10. Internally, computers use the binary (base 2) number system. The binary number system has only two digits, namely 0 and 1. Its lowest digit is 0 and its highest digit is 1—one less than the base of 2.

As we will see, binary numbers tend to be much longer than their decimal equivalents. Programmers who work in assembly languages and in high-level languages like Java that enable programmers to reach down to the machine level, find it cumbersome to work with binary numbers. So two other number systems—the octal number system (base 8) and the hexadecimal number system (base 16)—are popular primarily because they make it convenient to abbreviate binary numbers.

In the octal number system, the digits range from 0 to 7. Because both the binary number system and the octal number system have fewer digits than the decimal number system, their digits are the same as the corresponding digits in decimal.

The hexadecimal number system poses a problem because it requires 16 digits—a lowest digit of 0 and a highest digit with a value equivalent to decimal 15 (one less than the base of 16). By convention, we use the letters A through F to represent the hexadecimal digits corresponding to decimal values 10 through 15. Thus in hexadecimal we can have numbers like 876 consisting solely of decimal-like digits, numbers like 8A55F consisting of digits and letters and numbers like FFE consisting solely of letters. Occasionally, a hexadecimal number spells a common word such as FACE or FEED—this can appear strange to programmers accustomed to working with numbers. The digits of the binary, octal, decimal and hexadecimal number systems are summarized in Fig. E.1–Fig. E.2.

Each of these number systems uses positional notation—each position in which a digit is written has a different positional value. For example, in the decimal number 937 (the 9, the 3 and the 7 are referred to as symbol values), we say that the 7 is written in the ones position, the 3 is written in the tens position and the 9 is written in the hundreds position. Note that each of these positions is a power of the base (base 10) and that these powers begin at 0 and increase by 1 as we move left in the number (Fig. E.3).

Binary digit	Octal digit	Decimal digit	Hexadecimal digit
0	0	0	0
1	1	1	1
	2	2	2
	3	3	3
	4	4	4
	5	5	5
	6	6	6
	7	7	7
		8	8
		9	9
			A (decimal value of 10)
			B (decimal value of 11)
			C (decimal value of 12)
			D (decimal value of 13)
			E (decimal value of 14)
			F (decimal value of 15)

Fig. E.1 | Digits of the binary, octal, decimal and hexadecimal number systems.

Attribute	Binary	Octal	Decimal	Hexadecimal
Base	2	8	10	16
Lowest digit	0	0	0	0
Highest digit	1	7	9	F

Fig. E.2 | Comparing the binary, octal, decimal and hexadecimal number systems.

Positional values in the decimal number system			
Decimal digit	9	3	7
Position name	Hundreds	Tens	Ones
Positional value	100	10	1
Positional value as a power of the base (10)	10^2	10^1	10^0

Fig. E.3 | Positional values in the decimal number system.

For longer decimal numbers, the next positions to the left would be the thousands position (10 to the 3rd power), the ten-thousands position (10 to the 4th power), the hundred-thousands position (10 to the 5th power), the millions position (10 to the 6th power), the ten-millions position (10 to the 7th power) and so on.

In the binary number 101, the rightmost 1 is written in the ones position, the 0 is written in the twos position and the leftmost 1 is written in the fours position. Note that each position is a power of the base (base 2) and that these powers begin at 0 and increase by 1 as we move left in the number (Fig. E.4). So, $101 = 2^2 + 2^0 = 4 + 1 = 5$.

For longer binary numbers, the next positions to the left would be the eights position (2 to the 3rd power), the sixteens position (2 to the 4th power), the thirty-twos position (2 to the 5th power), the sixty-fours position (2 to the 6th power) and so on.

In the octal number 425, we say that the 5 is written in the ones position, the 2 is written in the eights position and the 4 is written in the sixty-fours position. Note that each of these positions is a power of the base (base 8) and that these powers begin at 0 and increase by 1 as we move left in the number (Fig. E.5).

For longer octal numbers, the next positions to the left would be the five-hundred-and-twelves position (8 to the 3rd power), the four-thousand-and-ninety-sixes position (8 to the 4th power), the thirty-two-thousand-seven-hundred-and-sixty-eights position (8 to the 5th power) and so on.

In the hexadecimal number 3DA, we say that the A is written in the ones position, the D is written in the sixteens position and the 3 is written in the two-hundred-and-fifty-sixes position. Note that each of these positions is a power of the base (base 16) and that these powers begin at 0 and increase by 1 as we move left in the number (Fig. E.6).

For longer hexadecimal numbers, the next positions to the left would be the four-thousand-and-ninety-sixes position (16 to the 3rd power), the sixty-five-thousand-five-hundred-and-thirty-sixes position (16 to the 4th power) and so on.

Positional values in the binary number system			
Binary digit	1	0	1
Position name	Fours	Twos	Ones
Positional value	4	2	1
Positional value as a power of the base (2)	2^2	2^1	2^0

Fig. E.4 | Positional values in the binary number system.

Positional values in the octal number system			
Decimal digit	4	2	5
Position name	Sixty-fours	Eights	Ones
Positional value	64	8	1
Positional value as a power of the base (8)	8^2	8^1	8^0

Fig. E.5 | Positional values in the octal number system.

Positional values in the hexadecimal number system			
Decimal digit	3	D	A
Position name	Two-hundred-and-fifty-sixes	Sixteens	Ones
Positional value	256	16	1
Positional value as a power of the base (16)	16^2	16^1	16^0

Fig. E.6 | Positional values in the hexadecimal number system.

E.2 Abbreviating Binary Numbers as Octal and Hexadecimal Numbers

The main use for octal and hexadecimal numbers in computing is for abbreviating lengthy binary representations. Figure E.7 highlights the fact that lengthy binary numbers can be expressed concisely in number systems with higher bases than the binary number system.

Decimal number	Binary representation	Octal representation	Hexadecimal representation
0	0	0	0
1	1	1	1
2	10	2	2
3	11	3	3
4	100	4	4
5	101	5	5
6	110	6	6
7	111	7	7
8	1000	10	8
9	1001	11	9
10	1010	12	A
11	1011	13	B
12	1100	14	C
13	1101	15	D
14	1110	16	E
15	1111	17	F
16	10000	20	10

Fig. E.7 | Decimal, binary, octal and hexadecimal equivalents.

A particularly important relationship that both the octal number system and the hexadecimal number system have to the binary system is that the bases of octal and hexadecimal (8 and 16 respectively) are powers of the base of the binary number system (base 2). Consider the following 12-digit binary number and its octal and hexadecimal equivalents. See if you can determine how this relationship makes it convenient to abbreviate binary numbers in octal or hexadecimal. The answer follows the numbers.

Binary number	Octal equivalent	Hexadecimal equivalent
100011010001	4321	8D1

To see how the binary number converts easily to octal, simply break the 12-digit binary number into groups of three consecutive bits each and write those groups over the corresponding digits of the octal number as follows:

100	011	010	001
4	3	2	1

Note that the octal digit you have written under each group of three bits corresponds precisely to the octal equivalent of that 3-digit binary number, as shown in Fig. E.7.

The same kind of relationship can be observed in converting from binary to hexadecimal. Break the 12-digit binary number into groups of four consecutive bits each and write those groups over the corresponding digits of the hexadecimal number as follows:

1000	1101	0001
8	D	1

Notice that the hexadecimal digit you wrote under each group of four bits corresponds precisely to the hexadecimal equivalent of that 4-digit binary number as shown in Fig. E.7.

E.3 Converting Octal and Hexadecimal Numbers to Binary Numbers

In the previous section, we saw how to convert binary numbers to their octal and hexadecimal equivalents by forming groups of binary digits and simply rewriting them as their equivalent octal digit values or hexadecimal digit values. This process may be used in reverse to produce the binary equivalent of a given octal or hexadecimal number.

For example, the octal number 653 is converted to binary simply by writing the 6 as its 3-digit binary equivalent 110, the 5 as its 3-digit binary equivalent 101 and the 3 as its 3-digit binary equivalent 011 to form the 9-digit binary number 110101011.

The hexadecimal number FAD5 is converted to binary simply by writing the F as its 4-digit binary equivalent 1111, the A as its 4-digit binary equivalent 1010, the D as its 4-digit binary equivalent 1101 and the 5 as its 4-digit binary equivalent 0101 to form the 16-digit 1111101011010101.

E.4 Converting from Binary, Octal or Hexadecimal to Decimal

We are accustomed to working in decimal, and therefore it is often convenient to convert a binary, octal, or hexadecimal number to decimal to get a sense of what the number is "really" worth. Our diagrams in Section E.1 express the positional values in decimal. To convert a number to decimal from another base, multiply the decimal equivalent of each digit by its positional value and sum these products. For example, the binary number 110101 is converted to decimal 53, as shown in Fig. E.8.

To convert octal 7614 to decimal 3980, we use the same technique, this time using appropriate octal positional values, as shown in Fig. E.9.

To convert hexadecimal AD3B to decimal 44347, we use the same technique, this time using appropriate hexadecimal positional values, as shown in Fig. E.10.

Converting a binary number to decimal

Postional values:	32	16	8	4	2	1
Symbol values:	1	1	0	1	0	1
Products:	1*32=32	1*16=16	0*8=0	1*4=4	0*2=0	1*1=1
Sum:	= 32 + 16 + 0 + 4 + 0s + 1 = 53					

Fig. E.8 | Converting a binary number to decimal.

Converting an octal number to decimal

Positional values:	512	64	8	1
Symbol values:	7	6	1	4
Products	7*512=3584	6*64=384	1*8=8	4*1=4
Sum:	= 3584 + 384 + 8 + 4 = 3980			

Fig. E.9 | Converting an octal number to decimal.

Converting a hexadecimal number to decimal

Postional values:	4096	256	16	1
Symbol values:	A	D	3	B
Products	A*4096=40960	D*256=3328	3*16=48	B*1=11
Sum:	= 40960 + 3328 + 48 + 11 = 44347			

Fig. E.10 | Converting a hexadecimal number to decimal.

E.5 Converting from Decimal to Binary, Octal or Hexadecimal

The conversions in Section E.4 follow naturally from the positional notation conventions. Converting from decimal to binary, octal, or hexadecimal also follows these conventions.

Suppose we wish to convert decimal 57 to binary. We begin by writing the positional values of the columns right to left until we reach a column whose positional value is greater than the decimal number. We do not need that column, so we discard it. Thus, we first write:

Positional values: 64   32   16   8   4   2   1

Then we discard the column with positional value 64, leaving:

Positional values: 32   16   8   4   2   1

Next we work from the leftmost column to the right. We divide 32 into 57 and observe that there is one 32 in 57 with a remainder of 25, so we write 1 in the 32 column. We divide 16 into 25 and observe that there is one 16 in 25 with a remainder of 9 and write 1 in the 16 column. We divide 8 into 9 and observe that there is one 8 in 9 with a remainder of 1. The next two columns each produce quotients of 0 when their positional values are divided into 1, so we write 0s in the 4 and 2 columns. Finally, 1 into 1 is 1, so we write 1 in the 1 column. This yields:

Positional values: 32   16   8   4   2   1
Symbol values: 1   1   1   0   0   1

and thus decimal 57 is equivalent to binary 111001.

To convert decimal 103 to octal, we begin by writing the positional values of the columns until we reach a column whose positional value is greater than the decimal number. We do not need that column, so we discard it. Thus, we first write:

Positional values: 512   64   8   1

Then we discard the column with positional value 512, yielding:

Positional values: 64   8   1

Next we work from the leftmost column to the right. We divide 64 into 103 and observe that there is one 64 in 103 with a remainder of 39, so we write 1 in the 64 column. We divide 8 into 39 and observe that there are four 8s in 39 with a remainder of 7 and write 4 in the 8 column. Finally, we divide 1 into 7 and observe that there are seven 1s in 7 with no remainder, so we write 7 in the 1 column. This yields:

Positional values: 64   8   1
Symbol values: 1   4   7

and thus decimal 103 is equivalent to octal 147.

To convert decimal 375 to hexadecimal, we begin by writing the positional values of the columns until we reach a column whose positional value is greater than the decimal number. We do not need that column, so we discard it. Thus, we first write:

Positional values: 4096   256   16   1

Then we discard the column with positional value 4096, yielding:

Positional values: 256   16   1

Next we work from the leftmost column to the right. We divide 256 into 375 and observe that there is one 256 in 375 with a remainder of 119, so we write 1 in the 256 column. We divide 16 into 119 and observe that there are seven 16s in 119 with a remainder of 7 and write 7 in the 16 column. Finally, we divide 1 into 7 and observe that there are seven 1s in 7 with no remainder, so we write 7 in the 1 column. This yields:

```
Positional values:   256      16      1
Symbol values:     1        7       7
```

and thus decimal 375 is equivalent to hexadecimal 177.

E.6 Negative Binary Numbers: Two's Complement Notation

The discussion so far in this appendix has focused on positive numbers. In this section, we explain how computers represent negative numbers using *two's complement notation*. First we explain how the two's complement of a binary number is formed, then we show why it represents the negative value of the given binary number.

Consider a machine with 32-bit integers. Suppose

```
int value = 13;
```

The 32-bit representation of value is

```
00000000 00000000 00000000 00001101
```

To form the negative of value we first form its *one's complement* by applying Java's bitwise complement operator (~):

```
onesComplementOfValue = ~value;
```

Internally, ~value is now value with each of its bits reversed—ones become zeros and zeros become ones, as follows:

```
value:
00000000 00000000 00000000 00001101

~value  (i.e., value's ones complement):
11111111 11111111 11111111 11110010
```

To form the two's complement of value, we simply add 1 to value's one's complement. Thus

```
Two's complement of value:
11111111 11111111 11111111 11110011
```

Now if this is in fact equal to –13, we should be able to add it to binary 13 and obtain a result of 0. Let us try this:

```
  00000000 00000000 00000000 00001101
+11111111 11111111 11111111 11110011
-------------------------------------
  00000000 00000000 00000000 00000000
```

The carry bit coming out of the leftmost column is discarded and we indeed get 0 as a result. If we add the one's complement of a number to the number, the result would be all 1s. The key to getting a result of all zeros is that the two's complement is one more than the one's complement. The addition of 1 causes each column to add to 0 with a carry of 1. The carry keeps moving leftward until it is discarded from the leftmost bit, and thus the resulting number is all zeros.

Computers actually perform a subtraction, such as

```
x = a - value;
```

by adding the two's complement of value to a, as follows:

```
x = a + (~value + 1);
```

Suppose a is 27 and value is 13 as before. If the two's complement of value is actually the negative of value, then adding the two's complement of value to a should produce the result 14. Let us try this:

```
a (i.e., 27)          00000000 00000000 00000000 00011011
+(~value + 1)        +11111111 11111111 11111111 11110011
                     ------------------------------------
                      00000000 00000000 00000000 00001110
```

which is indeed equal to 14.

Summary

- An integer such as 19 or 227 or –63 in a Java program is assumed to be in the decimal (base 10) number system. The digits in the decimal number system are 0, 1, 2, 3, 4, 5, 6, 7, 8 and 9. The lowest digit is 0 and the highest digit is 9—one less than the base of 10.
- Internally, computers use the binary (base 2) number system. The binary number system has only two digits, namely 0 and 1. Its lowest digit is 0 and its highest digit is 1—one less than the base of 2.
- The octal number system (base 8) and the hexadecimal number system (base 16) are popular primarily because they make it convenient to abbreviate binary numbers.
- The digits of the octal number system range from 0 to 7.
- The hexadecimal number system poses a problem because it requires 16 digits—a lowest digit of 0 and a highest digit with a value equivalent to decimal 15 (one less than the base of 16). By convention, we use the letters A through F to represent the hexadecimal digits corresponding to decimal values 10 through 15.
- Each number system uses positional notation—each position in which a digit is written has a different positional value.
- A particularly important relationship of both the octal number system and the hexadecimal number system to the binary system is that the bases of octal and hexadecimal (8 and 16 respectively) are powers of the base of the binary number system (base 2).
- To convert an octal to a binary number, replace each octal digit with its three-digit binary equivalent.
- To convert a hexadecimal number to a binary number, simply replace each hexadecimal digit with its four-digit binary equivalent.
- Because we are accustomed to working in decimal, it is convenient to convert a binary, octal or hexadecimal number to decimal to get a sense of the number's "real" worth.
- To convert a number to decimal from another base, multiply the decimal equivalent of each digit by its positional value and sum the products.
- Computers represent negative numbers using two's complement notation.

• To form the negative of a value in binary, first form its one's complement by applying Java's bit-wise complement operator (~). This reverses the bits of the value. To form the two's complement of a value, simply add one to the value's one's complement.

Terminology

base	digit
base 2 number system	hexadecimal number system
base 8 number system	negative value
base 10 number system	octal number system
base 16 number system	one's complement notation
binary number system	positional notation
bitwise complement operator (~)	positional value
conversions	symbol value
decimal number system	two's complement notation

Self-Review Exercises

E.1 The bases of the decimal, binary, octal and hexadecimal number systems are _____, _____, _____ and _____ respectively.

E.2 In general, the decimal, octal and hexadecimal representations of a given binary number contain (more/fewer) digits than the binary number contains.

E.3 (*True/False*) A popular reason for using the decimal number system is that it forms a convenient notation for abbreviating binary numbers simply by substituting one decimal digit per group of four binary bits.

E.4 The (octal / hexadecimal / decimal) representation of a large binary value is the most concise (of the given alternatives).

E.5 (*True/False*) The highest digit in any base is one more than the base.

E.6 (*True/False*) The lowest digit in any base is one less than the base.

E.7 The positional value of the rightmost digit of any number in either binary, octal, decimal or hexadecimal is always _____.

E.8 The positional value of the digit to the left of the rightmost digit of any number in binary, octal, decimal or hexadecimal is always equal to _____.

E.9 Fill in the missing values in this chart of positional values for the rightmost four positions in each of the indicated number systems:

decimal	1000	100	10	1
hexadecimal	...	256	...	...
binary	...	...	...	...
octal	512	...	8	...

E.10 Convert binary 110101011000 to octal and to hexadecimal.

E.11 Convert hexadecimal FACE to binary.

E.12 Convert octal 7316 to binary.

E.13 Convert hexadecimal 4FEC to octal. (*Hint:* First convert 4FEC to binary, then convert that binary number to octal.)

E.14 Convert binary 1101110 to decimal.

E.15   Convert octal 317 to decimal.

E.16   Convert hexadecimal EFD4 to decimal.

E.17   Convert decimal 177 to binary, to octal and to hexadecimal.

E.18   Show the binary representation of decimal 417. Then show the one's complement of 417 and the two's complement of 417.

E.19   What is the result when a number and its two's complement are added to each other?

Answers to Self-Review Exercises

E.1   10, 2, 8, 16.

E.2   Fewer.

E.3   False. Hexadecimal does this.

E.4   Hexadecimal.

E.5   False. The highest digit in any base is one less than the base.

E.6   False. The lowest digit in any base is zero.

E.7   1 (the base raised to the zero power).

E.8   The base of the number system.

E.9   Fill in the missing values in this chart of positional values for the rightmost four positions in each of the indicated number systems:

decimal	1000	100	10	1
hexadecimal	4096	256	16	1
binary	8	4	2	1
octal	512	64	8	1

E.10   Octal 6530; Hexadecimal D58.

E.11   Binary 1111 1010 1100 1110.

E.12   Binary 111 011 001 110.

E.13   Binary 0 100 111 111 101 100; Octal 47754.

E.14   Decimal 2+4+8+32+64=110.

E.15   Decimal 7+1*8+3*64=7+8+192=207.

E.16   Decimal 4+13*16+15*256+14*4096=61396.

E.17   Decimal 177
to binary:

```
256 128 64 32 16 8 4 2 1
128 64 32 16 8 4 2 1
(1*128)+(0*64)+(1*32)+(1*16)+(0*8)+(0*4)+(0*2)+(1*1)
10110001
```

to octal:

```
512 64 8 1
64 8 1
(2*64)+(6*8)+(1*1)
261
```

to hexadecimal:

```
256 16 1
16 1
(11*16)+(1*1)
(B*16)+(1*1)
B1
```

E.18   Binary:

```
512 256 128 64 32 16 8 4 2 1
256 128 64 32 16 8 4 2 1
(1*256)+(1*128)+(0*64)+(1*32)+(0*16)+(0*8)+(0*4)+(0*2)+(1*1)
110100001
```

One's complement: 001011110
Two's complement: 001011111
Check: Original binary number + its two's complement

```
110100001
001011111
---------
000000000
```

E.19   Zero.

Exercises

E.20   Some people argue that many of our calculations would be easier in the base 12 number system because 12 is divisible by so many more numbers than 10 (for base 10). What is the lowest digit in base 12? What would be the highest symbol for the digit in base 12? What are the positional values of the rightmost four positions of any number in the base 12 number system?

E.21   Complete the following chart of positional values for the rightmost four positions in each of the indicated number systems:

	1000	100	10	1
decimal				
base 6	...	...	6	...
base 13	...	169	...	...
base 3	27	...	...	...

E.22   Convert binary 100101111010 to octal and to hexadecimal.

E.23   Convert hexadecimal 3A7D to binary.

E.24   Convert hexadecimal 765F to octal. (*Hint:* First convert 765F to binary, then convert that binary number to octal.)

E.25   Convert binary 1011110 to decimal.

E.26   Convert octal 426 to decimal.

E.27   Convert hexadecimal FFFF to decimal.

E.28   Convert decimal 299 to binary, to octal and to hexadecimal.

E.29   Show the binary representation of decimal 779. Then show the one's complement of 779 and the two's complement of 779.

E.30   Show the two's complement of integer value –1 on a machine with 32-bit integers.

GroupLayout

F.1 Introduction

Java SE 6 includes a powerful new layout manager called GroupLayout, which is the default layout manager in the Netbeans 5.5 IDE (www.netbeans.org). In this appendix, we overview GroupLayout, then demonstrate how to use the Netbeans 5.5 IDE's Matisse GUI designer to create a GUI using GroupLayout to position the components. Netbeans generates the GroupLayout code for you automatically. Though you can write Group-Layout code by hand, in most cases you'll use a GUI design tool like the one provided by Netbeans to take advantage of GroupLayout's power. For more details on GroupLayout, see the list of web resources at the end of this appendix.

F.2 GroupLayout Basics

Chapters 11 and 22 presented several layout managers that provide basic GUI layout capabilities. We also discussed how to combine layout managers and multiple containers to create more complex layouts. Most layout managers do not give you precise control over the positioning of components. In Chapter 22, we discussed the GridBagLayout, which provides more precise control over the position and size of your GUI components. It allows you to specify the horizontal and vertical position of each component, the number of rows and columns each component occupies in the grid, and how components grow and shrink as the size of the container changes. This is all specified at once with a GridBagConstraints object. Class GroupLayout is the next step in layout management. GroupLayout is more flexible, because you can specify the horizontal and vertical layouts of your components independently.

Sequential and Parallel Arrangements

Components are arranged either sequentially or in parallel. The three JButtons in Fig. F.1 are arranged with sequential horizontal orientation—they appear left to right in sequence. Vertically, the components are arranged in parallel, so, in a sense, they "occupy the same vertical space." Components can also be arranged sequentially in the vertical

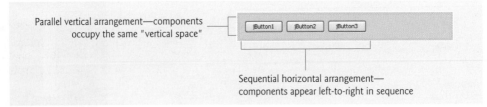

Parallel vertical arrangement—components
occupy the same "vertical space"

Sequential horizontal arrangement—
components appear left-to-right in sequence

Fig. F.1 | JButtons arranged sequentially for their horizontal orientation and in parallel for their vertical orientation.

direction and in parallel in the horizontal direction, as you'll see in Section F.3. To prevent overlapping components, components with parallel vertical orientation are normally arranged with sequential horizontal orientation (and vice versa).

Groups and Alignment

To create more complex user interfaces, GroupLayout allows you to create groups that contain sequential or parallel elements. Within a group you can have GUI components, other groups and gaps. Placing a group within another group is similar to building a GUI using nested containers, such as a JPanel that contains other JPanels, which in turn contain GUI components.

When you create a group, you can specify the alignment of the group's elements. Class GroupLayout contains four constants for this purpose—LEADING, TRAILING, CENTER and BASELINE. The constant BASELINE applies only to vertical orientations. In horizontal orientation, the constants LEADING, TRAILING and CENTER represent left justified, right justified and centered, respectively. In vertical orientation, LEADING, TRAILING and CENTER align the components at their tops, bottoms or vertical centers, respectively. Aligning components with BASELINE indicates they should be aligned using the baseline of the font for the components' text. For more information about font baselines, see Section 12.4.

Spacing

GroupLayout by default uses the recommended GUI design guidelines of the underlying platform for spacing between components. The addGap method of GroupLayout nested classes GroupLayout.Group, GroupLayout.SequentialGroup and GroupLayout.ParallelGroup allows you to control the spacing between components.

Sizing Components

By default, GroupLayout uses each component's getMinimumSize, getMaximumSize and getPreferredSize methods to help determine the component's size. You can override the default settings.

F.3 Building a ColorChooser

We now present a ColorChooser application to demonstrate the GroupLayout layout manager. The application consists of three JSlider objects, each representing the values from 0 to 255 for specifying the red, green and blue values of a color. The selected values for each JSlider will be used to display a filled rectangle of the specified color. We build the application using Netbeans 5.5. For an more detailed introduction to developing GUI applications in the NetBeans IDE, see www.netbeans.org/kb/trails/matisse.html.

Create a New Project

Begin by opening a new NetBeans project. Select **File > New Project....** In the **New Project** dialog, choose **General** from the **Categories** list and **Java Application** from the **Projects** list then click **Next >**. Specify `ColorChooser` as the project name and uncheck the **Create Main Class** checkbox. You can also specify the location of your project in the **Project Location** field. Click **Finish** to create the project.

Add a New Subclass of JFrame to the Project

In the IDE's **Projects** tab just below the **File** menu and toolbar (Fig. F.2), expand the **Source Packages** node. Right-click the `<default package>` node that appears and select **New > JFrame Form**. In the **New JPanel Form** dialog, specify `ColorChooser` as the class name and click **Finish**. This subclass of `JFrame` will display the application's GUI components. The Netbeans window should now appear similar to Fig. F.3 with the `ColorChooser` class shown in **Design** view. The **Source** and **Design** buttons at the top of the `ColorChooser.java` window allow you to switch between editing the source code and designing the GUI.

    Design view shows only the `ColorChooser`'s client area (i.e., the area that will appear inside the window's borders). To build a GUI visually, you can drag GUI components from the **Palette** window onto the client area. You can configure the properties of each component by selecting it, then modifying the property values that appear in the **Properties** window (Fig. F.3). When you select a component, the **Properties** window displays three buttons—**Properties**, **Events** and **Code** (see Fig. F.4)—that enable you to configure various aspects of the component.

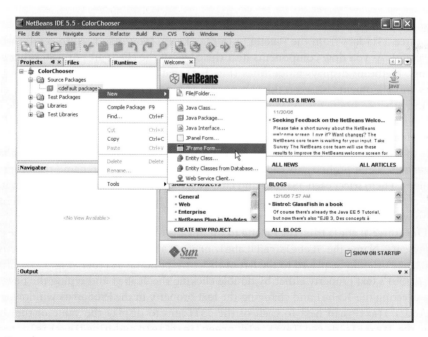

Fig. F.2 | Adding a new **JFrame Form** to the `ColorChooser` project.

Projects tab   ColorChooser.java shown in **Design** view   client area   **Palette** window

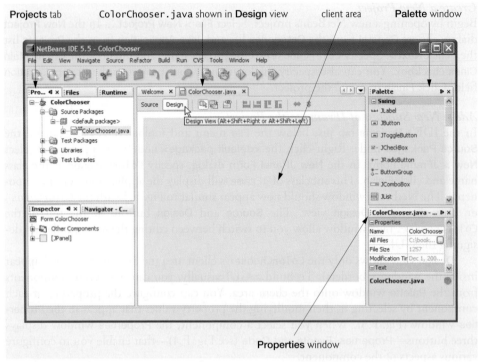

Properties window

Fig. F.3 | Class ColorChooser shown in the Netbeans **Design** view.

Build the GUI

Drag three JSliders from the **Palette** onto the JFrame (you may need to scroll through the **Palette**). As you drag components near the edges of the client area or near other components, Netbeans displays guide lines (Fig. F.4) that show you the recommended distances and alignments between the component you are dragging, the edges of the client area and other components. As you follow the steps to build the GUI, use the guide lines to arrange the components into three rows and three columns as in Fig. F.5. Use the **Properties** window to rename the JSliders to redJSlider, greenJSlider and blueJSlider. Select the first JSlider, then click the **Code** button in the **Properties** window and change the **Variable Name** property to redSlider. Repeat this process to rename the other two JSliders. Then, select each JSlider and change its maximum property to 255 so that it will produce values in the range 0–255, and change its value property to 0 so the JSlider's thumb will initially be at the left of the JSlider.

Drag three JLabels from the **Palette** to the JFrame to label each JSlider with the color it represents. Name the JLabels redJLabel, greenJLabel and blueJLabel, respectively. Each JLabel should be placed to the left of the corresponding JSlider (Fig. F.5). Change each JLabel's **text** property either by double clicking the JLabel and typing the new text, or by selecting the JLabel and changing the **text** property in the **Properties** window.

Add a JTextField next to each of the JSliders to display the value of the slider. Name the JTextFields redJTextField, greenJTextField and blueJTextField, respectively. Change each JTextField's **text** property to 0 using the same techniques as you did for the JLabels. Change each JTextField's **columns** property to 4.

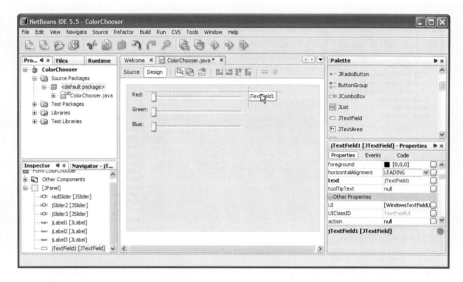

Fig. F.4 | Positioning the first `JTextField`.

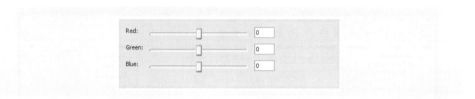

Fig. F.5 | Layout of the `JLabels`, `JSliders` and `JTextFields`.

Double click the border of the client area to display the **Set Form Designer Size** dialog and change the first number (which represents the width) to 410, then click **OK**. This makes the client area wide enough to accommodate the `JPanel` you'll add next. Finally, add a `JPanel` named `colorJPanel` to the right of this group of components. Use the guide lines as shown in Fig. F.6 to place the `JPanel`. Change this `JPanel`'s background color to display the selected color. Finally, drag the bottom border of the client area toward the top of the **Design** area until you see the snap-to line that shows the recommended height of the client area (based on the components in the client area) as shown in Fig. F.7.

Editing the Source Code and Adding Event Handlers

The IDE automatically generated the GUI code, including methods for initializing components and aligning them using the `GroupLayout` layout manager. We must add the desired functionality to the components' event handlers. To add an event handler for a component, right click it and position the mouse over the **Events** option in the pop-up menu. You can then select the category of event you wish to handle and the specific event within that category. For example, to add the `JSlider` event handlers for this example, right click each `JSlider` and select **Events > Change > stateChanged**. When you do this, Netbeans adds a `ChangeListener` to the `JSlider` and switches from **Design** view to **Source** view where you can place code in the event handler. Use the **Design** button to return to **Design**

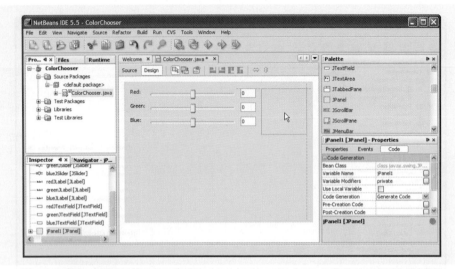

Fig. F.6 | Positioning the JPanel.

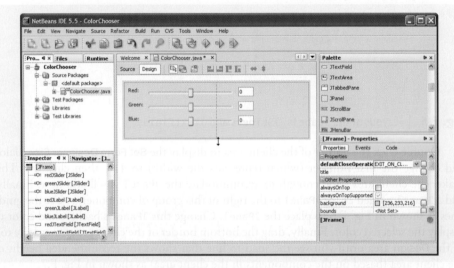

Fig. F.7 | Setting the height of the client area.

view and repeat the preceding steps to add the event handlers for the other two JSliders. To complete the event handlers, first add the method in Fig. F.8. In each JSlider event handler set the corresponding JTextField to the new value of the JSlider, then call method changeColor. Finally, in the constructor after the call to initComponents, add the line

```
colorJPanel.setBackground( java.awt.Color.BLACK );
```

Figure F.9 shows the completed ColorChooser class exactly as it is generated in Netbeans "in the raw." More and more software development is done with tools that generate complex code like this, saving you the time and effort of doing it yourself..

```
 1   // changes the colorJPanel's background color based on the current
 2   // values of the JSliders
 3   public void changeColor()
 4   {
 5      colorJPanel.setBackground( new java.awt.Color(
 6         redJSlider.getValue(), greenJSlider.getValue(),
 7         blueJSlider.getValue() ) );
 8   } // end method changeColor
```

Fig. F.8 | Method that changes the colorJPanel's background color based on the values of the three JSliders.

```
 1   /*
 2    * ColorChooser.java
 3    *
 4    * Created on December 2, 2006, 9:25 AM
 5    */
 6
 7   /**
 8    *
 9    * @author  paul
10    */
11   public class ColorChooser extends javax.swing.JFrame
12   {
13
14      /** Creates new form ColorChooser */
15      public ColorChooser()
16      {
17         initComponents();
18         colorJPanel.setBackground( java.awt.Color.BLACK );
19      }
20
21      // changes the colorJPanel's background color based on the current
22      // values of the JSliders
23      public void changeColor()
24      {
25         colorJPanel.setBackground( new java.awt.Color(
26            redJSlider.getValue(), greenJSlider.getValue(),
27            blueJSlider.getValue() ) );
28      } // end method changeColor
29
30      /** This method is called from within the constructor to
31       * initialize the form.
32       * WARNING: Do NOT modify this code. The content of this method is
33       * always regenerated by the Form Editor.
34       */
35      // <editor-fold defaultstate="collapsed" desc=" Generated
36      private void initComponents()
37      {
38         redJSlider = new javax.swing.JSlider();
39         greenJSlider = new javax.swing.JSlider();
```

Fig. F.9 | ColorChooser class that uses GroupLayout for its GUI layout. (Part 1 of 6.)

```
40        blueJSlider = new javax.swing.JSlider();
41        redJLabel = new javax.swing.JLabel();
42        greenJLabel = new javax.swing.JLabel();
43        blueJLabel = new javax.swing.JLabel();
44        redJTextField = new javax.swing.JTextField();
45        greenJTextField = new javax.swing.JTextField();
46        blueJTextField = new javax.swing.JTextField();
47        colorJPanel = new javax.swing.JPanel();
48
49        setDefaultCloseOperation(javax.swing.WindowConstants.EXIT_ON_CLOSE);
50        redJSlider.setMaximum(255);
51        redJSlider.setValue(0);
52        redJSlider.addChangeListener(new javax.swing.event.ChangeListener()
53        {
54           public void stateChanged(javax.swing.event.ChangeEvent evt)
55           {
56              redJSliderStateChanged(evt);
57           }
58        });
59
60        greenJSlider.setMaximum(255);
61        greenJSlider.setValue(0);
62        greenJSlider.addChangeListener(
new javax.swing.event.ChangeListener()
63        {
64           public void stateChanged(javax.swing.event.ChangeEvent evt)
65           {
66              greenJSliderStateChanged(evt);
67           }
68        });
69
70        blueJSlider.setMaximum(255);
71        blueJSlider.setValue(0);
72        blueJSlider.addChangeListener(new javax.swing.event.ChangeListener()
73        {
74           public void stateChanged(javax.swing.event.ChangeEvent evt)
75           {
76              blueJSliderStateChanged(evt);
77           }
78        });
79
80        redJLabel.setText("Red:");
81
82        greenJLabel.setText("Green:");
83
84        blueJLabel.setText("Blue:");
85
86        redJTextField.setColumns(4);
87        redJTextField.setText("0");
88
89        greenJTextField.setColumns(4);
90        greenJTextField.setText("0");
91
```

Fig. F.9 | ColorChooser class that uses GroupLayout for its GUI layout. (Part 2 of 6.)

```
92          blueJTextField.setColumns(4);
93          blueJTextField.setText("0");
94
95          javax.swing.GroupLayout colorJPanelLayout =
new javax.swing.GroupLayout(colorJPanel);
96          colorJPanel.setLayout(colorJPanelLayout);
97          colorJPanelLayout.setHorizontalGroup(
98             colorJPanelLayout.createParallelGroup(
javax.swing.GroupLayout.Alignment.LEADING)
99             .addGap(0, 100, Short.MAX_VALUE)
100         );
101         colorJPanelLayout.setVerticalGroup(
102            colorJPanelLayout.createParallelGroup(
javax.swing.GroupLayout.Alignment.LEADING)
103            .addGap(0, 100, Short.MAX_VALUE)
104         );
105
106         javax.swing.GroupLayout layout = new
javax.swing.GroupLayout(getContentPane());
107         getContentPane().setLayout(layout);
108         layout.setHorizontalGroup(
109            layout.createParallelGroup(
javax.swing.GroupLayout.Alignment.LEADING)
110            .addGroup(layout.createSequentialGroup()
111               .addContainerGap()
112               .addGroup(layout.createParallelGroup(
javax.swing.GroupLayout.Alignment.LEADING)
113                  .addComponent(greenJLabel)
114                  .addComponent(blueJLabel)
115                  .addComponent(redJLabel))
116               .addPreferredGap(
javax.swing.LayoutStyle.ComponentPlacement.RELATED)
117               .addGroup(layout.createParallelGroup(
javax.swing.GroupLayout.Alignment.LEADING)
118                  .addGroup(layout.createSequentialGroup()
119                     .addComponent(blueJSlider,
javax.swing.GroupLayout.PREFERRED_SIZE, javax.swing.GroupLayout.DEFAULT_SIZE,
javax.swing.GroupLayout.PREFERRED_SIZE)
120                     .addPreferredGap(
javax.swing.LayoutStyle.ComponentPlacement.RELATED)
121                     .addComponent(blueJTextField,
javax.swing.GroupLayout.PREFERRED_SIZE, javax.swing.GroupLayout.DEFAULT_SIZE,
javax.swing.GroupLayout.PREFERRED_SIZE))
122                  .addGroup(layout.createSequentialGroup()
123                     .addComponent(greenJSlider,
javax.swing.GroupLayout.PREFERRED_SIZE, javax.swing.GroupLayout.DEFAULT_SIZE,
javax.swing.GroupLayout.PREFERRED_SIZE)
124
.addPreferredGap(javax.swing.LayoutStyle.ComponentPlacement.RELATED)
125                     .addComponent(greenJTextField,
javax.swing.GroupLayout.PREFERRED_SIZE, javax.swing.GroupLayout.DEFAULT_SIZE,
javax.swing.GroupLayout.PREFERRED_SIZE))
126                  .addGroup(layout.createSequentialGroup()
```

Fig. F.9 | ColorChooser class that uses GroupLayout for its GUI layout. (Part 3 of 6.)

```
127                        .addComponent(redJSlider,
javax.swing.GroupLayout.PREFERRED_SIZE, javax.swing.GroupLayout.DEFAULT_SIZE,
javax.swing.GroupLayout.PREFERRED_SIZE)
128
.addPreferredGap(javax.swing.LayoutStyle.ComponentPlacement.RELATED)
129                        .addComponent(redJTextField,
javax.swing.GroupLayout.PREFERRED_SIZE, javax.swing.GroupLayout.DEFAULT_SIZE,
javax.swing.GroupLayout.PREFERRED_SIZE)))
130             .addPreferredGap(
javax.swing.LayoutStyle.ComponentPlacement.RELATED, 9, Short.MAX_VALUE)
131             .addComponent(colorJPanel,
javax.swing.GroupLayout.PREFERRED_SIZE, javax.swing.GroupLayout.DEFAULT_SIZE,
javax.swing.GroupLayout.PREFERRED_SIZE)
132             .addContainerGap())
133        );
134      layout.setVerticalGroup(
135         layout.createParallelGroup(
javax.swing.GroupLayout.Alignment.LEADING)
136            .addGroup(layout.createSequentialGroup()
137            .addContainerGap()
138            .addGroup(layout.createParallelGroup(
javax.swing.GroupLayout.Alignment.LEADING)
139                .addComponent(colorJPanel,
javax.swing.GroupLayout.PREFERRED_SIZE, javax.swing.GroupLayout.DEFAULT_SIZE,
javax.swing.GroupLayout.PREFERRED_SIZE)
140                .addGroup(layout.createSequentialGroup()
141                    .addGroup(layout.createParallelGroup(
javax.swing.GroupLayout.Alignment.LEADING)
142                        .addComponent(redJSlider,
javax.swing.GroupLayout.PREFERRED_SIZE, javax.swing.GroupLayout.DEFAULT_SIZE,
javax.swing.GroupLayout.PREFERRED_SIZE)
143                        .addComponent(redJTextField,
javax.swing.GroupLayout.PREFERRED_SIZE, javax.swing.GroupLayout.DEFAULT_SIZE,
javax.swing.GroupLayout.PREFERRED_SIZE)
144                        .addComponent(redJLabel))
145                    .addPreferredGap(
javax.swing.LayoutStyle.ComponentPlacement.RELATED)
146                    .addGroup(layout.createParallelGroup(
javax.swing.GroupLayout.Alignment.LEADING)
147                        .addGroup(layout.createSequentialGroup()
148                            .addGroup(layout.createParallelGroup(
javax.swing.GroupLayout.Alignment.LEADING)
149                                .addComponent(greenJLabel)
150                                .addComponent(greenJSlider,
javax.swing.GroupLayout.PREFERRED_SIZE, javax.swing.GroupLayout.DEFAULT_SIZE,
javax.swing.GroupLayout.PREFERRED_SIZE))
151                            .addPreferredGap(
javax.swing.LayoutStyle.ComponentPlacement.RELATED)
152                            .addGroup(
layout.createParallelGroup(javax.swing.GroupLayout.Alignment.LEADING)
153                                .addComponent(blueJLabel)
154                                .addGroup(layout.createParallelGroup(
javax.swing.GroupLayout.Alignment.TRAILING)
```

Fig. F.9 | ColorChooser class that uses GroupLayout for its GUI layout. (Part 4 of 6.)

```
155                           .addComponent(blueJTextField,
javax.swing.GroupLayout.PREFERRED_SIZE, javax.swing.GroupLayout.DEFAULT_SIZE,
javax.swing.GroupLayout.PREFERRED_SIZE)
156                           .addComponent(blueJSlider,
javax.swing.GroupLayout.PREFERRED_SIZE, javax.swing.GroupLayout.DEFAULT_SIZE,
javax.swing.GroupLayout.PREFERRED_SIZE))))
157                     .addComponent(greenJTextField,
javax.swing.GroupLayout.PREFERRED_SIZE, javax.swing.GroupLayout.DEFAULT_SIZE,
javax.swing.GroupLayout.PREFERRED_SIZE))))
158             .addContainerGap(javax.swing.GroupLayout.DEFAULT_SIZE,
Short.MAX_VALUE))
159       );
160       pack();
161    }// </editor-fold>
162
163    private void blueJSliderStateChanged(javax.swing.event.ChangeEvent evt)
164    {
165       blueJTextField.setText( "" + blueJSlider.getValue() );
166       changeColor();
167    }
168
169    private void greenJSliderStateChanged(
javax.swing.event.ChangeEvent evt)
170    {
171       greenJTextField.setText( "" + greenJSlider.getValue() );
172       changeColor();
173    }
174
175    private void redJSliderStateChanged(
javax.swing.event.ChangeEvent evt)
176    {
177       redJTextField.setText( "" + redJSlider.getValue() );
178       changeColor();
179    }
180
181    /**
182     * @param args the command line arguments
183     */
184    public static void main(String args[])
185    {
186       java.awt.EventQueue.invokeLater(new Runnable()
187       {
188          public void run()
189          {
190             new ColorChooser().setVisible(true);
191          }
192       });
193    }
194
195    // Variables declaration - do not modify
196    private javax.swing.JLabel blueJLabel;
197    private javax.swing.JSlider blueJSlider;
198    private javax.swing.JTextField blueJTextField;
```

Fig. F.9 | ColorChooser class that uses GroupLayout for its GUI layout. (Part 5 of 6.)

```
199    private javax.swing.JPanel colorJPanel;
200    private javax.swing.JLabel greenJLabel;
201    private javax.swing.JSlider greenJSlider;
202    private javax.swing.JTextField greenJTextField;
203    private javax.swing.JLabel redJLabel;
204    private javax.swing.JSlider redJSlider;
205    private javax.swing.JTextField redJTextField;
206    // End of variables declaration
207
208 }
```

Fig. F.9 | ColorChooser class that uses GroupLayout for its GUI layout. (Part 6 of 6.)

Method initComponents (lines 36–161) was entirely generated by Netbeans based on your interactions with the GUI designer. This method contains the code that creates and formats the GUI. Lines 38–93 construct and initialize the GUI components. Lines 95–161 specify the layout of those components using GroupLayout. Lines 108–133 specify the horizontal group and lines 134–159 specify the vertical group.

We manually added the statement that changes the colorJPanel's background color in line 18 and the changeColor method in lines 23–28. When the user moves the thumb on one of the JSliders, the JSlider's event handler sets the text in its corresponding JTextField to the JSlider's new value (lines 165, 171 and 177), then calls method changeColor (lines 166, 172 and 178) to update the colorJPanel's background color. Method changeColor gets the current value of each JSlider (lines 26–27) and uses these values as the arguments to the Color constructor to create a new Color.

F.4 GroupLayout Web Resources

weblogs.java.net/blog/tpavek/archive/2006/02/getting_to_know_1.html
Part 1 of Tomas Pavek's GroupLayout blog post overviews GroupLayout theory behind.

weblogs.java.net/blog/tpavek/archive/2006/03/getting_to_know.html
Part 2 of Tomas Pavek's GroupLayout blog post presents a complete GUI implemented with Group-Layout.

java.sun.com/javase/jdk6/docs/api/javax/swing/GroupLayout.html
API documentation for class GroupLayout.

`wiki.java.net/bin/view/Javadesktop/GroupLayoutExample`

Provides an Address Book demo of a GUI built manually with `GroupLayout` with source code.

`java.sun.com/developer/technicalArticles/Interviews/violet_pavek_qa.html`

Article: "The Next Wave of GUIs: Project Matisse and NetBeans IDE 5.0," by Roman Strobl.

`www.netbeans.org/kb/50/quickstart-gui.html`

Tutorial: "GUI Building in NetBeans 5.0," by Talley Mulligan. A walkthrough of building GUI applications in Netbeans.

`testwww.netbeans.org/kb/41/flash-matisse.html`

Flash demo of the Netbeans Matisse GUI designer, which uses `GroupLayout` to arrange components.

`weblogs.java.net/blog/claudio/archive/nb-layouts.html`

Flash-based `GroupLayout` Tutorial.

`www.developer.com/java/ent/article.php/3589961`

Tutorial: "Building Java GUIs with Matisse: A Gentle Introduction," by Dick Wall.

`myeclipseide.com/enterpriseworkbench/help/index.jsp?`
`topic=/com.genuitec.eclipse.dehory.doc/doc/quickstart/index.html`

Tutorial: "Matisse4MyEclipse—Swing RCP Development Quickstart," from MyEclipse. Introduces a version of the Matisse GUI designer for the Eclipse IDE.

Java Desktop Integration Components (JDIC)

G.1 Introduction

The Java Desktop Integration Components (JDIC) are part of an open-source project aimed at allowing better integration between Java applications and the platforms on which they execute. Some JDIC features include:

- interacting with the underlying platform to launch native applications (such as web browsers and email clients)
- displaying a splash screen when an application begins execution to indicate to the user that the application is loading
- creating icons in the system tray (also called the taskbar status area or notification area) to provide access to Java applications running in the background
- registering file-type associations, so that files of specified types will automatically open in corresponding Java applications
- creating installer packages, and more.

The JDIC homepage (jdic.dev.java.net/) includes an introduction to JDIC, downloads, documentation, FAQs, demos, articles, blogs, announcements, incubator projects, a developer's page, forums, mailing lists, and more. Java SE 6 now includes some of the features mentioned above. We discuss several of these features here.

G.2 Splash Screens

Java application users often perceive a performance problem, because nothing appears on the screen when you first launch an application. One way to show a user that your program is loading is to display a splash screen—a borderless window that appears temporarily while an application loads. Java SE 6 provides the new command-line option -splash for the java command to accomplish this task. This option enables you to specify a PNG, GIF ot JPG image that should display when your application begins loading. To demonstrate this new option, we created a program (Fig. G.1) that sleeps for 5 seconds (so you can view the splash screen) then displays a message at the command line. The directory for this example includes a PNG format image to use as the splash screen. To display the splash screen when this application loads, use the command

```
java -splash:DeitelBug.png SplashDemo
```

```
 1   // Fig. G.1: SplashDemo.java
 2   // Splash screen demonstration.
 3   public class SplashDemo
 4   {
 5      public static void main( String[] args )
 6      {
 7         try
 8         {
 9            Thread.sleep( 5000 );
10         } // end try
11         catch ( InterruptedException e )
12         {
13            e.printStackTrace();
14         } // end catch
15
16         System.out.println(
17            "This was the splash screen demo." );
18      } // end method main
19   } // end class SplashDemo
```

Fig. G.1 | Spash screen displayed with the -splash option to the java command.

Once you've initiated the splash screen display, you can interact with it programmatically via the `SplashScreen` class of the java.awt package. You might do this to add some dynamic content to the splash screen. For more information on working with splash screens, see the following sites:

```
java.sun.com/developer/technicalArticles/J2SE/Desktop/javase6/
    splashscreen/
java.sun.com/javase/6/docs/api/java/awt/SplashScreen.html
```

G.3 Desktop Class

Java SE 6's new `Desktop` class enables you to specify a file or URI that you'd like to open using the underlying platform's appropriate application. For example, if Firefox is your computer's default browser, you can use the `Desktop` class's browse method to open a web site in Firefox. In addition, you can open an email composition window in your system's default email client, open a file in its associated application and print a file using the associated application's print command. Figure G.2 demonstrates the first three of these capabilities.

The event handler at lines 22–52 obtains the index number of the task the user selects in the `tasksJComboBox` (line 25) and the `String` that represents the file or URI to process (line 26). Line 28 uses `Desktop static` method `isDesktopSupported` to determine whether class `Desktop`'s features are supported on the platform on which this application runs. If they are, line 32 uses `Desktop static` method `getDesktop`, to obtain a `Desktop` object. If the user selected the option to open the default browser, line 37 creates a new `URI` object using the `String` input as the site to display in the browser, then passes the `URI` object to `Desktop` method `browse` which invokes the system's default browser and passes the `URI` to the browser for display. If the user selects the option to open a file in its associated program, line 40 creates a new `File` object using the `String` input as the file to open, then passes the `File` object to `Desktop` method `open` which passes the file to the appropriate application to open the file. Finally, if the user selects the option to compose an email, line 43 creates a new `URI` object using the `String` input as the email address to which the email will be sent, then passes the `URI` object to `Desktop` method `mail` which invokes the system's default email client and passes the `URI` to the email client as the email recipient. You can learn more about class `Desktop` at

```
java.sun.com/javase/6/docs/api/java/awt/Desktop.html
```

```
1   // Fig. G.2: DesktopDemo.java
2   // Use Desktop to launch default browser, open a file in its associated
3   // application and compose an email in the default email client.
4   import java.awt.Desktop;
5   import java.io.File;
6   import java.io.IOException;
7   import java.net.URI;
8
```

Fig. G.2 | Use `Desktop` to launch the default browser, open a file in its associated application and compose an email in the default email client. (Part 1 of 3.)

```
 9    public class DesktopDemo extends javax.swing.JFrame
10    {
11       // constructor
12       public DesktopDemo()
13       {
14          initComponents();
15       } // end DesktopDemo constructor
16
17       // To save space, lines 20-84 of the Netbeans autogenerated GUI code
18       // are not shown here. The complete code for this example is located in
19       // the file DesktopDemo.java in this example's directory.
20
21       // determine selected task and perform the task
22       private void doTaskJButtonActionPerformed(
23          java.awt.event.ActionEvent evt)
24       {
25          int index = tasksJComboBox.getSelectedIndex();
26          String input = inputJTextField.getText();
27
28          if ( Desktop.isDesktopSupported() )
29          {
30             try
31             {
32                Desktop desktop = Desktop.getDesktop();
33
34                switch ( index )
35                {
36                   case 0: // open browser
37                      desktop.browse( new URI( input ) );
38                      break;
39                   case 1: // open file
40                      desktop.open( new File( input ) );
41                      break;
42                   case 2: // open email composition window
43                      desktop.mail( new URI( input ) );
44                      break;
45                } // end switch
46             } // end try
47             catch ( Exception e )
48             {
49                e.printStackTrace();
50             } // end catch
51          } // end if
52       } // end method doTaskJButtonActionPerformed
53
54       public static void main(String args[])
55       {
56          java.awt.EventQueue.invokeLater(
57             new Runnable()
58             {
```

Fig. G.2 | Use Desktop to launch the default browser, open a file in its associated application and compose an email in the default email client. (Part 2 of 3.)

```
59              public void run()
60              {
61                  new DesktopDemo().setVisible(true);
62              }
63          }
64      );
65  } // end method main
66
67  // Variables declaration - do not modify
68  private javax.swing.JButton doTaskJButton;
69  private javax.swing.JLabel inputJLabel;
70  private javax.swing.JTextField inputJTextField;
71  private javax.swing.JLabel instructionLabel;
72  private javax.swing.JComboBox tasksJComboBox;
73  // End of variables declaration
74  }
```

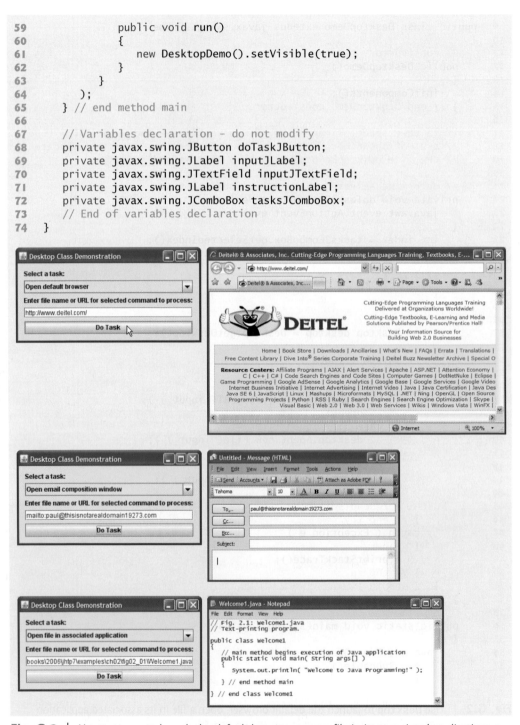

Fig. G.2 | Use `Desktop` to launch the default browser, open a file in its associated application and compose an email in the default email client. (Part 3 of 3.)

G.4 Tray Icons

Tray icons generally appear in your system's system tray, taskbar status area or notification area. They typically provide quick access to applications that are executing in the background on your system. When you position the mouse over one of these icons, a tooltip appears indicating what application the icon represents. If you click the icon, a popup menu appears with options for that application.

Classes `SystemTray` and `TrayIcon` (both from package `java.awt`) enable you to create and manage your own tray icons in a platform independent manner. Class `SystemTray` provides access to the underlying platform's system tray—the class consists of three methods:

- static method `getDefaultSystemTray` returns the system tray
- method `addTrayIcon` adds a new `TrayIcon` to the system tray
- method `removeTrayIcon` removes an icon from the system tray

Class `TrayIcon` consists of several methods allowing users to specify an icon, a tooltip and a pop-up menu for the icon. In addition, tray icons support `ActionListeners`, `MouseListeners` and `MouseMotionListeners`. You can learn more about classes `SystemTray` and `TrayIcon` at

```
java.sun.com/javase/6/docs/api/java/awt/SystemTray.html
java.sun.com/javase/6/docs/api/java/awt/TrayIcon.html
```

G.5 JDIC Incubator Projects

The JDIC Incubator Projects are developed, maintained and owned by members of the Java community. These projects are associated with, but not distributed with, JDIC. The Incubator Projects may eventually become part of the JDIC project once they have been fully developed and meet certain criteria. For more information about the Incubator Projects and to learn how you can setup an Incubator Project, visit

```
jdic.dev.java.net/#incubator
```

Current Incubator Projects include:

- FileUtil—A file utility API that extends the java.io.File class.
- Floating Dock Top-level Window—A Java API for developing a floating dock toplevel window.
- Icon Service—Returns a Java icon object from a native icon specification.
- Misc API —Hosts simple (one method, one class type of) APIs.
- Music Player Control API—Java API that controls native music players.
- SaverBeans Screensaver SDK—Java screensaver development kit.
- SystemInfo—Checks the system information.

G.6 JDIC Demos

The JDIC site includes demos for FileExplorer, the browser package, the TrayIcon package, the Floating Dock class and the Wallpaper API (`jdic.dev.java.net/#demos`). The source code for these demos is included in the JDIC download (`jdic.dev.java.net/servlets/ ProjectDocumentList`). For more demos, check out some of the incubator projects.

Mashups

Introduction

Building web application mashups is one of the signature topics of Web 2.0. The term mashup originated in the music world—a music mashup is a remix of two or more songs to create a new song. You can listen to some music mashups at www.ccmixter.org/. A web application mashup combines complementary functionality, usually accessed via web services (Chapter 28) and RSS feeds (www.deitel.com/rss and www.rssbus.com) from multiple web sites. You can create innovative and powerful Web 2.0 mashup applications much faster than if you have to write your applications from scratch. For example, www.housingmaps.com combines Craigslist apartment listings with Google Maps to display on a map all of the apartments for rent in a neighborhood.

Popular Mashups

Figure H.1 shows some popular mashups.

URL	APIs	Description
Popular Google Maps Mashups:		
www.mappr.com/	Google Maps, FlickR	Find photos of sites across the US.
www.housingmaps.com/	Google Maps, Craigslist	Find available apartments and homes by neighborhood. Includes prices, pictures, the address and rental-agent contact information.
www.broadwayzone.com/	Google Maps	Find the locations of theaters in New York City and the shows playing at each theater. Links to details about the show, ticket information and subway directions.

Fig. H.1 | Popular mashups. (Part 1 of 2.)

URL	APIs	Description
www.cribseek.com	Google Maps	Maps with properties for sale.
www.shackprices.com/	Google Maps	Find the approximate value of your home based on recent home sales in your area.
www.mashmap.com/	Google Maps	Click on a theater on the map to find movies and show times.
paul.kedrosky.com/ publicloos/	Google Maps	Find public restrooms in San Francisco. Includes the address, a rating and comments about each restroom.
Other Popular Mashups:		
www.doubletrust.net	Yahoo! Search, Google Search	Combines Yahoo! and Google search results into one page.
api.local.yahoo.com/eb/	Yahoo! Maps	Find the location of events (by date) in a geographical area.
www.csthota.com/geotagr	Microsoft Virtual Earth	Store and browse photos by geographic location.
www.kokogiak.com/ amazon4/default.asp	Amazon Web Services	Add Amazon items to your wish list, put the link to a book into your blog on Blogger, add a link to your del.icio.us bookmarks or look for the book in your local library.

Fig. H.1 | Popular mashups. (Part 2 of 2.)

Now that you've read most of *Java How to Program, 7/e*, you're probably familiar with API categories including graphics, GUI, collections, multimedia, databases and many more. Nearly all of these provide enhanced *computing functionality*. Many web services APIs provide *business functionality*—eBay provides auction capabilities, Amazon provides book sales (and sales of other types of products, such as CDs, DVDs, electronic devices, and more), Google provides search capabilities, PayPal provides payment services, etc. These web services are typically free for non-commercial use; some impose (generally reasonable) fees for commercial use. This creates exciting possibilities for people building Internet-based applications and businesses.

APIs Commonly Used in Mashups

We have emphasized the importance of software reuse. Mashups are yet another form of software reuse that saves you time, money and effort—you can rapidly prototype starter versions of your applications, integrate business functionality, integrate search functionality and more. Figure H.2 shows some APIs commonly used in mashups.

API source	URL	Functionality
Google Maps	`www.google.com/apis/maps/`	Maps
Yahoo! Maps	`developer.yahoo.net/maps/`	Maps
Microsoft Virtual Earth	`virtualearth.msn.com/`	Local search, maps
Amazon	`aws.amazon.com/`	E-commerce
TypePad ATOM	`www.sixapart.com/pronet/docs/typepad_atom_api`	Blogging
Blogger ATOM feed	`code.blogspot.com/`	Blogging
Flickr	`developer.yahoo.net/flickr/index.html`	Photo sharing
YouTube	`www.youtube.com/dev`	Video sharing
PayPal	`developer.paypal.com/`	Payments
del.icio.us	`del.icio.us/help/api/`	Social bookmarking
Backpack	`backpackit.com/`	Event scheduling
Dropcash	`www.dropcash.com/`	Fundraising organizer
Upcoming.org	`upcoming.org/services/api/`	Syndicate event listings
Google AdWords	`www.google.com/apis/adwords/`	Manage Google AdWords advertising programs
eBay	`developer.ebay.com/common/api`	Auctions
SalesForce	`www.salesforce.com/developer/`	Customer Relationship Management (CRM)
Technorati	`developers.technorati.com/wiki/TechnoratiApi`	Blog search

Fig. H.2 | APIs commonly used to make mashups.

Deitel Mashups Research Center

Our Mashups Resource Center, which is located at

> `www.deitel.com/mashups/MashUpsResourceCenter.html`

focuses on the enormous amount of free mashup content available online. You'll find tutorials, articles, documentation, the latest books, articles, blogs, directories, tools, forums, etc., that will help you quickly develop mashup applications.

- Check out the newest and most popular mashups, including scores of Google Maps-based mashups showing you the locations of theaters, real estate for sale or rent, properties that have sold in your area, and even the locations of the public restrooms in San Francisco!

- Search ProgrammableWeb for mashups by category.

- Check out the Flickr APIs for adding photos to your applications, updating photos, replacing photos, example requests, and asynchronous uploading.

- Check out the article: "Building Mashups for Non-Programmers."

- Check out the Smashforce tool that enables Salesforce.com users to mashup applications such as Google Maps with their Multiforce and Sforce enterprise applications.

- Find mashup sites such as ProgrammableWeb, Givezilla, Podbop, and Strmz.

- Check out IBM's Enterprise Mashup Tool.

- Check out the search and mapping APIs from Microsoft, Yahoo! and Google that you can use in your mashup applications.

- Use Technorati APIs to find all of the blogs that link to a specific web site, search blogs for mentions of keywords, see which blogs are linked to a given blog and find blogs associated with a specific web site.

- Use the Backpack API to help organize tasks and events, plan your schedule, collaborate with others, monitor your competitors online and more.

Deitel RSS Resource Center

RSS feeds are also popular information sources for mashups. To learn more about RSS feeds, visit our RSS Resource Center at `www.deitel.com/RSS/`. Each week, we announce the latest Resource Center(s) in our free e-mail newsletter, the *Deitel Buzz Online*:

> `www.deitel.com/newsletter/subscribe.html`

Please send suggestions for additional Resource Centers and improvements to existing Resource Centers to `deitel@deitel.com`. Thanks!

Mashup Performance and Reliability Issues

There are several challenges when creating mashup applications. Your applications become susceptible to traffic and reliability problems on the Internet—circumstances generally beyond your control. Companies might suddenly change APIs that your applications use. Your application is dependent on hardware and software capabilities of other companies. Also, companies could impose fee structures on previously free web services or could increase existing fees.

Mashup Tutorials

This and the next several sections list extensive mashups resources from our Mashups Resource Center. Once you've mastered web services in Chapter 28, you should find building mashups straightforward. For each API you'd like to use, just visit the corresponding site, register and get your access key (if one is required), check out their sample implementations, and be sure to honor their "terms of service" agreements.

`www.programmableweb.com/howto`

Tutorial: "How to Make Your Own Web Mashup," from Programmableweb.com, is a 5-step tutorial for making a mashup. Topics include selecting a subject, finding your data, weighing your coding skills, signing up for an API, and starting to code. Includes a list of available APIs.

`blogs.msdn.com/jhawk/archive/2006/03/26/561658.aspx`

Tutorial: "Building a Mashup of National Parks Using the Atlas Virtual Earth Map Control," by Jonathan Hawkins, shows you how to display pushpins on a Microsoft Virtual Earth map. Includes a brief tour of the application and a step-by-step guide to build this application (includes C# code).

www-128.ibm.com/developerworks/edu/x-dw-x-ultimashup1.html?
    ca=dgrlnxw07webMashupsPart1&s_cmp=gr&s_tact=105agx59

Tutorial: "The Ultimate Mashup—Web Services and the Semantic Web." This six-part tutorial from IBM covers the concept of mashups, building an XML cache, RDF, Web Ontology Language (OWL), user control and more. The tutorial is primarily for IBM employees; others must register.

conferences.oreillynet.com/cs/et2005/view/e_sess/6241

Download the Mashup presentation from the O'Reilly Emerging Technology Conference.

www.theurer.cc/blog/2005/11/03/how-to-build-a-maps-mash-up/

Tutorial: "How to Build a Maps Mashup," by Dan Theurer. Includes the JavaScript code and a sample mashup application.

Mashup Directories

www.programmableweb.com/mashups

ProgrammableWeb (www.programmableweb.com/mashups) lists the latest mashups, APIs, and web platforms news and developments. It includes a directory of new mashups, the most popular mashups, and more. Search for mashups by common tags including mapping, photo, search, shopping, sports, travel, messaging, news, transit and real estate. Check out the Web 2.0 Mashup matrix with links to numerous mashups. For each site, you'll find the mashups that have been created with the other sites in the matrix.

www.programmableweb.com/matrix

ProgrammableWeb includes a Web 2.0 Mashup matrix with links to numerous mashups. For each of the sites listed, find the mashups that have been created with the other sites in the matrix.

googlemapsmania.blogspot.com/

Lists numerous mashups that use Google Maps. Examples include Google Maps mashups with US hotels, public transit information, UK news and more.

www.webmashup.com

An open directory for mashups and Web 2.0 APIs.

Mashup Resources

code.google.com/

Google APIs include Google Maps, Google AJAX Search API, Google Toolbar API, AdWords API, Google Data APIs, Google Checkout API and WikiWalki (Google APIs used in Google Maps).

www.flickr.com/services/api/

APIs available from Flickr include updating photos, replacing photos, example requests and asynchronous uploading. API kits include Java, ActionScript, Cold Fusion, Common Lisp, cUrl, Delphi, .NET, Perl, PHP, PHP5, Python, REALbasic and Ruby.

developers.technorati.com/wiki/TechnoratiApi

APIs available at Technorati include CosmosQuery, SearchQuery, GetInfoQuery, OutboundQuery and BlogInfoQuery. New and experimental APIs include TagQuery, AttentionQuery and KeyInfo.

mashworks.net/wiki/Building_Mash-ups_for_Non-Programmers

Article: "Building Mashups for Non-Programmers," from MashWorks. Gives non-programmers sources for creating mashups, such as links to mapping services and examples of mashups created by non-programmers using both Google Maps and Flickr.

Mashup Tools and Downloads

mashup-tools.pbwiki.com/

Mashup Tools Wiki is a developer's source for tools and tips for building technology mashups.

`news.com.com/2100-1032_3-6046693.html`
Article: "Yahoo to Offer New Mashup Tools," by Anne Broache. Discusses Yahoo's announcement that it will provide APIs for doing mashups through its Developer's Network. In addition, Yahoo will also set up an Application Gallery for viewing programs created with the APIs.

`www.imediaconnection.com/content/10217.asp`
Article: "Marketing Mashup Tools," by Rob Rose. Discusses using mashups for marketing on web sites. Topics include site search systems, e-mail campaign management, content management systems, web analytics systems and what to consider when mashing up these tools.

`datamashups.com/overview.html`
Free Tool: DataMashup.com is a hosted service that offers an open source tool (AppliBuilder) that allows users to create mashups. A demo is available.

`blogs.zdnet.com/Hinchcliffe/?p=63`
Blog: "Assembling Great Software: A Round-up of Eight Mashup Tools," by Dion Hinchcliffe. Discusses what mashups do, API source sites such as ProgrammableWeb, and his review of eight mashup tools including Above All Studio (from Above All Software), Dapper (an online mashup tool), DataMashups.com (good for small business application mashups), JackBuilder (from JackBe)—a browser-based mashup tool, aRex (from Nexaweb), Process Engine (from Procession) for task automation, Ratchet-X Studio (from RatchetSoft) for rapid application integration, and RSSBus (from RSSBus) for creating mashups from RSS feeds.

`www.ning.com`
Use this free tool to create your own "social applications." Check out some of the applications people have created using Ning including a map of San Francisco Bay area hiking trails, restaurant reviews with maps, and more. Ning was co-founded by Marc Andreessen—one of the founders of Netscape.

Mashup Articles

`www.factiva.com/infopro/articles/Sept2006Feature.asp?node=menuElem1103`
Article: "Mashups—The API Buffet," from Factiva. Explains what mashups are and how they are created.

`www-128.ibm.com/developerworks/library/x-mashups.html?`
`    ca=dgr1nxw16MashupChallenges`
Article: "Mashups: The New Breed of Web App: An Introduction to Mashups," by Duane Merrill. Discusses what mashups are, types of mashups (mapping, video, photo, search, shopping, and news), related technologies (such as architecture, AJAX, web protocols, screen scraping, semantic web, RDF, RSS and ATOM) and technical and social challenges.

`ajax.sys-con.com/read/203935.htm`
Article: "Mashup Data Formats: JSON versus XML/XMLHttpRequest," by Daniel B. Markham. Compares the JSON (JavaScript Object Notation) and XML/XMLHttpRequest technologies for use in web applications.

`www.techsoup.org/learningcenter/webbuilding/page5788.cfm`
Article: "Mashups: An Easy, Free Way to Create Custom Web Apps," by Brian Satterfield. Discusses resources for building mashups. Lists several mashup sites including Givezilla (for nonprofits), Podbop (MP3 files and concert listings) and Strmz (streaming video, video blogs and video podcasts).

`www.msnbc.msn.com/id/11569228/site/newsweek/`
Article: "Technology: Time For Your Mashup?" by N'gai Croal. Discusses the history of mashups, music mashups, video mashups and web apps.

`www.slate.com/id/2114791/`
Article on newsmashing—a mashup of blogs with the news stories to which they refer. This allows you to see a complete article and read related commentary from the blogosphere.

images.businessweek.com/ss/05/07/mashups/index_01.htm
Business Week Online article, "Sampling the Web's Best Mashups," listing popular mashups.

www.usatoday.com/tech/columnist/kevinmaney/2005-08-16-maney-google-mashups_x.htm
Article that discusses the proliferation of Google Maps mashups.

www.clickz.com/experts/brand/brand/article.php/3528921
Article entitled "The Branding and Mapping Mashup." Discusses how mashups are used to bring brands to users based on location. For example, users can find the cheapest gasoline in their area.

www.usernomics.com/news/2005/10/mash-up-apps-and-competitive-advantage.html
Article: "Mashup Apps and Competitive Advantage: Benefits of mashups including user experience."

Mashups in the Blogosphere

web2.wsj2.com/the_web_20_mashup_ecosystem_ramps_up.htm
Dion Hinchcliffe's (President and CTO of Hinchcliffe & Company) Web 2.0 Blog discusses mashups. Includes a nice graphic of the Mashup Ecosystem.

www.techcrunch.com/2005/10/04/ning-launches/
Blog that follows Web 2.0 companies and news. This posting talks about Ning, a free tool you can use to build social applications.

www.engadget.com/entry/1234000917034960/
Learn how to make your own Google Maps mashups.

blogs.zdnet.com/web2explorer/?p=16&part=rss&tag=feed&subj=zdblog
ZDNet blog posting titled "Fun with Mashups." Includes links to several mashups.

Mashup FAQs and Newsgroups

groups.google.com/group/Google-Maps-API?lnk=gschg&hl=en
Google Maps API newsgroup on Google Groups. Chat with other developers using the Google Maps API, get answers to your questions and share your applications with others.

www.google.com/apis/maps/faq.html
Learn how to use the Google Maps API to create your own mashups.

programmableweb.com/faq
Mashups FAQ on ProgrammableWeb provides an introduction to mashups and APIs and discusses how to create your own mashups and more.

Index

End User License Agreements

Prentice Hall License Agreement and Limited Warranty

READ THE FOLLOWING TERMS AND CONDITIONS CAREFULLY BEFORE OPENING THIS SOFTWARE PACKAGE. THIS LEGAL DOCUMENT IS AN AGREEMENT BETWEEN YOU AND PRENTICE-HALL, INC. (THE "COMPANY"). BY OPENING THIS SEALED SOFTWARE PACKAGE, YOU ARE AGREEING TO BE BOUND BY THESE TERMS AND CONDITIONS. IF YOU DO NOT AGREE WITH THESE TERMS AND CONDITIONS, DO NOT OPEN THE SOFTWARE PACKAGE. PROMPTLY RETURN THE UNOPENED SOFTWARE PACKAGE AND ALL ACCOMPANYING ITEMS TO THE PLACE YOU OBTAINED THEM FOR A FULL REFUND OF ANY SUMS YOU HAVE PAID.

1.GRANT OF LICENSE: In consideration of your purchase of this book, and your agreement to abide by the terms and conditions of this Agreement, the Company grants to you a nonexclusive right to use and display the copy of the enclosed software program (hereinafter the "SOFTWARE") on a single computer (i.e., with a single CPU) at a single location so long as you comply with the terms of this Agreement. The Company reserves all rights not expressly granted to you under this Agreement.

2.OWNERSHIP OF SOFTWARE: You own only the magnetic or physical media (the enclosed media) on which the SOFTWARE is recorded or fixed, but the Company and the software developers retain all the rights, title, and ownership to the SOFTWARE recorded on the original media copy(ies) and all subsequent copies of the SOFTWARE, regardless of the form or media on which the original or other copies may exist. This license is not a sale of the original SOFTWARE or any copy to you.

3.COPY RESTRICTIONS: This SOFTWARE and the accompanying printed materials and user manual (the "Documentation") are the subject of copyright. The individual programs on the media are copyrighted by the authors of each program. Some of the programs on the media include separate licensing agreements. If you intend to use one of these programs, you must read and follow its accompanying license agreement. You may not copy the Documentation or the SOFTWARE, except that you may make a single copy of the SOFTWARE for backup or archival purposes only. You may be held legally responsible for any copying or copyright infringement which is caused or encouraged by your failure to abide by the terms of this restriction.

4.USE RESTRICTIONS: You may not network the SOFTWARE or otherwise use it on more than one computer or computer terminal at the same time. You may physically transfer the SOFTWARE from one computer to another provided that the SOFTWARE is used on only one computer at a time. You may not distribute copies of the SOFTWARE or Documentation to others. You may not reverse engineer, disassemble, decompile, modify, adapt, translate, or create derivative works based on the SOFTWARE or the Documentation without the prior written consent of the Company.

5. TRANSFER RESTRICTIONS: The enclosed SOFTWARE is licensed only to you and may not be transferred to any one else without the prior written consent of the Company. Any unauthorized transfer of the SOFTWARE shall result in the immediate termination of this Agreement.

6. TERMINATION: This license is effective until terminated. This license will terminate automatically without notice from the Company and become null and void if you fail to comply with any provisions or limitations of this license. Upon termination, you shall destroy the Documentation and all copies of the SOFTWARE. All provisions of this Agreement as to warranties, limitation of liability, remedies or damages, and our ownership rights shall survive termination.

7. MISCELLANEOUS: This Agreement shall be construed in accordance with the laws of the United States of America and the State of New York and shall benefit the Company, its affiliates, and assignees.

8.LIMITED WARRANTY AND DISCLAIMER OF WARRANTY: The Company warrants that the SOFTWARE, when properly used in accordance with the Documentation, will operate in substantial conformity with the description of the SOFTWARE set forth in the Documentation. The Company does not warrant that the SOFTWARE will meet your requirements or that the operation of the SOFTWARE will be uninterrupted or error-free. The Company warrants that the media on which the SOFTWARE is delivered shall be free from defects in materials and workmanship under normal use for a period of thirty

(30) days from the date of your purchase. Your only remedy and the Company's only obligation under these limited warranties is, at the Company's option, return of the warranted item for a refund of any amounts paid by you or replacement of the item. Any replacement of SOFTWARE or media under the warranties shall not extend the original warranty period. The limited warranty set forth above shall not apply to any SOFTWARE which the Company determines in good faith has been subject to misuse, neglect, improper installation, repair, alteration, or damage by you. EXCEPT FOR THE EXPRESSED WARRANTIES SET FORTH ABOVE, THE COMPANY DISCLAIMS ALL WARRANTIES, EXPRESS OR IMPLIED, INCLUDING WITHOUT LIMITATION, THE IMPLIED WARRANTIES OF MERCHANTABILITY AND FITNESS FOR A PARTICULAR PURPOSE. EXCEPT FOR THE EXPRESS WARRANTY SET FORTH ABOVE, THE COMPANY DOES NOT WARRANT, GUARANTEE, OR MAKE ANY REPRESENTATION REGARDING THE USE OR THE RESULTS OF THE USE OF THE SOFTWARE IN TERMS OF ITS CORRECTNESS, ACCURACY, RELIABILITY, CURRENTNESS, OR OTHERWISE.

IN NO EVENT, SHALL THE COMPANY OR ITS EMPLOYEES, AGENTS, SUPPLIERS, OR CONTRACTORS BE LIABLE FOR ANY INCIDENTAL, INDIRECT, SPECIAL, OR CONSEQUENTIAL DAMAGES ARISING OUT OF OR IN CONNECTION WITH THE LICENSE GRANTED UNDER THIS AGREEMENT, OR FOR LOSS OF USE, LOSS OF DATA, LOSS OF INCOME OR PROFIT, OR OTHER LOSSES, SUSTAINED AS A RESULT OF INJURY TO ANY PERSON, OR LOSS OF OR DAMAGE TO PROPERTY, OR CLAIMS OF THIRD PARTIES, EVEN IF THE COMPANY OR AN AUTHORIZED REPRESENTATIVE OF THE COMPANY HAS BEEN ADVISED OF THE POSSIBILITY OF SUCH DAMAGES. IN NO EVENT SHALL LIABILITY OF THE COMPANY FOR DAMAGES WITH RESPECT TO THE SOFTWARE EXCEED THE AMOUNTS ACTUALLY PAID BY YOU, IF ANY, FOR THE SOFTWARE.

SOME JURISDICTIONS DO NOT ALLOW THE LIMITATION OF IMPLIED WARRANTIES OR LIABILITY FOR INCIDENTAL, INDIRECT, SPECIAL, OR CONSEQUENTIAL DAMAGES, SO THE ABOVE LIMITATIONS MAY NOT ALWAYS APPLY. THE WARRANTIES IN THIS AGREEMENT GIVE YOU SPECIFIC LEGAL RIGHTS AND YOU MAY ALSO HAVE OTHER RIGHTS WHICH VARY IN ACCORDANCE WITH LOCAL LAW.

ACKNOWLEDGMENT

YOU ACKNOWLEDGE THAT YOU HAVE READ THIS AGREEMENT, UNDERSTAND IT, AND AGREE TO BE BOUND BY ITS TERMS AND CONDITIONS. YOU ALSO AGREE THAT THIS AGREEMENT IS THE COMPLETE AND EXCLUSIVE STATEMENT OF THE AGREEMENT BETWEEN YOU AND THE COMPANY AND SUPERSEDES ALL PROPOSALS OR PRIOR AGREEMENTS, ORAL, OR WRITTEN, AND ANY OTHER COMMUNICATIONS BETWEEN YOU AND THE COMPANY OR ANY REPRESENTATIVE OF THE COMPANY RELATING TO THE SUBJECT MATTER OF THIS AGREEMENT.

Should you have any questions concerning this Agreement or if you wish to contact the Company for any reason, please contact in writing at the address below.

Robin Short
Prentice Hall PTR
One Lake Street
Upper Saddle River, New Jersey 07458

License Agreement and Limited Warranty

Using the CDs

The interface to the contents of the Microsoft® Windows® CD is designed to start automatically through the **AUTORUN.EXE** file. If a startup screen does not pop up automatically when you insert the CD into your computer, double click on the **welcome.htm** file to launch the Student CD or refer to the file **readme.txt** on the CD. To launch the interface of the Linux® CD double click on the **welcome.htm** file to launch the Student CD.

Software and Hardware System Requirements

- 500 MHz (minimum) Pentium III or faster processor; Sun® Java™ Studio Creator 2 Update 1 requires a 1 GHz Intel Pentium 4 processor (or equivalent)
- Microsoft Windows Server 2003, Windows XP (with Service Pack 2), Windows 2000 Professional (with Service Pack 4) or
- One of the following Linux distributions: Red Hat® Enterprise Linux 3, or Red Hat Fedora Core 3
- Minimum of 512 MB of RAM; Sun Java Studio Creator 2 Update 1 requires 1 GB of RAM
- Minimum of 1.5 GB of hard disk space
- CD-ROM drive
- Internet connection
- Web browser, Adobe® Acrobat® Reader® and a zip decompression utility